Jean-Jacques Rousseau

Emilius and Sophia

Or, a new system of education

Jean-Jacques Rousseau

Emilius and Sophia
Or, a new system of education

ISBN/EAN: 9783742800442

Manufactured in Europe, USA, Canada, Australia, Japa

Cover: Foto ©Andreas Hilbeck / pixelio.de

Manufactured and distributed by brebook publishing software
(www.brebook.com)

Jean-Jacques Rousseau

Emilius and Sophia

THE

CALIFORNIAN

A WESTERN MONTHLY MAGAZINE.

JULY--DECEMBER, 1880.

VOLUME II.

SAN FRANCISCO:
THE CALIFORNIA PUBLISHING COMPANY,
No. 202 Sansome Street, corner Pine.

CONTENTS.

POETRY.

THE CALIFORNIAN.

A WESTERN MONTHLY MAGAZINE.

VOL. II.—JULY, 1880.—No. 7.

THE GREAT BRONZE GOD.

It was near nine o'clock, on one of the sunniest, brightest mornings that ever transformed the Yokohama Bay ripples into diamonds or fringed Fuji-yama's robe of snow with purest gold. We were going to interview Daibutz, the great bronze Mogul of the Buddhist gods. We had heard much of Daibutz. Every Japanned American we met wanted to know if we had seen him, and every other one confided to us religiously that we ought to see him; but for three days previously an anti-Buddhist weather-clerk had dampened our enthusiasm, taken the starch out of our plans, and imprisoned us with floods of "moist, unpleasant" rain. On this Sunday morning, however, all was serene, from the meteorological outlook to the tempers of those concerned; and, blue skies eliminating blue spirits, we cheerfully prepared for departure—we embracing Doctor and Mrs. Eldridge, patron saints of Americans in Yokohama, and a party of American ladies and navy officers, recipients of their hospitality.

A dozen *jinrikishas* waited before the door, and two dozen coolie biped steeds lounged picturesquely and otherwise in waiting. A word as to these phenomenal conveyances, since this journey, like all others in Japan, depended solely on them. They are to Japan both street-cars and carriages, and are as curious a style of vehicle as civilized people can well imagine. They are simply huge perambulators, in which grown folk are trundled about pretty much as babies are at home, only the delectable and dilatory nurse-girls are replaced in Japan by small, muscular, bow-legged, and scantily clad coolies. You employ an oriental tandem of one, two, or three of these coolies at a time, according to your weight, the distance to be traveled, and the roads. The Japanese, who are as a race small and slender, frequently ride two, and even three, in one *jinrikisha*, and, when they do, the general "baby-wagon" air makes it strongly suggestive of huge twins or monster triplets. American dignity, however, airing itself abroad, rises superior to Japanese economy, and your globe-trotter invariably makes the *jinrikisha* game a game of solitaire; consequently, they are not the most sociable things in the world, particularly in view of the fact that, the law requiring them to travel in single file to avoid collisions, conversational indulgence is attainable only by means of a speaking trumpet or a peripatetic telephone.

The coolies are a curious class. They seem so like animals, with their bare legs, feet, and heads, their dogged indifference to the weather, going bare-footed and bare-legged in the snow storms, and their monkey-like chattering in voices which are always unnaturally hoarse or shrill, that it makes you almost uncomfortable to think that they, too, are of flesh and blood, and may possibly have souls—curious foreign souls, to be sure—to be saved. They have an odd habit of going along quietly enough when they have a single vehicle in charge; but when a long line of them are traveling together, and the first one comes to a bridge, a rut, or any obstruction, large or small, in the road, some heathenish sounding word is passed along the line, and bellowed, groaned, hooted, and howled to the end, making the wildest succession of noises ever heard outside of a boiler factory or of a Methodist camp-meeting. But they never kick and never shy, nor do they explode or run away. When we were finally ensconced in our queer, but royally comfortable, low-backed cars, it was with a feeling of perfect confidence in the brown and muscular motors, who only waited for steam to be turned on to fly like mad over a strange and lovely country, and under the bluest sky that ever smiled on a pious visit to the god of somebody else's ancestors.

Our way led first through the narrow and populous by-streets of Yokohama, with their low, smooth-planed, unpainted, windowless houses, with doors and walls that slide so that the entire front of the house is taken out and set on one side in all but the most unpleasant weather. If there are any nails in a Japanese house, they are invisible. Everything is grooved, fitted, smooth sliding, and, as they are a cleanly people, their houses, as you pass them, are something exquisitely neat and dainty to look at. The dresses are as quaint and curious as the houses. Their general costume is a very lazy one, and is utterly incompatible with hurried movements or violent exercise of any kind. It is well that this is so, for in a Japanese dwelling any sudden motion would be liable to send you through the inner walls, which are composed entirely of small, translucent paper panes, set in very delicate wooden frames. One good, energetic American, in a fit of absent-mindedness, could walk through a whole block of Japanese houses and never feel that his progress had been interfered with.

As we passed over the simple, substantial, arched granite bridges that spanned the canal, which is everywhere in Yokohama, the swift quietness of the easy-rolling *jinrikishas* was broken by the sound of wooden clogs, which clicked like castanets and clattered like the bones of the minstrel end-man, as the numerous passers-by tripped along in a slow, pigeon-toed, and not ungraceful fashion. The people are quaint, composed, easy-going little folk, and understand being clumsy in the most graceful possible way. Almost everything in Japan is diminutive and infantile. Their carriages are like baby-wagons; their ordinary costume bears a strong family likeness to an infant's swaddling clothes; the houses are like play-houses; their childen like funny *bric-à-brac* dolls, and unreasonably near of a size; even in their graveyards, the head-stones are from six to twelve inches high, and so close together as to give the idea that they must have been buried standing, and in defiance of the cubic air ordinance at that.

These and many more things struck us as we wound through devious highways and by-ways in the suburbs of Yokohama, past the picturesque tiled roofs and the cunning, wide-open little houses, by fathoms of blue and white china exposed in the little open recesses they call shops, and long distances of gay-colored, cheap curio and clothing bazars, often past a stock of mixed, common, and inferior foreign goods, jarring like a false note in a harmonious strain, stared at by blear-eyed old women and smiled at by young ones, unnoticed by the men and pursued with shouts by the children, until finally we rolled over the last bridge and found ourselves suddenly trundling along the muddy embankments that raised us above the level of the low, intentionally overflowed, terraced rice fields. These last, we were told, were soon to bud and blossom as the rose; but this was only a prophecy, and they were still for us a monotonous, unvarying set of rich, black mud-flats. True Californians never pin their faith on overflowed lands. The somber monotone of the rice fields was relieved here and there by picturesque little black, conical, thatched cottages, nestled among slender green trees, while children in richly colored rags played and shouted around them. Despite the cloister-like characteristics of the *jinrikisha*, our good lungs and high spirits kept us from feeling completely isolated, and the air was laden with comments, witticisms, and snatches of song, with a jollity that made our long single file strikingly like the mother-in-law's funeral to which a navy officer compared it. The tea-house girls viewed our good time with sympathetic smiles. Tea-houses are everywhere in Japan. They sprang up like mushrooms under our feet, and gentle handmaidens, in gray and navy blue garments lined with red, stood at the roadside and besought us in silver-voiced chorus to pause and enter. But we were fresh from the best of breakfasts, and relentlessly bent on interviewing Daibutz, and even the persuasive tea-house girl could not turn us from our fell pursuit—at least not then. It was long before we could decide which were the more numerous in Japan, the tea-houses or children, but at last the children took the palm. They crowd the streets of the city. You expect that; but in the alleged lonesome and quiet country they swarm like bees by the roadside, and swoop down upon you in bands and armies. Their shrill-voiced "ohio," which is "Jap" for "good-day," and their funny, patched, gay-colored clothes, pursue you like a decorative nightmare, turn where you may.

But children and tea-houses were alike forgotten when a turn in the road brought us suddenly into the presence of Fuji-yama—that peerless mountain, worshiped by the Japanese and a beautiful memory to all who have seen it. This day it loomed up against the delicate blue sky, a great, lone, white cone, so near you could almost touch it, so grand, so pure, so dazdingly white that the sight of it was awesome. Far down its side faint, blue shadows gave it shape and blended with the olives, yellows, and browns of the trees, low hills, and rice fields in the foreground. It was very beautiful, and we succumbed to its spell, wondering no longer at the mountain idolatry of the queer, impressionable little people around us.

A few more turns and we began to feel sensible that we had advanced somewhat on our road. Distances in Japan are largely a matter of temperament. It is from nine to eighteen miles from Yokohama to Daibutz, according to the company, the weather, and the digestion. One bilious man assured us that it was twenty.

The true American abroad, as at home, is accustomed to gauge distances by his pocket-flask, and by the time those trusty pedometers said half way, we were contented to give the mud-stained coolies their hard-earned rest, and at last yield to the solicitations of the ubiquitous and inviting tea-house. The *jinrikishas* rolled into a small court-yard, and we bundled out and seated ourselves on a very low verandah that bounded the court-yard on three sides. Presently we crossed it, and sat cross-legged on soft mats in one of the pretty, little paper alcoves, utterly destitute of furniture, that yawned invitingly all around the court—this in response to voluble, sweet-voiced, coquettish, and unintelligible greetings from low-bowing Japanese maidens, headed by a horrible *duenna* with blackened teeth. They brand them this way in Japan for having committed matrimony, though even that is not sufficient to make them keep their mouths closed. Leaving their sandals on the verandah, they glided noiselessly about in stocking feet, bringing us astringent and unpalatable Japanese tea in dainty, fragile porcelain bowls, served on pretty lacquer stands, with a *sauce piquante* of oriental *salaams* and smiles, and an accompaniment of reasonably good confectionery.

Japanese girls are lovely in the best style of decorative art, with their bright black eyes, pretty painted faces, the simple straight *kimono*, or dress, made of fine silk and red lined, the *obi*, or sash, made of rich, thick, brocaded silk, wound round and round the waist, and the small shapely hands and plump smooth arms disclosed by the falling away of the loose sleeve. But their crowning glory, the climax as it were, is the superstructure which adorns their pretty little heads. It is the abundant shining black hair dressed in picturesque spread-eagle fashion, with gay *crêpe* bands wound in and out among the tresses, and stabbed with many long curious gilt daggers and pins. The *ensemble* is beautifully grotesque, and it is hard to believe them anything but phenomenal peripatetic decorations.

Our repast having been finished, the paying of the insignificant bill, and the bestowal of a few cents of *pour-boire*, brought such prostrations and such bumping of winged heads on the floor as quite distressed us, and we made all possible haste to our *jinrikishas*, and were soon spinning along toward Kamakura and Daibutz. Once more over the paddy fields, and anon over and among low green hills, through narrow paths where a chance motion would start a crimson shower of odorless petals from the tall bloom-laden camellia hedges, or bring one in contact with the graceful bamboo fences, into which the young shoots still growing are woven, making barriers too lovely to do anything but shut out sentiments or imprison emotions. The hills are thickly wooded, and in the loveliest spot on every hillside you will always find a Buddhist shrine. Sometimes it is hollowed out of a rock, sometimes carved in the stump of a tree, sometimes built of wood or stone, and always containing one or more rudely carved stone or wooden images of Buddha. About the shrine there are often piles of smooth, round stones, offerings of the faithful—sometimes garments, and frequently sandals, proffered by suffering wayfarers with a prayer for the ease of pain.

On this day the distance to Daibutz was but nine miles, although the roads were heavy. At early noon a last turn through the paddy fields and a last pull over the hill brought us to Kamakura, beyond which is Daibutz.

At Kamakura we traveled a long mile through a densely populated street, and kept our fingers in our ears through just one mile of continuous, prolonged "ohio." Thence through a magnificent avenue of stately trees, where before us lay the sea—our first glimpse of it since leaving Yokohama, and at our left the grand old black, red, and pagoda-topped temples of Kamakura. Leading straight from the temples to the sea, there stretches a broad granite way, with scattered trees on either side, down which, in times long gone by, the high priests, in full panoply, went once a year to the seaside to perform religious rites now quite abandoned and almost forgotten. We went from the grand avenue across an open stretch of country by the seaside, then among the trees again, and suddenly into a lovely little village nestled among the hills and out of all sight and hearing of the sea.

But we looked in vain for Daibutz. We were told that we were not to dash rudely, with giddy heads, empty stomachs, and whirling *jinrikishas*, into the presence of the god. So the procession came to a halt in front of the regulation tea-house, where, after a glass of dry Mumm (quite a rarity in the East, where they usually drink Heidsieck) and a bite of something from our host's special "Jap," who had gone before, we were ready to interview anybody, our minds full of romantic expectation and our hands of chicken sandwiches. A stroll of five minutes through the romantic by-paths sufficed to dispose of the sandwiches and bring us to one of those huge, pagoda-topped gates, flanked by gorgeously painted rainbow gods in cages, which invariably denote the entrance to a Buddhist temple. The tree-bordered, gray stone walk that brings you to Daibutz was skillfully contrived, so that, without any previous glimpses, a sudden step brought us full into the presence of his bronze majesty, in the very spot where he has rested immobile for over six hundred years. He loomed up right before us, a colossal figure of Buddha, represented sitting, oriental fashion, on a tremendous granite platform. His great hands were lying palm up on his enormous lap, and the sitting posture and the inadequately low pedestal made the figure look so disproportionately broad that it was at first difficult to realize its height. But a glance at the surrounding trees and buildings over which it towers, and the feeling of being microscopically minute which crept over us, soon brought us to a sense of its size. It bears a strong family likeness to all other images of Buddha, but its proportions render it unusually impressive, for while the non-superstitious American mind can rise superior to the toy idols of the mantelpiece, a god forty-four feet high and eighty-seven in circumference, with an eight-and-a half-foot face, a thirty-four-foot knee, and a thumb three and a half feet in circumference, is not to be sneered at. Huge earrings and a close-fitting, bead-like head-dress give it rather an Egyptian air. There is a legend that the god was ordered by a pious empress of Japan, who commanded contributions of copper coin from all the faithful, and received enough to melt over into this immense image. We were struck at once by the discolored appearance of the bronze, which is gray, mottled, and weather-beaten from the suns and storms of six centuries, and then by the wonderful expression of the figure, which is the embodiment of majestic repose. It is somehow more natural to look to the texture than to the meaning of any oriental work of art, and their intelligent expression of an idea was always a surprise. In our lordly way, we expected skill rather than ideas from them, but acquaintance with them very soon changed that misconception. Like all images of Buddha, Daibutz repays study. It is artistically valuable as the almost perfect expression of a grand idea—the idea of divine repose. There is nothing dull in its immobility, yet nothing sphinx-like behind its serenity; no riddle to unravel or to vex you. It is simply the perfection of philosophy—a passionless calm. It is the perfect development and perfect gratification of all the faculties; the consequent absence of desire or unrest. Those who study and love it fancy that the spell of its quiet serenity descends upon them and fills them, like hasheesh or the lotus, with a sense of perfect peace. Our merry crowd were each and all just a little touched by the grand old god, and before we left we had mutually confessed feelings of respect and admiration for him, and unanimously resolved that he should adorn our parlors were he only a few degrees smaller. We were then shown to a small dark door, which led (for the image is utterly hollow) into its very bosom, which is fitted up in a rude way as a temple. A break-neck climb up a vertebral stairway took us to the small window which made darkness visible, whence we could look on the comparatively Lilliputian grove, which affords shelter to picnic parties and makes a short-waisted background to the sixty odd feet of Daibutz and pedestal.

While in the interior it seemed incredible that this monstrous image could be the work of the puny Japanese. It was cast, we were told, in sections, and the parts so joined as to appear one casting. The bronze of which it is made is excellent in quality, containing considerable gold. Gold was once very cheap in Japan, and as late as 1600 they exchanged gold for silver, weight for weight, with the Dutch.

This information, and much more besides, was imparted to willing listeners by the one or two of the party who were old residents, while we went through the next step in the programme. That was to climb a ladder, scramble over his thirty-four feet of bronze knees, and recline on his tremendous thumb while we were being photographed. There is room on his hands for a party of a dozen, and one can never realize his photographed insignificance till he sees himself perched, flea-like, on Daibutz's thumb-nail.

A few years ago an enterprising Yankee, a New Yorker this time, tried to buy the god, with the idea of taking it to pieces for transportation, and putting it up and exhibiting it in New York. As the church was in a tight place, Daibutz was bargained for and almost sold, when the English in Japan made such an outcry against the vandalism that the government put a stop to the sale. *Bric-à-brac* gods and empty pockets strongly tempt the sacrifice of one and replenishment of the other.

But by the time our first surprise was over, and we were ready to philosophize, we were also ready to eat, and the proposing of lunch, or "tiffin," as they call it in the East, was very warmly seconded. So, with a last, long look at divine Daibutz, a parting glance at the sun-bathed scene, and a sigh for the peace that passeth understanding, we returned to "tiffin" and the tea-house. It was with a sense of contentment emulating Buddha's that we bundled into our comfortable *jinrikishas*, and unanimously voted a return home by the *tokaido*.

The *tokaido* is the great highway of Japan—a wide road leading half around the island, skirting the sea, and almost one continuous, densely populated street. A few short cuts across the rice fields brought us there just as the crescent moon was rising, the *jinrikisha* coolies lighting their paper lanterns, and fair Fuji-yama shining, chill and faint and white against a cold, gray sky. The trees stood out in fantastic silhouette, the Japanese lanterns in front of the *jinrikishas* cast yellow rings of light, the new moon shed a faint, sweet half-light, and distant Fuji-yama melted quite away, as we bowled rapidly home. The semi-transparent Japanese houses showed tea-box pictures as we passed them. The shrill voices of the children were heard no more, and the grunting and screeching of the coolies was all that broke the silence. As for our party, the married folk were all napping, and the young people had reached a stage of sentimentality, born of twilight and champagne and decorative effects, that made the shouting of sentiments a barbarism and the lonesome *jinrikisha* a deadly failure. And so we rolled along, while the captain behind sang "Love once again," and the midshipman in front sang something concerning "Breaking hearts that break in vain," till the flashing of waters, the crossing of many bridges, and a new activity in the streets, told us that we were once more in Yokohama.

MINNIE D. UNGER.

SAINT BARTHOLOMEW.

"There was no discord. It was music ceased."

CHAPTER I.

The usual rush for the morning boat, the breathing spell crossing the bay, again the bustle on the Oakland wharf, and two young women, Mrs. Alston and her sister, Miss Grey, started "East" on the overland train one morning in early May, beginning a journey of three thousand and odd miles with the peaceful security known only to American women.

As the train moved slowly off, Mrs. Alston, the elder of the two and a widow, sat with her two-year old baby, Elsie, in her lap, awaiting a general subsidence of things. Opposite was the nurse, grasping with undue vigor shawl-straps, satchels, and lunch-baskets, while an unmistakably Irish foot was planted squarely on a large valise, as the only means left her to indicate her mistress's rights. Miss Grey leaned far out the window, energetically waving a rather limp handkerchief to the receding group of friends on the platform; then, raising her eyes, took a last, long look at the bright, shimmering bay, and, opposite, the "Western Queen" herself—poor, ugly, conceited, true-hearted little Frisco.

"Nell, are they out of sight? And are we going so rapidly that no one could jump on board by any possibility?" asked Mrs. Alston, earnestly.

"Yes, O suffering dame!" laughingly replied Nell, drawing in her head; and then, looking at her sister, she burst into a merry laugh.

"Might I inquire into the somewhat mysterious cause of your amusement?" said Mrs. Alston, with unrelaxed severity.

"Oh, Agnes! You are the most pitiful looking creature I ever saw; sitting there so pale and resigned, and trying to look cheerfully thankful for all favors received, surrounded by——"

"Miss Grey, if you say a single word about Marius and those ruins, I feel that I shall go mad! Cousin Arthur said it twice, Uncle Phil three times, and Mrs. Gratton once. Who was the creature, anyhow? No, don't tell me now: reserve it for the stagnation of the plains."

"I am proud to relate that Carthage entered not into my thoughts; I was only going to refer to our luggage. Has it struck you that it might come under the head of voluminous?"

"Not at all. It only seems so because we had these things thrust upon us by misguided friends," said Agnes, looking with aversion at her left hand, that held a pink and yellow paper windmill for Elsie, and then at her right, which contained a large bouquet of California's most exquisite blossoms, robbed of as much beauty as the florist's sacrilegious hand could well accomplish at a day's notice.

"Why on earth people—good Christians, too—will show so little discretion in the selection of farewell gifts, I can't imagine," rejoined Nell, glancing in her turn at her hands, which grasped respectively an immense box of bonbons and a package of novels, slipped into her hand by jolly, kind-hearted Uncle Phil (who had been a father to her since her early orphanage), with the words:

"There, my little girl, I hope you will like them. I confess I've had a great struggle trying to think of something that is solid, and yet a woman could understand. I stayed awake two nights, and searched the bookstores six times, but I think I have made a good job of it."

"No one but a man could have thought of that pink and yellow monstrosity," continued Nell, throwing all their gifts up into the rack above their heads, and giving an unnecessary poke to the windmill.

"It seems so ungrateful to act so, after all their kindness," remarked Agnes, with a perceptible shade of impenitent satisfaction in her voice.

"I do believe that the best part of men-folks remains forever undeveloped, in all its simple, healthy, blundering, school-boyishness. A woman's goodness grows up, and wears a chignon and train; a man's is always dressed in a gingham pinafore and brass-toed boots," said Nell, sententiously.

"Much, doubtless, might be said on the subject, but, as I perceive the oracular creeping into your tone, I must ask you to postpone it and tell the porter to come to me," interrupted Mrs. Alston, acting upon principles educed from a long experience with Nell's enthusiasm.

The porter came smilingly forward, with a view to the untested possibilities of the party.

"What the first days of our trip would have been without our gem of a porter, Rufus, I shudder to imagine," wrote Nell, per postal-card, to her brother in San Francisco.

After the party were comfortably settled and order reigned, they became suddenly conscious that the car contained other inmates; and Agnes's well traveled eye took in, with satisfaction, the fact that there were only two ladies besides themselves. "Which means," she explained to Nell, "a chance to wash your face before afternoon, and an amount of chivalrous attention from the gentlemen which we can regulate."

One of the two ladies had the section next their own. She was a stout, active little woman, with big, innocent blue eyes; a fresh, girlish face contrasting somewhat pleasantly with her snow-white hair. With her was a little girl who called her "Grandma." Both seemed inclined to cultivate everybody's acquaintance, but Agnes studiously avoided any contact, even of the eyes, until she was sure of her ground. The other woman sat farther down the car. She was a young married lady, with a masculine stamp of feature that made Nell instantly study the husband's face for traces of the suggestive consequences; but, although "of his port as meke as is a mayde," he seemed very peaceful and happy withal. Directly opposite was a courtly lookly old gentlemen, with an air of rigid conservatism that was preëminently respectable. The very way in which his hair was brushed, and the manner in which he put his gold eye-glasses upon the bridge of his delicate nose, and opened and read his many newspapers, breathed the very essence of patrician self-respect. He appealed directly to Mrs. Alston's nice taste, and he was immediately relegated to her list of knights, Nell declaring him too orthodox for her taste, and she parted with his vassalage without a murmur. Diagonally opposite, and in the corner, was a man with his hat pulled well over his face, evidently bent on finishing his interrupted morning nap. His hands were very thin and white, and lay listlessly folded one upon the other. Every little while Agnes and Nell observed a small, red-haired, sour-visaged man enter the car, look solemnly at the sleeping figure, and then walk away, to return in a few moments and repeat the act. By and by, Nell noticed her sister's continued silence, and found that she was dozing, with the morning's journalistic salad of "battle, murder, and sudden death" in one hand and a bottle of smelling-salts in the other, which combination suggested to Nell Victor Hugo's conceit that "the mouse *plus* the cat is the revised and corrected proof of creation."

Soothed by the generally drowsy appearance of the car, Nell closed her eyes, leaned her head against the window-frame, and soon fell asleep. She awoke with a start, to find fastened upon her a pair of large, almost black, eyes, belonging to the man in the corner, who had wakened from his nap, uncovered his face, and sought amusement in studying the two oddly contrasted faces that belonged to the sleeping figures across the aisle—the older one pale, fine-featured, with a rare purity pervading it, combined with an unexpected revelation of strength in the thin, firmly closed lips; the young girl's, an irregular face with odd proportions, but full of rich coloring, from the curly auburn hair to the full, sensitive lips, that seemed to quiver and speak even as she slept. When Nell found this stranger quietly studying her face, she flushed hotly, and sat up very straight, for it takes three days' travel to level all the conventionalities of ordinary life; once down they stay so, and overland travelers luxuriate in a primitive unrestraint to which we can only imagine a parallel in the age of Cave-dwellers.

They were nearing Sacramento, and, as usual, it became oppressively warm; so Nell opened her window and looked out at the sea of waving wheat that met the horizon, and then at the brilliant carpet of orange eschscholtzia, purple iris, yellow cowslips, and blue "baby's eyes," that lay beside the car track. As Nell, her heart in her eyes, looked her farewell to California's loveliest phase, Agnes awoke; and, under cover of attending to one of her demands, Nell ventured another glance at the black-eyed stranger. He was reading, which gave her an opportunity to look fairly at him for the first time. A look of what seemed to Agnes recognition leaped into Nell's face, and made her ask, "Well, Nell, who is it?"

"Saint Bartholomew," said Nell, in a low tone of quiet conviction.

"If you are going to have one of your enthused reveries, I wish you would put your head out of the window, and let the winds have the benefit of it. I am not strong enough."

"'Lauk-a-mercy on me, this is none of I!
But if it be I, as I do hope it be——'

Then I see a ghost!" continued Nell, without removing her eyes from the stranger's unconscious face. "Agnes, do manage to turn your head so that you can see that—that man in the corner."

"Well, a fellow-creature evidently consumptive. Poor thing!" was Agnes's indifferent verdict.

"And I see the Saint Bartholomew of Raphael's earliest conception of the Last Supper, painted in the full idealism of his youth. It is exactly the dark, Hebrew skin; the full, square-cut, black beard; the large, sad, black eyes; the well cut nose and mouth; the curly, intelligent hair——"

"There, Nell, that will do. When you begin to expatiate on 'intelligent hair,' I confess an inability and disinclination to follow you further," interrupted Agnes, beginning to read her newspaper; so Nell was left to pursue her raptures alone, which culminated in a stealthily drawn sketch of Saint Bartholomew's head.

After passing through Sacramento's heat and dust, the temperature became more comfortable, and the party served their first meal amid the usual drawbacks attendant upon such an event. Rufus was feed to appear oblivious to the burning of a small alcohol lamp; the lunch baskets were brought into requisition, and cold turkey, pickled lambs' tongues, sandwiches, tea, and claret, filled the bill of fare. Elsie was treated to the usual diet for overland children—boiled condensed milk. Agnes declared an armistice and offered the young old lady, a Mrs. Reddington, a cup of tea, with a friendly smile; so the parties were bound by a subtile tie. Mrs. Reddington was an interestingly stupid woman, with a quota of practical sense that seemed almost incompatible with her remarkable immaturity. She had traveled much, but her nature was impervious to the power of assimilation. She was constantly saying trite things, with an air of delighted discovery that was perfectly irresistible to Nell's keen sense of the ridiculous. Her admiration for Agnes soon knew no bounds; in her feeling toward Nell there was an instinctive reservation that might perchance embrace an unforeseen development.

The train now wound its way through the foothills of the Sierra, covered with redwoods, madroños, bays, and pines. Higher up the mountains there are no trees but the pine, through which, in the windings of the route, can be seen grand sweeps of country stretching far into the blue distance. Hungrily the eye clings to this last glimpse of green, with a full sense that the gray desert lies ahead, which almost obliterates the sights' memory of color.

"Do you know, Miss Grey, I am very much interested in that invalid whose section is opposite mine in the car?" said Mrs. Reddington, as she and Nell sat on the steps of the platform in the waning light, breathing the fresh pine-scented air, and watching the rugged grandeur of the landscape as they flew over the mountains.

"Indeed?" absently inquired Nell, wrapped in the great joy of the wild beauty about them.

"Yes, indeed. I never saw a man so wretchedly lonely in all my life. Rufus says that he is a very wealthy invalid, traveling with his valet, that horrid, greenish colored little fellow that pops in and out of the car every second. He is dying of consumption, and as sure as we don't rouse him, he will die on our hands. I feel it."

"I'm sure I'm willing to turn myself into an itinerant circus company for his benefit, if he will only postpone his *finale*," said Nell, roused from her reverie.

"I have made up my mind to speak to him to-morrow at all risks," exclaimed Mrs. Reddington, heroically.

"Do you then fear contagion?" asked Nell, with apparent innocence, enjoying the situation, although there was present no third person to catch the reflection of the fun.

"Oh, no. The disease is not catching, my dear; remember that. My only fear was that he might not like it, he seems so frigid. Do you think it would do to offer him some of my hoarhound candy (I always carry it) when he has one of those coughing spells? It will not hurt him, and it will break the ice."

"Well, scarcely, Mrs. Reddington. I would venture to suggest that we ignore utterly the fact of his ill health. Nothing would please him more than to put him on a level with healthy animals in general. Suppose you ask him to get you a bit's worth of a necessary anything at some station. Even if the valet gets it, the effect is the same, and the *sesame* will have been spoken."

"Why, how on earth can you tell what he likes or dislikes? You never knew him, did you?" asked the old lady, looking wonderingly into Nell's face.

"No; but I have met a representative of his type, and a very few general laws serve to classify us, notwithstanding a difference of idiosyncrasy," answered Nell, mischievously.

"Oh!" lucidly remarked the old lady, a confused idea of printing machines and Congressmen running riot in her literal brain.

After a long silence, spent by Mrs. Reddington in making mental note of Nell's remark to ask an explanation of her good-natured husband at some future day, they were roused by the usual "slowing up" of the train as it neared "Cape Horn." The train seemed to totter for an instant, and then stand on the verge of an abrupt precipice two thousand feet in height; from which it is a thrilling sight to look down through the fading light, into the beautiful, river-laced *cañon* below, that seems, in the weird light, a valley of crystal-streaked malachite.

"It does not compare with the sunlight view. The effect of color is largely lost to us now, as also the grades of distance, the atmospheric effect of which is the rarest feature in your Californian views," said the courtly old gentleman, whom Nell had christened "Chesterfield," as the train wound slowly on, and the many passengers, who had come out "to see the sights," were returning to the close, dimly lighted cars.

"I suppose not, sir, but it is grand," answered Nell, resenting his iconoclastic spirit and the implied superiority.

"I can scarce refrain from a smile, when from this my mind runs back to Switzerland and the Tyrol and some effects I have witnessed there. I wish you may some day see their duplicates, mademoiselle," he continued, as, bowing impressively to the two ladies, he went in.

"I hate him, and I did the moment I saw him," cried Nell, savagely, to the startled Mrs. Reddington. "The old pedant! 'Oh, you are sick of self-love, Malvolio, and taste with a distempered appetite.'"

"Well, for my life, I can't see what excites you. I never saw a nicer old gentleman in all my travels, and so polite, too," exclaimed the astonished old lady.

"If there is any one thing I detest, it is a chronic dissatisfaction with everything present, and a systematic deluge of contrasts. 'Witness effects,' forsooth! I suppose he 'witnesses' the love and hate, joy and misery, deaths and sadder births, the world is full of, and never feels anything," wrathfully continued Nell.

"Let's go in, Miss Grey; we're sure to catch our deaths out here," interposed Mrs. Reddington, a little frightened.

"You are certainly one of Nature's enthusiasts, Mrs. Reddington," said Agnes, in her graceful way, upon their return to the car.

"Yes, indeed. I always make it a point to miss nothing in traveling, because people always ask if you saw so-and-so, and it does sound so stupid to say that you have not. As the poet says, 'Live and learn.'" And the old lady smiled brightly at the aptitude of her quotation, as she combed and braided her granddaughter's hair, preparatory to putting her to bed. "And now I must put this little chickabiddy to roost," she continued, turning the child's head around on the pivot of one stiff, little braid, to kiss her.

They were all exhausted by the first day's restraint; so Rufus made up the sections, and soon each of the two ladies and her charge disappeared behind the green and yellow curtains.

Time, courage, persistence, Rufus, and the step-ladder, at last succeeded in landing Nell in the berth above her sister, where, within ten minutes, she was converted into a mass of bruises, in her efforts to pack herself away with some degree of decency, comfort entering not into the proceedings. Just as she began to get over the first agonizing fear of suffocation, Elsie awoke and stayed awake for hours. She did not cry, but prattled, laughed, and played in the most aggravatingly charming way. At last Nell leaned down from her perch, and said, "This is nice, eh, Agnes?"

"Intrinsically cheerful, Nell."

"There is some comfort in the fact that the infant is not howling all this time; as it is, she only disturbs us," said Nell, consolingly.

"She is excited. She will rest quietly by to-morrow night. By the way, Nell, how is the question of matrimony now?"

"Below zero," whispered Nell, fiercely, "and from this date shall be subject to no more variations in my mind. Agnes, there is no use denying the fact, the human soul is not worth the trouble it takes to raise an infant."

"You are a hopeless pagan," answered Agnes, with such unusual fervency that it toppled Nell's pending arguments.

Then followed a weary interval, during which Elsie was the only one of the three who fully enjoyed the gift of life.

"Look here, Agnes; do you think we could manage to smother her without being found out?" asked Nell, leaning down behind the curtain again, trying to get a little fun out of the situation, and realizing how unalterable was Agnes's rigid rule of insisting upon sleeping with her child, however detrimental to her delicate health. It was one among the many decrees that encompassed her individuality. So passed the hours, with frequent chat between the sisters, until finally Elsie slept, and peace fell upon the weary party.

Chapter II.

"Did you note the world of snores that encompassed us last night, Agnes?" asked Nell, the next morning, after breakfast.

"No. I don't think I brought any great amount of analytic mental force to bear upon the fact, as I suppose you did," answered Agnes, with her usual quiet sarcasm, in which Nell had been acute enough long ago to detect a sufficient tinge of envy to warrant her ignoring the acerbity.

"Of course I did, and had great fun out of it, too. I counted six distinctive snores—two fat, jolly ones; a thin, irascible one; an erratic one; an expressive, conversational one; and Chesterfield's, for, let me tell you, he out-snores them all," announced Nell, with malicious triumph. "I grant it was a high-bred snore, clear and even-toned, and suggestive of gout, apoplexy, and port wine, and other aristocratic causes and effects, but it was a snore."

"I wish you would please tell Rufus and Mary to come to me," said Agnes, as if she had not heard Nell's dissertation; then, as the nurse and porter came, she continued: "Mary, take Elsie where I can neither see nor hear her until dinner time. Rufus, take those magazines to that invalid gentleman in the corner, and ask him if he would like to look over them." She raised the barrier of *Harper's Bazar* between herself and her sister's battery of questions, which, however, was soon lowered, as Saint Bartholomew approached, and, bowing with a slow grace to Mrs. Alston, said in a somewhat high-pitched, but sweet-toned voice, "I believe I am indebted to you, madam, for this thoughtfulness," indicating with a quiet gesture the books that he still held, "and I must thank you sincerely for your kindness." Bowing again, he returned to his seat.

"First class in manners, stand; and, Saint Bartholomew, go up head!" whispered Nell, with such a comical grimace that even the smileless Agnes relaxed for a second.

"I declare I'm real envious. You have roused the lion first, although Miss Grey and I plotted vigorously last evening," said Mrs. Reddington, leaning over and speaking in low tones.

"An ounce of action is worth a pound of plot, Mrs. Reddington. The man is a gentleman, lonesome and ill, and we may serve to relieve the monotony of his journey. Why should we not?"

"Yes, indeed. I agree perfectly," said the old lady, leaning back, lost in the contemplation of Mrs. Alston's vigor of mind, which seemed all the more forcible against the mysterious background of Nell's words and moods.

"Imagine what Uncle Phil has given me in the book line," cried Nell, as she opened the package given her the day before.

"*Helen's Babies* and *That Husband of Mine*," answered Agnes.

"Would it were. Listen. First, *Ossian's Poems*. Now, if there is anything as stupefying as opium, it is this unknown lunatic's poetry. Second, *Pilgrim's Progress*. As though I had not been raised on that and the bottle, right under his eye, too, until I reached the age of discretion and beefsteak! Third, *Proverbial Philosophy* by the only man who could have perpetrated the crime. Now, what could be more crisp and more cheerful for car reading? Fourth (the clerk must have prompted him), *Ethics of the Dust*. I shall ask him if suggested by our linen dusters and veils. There is not a readable thing here. Uncle is the dearest old soul I ever met, but as a literary caterer to a progressive maiden of twenty summers, he is a failure—an abject failure." And Nell ceased for want of breath.

Agnes handed her *The Lady's Journal* without a word of comment, knowing it contained matter of absolutely no interest to her fashion-hating sister. There was an element of refined cruelty in this reserved woman's complex nature, which was never recognized by her male friends, and by but few of her own sex. There was about her a lack of the coloring of gladness, that seemed, to the analytic, but part of the fascination of her picturesque dignity, but which marked a pitiful "penury of soul." She was charitable when no contact was exacted which might soil her white hands and morals. She loved her child as she had loved her husband, with a rigid, patient attention to every duty, mathematically, gracefully. She had read and thought, but considered it outside the province of a woman to lay claim to either. Nell's quick perception had probed to the limit her sister's character, and she had learned to avoid any close contact with its coldness and artificiality. A repulsion, born of the knowledge that she was understood, caused Agnes to build still higher the wall between herself and her clear-headed sister, which Nell respected perfectly, but with a touch of pity tingeing the feeling. Strangely different were these sisters, and a year's close contact had heightened the faults of both. The hours passed; the passengers slept, ate, talked, and stared in an endless routine. People were beginning to be very polite to one another, and card cliques were being formed that lasted to the journey's end.

"Nell, at the next station where we stop over three seconds, I wish you would see if the 'city' contains anything but saloons, and try to buy me a tooth-brush. I can't find mine, high or low." Such was the stagnation of Nell's mind at this period of the journey, disappointed at the failure of her mine of reading, and weary of the monotony of the desert outside, that her sister's request thrilled her soul with the possibility of an adventure.

After passing many stations that bore no evidence of the presence of a tooth-brush, the train stopped for half an hour at a settlement that looked more promising than usual. So Nell walked demurely through the groups of rough looking men lounging about the platform, and zealously avoided the knots of squatting Indians, fantastically dressed and painted, who were all engaged playing games of cards not unknown among the Western Whites. Nell found a comparatively harmless looking store, whose front was covered with a patchwork of signs, announcing that within could be found the Justice of the Peach, the Doctor, Wells, Fargo & Co.'s agent, the telegraph office, a few select groceries and drugs, and an unrivaled stock of dry goods. Peering in cautiously, to see if it was not a saloon in disguise, but seeing a notice of nothing more desperate in character than "ginger-pop," Nell entered, after a reassuring glance back at the train.

"What'll yer hev, miss?" shouted, in genial tones, the swarthy giant behind the counter, coming forward at a bound, to Nell's astonishment. It took all her courage away to determine not to flee ignominiously, and then all her reason to recollect what she wished to buy. There was only one tooth-brush in the store, telling the tale of either a very small demand or a lamentably stinted supply, and as Nell rubbed her thumb over it testily, she heard some one approach from behind and inquire of the clerk, "Have you any tooth-brushes?" Her heart gave a great bound and then stood still, as she recognized Saint Bartholomew's quiet voice. And there was only one tooth-brush!

After an instant spent by the three in silence, Nell burst into a merry laugh, and, turning, held up the brush and said, "This is the only one in town. Please take it. We can wait," with such a quizzical expression in her blushing face that the stranger broke into a hearty laugh, in which the jovial clerk joined them with such a shout that Nell's feeling of terror returned. After a little courteous demurring between the two purchasers, it ended by Nell's buying it for the sum of two dollars; for the clerk realized the capabilities of the situation, and named the price with unblushing effrontery.

"Wa'al, I'll be 'tarnally gummed if ever I see anything ez comical ez that," yelled the giant behind the counter, with another roar of laughter that Nell and her companion heard half way to the train.

"I shall give myself the pleasure of seeing you back to your party," he said, quietly.

As they reached the platform, they were surrounded by three or four Indian women, all crying, "Papoose, one bitty."

"Do they really want to sell them as cheap as that?" asked Nell, wonderingly, while a compunctious thought of Elsie flashed across her mind.

"Oh, no; but those mysterious looking humps on their backs are their papooses, strapped to boards, and covered with shawls or pieces of blanket; and for the exorbitant sum of one bit they uncover to the world's cold gaze their faces," answered Saint Bartholomew, with a smile, tossing a piece of silver to one of the squaws, who instantly slipped the board over her shoulder, and, lifting the rags, showed a very hearty little warrior, sleeping soundly. As other passengers pressed around to see the papoose, the mother quickly recovered its face, and, shaking her head with a hideous grimace, said, "No, no. No bitty, no see papoose," and shuffled off, satisfied with her day's returns.

"Cooper never could have seen Piutes, or else his powers of idealization have been grossly underrated," said Nell, with a shudder, as they entered the car.

"May I make you acquainted with my sister, Mrs. Alston?" introduced Nell, as they rejoined the party.

Taking a card from his note-book, Saint Bartholomew said, handing it to Agnes, with a smile, "In the absence of any other means, permit me."

Agnes glanced at it, and read, "Morse Winter."

"Miss Grey, my sister, Mr. Winter. Now, tell me the success of your commission, Nell," she added, with a tremor of sweetness in her voice that Nell was used to in the presence of strangers.

As the train moved on, they fell into lively conversation, in which Mrs. Reddington soon joined, and time flew quickly by until bed-time.

"There is a touch of monotony in pickles and cold turkey three times a day, Agnes," said Nell, plaintively, after breakfast the next morning.

"True; but I am not strong enough to stand the rush and scurry of station meals, nor the probability of fricasseed cockroaches; so I see no alternative," answered Agnes, beckoning to Rufus, who cleared away and "washed up" daily, for a trifling consideration administered every morning.

"What a lugubrious creature you have in the way of a valet, Mr. Winter," said Nell, as he joined her soon after, sitting opposite Agnes and Chesterfield, who were immersed in European travels.

"Yet Jeremiah is a pearl beyond price, Miss Grey; faithful, true, and tender-hearted as a woman. His doleful face is the strongest bond between us; it cheers me to look at him, because he succeeds in looking so very much more miserable than I ever feel, even at my worst; and sometimes I am very like a perambulating tombstone, too," laughing with a little bitterness that Nell hastened to drive away by leading him to tell of his home and travels. He had spent the last eight years of his life in traveling hither and thither in the hope of escaping his doom, which was hereditary, and now, in his thirty-eighth year, he had given up in despair, and was returning to his old Boston home, where his mother awaited him with a bright, sweet patience and long-abiding love that was this man's religion. Much of this and more he told Nell, who listened as women do, drawing him unconsciously on by the subtlety of her sympathy. When she told him of the resemblance she found in his face to Saint Bartholomew, he said, "Well, that's odd! Three years ago I met a musty old German professor in Berlin, who told me the same thing. I hope my end is not going to be quite so disastrous as that poor old saint's, whose only virtue was the manner of his death." Then, after a pause, he said, "I feel distinctly angry at you, Miss Grey, this minute, for making me serve up to you such an enormous dish of the *ego*."

"That remark is the only one containing the true essence of egotism, Mr. Winter," answered Nell, a trifle coldly. "Your story is a phase of life, a fragment of a grand whole, and, as such, interests me."

Instantly resenting her change of mood, he answered, "You are ungenerous; you give nothing in return. That is why I feel it."

"It never, then, struck me that it takes more generosity to listen than to tell," she answered, archly.

From personalities the two drifted off into the broad sea of generalities, and he was surprised to find in this girl, this child, as she seemed to him, a depth of thought and brilliancy of fancy that made him look to his laurels. As he bowed over her hand that night, after another of these "soul-wanderings," as she called them, she looked up into his face, and said gravely, "I must thank you for paying me the compliment of forgetting for an hour that I am a woman. Good night."

"Good night, Jane Eyre," he said.

The next morning they arose early, to be in readiness to change cars at Ogden. To Mrs. Alston's surprise, the nurse did not make her appearance to dress Elsie. After a careful hunt it was found that she had disappeared and was not to be found on the train. The conductor recollected that he thought he saw the figure of a woman leave the car at Kelton, run down the platform, and disappear into the darkness beyond. The train being in motion, he had no time for investigation, but Agnes felt convinced that the fugitive was the nurse, and she accepted the trying situation with her usual grace, but with a shade of added irony in her tone when she addressed the cheerful, sweet-natured Nell. At Ogden they telegraphed back, and received answer that no such person as the nurse had yet been seen, and her whereabout remained forever a mystery.

A last fee to Rufus transferred the party to the cars of the Union Pacific, where the fact that he went no farther on the line obtruded itself, as he bade them good-bye with true negro condescension.

The occupants of the car found themselves in exactly the same relative positions that they were in on the Central Pacific, as is generally the case.

Jeremiah became from this time Elsie's slave, to the intense amusement of everybody. For it was irresistibly comical to see the efforts of the quiet, melancholy little man to keep his mood parallel with mad-cap Elsie's, who seemed to comprehend the full possibilities of the situation.

"Mr. Winter, I think we are indebted to you for these grateful attentions on the part of Jeremiah," said Agnes, toward afternoon, as they sat playing cassino with Nell and Mrs. Reddington.

"Not in the least, Mrs. Alston, although I'd be only too glad to be of some use in these calamitous times. It was his own idea, without a word of explanation to me. I have been hugely pleased at this sudden move on the part of the old fellow. After this nothing will surprise me."

"It means something, I'm convinced," said Nell, ambiguously, with a curious smile.

"He must be very unhappy; I never have seen him laugh yet," said Mrs. Reddington, losing, as she always did, her "little cassino."

"Laugh! Why, my dear madam, I have known old Jerry fifteen years, and I never even saw him smile but twice. The first time was when his wife died and he broke his leg within two days. When I demanded the reason of his ill-timed mirth, he said, 'Because, Mr. Morse, I feel that the Lord has not forgotten me, humble worm that I am.' Poor fellow! he has a terrible chronic disease, which he inherited, and —"

"Gracious me!" interrupted Mrs. Reddington, excitedly, "and that child has been with him all the morning!"

"The disease, I grant, is contagious, but Elsie is safe; it is called Puritanism," replied Mr. Winter gravely, saving an ace with great precision.

"What was the second occasion of his smiling?" asked Nell.

"When we were on one of those disgraceful tugs in the English Channel, and Jerry was very sea-sick. Immediately after a very severe paroxysm of agony I think he smiled. I may be mistaken; but my impression is that it was a smile."

"Sea-sickness never made me smile," said Mrs. Reddington, looking with sudden curiosity at Jeremiah.

Nell played the game through; then giving up her hand to Chesterfield, she took a magazine and sat in Mr. Winter's empty section, where Elsie and her meek slave soon followed.

"Jeremiah," said Nell, suddenly, facing him as he sat on the floor playing marbles with his little tyrant, "tell me what happened to Mary. Come, be honest!"

The little man started and stared in absolute horror at Nell, and, in a slow whisper, he said, "Woe is me now! for the Lord hath added grief to my sorrow. Oh, please, miss, if you knew the tribulation of my soul since this mornin' ——"

"There, that will do; don't preach. Tell me all about it."

"It was in this wise, miss," he continued, still staring in wonder at Nell: "firstly, I found in brotherly talk with this Mary that she was a human soul led astray by the Romish Church into the paths of ——"

"Please skip that part, Jeremiah, and go on with your secondly," said Nell, controlling her rising laughter.

Too accustomed to such a reception of his dissertations to be much disturbed, he continued:

"Well, you see, Miss Grey, I sought to bring a little of the light of true righteousness into the night of her gropin' soul, and exhorted with her considerable; and last evening, to better show to her the awful sinfulness of her ways, I took to tellin' her of the suddentness of death and of what might happen any minute to her, considerin' the ways of enjines, and Indians infesterin' the plains, and buffaloes and wolves, and Devil's Gates and Slides ahead; and I'm sorrier than I can tell, miss, but I think this last dun it. Consarn her superstitions!" cried he, made human by his intense self-reproach.

After setting his mind at ease, Nell dismissed him, and then gave vent to her laughter, to the surprise of the absorbed card-players. She called Mr. Winter, and, amidst little ripples of laughter, that ran before and after and over her sentences, she managed to tell the tale of the lost Mary. Jeremiah's morbid anxiety to compensate in some measure for the ill effects of his missionary work was so humble that he was forgiven by all concerned, although Nell vowed that the scenery was a blank to her for two days, and her thoughts could not soar above the responsibility of the condensed milk and alcohol lamps.

One morning, after an unusually severe effort to amuse Elsie with a handkerchief tied into manly shape and baptized "Romeo" (although a prejudice of color changed it to "Othello" toward the journey's end), and a worsted doll termed "Juliet," and just as Nell was rendering with great truth and delicacy the "balcony scene," Elsie broke into a long, persistent wail, that bespoke such an utter lack of proper interest in the matter in hand that Nell calmly opened the window near her, and pretended to toss out the weeping child, with such a look of desperation that Mrs. Reddington sprang to her feet, seized Nell's arm, and said, trembling with excitement, "What on earth are you going to do, Miss Grey?"

"I purpose putting this—this—thing out of the window, to grow, 'like a wayside flower on the highways of usefulness,' as Tupper says happiness does," Nell answered, with a calm fiendishness that sent Mr. Winter out of the car with a shout of laughter.

"Are you mad to act so?" continued the righteously aroused old lady.

"I think you have diagnosed the malady; I was mad, but your words have brought me to my senses, and I'll bear with this 'death in life' a little longer," Nell answered penitently, ignoring her sister's frowning disapprobation, and reveling in the fact of Mrs. Reddington's obtuseness. From that hour she eyed Nell with suspicion, and never allowed her granddaughter to be alone with her if she could help it, for the child was blind to Nell's idiosyncrasies and worshiped the sprightly young lady, much as she did a marionette show. Winter returned in a short time, followed by a sturdy, rosy-cheeked young girl, whom he introduced as Polly, who was traveling with her mother, second class, and who would take charge of Elsie. Nell sank back, after placing the child in Polly's strong arms, and looking up into Winter's face, said, "I can't thank you all in one day for your thoughtfulness, but I will dedicate certain hours of my after life to singing a daily *Benedictus* composed in commemoration of this event."

"Give me all the time otherwise wasted on poor Elsie, and I'll call it quits," he answered, taking his seat beside her.

"Done!" cried Nell, "and now I am going to beat you twenty straight games of euchre. Get your pack, please; Elsie chewed up our jack of hearts." They chaffed each other mercilessly during the usual incessant round of card-playing that forms nine-tenths of the existence of overland travelers. He caricatured, with a skilled hand, their fellow-passengers, to which Nell added doggerels, he playing the Scotch reviewer with a severity that ended in many a long drawn battle. Often they fell into serious mood, and followed the will o' the wisp of the mind whithersoever it might lead. Nell began to feel that she had a strange influence over the world-worn man. Between the intervals when they were together he sat looking from his window at the great lonely waste stretching to the horizon on every side, with his face sunk into an expression of utter weariness that made plain the ravages of the disease that was sapping his life away. Then turning his head a little, he would watch Nell a few minutes, and, rising, would go to her side, and slowly and imperceptibly a great goodly warmth came into his face and manner, and he was young and strong again.

Mrs. Alston was one of those women who think that a man—a lover, if possible—is one of the essentials to the proper surroundings of a young lady, and the greatest pleasure of her life was the fostering of a match. Once in her life she had striven to further the suit of a man who loved and courted Nell, whose clear eyes detected her sister's furtherance, and the few decisive words she thereupon spoke decided Agnes never again to disturb her own peace by any further active interference in Nell's affairs of the heart. Agnes's instinct quickly caught the charm that bound Winter to her bright, sunny-natured, and healthy-minded young sister, and recognizing the probability of at least a flirtation, she accepted the situation with well controlled interest. So Agnes frequently withdrew to Mrs. Reddington's section, where she and that good lady were eloquently entertained by Chesterfield, who held forth on the scenery, consulting his guide-book every few minutes, for he was that greatest of bores, a statistical traveler.

Slowly the train swept over the weird, dreary plains, that seem not of the world nor for it—a great anomaly, ghost-like in its wide separation from all precedent. As they neared the summit of the Rocky Mountains it grew very cold, which is the sole indication of the long, wonderfully gradual climb.

On the morning of the fourth day, as Nell climbed down from her perch, she was surprised to find that Winter's section was still shrouded in its curtains. He was generally up and dressed by daylight, being unable to breathe easily in the narrow berth. As noon approached, and still he did not appear, Nell waylaid Jeremiah and asked the cause.

"He's had one of his bad spells, miss. He says it's the scarcity of the air, or somethin' like that, up on these mountains, and he has been havin' a terrible time all night. If he has a hemmyrage it will go hard with him, poor boy! The doctor, in the next car, came in, and told him to lay quiet until this evening, when we are over the highest part."

This news soon spread through the car, and a hush fell upon its inmates. During the afternoon Jeremiah brought a note to Nell, who tore it open quickly, almost anticipating a last will and testament, but found this:

"MY DEAREST FOE:—Do you all intend to drive me slowly mad by this hideous silence? If I do not hear that ringing laugh of yours within ten minutes, I'll get up, and the doctor, Jerry, and the consequences can take care of themselves. I now give you an order for three complimentary epitaphs, from which I'll choose one, and file it for either immediate or future use. Would you care if it proved the former?

"MORSE WINTER."

Nell could read interlined all the man's acceptance of possible danger, founded upon an indifference that chilled her strangely, while the flippancy of his last question jarred upon her somewhat tragic mood. After a moment of rigid self-inspection, she threw off the result of it by writing the epitaphs, to the undisguised horror of Mrs. Reddington. Nell assured her that it was a well known stimulant, and the effect upon the dying was wonderfully bracing. The old lady sank back in utter despair at Nell's heartless depravity, which scene the latter shortly described beneath her specimen epitaphs, and soon she had the pleasure of hearing a smothered laugh come from the curtained section.

At Cheyenne, where the train stops thirty minutes, Jeremiah brought word that his master felt better; so Nell, with an abrupt change of mood, seized Mrs. Reddington's little girl, and jumped from the platform into the great drifts of snow that surrounded the train, and had a game of snow-balling, which was a novelty to the two California-born girls. They returned to the car wild with fun and mischief, and with their hands full of snow-balls, which were ignominiously ordered out of the windows by their orderly elders. All that afternoon and night they were on the down grade, as imperceptibly gradual as is the long climb to the summit.

The following morning Winter made his appearance, with signs of his recent suffering written in his unnaturally luminous eyes, and the bright spots burning on his wan cheeks. Nell looked over, and nodded with a smile her greeting, and in a moment he was with her.

"You shall not skip around in this way, Mr. Winter. Let us go to you, please," said Nell, instinctively avoiding meeting his eyes.

"What made you lasso me with that smile of yours, and drag me over, then, mademoiselle? Answer me that," he said, with an odd ring of excitement in his usually quiet voice.

All the morning Nell found it hard to keep the conversation on safe grounds, for there was in his every act and word a subtle purpose that her intuition met half way, and challenged by her cool self-possession. After lunch, as the weather was cool and sunshiny, Nell escaped with Elsie to the back platform, where, theirs being the last car, they were undisturbed. In a short time they were joined by Winter, to Nell's discomfiture.

"You know you ought not sit out here, after your illness of yesterday," she said, peremptorily, as he quietly seated himself beside her on the steps.

"Why, pray? The sun shines out here now, and the car seems so dreary." Then, seeing a shade of scorn flit over her expressive face, he hastened to add lightly, "Fresh air at this altitude will not hurt me, Miss Grey; it does me good."

"Then, if you will stay, I instate you as my agent in the present exhibition; for at every station the settlers' children flock around us in wonder, thinking Elsie and I are a superior style of papoose and mother, done up in this scarlet shawl. Now, my idea is to enrich the the family coffers by exhibiting her at the usual rates. Does my agent think it feasible, not to mention honorable?"

"I recognize no earthly honor but that of being near you," he said, with stubborn purpose.

After a pause, Nell, bent on punishing him, dreamily murmured, "My whole soul is translated into a longing to see face to face my ideal—ideal——"

"What, Miss Grey?" he asked, earnestly.

"Buffalo, Mr. Winter. I have suffered all the ills that alkali plains and prairie lands are heir to, and have not yet seen a coyote or a buffalo. My geographies led me to believe from infancy that they abounded here."

"Buffaloes are not often seen from the trains these days, but still we may see a herd before we get to Omaha," he answered, coldly; then after a moment's pause he turned to her abruptly, and said, almost fiercely, "I do not understand you, Miss Grey."

"Then I will explain myself, Mr. Winter," said she, thoroughly aroused, and looking him fully and coldly in the face. "I have recognized the change in your manner since yesterday, and can only say I regret it very deeply. Threadbare sentimentalities I have no tolerance for, and I plainly foresaw your drift. Life is too real to me to treat any phase of it frivolously. I am willing to run over with you the whole philosophy of sentiment, from Plato to Gail Hamilton; but any further session of conventional nonsense, I veto."

"I willingly grant you a large amount of perception, but there are some things veiled from even your clear sight," he said, gravely.

"Not in the least," she exclaimed. "In plain English, you intended to amuse yourself by changing our honest friendship into a modern, comfortable, noncommittal flirtation, and—and I'm disappointed." And she ended weakly, with a tremor in her voice, and an uncomfortable consciousness that she had not always exacted this transcendental truthfulness from every man she met. They faced each other for one short moment, her face flushed and quivering with excitement, and his filled with wondering admiration and a twinkle of intense satisfaction at her odd impetuosity; seeing which she bit her lips and felt generally absurd and miserable, although something within her made her feel a vague and undefined sense of justification.

"My little friend," he presently said, very gravely, "I thank you for your earnestness, but I owe it to myself to say that you wrong me, at least in the spirit of my actions, even if the letter was unworthy of you. I am a very simple sort of man. I really have no notion of what women like or dislike. I act only at the dictation of my feelings. I never felt this way before, and hence I never acted so before. It is all new to me; I'm sorry I made a mistake. But," after a pause, "do you think you can trust me now?"

"Certainly. I shall be glad to meet you on the old ground during the rest of our journey," said Nell, feeling that her ready phrases were no match for this man's quiet simplicity, and that her fears had outrun her judgment. "And now I must go in, as Elsie has gone to sleep, and I'm afraid she will take cold," continued Nell, preparing to rise.

"One minute, Miss Grey. May I suggest to you that these shabby words and acts of to-day are not fair representatives of what is behind it all—a power that has courage to try some day for a victory?"

It was the man's turn now to flush, and she was very still and held her colors well. Then both arose, and the movement broke the charm, and, in a voice harsh with a sudden bitter self-scorn, he cried, "A fool, an arrant fool, to stand and talk to you of victory with one foot in my grave!" adding, in a voice full of tenderness, "I keep forgetting it somehow, child; since I met you I feel that life must be meted out to me as it is to other men. Run in now, little girl. You are sure we are friends?"

"Sure," she answered, very quietly.

He stooped and kissed the sleeping child in Nell's arms, and then she went in.

ANNA ALEXANDER.

HOW DR. WHITMAN SAVED OREGON.

The name of Dr. Marcus Whitman is not found in the *American Cyclopædia*, strange to say, and yet it is one that should be inscribed upon the roll of the nation's patriots. It has made its mark in history, and saved the United States a rich empire on the North Pacific that was on the verge of being lost to us from want of knowledge and interest on the part of those in authority at Washington. Only for his patriotic efforts and personal sacrifices, the Ashburton treaty would most likely have disposed of the great region of the Columbia as of trifling importance, and, knowing his services and recognizing his patriotic devotion, his name will be ever held in tender regard by the people and States of the great Columbian valley.

I remember well, a third of a century ago, reading of the "Whitman massacre," not thinking that shortly after my own life would be located on the far western shore, and the history of Whitman be a household word with me and mine. But so it is; and while my pen often indites sketches of the history of the Western Coast, there is no theme it can find more interesting than to trace the causes of early settlement, and the careers of those adventurous souls who were first in threading the pathless wilds of the middle continent, and were sometimes martyrs to both faith and patriotism. The romance of history lies in these opening chapters that offer views of the future, where man and nature are in wildness, and civilization itself comes in half savage garb to conquer barbarism.

It may be interesting to cultured minds to look back through almost half a century, and see what changes time and man have wrought on the North Pacific—to glance down the vistas, from the era of savagery to the present time, and study the romance of history, as well as the grand results of civilization. There is no romance to compare with the adventures, and often with the sorrows, of those who have led the march of empire westward, and that it flowed hither as it did in 1843 was due chiefly to Dr. Marcus Whitman; and thenceforward it has swept, as in a resistless tide, that to-day makes the Columbian region great in its present and imperial in the promise of its future.

Half a century ago this vast region was in its aboriginal condition, occupied by native tribes and undisturbed by the hand of man, except that the Hudson's Bay Company had its stations and its hunters, agents, and trappers everywhere, doing their best to make money out of traffic with the natives, and carefully avoiding interference with their life and habits. Their spring brigade from Red River worked its way across the mountains, to come sailing down the Columbia in fleets of *bateaux* manned by Canadian *voyageurs*, whose advent was accompanied by semi-barbaric features, and constituted the grand event of the year. Once or twice a year, some trading vessel belonging to the Company came around the world by way of the Sandwich Islands, entered the Columbia, and battled its way against the currents to Vancouver.

About this time some Indians of the Flathead tribe, whose home was on the headwaters of the Columbia (in north-western Montana, whence it makes a grand circuit northward and westward to avoid the Bitter Root Mountains, bending southward in a wide detour to reach the confluence with Snake River), heard from some wandering trapper and hunter a story of the Christian's belief in God, and, impelled by their desire for information, four of the tribe made their way, in 1832, eastward to St. Louis. There they met Catlin, the celebrated naturalist and artist, and through him the religious world was made aware of the spiritual famine of the far western tribes, and it resulted in sending missions to Oregon by both the Methodist and Presbyterian Churches.

The American Board organized an expedition in 1835 to prospect Oregon, and locate a mission, if desirable. Of this expedition was Dr. Marcus Whitman, a physician, described as a person of easy-going ways, somewhat uncertain in forming opinions, but steadfast in them when formed—bold in carrying out his plans when matured, either in business of the mission or in his medical practice, and in the latter generally successful. He and Rev. Mr. Parker made their way, on this errand, to the great American rendezvous, on Green River, this side of the Rocky Mountains. There they met with a party of Nez Perces, who offered to pilot them to the Columbia River. They then manifested the friendliness that has always characterized the majority of the tribe, and offered inducements for the establishment of a mission among them. This resulted in Mr. Parker going on to survey the land and look for a suitable location, while Dr. Whitman retraced his steps to make favorable report to the Home Board.

In 1836, Dr. Marcus Whitman and Rev. H. H. Spaulding, and their wives, made an adventurous journey across the continent with wagons as far as Boise, reaching the Columbia, and receiving assistance from the Indians to build a station on the Walla Walla River, where Dr. Whitman settled as missionary to the Cayuses and Umatillas, while Mr. Spaulding went eastward to make his home with the Nez Perces. The missionaries and their wives went at first down the Columbia, and were handsomely received and entertained by Dr. McLoughlin, Chief Factor of the Hudson's Bay Company, who, considering the circumstances and the jealously felt concerning American influence, was liberal in offering hospitality and supplies.

W. H. Gray came with the company as financial agent, and has written a history of Oregon that is valuable, as it contains many important details, and I rely much on it for facts and dates. In his book he gives a charmingly wild and picturesque view of the great American rendezvous at Green River, and, as this aims to be a panoramic sketch, we must not overlook this vision, characteristic of the plains at that early time.

The missionaries traveled with a caravan, and word had gone on ahead concerning them; and two days before they reached the rendezvous they were met by a party of Indians and White Men, who rode out to give them greeting, and a wild, barbaric greeting it was, savage yells and a fusillade that sent rifle bullets screaming above their heads, and a charge into camp that would have terrified them, only some of the party understood and explained the rude etiquette of the desert to the rest.

That night they camped on the summit of the continent, Mr. Gray says, a high land about thirty miles south of Wind River Mountain, from which vicinity waters flow by the channels of the Columbia, Colorado, Missouri, and Saskatchawan to the four quarters of the continent. That is alone a picture that stamps itself upon the memory with great force and vividness.

Crossing the mountains, they wended their way down the *cañons* to the beautiful valley of Green River, where Bridger's trading fort was long located, a charming oasis set in this wilderness of desert plains and inhospitable ranges, verdant and blooming, and just then alive with the presence of fifteen hundred Indians, traders, trappers, and representatives of every kind of civilization. It happened that the nomadic tribes were just then at peace, and they had met here as the neutral ground of that wide, wild region. Here were log huts or houses for traders, there rude shelters for hunters, there were tents of travelers, like our missionaries and their wives, and hither had also wandered an English baronet, who found it convenient to absent himself from civilization and its attendant extravagance while his estate was being nursed back to a paying basis. Here were hunters, trappers, and traders, with their Indian wives; men who had strayed off from civilization, and were astonished to be brought face to face, so many thousand miles from home, with men and women of culture, who were carrying the older civilization across the continent. Here were the camps, store, and equipments of the American Fur Company, and beyond them, for six miles up the stream, were the camp-fires and lodges of Hannacks, Nez Perces, and Flatheads, the homes of the last named a month's journey to the northward. Everything indicated that it was an armed truce; every tribe and company maintained strict guard, and was prepared at any moment to arm in self-defense. The different tribes united to give the strangers a view of savage display by turning out in all their paint and feathers, armed with all sorts of weapons, and ornamented with every kind of barbarous finery, mounted on their horses, marching in procession five hundred strong, and indulging in the whoops and yells that suited the wilderness. Such was the wild scene our travelers came upon as they journeyed toward the setting sun, and we may believe that they wondered to find themselves so far from all their kind, and so removed from all culture and social arts.

But we must pass over in haste the final settlement of the missionaries, the jealousy of the Catholic priesthood, the generous conduct of Governor Ogden and Dr. McLoughlin, of the Hudson's Bay Company—the latter of whom especially deserves well of all Americans, for the kindness shown the early comers; that, too, when reproached by the Company for favors shown them, and held responsible therefor. We have to do with a period six years later, during which time the missions appeared to do much good, and conferred great benefit on the Indians.

It was in the fall of 1842 that rumors reached Whitman that the Columbia River region was about to be abandoned to Great Britain. Such was the boast of the Catholic priests, and such the cautious acknowledgment of the officers of the Hudson's Bay Company, and such was the actual fact. Whitman was at his mission of Wailatpu, near the present site of Walla Walla. He held in high esteem the country we now occupy, though he had no adequate conception of its worth; he did not know the value of the land around him, where to-day the waving wheat fields and exuberant crops speak of the richest fertility; but he knew that this wide domain was priceless in its value to coming generations. All the patriotism in his nature was stirred at the thought that the ignorance of the Government might lead to its abandonment, and he and others find themselves residents on foreign soil. It was winter, but men of his class care nothing for seasons; snow covered the middle continent, but he was determined to save the Pacific north-west to his country, and therefore adventured this midwinter journey across a frozen world, daring all that Nature could do to bar the way, desperate in his determination that the Oregon should flow toward the sea only past shores protected by his country's flag. That was the ruling motive, and the man who planned and executed this expedition, and clutched this grand region, by so doing, from the grasp of Britain, deserves an honorable name in that connection as long as his country has a history.

Dr. Whitman's companion on this terrible winter journey was General A. L. Lovejoy, one of the oldest residents of Oregon, who furnishes Mr. Gray an account of this memorable journey. He says: "I often had conversations with the doctor, touching the prospects of this coast. He was alive to its interests, and manifested a warm desire to have this country properly represented at Washington, and, after some arrangements, we left Wailatpu October 3, 1842 overland for the Eastern States. We reached Fort Hall in eleven days, made some purchases, took a guide, and left for Fort Wintee, changing from a direct route to one more southern, through the Spanish country, *via* Taos and Santa Fé." On their way to Wintee they met terribly severe weather, and heavy snows retarded progress. Thence they proceeded to the waters of Grand River, in Spanish territory, procured supplies, and took a guide for Taos, New Mexico, and, vainly baffling with terrific snow storms on table lands, found refuge in a deep ravine. After vain efforts to proceed, Whitman returned, and procured a better guide, who knew the country, when they fought their way, at a snail's pace, to Grand River. This stream was frozen on each side, had a rapid current, and was crossed by leading their animals to the brink of the ice, pushing them into the stream, and leaping in after them. Battling across to the farther side, they scrambled upon the ice, dragging the animals out as they could; after which perilous feat their frozen garments and half frozen limbs were thawed and warmed by a comfortable fire. It was thus they worked their way southward and eastward through New Mexico, to the headwaters of the Arkansas River, at Bent's Fort, where they arrived in January, 1843. Great physical strength and iron constitutions carried them through it all.

Tyler was President and Webster was Secretary of State. The Ashburton treaty was in progress, and not much interest was felt in the north-western boundary. Little was known of that distant region, and from English sources the assurances were positively made that the country was comparatively worthless, more valuable for hunting and trapping than for all civilized uses. This was the condition of affairs when Whitman reached the capital. It was all but conceded that privileges on the north-east coast, in respect to fisheries, should offset the surrender of the Columbia River region to Great Britain. Governor Simpson, of the Hudson's Bay Company, had reached Washington, had interviewed Webster, and managed to leave this impression on his mind. There was no living man to plead for Oregon and tell the truth fearlessly, until, "in the dead of winter, an awkward, tall, spare-visaged, vigorous, offhand sort of a man appeared at the Department in his mountain traveling garb, consisting of a dark-colored blanket coat and buckskin pants, showing that to keep himself from freezing he had been compelled to lie down close to his camp-fire while in the mountains, and on his way to Washington he had not stopped for a moment, but pushed on with a vigor and energy peculiarly his own." This man had been tauntingly told that *it was impossible for his Government to be informed so as to prevent the surrender of Oregon*, but he had surmounted impossibilities and was there in person to make known the facts.

Entirely unmindful of his rude garb and weather-beaten looks, Whitman sought an interview with the Secretary of State, gave his object, and stated the plans and purposes of the British Government. He had hardly made his object known when Webster interrupted him: "But, doctor, you are too late; we have just about traded Oregon off for a cod fishery." His first interview failed to make any strong impression. Webster had made up his mind that there was actual value in the fisheries, while he knew nothing about the Columbia River region, and at best there never had been any benefit apparent from the claim to ownership. But Whitman had not crossed a continent through winter snow and ice to be balked in a single interview. He sought the presence of the President, and, wild man as he appeared, dressed in blanket coat and skins, he interested John Tyler in his cause, and procured a hearing for himself and for Oregon. It is true that John Tyler is considered the least among the Presidents, and his name is not fragrant with great and good deeds, but we owe him this much consideration—to recognize that only for his influence the Ashburton treaty would have gone as already planned, and the national domain have lost the great wealth and glory of the galaxy of States to be formed from the Pacific north-west.

Only for the perils encountered by Dr. Marcus Whitman the result would have been entirely different; the British flag would still wave over Fort Vancouver, and over many a broad league of land besides that now shelters under the American flag. We do not need to particularise his efforts to win this great success; but he did win, and we reap the benefits as a nation to-day. After his cause was won he presented himself to the American Board, to be censured for leaving his station and causing such expense; but, since then, the successors in that Board claim the glory of his act and sanction the deed. He sold his little property and went westward, preaching on the frontiers the nature of the far distant west, and enlisting about eight hundred and fifty sturdy frontiersmen and their families to accept his pilotage across the continent of wildernesses, to make homes on the western shore. That was the commencement of emigration in force to Oregon. Thousands followed where they led, and Dr. Whitman perhaps at last fell a victim to his patriotism, for a later emigration carried disease into the country, that spread among the Indians, and so poisoned their minds that, with their native superstition, they one day massacred his family, to find that they had thus destroyed their brightest hopes and murdered their steadfast friend. This happened after eleven years of devotion to his work and their interests, and to-day we hear occasionally that among early pioneers contribution is being made to raise to his memory a monument on the spot where he lived, labored, and died. It grows so slowly that we may doubt if it will ever suffice to record the acts that grace his memory.

Over the region where Whitman wandered, searching for a fertile location, and half doubtful if any spot would answer, stretch the most fruitful grain fields of the continent. Every acre of upland and bottom is fertile, and railroads are pushing their way there to relieve the toiling river steamers of work they cannot do. The years have been revealing the resources of this grand region slowly and reluctantly, but they have not fully done their work of revelation yet, for the ranges that look down on Walla Walla blossom with precious ores, the hills near by are lined with coal deposits, and, far and near, the valleys and the uplands invite coming population and offer untold wealth. The herder retires before the agriculturist; but flocks upon a thousand hills respond to the labor of the farmer, to yield millions. The work of development has just commenced. It is to be regretted that Dr. Whitman could not have lived to see this day, and receive from a grateful country the plaudits he so well earned as a patriotic American. It is mournful to remember his fate; but it is better to have so labored and accomplished, even if to meet so terrible a death, than to have expended a lifetime among the world's older civilization, toiling in monotonous ways of peace and profit, without having done any deed to rival the heroes of all time, or left any remembrance of great endeavor.

Mr. Gray, who was with Whitman in 1836, tells how they surmounted every obstacle, and stood at last upon the western acclivity of the Blue Mountains. There they overlooked the great region of the Columbia, spread beneath and before them, and took in the grand *coup d'œil* of hills and uplands, valleys and distant mountains, including the *sierras* of the Cascade Range, that were lifted in the west, crowned with panoplied snows of Hood, Adams, Saint Helen's, and Rainier—an unsurpassed and glorious view; but the pioneer missionary of 1836 could not dream that the settler of 1880 would find all modern conveniences and civilized usages at command, and possess the means, by telegraph, to communicate with the uttermost parts of the earth. S. A. CLARKE.

A LEGEND OF COAHUILA.

I.

Over the mountain the moonbeams peep
At the stilly lake below;
Into the shadows they softly creep,
And gleam where the ripples flow.
The winds are hushed, and the woods are still
And weird in the mellow glow;
"O Night!" I cry, and a whispered sigh
Steals back from the peaks of snow.

High on a bank, where rocky steeps
Fling shadows out to meet the spray,
A woman sat, with eyelids drooped
And heart-strings trembling timidly.
Anon her eye, with wistful glance,
Stole out along the lake's expanse;
Or, startled by the restless flow
Of cave-pent surges deep below,
She listening bent, and, waiting there,
The stars grew pale and seemed less fair.
The while she watched, along the shore—
Full sweet, a song she knew—
The music of a dipping oar
Broke faint, and nearer drew;
And leaning, timid, from the cliff,
The maiden watched a fragile skiff,
Which onward through the shadows sped.
"'Tis Pedro's oar," she softly said,
And downward through the leafy cover
Sprang eagerly to meet her lover.
No sooner leaping to the shore—
The youth had dropped his gleaming oar—
Than, stealthy, from the shaded bank
O'ergrown with vines and creepers rank,
A savage figure glided out;
And ere the youth could turn about
Another and another sprang,

Like crouching tigers, from the brake,
And out along the stilly lake
The cruel Indian war-cry rang.
A moment, deftly, blow for blow,
With sinewy arm and corded frown
The gallant boatman faced his foe
And beat their murderous weapons down.
Now in the foam, now out again,
Now struggling on the sandy plain,
Decided ere it yet began,
The fierce unequal contest ran.
Meanwhile, above, in wild dismay,
The startled maiden trembling stood,
As sudden through the silent wood
Outrang the clamors of the fray;
And near her in the moonbeam's ray,
His face all dark, his eyes aglow,
A stranger watched the scene below.
Unmoved alike by cry or call,
He stood before her, stern and tall,
And silent gazed upon the tide.
"Oh, save him, save him!" faint she cried.
But mute and fierce, like one who hears
A demon's whisper in his ears,
He paused, and, turning, seized her hand:
"Dost promise this: my bride to be
If I shall rescue from the strand
This hapless youth who comes to thee?"
A tremor, born of anguish, stole
Its icy current to her soul
As faint she spake: "I promise all—
But hasten, hasten, ere he fall."
With one quick bound he cleared the stone,
And darting downward through the zone
Of circling shadows, rock, and branch,
He fell as falls an avalanche
Upon the startled savage foe.
In death already one lay low;
But faintly now and hotly pressed,
The life-blood gushing from his breast,
A moment more, and Pedro's brand
Had fallen from his stiffening hand.
Two wily figures fierce beset
The dauntless boatman struggling yet,
When Felix sprang with giant stride
Across the sand-cove to his side.
So close they fought, nor friend nor foe
His presence marked till one deft blow
Along the glittering strand laid low
The foremost warrior of the twain;
And, leaping quick, he struck again,
But lithe beneath his whistling blade
The savage darted to the shade
Of drooping branches, still and weird,
And in the darkness disappeared.
Thus, like a whirlwind on the shore,
The combat rang, and all was o'er.
But low beneath the broken moon,
The yellow sands were rent and strewn

With stilly things; and, bended fair
Above one prostrate figure there,
  A woman knelt, whose piteous cry
Went out upon the still night air:
  "Speak, Pedro, speak! Thy Lola's nigh."
And, pleading thus, she could not hear
The voice of him who, bending near,
  Spake tenderly: "He will not die."

II.

'Tis twilight hour, and softly now
  The day-god hides his ray;
His finger tips the mountain's brow,
  And low, and far away,
The yellow mists of summer-tide
  Are shifting into gray.
Along the plain the shadows creep,
  And sweet, and everywhere,
A hundred voices mellow deep
  The twinkling twilight air.

Hard by her father's open door,
Where vines and blossoms, clambering o'er,
Formed many a bower and cool retreat,
A lover mused at Lola's feet.
"How sweet to be," he softly said,
"At thy dear side when day is done!
The world's a song, my peerless one;
'Tis all a song when thou art near.
But how—Sweetheart, what means the tear
A-glitter where thy lashes play?
Why turn thy beauteous head away?"
While thus he spoke a far refrain
Of hoof-beats echoed o'er the plain.
Now faint and soft, now loud and clear,
They reached the maiden's startled ear;
And ere her lover's eye could read
  The sudden pallor on her face,
A gallant rider reined his steed
  Before the leaf-strewn hiding place,
And, quick dismounting, crossed the wood,
And 'neath the vine-clad trellis stood.
Upspringing quick, a glad light shone
On Pedro's cheek, as in his own
The stranger's hand he warmly grasped.
"A brother's hand by thine is clasped,"
He grateful said, and turning back
Along the arbor's winding track,
He led the youth to where the maid
Sat silent in the deepening shade.
With piteous eye and rigid face
The maiden paused a moment's space,
Like one bewildered—where to go;
And then more calmly, rising slow,
She cast herself—unheard his call—
At Pedro's feet, and told him all.
Quick turning on the silent youth,
He fierce began: "And this, forsooth,

Thy friendship is! Didst think that I
At such a price my life would buy?
That craven I would still live on
With love and hope and honor gone?"
Like one whose lips their speech deny
He sudden stopped; and, mounting high
O'er pallid cheek and fixèd eye,
His passion burned—a rigid stain;
But, ere it broke in words again,
With gentle touch a hand was lain
Upon his arm, and Felix spake:
"Think not I come thy wrath to wake.
When low that night upon the shore
I saw thy loved one bending o'er
Thy wounded form, and to thine ear
Speak wild, sweet words thou couldst not hear,
E'en then a pang my bosom knew
That I should wrong a love so true.
She is thy bride—her hand is free.
Thy heart shall judge 'twixt thee and me."
He bent a moment, still and pale,
Above the mossy trellis rail,
Where white a little hand was pressed;
And, raising softly to his breast
The fragile thing, turned quick away
Amid the shadows' gathering gray;
And lo! as down the valley's track,
The beat of hoofs came floating back,
The stars crept out, and, weird and shrill,
A night-bird whistled from the hill.

D. S. RICHARDSON.

FEMALE BOHEMIAN LIFE IN BOSTON.

M—— and myself are Bohemians. Now, don't let that last word bring up to your mind visions of handsome, careless youth with marvelous mustaches, innumerable unpaid debts, and shiny broadcloth; youngsters whose curling locks smell of tobacco smoke, who live like kings one day, and like beggars the next; because, if you do make up your mind to that sort of thing, you will have to undo it again, for M—— and I are women. We live in a womens Bohemia, which, though it knows not the delights of strong pipes, strong cheese, and strong drinks, nor yet of an occasional High Jinks, is still enjoyable. We are not sisters, nor yet cousins; in fact, we never saw each other till we met in the train as we were speeding toward Boston. That mysterious something which makes women was so confidential on a railway train made each of us confess to the other why we were on the way to the "hub of the universe." It seems we both were tired of living in the small country town we had always known, that both came to Boston to be rid of the everlasting "muck-rakers" of the village, that each wanted to be somewhere out of the sight and sound of gossip, of green worsted tidies and neighbor Jones's rheumatics, and so each had sought to drown herself, mentally, in the great city of Boston.

Neither of us knew exactly where she was going, and so we both went together, and together we have stayed ever since. We soon found comfortable quarters in a pleasant street—comfortable, not elegant, nor even pretty. We are up four flights of stairs in a respectable but obscure lodging house, whose good tempered landlady we have cajoled into letting us keep house on her fifth floor. Our "castle in the air" consists of three rooms, rented for a very low price (for neither M—— nor I is possessed of much of this world's goods), a parlor, bedroom, and a kitchen. The parlor has yellow paper on the walls, and the carpet is green and red; but the sun shines brightly in at the dormer windows, which are adorned with white curtains, an ivy, and a bird. M——'s sketches and studies hang on the walls, while my piano with its well-worn music fills one side of the room. M——'s easel stands in one window, and opposite my piano is our bookcase, a model of elegance. It is a dry-goods box, with three shelves, painted in imitation of lacquer-work, and a curtain of our joint handiwork hangs over it, to keep our precious books from dust and harm. On it are plaster casts of Mercury and the Venus of Milo, and some fancy Japanese fans. A cheap cotton flannel curtain hangs in the doorway between this homely little room and our bed-room, and across the hall is our kitchen—into whose mysteries you are not to be initiated. You must be satisfied when I tell you that M—— and I take turns at the cook-stove. One week I lie in bed in luxurious ease till the odor of coffee bids me arise; and the next, I rise early, build the fire and cook breakfast like a veritable "Biddy," and when it is ready I enter the parlor where M—— awaits me, and, with a low bow, I say, "Breakfast is served, miss," as though I had never done anything else all my life long. We both wash the dishes, make beds, etc., and then start off to market. We find the stairs a great nuisance—for there is no elevator or dumb waiter in the house. To avoid making any unnecessary trips from the cellar to our attic, we have rigged a bell, whose handle is a string, which hangs outside the house and ends in the back yard; whenever the butcher or baker or candlestick maker wishes to leave anything for us, he rings the bell, and we lower a basket from the back window to receive the article. The first time we tried the experiment, M—— piously exclaimed, with folded hands and upturned eyes, "Truly, laziness, not necessity, is the mother of invention."

M—— goes every day, for three or four hours, to paint at the Art School, while I spend that time in practicing my singing lesson—for we both belong to that class of women, who, to use the sarcastic words of a "down east" friend, are "*pursuin' somethin'*." Our evenings we spend together. Sometimes we go to the theater; for, in Boston, wherever it is proper for women to go at all, they can go unattended by gentlemen. We occupy cheap seats, and enjoy the performance quite as well as if we sat in a box and had some elegant young man, in swallow-tail and glasses, to talk to us during the fine parts of the play, and leave us for a drink in the intermissions. Sometimes I go to a concert alone, for M—— does not like music, but I have her escort to and from Music Hall. On entering the building I cast my eye about for some staid looking couple, in whose wake I follow closely, and so slip into my seat quite unobserved. When the concert is over and I emerge with the crowd from the doors, I am sure to hear M——'s voice saying in my ear, "'Av a 'ack, miss?" and, taking her arm, away we trudge homeward, without the smallest fear of any naughty man who might stare at us, or any dread of Mrs. Grundy. We are too obscure and insignificant to be worthy of her notice, and for this we are duly thankful.

Sometimes in the early evening, after we have washed our tea-dishes, we take a walk down Beacon Street, for the purpose—the deliberate purpose—of staring into people's windows that we may get a glimpse of the life we read of, but with which we never come in contact. Sometimes we see through parted curtains a family seated at dinner; a comfortable papa and satisfied mamma, blooming daughters and terrible young boys. We fancy we can hear them talk, and can almost taste the coffee that is served in the dainty cups. Sometimes we see children with eager faces pressed against the window pane, watching for the belated papa, straining their eyes to be the first to catch a glimpse of him. At last we see him approaching, and so do the children, for they have left the window and cluster around the door, and as papa opens it we hear, for we have actually gone up two or three of the marble steps on purpose, "My first kiss, papa!" "No, mine!" "No, mine!" from half a dozen rosy lips. And then the door closes, and we hear and see no more of them. M—— does not say so, nor do I, but I am sure each feels a little pang at the sight, and envies the father of these lovely children the privilege of feeling their loving arms about his neck and of caressing their chestnut curls with such tender touch. Instinctively we move away from the house, each busy with her own thoughts. And I wonder if M—— thinks, as I do, of what might have been once for us, in our younger days, before the crows' feet came to our eyes and the gray hairs to show faintly on our brows, but for our own folly. But we are both too hale and hearty to sentimentalize long; so, by the time a few brisk steps have brought us to our next well lighted house, "Richard is himself again," and we are ready to appreciate what we see within. The windows are high, and so we stand on tiptoe on the carriage block, balancing ourselves as best we may, to see our Mr. Jarndyce—for all our unknown friends have names and histories wholly of our invention. He sits in a large easy chair before an open fire, surrounded by miles of books. A student lamp spends its soft light in illuminating his silver hair, and the expression of his face is so contented and peaceful that M—— and I carry pleasant reflections of him into our dreams at night.

M—— and I are very economical. I often think, when I am sponging and brushing my old suit, how Ganymede would laugh at our wardrobes—Ganymede who delights in elegant costumes! A cheap flannel suit is our every day garment in winter, and is made by our own hands. I fit M——'s for her, and she returns the favor for me. We have each a cheap black silk, which we keep folded and put away for very extra occasions, and which is our sole "company gown." Our gloves are castor beaver, our hats double back-action, reversible affairs, which serve as hats in the daytime, and, by adding a pair of ribbon strings and a flower or two, as bonnets in the evening. In summer, the flannel suit worn in the winter is washed and turned, and made over into a "scramble dress" for the mountains, for we spend July and August with M——'s old maid aunt in Jefferson, New Hampshire. We even carry our economy so far as to do up our own pocket handkerchiefs and aprons, for washing costs a great deal here—even the "cheap" Chinese laundries are so only in name. I never shall forget the first time we played washerwomen. It was my week at playing lady; so, as M—— proposed the plan, I let her carry it out, and without a qualm of conscience I saw her march toward the kitchen with her arms full of handkerchiefs, her sleeves rolled up above the elbow (and, in spite of her forty years, her arms are very pretty). She had a look of triumph in her eyes and a strength in her gait and motion that seemed to imply power to play marbles with mountains. I heard the water run into the tubs, and the splash of her arms in the suds; I heard much rubbing and then a pause, then a forlorn "oh, dear," and, on rising to find out what was the matter, I saw a most ludicrous sight. On the floor sat M——, beside her the tub, upset, and its contents of suds and pocket handkerchiefs floating around the floor of our little kitchen. Poor M—— had suds in her hair and eyes; her neat cambric dress was soaked; her arms were burned, and her two pretty feet were thrust out before her in the puddle of suds, in a most dejected attitude. Of course, I laughed and she cried. She said I was heartless, and I replied, picking her up, that she was too small and frail for such work, and that henceforth my brawny arms should wash the handkerchiefs. And so I have been installed as laundress to her royal majesty M——.

Although Bohemia is a large place, we have very few friends, and the number of our gentlemen friends is just two. One is a man of some fifty years of age, who was an artist of great promise in his youth, but paralysis has so withered his arms that for years his paints and brushes have been useless to him. He is M——'s particular friend; and to see those two, on a rainy afternoon, trot off under one cotton umbrella, to see an exhibition of etchings, makes my old heart rejoice, they seem so happy. I wonder what made me write *old* heart, for M—— is some ten years older than I; but she is so little and pretty, and I so large and gaunt and awkward, that I feel as though she were some pretty kitten put under my protecting care. When they return home from the exhibition, Jones seems another man. He is very enthusiastic about the etchings, very well pleased with his company, and then he suddenly falls into silence, sits quiet for an hour or so, and then leaves abruptly. I shake my prophetic head at his retreating figure, and say to M——, as the echo of his footsteps dies away, "My dear M——, if you go on at this rate, you will be inspiring that poor old Jones"—she looks aggressive at hearing him called poor and old—"to paint with his toes next. Don't you see how he mopes and broods, and gazes in silence on his patched boots, as if speculating on the capacity of his toes for learning to handle a paint-brush?" But M—— only blushes and laughs at my nonsense, and I inwardly resolve to confide to Jones, at my next opportunity, that if he ever carries off M——, he will have to take me too, and I know that will frighten him off, and I shall own my M—— in peace. *My* friend's name is Robinson. M—— says he is a "snuffy old widower," but that is wholly in revenge for my calling her Jones "poor old Jones." Robinson's only joy is in his violin. He sometimes comes to our sky parlor, and we play duets and sing songs, with violin *obligato*. Such visits I enjoy very much, but poor M—— rushes frantically out of the room, and seeks refuge in the society of a lame seamstress, who lives on the first floor, and begs to be allowed to help her in her endless sewing, that she may drown the sound of the scraping and squalling going on above.

In the early summer we take rides in the open horse-cars to some of the suburbs, eat our supper under some out-of-the-way tree, stroll among the pretty gardens for a while, and come home by moonlight; or we take a sail—no, a *steam*—down the harbor, and refresh ourselves by strolling on the sands and poking pebbles with our parasols. And this is our life in Bohemia! We are happy, perfectly happy, because we are free to do as we like. We find pleasure in small things, and happiness in being busy. M—— is devoted to her art, and I to my singing, and each to the other, and so runs our world away. I suppose my fashionable young lady readers of the Golden City have by this time turned their aristocratic noses at least a foot into the air, and each of them pities us because we know not the delights of kettle-drums and flirting with Presidio officers, and perhaps, in the compassion of their hearts, they wish they might do something to show us the utter depravity of such a life as ours. They certainly have a right to despise our Bohemian ways, and to thank heaven they are not as we are. My only reply to them is that

"John P.
Robinson, he
Sez they didn't know *everything* down in Judee."

MELLIE A. HOPKINS.

THE MYSTERIOUS HAND.

It was in the year 1861, shortly after the commencement of hostilities between the North and South, that I found myself a passenger from Gibraltar to Southampton, on one of the Peninsular and Oriental Company's steamships. With the exception of a young English *attaché*, a personal friend of mine, the passengers were composed of British officers, ordered home to join their regiments, in anticipation of a war between Great Britain and the United States, growing out of what is called the *Trent* affair; two Southern envoys—namely, Messrs. Slidell and Mason—*en route* for England and France, having been forcibly taken from the British steamer *Trent* by the commanding officer of an American man-of-war.

I am invariably sea-sick when on the ocean. On this occasion I was, as usual, confined to my state-room, where I was visited by the young Englishman referred to, who, after sympathizing with my affliction, very kindly said to me, "Be careful, my dear fellow, when you come out to the cabin. With the exception of ourselves, all the passengers are British officers, ordered home to join their regiments. War between the United States and Great Britain, although not declared, is imminent, and 'our fellows' have got their fighting blood up, and you being the only American on board, they will naturally want to pitch into you, and will do so on the slightest provocation. So be careful, for heaven's sake!"

I was too sea-sick to pay much attention to my friend's warning, feeling perfectly well convinced that no human "pitching in" could be much worse than the terrible pitching up and down of the ship, then laboring in the trough of a heavy sea. In fact, I very soon forgot all about it.

In a couple of days, however, I found myself seated at the dinner table, immediately opposite the Honorable Colonel Anneslie, of the Scots Fusiliers, his regiment being a portion of the household troops, then in London. After a formal introduction, the subject of the anticipated difficulty between the two nations was introduced by Colonel Anneslie, by his asking me what I thought of the insult Great Britain had received. I replied that I saw nothing that diplomacy between two kindred nations could not remedy. The Colonel expressed surprise at my remark, adding that "no nation like that of Great Britain could submit to such a slap in the face without drawing the sword." I smiled, and said a military man would naturally feel that the arbitrament of the sword was the proper method of disposing of such a difficulty, but that men of peace preferred to resort to every other remedy before that of blood-letting. By this time many of the officers had left their seats, and were eagerly listening to the conversation. Much to the horror of my young English friend, who, in the kindness of his heart, had taken his seat at my side, in order to shield me as much as possible from what might prove to be an outburst of indignation on the part of his countrymen, I then said:

"With all due respect for your sentiments, Colonel, permit me to add that the views which I have expressed are sustained by the highest living English authority on International law—namely, your own Mr. Phillimore—who, in a communication to the London *Times* of a recent date, which I perused at Gibraltar just before coming on board, says, if my memory is not at fault, that the American naval commander was not only justified in taking from the *Trent* Messrs. Slidell and Mason, but would have been justified in carrying the *Trent* into the port of New York."

Several officers immediately jumped to their feet, exclaiming to Colonel Anneslie, in tones which indicated their excited feelings, "Present me! Present me!" After which a captain, whose name I have forgotten, but who must have stood over six feet in his stockings, said to me, in a tone of sarcasm which he evidently took no pains to suppress:

"I beg your pardon, but is it not possible that you have made a mistake in the paper to which you have referred? Instead of the London *Times*, which we certainly had an equal opportunity with yourself to peruse before sailing, have you not given us the benefit of some article you have been reading in the New York *Times?*"

I told him I thought not. I perceived, however, that, without an exception, these gentlemen evidently thought I had been making a fool of myself, and so bewildered is a person from the effects of sea-sickness that I began to fear I had, when Colonel Anneslie, as if to set the matter at rest, directed one of the junior officers to step to the captain's cabin and ask him if he had the latest London *Times* received at Gibraltar before sailing. Not a word was said until the young officer made his appearance with the London *Times* in his hand. I was feeble and nervous, and my nervousness was augmented by my English friend at my side making a remark to me, in the honesty of his feelings, in a low tone, not at all complimentary to my common sense or prudence. I felt as if I should have fainted with joy as the subaltern, in handing the paper to Colonel Anneslie, remarked in a suppressed tone, but sufficiently distinct for me to catch the words:

"By Jove, he is right; there's Phillimore's opinion!"

Mr. Philimore's communication was then read aloud, and the true character of a British gentleman was made conspicuous by the courtesy and kindness promptly displayed and extended toward me during the voyage to Southampton. There Colonel Anneslie called me to the side of the ship to witness the arrival of the Scots Fusiliers, who had just come down from London, to embark for Canada on their warlike mission, and who, recognizing their Colonel as they were ascending the side of the transport, placed their forage caps on their rifles and cheered their commander, just as he said to me:

"Allow me to present to you my regiment, and at the same time to regretfully bid you farewell."

On leaving the steamship at Southampton, I discovered to my great regret that all the berths on Cunard steamers to sail for the next month had been taken up for British officers and their wives, and that my only chance to get to New York was to take passage on the German steamer *Bremen*, just arrived, which would sail in three days. On this vessel I secured passage for myself and family.

Sauntering back to my hotel, I espied a natty little craft in the dry-dock, which, on inquiry, turned out to be the Confederate cruiser *Nashville*, undergoing repairs. The officer of the deck, who appeared to be a stripling of eighteen or nineteen years of age, wearing a pea-jacket and cap ornamented with gold braid, was nervously pacing the deck. As I stood on the wharf, this youngster was joined by two others similarly uniformed. The impression then made on my mind was that the *Nashville* was officered by young, enthusiastic, and determined men.

I remained at the dock long enough to take a mental observation of her armament, which consisted, as nearly as I could judge, of a swivel bow-gun, probably a twenty-pounder, and two others, probably ten-pounders. I was about leaving for my hotel, when an officer, who subsequently proved to be the chief engineer, approached me, and, in the frankest manner possible, said:

"You are an American, I perceive."

I replied affirmatively. He then invited me on board, which invitation I declined. He repeated the invitation, stating that the other officers would be glad to see any American. I begged to be excused, as I had some purchases to make, etc. He then told me that he and the second engineer were New Yorkers—that their families lived in the city of New York, and he wished me to take a couple of letters, containing money, to their wives. I told him the United States Government had sent instructions to Europe, warning all Americans against being the bearers of letters from or to parties in arms against the Government, and, trivial as the service might seem, I regretted exceedingly that I could not comply with his wish.

I parted with him, and was nearing my hotel, when I heard footsteps coming rapidly behind me. Turning around, I discovered my new acquaintance, the engineer. He approached me, and, in an agitated voice, said:

"Do you purpose returning to New York on the *Bremen?*"

I told him I did.

"Have you paid for your passage?"

I replied in the affirmative.

"I am sorry," he added, and was about leaving me, when he turned quickly, came up close to me, and, in a low voice, said, "Forfeit your passage money; do not go by the *Bremen*. We are here expressly to burn the *Bremen*. We have an authenticated list of her cargo. She has on board eight hundred boxes of Prussian rifles for the Federal Government. In twenty-four hours we will be out of the dry-dock. Two hours after the *Bremen* starts for New York, we shall be in pursuit. The *Nashville* is fast; we shall rapidly overhaul, burn, and sink the *Bremen*. We shall bring back to Southampton all her passengers, but their baggage will be lost."

I thanked him for his information, and we parted. I was plodding along, bewildered, in a measure, by my situation, and contrasting, unfavorably to myself, my refusal to take charge of a letter to a poor woman in New York, who was, perhaps, suffering from want of the money it contained, with the anxiety her kind husband had displayed to save me from the horrors of perhaps a deadly conflict at sea. I had half a mind to go back to him, and take his letter and its consequences, when I ran against Captain Wessels, of the *Bremen*. I felt it my duty to communicate to him the information which had so strangely come to my knowledge. He was very much agitated.

"How long," said he, "will it take you to get your family down to the steamer?"

"Twenty minutes," I replied.

"I give you half an hour. Forty minutes from this moment" (pulling out his watch) "we shall be under way."

In twenty minutes my family and baggage were on board. In ten minutes more, every passenger going by the *Bremen* was on her deck. The gang-plank was hauled in, fastenings cast off, the tinkle of a bell was heard, we backed out from the dock, another tinkle, and we were under way. I looked at my watch. Forty-five minutes had elapsed since I had been conversing with the captain in front of the hotel. Fortunately, the steamer's fires had not been put out from the time of her arrival, a few hours before.

The *Bremen* was a stanch craft, and officered by hardy men of experience. As much steam as she could safely carry was given her, and we rapidly left behind us the shores of old England. That night Captain Wessels told me that everything he possessed in this world was on board the steamer; that he was largely interested in the safe delivery of the eight hundred boxes of arms; that the *Nashville* was very fast, and, in fair weather, could overhaul us with our twenty-four hours' start; that if she did, he would fight her with steam as she came alongside, and would scald to death every human being on board, if possible. Here, I could not help but think we stood a chance of having a broil converted into a boil, with somebody cooked, gratis. I should be telling an untruth if I stated that I relished the prospect.

For forty-eight hours we boomed along in splendid style, when a gale of wind sprung up, which, although favorable to our prospect, nevertheless tried the metal fastenings and cordage of our gallant iron craft. In such a heavy sea the *Nashville* could not live, the captain said, which consoled us for the rolling and tossing, the loss of meals, and general discomfort of everything around us. On the ninth day, the captain, in honor of our escape from the *Nashville*, gave us a "jolly spread," with fine old Rhenish wine, and other accompaniments. Songs were sung, and toasts were drunk in memory of "Faderland," "Our Fritz," etc.; for, with the exception of two ladies, my family and myself, the passengers were all German students, *en route* to join the Union army. On the tenth day, about noon, when on the banks of Newfoundland, there was a tremendous crash, which shook the vessel from stem to stern. Steam was let off rapidly, the vessel stopped. Orders were imperatively given in tones which seemed to combat with the elements; there was a running back and forth on deck overhead, a dragging of blocks and cordage and rattling of chains. The vessel, having lost her momentum, began to roll and pitch and toss fearfully. The weather was bitterly cold, our sails frozen and unmanageable, a tremendous sea was rolling, our machinery disabled; we were at the mercy of the elements. The good ship *Bremen* gradually settled to her larboard side, the seas began to roll over us, the hatches were battened down, the deadlights secured; we were in utter darkness, and inclosed in an iron prison. A feeble light was, after a time, obtained, and swung in the cabin, but no preparation of food was thought of. The cook and waiters seemed to have stepped ashore. For hours no one came to communicate with us. At last, a solitary waiter appeared, and placed some bread, cold meat, and water on the table. We questioned him; he answered not, looked frightened, and disappeared. This state of things was kept up for twenty-four hours longer, when, finding things getting no worse, we began to think matters were more likely to improve.

About seven o'clock of the night of the eleventh day out, Captain Wessels, for the first time since the accident, entered the cabin and took his seat at the head of the table. He looked sad, gloomy, and exhausted. Although he had been so long without food, I noticed he was not eating. Not a word was uttered by any of the passengers. I approached the captain, and, quietly seating myself at his right, said, in tones as firm as I could command:

"Well, captain, how does it look?"

He did not immediately reply nor look at me. Thinking he had not heard me, I was about to repeat the question, when he gently placed his hand on mine, and with an expression so sad, so mournful, that I shall never forget it, replied:

"I will tell you. No small boat can be launched, or can live, in such a sea as is now raging. Our machinery is disabled beyond repair. Our sails are frozen and unmanageable. We have sprung a leak on the larboard quarter. Our pumps are broken. The water is gaining on us with such rapidity, that, if the wind does not shift before midnight, so as to throw us on our starboard, and thus enable us to pass a sail over the leak on the larboard, we will be at the bottom when that hour arrives. Now, go to work, cheer up your fellow passengers, particularly the poor ladies and children. Good night. If we should never meet again, believe that I have done all in the power of a human being to save the ship and the precious lives intrusted to my care. May the great God have mercy on us all!"

He then left the cabin and went on deck. The passengers had been attentively watching us. I turned to them, and although, as I was told afterward, my face was as pallid as that of a dead person, I exclaimed:

"Cheer up, cheer up; by midnight we shall be out of trouble."

German songs were then sung by the students, affording me an opportunity to quietly slip away to my state-room, my family having preceded me. On entering my state-room I locked the door, took out the key and placed it under the pillow on which the head of my darling boy was resting.

I awakened him, and told him to rise and kneel with me. He did so. I said, "Now, my child, it is my duty to say to you that we are in great, very great peril. God alone can save us. Pray fervently to him to spare us—to spare all in this ship."

The child did so; we prayed together, and if prayers ever went up from the heart, those prayers did. A few moments afterward, the boy was fast asleep, and, strange as it may seem, a feeling of drowsiness gradually crept over me. I have heard it said that persons on the eve of execution have been known to sleep soundly. I think I can account for it. Hope and fear have given way to resignation—a quiet submission to the will of Providence. Be that as it may, I soon fell asleep, and slept as soundly as I ever did in my life, until suddenly awakened by what appeared to be a heavy blow against the larboard quarter of the ship. In an instant I realized the situation. I thought my hour had come, and, with all my faculties alert, I calmly awaited the awful sensation of sinking to the bottom. Even in this terrible moment there was a consolation in knowing that all who were dear to me in this life would not be separated from me in death—that we would go down, down together. The vessel, however, gradually careened from the larboard to the starboard. Pulling and hauling, shouting and running, were heard overhead. It wanted half an hour to midnight. The wind, as by a miracle, had suddenly shifted from NNW to NNE. God was in the elements. The Mysterious Hand was visible! We were saved!

In five days afterward we were at our dock in New York. With the exception of myself, who was in the consular service, the passengers were rigidly searched for letters, but none were found. Mr. Seward was informed by me of the locality of the *Nashville*, and a man-of-war was promptly dispatched to look after her.

George V. Brown.

THE INTEROCEANIC CANAL.

A residence of four years on the Nicaragua and Panama transits, in the interests of American transportation companies, and a practical familiarity with the navigation of both oceans to the *termini* of these transits, naturally led me to take a special interest in the subject of an isthmus ship canal, when the San Francisco Board of Trade took the initial step, which resulted in the appointment of a committee to consider and report upon the practicability of the proposed Nicaragua and Panama projects. The report of that committee, of which I had the honor to act as chairman, is before the public. It is now proposed to make other considerations, inseparably connected with the subject, but which are foreign to the purpose of the

Board of Trade report, the special subject of this article, premising, however, that the ideas herein advanced are entirely personal.

I can recall the day, many years since, when, after a tedious voyage round the "Cape of Storms," I stood, for the first time, on the shores of that magnificent inland sea, Lake Nicaragua. Fresh in my mind were the weary months I had passed in reaching this spot. When I realized that this splendid sheet of water was connected with the Atlantic by a navigable stream, and that I was only eight days' travel from New York, the idea occurred to me with magic force, that, at some future day, the genius of the age would supplement the work of nature, and no more should the mariner be called upon to battle the tempestuous waves of the Southern Ocean to reach the spot whereon I stood—*only twelve and a half miles* from where I had left the *White Falcon*, two hours before, afloat on the Pacific.

In later years, *en route* from Virgin Bay to Granada, by lake steamer, when passing the location of the now projected canal, I have, with curiosity, followed the setting sun, almost until it dipped into the waters of the Pacific, and never without thinking how little the Almighty had left undone in the work of an interoceanic canal through Lake Nicaragua. The reader will not wonder that the subject has been of more than passing interest to me ever since.

The political consideration of the interoceanic canal question is of vast importance, and applies equally to either route. This international highway will be truly the "key of the Pacific," and our country should not permit it to pass under the dominating influence of any foreign power. It is vastly more important that *any* canal, which shall unite the Atlantic and the Pacific, should be controlled by the United States than it was that the Suez Canal should be controlled by Great Britain. This great highway, wherever and whenever constructed, should therefore be under the predominating influence of our own, acting jointly with the local government through whose territory it passes.

The English Government had no hesitation in purchasing the control of the Suez Canal. *Not having built it, England had to buy it*, and, like England, if we do not build we must purchase a controlling interest. We might, perhaps, depend upon treaties with the maritime powers, guaranteeing its neutrality; but, in the exigencies of war, treaties are often ignored, and the managing control of such a work holds the key of the position; a few hours would suffice to render the canal useless for months. The action of President Hayes in this matter will meet with the approval of all patriotic Americans, who recognize the fact that, if we are not inclined to fight unless it is necessary, we are nevertheless *ready to do so when our interests are threatened*. The actual existence of a large standing army and navy is not needed to give weight to the principles enunciated by President Hayes. Our country has the power in reserve to command the respect of foreign nations, and if we can justly say to them, "our citizens own the major portion of this work; its protection is a vital necessity to our country; and we shall maintain a protectorship over it, as a special duty"—if we can rightfully thus assert, no foreign power will question our right, unless under circumstances which would render it advisable and unavoidable to submit the question to arbitration or to the issues of the sword.

Of equal interest to us is the method by which this great work shall be constructed. Our Government having officially indorsed the Nicaragua route, it would appear proper that it should construct it as a Government work, to be free for American tonnage, and charging an equitable toll on all foreign tonnage, other than Nicaraguan. Our merchants feel that the opening of an interoceanic canal should be to them a guarantee of moderate freights between the Pacific Coast and our Eastern seaboard, as well as Europe. They view with apprehension the possibility of a combination with the great freight monopolies which now control our inter-State commerce.

On the other hand, Government works are prosecuted so slowly and so expensively, and their continuance is so dependent on the caprices of the party in power, that this idea has little to recommend it, except the single consideration just named. Consequently, we must aim to reach a method by which the construction can be so assisted by the Government that the latter shall have a distinct and overpowering voice in the tonnage tax to be charged, thus insuring the result aimed at: a work for the mutual benefit of the investors and of the world's commerce. The committee of the Board of Trade have this same object in view when they "urge the absolute necessity of regulating the tonnage tax by means of an International Convention, in which all the maritime nations shall be represented; the tonnage tax thus levied, being unchangeable, except by a majority of the signatory powers." The advantage of this excellent recommendation is rendered somewhat questionable by the equal facility which such an arrangement would give the powers for interference with other details in the management of the canal, and would hardly be available except as accompanying a treaty of neutrality, covering the canal itself and its approaches within a specified distance—say one hundred nautical miles.

Admitting the obvious necessity that our Government should rightfully claim a voice in the management of the canal, it is equally obvious that this right can only be attained by rendering such pecuniary assistance as will insure it unquestioned. Inasmuch as the results of public subsidies to transportation companies, in our country, have not been such as our people were led to anticipate, the idea of any government subsidies has few friends; in fact, our State has prounced emphatically against them. Nevertheless, in this exceptional case, our Government could safely guarantee the interest on the construction bonds of the Interoceanic Canal Company at a low rate of interest (say five per cent.) during the period of construction, to be issued in four equal installments for the amount named by the Government survey, including contingency estimate and no more; the period of construction to be limited to six years from breaking ground. The interest on these bonds should terminate at the end of the period so fixed, and said interest should be repaid by a sinking fund within double the time, or twelve years. This would at once give the bonds of the Company a standing throughout the world, and even this limited assistance might only be accorded with the agreement, expressed on the face of the bonds, that the Government, in consideration thereof, should fix the tonnage tax at a rate which should not net the Company less than seven per cent. per annum.

There appears to be no reason why our Government should not, and every reason why it should, assume such a position toward this great project. This would insure the early completion of the work and ultimately cost the country nothing, while we should sooner receive the vast benefits which the canal would confer on our commonwealth and the whole Pacific Coast.

Surprising as it may appear, there are a few who question the value of an Interoceanic canal to San Francisco, and fear that it would divert commerce from our port. The commerce with our Eastern seaboard, which now merely passes through this city, might, in some instances, leave us for the canal route, as it also possibly might be transferred to the Pacific terminus of the North Pacific Railroad, now being constructed. But it is of little benefit to us that a cargo of tea is here transferred from ship to car. A few merchants, who now realise a profit in the Cape Horn trade, might find that business injured by it, but the new avenues that would be opened to them should far more than compensate. The owners of sailing ships also recognize the fact that, although the Nicaragua Canal would be available to them, the decreased distance would gradually give screw steamers of large tonnage an increased advantage. These two interests value our commercial isolation for such exceptional reasons as only prove the rule of the greatest advantage to the greatest number.

Let us now consider the enormous advantages. Almost in vain has our commerce beaten against the shores of China for thirty years. China does not want the products of our soil, and we do not want her population. Europe, on the contrary, wants *all that we can produce*, and a desirable European immigration is one of the great necessities of the Pacific Coast. With the completion of the canal, we can reach European markets in twenty-five days, and our Eastern seaboard in eighteen days, while our Gulf ports can be reached in fourteen days. Freights will be carried to Europe at rates now paid to Hongkong, and steerage passengers can be brought here at an expense of about thirty-five dollars each. The saving effected in handling our present average wheat crop will alone amount to two million one hundred thousand dollars per annum. The development of Nicaragua will also create a large and profitable commerce with our port. The construction of the canal will not only draw upon us for our surplus labor, but will create an immediate demand for our lumber and many products of our soil. In this connection it is necessary to state that, although Nicaragua is abundantly supplied with woods, they are mostly hard, cabinet varieties, more valuable than ours, but not adapted to such purposes as canal construction would require. The resources of that magnificent, but almost virgin country, would receive rapid development, and there is nothing grown there that we are not daily purchasing. Those who entertain exaggerated ideas of the value of Chinese commerce can see nothing in the construction of this great work that tends to decrease the probabilities of our success elsewhere. The canal would open other, and, it is submitted, vastly more encouraging, fields for our commercial and our industrial enterprises. Viewed in any light that candid investigation can place on the question, it offers the greatest advantage to our commonwealth and the whole Pacific Coast. Our people are as yet comparatively ignorant of the subject. Our producers, who, of all others, are the most interested, have not had their attention called to the immense advantages offered them in this beneficent enterprise. Did they realize it, they would, as one man, urge its construction with the least possible delay. We are the community most interested in this question, and we know the least regarding the advantages it offers. In the language of the Board of Trade report, there is, in the project, "Prosperity for our producers, profit for our merchants."

It is not within the scope of this article to enter into a discussion of the merits of the two projected routes for an interoceanic canal, but a few ideas present themselves as worthy of note in this connection. In the many technical discussions which have claimed my attention, I have been impressed with the fact that projectors and engineers are, in such arguments, much like attorneys, seeking only to develop the unfavorable points in other projects, and the favorable points in their own. Thus we find Count de Lesseps dwelling upon and exaggerating the difficulties of the Nicaragua route, while complacently passing over, as minor affairs, the stupendous obstacles that bar the way to success in his Panama scheme. It is a notable fact, for which proof can be furnished by the writer, that *Count de Lesseps's autographic signature appears on an application to the Nicaraguan Government for a concession to construct the very work he now pronounces against;* and the "Blanchet Concession," failing of passage in the Nicaraguan Senate by only one vote, we find him subsequently taking up the "Wyse Panama Concession," far less favorable in terms. Comment is unnecessary, and the inference is left to the reader.

The Eads project for an isthmian ship railway claims a few remarks at our hands. Doubtless it is *feasible* to build a railway on which a ship can be transported; but I have yet to learn of the first ship-builder, ship-owner, or ship captain who would allow his ship to be thus treated, full of cargo. The water is to the ship what the foundation is to the house; deprived of its foundation, a loaded ship would be ruined, and the larger the ship the more impracticable does the scheme become. No mechanical contrivance, when the ship is out of water, can transfer the enormous weight from the keel, where it is *not* intended to rest, to all parts of the water-borne lines, where the principles of naval construction require that it *shall* rest.

The Channing scheme of transporting ships in *caissons* filled with water is more reasonable, but still impracticable, because it would be impossible to keep such a structure water-tight in transporting it over grades, and with foundations liable to settle from the enormous weight. The wear and tear of such structures in a tropical climate would also be immense. These ideas are the natural efforts of ingenious minds to avoid the difficulties which are encountered in all interoceanic canal projects, and they only prove, as Count de Lesseps says, that "great engineers are often mistaken." They also indicate the great and increasing interest which is being developed in the question we have been considering.

The prediction is a safe one that, before many years elapse, instead of regarding it as a problem of the future, the Nicaragua interoceanic ship canal will have become an accomplished fact. Its completion will be the dawn of a new era in the development of the Pacific Coast. It will rapidly increase our mercantile marine, it will enhance the prosperity of our commonwealth, which halts in its onward march of industrial and commercial development, for reasons which are patent to close observers. Furnishing an avenue, open to all, for the cheap and rapid transportation of the varied products of our soil, it will quicken the energies of our producers, encourage the enterprise of our merchants, and inaugurate an era of prosperity on the shores of the Pacific. In the eloquent words of the Board of Trade report, "God speed the day when the Pacific shall be wedded to the Atlantic! It will be a happy day for our children, for our country, and for the world."

WM. LAWRENCE MERRY.

SATIN VERSUS SACKING.

In the April number of THE CALIFORNIAN appeared an article headed "Americanism in Literature." It occurs to us that a better title would have been "Walt Whitman;" therefore, the secondary matter, prefacing the direct treatment of the author of *Leaves of Grass*, will not be here considered. When the writer of the paper before us, after a circuitous journey, finally arrives at the true subject, his path becomes as straight as it was crooked before. He expresses doubt as to the possibility of a literature distinctively American, but none whatever as to the false position of our modern *Ossian*. It may prove wholesome for us to follow the main points of argument, as nearly as may be, in the order of their advancement:

First, the writer declares his intention to cast no reflection upon the "personal sincerity," the "perfect good faith," of Whitman—generously relegating him to the pitiable company of "unconscious *poseurs*." To have left him there would seem to have been punishment enough; but, further on, he is abruptly recalled, and both he and the reader are startled with the charge of the "meditated acting of a part." At a single stroke, the modest hues of sincerity are changed into the "proper colors of affectation and masquerade." Perhaps these antagonistic positions sufficiently neutralize one another to allow us to proceed, without further comment, to point number two:

"He [Whitman] addresses an exceedingly cultivated age in the artistic language of barbarism." Fortunately, the rude bard is not compelled to bear this heavy accusation alone. On either side are placed supporters mightier than himself. "He rouses, in a perfectly unbiased critic, something of the same amazement as might result from seeing some native of our great West robed in the garb of an ancient British harper, and chanting, with picturesque solemnity, the most eloquent passages of Carlyle and Emerson." If these latter, at their best, sound "barbaric yawp," we need not stay to commiserate the third singer. We suspect that the writer was led into this particular contradiction through the overpowering effect upon him of certain articles coming under the general designation of "dry goods." He was blinded, probably, by the glare of Whitman's red flannel; consequently, he threw over him the more pleasing garb of the British harper, which, as may be believed, caused him to sing surprisingly exalted strains. Of this, more hereafter.

The writer continues: "One need hardly fear the charge of dogmatism in asserting that all Mr. Whitman's work, from beginning to end, is absolutely without art." If any attempt is made to prove this assertion, it is very indirect, and, as nearly as we can discern, amounts to this—*viz.*, that Whitman has ignored the present "exquisite degree of development" of the "metrical and rhythmical structure of English verse." Should this prove convincing to the reader, we do not care, for the time being, to disturb his easily earned repose.

Again: "He [Whitman] glorifies the ignorant masses; but," is it added, "he is by no means of them." He does not do this well; he does not even "partially represent their rude life;" for, to accomplish this, requires "sunny honesty," "candid heartiness," "limpid, unostentatious directness," and, of course, rhyme and meter—all of which are denied to be in his possession. But where does the critic find authority for this statement so positively made? True, Whitman finds music in the sounds of humble toil, and sees beauties among the lowly scenes of life, whether in olden homes or in the wilds of the West. Is it because he so frequently sings of these that he is said to "glorify the ignorant masses?" Such is the conclusion to which we are driven.

As to the last point (with which we believe the gist of the article concludes)—*viz.*, that a man of European culture cannot be a democrat—we will rest upon the assurance that it carries with it, as its predecessors may have done, its own answer.

After this brief array of inconsistencies, which are made to constitute the substance of a magazine article, let us turn to our writer's volume of verse, published some two years ago and the causes of their occurrence may, by this means, be readily discovered. Men, be they learned or unlearned, speak plainly enough when they have something important to say. Their diction is then straightforward, as a rule, and one idea is not apt to endanger, much less to contradict, another. Says a great critic, "The one unpardonable sin in a versified composition, next to the absence of meaning, and of a true meaning, is diffuseness." As one opens and peruses *Fantasy and Passion* with this maxim in mind, he finds many an opportunity for its application. The long, sonorous words and the pyramidal exclamation points multiply—each moving, or stationed, according to the strict tactics of rhyme and meter. The performance is acceptable as a parade. The veteran, however, sees small preparation for the stern hour of battle. The subjects that open the volume, and occupy it for forty-three pages, all belong out of doors—some on the earth, others in the air, and others still in the writer's imagination; but they are portrayed by one that has studied them from his parlor window. The atmosphere of the house is too strong for the perfumes of Nature. The clouds lead from "earth to sunset lands,"

"As *stately stairways* to imperial halls."

The spaces between the apple trees appear as "*aisles*," the leaves of the roses have a surface of "*satin*," and the ferns are

"Delicate, supple, frail as *lace*."

Ivy, ferns, leaves, clover, grapes—all are clipped or pulled up by the roots, and brought into the drawing-room to languish in the tyrannic, ever-uppermost presence of "velvet" and "brocade." Human kind and the creatures beneath are not exempt; no more are personified abstractions. The young lady in Seville recalls a product of the loom; she has

"A drowsy smile, two dimpling cheeks, and two
Fathomless *velvet* Andalusian eyes."

The tigers in the jungle suggest a textile fabric. They are exhibited to us

"With sleek, striped shapes of massive size,
Great *velvet* paws, and lurid eyes."

Even poor Poesy cannot escape. Meeting Genius, she

—"lures him with her *velvet* glance."

This writer prints seven stanzas entitled "An Interior." With nearly equal propriety, he might have so styled some seven times seven pages. It is not easy to perceive how one with this dress-maker's bias, this *penchant* toward the millinery department of literature, can afford enlightenment or pleasure concerning things of Nature. The bent of mind would seem to forbid it. As long as the rock-maples, covered with the glory of autumn, suggest no more than

"Great gorgeous tapestries out of Eastern lands,"

and toads, seeking their insect supper in the grass or among the cabbages, rise to the foreign distinction

"Of thick-lipped slaves, with ebon skin,
That squat in hideous dumb repose,
And guard the drowsy ladies in
Their still seraglios."

we have little hope of penetrating what Goethe was pleased to style the "open secret." Not only is this writer's genius a thoroughly in-door one, but it haunts the chambers of dwellings of far-off lands. He does not even sing of the kind of house in which he himself lives:

"A chamber where the wainscot woods
Are rich with dark shapes, oddly mold,
And where the time-touched arras hangs
In blendings of blue, green, and gold;
And, dimly pictured, gleam the walls,
With here bluff huntsmen, all at tryst;
Here mounted knights; a falcon here,
Wide-winged upon a lady's wrist."

It is in such an apartment that he is most at home, and from which, in our judgment, he looks out upon and seeks to catch the life of the fields, forests, and flowers of New England. Is there any escape here from artificiality—the thing that the writer himself so strongly condemns in Whitman? Artificiality of form is indeed reprehensible, but what shall be said when the very essense, the spirit, is the result of machinery as real as that of a carpet-loom? We have not space to quote largely. The volume is open to whomsoever will take the trouble to read and try the strength of our position. If it be admitted that the author of *Fantasy and Passion* is constitutionally incapable of appreciating the hidden beauties of Nature (without which gift no man can be a poet), there remains little need of considering his language—his form. But, inasmuch as he insists so strenuously upon that point, let us make a few short selections from his writings:

"WINDS.

"O invisible lives, that aimlessly,
With mutable voices, fare
Mysteriously and tamelessly
Through the altitudes of air,
When I welcome lofty dreams of you
Amid hours of calms or storms,
I discern evanescent gleams of you
As divine phantasmal forms!

"Here, grouped in superb frigidity,
The blasts of the North repose,
Proud spirits of intrepidity,
Whose wings with clangors unclose.
In their saturnine eyes crepuscular
Cold hatreds bitterly glow;
In the girth of their dark arms muscular
Sit shipwreck, ruin, and woe.

"Thus, haughty in dread immobility,
Or lurid in arrogant might,
Exultant in soft volubility,
Or languid in drowsy delight,
Sublimely, serenely, or dismally,
Weird throngs, you glimmer and go
Where spectrally loom and abysmally
The realms that my visions know."

Diffuseness outdone! Whether there be more wind in "the altitudes of air" than in the above stanzas is a serious question. But let us take a more substantial subject, bending the vision carefully toward the North Pole:

"Here Silence, like a monarch, reigned immensely;
The quintessence of Cold was here no less;
Each utter as before God spake intensely
And visible things leapt out of nothingness—
A land wherewith no living sign was blended,
A white monotony of weird device,
One towering lateral torpor, chaste and splendid,
One monstrous immobility of ice."

Such is the home of the "Iceberg." Several more equally unmanageable stanzas under this title ought to be presented, but the lack of space forbids. Is it not evident to the most careless reader that these ponderous words are too heavy for the ideas that lie beneath them? No man with false teeth would dare attempt to read them aloud. To study Swinburne does not necessarily reward the student with the power to achieve his special success. These lines scan well; the tape-measure attests their accuracy, or, as the author would have it, their *art*; but do they approach the mold of verse that "*cultured American men and women*" are waiting to "gladly and proudly recognize when it really appears?" If so, in mercy to the barbarous present, may the day of appearance be long delayed! We may be stricken with fogyism, the star of our birth should, perhaps, have risen ages earlier; but we hazard the cry, "Better meaning than measure; better sense than sound." "Winds" and "Icebergs" are rather stern subjects. The gentle moonshine demands, however, like treatment at the hands of this rhyming surveyor in the field of letters:

"Wide tracts of cloisteral forest-land, I know,
Are welcome to that luminous heart of thine,
Where, under murmurous branches, thou most throw
Dim palpitant arabesques of shade and shine."

Whatever the theme, the reader fails not to have his mouthful. If music is to be found in any particular kind of poem, surely it should be in a barcarolle or a cradle-song. *Fantasy and Passion* contains two pieces severally so named. Below one may read two of those stanzas, entitled "Barcarolle:"

"With strange, half-proud humility,
With sumptuous tranquillity,
Thou art lounging, sweet, at my flattered feet, in statuesque immobility;
Against thy bosom's chaste, superb repose
One heavy blood-red, *velvet*-petaled rose."

On second thoughts, it has occurred to us that we may be gladly excused from furnishing the concluding stanza. The "Cradle Song" is not so prodigiously polysyllabic, but offers, to our our ears, no more melody.

The school to which this writer belongs we believe to be founded in error—namely, in the confusion of the two arts, poetry and painting. These arts are exceedingly jealous, and one cannot encroach upon the boundaries of the other without detriment to both. Word-pictures are endurable only when they exhibit something more than could have been touched on by the brush. This power of suggestion is very rarely discoverable in the author under consideration. He contents himself with doing what is properly the painter's work. The position is false at the start, and, being held with dogged pertinacity, becomes, in the end, other than a source of pleasure. The painter defeats the poet. A stanza like the following, because of the overdye of detail, portrays a tea-rose taken from a chromo, or from the milliner's window, rather than from the garden:

"Half tinged, like some dim-yellow peach,
Half like a shell's pink inward whorl
That sighs its sea-home after,
Your creamy oval bud lets each
Pale outer petal backward curl,
Like a young child's lip in laughter."

Children do not laugh with their lips curled backward, by the way; but then "laughter" rhymes faultlessly with "after." Again:

"Frail germ of strength, I scan with eager heed
As from the summer sward I lift you up,
The tawny oval of your polished head
Bulging so sweetly from its rugged cup."

Certainly this is the way an acorn looks, but was it worth while to say so? Our writer devotes his energies to petty particularizing, to overwrought niceties of description—a strong indication that the poet is not born, but made. Be the poems ever so accurate, they have the manufacturer's stamp on them. Nature is brought into the house, and there worked over and over, until her freshness is lost, and nought remains to be seen save the misapplied skill of the artisan. Fantasy there is in this volume, but Passion we have not been able to discover. The cast of mind forbids that. The poet of Man or of Nature could not write three sonnets under the several names of "Satin," "Velvet," and "Brocade." The eye does not roll in fine frenzy over silks and satins; the shimmer of fine fabrics bears not the least resemblance to the fires that flame upon the altar of inspired song. Of course, many excellent lines are to be found threading their way through the entangled syllables of the little book before us. A cultured writer could not well avoid making occasional happy hits in the course of two hundred pages, but this by no means proves that the author really had anything to say to the world; and this is, as has been said, the real issue. Too much *satin*—such is the verdict after each perusal. The handiwork of Nature reaches perfection as it descends to the manual dexterity of the clever workman. The lily

—"bursts from soilure and decay
In taintlessness of alabaster calm."

The butterfly

—"soars fluttering, breeze-assailed,
Gay as those flowery gondolas that slid
Through sculptured Venice in old days, and trailed
Brocades and *velvets* where they softly sailed."

The grapes

—"dream of some old ducal board,
Blazing with Venice glass and costliest plate,

Where princely banqueters caroused in state;
And through the frescoed halls the long feast roared.

"Or how *brocaded* dame and plumed grandee
Saw [their] imperial-colored fruit heaped up
On radiant silver, or in chiseled cup,
Where some proud marble gallery faced the sea."

The ivy has

"Masked beauteous dames through arrased chambers glide,
With lazy, graceful staghounds at their side."

Or maids

"In *velvet* and *brocade*, in plumes and *silk*,
With falcons, and with palfreys white as milk."

Word-wrought fashion plates cannot deceive, though they be labeled poems of nature. No more can frigid and contorted addresses to mankind escape detection, though shielded by the placard of "Passion."

"I have sought the intensest ways to best adore you;
I have laid my soul's last treasure at your feet;
Yet I tremble as in thought I bend before you
With abasement and abashment and defeat,
Knowing well that all the love I ever bore you
Is requital weak of worth and incomplete."

This is the first stanza of a piece entitled "Adoration," and all but the last that we shall offer from this writer. Though we have ever believed his volume to be a cleverly constructed failure, we should have continued to hold our small peace had he not forced us to speak by this recent aimless dab at Walt Whitman. In justice, both to the author and to the reader, we will not dismiss him without quoting two pieces in full.

"CHIAROSCURO.

"The garden, with its throngs of drowsy roses,
Below the suave midsummer night reposes,
And here kneel I, whom fate supremely blesses,
In the dim room, whose lamplit dusk discloses
Your two dark stars of eyes, your rippled tresses,
Whose fragrant folds the fragrant breeze caresses.

"White flower of womanhood, ah! how completely,
How strongly, with invisible bonds, yet sweetly,
You bind, as my allegiant love confesses,
You bind, you bend, immutably and meetly,
This soul of mine, that all its pride represses,
A willing falcon in love's golden jesses.

"To me such hours as these I breathe are holy;
I kneel, I tremble, I am very lowly,
While thus dear consecrated night progresses,
And faint winds through the lattice vines float slowly
From all high starriest reaches and recesses—
Night's heavenly but unseen embassadresses."

Now, if Miss Chiaroscuro stayed to hear this effusion through, she certainly exhibited more patience and courtesy than characterizes the average of young ladies in America. Poetry can be made by recipe, as well as cake or pie. Search the cook-book of letters, reader, and by carefully applying the principles found there you shall succeed in literary pastry as well as the most famous caterer.

"SATIN.

"No moonlit pool is lovelier than the glow
Of this bright, sensitive texture, nor the sheen
On sunny wings that wandering sea-birds preen;
And sweet, of all fair draperies that I know,
To mark the smooth tranquillity of its flow,
Where shades of tremulous dimness intervene,
Shine out with mutable splendors, mild, serene,
In some voluminous raiment white as snow.
For then I feel impetuous fancy drawn
Forth at some faint and half-mysterious call,
Even like a bird that breaks from clasping bars;
And, lighted vaguely by the Italian dawn,
I see rash Romeo scale the garden wall,
While Juliet dreams below the dying stars."

This satin is astonishing stuff. The visions it starts before the eyes that gaze worshipfully upon it are hardly to be credited. It works like magic, being a sort of patent medicine to ease whatever disturbance affects the mind. "No family should be without it."

If the author of *Fantasy and Passion* had little to say in his book, much less was he prepared, in a magazine article, to assail a great, rude genius, far above his comprehension. Let us endeavor briefly to examine our huge roll of sacking, and see if it does not possess certain attractive properties, though placed side by side with "tremulous," "mutable," "voluminous" folds of satin. In a published letter to Emerson, written in 1856, may be read the following bold passages, which strike the key-note of the author's character and of his labors:

"There is no great author; every one has demeaned himself to some etiquette or some impotence. There is no manhood or life-power in poems; there are shoats and geldings more like. Or literature will be dressed up, a fine gentleman, distasteful to our instincts, foreign to our soil; its neck bends right and left wherever it goes; its costumes and jewelry prove how little it knows Nature; its flesh is soft; it shows less and less of the indefinable, hard something, that is Nature.

It is no marvel that the man that speaks thus familiarly of the

—"hidden ground
Of thought and of austerity within,"

should be incomprehensible to a player upon the surface. It is no wonder that the writer that inveighs so severely against the foreign gloss, the shimmering costumes, cheap ornaments, and mincing gait of much of our literature, is condemned by a rhymer that might have sat at the feet of Herr Teufelsdrockh, and been dubbed, by the queen of French fashion, Noble Knight of the "Vestural Tissue." A plea for manhood, for genuine masculinity, in letters as well as in life, has Walt Whitman sounded from first to last. He has pushed his language to extremes, has spoken savagely, at times; yes, all but brutally. Nevertheless, we believe that he has erred upon the side of truth. And who shall say that the hard Saxon of his *Leaves of Grass* was too harsh a medicine for the milk-and-water disease in literature—symptoms of which are developed in such volumes as *Fantasy and Passion?* A man of unflagging faith, of deep and steadfast earnestness, a close student of the living world about him, a man exceptionally strong in mind and body, filled with the ceaseless energy of perfect health—it is not surprising that he was unable to listen silently to the smooth, sickly babble, the polished and perfumed insipidities, daily offending his ears. While we would not defend his violence *in toto*, we fear that the intent of its use has not been universally perceived. As we understand *Leaves of Grass*, it is a protest against sham of every kind and description; and when the lamentable prevalence of sham is considered, there is certainly strong ground for palliation of much of its unbridled freedom and vehemence of language. Perhaps, nothing short of Whitman's liberty of speech could be expected to send the dandy writers, the champions of equal daintiness and deceit, to the shades where they rightfully belong. "Down with scribbling fops and fools! Give us men and women—creatures fit to dwell in a world of infinite beauty and perfection. Away with weaklings and counterfeits, and fill their places with honest, wholesome beings, to associate with whom is not contamination. Let men open their eyes and ears, and learn that it means something to be alive." Such we conceive to have been the central thoughts of this author's aim in addressing his fellows. Was he fitted to carry out his design? First comes his firm faith:

"Endless unfolding of words of ages.
And mine a word of the modern, a word *en masse*,
A word of the faith that never balks."

Next appears his earnestness:

"I do not say these things for a dollar, or to fill up the time while I wait for a boat."

"O truth of the earth! O truth of things! I am determined to press the whole way toward you.
Sound your voice! I scale mountains, or dive in the sea, after you."

No one could be more absorbed in his work—no one more anxious, if possible, to utter his feelings and ideas. If his language is at times forced, it may be for the reason that the thought has pushed it too hard in its effort to find a voice. This author seeks to interpret the hidden meaning of everything that comes under his observation, be it of rare or of commonest occurrence. Important matter is confided to him from all sides, and he strives to repeat it. He would be the world's mouthpiece:

"It is you talking just as much as myself; I act as the tongue of you.
It was tied in your mouth; in mine it begins to be loosened."

As with man, so with Nature:

"I hear you whispering there, O stars of heaven, O suns, O grass of graves! O perpetual transfers and promotions, if you do not say anything, how can I say anything?"

This man is sensitive to the slightest impression of Nature; and he is perpetually amazed at, and confounded by, phenomena that, because of their familiarity, we are wont to pass unnoticed. Of course, to such a mind, the problem of life ever deepens, but his cry of impassioned inquiry still sounds on. He may be baffled, but he neither desists nor complains. He is an utter stranger to discouragement or any morbid sentiment. Often he is mad with very health—intoxicated with the unspeakable riches of his being:

"To behold the day-break!
The little light fades the immense and diaphanous shadows;
The air tastes good to my palate."

"The atmosphere is not a perfume; it has no taste of the distillation; it is odorless.
It is for my mouth forever—I am in love with it.
I will go to the bank by the wood, and become undisguised and naked;
I am mad for it to be in contact with me."

The poet insists that one is not half a man or woman when the body is incapable of enjoying the gentlest and most secret influences of earth, air, and sky. He adores health—the nice balance of the mental and the physical that proclaims the perfect creature. The animal side of man is so grossly neglected and abused, entailing thereby such wretched frustration of the grand and glorious design for which he was called into existence—men are so frequently failures, wrecks, incapable of noble effort, of intelligent appreciation of the privileges proffered them—that this poet all but deifies the flesh, as he cries with a loud voice,

"Oh, my brothers, in the name of your Maker, attain to every possible perfection; be whole, be strong, be pure and sweet—open to the influx of the glorious life that stunted, deformed, diseased beings can never taste. Obey the laws of your being in the face of all criticism, and you will no longer know yourselves, so mighty, so splendid shall you become."

So worshipful a thing does the human body appear in the eyes of this vigorous, full-voiced, free, and intrepid singer, that it is impossible for him to understand how anything obscene can be thought or said concerning it. That his enthusiasm again and again carries him too far is by no means disputed; but that the intent is touched with impurity cannot for a moment be believed. The bounds of enthusiasm are unlimited. If those profoundly in earnest did not sometimes say that which were better unspoken, we would miss many another utterance of incalculable value. We are shocked by certain passages in *Leaves of Grass;* but the fire that prompted them has rekindled besides so much wisdom and beauty, that, on the whole, we would rather refrain from, than indulge in, censure. Such a poet must err occasionally in his search for, and presentation of, so many bold and startling truths. It is easy enough for a writer, every breath of whose passion is manufactured to meet the present need, to keep within the proprieties of a Sunday-school pamphlet; but Walt Whitman, whatever else he may be, is something more than one of these upright, self-moving machines, that grind to order chaffy grists that were better spilled than taken from the mill.

"Smile, O voluptuous, cool-breathed earth!
Earth of the slumbering and liquid trees!
Earth of departed sunset! Earth of the mountains misty-topt!
Earth of the vitreous pour of the full moon, just tinged with blue!
Earth of shine and dark, mottling the tide of the river!
Earth of the limpid gray of clouds, brighter and clearer for my sake!
Far-swooping elbowed earth! Rich apple-blossomed earth!
Smile, for your lover comes.
Prodigal, you have given me love. Therefore I to you give love.
O unspeakable, passionate love!

The relation between this writer and Nature is as intimate, and the feeling as tender, as that subsisting between a youth and the maid of whom he is enamored.

"You sea! I resign myself to you also;
I guess what you mean.
I behold from the beach your crooked, inviting fingers;
I believe you refuse to go back without feeling of me."

It is exceedingly difficult for us to understand how the reader of such lines can harbor a suspicion, even, that the sentiment is feigned. If the hot fire of sincere, unrestrained passion does not scorch these pages as it passes them over, one by one, we are wondrously deluded. The red, bounding blood of the man behind flows through these stanzas from first to last. Tame words are out of the question; the language must be extravagant. Excessively *wild* it may be; but—heaven be praised!—it is *alive*, carrying with it the quickening power without which poetry is impossible.

"Press close, bare-bosomed Night! Press close,
Magnetic, nourishing Night!
Night of south winds! Night of the large few stars!
Still, nodding Night; mad, naked, summer Night!"

If we are competent to decide, there is more inspiration in the above four lines than in any forty pages of such books as *Fantasy and Passion.* No inlaid work here, no mother-of-pearl or carving in ivory; but the full, impetuous gush of song as it descends from the fountain-head. This is not painting, much less chromo-printing; but the free sketch of the master, as accurate as it is comprehensive and suggestive. Instead of beholding such a picture through a magnifying glass, one can, after the first glance, see deepest into it with closed eyes.

And is Walt Whitman no artist? None but artists know the boundaries of their particular art; and herein lies the crucial test. Very seldom does our singer, when he is singing, fail in this regard. It is when he is laying down some fact too rank for aught but the harshest prose that he quits the domain of poetry; and there is justice in the proceeding. That his crashing sallies of rejoicing in masculinity, in strength, in the lionhood of mankind, and his blacksmith's blows dealt against the neutrality and namby-pamby element prevailing so largely among those who should be his fellows, his equals—that these necessarily prosaic efforts are rightly conjoined with the beauty and grace of poetry proper, is hardly to be maintained. The teacher of disturbingly plain, practical truths may shift himself too suddenly to the side of the exalted poet, chanting lays of charming mystery; but surely this does not destroy. It rather confirms the respective capacities employed in the one and in the other. Whitman is poet not only, but law-giver. Many a lesser writer would have separated matters that he has seen fit to send forth together. Nevertheless, when a man *has anything to say*, his method is of secondary consideration. We have this one cause for redemption of a multitude of offenses—*viz.*, that when this author determines to write poetry, the result is not a disappointment.

Again we ask, is it true that "all Mr. Whitman's work, from beginning to end, is absolutely without art?" The writer of this assertion was, as we have shown, thinking of the clothes of poetry. Whitman neither rhymes nor cuts his lines by the yard. This is the gist of the accusation. The fact of his mastery of rhythm is entirely overlooked. Will any one, sensitive to the music of speech, say that the appeals to the "Night" and to the "Sea," above quoted, are not as far removed from prose as if the lines were marked off by a carpenter's square, and tasseled with syllables that jingle each to the tune of its mate? This blunder of our critic is an additional testimonial to the subtlety of the melody of Whitman's diction. He was read by the eye, not by the ear. Let the reader listen for a moment:

"I hear the workman singing, and the farmer's wife singing;
I hear in the distance the sounds of children, and of animals early in the day;
I hear the inimitable music of the voices of mothers;
I hear the persuasions of lovers."

Is there no skill to be detected in this language, not to mention the native grace of the ideas? One quotation more, from the "Poem of the Dead Young Men of Europe," and we rest this part of the argument:

"They live in other young men, O kings!
They live in brothers, again ready to defy you.
They were purified by death—they were taught and exalted.

"Not a grave of the murdered for freedom but grows seed for freedom; in its turn to bear seed,
Which the winds carry afar and re-sow, and the rains and the snows nourish.

"Not a disembodied spirit can the weapons of tyrants let loose
But it stalks invisibly over the earth, whispering, counselling, cautioning.

"Liberty! Let others despair of you. I never despair of you.

"Is the house shut? Is the master away?
Nevertheless be ready—be not weary of watching.
He will soon return—his messengers come anon."

Where the body of Whitman's subject-matter is of the coarsest material, he does not neglect a certain indefinable delicacy of construction; while in his purely poetic strains, this skill rises to a degree of excellence that may well compensate for the absence of strict meter and rhyme. So much for Mr. Whitman's "mere antique license."

And now a word more as to his self-consciousness. He certainly believes in himself—a very essential requisite for one who is to undertake any kind of work whatever. But when Whitman introduces, with characteristic rush, his burly, magnetic personality, if we understand him, he brings a pressing multitude of his fellows with him.

"These are the thoughts of all men in all ages and lands; they are not original with me.
If they are not yours as much as mine, they are nothing, or next to nothing."

"In all people I see myself—none more, not one a barleycorn less;
And the good or bad I say of myself I say of them."

After all, Whitman's egotism amounts to no more than this, that he is a native son of the soil, a child of Nature, and as good as "you, whoever you are." He goes to Nature for his example.

"I see that the elementary laws never apologize.
I reckon I behave no prouder than the level I plant my house by, after all."

Grant that our *Ossian* is self-sustained and ready to say so; it is because he is a *man*, not because he is Walt Whitman.

"Any man or woman shall stand cool and supercilious before a million universes."

"I cock my hat as I please, indoors or out," he says to "trippers" and "askers," but the dumb beast can humble him:

"The look of the bay mare shames silliness out of me."

It is because he "sees through the broadcloth and gingham," and, let us add, the *satin*, *velvet*, and *brocade*; it is because he understands the actual worth of those "who piddle and patter here, in collars and tailed coats," that he is so often tempted to glory in himself. However, he retracts as often, and the simplest creature or thing of earth causes him wholly to forget that he is

"Walt Whitman, an American, one of the rough—a kosmos."

The red-necktied trickster in thought, speech, or behavior finds him untamable as a buffalo; but the infant in slumber holds him spell-bound:

"The little one sleeps in its cradle,
I lift the gauze and look a long time."

And this leads us, after so lengthy a diversion, to the mention of still another among the many qualifications that fit this author for the office of a poet—*viz.*, that of broad sympathy. Faith, earnestness, sympathy—add to these acute powers of perception and a peculiar gift of language, and the result must be some sort of a poet created by One higher than himself, the creature. It is only with artificialities, with things wherein never flow the juices of life, things inherently dead, that Whitman finds no bond of union:

"When a university course convinces like a slumbering woman and child convince,
When the minted gold in the vault smiles like the night-watchman's daughter,
When warrantee deeds loafe in chairs opposite, and are my friendly companions,
I intend to reach them my hand, and make as much of them as I do of men and women."

Herein may be gleaned his attitude toward the world. It is manifest on every page of his book that whatever comes from the Maker of us all, and of all that surround us, touches him to the quick; whatever exhibits, in its ordained way, the fathomless manifestation of *life*, has fascination for him forever:

"And the cow crunching with depressed head surpasses any statue.
Oxen that rattle the yoke or halt in the shade, what is that you express in your eyes?
It seems to me more than all the print I have read in my life."

Comparisons are odious; nevertheless, they may be edifying. Let us hear what the author of *Fantasy and Passion* has to say about cows. Take a stanza from the piece entitled "Clover."

"Here, too, the massive, lazy cow, star-eyed,
Thrusts down her dark, moist nose, and all day long,
By your delicious feast unsatisfied,
Crops with rough, florid tongue your honeyed throng,
Lashing off flies with her tail's restless thong."

Here is the eating machine. She is minutely pictured from tip of tongue to tip of tail; but what have we learned or felt from this visit to the familiar tenant of the summer field? What hint did we get to repay us for the tramp and the time? Under such guidance, will the "yellow primrose" ever appear anything more than simply the "yellow primrose?" There is a difference between looking even at a cow and really seeing her. The rare vision and love of the poet for the object of his gaze must first be, or nothing will be told us:

"I think I could turn and live with animals, they are so placid and self-contained;
I stand and look at them sometimes half the day long."

One that speaks thus is a receiver of impressions, and may become a translator of hidden meanings; in other words, a poet. He will probably consume little time in wheeling about platoons of stiff-backed, brass-buttoned stanzas; he will the rather think down into the matter he is to reveal until the burrowing thought brings its own tongue. Does he undertake to describe, the picture will be living; not a dry, prolix enumeration of surface peculiarities evident to the most careless observer. The imagination of the true poet moves in a bee-line; and perhaps the grand cause of its enchaining power is the rapidity with which it acts upon the feelings. While it points to some one central truth of exceeding beauty, its magic hand beckons into our presence a host of companions scarcely less delightful. Within this subtle power of provocation is secreted the very aroma of poetry.

"Outlines!" cries Whitman, "outlines!" The sketch is free and apparently careless, but, as the eye rests longer upon it, the detailed picture comes out, feature by feature, into final completion. The first faint streak of dawn is all at first; but patiently the dim tint spreads and deepens, until at last it is universal day. In abstract thought, as in description or narration, Whitman draws few lines; and we believe this method, while it is the most difficult, is the most effective employed in the art of poesy. Hammerton goes further; he declares that in the realm of painting, also, sketches equal finished pictures. Let us examine Whitman's narration of the visit of a slave to his house:

"The runaway slave came to my house and stopped outside.
I heard his motions crackling the twigs of the woodpile.
Through the swung half-door of the kitchen I saw him, limpsy and weak,
And went where he sat on a log, and led him in and assured him,
And brought water, and filled a tub for his sweated body and bruis'd feet,
And gave him a room that entered from my own, and gave him some coarse, clean clothes;
And remember perfectly well his revolving eyes and his awkwardness,
And remember putting plasters on the galls of his neck and ankles.
He stayed with me a week before he was recuperated and passed North.
I had him sit next me at table. My firelock leaned in the corner."

The tyro will, perhaps, believe such writing an easy task; but this, we apprehend, will not be the judgment of him who has had experience. That is a master-touch—"the revolving eyes" and the "awkwardness;" so, too, that at the close—the "firelock leaned in the corner." The volume before us abounds in like passages, evidencing the sharp perception, the aptness of language, and the patient thoughtfulness of the true poet. The omnibus-driver, with his "interrogating thumb;" the carpenter's foreplane, whistling its "wild, ascending lisp;" the mocking-bird, as he "sounds his delicious gurgles, cackles, screams, weeps;" the herds of buffalo that "make a crawling spread of the square miles far and near"—all proclaim that Whitman is an intimate of men and things, that he learns much from even the least of them, and that he can make his chosen communications attractive, as well as beneficial, to his fellows.

We cannot leave this champion of naturalness, this athlete-lover of life, passionate, independent, resistless adorer of naked truth and beauty, without the following lines of characteristic pregnancy of suggestion and most exquisite tenderness:

"A child said, What is the grass?—fetching it to me with full hands.
How could I answer the child? I do not know
What it is any more than he.
I guess it must be the flag of my disposition, out of hopeful green stuff woven;
Or I guess it is the handkerchief of the Lord,
A scented gift and remembrancer, designedly dropped,
Bearing the owner's name some way in the corners,
That we may see and remark, and say, Whose?

"Tenderly will I use you, curling grass;
It may be you transpire from the breasts of young men;
It may be if I had known them I would have loved them:
It may be you are from old people, and from women,
And from offspring taken soon out of the mothers' laps—
And here you are the mothers' laps.

"The grass is very dark to be from the white heads of old mothers,
Darker than the colorless beards of old men,
Dark to come from under the faint red roofs of mouths.
Oh, I perceive after all so many uttering tongues,
And I perceive they do not come from the roofs of mouths for nothing.

"I wish I could translate the hints about the dead young men and women,
And the hints about old men and mothers, and the offspring taken soon out of their laps."

It has been endeavored to show that the writer of "Americanisms in Literature" was not equal to the task assigned. To allow his internecine propositions to fall foul of one another, to their own destruction, was a simple, and we trust a satisfactory, process of proving the correctness of the position taken. Furthermore, a hasty inquiry into the causes of his failure has been instituted. This could be most readily done by an examination of his mental characteristics as recorded in the volume given by him to the world, and by a survey of Whitman's genius depicted in like manner. The plan that he himself avoided in dealing with Whitman we have adopted in our discussion of both writers—*viz.*, that of making extracts from their published works. We have not, however, employed "the cheap means" of selecting "most ill advised passages" as illustrations. On the contrary, the effort has been to quote only such passages as were calculated to afford, as far as they extended, a characterization of the volume entire. Full justice cannot be expected in so short a paper. We may have been too severe upon the one hand, or too lenient upon the other. The author of *Fantasy and Passion*, however, certainly cannot censure any of our chance hard words; for it is he who says, "His glimpses of perfect sanity are sometimes Mr. Whitman's most unfortunate points."

We believe that he should not have spoken; and we also believe that, had *Leaves of Grass* exhibited vastly more "ocean turbulence," and had its author been a far more "terrifying maniac," still would "cultured American men and women" have welcomed both as a relief from, and a rebuke to, Rosetti-isms thrice reduced and piping rhymesters prostrate with chronic mediocrity. ANTHONY THRALL.

THE NAVAL RESOURCES OF CHINA.

It may with safety be assumed that prior to the years 1860-61, the guns, rifles, or munitions of war, manufactured upon foreign principles, in the possession of the provincial authorities of China, were almost useless. The lesson that the mandarins then received from the allied armies was not lost upon them. They saw that, despite the number of men they could bring into the field, the superiority of arms of precision, combined with skill in military tactics, enabled the western soldiers to become conquerors; and although Tseng Kwo Fan and the General, San Ko Lin San, in their memorials to the Dragon Throne, informed his majesty that his troops were utterly defeating the barbarians, and that the latter would never reach the imperial city of Peking, the Chinese learned to their cost the falsity of these representations. The western cannon which were found in the Taku forts upon the entry of the British troops were of Dutch and British make, small twelve-pounders, such as are used for signal guns upon vessels. A few, however, were of superior caliber, and were possibly of Russian manufacture. The rest of the guns were of Chinese origin, and it has been stated by officers engaged in the attack that the defense made by the Chinese, when we consider the weapons used and their disadvantage in point of inferiority of equipment, was a matter of great surprise. It was at the storming of the Taku forts that the Armstrong gun was first used in action. The Chinese troops were also armed with a few smooth-bore muskets—these articles, in common with the cannon, having been purchased at Hongkong or Singapore, and conveyed along the coast to the north in junks.

The armament of the Chinese forces received an impetus in the march of improvement immediately upon the outbreak of the celebrated Taiping rebellion. This rebellion caused the imperial generals and viceroys to search for persons who would supply them with arms. Numbers of European merchants engaged in the traffic, and a vast quantity of worthless, rejected muskets were foisted upon the officials. Sales were also made to the Taiping leaders, and in several instances large fortunes were realized by those interested. The repairs of these arms becoming necessary, the attention of Li, commanding general, who was then known as Li Futai ("Futai" meaning governor), and who is probably better known to the reader as Li Hung Chang, Governor-General of Chihli, was drawn to the want of an arsenal. Shot and shell of semi-foreign make were being turned out of small foundries at Shanghai for the use of the imperialists, but it was reserved for an official by the name of Fêng, in the year 1865, to establish, by authority from the central government, a yard for the building of vessels of war, and an arsenal for the manufacture of small arms and cannon. The whole of this undertaking was under the auspices of Li, who, at this period, having been removed from his office of Futai of Kiangsu (*i. e.*, Governor), was conducting operations against the Nienfei rebels, in the northern provinces, and required all the munitions of war he could obtain. The locality chosen is near Shanghai, in the province of Kiangsu, being distant from the foreign settlements about five miles. It was formerly the site of an old temple, and to this day is called "Kaou Chang Meaou." In official documents its title is the "Kiangsu Chi Chi Fang," or "the province of Kiangsu machinery depot or factory." It covers an area of five hundred *mow* of ground, each *mow* equaling one-sixth of an acre. It has a dock for ship-building purposes, and large machine shops for the manufacture and repair of Remington pattern rifles, capable of turning out, if pushed, about five hundred rifles per week. The machinery is of the most perfect kind, comprising every requisite for boring, fitting, and turning barrels; also wood-working machinery, for the stocks and butts of the rifles, and the manufacture of cases for transportation, and everything needful for the general work required. This branch is at present time entirely under Chinese superintendence, the Englishman who supervised the rifle factory having been sent home. The work turned out has elicited the admiration of all military and naval officials of various nationalities who have visited the arsenal. The same may be remarked of the department for the manufacture of rifled cannon. Within the past three years an experienced person has arrived from the Woolwich Arsenal, and the result of his labors was lately shown at the proof of some six 64-pounders of the Woolwich type (Fraser pattern), the test being eminently satisfactory. These guns were constructed from raw material, the steel and iron having been imported from Europe. The machinery, steam-hammers, converting crucibles, and retorts are capable of turning out 25-ton guns. Everything is of the most improved type, the rejected patterns having been either sent to the arsenal at Tsi Nan Foo, Shantung province, or used for old metal.

For the construction of iron-clad ships, there is machinery for bending, planing, boring, and riveting iron plates up to ten inches thick. A portion only of this has been erected, but it remains for the rising generation of enlightened officials to build an iron-clad. A sample iron turret ship was built by the foreign engineers and naval constructors attached to the department, but she was not found to possess seagoing qualities upon trial at the mouth of the Whangpoo, and she now rides at anchor, a sort of white elephant. In all, the vessels constructed at this arsenal number seven, two of them being ship-rigged frigates of 2,000 tons burden, mounting 24 guns (Krupp 20-pounders) as a broadside battery, one bow and one stern-chaser of 9-inch caliber, Vavasseur pattern, all breech-loaders. The other ships are either brig or schooner rigged, some of them having Krupp 40-pounders, and the others brass 12-pounders, cast at the arsenal at Nanking. The whole of the naval force associated under the direction of this province's authorities is as follows: 2 frigates of 2,000 tons, 500 horse-power, 26 guns each; 4 gun vessels of 600 tons, 150 horse-power, 6 guns each; iron turret vessel of 150 tons, 80 horse-power, no gun; in all, 7 vessels of 6,550 tons, 1,880 horse-power, 77 guns, and manned by 2,000 men. The arsenal also manufactures shot and shell, and has been actively employed for over twelve months past in turning out war material for Tso Tsung Tang, the conqueror of Kashgar, and the Governor-General commanding the troops in the northwest.

Attached to the Shanghai arsenal are extensive works for the manufacture of gunpowder, ignition fuses for mines, and torpedoes, percussion caps, signal and war rockets, and a small building used for sulphuric acid chambers. These mills are capable, when required, of turning out from ten to twelve tons of powder per week, rifle, pebble, and prismatic. The charges are here worked into cartridges, used for Remington, Snider, and the various arms, and also for heavy guns. The whole establishment is under the superintendence of two Englishmen, but rapid strides have been made by the natives in acquiring the methods for the manipulation of the dangerous substances. The raw materials—*viz.*, saltpeter, sulphur, and the various chemicals—are nearly all imported. The charcoal used is burned at the works, from the Chinese willow. A constant strain has been placed upon the factory for nearly a year, excessive demands being made upon its resources to supply the army in the north-west. The sum of 60,000 *taels* ($80,000) is appropriated every month from the customs revenue for the maintenance of this establishment, which employs 700 hands.

The arsenal at Nanking was established under the direction of Dr. Macartney (now interpreter for the Chinese Legation in England), assisted by an able staff of foreign artisans; but these gentlemen were removed from time to time, and the whole of the machinery, which is very costly, is now worked entirely under Chinese superintendents and by Chinese workmen. This arsenal furnishes brass and steel guns, percussion caps and fuses, and the work shown is very creditable. The two arsenals at Tientsin are also supplied with heavy machinery for effecting repairs to rifles and marine engines, as well as for general repairs; and also a factory has been recently established at Hai Quan-Sz (in a temple on the plain outside of the city of Tientsin, where the treaty of 1860 was signed), for construction of telegraphic machines, torpedo connections, fuses, and rifles. The main arsenal employs from 500 to 600 men, under the supervision of three Europeans, assisted by Chinese, who have received their training at the Shanghai arsenal. The gunpowder works are on a large scale; every description of powder, cartridges, shells, rockets, and munitions of war, is made here. These works were first started in 1865, by Chung How, the now disgraced Chinese Envoy. They have been much enlarged and improved upon by Li Hung Chang, Viceroy of Chihli, who also holds the rank of Superintendent of Arsenals and Naval Affairs for the Empire. The cost of maintenance is probably $100,000 per month.

A torpedo school, for instruction of Chinese cadets, was established in Foochow in 1877, but has been removed to Tientsin. The pupils show a marked proficiency in the manipulation of the system of torpedoes and telegraphy attached to the Taku forts. They also work the line of wire connecting Taku with Tientsin, and thence on to the Viceroy's palace. Regular examinations are held quarterly by the Viceroy, who awards honors to those distinguishing themselves.

To the Foochow dockyard must be awarded the honor of the construction of the only war vessels China possesses, with the exception of those constructed in England, to be hereafter referred to. This vast and costly undertaking was first originated by Ting Futai, under the management of M. Prosper Giquel, Lieutenant Vasseaux, of the French navy, and afterward Commissioner of Customs at Hankow and Ningpo, and who, during the Taiping rebellion, raised and commanded a force known as the French contingent. The whole establishment was officered by Frenchmen, excepting the naval instructors, Captain Carroll and Mr. Harwood, gunner. This dockyard is used only for the purpose of ship-building. It has built no less that twenty-seven gun vessels and transports; some of them, to be enumerated hereafter, are really formidable ships. With the exception of the corvette *Yangwoo*, and the gunboats Nos. 6, 7, and 8, which possess engines built in Scotland, after models in use in the English navy—*viz.*, direct acting horizontal, with fighting boilers—the other vessels have all low-pressure upright engines, similar to those used in the merchant navy. Ten of these engines were built in France, at the *ateliers* of the Société Forges de Lyons and the Société Marine de Marseilles, but were fitted at the Foochow dockyard. All the boilers were constructed by native artisans. Of these ships, eighteen were built under the supervision of the French artisans, but in 1876 their services were dipensed with, and the remaining nine were constructed by the Chinese themselves. The following may serve as a classification of their fighting capacity:

No.	Class	Guns.	Calibre.	H.-P.	Tonnage.
1.	Transport	4	18	180	700
2.	Gunboat	4 1	18 60	80	150
3.	Gunboat	4 1	18 60	80	200
4.	Gunboat	4 1	18 60	80	200
5.	Corvette	10 2	40 100	300	800
6.	Gunboat	6 2	40 100	200	900
7.	Gunboat	6 2	40 100	200	900
8.	Gunboat	6 2	40 100	200	900
9.	Transport	2	40	180	500
10.	Transport	2	40	180	500
11.	Transport	2	40	120	500
12.	Transport	2	40	120	500
13.	Gunboat	6 2	40 100	120	900
14.	Gunboat	6 2	40 100	150	900
15.	Gunboat	6 2	40 100	150	900
16.	Transport	No guns.		120	500
17.	Transport	No guns.		120	500
18.	Transport	No guns.		120	500
19.	Gun vessel	6	40	180	500
20.	Gun vessel	6	40	180	500
21.	Gun vessel	6	40	180	500
22.	Ram model	10 2	40 100	200	800
23.	Transport	4	40	120	500
24.	Transport	4	40	180	500
25.	Transport	4	40	120	400
26.	Composite vessel.	Building.		200	800
27.	Composite vessel.	Building.		200	800

The armament is mainly comprised of 40-pounder Vavasseur breech-loading guns and Armstrong and French type 100-pounder muzzle-loaders. The small 12-pounders are brass guns, cast at the Nanking arsenal. These vessels all carry Remington small arms, and are manned entirely by Chinese, under native commanders and engineers, no foreigners being employed whatsoever. Their average speed is ten knots, Nos. 5, 6, 7, and 8 steaming with improved engines, making fourteen knots. As a rule, they are all brig rigged, except the corvette No. 5, which has the full rig of a ship. Nos. 1 to 25 are built of wood, teak being used entirely in their construction. Nos. 26 and 27 have iron frames, with teak planking.

The ships have their various stations at the treaty ports, and are under the supervison of the Port-Admiral of the place where located. There is, however, a General-Admiral, but he is entirely subordinate to the officials of the dockyard. A system of signals, by means of which communication between the ships can be sustained, has been arranged. At the present time the largest part of the fleet is commanded by young men, who were trained upon a sailing ship, the *Kienwei*, commanded by Captain Tracy, of the English navy, and who afterward proceeded upon a cruising voyage to Singapore, India, and Japan, in the steam corvette *Yang Wu*, under the guidance of English naval instructors. These young men are nearly all natives of either the Kwantung or Fohkien provinces. They have attained a remarkable proficiency in navigation and gunnery, and their efforts to organize the Chinese navy have been attended with great results. The writer can vouch for several of these embryo Chinese Nelsons, inasmuch as he has made several passages in the gunboats under their command. Prior to assuming captain's duties, they all pass through trials as first and second lieutenants. The vessels were originally commanded by Chinese, who bore excellent reputations as coast pilots, steering the ships from point to point on the coast, but never losing sight of land. These gentlemen are being gradually supplanted by the trained men, much to their disgust.

The hands of the captains are somewhat tied by the manner in which naval affairs are administered in China. Each mandarin who has some hanger-on round the coast ports sends candidates for all positions, even to those of cook and sweeper, on board the ships. The captains, of course, are still under the spell of the old custom, which cannot be yet removed, and they have to drill these nominees into ship ways. The captains' salaries range from 150 *taels* ($200) up to 500 *taels* ($700) per month. Their allowances, with which to find the ship in oils, paints, blocks, rope, and all requisites, except coal, varies according to the size of their command. A vessel's allowance would be from $500 to $1000, according to her tonnage. Should any be detached as guard-ships at treaty ports, the wear and tear is nothing; then the allowance lines the captain's pockets.

Upon the whole, the ships of the Foochow division may be considered as the most effective, both in point of drill and in fighting capacity, with the exception of the new "Greek alphabet" gun vessels. This type of war ship has excited universal comments in the naval circles of every country. They were all built by Messrs. C. Mitchell & Co., and the engines by Messrs. Thompson, of Newcastle-on-Tyne, England, from the designs of Mr. Rendel, of the eminent firm of Sir W. J. Armstrong & Co. The *Alpha* and *Beta* are each of 300 tons burden, and carry a 26½-ton Armstrong gun, capable of penetrating a 12-inch armor plate. These two gunboats arrived in China in March, 1877, and are now stationed in Formosa, at the port of Taiwan-foo. The *Gamma* and *Delta* carry each a 12-inch 38-ton gun, firing a projectile of 800 pounds, with charges of 130 pounds of prismatic powder, and can penetrate 19-inch armor. Their dimensions are as follows: 115 feet long; 30 feet beam; mean draught, 8 feet with a 3-foot freeboard. Their displacement is 400 tons. The engines are twin-screw of 270 horse-power, and are capable of steaming 9 knots per hour. They are schooner-rigged, with tripod masts, and can carry sufficient coal to work at full speed, using 14 hundred-weight per hour, for seven days of twenty-four hours. The *Epsilon*, *Eta*, *Theta*, and *Zeta* models are a further advance upon the original type. They measure 127 feet long, 29 feet beam, with a draught of 9 feet 6 inches, and their displacement is 440 tons. The propelling power consists of twin-screw horizontal engines, capable of driving them 10 knots, and, by reason of their possessing bow-rudders and fine lines, they can also steam 9 knots backward. The bunker capacity is 70 tons, and the consumption of coal 6 hundred-weight per hour. They are schooner rigged, with tripod masts. Although the *Epsilon* series carry only 35-ton guns, owing to the advance made by Messrs. Armstrong in the power of ordnance relative to weight, the new 35-ton is equal in power to the 38-ton gun, with a 250-pound battering charge. The 35-ton gun's projectile has a velocity of 1,925 feet, equal to 400 foot-tons energy per inch of circumference. With a 235-pound charge the new 35-ton gun has one-fifth more penetrating power than the old 38-ton, the figures showing 356 foot-tons per inch as compared to 300. The high initial velocity of the 35-ton gun causes the trajectory of its projectile to be very flat, and thus gives the gun a much better chance of hitting any object, and also increases the range. With the exception of the Italian war ship *Duilio*, with her 100-ton Armstrong guns, and the British turret-ship *Devastation*, with her 80-ton Woolwich guns, the Chinese government possesses the most powerful guns afloat. The main feature of all these gunboats is the great gun which is placed on line with the keel in the bow, and is mounted and worked entirely by hydraulic machinery. Five men work it efficiently. There are no chains, cog-wheels, or gearing—not even a gun-carriage. The gun lies on the deck between two great beams, with two pistons sliding upon them, which take hold of the trunnions, and there is nothing more to be seen. The captain of the vessel stands behind a splinter-proof cabin, and can aim and work the gun, steer the vessel, and regulate her speed, by means of levers. In addition to the heavy guns, two 12-pounder breech-loading Armstrongs and one Gatling gun are carried aft. All the vessels are built of steel, and have four transverse water-tight bulkheads, with a horizontal under-water deck protecting the magazines. The whole of the machinery, engine, boilers, and hydraulic, are below the water-line. The commanders, officers, engineers, and crew are all Chinese, and number fifty all told. The captains have been pupils of the Foochow school-ships, and are fully competent to take their commands. Their station at present is at Tientsin. Gun practice and drill is had each day, and a good state of efficiency prevails. It may be stated that all the little ships steamed out from England, and, owing to the interest displayed by the Admiralty, officers of the British navy were permitted to assume command. The voyage throughout were perfectly successful. They encountered heavy gales in the Bay of Biscay, but proved excellent sea-boats, thus demonstrating the fact that this class of war-ships are capable of making voyages on the open seas.

In addition to the vessels mentioned before, the province of Kwantung has some small steamships, used chiefly for the suppression of piracy and for revenue purposes, but which could be adapted for the purposes of war if necessary, being fairly armed. Four more of the "Alphabet" fleet are about to be built, by order of the Viceroy of the "Two Kwangs," for coast defense. It may be safely asserted that this large fleet of ships places China in a very fair position as regards her naval equipment. Her vessels are good, and their armaments excellent; but what she needs most is men to command her sailors. Discipline is lax, although bravery is common among the men, who are all drawn from the maritime provinces, and three-fourths of whom have served upon foreign steamers and ships, and are acquainted with nautical usages. It would be invidious to make any comments upon the part China may play in a naval engagement, but foreign nations, in the event of war, would not find victory in 1880 as easy as they found it in 1860 and 1861.

HENRY D. WOOLFE.

SEVEN LETTERS.

I have had no little difficulty in finding a title, from the uneasy consciousness that the unprofessional reader, when he sees anything relating to music, shies at the idea of a dissertation on the chord of the diminished seventh, and that the professional, discovering nothing technical, will throw it aside with the ominous, muttered word, "Trash!"—than which nothing can be more mortifying to the aspirant for literary and musical honors, since it classes his work with "Cruel as the Grave" and "La Harpe Eolienne." On the other hand, I have no desire to delude the unwary into fancying that they are about to gain some recondite piece of information. I have nothing to say about the Seven before Thebes, nor the seven bodies in alchemy.

The atrocious crime of being a *dilettante* I attempt neither to palliate nor deny. Since all is vanity, in a more personal sense than the Preacher's, I confess to believing that the *dilettante* is a sort of musical epicure, enjoying all finer flavors, if I may use the word, that escape the professional musician, except in a few rare instances; for the *dilettante* has a sort of veneer—a superficiality—which makes him despised by the masters of the craft, but which nevertheless gives him an advantage over them, in that he brings to the enjoyment of the great composers' works a slight knowledge of other arts, a broader culture, that may interweave with music, and raise his appreciation and his ideal proportionably. The more we read and study and live, the deeper and wider and higher becomes the meaning of the greatest of all the arts, named from the Muses themselves; and what the *dilettante* loses in the mechanical he gains in the poetical. It strikes the outward observer that a petty quarrel over two piano makers, or over precedence in a dressing-room, is unworthy of the enviable title of artist, and it would almost seem that there is something belittling to the soul in making a slave of the goddess who should be worshiped, until at last all that is seen of her is her market value in the concert hall or the opera house.

But the indignities that poor Music suffers at the hands of those whom she has divinely gifted are not her only wrongs. There is a large class of human beings by whom she is despised and ignored. Of such is John Stuart Mill. I fancy that he expressed the opinion of many wise, and learned, and narrow men—narrow, because they shut off and refuse to cultivate one side of their nature, and so deprive themselves of a means of recreation and refinement that would develop them, who can say how many fold?—when he said that he had examined music and discovered that it was based on only seven letters or notes, and the combinations must manifestly be so few and so monotonous that he decided to waste no time over such trivialities. I think the poor, weary, repressed economist forgot, or did not accept, the theory of the evolution of great things out of small. From those seven letters has sprung a whole literature of the emotions; and in an infinite variety of tones, from the faintest pressure of the violin bow on the strings to the sublime swell of the organ, is found expression for all the joy and grief, the pathos, passion, despair, the consolation and religion of suffering humanity. Lord Brougham, who roared out "Stop that nuisance!" to the crestfallen amateur pianist, would have been comforted and sustained by Mill's enunciation of his convictions on this subject, as well as the amiable hostess who said to the young lady waiting for the gentlemen to finish knocking about the billiard balls before she began her song, "Go right on, dear, I don't think they will mind," with a fine unconsciousness of sarcasm.

What is to be done with these Philistines? They cause the artistic to writhe with anguish; yet they are really not much worse than those who profess an intense scorn for what they call "classical" music, heaping together under one indiscriminate head incongruous authors like Bach, Haydn, Beethoven, Mendelssohn, Chopin, and Schumann, while they listen with delight to such worthless proofs of time and talent wasted as a "Silvery Shower," or a "Cascade of Pearls," compositions of about as much value in music as the poems of the "Sweet Singer of Michigan" possess in literature. We must perforce regard these unfortunates with the same regretful pity that we bestow upon the benighted being who glories in his preference for the jokes of the end man in a minstrel show, declaring that Booth's "Iago" puts him to sleep.

Perhaps this false musical taste proceeds in a great measure from a defective musical education. When our children begin to read and recite, we would scarcely give them doggerel and dime novels to enlarge their vocabulary and develop their minds. There is plenty of easy and well written music for the little fingers and quick childish brains to learn and grow upon.

That, in spite of our persuasion to the contrary, America is not yet a musical nation, musical foreigners soon discover. A certain German music teacher gauged the general public in giving the following direction to a pupil who was practicing for a public performance: "Be sure to strike the last note of your runs clearly and distinctly; they will not know what false notes come between." My conscience should smite me for passing on this bad advice, which probably in the Fatherland no one would dare to give, for there they expect good music or none.

Surely, of this there is a wide range from which all may choose; there is more than enough to satisfy every individual taste. There is the strong, healthy classicism of Johann Sebastian Bach, and Handel, and the many-sided genius of Mozart, with his merry, delicate face, such as we fancy must have belonged to his own "Cherubino." We hear his motto running through all his music, *dum vivimus vivamus;* yet occasionally comes a tinge of melancholy, as if he had caught the echo of the minor chord that vibrates under and throughout Nature's gladness if we had but the ears to hear it, from the yearning of the restless sea to the shudder that creeps up the trees before the bursting of a thunder-shower, or the

"Wild wind symphonies that moan and die
On hemlock harps with such a sad refrain.'

Passing these, we have Beethoven, the giant, the "generalissimo von all," as a German friend of mine quaintly expressed it. He is an inexhaustible mine, like Shakspere. Tender, caressing, gloomy, passionate, sublime, he probes the human heart. "Study the *Appassionata Sonata,*" said my friend; "into that he has put all his sorrow." And it is the sorrow of a vigorous, large-hearted nature, the sorrow of a Prometheus suffering for mankind, utterly different from the morbid, introspective melancholy of Chopin, which is like that of a beautiful consumptive girl; for modern genius is essentially subjective, and as such essentially feminine. Chopin has made his own the *Nocturne* first tried by Field, and has left us treasures of dreamy melodies to be learned by heart and played in the twilight; fancies now overlaid with a delicate, fairy-like tracery, again, as in the *C minor* and the *Lamento,* breaking into stormy, rebellious passion, wild with all regret. His "Funeral March" has found a worthy translator into language in the glowing and enthusiastic pages of Liszt's tribute to his dead friend:

"Only a Pole could have written this. The solemn and heart-rending sight of a whole nation weeping over its own death is found here in the funeral knell that seems to attend it. All the feeling of mystic hope, of religious appeal to superhuman mercy, to infinite clemency, and to justice that keeps count of each grave and each cradle, all the lofty resignation which has shed the light of aureoles on so many sorrows and disasters borne with the heroism inspired by the martyrs, ring in this chant with a despairing supplication. The purity, the holiness, the resignation, the faith, and the hope in the hearts of women, children, and priests, echo, shudder, and tremble with ineffable vibrations. We feel that it is not a lament for the death of a hero whom other heroes will avenge, but that of a generation which has succumbed, leaving behind only women, children, and priests. And this melody is so unearthly sweet, so softened, as it would seem, by distance, that we listen in stillness, as if it were sung by the angels themselves around the Throne. No cries, no hoarse groans, no impious blasphemies, no furious imprecations disturb the wail that is like a seraph's sigh. The antique spirit of grief is shut out. Nothing recalls the fury of Cassandra, the abasement of Priam, the frenzy of Hecuba, the desolation of the Trojan captives. In the survivors of the Christian Ilium a proud faith surmounts the bitterness of suffering as well as the weakness of prostration; their sorrow shakes off its frailty, and, rising from the ground watered by blood and tears, lifts itself towards the Judge of all, imploring him in such poignant prayer that, as we listen, our hearts break under a sublime compassion."

This inspired composition was arranged for the orchestra, and given in that form, for the first time, as part of Chopin's own funeral service. Would that I had been spared the infliction of its repetition on an occasion that shall be nameless. Chopin was above all original. He might have quoted of himself Alfred de Musset's line:

"Mon verre n'est pas grand, mais je bois dans mon verre."

His works are not for the many; in that, as in some other ways, he brings Keats to mind. Like all men of genius who fail with the public, he prided himself on pleasing the esoteric few.

"I am not fit to give concerts," he said to an artist friend. "The public intimidates me, the breaths stifle me, the curious looks paralyze me, I am dumb before all those strange faces; but you were made for it. When you fail to win the public you can overwhelm it."

Who could do justice in words to his polonaises and mazurkas, his waltzes, that are like lovely, heart-broken women, wearing a brave front before the world!

It seems strange that those people who reiterate that they "like a tune" fail to hear the melodies scattered through all of Schubert's works, and repeated often enough to make an impression on even Napoleon Bonaparte, according to Madame de Rémusat's account. Most people know Schubert only through his "Serenade," which has been half ruined by one of those who rush in where angels fear to tread, and arranged as a duet and sung to admiring audiences. Most lovers would object to having a high tenor join him unexpectedly in imploring the lady of his love: "Let thy pity then restore me, bid my heart be still." But every art must suffer from straining after cheap effect. To those who know them, nothing can equal the creepy chill that runs over one at the suspense and horror in the *Doppelganger;* the hurried clatter of horses' hoofs, and the mysterious sweetness of the phantom's seductive invitation to the terrified boy, in the *Erl-King.* Faust's "Gretchen" herself sings her wretched song before her spinning wheel: "My heart is heavy, my peace is gone." Who can fail to be touched by the exile's desolation in the "Wanderer," after the "Serenade" better known, perhaps, than any other song of his. The light, balancing air, that he has set to Heine's "Fisher-maiden," should make it popular, unless it is that the English translations of most of these exquisite gems, in trying to preserve the rhythm, have travestied the inimitable, simple grace of the original poems, and have become a mere tissue of affected nonsense. Only a poet can translate a poet.

We cannot all have voices, alas!—and for instrumentalists to gloat over, Schubert has given his beautiful *Momens Musicals*—real inspirations—his wild impromptus and fantaisies, and some fine sonatas, besides chamber music and symphonies, like all the great masters. I say all, but indeed they can nearly be counted on the fingers, while the name of mediocrity is legion. I have given most space to the German school because of its wider scope and abundance of piano music. Italy, the land of melody, has done more for the human voice than for other branches of the art, as Bellini, Donizetti, and Rossini can testify. They wrote for the old, florid school of singing, that made artistic training and hard study a necessity. The new Wagnerian opera requires a perfect orchestra rather than perfect vocalists, and a wide chest and deep lungs are apparently the only things needful for success in *Tannhaüser* and *Lohengrin.* Most of the German voices sound tired.

It is a pity that a superficial veneer of some operatic tricks should have taken the place of thorough grounding and development of the voice. Flexibility in its highest degree is a long, steady, sustained note, without the trembling and vibration that very many take for expression, but that, in reality, is inability to hold a pure note. The smoother the execution, the more perfect the singing of even the simplest ballad. The "h" might almost be called the shibboleth of singers, as it is of Englishmen. Ask almost any vocalist to execute a rapid passage, and you will hear an excellent imitation of laughter, though far from intended. If we only knew it, the audible escape of the breath in a vocal run is just as unpardonable as the sudden jerk and lifting of the hand in playing a piano scale. But it is such a common fault that it is painfully apparent only to those who have been warned against it; and perhaps the consciousness of their defective style causes singers generally to prefer the staccato, which, after all, is only a trick, and no certain proof of a good school.

The universal rage for *opéra bouffe* has had a bad effect on all classes of music in quickening the time. We must hold M. Offenbach responsible for turning the *andante* into an *allegro,* and the *allegro* into a *presto,* so that when a real *prestissimo* comes, the brass brays, the reed instruments gasp, the strings saw frantically, the notes, right or wrong, hurry on helter-skelter. It is who shall get to the end first, and the big drum and the cymbals come in with a clash that covers the discord made by those who have fallen behind in the rush, as they drown the shrieks of victims of the *mêlée,* and in confusion worse confounded we imagine that we have heard something very grand.

The *bouffe* composers are rapacious, too. Not content with gathering in street songs from the *cafés chantants,* they dive for tiny pearls of melody in the great ocean of sweet sounds that genius has left us, and debase the gem by the ignoble setting. There are strains in *La Belle Hélène* that are distinctly Mendelssohn; and even Gounod is not above laying hands on the *Largo* of the third Beethoven *concerto,* for the opening of Faust's great air, "Salve Dimora"—flat burglary as ever was committed.

I know that the *Larghetto* of Beethoven's second symphony, and the *Andante* of his fifth, have been used in the same unceremonious fashion, though by whom I cannot at this moment say. The author of the "Turkish Review," or "Patrol," as it is indifferently called, made a raid on one of Beethoven's marches, and, considering the immense possibilities of plunder, came away with a very small portion. As he grows older he may grow bolder, however; although from his point of view it is, perhaps, better as it is, since the public went into ecstasies over it, and, as Holofernes says, "*Satis quod sufficit.*" There was a man who set Rossini's air, "Di Tanti Palpiti," to a comic song, enumerating the joys and woes of the matrimonial duet, but he gave his original the credit of the composition, apparently struck with the appropriateness of *tanti palpiti* to wedlock.

It may be that something of the indifference of the world to absolute beauty is owing to the lack of enthusiasm on the part of those who are privileged to be its interpreters. Few possess the humility, combined with absorption in their art, that animated a certain string quartet in Paris. They laid down for themselves the axiom that beauty is always recognized, and if it is ignored, the fault lies not in the object, but in the manner of its presentation. Full of this idea, they studied one quartet by a great German composer until they felt themselves able to do it justice before the world. It was a failure. Not at all discouraged, they decided that they had not brought themselves to the necessary perfection, and worked harder than ever, until, after more than one rebuff, they forced the appreciation of their masterpiece from the most recalcitrant. But such patience is a rare gift. The constant hurry in which we live, the continual inventions for the increase of speed in travel and personal communication, infuse a corresponding impatience to finish a thing and lay it aside, when, perhaps, we have merely glanced at the outer husk, not dreaming of the inner fruit. Perfection in morals, science, or art is dependent on close study, earnest application, and a high ideal. In the press of everyday life we lose our grasp of the ideal, retaining it best, perhaps, in music, the most ethereal of all the arts. Now, suppose the passion for realism, that has set the world crazy, were to take possession of the realm of sound, as it has of literature and painting, what an insufferable din would deafen us. No music of the spheres "still quiring to the young-eyed cherubins," but the rumble of carts and drays, the roar of the mill-dam, the creaking and groaning of machinery, the brutal growls and drunken shrieks of the populace, since in realism is recognized only the graphic portrayal of the lowest and most degraded types, and the more revolting the picture, the greater the artist, to our perverted taste. We live in an age when the widest publicity is given to crime, and if innocence is ignorance of evil, the youngest child can hardly hope to wear the name. With our mental palate jaded by its daily food, for our relaxation and amusement we require something still more highly flavored, as the oldest resident of India eats the hottest curry. Singing men and singing women we have in abundance, but the one concerning whose private life are circulated the most piquant details is the one that wins our plaudits and our flowers.

The usual theory of musical matrimony is that the irritable, high-strung nerves inseparable from genius, the revolt from the laws that govern ordinary mortals, the large share of individuality claimed by the public, go to the tempering of a steel that will at last strike fire from the coldest flint, and straight the matrimonial tinder is in a blaze. Yet one noble exception springs instantly to mind—the ideal union of Robert and Clara Schumann, the composer and his best interpreter.

But then there are composers and composers. The poet sings of Prince Agib, who wrote a lot of ballet music in his teens, and whose devotion to the art was so extreme, though apparently an amateur, that

"He would diligently play
On the Zoetrope all day,
And blow the gay Pantechnicon all night."

The wretched victim who lived within earshot must have had reason to exclaim, with Ducis's Hamlet:

"Hélas! mon cher Norceste.
Je me suis élancé hors de mon lit funeste."

Rossini, who composed in bed, was similarly affected by hearing his favorite air ground under his window on a barrel-organ. He appeared before the astonished "organist" in a very sketchy toilet, and, giving a few vigorous turns to the crank, cried:

"*Così! così!* Never play my air again unless you play it as I do."

It is of Rossini that the story is told of his making a visit to Beethoven, who refused to see him, "because," using a very material metaphor, "Rossini never treats his friends to anything but dessert."

The Germans call him the head confectioner, but the Italians return sneer for sneer, and hiss *Tannhauser* whenever they get an opportunity.

So school rivals school, in art, science, philosophy; discord clashes on discord, to melt at last, we hope and pray, into one great harmony, that shall thrill through all eternity.

HELEN MORSE LAKE.

THE DEATH OF THE SUN.

I.

"By the Golden Gate."

The dying, dying Day,
Sighing his soul away on Ocean's breast,
Without a pang for sovereignty's lost sway;
Smiling adown the west,
Sinking so calmly, as a king should do,
Unfaltering, to his doom;
Nobly environed—royalty's own hue
Emblazoning his tomb.
Glories of purple and of living gold
That dazzling bier enfold,
Burning with splendor to which light is dim.
Now riseth up the haze of far-off seas,
And soft, in monotone, borne on the breeze,
Soundeth a dirge, chanted by wavelets o'er,
Where ever, evermore,
Pulses the throat of the unresting tide,
That moans, like lost, imprisoned soul,
Impatient of control,
With hands outstretched as one, alone,
Whose hopes are all undone.

Colder the chill wind blows;
For loss of him
Dark grows the brow of princely Tamalpais,
While the departing one
Smiles yet more faintly o'er the waters wide.
Clouds, violet and rose,
Wreathe him with beauty, fondly, ere he dies;
Once more he glances o'er the wailing wave,
And then descends, majestic, to his grave.
Wail on! Wail on! Wail on! Our king is dead!
Darkness and desolation, drear and dread,
The mourning earth, as with a pall, o'erspread.

II.

"By the Sacred River."

Hark! On the coast
Of far Cathay—of India's gem-strewn shore—
From an unnumbered host
Pæans of welcome and of joy up-springing;
Heaven's glowing arch,
With freshest notes of life and gladness ringing,
And lo! our vanished king, still grandly living,
And yet more glorious in giving—
Still, in triumphal march
Onward, the monarch of more dazzling skies—
Still, in his high emprise

Of constant duty, eloquently telling
Of dearest hopes in Christian souls indwelling
By grace profound —
Emblem of mortal life, immortal glory,
Unmatched in story.

ISABEL A. SAXON.

A STRAIGHT MANZANITA.

"You will find it," replied Mr. Burton, slowly, "when you find a perfect woman."

"Then," said I, a little coldly, "I shall not be skeptical as to my ultimate success."

The afternoon was slowly mellowing into dusk. I had been to the village, several miles distant, for my mail, and had found Burton there on a similar errand. Both of us were enthusiastic pedestrians, and we had both walked, although horses were abundant. As our errands were finished about the same time, and as our way home was in common for nearly three miles, we started together, as we had many times before. Our path lay for some distance through copses of manzanita bushes, whose limbs were twisted in a hundred eccentric shapes.

"I have been looking for some time," I had said, "for a manzanita limb straight enough and long enough for a walking stick."

His answer jarred upon me. I knew that he was cynical in regard to women; but I did not like his sneer. It seemed uncalled for and unmanly.

He was greatly my senior, being over sixty years of age, while I was six and twenty. I had been graduated at college some two years previously, and although I had enough money for my immediate wants, I had felt the necessity of activity. I was an orphan, with no ties to bind me to any place since both my sisters had married, and after traveling for a year or more I had come to California. I commenced the study of the law, as is usual with most young men of means whose talents seem to incline in no particular direction. The natural ardor of my disposition made me pursue vigorously anything I undertook; but, fortunately or unfortunately, my career as an advocate was terminated, or at best suspended, by an affection of the eyes. My physician forbade me to proceed with my studies, and as, with my disposition, it was impossible for me to remain inert, I had purchased a farm next to that of Mr. Burton, and was essaying, with indifferent financial success, the *rôle* of an amateur farmer. In my leisure I had written some, and, out of three articles which I had forwarded to a leading magazine, one had been accepted and the other two had been returned as "not available." So I might claim to be one-third of a *littérateur*.

Mr. Burton, as I have said, was my next neighbor. I had met him in the village soon after my arrival, and our common taste for walking had thrown us together frequently as we returned from the town. It was easy to see that his was a strong and rugged character. While he was not an educated man, in the restricted sense of having a classical education, he had read much and thought more. His ideas were original, and his expressions at times had a force and newness which were startling. His conversation was healthful and invigorating, save on that one subject—woman. Upon any allusion to the gentler sex he was silent or bitter. I had, of course, never asked the reason of this. His natural dignity would have repelled curiosity, even if I had so far forgotten myself as to seek an explanation of that which he never offered to explain. But to me, who had almost chivalric ideas of the grace, purity, and dignity of womanhood, these slurs were the more irritating because they appeared unworthy of him and inconsistent with his character, as I had outlined it to myself.

These walks had extended over several months, and during that time we became quite well acquainted. Several times, when we had reached the point where our paths diverged, I had invited him to call on me, and, while he thanked me courteously, I had noticed that he never accepted; nor did he ever extend to me a similar invitation. There was a perceptible reserve which extended not only to himself, but to his home. Once, indeed, he had been at my house when I had imported some new varieties of fruit trees and had invited him to try one of each kind on his place. He stayed but a few moments, however, and insisted on paying for the trees which I gave him. I respected his reserve, and never sought to draw aside the veil. It so happened, however, that the next time I visited the village after the remark about the manzanita I did not see Burton at the post-office as usual, although we had agreed to go at the same hour on the days the mail came. The post-master was a bustling, talkative man, who united with his official functions the occupations of a storekeeper, apothecary, and general merchant. As I made some slight purchases, I asked:

"Has Mr. Burton been in town this afternoon?"

"No, sir; haven't seen him, sir. One dollar and a half. Anything else? Oh, yes!—the coffee. Burton's a queer man, ain't he? Lives there with his daughter and an old servant; wife's dead, I believe. One good thing: never runs an account; always pays cash. You'll find that a first-class article. I ought to charge more'n I do for it. Shall I tell him you asked for him if he comes in?"

Mr. Heesum, a gentleman from Missouri, volunteered this: "The gal's been away to school for a powerful long time—jest got back this summer. They haint very sociable folks nohow. I heerd that the gal rides horseback a good deal on the old man's place; but they don't nobody see her anywhere else."

As the conversation threatened to become general, I gathered up my parcels and hurried away. As I walked along the path on my way home, I could not help thinking of this man, who seemed so noble hearted, so genuine and worthy, and whose life had yet evidently been blighted as by some biting frost, or perhaps scorched like a noble tree by some consuming fire. My path wound in and out among the warped bushes, now dropping the ripened berries as their twisted limbs were stirred by the autumn breeze.

"Poor fellow," I thought; "it is a sad experience, surely, which suggested such a simile."

For a few days after this, I was busily occupied. There had been a copious fall of rain, and the land was left in fine condition for plowing. Every man and every horse on the place was pressed into service, and foot by foot the rich earth was turned to the sun and breathed a freshness and an inspiration which no poet has ever imprisoned in his song. Whatever my shortcomings may be, I was never afraid of work, and I did not shrink from my full share of it now. Labor of which one can see the immediate product as he works has always an exhilaration. I was young, athletic, active, and as I breathed the sweet air, enjoying each draught as one drinks fragrant wine, and called to my horses as they now and then deflected from the furrow, and bore down upon the handles, I felt like a veritable god plowing the soil of a new world. There is one intoxication which is pure: it is the exaltation which a healthy organism feels in congenial labor. But the beverage is so strong that men nowadays are seldom drunk of it.

As I was turning my team at the end of a furrow, one fine morning, my hat accidentally fell off, and, before I could rescue it, was trodden under foot by the horses as they swung into position, and was also torn across the rim by the plow. As the inside was not soiled, I put it on my head again, caring little for its disreputable appearance, for it matched admirably my muddy boots, blue overalls, and blowse shirt. I had just chirruped to the horses again, when I saw one of the hired men, who had been repairing a fence, running toward me across the field. He came up panting.

"Shure, Mr. Lawton, there's the dhivel to pay up at the barrun."

"Why, what's the matter at the barn, Dennis?"

"Some fule left the gate of the corral and the pasthure both of 'im open, and the Jarsey carruf has got out into the woods."

I began to think that Dennis's designation of the situation was not exaggerated. This Jersey calf was a pure "blood," and had cost me considerable money. Hastily leaving Dennis to continue the plowing, I hurried to the barn. The only horse not in use on the place—I had forgotten this one when I said they were all in service—was a venerable relic of a past age, left by the previous owner because he was not worth taking away. We called him "The Flying Dutchman," partly in derision at his speed, and partly because one could see the sun through his ribs. As there was no choice I saddled the "Dutchman" and started in pursuit, if such it might be called. I could not help laughing at my appearance. I tried to compare myself to Don Quixote, but had to confess that the odds were in favor of the old knight. After a couple of hours' search I found the missing calf near Burton's place, half a mile or so beyond the road which led to his house, and secured it with a rope which I had brought. Turning the "Dutchman's" head once more toward home, I commenced retracing the way, leading the calf behind me. We crept slowly along the outside of Burton's fence, which, with mine connecting, led in a straight line to my barn.

A few rods before arriving at the road that led to Burton's house, a thick growth of underbrush obscured the view, both of the road and of the gate, although our immediate pathway was clear. I had been humming an old college song for some distance back, but, just before I emerged from this thicket, the melody, or lack of melody if you will, took such possession of me that I suddenly burst into a rollicking chorus with the full power of my lungs. There was an affrighted snort, a sudden pawing of an animal's feet, and I emerged just in time to see a horse, with a side-saddle on, tearing up the road, while a young lady in riding-habit, who had evidently dismounted to open the gate, stood looking at the disappearing courser.

I suddenly became aware of my ridiculous appearance and my unconscious offense. The young lady turned and looked at me; and we, all three of us, came to a standstill and mutely returned her gaze. I hesitated to speak, hardly knowing whether she would regard me, or the "Dutchman," or the calf, as the responsible head of our trio. At last, conscious that I ought to speak, I broke the silence with a desperate effort.

"Miss, I'm—I'm very sorry. If you will hold the calf, I'll try to catch your horse."

"I will *tie* the calf for you," she said, with the suspicion of a smile, "if you will do me that favor."

"Excuse me," I said, coloring.

What a stupid fool I had been! She had probably thought me a clown before I spoke; she would be convinced of it now.

I dismounted and tied the calf, then cut a bough from the first bush at hand with which to urge my horse, and was again quickly in the saddle. I had not before attempted to make the "Dutchman" trot, but now I lashed his sides until, with a reproachful groan at each step, he quickened his rheumatic gait. In the mile which intervened before I came upon her horse, feeding quietly in a glade, I had ample time to reflect upon my stupidity and my ridiculous appearance. To tell the truth, I cared less for the latter than the former. My costume, except my disfigured hat, was such as farmers usually wear, although the *tout ensemble* of the trio, as we burst upon the young lady in her first resentment, must have been such as to inspire her contempt or amusement, and probably both. But that boyish song! And, above all, my request that she should hold the calf—that was inexcusable. My only thought had been that I could not pursue the horse with that incumbrance. I had been thoroughly embarrassed for the first time in my life, and I voted myself a remarkable donkey.

Her horse was a gentle animal, although high spirited, and I had little difficulty in securing him when I reached the spot where he had stopped. Thus far I had been thinking chiefly of myself and of my plight. But as I turned back I half forgot my chagrin, and my mind reverted to the figure waiting at the gate. I had seen her only a moment. She had spoken but one sentence. Yet there lingered a very distinct impression of grace and beauty, and the soft ringing of a pleasant voice.

"Of course," said I to myself, "this is Mr. Burton's mysterious daughter, and I presume I have made her an enemy for life. But, by Jove, I wonder at her father's skepticism!"

On arriving at the gate I found her waiting, and as I assisted her to mount, she said:

"I have caused you a great deal of trouble."

"Don't say that, I beg, Miss—Miss Burton, I presume——"

She bowed assent to the name.

"——because it was my stupidity in coming upon you so suddenly, that caused the whole trouble."

She thanked me again for getting her horse, then rode swiftly toward her home, while I and the "Dutchman," followed by the calf, resumed our path by the fence. What my sedate companions thought as we made our slow way through the woods, I know not; but my own feelings were an admixture of chagrin and pleasure. At last I reached home, and as I dismounted I was about to throw away the bough, which I had cut by the gate, when it arrested my attention. It was a straight manzanita limb, of the proper length and thickness for a walking stick. Burton's words came to me with a rush, and for a moment I was utterly bewildered. I was not a believer in signs, and I soon recovered myself and dismissed the matter as idle. But it kept recurring and I could not banish it from my thoughts.

Some two weeks after this, I sat on my veranda, watching the sun set. Across the long valley the slant rays were broken in golden shafts, and in the far distance the mountain was purple and amethyst, now and then suffused with rosy light. The whole scene was constantly changing, and the day was fainting, dying in a swoon of color. Up the road I heard the rhythmic rise and fall of a horse's feet, and soon Mr. Dorkins had reined up in front of me. Mr. Dorkins, Mr. Burton, and one other, had for a number of years composed the board or committee who were charged with the management of the district school, being the three of all the neighborhood most proficient in the "three r's" of traditional renown. At the last election, some four months prior to the time of which I am writing, the third committeeman had declined a reëlection, and Mr. Burton had suggested my name. Probably owing to the *prestige* which I had acquired when it became known that I had "been to college," I was elected.

Mr. Dorkins was a practical farmer, of good judgment and excellent intentions.

"I hadn't much show at eddication myself," he told me once, apologetically, "but I'm going to make scholars of my children if it takes 'em five years apiece."

On this particular afternoon, Mr. Dorkins, in the manner peculiar to country people, to whom time never seems an object, opened the conversation on matters entirely alien to his errand.

"Ground looks pretty well, Mr. Lawton. I reckon you'll have a right smart yield next season."

"I hope so, Mr. Dorkins. Everything seems very favorable."

Then a running talk followed on the weather, prospects, politics, and so forth, Mr. Dorkins sitting the while, or rather reclining, upon his horse, with one foot out of the stirrup. At last he gathered up the reins as if to depart; then, turning to me as though he had just thought of something incidentally, he said:

"Oh, by the way, the teacher was over to my house this evenin' about three o'clock, bein' as I was nearest to the school. His father's took sick very sudden, and so he's went home. I reckon you and Mr. Burton better come to the school to-morrow, and see what we can do for a new teacher to start in Monday. I'm goin' to town to-night, and I'll see what sort of timber they've got fo make a teacher of, if you'll see Mr. Burton and tell him to be on hand."

"All right, Mr. Dorkins," I said, with my heart throbbing unaccountably. "I think I can either go down to Mr. Burton's or send word. What hour to-morrow?"

"Waal, how'll three o'clock suit?"

"That will be perfectly convenient for me."

"Waal, then, I must be goin'," and he rode off at a brisk gallop.

I went to my room, and for the first time in several months I donned a black suit, and dressed myself as immaculately as if about to make a round of calls in a fashionable metropolis. Half an hour's walk brought me to Mr. Burton's house, and as I went up the steps to the door I saw through the window, the curtains being up, the father ensconced in an easy chair, and the daughter seated by the table reading to him. They did not hear me until the old servant, evidently long unused to callers, ushered me unceremoniously into the room. Mr. Burton came forward as soon as he saw me, and received me hospitably.

"Helen," he said, "this is Mr. Lawton, to whom you are indebted for having a horse to ride home the other day."

It was an unlucky allusion, but he spoke so frankly that I saw she had not told him of the ridiculous figure I had cut in that adventure, a delicacy which I appreciated. With feminine tact, she answered without referring to this unfortunate reminiscence.

"Mr. Lawton is a neighbor, also, I believe. We are so unneighborly, though, that I know very few of those about us, even by name."

"True, child, it is true," said he, with a tired look for a moment in his face; then, remembering himself, he added, "Be seated, Mr. Lawton. The child and I were reading *Elia.* What a quaint humor runs through all these essays."

I was surprised to see Burton appreciate the humor of Lamb. I had expected in my innermost heart to find his house very like a dungeon, and I found myself in a home which possessed all the accompaniments of refinement. There were books on the table and on the long shelves across the room — books which had the easy air of constant companions, and not the uncomfortable rigidity of formal acquaintances. Between the windows was a piano, although I would have confidently asserted before this evening that there was not one in the county.

I was able to tell them some bits of gossip about the genial essayist, which I had picked up in Europe, and in which they were much interested.

"The child reads to me every evening" — always "the child," although she was a woman of twenty, very beautiful, too, I thought, as she sat near the old man.

The conversation drifted on naturally from this beginning, Miss Burton never taking the lead, yet always giving it new impetus by some opportune remark. I stated my errand presently, and after Mr. Burton had assented to the appointment for the next day, I rose to go, when he motioned me to my seat, saying:

"The child sings to me every night, Mr. Lawton. Perhaps you wouldn't mind——"

"Mr. Lawton may not care for singing, father," she interrupted, quietly, with a little color.

Of course I protested that I was very fond of it, and Burton added:

"I can't allow Mr. Lawton to deprive me of that, child," always speaking gently, as if a rough tone might frighten her. He was like another man to me.

She sang several selections, intelligently, and in a voice not of great strength, but of much sweetness and purity.

When I took my departure, Burton followed me to the door, and, coming out under the clear starlight, he stood a moment with me in silence.

"The child is right," he said, presently; "we are too unneighborly. We have enjoyed your call, Mr. Lawton, and we would be glad to have you come again. I should have asked you before, but I am an old man, and old men are sometimes *forgetful*," with the same expression I had noticed earlier in the evening. "You must remember that old men are sometimes forgetful."

As I walked home the stars seemed to twinkle with very glee. I had discovered an unexpected land. I had not supposed there was such a home within thousands of miles, and suddenly I found that for months I had hungered for just such friends. But I could not understand it. How unlike the Burton of my walks was this tender old man, whose eyes followed everywhere the form of this young girl.

I accepted Burton's invitation, and frequently walked over to his house of a pleasant evening. Helen had been home some six months now, and I fancied Burton's cynicism was losing its hold upon him. Once, as we walked home from the post-office, I read him a portion of a letter from one of my sisters. She had recently commenced housekeeping, and was all enthusiasm.

"I like to think of her so pleasantly situated," I said. "With her taste, she will make a paradise of her new home."

"Yes," he replied, appreciatively, "it is a pleasant picture you have shown me. I have no doubt she will be very happy."

The next time we walked out from the town it was Saturday afternoon.

"Helen has a friend with her for a week or so, one of her former classmates. We should be pleased to have you dine with us to-morrow afternoon, and spend the evening."

I accepted with pleasure, and several times during her friend's visit I made one of the little company that gathered around the fireplace. The winter rains had commenced in earnest, and the storm outside beat wildly at the pane, or shrieked in angry gusts as it circled around the house, seeking vainly an entrance to the cheerful room. I could see that Burton was undergoing a change in this new environment. He was waking from some dream that had held him in terrible subjection. His eyes were always upon Helen, as though he feared that she might vanish, leaving him only the phantoms of the dead past again. I could see that he grew more gentle, and he soon ceased to utter his customary sneer at women. The current of his life left its angry struggle with the rocks, and flowed restfully and in peace, at last. Day by day I saw this change wrought in him, and I knew the influence which had breathed its benediction upon his tired life.

In the spring, business called me to San Francisco, where I remained nearly a month. I renewed many pleasant acquaintances, and for a time enjoyed a return to the gayeties with which I had once been surfeited. A reception, to which I had received cards, was to be given the evening before the day on which I had decided to return to my home, and as it was reported that a "grand affair" was expected, I resolved to attend. Just before supper I found myself talking to the host, who, probably from a polite desire to entertain me, displayed much interest in agricultural matters, and drew me on to explain some experiments I had made in hop culture.

"Have they proved successful?" he asked.

"Sufficient time has not yet elapsed," I replied, "but Mr. Burton, who is a practical farmer, and who has joined me in the experiment, is very hopeful."

"Let me see. Burton? I wonder if that isn't the one that I know. He lives somewhere up there. What is his first name?"

"Chauncey."

"The same one. We are from the same town East, and were boys together. Poor fellow! He married a beautiful woman, but she ran away with a young scamp—eloped. Burton was a fine fellow, but this seemed to——"

Here the hostess came up, and requested her husband to escort some lady to the supper-room, and he excused himself without finishing his sentence. I soon after sought an opportunity to say good-night, and left the house. I reached my room at the hotel, and heard the great clock strike one as I entered the door. I mechanically lighted the fire, and seated myself in front of it. I sat there five hours, unconscious of the time. I had admired Helen Burton from the moment I first saw her; but now, for the first time, I knew that I loved her, passionately and with my whole being—now, when I knew the terrible shame which was her heritage. I thought I understood it all now—Burton's cynicism, their reserve, everything. I could read the whole story: Burton, left with his child, had sought California because of its distance, and that the innocent child, forsaken by its mother, might never know of her existence. The father might forget the past when he gazed upon the daughter; but could I?—would my sisters, my relatives? I had inherited a proud, unspotted name. My family was a leading one in the eastern State where they had lived so many generations, and they gloried in the long line of proud and aristocratic men and women whose reputations were unsullied. What would they say if I should wed this girl, whose mother had brought dishonor upon her house? I had inherited this family pride. Could I bear it myself, to see the world's sneer, to see people point their fingers at her while they told her story. She was pure, noble, true; she was innocent of wrong herself; it was not her fault—no one could say that it was her fault. No one could say a word against her, or find one flaw in her pure, sweet life. But could I ever forget that terrible birthright? And if I, with my illimitable love, must always remember it, could I expect that others would overlook it?

When the morning light came in at the window I still sat there, with a great pain at my heart. The fire had died away, and the ashes alone remained; so, it seemed, had died away the warmth of my life, leaving nothing but ashes. I arose, and with bitter thoughts commenced preparing for my return. In the corner stood the manzanita stick which I had brought to the city to have made into a cane, and I noticed that in cutting one of the knots the workman had been unskillful, and the stick had a crooked and jagged appearance. Acting upon an impulse which I regretted a moment after, I broke it in two, and cast the pieces into the grate.

The boat on which I was to leave San Francisco would not start from the wharf until afternoon, and I spent the day miserably enough, with no companions but my thoughts. I walked the streets, then dropped in at the libraries, then walked the streets again, but all the time grappling with a foe I had never encountered before—indecision. At last the afternoon came, and I went on board the steamer, and sat watching the people as they came on—watching, but not seeing them. Presently the boat swung slowly out into the stream, then, gathering force at each breath of its iron lungs, it swept majestically by the long wharves, past lonely Alcatraz, into the warmer air of the upper bays. I sat in the stern of the boat, and near me an old farmer was discussing some project with his wife.

"I know it won't suit Ben's folks," he said, "but if we think it's right, it's our duty to do it. The only way to do when you're in doubt is to do what your conscience tells you to. We can't expect to suit everybody."

Finding either the air or her husband's homely wisdom too bracing, the woman went into the cabin, the man following, and I saw them no more. It was a commonplace, a truism—"Do what your conscience says is right, even if the world is not suited"—but there are times when human nature grasps at a truism; crises when, in a chaos of disconnected circumstances, man gropes for a generality.

I arrived at the village about noon of the second day, and, taking the familiar path, I was soon in the woods. Here, at least, there was no indecision. Everything lived out the fullness of its life, in a confidence born of an exquisite relation to the harmonious whole. The mistletoe clustered in the branches of the lordly fir; the aristocratic madroño glittered with saffron dress; side by side grew the gaudy eschscholtzia and the maidenly nemophila; while, over all, the noonday sun held resolutely to its course. It is only man, after all, who erects factitious standards, who curbs the truth and beauty that seek to blossom in his nature, who is ashamed to face the universe in the simplicity and honesty of his natural self.

When I came to the point where the paths diverged, I took the road that led to Mr. Burton's. A short walk brought me to the house, and as I passed up the front steps I heard some one playing at the piano. Nature seemed listening, so still was the bush, as the notes of one of Mendelssohn's divine conceptions floated off upon the midday air. Within the house, the player, filled with the spirit of the music, did not hear my step until the old servant ushered me into the room, and I stood before her. When she saw me, there was a momentary look of glad surprise, quickly repressed; then, coming forward, she welcomed me.

"I am glad to see you. I did not know you had returned."

She lifted her eyes as she spoke, and, as I gazed into their pure depth, I felt ashamed of the weakness that had doubted.

When we came out on the wide porch, two hours afterward, the birds, no longer sheltering from the heat, filled the air with their ecstasies. Looking across the long vineyard, I could see Burton slowly returning to the house.

"Helen," I said, speaking the name for the first time, with a delicious sense of newness, "I must tell your father of this."

"You must tell him," she answered. "But I thought you knew—he is not my father; he is my uncle, although he has been like a father to me from my infancy, and I have always called him so, as it seemed to please him. My own father died when I was a year old, and my mother was buried, I am told, less than three months afterward."

I could not help feeling a thrill of joy. Although my love for Helen had conquered in the struggle which had taken place in my mind, I could not repress a feeling of pleasure. I knew it was unworthy of me, and yet, as we stood watching the glory of that afternoon, as it appeared in the hues of our new love, I thought of the story I had heard of Burton's life, and was glad that Helen was not his child. I felt this thought to be unjust to my friend, as she continued:

"He has always been kind and good to me. I have no recollection of any relative excepting him, not even my own father and mother. Sometimes I think he must have had some bitter experience, as he never alludes to the past; but I have never asked him. He has always been gentle and kind to me."

When Burton came up we all went into the house together, where I soon told him of my love for Helen, and that she had promised to be my wife. He sat with his face buried in his hands. At last, rising, he went to her, and placing her hand in mine, he said, with a broken voice:

"Child, it is hard for me—very hard—to give you up. You have been a revelation to me—you have taught me faith where I never expected to believe again." Then, almost fiercely, after a pause: "Be true to him, child; have no thought that is not his, no wish that he does not know. Pray God to keep your heart true to him."

There was evidently a great struggle in his mind. The past had risen up convulsively; but he conquered it at last, and for the last time.

"You cannot know," he said; "it is best you should not know. This is all very sudden to me, and I forgot myself. I am an old man, and it was very sudden."

Then, stroking her hair, with infinite tenderness, and drawing her to him:

"May God reward your love by its long continuance." CHAS. H. PHELPS.

WITCHCRAFT.

How incredible would it appear to us, living in this enlightened age, that for several hundred years the world firmly believed in the existence of an easily acquired evil ascendancy over all creation, that enabled human beings to work untold mischief to their kind, and even subvert the laws of nature, did we not take into consideration the fact that so few had been the discoveries of science—so limited was the knowledge of men in regard to those very laws which they supposed had been infringed—that effects could not as in these days be traced to their real cause, and much that was the inevitable result of the action of great and now well known principles, such as physics and chemistry, came very naturally to be regarded, in a superstitious era, as the work of some power greater even than that of nature. During the fourteenth, fifteenth, and sixteenth centuries the popular idea of the rites and ceremonies indulged in by the disciples of witchcraft was the same, in its principal features, throughout all the nations of Europe, and it formed a belief so fanciful that it is easy to conceive its having sprung originally, as it must have done, from minds that were not only unenlightened and uneducated, but the imaginings of which were distorted equally by superstition and disease.

It was believed that myriads of demons—who not only multiplied among themselves, but were daily increased by the souls of wicked men, still-born children, and all who died a violent death—filled the whole earth, exciting whirlwinds and tempests when they met in great numbers, destroying the beauties of nature and the works of men's hands. They were often drawn in at the mouth and nostrils, and tormented those they thus entered with pains and diseases. All these demons were for a stated period at the command of any mortal who would sign away his soul to the Prince of Darkness; and all that the witch or wizard desired them to do was, with the exception of any *good* action, swiftly performed. General meetings, or "Sabbaths," as they were called, took place at the will of Satan, and were always named for a Friday night, or rather Saturday morning, immediately after midnight, the place generally chosen for assembling being one where four roads met, or in the neighborhood of a lake. Upon the spot selected nothing, it was said, could ever grow again, the earth being burned and rendered sterile by the hot feet of the demons. All witches and wizards who failed to attend these meetings were lashed, by order of Satan, with a whip made of serpents and scorpions. Broomsticks were supposed to be the steeds of French and British witches, but in Italy and Spain the devil himself, in the shape of a goat, was thought to carry them on his back from one place to another. No witch, when going to a Sabbath, could leave her home by a door or window; her only practicable exit was thought to be by key-hole or chimney, and during her absence an inferior demon was said to take her form and lie in her bed, feigning illness. The votaries of the Black Art once assembled, the ceremony first performed was to kiss the devil, who took the form of a goat for the occasion. This was followed by an examination of those present, to see if they were stamped with the devil's mark, and those who were not received it from the master of the ceremonies, as also a nick-name, their own cognomens, because bestowed in holy baptism, never being pronounced by his satanic majesty. Then they would sing and dance furiously, till some one anxious to join them arrived, when they would be silent till the new-comer denied his salvation, kissed the devil, spat upon the Bible, and swore obedience to Satan in all things. These forms of initiation were followed by more dancing and singing. Those who had not been mischievous enough were flogged with thorns and scorpions by their master. A multitude of toads danced for their amusement, and for reward were promised a feast of unbaptized babes, and the meeting ended with a banquet of viands too disgusting to enumerate. When the cock crew they all disappeared, and their Sabbath was at an end.

The first impetus given to the destructive wave of superstitious belief in these things, which, gathering strength as it rolled on with the passing centuries, caught up in its progress and carried into the awful sea of eternity so many thousands of unhappy beings, dates as far back as the time of Moses, a period when, the chosen people being placed in the midst of idolatrous nations, it was deemed necessary, in order to keep them separate and distinct, to punish severely all those who exhibited any tendency to consult the oracles of the heathen, or appeal to their false gods. Such acts, it was seen by an all-wise Power, would have led them in time to renewed idolatry; and in order to save them from further back-sliding, the famous command was given forth, "Thou shalt not suffer a witch to live!"—a command which became, centuries later, the watchword of the superstitious, the fanatic, and the maliciously inclined. To the vast number who were for several hundred years zealous in their condemnation of witchcraft, quoting Scripture as their authority, it seems to have signified nothing that the literal meaning of the Hebrew word translated "witch" was a poisoner, a diviner, or fortune-teller—a being very different from the more modern so-called witch—and that those denounced by the Mosaic law were not pronounced by the Divine Word possessed of any especial power, but were more probably considered punishable for the mere desire or more criminal *pretense*, so dangerous at that period to the religious welfare of the favored Hebrews, of the ability to foretell their Creator's will and to usurp His authority. Thus, led into error by an incorrect reading of this scriptural injunction, men began to attribute every wondrous appearance in nature, or unusual distortion of the human frame—in short, all phenomena of mind and matter—to the exercise of an unholy influence wielded by some malignant mortal.

It came to be in time that any individual whose heated or diseased imagination conjured up spectres, or caused him to believe himself a wolf or tea-pot, instead of being called a lunatic or hypochondriac, and treated medicinally as such, was said to be bewitched; that every child who had an epileptic fit, or was thrown into convulsions by excess of terror, was pronounced under the influence of one of these so-called witches. And nothing was easier than to find some person or persons at whom to point the finger of suspicion. It was quite enough for a woman to be old and ugly, or poor, or ill-tempered, to fall under the ban; and let her have uttered a word that could be construed as a menace, or have looked upon the afterward afflicted person with steady gaze, or have mumbled anything unintelligible in his presence, or even expressed an opinion, favorable or otherwise, upon the state of his health, and sufficient evidence against her was considered to exist to justify her arrest and trial for witchcraft. Indeed, it is upon record that one old woman was burned in Scotland upon this charge, because a cat, which the witnesses *believed* to be the devil, was seen to jump in at her window. No other testimony was thought necessary to legalize her condemnation.

It is not surprising that any one once accused of the absurd practices appertaining to witchcraft very rarely escaped with life, when we take into consideration, not only the false evidence that malice or the excited imaginations of the over-zealous might bring against them, but the ridiculous tests of their guilt which were considered sufficient to convict them. The most common mode of discovering a witch, by the ordeal of "swimming," consisted in tying together, crosswise, the thumbs and big toes of the accused, and in this cramped condition the body was drawn through the water by a rope. If it floated, as was almost invariably the case—a body in this position, being placed carefully upon the back, offering a strong resistance to the water—the victim was considered guilty; for, having renounced their baptism, the element with which the sacrament had been performed was supposed in turn to renounce them. Many are the cases in which, convicted by this test, unfortunate wretches have been torn to pieces by the mob, without the ceremony of judicial trial and condemnation. But those poor creatures who sank beneath the surface of the water were not always, even if they escaped drowning, let off by their persecutors, for ofttimes other ordeals were then resorted to, on the plea that escape from the first was insufficient evidence in their favor. One most barbarous test, often employed, was to find, by pricking with long pins, the devil's mark upon the person of the accused, a spot which was supposed to be without feeling and to yield no blood. This method was much affected during the middle of the seventeenth century by a man called Matthew Hopkins, who, styling himself Witch-finder General, took upon himself to make periodical tours of the English counties of Norfolk, Essex, Huntingdon, and Sussex, hunting out witches. His claims of twenty shillings a town, expenses of living for himself and two assistants, with carriage fare, were always allowed by the authorities, and in one year alone sixty people were brought to the stake by his efforts. Another of this man's witch-tests was to place the suspected persons cross-legged on a stool, binding them to it if refractory, and keeping them in that constrained position, without meat or drink, for twenty-four hours. It was thought that during this time one of their imps or familiars, as the demons who served them were were called, would come in the shape of an insect to suck their blood; and if any of those watching saw a fly, moth, or other insect, enter the room and light upon the accused, and it could not be caught or killed, the suspected was adjudged guilty, and sentenced forthwith to be hanged or burned. Yet another method resorted to by this man was to make the poor victim repeat the Lord's Prayer, and one word missed or pronounced incoherently, which it was more than probable would be done under the strain of great trepidation, sealed their fate irrevocably.

It is gratifying to know that this trader upon human misery fell a victim to his own toils. His great rapacity weakening his influence, the populace began to see that no one was safe from his persecutions, and, rising in anger, accused him of being a wizard himself. An old jest, that by magic he had cheated the devil of a memorandum book, in which were entered the names of all the witches in England, became the charge brought against him. He was put to his own test of swimming, and although it is not known whether he was drowned, or floated and was executed, it is very sure that we hear of him no more.

But these ordeals were not the hardest trials which so many unfortunates were forced to endure. Numerous are the instances in which the accused, when they persisted in denying an alliance with the devil, were subjected to the severest torture; and few had sufficient nerve to endure their frightful agony, but, in their frantic desire to escape further suffering, would confess, as desired, to even the most preposterous charges made against them. Confessions thus extorted were almost invariably retracted as soon as the torture was suspended, but were nevertheless regarded as proof sufficient to warrant the execution of the self-convicted criminal, for all such retractions were deemed a sure sign that Satan had again gained possession of one whom penitence, rather than pain, had instigated to confession. The fact that a person was thus proved to be a wizard or a witch did not by any means invalidate their testimony against others, but was rather thought to increase its value, upon the principle, we suppose, of setting a thief to catch a thief; so that those who wielded the torture had but to prompt the sufferer to accuse some one else of the crime of witchcraft, or their own ill-will lead them to wish that others should experience what they were enduring, and any number of innocent beings would at once be placed in jeopardy of their lives. Moreover, even the worst criminals and most abandoned characters were permitted to give testimony in all cases of witchcraft, and lawyers admitted as evidence some mischief that could be proved to have followed close upon a threat or openly expressed desire for revenge. We read of one case in which an old woman, her son and daughter, were executed because a lady, whose harsh conduct toward her had provoked her wrath, died *one year and three months* after the poor creature had been heard to curse her persecutor.

Thus was opened to the jealous, the revengeful, the avaricious, and the maliciously inclined, an easy and efficient mode of getting rid of a rival, an enemy, or any obnoxious individual; and there can be little doubt that many took advantage of the opportunity, sending shoals of wretched beings to the stake to gratify their varied purposes.

As the crime of witchcraft became notorious, and the torture-elicited confessions of those who had owned to having made a compact with Satan were given to the world, it is reasonable to believe that many people became possessed of the desire to profit by such unlimited power as the devil was said to grant to his servants; and that in attempting the spells which those convicted of witchcraft had confessed to having used, they were detected in the act, tried, and found guilty of a crime they had merely been essaying, and so greatly increased the numbers of those who suffered. Others, again, no doubt, mistook their own superstitious fears, and really believed themselves guilty, through ignorance of the nature of the accusations against them, for we read of one man, who called himself a warlock, or wizard, because he had seen the devil dancing like a fly about the candle, and also of an old woman, who, thinking herself a witch because she had been called one, proved her simplicity by asking the judge upon the bench if one might be a witch and not be sure of it one's self. So firmly fixed in the minds of the masses did the belief in witchcraft at last become, and so great the popular horror of its votaries, that when a person, by some unusually lucky chance, escaped conviction, they were avoided as the pestilence, and ofttimes left literally to starve, for none would give them work or help them in any way. Therefore, very many, when once the taint of suspicion was upon them, chose rather to accuse themselves and die, than live the wretched, isolated life that they knew was before them. Taking into consideration the voluntary confessions of these poor beings, who, with the intention of convicting themselves (as we read in *Mackenzie's Criminal Law of Scotland*, published in 1678), gave the rein to their wildest fancies, and also the avowals of intercourse with Satan extorted from those subjected to torture, we cannot wonder that the simple minded and credulous, of all ranks and degrees, should have been imbued with a belief in this gross delusion, wild and impious though it must seem to our more enlightened understanding.

It was not by the civil authorities alone that the existence of this diabolical art was acknowledged, and its supposed disciples regarded as the worst of criminals. The different religious sects also believed most firmly in the possibility of a league between man and the devil, and the more devout was an ecclesiastic, the more earnest and frequent were his appeals to his flock to do all in their power to exterminate, even by the harshest measures, the terrible evil which had taken root in their midst. But, although at an early period of the Church of Rome capital punishment was assigned to those supposed to have accomplished by sorcery the death of others, or by false prophecies to have made innovations in the State, it is now generally believed that the charge of necromancy and witchcraft was oftener made with some political object in view than for any strictly religious reasons. And it is yet more certain that the frequent anathemas launched forth at a later period, by the various Popes, against all dabblers in the Black Art, were turned by the zealous into instruments for the extermination of those heresies and schisms which at that time were springing up everywhere over the civilised world. Yet, in spite of all this, we are not justified in doubting that many generations of Christians and churchmen really had firm faith in the possibility of such practices, but should rather believe that extreme fanaticism led not only the Church of Rome, but each of the new sects, to suppose all other denominations not merely mistaken in creed, but absolute worshipers of the devil, so that in persecuting each other they but followed out their earnest convictions of what was right.

A case in point is that of the Stedinger, a brave people who occupied, in the eleventh century, the district between the Weser and the Zuyder-Zee, who had attained a high degree of civil and religious liberty, and were successful in repelling the Normans and Saxons. In 1204 this community refused to pay tithes to the clergy, who had forced themselves into their peaceful retreat, and the Archbishop of Bremen applied to Pope Gregory IX. for his spiritual aid against them. A crusade against the Stedinger, for being "abominable witches and wizards," was preached in all that part of Germany; their country was invaded by an army of four thousand men, under the Duke of Brabant, and the spirit of fanaticism giving nerve to the arm that had hitherto tried in vain to subdue them, the whole race was exterminated.

Again, in 1307, when, by their wealth, power, pride, and insolence, they had raised up enemies on every side, this absurd, yet effectual charge was brought against the Templars. It was said that they had sold their souls to the devil, and that when a novice was admitted into their order he was forced to renounce his salvation and spit upon the cross. It was also asserted that when a knight died, his body was burned into a powder, and mixed with wine, which was drunk by every member of the order. When put upon the rack, hundreds confessed to even the most preposterous charges against them; but, though they denied it all when relieved from torture, this fact only made the popular fury against them all the greater, as they were looked upon as relapsed heretics. In 1313 the the last chapter of their history was closed with the burning of the Grand Master, Jacques de Molay, and his companion, Guy, Commander of Normandy.

We have a very sad instance, however, of this cruel charge being brought forward, not by those sincere in their fanaticism and mistaken zeal, but solely to compass political ends and gratify national jealousy and hatred, in the well known story of Joan d'Arc; for, though the masses of the English believed her a sorceress, and the lower orders of the French an inspired heroine, yet the better informed on both sides considered her but a tool in the clever hands of the celebrated Dunois. About the same period a similar instance occurred in the trial of the Duchess of Gloucester, accused of consulting witches in order to compass the death of her husband's nephew, Henry VI.; but we can easily trace the real cause of the charge to the deep hatred between the Duke of Gloucester and Cardinal Beaufort. Again, the same pretext was used by Richard III. to destroy the Queen Dowager, Jane Shore, and the Archbishop of Canterbury.

Very terrible were the consequences of the celebrated bull against witchcraft issued by Innocent III. in 1488, and of the various manifestoes of his successors. Inquisitors, armed with apostolic power to convict and punish, set to work, all over Europe, hunting out witches. Comanus burned, in Italy, forty-seven poor women in one province alone; and in Germany, which, with France and Switzerland, suffered most during this crisis, Sprenger destroyed them at the rate of five hundred a year. From the year 1610 to 1640 executions, instigated by these bulls, took place at Bamberg, in Bavaria, at the rate of one hundred annually. But the records of Würzburg, from 1627 to 1629, are the most frightful. The list of victims during these two years contains the names of one hundred and fifty-seven persons, of both sexes and all ages, including many very young children and thirty-two poor vagrants. What is said to have kept up the delusion in a great degree, not only in this city, but all over Europe, was that numbers of diseased and hypochondriac people, believing in the crime and mistaking their own symptoms, came forward voluntarily, and accused themselves of witchcraft. In Geneva five hundred persons were burned, under the name of Protestant witches, during the years 1515 and 1516. In the district of Como, one thousand unfortunates suffered death in the year 1524. The number of victims in France was so great that it has never been computed; and in Spain and Portugal, where the Inquisition alone took cognizance of the crime, the numbers are likewise unknown. But it is safe to believe that in the former country, at least, so long the home of a superstitious race that the people could not fail to imbibe something of their Moorish neighbors' faith in spirits, good and evil genii, spells, charms, and philtres, the sufferers were numerous.

It was not till fifty years after the bull of Innocent III. that any severe enactments against sorcery were made by the English Parliament. The first statute that specified the particular crime of witchcraft was passed in 1541, but the persecutions may be said to have fairly begun in 1562, when a statute of Elizabeth recognized witchcraft as a crime of great magnitude. During the next half century we read of numerous trials and convictions throughout Great Britain; but it was not till the accession of James I. to the English throne, in 1603, that this mania reached its height, not only raging more fiercely than ever before in the realm of this superstitious king, but reaching its climax at the same period in all the other countries of Europe. As the Scotch are a people renowned from earliest times for their powers of imagination and their belief in the existence of goblins, wraiths, kelpies, and other spiritual beings, it is not astonishing that the monarch who sprang from them should, in uniting the thrones of Scotland and England, have imbued his new kingdom with much of the superstition prevalent in his native country. Great was the interest he manifested in all cases of witchcraft, and his famous work on Demonology was for many years not only quoted as an authority beyond which no judiciary should wish to search, but the methods recommended by it for the detection of the witch or wizard were acted upon throughout the land. Written for the good purpose of rooting out what was considered a terrible evil, this book proved as efficacious as the bull of Innocent III. in spreading it and keeping it alive; for, just as morbid affections of the mind, which depend upon the imagination, become more common by the public attention being drawn to and fastened upon their symptoms, the prevailing mania spread the more rapidly as the severity of the inquiries and number of the punishments increased. Among the innumerable cases of witchcraft that occurred during the reign of this king, the following famous trial of the witches of Lancashire is one of the most interesting:

About the year 1634, certain rumors, emanating from a boy called Robinson, the son of a wood-cutter who lived upon the borders of Pendle Forest, reaching the ears of the local magistrates, the youth was called up for examination. His story was most extraordinary. He said that one day he had seen in the forest two greyhounds, which he tried to start after a hare, and he was about to strike them with a stick, as neither would move, when they suddenly changed into a woman and a boy. The former offered him money to sell his soul to the devil, but he refused. She then took out a bridle and shook it over the head of her companion, who turned into a horse; upon which she seized the narrator in her arms and rode off with him, over bogs, fields, and rivers, till they came to an old barn. Entering the barn, they found within seven old women, pulling at seven halters which hung from the roof—a rain of meat, bread, and other edibles falling around them as they pulled; and upon this food they afterward feasted. The boy, Robinson, had recognized many of the women as living in the neighborhood, and upon his evidence they were at once arrested. About twenty persons were thrown into prison, and eight were condemned and executed without further testimony. Many years later, this same Robinson confessed that he had been bribed by his father and other persons to give false evidence, in order that they might gain large sums by threatening those who were rich enough to buy them off; but not one of the wretches who concocted this plot was ever brought to justice. This event supplied the material with which Ainsworth built up his lively and interesting romance, entitled *The Witches of Lancashire*.

In 1669 the epidemic fear of witches, having found its way into the distant country of Sweden, showed itself in its most malignant form. The king having been informed that the little village of Mohra was troubled with witches, a commission of clergymen and laymen was appointed to visit the place. Upon their arrival, a sermon was first preached, which greatly affected the common people, and afterward a charge read to them to come forward and declare the truth as to all cases that they knew of among them. Men, women, and children promised, weeping and sobbing, to tell all they had heard and knew; and the next day seventy persons, including seventeen children were denounced. When put to the torture, they all confessed their guilt; and one little girl, who no doubt had experienced in a dream all that she thought had really happened to her, swore positively that she had been carried through the air by witches, who had let her fall to the ground from a great height when she uttered the name of Jesus. The devil very kindly picked her up, and healed a big hole which the fall had made in her side. Her mother's statement that the child, till the day named, had had a great pain in her side, at once convinced the judges of the truth of the story. It is very easy for us to trace the source of other absurd details given by these poor little children to the well known imaginative powers of sensitive youthful minds; but the commission no doubt thought they were exhibiting not only much zeal, but great wisdom, in sending the whole number to the stake. And, in addition to these, fifty-six more children were found guilty of witchcraft and sentenced to imprisonment and public whippings.

The New World was also, about the same period, visited by its first and last attack of this description. The daughter of a mason, named Goodwin, had, no doubt, been brooding upon the stories which had found their way across the ocean, and in consequence imagined herself bewitched by an old Irish woman called Glover. This poor old creature, not being able to repeat the Lord's Prayer without a mistake, was found guilty and executed. Very naturally, the fears of the colony becoming excited by this discovery of a witch in their very midst, all the nervous women were attacked with hysteria, the suffocation peculiar to which they at once attributed to the devil, who, they said, was sticking balls in their windpipes to choke them. Working upon each other's imaginations with various stories until they set themselves into fits, they began to have visions in which witches appeared to them and tempted them to join their ranks. These phantasms took the forms of neighbors and friends; and upon the testimony of those who thus beheld them, two hundred, of all ages and conditions, were arrested and convicted. Nineteen were executed, one of the victims being a child only five years old, who was said to have been seen in company with the devil, and to have bitten with its little teeth those who refused to sign a compact with his majesty. They even went so far in their madness as to try and execute a dog for a like offense.

But when people saw their nearest and dearest snatched from them, a revulsion of popular feeling set in, or rather the delusion began to take a different form. The community commenced to think that the devil might be putting false testimony into the witnesses' mouths, for the destruction of the innocent; and in order to thwart him in this purpose, all prosecutions were stopped, and even those who had confessed were released. Judge and jurors openly expressed their penitence, for they now looked upon those who had suffered as the victims, instead of the accomplices, of Satan. Public attention being gradually drawn to other matters, and the imaginative recovering from their affright, no more was heard of people being bewitched; and so, in time, the subject dropped and was forgotten.

Yet at this very epoch, when the minds of men seemed to be hopelessly clouded by superstition, a light was generating which would ere long dispel the gloom, and in time illuminate all the world. It shed its first beams upon Germany, England, and France, gradually increasing in brightness till the middle of the eighteenth century, when witchcraft began to be looked upon as an exploded doctrine.

Even when the witch mania was at its height, the spirit of the age was changing, slowly, silently, but surely. Subjects, formerly thought too sacred and holy for the consideration of any but the clergy, now began to be discussed by the many; and learned writers, who challenged the very possibility of this crime, arose on every side. The invention of printing, and many new discoveries in science, did much to assist the growth of this new order of things. The year after the Restoration (1662), the Royal Society, which had taken its rise at Oxford from a private association, was formally incorporated by royal charter, and began to publish its transactions. About the same time, the French Academy of Sciences was also founded; and the Germans, in imitation, established a similar institution at Leipsic. The celebrated *arrêt* of Louis XIV., commanding that a number of poor shepherds, who were under arrest in Normandy, should be released and protected, was the severest blow of all to the superstition, and one from which it never recovered. A belief so deeply rooted in the minds of the ignorant many could not, of course, be eradicated all in a moment by the arguments of the enlightened few; but the evil was soon greatly ameliorated by the changes in the laws of the different European nations, which began to deprive the magistracy of their former unlimited powers for the destruction of supposed witches. In England and Scotland, up to the year 1665, there was little diminution of the popular mania; and in 1649 an act was passed in the former country, confirming a statute of Queen Mary, not only enacting severe penalties against witches, but against all those who covenanted with them, or sought their aid in any way. During the next ten years, four thousand persons suffered; but after this the executions were few. The last one which occurred in Great Britain was in 1718. The penal statutes were all abolished soon after, and in 1736 was annulled the famous one enacted many years before by James I.

Germany, for all that its advancement in science and learning had been very great, bears the odium of having presented to the rest of the world, in astonishing and disgusting contrast with the altered and improved spirit of the times, the last of these horrid spectacles. In 1749, some young women of a convent in Würzburg imagined themselves bewitched, because they suffered from fits, felt the suffocation of the now well understood hysteria, and one of them evacuated from different parts of the body some needles she had swallowed. One Maria Renata Sauger was accused of bewitching them, and arrested. At her trial, the girls swore she had been seen to climb the convent walls in the shape of a pig, and, drinking the wine in the cellar till she was intoxicated, start up in her own form; that she prowled about at night in the shape of a cat; that as a hare she had milked the cows dry; and, finally, that she performed as an actress in a Drury Lane theater in London, and returned to Würzburg on a broomstick the same night. She was condemned, upon this evidence, and burned alive in the market-place of the city.

Although this is the last example on record of the terrible effects of one of the most frightful epidemics which ever visited the earth; yet, like some rank weed, which, having introduced its roots into the ground, can never be eradicated, many fibers of this tenacious belief in witchcraft still cling to the soil where it once luxuriantly flourished. As late as 1785, the sect of Seceders, in Scotland, were in the habit of introducing among the sins—national and personal—annually confessed from the pulpit, "The repeal by Parliament of the Penal Statute against Witches, contrary to the express law of God." In Ireland, the statute against it has not even yet been abolished, but it is, of course, considered a dead-letter in the law. The belief also lingers in Sweden, and to this day is very prevalent among the lower orders of the French and in the north of England, but the doctrine is nevertheless virtually a thing of the past, and beyond all hope of a revival. Its strongest foothold is at present in the minds of the grossly ignorant, and while intellect and knowledge remain, as they are now, the ruling powers in all civilized parts of the earth, it can never regain a firmer hold upon mankind than is allowed to any of those innumerable small superstitions which occupy a corner in nearly all men's minds, yet have no serious influence upon their lives.

CONSTANCE MAUDE NEVILLE.

THE HOMESTEAD BY THE SEA.

The sighing and respiration of the great sea to-day was wonderfully soothing, until there was a series of dull explosions, like the percussion of far-off gunnery. One may hear these sounds on a still midsummer day, or at midnight, when the sea is pulsing and breaking along the shore line. It required two hours to find out the secret. Along these chalk cliffs there are great caverns, wind and wave worn. Standing near the mouth of one of them, a "boomer" came surging along, and placed its watery seal over the mouth, driving and pressing the atmosphere before it. When the seal was broken there was an explosion like a gun seaward. The turn of the tide is frequently marked by a series of these boomers, and then there is a suggestion of a park of artillery under the cliffs, and the long roll is beaten along the shore. All discoveries are simple enough when once the secret has been found out. How many men walk along the edge of a discovery all their lives, and never quite enter into the promised land! Some blundering successor stumbles into the fruition of the great secret. There are men within bow-shot of prizes as magnificent as ever crowned human research; but they will go no farther. Columbus rested at the Antilles; the continent was just beyond. If you have got as far as the islands, it may be well, before you give up the search, to look at the sea-weeds and drift-wood, whether they do not come from the mainland. Having gathered and cooked the mussels, you might as well stay and eat them as to have another eat them and throw the shells after you. Charles Lamb discourseth about the mussel wisely: "Traveling is not good for us; we travel so seldom. How much more dignified leisure hath a mussel, glued to his impassable rocky limit, two inches square! He hears the tide roll over him backward and forward twice a day (as the Salisbury coach goes and returns in eight and forty hours), but knows better than to take an outside place on the top of it. He is the owl of the sea, Minerva's fish, the fish of wisdom." And yet the mussel can travel, and if detached will seek out a new location, and by means of its silken beard, or byssus threads, which it can weave in a few minutes, anchor itself anew to the rock. It has two enemies: The whelk, a sort of univalve mussel wolf, which bores a hole through the shell about the size of a pin, and sucks the life out; then there is a species of sea-gull which, when all other resources fail, plucks off the mussels, and, rising high enough, dashes them on the rocks; from which circumstance Æsop may, or may not, have invented his story of an eagle dashing a tortoise on the shining crown of a bald-headed man.

Yonder, where the surf frets the shore and pencils a dark line of kelp, look for the star-fish and the limpet, and for mosses in ultramarine and carmine such as no florist can match from his garden. And what is the sea but a great treasure-house of palms and ferns, of corals, and of lilies which no eye hath seen, and royal highways, under whose arches there is an eternal procession of living things, and glorious mausoleums for the dead? This maritime discourse was somewhat abbreviated, because the youngster for whose benefit it had been made suddenly disappeared behind the rocks. He had begun some experiments on his own account. He had found out that the abalone which cleaves to the rocks has a wonderful suction, and the pinching of his finger between the shell and the rock, as in the vice of a blacksmith, extorted a wholesome yell and kept him in a grave and thoughtful frame of mind for five minutes. Anemones abound in all the rocky pools, spongy, unfolding at the top and closing quickly at the touch, the lowest form of sentient life, but knowing what is what. This youngster takes his second lesson in natural history by dropping in a mussel, when the anemone closes over it, and a few minutes thereafter throws out an empty shell-fish; but when the young rogue dropped in a stone, it was thrown out in a contemptuous way, as if the anemone long ago understood the trick and was not to be deceived by naughty boys.

The star-fish comes in with the drift, as if he were altogether helpless; but, dull and inert as he seems, he watches tides and opportunities. Like the whelk, he loves the bivalve mollusk, but does not bore for it. There is a theory that he folds his five fingers affectionately around the clam or oyster, and then, by the aid of a sort of marine chloroform, secures an opening, when in goes one of the five fingers, and the mollusk is forced to shell out. There is a beautiful combination of persuasion and force. The sedative is tried first, and the pressure afterward. It is a pity that some such process could not be tried on that class of human mollusks whose shells have closed over their millions with an unrelenting grip. Some day their empty shells may be cast up on the other shore. It might be better for them that a star-fish should insert one of his fingers before the drift period begins.

In the chalk bluff, more than forty feet from high-water mark, is the vertebræ of a whale distinctly outlined. This monarch of the seas selected his tomb with some reference to the fitness of things. The Egyptian monarchs built for themselves granite tombs; but the whale lay down on the ooze, and the infusoria of five thousand years or more built around and above him. He was grandly inurned, and lifted up out of the sea by such a force as no living or dead Pharaoh could command. In the matter of royal sepulture, it is certain that the whale had an immense advantage. But after three or four thousand years, the defunct monarchs of sea and land are mainly valuable for bone-dust, and are rather poor fertilizers at best. From the hill one may see whales gambol in the Bay of Monterey, in the early spring months. What a great laundry establishment these fellows might set up, if they only knew how to utilise their power! At present, these columns of spray blown into the horizon are only picturesque. There is a grave suspicion that the friend, whose Mongol servant blew the spray from his mouth into the sponge to be set for bread, would have much preferred that the whale had performed that office. Years ago, one of these monsters was seen floundering about in the bay all day long, as though in great distress. The following night he drifted ashore, dead. The great hulk had no mark of the sword-fish or the whaleman's lance. The sailors said that he was worried, teased, and finally hunted to death, by a fish called a "bummer." How strikingly human-like was this experience of the dead mammal!

There was a strange fascination about two wrecked vessels, whose timber heads could be seen above the sand. Sometimes, in a storm, they would get adrift. So weird like and mysteriously did they rise and fall on the surging sea, appearing and disappearing, thrusting their timbers out like arms imploring help, that one might fancy they were the spirits of these lost vessels coming back to protest against this broken rest. How strangely they accented the storm! When it subsided they would bring up at the old place, and the sand would bury them again. There was an odd genius in the town who claimed these wrecks by preemption. When his finances were low, and creditors pressed for small bills, he made his payments conditioned, as to time, on the coming of the next storm which would unbury the wrecks. Providence saved him a deal of hard shoveling, by raising the wind for him. Then he drew out copper bolts enough from the wreck to liquidate his bills, but gathered no surplus. Hath not many a mine been exhausted by indiscreet development? As long as that copper lasted, "Bob" paid his debts periodically. If he has not yet drawn his last copper bolt, he is still entitled to the financial confidence of this trading and huckstering world.

These round holes in the hard rocks are deftly wrought by the *Pholas*, a little bivalve, which, by means of its rasping shell and strong, elastic foot, keeps up the attrition, grinding away day and night until his excavation is perfect. It fits him on all sides, and he is content to live and die there. How much better is his condition than that of round men who have been trying all their lives to fit themselves into square holes, and square men who never could adjust themselves to round holes. The *Pholas* has found his place, and therefore may be ahead in the race. There was a famous theologian of the last century, who, sitting at his desk year after year, wrestling with problems which neither he nor any other mortal ever understood, ground the floor of his little study, by the attrition of his feet, until it was nearly worn through. His footprints are still preserved as sacred relics. Nor ought the inquiry to be pressed now whether the hole which the *Pholas* wrought with his foot, or the hole which the theologian ground with his foot, was the better or more permanent one. If the question is at all pertinent, it may be ripe for an answer a thousand years hence.

When the tide is out, one may find the razor-fish, so called because the shell resembles the handle of a razor. If laid hold of suddenly, the chances are that before he can be drawn out he will slip out of his shell, leaving that empty in the hand, while the "soul and essence" of him has gone down half a fathom into the sand. Yet is he not more slippery than many an individual, who, when pressed to do some magnanimous deed in behalf of the community, slips out of his shell, and, losing the grip, you can no more find the soul and essence of him than you can find the soul of this razor-fish, which has gone deep into the muck and sand. In either instance, the empty shell is only the sign of the thing wanted.

If it were not for this eternal scene-shifting, the monotony of the sea might be oppressive. But every change of the wind, and every drifting cloud across the sky, gives a new blending of color and tone. If to-morrow the south wind shall blow, or a gale come piping down from the north, the face of the deep will have been created anew, as much so, in an æsthetic view, as if it had been poured out for the first time on the surface of the globe. Is there not a perpetual series of creations on both sea and land? The waters are taken up in the clouds, and poured out again. Mountains are disintegrated, and go down to the valleys, but other mountains are lifted up out of the sea and out of the arid plains. Climbing a hill, more than four hundred feet above the surface of the water, and five miles inland from the present shore line, one may find thousands of marine shells, many of mollusks not yet extinct as species, and read on the face of this conglomerate, as in an open volume, the record of a physical creation, whether by the subsidence of the sea or the elevation of the land, as fresh geologically as if all this had occurred but a century ago. This world of waters creates no sense of isolation. Observe, too, that whoever has been born and bred by the shore will evermore look out on the sea and be glad. A sail is better than a horse, and the breaking of the waves hath more majesty and a diviner music than any organ touched by human hands. *Mem.:* the man who has gone over the rocks, and is filling his pockets with mussels in a furtive sort of a way, is from the interior. He wants salting. He is looking out drift wood, and will strike a match presently. Let him fancy, if he will, that his feast is fit for the gods. To-night he will probably dream that one of these wrecks, covered with barnacles and sea-weed, has rolled over, and is lying athwart his capacious diaphragm.

The Patriarch went out into the fields at eventide. Was it any the worse for him that his meditations were gilded with a touch of romance? What if he thought less of the lilies of the field, and more of the veiled lily from Nahor? Was not that human? So we go down to the seashore as the soft twilight comes on apace, and think it no worse that the voices of lovers blend with the cadence of waters. If there is no higher inspiration for them, let Isaac speak to Rebecca. It is little to them that there is a blush in the horizon, and that a moment ago the sea was opalescent, and the mountains put on and put off their royal vestments of purple.

This homestead by the sea was an accident. It was the result of a bit of facetiousness, that had a solemn termination, as it were. Riding past the court-house in Santa Cruz, nineteen years ago, when that town had not as many hundred people, the wag of a sheriff was dividing his time between crying a ranch at public sale, to close an estate, and whittling a stick. No bids for the last hour. Would the citizen on horseback halt a minute and accommodate him with a bid, just to relieve the dullness of the occasion? The last bid was raised five dollars. What did that madcap of a sheriff do but slap his hands together and declare that the estate was sold. There have been earthquakes which were inconveniently sudden, and thunder-claps from a clear sky; but such an investiture of real property had not been known in many a day. The sheriff shut up his jack-knife; the bystanders closed theirs, and they all went round the corner, as they said, to consult a barometer—a proceeding which that official never did fully explain. When one has been overtaken by a surprise, a climax, or even a joke, which has at the bottom of it such a flavor of real estate, it is best to sleep on it for one night, and take a fresh view of the situation on the following day. Does not the ideal country estate in some way enter into the sleeping or waking dreams of most sanguine men? There are to be many broad acres, parks, and fountains, orchards drooping with fruit; vineyards creeping up the hillsides; a trout stream in which "chubs" greatly abound; a capacious mansion, with hospitable doors swinging open as if by instinct on the approach of friends; barns filled with fragrant hay; thoroughbred stock, from the horse down to the dog and cat; Alderney cows, coming up at night with cream in their horns, mild-eyed and gentle, with breath as sweet as the white clover they had eaten; gilt-edged butter, not handed round in pats as large as a shilling, for admiration, but set forth in solid cubes, like gold which had been honestly assayed and run into ingots; strawberries perennial, and always smothered in cream; bellflowers and pippins, ripening in the autumn sun; scientific farming, not for profit, but just to demonstrate how it can be done; long, tranquil days, restful and full of indescribable peace, when bees go droning by, and the perfume of the orchard comes in at the open windows. That is pretty nearly an outline of your dream, with some minor variation of details thrown in; such, for instance, as a great chamber looking toward the rising sun, where the one epic poem of the nineteenth century is to be written. Are there some twinges of pain about the heart that this dream has never been quite realized? Consider for a moment that heaven, so far as it relates to this world, is for the most part an ideal conception. It is not what one has reduced to possession, but what he hopes to have. Now, one can put a great deal of heaven into the ideal country home, and not realize largely on the investment. If the strawberries cost a dollar apiece, and the favorite horse has a trick of putting his heels up toward the stars, the chickens stagger about with the gapes, and the phylloxera browns the vineyard as if a subterranean fire had been burning at the roots, these touches of realism may chasten the expectations somewhat, and at the same time serve to plant the amateur farmer more firmly on his feet. It is a pity that the world could not be enriched by the experience of the gilt-edged farmer from the city. What is most wanted is a book of failures—an honest filling in of the blanks between the ideal and real country life.

A survey of the new purchase disclosed a number of particulars; and, among others, that a dead man's preëmption claim, when sold under the form of law, passes a rather shadowy title to the buyer. It was needful to become a constructive preëmptor, and to exhort a number of impenitent squatters to early penitence and reformation. The Saxon's hunger for land is generally matched by his appetite for land-stealing. If two parcels of land of equal area and value be shown him, one already claimed and the other open to settlement, the chances are that this descendant of ancient land-robbers would much prefer to pounce on the land already occupied, and fight it out. If he is not reconstructed in his inmost soul, he will always be wanting his neighbor's vineyard. The new purchase met all æsthetic requirements. It was on the edge of the town, and hardly more than a mile from the sea. It had a grove in the foreground, a trout stream on either side, with a fringe of tall redwoods, a backing of mountains, and a water view comprising the whole of Monterey Bay, and as much of the ocean as the eye could reduce to constructive possession. Not a fence to mark a boundary; but the two-room shanty, with its great stone chimney on the outside, loomed up like a palace. There was a fire-place which yawned like an immense cave. An old rifle-barrel, planted in the chimney, served well enough as a crane. The opening at the top was liberally adjusted for astronomical observations, but had been slightly abridged by the nest of a pair of gray wood-squirrels, which kept up a perpetual racing on the dry roof at night.

It is not probable that the primitive man had any such house to await his coming; and, having his constitution adjusted to a tropical climate at the outset, he had little use for a stone fire-place where the back-log lasted a week. It would furnish a curious commentary on the evolution of dwellings if one could establish the fact that the first house was built of *adobes*, like those which one now sees along the bluff of the Branciforte, and which have more than one quality of the perfect country house. A breast-work of earth might have been raised first, to break off tempests; afterward, it would have four sides, then perhaps a thatch of palm leaves—and the primitive *adobe* dwelling stood in its glory. In such a habitation the sun could not smite by day, and only the fleas could smite powerfully at night. If any learned archæologist finds fault with this theory, let him make a better one out of *adobes* if he can.

It was an odd circumstance that the grove had been the chosen place for many a camp-meeting, the board buildings still remaining; while on the opposite side an eccentric African had occupied for many years a hut, and led a sort of mystic life. He was skillful in compounding simples, the potency of which was greatly increased by his incantations. It was even said that he had the gift of hoo-dooing, and always kept the roughs at bay by threatening to fix his eye on them. There was a trace of orthodoxy in his methods—since if the wicked cannot be won by love, they can sometimes be scared into decency by sending the devil after them. Here were signs of grace on one side, and diabolism on the other. But neither effected much in "Squabble Hollow," two miles beyond. It is a pity that the African had not done a little hoo-dooing up there among the pioneers, so that the reign of peace might have set in at an earlier day. It is quiet enough now, because Time, with his scythe, has cut a clean swathe there.

If one has planted his own orchard, he will eat the fruit with greater satisfaction. He will have an affection for the trees which he once carried under his arm, and will trim them tenderly in the spring. Whoever ate the cherries which he bought in the market with such secret satisfaction as those which he plucked from his own trees in the early morning? If your neighbor invites you to his cherry orchard, he honors you above kings. It is doubtful if royalty ever poised itself on a rickety chair, or reached for cherries so deftly as that school-girl, who read her graduating essay, with pendent blue ribbons, last month. She is not greatly changed now, except that her mouth has increased about a hundred per cent. Every tree which one sets with his own hands is better than those which the hireling and stranger have set. He establishes secret relations with it, communes with it, eats of the fruit as if the tree itself rejoiced in bestowing such a benediction. When the apples fall to the ground, in the still autumn day, it is as if they dropped from the opening heavens. Every one is the symbol of wisdom, and hath, in its malic acid, a subtile essence, which carries health to the morbid liver. And no individual is ever wise when that organ is in trouble, or, at least, he has an unhappy way of expressing his wisdom. From this sanitary point of view, it will accord with a healthy conscience if a little cider mill is set up under the wide-branching oak hard by. If you have any scruples, you need not taste of the cider, but you can smell of the pomace, and note how the bees and yellow-jackets are drawn to it for honey. The bees go in a straight line to a knot-hole in the dead top of a redwood tree. The taking up of a wild swarm, which had stored honey in another tree, was not a happy experiment. When the tree came down, there was a black, boiling mass of enraged bees. No lack of honey. But, if one wishes to know what is meant by the "iron entering into the soul," let a dozen bees go under his necktie, and prod him along his back—the last one, by way of a tiger, prodding the tip of his nose, because at that very instant one must sneeze or die. How can one tell what is sweet except there be some bitterness in contrast? It was evident that old dog "Samson," who dropped his tail and yelled when the bees lit on him, was not given to much philosophical reflection; but the speed of that disconsolate cur was mightily helped on his way back to the kennel. If an invitation were now extended to him to take up another hive, he would do nothing more than wave his tail and send regrets.

That platform in the grove is maintained for the benefit of free speech, with reasonable limitations. Clerical and political orators have had their day there. In short, it is the platform of all nations, newly consecrated every summer by the rhythmic feet and gleesome voices of childhood. Then, if ever, the oak and madroño spread their branches of perpetual green over such more tenderly, as symbols of the immortal freshness of youth. Is not this succession of life from chaos eternal, and the race itself only in its infancy? Neither the woodman's axe nor the fire could take the vitality out of that redwood stump, for the saplings have sprung out of its clefts, and the old roots are sending these new spires up toward the heavens. As little does the destruction of a nation affect the genesis of the race, or its everlasting succession. The orchard is the symbol of peace, abundance, the mellowness of life. It is the sign of a gentle civilization grafted on to the wildness of nature. The wild blackberry and strawberry, which grow along the fences and hedgerows, have an aboriginal flavor. When they are domesticated they are a hundredfold better. The wild trees of the forest take to themselves new qualities when set in the open grounds. The ship built of "pasture oak" is a better craft, because the toughness of fiber of such trees was gained in the open field, where they had given shelter to ruminating cows. Was not the yew tree, which grew about the ancestral homes generations ago, chosen for the cross-bow because of its toughness and elasticity? This solitary ash by the fence is more lithe and graceful for its introduction to domestic life; and this wide-branching oak before the door, casting now its shadows aslant, made handsome obeisance to the earthquake, sweeping the ground with its lateral branches. Not a fracture of one of its elastic limbs; but that ancient stone chimney rumbled fearfully, and stood apart in moody isolation. When the dog abandons the civilized community and hears no human speech, he loses his bark. The lowest type of humanity has only a few guttural sounds. The civilized master follows the condition of his dog—that is, if he be cast on some solitary island, he gradually loses his speech. Dog and man have finally gone back to dumb nature. Why is the fruit of the ancient pear tree, standing by some deserted homestead of ante-revolutionary days, more acrid and pungent than it was a hundred years ago? It had lost association with human kind. If one could grasp the sweeter subtleties of Nature, he might find a gracious accord, a point of sympathetic contact, where the mellowness of the individual, the rich and generous juices of his nature, give a finer quality to the fruits of the trees which he has planted. Something may come back to him, also, in the aroma of the orchard, helping him by its fragrance to a gentler and more thoughtful life. W. C. BARTLETT.

A MOUNTAIN FIRE.

A long, low murmur on the midnight air,
As of the tide upon some far-off shore;
A swell among pines standing tall and fair,
A whisper as of danger leaning o'er;
A strange light growing up the hollow sky,
Eclipsing the white glory of the moon;
A signal flag on the wind streaming by,
Of wreathen smoke outflung, has followed soon.

Out of the darkness starts a tongue of fire,
Wrapping the white trunk of some dead old pine,
Mounting in fierce and absolute desire
To reach the glowing heavens' altar-shrine.
The dark is flooded with the crimson light,
The green pines shiver in the fire's roar,
The scene of grandeur grows upon the sight,
And the wide, doming heavens arch it o'er.

The hollow circles of the smoke uproll
Against a sky of palpitating flame,
Wreathing above the pines, scroll upon scroll
Swelling and rising in the crimson stain.
The moon is dead; the stars' green points of light
Merge in the drifting sparks that fill the night;
And the great flames sweep upward fold on fold,
Till the dark mountain stands swathed round with gold.

MAY N. HAWLEY.

IN EARTH'S SHADOW.

The world's sad petrels, dwelling evermore
On windy headland or on ocean floor,
Or piercing violent skies with perilous flights
That fret them in their palaces o' nights,
Breaking enchanted slumber's easeful boat
With shudderings of their wild and dolorous note,
Above the billows haggard with the moon,
And faint with fantasies of nightly noon;
There lies for them not anything before
But sound of sea and sight of soundless shore,
Save that a whisper through the night makes way
With glimmering wings prophetic of the day;
Then for a golden space the shades are thinned
By singings of the rosy-footed wind;
But soon the dark comes, wilder than before,
And swift around them breaks a sullen roar;
The tempest calls to windward and to lee,
And—they are sea-birds on the plaintive sea.

CHARLES EDWIN MARKHAM.

THE PROTESTANT HERO OF THE XVII. CENTURY.

The admirers of Gustavus Adolphus have woven around his name a wreath of legends and traditions more appropriate for the saint than for the great political and military leader. Enthusiastic Protestants have surrounded him with an ideal glory. They have delighted to think of him as the heroic champion of their faith. They would make him in Protestant tradition what Godfrey of Bouillon and Saint Louis have become in Catholic tradition. This is going too far. He undoubtedly accomplished for Protestantism "a work which no other man then living in Europe would or could have accomplished." He saved for Germany the results of the Reformation; yet our interest in his life and character is not based solely upon his achievements in behalf of Protestantism, but as well upon the fact that he led his people to the height of their national glory.

The first historic glimpse which we get of this nation shows it to be a part of the ancient Scandinavian people, which, though everywhere speaking a common language, was yet without a common government. It was governed, not by one king and one parliament, but by many kings and many parliaments. But in the ninth century the numerous petty kingdoms yielded before an irresistible tendency to centralization, and out of the multitude of little states arose the three kingdoms of Denmark, Norway, and Sweden. A little later, in the thirteenth century, began the differentiation of language. The Danish and Swedish came to be recognized as separate languages, distinct from one another, and distinct from the mother tongue. In the fourteenth century an effort was made, prompted by royal ambition, to unite the three kingdoms under one government. The union effected was called the Union of Calmar. This lacked strength, because it was formed in opposition to the tendency of developing nationalism; Sweden, especially, was dissatisfied in being considered merely a province of a great Scandinavian kingdom, and under the tyrannical rule of Christian II. this dissatisfaction culminated in revolt. The yoke was no longer endurable, and the terrible execution of Stockholm, in which between eighty and ninety of the first men of the nation perished, taught the people how merciless was the hand that sought to guide them. Gustavus Wasa, a son of one of the murdered noblemen, led the revolt. He determined to free his countrymen, and lift them once more to national independence. He succeeded, and in 1523 was chosen King of Sweden. This was the grandfather of Gustavus Adolphus.

In order fully to comprehend the development of personal character, we must know not only the person's relations to his contemporaries, but also the characteristics of those from whom he is descended; for, however far we may still be from a just appreciation of the law according to which faculties of the soul are inherited, "there exists undeniably a link between generations—a relation such that, if parents and ancestors had not been as they were, the children would not have become such as they are." Yet the child may be unlike the parent. A virtue of the father may reappear as a fault in the son; for example, economy may become avarice, and generosity may pass into reckless prodigality. Of a complete, well-rounded nature in the father, some of the children may receive merely a fragment, a power in some given direction, and this power, through the lack of mental balance, may be inadequate to insure a successful life. Thus it happened in the elder sons of Gustavus Wasa. Eric became a brilliant maniac, and John a religious fanatic. But in Charles IX., the youngest son of the old king, the powers of the father seem to have been once more united, and in Gustavus Adolphus, the son of Charles IX., we have "the ripest fruit of the Wasa tree."*

When Gustavus Adolphus was born, in 1594, his cousin, Sigismund, the son of John, was King of Sweden. For the family of Charles IX. there was hardly a way to the throne, save through a revolution which should overthrow the legitimate sovereign. Such a revolution came. Sigismund had been trained by Jesuits, and he adhered to their teachings. In 1593 the Council of Upsala determined the future policy of Sweden in the interests of Protestantism, but the principles and prejudices of Sigismund made it impossible for him to support this policy. The result was war—war between the nation and its king. The nation was victorious. Sigismund was deposed, and in 1604 the crown was placed on the head of Charles IX. By this the young Gustavus Adolphus became heir to the throne of Sweden.

---

* Svedelius, "Om Konung Gustaf II Adolfs Karaktersutveckling, skildrad under den tidigare delen af hans lefnad," 6.

During these years of civil war, Gustavus Adolphus was receiving his childhood impressions, and, for a lively and precocious mind like his, these impressions were not without importance. He heard of insurrections and battles, of treachery and defeat, of bigotry and persecution. He saw the earnestness of his father and of those who supported him, those whose lives and well-being hung on the issue of their cause. He saw men who had thus been willing to venture everything for the welfare of their country. He caught their spirit. He learned what it meant to be king. He learned, moreover, that he was a prince, and that he might might soon expect to bear the burden of kingly authority. He had, as a boy, a certain arrogance, but arrogance tempered with a sense of justice. With a weak, indulgent father and a fond and doting mother, he might easily have become a spoiled child; but he was not his mother's favorite, and under the severe domestic rule of Charles IX. there was little danger of undue indulgence. He was kept at his studies under strict discipline; but at length his independent spirit revolted. His governor, Otto von Mörner, wrote, on one occasion, that "Herr Gustavus Adolphus, who was then in his fifteenth or sixteenth year, would no longer consent to be disciplined, but held chiefly to those who granted him his free will with women, card-playing, and the chase, as well as in military exercises." He had outgrown the narrow discipline of a pedagogue. His nature demanded freedom, just as the nature of every boy, or every young man, at a certain period, demands freedom, if he is to attain the highest type of intellectual or moral development; and it would have been only natural, if, in seeking this freedom, in breaking loose from the hampering chains of a narrow and short-sighted discipline, he had been led into excess. And John Skytte, who had been his instructor for nine years, seems to have appreciated this danger. Having been sent on a foreign mission in 1610, he wrote, during his absence, to the young prince, warning him from the follies and vain pleasures of youth. "The words," says Professor Svedelius, "contain no reproaches for faults already committed, but it can be read clearly enough between the lines that the instructor regarded the warning quite necessary. If we add Skytte's warning to the complaint of Otto von Mörner, there may appear some reason for presuming that Gustavus Adolphus, during a certain part of his early youth, passed through, as it were, a period of recklessness."

This period of moral recklessness in the life of Gustavus Adolphus did not continue long or make any very lasting impression on his character; neither were the energies of his mind so diverted as to hinder materially his intellectual development or the acquisition of knowledge. "Soon came the Danish war and his father's death, and he found other things to think of than women and card-playing." In 1611, at the age of seventeen, he ascended the throne. Henceforth, the business of war and government demanded his attention. His opportunities for undisturbed study were gone, yet these had been so well improved that he spoke with great facility Latin, German, Dutch, French, and Italian. He understood English and Spanish, had a certain knowledge of Polish and Russian, and is said to have been by no means ignorant of Greek. He prized above all other ancient classics the writings of Xenophon and Seneca. Hugo Grotius's *De Jure Belli et Pacis* was his companion even on his distant campaigns. He became a man of liberal culture, and was always zealous for the advancement of learning in his kingdom. Like many other young men, he passed through a period of verse-making. His love-songs are still extant, or some of them at least, but the memory of the fortunate being who inspired him to sing has passed away. The best and best known of his poetical productions is the celebrated battle hymn, sung by his army on the eve of his last battle. The original is in German.*

These verses, and his love-letters to Ebba Brahe, suggest that Gustavus Adolphus, as a young man, felt something of that languishing sentimentality, "that depression of spirits, that melancholy peculiar to the youthful heart, which many are certainly fortunate enough not to know, but which in others gnaws at the heart in the midst of the age of gladness." He was not moon-struck, but there was a little place in

---

* In *Kongl. Vitterhets Historie och Antiqvitets Akademiens Handlingar*, part XXVI, new series, appears an article by Johan Wilhelm Beckman, in which this hymn is critically examined, and the following given as the original text:

Verzage nicht, du Häufflein klein,
Ob schon die Feinde willens seyn,
  Dich gäntzlich zu verstören,
Vnd suchen deinen Vntergang,
Davon dir wird gantz angst vnd bang,
  Es wird nicht lange wehren.

Tröste dich dess, dass deine Sach
Ist Gottes, dem befehl (!) die Rach,
  Vnd lass es jhn nur walten,
Er wird durch einen Gideon,
Den er wol weiss, dir helffen schon,
  Dich vnd sein Wort erhalten.

So wahr Gott Gott ist, vnd sein Wort,
Muss Teuffel, Welt vnd Hellenpfort,
  Vnd was dem thut anhangen,
Endlich werden zu Hohn vnd Spott,
Gott ist mit vns, vnd wir mit Gott,
  Den Sieg wolln wir erlangen.

his soul for the romantic softness of youth. This element of his nature finds expression in his love affair with Ebba Brahe, which was an important event in the development of his character. On either side there was deep sincerity and purity of purpose. She was a young woman of noble birth, of physical beauty, of amiable temper. With her he proposed to share his throne. He was nineteen; she was seventeen. But, in spite of them, the line of Shakspere is true:

"The course of true love never did run smooth."

The Queen Dowager was unwilling that a woman not of royal blood should be lifted to the throne of Sweden, and, either through her opposition or some other influence, the vows of betrothal were broken, and Gustavus Adolphus descended from the noble purity of his relations with Ebba Brahe to become the paramour of Margaret Cabellau. In referring to this event, I would not be understood as intimating that the man whom the Protestant world has been wont to regard the purest and noblest character of his age, was, after all, only a degenerate libertine. This manifestation of human weakness, says a Swedish historian, was merely "a passing aberration, but not the beginning of a lasting slavery of the character to the passions. That romantic mood, which is reflected in his love for Ebba Brahe, changes into the intoxication of sensuality in his connection with Margaret Cabellau, but was in its ideal form, as in its abasement, merely a *stadium* of development, through which Gustavus Adolphus passed in order afterward to raise himself to that standpoint whence the relations of life were conceived less ideally, but more truly, and the sacredness of fidelity appeared worthier than the charms of love." From this we see—and here I borrow the words of one who has studied the life and character of the king more profoundly than any one else—from this "we see that even he was like many others, wherefore the others ought also to be able to be like him; that is to say, to grow better with time. But, unfortunately, it is not unusual that men grow worse the longer they live. The pangs of remorse are sometimes the feelings of the aged, when he cannot escape the better memory of his departed youth. But when I consider the whole of Gustavus Adolphus's development, this conviction urges itself upon me, that this man, when he fell by Lützen, was not merely a more experienced man, wiser and riper in understanding, but also morally ennobled, a purer and more exalted character, than when he first began his public life. His character grows continually upward—it rises ever higher; the temptations are increased, but the more earnest the moral work becomes, the stronger is developed the power for good. That which is morally great in Gustavus Adolphus is not that he was from the beginning, or became in time, an ideal saintly character. Such he never was. But his greatness is this, that he became ever better and better, ever purer, and this the more the allurements of the world tempted. The temptations for the youth in the home of his parents were moderate, but they were greater for the hero of Europe, in the exultation of triumph, under the caresses of adulation, among the most enchanting pleasures of ambition, in the web of political projects, where interests crossed each other, so that the choicest thought and surest will were needed, in order that the distinction between right and wrong might not be entirely confounded."*

Turn now from the personal character of Gustavus Adolphus to his political policy. To understand this, we must understand the spirit of his times, and the circumstances under which he ascended the throne. These were not propitious. In the beginning of his reign, the king was not the only sovereign in the kingdom. The principle that a king might divide his kingdom at will among his sons was not entirely extinct. There were reigning dukes, who had sovereign authority within the limits of their respective territories. The southern and richest portion of the Swedish peninsula was in the hands of the Danish king. The nation was oppressed with poverty. The king was poor, and the peasants were poor. Whatever wealth there was in the country was in the hands of the nobles, who were free from taxation. Thus the burden of government pressed all the more upon the peasants, which led to discontent and insurrection. All over the country there was lack of law and order. The rich crowded the poor nto deeper poverty. Reckless bands of mercenary soldiers, roaming from place to place or quartered in the villages, robbed the industrious of their gains. The poor cried for help, the oppressed demanded justice, and the descendants of those whom Charles had beheaded for their treason called for vengeance. There was war with Denmark, war in Russia, and Sigismund, King of Poland, was striving to regain his seat on the Swedish throne. He was allied with the most powerful princely houses of Europe. He had around him, in Poland, a body of Swedish nobles, who had been driven into exile. Through these he scattered among those at home the seeds of discord and civil strife. To govern Sweden under such circumstances, to

* Svedelius, 15.

win the support of the nobility, to rouse in the people patriotism and the spirit of self-sacrifice, was no easy task, even for an old and experienced ruler. But here a mere boy, a lad of seventeen, was called to shape the policy of the nation. It is true that at his side stood Count Axel Oxenstjerna, as Prime Minister, but Oxenstjerna himself was little more than a boy. He was still under thirty, and in all important matters of policy yielded to the king.

With this state of affairs, Gustavus Adolphus began to reign. His work was difficult, and he appreciated the difficulty. He realized what perils he had to face. Of these the presence of the enemy moved him least. In the face of Tilly's troops, and before Wallenstein's batteries, he was always cool, always unconcerned about his personal safety. But when, as a young man about to ascend the throne, he reflected on the affairs of Sweden, on the wars on all sides, on his father's approaching death, he was troubled; he shrunk from the great responsibilities; he "wept that it should be his fate to bear such burdens." Here there was bravery, but not arrogance.*

When we remember that three of the four wars in which he engaged were an inheritance from his father's reign, we see to what an extent his policy was conditioned by the circumstances of the kingdom when he became king. The natural boundary of Sweden on the south is the Baltic, but when Gustavus Adolphus ascended the throne, the southern portion of the peninsula was in the hands of the Danes, and Denmark was at war with Sweden. Here, then, we may see clearly the first point in Gustavus Adolphus's foreign policy. It was this: to end the Danish war, and, in doing so, to get possession of the rich provinces in the southern part of the peninsula. And to this he at once directed his attention. As soon as his first parliament was over, he took the field; but his first military exploits were not brilliant. There was nothing in them to dazzle the mind and spoil a hero. The war was ended by a treaty, in January, 1613, but the borders of the kingdom were not materially extended. Gustavus Adolphus failed to win the first great point in his policy. The first year of his reign was an apprenticeship; his labor brought small returns, but the experience was valuable. It prepared him for later work. There was much in it to inure him to hardship, much to make ambition reasonable. He learned what it costs to wage war—what incalculable labor, what never-resting thought, what untiring watchfulness. But in this campaign he showed certain traits of the barbarian; as, for example, in the plundering and burning of Christianople; yet he learned so thoroughly the uselessness of barbarity, that in his later wars he was celebrated for his mildness and just dealing.

In this, his first war, as throughout his career, Gustavus Adolphus showed a liking for bold throws. While at times he appears the most cautious of men, on other occasions he is the most audacious of political gamblers. In his game with Russia he staked the future of his nation. Here he pursued a policy which seems to us strange and difficult to be understood. In the civil wars in Russia, which preceded the elevation of the family of Romanoff to the Russian throne, in 1613, this nation appeared on the the verge of dissolution. The Swedes were in power at Novgorod, the Poles held Smolensk and Moscow, and the throne was repeatedly claimed by false pretenders. While a deposed czar entered Warchau in triumph, a Russian embassy appeared in Stockholm, asking a Swedish prince for the throne of Russia. Hatred of the Poles united the majority of the nation in this demand. Here it was proposed either to make Charles Philip, the younger brother of Gustavus Adolphus, ruler in Russia, or to allow the King of Sweden to wield the Russian scepter together with his own. It was clear that Gustavus Adolphus favored the second alternative. He was not zealous in the cause of his brother, and the Queen Dowager was reluctant to have her favorite son go among such a rude and warlike people as the Russians. Thus there was delay, and when finally Charles Philip landed in Russia to claim the offered throne, the Russians in Moscow had chosen Michael Romanoff. At first thought, the policy of Gustavus Adolphus in this matter appears worthier of an adventurer than of a shrewd statesman. But, whatever might have been the effect on Sweden's future, had Gustavus Adolphus been firmly established on the throne of the czars, it is certain that through his policy he looked only to the safety and welfare of his people. He intended merely "to avail himself of the internal confusion of Russia in usurping a portion, greater or less, of the Russian territory, or the whole of it, in order to cover Sweden's frontier, and fortify its power in the eastern provinces; and when the throne of Russia was offered to the royal family of Sweden, he seized this opportunity to increase the Swedish power at Russia's expense." If the Russians hoped to build up their declining nation by giving the scepter into the hands of the King of Sweden, they were miserably fooled. He thought less of nothing else, and, looked at from a patriotic Russian point of view, his pol-

* Swedelius, 27.

icy does not appear in the purest light. The saint which men claim to see in him later was not developed. His dealings with the Russians at this time were worthy of a Machiavelli or a Bismarck. But, judged from a narrow Swedish point of view, we see no motive but Sweden's rights, Sweden's advantage, Sweden's glory. He was willing to become czar—in fact, there are state papers on Russian affairs, issued by him while he bore this title—but he was not willing to accept and hold a new crown, if thereby he would be obliged to neglect the real interests of his own people. Here the well-being of his nation was the primary consideration; personal gain and personal ambition were secondary. That the czar should be a Swede was not so important for Gustavus Adolphus and for Sweden as that he should not be a Pole. Russia, trampled beneath the feet of two hostile nations that were making war on her soil, was comparatively powerless. In the south, Polish influence predominated; in the north, Swedish. The Poles had been enemies of the Swedes since the wars of Sigismund and Charles IX., and the question of succession came to the mind of Gustavus Adolphus as a proposition not only to build up Swedish against Polish influence in Russia, but also "to secure an advantageous position in opposition to Russia itself." And, after the question of succession was dropped, the policy of Gustavus Adolphus looked to the obtaining of such a position through a treaty of peace. But for three years such a peace was impossible.

Finally, in 1617, came the treaty of Stolbova, and Sweden won the position desired. Gustavus Adolphus returned from this, his second, war a conqueror. Although he had not retained the title of czar, he had accomplished what he had hoped to accomplish, by accepting the offered throne: he had carried out the second great point of his policy. He had won vast possessions east of the Baltic, and east of these he had established a safe frontier against the Russians, who were entirely shut out from the sea. He had taken the first step toward the realization of a project for which he fought with more or less earnestness throughout his life—the project to make the Baltic an inland sea of the Swedish dominions. And this project was kept in mind during his third war—that with the Poles; and also during the last and greatest undertaking of his life—his campaign in Germany.

The policy of Gustavus Adolphus toward Poland was the ancient policy dictated by the nation to his father. It looked to the maintenance of national independence, and the preservation of the Protestant faith. The Swedish people had stated to Sigismund, the rightful heir to the throne, the conditions under which he might continue to be their king. He failed to fulfill these conditions, and Charles IX., the uncle of Sigismund and father of Gustavus Adolphus, was put in his place. Sigismund, however, though deposed in Sweden, was still King of Poland, and still claimed the Swedish throne. He fought to carry out this claim. He was a Catholic, and his political principles were those of the Jesuits. But the Swedes were Protestants, and naturally demanded a Protestant king. Gustavus Adolphus was able to meet this demand, and his policy toward Sigismund was made plain to him by the enthusiastic support of his people. They demanded that Sweden should remain independent of Poland, and be ruled by a king of their own faith. When, therefore, Gustavus Adolphus fought for his throne, and for a recognition of his right to it, he was acting in accordance with the wishes of the people: and in this part his policy toward Poland had the indorsement of the nation. But he aimed at more than this. He had little faith in the so-called natural boundary of Sweden as its line of defense. He wished land beyond the Baltic, as a bulwark against Poland—a continuation, as it were, of the eastern provinces which had been confirmed to him by the treaty of Stolbova, and which served as a protection against Russia. This, then, was the second of the determinative features of Gustavus Adolphus's policy toward Poland. The plan proved difficult of realization. The war and the negotiations dragged on from year to year. Other interests in other quarters demanded attention. Still, a permanent peace was impossible. At length Gustavus Adolphus was imperatively demanded in another field; and finally, in 1629, he made a truce of six years, and obtained from Sigismund a practical recognition of his claims. He obtained also certain territory south and east of the Baltic—certain cities and ports, from which he drew a portion of the revenue that supported him in his next great undertaking.

With the close of the Polish war, we reach a point in the career of Gustavus Adolphus where he rises from the position of actor in the comedy of national politics to play a part in the tragedy of international politics. In this latter *rôle* he is generally known. The Protestant Revolution of the sixteenth century left Europe divided into two great parties, with no prospect of peace between them, but in the so-called Peace of Augsburg the sure conditions of a future war. This war came in the seventeenth century. It began in Bohemia in 1618, and was ended by the treaty of Westphalia in 1648.

From the small beginnings of a provincial insurrection, it grew to be a general European war. The whirlwind, which gathered up a few straws on the plains of Bohemia, increased as it advanced toward the west, its increasing circles sweeping wider and wider, and leaving behind a broader and broader track of desolation. One nation after another was drawn from its isolation and plunged into the scene of universal confusion. The great revolution led by Luther seemed about to be followed by a reaction that would destroy forever the influence of Protestantism in Europe. The Protestant princes of Germany had endeavored to resist the advance of the Imperialists, and been defeated. They turned to foreign powers for support. Christian IV., of Denmark, wanted to be a hero. He was jealous of the rising power of Gustavus Adolphus. He espoused the cause of the Protestants, and became their champion. He led an army to Germany for their defense, but he led it only to defeat and disaster. This was in 1626. After this their cause was more hopeless than ever; they were without a superior leader, their armies were everywhere defeated, and discord reigned in their councils. In this state of affairs, all eyes turned toward Gustavus Adolphus. He was now about thirty, and thus in the full vigor of early manhood. His character had ripened under the serious business of war and government; and there was, as Geijer says, no nobler name in Europe than his.

He had watched with interest and anxiety the course of the conflict, had seen with regret the mistakes and follies of the Protestants, and was willing to become their leader. But while the Polish war continued, his hands were tied. The six years' truce was made toward the close of 1629; in 1630 he was free to begin his German campaign. The story of this campaign is familiar; every one who has read the history of the Thirty Years' War remembers without difficulty the events attending the participation of Gustavus Adolphus—how he called together the estates of the kingdom in Stockholm, and commended to them his little daughter as their future queen; how he took on board his little army of thirteen thousand men, and left his country forever; how, on landing in Germany, he thanked God for the safe voyage, and prayed for the triumph of what he considered to be right; how he met the superior numbers of the enemy; how he scattered the forces of Tilly, and marched unhindered through the middle of Germany; how he fell at Lutzen, and at his death won a victory over Wallenstein. All this we know, but when we undertake to find out the motives which led Gustavus Adolphus to participate in the Thirty Years' War, to determine how far these motives were religious, and how far political—in a word, to explain this part of his policy, we have to do with one of those historico psychological questions which can never be fully answered. However, from his character and utterances, and from the character of the war in which he was called to engage, we can arrive at a tolerably satisfactory conclusion. In the light of recent researches in the history of his reign, it is not possible to doubt that, during his later years, Gustavus Adolphus was a sincere, earnest, religious man. The Thirty Years' War was not purely a religious war, but it was one in which ecclesiastical and political interests were so intertwined and interwoven that they could not be separated one from the other; and the danger which menaced Sweden, in the event of a complete triumph of the Imperialists and Catholics in Germany, threatened not merely Sweden's political, but also her religious, freedom. But from the Council of Upsala, in 1593, and the days of the nation's triumph over Sigismund, the leading article in the religious, as well as in the political, policy of Sweden was independence; and the policy of Gustavus Adolphus was the policy of his people. Therefore, to deny that he was actuated by religious motives shows a failure to comprehend the true character of the king, and his relation to the events of his time. He was a religious man, and a thorough Protestant; and he desired to foster the religious interests, not only of his people, but also of the Protestants in Germany, and this desire was a determinative motive to action.

While we thus attach considerable importance to religious interests, and see in them a religious motive, it is not thereby said that they furnished Gustavus Adolphus all, or his chief, motives for engaging in the Thirty Years' War. He was not a religious reformer, or "Protestant saint;" he was a ruler, a warrior, a statesman, and as such the political well-being of his country lay near his heart. He saw the advance of the Imperialists, the helplessness of the Protestants in Germany, the miserable failure of the drunken King of Denmark; he saw that only one step more was needed on the part of the Imperialists to rob him of his independence, and that Wallenstein, by his endeavors to get possession of Stralsund, and thus of the Baltic, was preparing to take this step. For Gustavus Adolphus, in view of this condition of things, to have refused to advance, to have retired within the borders of his kingdom, there to attempt his defense, would have been to abandon the policy he had thus far followed with success—the policy of making his line of defense beyond the Baltic. And in this case he believed that this was the only safe policy; and, having encouraged and aided Stralsund to hold out against Wallenstein, he entered Germany to carry it out. Here, then, was a political motive. While Gustavus Adolphus held to the policy which he had pursued toward Russia and Poland, he had at the same time other and more comprehensive plans. The prospect of a line of provinces along the eastern and southern shore of the Baltic, united with Sweden and under the immediate control of the Swedish Government, was, it is true, not an unambitious prospect. But he looked to other ends. He looked to the union of Sweden and Brandenburg, to the building up of a great Protestant power in the north of Europe, which should give unity and direction to Protestant Germany and Scandinavia, and form not merely a counterpoise to the Hapsburg power in Austria, Spain, and Italy, but be the controlling power of Europe.

BERNARD MOSES.

MODERN MONTEREY.

Ruskin recently spoke of the resemblance existing between a duck and a snake, implying, perhaps, relationship at some long-passed day. Ducks and snakes are both stupid animals, and have no souls. A bird, however, has a soul, and I could easily believe it to be related to the human family, if it were only for having in common the one trait—the irresistible desire to flit when the spring time comes. No matter how soberly and sincerely I say to myself all through the winter, "I shall not want to go anywhere next summer; that will be a saving, and I can get me an elegant summer suit." But when the spring time comes, I find that that part of my soul which is related to the bird grows very restless, and before the summer is far in the land I have forgotten all about the elegant suit, and am flitting somewhere.

This year it was to Monterey. It was not the first time my steps had turned that way. I had been there many times before, and I have learned to love the old place, which holds so much of interest to the American people. Historical associations alone, however, have never yet made any place pleasant or desirable to live in; but in Monterey nature has done much, though art and improvement, until quite recently, very little, to make the town and the surrounding country attractive.

In regard to its earlier history the main difficulty is to know where to begin to speak of it. That Juan Rodrigues Cabrillo must have passed the harbor in his cruise of 1542; that Viscayno landed here, and took possession for the Spanish king in 1602; that Father Junipero Serra reached Monterey in 1770, with the good ship *San Antonio*, and on the second of June celebrated the first Mass under the trees—we have all heard and read so often that I am afraid of being "choked off" by the editor if I attempt to say it again. Still, there is some excuse for lingering a moment over the arrival of the good priest, Junipero Serra, for he built the beautiful Mission of San Carlos, in Carmel, the lovely little valley with its stretch of shining white beach, and its remnants of Mission garden and old orchards. And, besides, the very tree under which the altar was erected for the serving of the Mass is still spreading its broad shadow over the earth, and the tree still standing there is proof that the whole story is true, if even it had not passed into history as a fact. He came ashore; upon first landing, brought thirty-eight out of the fifty of the ship's crew, monks and sailors, with him; and, after declaring the land the property of the King of Spain, took spiritual possession of the realm for his church. The ground must have undergone considerable change since then, for where the ugly wooden cross stands to-day, marking the spot where this first Mass was said, a little run, or gulch, has washed its way deep into the soil, and the slope by the tree, where the worshipers would naturally have knelt, is so narrow that thirty-eight people could not possibly have crowded around, unless some of them had descended into this gulch, a proceeding neither dignified nor practicable, either then or now. The tree from which the bell was suspended that bright June morning has toppled over, and the trunk is now lying prone in the tiny stream it had so long overhung.

Monterey itself should be viewed afoot. This advice is not an insinuation against the state of the streets, though the truth is that every street has a gully running through the center. The streets are wide enough, however, and one can drive either to the right or the left of the ravine, and, as my brother philosophically remarks, these gulches will be of considerable help in building the sewers. Some of the older streets run in any and every direction that happens to suit; the newer ones run due east and west, north and south. Monterey has grown of late, in both size and importance; but the newly erected American residences, I am glad to say, have nothing of the rectangular, hard-cornered look about them which new American houses are apt to have. A spirit of veneration for the traditional quaintness of the old capital seems to have mercifully guided the hand of the designing architect, and the result is that the modern features of the town blend harmoniously with what was already there when the Americans came. And surely, what they found there could not have been so utterly despicable. The place had been the residence of the Spanish governors for fifty years, of the Mexican governors for twenty-five. To be sure, we know how far removed from the center of civilization California was in those days; still, there were men of character and distinction among the long line of governors, priests, generals, who once dwelt here—men whose mark it is neither easy nor altogether desirable to efface.

Many of the *adobe* houses, solid two-storied buildings, lie in the midst of large gardens, surrounded by high walls built of *adobe*, or the chalk-stone found in the vicinity. When built of chalk-stone, the upper portion is frequently of hard-packed earth, overgrown and covered with shrubs and weeds; when raised of *adobes* alone, they are always finished with a layer or two of red tiles, and above, and out from behind these gray walls, with their red edge, crowd the green foliage of tree and bush, and the tender pink and golden yellow of apple-blossom and the cloth-of-gold rose. The gate is grated, permitting a broad view of the garden, and a glimpse of the interior of the dwelling, if the hall-door happens to be open, for the gate is always just opposite the front door of the house. A number of houses are but one story high, and they are the coziest of all, the generous veranda promising shade and coolness for the summer-time, the heavy walls and deep fire-places insuring warmth and comfort for the winter months. Many of the less pretentious houses have no fire-place at all, except the apology that serves for culinary purposes. The climate is so mild that there is no suffering from actual cold—it is only the uncomfortable sensation creeping over one on a long, rainy day, that needs to be banished by looking at a cheerful fire.

Quite a number of the wealthy prominent Americans, lately removed to Monterey, have bought some of the better preserved of the old *adobe* structures, and have converted them into desirable and attractive homesteads; for, no matter how indolent and non-progressive the Spanish population may have been, there is one element in this sleepy old place which never stood still—the plants and flowers of field and garden. They took no holiday, summer or winter, these thousands of roses, lilies, vines, and trees; they kept right on growing, growing, growing, till they have covered houses, fences, ruins, with a tangle of scarlet, gold, and purple blossoms. In the garden of a Madame Bonifacio (I beg pardon for growing personal—I do not know the lady, but I want other tourists to enjoy what I saw), there is a trellis over the walk, from the hall-door to the gate. The entire trellis is covered with a rose, yellowish in color, the size of a breakfast-saucer, and crowded with blossoms. The stem of this rose is a tree, as large round as the neck of an ordinary sized man. This must be seen to be believed, I know; but it's there.

Pretty well back, on something of an eminence, stands Colton Hall, named after the first American *alcalde* under the military administration of General Riley. It was originally designed as both a town-hall and a school-house, and answers the latter purpose still. No one will ever go into raptures over its architectural beauties, though the building is quite large, built of the handsome light chalk-stone, and well finished. Here the first California Constitution was framed, in September, 1849; it is really the cradle of our State laws—and a good sound cradle it looks to be, even to this day. Beside it stands the jail (ominous juxtaposition), built of imported stones. The cause of the distinction enjoyed by the jail (to be erected of imported stone, when native chalk-rock was good enough for the town-hall) was in reality a bad augury for Monterey; for, during the time that government had its seat here, these stones were sent for to build a dry-dock with. As soon as it was decided that the Legislature and the State Government should be removed to San José, this project was abandoned, the stones were used to build the jail with, and, soon after, Monterey entered upon the long sleep from which it is only just awaking.

Closer in, is a long, two-story, shaky *adobe* building, bearing every mark of old age about it, without having yet advanced to the dignity of a ruin. This is the Presidio of Spanish times, the *cuartel* of the Mexican *régime*, and the soldiers' quarters of the beginning of our own Government. It lies in the heart of the town, abandoned and deserted, save for a room or two in the lower story, where otherwise homeless wanderers at intervals take up their abode. The fort itself, and the *casamata*—the place where the powder and shot were stored, and the cannon were kept—are out on the hill, to the west of the town; and, as I had a great curiosity to inspect these relics close by, we wended our way through the busy streets, and were soon ascending the hill. On the lower terrace, overlooking the Bay of Monterey, stand the remains of thick *adobe* walls, with a heavy, blackened log protruding here and there from the heaps of *débris*. This is the *casamata*. No other traces of older fortifications are visible on this plateau; but back of this, on the summit of the hill, there is still a solitary cannon, pointing its warning finger at the bay. Steep as the climb was, we mounted to the rampart and descended into the interior. The earthworks had been star-shaped. From the main road at the foot of the hill, I had often noticed a low roof, barely visible above the outer walls. Now I had the gratification of seeing it near by, at last, and found that it was the blockhouse—the last resort of the garrison, had the outworks ever been taken. The sturdy old thing looked defiant even now, with its notched loop-holes and impenetrable timbers; but out of the low entrance-door hung wisps of hay and bundles of straw, showing that it had degenerated into a mere storehouse for the abundant grain that now grows around it. A little farther back, but well protected by the cannon of the fort in former times, are the ruins of the soldier's barracks, with no signs of life about them, save that a lizard glides swiftly by over fallen logs and decaying timbers. The officers' quarters were in better condition, and we mounted the stairs that led, on the outside, to the upper story. Messieurs the officers had been comfortably fixed, as usual, I'll warrant; large, well lighted rooms, fire-places, and the most magnificent view imaginable. Standing on the rude balcony, which the landing of the stairs forms in front of the house, one gets a wide look across bay and city. Over these placid waters there, the *Savannah* came gliding, on the second of July, in 1846; and on the seventh of the same month the stars and stripes were raised by Commodore Sloat, right here in front of us, over the old Mexican *casamata*, and yonder in the town, over that rambling, two-story *adobe* house I spoke of before. The Mexican people were well enough satisfied to accept the Americans and their rule, so far as I could learn from Don Rosario Duarte, who came with Commodore Dupont on the *Cyane*, as American marine, though a Spaniard by birth; but their rulers were wide apart and divided in their opinions on this point. Governor Pio Pico, in his little speech, anathematizes the "hordes of Yankee immigrants who have already begun to flock into the country, and whose progress cannot be arrested."

"Already," he exclaims, "the wagons of this perfidious people have scaled the well-nigh inaccessible summit of the Sierra Nevada, crossed the entire continent, and penetrated to the fruitful valley of the Sacramento. What that astounding people will next undertake, I cannot say; but in whatever enterprise they do embark they will be sure to prove successful." Thank you, friend Pio Pico, we have endeavored to verify your kind predictions. Don Mariano Guadaloupe Vallejo showed a great deal more "savey" on this occasion. He said: "Why should we shrink from incorporating ourselves with the freest and happiest nation in the world, destined soon to be the most wealthy and powerful? Why should we go abroad for protection when this great nation is our adjoining neighbor? When we join our fortunes to hers, we shall not become subjects, but fellow-citizens, possessing all the rights of the people of the United States, and choosing our own Federal and local rulers."

The only things in the way of treasure that our soldiers got in the city of Monterey at the time of its bloodless capture, were one hundred and fifty pieces of ordnance—cannons, large and small—which are at present decorating street corners and serving as hitching-posts. They are stuck in the ground, without much attention to "heads or tails," and remind one—I don't mean to cast reflections—of the bravado of most Mexican military: ferocious of aspect, but utterly harmless, and incapable of doing serious injury. The heaviest two pieces are "planted" in front of the Monterey Whaling Company's office, near the fort, as if they had proved too heavy for further hauling. Next to this house (the Whaling Company's) stands a red brick building, of many memories. It was built, very early, by Mr. Dickenson, one of the party who came in 1846, just ahead of the Donners, and barely escaping their horrible fate. He had with him his wife and two daughters, young ladies who were greatly sought after, and much courted and flattered. The boldest admirer they ever had, however, was an enormous grizzly, who forced his way into their room one night, and insisted on making them a friendly call anyhow, no matter how strongly they objected. Young ladies had lungs in those days, as well as now, and I can imagine how their cries and screams rang through that old brick house. One of the young ladies, married long since, lately presented a brick from the wall of this building to the Society of Pioneers.

The surroundings of Monterey could not well be more beautiful if they had been gotten up to order. Hills, gently rising, the chain broken here and there by a more abrupt peak, environ the city, crowned with dark pines and the more famous cypress of Monterey *(Cupressus macrocarpa)*. The Lomalto is a bald peak, with a lower peak, more gently sloping, for its neighbor. The whole was formerly called the Cerro San Carlos—for to this Holy Charles seems to have been assigned the guardianship of Monterey and the Carmel Mission. To the right, or west of us, as we stand facing the bay, is the hill bearing the remains of the old fort, beyond which winds the road to Point Pinos and the light-house; to the left of us, east, lies a forest of pine and live-oak, and above the trees waves the flag from the tower of the new Hotel del Monte. Before us the bay lies calm and blue, and away across, on a light day, even without the aid of a glass, can be seen the town of Santa Cruz, an indistinct white gleam on the mountain side.

And now, having devoted the whole morning to historical researches—which led to the discovery of an owl, a mole, and several lizards, among the ruins of the fort—let us follow the waving of the flag, which beckons us out of the "dark forest-green." A short mile from the heart of the town lies the new hotel, over which these crazy, sleepy old Montereyans are fairly going wild. There are two roads by which to reach the place, one along the sea-shore, while the other, a longer drive, takes us by the handsome Catholic church, across one or two narrow lagoons, and past the ancient, as well as modern graveyard. Whichever way we drive, we enter directly into the forest—not "grove," as these horrid people call it, but veritable, venerable, old-fashioned forest. Pines *(Pinus insignis)*, trying their best to reach the stars, are intermingled with live-oaks of singularly tall, straight growth *(Quercus agrifolia)*. There is nothing gnarled or stunted about them; no bleak wind has ever crippled their growth, or distorted the solid trunk into weird, repulsive shapes. Evenly the long, low-hanging branches spread on every side, giving shade and protection to hundreds of flowers and ferns. A thick carpet of native grasses serves them for bed, and the poison-oak, the bane and pest of most California country resorts, is conspicuous only by its entire absence.

The horses seem to check their speed of their own accord as they enter this solemn forest dome, and I am just about to make myself ridiculous, by the suggestion that they are listening to the peculiar, low, soothing whisper that the wind breathes through the tree tops, when a cry of surprise cuts off my brilliant remark. A fairy castle has just risen out of the ground, or dropped from the skies, and rests airily among the trees in the distance. I was afraid to breathe when I saw it first, for fear of dispelling the vision; but, as we approach, the thing assumes more solid lines, a more substantial shape, and I find that we are right in front of the much-talked-of new hotel.

Who planned the place, or laid it out, in the common parlance of mortals, I don't know. I don't know what it costs, and don't want to know. Don't, for pity's sake, let us destroy the few æsthetically romantic impressions that are graciously vouchsafed us in this land of dollars and cents. Let us enjoy the rare pleasure of ranging around and through the place without giving heed to the fact that the architect's rule and the carpenter's square were employed in its construction. For the information of those prosaic beings who *must* have feet and inches, let me say that the building is very nearly three hundred and seventy-five feet long, three stories high in some parts, four in others. The whole, on closer inspection, seems a happy mixture of forest château, Italian villa, and old English country seat, though they call it, I believe, Queen Anne or Eastlake style. Outside are the spacious verandas of the Italian villa, inside are the wide halls and generous fireplaces of the English manor-house. Outside, the lofty forest, the blue waters of Lake Como (*vulgo*, Laguna Segunda) blinking through the trees, and the white beach of the ocean in the distance, form incomparable scenery. Inside, the broad staircases, the many-shaped windows, each framing in a sylvan view, the variously arrayed rooms in the different towers, the manifold entrances and exits, always leading into forest-green, make the house picturesque. Now, I don't really know whether interiors can be picturesque—I don't know whether artists allow that term; but I insist that "picturesque" is the only correct word to apply to the inside of that building.

A drive is to be constructed from the east of Monterey, along the beach, by the whaling station, all the way around Point Pinos and the light-house, along Moss Beach, to Cypress Point, to the old Mission, and across the country, back again to the hotel. A Cliff House is to be built on the highest, most wildly romantic spot near Point Cypress—a resort for the people at the hotel and for "citizens at large." The fact is, that if any one undertakes the entire drive in one day they will want some kind of a resort on their way. There is also a race-course near the hotel, and all the walks and drives, near and far, are being constructed of gravel brought from Soledad. Of this large tract of land, small tracts will be sold to people who wish to establish a permanent summer residence in the country. Some of the land in the vicinity of the hotel has been divided off for this purpose also, and so near to it that people who are afraid of the drudgery of housekeeping can take their meals at the hotel.

California enterprise, by the way, was never better illustrated than in the erection of this hotel. On the fifteenth of January, of this year, the giants of the forest held undisputed possession of the ground which the house now covers. On the first of February the architect arrived with his force of men. At the time of the present writing (May 15th) there are over three hundred men still at work in the house and on grounds; and on the third of June, before this paper is laid before the reader, the hotel will be thrown open to public.

It was a day of rare enjoyment that I spent there; and as I, like the cook, Frederika, in *Old Mamselle's Secret*, always think of others, I gathered what I could of the many wild flowers growing there, for the benefit of those who take an interest in our California flora, and brought them home to Dr. Behr, who has kindly given me the botanical names of the different varieties my basket held. They are the *Aquilegia*, *Viola aurea*, *Orthocarpus*, *Castilleja*, *Convolvulus*, *Collinsia*, *Eschscholtzia*, and others, which I had carelessly so mutilated as to be unrecognizable. The backward season has been more severely felt by the butterflies than the flowers, and there was not so great a variety as there should be. But among those who have their home and being there the Doctor mentions these: *Anthocharis sara*, the *Melitæa*, *Canongrepha Californica*. And *à propos* of the Doctor, he is really heaping coals of fire on my head, for I once cut very deeply into his scientist heart. When it came time for my usual spring-flitting, several years ago, he said to me:

"Toward the south, where you are going now, there is a blue butterfly which has not yet been classified. If you bring me a specimen of this butterfly it shall be named after you. I promise."

It must be admitted that the Doctor understands a woman's nature, at least as well as that of a rattle-snake or a tarantula-hawk. He did not say, "Madame, I expect you to devote a few spare moments to the advancement of science in our new country." He simply stimulated my activity by promising that my name should ride down to posterity on the back of a blue butterfly. Well, I stopped at San Luis Obispo, climbed the height of the Santa Lucia Mountain, and almost the first thing I saw was a magnificent blue butterfly. My escort captured it, after some trouble. It was cruelly impaled on a pin, which I stuck, for better security, into the log upon which I had sat down for a rest. On my return to the city I hastened to Dr. Behr, told him where I had found the blue butterfly, and described it most minutely. The Doctor rubbed his hands in high glee:

"The description is correct," he said, nodding; "it must be the right thing. The whole tribe shall be called by your name now. But where is the specimen? Let me have it."

"What, the butterfly?" I asked. "Oh, that's on the top of the Santa Lucia Mountain. I came away and forgot it there."

You should have seen the Doctor's face! Out loud he said nothing, but I'd give something pretty to know what his private opinion was just then of women in general and myself in particular.

No Monterey trip is complete without a visit to the old Mission. A lovely spot, this narrow Carmelo Valley, stretching down to the sea, or the bay rather, which takes its name, I suppose, from the Carmel River emptying with it. It is a pity that these old places are allowed to go to decay. This building here, at least, might be preserved, if not restored, as it is built of stone—the light yellow chalk-stone of the country. The roof has most all fallen, but the architecture and construction of old buildings would disgrace no builder of the present day. It has the slightly Moorish tone which I imagine I can discover in all these places built by the Spanish *padres*.

The bells are gone from out of the towers, but the delicately wrought cross on one still points to heaven. Of the twelve arches which originally spanned the nave, some are quite solid, and could easily support a roof; and if the whole were restored, it would be one of the grandest monuments we could bequeath to grateful generations coming after us.

No wonder Father Junipero Serro loved the spot so well that he wanted to be laid to rest here, where he had performed so important a part of his life's labor. The land was rich with the grain he had sown, and the docile Indians who trimmed his vines in the Mission garden loved him, perhaps, more devotedly than their newly given God, for they could not see Him, while the good *padre* provided for them as a father does for his children. But now comes the knotty point, over which there has been so much contention. That the *padre* was buried inside of the old church, there seems to be no doubt. The question is, what became of his bones? Long after the mission system "had outlived its usefulness," the bishops of San Luis, Los Angeles, and San Juan Bautista, came in solemn state to remove the sacred remains to a place not so dilapidated as the Mission church had become. To their consternation, they found nothing to remove; and, though the story was hushed up as much as possible, all sorts of rumors went flying among the superstitious Catholics of Spanish and Indian blood, as to what had become of the good father's bones. Having some curiosity on the subject myself, I once more sought my oracle, Don Rosario Duarte, and asked what he thought had become of this pious man's ashes.

"That," he said, "I can tell you. My mother-in-law, who died ten years since, at an advanced age, has told me a hundred times of the deputation of high officials and humble monks who came all the way out from Spain to carry back with them the bones and ashes of Father Junipero Serra. There are still three of the old Mission Indians living here in town. One of them, a woman named Yumesa, will corroborate my statement, for she claims that she can recollect how every one of the *caballeros* and *monjes* comprising this deputation looked.

I tried my best to find Yumesa, not because I doubted Don Rosario's word, but because I wanted to see what a real, live Mission Indian looked like. I failed to discover her; but of the thousands who will flock to Monterey in the course of this summer, I hope that some one may make it a special task to find and interview Yumesa. JOSEPHINE CLIFFORD.

NOTE BOOK.

TO THE NEED OF A HISTORICAL SOCIETY upon this coast, we had occasion to refer last month in reviewing Governor Burnett's *Recollections*. A correspondent takes us to task for the following language used in that connection:

"There is material in the history of the Pacific Coast which is rapidly being lost for want of some organization to systematically collect and preserve it, but which, in the future, if so collected, some historian would gather into a story as dramatic and fascinating as that of Prescott or Macaulay. Perhaps, however, we should be thankful that, in the absence of any organized effort to rescue this fast perishing tradition, there are occasional disconnected publications which may in some manner preserve it."

Our correspondent points, with just enthusiasm, to the collection made by Mr. H. H. Bancroft, of San Francisco, who has expended large sums of money, and much valuable time, in securing every book, pamphlet, or relic which would throw light upon the history of the Pacific States, and who, by means of an extensive correspondence, has reduced to an available form the personal experiences of hundreds of individuals.

"In no State," says our correspondent, "has so much private enterprise, capital, and ability been expended in the pursuit of the very object to which you allude."

This letter comes very opportunely, to give point to our suggestion. We were aware of the collections made by Mr. Bancroft, and by at least one other gentleman, and the success which had attended their efforts seemed to us to show the necessity of an organization. Individual effort, even where it is as public-spirited and as magnificent as in the case cited, is always limited by the will, by the other engagements, and, finally, by the life of the person making it. Private collections also are liable to disintegration, and the vast labors of a single lifetime may come to naught simply because at the moment there is no one to keep the results intact. Furthermore, such collections should be public, should be accessible to all persons. A historical society alone can accomplish this. There are thousands of persons who came here in early days whose lives were eventful. Their deeds, taken collectively, constitute our history. Many of these are aged, and in a short time the hand that now can write will forever lose its cunning. The death of every such man, with his life-story untold, is a public calamity. An organization, with a bureau of correspondence, might yet preserve much of that which otherwise will soon be forever beyond our reach. It is not only selfish, it is extremely impolitic, to leave to individual effort that which is public concern. That there are organizations which were generally expected to display an interest in this matter we know, but that any interest has been shown outside of the individual instances cited we have yet to learn.

CADET WHITTAKER does not appear to advantage in the light of the investigation into the West Point "outrage." It is clearly established that Cadet Whittaker has attempted a colossal fraud on the good people of the country. From the first it was a source of wonder that a person within calling distance of aid should passively submit to the treatment to which he claimed to have been subjected. Possibly the worst feature of the whole affair is the damage which it will do to the Military Academy. The fact that Whittaker was a colored cadet was enough to awaken in the minds of many well-meaning persons a belief in the most extraordinary stories which he might choose to invent, and this credulity was heightened by the prejudice which the graduates of the Academy have fostered by their pretensions at *caste* and superiority. The supercilious bearing of many officers has done incalculable injury to the system which produced them. This is very natural, and, to an extent, not illogical. Cadet Whittaker's case came at an inopportune time to inflame this prejudice. This is much to be regretted, as the history of our late war, as indeed of every war, shows the superiority of the professional soldier. While there were deeds of gallantry and no little military talent found in individual civilian soldiers, it must be confessed that the great generals were graduates of the Military Academy. If this be so, a country with such vast possessions to defend as are held by the United States cannot afford to neglect any precaution, at least so long as men continue to think that cutting each other's throats and shooting off each other's heads are the best means for the settlement of disputed questions. We do not expect a man to be a good doctor who has not been graduated at a medical school, nor a successful minister who has not attended a theological seminary. We train our business men from boyhood. In every branch of life we advocate special training as a prerequisite to excellence. It is equally necessary with the profession of arms. If we would win in the supreme moment of conflict, we must train some men through long years for that moment. Cleverness, aptitude, will not at the time supply the place of this experience. It is probable that the efficiency of the West Point Academy in many ways may be increased. It is certain that the graduates may assist the institution, as well as their profession, by abating somewhat their arrogance. But the inefficiency, if any, may be remedied, and the arrogance is merely a silly pretense, while the fact still remains that war may come, as war has come, and that in such event the country will need the bravery, experience, and genius of these men who seem so useless in time of peace. After a war the nation rewards its soldiers with unstinted honors. Before the war, while peace remains, it is grudging and parsimonious.

THE COMMENCEMENT EXERCISES at the University of California were largely attended. It is a pity that the entire population of the State cannot be brought together at Berkeley once a year to see the work which is done there. One notable event connected with the graduation of the class of this year, is the fact that the highest honors are borne off by two young ladies. The class is a large one, and the advocates of the idea of feminine intellectual inferiority will have difficulty in explaining this preeminence. One of the young ladies has already acquired an enviable reputation upon this coast as a writer. The President of the University called attention to the necessity for endowments to assist needy students, and for other purposes. It is worthy the consideration of our rich men that a sum which they would hardly miss, would yield a sufficient interest to be a perpetual benefaction in assisting poor young men and women to complete their studies; and it is certain that no investment would yield a greater return of real pleasure and satisfaction.

SECRET SOCIETIES have grown with remarkable rapidity during the last few years, especially in America. The time when there was but one of these societies is within the memory of many persons now living. To-day they are numerous, and comprise such an extensive membership that we are surprised that no writer on social science has mentioned them as curious phenomena of the times. We live in an age of cooperation, in a gregarious century. Every undertaking of magnitude is accomplished by an aggregation of force and capital. We believe these societies are accomplishing a vast deal of good. It may be admitted, for the sake of argument, that the secrets they profess to teach are unimportant, that their mysticism is an innocent dev[ice for] retaining the interest of their members. We may safely assume that their mysteries are merely ritualistic, and form no argument either for or against the societies, any more than the ritualism of organizations which do not sit with closed doors. But, looking at the practical working of these orders, we find two phases prominent, the pecuniary and the social. The proportions which either assumes are different in the several societies. In some the pecuniary aspect is omitted, except in the form of charity. In others it is the most prominent feature, and takes the form of life insurance, benefits, and so forth, according to the constitution of the order. Certainly there can be no objection either to charity or to that wise provision which seeks to anticipate and avert the evils of the future. But it is the social aspect which we most commend. Men are too apt to get into ruts. We should welcome anything that will bring them together. The scholar may always learn from the laborer, and the laborer may get an insight into newer and higher things from a few moments' conversation with the scholar. It is at once a reciprocal duty and privilege with men to break down clannishness. An intellectual man who holds himself aloof from his less learned fellow-men, loses something of the fullness of true education and culture. He becomes a mental snob. With him it is all head development. He cannot perceive the grandeur in the character of this unlettered man, who would not do a mean action for the universe. Neither can he appreciate the marvelous practical information of this other, who is a close observer of Nature and her laws. We have no patience with unvarying standards to which all men must conform. Our modern education tends too much that way, and we must get out of our little manner of thinking that our talents are the only talents, and that our learning is the only knowledge. A man should be able to appreciate the true nobility of a dog. We need more catholicity; and anything which will bring men together, which will break down arrogance, pretense, and sham, which will build up courtesy, appreciation, and tolerance, and, above all, which will teach that there is no imperialism in excellence, no one virtue that may dominate the rest in purple, we should be prepared to welcome.

CORRUPTION IN AMERICA is a favorite theme for English sneers. We are frequently assured that our system of popular enfranchisement is a failure, because votes are bought and sold by the wholesale. In view of the air of placid virtue with which these charges against us are made, it may be well to inquire what becomes of the vast sums of money which were openly acknowledged to have been expended during the last election in England. It is no secret that a seat in Parliament costs a man a handsome amount. Figures are given which seem marvelous to our American ears. We were told the exact amount that one wealthy lady was about to expend for one young aspirant. What is most singular is that this seems to be taken as a matter of course. It would go hard with a candidate here who was accused of buying his way into place; but it seems to create no prejudice against an aspirant with our English cousins.

THE MONROE DOCTRINE may become a source of serious entanglement before we are through with it. It is hard to see how the United States can permit a canal to be built between the two oceans, unless it is subject to American control. In case of war, it would prove disastrous to our shipping to have the canal in the possession of enemies. But have we the right to insist that no one else shall build the canal, unless we propose to do it immediately ourselves? Have we the right to stand in the way of the world's development, except by virtue of some superior claim to forward that development? A "dog in the manger" policy is unworthy of a great nation. If we are not rich enough, or enterprising enough, to complete this great undertaking, we have no moral or legal right to prevent others from doing it. We believe the Monroe doctrine should be enforced; but we believe, as a corollary to this, that America herself is bound to construct the canal without delay.

SUMMERING HAS COMMENCED. The hills were never more beautiful, the valleys never more inviting, and they are so near, so accessible, that no one who stays at home, and has dyspepsia all next winter, can claim the right to grumble at his fate. We are apt to forget about a vacation in California. Nature does not remind us of it, and we go on from year to year to work until we stop, suddenly. Men must learn this lesson of rest. They must be made to see the economy of occasional idleness, the wasteful prodigality of overwork. And it is not merely rest we need. We must have change of air, water, scenery, inspiration. If we cannot go to the watering places—and it is a mistaken idea that we must huddle together in the country just as we do in the city—we can pitch our tent in the aromatic forest, beside the restful stream. There will not be a night for three months in which we cannot sleep in the open air with impunity, if we go over the first ranges of hills from the coast. We need no books; what we want is a fishing-pole and a gun. We can study Nature's picture in a book when we are at home and cannot see Nature herself. One month of this out-door life is worth all that a man can earn in the other eleven months, for it gives him the impetus to earn it. And the hearty man who comes back at the month's end will do better work in his eleven months than the unnerved man who went out under the trees would have done in the round year by remaining at home.

SCIENCE AND INDUSTRY.

THE MICROSCOPE IN BOTANY.

The microscope is constantly enlarging its field of usefulness, and is adding, day by day, new triumphs in the direction of original research. It has recently given to the world a new and more certain mode for determining the geological structure of rocks; and the fact is now announced of a discovery of equal importance in connection with the life and growth of plants. As, in the first case, many of the universally accepted theories of geologists were brushed aside, so, in the present instance, theories which botanists had supposed to be well established are completely overthrown. It appears that Professor Prinsheim, of Berlin, has recently been studying the green coloring matter in the leaves of plants, known as chlorophyl, and the cells in which it is contained. Botanists have heretofore assigned to this substance the work of absorbing from the atmosphere, during the night, carbonic acid gas, retaining the carbon for the sustenance and growth of the plant, and returning the free oxygen to the air to make good the deterioration of that element through the respiration of the animal creation. Now Professor Prinsheim has demonstrated, by the aid of the microscope, that chlorophyl does not perform that work, but that the carbon in the atmosphere is appropriated and assimilated through the medium of a balsam-like substance in the plant, heretofore unknown, to which he gives the name hypochlorine. This newly discovered substance, when under the influence of sunlight, has a strong affinity for carbonic acid; and it further appears that the heretofore supposed active chlorophyl is merely a passive agent—a sort of curtain, screening the hypochlorine from the direct or too powerful influence of the sun's rays, so that it may do its work with regularity and moderation. The Professor has shown, by experiments, that if the intensity of the sun's rays is materially increased by any optical apparatus, the chlorophyl screen, or regulator, is found too feeble to protect the hypochlorine in its proper work, and oxidation sets in so rapidly that both chlorophyl and hypochlorine are rendered inert, and the plant dies. This discovery opens an entirely new field for botanical research, and furnishes additional evidence that plants have a regulator of vital forces, corresponding more nearly than the simple chlorophyl to the heart and lungs of animals, and further proof is gained in the direction of a unity of life between the animal and vegetable kingdoms.

SCIENCE NOT ATHEISTIC.

The Lord Bishop of Carlyle, in discussing the theories of matter, in regard to their possible atheistical tendencies, holds that all physical science is compelled, by its very nature, to take no account of the being of a God; for, as soon as it does so, it trenches upon theology, and ceases to be physical science. Such investigations are, by agreement, conversant simply with observed facts, and conclusions drawn from such facts. But because investigators proceed in that manner, they do not, either in fact or by implication, deny the existence of God. "Take," he says, "the case of physical astronomy: To the mathematician, the mechanics of the heavens are in no ways different from the mechanics of a clock. It is true that the clock must have had a a maker; but the mathematician who investigates any problem in connection with its mechanism has nothing to do with him as such. * * * But he does not deny his existence; he has no hostile feelings toward him; he may be on the very best terms with him. * * * Precisely in the same way, the man who investigates the mechanics of the heavens finds a complicated system of motion, a number of bodies mutually attracting each other, and moving according to certain assumed laws. In working out the results of his assumed laws, the mathematician has no reason to consider how the bodies came to be as they are; that they are as they are is not only enough for him, but it would be utterly beyond his province to inquire how they came to be so. Therefore, so far as his investigations are concerned, there is no God. * * * Still, they are not atheistic; and he may carry on his work not merely without fearing the Psalmist's condemnation of the fool, but with the full persuasion that the results of his labors will tend to the honor and glory of God."

THE CIRCULATION OF HUMAN BLOOD MADE VISIBLE.

Dr. C. Huter, a German microscopist, has constructed a simple device by which the circulation of the blood is made visible in a human subject. His method is as follows: The head of the subject is placed in a frame, with which is also connected a microscope. The head and instrument are so placed that the lower lip may be slightly drawn out, and its inner portion fixed uppermost upon the stage of the microscope. A strong light is then thrown upon the surface of the lip, the light being intensified by use of a condenser. Thus arranged, the instrument is properly focused upon a small superficial blood-vessel, when the observer may plainly see the endless procession of blood corpuscles passing through the minute capillaries, the colorless ones being distinctly identified as little white specs, more or less thickly dotting the main body of the red stream of blood. This device may often prove of considerable importance to the medical practitioner, by enabling him to carefully note the variations in the blood flow, and the relative proportions of the white corpuscles in that fluid. This is the first instance where the flow of the vital fluid of one human being has been made visible to another. Observations as to the character of the blood have heretofore been made upon that fluid after it has been drawn from the subject, and, of course, under circumstances very unfavorable for accurate determination.

HOUSE FLIES.

The common house fly belongs to the order of diptera, from the Greek *dis*, "twice," or "two," having reference to the distinguishing characteristic of two wings only. They are also specially marked as having the mouth in the form of a proboscis, with a sucker. Flies, though often seriously annoying, are extremely useful as scavengers, and thereby preventers of disease. There are several distinct species of what are known as house flies, two of which are more numerous than all others combined. One of them, the most common and numerous, is known to scientists as the *musca domestica*, and fortunately this is the least annoying, except for its great numbers. The other is known as *stomoxys*, or the piercing fly. It makes its presence known, and may be distinguished from the more common one, by its somewhat stinging bite, for it is able, by its peculiar proboscis, to pierce the skin, which the more common fly cannot do. Dr. Livingstone has made known the existence, in Central Africa, of one of the most extraordinary insects of this kind yet discovered. It is called by the natives *tsetse*, a word the pronunciation of which probably sounds much like the noise produced by the insect in its flight. Though not larger than our common household pests, it is described as a really terrible insect, whose sting is absolutely fatal to several of the domestic animals, but comparatively harmless to man. So deadly is its poison that when a very small number of these flies attack an ox, or a horse, or a dog, the animal soon begins to stagger, becomes blind, swells up, and finally dies in convulsions. And yet it is said that this deadly poison is simply annoying, but not fatal, to either man, the pig, the goat, or to wild animals generally. The discovery of some antidote to the sting of this venomous fly would bring wealth and glory to the discoverer. Dr. George Macloskie, of Princeton College, has recently been making the *stomoxys* a matter of special study. He has discovered that it has one very bad habit, for which the common house fly has sometimes been unjustly blamed. This habit is described as follows: The piercing fly was often observed to have her head and proboscis covered with eggs. That they were not her own was evident from their different shape, and from the fact that they were attached to the wrong end of the insect. Further observations showed that these eggs developed into anguillula worms, resembling paste eels. Here, then, we have one of the ways in which this fly defiles articles of diet, etc. The house fly alone has a retractile proboscis, that folds up and is drawn into the head. The lower end of the proboscis consists of a knob, and contains the lips and a series of forked half-rings, by means of which that fly rasps the surface from which it gathers food. The teeth of the house fly form a single row of five or six on each side of the mouth, while the blow fly has as many as thirty teeth, arranged in three rows on each side. The Doctor remarks that the structural resemblances of the crayfish, the cockroach, and the fly are very similar.

SPONGE UNDERCLOTHING.

An inventor has patented a new kind of cloth, which consists simply of sponge. The sponges are first thoroughly beaten, in order to so crush all the mineral and vegetable impurities that they may be readily removed by washing. The sponges are then dried and carefully cut with a sharp knife into thin sections, which are subsequently sewed together. The fabric thus prepared is free from the danger which sometimes arises from the absorption into the system of poisonous dyes. A garment made of such a fabric absorbs without checking the perspiration, and thus diminishes the danger of taking cold. It is a bad conductor, and therefore helps to maintain a uniform surface temperature, and it can be more readily cleansed than ordinary woolen garments. Its flexibility also greatly diminishes the liability to chafing.

A GROWING TASTE FOR ART.

The progress made in the direction of improving the quality and finish of the various products of skill and industry, in this country, gives unmistakable evidence of a growing taste for art among our people. There are now but few dwellings, among even the poorest, where there is not some evidence of a love for the beautiful in the way of decoration. To satisfy this demand, the chromo has been advanced to a near approach to a fine art, and is now largely employed for the adornment of walls where circumstances will not admit of more elaborate and costly productions. Articles of virtu, more or less expensive, are found in almost every dwelling in the land. The decorative artist is in large demand in nearly every line of mechanical product. The furniture and fixtures in our houses and in our public buildings, the railroad car, the steamers upon our bays and rivers, all bear, more or less, the impress of the taste and genius of the decorator. Even advertising, and especially railway advertising, in response to this universal demand, seems to be laying claim to recognition as a fine art. The passenger departments of some of our leading roads lavish the highest skill of writers, artists, engravers, and printers upon productions setting forth in the most attractive manner the advantages and attractions of their several routes. But perhaps the most noticeable of all is the rapidly increasing demand for decorative table wares. During the past two years the advance made in meeting the wants of the public for artistic form and beauty in table service has been far greater than during any previous similar term. Twelve years ago one man was able to perform all the decorative work for the numerous establishments for the manufacture of fine wares in Trenton, New Jersey. Since that time the number of decorators has annually increased, until there are now not less than three hundred in that city, fully employed. Some of the work turned out is very superior, vases being produced worth from $100 to $500. Catering to the increased demand for home decorations, artistic and original designs, in both shape and ornament, have been produced, equal or ranking near to the most beautiful of similar productions in Europe. Our industrial expositions, our museums of art, and our schools of design have accomplished the most of what has already been done to create a taste for the beautiful in this direction; but we need more art schools to educate our people to a still higher appreciation of the beautiful in art. The fullest success of our industrial and commercial interests depends largely upon such education. It has been truly said that "Beauty, combined with utility, gives a commercial value not otherwise obtained."

HOUSEHOLD FURNISHING.

The social life of ancient times differed materially from that of our own in almost every aspect. Yet, although personal habits have changed, the ordinary wants of men remain about the same. The form and style of dwellings, and of their furniture—such as beds, chairs, lounges, tables, cabinets, etc.—have essentially changed in style, but have ever maintained a certain identity of form and use—more nearly so than articles of clothing. The carpet, stove or range, and the plate-glass mirror are about the only novelties—save Yankee notions—which have been introduced into modern dwellings. Of late, there has been a growing taste for the antique, and old attics, lumber-rooms, and even second-hand furniture stores, have been ransacked over and over again for antique designs, or real articles for house furnishing or decoration—said articles consisting mostly of old desks, ancient chairs, antique sofas, tables, cabinets, etc. Old crockery, cracked and nicked though it may be, has been made to do duty again, and even modern wares, new from the store, have been submitted to long baths in dirty, mineralized waters, to give them an appearance of antiquity. Such is the inevitable rule of fashion. Articles of furniture made previous to the advent of the present century, promising any kind of artistic value, are now difficult of procurement, while many old designs have been imitated by clever amateurs and introduced as antiques. The *furor* in this direction, however, is now fast giving way, and new designs are sought for, but varying largely from anything *heretofore* met with. The traditional parlor set, bearing marks of uniformity, is now rarely seen, especially in our Eastern dwellings. Variety is the order. Fancy tables, with standards of gilt or ebony, and tops upholstered with plush or raw silk, and sofas and chairs upholstered mostly as odd pieces, are the style. The new designs in upholstering are mostly of Persian patterns, Japanese figures, or floral designs; the last two are especially liked for chamber sets. There is a marked difference between American and English furniture. We follow more nearly the French. English articles of manufacture, of all kinds, are designed with a view to durability and strength. American productions are made attractive as well as durable, and in variety, design, uniqueness, and practicability, far exceed the English. Americans display superior taste in the gracefulness and beauty of their work in nearly every line. This fact is accounted for partly from superior inventive genius, as displayed in the patent office records of the two countries, and in part from the superior education of our workmen, and their freedom from the conventional rules which are so arbitrary in English workshops. There appears, just now, a strong aversion to casters on furniture, at least as these motive facilities are usually made to appear. Chair-legs especially, and indeed all kinds of furniture legs, with casters affixed in the usual way, are very awkward and unpleasant to look upon. A six or seven-inch leg, turned or carved into all sorts of beautiful shapes, with a sudden taper down to where the caster begins, is a horror to any one possessed of good taste. When casters are absolutely needed, they should be inserted into hollow feet, where their unsightly forms will be hidden from the eye.

ART AND ARTISTS.

ARTISTIC PORTRAITURE.

Not long since there appeared in one of the issues of the *Art Amateur* a reproduction of a photograph taken on the Isle of Wight, by Mrs. Cameron, a lady whose success in photography has elicited the praise of all who have seen her work. But few specimens have reached this country. The one referred to, however, is a sufficient guaranty of the lady's artistic ability, and justifies the reputation she has earned for herself among art lovers. In choice of subject she seems particularly happy, while for grace of composition and breadth and simplicity, in the management of draperies and light and shade, her work rivals many of the masters. It is probably safe to claim for some of our American photographers as high a degree of mechanical excellence as that attained by any other people. That which is yet most required is artistic treatment. Of course, very much depends upon the subject, and the willingness of the sitter to abide by the better taste and judgment of the operator. It is rare to find such models. Ordinarily, the sharper the picture and fewer the shadows, the more satisfactory it is. Many see in shadow only dirt, and the more screens employed to illuminate, by false reflections, the shaded side of a subject, the more it is to the sitter's liking; for this reason, photographs are rarely of interest except to those personally acquainted with the subject. With Mrs. Cameron's work it is different; in addition to the value they possess as likenesses, their artistic qualities are of so high an order as to command the admiration of all. Our portrait painters might also profit by a careful study of this lady's work. How many American portraits would find purchasers if forced upon the market? Yet almost fabulous prices have been paid for pictures of unknown persons, on account of their artistic merit. At the recent sale of the Demidoff collection, at San Donato, a portrait by Van Dyke brought $30,000, and one by Rubens $16,000. The reputation of these artists no doubt greatly influenced the sale, though there are like instances in which both artist and subject have been unknown. Since it is the aim to combine art and utility in all other departments of manufacture, would it not be well to try to effect the same combination in portraiture? Justice to the artist, however, compels us to admit that the absence of art in portraiture is oftener the fault of the patron than the painter. In no other branch of picture-making is the artist so hampered. He is frequently compelled to yield to the notions of others, which are oftener at variance with the generally accepted ideas of taste and treatment, and can therefore not be held wholly responsible.

ANIMALS IN MOTION.

Few events have excited greater interest among artists and those interested in animal life than the exhibition given at the Art Rooms, early in May, by Mr. Muybridge, illustrating the movements of the horse and other animals in rapid motion. By the application of electricity to a series of cameras placed at short intervals, and equidistant from each other, Mr. Muybridge has succeeded in obtaining a succession of instantaneous photographic impressions, illustrating the positions of an animal during all the stages of a stride. When first produced, these plates excited much skepticism and ridicule. Taken singly, they are entirely deficient in grace, and convey no impression of movement whatever; but when made to follow each other in rapid succession, by means of the zoögyroscope—a revolving disc, from which the impressions are projected upon a screen—the effect is so startling as to convince the most skeptical of the accuracy of the plates. The principle has been applied with equal success to horses, cattle, and dogs, and also to the flight of birds and quick movements of men. The inventor, in his enthusiasm, predicts a great revolution, not only as regards the rearing and training of horses for speed, but in the matter of their representation on canvas. That a horse in running never assumes the position given it by artists may, perhaps, be accepted as a demonstrated fact. Also, if it is the intention of the painter to convey the idea of rapid movement, it is equally certain that no single position of the animal developed by photography will serve his purpose. Movement in the horse is presented only by the rapidity with which one position follows another, as demonstrated by the zoögyroscope. The artist can employ no such artificial means, but is necessarily limited to a single attitude, and must, therefore, compromise upon some pose that will convey to the eye the same impression that accompanies a rapid succession of positions in nature. In other words, fact must be sacrificed to impression. How well artists have succeeded in conveying this impression has been many times proved by the readiness with which the smallest children interpret their intentions. Putting aside all prejudice in favor of previously accepted notions, we fail to see how Mr. Muybridge's discovery will greatly affect art as regards the movement of animals.

THE EPIDEMIC.

From a perusal of Eastern periodicals, it would seem that our California artists have no special cause for condolence on the ground of adverse criticism. The epidemic which manifested itself so strongly during the late exhibition was, it appears, not local, but attacked with equal virulency art writers all over the country. From the north, south, east, and west, the outcries of the afflicted are audible, and the manifestations are so alike that one is prone to attribute the disease to some cause not in the control of picture-makers. Professor Jevons might find in it fresh evidence of the truth of his "sun-spot" theory; or perhaps the planetary conjunction has adopted the art departments of the press as a kind of safety-valve for the diffusion of any superfluous influence not specially allotted to the various phenomena that are to manifest themselves according to programme during the coming year. In New York, critics are divided on the question of the Academy and the Society of American Artists, and assail strongly those leagued with their enemies. Boston, with its well-known complacency, spares its own, but claims that an artist to be recognized must first gain its approval, and therefore has little sympathy to bestow upon those outside its charter limits. Faint pipings are heard from all parts of the Far West. It is perhaps too soon to determine what will be the effect of all this commotion upon the future American school. Many, for the time being, may be discouraged; but probably, when the heavenly bodies shall have recovered from their dissipations, harmony will be once more restored between the pen and brush.

THE NEW YORK EXHIBITIONS.

Citizens of New York are much to be envied on account of the facilities afforded them for the enjoyment of the fine arts. As a metropolis, it is naturally sought by a majority of our best artists, who there find a wider field for the disposal of their works; and likewise the foreign pictures that seek an American market are there first offered to view. The past winter seems to have been unusually prolific as regards art display. In addition to the usual exhibits at the galleries of dealers, where many works of the best modern French painters have been shown, no less than five exhibitions have been given by the various societies. Until quite recently, water colors have met little encouragement in this country. They now seem to have gained a firm foothold in

New York, and their exhibitions excite much interest. The one given during the past winter has been generally well received by the press. Among the contributors are many familiar names, while others, quite new to the public, are spoken of as doing creditable work. At the Salmagundi Club exhibition, in black and white, the works of Shirlaw, Smiley, Abbey, Kappes, Reinhart, and the numerous other excellent contributors to the Scribner and Harper magazines, were to be seen. It is mainly to the members of this club that we are indebted for those pleasant articles relating to the Tile Club. The showing of the "Society of American Artists," though excellent in many respects, and exercising a healthy influence upon American art, was not regarded much in advance of their last year's exhibition, except in the department of sculpture. At the Academy, the exhibition was regarded not quite up to the average, though comprising a large number of pictures. Messrs. Fuller, of Boston, and Winslow Homer received special mention, the first for a portrait of a boy reading, and the latter for some negro studies and a camp scene. Perhaps the most interesting of all the exhibitions was the loan collection, embracing works of the old masters and modern pictures by foreign and American artists, brought together on the occasion of the opening of the Metropolitan Museum, in Central Park. A writer in *Scribner's Monthly* dwells with special pleasure upon the fact that, instead of being eclipsed by comparison with the works of so many eminent foreign painters, as many feared would be the result, American art stood the test very satisfact- ily. This is certainly encouraging to our painters, and promises well for the future.

THE LOAN AND ART EXHIBITION.

Several loan exhibitions of pictures from private galleries have been given in San Francisco, under the auspices of the Art Association, but to the people of Oakland belongs the credit of introducing to our coast the first general loan exhibition, embracing all articles of interest, historical as well as artistic. The success of the enterprise was much doubted at first. The projectors anticipated difficulty in finding in our young community a sufficient number of articles of interest to make an exhibition that would prove attractive to the public. The result, however, was most gratifying, not only to the enterprising ladies who had the affair in charge, but to the large number who attended during the two weeks of its continuance. Notwithstanding a little doubt on the part of some as to the authenticity of a few of the articles displayed, as a whole the exhibition was instructive as well as interesting. All tastes might have been gratified by a visit, from that of the historian and antiquarian even to the epicurean. Imagine one of the latter contemplating, for instance, a tooth and part of the jawbone of the great consul and *bon vivant*, Lucullus. The identical bone and ivory that eighteen hundred years ago, enshrouded in the presumably fat cheeks and firm lips of the conqueror of Mithridates, served on so many occasions in the mastication of roasted dog and succulent pig, stuffed with asafœtida. The sight of it recalls to mind that great feast given his friends, which cost the owner upward of fifty thousand *denarii*—a sum so great that historians regard the fact of sufficient importance to be transmitted to all posterity. Our barbarous ancestors, clothed in skins, gathered oysters on the coast of Britain for that very occasion, and all the then known world was taxed for contributions of beast, bird, and fish. When we realize that this bit of bone was perhaps the first to pierce each delicacy served on that occasion, our reverence for Lucullus is not only enhanced, but our gratitude to the ladies of Oakland for the exhibition surpasses expression. Near by lay a dish from which the Great Frederick—the founder of the German empire—supped; perhaps one of the set from which the enraged father selected a missile to hurl at the head of poor Wilhelmina, because she loved music. Under the same category of epicurean reminders may be classed also the punch-bowl of George I., Napoleon's tumblers, and some of Louis Philippe's chinaware. Among the many articles of historical interest might have been seen lying side by side, on a Japanese table, the skulls of two of the incas of Peru—men who planned a civilization of their own, remarkable and even instructive to the proud princes of the Old World. One involuntary hopes that the owners had the good fortune to die before Pizarro and his gold-seekers first placed foot within the bounds of their peaceful, happy empire. There were relics of all ages, from embalmed child of ancient Thebes to the brass warming-pan "one hundred years old." Old Greek weapons were compelled, for the time being, to keep company with vulgar modern cannibal war-clubs. A bit of curtain from the bed of the beautiful and romantic Queen of Scots divided one's attention with an autograph letter of the proud Elizabeth—a letter written by the same hand that signed the fatal warrant. Here, a lock of Washington's hair caused the American heart to palpitate, and there lay Washington's razor. *If* that great man ever did mutter an unrecorded oath, perhaps this quiet little instrument was the cause of it. Old portraits, books, and manuscripts, autograph letters of historical personages, *bric-à-brac* and curios from everywhere, embracing *scarabæi* and sacred bugs from Egyptian tombs, and silver heads and pottery from American *tumuli*; bronzes, draperies, furniture, and pictures saluted the visitor from all sides. Of the latter, little can be said. With a few striking exceptions, the gallery was composed of imported copies, too often seen to excite interest. The exhibition will be remembered by all who attended, and will encourage still greater achievements in the same direction.

AUCTION PICTURE SALES.

A few years ago it was the custom among our local artists to dispose of their pictures at auction. Every year a combination sale was held, to which each painter was invited to contribute one or more works from his easel. Money was then more plenty, and taste not as critical as it is to-day. Pictures, good and bad, were sure to bring under the hammer all they were worth. It soon became known in the East that California offered a rich field for such sales, and, as a natural consequence, car-loads of pictures rolled overland, and were thrown upon the market. In nearly every instance these pictures belonged to what is called the commercial order, for the manufacture of which several establishments exist in New York, where many men are employed, and from twelve to sixteen copies of a single work produced in a day, to be distributed as originals to the different markets in the United States. With rich looking, cheap frames, and not unfrequently the names of celebrated artists attached to them, they commanded a ready sale. One year, it is stated, no less than twenty-three hundred of these pictures were offered to the San Francisco public through a single auction house. To-day a large portion of the "gems" that adorn our residences belong to this class, and, in many instances, are prized as valuable originals. Picture buyers naturally waited for these sales, hoping to secure cheap bargains, and the artists, in order to compete with the imported stock, could not afford the time and care necessary to the making of a good picture. They painted auction pictures, to be sold at auction prices. In every instance, however, the purchaser who imagined he was trading upon the necessities of painters, received all he was entitled to for the small prices paid. At times our artists offered their best work, but the public, from a distrust, engendered through the former practice, failed to respond to the extent the pictures deserved. Since then, purchasers have been patronizing the studios and exhibitions. By this means they secure conscientious work, and the artist receives just remuneration. During the past two years of depression, art has been at a standstill, and, in consequence, some of our best painters are seeking other markets, while many have been obliged to resort to teaching and illustrating. In our opinion, the worst effect of the "hard times" is the revival of the custom of selling pictures at auction. The sale held May 19th, at the rooms of Newhall & Co., in which several well known artists participated, cannot be regarded a success. In a few instances, however, the prices realized were sufficient to warrant an expectation of better times in the near future. With these encouraging signs, artists will probably find it unnecessary to continue this method of disposing of their productions. The practice is apt to degenerate into simply a picture-making business, and not only cheapens the work of those who participate, but works an injustice to those who labor conscientiously and earnestly for the advancement and the elevation of art.

BOOKS RECEIVED.

THE NORTH AMERICANS OF ANTIQUITY: Their Origin, Migrations, and Type of Civilization. By John T. Short. New York: Harper & Brothers. 1880. For sale by Payot, Upham & Co., San Francisco.

American antiquarian knowledge has received vast accessions from the patient investigations of the past few years, and the volume before us gives, in a popular and fascinating form, the results of these studies. The author pays a just tribute to our eminent Californian historian, Mr. H. H. Bancroft, and, indeed, makes copious extracts from, and references to, that gentleman's exhaustive work, *The Native Races of the Pacific States*. After discussing the antiquity of the Americans, and reviewing the evidence, Mr. Short says:

"We have seen that as yet no truly scientific proof of man's great antiquity in America exists. This conclusion is concurred in by the most eminent authorities. At present we are probably not warranted in claiming for him a much longer residence on this continent than is assigned him by Sir John Lubbock, namely, three thousand years. Future research may develop the fact that man is as old here as in Europe, and that he was contemporaneous with the mastodon. As the case stands in the present state of knowledge, it furnishes strong presumptive evidence that man is not autochthonic here, but exotic, having originated in the old world, perhaps thousands of years prior to reaching the new."

The various theories as to the colonization of the continent are subject to a rigid scrutiny, and two chapters are given on the Indian traditions bearing upon this point. An able comparison of crania is instituted, in the course of which occurs a description of the curious habit of head-flattening, in various nations, both in America and the old world. A very interesting chapter is the one on the Ancient Pueblos and Cliff-dwellers, from which we extract:

"The descriptions of them seem more suitable to form parts of the most romantic works of fiction than of sober and scientific memoirs from the pens of governmental explorers. One hundred miles westward from the ruins of the Chaco lies the Chelly Valley or *Cañon*. The Chelly is one of the tributaries of the Rio San Juan from the south, having its source in the Navajo country. The Chelly *Cañon* is described as from one hundred and fifty to nine hundred feet wide, with perpendicular sides between three hundred and five hundred feet high. Simpson, in 1849, found several caves built up in front with stone and mortar in a side *cañon*."

The United States party explored the Mancos River in Colorado:

"One of the first cliff houses discovered by the explorers is a most interesting structure, the position of which, six hundred feet from the bottom of the *cañon* in a niche of the wall, furnishes a strangely significant commentary on the straits to which these sorely pressed people were driven by their enemies. Five hundred feet of the ascent to this aerial dwelling was comparatively easy, but a hundred feet of almost perpendicular wall confronted the party, up which they could never have climbed but for the fact that they found a series of steps cut in the face of the rock leading up to the ledge upon which the house was built. This ledge was ten feet wide by twenty feet in length, with a vertical space between it and the overhanging rock of fifteen feet. * * * His next discovery in the face of the vertical rock, which here ran up from the bottom of the *cañon* and at a height of from fifty to one hundred feet, were a number of nestlike habitations, one of which is figured in the cut.

"The cliff-house in this case was reached by its occupants from the top of the *cañon*. The walls are pronounced as firm as the rock upon which they were built. The stones were very regular in size, and the chinkings-in of small chips of stone rendered the surface of the wall remarkably smooth and well finished. The dwelling measured fifteen feet in length, five feet in width, and six feet in height. A short distance below this little dwelling, five or six cave-like crevices were found walled up in front with perfect walls, rendered smooth by chinking. Three miles further down the *cañon*, the party discovered, at heights ranging from six to eight hundred feet above their heads, some curious and unique little dwellings sandwiched in among the crevices of the horizontal strata of the rock of which the bluff was composed. Access to the summit of the bluff, a thousand feet high, was obtained by a circuitous path through a side *cañon*, and the houses themselves could only be reached at the utmost peril—of being precipitated to the bottom of the dizzy abyss—by crawling along a ledge twenty inches wide and only high enough for a man in a creeping position. This led to the wider shelf on which the houses rested. The perfection of the finish was especially noticeable in one of these houses, which was but fifteen feet long and seven feet high, and with a side wall running back in a semicircular sweep. In every instance the party found the elevated cliff-houses situated on the western side of the *cañon* with their outlook toward the east, while the buildings at the bottom of the *cañon* were indiscriminately built on both sides."

A full account is given of the interesting discoveries in Arizona and New Mexico. The book is handsomely illustrated, and a valuable accession to current literature.

THE BOY TRAVELLERS IN JAPAN AND CHINA. By Thomas W. Knox. New York: Harper & Brothers. 1880. For sale by Payot, Upham & Co., San Francisco.

Mr. Knox has made an entertaining book, not only for boys, but for children of an older growth. The book is filled with pleasant description, and with a variety of incidents. As a specimen of the book-maker's art it does much credit to its publishers. It is profusely and beautifully illustrated, the subjects being furnished by the scenery, buildings, works of art, and curious sights in the countries visited.

ODD OR EVEN? By Mrs. A. D. T. Whitney. Boston: Houghton, Osgood & Co. 1880.

One who lives to reach the end of one of Mrs. Whitney's sentences is usually repaid for the time expended, and *a fortiori* one who reaches the end of a work from her pen is not frequently disappointed. The book before us is not an exception to the rule. It abounds in strong characterizations, and the story is, on the whole, well sustained. The plot is laid in an out-of-the-way place, and the people are not of the every-day type. There is a certain freshness about the book, which even the writer's tendency to stop and moralize every now and then does not destroy.

CONFIDENCE. By Henry James, Jr. Boston: Houghton, Osgood & Co. 1880. For sale at the book stores.

Confidence is the name of a somewhat plotless novel by Mr. James, in which he introduces a number of aimless people, with nothing to do, and, what is worse, nothing to talk about. The chief end of their delightfully vacuous existence seems to be what the author calls "ingenious remarks," some of which, to be sure, are sprightly enough, but which, spread over three hundred and fifty pages, grow wearisome to the spirit. We are assured that the characters are different, one from the other, yet they are all patiently laboring after "ingenious remarks" in a very similar manner, the ideas, and even the structure of their sentences, being identical, and the conversation of each of the several characters bearing a striking resemblance to the asides and connecting clauses of Mr. Henry James, Jr.

YOUNG MRS. JARDINE. A novel. By the Author of *John Halifax, Gentleman*, etc. New York: Harper & Brothers. 1880. For sale by Payot, Upham & Co., San Francisco.

It requires courage to write a book, nowadays, in which the sentiment is healthful and the characters are healthy. Modern fiction, like modern society, is pre-[illegible], and wears a liver pad. Your latter-day hero is *blasé*, and your latter-day heroine is eccentric. The book before us takes us back to a few such simple ideas as love, truth, honor, and embodies them in strong personifications. There is a refreshing optimism which abounds on every page, although now and then degenerating into "gush." There is no striking originality in the story or the people it tells of. Roderick Jardine incurs his wealthy mother's displeasure by marrying his dowerless cousin, and the book is chiefly an account of the love, life, and struggles of this young couple. Roderick is unused to poverty, is ashamed to work at first, and learns the lesson with some bitterness of heart, coming out nobly, however, at the last. "Young Mrs. Jardine," who is, perhaps, a trifle overdrawn, is an unselfish and devoted character. We have no hesitation in pronouncing the book worthy of the high reputation of its author.

SCIENCE PRIMERS. *Introductory*, by Professor Huxley, F. R. S. New York: D. Appleton & Co. 1880. For sale in San Francisco at Appleton's agency, 107 Montgomery Street.

This little book is intended as an introduction to an extended series of scientific primers, designed for young minds, and is appropriately filled with definitions and explanations of rudimentary principles. It will be followed by a succession of primers, in various departments, by the most eminent specialists. The illustrations are drawn from familiar sources, and abstractions are either simplified or omitted.

A PRIMER OF AMERICAN LITERATURE. By Eugene Lawrence. New York: Harper & Brothers. 1880. For sale by Payot, Upham & Co., San Francisco.

Mr. Lawrence has covered a large field in an amazingly short space in the little book before us. Of its value it is sufficient to say that the author of *Historical Studies* has maintained his reputation in this last effort.

FRANKLIN SQUARE LIBRARY. New York: Harper & Brothers. 1880. For sale by Payot, Upham & Co., San Francisco.

The enterprising firm of Harper & Brothers have issued several numbers of this series. The titles indicate the field covered by the "Library," and the prices are annexed to show how cheaply one may read if he has the desire.

No. 107.—*The 19th Century*. A history. By Robert Mackenzie. Price, 15 cents.

No. 109.—*A Sylvan Queen*. A novel. By the author of *Rachel's Secret*. Price, 15 cents.

No. 110.—*Tom Singleton, Dragoon and Dramatist*. A novel. By W. W. Follett Synge. Price, 15 cents.

No. 111.—*The Return of the Princess*. A novel. By Jacques Vincent. Price, 10 cents.

No. 112.—*Russia Before and After the War*. By the author of *Society in St. Petersburg*. Translated from the German (with later additions by the author) by Edward Fairfax Taylor. Price, 15 cents.

No. 113.—*A Wayward Woman*. A novel. By Arthur Griffiths. Price, 15 cents.

No. 108.—*Barbara, or Splendid Misery*. A novel. By Miss M. E. Braddon. Price, 15 cents.

No. 116.—*For Her Dear Sake*. A novel. By Mary Cecil Hay. Price, 15 cents.

UNTO THE THIRD AND FOURTH GENERATION. By Helen Campbell. New York: Fords, Howard & Hurlbert. 1880. For sale by A. L. Bancroft & Co., San Francisco.

THE LITTLE MOUNTAIN PRINCESS: A Sierra Snow Plant. By Ella S. Cummins. 1880. Boston: Loring, publisher. For sale by A. L. Bancroft & Co., San Francisco.

OUTCROPPINGS.

THE ALCHEMIST.

The lamp was turned low, and the measured breathing of the watcher told that he slept. I was in that exasperating half-asleep state, so familiar to the invalid, which has all the accompaniments of slumber except its comforts, when the door softly opened and a mysterious individual entered, who silently motioned to me to follow him. With unreasoning obedience I complied. My guide led me through a number of halls and passages, all strangely unfamiliar to me, and at last entered a small room dimly lighted by the dull red flame of a smoky lamp. The disordered state of things, and the general aspect of the room marked it as the laboratory of a man of science. The tables, chairs, and even the floor were piled with dusty volumes, and with numerous mechanical contrivances which puzzled me with their apparent uselessness. In a corner of the room sat what I supposed, at first glance, was a man. My guide, however, checked the polite obeisance I was making in that direction, and going to the corner drew the chair and its occupant to the centre of the room. The figure was, to all appearance, the corpse of a young man. I turned to my conductor for information, and he explained:

"Know that I am the possessor of a secret which far surpasses the embalming process used by the ancient Egyptians in preserving their dead, though I admit it was in endeavoring to discover their secret that I obtained mine. I have had for many years a suspicion—nay, I may say a belief—that it would be possible to cause a body to retain all its mental faculties intact if subjected to this process, which can scarcely be called embalming. This object once attained, we find an agent in electricity which, properly directed, endows the subject with a kind of life and activity, subservient, in some degree, to the will of the operator, and capable of performing wonders. It was many years before I was able to secure material for the carrying out of my plan. It is necessary that the party honored by this distinction should be in the enjoyment of health at the time of his demise, and that the immediate cause of his death be not so violent as to impair any of his mental faculties. I could, of course, have lured some unsuspecting curiosity-seeker into this room, and quietly and unceremoniously dispatched him in some manner best suited to the furtherance of the project in hand. But this course was open to the objection that my further experiments would have been interrupted by the technicalities of legal investigation; and, besides, I have conscientious scruples against such a plan. It meets with much opposition from the ignorant, and would probably result eventually in the elimination of its advocates."

I heartily approved of these arguments, and a feeling of relief, not to say complacency, stole over me which I had not experienced before since entering the room. I accordingly listened with more assurance as the alchemist continued:

"This is the body of a young poet, who terminated his brief sphere of uselessness about six or eight months ago. There was much disagreement among the physicians concerning the cause of his sickness. Whatever it may have been, I decided that it left him in every way qualified for my purpose. On pretense of taking his remains to his distant friends, I secretly removed them to this apartment, and they have been instrumental in assisting me to elaborate the theory which has been the study of my life. The *cadaver* has been subjected to my preparation, and by placing him under the influence of an electric current, I am usually able to elicit from him remarks upon any subject which may be spoken in his ear by the operator. Unfortunately, owing to the unnatural bent of his intellect, he has an uncontrollable predilection for putting all of his conversation into verse. This eccentricity nearly caused dire disaster at one time, when, without thinking, I asked his opinion on some topic connected with the Turko-Russian war. The unusual exertion attendant upon his efforts to find rhymes for some of the proper names nearly proved fatal, and indeed occasioned a double compound fracture of the inferior maxillary bone, which even yet interferes seriously with his pronunciation. Another peculiarity, which is probably also owing to the flighty nature of his feeble intellect, is this: he very often evades the subject given him entirely, and prates volubly of something in no way connected with it. I simply mention these things that you may understand before he begins that whatever is peculiar in his compositions is due to his paucity of brains, and not to anything I have neglected or overlooked in my preparation."

The alchemist then connected an electric battery with the body of the young man, and, turning to me, asked if there was any subject I would like to hear discussed. It suddenly occurred to me that I was down on the bills for a poem at the next meeting of the literary club to which I belonged, and I determined to utilize this electric poet and turn his gibberish to account. Accordingly I murmured the name of the author who was to receive a panegyric at my hands. There was a preliminary chattering of teeth, a slight grating of the injured jaw-bone, and the ghastly orator began, not, however, on the subject I had proposed:

A monster lived near Hampington,
  John Thompson was his name;
And rarely he was seen of men,
  Yet wondrous was his fame.
'Twas said he was the strongest man
  That ever drew a breath;
He carried carnage in his path,
  His very look was death.
The pathway to his forest cave
  Was dark with human gore,
And those who trod that gloomy path
  Found exit nevermore.
And thus John Thompson grew to be
  A hero of renown;
His deeds were told with bated breath,
  And spread from town to town.
And yet it was a noted fact
  That no two living men
Had ever, *at the same time*, seen
  This monster or his den.
But once there came to Hampington
  A modest looking man,

A man whose brow had changed its hue
   Beneath the weather's tan;
A hermit he, who, by his mien,
   Showed that he had not been
In man's society for years,
   From lack of kith and kin.
He entered at the tavern door,
   And sat down by a man
Who was relating bloody tales
   As only such men can.
He said, "It's mighty clear to me
   That something must be done.
This makes three days we've searched the woods
   For Widow Johnson's son.
I'll tell you how it looks to me:
   The lad's got lost, you see,
And wandered through the woods all night,
   Or slept beneath a tree.
This cannibal—he's nothing else—
   Came on him there alone,
And choked the helpless boy to death,
   Or bruised him with a stone.
Tom Dawson said he thought he heard
   A scream of pain and fright,
As he was going through the woods
   Toward home, the other night.
He looked around and saw a man,
   Full ten feet high or more,
Go swiftly by, and in his arms
   A human form he bore.
I never could believe the things
   They say that man has done;
But now I know John Thompson well
   Deserves the fame he's won."
The stranger listened with a smile,
   Until he heard the name;
And then he laughed so long and loud,
   The man was filled with shame;
And, rising, in an angry tone,
   He said, "I'd like to know
Why you should laugh as though the tale
   Related were not so?"
The hermit checked his mirth awhile,
   And said, "I ought to claim
Some interest in this strange affair—
   John Thompson is my name.
And do I look as if I lived
   By eating helpless men?
And is my form a giant form?"
   And then he laughed again.
"I found the lad beneath a tree—
   Thus far your tale is true;
I also took him to my cave,
   And nursed him all night through.
To-day I brought him to his home;
   He is alive and well;
Whatever else you wish to know,
   I leave for him to tell.
But now, before I leave you, sirs,
   Pray learn this task of me:
To credit not, too hastily,
   What other people see.
Believe but half that you may hear
   Of slander, and repeat
It not at all to any one
   That you may chance to meet.
For scandal never is confined
   To what is strictly true;
Thus men get famous for the deeds
   That they could never do."
John Thompson passed the open door,
   And went upon his way;
But Hampington has not forgot
   His lesson to this day.

At this point the alchemist broke the circuit, the poet's jaw dropped, and his voice died away. I was disappointed. It was James Thomson, the poet, whose eulogy I had expected. I said as much to the alchemist, and inquired:

"Do you think a repetition of the name would result more favorably?"

"That is an experiment," he replied, "which I have never deemed expedient heretofore, but you may try it if you wish."

Thereupon he reconnected the circuit, and I said, in a distinct voice:

"James Thomson, author of *The Seasons*."

A look of great perplexity passed over the pallid features of the *cadaver*. He was evidently beyond his depth. He muttered a few disconnected, unintelligible words, and then suddenly fell to the floor in a limp and motionless heap. I gazed with much disquietude upon the face of the alchemist as he arose from an examination of the prostrate figure. He turned on me in a fury.

"You did it! Well, you shall supply my loss."

He hurried to the table, and, mixing some drugs in a cup, bore down upon me with a look that made my blood run cold.

"Drink it!" he cried; "you must!"

I was as helpless as the dreamer who sees, or, what is worse, feels, the approach of some terrible calamity which he is powerless to avert. I struggled to rise, and with the effort awoke, to find the watcher standing by my bed with a sleeping potion in his hand, saying, in a voice of authority:

"Drink it; you must. You will sleep better after it."

It is needless to add that I took it with an alacrity that astonished him. WM. A. CALDWELL.

A HOMELY HEROINE.

It is surprising in what humble garments true heroism clothes itself sometimes, even in this garish, boastful, show-making city of ours. And there is a great deal of quiet, unostentatious heroism to be found here, I can assure you. I myself stumbled on a heroine one day, quite unexpectedly, in a little dust-covered, wind-beaten house, away out on Market Street.

In some manner—the details would only tire the patient reader—I had become possessed of a claim against the land on which this more than modest structure had been erected; and as I had never seen the place nor the occupants, I ventured out in that direction one morning, and was not over well pleased to note the insignificant appearance of the whole possession. I had understood that the inmates of the house were a couple of "hard-working Irishwomen;" and as I stood at the door waiting for admittance, and vaguely wondering how a brawny fisted, hard-working Irishwoman should have the patience to lay out a miniature flower-garden, such as I saw at my feet, amidst the Market Street sand-dunes, I was startled by a subdued voice saying, "Good morning, ma'am," right at my elbow. I looked around and down on a tiny figure, clad in worn, but clean, mourning; a pair of shrewd, yet honest, brown eyes peered up into my face, and a small, labor-hard hand pushed back the slightly gray hair from a narrow face, marked deeply with lines of care, but showing traces of former beauty.

Evidently the woman had been accustomed to mentally view me in the light of an ogress, or a female Shylock, for I could read as much surprise in her face as there was possibly expressed in mine, and her features brightened perceptibly as she, after a keen look at my face, flattened herself against the wall to admit of my passing into the parlor. It was a mere box, was this parlor; but old as the scant furniture was, it was guiltless of even a speck of dust, and the muslin curtain at the single window was white as soap, water, and earnest manipulation could make it. Above the old-fashioned sofa hung the photograph of a woman whose handsome features fascinated me. I seemed to discover a resemblance to some one I had long since known and half forgotten; but when I turned around and looked into the face of the little woman who stood behind me, I found that it was her face to which this one bore so vague, and yet so strong, a likeness. Moreover, I discovered that it was this photographed face, and these same large, still eyes, *after* they were closed in death, that had made a heroine, and almost a martyr, of my new acquaintance, poor little Miss McGrew. For the husband of her handsome sister, shortly after his wife's death, had shown such unmistakable symptoms of coming insanity that she had to "give up her situation wid a real nice family" to come to her dead sister's home and look after "the childer."

The poor man had loved his wife, in life, devotedly, but without any jealousy; after her death, however, he fell into the delusion that she had deserted him for another, and he would sit crouched behind the window-blinds for hours, waiting for the man to pass who had married his Nora. After having made two or three descents on the wrong man, and gotten his name well up for a lunatic, Miss McGrew, in her trouble and helplessness, went to the Bishop, who sent one of the priests home with her to examine into the state of affairs. Unfortunately, it was the same priest who had officiated at the dead wife's funeral, and the husband suddenly bethought him that it was this very priest whom his Nora was now married to; and for many days the reverend Father's head stood in imminent danger of separation from his body. When the priest failed to restore the man to reason, the good Bishop himself tried to speak rest to the troubled soul; and, instanter, it was the little old Bishop himself who had lured his handsome Nora from his side, and had made her his own wife.

Through all this trouble, Miss McGrew had the sole care of the wretched husband and the three children; and not a night's sleep nor a day's rest did she get, sleeping always beside an open window, behind a barred door, and with "the childer" just within her grasp, to throw them out of the window in case their crazy father should make a sudden attack on them all. After a while, the Bishop saw to it that the man was placed before a proper commission, who declared him insane and removed him to Napa.

But this was really only the beginning of my heroine's troubles. After this came long years of struggle with poverty and sickness, and, at last, death. The sum she had laid aside during her years of "living out" was not over large; the brother-in-law had had nothing to leave his children when he went into his living tomb at Napa but the piece of ground on which the house now stood. Realizing that she must be both father and mother to her sister's children, she gathered up the remnants of her little savings and built this place, so they might have at least a roof to shelter them. She worked at everything and anything she could get to do; had a roomer sometimes in this "best room;" took in sewing, washing, ironing—anything to keep the wolf from the door, and educate "the childer," as she knew it had been her sister's ambition to do. With the aid of the Sisters and the Fathers, the two girls, as well as the boy, were making such progress that she was proud of them, particularly of the boy. It had been such a sore struggle to keep them together in their little home, that her heart grew quite light as the time came near when the boy would be able to help her earn a little, for it looked as if she could hardly hold out much longer. The wants of the children had grown with their bodily growth, and already there were debts here and there, trifling in themselves, but of considerable magnitude to little Miss McGrew, to whom they looked like mountains that *must* be climbed over.

When the boy was sixteen, he commenced ailing. He was growing too fast, she said—was listless, had no appetite; and I can fancy his mite of an aunt preparing little dainties for him to eat, coddling him up generally, but still trying to impart some of her own energy to him. It was useless. After a long sickness, and before he was seventeen, he died.

I had been studying her face during her narration, as I have a habit of doing with people who interest me, when I saw the poor lips tremble, and the quick tears spring into the clear brown eyes. I turned to look out through the open window, for I could not trust my voice just then, and we both sat for a moment in silence.

After the boy's death, and to cover the expenses of the doctor's attendance and the funeral, she had contracted the first heavy debt, which had nearly, through mismanagement, swept away the little possession she had so faithfully tried to save up for the children, and which was the only home she could ever hope to have after a life of honest toil and self-sacrificing devotion. Not that *she* ever thought she had been sacrificing herself—bless you, no! She didn't think she had been doing anything more than was just her ordinary duty. It never entered her mind that she deserved special sympathy or commendation for anything she had done and suffered. She was too busy bridging over the abyss from day to day to know anything of sentiment or maudlin self-pity. It was a constant question of existence with her, and for her and the children, too; and to exist meant, with Miss McGrew, to live honestly, and without a debt at the corner grocery.

She said the most severe trial to her had been a sum of eighty dollars, which she had once been compelled to borrow from another girl, who had "worked out," like herself, as she needed the money for taxes. She said she had felt certain that she could repay the money in the course of the year, if she had to live on bread and water to do it. But then had come the boy's lingering sickness, and she could not pay it off. It so happened that the girl came to need the money herself, but she never once asked Miss McGrew for it, and this, she said, made her feel all the worse. If the girl had clamored for it, and blustered about it, she would, perhaps, not have felt so badly. But at last, when the little home had been mortgaged, and what she considered a large sum of money had come into her hands, she had the great satisfaction of paying off the patient creditor.

"And I carried the money to her myself," she said, with sparkling eyes; "and I made her take a twenty-dollar piece for interest, though she wouldn't hear to it at all, dear soul; but I made her take it, for all that."

Just then the other of the "two hard-working Irish women" came in, the second eldest of "the childer"—a slender, white-faced girl of sixteen, who was teaching in Father Gallagher's school, the aunt told me with some pride, and bearing her share of the labor quietly and uncomplainingly as the aunt herself.

After having resisted all invitations and temptations to take dinner with them—"a cup of tea, at least; well, then, a glass of milk"—I arose to take leave; and plunging back into the rattling, driving, never-stilled stream of life that passes close by the very door of the house, I fell to wondering whether any, and what kind of a monument would ever be raised to my little, homely heroine.

C. J.

WOOING.

Were I a bird, to sing I'd seek
  Such notes, entranced you'd listen;
A breeze, I'd never quit your cheek;
  A sunbeam, I would glisten

In either dark and liquid eye,
  Persistent as a lover;
Where rosy lips with fragrance sigh,
  A butterfly I'd hover.

Were I a moonbeam, I would creep
  Where envious shadows hide you;
With silver silence spell your sleep,
  And sleep, myself, beside you.

Were I a star, one golden dart
  From out my shining quiver
Should pierce your shy and tender heart,
  And make you mine forever.

But one can only sit and write,
  In halting rhymes confessing;
Bird-notes, breeze-kisses, starry light
  Convey a subtler blessing.

I've wooed you roughly, love. Perchance
  They'll teach me how to render
A subtler homage, word, and glance—
  Your heart is shy and tender.

EVELYN M. LUDLUM.

A ROMANCE OF EAGLE LAKE.

Eagle Lake forms one of a chain of lakes lying within the limits of Kosciusko County, northern Indiana. Upon its western shore there rises an elevated portion of land, known as the Summit, which, in the early days of the country, became the scene of a tragic occurrence. A huge oak crowns its apex, in whose topmost branches eagles built their nests, from which circumstance the lake thus overshadowed gained its name. At this period, Indians traversed wood and prairie in untamed freedom. The sun rose and set in as resplendent glory then as now. Nature is no respecter of civilization: she spreads her bounties in like beneficence upon the rude hut of the savage and the costly palaces of well ordered society. Through contact with invading settlers, the spirit of traffic had become awakened in the minds of the natives, blinding their vision to results of the future. Not unfrequently marriages occurred between them, by which means valuable tracts of land fell into the possession of the Whites. To this day, many influential families of the West thus trace their ancestry.

The country at this time was divided among the several tribes in accordance with stipulations of savage warfare. The Miamis held divisions contiguous to the Wabash River; the Pottawatomies retained possession of lands lying north of Lake Michigan; while the Winnebagoes occupied the portion of country extending from Fort Dearborn (now Chicago) to Rock River, still farther to the northward, bordering upon the possessions of the Sioux, and lesser tribes of Sacs and Foxes. Trading posts were conveniently situated near navigable streams, upon whose waters glided, in noiseless succession, Indian canoes, loaded with commodities of trade and barter. A dip of the oar, a ripple of waves, a slippery landing amid tangled vegetation, and the cargo has reached port. Such, it may be presumed, were among the rudimentary beginnings of Western commerce. Numbers of men were employed by the companies, upon whom devolved extended journeys into unexplored regions. These men were selected with a view to fitness for their positions. They were men who loved these solitudes, the so-called cultivation of the races failing to supplant the desire to worship truth in accordance with the dictates of conscience; and upon these wide-spreading prairies, and amid the pathless woods, freedom in undisturbed serenity reigned. Laws of being alone controlled action. Individuality became a stern necessity. Every man's life was held at hap-hazard, for whose maintenance he himself was responsible.

At the close of a chill day in November, a young man, weary and travel-worn, arrived at Prairie Creek settlement. Something in this man's appearance excited curiosity and comment among the idlers there congregated.

"This solemn-faced aristocrat to brave the wilderness!" they said. "Why, in six months' time his head will serve as a foot-ball for young papooses."

Time passed. The young man's name was registered upon the dingy ledgers of the traders as John M. Hamilton. Whence he came, or from what motive, remained a mystery. If his employers knew of his antecedents, it was their own secret; and, in those days, neither distinctions of class nor testimonials of character were considered necessary. There stood the competitor: let his deeds speak for him. Unmistakably, every lineament of form and feature in this stranger indicated a degree of refinement unusual to the time and place. Instinctively he held himself separate and apart from his associates, preserving a reserved silence relative to every event of his former life. With dog and gun he roamed forest and plain. His moods were incomprehensible to the careless settlers, who familiarly recounted the story of their lives and adventures to whomsoever would listen. Yet beneath his gravity of demeanor a certain restlessness betrayed itself. It was evident, throughout the weary months of waiting which followed his arrival, that he longed for action. Therefore, when, in the spring of 1832, he, with a select number, was detailed for a trading expedition to the head-waters of Rock River, his countenance for the first time brightened with the clear, keen light of a daring spirit. His idle life had indeed become almost insupportable; added to which, a strange story gained credence among the settlers, no one knew how, or from what source it sprang, that this quiet, self-contained man was really a son of Alexander Hamilton, who, through domestic unhappiness, had fled to the wilderness. A wild, giddy wife, it was whispered, had dishonored his proud name.

The country at this time, through its natural advantages alone, was regarded as the very El Dorado of the West. Its virgin soil remained as yet undisturbed. In primeval grandeur, its forests bowed but to the sweeping winds. With a view to the preservation of trails, the

Indians kept exterminated, by fire, obtrusive underbrush, thus securing inviolable, canopied vistas, producing a weird effect of a world inclosed within a world. Robin Goodfellow, in fairy circle, might well have held high carnival within these courts. Tracery of sunlight, or the paler gleam of moonbeams shining through interstices of fluttering leaves, conspired to create an impression of unreality never realized under conditions of unobstructed space. Through the forest glades, at this season carpeted with delicately tinted violets and the yellow lady's-slipper, to which the fruitful strawberry plant added its quota, along the prairie's border, bewildered in mazes of narrow, sinuous trails, crossing and recrossing, suddenly developing in fine open plains, always upon the alert through fear of wild animals or hostile tribes of Indians, Hamilton and his company passed, halting at length upon the banks of an unknown stream. No such waters were designated upon their map of guidance, yet they were cool and refreshing to the wearied party as falling dew to the parched earth. It was a spot peculiarly adapted to repose. The elements were redolent of sweets; a very wealth of verdure made heavy the air. Miasmatic dullness settled upon them, relaxing their activities, and stealing away their senses in a lethargy of death. Hamilton first succumbed to its debilitating influences, refusing the usual restoratives to which his more experienced companions resorted, begging simply to be left for an hour's rest, when he would follow in their trail. The birds trilled their softest lays, swaying branches waved their lullaby, drowsy sleep mastered him. Spots of red deepened to crimson upon cheek and brow, one of the malarious fevers prevalent in the new country racked his frame. He lay within a sheltered grove, beside the gurgling stream, yet no drop touched his lips, no cooling moisture laved his brow. His companions, as fate would have it, became entangled in a labyrinth of trails, from whose meshes for days they sought egress. A day and a night thus passed, in which he remained insensible to suffering or to the ravings of delirium. The pitying winds alone listened to his lamentations. Tenderly the name of Alma lingered upon his lips, smiles vainly struggling for mastery over convulsive pain. "My love! My darling!" was softly uttered, as he sank into momentary calm, interluded by the mournful swell of the breeze, when again loud tones of menace and of expostulation startled the stillness, dying away in a wild "Ha, ha!" of maniacal laughter. A hush as of death succeeded. Sun-streaks fell across the pallid face of the sleeper. Gradually its lines of sufferings relaxed, his respiration sank to uniform regularity. The fever had spent its force, and he lay in undisturbed repose.

Upon this predestined morning, Naketah, the rarest gem in the renowned chief Black Hawk's encampment, with dejected mein stepped into her canoe for a day's quiet meditation. Her eyes were heavy with tears. Only one short month would elapse when she would be given in marriage to Checosa, the cruel chief of the Sioux. Black Hawk, seeking to ally the northern tribes, had so willed it. In the grand council of the preceding day, presents of wampum and cloth of tinsel had been interchanged, and fire-water had been drunk in ratification of the contract. Thus it chanced that the lithe-limbed Naketah sought refuge in the distant wood. The sunlight glistened as with gradually brightening countenance she glided down the stream. A light song rose to her lips, dying away in saddening thought. Here, at this point, appeared a quiet retreat—a thickly wooded grove, where she would rest from the unwonted lassitude which oppressed her. The gay-hearted Naketah was all unused to sorrow. Her rare beauty, appealing even to the savage breast, had hitherto protected her from cares, which, alas! now entangled her in inextricable woes. Sobs and tears rent the air. She swayed back and forth upon the mossy bank, where, in abandonment to her grief, she had thrown herself. With ominous cry, sparrow-hawks circled above her head. She watched with stifled breath their hateful movements. They reminded her of Checosa, the rapacious chief of the Sioux, at recollection of whose deeds of blood a light of fire came into her clear, liquid eyes. Swift as thought she bent her bow, bringing to her feet a fluttering hawk. Hush! The sound of a human voice surprises her. She starts to her feet, standing like a wild gazelle poised for flight, when lo! her eyes fall upon form of the white brave, whose repose she has disturbed. She remains transfixed in wonder and awe. A faint smile and wave of his hand reassured her. Slowly, half bashfully, she approaches and bends over him. His feverish lips feebly articulate "water." She flies to the stream, places the cooling draught to his lips, and soothingly laves his brow.

In the languor of recovery, Hamilton wonders if at last he has reached Arcadia's fabled grove. As admiringly his gaze follows the supple form of the maiden, smiles return to his lips, pleasure beams in his eyes; he sits upright, and partakes of dewy berries which this dusky goddess provides. But sadness at length returns to the heart of this sweet Indian maiden. Silently she sits apart. He, with gentle consideration, soon draws from her guileless utterances the cause of her sorrow. Chivalric impulses burn within his breast, as, midst fast falling tears, she recounts her story. He soothes her with grateful assurances of sympathy and solemn vows of deliverance. At close of day, wrapped in his blanket, pale and wan from exhaustion, Hamilton and the maiden were borne upon the smooth-flowing waves to the encampment of Black Hawk, chief of the Winnebagoes, where the white brave was hospitably received, and where, with renewed violence, again his fever returned.

A fortnight has passed, and still he lies prostrate. To Naketah the days are numbered. How now shall the white brave defend her, she laments; what power shall avert her doom?

"Naketah," whispers the sick man.

Instantly she stands at his side.

"How long is it now?" he questions.

"At full of the moon, arrayed in wampum belt and eagle's plumes, Checosa, the Sioux chieftain, comes," sighs she.

"What then, Naketah?"

"The hunt, the feast," she sadly replies.

Joy sits upon the countenance of Hamilton.

"Come closer, sweet one. Listen. In the long days that I have been silent I have devised a plan of escape. Look into my eyes, dearest. Do you not see the light of hope glowing there? Array yourself in beaded sandals, as if for the bridal. When they are away at the hunt, upon the plea of gathering wild honey to crown the feast, steal to the grove beside the river. There wait. From my couch I have observed a pony, the fleetest of his race, tethered to a sapling."

Naketah uttered a cry of delight.

"It was for my bridal," she said; "this coal-black pony was to bear me to the land of the Sioux."

Eagerly, he continued:

"I will seize my opportunity, and before night I will be with you, when we will fly to a place of safety."

Successfully overcoming difficulties, Hamilton, accompanied by Naketah, swiftly retraced his journey to the settlement. Many solitary hours of his first arrival had been spent upon the summit previously mentioned, overlooking Eagle Lake. At various times he had explored its surroundings, fascinated by its absolute loneliness. The breath of God alone filled its heights and depths. His great thought lay manifest in grand provision! Saccharine substance and honey dew lured insects innumerable, and the wild mandrake hung in golden fruitage beneath its sheltering foliage. Like turreted battlements, dense tamarack forests reared their branches to the sky, extending northward into as yet unexplored regions. To this spot, then, he would wend his way. For a time secrecy was desirable—here, with his dusky bride, he would pitch his tent. His unexpected arrival at the settlement was readily accounted for—rumors of his illness, and probable captivity or death, having reached them. His appearance, therefore, was hailed with expressions of relief.

In the security of this forest, Hamilton and Naketah established their household altar. A canoe had been provided from the settlement, in which, through the long summer days, the happy Naketah searched every nook and sheltered cove about the lake, returning at nightfall laden with fish, which, in Indian fashion, was dried and preserved for use. Also, she gathered from adjacent trees the fragrant spice-wood, and plucked from lowly beds the coral wintergreen berries. With deft hand, she kneaded the corn into palatable cakes. Again, for hours she sat upon the Summit, watchful of the eagle's flight. In her perfect content, the land of the Winnebagoes had faded to a dream; only now was life worthy of remembrance. Never, she mused, would the cruel Sioux chieftain claim her for his bride. She clapped her hands in an ecstasy of emotion, by such unusual sound hastening the eaglets to their eyries and causing a fluttering of wings among numberless tiny insects. Shadows upon the waters deepened. Time flies swiftly when joy rules the hour.

That very evening, as they sat beside their cabin door, Hamilton explained to her the probability of a war between the Whites and the northern tribes, headed by the Winnebago chief, Black Hawk:

"And during my absence, wait quietly within your cabin. Remain within call upon my return. Heed well my words. Though at present no danger threatens, yet I would have nought happen to my Naketah."

And well she kept her promise. But who shall take a bond of fate, or through obedience to mortal mandate evade its dread decrees? Naketah sat upon the braided mat, in careful arrangement of her slender stemmed rushes, and while with deft fingers they were interwoven, she sang a low murmuring lullaby, as if to baby ears, when thought of her happiness dawned anew upon her.

"Oh, my beautiful, my brave! who, like the strong limbed sycamore, towers grand among men. Oh!——"

A stealthy footstep startled her. With a thrill of terror she crawled to her loophole, when there, with evil eye, appeared the cruel Sioux chief. With the bound of antelope she cleared her cabin door, and, before discovery, reached the shore where lay concealed her light canoe. She pulled for life, and all that life held dear. Yells and imprecations followed her escape; an arrow whizzed past her cheek. With brave intrepidity she continued her course; she struggled hard for love and life. A second missile foundered her bark. She turned upon her relentless foe with a wild shriek, reaching out her arms imploringly toward the Summit. A final shaft from the pursuer's hand silenced her voice forever. At that moment a shot reverberated along the shore, and the revengeful Sioux chieftain breathed his last. Returning to his cabin, and finding Naketah absent, Hamilton ascended the Summit in search of her, when the scene there brought to its close opened upon his gaze. Alas, for the beautiful Naketah! the pride of her race, and the true love of Hamilton. But a ripple marked the spot where she vanished forever.

A year had passed since Hamilton's second disappearance, when again in strangely altered guise he stood among the settlers, "with them, but not of them." His travel-stained garments indicated conditions of toil and hardship. His usual reserve had settled into impenetrable gloom. But one person, if any, ever knew of his whereabouts, and this man, almost as taciturn as himself, kept his counsel. Though still living, no word has ever passed his lips. It appears, indeed, that Hamilton possessed a strange power over all with whom he came in contact, imbuing them with something of his own nature. Soon a cabin was erected on the Summit of Eagle Lake. It was here that the tragedy which at last wrecked love and hope was enacted—it was here that he would live and die. Never again did his presence disturb the settlers' gaze. Rumors of a tall form, pacing unwearily the Summit's height, reached them, an occasional shot reechoed through the tamaracks. Such were the only tokens by which ever living soul, save one, had knowledge of John M. Hamilton.

In the summer of 1838, his death occurred, and, according to directions, he was buried upon the Summit made memorable by the events here recorded. In 1858, twenty years from the date of his death, when Prairie Creek settlement had become transformed into a flourishing town, there arrived at its principal hotel a stranger of distinguished appearance, closely resembling, as the older inhabitants at once took cognizance, the recluse of Eagle Lake. Making inquiries concerning the life and death of the person known as John M. Hamilton, he visited his place of rest, securing in his own right its surroundings from disturbance.

MARTHA CORNELL WOODWARD.

WITH HEARTS OF FIRE.

"Bessie, I wish you would write me a story of an opal."

I have a bad habit of scribbling, and whenever I am irritable, nervous, blue—being a woman, I plead guilty to all these inexcusable states of body and mind—my feelings very often find vent at the point of my pen, certainly a safe and harmless way of working them off. My friends, knowing my habit, often importune me to write upon some special subject, suggested, perhaps, by an incident in their own lives or those of their friends. So I was scarcely surprised to hear the request. We had been sitting in the moonlight, discussing the prevalent superstition regarding opals. The incessant noise and clamor that had filled the busy streets all day had subsided, and the passing of street-cars, the occasional rumble of a carriage, did not disturb us. The moonlight silvered the church spire on the opposite side of the square, and made the leaves on the trees shimmer and gleam like a transformation scene, and then, stealing up to the window where we were sitting, glorified the face bending over me, as the lips parted to prefer the request. The dear, beautiful face! How I wish you could see it as I saw it at that moment. The rippling golden hair, brown in the shadow, silvery in the moonlight; the dancing, laughing eyes of blue, the sweet, womanly mouth; the parted lips, through which gleamed the white, even, perfect teeth. In the open palm lay a ring, two diamonds shooting out steady bluish rays, and between them, beating, throbbing, smouldering, like a soul in pain, sometimes red as the fiercest heart of flame, then paling until almost colorless, was an opal. Watching its heart of fire, the story came to me:

The vesper bells chimed softly out through the twilight of a sultry day, echoing down the narrow valley, throbs of silvery sound dying away among the foot-hills, waves of sweet silence. The door of the little church stood open, and one form after another glided softly in, and kneeling before the shrine of some best-loved saint, made, with trembling fingers, the sign of the cross over a breast mayhap weary of battling with the pains and disappointments of life, and, closing eyes full of unshed tears, murmured, with quivering lips, a prayer. Around the altar hung clouds of incense, the lamp that is ever burning shone like a star amid the dusk and shadow, and the tones of the organ beat through the silence like the anguished throbs of a stricken soul. Just as the last tremulous tones were dying away, from the window of the confessional, in a shadowed niche at the side of the chancel, gleamed, for a single moment, a glance from eyes that seemed to search every nook and corner, and penetrate every dusky shadow. It was only for a moment, and was instantly withdrawn, as a tall, slender figure entered, shrouded in lace, despite the closeness of the evening, and, passing rapidly up the aisle, along which her trailing skirts swept with a ghostly sound, knelt at the confessional, and buried head and face in the tightly clasped hands. They were small shapely hands, covered with sparkling jewels, and as, after a moment of silence, she raised her head, the lace partially falling, you could see tresses dark as night and a cheek satin smooth, crimson and hot with intense feeling—the glorious eyes, full of dangerous fire, the red lips trembling with excitement. It cannot be religious fervor; it is no holy enthusiasm that calls that panting fear into those eyes, that makes the breath come in quick, short gasps, and the bosom heave like a frightened bird. Listen, she speaks! The voice is so low the waiting priest bends his head lower to listen:

"Angelo, be quick; I can stay but a moment. I have brought the jewels; here they are. Take them, and I must go. I may be watched and followed. Oh, what would become of you—of us both—if we are discovered!"

While she speaks, she has torn the sparkling rings from her fingers, the diamonds like drops of liquid light from her ears; and unclasped from the slender throat a necklace of opals, wondrous, priceless stones, that gleam even through the shadow with a red, dangerous light. Over the dark, bared head bend locks that are fair; into the dusky eyes shoot glances from others, blue as the spring-time violets, but beaming with all a man's passionate adoration. The voice that answers hers shakes with its fathomless depth of feeling; and her tiny hands are clasped so hard that she almost cries out as she strives to draw them away.

"My darling, my poor frightened dove, what is there to fear? Surely no one would follow you to the confessional. See! I have the jewels—Gods! what are these stones that jeer and gibe at me? There is something mocking in their gleam."

"My opals! Oh, Angelo, they were his wedding gift to me. 'Tis said they bring misfortune. What if he suspect? It will be death to us both."

"How nervous you are, my own. Courage, courage, now just as we need it most, when we have but to take a single step and we may belong to each other. Oh, the heaven of that thought! My brain whirls with its mad delight. Let me have one kiss to assure me it is true, and I am not dreaming."

As he touched her lips, she almost shrieked, as she shrunk away from him, shuddering, as with cold.

"I must not wait longer. Be careful of the jewels—they are our all. At ten precisely, in the acacia grove. Till then, adieu; do not fail me. I tremble—I am afraid."

"Benedicite, daughter!" and the curtain of the confessional fell, and the graceful form moved quickly, noiselessly away.

Left alone, the young priest, with trembling hands, removed his surplice, and stooped to gather up the jewels and place them in an inner pocket of his long coat. As he touched the opals, he started suddenly, dropping them again in nervous haste.

"Pshaw! how foolish I am; and yet I could swear they laughed at me. 'Tis but a superstition—there is nothing in it. We cannot be discovered. Don Pedro knows nothing—does not even suspect that I love his beautiful wife. Only a few hours more, and she will be forever my own—my own—my own."

He picked up the jewels, placed them securely in his pocket, and went out, carefully closing and locking the door. He passed swiftly along, singing softly, as was his wont, an Ave Maria, not surely because holy thoughts filled his mind, for his heart beat fiercely with mad, uncontrollable passion. Stop! Was that a stealthy footstep? He is passing the acacia grove, from which, in a short hour, he is to fly, carrying his heaven with him; he shivers with a sudden fear—a sense of some undefined presence, some unseen danger. He is no coward, and turns to meet it, only to find himself held in a grasp strong as death, and confronted by the husband of the woman he loves.

"Now make your peace with heaven, if so be you can, for, by my soul, in one instant I will send you into eternity. The Spaniard is not blind—he can see; but he can wait until he strikes surely. Give me the jewels. They were my gift to her when she became mine, and she shall never be yours—never, never. Now pray, if your guilty lips can frame a prayer. I raise my hand; when it falls, you die."

It had come, then; it was as she said—the opals had brought misfortune. By the moon's soft light, which was just then rising, he could see them lying where the haughty Spaniard had thrown them, gleaming at him with their impish faces. How tender the moonlight seemed! He wondered if she sat where it could illuminate her wondrous beauty. His lips moved to frame a prayer. It was only this: "My love! my love!" Even in this supreme moment, his thought was of her. He grasped the merciless hand that was stretched high above him:

"Wait! I have a favor to ask. Spare her; she is innocent; I alone am guilty."

The face of a demon could not be darker than the one that bent above him:

"Spare her? I will send her to you; you shall not be separated long." And swiftly the uplifted hand descended.

The moon rose higher and higher, its soft radiance piercing the densest shadows of the acacia grove, where a face fair and peaceful lay upturned to its caresses. The musical, silvery chimes struck ten. Almost at the same instant a veiled, shadowy figure entered the wood, and stole noiselessly along toward its deepest shade. The dark eyes were filled with a slumberous light; one burning spot burned on either cheek; the breath came in quick, choking gasps, and the slender fingers that held the lace covering round the shapely head and throat clasped and unclasped in a quick, spasmodic way.

"I am sure no one saw me, and yet I cannot rid myself of the idea that I am followed. Why can I not shake off this horrible depression? Oh, my love! my love! What would I not dare for you!—what would I not give for you! My life, if needs be, a thousand times over!"

The heart of the wood is reached. It is all so still, so dark, she is afraid. She whispers, scarcely above her breath:

"Angelo! Angelo!"

"He is here, my love!" and from behind a dark acacia a tall form comes quickly toward her.

What is this sudden terror? She cannot speak; she is dumb. One glance into the face bending over her, one shriek, and she turns to flee. A grasp like iron holds her and drags her swiftly back.

"You come to seek Angelo. He is here. Look, he is waiting for you. He trusted you so fully, you know: he was so sure you would come; he is sleeping while he waits. And see! he has brought you jewels for your bridal. Look how they gleam—how like their red hearts are to drops of blood! Let me clasp them on your neck, my beauty, that he may see them when he wakes."

In a dark horror, as of one in a dream, she gropes to where his fair dead face smiles up to her. She tears the opals from her throat. Yet they gleam red—red with blood—his blood! No need for the murderous knife to do its work. With one wild cry startling the stillness of the night, she goes to join her lover, while the pale moonbeams rest tenderly on two white faces in the heart of the acacia wood.

But what became of the opals? Rap, rap, at the door.

"Will you have the gas lighted, madam?"

Flash after flash shoots up, and falls upon the ring still lying in the outstretched palm. Is it fancy, or does it change and darken, like a drop of blood?

A.

HINTS TO CONTRIBUTORS.

1.—Write your article *in ink*, on one side only of the paper.

2.—If you cannot write legibly yourself, have your article copied. Pay particular attention to proper names and technical phrases.

3.—If you desire your article returned, inclose stamps for that purpose.

4.—Condense.

A NOCTURNAL CONCERT.

The voice of Nature never yet was still.
When comes the night, and darkness, deep, profound,
Clothes all the earth, then list. A noisy sound,
From some deep-sleeping pool, your ears will fill;
Ten thousand hammers, wielded with sturdy will
On muffled anvils, seem to strike and pound
Like that click, clank, of hammers when they bound
From hardened steel. At intervals a shrill
And scarce note disturbs your listening ear:
These are the sounds that issue from the throats
Of those wet warblers of the tarns and fens—
Those chorus singers of the marsh and mere,
Who serenade the stars with their harsh notes,
In symphonies no mortal creature kens.

ALVAN PENDLETON.

COMPENSATION.

I thought she had all things to make her life
What life should be—gracious and glad and sweet;
All earthly good seemed prostrate at her feet.
And I—my lot was one of daily strife
To meet my daily needs. To-day she'd call
It blest to take my life, so poor and small
To careless eyes, and at my feet would cast,
If only love could be so bought and sold,
All treasures of her present or her past,
Seeing the one great joy my life doth hold,
The sweetness that all sweetness doth enfold.
She cries, "O niggard Fate, you've given me naught!"
And I, my heart with happiness o'erfraught,
Cry out, "O bounteous Fate, you've given me all."

CARLOTTA PERRY.

HARVEST.

The valley slopes lie smiling in the sun,
Rich with the varied harvests of the year;
One light cloud floats upon the summer sky,
Reflected in the fountain falling near.
The poppies gild the distant mountain-tops,
The rose-breath from the garden freights the air;
Idly, I swing beneath the laurel's shade,
And wandering breezes lightly lift my hair.
The lark's sweet note is echoed from the lane,
The linnet warbles in the live-oak tree,
And in the far-off field the reaper's scythe
Lends its soft murmur to the melody.
Among the fragrant vines the wild bees hum,
A drowsy sound to my charmed ear doth come.

ALICE GARY COWAN.

ANNOUNCEMENT.

Commencing with the May number, THE CALIFORNIAN passed into the hands of its present owners, The California Publishing Company. It was not deemed expedient to change the name of the firm publishing the magazine until the commencement of a new volume. We take this opportunity, however, to say that we are encouraged by the success which has attended our efforts, and that in every legitimate manner we shall endeavor to improve the magazine. The high appreciation which has met our efforts shows conclusively the existence of a literary taste in this community, which we shall strive to please by making THE CALIFORNIAN the spiciest, breeziest, and best periodical in the country. Mr. A. Roman will continue as Business Manager.

THE CALIFORNIAN.

A WESTERN MONTHLY MAGAZINE.

VOL. II.—AUGUST, 1880.—No. 8.

CASA GRANDE.

There is no subject of greater interest to the intelligent mind than the unwritten history of the human race. We look back to our ancestors, who were probably no better than ourselves, with an innate veneration, common to all mankind. It is human to inquire into the past. We have a strong natural desire to know the early history of man as an inhabitant of the earth, and to speculate on the future. To us it is a subject of absorbing interest to inquire how we came to be here, and why. Were we created in our present shape, or are we the result of evolution from lower forms? It is now generally conceded that the human race has walked the earth for a much longer period than was formerly supposed. Darwin's well known theory of gradual advance from the lowest types to the highest is now assumed by many educated minds, and the subject has become so interesting that earnest men, in various parts of the world, are devoting their lives to its study.

It is to a certain extent humiliating to visit the British Museum, or to pass through the extensive galleries of the Louvre at Paris, and view the relics of ancient civilization there shown. It humbles our pride to be compelled to admit that in some things the ancients were our superiors, and that they had in daily service articles of use and ornament that we cute Yankees have reinvented and consider new. But there is a period still more ancient, of which we have but vague ideas, and of which we know but little. In Europe, evidences of the age of prehistoric man are being carefully collected, and all new facts bearing on the subject studied with the greatest interest. In the Eastern States of the Union, the works of the ancient mound-builders—of whom we have no history—are being as carefully investigated and preserved. Over the entire Pacific Coast, also, works of ancient man have been found. Although but little interest has been taken in them by our gold-hunting people, they are being collected by the wholesale to enrich the museums of other lands, when they should be preserved in our own.

The ubiquitous prospector, while searching for gold and silver, is often surprised to find remains of a prehistoric civilization in the most unexpected localities. There is little doubt that the whole country, including the wide-spread desert and mountain *cañon*, has been a scene of activity in years long past. And it is difficult to account for the facts, such as we find them, unless we assume that the unknown race was one of gold-hunters, like ourselves. There is no better theory to account for their selecting, with evident forethought, such a sterile and desolate country for an abiding place. Moreover, there are reasons to believe that they led a roving life, and were constantly changing. There is said to be a tradition among the Pueblo Indians of the south, to the effect that another race, known as the Montezuma tribes, went to Mexico in very ancient times from the north; and that the emigration was gradual, as if the nomadic race had been slowly driven southward by some unknown cause. In evidence of this, it has been shown that a line of ruins extends from the Gila River quite to the City of Mexico, with rather more obscure traces northward. At certain points the movement seems to have been for a time checked, and a stand made, which must have occupied a long period of years; for it may be shown that the ancient people built cities, engineered irrigating canals, erected *casas grandes*, prospected the hills for gold, silver, and copper, strewed the ground with broken pottery, lost their stone axes and shell ornaments, built mounds, and buried their dead.

It is historical that the Spaniards in Mexico found a mixture of races at the time of the conquest. The Pueblo Indians planted corn, beans, and pumpkins, and lived almost wholly on the fruits of agriculture, while the Montezumas were rich in gold, silver, and copper. Modern miners and prospectors have discovered a relation between these ruins and deposits of the precious metals—a clew to the richest spots in Arizona and New Mexico, revealed by the marks left by the ancient gold-hunters. Wherever they have found old ruins may be discovered, in nearly every case, valuable mines. A similar experience was made by the early explorers of the wonderful copper mines of Lake Superior. The best mines and the largest deposits of copper had been discovered and worked by an ancient and unknown race; in Arizona and New Mexico, old workings are not uncommon. Several instances are fresh in the mind of the writer. In the Valeria Mine, Arivaca District, Pima County, Arizona, a human skeleton, with tools of copper and stone, was found in an old shaft, from which a quantity of native silver has lately been taken. In the Pinal District, Pinal County, tons of litharge have been found, which in all human probability is the refuse of ancient furnaces, which have fallen into decay and all traces of them been lost. The same substance has been found elsewhere in Arizona. Another discovery of this nature has lately been made at a locality twenty-six miles north-east of Prescott, Yavapai County, Arizona, at the copper mines of Head & Richards. An old shaft was discovered, which had become obscured and nearly filled in by drifting sands. When cleared out it was found to be twenty feet deep, with a drift at the bottom fifteen feet long, in which lay hammers and gads of stone. J. J. Vosburgh, agent of Wells, Fargo & Co. at Globe City, was prospecting, in 1879, in the White Mountains of Arizona. On the highest peak, twelve thousand feet above the level of the sea, he built his evening camp-fire. In doing so, he noticed some Indian arrow-heads on the ground. Stooping to pick them up, he saw, scattered among the loose earth, a quantity of stone beads, some of them in an unfinished condition, an examination of which is a key to the mode of their manufacture. Some of these interesting relics have been sent to San Francisco for the State Museum, where they may be examined by those interested.

The ancient building known as Casa Grande, on the banks of the Gila River, is at the present time the most interesting of all the ruins left by the prehistoric people. Although there are many other ruins of less note which are worthy of careful study, this one is the best known, and is identified with the history of the country. The events which led to the discovery of Casa Grande may be briefly stated. When the Spaniards had conquered Mexico, and the first excitement was over, they began to turn their attention to the unknown north country. As we, at the present day, allow our imaginations to color the mental picture we paint of unexplored lands, so the victorious Spaniards listened eagerly to stories, invariably rose-tinted, which came to their ears from time to time. The El Dorado had not yet been discovered, in the existence of which the civilized world at that period had the most implicit faith; as a proof of which, the voyages of Sir Walter Raleigh, in 1595 and 1617, may be cited, and a number of Spanish expeditions well known to historians. It is not strange, therefore, that the Spaniards in Mexico should willingly equip expeditions to the unknown land. Rumors of cities of great wealth and splendor, and mines of gold, silver, and precious stones, reached Mexico from various sources. It is unnecessary to repeat here what has been so well told in a former number of this magazine. A well written and very interesting account of the expedition of Coronado, with a map of the route he took, may be found in the annual report of the regents of the Smithsonian Institution, for the year 1869, to which the reader is referred. The following extracts bearing on the history of Casa Grande are in part from that source.

In the year 1530, Nuno de Guzman, President of New Spain, became interested in a statement made to him by a slave, to the effect that he had seen in his native country, lying to the north of Mexico, cities nearly as large as the City of Mexico, in which streets were exclusively occupied by artisans in gold and silver. The Indian also stated that a desert intervened, which would require at least forty days to cross. The President having allowed his imagination to get the better of his judgment—a mistake too common at the present day—organized an army with the intention of conquering these cities in the name of Spain. When, however, he had reached Culiacan, a point in Mexico near the Gulf of California, in the present State of Sinaloa, he found the difficulties so much greater than he had expected that he abandoned the undertaking, and contented himself with making a settlement. Culiacan at the present day contains more than twelve thousand inhabitants. About six years afterward, in 1536, a party of Spaniards came to Mexico from the north. With them came also an Arab, or negro, named Stephen. This party was a remnant of the expedition of Pamphilo de Narvaez, which sailed from the West Indies, in 1528, with four hundred men and eighty horses, in four ships, to explore Florida, of which Narvaez was Governor, under commission from Spain. The expedition ended most disastrously. Shipwrecked, taken captive by hostile Indians and enslaved for years, treated with the greatest cruelty by their captors, this small party of four—probably the only survivors—finally made their escape, and reached Mexico as above stated, having crossed the continent northward, thence traveling southward through New Mexico and Arizona to Culiacan.

These men caused an excitement by the stories they told of cities they had seen, and of mythical mines of gold and silver, which led to the expedition of Coronado, in the year 1540. The adventures of this expedition have ofttimes been related—how the negro, Stephen, and a Franciscan friar, Marcos de Nica, with a party, were sent out in advance, to learn whatever could be ascertained of the seven cities; how the negro was killed, and the remainder of the party returned without discovering anything of special importance, yet feeding the flames by drafts on their imagination, inventing stories of golden splendors they had never seen; and how Coronado marched northward nearly to the present site of Omaha, and returned disappointed. All this is a matter of great interest, but has little bearing on the subject of this paper, and is only mentioned here on account of its connection with a secondary expedition, which was sent by Coronado, and commanded by Captains Melchior de Diaz and Juan de Saldibar, to explore a portion of the country.

This party had extended its exploration as far as Chichilticale, on the edge of the desert, six hundred miles from Culiacan. They met Coronado at Chiamena, and gave very discouraging accounts of what they had seen. This did not, however, deter Coronado from repeating the exploration, and visiting Chichilticale in person, which is described in the records in the following language:

"He was especially afflicted to find this Chichilticale, of which so much had been boasted, to be but a single ruined, roofless house, which at one time seemed to have been fortified. It was easy to see that this house, which was built of red earth, was the work of civilized people, who had come from afar."

This seems to be the first historical notice of Casa Grande.

Father Kino, in 1694, one hundred and fifty years later, visited the Gila River and Casa Grande. He found traditions among the Pima Indians dating back four hundred years. It was then a ruin. Another priest, whose name is not given, visited these ruins in the year 1764. Father Font was at Casa Grande on the third of October, 1775. He says:

"The Casa Grande must have been built five hundred years previously, in the thirteenth century, if we may believe the accounts given by the Indians. The house is seventy feet from north to south (Spanish feet), and fifty feet from east to west. The interior walls are six feet thick. We found no trace of stairways. We think they must have been burned when the Apaches destroyed the edifice."

In modern times, Casa Grande has been more frequently visited, and descriptions of it given. An interesting account may be found in *Notes of a Military Reconnoissance from Fort Leavenworth, in Missouri, to San Diego, California*, by W. H. Emory, published in Washington, in 1848. On the eleventh of November, 1846, Lieutenant Emory was encamped, with his command, eight or ten miles from the Pimos Villages. A party visited the Casa Grande, called by him Casa Montezuma. While riding, Lieutenant Emory asked the interpreter if the Indians knew the origin of these buildings. The reply was, "No. In truth, we know nothing of their origin. All is wrapped in mystery." The following is from his narrative:

"About the time of the noonday halt, a large pile, which seemed the work of human hands, was seen to the left. It was the remains of a three-story mud house, sixty feet square, pierced for doors and windows. The walls were four feet thick, formed of layers of mud two feet thick. Stanly made an elaborate sketch of every part, for it was, no doubt, built by the same race that had once thickly populated this territory, and left behind the ruins. We made a careful search for some specimens of household furniture or implements of art, but nothing was found except the corn-grinder always met with among the ruins and on the plain. Marine shells, cut into various ornaments, were also found here, which showed that these people either came from the sea, or trafficked there. No traces of hewn timber were discovered; on the contrary, the sleepers of the ground floor were round and unhewn. They were burned out of their seats in the wall to the depth of six inches. The whole interior of the house had been burned out, and the walls much disfigured. What was left bore marks of having been glazed. On the wall, in the north room of the second story, was found some hieroglyphics, which were carefully drawn, but the drawings have been lost."

Lieutenant Emory visited other interesting ruins, at one of which he found sea-shells worked into ornaments, and a large bead an inch and a quarter in length, of bluish marble, exquisitely carved or turned.

The writer of this article, in company with Professor George H. Cook, State Geologist of New Jersey, and S. P. Van Winkle, also of New Jersey, visited Casa Grande in April, 1879. This remarkable ruin lies about twelve miles from the flourishing town of Florence, Pinal County, Arizona. It stands on a wide-spreading *mesa*, rising slightly from the main road. The mesquite trees, although low, hide the building until it is nearly approached. For miles distant from the ruin the ground is spread with fragments of broken pottery, in such quantities that it is impossible to reject the idea that the site was at one time densely populated, where now utter desolation reigns. It is natural, under such circumstances, to speculate as to how the people lived; for, if the country was in the same state then as now, the question would be a difficult one to answer. The visitor has ample time to think the matter over from the time he first begins to observe the signs of human habitation until he reaches the building. With our party the conclusion reached was that the Colorado desert may have been once an inland sea, and the climate widely different from the present. It must be a consolation to those who intend to reside in that part of Arizona to feel assured that no violent earthquake could have happened for centuries, for the walls of Casa Grande are in such a condition that they could not withstand even an ordinary shock.

As the traveler approaches Casa Grande he cannot fail to be somewhat disappointed, the more so if he has taken a romantic or poetical view of the published descriptions of that noted building. Instead of the stately edifice he has pictured in his imagination, he beholds only a huge dun colored, almost shapeless mass, looming up strangely from the desolate plain. There is nothing architectural about the structure. It is, at best, but a mud house; though, as he examines it more closely, it seems more and more wonderful, and the mind is filled with conjecture as to the uses to which this great building may have been put, and why it stands so lonely and isolated. But, on examining the ground around about, it will be discovered that Casa Grande is but one of many similar buildings that were scattered city-like over the *mesa*. Fallen walls of houses older, or which were thrown down by some unknown cause, may be traced out, or detected by the characteristic concrete which lies in heaps at various points.

The following is a plan of Casa Grande, on a scale of twenty feet to the inch:

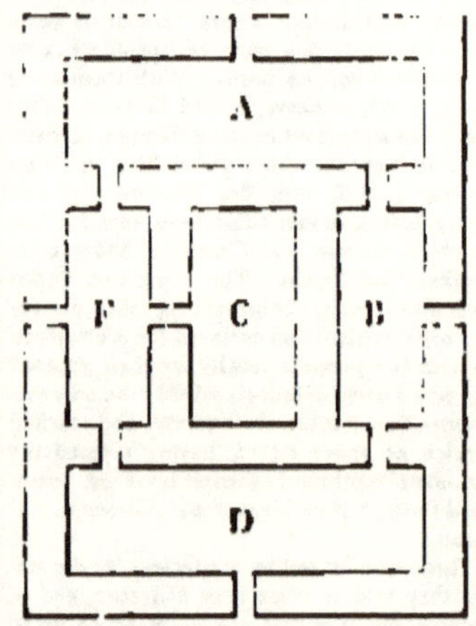

The walls were originally, as near as may be, four feet in thickness, the exact measurement being three and seven-tenths feet. The highest point, as the building now stands, is thirty-five feet. It was originally four or five stories high, each of which was eight feet from floor to ceiling. The extreme length, carefully measured, is fifty-eight and a half feet, and the width

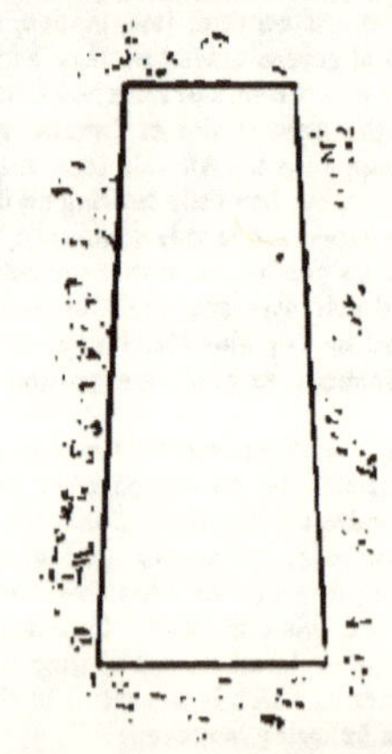

forty-three feet. In the north, south, east, and west faces of the building, there were narrow doors, centrally placed, through which entrance was made into the main compartments, and over each door, narrow port-holes, decreasing in width from the bottom upward. The foregoing cut gives the form of them, drawn to a scale of half an inch to the foot.

Some of these port-holes have been built in with concrete, as if they had been found to be unnecessary, or had been filled up for defense. The building faces nearly the cardinal points of the compass, the north and south walls bearing north, ten degrees east, which is nearly the true meridian. The interior must have been dark, as the light was admitted only through the before described port-holes. The inner room was, presumably, like a dungeon.

A chemical analysis of the concrete of which the walls are built reveals the secret why the building has for so many years, not to say centuries, withstood the action of the elements, and also the probability that the ancient builders had acquired the art of burning lime, although they were still in ignorance of the use of iron.

ROUGH ANALYSIS OF CONCRETE FROM CASA GRANDE.

Sand and matter insoluble in hydrochloric acid	74.00
Carbonate of lime	17.00
Iron and alumina	1.10
Water	4.80
Organic matter and loss	3.10
Total	100.00

It will be seen by the above analysis that the concrete contains seventeen per cent. of carbonate of lime, and it is fair to assume that part of the insoluble portion may be silicate of lime, a substance which forms in the hardening of mortars. There is no reason to think that the builders made use of the limestones so abundant in the immediate vicinity, but the scattered fragments of shells lead to the opinion that sea-shells were brought from the shores of the Gulf of California; although when the fact is considered that seventeen per cent. of the massive four-foot wall is lime, the expenditure of labor seems almost incredible. It may be that the soil of the *mesa* is in itself calcareous, and that the concrete was prepared much as ordinary adobe is at the present day. But this is not at all likely. It is more probable that lime was burned to mix with the building materials.

The inner surface has remained these long years intact, the smooth face showing no sign of decay. The little wrinkled marks, left when the surface dried, remain the same as when, centuries ago, the builder laid aside his tools, and the work was declared finished. Readers of works written by travelers in Egypt wonder at the accounts given of temple and tomb, whose pictured walls remain as fresh as if newly painted. They are inclined to think, if at all skeptical, that these statements are exaggerated. Yet here in Arizona we have evidences that, in the warm, dry climate, changes take place slowly. It is not easy to understand why the concrete walls should not last a thousand years as well as a hundred. Some parts of the outer surface remain as smooth as when left by the builder, while in others the tooth of time has gnawed unsightly cavities, like cancer spots. Why this should be the case has caused the writer much thought. For centuries occasional rain storms, and the continued action of the natural sand-blast, have gradually worn away the surface, and left their records on the old dun-colored walls. We are apt to overlook the importance of little things, and may forget that an incessant bombardment, lasting for centuries, may produce great changes, even if the missiles be only grains of sand. Professor William P. Blake read a paper before the California Academy of Sciences, January 15, 1855, describing the action of drifting sand as seen by him in the San Bernardino Pass. Even quartz was cut away. Hard minerals, like garnets, were found, in some cases, to have protected softer stones under their lee. After this action had continued for years, a stony finger was seen pointing to windward, with a garnet or other hard mineral at the tip. The writer has observed the same phenomenon in many localities in both California and Arizona, and lastly on the ancient walls of Casa Grande.

The central series of rooms was at least one story higher than the others. From A into E there is a port-hole in the second story, from room to room. From E into D there was originally a port-hole of the same size, but it has been filled in. From E to C there is a door, but none from C into B, instead of which there are several curious circular openings, from eight to ten inches in diameter, extending through the thick walls, and resembling modern stove-pipe holes. They are still perfectly smooth on the inside. What use these singular openings were put to can only be conjectured.

After making an examination of so remarkable a building, it was perfectly natural to speculate as to the uses to which it could have been put, and this is precisely what our party proceeded to do. It is amusing, even now, to remember how many suggestions were made, and how absurd some of them were. All were finally abandoned, and we were obliged at last to admit that no clew to the mystery had been discovered. One of the party suggested a grain warehouse, as the extensive irrigation works and the signs of a dense population indicated that large crops may have been raised. But this theory was rejected when it was seen how small the floor rafters were. Any one of the many rooms full of grain would have crushed the floors, if not the walls themselves. Another thought that the building had been a temple, or some kind of religious edifice; but the smallness and multiplicity of the rooms, and the still greater number of doors and port-holes, argued against such a supposition, although the mysterious central rooms and the unexplained cylindrical openings were suggestive of pagan rites.

The interior of the building has been burned out long ago; still the ends of the rafters are well preserved, having been deeply embedded in the walls. On digging them out, it may be seen that they have been cut with a blunt instrument, the marks of which are to all appearance just as they were made by the hand of the workman. It may be argued that the floor joists being of wood, and showing but little, if any, mark of decay, the age of the building may be overestimated. As an offset to this objection, however, may be cited the mining of cedar logs in the ancient swamps of New Jersey. Dr. Beesley, quoted by Professor Cook in the geological reports of the State, estimates the age of some of the fallen trees at fifteen hundred and fifty years. They are at the present time being split into shingles and sawed into lumber, to be used in building in the cities of New York and Philadelphia. The piles upon which old London bridge is built were driven five hundred years ago, and are still in a good state of preservation. One of the wooden piles from the bridge built by Trajan over the Danube was found to be superficially petrified, but the interior wood was sound after sixteen hundred years. The timber supports used by the ancient copper miners of Lake Superior are still remarkably sound and well preserved. But wood still more ancient has been found in Egyptian temples, which is known to be four thousand years old. Considering these facts, it is fair to admit the possibility of this remarkable antiquity having been built at a period very remote.

Several attempts have been made to discover a clew to the age and uses of Casa Grande by digging, but with indifferent success. A gentleman at Florence informed the writer that he had a piece of gold, resembling a coin, found within the ancient walls. A Mr. Walker made some excavations on an appropriation granted by the Legislature of Arizona. Others, from time to time, have made similar attempts, resulting, as before stated, in disappointment. Some visitors have said that a hollow sound could be heard in the inner room by jumping on the floor. It is quite evident that a portion of the walls have fallen inwardly, which may account for the sound, if it is true. Nothing of the kind, however, was noticed by the writer or party. Steps should be taken to preserve Casa Grande from the vandalism of visitors. Unless something be done to effect this end, it will eventually be carried off piecemeal. The Territorial Legislature should enact a law for its protection, and this cannot be done too soon.

HENRY G. HANKS.

MODERN ARCHERY.

With the antiquity of archery this article has nothing to do. From very early days, it has been the means of supplying man's wants in the chase, of fighting his battles; and to-day it furnishes a pastime, innocent, healthful, and fascinating. The fascination of the long-bow is something seemingly indefinable—growing, gaining on its votaries with each repetition of its use. After the probationary period of sore fingers, tired muscles, so far untrained, and other preliminary steps necessary to the acquirement of the art, comes, with increasing skill, the love of it, ever growing until so firmly rooted as to almost defy removal. The many difficulties to be overcome by the ambitious devotee are but so many incentives, and the more they block the way, the greater the perseverance, the more determined the efforts, until a satisfactory degree of skill is acquired. The bow of to-day is different from the bow of our childhood days in nearly every respect. No boy would be a boy without bow and arrow, and the fact of being its manufacturer undoubtedly added greatly to its value in the owner's eyes. Anything bendable was utilized. An old barrel-stave, or shapely sapling dried in the oven, answered every purpose; and with such crude weapons, the small boy has from time immemorial performed many creditable feats in shooting. That all boys are in a certain sense archers hardly excuses the wonderful tales related by the aged citizen of to-day of *his* shooting in the dim ages of the past. The citizen aforesaid is a grave and respectable member of society, renowned for his many virtues, and undoubtedly his word is as good as his bond. And yet of all the citizens of this class who appear on the archery range as interested spectators, but one is so far known who never killed a bird on the wing in boyhood days. The citizen invariably recounts his youthful exploits (as he remembers them), and if questioned as to killing game "on the move," as invariably answers affirmatively without the least hesitation. And the chances are he believes it. The writer has frequently requested a sample of skill from this description of spectator, and usually with the following result:

Citizen opens the ball: "How far do you call that?"

"Fifty yards."

"You make a great many misses. Not a very good shot, are you?"

"No, nothing extra. About fair to middling."

"Lemme try it once?"

"Certainly; but excuse me for saying you will probably be a little disappointed at first."

"That's all right. Watch this."

Citizen adjusts his eye-glasses, draws up the bow, nips the arrow between thumb and forefinger, lets go, and starts a tunnel in the ground about half-way to the target.

"Hardly steam enough that time. Try again."

Second effort results about the same, and citizen retires in disgust.

"So long since I shot a bow—rather out of practice."

"Just so."

His own efforts rather spoiling his stories, citizen falls back on aboriginal reminiscences. The Indian is always to be relied on as subject-matter for a yarn, and possesses the further advantage of not being on hand to test the accuracy of citizen's remarks:

"When I was a boy, I used to see Indians do some tall shooting. Knew one fellow who'd cut a sixpence out of a stick *every time* at a hundred yards."

"That so? Had good eyes, that Indian."

"Eh! What's that? What do you mean?"

"Nothing more than that you or I would need a telescope to see a sixpence a hundred yards off."

Symptoms of mental commotion evident in citizen's countenance. Decides that "perhaps it wasn't a hundred yards," gradually reducing the distance to a few feet under cross-examination—eventually hauling off for repairs, quietly muttering a candid opinion to the effect that "there's not much in that game, anyhow."

Little episodes of this sort rank among the fables of archery, and are expected whenever citizens of the said species visit the range, and they are very numerous. Another peculiarity very noticeable is that it seems impossible for the average spectator to enjoy the surroundings without more or less interfering with the participants. Archery is a pastime requiring intense concentration of the faculties on the one object, and many an arrow is sent wide of the mark through some thoughtless act of the spectator, which attracts the attention of the archer at the critical moment of "loosing," that otherwise would have found its way with unerring certainty to the mark. However unintentional the cause, the result is always the same; and this stray hint may not be amiss. Admitting that to the looker-on the sport may be tame, to the participant it has a zest and piquancy hard to explain, which is known only to the archer, but by him thoroughly understood and felt; and the fact that good shooting requires so much attention to the apparently trivial details only adds to the enjoyment felt as the flying shafts strike the mark.

The army of archers is daily receiving accessions from all ranks of life. It is a pastime which is suited to both sexes, from youth to age, and as it requires the open air and fair weather for its practice, it leads to health and happiness. Picturesque surroundings attract the eye, and the amount of physical exercise secured is not sufficient to be harmful, but rather of positive benefit, and more especially to those who lead sedentary lives, and it is from this class that most recruits are drawn. From looking on, one comes to inquire the cost of an outfit, and, once drawn in, the victim almost invariably becomes an ardent and enthusiastic lover of the gentle art. For a long time American archers were dependent on Great Britain for their outfits, and the relative merits of the foreign manufactures are well known among the fraternity. At this time, however, American bows are largely used, and are finding their way all over the country, to the gradual displacement of foreign makes of corresponding price and quality as fast as they are introduced. For beginners, probably the best bows used are what are known as "self-bows"—that is, bows made from a single stick. Of this class, the majority are lemonwood and lancewood. A good, serviceable bow to start with can be had for four or five dollars; half a dozen arrows, say as much more; arm-guard, finger-tips, and quiver, say three dollars—so that a total of twelve or fifteen dollars will fit out the intending archer ready for the range. A straw target, thoroughly made, with regulation painted facing, will cost say six dollars, but can be bought by a club, or a few friends joining together, for common use. Once the probationary period is passed, the archer will become ambitious, and desire a better bow—and here his taste can be gratified with a large variety to select from. What are known as backed bows, made usually from two different woods (occasionally three), abound in styles and numbers, at from seven to twenty-five dollars in price, according to quality, through the various grades. Snakewood, beefwood, partridgewood, lemonwood, lancewood, yew, and so forth, joined with ash or hickory for the back, are in common use here, and can be seen on any archery range. Perhaps the handsomest in appearance are the snakewood and hickory, the beautifully mottled dark wood contrasting well with the white. The more expensive bows of this class are marvels of finish and workmanship. Every part is wrought out to a certain scale so delicately graduated as to secure the best results in accuracy of shooting, elasticity, and strength. The yew, however, is the bow *par excellence*, and is unequaled in smoothness and elasticity of pull, quickness, and lack of tendency to "kick," noticeable in all other bows. The archer desirous of doing the handsome thing by himself can get a fine yew bow for two hundred and fifty dollars. Should that frighten the intending purchaser, perhaps a statement that a yew can be secured for fifteen or twenty dollars may be reassuring. The fortunate possessor of a fine bow is envied among archers less favored, but at the same time has a little extra care on his hands in giving it proper attention, although that should be done with every bow, whatever the quality. A frequent rubbing with an oiled rag is to the bow what careful grooming is to the race-horse; and the better taken care of, the better the results in every way, in either case.

Once provided with a satisfactory outfit, and having learned how to hold the bow, how to "loose," and other details, the question of advancement is simply one of practice. Systematic, persistent work in time accomplishes the desired result in the way of skill, and in a few months the novice becomes an expert at the shorter ranges. Many, in beginning, start at ten or twenty feet distance from the target, and practice until they become proficient enough to hit the gold (the bull's-eye) a majority of shots. As skill is acquired, the distance is gradually increased, until the archer is almost sure of "a hit" every time up to sixty yards distance, the limit for what is known as short-range shooting. Target shooting is practiced in "rounds," the usual shooting in this vicinity being at the "American round"—thirty arrows each distance, at forty, fifty, and sixty yards. With growing skill and experience, the archer, if ambitious, as is usually the case, seeks new laurels in attempting the "York round," the present national round of Great Britain and of this country in public competitions. To get any satisfactory scores at this round is a work of much time and practice, not to mention pedestrianism, as it requires two dozen arrows at sixty yards, four dozen at eighty yards, and six dozen at one hundred yards; and those who flatter themselves into the belief that they are experts at the American round shooting, are usually surprised to see how often they do not hit the target at the longer ranges. The walking required to retrieve the arrows shot at the York round is rather more than could be anticipated without reckoning. An archer shooting alone, and three arrows at an "end" (each time the bow is used), will have walked nearly three miles at the hundred-yard range alone. To attain a respectable degree of proficiency at the York round is a work of years, and requires ambition and persistency on the part of the archer, as progress seems provokingly slow. Of course there are those who develop unusual aptitude, as in all sports, and acquire a condition of effectiveness so much sooner than many others who shoot in company with them that the effect is rather depressing on the slower ones; yet the peculiar attractions of archery are likely to stir up the rear ranks to greater effort in such cases. Time will tell, and it is generally a matter of time, after all. The archer, facing the target for the first time at a hundred yards, is usually more or less surprised to see how it has seemingly diminished in size, notwithstanding the four feet of diameter are still there, inviting the flying shaft. There is, possibly, a little trepidation, more determination, and still more curiosity, as the first arrow is started on its way—an eager straining of the eyes, watching the flight, and accompanying guessing as to its landing place. Following the arc, the archer half expresses aloud the thought, "That went over." Same with the other shots, and, hurrying to the target to ascertain the result, nine times in ten the arrows will be found sticking in the ground far short of the mark—a rather puzzling demonstration of optical delusion. Finally, the eager archer hears the dull thud denoting a hit, and, as it is usually a difficult matter to see an arrow in the target from that distance, mental conjectures as to its proximity to the center abound until the certainty is known. The first hit recorded is usually the signal for lively work in retrieving, and it is safe to say the hundred yards of space are covered in a "go as you please" style, generally pleased to go in the least time possible. To find the arrow planted squarely in the golden bull's-eye sends a thrill of exultation through the archer, and the chances are that the echoes are awakened by a joyous shout. Many have the impression that target shooting is "tame fun." More than likely it is the spectator, but to the archer it always retains its attraction. There is just enough of the element of chance to keep one at it from day to day. If shooting in company, each strives to outdo the other. If shooting alone, the records of other archers are always waiting to be excelled, as well as one's own previous efforts, and every increase of score is wonderfully gratifying. Many times has it been asked of the writer, "What fun is there in shooting alone?" Plenty of exercise, more recreation, and always the scores hitherto made by one's self or others to be surpassed. The many would-be witty remarks on "child's play," "two sticks and a string," etc., fall on the archer's ear without effect. Many a time have fishing friends smiled condescendingly on the writer for his "bow and arrow notions," as they term them, profoundly impressed with the fact of so much valuable time being wasted. At the same the writer (who never fishes) perhaps wonders at the great sport of sitting all day by the lake side, with "nary a nibble." Can it be called an even thing? "Every man to his trade" is a good enough adage; and just now the particular trade in discussion is archery, to which we will return, allowing the preceding comparison to enter as a bit of digression, permissible under the circumstances.

Shooting at a painted target is far from being the whole of archery. The delights of "roving archery," as it is termed, are many, and combine, to the full, outdoor exercise, more or less skill with the long-bow, and a general good time. Take a congenial party, the favorite bow, a few common arrows, lunch perhaps, and start anywhere, unless some particular route is arranged, across the fields, climbing a hill or two, wandering at will in shade or sun. Squirrels are all around you, inviting a shot. Larks fly on all sides; blackbirds are in swarms around the marshy places. Shoot at anything that moves. You will find abundant opportunities, and the fact that you do not hit anything worth mentioning does not detract a particle from your enjoyment. Perhaps you plump an arrow into a squirrel. With the hit will come a start of surprise perhaps, but none the less is it the genuine sportsman's keen delight in the successful effort. It is a score, and will be hailed with shouts from all. There's no envy in the party—it suits all alike that you have hit. Suppose you have walked two, or three, or five miles. You may have shot a hundred times, with possibly a squirrel or two, or a bird, as the reward of your efforts. The game is valueless as such, but in your eyes it seems worthy a place in the game bag. A cool, shady place, invites a halt, and over the lunch you can discuss the good shots, rejoice in the successful ones, laugh at the failures. It is pleasant to lie full length on the soft grass, and rest after what may have been a fatiguing tramp. The twang of the bowstring is musical to you. There is no aching head from the noise and jar of the gun, no aching shoulder from the "kick." The slight recoil of the bow is unfelt, and the soft whistle of the flying shaft has not frightened the game after the first shot. It may be you have emptied your quiver at one squirrel, and, through poor marksmanship, failed to drive him from his hole, which only your approach to gather the arrows will do. His curiosity to ascertain what were the whistling darts sticking all around has given you abundant opportunity to slay him, although you have not improved it. After a refreshing *siesta* under some hospitable madroño, you resume the tramp. More fields, more hills, a departure from the line of march to get the benefit of a sudden discovery of a mark on one side or the other. It matters not if the bird or beast shuns your approach, and you lose the opportunity. The chase was there, the cautious movements to get a close shot; all the hunter's instinct in you has been aroused anew, and, if yielding to the lost chance, subsides only to rise again at the next discovery. And this for a day, with what result? With this result: You have spent the day with Nature, have tramped yourself into fatigue enough to appreciate and enjoy calm, peaceful slumber. Perhaps you are sunburned a little. That is a healthful sign.

One day of this kind will take the sting from many days of seclusion, counteract the effects of confinement, give new life to the delicate, and drive away the cares and troubles of business, or make them seem lighter when renewed. The gentleman of position in financial or mercantile circles may, in a moment of leisure, cast his eye over some enthusiastic recital of archery doings in the field or at the target, with perhaps a contemptuous smile, as he thinks "there's nothing in it." Eminently correct, good sir, from your standpoint. The long-bow would hardly seem fitting in the bank president's luxurious office or the merchant's counting-room—hardly suited to the broker's office.

There is very little of the dollars-and-cents connected with its use. You have no occasion for its services to aid in the acquisition of wealth in your business routine, directly; but indirectly you may have, and remain in profound ignorance of the fact. You, Mr. President, for instance, need some recreation. The gun has lost its charms; you cannot stand the hard work necessary to any degree of success with pleasure to yourself. You cannot shoot or fish at your homes; you can easily find room and space for target-shooting with the long-bow, however, and have never once thought of it. "Pshaw! that will do for children." That's so, and for grown-up children, too; and bear in mind there are hundreds of them practicing archery to-day all over this broad country. Gentlemen of your persuasion beyond the Sierra are indulging in the sport and never tiring—are finding in it a delightful relaxation from business cares. You won't think of your offices in bending the bow. There's too much else to occupy your mind then, and this very forgetting for the time being serves only to bring you to your work with more willingness—more capacity to handle it. This archery which causes you amusement when seen in others will cause you another sort of amusement when you once become its votary. It will never lose its charm, and in place of ridicule you will have only praise. Once you are drawn into its power, you are helpless. There is no other modern pastime that will fill its place. Age is nothing, dignity is nothing, position is nothing in archery. It is a solace for all, a most delightful relief and relaxation, and can be enjoyed alone as well as in company. Go and buy a bow, arrows, and target, and go at it. On the start you probably could hardly hit "the broadside of a barn;" but before very long you will be surprised to find what an interest you are taking in your improvement, and then will the "fascination of the long-bow" begin to exercise its power over you. From the contemptuous idea you will go to the other extreme, and wonder why you never discovered it before, why you could believe it so much nonsense, and why you considered it too ridiculous for a second thought. That will follow as sure as ever you attempt archery.

The footing already attained in this community by this pastime is very little understood. It has long been a mooted question, "Where do all the pins go?" and among archers the same question applies to bows. A single house in this city has imported and sold bows by the hundred, and yet there are very few recognized archers in comparison. Many a backyard is decorated with the bright colored target for private recreation, that to passers-by on the street, and even to "friends of the family," is unknown. Decorate *your* lawn in like manner. As you come down town, stop and get an outfit. Visit any convenient archery range, and watch the shooters (but *don't* tell any Indian or other tales of wonderful shooting). The necessary details as to holding the bow, arrow, etc., will be practically explained in a few minutes, though they are difficult to satisfactorily express on paper. The rest you must teach yourself, and in time you will find it a labor of love. It will grow upon you ever. Don't think you will soon tire of the pastime. Maurice Thompson, the father of American archery, says, "So long as the new moon returns a bent beautiful bow in heaven, so long will the fascination of archery keep its hold on the hearts of men."

Albert W. Havens.

SAINT BARTHOLOMEW.

Chapter III.

As they neared Omaha, Nell and Agnes sat listening to a very excited argument between the masculine young married woman and Chesterfield, on the practicability of Mill's ideas on the rights of women; and just as the radical young matron began to perceive how impregnable was Chesterfield's position, surrounded by the wall of his prejudices and platitudes, Winter called to Nell that there was a fine herd of buffaloes to be seen from his window. Nell was delighted, and drew a hasty sketch of the herd careering around ambiguously in the distance, touching it up with snow-capped mountains in the background, and a decidedly impossible Pawnee warrior in the foreground. When finished, Winter quietly remarked:

"I'm sorry you took so much care with your sketch, for I begin to fear that it is only a drove of cattle, after all."

"Not every-day cows?" indignantly cried she.

"Cows," said he, with humility.

Nell vowed vengeance, but a compromise was effected by his pointing out to her, during the day, numerous coyotes, deer, and prairie-dogs. Apparently the two had drifted back to a safe footing, but they

> —"lure greedily up
> All silence, all the innocent breathing points,"

with an instinctive dread of what they might develop. Nell caught him gravely studying her face, and, upon her raising her eyebrows interrogatively, he said:

"I am glad our tickets take us by different roads from Omaha to Chicago, because a short absence seems to solidify the fluids of our feelings, giving us a chance to handle them."

"Why do you say 'short absence?'" asked Nell, ignoring the under-current of meaning in his remark. "I thought our routes diverged permanently from this point."

"Mrs. Alston told me you were going to stop over at Chicago, for a rest of several days, and I shall be there one night, at any rate; so you will have another chance to torment me, if it will give you any satisfaction to know it," he answered, looking inquiringly at her as she bent over the shawl-strap, in the vain endeavor to smuggle therein all of Elsie's stray toys.

Before Nell could answer, Mrs. Reddington, Chesterfield, and other of their car companions, came up, and bade her the pleasant good-bye and *bon voyage* so ready on the lips of American travelers. Mrs. Reddington stood looking at Nell for a moment, with a very grave expression on her girlish face; then she said, "I'd like to speak to you one minute, Miss Grey." Then, as she took Nell to a quiet corner, she continued, in an agitated whisper:

"I can't help thinking I ought to tell you a discovery I have made about Mr. Winter. That man is desperately in love with you. You are too young and thoughtless to notice things much, but I have not lived all these years for nothing."

"Why did you consider it necessary to put me on my guard? Is there danger of hydrophobia?" asked Nell, laughing in spite of the old lady's earnestness.

"Oh, no; but I know just what a peck of trouble lovers are, with their tragic, ruffling ways, and I believe in getting rid of them as soon as possible."

"What course would you advise, my dear Mrs. Reddington, supposing such were the case?" said Nell, trying to look serious.

"There's only one way," she said, sighing, as if weighted by many experiences; "let them propose, and get done with it, or they will pester the very life out of you with turnings-up at odd times, and long, wearisome letters, and such things. I could see in a second that you don't care anything for the poor fellow; so you mind what I say, and you will be all right." And she bustled off, leaving Nell standing and looking after her, wondering whether the difference between them was one of kind or merely degree.

Polly was to continue with Agnes as far as New York, to the great satisfaction of both mistress and maid.

Winter saw Mrs. Alston and her party into their car at Council Bluffs, and, under cover of the general confusion, he stooped over Nell, and said, in low tones:

"Good bye, child. Half the time before we meet again will be a memory, the other half an expectation. Do you understand?"

She looked up into his eyes with a thrilling sense of comprehension, that made her catch her breath quickly; but she merely nodded, and he was gone.

As the train flew through the more cultivated lands of the middle West, the eyes of the travelers were gladdened by the homelike traces of humanity, after the dreary isolation of the plains. May had begun to spread her green carpets, and to run up on the tree-tops the signals of the royal advance of summer. These meager signs of coming beauty suggested, by contrast, the perfected luxuriance left behind in California's valleys, and the last grand sweep through the Sierra.

Inside the car there were many new faces, that caused a certain revival of restraint. Nell found time to finish a magazine story that she had commenced near Sacramento, while Agnes sat in speechless exhaustion, waiting for their journey's end.

The mere thought, by this time, of a lunch-basket, and its musty, indefinite contents, was nauseating, and gladly they emptied out of the window their remaining pickles, crackers, sardines, and turkey bones, and betook themselves to the attached dining-car, whose fare had, at least, the charm of novelty.

A few hours before reaching Chicago, Nell sat looking fixedly out of the window, struggling with the passion of a sudden conviction. Dreamily looking down the vista of her future, she had suddenly realized that its horizon was bounded by the walls of Chicago. There seemed no beyond, and then full upon her fell the thought of Saint Bartholomew. A familiar mystery to us all is the sudden cleavage of the consciousness into a duality, the twin parts of which are distinct as to their animus and independent as to their action—the one, a proud and critical representative of the soul's idealism; the other, a plausible embassador to plead the cause of humanity's weakness. One of these spirit-warrings stirred Nell's whole consciousness as the thought flashed upon her, "Can it be that I love this man?" A stranger, whom she had known scarcely five days? She, who considered that propinquity covered the whole ground of any mushroom growth of love—who named a true love a spiritual development that wrought slowly, as grind the mills of the gods? Then came the thought, made familiar to her by a close self-analysis, that her nature was of the kind that lives intensely in the present, and, looking back over her life, she could see her "tattered sympathies and sentiments dangling on every bush and fluttering in every breeze." This fancy, then, would rend as had done others of sterner stuff, and in a week she would, probably, glance back with a laugh to see it, also, caught on the wayside bramble. Wearily drawing her hand over her aching eyes, Nell dismissed the thought with a bitter sense of self-contempt that clung to her.

"Nell, please hand me my valise. We will be in Chicago in about an hour," said Agnes, brightening up at the prospect of a release from their narrow quarters, the soot, cinders, dust, and disorder, the alternate draught and suffocation, and the endless jar and rattle of the wheels.

"I suppose our two remaining clean collars must go on duty; notwithstanding which addition, there is a hopelessly seedy look about us, Agnes, and I doubt if we gain an *entrée* into any but a fourth-rate hotel."

"We have the conventional overland look. It is unique, and people recognize it instantly, and it makes us preëminently respectable," said Agnes, in reassuring tones, as she bade Polly pack away the well worn dusters.

As the city came into sight, a curious electric transformation swept over the car, changing its whole atmosphere, and tempering it to suit the great world's exactions. The party passed safely through the mazy routine of the depot, and they were soon seated in a hack and spinning through the streets to the hotel.

"Please, Agnes, when the clerk comes, answer all questions, for I can't recollect our names, origin, residence, destination, or anything else. I feel as if we had got traveling, and would be compelled to go on forever, round and round the globe," said Nell, throwing herself into an arm-chair in the hotel waiting-room.

When the clerk came, Agnes gave one of her characteristic orders, "Rooms, bath, lunch."

In the evening Agnes sat writing letters by the bright coal-fire, while Nell wandered restlessly about, with the mercury of a strange excitement running through her veins. At last she went into the hall, and, meeting a bell-boy, sent him to the office, weighted with an inquiry that brought back the answer, "Yes, miss, a Mr. Morse Winter and man, from California, registered this morning. Anything more, miss?"

This answer sent Nell into Agnes's bed-room to have a romp with Elsie, whom Polly was putting to bed. In a few moments, Agnes opened the parlor door, and said, in a voice touched with a shade more indifference than usual, "Nell, come in. Mr. Winter has called."

Nell followed her sister immediately, and, finding him standing by the fire, went up to him, and gave him her hand with her usual frankness and self-possession, but shrank back slightly, and flushed hotly, when his hand met hers with a jealous, gathering clasp, and his great black eyes kissed hers with a long, yearning look. She sank into a chair, completely unstrung by this wordless greeting, and he was the first to regain his self-possession. Turning to Agnes, who had seen everything, and was tingling with the recognition of a tragedy in process, he opened a desultory conversation, spiced with an occasional recollection of Mrs. Reddington, in which Nell soon joined. An hour passed, during which Jeremiah called to pay his respects, looking as somber as usual. With a tact and grace to which even Nell's sensitiveness could not take exception, Agnes begged to be allowed to finish her letters, and was soon deeply absorbed. A fire-alarm bell gave Winter the excuse for drawing Nell to the bay-window, behind the curtains of which they stood facing each other, totally oblivious to the repeated alarm.

"I wonder if you know what my joy is at seeing you once more?" he asked, in low, grave tones.

"Mr. Winter, let us leave unsaid much that may be regretted. It is best," she answered, quickly.

"Best! It is a word of the earth earthy. It implies the diplomate. It does not touch my mood, child," he answered, with gathering excitement.

"It is the superlative. Can your mood be beyond that?" she said, to allow him a chance to escape, if he would, through the door of commonplace.

He did not even hear her, for his next words were:

"The hours since we parted have made something very plain to me, Miss Grey—I love you! Please don't trouble yourself about it, child. I ask nothing from you; I only want the same recognition of it that you would give—if I may say so—the quiet beauty of a starlight night, or the perfume of a flower; they don't ask anything in return, neither do I. I just wanted to tell you about it—I really had to. And this hour will be so much to me in the days to come."

"You use the word 'days' advisedly, Mr. Winter, for I don't see how a true, lasting love can grow in a week. It seems impossible," she said, holding well in hand the leash of her feelings, and arguing more with her own fainting convictions than heeding his.

"'A wayward modern mind dissecting passion,' I see," he said, surprised at her words, but speaking lightly and smiling down at her; "sounding the coin I offer her to see if it's counterfeit! That is all right, little girl; if more of you women did it there would soon be less false money circulating. But," he continued, with a complete change of voice, "you can't measure my love with a yard-stick cut from the tree of your prejudice. I do not know how to make it clear to you, I'm sure. Some things must be taken on faith. Four-fifths of life is made up of things as intangible as electricity. Then, again," he said, dropping to a more comfortable level, "a journey of even a few days, in as close companionship as ours has been, is worth a year of evening calls under the gaslight. However it is, child, my love for you is the strongest, purest, most loyal my life has ever known; and I know the highest my nature is capable of. You shall see."

"It all seems plain enough, but sophistries are masqueraders," she said, in a slow, strained way, and so low that he only caught one word.

"'Sophistries!' You are a bit severe, I think, little one," he said, gravely.

"Oh, I did not mean you. I mean myself," was her quick, seemingly irrelevant answer.

"Do you know, Miss Grey, I think you are acting very strangely. I don't understand you. I am not sure that you have heard anything I have been saying to you," he said, wonderingly.

"Strangely? Have I?" she asked, in a startled way; then, looking up at him and giving her head the little toss she always did before saying anything very impudent, she said: "So you cannot imagine why I act so, can you?"

"I suppose it is because you don't believe one syllable I've been telling you."

"Your imagination is very dull to-day," she said, turning and looking out of the window. Then, facing him again, she said, kindly, "I do understand you perfectly, Mr. Winter, and I am glad my life is blessed by your respect and love; nothing sweeter or truer has ever touched it."

He bowed silently, with no thought of what she hid from him, for his ill health had given him opportunity for a wider knowledge of books than of people, and the feeling was so strong with him that she must not love him that it completely shut his eyes to a just reading of her actions. They continued with a tacit change of manner.

"I hope fate will cast our lives together before long, Mr. Winter," said Nell, pleasantly, with a full knowledge that the triteness of her words best hid her true feelings.

"If we meet again it will not be the work of any more classic a fate than Morse Winter, Esquire, for your sister has kindly given me your summer address, and as it is not very far from Boston, and she has invited me to do so, I would not be surprised if some day I should appear suddenly at a banquet like poor Banquo's ghost, a creature out of place." And he laughed a little bitterly.

"Please omit the green tarletan, gory gashes, and other scenic effects, and I can assure you you will be cordially welcomed."

"Mrs. Alston tells me you will spend the summer with friends at C——, but that there is quite a nice hotel in the town, so that Jeremiah and I may journey that way some day, when mother gets tired of seeing me about."

After a pause, he quietly took her hand and said, "You know, child, that the sure companion of my disease is hope; well, I confess to a hope—which I thought forever dead when I left San Francisco—that New York physicians may change their minds regarding my case, and say that all may yet be well with me, and then—"

Nell looked up at him with fast filling eyes, all her own pain forgotten in pity for him, blinded by the light of so false a hope.

"Well, good bye. I must not keep you; I am off in the morning. May peace and joy be with my little love!" So saying, he stood for a moment looking at her drooping head, and then, drawing her hand softly over his closed eyes once or twice, he gravely kissed it, and left the room after a few parting words with Agnes, who still sat by the fire, apparently oblivious to all surroundings.

"Good night, Nell," said Agnes, in a voice that entreated confidence.

"Good night, Agnes," replied Nell, in a voice that recognized it, and was firm in its negation.

Chapter IV.

At the end of a week, Mrs. Alston and her party arrived at the little mountain town of C——, Connecticut, where they were greeted by their cheery hostess, Mrs. North, with her usual cordiality. Professor North was a man of inherited wealth, whose life had been spent in scientific study and research, and whose greatest effort in the world of tangibilities was to keep his energetic and worldly little wife so occupied as to make her forget as much as possible his peaceful, earnest existence. C—— being his birthplace, he had built there a large, handsome summer residence, which his wife filled with their friends, for whose pleasure it was her greatest happiness to plan, and the whole house seemed flooded with the sunshine of her bright, warm nature.

Being a Californian girl, born and bred, Nell was at first assiduously courted by the gentlemen among the gathering guests in the light of a rare curiosity, and attentively studied by the ladies, with a view to imitation if proved of attractive metal, and circumspect criticism if not. Nell was soon the merry, pleasant favorite of them all, but slightly feared because she seemed impervious to any closer relationship, loving best to wander alone, or with the children of some of the guests, over the daisied meadows or pine-covered hills, where somehow the distance seemed bridged between herself and her "Saint Bartholomew," the weary, pain-racked man who appealed to her deep, strong nature as no man had ever done before; and whose influence seemed to grow faster as a memory than as a presence, until the future seemed one great hope that he would come to her, if only for an hour. She had faced, in her honest, healthy way, the fact of his fast approaching end, but it brought no true realisation of its pain, her temperament limiting her life of feeling to the present.

So the weeks flew by, filled with a round of gayety, and Professor North wandered with his testing-hammer among the rocks, with a heart full of quiet, grateful content. Among the guests was a young lawyer, a Mr. Black, whom Agnes soon selected to be the fittest subject for a summer flirtation for Nell, her love of intrigue conquering her sane memories of the past. Nell's frank, good-natured indifference was her best defense, and Mr. Black soon wearied of his suit, and left her to wander whither her mood led her, and, as Agnes expressed it, "to try to set up a reputation for oddity at the risk of chills and fever and being considered imbecile"—for poor Agnes's spirits were somewhat ruffled at Nell's reception of Mr. Black's attentions.

One early morning, toward the end of the fourth week after their arrival, Nell went to the breakfast-room to read till the rest came down. The butler entered and handed her several letters; three were home letters, whose superscriptions were as familiar as home faces, but a fourth sent the hot blood to her face, and then left it pale and quivering. It was the handwriting that had scored the euchre account, interlined her rhymes, and labeled her sketches in the weary crossing of the great desert; the quiet, unshaded letters, with capitals plain and without flourish, as if the hand that held the pen was too tired for ornament. Nell carried her letters, unopened, out into the morning sunshine, which leavens all tidings either of joy or sorrow. With the fascination of pain endurance, Nell left Winter's letter until after reading her Californian news; then she opened it. It ran thus:

"I am coming by Sunday evening's train. Keep a day or two free for a hungry man. Tease me, scold me, snub me, hate me, but let me see you once more.
"M. W."

A few homely words, but they seemed to put their arms about Nell and kiss her with a swift, deep passion, and she sprang to her feet with a little gasping sigh, and, following a very common instinct, off she started for the woods. She was young, and forgot her breakfast and her parasol. The sky looked a bit bluer than usual, the pines a trifle taller, the grass a little greener, the rose-tinted arbutus was certainly more fragrant, and surely no lark ever before sang its liquid seven-note trill as did the one that greeted Nell that morning. And then a sudden sense of great gladness of life came over her, and sent her bounding through the woods, laughing aloud for very ecstasy as she leaped over stumps and streams in a way that would have petrified Agnes could she have seen her. As she neared the edge of the woods, one of those electric changes that only such a nature is subject to came over her, and she threw herself upon the ground and sobbed passionately. After a time she stopped, and lay perfectly still; then, sitting suddenly upright, she shook herself impatiently, and said aloud:

"Helen Grey, you are a hopeless fool—go home!"

That night, after Agnes's light was out, Nell went into the room to have their usual evening chat, and in a voice thoroughly non-committal in its inflection, she said, "I received a note from Mr. Winter this morning; I suppose you remember him. He says he is coming up by to-morrow's train. I hope we can make it pleasant for the poor fellow."

Nell's was one of those natures that crave sympathy, as a flower does sunshine; but the sympathy must be perfect—an identity of soul-tissue that warrants an assurance of complete comprehension, that renders superfluous even a word, a look, or a hand-clasp. A lesser sympathy was met by an instinctive reserve that made her seem as cold and proud as her sister.

Agnes expressed her pleasure at again meeting Mr. Winter, which was very true, as the fair prospect of fresh possibilities of indulging in her favorite pastime of superintending love affairs spread before her. Being a little sleepy, she was off her guard, and began determining audibly whether they had better give him a picnic, to which Nell could wear a white muslin-cambric with a certain very picturesque hat, or a dinner, where Nell's dark green silk showed to best advantage her rich coloring, especially with a touch of coral and white lace at the throat.

"Why, Agnes, what on earth is the difference? If he could stand us a whole week in those hideous linen dusters and green veils, he will not care if we are dressed in gunny-sacks, tied in the middle," said Nell, whose mood made her more than ever "grandly independent of externals."

"I must say I should like Mr. Winter to see us respectably dressed for once. There is a way of doing everything, Nell—one right way; and the amenities of life are founded on large principles, that are seldom recognized by frantic cavilers after abstract truths," said Agnes, with as much resentful severity as was ever heard in her even-toned, refined voice.

"I promise, Agnes, I'll give up the gunny-sacks, only don't call me hard names. You shall make out a programme for me to dress by during his visit, and I'll follow it meekly to the hair-pin—and may heaven have mercy on my soul!" So saying, Nell bade Agnes good night, and went to her own room, with a strange pity in her heart for her sister, in whom she saw, every hour, such rare capabilities that lay dormant under the edict of her sovereign conventionality.

On Monday morning Winter called, and Nell went to the parlor, leaving Agnes and Mrs. North to follow at their leisure. She found him standing, with one hand resting on the back of a chair, and when she entered he did not speak nor move, beyond a slight gesture that bade her come to him, which seemed so familiar, as his illness had warranted many a reversion of courtesy between them. Nell went to him, and stood, white and still, facing him. He placed a hand on either side of her face, and, raising it, held it so, and her spirit quailed before the passion in his eyes, and she closed hers with almost a shudder.

"At last!" he muttered, with an intensity of feeling that told the tale of his inner life since they had parted.

Another silent moment, and they heard the ladies approaching, and, after the manner of the modern world, they were found seated, chatting merrily about past traveling experiences. Mrs. North's heart was immediately won by his quiet grace of manner and pale, worn face. Under cover of the general conversation Nell had a chance to study him, and she was shocked to see the changes a few weeks had wrought. What seemed more inexpressibly pitiful than all else was the stamp of entire hopelessness on face and manner. Nell knew that he did not wish to receive the many hospitalities that Mrs. North seemed determined to shower upon him, and so she fought valiantly for his peace, and he looked his gratitude.

The days flew by, spent by Nell and Winter in a world of their own, from which the other guests withdrew, almost impatient at this thrusting of a vision of death into their merry-making. Seeing him thus set apart, and spiritualized by the contrast, Nell rejoiced that of them all her spirit alone could reach his in a fellowship that bound them more closely every hour. Almost every day Winter spent at the Norths', Mrs. North's feeling toward him of reverential admiration growing every day, her tender heart being often wrung by absolute pain from her intense pity for him, while the Professor unconsciously drifted into an intellectual comradeship with him.

Many were the conjectures, but no one understood the relationship between Winter and Nell, for there had never been a word of love between them since his coming, and yet they all saw that he lived only in her bright presence. By common consent, they and the Professor were left to themselves, and the subject was generally dismissed with, "Well, it's beyond me!" which statement was literally truer than they imagined. Realizing that to gain Nell's confidence was impossible, Agnes contented herself with the scenic effect of the *ensemble*, and her sarcastic criticism of her sister's unconventionality was not often heard during those sunny days.

One day—a fair, sweet day in early June—the household went on a mountain-drive and picnic, leaving Nell, Winter, and Professor North on the lawn under the maples. The two men were engaged in a quiet discussion of some sort at a little distance from Nell, who sat leaning against a tree, surrounded by books, shawls, cushions, and a basket of fruit. As Jeremiah—who was always within sight of his "boy," as he called his master with democratic familiarity placed the fruit near Nell, and before he arose from his knees, he said, in a breathless kind of way, without looking at her:

"Save him, Miss Grey! Please save him; it's only you that can do it. You know what I mean."

"I know, Jeremiah, I know; but it is too late. Utterly hopeless—hopeless—hopeless," moaned Nell, shutting her eyes and leaning back wearily. Then sitting up suddenly, she said, with an imperious gesture, "There—you may go."

Jeremiah went away, with his hard, unwholesome little face broken up into quivering misery. Nell was soon joined by Winter, and together, in an amused silence, they watched the Professor, who was madly chasing butterflies, bare-headed and with a lack of dignity that was irresistibly funny.

"I seriously think it is all a mistake about man being a gregarious animal," she said at last, not taking her eyes off the zealous scientist.

"I think I catch your drift, but let's hear the oracle speak," he answered, watching her face with a deep, quiet content.

"Well, there's no denying the fact that this world is beautiful, always beautiful—even the brown earth, and the dead leaves, and the gray rocks. We humans are the disturbing element. Not each one alone, but it is the friction between two that upsets things and makes life hideous. Just look at Professor North; he is this moment perfectly happy, and I think he is the only one in the whole houseful who knows what lasting peace is, just because he does not pretend to be gregarious."

"Granted the disease; how about the remedy?" gravely inquired Winter.

"Pen each creature up in a separate acre of his own, and then peace would reign," she answered, promptly.

"I pass over the flaws in your brilliant argument. You apparently are not, then, an upholder of duty?"

"Duty is the screw that is loose in the human fabric. Men and women will always suffer so long as they acknowledge it as a leader. Now, confess, would not the world be a real jolly place if it were not for the blot of a brother here, a mother there, or a husband yonder?" continued Nell, with the comfortable assurance that she was always charming to this man who loved her, however perforated by sophistries her philosophy might be.

"Yes, child, it is so; and I've often wondered whether this same duty is a natural element in us, or an abnormal development of some narrow law of earth. Certain it is that an omission of duty causes us more misery than a brave doing of it; and—that brings me to a point I have shrunk from ever since I came up to C——. Pardon my intruding it upon this sunshiny day, but I think I had better have done with it."

"Certainly, Mr. Winter," said she, turning her head away quickly, conscious of the sudden dread that swept over her face, taking with it the bright coloring of her lips and cheeks.

"I told you in Chicago that I cherished a hope of recovery. Do you recollect?"

"I understand all, everything. I beg that you will spare yourself, and—me, the pain of explanations," she said, quickly, without turning her head.

"That hope," he continued, hardly noticing her words, and looking off to the horizon, "has gone from me—forever. With it, all else that binds me to earth, except my love for you and mother. There are not many to mourn, and my going will give little pain. Poor mother is used to sorrow, and used to my long absences from her. You—well, you will miss me, I suppose, a little while. I have not spoken of it to you, but I fully appreciate your noble sacrifice of yourself to give me a few sweet days of holy joy before I go out of life." A pause, and then he said, slowly, "I had hoped to live and try to win the chrism of your love. I wonder if I could have won you, child! I fear not, for there is a something about you that I have never been able to translate; it often puzzles me." Another pause, during which Nell made a sudden movement as if about to speak, and then he said, quickly, "I ask your pardon; I have no right to speak so to you; let it pass. I am happy, very happy, in loving you, and would not have it otherwise. Come, hand me Schiller. We have kept Wallenstein in a precarious position long enough."

And through the quiet hours he read to her, and she heard not a single word, but sat with her eyes, big and black with suffering, running over and over, with slow and painful precision, the outline of the pine-covered hills; and those hours took something from her that she missed through life.

The days lengthened into weeks, full of a joy such as had never touched her life before, and full of a sadness that stalked beside the joy like an ever lengthening shadow. Nell often felt that she ought not to deceive him, and must tell him of her love, but there always came over her a strange, prophetic instinct, of which pride formed no part, that bade her keep silent and suffer alone. The last day of his visit came, when he felt that his strength was fast failing him, and the rest of his life he owed to his mother, waiting for him without a murmur of reproach. He never left his hotel after nightfall, but this last evening he spent at the Norths', and it was late after he had bidden them all good bye, and stood with Agnes and Nell on the broad piazza in the bright moonlight.

Mrs. North had not been seen since, earlier in the evening, she had seen Winter lift little Elsie, and hold her closely to him, burying his white, haggard face in her sunny curls. The gentle-hearted woman had fled to her husband's library, where she sobbed out her grief on his shoulder.

"Oh, John, if you could have seen the poor fellow standing there with Elsie, saying good bye to life and its dead possibilities. It was the saddest sight I ever saw," and she cried again, while with one hand her husband patted her head soothingly, and with the other softly turned the page of the latest phase of the Ruskin-Whistler controversy, which lay on the table before him.

A curious numbness seemed creeping over Nell, who stood silently by as Agnes repeated her farewell in a voice whose usual pitiless composure was disturbed by a perceptible tremor of true feeling. Turning to Agnes, with a grace and dignity she never forgot, Winter said:

"Will you trust your little sister to walk to the gate with me, if she wraps up warmly, and I promise not to keep her long?"

In reply, Agnes drew from her shoulders a white shawl, and threw it over Nell's head, who felt a sudden dart of hate for her sister, when, from a force of habit that never forsook her, she arranged Nell's unruly locks about her brow with a few touches of her soft, white hand. With a fear that Agnes saw the flash in her eyes, Nell hastily kissed her, and, taking Winter's arm, they turned down the long, moonlight-checkered avenue. In unbroken silence they walked until they reached a rustic bench, midway between the house and gate. They seated themselves without a word, the great hush in the world external seeming to Nell but part of the numbness that was deadening her senses, and against which she struggled in vain.

"Nell, Nell," at last broke from him, "do you know that this is good bye forever?"

Her stiff lips motioned for words, and at last she said in a voice that sounded strange to her own ears, "Why?"

"Why, child? Because I met you too late, and because I am dying. Never again on earth after to-night, little girl."

"How long do you think you will live?" she asked, with a calmness that stung him.

"A few months, at the utmost."

She continued coldly, slowly, and evidently with great effort, and he was completely misled.

"You have never asked me to love you, nor to be your wife, but now I ask you. I beg you to marry me. Marry me to-morrow morning, and take me with you, to be there until the end."

"Do not tempt me into accepting the self-sacrifice. Do not, I say. I am not as strong as I used to be against temptation."

"Where is the sacrifice when I love you?" she asked, in the same wearied voice.

"Nell, I know you, and can see the great womanly pity that prompts you to this. I am not blind. If you loved me, you could not speak so calmly and coldly."

"No, you are wrong. There is something that has come over me this evening that seems like a spell. I can't break through it, and it is deceiving you."

"You are brave, child, but I cannot believe you."

As she sat looking at him it suddenly flashed upon her that she never would be able to convince him of the truth, and the thought roused her. She rose quickly, walked a few steps from him, then, returning slowly, she stood in front of him, saying, in low tones, that had a strange throb of entreaty in them, "Mr. Winter, I do love you. Please believe me. I have from the very first. Oh, please try to believe me."

Winter knew she was not acting, but he was also certain that her sympathy was ruling her present mood, and that he must be very firm, and not lose his head.

An imaginative temperament, in emergency, often mistrusts itself, and, in turning traitor to its own instincts, overshoots the mark. Nell read his incredulity in his quiet attitude, and, turning from him with a low moan, she threw her arms about a tree that was a step from them, and laid her face against the cold, dark trunk, in speechless misery. A moment of silence, broken only by the step of Jeremiah on the gravel, as he paced to and fro far down the avenue, near the gate, waiting for his "boy," and then Winter went to her, and, unwinding her clinging arms from the tree, he quietly took her to him, and said, with a great tenderness in his voice, "Listen, little girl, there must be no misunderstanding between us that might trouble your future. You have mistaken for love your sympathy for me. The strongest element in your nature is your wonderful sympathy. I saw it in every feature of your face the first time I looked at you, and I've seen it in every phase since then. Your sensibilities are so delicate that I believe you fairly lose your personality, for the time being, in that of another. I am many years older than you, Nell, and I know you better than you do yourself, and I know you do not love me."

Then, as she started from him, he held her, and continued:

"Hush, child, I have not finished yet. Do you think that, even if I were sure you loved me, I would bind you to my remnant of wasting life, and, after the end, to my memory? Most decidedly, no. I would not have you love me, even if I could. You must not, you shall not. Nothing would make my last days so utterly miserable as to think that my blind selfishness had given you any pain. Your future shall be worthy of you, and brimming over with all that life can give you."

As he spoke, Nell became very quiet, and the strange, prophetic ban of silence, that she had felt from the first, was made plain to her, and she knew that, for the sake of his peace, she must hide her suffering. She lifted her head, and tried to smile up into his face, but she could not control her quivering lips, and a sudden self-pity sent the hot tears slowly down her white cheeks.

"Child, I cannot see you suffer in this way. Tell me that I am not mistaken. Speak quickly, and say you do not love me," broke from him, in a voice sharp and thin from sudden pain. She breathed hard and slowly once or twice, and then whispered:

"You are right. I was deceiving you. I do not love you. Be at perfect peace regarding me."

"Are you sure?" he persisted, startled by her manner and quivering voice, so pathetic in its uncertainty.

She gave a quick look about her, with eyes like a hunted animal, and then said, rapidly, "Sure, very sure. Now, good bye. The night air is too damp for you. You must go—go quickly. We have been such good friends, have we not, Saint Bartholomew? Jerry will scold if I keep you any longer. Good bye," she continued, with an effort at her old bright manner. And in a moment he was gone. When the slow step retreated down the walk, was joined by another, and then died away in the distance, the silence was broken by a long, low moan, and the girl fled homeward up the avenue.

A month passed. One still, sultry morning, there came a letter to Nell from Boston, addressed in the small, delicate handwriting of a past generation of gentlewomen.

It contained these words:

"My son's spirit found rest last night, at midnight. Among his last words were these: 'Mother, dear, you will not forget to write a word to my little love?' He had great affection for you, my child. He would lie for hours and tell me of your winsome face and manner. He said you had a very superior intellect—almost masculine. I suppose that is the reason why you could not return my son's affection. It is a woman's mission to cultivate her heart rather than her brain, but, for the sake of his love for you, remember, dear, you have always, until the Father calls me, a friend and mother in

"ESTHER M. WINTER."

ANNA ALEXANDER.

UNDER THE SANDS.

The sunshine falls upon a golden strand
  Beside a sea that stretches far away,
  Where all the summer long, in careless play,
The peaceful waves come rippling o'er the sand—
So calm, so still, we cannot understand
  That ever sailors' wives should sit and weep,
  That ever they should wake while others sleep,
Because of tempests on the sea and land.
Ah! wait till winter waves assail the shore,
  And beat away this level floor of gold,
For where 'twas wrecked and buried years before
  A ghostlike ship shall lift its timbers old.
O sorrow of my heart, thou liest as deep!
Heaven grant no storm of time may break thy sleep.

SEDDIE E. ANDERSON.

SOME OF OUR EARLIER POETESSES.

It is among the *dii minores* that we discover a large proportion of our choicer verse. The glory of these lesser singers, when at their best, outshines all but the brightest effulgence of their superiors. Particularly in their scenic song do we repeatedly meet most glowing passages; and it may not be amiss to here renew our acquaintance with certain of them. The poetry of America does not suffer in the hands of such men as Gallagher on shore, and Sargent on the sea. For instance, the opening of "Miami Woods," by the former author:

"The Autumn time is with us! Its approach
Was heralded, not many days ago,
By hazy skies that veiled the brazen sun,
And sea-like murmurs from the rustling corn,
And low-voiced brooks that wandered drowsily
By purpling clusters of the juicy grape,
Swinging upon the vine. And now, 'tis here,
And what a change hath passed upon the face
Of Nature, where the waving forest spreads,
Then robed in deepest green! All through the night
The subtle frost hath plied its mystic art;
And in the day the golden sun hath wrought
True wonders; and the winds of morn and even
Have touched with magic breath the changing leaves.
And now, as wanders the dilating eye
Athwart the varied landscape, circling far,
What gorgeousness, what blazonry, what pomp
Of colors, burst upon the ravished sight!
Here, where the maple rears its yellow crest,
A golden glory; yonder, where the oak
Stands monarch of the forest, and the ash
Is girt with flame-like parasite, and broad
The dogwood spreads beneath, a rolling field
Of deepest crimson; and afar, where looms
The gnarled gum, a cloud of bloodiest red."

Again, from the "Falls of a Forest Stream," by another Western poet. Would that the mightier never wrote after a lesser fashion:

"O'er all there broods repose; the breeze
Lingers as it goes past;
The squirrel's foot sounds loud among
The leaves by Autumn cast;
And the lonely bird, whose glancing wing
Flits restlessly among
The boughs, stops doubtfully, and checks
The sudden burst of song.

"And silently, year after year
Is ushered in and goes,
And time, amid these quiet scenes,
No other measure knows,
But the wakening and the sleep of birds,
The dawn and shut of day,
And the changes of the forest leaves,
From budding to decay.

"The wilderness is still; the long,
Long sleep of ages gone,
With its unmoving presence fills
These distant shades and lone;
And changing dynasties, and thrones
Cast down, send hither brief
And fainter echoes than the fall
Of Autumn's faded leaf."

Such poets are not rare among us; their song, though wafted to no great distance, come fresh and fragrant as the very forest. But we have promised ourselves to devote this paper to the female poets. Maria Gowen, better known as Maria Brooks, and perhaps better still as Maria dell' Occidente, has been dead about thirty-five years. How many of the present generation are aware that this, their countrywoman, was pronounced by Southey to be "the most impassioned and imaginative of all poetesses." Mrs. Browning has since put England in a position to dispute the title with us; but the star of our own poetess is burning still. Beautiful throughout her being, in soul, mind, and body, gifted with those high and mysterious powers that so rarely take up their abode in the flesh, Maria Brooks must be remembered as one of the most wonderful of American women. A life of sorrow is too often the price of unusual endowments, and this suffering one paid it in full. At the age of fourteen, she was betrothed to a Boston merchant. We have not the space to give her after history. The reader may learn enough from these four stanzas, direct from her own heart:

"The bard has sung, God never formed a soul
Without its own peculiar mate, to meet
Its wandering half, when ripe to crown the whole
Bright plan of bliss, most heavenly, most complete.

"But thousand evil things there are that hate
To look on happiness; these hurt, impede,
And, leagued with time, space, circumstance, and fate,
Keep kindred heart from heart, to pine, and pant, and bleed.

"And as the dove to far Palmyra flying,
From where her native founts of Antioch beam,
Weary, exhausted, longing, panting, sighing,
Lights sadly at the desert's bitter stream—

"So many a soul, on life's drear desert faring,
Love's pure, congenial spring unfound, unquaffed,
Suffers, recoils: then, thirsty and despairing
Of what it would, descends, and sips the nearest draught."

Who would know whence comes the truly fearful passion of this author, let him read that strange romance, "Idomen, or the Vale of Yumuri;" then he will be prepared to take up her master-piece, "Zophiel, or the Bride of Seven." We shall not attempt a review of this poem, a marvelous mingling of the human and preterhuman, rich in all the colors of the Orient. Its sweep is all too wide, its passion too subtile, its language too luxurious, for any but the true lover of poetry. The reader can do no better than to study it as an entirety. We glance at the heroine, Egla, a Hebress, and pass on:

"He who beheld her hand forgot her face—
Yet in that face was all beside forgot;
And he who, as she went, beheld her pace
And locks profuse, had said, 'Nay, turn thee not.'
Placed on a banquet couch beside the king,
'Mid many a sparkling guest, no eye forbore;
But like their darts, the warrior princes fling,
Such looks as seem'd to pierce, and scan her o'er and o'er;
Nor met alone the glare of lip and eye—
Charms, but not rare; the gazer, stern and cool,
Who sought but faults, nor fault or spot could spy;
In every limb, joint, vein, the maid was beautiful,
Save that her lip, like some bud-bursting flower,
Just scorned the bounds of symmetry, perchance,
But by its rashness gained an added power,
Heightening perfection to luxuriance.
But that was only when she smiled, and when
Dissolved the intense expression of her eye;
And had her spirit-love first seen her then,
He had not doubted her mortality."

Passion is ever varying with this writer, and each change brings unexpected charm. The thought is always high and pure, and the diction forcible. Mrs. Brooks lived for a considerable time in Cuba, and there wrote perhaps the better part of her poetry. There, too, she was destined to die. Her farewell to this land of "dark-eyed daughters" comes to us with peculiar tenderness:

"Alas! I fear my native snows—
A clime too cold, a heart too warm—
Alternate chills, alternate glows,
Too fiercely threat my flower-like form.

"The orange tree has fruits and flowers;
The grendilla, in its bloom,
Hangs o'er its high, luxuriant bowers,
Like fringes from a Tyrian loom.

"When the white coffee blossoms swell,
The fair moon full, the evening long,
I love to hear the warbling bell,
And sunburnt peasant's wayward song.

"Drive gently on, dark muleteer,
And the light seguidilla frame,
Fain would I listen still to hear
At every close thy mistress' name.

"Adieu, fair isle! The waving palm
Is penciled on the purest sky;
Warm sleeps the bay, the air is balm,
And, soothed to langour, scarce a sigh

"Escapes for those I love so well,
For those I've loved and left so long;
On me their fondest musings dwell,
To them alone my sighs belong.

"On, on, my bark! Blow, southern breeze!
No longer would I lingering stay;
'Twere better far to die with these
Than live in pleasure far away."

More familiar to American readers are the writings of Elizabeth Oakes-Smith. "The Sinless Child" and "The Acorn" have given this author a popularity that her other poems, though as perfect in their way, could not have secured. Passion is not the first element one meets as one reads her little volume of verse. We the rather seek such words as hight, purity, the command of an exalted self, with which to picture the impression received. There is certainly power; but the fire that leaped along the lines of Maria Brooks is here a calm, tempered light, never dazzling, but always beautiful. It is the halo that surrounds the philosopher, the true thinker, trusting not only to the mind, but to the soul, to lead the way to truth. Intellectual as she is, the motto of Mrs. Smith is, "Instinct before intellect." This theory underlies the sweetness of "The Sinless Child," and we find it constantly recurring in all the varied writings of this pattern authoress. Poems, essays, novels, all reveal the same strong reliance upon the inner sense to perceive the true and the beautiful.

"The Infinite speaks in our silent hearts,
And draws our being to Himself, as deep
Calleth unto deep. He, who all thought imparts,
Demands the pledge, the bond of soul to keep;
But reason, wandering from its fount afar,
And stooping downward, breaks the subtile chain
That binds it to itself, like star to star,
And sun to sun, upward to God again.
Doubt, once confirmed, tolls the dead spirit's knell,
And man is but a clod of earth, to die
Like the poor beast that in his shambles fell—
More miserable doom than that to lie
In trembling torture, like believing ghosts,
Who, though divorced from good, bow to the Lord of Hosts."

The same voice is again heard in the sonnet, "Mental Solitude." Various as are the vehicles in which the genius of this author is carried to the world, we find none more suitable than the sonnet. The sonnet is, naturally, less used than those forms of verse where the writer is free from the restraint it imposes. Genius, however, has been pleased to lock it choicest treasures in the sonnet, from Dante down. May be it will, one day, again be fashionable to read it. We shall not speak so much of Mrs. Smith's familiar poems, preferring to ask the reader's attention to those somewhat neglected. None can fail to recognize the music of the upper air in the sonnet of the "Wayfarers:"

"Earth careth for her own. The fox lies down
In her warm bosom, and it asks no more.
The bird, content, broods in its lowly nest,
Or, its fine essence stirred, with wing outflown,
Circles in airy rounds to Heaven's own door,
And folds again its plume upon her breast.
Ye, too, for whom her palaces arise,
Whose Tyrian vestments sweep the kindred ground,
Whose golden chalice Ivy-Bacchus dies,
She, kindly mother, liveth in your eyes,
And no strange anguish may your lives astound.
But ye, O pale, lone watchers for the true,
She knoweth not. In her ye have not found
Place for your stricken heads, wet with the midnight dew."

In her dramas we believe Mrs. Smith to be at her hight. The student cannot but rejoice in them. The writer does not recall one "pretty" line in these writings; and when it is remembered that the author is a woman, the statement assumes somewhat of importance. No sparkle, no shimmer, no butterfly grace or spinning of cobwebs, but sober visions from the depths of thought. The poet looks in the face of her fellow creatures, and puts the one question, "What does it all mean?" She is ever searching, and the results of her inquiry are embodied in language worthy of the subject. Her peculiar cast of mind is strikingly exhibited in the little poem entitled "Presages:"

"There are who from their cradle bear
The impress of a grief,
Deep, mystic eyes, and forehead fair,
And looks that ask relief;
The shadows of a coming doom,
Of sorrow, and of strife,
Where Fates conflicting round the loom,
Wove the sad web of life.

"And others come, the gladsome ones,
All shadowless and gay,
Like sweet surprise of April suns,
Or music gone astray;
Arrested, half in doubt we turn
To catch another sight,
So strangely rare it is to learn
A presage of delight."

The reader may have read the "Ministering Spirits;" if so, he is asked to read it again:

"White-winged angels meet the child
On the vestibule of life,
And they offer to his lips
All that cup of mingled strife;
Mingled drops of smiles and tears,
Human hopes, and human fears,
Joy and sorrow, love and woe,
Which the future heart must know.

"Sad the smile the spirits wear,
Sad the fanning of their wings,
As in their exceeding love
Each a cup of promise brings;
In the coming strife and care,
They have promised to be there;
Bowed by weariness or grief,
They will minister relief.

"Lady, could the infant look
In that deep and bitter cup,
All its hidden perils know,
Would it quaff life's waters up?
Lady, yes, for in the vase,
Upward beams an angel face;
Deep and anguished though the sigh,
There is comfort lurking nigh—
Times of joy, and times of woe,
Each an angel presence know."

The poems of Mrs. Smith are addressed mainly to humanity, but Nature now and then receives a worthy tribute. A poem of Nature is selected for the closing quotation. The human element will intrude; and, after all, becomes, perhaps, the prominent feature:

"THE FIRST LEAF OF AUTUMN.

"I see thee fall, thou quivering leaf, of faint and yellow hue,
The first to feel the Autumn winds, that, blighting, o'er thee blew,
Slow-parted from the rocking branch, I see thee floating by,
To brave, all desolate and lone, the bleak autumnal sky.

"Alas! the first, the yellow leaf—how sadly falls it there,
To rustle on the crispéd grass, with every chilly air!
It tells of those that soon must drop all withered from the tree,
And it hath waked a sadder chord in deathless memory.

"Thou eddying leaf, away, away, there's sorrow in thy hue;
Thou soundst the knell of sunny hours, of birds, and liquid dew,
And thou dost tell how from the heart the blooms of hope decay—
How each one lingers, loath to part, till all are swept away."

A charming singer is Sarah Helen Whitman. She is filled with sweet sounds, and pours them forth as naturally as the bird. She has not the harmony of either of her sisters-in-song before mentioned; but she has their melody, and more. Not that she is over light—she is, on the other hand, thoughtful, though we may not say profound. She could write the "Ballads of the Fairies," and she could also write the "Hours of Life." She is a student, a genuine lover of her art; and what she touches she does not leave until it is finished. Whether her theme be lofty or low, the words follow one another like the strokes of a bell in the interpretation of her thought. She is a lyrist. Her instrument is the lyre, but she can also wake the grander voices of the organ. The arbutus itself is not more delicate than her description of it:

"There's a flower that grows by the greenwood tree,
In its desolate beauty, more dear to me
Than all that bask in the noontide beam,
Through the long, bright summer, by forest and stream.
Like a pure hope, nursed beneath Sorrow's wing,
Its timid buds from the cold moss spring,
Their delicate hues like the pink sea-shell,
Or the shaded blush of the hyacinth's bell,
Their breath more sweet than the faint perfume
That breathes from the bridal orange-bloom.

It is not found by the garden wall,
It wreathes no brow in the festal hall,
But it dwells in the depths of the shadowy wood,
And shines, like a star, in the solitude.
Never did numbers its name prolong,
Ne'er hath it floated on wings of song,
Bard and minstrel have passed it by,
And left it, in silence and shade, to die—
But with joy to its cradle the wild-bees come,
And praise its beauty with drowsy hum,
And children love, in the season of Spring,
To watch for its earliest blossoming."

Mrs. Whitman is always happy in her poems of Nature, endowing them usually with a human interest.

"No foliage droops o'er the woodpath now,
No dark vines swinging from bough to bough;
But a trembling shadow of silvery green
Falls through the young leaf's tender screen,
Like the hue that borders the snowdrop's bell,
Or lines the lid of an Indian shell.
And a fairy light, like the firefly's glow,
Flickers and fades on the grass below."

The description is continued with like exquisiteness of thought and diction; but the poem is not finished without these lines that fasten it to the heart:

"Yet sad would the spring-time of Nature seem
To the soul that wanders 'mid life's dark dream,
Its glory a meteor that sweeps the sky,
A blossom that floats on the storm-wind by,
If it woke no thought of that starry clime
That lies on the desolate shores of Time,
If it nurtured no delicate flowers to blow
On the hills where the palm and the amaranth grow."

With all our author's cheerfulness, the melancholy that will overlie the life of the sweetest singer has settled upon her own. The struggle to free herself from this shadow gave birth to her finest poem, "Hours of Life." Mrs. Whitman is not only gifted, but learned, and in this voyage of the soul from darkness into light, erudition is admirably mated with poetic skill. The following few lines may prove acceptable, though they convey but an imperfect idea of the complete poem:

"In the long noon-tide of my sorrow
I questioned of the eternal morrow;
I gazed in sullen awe
Far through the illimitable gloom
Down, deepening like the swift maelstrom,
The doubting soul to draw
Into eternal solitudes,
Where unrelenting silence broods
Around the throne of Law.

"I questioned the dim chronicles
Of ages gone before,
I listened for the triumph songs
That rang from shore to shore
Where the heroes and the conquerors wrought
The mighty deeds of yore,
Where the foot-prints of the martyrs
Had bathed the earth in gore,
And the war-horns of the warriors
Were heard from shore to shore."

The search is continued in the legendary haunts of many a land; when "wearied with man's discordant creed," the poet turns to Nature:

"A holy light began to stream
Athwart the cloud-rifts, like a dream
Of heaven; and lo! a pale, sweet face,
Of mournful grandeur and imperial grace—
A face whose mystic sadness seemed to borrow
Immortal beauty from that mortal sorrow—
Looked on me, and a voice of solemn cheer
Uttered its sweet evangels on my ear.

* * * * * * *

"Royally the lilies grow
On the grassy lea,
Basking in the sun and dew
Swinging in the breeze.

"Doth the wild fowl need a chart
Through the illimitable air?
Heaven lies folded in my heart:
Seek the truth that slumbers there—
Thou art Truth's eternal heir.

"Let the shadows come and go,
Let the stormy north wind blow,
Death's dark valley cannot bind thee
In its dread abode;

There the morning star shall find thee,
There the living God.
Sin and sorrow cannot hide thee,
Death and hell cannot divide thee
From the love of God."

Many a heart dwells fondly on the memory of a beautiful woman and poet, who, after comparatively a short life, purer even than anything she had written, died at New York some thirty years ago. Mrs. Frances Sargent Osgood was a delightful writer of prose, and a poet of no ordinary power; but her writing is like a veil between us and the author, behind which sits the woman, surpassing her loftiest utterance. One little poem may speak for her:

"SILENT LOVE.

"Ah! let our love be still a folded flower,
A pure moss rosebud, blushing to be seen,
Hoarding its balm and beauty for that hour
When souls may meet without the clay between!

"Let not a breath of passion dare to blow
Its tender, timid, clinging leaves apart;
Let not the sunbeam, with too ardent glow,
Profane the dewy freshness of its heart!

"Ah! keep it folded like a sacred thing—
With tears and smiles its bloom and fragrance nurse;
Still let the modest veil around it cling,
Nor with rude touch its pleading sweetness curse.

"Be thou content as I, to *know*, not *see*
The glowing life, the treasured wealth within—
To feel our spirit flower still fresh and free,
And guard its blush, its smile, from shame and sin!

"Ah, keep it holy! Once the veil withdrawn—
Once the rose blooms—its balmy soul will fly
As fled of old in sadness, yet in scorn,
Th' awakened god from Psyche's daring eye."

There are many of our female poets of whom we should speak; but anything like a complete review of this division of our subject would carry us far beyond the line allotted. The South has furnished her quota of women illustrious in prose and verse. Susan Archer Talley, Amelia B. Welby, Catherine Anne Warfield, Anna Peyre Dinnies, L. Virginia French, Rosa Vertner Johnson—all these are bright names. Miss Talley, a true descendant of the Huguenots, with a nature free as the winds and waters that were the playmates of her childhood, is a writer of decided character and merit. In one particular, she stands alone. Early in life she lost her hearing; and yet the music of her verse is such as satisfies the most sensitive ear. Shut out from the world, she turned within herself, and created a world of her own. Literature and the arts became daily sustenance; and her works thereafter attest a richness of intellectual and spiritual growth that is its own reward. "Ennerslie" is a poem, come from what source it may; but, from one hindered by so vital an infirmity as that of Miss Talley, it is indeed a triumph. Not only in the weirdness of the story, but in the harmony of its numbers, it rivals the creations of that master-artist, Edgar A. Poe. Two stanzas will suffice for illustration:

"Yet in that tower is a room
From whose fretted oaken dome
Weird faces peer athwart the gloom,
Mockingly—mockingly!
And there, beside the taper's gleam,
That maketh darkness darker seem,
As one that waketh in a dream,
Sits the lord of Ennerslie.

"Sitteth in his carvèd chair—
From his forehead, pale and fair,
Falleth down the raven hair,
Heavily—heavily:
There is no color in his cheek,
His lip is pale—he doth not speak—
And rarely doth his footstep break
The stillness of grim Ennerslie."

The critics are divided concerning the claim of Mrs. Welby. Poe declares that "she has nearly all the imagination of Maria dell' Occidente, with a more refined taste; and nearly all the passion of Mrs. Norton, with a nicer ear, and, what is surprising, equal art. Very few American poets are at all comparable with her, in the true poetic sense." This we believe to be the one extreme, and as far from the truth as the converse opinion that she is a happy compound of music and fancy. There was nothing in the life of this joyful woman to call up the passion that suffering awoke in the darkened heart of Mrs. Norton; neither could her nature have been as sensitive at the beginning. Passion and imagination do not strike us as characteristics of Mrs. Welby's poetry; but in native grace, spontaneous thought, and simplicity of diction, she stands on a level with the best of our authoresses. Her "Musings" is, in our estimation, not only an excellent exhibition of the author's peculiarity of genius, but a master production of its kind. Having read this poem, the reader is at once satisfied that the writer might accomplish much in other directions. The first two and last two stanzas must suffice for our quotation:

"I wandered out one summer night,
'Twas when my years were few,
The wind was singing in the light,
And I was singing, too.
The sunshine lay upon the hill,
The shadow in the vale,

And here and there a leaping rill
Was laughing on the gale.

"One fleecy cloud upon the air
Was all that met my eyes.
It floated like an angel there
Between me and the skies.
I clapped my hands and warbled wild,
As here and there I flew,
For I was but a careless child,
And did as children do.

* * * * * *

"I heard the laughing wind behind
A-playing with my hair—
The breezy fingers of the wind,
How cool and moist they were!
I heard the night-bird warbling o'er
Its soft, enchanting strain,
I never heard such sounds before,
And never shall again.

"Then wherefore weave such strains as these,
And sing them day by day,
When every bird upon the breeze
Can sing a sweeter lay?
I'd give the world for their sweet art,
The simple, the divine;
I'd give the world to melt one heart
As they have melted mine."

This necessarily imperfect paper will be brought to a close by a glance at the genius of Mrs. Warfield. The life of this lady has not been that of the true poet; but, in spite of her surroundings, she has disclosed certain qualities of mind rare among writers of either sex. The author of such a story as "The Household of Bouverie," and such a poem as "The Legend of the Indian Chamber," lifts herself by these productions to an honored place among the exponents of the tragic and the mysterious. Hers is a dangerous realm, but she travels it with steady step, and returns from her shadowy journeying unharmed, unwearied, and self-possessed. The reader does not need to know the story in order to appreciate this author's subtle command over the shapes of darkness, as it is exhibited in the last three stanzas of the "Indian Chamber:"

"Turned away the soul-sick stranger,
Traversed he the chamber high,
Where the Baron's awful aspect
Chained his step and fixed his eye.
Never from his memory perished,
Through long years of after life
In the camp, the court, the battle,
That remorseful face of strife.
Rooted as a senseless statue,
In his hand the cup of gold,
Lips apart, and eyes distended,
Stood the Norman Baron bold.

"High her cup the phantom lifted,
Flames within it seemed to roll;
Then alone these words she uttered,
'*Pledge me in thy feudal bowl.*'
Chained and speechless, guest and servant
Saw the Baron drain the draught;
Saw him fall, convulsed and blackened,
As the deadly bowl he quaffed;
Saw the Phantom bending o'er him,
As libation on his head,
Slowly, and with mein exulting,
From the cup of flames she shed.

"Then a shriek of smothered anguish
Rang the Indian chamber through,
While a gust of icy bleakness
From the waving arras blew,
In its breath the watchers shuddered,
And the portals open rung,
And the ample hearth was darkened,
As if the ice were on it flung;
And the lofty torches, waving
For a moment in the blast,
In their sconces were extinguished,
Leaving darkness o'er the past."

JOHN VANCE CHENEY.

PROTECTION OF ANIMALS USEFUL TO MAN.

Man has spread over the earth, and believes himself lord of it; but by his consumption, and still more by his waste, he has destroyed the balance of nature, and is depopulating both land and sea. He is a thriftless lord, who, if he continue his present habits, will leave a diminished heritage to his descendants. Now that the laws which govern life are to a great extent known, and the relations borne to each other by plants and animals are understood, it is in the power of mankind to check this loss by affording protection to all organisms which are useful to him, and also such as furnish food.

Protection against climate and inorganic influences is an important part of this protection, but will not be treated of here, since man recognizes its necessity as regards his domestic animals, while he is comparatively powerless in this respect as regards undomesticated, though useful, species.

Man's waste has lost the world many useful species, and, if not stopped, may lose many more. A few examples will prove this. The *rytina*, a marine herbivorous mammal, similar to the still existing manatee and dugong, the great auk, the dodo, and the solitaire, have all become extinct within comparatively recent times. The former, a native of Behring Sea, reached a length of thirty-five feet, and, from its cumbrousness, fell a ready prey to its Russian enemies, who slaughtered it so mercilessly that in less than a century what might have afforded a permanent store of food, through all time to come in a region where food is scarce, disappeared entirely from existence. The three others, birds with imperfect wings, unable to fly, but able to cope with their environment until the advent of man, were similarly hunted down by "those who go down to the sea in ships," and are now known only by pictures, bones, and relics. The gigantic moa birds of New Zealand have had a similar history, but in this case the Maori, instead of the Aryan, is responsible. Not only bones, but feathers and eggs, of these gigantic birds, some of the largest of which attained a height of from twelve to fourteen feet, have been found, and the natives have traditions of the moa-hunts in which they used to engage, surrounding the poor birds, and, with loud yells, driving them into a lake, where they could be killed from canoes without a chance to resist.

Many of the large quadrupeds now existing are destined, at the present rate of destruction, to complete disappearance, at least in their wild state, in a few generations. If the disappearance were confined to the larger *carnivores*, the loss could be endured. Mankind would probably prefer, on the whole, to view the lion, the tiger, and the bear in the safe retreat of a menagerie, rather than in their native wilds. But the extinction of the African elephant and the American bison will be a loss to mankind. Ruthlessly killed wherever met with, partly for the sheer pleasure of killing, partly for the sake of tusks that were once his defense, specialized for his own use, the elephant stands no chance in the struggle unless man have mercy. The bison once ranged from 62° to 25° north latitude, or from Great Slave Lake, in the north, to the north-eastern provinces of Mexico; while westward it extended to the Blue Mountains and the Sierra Nevada; and eastward it passed the Mississippi, and even the Alleghanies. Now it is limited to two small areas—one in western Kansas, north-western Texas, and the Indian Territory; the other about, and to the northward of, the sources of the Yellowstone. "At this present rate of decrease," says Allen, "it will certainly become wholly extinct during the next quarter of a century."

The elephant-seal (*Macrorhinus proboscideus*) was once common along the coast of Upper and Lower California, and abounded in many localities in the southern hemisphere, between 35° and 55° south latitude; but it was so persistently hunted, for the sake of its oil, that it disappeared almost entirely from our coasts, and became very rare even at Kerguelen Land, Heard's Island, and the Crozets. So scarce did it become that the chase was almost relinquished, and the result of only five undisturbed seasons was that in December, 1874, it was, according to J. H. Kidder, "very numerous" at the Crozet Islands.

In 1879 a schooner from San Francisco found nineteen of these animals on the coast of Lower California. At once the crew killed all but seven of the youngest, and they think it probable that the crew of another vessel killed the remainder.

The sea-elephant is the largest of the true seals, the males equaling, or exceeding, the almost equally unfortunate walrus in size. The facts given above tend to show that but a small amount of intelligent forbearance would enable this creature to again become abundant.

Even if the sheer waste of life indulged in by man for his whims, his pleasures, or his passions, were put an end to, and his destruction limited to what is required for food, it is certain that, without protection, and, in some cases, assistance, at the season of reproduction, many species required by him for food would not be able to keep up their numbers. Man recognizes this fact in the case of all such species of plants and animals as are immediately under his care, but usually ignores it in the case of undomesticated species, however useful they may be to him.

He is careful not to slay the cow with calf, or the ewe with lamb, but takes the fish when full of spawn, and gives neither seal nor whale a fair chance to reproduce its kind. He appears, in many instances, to have actually a notion that God will keep up the supply for his benefit, in spite of his efforts to put an end to it.

Yet the necessity for a "close time" for certain animals is beginning to be recognized. Already it is decreed, and, to a certain extent, observed, in the case of such beasts and birds as are denominated "game," and also with one of the most valuable kinds of food-fishes—the salmon. What is done is but the beginning of what will have to be done in this direction, if the supply is to be kept up.

That portion of our food which is derived from the land area of the globe is, in this respect, far more favorably situated than that derived from the water area. Although, unless care be taken to prevent it, such wild species of quadrupeds and birds as are useful to man are doomed to early extinction, yet at least he retains within his hands a less varied supply in his domesticated animals and plants.

But man's power over the water area is, and probably ever will be, more limited than over the land. The depths of the ocean are beyond his sway. The most that he can do is to traverse its surface with more or less safety, and to extend his rule around its shores. He cannot enter in and dwell there. The waters directly under his rule are only lakes, streams, and the borders of larger bodies of water. Yet his power, even over the harvest of the ocean, is, if intelligently directed, quite considerable.

As animal life in the ocean is under different conditions from that of the land, depending for respiration not upon the oxygen of the air, but upon that in the water, and for food almost entirely upon other animals, since plant life does not exist at great depths, man's efforts must be principally directed to keeping up the stock of animal food needed by the species upon which he feeds. That is to say, while upon the land he must keep up the supply of food-plants for the animals he feeds upon or requires, in the ocean his task is to keep up the supply of animal food required by species useful to him. To this end, a knowledge of the entire life-history, food, habits, and distribution of all kinds of marine organisms is needed, and this work is slowly, but surely, being carried on by unobtrusive workers scattered over the civilized world. When a full knowledge of these things is obtained, it will often be found quite feasible to protect any species in the reproduction of its kind.

This protection can be exercised in two ways. First, by ordaining a "close time," during which it shall be unlawful to catch the protected species; second, by artificial breeding. Most mammals and birds have a limited number of young, and, although it is possible to hatch the eggs of the latter artificially, yet, as the bird herself sits upon the eggs, the advantage is doubtful. But with fishes the case is different. The eggs, or ova, laid may often be tens or even hundreds of thousands in number, yet the species does not increase in numbers, even when man's hand does not tax it heavily. As the mass of ova is fertilized after it is laid, by the squeezing over it of the milt of the male, a large proportion is never fertilized at all. As the eggs are deposited upon the bottom of the stream or sea-bed, currents and storms, and the accidental passing of objects over the spot, cause many to be washed away and destroyed. Still larger quantities are eaten. Every predatory fish is on the watch for ova, and the little fishes get even with the large ones by devouring their spawn. Even the parent fish will, in many cases, devour her own offspring.

All this has been successfully remedied in the case of salmon, trout, and a few other fishes, and can as well be remedied in other cases. The ripe ova are gently pressed through the oviduct of the female, which is then released. The ripe milt of the male is pressed out over the ova, and carefully mixed, to insure fertilization. The ova are cared for in tanks, constructed to suit the habits of the species, and, after hatching, are placed in the water to take their chance. In this way, out of about sixteen thousand eggs yielded by a salmon of twenty pounds in weight, fifteen thousand may, according to our Fish Commissioners, be made to produce fish.

Apply the same ratio to other fish, and we shall begin to see how much can be done toward increasing the harvest of the waters, by at the same time supplying fish and finny food for fishes. Were this process followed methodically throughout the world with all the most useful species, the increase, if destructive agents were kept down, would be limited only by the power of the ocean to supply life.

The invertebrate habitants of the waters, some useful directly to us, all useful as food for fishes, can also be, to a great extent, protected. Though a "close time" can hardly be extended to them, the increase of the species can be cared for in the same way as is that of oysters —by beds, pounds, or preserves, within which they can multiply, free from enemies.

The *crustacea* (crabs, lobsters, shrimps) need no artificial fertilizing, since, as in birds and mammals, the ova are fertilized before extrusion, but they may advantageously be bred in ponds.

When those regions of the earth now held by savage, barbarous, or semi-civilized tribes falls into the hands of nations which have among them a few who study the actual book of life—and the time, judging by recent acquisitions, is not very far distant —we may hope that the protection of a "close time," during which they may bear and suckle their young, will be extended to such mammals as the bison, the elephant, the walrus, the elephant-seal, and the whale, and that all birds, except such as are notoriously injurious to man's interests, will be granted a term in which they can hatch their young in security.

Although plant life in general is essential to animal life, there are many plants which are deleterious in their nature, and more which are useless from man's point of view, since they do not furnish food for animals under his protection, or crowd out more useful plants. The protection of useful plants against their rivals is thus really the protection of animals against plants, because the prevalence of comparatively useless species is a check upon animal life. But besides these indirectly injurious plants there are certain plants possessed of toxic qualities, which, though no more inimical to rival plants than others not possessed of such qualities, cannot safely be allowed to flourish where domestic cattle are kept. As an example may be cited the *loco (Astragalus Menziesii)*, by which cattle in California are often poisoned.

The class of *fungi*, so protean in its forms and qualities, not only furnishes species which are poisonous to animals, but it also contains forms which live upon and often destroy animal organisms. Insects and fishes are frequently killed by molds, which multiply within them to such an extent that they are forced to succumb. The death of the former is often no loss in itself, so far as mankind is concerned, but the dead insects, filled with fungoid spores, are themselves a source of danger.

A glance in a fish tank will but too frequently reveal the ravages of *fungi*. Patches of mold may be seen upon the sides of the fishes—a miniature forest borne about with them as they swim. These are mischievous enough, but below them are still lower plants—agents of putrefaction—the vibrios, bacteria, and spirales, those mysteriously appearing living particles, which have been the mainstay of the believers in spontaneous generation. Many of these are the sure accompaniments of certain fevers, and in some cases the origin of the disease has been traced to them. While some doctors still deny this, and others as strenuously maintain that all diseases are caused by parasitic living cells, the germs of which are to be found in the air, the facts point to at least its partial truth, tending to show that while some diseases are caused by living agents, others are more probably caused by some alteration in the secretions of the body, induced by external causes.

In the words of Dr. Wythe: "Every agency of nature outside of the bodily organism, and every activity of body and of mind within the living structure, is capable of becoming a cause of disease, as soon as it disturbs the normal current of life, so that the number of causes is practically unlimited."

The protection of flocks, herds, and poultry from quadrupeds and ravenous birds is tolerably well effected by mankind, at least in civilized countries. The problem has to a great extent been solved, as it will have to be solved over the entire face of the globe, if population should largely increase; the larger beasts of prey are driven to the recesses of forest or mountain, or are exterminated, while the smaller are kept down with shot-guns and traps. It is not improbable that the only lions and tigers of some future generation will be those bred in captivity.

But the most dangerous enemies of ourselves and of our animals are not the vertebrata, but the myriad forms of insects, and those protean organisms, the internal worms. The insect has things very much his own way in the world—he is victor over the vertebrate, though worsted individually, by sheer numbers, power of reproduction, and ability to elude search. The tsetse fly, which renders large portions of Africa impassable by horses, oxen, and dogs, but does not attack man; gnats, fleas, lice, bugs, mosquitos, black-flies, ox-flies, the *Asilus crabroniformes*, are so many free parasites, living upon the bodies of animals and men, and for the most part sucking their blood; the chigo, free when young, is when adult parasitic on man and on his animals; the ichneumon larvæ feed upon those of the lepidoptera, and do not spare the silk-worm because it is useful to man; the curious young of the blister-beetles, known as triungulins, cling to bees and other hymenopterous insects, and thus obtain access to their nests and thrive on their honey; the gad-flies pass their early stages within mammals. These are but a few of the insects that exist upon other animals. Among the arachnida the lower forms *(Acaridæ)* are both troublesome and dangerous. Most mammals have their peculiar species of acari; the horse has two, which give rise to skin affections; man has the itch from another, bees are killed by another; ticks *(Ixodes)* attack dogs, sheep, and other quadrupeds, living free on the bushes until some mammal passes; birds swarm with acari. The crustacea, insects of the water, do for fishes and cetacea what the insects and arachnids do for birds and mammals, thus taking a sort of revenge for the consumption of free crustacea by larger animals. The isopoda live in the mouths and among the gills of fishes, taking toll from the food, while some penetrate the skin, and others prefer to live beneath the carapace of of higher crustaceans; the female lerneans, free when young, attach themselves by the mouth, when older, to the eyes, fins, or other parts of fishes, lose their limbs, and become swollen masses ending in two ovisacs, bearing upon their bodies the minute males, who retain their limbs and senses; while barnacles fix themselves on whales.

The internal worms are almost endless in their forms and in their metamorphoses. The filariæ, free when young, are introduced with food—or, more often, water—into the bodies of molluscs, fishes, amphibians, birds, and mammals, where they multiply exceedingly; and trematode-worms (flukes—*Monostomum* and *Distomum*), pass their entire lives as parasites, changing their hosts and changing their shape, and frequenting fishes, mammals, birds, and other animals. The whale, the sturgeon, the herring, the seal, the sheep, all are troubled with distomes in the liver, and man is far from being free from their presence.

Tape-worms abound in the digestive organs of almost every class in the animal kingdom, and their immature forms traverse the tissues, and become what are known as "cestoid" worms within such organs as the brain, the liver, the kidney, or the eye. The tape-worms of herbivorous animals pass their young stages in the water or on plants; those of carnivores inhabit their prey, and only become adult tape-worms when eaten by proper species. These various parasites, and many other forms, do not always kill. On the contrary, a healthy animal will often carry about many of them. Yet we have but to mention the dreaded *trichina* (a *nematode*, or round worm), and the tape-worm, to prove that they have the power to injure man. There can be no doubt that an excess of even the comparatively innocent kinds injures the host, or that a weakly organism may fail beneath its internal burden.

Now that the life-history of most of these dreaded parasites is known, it is possible to avoid their presence, and to this end the eating of uncooked or partially cooked food, and the drinking of water that has not been boiled, must alike be avoided. Heat kills the young of worms, as it does germs of all kinds; and, when we consider how abundant the ova of these parasites are, we may doubt whether man does not, to a great extent, owe his supremacy and increase of numbers to the fact that he alone, of all animals, subjects his food to heat. Good cookery, therefore, is, even from this point of view alone, a large part of the science of life.

The carnivores of the ocean, the sharks and rays, and the toothed cetacea, play havoc among our food-fishes, and need to be checked in their increase. This can be best done by utilizing them. Sharks furnish oil—one species is taken for its oil on the coast of California. Sharks' fins are a delicacy in China, and white races eat some of the rays. The flesh of sharks and rays would furnish good and cheap food for the poor.

When man needs any animal for food or in the arts, its numbers soon decrease unless he takes steps to prevent it, and, in the case of the sharks and rays, as well as of the dolphins, the decrease is a benefit to man, permitting more useful species to increase.

W. N. Lockington.

FRITZ REUTER'S LIFE AND WORKS.

"Qui vir, et dialectum patriam et sensus animi patrios callet; quem eundem Gratiæ ipsæ Musis conjunctæ jocis miscere seria docuerunt; cujus scriptoris quum alia opera tum etiam librum aureolum hunce OLLE CAMELLEN, Germania laudat universa."

A friendly Kiel critic of my first article (upon Groth, Ditmarsch, and Plattdeutsch, in the February number of THE CALIFORNIAN) seems to think that there is a thread of half apology running through it in behalf of the Low German, and ascribes it, in a charitable spirit, to my wish to overcome the supercilious "pride of the English race," toward a kindred but humbler tongue—a poor cousin, as it were. It may be that there was such a tinge unconsciously given to the essay; but if any prejudice exists in the American mind as to Low German (a premise I do not wish to concede), it has assuredly sprung from exotic seeds planted there by fastidious High Germans. There is a class of Germans who, in discussing Plattdeutsch with Americans, leave an incorrect impression as to the social *status* of the less cultivated tongue, not so much in the facts they offer, as in the impression left, to be derived from those facts. There is still another class, who (not being quite at ease as to their own educational ground) fancy that any suspicion of the *platt* in their language would be a social blot—a proof of vulgarity. Of this order was that lady, introduced in a modern German novel, who assumed to be an oracle in culture by reason of being the daughter of a professor, and who reproved her docile husband for saying *hippodrom*, instead of *hippotraum*, "because *drom* was so *platt!*" No language or dialect is in itself mean; nor can any dialect beget vulgarity; on the other hand, vulgarity degrades any language it employs, no matter how noble it may have been in origin. Tuscan has, ever since Dante and Boccaccio, been the cultivated language of Italy; but, for all that, the proud Venetian retained his own soft dialect. It accompanied him everywhere; even in his courts, where the pleadings were entered in Tuscan, the arguments of the advocates were in Venetian; and it proved the chief feature of as bright a period of the drama as Italy ever saw, when Goldoni wrote down his plays in his native idiom. Under such circumstances, no speech, or phase of speech, could be anything but dignified. Broad Scotch has never been relegated to an inferior social position. It has been the garb of lyric and elegiac poetry; it has been the solvent for wit in the drawing-room; it has intensified the humorous sally of the advocate, and has furnished its harmony to the lecture-room of the professor. So much for the dignity of dialect, provided, of course, we take dialect in its scientific and good sense, and do not confound it with disintegrating language. A bronze medal may not be of greater intrinsic bullion value than a debased coin; but, in that it is genuine, it is meritorious, which the greasy coin is not. Chinook is a tatter fit only for the worst days of Babel; Pigeon English is disgusting—Confucius himself would be contemptible if he attempted to converse in it. If ever a Chinese admiral blockades our harbor, and dictates a surrender in Pigeon English (and who can say what is in store for us?), he would probably be listened to with inextinguishable laughter.

Slang is distorted metaphor and corrupt speech at the same time, both of which vices, like a pair of bow legs, give it a harlequin, pigeon-toed air. Bret Harte's "Heathen Chinee" is simply a well arranged chain of slang; and he ought to have been ashamed to offer it in pawn for fame, when he had far better stuff in his scrip at the time. James Russell Lowell's *Biglow Papers* may be considered partly in the light of dialect, partly as an attempt to represent a peculiar local pronunciation, and partly as the angular wit of one class of American society—not precisely slang, and yet which looks at times very like the boldest order of slang. Artemus Ward wrote the *patois* of the billiard room and country hotel—an *argot* that would, and did, enable him to discuss the broadest questions of philosophy, politics, and art with the average crowd for which one has the bar-keeper "set up the drinks."

But I must return to my subject, having announced that my platform (a vile Americanism, *mein lieber Freund*) contains a plank for the due support of the social and literary dignity of all twigs of the great Teutonic or Gothic branch of articulate speech, whether written or unwritten. And, in one respect at least, I would suggest an advantage which the German has over the English limb of the Teutonic tree: when High German wears out in spots, as all languages are fated to do, by constant use, the High German has a choice lot of archaic material at hand, in the shape of Plattdeutsch, with which he can mend his tongue—expressions, phrases, constructions known to the elder Cethegi of the race, which can be used without violence to taste. But when our English tongue rusts out, we have nothing wherewith to patch it, except chunks of slang, or euphuistic soft-solder, imported from Gaul. It is interesting to notice the dainty efforts of the Laureate, now and then, to substitute an ancient word in lieu of a trite modern phrase, like old tiles set in a new chimney-piece; but it is evidence that the language is disintegrating.

In the former article I undertook to treat of thought worked into a quaint and novel language, under peaceful auspices, in "a land where all things always seemed the same," and where the poet would appear to have drawn the georgic tranquillity into his blood, and to have reinfused it into his verse and prose—a sort of Teutonic Theocritus, in fact.

Now, I must speak of a widely different character, laboring, if not in the same field, at least just over the hedge, and obtaining a different success, although reaching it by the same paths.

Groth's *Quickborn* is a felicitous chain of lyrics; and the work may fairly be placed as the first serious employment of the dialect in which it was composed for two centuries, if we leave out of consideration the dilettant efforts of Voss and a few others, who, in times past, for amusement, noted the possible capacity of the common tongue for literary effort.

Groth has written prose tales; but these efforts, so far as concerns the matter of them, might as well have been idyls; for verse would have suited eminently their pastoral character.

On the other hand, Fritz Reuter first appeared as a writer of verse. But though his *Läuschen un Rimels* won great success, and brought him a degree of provincial fame, I consider that collection as no evidence of brilliancy that would give promise of his future work. It was, as he says, an "assembly of street urchins," amusing from their dirty faces and mirthful ways, but with nothing to indicate what they would be when grown to manhood. They were like tavern signs, on which a great painter may have labored before his genius had been hailed by the world of culture.

And although Fritz Reuter wrote poems, and long ones, too, it is as the prose sketch-writer that he is to be deemed most successful. This is not to disparage his poetic talent, which blossoms out of everything he said or wrote. It is simply an attempt to establish an approximative standpoint from which to consider him in discussion. If Burns were to be taken as a Scotch type of Groth, the Ettrick Shepherd might bear some resemblance to Reuter.

Fritz Reuter was born in Stavenhagen, Mecklenburg-Schwerin, November 7, 1810. In the Rathhaus, where Fritz first saw light, the enthusiastic burghers, in 1873, placed a commemorative tablet to his honor, having, in 1865, already planted a "Reuter Oak."

The town is in the midst of a flat country, here and there a bit of rising ground called ostentatiously a mountain, with little lakes as resting places for the sluggish streams. The inhabitants, both gentle and simple, have their interests mainly centered in the crops, wheat being the staple—a land of slow-moving, reflective, perhaps a little sly, peasantry—men loath to grasp at new ideas, with a ponderously careful tread, as if progress were being made over wide furrows, with constant danger to the grain below.

Stavenhagen (*plattd.* Stemhagen) was ruled in those days, and for generations thereafter (1805-45), by Fritz's father, as *Burgermeister* (a sort of mayor, with certain criminal and other conciliatory jurisdiction.) Fritz's mother was one of those typical, patient invalids, full of kindness and cultivation, a queen *fainéante* in her household, carrying for scepter her knitting needles, regarded by all, high and low, with affection and chivalrous courtesy, elicited by her helplessness and bodily suffering. It was probably to her nature that Fritz owed his literary leanings, his powers of humorous observation, and his tact and gentle charity in expression. It certainly was not from his father that he drew any of these gifts. His father was a shrewd, common-sense official, full of plans which he carried out with success, bound up in his daily life and duties, and conscientious in performance, a man of stalwart power and passions, filling his part in life amply and creditably.

Fritz has, in "*Ut de Franzosentid*," given us a vivid picture of life at Stavenhagen in his infancy. With a masterly hand, he has drawn for us an outline of the Amtshauptmann (Prefect of District) Weber, a grand old figure, something of a tyrant in his way, looked up to by both burgher and peasant, and of his wife, a worthy counterpart. Then there is an "Uncle Herse," who, however, was no uncle at all, but who had that make-up of character and habits which brings the child inevitably to claim some irresponsible relationship with him—a man who was clever, who knew what the birds said, and could answer them—a treasure to any community of children anywhere. Then there was Fritz's mother's sister, "Tante Christiane;" there was Mademoiselle Westphalen; there was the "Watchmaker Droz," a *real* Frenchman (aus Neufchâtel), employed to teach Fritz a proper accent.

Fritz did not, for his first years, attend the public school, but took his lessons with his sister, Lisette, and his two cousins, Ernst and August. Finally, he went to a girl's school, "an owl among the crows." Uncle Herse taught him arithmetic and drawing; the town apothecary, Latin and history; his father, geography; and so his training went on, in a straggling way, until a theological student appeared in the house as a regular pedagogue. When Fritz was fifteen, he lost his mother by death, and, at about the same time, was placed at school in the little town of Friedland, Mecklenburg-Strelitz. Of his life there (it lasted three years), there is a quaint picture drawn in "Dörchlauchting."

At this time Fritz had thoughts of becoming a painter; his more prosaic father preferred the law. Neither was right; but Fritz gave to art a better chance than to jurisprudence. He was sent to the gymnasium at Parchim. In 1831 he went to the University at Rostock, "the up-and-down jump for every true Mecklenburger," as he terms it. In half a year he left Rostock for Jena, and became an altogether too gay member of the Burschenschaft there. It was here that he committed the offense which led to his subsequent conviction of an attempt at high treason, sentence to death, followed by commutation to imprisonment for life, then softened to thirty years, and finally remitted, after he had served seven years of misery, and had lost the flower of his days in aimless trifling within prison walls.

It was the misfortune of the young man that in those days the German governments comprehended so little the radical leaven which must, at a certain age, work into a ferment in the veins of most educated youth. Had Fritz played the same class of political pranks at an English university, perhaps the college dons would have looked after him with some degree of nervousness, and would have given him an admonition now and then; but to have ranked him as a criminal would have been, in their eyes, downright absurdity. In an American college, such talk or conduct might have brought a jocular criticism from the rhetorical professor, who, with his gibes, would have patronized the sophomoric reformer into conservatism. Dilettant radicalism has long been regarded by English and American professors as an amiable dronebee in the youthful bonnet, that must finish up a certain amount of buzzing before it assumes a duly conservative torpidity, or is kicked out of the hive altogether by ideas of a honey-gathering class.

The Germanic authorities in those days had, however, the blood of Kotzebue in their eyes, and they fancied every top-booted, velvet-coated, be-ribboned student to be a possible Karl Sand. They make cabinet ministers out of such stuff nowadays. Witness Baron Haymerle.

The prominent facts of Fritz's trouble are these: There was found to be a student conspiracy ramifying all the universities. Some silly fellows did actually commit an overt riot and sedition at Frankfurt. Fritz was captured in Berlin (he had left Jena, and had gone thither to study law), was tried, and commenced his seven years' life in the different military prisons (Festungen) to which he was relegated, finally winding up, as an act of grace, at Dömitz, under his own Grand Duke; and, at last, being freed altogether, on the death of the King of Prussia—a broken young man, with a passion for strong drink (Trunksucht) that never again entirely forsook him, but was the vampire of his life and powers.

In 1840, at the instance of his father, he went to Heidelberg to study jurisprudence; but, owing to his unhappy tendency to alcoholism, he was recalled, and started afresh on a new career as a farmer. Herein he might have succeeded but for his disease. At this time he met his future wife, Luise Kuntze. In 1844 he completed his education as a farmer; but his "Stromtid" was still a failure, for the old reason; and in 1845 his father died, having finally despaired of his son's reform, and making in his will a guarded testamentary trust, by the terms of which Fritz was not to touch his share of the succession until he had shown signs of freedom from the drink trouble for a term of years. Fritz never abstained for the period, and was never let into the possession of the fund.

He had one good friend, however, who held him patiently up during this period of his life, one Fritz Peters, to whose sympathy and care he probably owed his life, and to whom the public possibly owe his works. At this time he commenced to write—trifles, maybe, but it was a training for success.

In those days broke out the 1848 excitement. Of course the old Freiheit must began to effervesce in the veins of Reuter, and he attempted what we Americans would call "going into politics." He was a deputy at the Town's Diet at Güstrow, and then a delegate to the Assembly for both Mecklenburgs; but the movement never came to anything, and, indeed, that sort of business was not in Reuter's vein, as an incident would seem to show: He was acting as President of a Reform League established at Stavenhagen. Of course, the members had an agricultural slowness of comprehension. This was too much for the patience of so nervous a politician as Fritz, and, amid the regrets of the assembly, he laid down the gavel. He was pressed to give his reasons for declining the office. The good-natured burghers desired, if possible, to conform to his views, and retain him. But Fritz made for the door, and reaching it, shouted, "You wish to know why I leave?" There was a general stillness of expectation. "Ji sid mi all tau dumm, ji Schapsköpp" (you are all too stupid for me, you sheepheads), and vanished. Such a man was not stuff for a popular orator; at least, he would make small headway here in a Sand-lot demonstration.

At this time he started in vocation as a private teacher. Still the old trouble. His bride then married him, in hopes to reform him, and in 1851 they commenced life together at Treptow. The wife seems to have been a real helpmate and sympathizer. She never was able to say that she had driven off the arch enemy, but her presence probably kept the demon at bay most of the time.

Now it was that the poor fellow commenced his work as an author; and, to do so in the projected manner, it became almost necessary for him to relearn his Plattdeutsch. The trifles he had hitherto produced, of a doubtful merit and merely local interest, were in High German. Klaus Groth's *Quickborn* had but just appeared, and it struck the needy pedagogue that something of a similar character in the Mecklenburg dialect would be popular, at least within the boundaries of the duchies. In that country there is a great degree of popularity given to what we might call "yarns," for the want of a better word *(Geschichte)*. Fritz had been in the habit of versifying these, and, having collected a quantity, launched out with great rashness in business, as both publisher and author. These first endeavors he styled *Läuschen un Rimels*—"a mob of little street urchins, who, in ruddy health, tumble over one another, unrestrained as to æsthetic poses—jolly faces, laughing out from under tow locks, and finding, at times, their fun in the world's folly." The success of this venture was wonderful. The edition, consisting of twelve hundred copies, was sold off briskly, and, though his reputation did not yet pass beyond his native Plattdeutsch land, yet his success as an author was established. This work has a quaint dedication to his old, well-tried friend, Fritz Peters.

De Reis' nah Belligen followed—a story, in verse, of the adventures of Vadder Witt and Vadder Swart, two respectable peasants, who with their sons, Corl and Fritz, project and partially make a journey to Belgium, for purposes of culture and traveled experience. The excursion is one of ludicrous misfortune, winding up in the police station in Berlin, whence the party return home to be tongue-castigated by their less adventurous and more conservative wives. There is the thread of a love story, with Fritz and the sexton's daughter for hero and heroine, which terminates happily on the arrival home of the traveled party.

At about this time (1855) our author began the publication of a weekly journal, *Unterhaltungsblatt für beiden Mecklenburg und Pommern*. It was in this that he first introduced to his readers his most distinct and remarkable character, the jovial "*immeritirter Entspekter* Bräsig," who wrote characteristic letters to the journal about matters and things of interest to himself and the public. To any admirer of Dickens, who has not also read Reuter, it would be a pleasure worth a whole philological journey through High German, Low German, and Messingsch, to shake hands with the Inspector. It is impossible to give, in any language but his, the cream of his utterances. His style is his own. However, the character was, at this period, only outlined, and it was not until some some time later that Bräsig became an active mover in Reuter's fiction. On the German stage he became, eventually, a leading character—as marked, as definite, as our American "Joshua Whitcomb."

The journal lived but a year. The publisher left his affairs in disorder, and decamped for America. Fritz at this time took up his residence in New Brandenburg.

His next production was a tragic sort of idyl, *Kein Husing* (No Housing. *Anglice*, no right of settlement in the parish.) It was, in his own estimation, his chief work. A young peasant, desirous of marrying the girl whom he loves, is thwarted in procuring the legal solemnization of the marriage, for the reason that he is unable to furnish the necessary evidence that they will not become a charge on the public, it being necessary, under the local laws, that the pair should have a legal abode, and he, employment. He is prevented from this by the machinations of the young Squire, who has cast covetous eyes on the poor girl. The impatient desires of the peasant lovers getting the better of their prudence, the time approaches when their indiscretion becomes known. The young aristocrat and the peasant have a dispute; the peasant strikes the gentleman dead, and disappears as an outlaw; the young mother becomes an outcast, and goes crazy, and her infant boy, at her death, falls to the protection of the old servant, once the friend of the father. The father returns from America, and hears the story of his bride's death, and takes the child with him to his new home. The moral of the tale is the working of a *quasi* system of villeinage, which takes from the serf his freedom while he is practically at least *adscriptus glebæ*. While it is a *possible*, yet it can hardly be a *typical*, state of affairs, even in Mecklenburg.

Ut de Franzosentid next followed. This is in prose; and for freshness and delicacy of character drawing there can be nothing superior in sketch writing. Each person stands out as plain as if morally photographed, and there is variety enough, there are people enough, and material enough, to furnish up a three-volume novel.

There are no finer gentlemen in all Thackeray than Amtshauptann Wewer and Colonel von Toll. Uncle Herse would add a charm to Pickwick, if he only could be posthumously inserted, as binders sometimes insert a rare plate in a work for which it was not originally meant.

Mademoiselle Westphalen is as sweet a woman as ever was; and the peasant characters, headed by the miller, the rear brought up by the "Uhrmacher Droz," in his French regimentals, are wonderful in their way. The miller's daughter is a gem. In short, Fritz has cast a halo about the picture of his childhood; and in the center of it he has placed his sick mother, knitting away and receiving the chivalrous homage of the old Amtshauptmann.

Hanne Nüte (short for Master Johann Snut), or *de lütte Pudel*, is "*'ne Vagel un Minschengeschicht*," or tale of men and birds, which, if properly read to children, with becoming attention to dramatic recitation and onomatopy, in giving the human dialogue and the bird business, would prove a genuine delight to any healthy crowd of young persons we know—provided, of course, they knew the tongue.

The "Little Poodle" (so called on account of her curly head) is a good little child of a poverty-stricken family, the station in life of which puts her socially beneath Hanne, the son of the village smith. She is out with the children, tending the geese, when the old gray gander takes it into his head to bite the baker, a well-to-do, but bad man. The surly baker, indignant at the laughter excited, visits his wrath upon the innocent Little Poodle, when Hanne appears as her defender, and intervenes with a blow to the discomfitted baker. Hanne "gets it," on his return home, for his heroism. The course of true love is broken by the disparity of social *status*, and by Hanne's departure on his Wandering Year as apprentice.

He takes leave of his friends, and, among them, of the old rector, with whom he has a glass of wine, and who breaks into a spasm of enthusiasm over his own student life at Jena, to the great terror of his wife, who fears he may have taken a drop too much.

Hanne sets out. The birds convene; the duties are assigned as may best befit the different feathered families; and under the leadership of the solemn Adebor (stork), a general campaign of observation is entered upon for the protection of the Little Poodle's love interests. Hanne is exposed to various trials. Among his experiences, he is employed by a boxom young widow, who tempts him to stop and take up the abandoned sledge of her good man. She attacks him, after the manner of her sex, with good eatables; she pours out for him the most enticing cups of chocolate; she potters about him as he drinks it.

"Un leggt vör lütt Trurigkeit
Sick sacht in Hannern sinen Arm
Un de oll Jung'; de tröst't un ei't
Un dorbi ward em gor tau warm—
'T is mäglich von de Schockelor."

(And leans, her sorrow moving her,
So gently back on Hanne's arm:
And he—he plays the comforter,
And grows, unwitting, all too warm—
Quite likely 'twas the chocolate.)

But he is reminded by a sudden strain of the nightingale, who is in the bird conspiracy in in favor of the Poodle, of his sweetheart at home, and, forthwith, he starts up, tells the widow the truth, and quits her with just as little resentment in her heart as it is possible for a true woman to have, under the circumstances. He reaches the Rhine, and there he comes to grief. He is arrested for the murder of a poor Jew peddler, on the circumstance that some of the Jew's property is found on him. How the birds turn in and help him; how the widow befriends him; how the rich baker is found to be the murderer; and how Hanne and the Poodle become united, and how the stately Adebor looks down the chimney of the newly married pair,

"Dunn seggt hei: 'So is dit
Adjüs! Wenn't Frühjohr wedder kümmt
Denn bring' ick jug wat mit.
Passt up! Dat sall vör Allen
Grossmutter Schnutsch gefallen.'"

it being the custom in North Germany (as also detailed by Hans Andersen) for the storks to supply any call for babies, they, as importers, having a "corner" in that trade.

He also wrote at this period (1858–63), *Ut mine Festungstid.* This pathetic comic history of his prison life shows the man in a charming light. There is no bitterness in it—nothing but gentleness and humor. The military officers with whom he came in contact are all treated with fairness. There is no petty grumbling, and, while the account of the manly Colonel, a compatriot who was so thoughtful of the poor boy's situation, as related in the first part of his story, has something tragic in it, the scene of the kind, superannuated old commandant in charge of Dömitz, and his lovely family, would strike any one as the perfection of homely humor. It is quite likely that perhaps the military officers of that day were not as apprehensive of political danger as the civilians, and were, therefore, possibly less given to cruelty in the line of their duty.

The *Olle Camellen* series is probably the most pretentious of all Fritz Reuter's productions; and whatever criticisms might be thrown out as to the "sketchiness" of the stories, they are no weaker in that respect than the corresponding period in the labors of Dickens and Thackeray. It is on a plane with these two authors that we would place Fritz. His career did not extend as far, but his efforts are worthy the same order of praise. *Ut mine Stromtid* has in it the germ of a new *Vicar of Wakefield.* There is purity of delineation in every character. Dickens could never draw a gentleman well, Thackeray found it hard to color up his lady portraitures with proper intensity, but poor Fritz had a tact in both lines, which, if developed, would have made his books something wonderful.

After reading *De Olle Camellen*, one cannot but feel that in those little villages of Mecklenburg there are people the equal of any Scotch Covenanter or New England Puritan for rabid devotion to principle, and that throughout the wheat fields, and along the little ponds they call lakes, there is enough kindness of heart and delicacy of feeling to civilise all Russia and Turkey, if it could only be distilled into them. Germany will never drop to pieces as long as there are Havermanns and his kind to bind the sheaves together. A country that has so much force of character, morality, and shrewdness, lying, as it were, fallow in every farm and village, cannot be wondered at that it flings into fame in each generation its full measure of great men, and that, when its enemies commence to swarm, it finds a hero in every flaxen poll summoned from the plow or the stable.

As long as the Plattdeutsch oak flourishes, and the Plattdeutsch speech is uttered, so long will there be a German Empire and a German voice in the councils of worldly government. Fritz Reuter lived to see his writings eagerly read from one end of Germany to the other. He lived to enjoy the honors of aristocratic governments, without yielding a jot of his independence; to find his boyish vagary of a united Germany a reality, and to see the colors, for the wearing of which he took such severe punishment in his youth, the emblem of German victory. He lived to receive the favor and encomium of the great German Chancellor, whose wit and humor, and whose appreciation of wit and humor and their attendant pathos, are said to be as profound as his statesmanship. When the Franco-Prussian war broke out, Reuter was a practical patriot to the marrow, albeit there is a tenderness in the little lyrics which he then wrote which shows how deeply he appreciated the private woes that find their hot-bed growth on the field of battle. In the latter years of his life, however, his malady crowded more persistently upon him. His later volumes, while marked at times with flashes of the fire that makes his writings so charming, still show that the foul fiend was at his elbow more frequently than ever. The "Journey to Constantinople" is a bit of humorous romance, combining his own souvenirs of the tour made by him in 1864 with the comic adventures of two rival Mecklenburg families, who are supposed to make the excursion. It is only a half success, though in it there are still traces of the old spirit. "Dörchlauchting" (His Little Serene Highness) also appeared at about this time.

In 1874 he died, in the full enjoyment of a personal and literary popularity which only genius and national sympathy could explain. He had acquired a moderate fortune by his works, and had been settled for some years before his death at Eisenach. The disease which ended his life was some affection of the heart; but his morbid passion for alcohol was probably the remote cause.

I have not been able, in the foregoing slight biography, and in the one of Groth, to give a clear outline of the Groth and Reuter influence upon German social literature. The limits of a magazine article have already been too far trespassed upon. Nor have I, in either of the two Plattdeutsch essays, paid such regard to the bibliography of the two authors as, in these days of exact information, befits a review in any branch of literature. I must, however, refer the reader to Adolph Wilbrandt's biography of Reuter, to which I am indebted for most of the facts of Reuter's life. If one were to give an account of the Plattdeutsch reading clubs and social organizations that have sprung into existence in the last twenty years, it would be almost a literary history of North Germany. No such enthusiasm for any given branch of literature has been stirred since the days when Petrarch, Boccaccio, and their contemporaries labored for the spread of classical learning.

I must close this article, however, by saying that, if it seems to an English reader bold and unwarrantable in its enthusiasm, it is because I cannot bring Reuter out of the field in which he has flourished any more than I could transplant to California the oak which flourishes in his honor at Stavenhagen. One can bring across the ocean the hard, impenetrable pillars of Egypt; but the oak tree drops his leaves, and seems, after transportation, to be nothing but firewood.

DE EIKBOM.—THE PLATTDÜTSCH OAK.

AUS HANNE NÜTTE.

Ik weit einen Eikbom, de steiht an de See,
  De Nurdstorm, de brus't in sin Knast,
Stolz reckt hei de machtige Kron in de Höh;
  So is dat all dusend Johr west;
      Kein Minschenhand,
      De hett em plant't;
Hei reckt sik von Pommern bet Nedderland.

Ik weit einen Eikbom vull Knorrn un vull Knast,
  Up den'n fött kein Bil nich un Aext.
Sin Bork is so rug un sin Holt is so fast,
  As wir hei mal bannt un behext.

FROM HANNE NÜTTE.

I know of an oak by the shore of the sea;
  Through his boughs the north winds make moan;
High tosseth his mighty crown, proudly and free,
  The growth of full thousand years gone.
      No human hand
      His glories planned;
He stretcheth from Pommern to Netherland.

I know an oak tree all gnarly and scarred,
  Whose roots bill or axe never harmed;
His bark is so rough and his timber so hard,
  As though by some ban he were charmed.

Nichs heit em dahn;
Hei ward noch stahn;
Wenn wedder mal dusend von Johren vergahn.

Un de Kunig un sine Fru Künigin
Un sin Dochter, de gahn an den Strand:
"Wat deiht dat für'n mächtigen Eikbom sin,
De sin Telgen reckt äwer dat Land?
Wer heit em plegt,
Wer heit em hegt,
Dat hei sine Bläder so lustig regt?"

Un as nu de König so Antwurt begehrt,
Tredt vör em en junge Gesell:
"Herr König, Ji hewwt Jug jo üm nich d'rüm schert,
Jug Fru nich un Jug' Mamsell!
Kein vörnehm Lüd',
De hadden Tid,
Tau seihn, ob den Bom ok sin Recht geschüht.

"Un doch gräunt so lustig de Eikbom up Stun'ns,
Wi Arbeitslüd' hewwen em wahrt;
De Eikbom, Herr König, de Eikbom is uns',
Uns' plattdütsche Sprak is't un Ort.
Kein vörnehm Kunst
Heit s' uns verbunst,
Fri wüssen s' tau Höchten ahn Königsgunst."

Rasch giwwt em den König sin Dochter de Hand;
"Gott seg'n Di, Gesell, för Din Red'!
Wenn de Stormwind einst brus't durch dat dütsche Land,
Denn weit ik 'ne sekere Stad':
Wer eigen Ort
Fri wünn un wohrt,
Bi den'n is in Noth Ein sun beaten verwohrt."

But naught recks he;
A grand old tree
For another full thousand years he'll be.

The monarch, and with him his stately dame
And his daughter, walk on the strand;
"This oak, how mighty of girth and frame,
With branches that shadow the land?
Whose watch and ward
Hath so kept guard,
That his verdure thus gayly flaunts heavenward?"

As the King now seeketh an answer there,
Before him a working lad stands;
"Oh, Sire, the tree hath had little care
At yours, or the Queen's, or my Princess' hands:
No gentle folk
E'er watched the oak,
To guard it as sapling from harmful stroke.

"And now, the lusty old giant up-towers;
We Commons have tended him long;
The oak-tree, my Liege, the oak-tree is ours,
Of true Plattdeutsch nature and tongue:
No courtly wile
Hath grafted guile
On a growth ne'er fostered by royal smile."

Straightway the King's daughter gives him her hand:
"God bless thee, my lad, for thy word.
The storm-blast may roar through our German land,
I know who can refuge afford.
Who, bold and free,
Hold Liberty—
Such hearts, in need, must loyal be.

T. H. Rearden.

AN ADVENTUROUS NUN.

I have a young friend, still in his nonage, who joins to an independently decided bias in matters of taste an endearing docility in matters of action; or, with less art, in a Polonian sense, though he knows what he wants to read, he submits to the parental choice of books up to a certain limit. That measure full, however, nature's reaction sets in; *e. g.*, after a filial wrestle, during hours of toil-won leisure, with *Herodotus*, Rawlinson's, four volumes; *Plutarch*, Clough's, five volumes; *Gibbon's Rome*, Bohn's, seven volumes *(Oscito referens!)*, he appeared before me one day with the light of triumph playing, as it were, in a *nimbus* about his head, waving a small pamphlet, upon which was "the counterfeit presentment of two brothers" engaged in mortal combat. A prairie on fire was the background; the legend was: 'The Rival Redheads, or The Bloody Putty-Knife."

"And now, Philip, my king," cried the youth, "I shall wade knee-deep in gore!"

This gusto for the literature of the primal-elder curse, while it struck me as piquant in one whose tender heart—God love him!—would hardly permit him to shoot blue rocks at a match, though in more generous sport he holds his own creditably with experienced Nimrods, impelled me to send him the accounts of Charlie Parkhurst, the woman stage-driver, which were going the rounds of the newspapers a few months ago, hoping that her bold slaughter of the road agent, "Sugarfoot," would lure him to cast an eye of partiality over the whole history of the intrepid Amazon. But, alas! academic shades had corrupted my luxuriator in dime novels; the Blimbers were upon my Samson, "with a weight heavy as frost." He now only cared for the past; paralleling all this pale modernity with the ruddier life of our precedent fellow-worms; a habit of mind caught, perhaps, from the enforced Plutarch of his adolescence. His sole comment on the biography of Charlie Parkhurst was:

"She was nothing to Catalina de Erauso; *she* waded knee-deep in gore."

I was glad to perceive that amid the molded lodges of the past he still retained his old criterion of excellence. I myself had experienced quite a thrill of interest in the solitary Rhode Island girl, who, close-mouthed and strong-wristed, beat men at their own weapons, in an hour of man-milliners, when it is propounded that women are only retained on sufferance in the few trades and callings considered suitable to them. Hence it was that, in my reply to my academician's letter, I asked curtly in a postscript:

"Who, in the name of the Prophet, is Catalina What's-her-name?"

To which he responded:

"The Monja-Alferez, the Nun-Ensign. Floreat, 1615, or thereabouts."

After this I came into possession of such details about the Doña de Erauso as made me much doubt her authentic existence; but since Don Maria de Ferrer edited her autobiography, and Don José de Saban y Blanco mentions her in his *Tablas de la Historia de España*, and a picture of her, painted by Pacheco in 1630, is still extant, we must needs accept her as a moral monster, good for a study in psychological dissection, while we fervently trust the die that molded her has been broken long since. Save in inviolate modesty and a certain whimsical regard for effect, this Catalina had not the minutest quality of mind or heart belonging to a woman. She was brought up in a cloister of which her aunt was prioress, and where her parents doomed her to be immured for life. She submitted to conventual discipline till she was fifteen, when she began to perceive that, while the current of her being was dammed up into monastic stagnancy, it had the pulse and beat and precipitous leap of the torrent in it. The inner spirit did not sing, at the first movements of her discontent, with that distinctness which was to be desired. Like most of us, she knew better what she did not want than what she did. I say most of us, so as not to be invidious to the man who wrote, "I want to be an angel," who knew. Catalina could not say, "I want to be a soldier," as the obvious consequence of "I cannot be a nun." She even took the white veil, and her noviciate had almost expired, when a violent quarrel with a Sister showed her, as by inspiration, her true vocation. It appears that within the walls of the St. Sebastian l'Antiguo the church was decidedly militant, for the climax of the dispute was a severe beating administered by the nun to the novice. After this affront Catalina knew that she was made to kill—not the offending nun, but such of the human race as should come under her terrible displeasure. Sent upon an errand to the prioress's cell, she found there the keys of the convent, much more precious to her at that moment than St. Peter's own. All the wild beast in her panted and gathered its muscles for the bound that was to give it liberty. With cool foresight Catalina filched, besides the keys, money, needles, thread, and scissors. When the great outer door of the convent swung together behind her, she ran, perfectly ignorant of what direction she was taking, till she reached a chestnut grove, in the sheltered depths of which she fashioned her boy's dress out of the nine full petticoats of woolen *perpetuan* which women wore in Spain in the year of grace 1600.

Thus equipped, she followed the first road haphazard to the town of Vittoria, and boldly hired herself as secretary to her uncle, who, however, had never seen his remarkable relative. He wished to educate her, but Catalina, feeling that she had no time to lose in that way, moved on to court, then held at Valladolid. Here, by one of her audacious caprices, she entered as page to the king's secretary, who was the patron of her family. She served this gentleman till, as might be expected, her poor old father arrived at his palace gate to beg the secretary's assistance in recovering the fugitive Catalina. That enterprising virgin, overhearing her father's sobs and entreaties, instantly hired a mule and was off for Bilboa. In that city she called herself Francisco de Loyola, and soon fell into disrepute to the extent of being imprisoned for a month on account of a quarrel. After two or three years of liberty, by a foolhardy freak that one readily comprehends, however, she went to St. Sebastian, attended mass at the church of her own convent, and spoke to her former mates, the nuns. They thought her a stranger youth: "*Bien vestido et galan*," she says in her journal. One dares not hazard openly the conjecture that this description of her appearance by herself forever establishes her sex. Later she joined the expedition against the Dutch, commanded by Don Luis Fernandez de Cordova, and managed to sail to the Spanish Indies on the ship commanded by a maternal uncle, of whom she seems to have had as many as the Popes of her century had nephews. In engagements with the Dutch fleet she first saw active service, where the rattle of shot, the groans of the dying, the braying music, the hot curses, woke the slumbering war-lust in her, to rage unslaked, though more blood than would satiate a Faustina flowed by the act of her own unsparing hand. She might have been a Thug so bent was she upon making corpses.

When the Spanish fleet was to return to Spain Catalina robbed her uncle of what money she thought needful and escaped in the night, having decided to remain in America. She was placed at the head of a commercial house at Zaña, in Peru, but soon quarreled with a citizen of that town, who cut her face. Armed with a long *cuchillo*, she hid herself in the church and sprang on her antagonist, gashing his face terribly as she amiably asked:

"Which has had his face cut?"

Leaving Zaña for Truxillo a friend of the man she had mutilated met her there, and, endeavoring to avenge his comrade, was killed. Catalina took sanctuary in the cathedral, was rescued from justice by the influence of her master, Urquiza, who then gave her money and a recommendation to one Don Diego Solarte, a merchant of Lima. To Lima this tender nursling of the fairies accordingly betook herself, and in Don Diego's house tried the hazardous experiment of making love to the merchant's young sister-in-law. Don Diego, doubtless spurred on by his wife to make a good match for Dolores or Carmelita, sought to pin this Iberian Princess Badoura to a marriage. Like many a genuine wooer *au masculin*, who is only a naughty, naughty trifler, Catalina enlisted in a corps forming at Lima for the government of Chili, and was conspicuous by her absence at Don Diego's.

The name of the secretary to the Governor of Chili was Don Miguel de Erauso. Miguel was the name of one of Catalina's brothers who had left Spain for South America in boyhood. Upon inquiry this Miguel proved to be that Miguel, in the language of Inspector Bucket, and Catalina chose to become intimate with him, he in turn admiring her reckless daring. In the battle of Puren the Indians surrounded her company's banner. With sword and dagger Catalina, alone, fought for and retook the Spanish standard, cutting it from the very hand of a casique who had grasped it. She was covered with wounds, and was rewarded for her gallantry with the hard-won banner. It was then, too, that she was promoted to the rank of *alferez*, or vexillary. Having taken a Spanish renegade prisoner, Catalina hanged him to the next tree with the *sang froid* of a Tristan l'Ermite, but as a price was on the man's head the Governor had been anxious to have him taken alive, and the miscarriage of his project so vexed the excellent Chileno that he not only refused to confer the command of her company on Catalina, but disgraced her, and sent her to a dangerous garrison whose members even slept under arms. On her return from this rustication, she indulged in the pastime of slaughtering a banker in a gambling broil, and stabbing the Auditor-General of Chili through both cheeks; going to cool off in the monastery of San Francisco *comme à l'ordinaire*. Here the Governor's soldiers blockaded her for six months, during which time a young ensign visited her secretly, to request her services as second at a duel to be fought that evening beyond the walls. Though burning for adventure and chafing with *ennui*, she hesitated. Heaven knows what angel or devil interfered to hold her back through the momentary fear that her principal wished to lure her outside the walls and betray her to the Governor. These suspicions were soon allayed, however, and the two, wrapping themselves in cloaks, went at the appointed hour to the wood where the duel was to be fought. As the combat proceeded, Catalina continued to slouch her sombrero more completely over her face, as it was especially necessary that she should escape recognition, but when she saw her friend stagger from a wound, she cried:

"A cowardly traitor's blow," and was instantly given the lie by the other second. Two more swords were unsheathed and crossed, and Catalina's opponent fell, mortally wounded, and calling for a priest. Recognizing the voice, the tigress turned the dying man's face to the sky.

"Who are you?" "Don Miguel de Erauso," were the question and blasting answer that passed between the sister and her murdered brother.

Catalina's escape from the convent was into the province of Tucuman, by a road over the eternal snows of the wildest of the Andes. She performed this perilous journey with two malefactors fleeing from justice. In the frozen regions the travelers came upon two men, leaning against a block of ice, stiff in death, with a ghastly smile congealed upon their lips. Both Catalina's outcast companions succumbed to the rigors of the desert. Our heroine rifled their corpses of their valuables, and pushed on, telling her beads, "recommending myself," she tranquilly writes in her journal, "to the Holy Mother of God, and to St. Joseph, her glorious spouse."

At Tucuman she was hospitably entertained (we are forced to conclude that she was prepossessing in outward seeming); but for sole reward of so much love, she flirted with the daughter of the house, and consented to marry her, only mounting the inevitable mule the eve of the wedding. Leading the life of a desperado, through broils that with her always meant murder; spending nights and days in ferocious gaming; fighting among perdus in every expedition against the unhappy Indians; twice put to torture to compel confession of her crimes, but dumb as Leæna—she stood at last under the gallows, at Piscobamba. Here, it was said, a revelation of her sex would have saved her life, but the indomitable heart was incapable of crying for quarter; and, even as she warned the hangman not to bungle, her reprieve arrived from La Plata, where an insult to a noble lady, avenged by Catalina, had made powerful friends for her. Her next adventure was to carry off to a place of safety a young wife, who was surprised by her jealous husband with her paramour. This latter, being a bishop's nephew, the monks of the place confided the lady to Catalina's care. Just as the fugitive pair turned in at the convent, where the guilty woman's mother was a nun, the enraged husband, who was in hot pursuit, sent two carbine balls after them, which rent Catalina's collar, and cut off a lock of the wife's hair; but his horse was worn out, and Catalina was able the place the Doña in safety. This accomplished, it remained to give satisfaction to the Don, who was not exhausted, whatever his horse may have been, and who, in fact, bellowed for revenge. He surprised Catalina in the church, within whose precincts they fought, regardless of all but their rage, and the injured husband fell dead on the altar steps, Catalina at the same time reeling from loss of blood. The populace would have dragged her to prison, but the monks interfered, and nursed her back to life in the convent.

After her restoration to health, a wealthy, curled darling of Cusco incurred her mortal resentment, chiefly, it appeared, by his success in society, and his title of the New Cid, implying, as it did, unparalleled bravery. This frolicsome youth, who, probably, did not know the Spanish for the significant warning, "Let sleeping dogs lie," saw fit to feign to abstract Catalina's money one night at the gaming table. With a sudden movement the Alferez pinned the New Cid's hand to the table with her dirk. She drew her sword, but she was overpowered by numbers, wounded in the *mêlée*, and forced into the street. There her friends rallied about her, and the Cid's about him, and the two bands agreed to seek a proper arena in which to settle the quarrel. As they passed the Franciscan church, however, the Cid stabbed Catalina in the shoulder, while his friend's sword pierced her side. She fell, and the affray raged around her prostrate body. Life came back to her only to show her the Cid standing on the church steps, smiling disdainfully at the imminent defeat of her party. Stung to fury, Catalina dragged herself to her enemy's feet, and uprose, covered with blood, before her terrified enemy's eyes. He struck at her at random, and under his raised arm she planted her dagger surely in his heart. The two fell, grappling together, and rolled down the cathedral steps to the corpses below. This time she was nursed by Fray Luis Ferrer de Valencia, a monk, to whom, in the secrecy of the confessional, she revealed that she was a woman.

Although her life was saved, she knew there were vows of vengeance registered against her too numerous and deadly for her to hope to brave. Consulting her friends, she set out in a litter, under an escort of her own slaves, for Guamanga. The officers of justice often overtook her on the road, but, by dint of bullying some, and bribing others, she arrived in safety at her destination. Here the *corregidor*, acting under orders from the Viceroy of Lima, attempted to arrest the dangerous Alferez, but the Bishop of Guamanga interfered when Catalina's resistance became deadly, and removed the recalcitrant one to his own palace. Here she confessed to the prelate, and received absolution only on condition that she resume the dress of a nun, and enter a convent at Guamanga. At bay—for to consent was her sole escape from the gallows—Catalina yielded, and became a sister in the convent of Santa Clara. She was then twenty-eight years old.

After this she was, in a manner, famous. Great men in church and State visited her. She traveled in splendor, with a large and noble escort, and, after two or three years of conventual life, received permission from his most Catholic Majesty to return to old Spain, of which permission she immediately availed herself. Going from Cadiz to Seville, the curious crowd surged around her, cheering her under the name of "La Monja-Alferez." She solicited a recompense for military services in America, and was granted a pension of eighteen hundred crowns by Philip IV. She made a pilgrimage to Rome, where Urban VIII. reconciled her completely with the church, and authorized her, by brief, to wear a man's dress for the rest of her life, on condition that she respected God's image in her neighbor. Having been dined and wined by the princes of the Church of Rome, Catalina returned to Spain, and it is only known of her further that she drifted back to America in 1630. It seems that the only apology to be made for her is that quaint one offered by Octave Feuillet for his pet monster, Camors, which drew down such inextinguishable laughter on his head: "*Elle fut une grande pécheresse, mais elle fut pourtant une femme.*"

PHILIP SHIRLEY.

RAGS, SACKS, AND BOTTLES.

He wore a broad-rimmed hat, and his hair was long, and his whiskers bushy. He was a small man, and drove a mule that was also small, and so old that the memory of its youth must have been the merest shadow. The wheels of the little old cart were so loose on the axles that they would get themselves into the most unaccountable positions, sometimes lurching so far to one side or the other that wreck seemed inevitable. On such occasions, which were always unexpected, the little man had to lean the other way.

"Rags, sacks, an' bot-tels!"

Whoa, Beauty! Wonder what this gentleman wants. Want to sell some rags, sir? No? Could I ride with him? No use stoppin' a fellow—a business man—fer sech a question ez thet. In dead earnest? Well, well, well, well! Ef thet didn't beat him all holler. A fine, dressed-up gentleman a-ridin' through the streets in sich a fake ez thet there cyart—why, the boys 'ud guy me out'n my senses.

"Rags, sacks, an' bot-tels!"

Well, jump in, then, ef I *would* like ter hev a lift. Mebbe I was tired o' walking.

"Rags, sacks, an' bot-tels!"

He had a curious assortment of wares in the cart; under his feet, under the board that served for a seat, everywhere, mixed and mingled; gunny-sacks filled with strange things; a box for bottles, and cups with the handles knocked off; fragments of looking-glass; dainty old shoes run back at the heels and burst at the toes (he imparted to me in strict confidence the name of the young lady who had worn them—a great society belle); riff-raff and scum of finery, flimsiness, and poverty—a very curiosity-shop of exhausted economy and impatient extravagance gone to waste.

"Rags, sacks, an' bot-tels!"

It was the most doleful chant I ever heard. It employed but two notes, which he always struck with exact precision. There was no reference to a tuning-fork, nor clearing the throat, nor testing the vocal organs by running up and down the scale. The burden of the chant was on the key-note, the only variation being the dropping to the fourth on the first syllable of "bottles," and then resuming the old position in the scale on the last syllable. This gave the word a strange sound, and I did not recognize it; so I inquired its meaning.

"Bottles," he replied, looking surprised and somewhat contemptuous.

There were ale bottles and whisky bottles; a bottle the baby had used; bottles from the Rhine and Bordeaux; square bottles and round bottles; long bottles and short bottles; bottles of every nationality and pedigree; lean bottles and fat bottles; bottles with druggists' labels, and bottles without labels; dirty bottles and clean bottles—a ragged and hungry army of bottles that had been through many struggles, and that were destined for many more; bottles of strong principles, and bottles whose characters were so frail that they would crumble under the least touch of calumny or adversity—the fag end of all the disreputable bottles in creation.

"Rags, sacks, an' bot-tels!"

I noticed his keen little eyes carefully and rapidly scanning upper-story windows, throwing a quick glance into alleys leading into back yards; and the comprehensive look with which he regarded a clothes-line, with its burden fluttering in the wind, conveyed whole volumes of analytical discrimination.

Whoa, Beauty! He had caught a signal from a back stair, given by an untidily dressed, though good-looking, matron. Beauty came so suddenly to a dead halt that the cart wheels, which had been running peacefully along at a considerable inclination to one side, lurched over to the other, as if they wanted to rest themselves by standing on the other leg, and threw me violently against the little man.

"The streets," he said, in an apologetic tone, "is skimpety like, an' yer can't jess calkilate when you're a-runnin' a-foul of a rut."

The good soul! It was the crazy old cart that was at fault; but he would hide its infirmities, even at the expense of truth.

"Will yer set in the cyart," he said, "an' hol' Beauty 'gainst I come back? She's mostly purty gentle, an' mostn't run away; but she gits lively 'n strong at times, an' hez notions of her own, jess like a woman."

Beauty run away! Why, I have no idea such a thought had found place under her thick old skull for a quarter of a century.

As I awaited the return of the little man, my attention fell upon the patient and decrepit disguise of anatomy that stood so quietly in the patched and spliced shafts of the cart; and I could not help thinking that Beauty was made entirely of rags, sacks, and bot-tels. Her brown hide, patched and torn, and covered with the filth of the stable where she had lain, looked more like a sack than anything I had seen before. I was sure her ears were the dilapidated shoes of some broken down song-and-dance man, whose trumpery had gone to the rag-picker. I speculated considerably on what the old sack was stuffed with, and was forced to the conclusion that the great prominences all over her emaciated body were bottles; that the jagged ridge along the back was propped up by soda-water bottles, with the necks broken off; and there was no doubt in my mind that the lumps at the hips were Dutch bottles that were cracked, and fit for no other use. What kind of rags was Beauty stuffed with? A problem. But I thought the poor old stomach contained only rags that the junk dealer had refused—such as half-wool stockings, worn out at the heels and toes; old red-flannel rags, and rags that were mildewed and rotten; rags that had been rags for three generations, and sold because a stitch would no longer hold them together. Ah! but what kind of a soul had Beauty? Was it, too, made of rags, sacks, and bottles?—or was it woven of fine white thread? I think not the latter, but rather that it was composed of rags that had served for blisters, poultices, and ointments; rags from which all life and color had faded, leaving them blank, but white, for all that; rags that had felt all the privations to which rags can be subjected, that had been torn and tattered by the winds, left uncleansed all their natural lives, and that the rats and mice had eventually stuffed away in damp and dismal places to make nests of; rags that had served as handkerchiefs to conceal a sigh, or brush away a tear. There were sacks in the soul, too—empty dreams of emptier oat-sacks; and bottles in which flowers had been put, and left to wither when the water dried up.

"Rags, sacks, an' bot-tels."

The little man came out of the gate, lugging a sack full of rags and bottles. He deposited his burden in the cart, opened the sack, peered into it, buried his arm in its contents, and fetched up an empty bottle. This he deposited in the box, and repeated the operation until he had taken out all the bottles, leaving only the rags.

"Are rags dear?" I asked.

"Oh," he replied, with a shrug, "a business man can't growl about trifles, you know. Them rags'll weigh 'bout ten pounds."

"How much did they cost you?"

"Well, yer see, people wants all the money they kin git. Them people in there's mighty close." And he added, with a knowing look, "There's queer stories about 'em. An' then, times is purty close. They wanted twenty-five cents for 'em, an' kinder stuck to it like; but I warn't on the buy thet strong, an' when I got 'em down to fifteen cents, I tuck 'em."

As we jogged down the street, he continued his cry:

"Rags, sacks, an' bot-tels."

The house from which we had just made the purchase was apparently that of well-to-do people. There was neatly trimmed shrubbery in the garden, a smooth grass-plat, and flowers. The handle of the door-bell was silver-plated. My fancy clung to that house, with its slovenly matron, stood upon the door-step, on which was a mat bearing the word "Welcome," turned the handle, and entered. Then I found a rug at every door, but they were all woven of rags. There were rag carpets everywhere. Underneath the spotless white bed-spreads were quilts made of odd bits of cloth and rags from unimaginable sources. I was so disheartened in the search for something new, and fresh, and whole, that was hidden from outer sight, that I went down into the hearts of these people to find, perchance, a single thing that was not torn, and tattered, and empty; but a great night-mare there confronted me. It was a scare-crow, dressed in rags that it had worn so long they were falling off by piecemeal, exposing a frame that was warped and awry; that was split where the nails had been driven into it, and that was tied up with odds and ends of strings, and leather thongs cut from old boot-legs. Terrified with the spectacle, I hid myself in the innermost closet of that slovenly matron's (the mother's) heart, and there I was blinded by cobwebs and choked by dust. I stumbled upon a heap of ashes in a very dark corner. They enveloped me in a cloud. I was suffocating, and gasping for breath, when I was borne down into the ashes by a heap of rags, sacks, and bottles, that fell from above, and crushed me with the weight of a mountain. Struggling madly, I fought my way out. I gained the top of the mountain, and clambered down the side. I fell over something as I turned to leave. The darkness was oppressive, the dust suffocating. I felt at my feet in the utter blackness, and found, grinning, and ghastly, all dry, and parched, and shriveled, and whitened—a skeleton.

"Rags, sacks, an' bot-tels."

We did a driving trade that day. All the rags, sacks, and bottles in the town seemed to flock to us as to a haven of rest; for they must have known that a great future was opening up before them, in which, purified and transformed, they would come to occupy higher positions in [illegible] and serve nobler purposes. But we drove terribly hard bargains, and sometimes exhibited a meagerness of soul that was contemptible. It must be understood that we could not avoid this; for did we not have at home five or six little empty, tow-head bottles, that had to be filled *so* often? Did we not have five or six little bundles of rags that *would* shiver, and that *had* to be kept warm? And we loved them, even if people did say we were mean and hard-hearted; even if dogs did growl at us; even if we were cursed, and kicked, and driven out of back yards, drenched with dirty water the kitchen-maid had thrown upon us. But this occurred only once, and then there happened to be a silver spoon in the bottom of the dish-pan. It struck us scornfully, and fell to the ground, and we very slyly and very quietly put it into our pocket.

"Rags, sacks, an' bot-tels!"

The day's work was finally done, and the little man turned Beauty's head homeward. His business-like look went out, giving place to one of sadness and anxiety.

"My little girl is very sick," he said.

"Ah!"

"Yes, very sick. Most afeard she won't live long."

I accompanied him home. His house was a miserable hovel, with neither floor nor chimney. The furniture consisted of a broken table, an old chair, and a quantity of rags spread in the corner for a bed. The little man approached the bed, and, with womanly tenderness, stooped down and kissed a little bundle of rags almost buried in the pile.

"How is my little Mag?"

A wan, thin face smiled, and a weak voice replied, as two emaciated little arms sought his neck:

"Oh, papa, I'm *so* glad you've come. Give me some water, papa."

The little man held up her head, and she eagerly swallowed some water from a broken bottle.

"I've been so lonesome, papa—so lonesome. They all went away and left me, and a great big rat got on the bed."

"Where is the mother?" I asked.

"Dead," he replied.

I approached the little sufferer, took her tiny hands in mine, and found them cold. I kissed her forehead and lips, and found them hot. An indefinable horror was stealing over me, as if I stood in the presence of something invisible that was repulsive to nature.

"Papa," she said, "did you bring me any pretty rags?"

"Lots of 'em, Mag, lots of 'em. Whole heaps of 'em."

"Let me see 'em, papa. And—and will you make me a pretty rag doll?" she asked me, hesitatingly. "Papa can't make 'em as pretty as I can, and I am so weak I can't make 'em any more."

Her poor eyes sparkled as I rummaged the sacks for the finest and brightest rags, and made them into a very princess of rag dolls. She clasped it to her breast, and kissed it again and again, and laughed some, and cried some, and called it pet names, and said it was the prettiest doll she ever saw. Then she kissed me, and laughed and cried again. I asked her if she wanted something nice to eat, for I was prompted to this by the dreadful feeling that I could not understand. She shook her little flaxen head slowly, but sadly.

"Wouldn't you like a nice, big, round orange?"

A great, hungry eagerness came into her eyes, and the pale little face slightly colored.

"Oh!" she said, "an orange. I never tasted but one."

Somehow my eyes became so dim that I turned away, and discovered the rag-picker quietly crying. Then the truth came upon me, and overpowered me. There lay before me, on the bed of rags, a human being, drifting away. While church spires pointed proudly to heaven; while there were people in the world with generous but ignorant impulses; in the broad light of day, when the birds were singing, and the sun shining brightly; in the fullness of time, and by the grace of God; at the very footstool of the Throne in heaven, lay that little mortal dying—of what? *Starvation.*

Was I already too late? I rushed from the hovel, stunned and staggering, looking for Life; and, ringing in my ears, rousing every energy, was the solemn, funeral, heart-breaking cry:

"Rags, sacks, an' bot-tels!"

That was ten years ago. The little man and Beauty have long since passed away. My ward has just grown into lovely womanhood, pale, thoughtful, beautiful. I cannot imagine why the other boarders look at each other and smile when I kiss Mag "good night," and when she turns at the door, and throws me a kiss, with her eyes full of pure affection. But, somehow, the world is brighter than it used to be. I am greatly mortified to find a few gray hairs in my head, for I am afraid people will think I am getting old. I am told that I am much more careful with my dress than I was a few years ago. I am sure I feel younger than I did ten years ago. Those are very meddlesome boarders, and, comparing them with Mag, I care no more for them than for so many rags, sacks, and bottles.

W. C. MORROW.

FAILURE.

Long ago you said to me, "Sweet,
  A glorious kingdom before you lies;"
You pointed it out to my willing feet,
  You lighted the way with your loving eyes.

Many the triumphs the years have brought;
  Keen the pleasures, but keener the pain.
I stand by your side in the realm of thought,
  And I ask myself, is it loss or gain?

You give to me generous meed of praise,
  You give to me honor and trust, I know;
But you think with regret of my simple ways,
  My fond unwisdom of long ago.

Though I speak with the wisdom of gods and men
  (This is the bitter that spoils my sweet),
I know full well that never again
  Can I stir your pulse by a single beat.

You are not to blame. There is nought to be said;
  Ever by fate is our planning crossed.
I did the best that I could, love-led,
  For the sake of winning what I have lost.

CARLOTTA PERRY.

PROBABLE CHANGES IN AMERICAN GOVERNMENT.

I think it cannot be too often repeated that governments, in the main, are more the creatures of chance than of design. It will be found on reflection that the Federal American Government is no exception. We speak of the Constitution writers as the "founders" of our system. But we are too apt to mean the *creators* of it—having ungoverned freedom of action in its creation. They did not so understand their task. They knew it to be simply "the work of introducing into a country the best institutions which, in the existing state of that country, it is capable of in any tolerable degree." This was their work; but chance furnished the materials—a new country, divided into colonies; a practically republican (though not strictly democratic) state of society; the heritage (incubus or blessing?) of British electoral customs; an apparent tendency of society toward democracy all over the world, and a list not necessary to enumerate here. It does not belittle their achievement to understand, that chance furnished the occasion and the means. Other occasions and means for other political achievements—as great, if not similar—have at other times in the history of the world fallen to other men; but none have, like them, been grandly the masters of the moment. Political insight grows, if we remember that the first essential is to understand things as they are at present, their causes and consequences. If our Government be all expressed in the Constitution it is certainly the handiwork of one generation of men bearing no great mark of mutability. But let us ask ourselves these questions: Is it doing the same work for us that it did for its found-era? Is it doing our work in the same way that it did that of its founders? Is it doing our work in the very way that its founders would have wished it to do our work? Let us, in short, judge it as the founders were willing it should be judged in their day—in the same way that all governments must be judged—by what happens to man from men because of it; and no thinking man will honestly claim it is the handiwork of the Constitution writers, as they designed it to be in this day and under our circumstances. Chance has added materials which, in the hands of new men, have changed it (whether good workmen or not, let one hundred years hence answer), so that it is now, in many material respects, "a new thing under the sun."

It will be admitted, I think, that it was the design of the Constitution writers, above all other things, to give the United States of America a good government. But there was nothing Utopian in their schemes. Not even those among them who were most imbued with the prevalent notions of the "rights of man" supposed for a moment that it was practicable to establish and maintain either a pure democracy—that is, a government where all the adult males should directly meet in person and participate equally in all the affairs of government; or a pure representative democracy—that is, one in which each man has the same right to hold office as his neighbor, to take office by rotation or be chosen by lot. They understood that true freedom consisted in "laws made for the sake of liberty, not liberty merely to make laws." I am sure that they did not doubt that there was ignorance and vice as well as intelligence and virtue in the world, and always would be; and that if government were to be worth anything to man, were even to have power to maintain itself, it should in every sense be the ally of intelligence and virtue; that it should be "the sum of all its parts" (to use this true saying in its generally, but erroneously, understood meaning), that is to say, that if a majority of society should become ignorant and vicious, it would be a good thing that government should then contain a similar proportion of ignorance and vice, is a proposition the most influential and thinking men among them would have recoiled from. They knew that such a government must die itself, or be the death of society. Almost to a man, they would have said (even the black sheep among them, if there were any such) that in a corrupt state of society, or where ignorance on governmental affairs prevails, the good and intelligent men are entitled to hold the reins of government; and in every government, at all times, the best men have the best right to rule. It is the forward tendency of all forms of society to secure the best men as leaders. It is an ineradicable tendency; even mobs obey it.

So far as any man could then, or can now, see, the men at the head of affairs during the American Revolution, and in the Constitutional Convention, were fully and fairly the representatives of the American people in every sense. They had among them the wisest, the best, the most purely patriotic of the country; and I do not doubt they had among them many who were not wise, nor good, nor purely patriotic—to whom sounding phrases were more than truth, who were jealous of the power of abler men, and to whom place was more than country. But the substance of power had been in the best hands for many years previously, notwithstanding British errors and obstinacies, and had continued in such hands even during revolution. This had come through the British system of representation, suitable to a small or thinly populated country, where men of talent and virtue could not be "buried alive," as many such are to-day in this vast America. That was a system of more or less open and direct personal nomination and candidacy for office; occasionally, of course, there was a spontaneous movement of the minds of constituents in the direction of an eminently qualified man not directly seeking office. It differed from the British system of nomination and candidacy in minor matters, owing to the more democratic state of society, and to the more general privilege of the suffrage. But the suffrage was not universal at any time during the foundation of our Government; if any one has a different idea, he has but to read the electoral laws in existence at the time, and the first constitutions of the various States adopted after independence, to be convinced of his error. The judges, all the great State officers, and many of the minor officials, like sheriffs, were either appointed or elected by the Legislature. The legislative representatives in the lower houses, and purely municipal officers, were almost the only officials generally elected by the people throughout the States; but, for whatever office exercised, the right of suffrage was limited to property-holders and tax-payers. Thus a considerable number of persons, exclusive even of the large number of negro slaves, were excluded from any vote. This British system of personal nomination and candidature, engrafted on a more democratic and entirely republican state of society, by relegating the choice of administrative and judicial officers to the class most competent to judge of their qualifications, had given the best men in the country to the public service, had been found sufficient to carry the people through the perils of a revolution, and, it seemed plain, might safely be trusted for the future. Its features were imitated in the Federal Constitution. There was no supposition that in the latter it would ever be greatly changed; certainly no danger for the Government was feared in that direction. But there it has changed. There is the spot in the Constitution, which, in my opinion, has been shown by the history of our day to be weakest. The wisest men cannot be altogether wise.

Satisfied with the system of representation then in existence and working well, the Constitution writers wisely turned their attention to the apparent weaknesses of the federal republic they desired to found. They aimed to make it strong in three things: Against foreign enemies, against disintegration from domestic rivalry, against the ambition of any citizen or clique of citizens. These were its dangers. Could it be protected from them, it seemed clear that it must yield the American people the best fruits of government. That the framers of the Constitution succeeded, our history to this day attests to their sufficient honor. When their work was done they hoped, no doubt, that they had made a government which not only then did, but always would, "fairly well represent the existing state of society; would allow of change with the situation of the persons who should enjoy or be subject to it; in a word, would fit society as a man's clothes fit him, freely and fairly toward all parts, for the best interests of each and all."

Among the means which seemed essential to the well being of representative government the existence of parties was prominent before the minds of the Constitution writers. There was no doubt that parties were essential things for carrying on government. There was no doubt that the "watchfulness of the opposition" had maintained English liberty. So long as party did not degenerate into sectionalism, did not array State government against State government, it was all but essential. I do not doubt that many of the men who gave us our government, when, after its existence, they saw parties array themselves into opponents and supporters of the extension of the Federal idea, may have congratulated their country on the fact that here was a principle which divided all the people without regard to section; which gave them a cause of difference that would lead one party to watchfulness of the encroachments of central power, and another to watchfulness of the mutiny of sections. The two paths of tyrants to power in free States—centralization and division—were forever guarded. And there was ground for congratulation. Did they not save us from disintegration? Perhaps, too, they have saved or may yet save us from Cæsar and the Prætorian Guards.

But it was not the rule of party in close analogy to the English system (where distinction of ideas is everything and organization weak) which eventually established itself in America. The English system may have been good enough for the domestic management of a small state in the days of George III. It is wretched enough now if Mr. Hare, and Mr. Mill, and dozens of other thoughtful Englishmen, can be trusted. But for a continent, thinly populated though it may be, it never was a tolerable system. Party must have great cohesion to govern a continent. The English system became impossible almost as soon as we left off swaddling clothes. Down to the year 1820 there were no material changes in the State constitutions affecting the exercise of the suffrage. From that time forward the progress of a great change in the workings of our Government is apparent to any one who examines its history. It may be summed up in this way. I take from Mr. Seaman's book* the first three subdivisions; I have added the fourth:

1. The election of the Presidential electors came to be made by the people by general ticket.

2. Sheriffs and other county officers came to be elected directly by the people.

3. State officers and judges of courts of record came to be elected directly by the people.

4. The suffrage was made universal throughout the country, by which a large number of ignorant whites and blacks now participate in the election of nearly all officers of every grade whose appointment is not directly provided for by the Federal Constitution.

Following the first movement of this great change came the partisan nominating convention. The first of these conventions was held in 1824, in the State of New York, for the nomination of State officers. The first partisan national convention was held in the year 1832. These conventions now form an apparently permanent part of our system of government, as markedly American as any part of the Constitution. But they are not provided for in the Constitution, or controlled by our laws. And they were not imagined by the Constitution writers.

The change is accomplished now, and it is beyond recall. We are face to face with its results. If we examine them closely we shall find that the change has been a great one; and I

* *The American System of Government.* By Ezra Seaman. New York: Scribner & Co. 1870.

think it will follow that it is fruitful of other changes.

The government founded in this country was certainly intended to be the will of all the people, and the action of the best among the people. What is it now?

"It is the will of the dominant party, not the will of the people. Those of us who do not belong to the dominant party have no more voice in the Government than if we lived in France or Algiers."

I am quoting the words of the New York *Times:*

"We, the minority, are aliens—not in view of the law, but in view of the actual government of the country. Mr. Gladstone" (he had taken Mr. Lowe into the cabinet notwithstanding he did not follow his party in one particular) "may be of the opinion that the strength and right working of a government does not consist wholly in the number of its votes—that talent, debating power, sagacity, and high personal character still count for something, even to a government whose orthodox supporters are largely in the majority. We have got over all such obsolete ideas in this country. When a party has a large majority of votes"—

(No, I say, when it has any majority of votes whatever)

—"it can do anything it likes. It needs nobody's support, and scorns to look outside its own party lines for support. All it has to do is to feed its own followers well, and see to it that not the smallest nubbin of patronage falls to anybody who is outside the party fold. In this country party is the ruling power. The government is nothing but the ruling party. Whatever aids the party aids the government. The only proper and legitimate mode of aiding the government, therefore, is to aid the party. Whatever does that is right; whatever don't do that is all wrong. This fundamental principle of popular government has not yet penetrated the British mind. Parties in England think it worth while to conciliate the confidence and support of their opponents, as well as of their stanch supporters. *The general sentiment of the country* seems to them worth something and they try to get it on their side. * * How can a party be expected to maintain itself, if it is to be thus cut off from the full breasts of government patronage? What encouragement have politicians to work for a party victory, if they see any slices of its rewards coolly turned over to any who doubt its right to control in all particulars? What right has any party man to a judgment or conscience of his own? What business has he to set up for himself—to act upon his own convictions of duty, instead of following in the train of his party, content to obey its behests, and ask no questions?"

I am quite sure that that quotation states the nature of the practical sovereignty exercised over the American people of this day. And I am sure it is essentially a different thing from the government designed by the fathers of the country; that no hint of it is contained in the Constitution which came from their hands; that it would be as odious a thing to them as the limited monarchy from which they rebelled. We have the form of the government which they left us, but the substance for which they designed that form to be a protection has slipped from us utterly.

Let us examine our condition a little further. There was lately sitting in Chicago a body called the National Republican Convention. It was a partisan body, called for strictly partisan purposes; and later, we had another, called a National Democratic Convention, sitting elsewhere. These are the giants which contend between them for the possession of all of us, and one of them will, in time, seize us, wriggling more or less feebly, in its unyielding grasp. One or the other of them is the body of officers of government for the next four years. They are therefore the things which tell us what we shall be for that period; what measures of government we shall treat ourselves to; who shall be our masters; how our masters shall act towards us—they are the legislatures, the judiciaries, the executives, national prosperity, individual liberty, happiness, or misery, to many among us—more than the things at national capital and State capitals, county court houses and prisons, which we delude ourselves into thinking exist independently of them by the wisdom of our fathers and our own wills.

How came these bodies to possess this power? During the first century of our national existence there was practically one great question in American politics, which overshadowed and hid all minor differences of opinion. Now and then it may have been lost sight of for a moment, but, whether they remembered it or not, it was always present in the minds and hearts of the American people. It concerned their future as a nation. There could be but two opinions on it, and there could practically, therefore, be but two parties in the government. It assumed many forms, but it always meant "disintegration or cohesion." It could not be settled but by one of the bloodiest wars of modern times. And organization perfected itself, and partisanship deepened, as the struggle approached this final result. Thus there seemed to be but two great parties possible in America, and thus they necessarily came to be rigidly exclusive. It is well to remember this, however: these nominating conventions, as the supreme hierarchy of party, sprung into existence from inherent love of liberty and devotion to constitutional forms, on the part of the American people. They were the consequence of a revolt from "King Caucus," a system of hole-and-corner nominations indulged in by high officials, to the exclusion of the general body of citizens, contrary to the design of the Constitution and the spirit of all progress in government.

Did the revolt succeed in accomplishing its object, and are these nominating conventions a system in accord with the spirit of the Constitution? The revolt may have been successful for a time, and to a limited extent it may have lessened the power of Caucus; but he has now a surer grasp than ever, because it is partially hidden under the semblance of a representative system. And to the second part of my question I unhesitatingly answer that, however and with what purpose, good or bad, they were devised, these bodies are a clear infringement on the spirit of the Constitution. They are met ostensibly to nominate candidates for the Presidency. They offer you ultimately *two* men to choose from, and you must take your choice, however little you like either, or else be disfranchised. The Constitution intended you should elect the worthiest and best men among you in your several States as an electoral college, to freely deliberate upon the special suitableness of every possible man for the particular duties of that office, and freely exercise its so matured and unbounded choice for you, as the nearest and best approach to pure representative democracy, in this regard, that could be devised for this federal republic. But these partisan conventions have stepped in, and said, "No. There shall be no choice but such as we dictate. You may utterly abhor the selections we make for you to pick from, but pick you must, or refrain from voting. Your electoral college must contain only our tools, our nominees, and in no particular must it venture to act for you, but only for us." The man nominated may be a sound Republican or Democrat, and in that particular suit your tastes; but what if the issues between those parties are of no more importance for the time being to the country than one of "ins" and "outs;" what if both parties leave out of sight, or trifle with, some question uppermost in your mind—free trade or protection, Chinese or no Chinese, civil service reform or the "spoils system"—and offer you men with no decided policy in these present important questions? In that event—not an impossible, not even an infrequent one—the true influence which your vote should have on the selection of a President is absolutely lost. Where is the value of such a franchise for such an occasion? Whereas it was intended by the electoral college system set forth in the Constitution—and I do not doubt it would have resulted, if that system had been fully developed in just accord with its true intent—that the President chosen by it would represent all of the sound, and as many of the prevailing, political opinions of the country as it is possible for a single man to do. Not only in this particular is the operation of these partisan nominating conventions a gross departure from the spirit of the Constitution, but in another, and far more serious one. The Constitution declares that "no Senator or Representative, or person holding an office of trust or profit under the United States, shall be appointed an elector." Surely any one can see the objects of this provision without recurring to the explanatory literature on the subject, with which we are familiar. It means that the influence of high place, or of place or office of any kind, shall not sway the choice of the electoral college. It means that there shall be no cliques to snatch from the people's electors the unbounded choice; that it shall never inflexibly be limited to any oligarchy, bureaucracy, coterie, clique, or faction, holding among them, for the time being, the places of government. It means that such a prize shall be contended for by worthy striving of good men to gain the confidence of their fellow-citizens, and that all temptation or power to win it by intrigue, combination, bargain, rotation, or to the exclusion of anybody, shall be unavailing. But I say, and we all know, that, practically, these partisan conventions entirely override this purpose. "They have their birth in clique and faction of the narrowest and most exclusive sort." They are originated and controlled by the very men whom the Constitution expressly prohibits from interfering in any way with the free rights of the electors. A committee exists, calling itself, as may be, the National Republican or Democratic Committee. It is composed of "Senators and Representatives in Congress, and persons holding places of honor or profit under the United States," or by the certain proxies of such persons. This committee is the Propaganda Fide, or the St. Petersburg or Paris Central Police Bureau, of this republic, with its inquisitors, or spies, in every quarter, prompted by narrow fanaticism, or paid by the hope of its approval, diligent in spying the political movements—the very thoughts, so far as it is possible for any police system to spy all men's thoughts in any nation. It is perpetually in existence, as well served and as well informed as the most effective continental police bureau. It has its sub-committees, called State and County Committees, composed, like itself (if the party it represents has power of any kind in State or county), of the very men whom the spirit of the Constitution expressly forbids from influencing the free electors of the people. One or another subservient tool—pettifogging, half-educated lawyer, gin-mill keeper, or fanatical partisan—in almost every township throughout the whole country, knowing that his hopes of office, his good standing with the government that is, or will be, depends upon the favor of this its political police bureau, and being the center of a petty clique of "mouchards" feebler and stupider than he, reports to it, or its committee, the "state of feeling in his district," sayings at the tavern meeting, lies more or less about the number of his "supporters;" and, having thus secured its recognition as a worker, his power is assured within his sphere. He and his clique are the assured masters of the "primaries—meetings where the American people truly exercise their divine right of self-government." No one will deny that the "primaries" are at the heart of American government of this day. Not only the Presidential Convention, but every other nominating convention, springs from them. And they are nowhere hinted at, governed, or influenced by any constitution or law of the land. They are subject only to

> "The good old law, the ancient plan:
> Let him take who has the power,
> And let him keep who can."

Possessing so important a function in our government—take them one and all—in great cities and small towns, wherever their most important and engrossing pursuits gather the American people, and make their governmental form most directly important to them, these primaries are antagonistic to and inefficient for all good ends. They are often held in some obscure or, perhaps, disreputable tavern; almost always so that the very meeting place acts as a repellant against the influx of non-desirable (that is, respectable) citizens, "damned literary fellers," quiet, earnest thinkers, sober business men, undesirous of wasting time, and the like. The form of an election for county or State delegates to a subordinate partisan convention is gone through with, if the desirable element—that is "party tools," "henchmen," "heelers," "strikers," or other prettily named arms of the service—are in the majority. Should, by any accident, a sufficient number of respectable people attend a primary meeting, so that they could outnumber the hired ruffians of the party machine, the meeting is broken up by a fight, by stealing the roll, by the high-handed, open fraud of a so-called chairman, or other of many sufficient means, and the "delegates" are elected at another meeting. Generally, however, it is not necessary to resort to these means. The character of the place and the men at the bottom of the political ladder is quite sufficient to make those primaries entirely unattractive to respectable men. Such persons stay away. But an "election" is had of some sort for county convention, State convention, or national convention—all the same which. The doors are opened only by the political police bureau. The delegate must be well affected to the bureau. He must understand that to the bureau belongs the power of contesting his seat; and very certainly his seat will be contested if he is not ready to swallow the "slate" he well knows is prepared by the bureau for his digestion; unless, indeed, he happens to be one of a mob large enough for the time being to repel the political police, in which event gentler means are used, and he is *bought*, or his friends, if cheaper, are bought.

I should hesitate to give this view of these bodies if I held it alone. Many will agree with me. But the foregoing is merely a paraphrase of Mr. Sterne's* description, and I now quote from him exactly:

> "Every convention which springs from these meetings is packed. Farces! if such outrageous perversions of the rights of the people contained a single element of the ludicrous. The far greater number of the members of the convention are either directly bought with money or promises of office."

Or drunk with the intention of wrenching office from some candidate.

> "As a matter of accident an honest man"—

(that is, a man free from the trammels of the machine)

> —"may be returned to a nominating convention, but as a general rule, he is hopelessly powerless."

The bureau knows upon how many it can count. Every man has been watched, measured, bullied, wheedled, or bought at the right time during his progress from the depths to the doors of the convention, and a record carefully kept of the result. There will be no doubt or hesitancy, no opportunity for him to recall to his colleagues memories of the existence of honest purpose. He has no business there; he is not exactly an alien—he is a pariah.

Well, this picture is colored, it may be said. I admit it. The color, however, is the true color that the picture should have, only a little deepened, to give the real effect to weak eyes that otherwise would not see any picture at all. Yes, it is true that the members of the political police bureau often differ among themselves as to who shall govern us, and fail to make a slate, and the conventions themselves nominally decide upon the admissibility of their members; but I deny that in that event there is a free convention. The choice is still the choice of

* *On Representative Government and Personal Representation.* By Simon Sterne. Philadelphia: Lippincott & Co. 1871.

the bureau. Its members may not be able to unite on one man, but they differ only on this. They united long before the convention to forbid, or enfeeble, the consideration of any other man than the men about whom they dispute, or certain other alternates—perhaps, not literally by written agreement, but by identical spirit and purpose. If they forego their differences, and unite now on one man, it will be for "expediency." For his merit, his public worth and dignity, for their country's dignity, for his special fitness for the duties of the office? Pshaw! For the party. They are there before your eyes: "*Senators and Representatives, and persons holding offices of honor and profit under the United States,*" with all their blushing honors thick upon them. Unsafe sights for an electoral college, thought the Fathers. Here they must be helpless? Pshaw again! They frown, and their benchmen tremble. They raise a hand, and the benchmen are silent. They wave a kerchief, and the applause lasts, at their bidding, twenty minutes by the clock. Free men, freely choosing the worthiest and best suited among us for perpetual identification with the history of our country as our chief magistrate? No!—vassals as subservient as ever followed the proudest aristocrat; and, oh, how much meaner! The whole case is summed up in two narratives to be found in the morning's paper on the close of the Chicago Convention:

A delegate from Texas, one Mr. Stenigan, is speaking in that convention against civil service reform. He wants none of it, and indignantly asks, "What are we here for but to get offices?"

General Butler is being interviewed by certain Greenbackers anent their grievance of being obliged to take gold on the rare occasions when it is offered to them, and he explains how they were injured in this way: "In 1868 the chairmen of the Republican and Democratic National Committees agreed that the bonds should be paid in gold."

The Government of the United States consists, then, in effect, of these chairmen; or, perhaps, they are merely new officers under the Constitution, charged with the guardianship of the national honor, and properly responsible only to expediency and passion!

But they do give us one among the best! Sometimes; not always. And, even if always, our right is to cast our individual votes or direct influence for whom we each consider the very best. Nothing less than this is the honest or fair exercise of our suffrage. And all this it was intended we should have. Yet it is the fact, that the men who best represented the noblest aspirations of the American people for sixty years past never had a chance for their right place in American government—the highest in its gift. What would have been said by the Constitution writers had they been told that they were inaugurating a system which would exclude from the Presidency a Webster, a Clay, an Adams—scores of other tried men, the best in the land—and open it only to almost unknown mediocrities; and, worse than all, that the American people would regard this merely as a "curious fact?" I have heard some specious arguments for the approval of this "curious fact," but I am still guilty of the heresy of thinking that the best and most worthily prominent man in the country, to each man's thinking, should have each man's vote.

Let us consider, for a moment, the effect of these partisan aggregations on the conduct of their nominee in power. I condense a report in Mr. Stickney's recent book.*

Abraham Lincoln was as honest a man as ever filled any office. At the convention which nominated him an agreement was made between his friends and the friends of one Simon Cameron, of Pennsylvania, that if the Pennsylvania delegates should vote for Mr. Lincoln a seat in the cabinet should be given Mr. Cameron. Mr. Lincoln knew nothing of this agreement at that time. What followed was this: He was urged to fulfill the promise of his friends. His biographer, Colonel McClure, says he waited on him with letters from several prominent men, which "sustained me in the allegation that the appointment would disgrace the administration and the country, because of the notorious incompetency and public and private villainy of the candidate." Mr. Lincoln knew the protest to be well founded. He said, "All that I am in the world—the Presidency and all else—I owe to the opinion of me which the people express when they call me Honest Old Abe. Now, what will they think of their *honest* Abe when he appoints Simon Cameron to be his familiar adviser?" The appointment was made. Mr. Cameron became Secretary of War, and what might be expected followed. The most unblushing corruption was charged against him, and proved. Mr. Lincoln was, at last, compelled to summarily dismiss his secretary. And, of course, the dismissal was made in terms fitting the conduct which had been its cause? Here are its words:

"HON. SIMON CAMERON, Secretary of War—

"DEAR SIR: I have this day appointed Honorable Edwin M. Stanton to be Secretary of War, and you to be Minister Plenipotentiary to Russia.

"Very truly, A. LINCOLN."

---

* *A True Republic.* By Albert Stickney. New York: Harper Brothers. 1879.

This was not the end. The dismissed secretary wished to have it appear that he had not been dismissed at all, that he had voluntarily resigned his office, that his resignation had been regretfully accepted, and that he had been honorably appointed to another position where he, as a man of high personal worth, was fitly to represent a great nation at an imperial court. To make it appear so, it was necessary that the public records should be falsified, and that the President of the United States should be a party to this falsification. Colonel McClure says: "In my presence the proposition was made and determined upon to ask Lincoln to allow a letter of resignation to be ante-dated, and to write a kind acceptance of the same in reply. * * The record shows that Mr. Cameron voluntarily resigned, while, in point of fact, he was summarily removed without notice."

It may be said that a strong-minded President can resist the wrong influence of his party. Well, General Grant, was such a man; yet he did not. We all know, without stating them, the harsh charges that were made from time to time, with more or less justice, respecting the evil influence of the party managers over him; and his most ardent admirer cannot deny that some, at least, of those charges were probably well founded. The least grave of them was sufficient to cast a deeply to be regretted stain on the political, nay, personal, character of a chief magistrate. President Hayes unqualifiedly expressed his intention to carry out some measure of civil service reform, and, undoubtedly, honestly made his best effort to do so; but how lamentably he has failed. Mr. Garfield was nominated at the last Republican Convention for the Presidency. He is, beyond question, a man of high integrity and ability. Two men were proposed in the convention for nomination for the Vice Presidency, Mr. Washburne and Mr. Arthur. It cannot be denied that Mr. Arthur's career in office, so far as could be seen, has been that of a "machine" politician. A delegate arose in the convention and made an earnest appeal against his nomination, and in favor of Mr. Washburne's. He said, in substance: "The Republican party is pledged by its platform to civil service reform. Do not stultify yourselves. The people will think over your action quietly at their firesides." But to no use. Mr. Arthur was nominated, and Mr. Garfield's hands are tied. For Mr. Arthur represents the "machine," and Mr. Garfield cannot be elected without the aid of the "machine"—at least, the "machine" makes it appear he cannot be. He must bow to it if he shall be elected. And the Republican people who want civil service reform may think at their firesides *ad libitum*, but they can find no way of acting adversely to Mr. Arthur, so far as he represents the opposition to civil service reform, except by voting against Mr. Garfield. They must, consequently, vote with the "machine."

No one loves the "machine," or sees anything to admire in it, except those who live, or hope to live, by it. Yet our country is growing so large, and there are so many "offices to go around," that by one device or another the "machine" is always triumphant. From the highest federal office to the lowest State office political preferment is obtained, not by the display of marked or suitable qualities for doing the work of office as it should be done, but only by capacity for managing primaries and conventions according to the modes of the "machine." This is the ability which most certainly makes a successful politician in free America to-day. Straightforward, honest directness of purpose, with which the dreamers fondly characterize the ideal republican politician of an Anglo-Saxon republic, has given place, with us, to an Asiatic suppleness and skill in intrigue almost unexampled in political history.

That stronghold of individual liberty, the judiciary itself, has time and again been invaded and overcome by the spirit of partisan rule—a power greater and more despotic than was ever wielded by any Stuart of them all. In the Supreme Court of the United States it compelled a partisan and unrighteous division of opinion in the Dred Scott case. In the same court, two judges were appointed for the express purpose (according to common belief) of reversing a previous fully considered and solemnly made decision of that court on the constitutionality of the legal tender act. The decision was reversed, and the London *Times* declared, in effect, that no high court of judicature in any Anglo-Saxon country had ever before so disgraced itself. In the Electoral Commission, the judges of the same court, selected with a confident belief of all parties that some, at least, of them, by virtue of their high office, were far above partisanship, divided in opinion as they were respectively named Democrat or Republican.

No great war has arisen in which the Government has not found within the country a powerful organization, thwarting its steps in many important particulars; undermining its great reserve force of patriotic, moral support, by incitement to fanatical distrust. And although some men in every country may be found lukewarm toward the support of the government of their country in such an emergency, they are insignificant in power and number compared with the multitude (otherwise fair men) in the United States, who so act through force of the custom of always acting with but one party and knowing no bond of policy which can possibly unite them with any members of the other. It has been reserved for America to produce "Blue Lights" and "Copperheads."

Let us now glance for a moment at our system of legislative representation, and see how the rule of the majority, as we have adopted it, effectually tends to smother the real will of the people. I quote Mr. Dutcher:*

"A is the Democratic candidate and B the Republican before a constituency of, say, 23,000 votes. For A 12,000 votes are cast; for B, 11,000. A is said to represent the district, when, in truth, he represents only 12,000, and the 11,000 are not represented at all. They are said to be so; but let interests clash, or opinions differ, and he becomes their foe—their active opponent. Purely as a minority the minority receives no representation at all. Where there are many districts, and, consequently, many minorities, the aggregate of unrepresented votes becomes an astounding anomaly in a representative government."

Mr. Dutcher supplies the following actual computation, by which it has been found that fifty-eight per cent. of the entire vote cast secures all the representatives voted for, and forty-two per cent. fails to elect a single member:

In the Fortieth Congress there were 2,335,617 Republican and Democratic voters represented, out of a total vote of 4,005,573; thus there were 1,669,956 Republican and Democratic voters unrepresented; proportion, 58 to 42.

In the Forty-first Congress there were 3,524,335 represented, out of a total vote of 6,076,413; thus there were 2,552,078 unrepresented; and the result has been the same proportion practically ever since.

Now, if we could deduct from those supposed to be actually represented the number of persons who find themselves differing from their representative on important points of public policy, and who would never have voted for him at all had a chance to choose a better man, that is, a truer representative of their opinions, been allowed them, we should have a wonderful display of how nearly like the composition of a mob representative government may be.

Delegates to nominating conventions are elected on the same false principle as our legislative representatives, and thus minority opinions within the party fail to have their due weight in its deliberations.

It is very plain to me that a constant majority in the representative assemblies, so largely disproportionate to the actual majority of voters which elected it, tends to foster partisanship, to crush out minor differences of opinion, and to divide the country unnecessarily into merely two political organizations. The irresponsibility of the majority is so marked, and its power of rewarding its supporters so great, that it may maintain a powerfully cohesive organization, notwithstanding almost any errors and vices, except such as immediately, and plainly to the narrowest capacity, threaten serious injury to the government. Practically, each party has nothing to fear when in power so long as it satisfies the cravings of its orthodox followers, and avoids any greater excesses than its predecessor—which moderate requirement allows it a great limit of bad conduct, as we all know. The comparatively small number of "independents," who make majorities by voting with one party or the other, do so, in the main, without hope of obtaining office (for they know they are detested by both parties), and, being accustomed, for many decades past, to find "one party as bad as another," they grow weary of making changes, except upon very great provocation. Thus a majority, in the face of errors and excesses that would cause revolution in many other countries, can afford for a long time to ask Bill Tweed's question, "What are you going to do about it?" It is inevitable that such a system of representation, dividing, as it does, so large a country as ours into merely two parties, should lead to the partisan nominating conventions; that these bodies necessitate a rigid and exclusive system of party organizations, the keeping alive of partisan strife, and indifference to growth and progress in the minor affairs of government; and that this is the hot-bed of all the glaring evils and disgraces of American public life.

The corruption and incapacity of our public servants have been the subject of constant complaint with a large part of the American people for the last eighty years. Even in De Tocqueville's day it was loud and deep enough to attract his attention as an important problem for the future of the country. After stating the problem, he supposed he had solved it in this way (I change the order of his sentences, for the purpose of condensation):

"The mal-administration of a democratic magistrate is a mere isolated fact, which only occurs during the short period for which he is elected. * * * Corruption and incapacity do not act as common interests, which may connect men permanently together, * * * and it is impossible that they"—

(corrupt and incapable officers, holding offices for only short terms)

—"should ever give a dangerous or exclusive tendency to the government."

* *Minority or Proportional Representation.* By Salem Dutcher. New York: U. S. Publishing Company. 1872.

Whether or not he was right in sketching corruption and incapacity in this harmless light may be answered by each man for himself, and will be answered mainly according as he hopes to obtain office through the "machine." For my part, I see, in common with thousands of persons in the country, literate and illiterate, high and low, that corruption and incapacity under our present system are forming a most permanent bond of union among the vast majority of politicians. They may not transmit their power, in all cases, directly to their flesh and blood children, as corrupt and incompetent aristocracies would, for such children may not be in the true line of descent. But there is a line of descent as clearly marked and certain. The power goes, by our system, to the next generation of corruptibles and incapables.

Many well meaning persons habitually answer the foregoing, "Pessimist and croaker, the system is good enough. The fault lies in the large number of ignorant persons at present exercising the right of suffrage. But the common schools may be expected to educate the children of such persons into good citizens, which will purify our politics in their day." This apotheosis of common school education is very effective, especially with persons who possess only such an education, and are but slightly addicted to original thought. The general spread of primary education has done great things, and can do much for America. But there are things it cannot do. It did not prevent China from standing still for centuries, because, although it has been almost universal there during that time, it was not in the right direction morally. It leaned too much toward satisfaction with itself and its sufficiency for the purpose of carrying on the government. The government obtained extraordinary permanency because of its aid; but custom, thus so powerfully established in so important a factor in the national life, bound the national mind in shackles which inflexibly retracted its moral and intellectual growth. If the general spread of the minor branches of knowledge, at all times and under all circumstances, insures national progress, why is not China the foremost nation of the globe to-day? It is a fact, which nobody can dispute, that for the last ten years, at least, there has hardly been a Legislature in any State in the United States against which charges of bribery have not been openly made. Yet our legislators had the benefit of the general spread of education; few of them were absolutely illiterate. Politics were corrupt, and the men did not need to be better than it was the custom to be. If politics remain corrupt (and the certain growth of large corporations, private wealth, and financial enterprises of all sorts, will keep them corrupt, unless we make a great change)—if the rising generation of Americans are accustomed to hear such charges daily, to find one party but little better than another, to see men in high place known to be corrupt, and to have achieved their position despite their characters—will that generation not also deem "smartness" far more essential than integrity or capability in public affairs, and will the common school education save them from so thinking? It has not saved their political fathers. This reasoning will also apply to the great evil of excessive and continually changing legislation, which, even in De Tocqueville's day, led him to make the following prediction:

> "It may be apprehended that men perpetually thwarted in their designs by the mutability of legislation will learn to look upon republican institutions as an inconvenient form of society; the evil resulting from the instability of the secondary enactments might then raise a doubt as to the nature of the fundamental principles of the constitution, and indirectly bring about a revolution. But this epoch is still very remote."

At the time this was written there had been but one revision of the original State constitutions. If De Tocqueville had lived to see the numerous experiments in legislation since made, notwithstanding a half century of the common school system; to hear the tone of easy contempt for almost all politicians and political efforts adopted by the rising generation; to see labor riots all over the country, and the steady growth of a class of intelligent persons in the large cities abstaining from voting—he would not have looked for some revolution at a remote epoch. Above all things he would have said: The spread of common school education has not checked excessive legislation hitherto; how can it be expected to limit it in the next generation?

Sir James Fitzjames Stephen, whom everybody must admit to be a clear and cautious thinker, cannot see much to be hoped for in the future, with respect to true liberty, from the indefinite increase on the American Continent of numbers of essentially small-minded but thoroughly self-satisfied persons, and continually suggests to us that, notwithstanding the best the common schools may do,

> —"the number of people able to carry on anything like a systematic train of thought, or to grasp the bearings of any subject consisting of several parts, will always necessarily be exceedingly small in every country, compared to the whole population. * * * The incalculable majority of men form opinions without the consciousness that they have reached them by intellectual processes correctly performed, but are attached to them because they suit their tempers and meet their wishes, and

not solely and in so far as they believe themselves warranted by evidence in believing them true; whereas the work of governing a great nation"—

(and in the United States of the future we must necessarily have one of the most complex governments that ever existed)

—"requires an immense amount of special knowledge, and the steady, restrained, and calm exertion of a great variety of the very best talents which are to be found in it."

A very large number of persons who possess these talents, and are willing to devote them to their country's service, are now excluded from any possibility of doing so; and the tendency with the immense majority of half-educated people is, and always will be, either to doubt the existence of any such persons, or to deny the possibility of any better knowledge than their own on political matters—on the principle by which they maintain their religious views. Thus thousands of talented men, who in a smaller state would materially aid the government, in so great a nation (though still more essential) may be buried alive, and their influence weakened by the half educated masses.

Finally, Mr. Ezra Seaman (to my mind a very accurate and observing man), in speaking of the destiny of the United States as its waste places fill up, points out that

—"the success of the Territories has been owing to the great natural wealth and resources of the country, the virtues of the public land system, the munificent donations of Congress, rather than to any great wisdom in their Territorial legislation. The shocking election frauds and abuses, and the barbarous legislation, in Kansas, involved the Territory in civil war, and showed that the heterogeneous mass of people that settle new Territories are poorly qualified either to make good laws or maintain order and peace—which is quite a different thing."

He deprecates the absurd confidence felt in the permanency of our Government under the present mode of conducting it, and points out that

—"we must reform our system of elections and representation, and thereby make our Government a government of the whole people, instead of a government of the leaders of the dominant party; we must revive a spirit of patriotism and respect for the workings of our Government, and arrest the downward course of corruption and prodigality. That we shall continue to increase in numbers and industry, commerce and wealth, for a half century or more to come is certain, but unless these reforms are effected in our Government, our national interests will become so numerous and incongruous, our population so heterogeneous; the national character and sentiments, religious views and aspirations of the people of different sections so discordant, the bonds of union so weak; corruption and profligacy so rank and bold, and sectional and class ambition so rampant, that the American Congress will become a jarring and discordant mob, and it will be impossible to reconcile its elements, and prevent the flames of civil war from bursting forth, perhaps in several sections at the same time, with the eventual result of the division of the national territory into several different nations."

That I am right in asserting the imminence of a change, or changes, in American government, many things in our public sentiments and conduct abundantly prove. All revolutions proceed from a desire to put better men in office; and thus they are rightfully thought a part of the upward tendency of humanity. It would take a volume to enumerate all the signs of change. It suffices to ask, why do so many thinking men among us complain from day to day of the exclusion from political life of the best men among us, and point to the present constitution of parties as the cause? Books have multiplied on the subject. "How can we get the best work of our best men in our public offices?" is the cry of one class. And from the other extreme, in the midst of actual and threatened riot, we hear the baffled howl, "Democratic thieves and Republican robbers." If we had no other analogy, this is singularly like the phenomena which preceded the French Revolution. The thinkers and the proletariat alike decry the present state of things, and long for something better. There is nothing to fear, however, from the analogy. I, for one, see other signs in the times than this. I do not for a moment doubt the substantial and proud perpetuation of American democracy. These things, nevertheless, show the fears of thoughtful men, and the impulses of men who suffer. A state of society in which the best men rise to the top is the aim of both cries—of every movement that ever amounted to anything in political conduct. That this has been the steady aim of the American people for the past eighty years, their complaints, as I have before stated, distinctly prove. And that they did not earlier bend all their energies to its attainment is due, so far as I can discern the philosophy of history, to the fact that in that period they have have had other overshadowing work to perform, and by no means to apathy. It is a reason well in keeping with the practical turn of Anglo-Saxon communities for self-government. It is taking one thing at a time, and selecting the most important thing for the present time—a markedly Anglo-Saxon trait, giving promise of stability—as distinguished from undertaking to bring about the millennium at once, which we rather unkindly call Mexicanization—giving promise of instability. The great work of the first century of national existence is nobly accomplished. Already the glaring signs which differentiated Republican and Democrat are fading to kindlier and more delicate tones. We may, and perhaps should, always retain the really fundamental opinions which make us either, and be ready to assert them when the occasion arises. But there is now no distinctively great national problem to be solved by their aid. A minority of each party, not noticeable for activity in politics, has compelled the respectful attention of both parties toward a reform in the civil service. The demand may be trifled with for a while, but it will ultimately be complied with if we are faithful to it. It will have at least one result: it will teach us that there are other practical problems in government, upon which good men can unite to their country's advantage, without regard to differences on metaphysical theories respecting the nature of our federal compact. Let us not even for the moment deceive ourselves regarding the value of this reform in the civil service. Even the best scheme which can be carried will by no means cure all the evils we see. The examining or appointing board may yet be open to the intrigues of politicians, and the composition of legislative bodies will not be affected by it at all, for it must necessarily leave out of sight the qualifications of all but the inferior officers of government.

Must we, then, limit the right of suffrage, or the number of offices to be filled by popular election, in order to save the Government, as some are inclined to think? I am sure not. This is not the tendency of progress in government. Despite the provocation to such a measure which the gross judicial corruption in the State of New York during the Tweed *régime* gave to the intelligent agricultural classes of that State—always noticeably at variance in politics with the working classes of the large cities—a constitutional amendment giving the nomination of judges to the executive, as in the old days of the State, was voted down by a large majority of the farmers. And our immigrants nowadays, from all the western countries of Europe, have enjoyed in their own countries practically universal suffrage. Clearly this will not be the change.

I think the ultimate remedy will be found in a reform in the electoral system based on the representation of minorities in all assemblies—not disturbing the rule of the majority, but purifying it by recognizing the right of the all important shades of political opinion to representation in direct and true proportion to the numbers entertaining them. Already in the election of the New York Court of Appeals the cumulative vote has been tried with excellent results. Various other trials of systems of proportional representation have been made elsewhere, in this country and in Europe, and the subject has forced itself on Congress more than once. The poorer classes in the State of California, more largely interested in joint-stock corporations than the same classes elsewhere, lately adopted such a system for the election of boards of trustees in such bodies. There are sincere and intelligent friends of freedom, jealous of any danger to American democracy, who recognize the adoption of a true principle of represention as its hope and certain result. I have mentioned some of them. I should not omit to name one of the earliest and most consistent, Senator Buckalew, of Pennsylvania.* If this article shall succeed in interesting but one inquiring mind in the future of representative government, its defects will have been atoned for. Reforms in the civil service, in the system of Presidential elections, and in the composition of legislative assemblies, are surely probable changes in our Government near at hand. Let us be ready so to guide them that we may fitly supplement the great work left ready for us. Clinging to the Constitution as the core of American patriotism, I do not doubt we shall—to borrow again the noble words I have elsewhere quoted—forward its design: "laws made for the sake of liberty, not liberty merely to make laws."

JOHN A. WRIGHT.

FUTURE GARDENS OF CALIFORNIA.

The month of August brings a period of enforced rest to the gardens of California; for the earliest luxuriance of bloom has departed, and thoughtful gardeners have cut back the roses and other shrubs, so as to insure a later blossoming time. Fitly, therefore, we may now consider the whole field, and attempt in some degree to realize how much or how little of a success our garden has been. In these sultry summer days, we are apt to be moved with a sense of the

* *Proportional Representation.* By Charles R. Buckalew. Philadelphia: John Campbell & Sons. 1872.

shortcomings of the modern gardening system. Doubtless, it is true that this system is one of the indices of civilization (as the horticultural writers will have you believe); but, really, do we not occasionally trim, and water, and cultivate through somewhat too many tribulations? The garden plot must be dug and fertilized when the autumnal rains begin. Then comes the seed-sowing of early annuals, the planting of spring bulbs, the endless repetition of weed-battles. As spring brightens into summer, the hosts of the insect world haunt and worry that hapless garden; and as summer ripens into its royal prime, the era of irrigation begins, and the ardent horticulturist drags lengths of hose to and fro, soils his best clothes, and has minor and unrecorded adventures with what a reporter acquaintance calls the pluvial fluid. The perplexities of garden-lovers are so endless and amazing, each month bringing its own burdens, that it needeth all the first-born roses of May, the fragrant lilies of June, the regal asters of August, to be sufficient compensation. Perhaps, if we are wise, and study nature's ways, we shall gain some lessons which may help us toward simpler systems of gardening. Such a result were well worth a long and earnest search. If all who love blossoms toil as they should, what shall be the similitude of the gardens of the future California?

No one has yet made fairly visible to men the best which lies concealed, yet potential, in soil and atmosphere of this new land. Enough, however, has been done in favored spots by the pioneer floriculturists to warrant the fairest hopes of the future, as flowers become more a necessity of the daily lives of men. The comparative ease and rapidity with which flowers can be grown here are the encouraging features of the case. Our Eastern friends come and see our gardens, and begin to rhapsodize at once; they measure cream-tinted roses, and revel in masses of color from scarlet anemones and blue larkspurs. The exuberance of our earlier summer is a continual surprise to them. Our vines, they tell us, grow more in one year than those of the East do in three. Pleasant praise, certainly; but do we really deserve it, and have we as yet gained a full insight into the uses of our climate? Once, I remember, in a decayed mining camp of the Sierra foothills, I saw a pretty picture, which, if I describe it here, may serve to illustrate my thought. Where two small but musical streams united, there was, under the brow of a pine-covered mountain, a half acre of rich soil, somewhat rocky and sloping gently to the water's edge. A deserted house, slowly crumbling to utter ruin, a few orchard trees, bits of stone wall, and mossy fence-rails, were all which gave clear evidence of former human possession, except that, close by the old well, some nameless person, years before, had planted a Lamarque rose, and this rose had made for itself a kingdom in the waste and lonely place. It curved in an emerald wave, crowned with white foam, shining and beautiful, flowing softly over wall and pillar, clinging to brown cliffs, and winding about the silvery pines, until at last, by what secret art I know not, this ardent rose-vine flung its white banners to the breeze from the topmost tuft of a giant cedar. There it climbs and blooms today, as much at home as is the manzanita on the mountain slopes, and no garden of the lowlands ever had fairer roses. I hate to think that, perhaps, some of these days a lean, restless, practical fellow will come along and fix up the ruined shanty, clear out the old well, dig up our wild rose vine to make room for his onion-bed, and plant a vineyard on the shining slope of the hills, where now the carnelian-hued mountain lilies nod all summer long. If I ever hear of such a thing, I shall take another road when next I climb the Sierra slopes, to find the lovely blossoming nooks and the friendly homes of healthy men.

All this brings us slowly to the heart of our disquisition. California gardens, famous already for what can be done with them, and widely known as of almost ideal beauty, are none the less deserving of occasional censures—not for what they have, but for what they have not. They are so much already that we are inevitably led to hope that they will not rest upon their present laurels, but, sighing for new realms to possess, will develop into forms of as yet unimagined beauty. Our horticulturists must search for new plants, and they must study out new ways in which to use them, for we cannot follow blindly after the methods of other people. There are hundreds, and even thousands, of species of herbaceous plants, bulbs, shrubs, and vines, not as yet seen in our gardens, though they would add immeasurably to our floral treasures, and would render many new effects possible. But, leaving for the present this side of the subject, and forbearing to give any lists of the rarer garden plants, we simply desire to make a suggestion about a new kind of garden, which, if once fairly entered upon, would prove the cheapest and most effective of methods for suburban and rural homes.

Perhaps it is not generally known that a reaction against the geometric system of gardening is now in progress in Europe. This system depends upon massing flowers, and upon the copious use of foliage-plants. Ribbon beds are its culmination. It appeals strongly to the love of order and of bright colors. For parks and extensive grounds this method will always find defenders, and even admirers. But during the prevalence of ribbon-gardening hundreds of choice border-plants have dropped out of cultivation. Only brilliant plants which massed well were desired. The present reaction against the ribbon-bed system contemplates the revival of an interest in old-fashioned flowers, and the use of them in new and peculiarly charming ways. To be successful in this new and natural system of gardening requires a genuine knowledge of plants and a cultivated taste. The field which lies before the ardent floriculturist is wide enough to occupy the enthusiasm of a lifetime, and to utilize the surplus means of the owners of suburban homes from Del Norte to San Diego.

While we unfold the manner of these new-era gardens we desire as audience the thoughtful and plant-loving people of city and town, of hillside and hollow. You are to be told what is meant by the modern "wild garden" of the most artistic of living landscape gardeners. Truly it were worth while for us to realize the course that scientific floriculture is taking. The main thing now arrived at appears to be this: that we shall try to make plants at home, growing as naturally as weeds, and, indeed, taking the place of the latter. Near the house we may have a "tame garden," trim, neat, sedate, and even geometrical, an it please you. But further from the house, on the hillside of the suburban homestead, you shall, according to the new scheme, work on a different plan. Here, the greatest imaginable variety of trees, vines, shrubs, bulbs, and herbaceous plants, winter, spring, summer, and autumn bloomers, shall be planted and acclimatized as much as may be. We will grub out the poison oak, and plant English holly, American kalmias, and the new Himalayan rhododendrons. Vines of the Mexican and Peruvian highlands shall climb up the Australian trees, and hang in bright festoons above the groups of gorgeous Chilian and Cape of Good Hope bulbs. Moreover, these plants, which grow in a wild state without cultivation, will, in a large measure, take care of themselves in our hypothetical "wild garden" of California. The scheme has the advantages of cheapness and simplicity. Once fairly entered upon, and the charm of such gardens will be far beyond those of the geometric sort.

The primal law upon which the idea of a wild garden is based is that all the plants of any given isothermal zone could be made to thrive at any point of that zone. Take, for instance, the mean temperature, summer and winter, of sixty degrees. High up, on tropic mountains, and descending lower and lower toward the poles, reflecting with faithful sensitiveness the local agencies of winds and slopes, currents and exposures, this mean temperature of sixty degrees has, on each continent, its peculiar flora; and with proper care the horticulturist may acclimate in his chosen spot the beauties of the whole world-wide belt of similar conditions.

Here, in California, the widest range of ornamental plants known to any climate is possible, and ought, in the near future, to be made a visible fact. Let us, for instance, consider the resources at the command of sensible builders of rock-work, in which the highest art-feeling which moves the true landscape gardener may find full expression. Rock-work there is which has been mathematically built up with angular and polished fragments of stone, having, at set intervals, neat pockets of earth, for the torture of sickly plants, and the misery of unfortunate artists, who pass by, look over the fence, and turn away sighing. But rock-ledges, and wild mountain walls, artistically developed, clothed with clinging vines, brown wall-flowers, rosette-like echeverias, trailing sedums, thick-leaved mesembryanthemums, and undescribed quaintness everywhere, are hopeful guerdons of the future landscapes of California. Such rock-ledges we have seen in the Oakland hills, and such, let us believe, do exist in many hidden nooks, by fair mountain streams, near the homes of busy folk. But suppose—let us ask the gardening world of California—suppose that we had a greater variety of rock-work plants? Why not use, with artistic judgment, the alpine plants of Carniola, Syria, the Caucasus, the Alps, Pyrennees, and Apennines, the Grecian cliffs, the Himalayan hights, the Mexican Cordilleras, and the Bolivian Andes? Does any gardener in this State believe that our people use a tithe of the treasures at their command? Half an hour spent in reading the best European catalogues will be sufficient evidence of the floral wealth yet to be made our own in that fair future of which we have such abiding faith. The garden of the future in the coming California for those who truly love flowers will need for its development a varied surface of hill-slope and ravine, such as can easily be found in San Mateo, Marin, Alameda, Contra Costa, or Sonoma. From five to twenty acres of such land will be required. Near the house there might be a trim garden, and perhaps a small conservatory, but over the rest of the territory mountain plants of every land are to be coaxed into a sense of possession and security. The growth of our handsomest native shrubs, annuals and herbaceous perennials, should also be encouraged. There will be a constant succession of bloom upon such a homestead. Early bulbs and shrubs will begin first upon the warmer slopes, and, as summer advances, the northern ridges and the deep ravines will have their turn. In the whole year no day will be without its own peculiar charm; each hour, almost, will witness some new flowers unfolding. Many of the best shrubs, which, in less favored climates, need constant attention and expensive greenhouse treatment, can here be grown almost as readily as apple trees. Then, too, the immense variety of hardy bulbs now within the reach of the ordinary purse is an endless source of enjoyment. Crocuses, tulips, lilies, jonquils, daffodils, and gladioli, are only a beginning. One might have over twenty different species of the lovely anemones, and in dozens of distinct shades and colors. The ranunculus does well here, and the bulbs of Peru and Chili are perfectly at home on our hillsides.

Although, as we have hinted, a tract of varied surface, embracing about twenty acres, is best adapted to this sort of a wild garden, yet the happy possessor of a half acre need not utterly despair, for he can use the same principles in a lesser degree, and graceful Nature will come to his aid with her benign and gentle friendship. He may plant vines along the fences, and make piles of rock which shall seem to have a reason for their existence. He may choose only those plants which are at home in that region, and give them such care that they will take sturdy possession, in a liberal mood, even as they do on the hillsides. With such surroundings, the roots of the home itself run deeper, and bind more firmly, year after year. And, in all simplicity, it is fair and pure homes that California, or, indeed, any land worth the loving, needs now, and will forever need.

Charles H. Shinn.

JACK'S BOYS.

Jack Trevers is a "sure enough" man, as Two-shoes says. "Nobody didn't made him out of a nink-stand and put him in a book;" he is a veritable citizen of Lake County. It was a long time ago that he came here from somewhere, with three baby boys and no mother for them. He built himself a cabin on an unclaimed piece of land, about three miles from the village, and then tried to get work. At first, he would work only near home, so that he could see his children every night; but when Johnny got to be four years old, and Tom had reached the mature age of nine, he got a job of teaming, that kept him away all the time, except two nights out of the week and Sunday. By this time, Tom had learned to cook a little, and to assume the responsibility of the household. Willie, the second child, was a nervous, active fellow, and so wide awake and full of mischief he kept the whole family in an uproar. Johnny, the baby, was an unfathomable looking boy, fat as butter, fair as alabaster, and the laziest little mortal living. The nearest approach he ever made toward playing was to lie on his back and laugh while watching his brothers play. His laugh was the most spontaneous and irresistible upheaval of merriment ever listened to; it bubbled up like creamy lager, and overflowed through its inherent effervescence. Indeed, if it had required effort on Johnny's part, it never would have been. He was a beautiful child, but for his dirty, neglected appearance; and the mother whose loving pride would have rectified this was far away in the distant sky.

Now, these three children were in a great measure cut off from all social intercourse by reason of their having no mother. No one visited the house. Jack taught the oldest one to read a little, and bought him a few books. He was an industrious scholar, and when he could master a newspaper paragraph was firmly convinced that he knew a great deal. The fact of his being cut off from all other boys with whom he could measure his attainments led him into this very common error; but it had one good result—he placed great value on his learning, and felt the necessity of imparting it to the other boys. So he kept school for two hours each day, and in this way they all learned to read. When Jack was at home, he encouraged them in their studies, and began to teach them something of arithmetic and writing.

It was the desire of their lives to possess a clock, and great was their delight one evening when Jack brought one home. They set it up according to directions, and it started all right. They were much pleased with its tone in striking, and as Jack showed them the way to make it strike, the presumption is that they kept it striking pretty much all the time he was off on his next trip. Be that as it may, when he returned, the clock wouldn't strike at all. He questioned them, but their answers bewildered and finally threw him off the scent. He came to the conclusion that Johnny was right in thinking it was tired. If this was the case, it did not require much time to rest, and in resting it acquired the most unprecedented vigor; for, when he returned again, it would strike the hours, the half hours, and almost the minutes and seconds. It would strike a hundred times without stopping, and *encore* without being asked.

"Now, boys," said Jack, "I know you've been foolin' with that clock."

They all protested. Their faces were innocent as could be.

"That's strange," said he; "it must have been out of kelter when I bought it. Cohen swindled me on it. By hokey, I never touch that Jew that I don't get salted. Hang me if I don't go for him the next time I see him."

"You punch him good, Jack," said Willie (they all called him Jack); "if he don't need it for the clock, he does for lots of other things. Tom's coat, you paid eight dollars for, was shoddy, and fell to pieces as soon as it got wet; and that ten pounds of sugar you brought home last time only weighed seven—we weighed it; and Johnny's new boots are only just pasted together, and are all apart a'ready. You just give him fits. I wish I could be there to see you do it."

Jack was a good-natured man, but feeling that it was his duty to resent such an accumulation of injuries, he tried to nurse his wrath to keep it warm. And the boys helped him; they told him so many instances of Cohen's rascallity in their own small dealings, and abused him so roundly, that in the morning, when he left home, he was as nearly angry as he had ever been. Now, the merchant was an unprincipled villain, who had grown rich out of the necessities of the wretchedly poor community around him; and his extortions were crying aloud for redress. Alas for justice! Jack forgot his anger before he reached town. The day was so beautiful, the roads were so good, and his off wheel-mule, "Beck," never once thought to kick herself out of the traces for the entire three miles, something she had not omitted before within the memory of man. The lovely influence of all these things conspired to bring on his softest and most dreamy mood; and he fell to thinking of the Widow Cramer, on the old Harbin Road, and to wondering if she really smiled upon all men as she smiled on him; and if, and if—*ad infinitum*, for the subject was an inexhaustible one. He was roused out of Eden by hearing his "boss" speak to him: "Go to Cohen's this morning, Jack, and take up a load of hides you will find there; leave the quicksilver until your next trip."

"All right, sir." And he swung his team around in front of Cohen's store.

"'Ust you trive rount pehint te shdore, unt not geep your tam pucking mules in te vay of mine gusdomers," Cohen roared, in a voice quite different from that in which he addressed a man with money in his pocket.

"You come and put me around, won't you?" said Jack, as two red spots slowly gathered in his cheeks.

"Do it yourself, unt be hangt mit you."

"Not much, Mary Ann," drawled Jack, looking at him out of the corner of his eye, and leisurely swinging himself to the ground. "I'm as much of a man as you are. Do you want to try it on?"

"You're a tam peggar, mitout a tollar to your bocket."

"Don't say too much, Cohen, unless you've got the sand to try it on."

"I vish dere vas a law to hang such insolent peggars."

Jack was doing something to his harness—buckling and unbuckling straps, and making changes generally—casting sidelong glances at the merchant meantime. When he was through, he reached him in one bound.

"You black scoundrel," he said, "you have swindled me out of hundreds of dollars since I came to this country—every dollar earned by hard work. Not only that, but you've cheated poorer men than I am; and you've robbed widows and orphans. You suck up every cent set afloat in this community. You're a thief, by hokey. You'd go on the highway if you were not too cowardly. There's nobody you wouldn't rob; you'd steal acorns from a blind hog. But talk's cheap—I've got something better than talk." And with that came the first blow, and Jack administered it; the price of it was ten dollars. The first blow was all that cost anything, and that being over with, Jack limbered himself to his work in the most energetic style. The bystanders forbore to interfere, though the merchant called on them most piteously. When Jack had satisfied himself of the thoroughness of the job, he picked him up, as one does a puppy, and pitched him into the street, and then walked into the store after the hides. He brought out his arms full, and met Cohen in the door, who dodged round to the back porch, where he petted his bruises, among the jeers of a dozen heartless little street cubs, until his adversary had loaded up and departed.

Now, Jack's boys, being alone and seeing no one, heard nothing of the fight over which the community was rejoicing, until he returned from his trip to spend Sunday. Indeed, they had forgotten the matter, and so had he until he heard that irrepressible clock, hammering distraction into everybody that heard it—children excepted.

"She do beat natur' all holler, Jack," said Johnny; "and her never lets up, only to draw her breath sometimes. That clock's worth a million dollars."

"Has she been going that way ever since I left?"

"Bet yer boots. And her can keep it up for never and never, amen."

"Jack," said Willie, "did you see Cohen?"

"Yes, and I whaled him like blazes, too."

"WHAT!" came from all the boys, in the largest sized capitals.

Jack thought he detected something like consternation in this simultaneous explosion, and made up his mind to "lie low and keep shady" until he could find out more. Presently Tom and Willie stole off together, and in a few minutes one of them called Johnny. Jack stepped to a chink-hole and peeped out, smiling.

"I've got the deadwood on you fellers now," he said. But his smile disappeared as he noted their performances.

"Why, they are only trading with each other—swapping knives, or buttons, or trinkets." So he withdrew, and began to get supper.

The next day Jack spent in the woods with his axe; he was getting fuel enough to last the children a week. Of course they were with him—Tom and Willie playing, and Johnny on his back down in the grass near his father. Presently the big boys were out of hearing, and Jack sat down by Johnny, in a comfortable manner, and opened conversation in a free-and-easy, half confidential style.

"I've a notion," said he, "to buy me some hogs to fatten, so I can make my own meat. What do you say to it?"

"All right," said Johnny, bringing himself to a sitting posture. "You get some, Jack, and I'll feed 'em for you."

The idea of Johnny volunteering to do anything was a surprise; and Jack determined to buy them immediately.

"What kind of hogs do you want, Johnny?"

"Well, you see, Jack, I want spotted ones, and not too big. If they're big they'll eat so-o-o *much;* and a feller can't be always workin' to fill up horgs even if they *is* spotted."

"Well, I'll get little ones; at least, not very big," said Jack. "I'll get 'em, sure; and don't you tell the boys anything about it. Won't they be surprised, though? And I'll get you a little tin bucket to carry barley and water to 'em, and you can feed 'em three times a day by the clock."

"Yes; but that clock's no good to keep time. She's bully on the strike, Jack, bet your boots; but when it comes to keepin' time she won't pin herself down to it. You'll have to let her make the music, and buy another one to keep time."

"But if I buy the hogs, and *spotted* hogs at that, I'll have no money to buy another clock."

"Well, now, maybe you can fix our clock so she can keep time; *maybe* you can."

"It might be done," said Jack, reflectively. "What did you fellers do to her when you took her to pieces?"

"Well, Jack, I'll tell you." Here he put one grimy fist in his pocket, and, after a few moments of serious and reflective fumbling, produced, among a handful of dirt, strings, pins, and buttons, three little tarnished brass cog-wheels.

"You see we got her together all right, only there was five more of these than she needed; so at first Tom and Bill took two apiece, and only give me one. But when you told us you had pitched into old Cohen the boys called me out and 'vided up better for fear I'd tell you, and that's how I got three."

"Well, well, Johnny, you nearly ruined the clock, though."

"Not much; bet your boots, we made her strike, Jack."

"Well, well, *well*," said Jack, smiling more and more as he recalled, with fatherly pride, all the methods the boys had used for his deception. "Well, well, *well*, if you fellers just keep on you'll make first-class *lyars* after a while." He meant lawyers, but would have sworn he could not see the difference even if one had corrected him.

Jack was often troubled in his mind about Johnny's laziness, and sometimes rallied him on the subject.

"I'm afraid you don't like work, Johnny," he would say.

"Bet your boots."

"What! don't like work?"

"I 'spise it."

"How are you going to live without work?"

"What you got to do, you can't work for me?"

"Of course, I can work for you, now you are small, but after while you will be a man, and get married, and have children; what'll you do then?"

"Why, Jack, I'll keep you right along. I won't throw off on you, 'cos you're old. I guess you can work after you get old, can't you? Some mans does."

"Yes; but suppose I take a notion to get married myself, and have some more children to support; then you'd have to make your own living."

"If you was mean enough to do that I'd kill you, sure. I'd bust your crust quicker'n lightnin'. I'd—I'd—I'd give you a *leetle* the hottest time you ever heard of, bet your boots."

The other children shared Johnny's feelings on the subject of their father's second marriage. It was only a short time before that some thoughtless fellow had stopped with them all night, and by playing on their feelings had found out their repugnance to all thoughts of Jack's marrying again. So he told them there was a widow woman living on the old Harbin Road that was sweet on Jack, and advised them to look out for danger in that quarter. They looked out as the sequel shows.

The next evening after this precious piece of news, when Jack swung his mules from the main road and dashed to the barn in a sweeping trot, with harness rattling and bells jingling, not a boy met him; everything was silent. He was frightened instantly, and leaving the team standing, he sprung from the seat and rushed into the house. No, not into it, for on the threshold he encountered three little savages, armed with clubs and pitchforks, who demanded of him an explanation concerning his matrimonial intentions. In vain he tried to waive the question and pass into the room. Little Thermopylæ stood grimly defiant. The tears that washed clean channels down their dirty faces were no augury of weakness, but the reverse. Jack knew his boys were never fighting mad until they reached the blubbering point.

"Come now, boys, let Pap alone, won't you?" He called himself by this endearing epithet only in extreme emergencies, such as administering medicine, etc.

"*You* 'Pap,'" said Tom; "durn such a Pap as you are, a tryin' to bring a woman here to pound daylight out of us."

"Why, Tom, what you talkin' about? Don't you know you wouldn't have the kitchen work to do if you had a nice stepmother to do it for you?"

Here every club was raised, and they made a rush for his shins. He avoided them, and they resumed position in the door. Jack had hard work to keep from laughing at the picture they made; their round eyes peering savagely through their unkempt forelocks, like so many pup terriers; the determination they evinced—"sand," he called it, in speaking about it to the Widow Cramer afterward. His inclination to laugh was supplanted by another and better feeling. Their antagonistic attitude caused him to look at them with the eyes of his observation opened, and he saw what handsome, manly fellows they were, and what a pitiful appearance they presented in their dirty, neglected condition. A pain shot through his heart with a thought of the sweet mother who could never, from her high home, reach them with needed help.

"Boys," he said, "I never had a serious thought of marrying before, but, durn my hide, if I don't think it would be the best thing I could do."

"Then you ain't goin' to marry her, are you, Jack?" asked Tom, ignoring the latter half of his father's remark.

"No; not if you don't want me to."

"Well, we *don't* want you to." Blubbered out with intense vehemence.

"Well, then, I won't."

"Honest injun?"

"Yes; honest injun."

"Will you cross your heart?"

"I will *that*," suiting the action to the word.

And so ended the second edition (diamond) of the Pass of Thermopylæ; and sixty seconds afterward no one could have told that a people had seceded, a battle been fought, and a victory gained on that piece of ground. The combatants were swarming about the wagon, whooping like savages; swarming over the hay, trying to feed the mules; swarming on the mules' backs, and, by reason of their ubiquity, appearing to be about thirty boys instead of three.

In course of time Jack bought some hogs, spotted ones, and not too big. The barley had to be carried to them from the stable and the water from a running spring close by. The new tin bucket was bought, and the lazy boy installed in his position. Jack did not hope much from Johnny, but told the other boys not to interfere with him, and, above all, not to do his work; for the handiness of Tom and Willie had been a constant premium on Johnny's laziness. So Jack said to them:

"Now, don't you fel's take any notice of him; let him go it on his own hook; he'll do pretty well for a day or two, and then if he knocks off the hogs won't starve till I get home."

So Johnny began. He did well for several days. Jack made the next trip, and before undertaking another he was rained in, and the teaming season was over. Then he found a job of rough carpentering on a house about eight miles away, and as he worked early and late he could go home only every Saturday night and spend Sunday with his boys. On his first visit, Johnny was still working with his hogs, but showed symptoms of weariness. On his second visit, he met the young man nearly half a mile from the house. It was then dark. He saw a little bundle of something sitting by the road as he approached, and when it got up and took shape it was Johnny.

"Hello!" said Jack, "what's up?"

"Nuf's up, Jack; If you want me to feed your durn horgs any more, you'll have to get some barley."

"Why, thunder and Tom Walker, I left enough barley to feed them a month; what have you done with it?"

Not a word from Johnny.

"Did somebody steal it out of the barn?"

"Course not."

"Did Smith's hogs get in and destroy it?"

"*Course* not."

"Did you boys sell it and buy something with the money?"

"COURSE NOT. You must be a durn eejot."

Jack knew it was no use to fish any longer for the truth in that small pail of curdled milk, and dropped the subject. The fact, as he afterward discovered, was, that Johnny had put in one lazy man's day's work on the hogs. Feeding them had got to be such a dead weight on his mind he could not sleep more than fifteen hours a night for thinking of it; so he "resolved him a resolution," and taking his little bucket one morning, directly after breakfast, he commenced carrying the barley to them. By the most unprecedented exertion he had deposited the entire amount on hand in the pig-pen, and on the road leading to it, by dinner time. Then he ate and slept with a clear conscience, and had nearly a week to do nothing in before his father's return. But this was not the last of his mismanagement with the hogs. Jack bought more barley, and directed him to use it with great moderation. Johnny carried out these directions to the letter. Another week passed; the hogs were doing well; indeed, they were living off the mud in their pen, half of which was barley. And so for another week they did tolerably well, but had to work out of all proportion to the amount of food they got; in fact, their claim was pretty well panned out. The third week they stood on their hind feet, braced up against the top rail of the fence, peering amain, like shipwrecked seamen, for the sight of a sail. But no sail came. Thursday night of the third week arrived, and the spotted hogs were almost in a condition to fly; their bones were hollow, and from the light volatile way their hair stood on end it was evident that it was fast turning to feathers. As the night wore on they became deeply embittered against the ways of civilization, and unanimously agreed to climb the fence and decamp, which they accomplished successfully.

In the morning, when Johnny discovered his loss, he was uneasy. He cogitated many ways of informing Jack, and finally concluded to write him a letter. There was no paper in the house, and, if there had been, there was no ink. He thought with regret of how they had used up all the ink in their negro minstrel performance a few days previous, the traces of which were still visible in their faces.

"Charcoal would a done just as well," he said, "and would a wore off lots quicker; now I'll have to write my letter on a slate."

So he got a miserably jagged, three-cornered piece of what had been one, and bent his gigantic intellect to the effort of composition. Manifold were the forms addressing themselves to his mind as the suitable manner of communicating his bereavement to his father; such as, "Jack, you're horgs is run off;" or, "you'd better come and catch your durn horgs," etc. But he did not like the effect of too brief an announcement. It would sound like a gun, he thought. Oh, if he could only stretch it out, "like a pair o' gallusus, that would be bully." Then he got to thinking of how he had unbosomed himself to Jack on the occasion of his first hog catastrophe, and he decided in his mind that the form of expression he then used was particularly felicitous. It conveyed the necessary information without compromising him: "If you want me to feed your durn horgs any more you'll hev to get some barley."

"That's just it," he soliloquized. "Bully for me. I know just what I'd orter say."

So he wrote with many smearings and corrections:

"Derh JAR IF u want Eev o uRe durn baRly fed ule Hev to git Sum moRe HoRgs.

"uRe afexn sun JON."

Having finished this masterpiece he carried it out to the county road, about half a mile away, where he sat down and began to make dirt pies, while waiting for some one to pass with whom he could intrust his letter to his father. He had finished only two or three with scallops, indentations, etc., when he saw a wagon coming.

"Oh, crackey," he said; "there's a lot of misble women in it. I 'spise women worse'n horgs; worse'n *spiled* horgs, too. I'll not send my letter by them, bet your boots."

But when the wagon came alongside it stopped, and a sweet-voiced woman asked:

"Is this the road to 'Squire Lawson's, honey?"

As the boy looked up he saw the face of an angel; and why not?—for a loving mother-heart looked out of gentle blue eyes upon him for the first time in his conscious life, and a tender, musical voice called him "honey."

"Yes," said he; "this is the road, *sure;* I know it is, cos my pap works there, and I've writ him a letter, and please won't you take it to him?"

"What's your pappy's name?"

"Jack Trevers."

Here two little girls in the back of the wagon exchanged smiling glances, and looked at Johnny with more interest.

"I'll give it to him," said the lady, reaching for the piece of slate; "your letter'll go safe enough, honey; don't you be uneasy; and I'm much obleeged to you for directin' of us. Good bye."

"Good bye," said Johnny, with a sort of catch at the word, feeling as if he had let a bird go, when a little forethought might have detained it. The wagon rattled on, and Johnny stood in the road just where it had left him.

"Durn my luck," he said. "First I lost the barley, and then I lost the horgs, and now I've lost *them*—and they're worth all the rest put together, bet your boots. Durn my luck, durn everything."

Then he looked at his pies, and, kicking them out savagely, went home.

Polly Cramer was a sister to Mr. Lawson, and was now making him her first visit since he had moved to his present abode. Under her green sunbonnet was the kind, loving face about whose smiles Jack had asked himself several questions on the morning of his fight with Cohen. It was now Friday; let us suppose this artful creature (all widows are artful) had two days in which to exercise her enchantments on poor Jack. He went home on Saturday night as happy as a lord, notwithstanding he carried in his heart the nucleus of the blackest plot that ever demonized a man. On Monday (let us be circumstantial) he went back to his work. Some time in the middle of the week it began to rain *à la Californie*—that is, with no intention of stopping short of a month. Now, what more natural than that Polly should become fearfully uneasy at the prospect of such weather, and make up her mind to go home forthwith, while the roads were still passable. Lawson and wife opposed. Jack, the sly-boots, opposed. All to no purpose.

> "When a woman will she will, you may depend on't,
> And when she won't she won't, so there's an end on't."

"I think you are very foolish, Polly," her brother said, as she was leaving; "but if the water keeps coming down like this, you had better lay over at Jack Trever's for a day or two."

About eleven o'clock that day, as Jack's boys supposed (their clock was now about two months ahead of time, and gaining rapidly), a small covered wagon drove up to the house, and stopped. Two mangy little ragamuffins filled the door instantly, and the head of a third one thrust itself between the first two, like a huge bobbin of flax sprinkled with gold dust, and strained, and squeezed, and wriggled until it succeeded in dragging out into the light the fat butterball of a boy that owned it. This last was Johnny. His face was one transparent glory, filled with "welcome;" but he spake not yet.

"Howdy, boys," said the widow. "Is the folks at home?"

"*We're* the folks," said Tom.

"Well, now, is that so? Ain't you got no father nor mother to take care of you?"

"We got a father, and he's comin' home tomorrow night. But we ain't got no mother, nor we don't want none."

"Well, boys, it's powerful wet, and I'd like mighty well to stop a spell with you, till the storm is over."

Tom and Willie looked at each other. Here was a live woman coming into the house. What should they do? As is often the case in more momentous questions, Fate decided while they deliberated. Fate on this occasion manifested itself through Johnny. His little face was glowing with cordiality.

"Come right in," he said. "We've got two beds—we boys can sleep in one, and you girls in the other, and Tom can cook bully, bet your boots. I'll get a chair for you to climb down on, and Tom can take your horses to the barn. We've got lots of hay, bet your boots. Now jump out, and run in the house; and Willie, you make up more fire, quick."

He issued his orders with irresistible authority, and in a few minutes all were housed, and a bright fire roared up the chimney. The widow glanced around. Dirt and discomfort everywhere. It looked a hopeless job to renovate.

"Believe if it was mine," she thought, "I'd burn it down, and camp out till I got another."

Tom came in from the barn, and began to make preparations for dinner.

"Never mind, honey," said Polly; "I can cook my own grub. You sit you down."

Tom obeyed, and watched her—watched her with growing interest.

"Hanged if ever I saw a feller as handy as she is," he whispered to Johnny.

"Bet your boots," said Johnny.

Polly found the flour and yeast-powder, and made bread. When she first rolled the dough out, after mixing, she spread a thin layer of lard over its surface, and rolled it up again with her hands; then she flattened it out with the rolling-pin, and cut it into shapes. She saw some bacon, and guessed rightfully, that it was the only meat in the house. She seemed to be looking for something more.

"There's lots o' taturs under the bed," said Tom.

She peeled them to boil, and, having boiled them, and fried the meat, she mashed the potatoes, and seasoned them with bacon drippings, salt, and pepper. The biscuits were baked beautifully, and fell apart on being handled, to the surprise of the ex-cook, who could not imagine by what hocus-pocus such a result had been produced. There was a pan full of eggs sitting there, and the children wondered if she would cook some of them; but she did not. Dinner was a decided success, and so was supper. In the morning, before breakfast, Johnny pointed out the eggs:

"You can cook just as many of them as you want to," he told her.

"I'm going to make cake out of 'em, for dinner," said Polly.

"What is cake?" asked Johnny.

The girls looked up at their mother quickly.

"Well, the pore little creetur—Lord love its pretty soul! To think of its never tastin' a bit of cake. *I'll* make some for it, honey, and then it'll know."

Rosy May asked him if he ever ate any pudding.

"Don't know what it is," said he.

"Did you ever see a pie?"

"I've made lots of 'em, bet your boots."

"What out of?"

"Dirt," said Johnny, triumphantly.

The dimples began to dance around Rosy May's mouth, but she choked them to death at a glance from her mother; but Blossom doubled up her little body like a boomerang.

One word about the children's names. The mania for uncommon names is not confined to the *élite*, but pervades all classes. Polly had never read a novel, but when her first baby was born she would not listen to the common names suggested by her family. Having a tender admiration of flowers, her thoughts ran on the name of Rose. The baby was born in May. Why not call her Rosy May? She declared her intention timidly at first, but, meeting encouragement from the sentimental young damsels of the neighborhood, she proclaimed it boldly, in defiance of "her folks," who had insisted on Nancy Mariar, Sary Jane, Mary Ann, and the like. When, some two years after, baby number two made her appearance, it seemed impossible to find a name for her. "Melindy," "Lucindy," "Elmiry," and many others, were discussed and dismissed. The young mother's taste still ran in the vein of flowers. She had never heard of Lily, Daisy, Pansy, and so on, or she might have made a selection.

"Well," she said to her husband one day, "I'm clean beat out about a name for the pretty thing, and I'm just a-goin' to call her Little Blossom till she's old enough to pick out the kind of posey she wants to be called after."

So the baby was named Little Blossom, in utter unconsciousness that the great humanitarian had rendered it immortal in the person of the child-wife.

Saturday night brought Jack, who was greatly surprised to find Polly there, and not any too well pleased, to judge from his greeting. The boys noticed that he was grim and reserved, and they resented it.

"Just to think," said Johnny to the other two, out in the barn, on Sunday morning, "after she made us that cake, and I saved him a hunk of it, too. It's over there in the speckled hen's nest, wrapped up so's she won't go for it. I've a great mind to eat it myself, and not give him a bite, when he treats her so mean, and won't hardly speak to Rosy May and Little Blossom."

"*I'd* do it," said Will. "He don't deserve any. And give me a piece of it, Johnny."

"Not much, bet your boots, 'nless you'll give back my striped taw you won from me yesterday."

"Here comes Jack," said Tom. "Now, Johnny, you get the cake and give him. That'll fetch him, sure. See if he don't own up that she beats natur' all holler. Then he'll treat her good, and maybe she'll stay here."

Johnny was prompt to act on this advice, but when he had scrambled up to the speckled hen's nest, a volley of exclamations burst from him.

"Durnd if she ain't been and made a hole in it. She don't think of nothing but her stomach. I wish she had'nt any, I do. I wish she'd starve to death, bet your boots."

"Has she eat it all, Johnny?" asked Tom.

"No; here's about half of it left."

"Well, that'll do. Bring it down, quick, and give it to him. He's 'most here."

But what was their surprise when Jack refused the cake sulkily.

"Eat it yourself," he said.

Johnny ate it, but the tears rolled over his fat cheeks, and he expressed his opinion of Jack at the same time.

"Don't care if I did lose your horgs. You're no better'n a horg yourself. I wish I could lose *you*, bet your boots, durn you. I'd rather have Rosy May and Little Blossom and their ma than a pig-pen full of you. I don't like you, anyhow. I never *did* like you much. I'd a swapped you off any time for Rosy May and Little Blossom and their ma, bet your boots, durn you."

Jack took no notice, and the small tempest soon blowed itself out. All the next week it rained incessantly. The children played in the barn a good deal, and that relieved Polly of their presence, and gave her a chance to clean things. It is astonishing the change she wrought in one week. She unearthed dozens of flour sacks from under the beds, and washed them. She made each of the boys a shirt apiece, and two table-cloths, and a change of pillow-cases, and hand-towels, and dish-towels, all out of this one fruitful mine. She mended and washed the boys' clothes, cut their hair, and made them thoroughly tidy in appearance. Jack came, as usual, on Saturday, and brought a large bundle under his arm; but he was still sulky and disagreeable. The children "prospected" the bundle. It contained muslin, for sheets; ducking, for boys' pants and jumpers; material for shirts and other things. But they were unappeased and ungrateful. They talked about him behind his back, and pitied poor Polly, who could not leave, no matter how much she might desire to do so. It still rained and rained. The bottom had fallen out of the roads. It was impossible to tell how much longer she might have to claim Jack's churlish hospitality. The generous boys not only pitied her, but they began to love her, with reason. Ideas of order and cleanliness were dawning upon them. They did not want to be again submerged in dirt. Everything was so pleasant in the house. The meals were always on time, and always good. Out of simple things, and few, she contrived a variety that delighted them. From dried apples she made roll pudding, apple dumplings, plain apple pies, and apple custard; and just so of everything. Willie put his arms around her one day, when no one else was present, and told her he wouldn't take a thousand dollars for her *then*, and her price was raising every day.

When Jack came again, churlish and disagreeable as before, the rain was over, and the waters had run down. At breakfast, the next morning, Polly said:

"I reckon the roads ain't so bad but what I can get over 'em somehow. I've been here a mighty long time, and I s'pose I'd orter go."

"I s'pose you had," said Jack.

The boys were aghast. They had ceased to think of such a thing. "Oh, don't go," "Don't go," was all they could say. Polly looked at Jack.

"You're right," said he; "I think it's time you left."

Then all the children opened on him, like a pack of hounds.

"You ought to be ashamed of yourself, Jack," said Tom.

"Leave yourself, if you want anybody to leave," said Willie.

"We can do without you better than we can without Polly," said Tom.

"Just give us a chance to try it," said Willie. And plenty more off the same piece.

But Johnny was the champion who "fit, bled, and died" on this memorable occasion. The family had risen from the table, and were moving away, when Jack glanced around just in time to dodge a potato aimed by Johnny, and thrown with such force as to strike the opposite wall and scatter itself all over the room. The young warrior stood on one of his chair-rounds, leaning on the table with his left hand, and throwing with the other. Whack, *whack*, went the potatoes, Jack dodging all the time, until Johnny, reaching too far for his ammunition, bore so heavily on the ricketty old table that it fell, and he with it. Springing up, with his hair full of peelings and crumbs, he grabbed a fork, and threatened to throw that.

"Help! help!" roared Jack. "I call for a parley. Now, what do you fellers want me to do?"

"We want Polly to stay here," said Johnny, breathless, "and Rosy May, and Little Blossom, too; and we're agoin' to keep 'em, too—bet your boots."

"Well, now, Johnny, if Polly stays here I'll have to marry her; and then you'll have a step-mother to pound you round."

All the boys became conscious of that other fight instantly, and for a moment seemed vanquished. Johnny hung his head, but Tom spoke up like a man.

"Tell ye what it is, Jack, we was eejots then. We didn't know what we wanted. We've got more sense now."

"Well, what do you want *now?* I'll do anything for you in reason."

Tom glanced at Polly. She was sitting on on the side of the bed, with her handkerchief before her eyes, crying, he thought. Her shoulders shook with excessive emotion, and the old bedstead trembled like an aspen leaf. The little girls were up behind her, where they had taken refuge during the potato storm. It occurred to Tom now that perhaps it would be necessary to obtain Polly's consent to the marriage, as well as Jack's; so he went and put his arm around her neck and whispered in her ear. Polly's grief was convulsive for a moment.

"Will you do it, Polly? Say yes—just you say yes, Polly; that's all you've got to do."

"Do say yes, Polly," urged the other boys; "just one leetle, *leetle* yes; that's all you've got to do."

"Come here, Jack," said Johnny; "you ask her to say yes—she'll do it for you."

"Well, you lay that fork down first," said Jack.

Johnny put the fork down, and Jack advanced to do as he was bidden; but hesitated for the want of words.

"Ask her to say yes, Jack; she'll do it for you, I know. Say yes for Jack, Polly, won't you?"

"Say yes, Polly," said Jack.

And, with a last explosion of grief that seemed a compromise between a snort and a scream, Polly said "yes," and rushed from the room.

In a year after Polly said "yes," Jack's miserable quarter-section, that no one would have bought of him at the rate of a postage-stamp an acre, was covered with young grape-vines, the rocks were picked up and built into fences, and a garden was growing around the house; the spring-water from the hillside was led down to irrigate it; watermelons and muskmelons jostled each other on the aristocratic side of the house, while pumpkins, squashes, and cucumbers loafed around in lazy content near the kitchen quarters; mammoth beets poked their heads many inches above the soil; peas, sweet-corn, and string-beans grew and ripened as if it were the hight of their ambition to please Polly and the children. Before long, the ponies and spring-wagon Polly brought as her marriage dower were put to a good use. Five days of each week they carried Jack's boys and Polly's girls to the village school. The boys are getting to be strong, manly fellows, and "May" and "Bloss" are two of the sweetest little girls ever seen. Jack bought them a Mason & Hamlin organ the other day, on which they can wring out a few wheezy tunes; and the good fellow is just as proud of their accomplishments as if they were his own "young uns."

HELEN WILMANS.

THE MAID OF ST. HELENA.

Across the long, vine-covered land
She gazed, with lifted, shading hand.

Behind were hillsides, purple, brown;
Before were vineyards sloping down;

While northward rose, through golden mist,
St. Helen's mount of amethyst.

But forest, vine, and mountain bight
Were less divinely benedight

Than she who so serenely stood
To gaze on mountain, vine, and wood.

Her presence breathed in sweet excess
The fragrance of rare loveliness—

A simple beauty in her face,
And in her form a simple grace.

She was so perfect and so fair,
So like a vision, and so rare,

The air that touched her seemed to me
To thrill with trembling ecstasy.

Spell-bound, for fear she might not stay,
I stood afar in sweet dismay.

At last, she sang some olden song.
I did not know its tale of wrong;

I only knew the oriole's note
Grew garrulous within its throat—

It seemed so shameful birds should sing
To silence so divine a thing.

She faded, singing, from my sight,
A dream of beauty and delight;

And I, with unconsenting will,
Retraced my footsteps down the hill.

CHAS. H. PHELPS.

ABRASIONS ON THE NORTH-WEST COAST.

In the earlier years of our experience upon the western coast of North America, but especially of California, Oregon, and Washington, we discovered along the shore-line numerous markings and indications of what are generally supposed to be ancient sea-benches, formed by the wearing action of the ocean, and marking the uplifting of the immediate coast, not in a regular or uniform manner, but *per saltum*. But a more intimate acquaintance with the material of these supposed sea-benches, and comparisons with the effects of water and weather upon the present shores, constrained us to doubt the sole agency of water in their formation. It became evident, from a study of many of them, and from their absence on the flanking hills and mountains of the Bay of San Francisco, Santa Clara Valley, Napa Valley, Petaluma and Russian River Valleys, and in the Great Valley of California, and the valleys to the southward, that other forces, more powerful and more persistently uniform in action than water, shaped these flat-topped and generally rocky benches and plateaus. It is, however, equally evident that some of the smaller ones, which are composed of gravel, sand, and alluvion, have been formed by deposits from water, or under water; and perhaps in part by the modified power that sculptured the rocky terraces. This class may, however, be quite readily distinguished and separated from the former, and the examples are found only slightly elevated above the present level of the sea; and yet their characteristics are wholly different from the old sea-markings around the basin of the Colorado Desert, where the line of water level is very plainly drawn. But the predominant class frequently exhibits, on an extended scale, level plateaus of rock, whose section indicates every degree of inclination, plication, and contortion of its stratification, and an infinite variety of texture. Along the present coast line the face of these terraces, torn and worn by the action of the ocean, by wind, and by weather, present every feature of ruggedness, whilst the surface immediately beneath the water is even more broken, irregular, and jagged. Yet the surface of the terrace may be nearly as plane as a floor, with only a thin covering of soil.

These rocky benches, terraces, or plateaus were never formed by the action of water alone; and although much of the sharp outlines of this abrasion and terrace forming has been modified, and even obliterated, by subsequent causes (principally by water from precipitation, alternations of heat and cold, and the actions of ocean waters), yet the readily recognized examples are so numerous, and so consecutive, and so characteristic, that the necessity for a more powerful agent is demanded. That agency abraded the continental line of our western coast; it even cut through the western extremity of the Santa Monica chain of mountains, which then protruded far into the ocean, and thereby formed the larger and northern islands of the Santa Barbara Channel, where its terrace markings are clear and well defined to the practiced eye. So far as we can judge from our present knowledge, these terraces and horizontal planings may have been formed at any reasonable hight; either at the surface of the sea or above it, or yet, more likely, beneath it. If it is found beneath the surface of the sea, then the subsequent elevation of the land may have been *per saltum*, whereby the irregular wear of the rocky surface by water action was prevented. Familiar with the peculiar appearance of numerous examples upon our western coast, we have seized every opportunity to detect them upon the hill and mountain sides of our great valleys communicating with the ocean, without discovering any that are unmistakable. And on the voyage from Yokohama, down the coast of Japan and through the Inland Sea, we were constantly on the lookout for examples, and became satisfied from two or more undeniable presentations that similar action has wrought its mark upon the ocean outline of that coast.

In order that the reader may judge of the character of the coast-line terraces and sculpturing, we enumerate and briefly describe a few of the principal instances which we have seen upon the coast during a service of nearly thirty years, of which many were spent upon the water, whence the best views are obtained under particular conditions of atmosphere and verdure covering. A few, among numerous sketches, made either personally or represented by photographs, or obtained from the old explorers, indicate in a measure the general appearances of these markings. Commencing well to the southward—with which, however, we are not so closely familiar—we have detected no line of coast terrace or plateau whatever at the extremity of the Peninsula of Lower California, in latitude 23°. Between San José del Cabo and Cape San Lucas there are none. From Cape San Lucas toward Magdalena Bay, we have had no recent close view of the coast; but on the Island of San Margarita, and the great headland of San Lazare, forming the ocean bulwark to Magdalena Bay, and reaching twenty-five hundred feet elevation, we discovered no signs of terraces or horizontal markings on either the ocean or bay sides, unless the general features of Cape Redondo be considered of the terrace character. The precipitous faces of the high rocky barrier to this bay, combined with the deep bold water upon its ocean front, has either not permitted the terraces to be molded sufficiently deep, or the causes did not exist in force at this low latitude. Of the coast hence to Cape Colnett, in latitude 31°, we are unable to speak from recent personal experience. North of this cape, we have had very favorable opportunities to study the coast features, and have made many views to illustrate the numerous and well marked examples of terraces that are molded and planed in the flanks of the high rocky coast barrier and the adjacent islands. Cape Colnett itself is a good instance, and Vancouver has given a view of its *mesa*, or table, forming the headland, indicating the strata inclined at a large angle, whilst the surface is cut off quite level; this condition is confirmed by recent sketches made at our request. Two plateaus are well marked, the stratification of the higher being perpendicular; the surface of the lower is quite level, while the point open to the northward of Colnett also shows a horizontal surface. The point near Solitarios, in about latitude 31°32', is a well marked table of about one hundred and fifty feet elevation above the sea, with a lower table toward the extremity of the point, and visible where it bears east-south-east. Five miles south of Point Grajéro, about latitude 31° 35', a deep, *cañon*-like valley opens upon the ocean, and exhibits numerous and very sharply marked rock-terraces on both sides, and at all elevations, the highest reaching possibly one thousand feet. The *cañon* stretches well back into the mountains. The northernmost of the Todos Santos Islands, lying off Todos Santos Bay, in latitude 31°40', is itself a well marked, rocky, horizontal plateau, thickly covered with soil; while the southern island has two terrace marks, the lower corresponding to the level of the surface of the northern islet, and another and higher one near the summit of the islet, is about twice the hight above the sea. Even a lower terrace line may be traced about fifteen feet above the present sea level. Then, passing abreast the northern point of Todos Santos Bay, no less than four well marked, terraced, rocky points, projecting into the ocean, were sketched in the same view. Each point had other terraces of greater elevations rising inland, while to the northward stood out the well known Table Mountain, with its remarkable flat top twenty-two hundred and forty-four feet above the sea, and having a breadth of forty-eight hundred feet. In this single view, no less than thirteen terrace markings are exhibited, excluding Table Mountain. This vicinity is the best marked terrace formation that we know of on the coast, and the lowest one not more than thirty feet above the sea level. They are not made in soft soil, but appear as if a planing machine had cut them out of the solid flanks of the high ocean barrier. The coast line just south of the boundary between California and Lower California exhibits a single terrace, or *mesa*, stretching some distance southward. Upon the small rocky Coronados Islands we have not detected terrace markings; they are so small and isolated that atmospheric and water weathering may have obliterated their original characteristics. Northward, between Point Loma and San Juan Capistrano, a broad table-land, or *mesa*, from one hundred to three hundred feet elevation, and many miles long, is familiar to all who have traversed that route by stage. At certain locations on this extensive *mesa*, are gravel mounds of regular shape, for which we have in vain endeavored to find a cause in the movement of water. Their low, flat, rounding outlines are about two feet above the level of the land, from twelve to twenty feet in extent, and lie contiguous to each other over occasional large areas, ceasing abruptly and giving place to the usual flat surface. The fullest effect of their shape is seen at sunrise, with the long shadows filling the intervening depressions. They belong to the characteristic elevations of similar extent throughout the Great Valley of California and locally known as "hog wallows;" and may have similar origin to the elevation of "Mound" and other prairies in Washington Territory. When abreast San Pedro Hill, lying at the south-west angle of the extensive Los Angeles plains, the lines of terraces are particularly well marked; and in the spring especially so by the brighter lines of gay flowers on their comparatively level but narrow surfaces. The traces of these terraces are cut in very recent rock, and are readily detected in the detailed contour topography of the Coast Survey. The view which we have made shows five principal terrace lines, which the topographical sheet also indicates.

These five principal terraces are on the south-west face, but a greater number lie on the north-west part of the hill, whilst markings on the land, or eastern, flank of the hill are not traceable. The lowest terrace is about sixty-five feet above the sea, the second is one hundred and forty feet, the third is two hundred and sixty feet, the fourth is three hundred and sixty feet, and the fifth is five hundred and eighty feet; smaller, and less distinct ones, about seven hundred and eight hundred feet; and the other especially marked ones at nine hundred, one thousand, and twelve hundred feet. The hill-top itself is somewhat rounded, and, at the highest point, is fourteen hundred and seventy-eight feet above the sea.

The *mesa*, lying fifteen miles north-west of Point Vincente, and forming the western part of the Los Angeles plains, is a capital example of the flat terrace, and is reproduced on the coast line, under the southern flank of the Santa Monica range, at a point about twenty miles westward of Los Angeles. At the mouth of the Arroyo Santa Monica, the table, several miles in extent, has an elevation of about ninety feet, and terminates in a bold bluff on the sea-shore. Yet this table, being in places composed of sand and gravel, may have been formed, in part, by deposits from water. Point Dume, lying about twenty-five miles west-north-west from Point Vincente, is a very well defined table, where a projecting spur from the flank of the mountain range has been planed off for two or three miles, while toward the extremity a deeper grooving has been effected, and left the rocky head as a dome-shaped point, two hundred and two feet above the sea. At San Buenaventura, and hence toward Point Conception, we find numerous plateaus, but most markedly exhibited in the vicinity of the cape, where the bold spur from the seaward extremity of the Santa Barbara Mountains has been planed across, and given a generally level surface, one to three miles wide, with a rising, rocky head at the extremity. It is a counterpart of Point Dume, but more extended. The rocky bluff at the surface of this plateau, and in the *arroyos*, indicates great contortion, plication, and inclination of stratification; but the top is flat, and covered with a shallow depth of soil and gravel.

Among the islands of the Santa Barbara Channel, San Clemente and San Nicolas are both long, comparatively flat-topped ridges; but the principal feature of the island grouping is the remarkable parallelism of their longer ends, and also of the channels, which have been cut through the group lying immediately off the Santa Barbara shores, and forming the western prolongation of the Santa Monica Mountains; and this parallelism is continued in the coast line of the Santa Lucia Mountains, Monte del Buchon, Point Arguello to Point Conception, and the San Pedro Hill. The horizontal sculpturing of terraces is exhibited among the Santa Barbara Islands, when passing between Anacapa, Santa Rosa, Santa Cruz, and San Miguel, while the eastern island exhibits very definite proofs of the causes which produced the rock terraces. Anacapa Island, lying in the throat of the Santa Barbara Channel, and directly abreast the opening of the extensive valley of Santa Clara, consists of a narrow, five-mile ridge of coarse, dark gray sandstone. Two-thirds of its length, reckoned from the eastern extremity, has been planed off at an elevation of about three hundred feet above the level of the sea, while the western part rises to nine hundred feet in height; but the line of the level of the summit of the eastern part is visibly scored around the flanks of the western part, notwithstanding the deep gulches, with almost vertical sides, which cut from the summit to the bottom of the cliff. On the north-western flank of the Monte del Buchon, lying between San Luis Obispo Bay and Los Esteros, although cut by deep gulches, there are three very distinctly traced terraces, each several hundred feet in hight. No other point is more plainly sculptured.

The seaward flanks of the Santa Lucia range, between San Simeon Bay and Monterey Bay, for forty or fifty miles, have occasional terrace lines, but the precipitous and high face of the mountains, combined with the great depth of the water under them, has apparently permitted less abrasions than at the other more favorably situated locations; and, even if the sculpturing had been slightly effective, subsequent causes might have obliterated it. This is the boldest and most compact line of coast mountain barrier for a thousand miles, the greatest elevation (Santa Lucia Mountain) reaching sixty-two hundred feet, within a few miles of the ocean. At Santa Cruz Point, and hence to the northwestward, a pretty rocky table bluff exists, bordering the backbone of the mountainous peninsula of San Francisco. Thence to San Francisco we have several examples of the flat, rocky terrace. Before reaching Pescadero, "the general formation of the immediate sea-board, for twelve miles, is that of a table land, of three terraces, the lowest gradually sloping from the base of the second to the coast, which is exceedingly rocky and forbidding."

We need hardly mention other familiar and capital examples, such as Ballenas Point, and the vicinity of Point Reyes and Bodega Bay. Passing rapidly northward to Point Arena, in latitude 39°, we have examined the beautiful plateau at the light-house point, as well as the others toward Arena Cove; but the former is especially noticed, because a photograph of the point exhibits the stratification as almost perpendicular, and shows the present broken and very jagged condition of the cliff and low water level, arising from the action of water and weather. This point is a jutting-out from the coast mountain chain, where it makes a slight change of direction; and the terrace forming the point is about forty feet above the sea, covered with a very thin stratum of soil, and for a distance of half a mile a base line was measured by the Coast Survey, with a difference of level on the plateau of about two feet, while the same level is maintained further on the plateau among the timber. In this striking case, as in most of the others mentioned, the rock appears to have been absolutely planed off, and the different degrees of hardness of the layers in stratification had no apparent influence upon the mechanical causes at work; in the waterworn cliffs the hard layers are jagged rocks on edge, the softer layers are worn away. Other terraces near Arena Cove reach over two hundred feet elevation, and while the bluffs for miles exhibit every contortion of stratification, and every degree of hardness in the layers, the horizontal surfaces of the plateaus have been planed off.

The shores of Mendocino Bay, Points Cabrillo, Delgado, Table Bluff, and Cape Orford, all tell the same story. The latter bears a strong family resemblance to Points Dume and Concepcion, and for three miles south of the cape, to the mouth of Elk River, the terrace is a fine blue, hard sandstone abounding in fossil shells. About Capes Mendocino and Fortunas are one or two slight indications of terraces as viewed from seaward, but northward of these capes the trend of the coast line is changed, and the climatic conditions of the sea-board are very different from the lower coast. These climatic causes appear to have acted, and are to-day acting, more energetically than to the southward. Nevertheless, as we approach the Straits of Juan de Fuca we have evidences of a single line of flat-topped rocky terrace from Point Grenville to Tatoosh Island. Destruction Island, in latitude 47° 41′, is one or two miles in extent, bordered by rocky, bold cliffs, flat topped, and about seventy-five feet above the sea. There may be furrows across it, but if so they are not particularly noticeable from seaward. The bluff of the adjacent main shore possesses the same characteristics as the island, as shown by the view on the Coast Survey chart. Off Cape Flattery, in latitude 48° 24′, lies Tatoosh Island, one hundred and eight feet high, bold, rocky, and flat topped. From personal inspection we judge it impossible that water alone could have leveled it off so well, especially as its immediate surroundings at the water's surface are worn into the roughest rock shapes. Fuca's pillar and other rocks bordering the cape have the same general elevation. If there are terrace lines on the cape (which has an elevation of fifteen hundred feet) they are masked by the heavy growth of fir. With the outer shores of Vancouver and Queen Charlotte's Islands we are not familiar, but we have failed to find among the views and descriptions of the old or recent navigators any indications of terrace formation; the whole ocean flanks of these islands is cut by long, deep, narrow fiords. Nor have we found them for certainty among the inner passages of the Great Archipelago extending from Olympia in 47° to the mouth of the Chilkaht in 59°, although we have discovered and measured the direction and depth of the markings of ice action among the islands of Washington Sound, and the adjacent parts of Vancouver and Whidbey Islands, both in the well preserved and clean cut and very deep groovings, and in the presence of large numbers of erratic bowlders, while the glacial deposits are frequent on the shores of Admiralty Inlet, and particularly so on the Nisqually Plains. It must be borne in mind that these evidences lie in the line of the great straits nearly parallel with the ocean coast line, and with an intervening mountain barrier, nearly one hundred miles therefrom.

Of the orographical or geographical details of the shores of the Gulf of Alaska we know comparatively little. La Perouse, in approaching the coast under Mount Elias, thus describes it, although we must confess to receiving all his descriptions with a certain amount of reservation, and even distrust:

> "The mountains appeared to be a little distance inland from the sea, which broke against the cliff of a table land three hundred to four hundred yards high. This plain, black, as if burned by fire, was totally destitute of verdure. * * * As we advanced, we perceived, between us and the elevated plateau, low lands, covered with trees, which we took for islands. The table land serves as a base to vast mountains a few leagues within. Approaching the coast, we saw to the eastward a low point covered with trees, which appeared to join the table land, and terminate at a short distance from a second chain of mountains."

Middleton Island, in the Gulf of Alaska, in latitude 50° 30′, is the only flat-topped island mentioned or depicted by any of the old navigators. It is about seven miles long, north and south, with a breadth of three miles. The surface is comparatively low, quite level, and destitute of trees; the shores are craggy. Belcher says it does not exceed thirty feet in hight, and has a very soft, spongy soil, over micaceous shale, interspersed with quartz dykes. A recent navigator (1879) informs us that it is one hundred and eighty feet high, with bold cliffs, indicating various degrees of stratification, and yet the surface is leveled for its whole extent. The southern point of Kayak Island, in 59° 49′, is a high table rock, as described by Belcher. Long Island, off the harbor of St. Paul's, Kadiak, and Chiniah Point, south-east of St. Paul's, are flat topped and rocky, although not particularly well marked. Among the few of the Aleutian Islands which we have seen, or along the peninsula of Alaska, we observed no terrace formations such as we have hitherto described; and we fail to find among the navigators, up to 1855, views that indicate such features. To the far north, in the Behring Strait, the English and Russian views, and our Arctic whalers, represent the rocky Diomede Islands as bold, moderately high, and flat topped; as well as the East Cape of Asia.

The evidences of these coast terraces seem to be found in greater proportion between latitudes 30° and 40° than further to the north, and this may, in a measure, be fairly accounted for. Since the period of uprising succeeded the terrace formation general and local climatic changes have, doubtless, taken place, tending to the destruction of the terraces, and as they were sculptured in sedimentary rocks most of their finer moldings have been obliterated. Throughout the coast line, below latitude 40°, we find that after the terraces had been elevated, the disintegration of the higher lands took place with greater activity than at present; and yet the material was carried downward without great violence, and formed long, gently inclined slopes from the base of the mountains toward the shores, or into the valleys. One of the finest examples of this characteristic feature is in the Valley of the Santa Clara, east of San Buenaventura; another, is the Valley of San José, Lower California; while innumerable examples abound on a smaller scale along the flanks of our mountains. Such results may have taken place under a climate of great heat and excessive moisture, with increasing precipitation, but without downfall of rain to create torrents, whilst disintegration was assisted by the cold weather of winter. Subsequently, these gently sloping deposits were cut through by torrential forces, which are yet at work, but on a decreased scale. On the immediate coast line many cases may be seen where these long sloping deposits of disintegrated material have been cut through by subsequent torrents, and are now being undermined and washed away, so as expose the flanks of the mountains from which they were formed. A notable example is that just north of Judas Head, on the island of Margarita.

But in all the instances of terrace formation which we have mentioned, and in many others not enumerated, we find one prevailing feature, regardless of the dip, or direction, or variable texture of the stratification of the rocks. A nearly level surface of rock, with a comparatively thin layer of soil thereon; the plateaus sometimes miles in extent, bordering the coast with jagged cliffs, whose bases illustrate the present action of water and weather. Above these plateaus are frequently others stretching in shore, and narrow lines of terraces which reach elevations of certainly twelve hundred hundred feet above the sea. While the general plateau is level, or partially so, there are frequent indications that broad groovings have been made across such plateaus as project far out from the line of mountains. This is notably so at Point Dume, Point Concepcion, Point Arena, and Cape Orford, and across the ridge of Anacapa. And it is noticeable that these plowings or groovings run with the general trend of the barrier of the coast line, sculpturing and featuring the lower headlands and the islands. They are not seen in transverse straits like Juan de Fuca, nor in the great fiords forming the interior ocean water communication from latitude 47° to 59°, nor in the *cañon*-like valleys of rivers like the Columbia, nor in the Great Valley of California, but are the handwriting upon the face of the main coast line and adjacent islands, except on high bold cliffs rising very steeply to great elevations from the deep waters; and so far as our personal examination extends they are not plainly exhibited on the Aleutian Islands, nor below latitutude 30°.

These prominent features and conditions have compelled us to believe that more effective and more regular agencies were at work to form them than are now at work so universally. The upheaval of the continental shores by subterranean action cannot produce such terraces and plateaus. If the north-west shores of America were to-day raised two hundred feet, we know, from the characteristics of the coast line and the depths bordering it, that similar results would not necessarily be among the consequences, although there may possibly yet remain sub-surface terrace marks from the ice-belt period. The horizontal crushing and consequent uprising of the line of surface-yielding would not produce them; and it is believed that no continuous levels can be traced along the coast indicating uniformity of upheaval. The action of water will not account for them; whether by "continual dropping," or by violent currents, or by storm, water first wears away the soft and more friable parts, leaving the harder with irregular jagged surfaces and masses. These irregular outlines and borders, if upheaved above the level of the sea, would not wear away regularly by the action of the weather; the irregularities would in time be partially or even wholly filled with disintegrated material, but the general surface of the rock would never bear the impress of having passed under a planing machine, as in many of the examples we have enumerated.

To account for the existing conditions we must be guided in great measure by experience; and judging from our knowledge of present local glacial action we can safely appeal to the action of ice moving slowly but irresistibly as a great planing and molding machine; its current of movement mainly controlled by the great, high, rocky barrier of the north-west coast line, perhaps influenced by islands and elevations of land not now existing, by oceanic and ice-mass forces no longer acting as such. From the evidence of the sculpturings along the coast barrier we may suppose a great ice belt to have existed contiguous to the continental shores, and forced southward parallel therewith, possibly by a great return Japan current, combined with the accumulated mass pressure at the north. And it is logical to suppose that this icy coast barrier existed at the same period as the great ice sheet that covered the adjacent continent. The mechanical effects of the coast belt of ice are those we see exhibited upon the ocean coast line and upon the islands adjacent; the effects of the ice sheet over the land are exhibited in some of the gorges opening upon the shores, and on the mountain ranges. All the groovings on Vancouver Island, on the islands of Washington Sound at the southern extremity of the Gulf of Georgia, and on Whidbey Island, together with the erratic bowlders and the glacial detritus in all that region, point to the mechanical agent as moving southward; and if we accept the theory of an ice sheet over the continent, or over a part thereof, and an ice belt contiguous to the continental shores, we can readily understand, from our present knowledge of the formation and movement of glaciers, that this coast barrier of ice moved as a great stream from the northward, probably with extreme slowness, but with certainty and with irresistible force through a prolonged period. Moreover, a body of ice bordering the shores of the continent would do its work more or less effectually, and at greater or less depth, according to the predominance of any given factor or factors, so that we can understand how terraces of different elevations may have been formed during that period without any relative change of the level of the sea and adjacent coast, although the same general effects would have been produced if the land had been rising or subsiding. And, moreover, the mass of ice resting on the land, partaking in part of the movement of the great ice belt, may have done similar work even above the level of the sea to what may have been done beneath its surface. Thus these terraces and plateaus do not necessarily indicate the different steps of the elevation of the continental shore; and instead of resorting to the theory of great and violent upheavals, *per saltum*, we see how the elevation may have been gradual, and even after the greater part of the terraces had been formed. This gradual movement of elevation is indicated by the present level character of the plateaus, or, when broad, by their slight inclination. We do not propose at this time to offer any explanation as to how this great ice belt was formed, or whether it extended far into or across the Pacific Ocean. Its course, from the evidence on the coast line, was parallel, or nearly parallel, with the continental shore, and we are constrained to believe that, as a great body ruptured from the continental ice sheet, it moved slowly to the southward by the combined forces of the ocean currents, the prevailing winds, and by the pressure of the great ice mass from the northward.

To the northward it is reasonable to suppose that the great ice belt lingered longer than at the south, and we know that the present home of the glaciers of the north-east coast is in the region adjacent to the Gulf of Alaska and its connecting waters, where there are wonderful exhibitions of this phenomenon. When the ice barrier was being dissipated, the destructive agencies of great seasonal changes and excessive rainfall were much more active, persistent, and wearing. Above latitude 40° we do not find the long, gently sloping surfaces of disintegrated material before referred to. As we advance northward, even the steep, sloping hillsides give way to the fiord-like coasts of Vancouver and the islands of the Archipelago Alexander. There, violent storms, excessive moisture and precipitation, and large thermal changes are producing a hundred fold greater effects than to the southward, and obliterating whatever evidence existed of the terrace or other formations. Or the terraces may have been but partially developed on account of the movement of the ice belt not closely following the trend of the coast line, or deflected therefrom at given localities by the seaward pressure of the continental ice sheet, or not exhibited on account of a subsidence of part of the north-westernmost parts of the coast.

And here we had intended to close; but upon recent, although comparatively limited views of the former water-level markings of the Colorado Desert and in the Salt Lake Basin, we were struck by the similarity, or parallelism of action, that sculptured the boundaries of the latter with that graving tool which etched the Pacific Coast line in the same latitude. In these cases two distinctive forms of action have been at work, although not necessarily at the same period. The old ocean level of the Colorado Desert is as sharply and clearly defined as if the waters had been drawn away from this basin but yesterday, and the boundaries bear the characteristic markings which would be expected should some of our more protected coast line be suddenly and uniformly raised, or the ocean level depressed several hundred feet without catastrophic action. The markings of the old ocean level are on a level with the present surface of the ocean, and no elevation of the land has taken place. No terraces are seen on the eastern shore of this ancient arm of the Gulf of California. Above the line of the sea-level the surface exhibits a washed-out line of sand and gravel; below it the soil is fine, with a comparatively regular surface, and full of marine shells. On the other hand, many of the peculiarities of the Salt Lake Basin (so far only as we have seen, and speaking, therefore, with great reserve) indicate that water above was not the means which effected the sculpturing seen on the lower part of the rocky flanks of the mountains from Promontory to Ogden. As observant travelers well know, the different levels of the lake are plainly scored and cut as narrow lines and terraces into the hard, rocky material of the mountainous shores. They are upon a much smaller scale than upon the Pacific Coast: nevertheless they seem to certify that here similar agenies were also graving its rocky walls, and certainly that the forces were wholly different from those formerly at work in the Colorado Sea. While there may have been no great current to move an ice mass, yet the force of the wind could in part have aided to slowly carry the mass of ice grinding along its borders.

GEORGE DAVIDSON.

A TRIP INTO SONORA.

Clouds hung low and threatening on an afternoon in last March, as we drove out of Tucson and took the road up the Santa Cruz toward Sonora. "We" consisted of Flory, a mining expert, who originally hailed from Georgia; the Professor, who spoke Spanish; Story, from San Francisco, who wore glasses in a gold frame; and myself. Our driver was a young Mexican with a troublesome name, beginning with Don and a long bugle-blast of vowel-sounds thundering in its wake; so we dubbed him "Colonel Miranda" at once. A liberal supply of colored woolen shirts, blankets (for the nights were still cold on the *mesas)*, a lunch basket, pistols, ammunition, and snake-antidote constituted the chief part of our outfit. By the time we had reached the first *posta* night had fallen with the rain, and the road was becoming slick and heavy. The valley of the Santa Cruz, from Tucson to the Sonora line, seventy-five miles, is a soft volcanic or alluvial soil, with occasional alkaline traces, and cotton-wood, mesquite, cactus, and palo-verde here and there, which, with occasional fields of socaton and scout-grass, form the vegetable growth.

As the night advanced the rain fell more heavily, and as our team was a pair of lazy mules, we crept along the *mesa* slowly from the first, getting slower all the time. When ten miles out, the Professor and Flory concluded to walk on to the next *posta*, and send back a team to meet us. It was eleven o'clock; the rain fell quietly, but surely, and toward midnight, after talking over a range of subjects as wide as Don Juan dreamed of, Story and I feel asleep. We were awakened by the scraping of limbs against the stage, and the stopping of the team. In his faith that the mules were too lazy to leave the road, Colonel Miranda had fallen asleep, and was served as those who rely on faith generally are. They had wandered far away from the road while we slept. He got out, looked around till he saw we were lost, yawned, and climbed to his seat, prepared to let things happen. Neither of us could talk with him. I got out in the rain, and, by striking matches, followed the trail as we had come, and at last found the road. It would have been quite impossible to recognize it after such a rainfall had not a wagon, with a pole under the axle of a broken shaft, passed, making a broad, deep cut. We were thankful for the misfortunes of others. As it was now too dark to travel we stopped in the road to wait for day, or the other team, and all of us soon fell asleep in the vehicle. During the night I was awakened by the presence of foreigners. These were coyotes; not one or two, but a dozen, at least. The rain had ceased. They whisked their dusky forms here and there, whining not entirely unlike city dogs when striking up an acquaintance and asking after the health of the family. I could hear their light, stealthy foot-falls as they trotted back and forth. While it was as difficult to see one as a minnow in a deep pool, I could easily smell them without a lantern. By odor it was high noon; the air was full of asafœtida and brimstone. At length one of them took the chair, and called the meeting to order. He set the tune in a long howl, and the others struck in. It seemed to say, "Squire, hear us do 'The Battle of Prague.'" It may have been that they mistook Story's snoring for music, and were politely helping him. I leaned out of the window and began a speech of thanks. There was a rustle, that died away out on the *mesa* into a subdued whisper, followed by the stillness of the grave. The serenade was over.

Day dawned, and we moved on slowly. Story growled at the Colonel; the latter didn't resent it. Two hours after we found Flory and the Professor, who had camped at a small house without touching the *posta*. We had traveled thirteen miles in sixteen hours. It was five miles yet to the *posta*. The rain had ceased, but there was plenty of water on the ground. We set out on foot, leaving Colonel Miranda to persuade the lazy mules along at the reckless pace of two miles to the hour. First, we started off with our dress-parade step; after half a mile we pulled up our pants' legs; two hundred yards farther we put them higher, and kept on till they were knee-breeches. The mud was sticky, and each foot carried along a farm with it. Had we passed over an Irish farm we would have bankrupted the proprietor by taking away all his soil. True, we could have scraped it off after crossing his three acres, and he could have shoveled and carted it back in two months. We needed either a balloon or a bateau. Story was rather fat. Soon his coat came off, then his vest, then his collar and overshirt, while he seemed on the eve of one of Falstaff's great thaws. Besides this, he was short-legged, so that when he would move one foot past the other, a passing promontory would collide with a reposing continent, and stick fast. It was *adobe*. The Professor, however, was made for wading, and could swing one foot around out through the country and bring it in when he wished to step.

All day we were climbing the valley of the Santa Cruz, and toward sunset reached Calabasas—the realization of Martin Chuzzlewit's Eden. Somewhere back in the cob-webbed past the King of Spain issued a grant of this tract, of seven leagues of land, to some old son of the conquest, who gave it the name of Calabasas (little squashes). From the grantee it has come down through all the tangled mazes known to the statutes of descent, distribution, and alienation, till it reached the hands of the company who now own it. Where the valley is nearly surrounded by mountain peaks they laid out the city of Calabasas, and put down the foundation of a hotel. We found, beside the incipient hotel, one small brick building, one *adobe*, and an artesian drill that had grown tired of plunging into dry dirt, and leaned over to rest. A mist was falling, the nearest approach to rain they had had in two years, while clouds crept along the valley and up the mountain sides, to scatter and weave their wraiths of thin, pale mist, in ghostly legions, around the eternal crags. Darting through broken clouds to the westward, the sunshine lit up a small cloud, poised against the mountain's breast, from center to circumference with all the colors born in the prism—a rainbow that had no bow—and retained its changing and recurring tints as the heavy folds, rolling through and about each other, crept up the mountain side. It was a moving volume of color—the unfashioned elements of the Bow of Promise—a mass of glory no painter could catch, sweeping up to the cold peaks to die. Thus the mist closed over the sun, and the sober-hued scene was unbroken, as we gazed from valley to hill. It was a beautiful, a remarkable phenomenon. Flory said it was a rainbow "dumped;" the Professor, who used to be on a newspaper "staff," said it was "pied;" while Story remarked that, as this was a new country, he guessed they hadn't "got molds yet to run 'em in."

The scenery about Calabasas is very beautiful. The windings of the Santa Cruz can be traced by the thin fringing of cottonwoods; indeed, at this time, that was the best proof of where the river ran, as that concern had about gone out of business. It was navigable up to the Calabasas landing—by small fish and tadpoles; but even for them it was the head of navigation. Down the valley, hiding among the cottonwoods, stand the crumbling ruins of the old Mission of Tumacocori. From present indications, the city of Calabasas will have to wait half a dozen centuries for its greatness. The river will first have to grow; then they will need an artificial rain-fall, as nature don't attend to that; and the commercial value of its staple—mule rabbits—must be enhanced, for it is a regular rabbit orchard.

Night fell after leaving Calabasas, Story and I going to sleep on the back seat. We were still climbing up the northern side of the "divide" between the valleys of the Santa Cruz and the Magdalena, and the last we remembered ere we went to the "arms of Murphy" (this joke by the Professor) was the slow, weary hauling of the vehicle. Deep were the slumbers on the back seat. Dreams—those wayward phantasies of the half-death of life—stole upon us. We were working a pole-boat up a rugged, swift stream, as I had often seen done in the Cotton States, and the heavy barge, in its concussion with the water at every shove at the pole, seemed to make something complain, and while we were trying industriously in the interest of science to discover whether it was barge or water that thus "spake out in the meeting," the river changed, and the stream began to run down hill toward its original source. Here was a new problem—what had wrought this disturbance? In sheer inability to account for it upon any acknowledged scientific principles, I took refuge in the nursery lore of long lost years, and believed that Tony Bucher had raised up the channel of the river at its mouth. Tony was one of those accommodating creatures who would do anything for any one if requested, but nothing for himself except lie in the shade and tell stories. Clearly did I remember how, in childhood, I had listened with open-eyed wonder to his recital of how he had once carried a steamboat on his back from one river to another on a wager of a pound of tobacco, and how, finding a well without bucket, rope, or windlass, and being thirsty, he picked up the hole and drank till his thirst was quenched. I blushed then, and perhaps did again in my dream, at the nation for not making him President. The barge was now rumbling down the whirling, roaring stream. Then I heard something like pattering feet, that grew more and more distinct, frequently broken into by Apache yells. I was awake now. The patter was from the feet of the wiry Mexican horses, while the Apache became none other than Colonel Miranda. We had crossed the "divide," and were "punching the breeze" for the valley of the Magdalena. Story was snoring a resonant bass to the hoof-falls and rattle of wheels. "The pale moonbeams, piercing the thin tissue of fleecy clouds overhead," as we used to observe in school while "doing" Spartacus, cast a weird light over the scattering mesquite trees, that seemed to whisk by us on their way to the northward. Colonel Miranda had been taking numerous astronomical observations through a bottle that was slanderously charged on the label with having harbored Muscat. We suppose they were entirely satisfactory, from his remarks, thrown out upon the chill air, "Hoop-la, ya-ya, Santa Maria," etc.

Agua Sacra was reached at two o'clock in the morning. This is the station of the Mexican "Coast Guard," consisting of two *adobe* houses, thatched with straw, and a small corral. The post-horses were out, and could not be found at night. We asked for feed for our team, intending to push on, after an hour's rest, to the next *posta*. The *Guarda de la Estacion* had none; never had any since he could remember. The horses are turned out, with the advice to help themselves, as the country lay before them, with plenty of freedom, if not grass. Travelers generally receive the same large-hearted invitation. Flory remarked that there was nothing small about Mexican hospitality. Story, who had now rounded to in his almost interminable bass, and crawled out from his snuggery, cut his cables and rashly shouldered the responsibility of a pun on the size of Mexican *horses;* the Professor began looking among the bottles and pistols, evidently puzzled in deciding which size was most suitable to the defense. Here Story, perceiving the drift of affairs, observed that he guessed Flory's remark was all right, and that he would withdraw his amendment. The Professor now became resolute, and assured us he would "develop things." Peering into the hut of the "Coast Guard," we supposed him to have had the following conversation. As it was in Spanish—a tangled mystery to us—we are left in a sea of conjecture; for the Professor ever afterward stoutly refused to tell us, always remarking, "Oh, well, it's no matter:"

Professor—"Hello, friend! Got any feed?"

Coast Guard—"Suppose we have. What then?"

P.—"That's good. We want some. Got plenty of money." Something in the region of his pocket jingled.

C. G.—"Glad to hear you are flush, Colonel."

P.—"Well, what about the feed?"

No answer. Two minutes elapsed.

P.—"What about the feed?"

Two minutes more and no answer.

Here the Professor sat down on a stool, remarking, *sotto voce*, in English:

"He'll come to. You just 'hold your horses' and trust to me. He's thinking it over."

Another minute passed.

"*Amigo*, what about the feed?"

Another pause in the stillness of hushed expectancy. Then came the answer from the dark recess of the hut: "Gua-ya-yah! Gua-ya-ya-yah! Gua-u-u-wa-u-u! Ga-u-u-w!"

This was in good English. A snore is the same in all languages. He was in the "arms of Murphy," and the Professor's smile shone under a cloud for two days, and ever afterward he has spoken of Mexican courtesy as belonging to the paleozoic age.

That night was passed in blankets around a fire. When day dawned, we had company. One of the Guard, perhaps the one that held the animated discussion with the Professor, was standing by the fire, blanketed, belted, and pistoled. I have seen handsomer men, but never one whose face will remain with me longer. I have seen it often in my dreams since. It was an epitome of villainy. As a precautionary movement, Flory passed the *mescal*, and then the expanse he would have called his face became transformed. The *cañons* and copses where the brigand expression lurked filled up and cleared away with the sunshine of a smile that was pleasant, and so much in contrast with his ordinary expression that it would provoke confidence. He examined the heavens through the bottle and became sociable. Story dubbed him Blucher, because as he rode away he reminded him of the old Prussian's appreciation of London on first view, "Lord, what a city to sack!" He was social, especially with the Professor; indeed, to the extent of examining his luggage. Whether this attention—from which the rest were exempt—had any special reference to the Professor's boast, in their late interview, about "plenty of money," we will never know, as we had only that coincidence, together with a lurking smile that nestled in his scraggy beard and played like sunlight ripples in the aforesaid *cañons*. All of us liked Blucher, except the Professor. How long we would have had to wait is just such a thing as would cause Dundreary to exclaim, "No fellah can tell," had not Don Conrado Aguirre, a wealthy sheep-herder come along. He had some connection with the stage company, and moved up the lazy *Guarda de la Estacion* to something like life. Don Conrado breakfasted with us, and in his kindly attentions, frank, open manners, and cordial bearing, left a memory of himself in the minds of the party not soon to fade.

Out from Agua Sacra fifteen miles we overtook Blucher, who was on horseback. The stage was rattling rapidly along, and Blucher had to gallop to keep up. He turned up a bottle, and "irrigated" without breaking his pace, and the frown that stole in among his grizzly whiskers and climbed up under the shadows of his *sombrero*, made a darker gloaming in the *cañons*. Night was again falling as we rode into Magdalena, the Colonel yelling, "Ha-ha! Yo-yo!" and cracking his whip like pistol shots over the mules' backs. Dogs, people, *burros*, and hogs got out of the street—or took chances. The bells of the Catholic church were ringing and clanging from the tower in the starlight. As ministers of the priesthood they recalled the words of "The Bells:"

> "The people, ah, the people.
> They that dwell up in the steeple
> All alone,
> And who tolling, tolling, tolling,
> In that muffled monotone,
> Feel a glory in so rolling
> On the human heart a stone."

Here we found a town of three or four thousand inhabitants—at least, that is what they told us. As it was night, we did not take the census. We merely got a supper of *frijoles*, *tortillas*, and scrambled eggs, and a box of cigars. The latter cost two dollars and a half, and could not be purchased in Tucson for less than seven dollars. It was with sadness that we here parted with Colonel Miranda—but the sadness was all on the part of the Colonel. *Cocheros* that sleep both day and night, when not "filling up," are a luxury to be dispensed with. While he was getting full he remained awake, and far be it from me to say aught against his work during those fitful moments of faithful labor. The Professor thought he could gauge the flow of *mescal* to such a scientific nicety as to keep the Colonel in a rosy-hued stage of getting drunk all the time; but the Colonel's mechanism, under the influence of his national drink, was as irregular as the time of a repaired watch. He would just amble along in the most orthodox way imaginable for a while; then, without any perceptible warning, would dash off into a big drunk, and, turning his muscadine-looking eyes toward the Professor, would yield him the reins, and fall off into sleep with the remark, "Brofezer, you jis drove while I slepe—slep none in a week." At least, this is what Story said was a liberal translation of his remarks. While sober he let things happen; his eyes looked far away into the green pastures of ideality, and his lips murmured snatches of some serenade that had been on duty centuries ago in the bowered courts of Granada.

We had another *cochero*, an old friend of the Professor, and the object of his most stilted laudations. We never knew whether this was intended as a sarcasm, or was the result of misplaced confidence. He was the noisiest driver on earth. "Ya-ya-ya! Hoop-la! He-he-he! Hi-hi-hi! Yoh, yoh, yoh!" rolled in one unbroken stream from him. As the preachers say, he "labored" his way. All night long he rained ejaculations. Beginning early, in a mist of complimentary ones, it gradually deepened as the train got slower, till during the latter part of the night it rained "big guns." It discounted a coyote convention. It let up only once, when he missed the road, and had to get out and look up the estray. As soon as he was straight again, the windows of his heavens were opened, and the deluge got to business again. Sleep was impossible. As day was struggling for existence we tried to sing one of those simple ballads of youth. Story struck in with a bass not to be mistaken even in a Centennial chorus by those who had ever been near him while he slept. Flory gave us the variations of the "Chamounix," while the Professor trailed in as if afraid to take the lead in anything but buying feed from a Coast Guard. Then there arose on the air a volume of chaos. It was our *cochero*. His soul was moved to music, too. In less than two bars all our guns were spiked, musically speaking, and the *cochero* camped upon the field. At first he tracked the tune, and, in the main, kept to its general direction, though he recognized no grooves. As soon as we ceased he drifted away upon a billowy sea of improvisations, in reckless defiance of the musical compass. He was reveling in a bath of music—of his own make. In the gray dawn we saw the coyote, with tail between his legs and raised bristles, skulking away, growling, behind sage-brush, while mule-rabbits fled for dear life, terror flashing from their peaceful rumps, as they glinted hastily, in long leaps, over the stum brush. There was nothing like it in rabbit experience or tradition. The folklore of this numerous and prosperous family gives no account of anything so like the time spoken of in Genesis, when chaos had it all its way. They had evidently not heard Senator Logan's great effort on the Constitution. "*Sauve qui peut*" was written upon everything that could run or fly. It had a moving effect, this song.

I wish to say a word for the Mexican *cochero*. As I have seen him in action, I claim the privilege and the pleasure. I am aware that I tread on semi-sacred ground, for the *cochero* is popular the world over, and I have often heard stories of his social prowess at stations and on the "upland lawn." The *cochero* is not pretty, but he is picturesque and memorable. Neither is he timid. The rolling clouds of dust have for him a charm, while the hottest summer sunbeams just glance off him without injury, and go frying away. He loves *mescal* and cheese. He has a voice of great endurance, and a tongue that never tires. He is generally two, one to hold the reins and yell, the other to use the whip and throw stones. Every few miles he loads up half a bushel of them, the size of goose eggs, and the way they whiz, and pelt, and ricochet about from haunch to ears, is tantalizing to the mules. They dread rocks more than whip or yells. The *cochero* loves music, and, though his taste is not always faultless, his devotion soars above reproach. He is original, and has never been known to follow a tune. He despises that mediocrity of musical power that cannot make its own music on the spur of the occasion. He would "draw" a house in a large American city—but wouldn't promise to hold it long. The coyote fears him only when he sings. That animal's style of getting out of hearing says as plainly as if he spoke in Low Dutch, "There he is, sawing bones again." The *cochero* feels kindly to his passengers, and gives them all kinds of information they wish, unless they become unreasonable and demand accuracy. The Professor asked one for information, and got it:

"How far is it to Hermosillo?"

"A little way."

"Is it a league?"

"Yes."

"Five leagues?"

"Yes."

"Three leagues?"

"Yes."

"Seven leagues?"

"Yes."

"How far is it?"

"Not far."

"Ten leagues?"

"Yes."

"Fifteen leagues?"

"Yes."

"Forty leagues?"

"Yes."

"How many then?"

"Right out yonder."

"Can we get there to-night?"

"Yes."

"By to-morrow night?"

"Yes."

"It will take us a week, will it not?"

"Yes."

"You know exactly how far it is?"

"Yes."

The Professor said something about truth, but as the *cochero* had drifted away into one of those labyrinths of noise, it was lost on him. This was his old friend.

The team usually consists of six horses or mules, two at the tongue, with four abreast. The roads are hard and level, and they average about seven miles to the hour. The stages are often rheumatic relics of patriarchal times, broken here and there, and lashed up with rawhide, one of the staple commodities of Mexico. When anything is needed, "rawhide" flashes into the Mexican mind like a healthy and decided jack-fish into a clear pool, and then follows a somewhat abbreviated and second-class schedule trailing slowly behind. If Mexican children are like the American animal, the following scene may not unfrequently occur:

Teacher—"José, what is the staple commodity of the United Mexican States?"

Boy—"Rawhide."

T.—"What did Cortes cross the ocean in?"

B.—"Rawhide."

T.—"Of what are stage-coaches made?"

B.—"Rawhide."

T.—"What are the elements of cheese?"

B.—"Rawhide."

T.—"What is money made of?"

B.—"Rawhide."

This may account for the irreverent way Arizonians have of speaking of Mexican silver as "rawhide." These people may, and do, in fact, at times, make mistakes in laying all frailties, as well as special virtues, at the door of rawhide; but the practical small boy, the world over, spies out the chances, and in that country cannot fail to attain a decent average by relying upon that popular stage-coach material, and yelling "rawhide" as often as confronted by an interrogation. At length this thought becomes the deepest groove in the intellect, and he is nationalized.

Early in this memorable night a little incident occurred worthy of notice. The night was dark—overcast with clouds—and it was with difficulty the road could be distinguished on the alkaline *mesa*. To prevent the recurrence of our first night's mishap, Flory had purchased a hand-lantern and a dozen candles. Before our *cochero* had gathered his clouds, and began to rain such floods of ejaculations, it was decided to light the lantern, and hang it over the dashboard, so as to throw the light to the front and upon the road. One was to hold the strap, which was fastened to the handle of the lantern. Its preparation was in the hands of Story and the Professor, who were riding on the front seat with our reservoir of music. After preparing it, the Professor let it down quietly over the iron rim of the coach. Riding on two hundred yards in a gloom as profound as before, Flory leaned forward, and the following interesting conversation took place:

Flory—"What's the matter? Light out?"

Professor—"Believe it is. Pull her in, Story."

Story—"Pull her in? Pull her in yourself."

Professor—"How the mischief can I?"

Story—"By the strap, of course."

Professor—"Pull her in by the strap yourself."

Story—"Where is it?"

Professor—"Blamed if I know."

Story—"Neither do I."

The stage stopped, and all looked and felt for the lantern. Flory got out and looked under the coach, and then remarked:

"By Jove!"

Looking in the direction his dusky arm pointed, there was the lantern, two hundred yards back in the wood, faithfully performing its duty. It looked lonely. The Professor gazed at Story, while the spectacles of the latter were turned upon him; and, catching the faint show of light from a star peeping through a break in the clouds, disclosed a face of blank gravity. It was a face that always inspired confidence. The Professor was one day trying to settle with a *señora* for a dinner for the party, but she distrusted him and a piece of American silver. The Professor could not make her believe. Story turned upon her his look of confirmation, remarking,

"Oh, it is all right; it's good."

Though she knew not one word of English, she was convinced. The Professor afterward remarked, that in that trying hour Story's face, behind his glasses, looked like an affidavit, *jurat* and all. Story thought the Professor held the strap of the lantern, while the latter was equally sure it reposed in the trustful hands of Story, and when he sent the lantern over the dash, concluded that his part of the enterprise was over, and dismissed it from his mind. Story, also, dismissed the subject; and so complete was their mutual confidence that they would have reached Hermosillo believing they had traveled all night by the light of that lantern. That morning we had a real Mexican *posta* breakfast—not one of those flanked by American adjuncts, and its individuality destroyed by the presence of the foreign element. It was distinctively Sonorian and sternly patriotic. The *Guarda de la Estacion* had a wife and five children that ranged along down from a six-year old, like little stairs, to the wee dusky-limbed fellow rolling about the dirt floor. There was no chimney, fire-place, or range, nor, as the solemn old Be-It-Enacteds of the nation would say, "anything of like kind or purpose." A fire burned among some rocks in the center of the house; a piece of sheet-iron lay across them, upon which the *señora* cooked *tortillas*. These are their waifers of wheaten bread, and are good, when one gets to liking them. The *frijoles* were warming in an earthern pot. She scrambled a dozen eggs, and made coffee in an antique tin. There were no chairs nor table in the house; no bed; no furniture. The only comfortable things we saw were a pig and two hens sitting in one corner. Breakfast was served on a palm mat, spread on the ground; we crouched about it in the best way we could, and while we ate felt that we were living in the third century before Christ. All that day we kept a look out for a Rebecca at a well, and would, perhaps, have found her—had there been a well. Two and a half dollars would have been a good price for everything in the room. Here, at last, I had found a family prepared for burglars. They had only to say, "Help yourselves, gentlemen," and the burglars would have been poorer. Story said he liked *tortillas* in the abstract, but, in a practical way, they made him think all the time that he was eating his napkin. *Frijoles* are the national dish of Mexico. While the raw vegetable in size, color, and general direction of taste resembles the southern peas, under Mexican manipulation they acquire a flavor the others never attain. The Mexican cook directs her almost undivided science to this dish. The *frijol* is wholesome and nourishing, and fattens like beer. Flory said that he had a friend who bought another and larger chair every six months for the first year and a half of his stay in Mexico, and then got mad, and had an eight-foot bench made, and camped on that. Fortunately, however, for these people, *tortillas* and *carne seca* counteract the tendencies of the *frijol*.

The Professor was the "rustler" of the party, and he *could* rustle. He demonstrated that at Aqua Sacra. We never held him responsible for results; if he *rustled* we were satisfied. If he got into trouble for us we freely forgave him. Having stopped to change horses at a *posta*, he made known to the *señora* that we wished dinner. She had nothing. No eggs, no chickens, no nothing, but *carne seca* and *frijoles*. She, however, had a pretty, dark-eyed daughter, with a wealth of blue-black hair, cupid-bow lips, and teeth that were perfect. He began praising her beauty. He was coquetting for dinner—the courteous, chivalric Professor. The *señora* said she was looking for a rich husband for her daughter; whereupon, the Professor remarked that he was going below to buy a mine, and on his return would bring a *padre*, and take *Señorita Dolores* away in legal form. He was accepted, and smiles, *tortillas*, coffee with sugar, eggs, and steak, soon graced a small table, supported by a mournful dog; at least, he sat under the table all the time unmolested. We found him there; we left him at his post. After dinner the Professor engaged the mother and daughter in a pleasant chat. We asked him to interpret for us, as we wanted to say something to the pretty girl—only a few remarks. To this he replied, "Not I," and, smilingly, went on with the talk. We were in trouble—wall-flowers in the desert. There was only one Spanish phrase in our united vocabularies; only one shot in our locker—so to speak—and Flory owned that, all unbeknown to the basking Professor. Flory was desperate, and, turning to the *señora*, in the most serious way said:

"Señora, este caballero tiene una esposa y cuatro hijos con cabello robio en Tucson." (Madam, this gentleman has a wife and four red-headed children in Tucson.)

The sun of the Professor's popularity set suddenly in a great black night, and left not even a gloaming. True, a sickly, sold-out smile spread over the evening sky of the *señora's* face, but it had none of the rosy tints of the dying day in it. Dolores wrapped her *reboso* about her head, cast one swift, dark, reproachful glance at the Professor, whose face had taken on the lightning-bug glow of his whiskers, then swept it flashing indignation toward Flory, and rushed away to weep bitter tears over the shattered castle of an hour's dream. The Professor vowed it was a falsehood, and when the thunders still gathered in the maternal face, he pronounced it a thin joke, and when that failed, he wanted to go—wasn't in a particular hurry; only wanted to go. As the team was not ready, he went out and studied a solemn looking crow on a picket, and had company enough.

The day we reached Hermosillo was a field day; that is, we had reached the plains where antelope graze and mule-rabbits are numerous. It was a beautiful sight to see a herd of the former dash away, bounding gracefully as the sweep of billows for miles across the open, grassy plain, to become a scarcely undulating speck in the distance, and thus go out. It almost lulled one to repose to see the graceful sweep of their delicately fashioned bodies, clearly defined against the yellowish brown of the sacaton, heading across the vast plats for almost an hour in an unbroken gallop, as regular as the movements of an accurately adjusted machine, it seemed so without exertion and flurry. Just as we are enjoying the picture of bounding antelope, yellowish sacaton plains, fringed in the distance by the dark mesquite, and overlooked by solemn, sun-scorched mountains, a mule-rabbit springs from behind a clump of bushes and strikes off. At first it is an easy gallop, with an aristocratic *nonchalance*, his tall ears reared aloft like small sails, and so thin that the sunlight peeped through them with a pinkish hue, added to the usual gray-white. Bang! goes a pistol, and the grass near him quivers. He stops and looks back, his eyes glaring like two small burglar lamps. Bang! goes another shot, that tears up the gravel under him. Then he lays aside the aristocrat and gets to work. By the time the gravel begins to fall, he is twenty yards away, his sails furled, the masts upon which they are rigged are laid flat upon his back, and buoyant, restless, impulsive life has taken possession of his feet. At every spring, a thin mist of dust flies up behind, through which his long form is seen bounding, six feet at a spring, and too rapid to count. Bang! bang! bang! go the other pistols, but it is no use. He is on fast schedule time, and in half a minute the white expanse of rump flashed over a distant bunch of grass and was gone. We shot away several boxes of pistol cartridges, with no other result than some fast time. It generally takes one shot to arrest attention; the second one produces the work, while the third and fourth are thrown away. No man could hit one with a pistol when "down to his knitting," though the ever present flag of truce carried aft is a good mark.

Much has been said about the fleetness of the coyote, but, after all, the Sonora mule-rabbit presents the greatest possibility in the way of unutilized, unreclaimed adaptability of lightning express capacity on record. We never hear of a tired one. Set him going on the largest *mesa*, and make your nicest calculation—he will be gaining on time as his form whirls, like a gray speck, out of sight behind the impediments two miles away. Walk the distance, and you will take an oath it is five. He never slinks, like the coyote, and his tail is not in the way. It is a perpetual flag of truce, protesting against war and praying for the millennium. His soul loathes personal encounters. The coyote will attack a few weak and defenseless creatures—especially if they are dead—but the mule-rabbit attacks nothing. He has one invariable method of settling controversies. He is a proof of the compensations of nature. His capacious ears can hear the whispers of danger three miles away, and though it approaches on the wings of the storm, when it gets there he is studying the rainbow hues of the sunlight shining through his ears in a valley on the other side of the "divide." All his powers are concentrated in his capacity to run, and were this capacity divided and distributed in equal portions, he would possess the most perfect and rounded character on earth; he would have the strength of an ox, the patience of all the sons of Job, and the self-assurance of the average Congressman. One would suppose, after witnessing a few of these bounds, so full of life and vigor, that he was tenacious of life. A greater mistake could not be made. The Professor, who is something of a naturalist, assured us that a bird-shot through the tip of his right breast will break his left hind leg. We believe he is the victim of his capacities. The chief business of his eyes and ears is to keep a lookout for danger; when they find it they send a kind of telegraphic message to his legs, and they then take charge of the situation. He has no choice in the matter, being, so to speak, in the hands of his legs.

Hermosillo, the capital of Sonora, is a beautiful city of nine thousand inhabitants, situated on the Rio Sonora, and surrounded by groves and fields, save on the south, where a bold rock rises several hundred feet above the valley. It overlooks the town, and is said to have been a strategic point during the revolutions. The palm of victory was accorded to him who got possession of it. The city has some pleasant residences, while a plaza, set with orange trees, nestles in the heart of the town. It is the headquarters of the military division of Sonora. But such a military! We saw them on parade, and will take the spectacle along as a fragrant memory. Beginning at the spruce white cap, you pass down the apologetic features of the long blue coat to the greasy linen trousers and *guaraches*, or sandals. These are mere rawhide soles, from which strings (also rawhide) pass up between the toes over the unwashed feet, and fasten around the ankle. Traveling from head to foot there is an increase in geometric ratio of shabbiness. The soldier seemed to regard his feet as distant and foreign provinces, that are scarcely worth attention. While in line we noted the Mexican law of variety in the slant of guns and the angle of feet, that ranged from a broad turn-out to a most decided pigeon-toe.

It was necessary, up to a few years ago, to keep a considerable force on hand to prevent revolutions. Politics was then a matter of mere personal following, and the leader had but to beat a drum upon the plaza and a thousand men would rally to his fortunes. These revolutions were never as serious as supposed by the outside world, as every step the news traveled added to its magnitude. In America revolution means bloodshed, and plenty of it; here it means a political change, with a sauce of lawlessness. But be this as it may, they are in Sonora almost, if not actually, things of the past. Most of the inhabitants of this State live in towns. The better, informed class are bitterly opposed to these outbreaks, while the lower class are learning that peace and protection to person and property insure development, prosperity, wealth, and happiness, and have so far changed that they, in the later revolutions, fled in great numbers from the leader into the mountains and out of the trouble. Those who understand the temper of the Sonorians now have but little apprehension for the future. American capital and energy are going into Sonora in considerable quantities, and already begin to show signs of their impress upon the order of the country. From what we have seen of the Mexican character, we are induced to believe they went into these revolutions more from a sense of duty to country than from a lawless instinct for plunder. This love of country and pride of native soil is a strong and prominent trait of the Mexican. His excesses are chiefly the fruits of ignorance, now rapidly passing away in Sonora under the attrition of American ideas and precedent. Scattered over Sonora are some of the richest mines and mineral deposits on the globe, and not a few are to-day being successfully operated by Americans. While traveling through Sonora a distance of six hundred miles, we were never molested or ill treated; on the other hand, we were as well received as the poverty of the people would warrant. We saw nowhere any evidence of hatred toward Americans. It may have existed, but, if so, it was so concealed as to defy our search for it. The number of Americans there mining and ranching is larger than we expected to see. While there, Mr. Doyle, of San Francisco, purchased a large mine for $200,000, as we learned, and an Eastern firm purchased three-fifths of the great Mulatos lead, perhaps the largest body of free milling gold ore in the world. Up to a few months ago the Apaches held the great chain of the Sierra Madre, and not only kept operators out, but drove away many who were engaged in mining in those rich districts. Now they are in turn driven out, and the American prospector, with his stout heart and unerring rifle, is here to bring to light the precious metals, and give the Apache such a reception as he don't fancy. The Apache rule in the Sierra Madre is over.

The mining law in Mexico is largely derived from the *Ordenanzas de Mineria* of Spain, and, in many respects, is superior to ours. They require work to be carried on eight months in the year; but the political officer has the power, upon a sufficient showing, to grant a prorogue for eight months, which means a practical suspension of that provision of the law as to the particular property. It would transcend the limits of this paper to go into any detailed statement of the peculiar features of this system. Suffice it to say, that as mining, under Spanish domination and since, has been one of the most important industries of Mexico, it has been kindly recognized and carefully fostered by the laws.

At Hermosillo we met Don Carlos Plitz, a native of Germany, and for many years superintendent of mining in California and Nevada, and who now owns and operates a mine at Chipinaña, near Ures, and from whom we learned many interesting features of practical mining in Sonora. Years ago there grew up a kind of mining law, founded upon peculiar necessities, that is in force to-day. By it the superintendent of a mine has certain civil jurisdiction, subject to the revision of the highest judicial officer of the district, and criminal jurisdiction to the extent of a committing magistrate. He can assume jurisdiction of controversies among the miners, settle disputes, impose small fines, punish offenders, and, in fine, has such powers of local police as are necessary to protect his interests. As the miners are generally remote from towns and cities, where the regular officers reside, the necessity for this power is apparent. The superintendent generally keeps a store near the mine to supply the miners, and the law prescribes a system of bookkeeping between them. Instead of figures they use signs, adopted by legislation, and which, for the illiterate miner, is a protection. The scale is briefly thus:

[sign] equals three cents.
[sign] equals half a bit.
[sign] equals a bit, or 12½ cents.
[sign] equals half a dollar.
[sign] equals one dollar.
[sign] equals five dollars.
[sign] equals ten dollars.

At the opening of every month each hand is furnished a *boleta*, or bill in blank, upon which the superintendent, under the miner's eye, places the price of everything purchased at the time, and also charges it on his books. This *boleta* is kept by the miner in a hollow stick, or quill, and protects him from false charges. So then if, at the end of a month, a miner's *boleta* stands thus:

Y0/X00··/Y0X//

he knows that he owes $33.40⅙, and if the bookkeeper has more charged it cannot be collected. If this miner is receiving $30.00 per month, the excess of $3.40⅙ is carried on to the *boleta* for the second month, and he is to that extent a peon, and belongs to the creditor till it is paid. Or, more properly, the creditor has a lien upon his person for the debt. If he runs away he may be arrested anywhere in the republic, and returned to the creditor, who adds the charges and expenses to the debt owing by the peon, to be worked out, or his life spent in the effort. In the hands of shrewd, unprincipled men they generally do the latter. The system is fine—at least, for the owner of the store. For the peon it is quite another question. The Mexican legislator, perhaps, reasons that the laborer has his *boleta* to show him his financial latitude and longitude, and if he puts his head in the halter it's his own affair.

We left Hermosillo, with its *adobe* walls and beautiful orange, citron, and lime groves, at night, taking a conveyance for Guaymas. Soon we were all asleep, the rumbling of the vehicle over the smooth, hard road making a gentle lullaby. Nothing disturbed us but a *bronco* horse, that concluded that thirty-five miles was enough for one night, and set to kicking. He kicked his partner loose and out of the road, then did likewise to both wheelers, and was paying his respects to the front of the hack, when we got out. There were steps to the sides, but we preferred to get out behind. A piece of trace singing by, on its way out of the country, didn't disturb us. The road was hard, and we lay on each other, Story and Flory on top of me. Mine was a fine strategic position. Both the others would get it first, so I begged them to be still. Coming down, as they did, they weighed a ton; a mad *bronco's* heels would weigh two. Things were flying around generally, and the hack conducting a masterly retreat, every kick threatening to run over us. We moved out to one side. The Professor was all this time coolly standing out of danger's way, and advising us to be quiet, that the *bronco* would quit after a while.

During all next day, till four in the afternoon, we dashed along through clouds of dust, whirling up from the powdered road-bed. We had four horses to the hack; four others were driven ahead, while two extra third and fourth assistant drivers cantered alongside our horses, yelling, throwing sticks and stones, and popping whips. Every twenty miles we halted at *postas* to rest a few minutes and let the animals drink. Don't imagine that we were traveling in state. Horses cost little here, and we had given the owner of this outfit a small sum to put us in Guaymas by the evening. Could we have gone by proxy, we would have hired a Pima Indian for a dollar a day, and he would have made the round trip in three days. He stands not very far behind the coyote on questions of personal transportation. These are queer people. They take a pride in being guides, and as such are invaluable and faithful to the utmost of human nature. One will make a contract to travel in the mountains with you. You ride; he foots it in preference. He is skirmisher, vanguard, vidette, cook, and general utility man. With his rifle and wallet of provisions, he climbs mountains and strides over plains without a long breath. You can sleep in safety alone with him one hundred miles from a house. He is the incarnation of faithfulness, until you return, settle with him, and give him his discharge. When the obligation is ended, he will steal your knife, a piece of tobacco, or anything, if you are not looking. His faithfulness dams up a reservoir of plundering, covetous wishes that, surging for an outlet, slop over at once when the obligation is ended. He then hoists the flood-gates. He never makes long contracts. Under a long one, he would get so full as to be in danger of an explosion.

After several days spent at Guaymas, Story shipped to San Francisco, and we returned to Hermosillo, where Flory purchased a mule, spurs, hair-rope, blankets, slung his Winchester across his saddle, and started for the mountains. Flory is good rider. We saw him tried. A bucking mule meets its match when it starts to the mountains with Flory. The Professor and I returned at our leisure to Tucson; but of this trip we say, as did the historian who came to two hundred years of which he was ignorant, and disposed of it by writing, "Nothing of importance occurred."

JAMES WYATT OATES.

NOTE BOOK.

CONVERSATION was one of the occupations in which our good great-grandfathers and great-grandmothers found much solace. It is a pleasant picture, this courtly group, with their grand manners and their fine talk—somewhat stilted, perhaps, but as full of stately courtesy as language can hold. Conversation comes of leisure, and nowadays we have no leisure. We must go straight at a thing, must probe it without indirection to its depth. As a result, we have small-talk and discussion—but no conversation. The discussion is to *convince;* the small-talk is a pitiful bridging over of the present moment until the work comes—it is an admission that we have neither time nor inclination to bestow anything of value upon the present occasion and company. All our democratic tendencies are polemic. Dr. Johnson, notwithstanding his loyalty, was at heart a democrat, and he was a confirmed disputant. To constitute true conversation, several elements must combine. There must be no heat—the cudgel must be thrown away—for minds will not become friends so long as there is antagonism. Then there should be knowledge—not necessarily profound, but enough to keep abreast of the subject—for haphazard opinions, formed and expressed on the moment, are utterly valueless. But most important in true conversation is honesty—the intellectual rectitude which is imperceptible, intangible, but which is always recognized and respected. It is impossible to converse—to do anything more than talk—with a man who does not believe what he asserts, who is moved to advance ideas for their novelty, their brilliancy, or, for that matter, if he does not believe them, for their truth. Intellectual and moral honesty should coexist in conversation. Mutual respect and self-respect should both be present. Then interchange of opinion becomes possible, and this seldom, if ever, takes place in discussion. It is a great pity we cannot have more calm, dispassionate conversation. If I have half thought out a subject and am stopped by my limitations, and my neighbor has also come half way on the other side, it is a pity that we cannot help each other to a full understanding—that we cannot get together without each contending vehemently that his half is the whole.

THE BRADLAUGH CASE, as was foreseen, ended by the adoption of Gladstone's resolution, admitting the former to take the affirmation and to his position in the House of Commons. This resolution was made a standing rule for future cases. Except for the erratic course of Bradlaugh himself this result would have followed as a matter of course. That Bradlaugh was a person of unusual insignificance, a demagogue who appeals only to the element of discontent, simplified and abstracted the questions involved, and made the triumph of common sense the greater, inasmuch as there could be no suspicion of any personal favoritism to Bradlaugh himself. By the decision reached it is practically settled that the choice of a representative is with the constituency alone, and that this choice, once made, shall not be rendered inoperative by any religious impediments or obstructions. If Bradlaugh had been rejected it would have defeated the expressed wishes of the borough which elected him, and this solely on the ground of a religious disqualification. While we entirely disagree with Bradlaugh's belief, or, rather, lack of belief, in regard to the existence of a God, we fail to appreciate how such difference can bear upon the question of the right of a constituency to elect him as their representative, or his right to sit if elected. We may impugn the taste of a people who desire to be represented by such a member, but it is for them, not for us, to choose. That this doctrine should have been vigorously contested in a country where, a few years since, the daughter of a clergyman was refused permission to put the word "Reverend" on her father's tombstone because he had not belonged to the official church, is not strange. But that the resolution was adopted, and religious disqualification forever abolished, is a credit to the distinguished statesman who is at the head of the English Government, as well as to those who aided him by word and by vote.

A POLITICAL ARTICLE appears in this number of THE CALIFORNIAN, and, during the discussion consequent upon a Presidential election, other political contributions are promised from the pens of our most able and distinguished writers. In its higher sense we recognize the question of government as of the first importance, and believe that our columns should be open to calm discussions of political matters. We recognize the right of all sides to be fully heard, and we presume that it is unnecessary to announce that the writers whose names are appended to the several papers are alone responsible for the sentiments therein contained. We shall not prune or distort articles to make them conform to our own convictions; nor, on the other hand, shall we consider ourselves in any way bound by the opinions or statements of the contributors.

THE ONLY STANDARD IN ART seems to be the individual tastes of a majority of cultivated people. That art has been subject to fashion and to the wildest vagaries, the history of all time abundantly establishes. Of late years, however, the idea has been gaining ground that art should copy nature, and that pictures should, in some degree, resemble the objects they are intended to represent. Now, the editor of this magazine has no pretensions as an art critic, and out of the plenitude of his modesty has relegated the "Art and Artists" department to an eminent specialist, who, in all probability, would promptly expose our "fallacies" if we were to submit this note. But, nevertheless, we adhere pugnaciously to our theory, that nature is distinct, well defined, definite, satisfactory. The atmosphere may sometimes soften outlines, but it rarely makes a tree look less like a tree than before; and if occasionally this effect is produced it is a rare and by no means a constant mood.

We are led to make these remarks from a careful examination of several numbers of a leading magazine, to which the most eminent writers contribute, and which is edited with remarkable discrimination and ability. No expense is spared in the endeavor to make the illustrations entirely worthy of the articles, the authors, and the publication. The first picture to which we turn, in the number before us, looks dizzy. Carefully covering up the print with our hand we try to make out the subject without consulting the name. After some study we decide that it is a duck-pond, with a girl in the center of the water. How she got there or why she remains is not clear. A friend is called in, who pronounces the "water" to be clover, in which the maiden is standing. We are both agreed on the femininity of the central figure. Removing our hand, we find the subject to be something which is entirely foreign to our conjectures. With the aid of the name we slowly make out of the nebulous mass the form and shape that is indicated in the text. Thinking the artist may have desired to delineate one of Nature's hazy moods above referred to we turn to other engravings, with much the same result. Now, is this art? Our art editor would, probably, answer, "Yes;" and would, no doubt, wander off into a technical explanation which we would not understand, but which, we are charitable enough to admit, would mean something intelligible to him. But, after he had finished, these questions would not have been answered satisfactorily: "Does it resemble anything in the heavens or on the earth?" and "Why make everything with such indistinctness, when Nature herself is so only at intervals?"

SCIENCE AND INDUSTRY.

USEFUL SHAMS.

One of the most noted features of modern industry is the ingenuity and skill displayed in devising cheap substitutes for rare or expensive articles in general demand. Celluloid may be instanced as one of those modern inventions which has been very largely employed as a substitute for various kinds of raw material. It is, perhaps, best known as a substitute for ivory. For many of the purposes for which that material has been employed, celluloid, although an imitation, a sham, is really better than the ivory itself, as it possesses not only all the strength and elasticity of that material, but it is also free from any tendency to warp, and does not discolor with age. The applications of celluloid are so various and well known that they do not need enumeration here. Among the other products which have also been successfully imitated are meerschaum, horn, and coral. These imitation products are manufactured from the pulp of potatoes, turnips, or carrots, treated with sulphuric acid, and are fully equal in every useful respect to the genuine articles. The manufacture of imitation precious stones has also become quite an important industry. Diamonds are now so perfectly imitated that, when properly cut, their refractive power is almost equal to the genuine article of the first water. Some artificial diamonds which were exhibited in the same case, side by side with real diamonds of the first water, attracted much attention at the late Paris Exhibition. The real diamond has been produced on a small scale by artificial means; but whether the process can be made profitable remains to be proved. Any person can convert a diamond into charcoal, but it is not easy to reconvert that coal into a diamond. Artificial pearls are so skillfully made as to deceive all but the most practiced experts. The natural alizarine of madder, which a few years ago represented an agricultural industry amounting to $10,000,000 a year, is now almost entirely superseded by a chemical product which can be made for one-third the price of the former, and equally as good in quality. The analine colors have not only supplanted those of former products, but they have added to our textile fabrics a great number of formerly unknown but most beautiful shades. The value of the annual product of these artificial dyes—all the products of the chemical laboratory—is now fully $16,000,000. The ultramarine of to-day—a substitute for that of a few years ago, which was prepared from lapis-lazuli at a cost of about $400 to the pound—is now produced for twenty-five cents per pound, while the annual consumption has increased from a few hundred pounds to over eleven thousand tons. The ladies may be both interested and astonished to learn that even ostrich feathers, the coveted court plumes of fashion, are not all plucked from the king of birds. Imitations of spun glass and silk on a celluloid quill are the "shams" which are nowadays often imposed on ladies for one-fifth of the cost which they would have to pay for the genuine article. The costly animal product known as "eider down" is rapidly being replaced by a much cheaper and a really better vegetable product obtained from the silky coverings of certain seeds. The qualities which recommend this "sham" are immunity from the attacks of moths and other vermin, and a lightness, elasticity, softness, and warmth equal to the genuine article. The above, and some other articles which might be mentioned, may be included under the general head of "useful shams," as contradistinguished from the many mischievous and hurtful imitations which are now being imposed upon the public. The former are a result of legitimate manufacturing ingenuity and scientific skill, and furnish cumulative proof of the rapid strides with which skill and science are invading the domain of nature in searching out useful substitutes for the more expensive raw materials and articles of general use and demand.

ELECTRICITY IN CYCLONES.

Professor John H. Tice, a well known meteorologist of St. Louis, has recently been studying the phenomena connected with the storms which have lately passed over portions of Missouri, and other Mississippi States, with very desolating effects. One of the phenomena connected with the Marshfield tornado was the manifest presence of a wave, or wash, of water, which swept along the storm-track, sometimes furrowing the ground in its progress. One of the most marked peculiarities connected with this special phenomenon was the fact that its presence was more apparent where the course of the storm *ascended* a hill, than when it passed over either descending or level ground. Fibrous roots, tufts of grass, bushes, etc., were left pointing *up* the hill, instead of down. Such would naturally be the case where a column of water was carried along in the tubular vacuum produced by a whirlwind—the lower portion of the column would naturally strike rising ground, and pass lightly over that which was descending or level. Again, it is said there was little or no wind outside of the immediate "whirl," and the tornado generally passed over wooden roofs, doing very little damage, but utterly demolishing any roof in its track which was covered with tin or iron. A mill, situated a quarter of a mile from the center of disturbance, had its iron chimney torn away and hurled to quite a distance. The cupola of another building, which was covered with tin, was completely wrecked, but the wooden roof over the main portion of the structure was uninjured. The bodies of trees were stripped of their bark, the ends of the green branches denuded of both leaves and bark and rifted into fine fibres—literally broomed out at their extremities—while the dry limbs were not seriously disturbed. Effects such as these can be accounted for only by the presence of an unusual quantity of electricity, which attacks iron and leaves undisturbed the wood work connected therewith. Under its influence, the sap beneath the bark of trees, and in their smaller branches, may be instantly converted into vapor, expanding some two thousand times in volume, with such an explosive force as to throw off the bark, shatter the trunk and larger branches, and split the green twigs into fibers. The conditions required to produce a cyclone is an almost total absence of atmospheric disturbance over a wide area, united with a high temperature. The heating of the lower stratum of air causes it to rise, when, of course, there is a rush of air from all sides to the center of disturbance. This naturally generates a whirling column, which immediately commences an onward motion, both motions constantly accelerating in rapidity and violence until a point beyond the original disturbing causes is reached. These sudden changes of temperature and violent disturbances of the atmosphere are competent to generate and set in action electric forces of the most extensive and intense character. If the moving column chances to pass over a body of water, the vacuum created in the center of the whirl is filled with a column of that element, which, in its onward motion, might produce such phenomena as were witnessed at Marshfield. "Cloud-burst" is a name given to a class of phenomena altogether distinct, and produced in a manner quite different, from the above.

SCIENCE IN FLOUR MANUFACTURE.

Until recently it was believed that the only thing to be sought for in the production of a good article of flour was a more or less fine disintegration of the kernels of wheat. As long as millers held to the theory that "grinding" was all that was required, a large percentage of the flour had its nutritive powers greatly reduced by being ground to an impalpable dust. Science, by aid of the microscope, has shown that no really good bread can be made from flour, in which any large portion of the starch globules have been thus broken down. The rising of bread is due to the starch globules, which remain whole, while the dust from the disintegrated ones, by souring, impairs the lightness and sweetness of the loaf. It is but recently that these facts have been made known to millers, and since that time they have been discarding their old theories and machinery, and devising improvements with the view to *separating* the the starch globules, rather than *pulverizing* them. Another important advance in this industry consists of an improvement in bolting machines. Until recently the bran was separated from the flour by a powerful air-blast, which blows off the light particles of bran. Considerable power is required for this process, and although it is carried on in a closed room, there is not only a great waste of the finer particles of flour, but the impalpable dust penetrates every part of the mill, and often gives rise to destructive explosions. By a recent invention, electricity is made to take the place of the air-blast. Just over the wire bolting-cloth, which has a rapid reciprocal motion, a number of hard rubber cylinders are kept slowly revolving and rubbing against strips of sheepskin, by which a large amount of frictional electricity is evolved. Then, as the middlings are sieved by the reciprocal motion, the lighter bran comes to the top, whence, instead of being blown away by an air-blast, it is attracted to the electrically-charged cylinders, as light substances are attracted to a piece of paper, or a stick of sealing wax, which has been smartly rubbed. The removal of the bran from the rollers and its deposit on one side are readily effected, while the flour is carried in another direction. The separation is thus made complete, with very little loss or dust. Still another device has also been introduced to remove from the wheat, before being ground, small pieces of iron, which, despite the utmost care, will find its way into the grain, working great injury to mill machinery. This trouble is now remedied by the use of a series of magnets, directly under which all the grain is made to pass. These magnets readily capture all the stray pieces of iron from the wire bands used in binding; and they have also revealed the singular fact, that, of the scraps of iron and steel which find their way into the grain, fully one-third are something besides the binding wire. They are of larger proportions, of varying character, and much more hurtful to the machinery than the wire. Thus it is that science is constantly coming to our aid in all our varied industries, lightening the labor of the workman, decreasing the cost of products, and in every way improving all the various processes which are involved in the improved and constantly advancing civilization of the age.

AMERICAN PLATE GLASS.

The manufacture of plate glass is quite a new industry in this country. There are as yet but four companies in operation. The pioneer and the largest works of the kind is located at New Albany, Indiana. It occupies twenty acres of ground, and employs $1,000,000 of capital. Connected with the works, and under the same management, is another, known as the De Pauw Plate Glass Works, with a capital of $750,000. These two establishments give employment to upward of one thousand persons. The Ford Plate Glass Works, at Jeffersonville, is operated by a capital of $600,000, and the Crystal City Works, near St. Louis, employs a capital of $750,000. This industry is an important one, and as yet furnishes but a very small portion of the plate glass consumed in the country. That it is profitable may be inferred from well authenticated reports that the most strenuous exertions have been made, by importers and foreign manufacturers, to crush out the business of home manufacture. It is said that efforts have been made, by a combination of those interested in the foreign manufacture, to purchase all the American factories, with a view to tearing them down, and establishing a monopoly of the business in the hands of the foreign manufacturers. Large sums of money, it is also said, have been spent in sustaining a strong lobby at Washington, to bring about either a material reduction or a total abrogation of the tariff on foreign plate glass. It is to be hoped that a business of so much and such growing importance will be fostered by the Government until it shall be able to take care of itself, an advantage which, under proper auspices, it will reach in a very few years.

THE MICROSCOPE IN GEOLOGY.

In no department of natural science has the student heretofore been compelled to tread with more uncertain step than in that of lithology. The interpretation of general geological phenomena has been quite satisfactorily given by Lyell; while the significance of organic remains in the sedimentary rocks has been quite as clearly unfolded by Buffon. But it is only recently that the geologist has been able to study the mineral constituents and minute structure of rocks, so as to decide with any degree of certainty in regard to rock-genesis, or rock-formation. In past times, if we gave a geologist a piece of rock for examination, he would tell us it was quartz, or granite, or trap, as the case might be. He might, perhaps, tell us it contained some kind of metallic substance, and with the aid of the crucible he would be able to tell us how much of the various metals it contained. But ask him about its mineral structure, how it was built up, the forms, nature, and relative condition of its component parts, and he could tell us little or nothing. Through this ignorance of the building up of rocks, great confusion has existed in regard to the whole subject of petrology, and rocks of widely different natures have often been classed by our most learned geologists under the same name. Various methods of investigation had been employed to reach more accurate determinations. The microscope had been brought into requisition in the ordinary way of its use. Chemistry had been invoked, and its searching analysis employed to unveil the secret workings of nature in building up the stony foundations of the earth, but all with little success; and the geologist had about concluded that any further progress in this special department was at an end. Just at this time Mr. Henry Clifton Sorby, an English geologist, resolved to apply the microscope in a new direction. He took thin scales of various rocks, ground them down into exceedingly thin plates, carefully polished these plates, or sections, on both sides, and mounted them on glass slides for examination, by either transmitted or by polarized light, with the view of determining how much they would thus be able to tell of their own history. He worked patiently for a long time in this direction before he reached any satisfactory results, and it is now only some ten or twelve years since he was enabled to announce to the world that what the spectrum had done in revealing the composition and condition of the distant stars, the microscope, in his hands, was doing for the rocks and sands under our feet. A new and wide field of research was at once opened up, and great numbers of earnest students availed themselves of the opportunity, until now we are able to study not only the intimate structure of coarse or distinctly crystalline rocks, but also to investigate, with the utmost exactness, even the almost infinitely small crystalline structures, determine the form, nature, and position of their granules, study at our leisure the minutest details of their structure, and thus reach most accurate conclusions in regard to their genesis. The microscope is thus becoming not only a great aid, but an indispensable requisite, to the study of geology. It has already thrown a flood of light on a class of rocks that have hitherto been most obscure; it has introduced system where before all was vague and indefinite—in fact, it has quite revolutionized that branch of geology to which this new mode of study has been applied. By this mode of examination, the observer is often astonished to find that a piece of rock, which to the naked eye, or even when examined in bulk by a powerful glass, seems perfectly uniform—of one color and one type—really contains three, four, and perhaps five or more types. By the study of sections, prepared as above, the mining expert is now far better able than ever before to trace the continuity of either vein or wall rock, and note with certainty the minutest change in the rock through which he is working.

A NEW SKATING SURFACE.

An English inventor, after much study and experiment, has, quite recently, devised an entirely new skating surface, which he calls "crystal ice," and which consists of a mixture of various salts, mostly, however, sulphate of soda, which crystallize at ordinary temperatures. This preparation, which is comparatively cheap, is simply spread out, in a plastic condition, from an excess of water, upon an ordinary floor. As soon as the excess of water evaporates the substance becomes crystallized, presenting a surface much resembling ice, quite as hard, and upon which ordinary ice-skates may be used with about equal facility as upon a water-frozen surface. When "cut up" by skaters, its surface can be readily smoothed by a steaming apparatus, and the floor, when once laid, will last for years. It is obvious that such a floor must have many advantages over artificial ice and floors for roller-skating. It is said that the mixture of salts used contains about sixty per cent. of water of crystallization; hence, after all, the floor consists mostly of solidified water. The above facts are obtained from *Nature*, of June 5th, in which it is further stated that a small experimental floor has proved such a complete success that a large skating rink is to be immediately constructed upon this principle.

LUMINOUS PAINT NOT NEW.

Much is being said, just at this time, in regard to the utility and novelty of a luminous paint recently invented by Mr. Balmain. But now comes *Nature*, of June 10th, and informs us that the Japanese were acquainted with the art of luminous painting nine hundred years ago. That publication gives a translation from a Chinese book, written about that time, from which it appears that one Su Ngoh had a Japanese picture of an ox which, it was said, left the frame every day to graze, and returned every night to sleep within it. This picture finally came into the possession of one of the Chinese Emperors, who showed it to his courtiers, and asked for an explanation, which none of them could give. At last a Buddhist priest informed the Emperor that the Japanese found a substance in a certain kind of oyster, out of which they manufactured a paint which was invisible by day, but luminous by night. The explanation was given by the writer of the book, that when it was said the ox left the picture by day to go a-grazing, it was simply under-stood that during the day-time the figure was invisible.

ART AND ARTISTS.

THE LOCAL ARTISTS.

In ordinarily prosperous years this is the season artists devote to those pleasant pilgrimages to Nature's shrines, in search of inspiration, motives, and the many enjoyments that are their birthright. We don't begrudge them their pleasures, but their absence is, no doubt, much felt by regular visitants to studios and places of exhibition. This year has been, to a certain extent, an exceptional one. Some of the studios are vacant, and, we regret to say, are likely to remain so, their former occupants having sought other fields for their labors. Hill is in Boston, Keith in Philadelphia, and we learn that Nahl and Tojetti are on their way to Europe. Messrs. Yelland and Strauss are in Oregon wrestling with Nature; likewise Mr. Bradford, whose objective point is Mount Hood. But the majority of our art devotees may still be found in their ateliers, working upon subjects the city and vicinity afford, or enjoying a quiet time in anticipation of renewed efforts later in the season. Few works are being placed on view owing to the unfavorableness of the times. The chief attraction of late among local pictures on public exhibition has been Mr. Yelland's view of the Golden Gate, to be seen at the gallery of Morris & Kennedy, on Post Street. This picture is regarded as Mr. Yelland's best work. It embraces all the excellencies of his former pictures, and shows a marked improvement in treatment. The subject is largely and simply composed, rich and harmonious in color, and is remarkable for care in detail, combined with breadth and comprehensiveness. Mr. Brooks has on private exhibition at his studio a recently finished life-sized picture of a peacock that commands the admiration of all who have seen it, and is, likewise, pronounced the *chef-d'oeuvre* of this conscientious painter. Mr. Perry has completed another of the excellent and characteristic subjects entitled "Solitaire." A handsome lady seated at a Japanese table, and surrounded by a beautifully painted assortment of *bric-a-brac*, is amusing herself at the game of solitaire with cards. The subject is treated with great care and minuteness, and is excellent in color and composition. Mr. Bradford, also, has several fresh works, principally Yosemite views, painted from studies recently made in the Valley, and characterized by all the excellencies of that widely known painter. Bouvy is engaged upon a subject representing a procession of chanting monks, winding down a stairway to attend service. The chief interest in the subject will be in the portrayal of character and facial expression, in which Mr. Bouvy excels. Hahn is painting some Jersey cattle for Mr. A. K. P. Harmon. R. J. Bush has in his Oakland studio two unfinished pictures that promise well—"A Spring Reverie," representing a pretty blonde girl pausing in the arrangement of a mass of flowers to contemplate a rose bud; and "The Little Tea Merchant," for which a picturesque little Oakland character posed. Deakin has just finished a picture of Cluny Castle, in Paris, on an order; and Denny, one of the yacht *Chispa*, also an order. In the "Latin Quarter" little seems to be doing. Mr. Ris has been working on a fine Oregon subject, which does him credit. Tavernier and Strong are devoting themselves largely to illustrating and preparatory work for coming pictures, and Mr. Robinson has been engaged upon an order from Dr. Toland. Otherwise, these gentlemen seem to be enjoying their *otium cum dignitate*, and reserving their powers for a more favored season. Mr. Cleenewerck, a comparatively recent arrival, has on view in the galleries several excellent pictures of the Munich order, landscapes and still life.

THE BEGINNING OF AN ART ERA.

It is gratifying to observe that the American people have awakened to a realization that there is something to achieve beyond the bare acquisition of wealth. It would seem that the long delayed inauguration of an American art era has been at length established. The present rage for decorative art is but a prelude to the introduction of those adornments of a higher order that are so sadly missed by visitors from the eastern hemisphere, and which add such a charm to the time-worn cities of Europe. Several of our leading cities are now engaged in a generous rivalry for the possession of art treasures. Museums of antiquities and articles of historical interest have already been started in New York, Boston, and other cities, and at present an unusual interest is manifested in the embellishment of our parks and public buildings with statuary, and in the introduction of a more picturesque and artistic order of architecture. Time will be required to effect the desired transformation, but the public-spiritedness that characterizes the day will soon work great changes. As a nation, we, at present, are just emerging from our "teens." We have passed through the period of youth, with its innocence and friskiness, and are beginning to awaken to a realization of the fact that there are many things not dreamt of in our philosophy. That assurance, begotten of a sturdy frame and vigorous physique, will soon give place to a more matured confidence, based upon cultivation, and a consciousness of equality with the world in those respects that distinguish manhood from immaturity. The recent general direction of thought and attention to the higher arts, as manifested in the disposition to beautify our cities, and establish museums, galleries, and art schools accessible to the public, may be regarded one of the strongest evidences of our certain and rapid development; and it is only a question of time when our country will abound in monuments of taste and refinement. Already we possess many valuable private collections of pictures, and in several instances magnificent endowments have been bestowed by wealthy citizens for the establishment of public galleries. These institutions seem to be ably conducted. Art schools are also springing up all over the country, and facilities for education in that department are increasing so rapidly that probably before many years our youth will find it unnecessary to go abroad to prosecute their studies. For all this we are wholly indebted to private munificence. Little or no encouragement has been received from Government, and none, perhaps, was to be expected. Republics are not only "ungrateful," but are slow to bestow favors even upon their own. The fifty million guardians of the treasury are too directly interested in the national fund, and are too little in sympathy with art education at the present time to be willing to grant any sum for such purposes. France is a remarkable exception. With her the cultivation of art is second nature. Force of habit, acquired under the old monarchy, and the consciousness that to art, perhaps, more than any other cause, she owes her present greatness and prosperity, will long serve to keep alive the interest. Of the French people, however, it may be said with truth that their fondness in this direction is deep-seated—in fact, a national trait, and not based altogether upon self-interest. The generosity they have shown in the bestowal of casts and art treasures upon foreign institutions, as instanced by her liberal donation to the San Francisco Art Association, and the national gift of the great Bartholdi statue of Liberty, to be erected in New York harbor, are evidences of her disinterestedness. Many years will elapse before a like state of affairs will be found in our republic. Looking at the matter from the standpoint of art, it is, perhaps, to be regretted that our present Government was not antedated by a century or two of aristocratic rule. As it is, our only resource is to look to the cultivated and wealthy in our midst for donations wherewith to foster and encourage the art tendency of the day.

WOMEN PAINTERS.

It has been claimed heretofore that women are naturally unqualified to become great artists—that is, to attain as great excellence as lies within the power of the other sex. No special reason seems ever to have been given, but the matter has been accepted by many as a truism, based probably upon the fact that history furnishes the names of no female Raphaels and Angelos. The injustice of this is at once apparent, since a glance at the past reveals the impossibility of their ever having entered the lists as competitors for art and fame, on account of the many restrictions put upon them socially, and the unchivalrous notions of their inferiority that it was the custom to entertain formerly. In these modern progressive and more enlightened days, those restrictions have been greatly removed, and woman has begun to assert herself in a manner that is rapidly gaining for her an acknowledgment of equal capacity with man in many departments from which she was formerly excluded. Especially in art has she demonstrated her capabilities, not only as a decorator, but in the higher branch of picture-making. It is true the world has yet produced but the one Rosa Bonheur and the one Mrs. Elizabeth Butler, but when we consider that hardly one out of a hundred male artists acquires more than a national reputation, we have no reason to exact a greater proportion of genius from the limited ranks of woman artists. Especially in the last few years have women asserted their powers. The *Magazine of Art*, in a London article entitled "Pictures of the Year," bestows the greatest praise upon Mrs. Butler's picture, "The Defense of Rorke's Drift," a historical incident of the Zulu war, lately on exhibition at the Bond Street gallery of the Society of Fine Arts. Considering the fact that Mrs. Butler's picture was exhibited in direct competition with another of the same subject, painted by the famous French artist, M. de Neuville, her work must have been of a very superior order to excite any kind of favorable criticism. The writer, however, goes further than this. In comparing the two, he says, "his (De Neuville's) may be pronounced to be more pictorial, hers to be more intensely characteristic; his executive dash is supreme, but more vivid and significant is her reserved power." Further on, he speaks of the competition as having been a very close one, and of great interest to the public. At the Grosvenor Gallery, in London, this year, nearly one-fourth of the contributors are women; and in the French Salon a large number of the sex is also represented. It may be gratifying to Americans to know that among the latter an American lady, Miss E. J. Gardiner, occupies the foremost place, having a picture on the line which is highly spoken of. In our numerous American schools, lady pupils preponderate, and many of them display talent. Of these, only a few will acquire much skill, but probably that number will be sufficient, proportionately, to prove that their capabilities are in no sense inferior to those of the opposite sex.

GREATNESS IN ART.

It is often a cause of surprise that during the past centuries—since the *Renaissance*, in fact—among the thousands who have devoted themselves to painting the names of so few are preserved to posterity as being great. Of good painters each generation can boast many, and probably it may be said with safety that our age is especially favored in this respect. Only at long intervals in the catalogue of painters do we find names to which the prefix "great" can be applied unhesitatingly, and considering all the qualifications necessary to perfection in an important work of art, possibly no one can be mentioned whose skill, in every respect, surpasses criticism. As colorists many of the old masters have never been equaled. Others excel in composition, in form, technique, or *chiaro-oscuro*; but what master combines the highest attainable degree of excellence in all these respects, with vividness of imagination, and that delicacy of organization which proclaims the poet, and enables one to grasp and depict those subtile qualities of nature, whose presence in a picture at once stamps its superiority? Indeed, considering the almost superhuman power necessary to perfection in painting it is a cause of wonderment that any should ever have earned for themselves the appellation of "great;" and we are no longer astonished that years of study are required for the attainment of even a passable degree of excellence. Notwithstanding all this, it would appear, from the large number who to-day enjoy world-wide reputations, that in the future history of art relating to our era there will be no want of names entitled to distinction; and, possibly, unbiased historians of the future will accord to some of our contemporaries places as high in the temple of fame as those occupied by some of the so-called old masters. The truth of the adage, that "a prophet hath no honor in his own country," has been frequently demonstrated as applied to other callings. Would it be unreasonable to presume that our august selves may be victims, possibly, to that same perverse and inexplicable human trait which prompts one to deny to familiars their due, and sets us groping through the past for objects of adoration. We are aware that even to suggest such a possibility is rank heresy, and a violation of that "unwritten law" which grants to the old painters inimitable superiority; yet, without wishing to deny the past its undoubted excellence, we venture to claim that, perhaps, some of the men of latter days are equally great, and eventually will be so adjudged.

THE METROPOLITAN MUSEUM.

The Metropolitan Museum of Art was organized in New York about nine years ago, dependent entirely upon private contribution, and has already formed the nucleus of an important collection that will increase in value and interest with time, and eventually redound to the credit of the city. It seems to be the intention of the directory not so much to form a museum of curiosities as to gather together representative works of art and art industries, that will not only possess historical value, but will be of service for educational purposes, and for the encouragement of like industries in America. In the spring of 1879 the museum was moved to its present quarters in Central Park. Here many important acquisitions have been made by purchase and donation; among the latter, a valuable collection of coins, presented by Mr. Joseph Drexel, of New York, very recently, and valued at $30,000. The contributions received thus far amount to $350,000, nearly a fourth of which is the gift of the trustees of the institution. The opening of the museum that took place in the spring was one of the events of the day, embracing, in its display, a large number of valuable pictures, loaned for the occasion; and since then, upon those days when no charges for admission have been made, the attendance has averaged ten thousand people, proving not only the public appreciation, but that the museum supplies a long-felt want. Much comment, favorable and unfavorable, has been passed by the press upon a collection of old Dutch and Flemish pictures purchased by the directory. If it be the intention of the society to limit their purchases greatly, perhaps this money might have been more satisfactorily expended. However, as the representative work of the people and an era in art, such a collection would seem to possess great interest. One of the most important exhibits to be seen in the museum is the Cesnola collection of antique pottery, showing the origin of all Greek art, and wonderfully rich in its extent and variety of art-form, as well as antique portrait heads. Mr. Cesnola, from whom the collection derives its title, is director of the museum. A large collection of oriental porcelain, purchased of Mr. S. P. Avery, occupies a prominent place in the exhibit, also; and a collection of laces and embroideries, contributed by a lady who reserves her name, excites much interest among those who have taste to appreciate them. As yet the museum seems to be little more than a beginning, considering variety, but the gentlemen in charge, whose enthusiasm increases instead of abates, will spare no pains as often as opportunity occurs to increase its attractiveness and render it more complete. To further the objects of the institution steps have been taken to establish an industrial school in its connection. A liberal New York gentleman, Mr. Auchmuty, has offered the use of a large piece of ground at First Avenue and Sixty-seventh Street, free of rent for three years, and will erect, at his own expense, a suitable building for the schools, which he proposes to start and keep running for three years. We learn that the proposition has been accepted, and that work will at once be commenced upon the buildings.

THE SEPTEMBER EXHIBITION.

At a meeting of the artists, held some time in the spring, it was decided to recommend to the Directory of the San Francisco Art Association to hold a third exhibition of pictures each year, to take place in September, and to comprise mainly loan works from private galleries, each local artist being permitted to exhibit one picture. The object of the resolution was to increase interest in the Art Association, which, from the stress of the times, had begun to flag; also to afford the supporters of that institution greater return for their contributions, as well as to increase the much needed revenue. Of late it has been the custom to give two exhibitions annually, one of pictures from local studios in the spring, and a winter display of the work of pupils connected with the Art School. Much is anticipated from the September display, and if our wealthy citizens respond as readily and willingly as on former occasions, we may look forward to a treat. Notwithstanding our remoteness from art centers, there are to be found in our midst many works of a high order of excellence, from both American and foreign studios, which would form an exhibition not easily surpassed. Some of these, comprising the works of Troyon, Corot, Gérome, Bouguereau, and many others possessing world-wide reputations, have been exhibited on former occasions, but so long a time has elapsed since that art lovers and the public generally will hail their reappearance with fresh enthusiasm. Many more recent acquisitions of art wealth to the community have been made also, and, if properly applied for, will no doubt be generously loaned. Such an exhibition will afford great pleasure, as well as instruction, to Californians, and will prove interesting as an exponent of the art taste of the community. Some of our artists may feel a little hesitancy in placing their work in direct competition with pictures of such standing, but it is to be hoped that each one will be represented; and no doubt, in many instances, it will be found that, as at the Metropolitan Museum, in New York, instead of suffering greatly by the comparison, they will command a higher appreciation.

AN ART EXCURSION.

Acting upon a hint furnished, no doubt, by the Tile Club excursion in a canal-boat up the Hudson River, an account of which appeared some time since in *Scribner's Monthly*, a wealthy gentleman of New York has extended an invitation to the members of the Artist Fund Society, of that city, to make a canal-boat excursion to Niagara Falls. He proposes to defray all expenses, making all the stoppages desired, and secure hotel accommodations for the party *en route*. It is the intention to ascend the Hudson under tow to Albany, and proceed by the Erie Canal to the Falls, where the party will remain three days, and return to New York in drawing-room car. The Society consists of sixty-five members, of which number about forty artists have accepted the invitation, each one of whom will paint a picture from sketches made during the trip, and present it to the host. The twenty-first of June was settled upon as the time of starting. Among those intending to participate are many of the most prominent New York artists, so that the gentleman, in addition to the pleasure to be derived from such an excursion, will become the possessor of a valuable collection of representative American pictures. It is to be hoped that the public will become participators in this, as in the Tile Club excursions, by means of some of our periodicals.

BOOKS RECEIVED.

History of the Administration of John de Witt, Grand Pensionary of Holland. By James Geddes. Volume I. 1623–1654. New York: Harper & Brothers. 1880. For sale in San Francisco by Payot, Upham & Co.

When the Dutch Republic burst its Spanish swaddling clothes there sprang into national life a class of educated, shrewd, clever (perhaps not always grand) statesmen, of whom John of Barneveld, of the gentle stem of Oldenbarneveldts, whose heroic career has been traced by Motley, and Cornelius and John de Witt may be regarded as fair types. Holland in those days cultivated the traits of the *bourgeoisie* with the same tenderness that is bestowed upon tulips; and when the burgher towns grew too powerful for the blunt administration of the Dircks and Florenses, Counts of Holland, who took toll from the mercantile barges that floated on the sluggish streams, and compelled the merchants to break bulk and to open markets upon their castellated mud-banks, the government practically devolved upon the proud burghers who conducted those same markets, and who had established their warehouses around the falling fortresses of their liege lords. These burghers were commercially aristocratic. In their way, they felt themselves quite the peers of feudal barons, whose castle were garrisoned, but whose lives were warfare, unsoftened by the elegances of life. Burghership had its honors, its duties, and its dangers. The routine of their town and village functions, enlarged when it came to administration of the province, and crowned by the States General, made them trained diplomatists. Their sons aspired to be civilian doctors of laws; and if ever a body of men understood international jurisprudence as part of their daily life and manners, it was the colleagues of De Groot and their successors. These men were no worse sailors than they were advocates in chancery; and an amphibious statesman, whose eye was as searching when resting on the rigging and equipage of a man-of-war as when engaged in parsing the language of a treaty, was a dangerous personage to have as antagonist in the conflicts of nations for supremacy, either on land or sea. Of this stamp of ability were the De Witts—uncompromising aristocrats, burghers, lawyers, diplomates, statesmen. Holland and its associate provinces were in those days governed by an oligarchy of such cultured, half mercantile, half juristical elements, with a popular class below, jealous of the hands that guided their government, and with a royal power threatening them from above, in the shape of the House of Orange, which, besides the prestige of feudality, was surrounded by the glamor of having snatched from the Spaniards, and successfully defended, the liberty and autonomy of the nation. For the Dutch of those times (1650–72), the reigning Prince of Orange was the Man on Horseback, and it was the life-long business of John de Witt to prevent his entry into the Stadtholdership, a task in which the Grand Pensionary was successful only during the minority of the Prince; and when, finally, William (afterward King of England) came to manhood, the hero-worship of the populace, and the threatening success of the Grand Monarch, proved too much for the lawyer burgher, and John and his brother, Cornelius, met death as a propitiatory sacrifice on the entry of William into his hereditary office of Stadtholder. The De Witts were, from father to son, the objects of Orange fears. Old Jacob, their father, had been virtually disfranchised by the father of William. He had even been a prisoner, suffering for his principle. But when John became Pensionary (1652), William was an infant in his nurse's arms, and so the field was clear for the young patrician lawyer. The Dutch had won distinguished naval renown, which, however, was likely to be impaired by the energy of Cromwell. With Cromwell, therefore, John de Witt managed a peace (1654), and secured additional guaranties that the Orange family should be kept out of power. This was good while it lasted; but Cromwell died, and the Stuarts returned, and the Stuarts were relatives and allies of Orange. So the energetic Pensionary turned to France (1664) for aid against the restored English dynasty. But the peace with France could never be sincere, and De Witt attempted a fresh alliance with England (1667) against France. What sort of an ally Charles II. would have been as against France, we, of this day, can hardly imagine. Had, however, the then English Government made solid terms with the Pensionary and kept them, and prevented William from taking the Stadtholdership, it is hardly likely that the Stuart dynasty would, twenty years later, have been driven into exile. But Louis XIV. invaded the Provinces: the Provinces, in terror, re-established the Stadtholdership; and (1672) the two De Witts, John and Cornelius, were massacred, the one (Cornelius) in prison, and the other (John) while visiting him. Our present historian has selected the half century ending with the death of John de Witt as the subject for his history, making the Grand Pensionary the chief figure, and Volume I. ends with the peace with Cromwell. In reading the book one is somehow dimly reminded of the American Adams family. Making allowances for differences in epoch and race, one finds the same uniformity of talent, the same coldness of purpose, and the same lack of personal favor with the populace. The author has made his work a matter of industrious study, and clothes his historical outlines with as much warmth as the subject will permit; indeed, if there is any defect in style, it is, perhaps, an over partiality to the dramatic present in narration, and to a semi-prophetic way of lighting up the immediate incident that is being told with a reference to the future events. The book is one that every cultivated reader of a political turn in this country will enjoy, and take as a lesson in politics.

THE LIFE AND WRITINGS OF HENRY THOMAS BUCKLE. By Alfred Henry Huth. New York: D. Appleton & Co. 1880. For sale in San Francisco at Appleton's Agency, 107 Montgomery Street.

Henry Thomas Buckle was a man with an object. To the accomplishment of the purpose which he had in view he gave his time, his energy, his private fortune, his most generous enthusiasm, and, eventually, his life. That purpose was to write a history of civilization, which should be not merely, as other histories had been, a dramatic narration of events, arrayed in chronological sequence, but an exegesis of the laws which regulate the movements and affect the opinions of men. For, with Buckle, civilization was the result of causes; the human intellect moved in the realm of law: and human actions, though as individual as the apparent vagaries of a comet, were yet in subordination to a general system. Upon the threshhold of this work he discovered that it was too vast for one life, and his first limitation upon his original plan was to confine his history to England as a nucleus, treating other lands incidentally and by way of illustration. In breadth of thought, in capacity for generalization, in honesty of mind, and in singleness of purpose, he was eminently qualified for the undertaking he had planned. But, on the other hand, there were obstacles which would have dismayed another. His health was delicate from childhood, and, as he finally discovered, was unequal to the task; his education had not been such as the general opinion would have pronounced sufficient for the necessary researches; old prejudices would have to be combated, new paths opened; and ultimate success would expose him as a target, if not to ridicule, to aversion and hatred. But Buckle was a pioneer, made of the "undaunted mettle" which, in the field either of action or of thought, presses on in defiance of obstacles. The first volume of the Introduction to his history (1857) took the world by surprise. The doctrines announced were antagonistic to many accepted ideas, which, as they were acquired by heredity, seemed the more established and unassailable. But, as Buckle himself remarks—for he never affected to be unaware of his ability—"the people of England have such an admiration of any kind of intellectual splendor that they will forgive, for its sake, the most objectionable doctrines." As had been foreseen, the book was immediately and bitterly attacked; but such was the beauty of the style, which Buckle had for a series of years assiduously cultivated, and such the force of the argument, that the author rose at once from obscurity to fame. Letters poured in upon him, which showed that his work was read and appreciated by the thinking and by the laboring classes alike. That Buckle fell into some errors, that he pushed some doctrines too far, that he did not push others far enough—all this may be admitted without detracting from the merit of his work. It is often asserted that Buckle has been left behind; but so has Newton in science, so has Edwards in theology, so have all pioneers in every line of thought and activity. In 1861 his second volume appeared—still a part of the "Introduction," in which he was deducing the general laws by which the history itself was to be written. His health now failing, he embarked for the Orient, taking in charge two boys, of whom his biographer was one; and in 1862 he died in Syria, in his early manhood, with his projected history no further completed than the "Introduction." Of his personality Mr. Huth gives us pleasant glimpses. Of his contemporaries, Mill most excited his admiration, by the accuracy of his intellectual methods. Whatever mistakes we may detect, or imagine we detect, in Buckle's work, certain it is that no man was ever more honest in conviction or more fearless in avowal. The brilliancy of his style, the fervor of his enthusiasm, the grasp of his mind, and the extent of his information, gave him a hold upon modern thought which is remarkable, when we reflect that all that he wrote was little more than a fragment.

SKETCHES AND STUDIES IN SOUTHERN EUROPE. By John Addington Symonds. 2 vols. Harper & Brothers. For sale in San Francisco by Payot, Upham & Co.

Here are two volumes by a man of letters in the truest sense, and a fine observer of society and men. Southern Europe has been not inappropriately called "the home of history." To a man of Mr. Symonds's scholarly abilities and impressionable spirit the lands bordering on the Mediterranean Sea must be full of historic and poetic suggestions. Those who have traveled will find in these volumes a new interest in their former experience, and those who remain at home will be inspired by true sympathy of thought, feeling, and imagination to travel without leaving their native shores. The beauty, refinement, and fervor of the author's style remove him far from all mere chroniclers, and make his studies at once a feast to the eyes, the mind, and the heart. Those who are familiar with Mr. Symonds's "Studies of the Greek Poets" will discover here the same spirit and tone applied in other directions and to other themes. The essays cover a wide range of thought, and are a striking illustration of a mind enriched by generous culture. The essay entitled "Love of the Alps" will be esteemed singularly beautiful for its genuine touches of nature, human nature, and human life. Upon the other hemisphere of thought, the essay on "Lucretius" will furnish a study for all reflective minds on the grounds and conditions of human knowledge, and the reappearance of the theory of the Roman poet in Tyndall's Belfast address, showing that ontological speculation has made no advance in twenty centuries; the chief difference between the Moderns and the Ancients being that we know better the depths of human ignorance. These volumes are printed in a manner altogether worthy of the author's pure style.

THE GODS AND RELIGIONS OF ANCIENT AND MODERN TIMES. By D. M. Bennett. Vol. I. New York: Liberal and Scientific Publishing House. 1880.

This heavy and bad-odored volume belongs to the *Truth Seeker Library*: a library made, we suppose, for the benefit of that particular class who cannot find truth in the general treasuries of human life and thought, where other people do. The writer was serving out a sentence in the Albany Penitentiary for violating the law concerning immoral and obscene publications. If the gods had not been a gossipy and scandalous set, they would never have let the writer into their company. But he got in, and he has managed to tell all he heard; though not all, for we are assured that there is another volume to come—from which may all the gods deliver us. D. M. Bennett belongs to the lowest rank of that class of writers—or printers, rather, for he is in no sense a writer—who make books by the rod; when one is needed it is easily got by cutting off a piece. This book is the climax of stupid conceit. The author approaches a great theme—the theme that gives the thread of history and the key to human progress—with an air of disgusting familiarity, and patronizes Carlyle by telling him that he is "quite correct," and twaddles on about "getting up the different systems" of religion, as if a religion could be made to order. We know nothing about the author's guilt or innocence concerning the matters charged against him, and for which he was imprisoned; but the presumptions raised by this book are that his punishment was just. As a clew to the history of the religious sentiment, or as a guide to the comparative anatomy of religion, or even as a decanter of information from which to decant the cheapest intelligence, the book has no value. It would be far better to study the dictionary to get an idea of the Homeric poems, or read the alphabet "from A to Izzard" to get the secret of the "Oration on the Crown."

CRITICAL ESSAYS AND LITERARY NOTES. By Bayard Taylor. New York: G. P. Putnam's Sons. 1880. For sale in San Francisco by A. L. Bancroft & Co.

Although not in any sense a genius, few men ever wrote more pleasantly or were welcomed by the public with more appreciation than Bayard Taylor. This last and posthumous volume gives us a glimpse of his literary work in a line different from that in connection with which he is ordinarily remembered—namely, that of book reviews and essays on authors. To say that these are discriminating is to do scanty justice to the accuracy of the judgment and the nicety of the criticism therein displayed. A large number of authors and books are treated, most of them very briefly; yet in each essay or note a vivid impression is left on the mind of the point which the critic desired to make. One thing is conspicuous in all—*i. e.*, a spirit of utmost fairness. There is no hypercriticism. A desire is evident to consider the value of the best work of the author under review, and that work is stated at its best, with entire candor and friendliness, even in those cases where the conclusions are unfavorable. These considerations combine to make these essays models in the art of thoughtful and impartial criticism.

A FOREIGN MARRIAGE, OR BUYING A TITLE. A novel. New York: Harper & Brothers. 1880. For sale at the book stores.

A Foreign Marriage, or Buying a Title, naturally suggests the record of one of those mercenary affairs, with money on one side, title on the other, and scheming on both, which can but result in sublime misery for all concerned, love being an entirely secondary consideration to worldly advancement. The facts of the story do not quite bear out the supposition. A young Italian nobleman and a wealthy American girl became interested in each other before either knows who the other is, and as the acquaintance continues, naturally fall in love, are married, and are blissfully happy for a time, quite in the manner of ordinary love matches. The Prince amuses himself after the fashion of his country by flirting with his neighbor's wife, and, as a result, kills the husband in a duel. The little Princess, in view of the shocking event, visits the church of St. Mark in a pensive mood, and absolutely refuses to drive again with her husband in the Cascine! (It was in the Cascine that the jealousy of the husband had been aroused.) The Princess then relapses into a tender melancholy, and finds her happiness for the rest of her life in devoting herself to the care of her son. Whether her husband still holds any place in her affections we are not distinctly informed. The plot is weak and rambling. With an abundance of cause there is very little effect. The principal characters are utterly spiritless and uninteresting, and their conversations entirely vapid. The best work in the book is the delineation of some of the minor characters. Mrs. Jefferson, the vulgar American resident, is very well drawn; and Hannah Stort is a representative woman, strong and symmetrical. The old Count Carmine Guigione, "fresh, dainty, and smiling," too, leaves a distinct impression of his personality. The writer shows great familiarity with famous sights in Florence, where the scene is principally laid. Some of the descriptions are exceedingly well done, as the Giglio Palace and the Church of St. Mark. The narration of the various fêtes is life-like and interesting. There is something too much of description, however. The long lists of objects described having no bearing on the story grow exceedingly monotonous. One always resents too much time being taken away from the actors in a novel. The people must always be preëminent. If we grumble at too much "jew" in *Daniel Deronda*, shall we not much more condemn too much familiar Italian scenery in a feebler writer?

LAWS AND REGULATIONS OF SHORT WHIST. Adopted by the Washington Club of Paris, compiled from the best modern authors, etc., with maxims and advice for beginners. By A. Trump, Jr., New York: Harper & Brothers. 1880. For sale in San Francisco by Payot, Upham & Co.

In these days of "booms" the game of whist has not been exempt, and the last few years have added largely to the literature of this favorite amusement. The book before us is a compilation of the rules which are usually accepted by players, and follows generally in the wake of Cavendish, Pole, and earlier authorities. A few new rules are given, not found in previous works. The lovers of whist will find it a satisfactory compendium.

SANTA CRUZ AND MONTEREY. Illustrated Handbook. Compiled by Henry Myrick. 1880. San Francisco: News Publishing Company. For sale at the book-stores.

OUR POLITICAL PARTIES. By Benjamin F. Teft, D. D., LL. D. Boston: Lee & Shepard. 1880.

HARPER'S HALF-HOUR SERIES. New York: Harper & Brothers. 1880. For sale in San Francisco by Payot, Upham & Co.

Life of Charlemagne. By Eginhard. (Translated from the text of the *Monumenta Germaniæ*, by S. E. Turner.)

The Right Honorable William Ewart Gladstone. A biographical sketch. By Henry W. Lucy.

Tales from the Odyssey. For Boys and Girls. By "Materfamilias."

Fellow-Townsmen. A novel. By Thomas Hardy.

FRANKLIN SQUARE LIBRARY. New York: Harper & Brothers. 1880. For sale in San Francisco by Payot, Upham & Co.

No. 117.—*Prince Hugo.* A novel. By Maria M. Grant.

No. 118.—*From Generation to Generation.* A novel. By Lady Augusta Noel.

No. 119.—*Young Lord Penrith.* A novel. By John Berwick Harwood.

No. 120.—*Clara Vaughan.* A novel. By R. D. Blackmore.

THE PRODIGIOUS ADVENTURES OF TARTARIN OF TARASCON. Translated from the French of Alphonse Daudet, by Robert S. Minot. Boston: Lee & Shepard. New York: Charles T. Dillingham. 1880. For sale in San Francisco by Billings, Harbourne & Co.

EASTWARD, HO! OR ADVENTURES AT RANGELEY LAKES. A book for boys. By Captain Charles A. J. Farrar. Boston: Lee & Shepard. New York: Charles T. Dillingham. 1880. For sale by Billings, Harbourne & Co., San Francisco.

THE VIRGINIA BOHEMIANS. A novel. By John Esten Cooke. New York: Harper & Brothers. 1880. For sale in San Francisco by Payot, Upham & Co.

THE HYSTERICAL ELEMENT IN ORTHOPÆDIC SURGERY. By Newton M. Shaffer, M.D. New York: Putnam's Sons. 1880. For sale in San Francisco by A. L. Bancroft & Co.

THE LIFE OF HIS ROYAL HIGHNESS THE PRINCE CONSORT. By Theodore Martin. Vol. V. New York: D. Appleton & Co. 1880.

OUTCROPPINGS.

A LEGEND OF FORT ROSS.

"Fair voyage, Captain, and safe return," cried the Commandant of Fort Ross, as his boat left the side of the frigate, and moved toward the shore. "In three months I shall expect you back."

"Do so. Success to the colony in the meantime," replied Captain Kotzebue, waving his hat as the distance increased between the boat and his ship: and the latter, with a freshening breeze, stood out to sea, while a parting cheer arose from the crowd of settlers lining the beach. One, however—a stalwart young man, with heavy, expressionless features, and dark, brooding eyes—took no part in the cheering, but, standing with folded arms a little apart from the others, regarded the departing vessel with a gaze of silent intensity. Him the Commandant addressed the moment he stepped on shore.

"What, Feodor, you here! I thought you were unwell."

"I am better now, your Excellency," replied the young man, quietly and respectfully.

"Your recovery is rather sudden," observed the Commandant, dryly, looking at him askance.

The suspicion implied by the tone and manner of the speaker caused an anxious, hunted look to come into Feodor's mournful eyes, which the officer noticed: whereupon, being naturally averse to the inflicting of unnecessary pain, he hastened to add, kindly:

"Never mind, however. I am glad you have recovered. You may resume your duties now, if you feel able."

Feodor bowed, and looked relieved, while the Commandant, walking toward his quarters, muttered:

"I never could make him out. He is a strange fellow."

Both assertions were certainly true. Feodor undoubtedly was a strange fellow; and since the morning, months ago, when he had first appeared, wet and dripping, at the settlement, claiming to have been lost overboard the night previous from a Russian whaler, nobody had ever been able to "make him out." His appearance and story seemed so equivocal that the commander would doubtless have taken measures ere long looking to a thorough investigation of his case had not the castaway, during the first week of his stay at Ross, proved himself such a valuable addition to the working force of the settlement that its ruler was loath to discover any reason for depriving himself of so valuable an assistant. As it was, affairs were allowed to remain *in statu quo*.

Feodor—by this name was he called—showed himself to be intelligent, industrious, faithful, and obedient; never interfered with others, and attended strictly to his own business. Thus had time passed until the arrival of Captain Kotzebue, in the spring of 1824, with orders from the Russian Government to assist the settlers at Ross in every manner possible. Finding, however, upon his arrival, that his services would not be in request for several months, he put to sea again almost immediately, for a cruise to San Francisco and the Sandwich Islands, while at the settlement, after his departure, the days and weeks dragged by in the dull and lifeless fashion natural to existence in a spot so remote from the world and its excitements. The Commandant and his officers, when not occupied in the performance of duty, spent their time principally in calculating the shortest possible period necessary for Kotzebue to complete his cruise and return. There was another, also, who, from the questions he occasionally asked, appeared to take considerable interest in the probable date of the frigate's reappearance. This was Feodor. He had, since his sudden recovery from his more sudden illness, been as efficient and faithful a follower as previously, and the Commandant's confidence in him increased daily. But it was destined to receive a severe shock. On the morning when the white canvas of the vessel was at last visible in the distance, Feodor sought an audience with his commander.

"Well, Feodor," said the officer, as the young man entered his presence, "what can I do for you?"

"I am come, your Excellency, to ask leave of absence."

"I fear it is impossible, my good fellow; but how many days do you wish?"

"Three or four weeks."

"Weeks! In the names of all the saints, man, where do you intend to go—in this wilderness?" demanded the astonished officer.

"Somewhere in the interior, Excellency, hunting," answered Feodor, letting his eyes fall beneath the other's intent gaze.

"But what sudden whim is this?" resumed the Commandant. "You have said nothing concerning it heretofore."

"No, your Excellency, but I have thought much. You have been kind enough to notice my indifferent health during the last few weeks. This expedition would, I am sure, restore it."

"I doubt it, Feodor," replied the officer. "Hardship and exposure are not likely to cure illness of any kind. No, no, my friend. We must do what we can for your health here at the fort, for it is impossible to grant leave to any one at present. The frigate is in sight, and will reach her anchorage before dark; and, until she sails again, we shall be only too much in need of whatever assistance you are able to give. Afterward, it shall be as you wish."

A strange look, half mirthful and half terrible, came for a moment into Feodor's brooding eyes; but he said nothing further, and, with a submissive bow, left the room. A few hours later, however, the Commandant found, to his indignation, that the young man had quietly taken his gun and a supply of ammunition, and left the settlement. Why he had chosen to go thus, could not be determined; but gone he was, and for many a long day the settlers saw nothing of him. However, the presence of Kotzebue and his crew served to divert, at least in a great degree, the thoughts of both Commandant and subordinates from the conduct of their late fellow-colonist; and as the weeks and months flew by, under the reviving influence of the new life, borrowed, so to speak, from the frigate, and the time of the vessel's departure drew near, their minds had still less leisure in which to dwell upon the fortunes of the fugitive. At length the whirl of excitement ended; the day fixed as the utmost limit of the frigate's stay arrived and passed. Night had come, the final farewell had been said, crew and Captain were embarked, and only waiting for the momentarily expected breeze. The fog crept slowly in, hiding the vessel from sight, and the throng of settlers lining the beach turned reluctantly to their domicils. Among them was the Commandant, who could not repress a feeling of lonely sadness as he thought of his departing guests. From this, by a sudden transition, his mind turned to the desertion of Feodor, and its sadness gave place to indignation. No sooner had he reached his quarters than he summoned his second in command.

"Lieutenant," he said, as the officer entered, "to-morrow we must commence search for traces of the deserter, Feodor."

The Lieutenant suppressed a smile as he replied:

"It is unnecessary, Colonel. Feodor is here."

"What! Here?"

"In his cabin."

"When did he return?"

"While you were on the beach. He has, however, been wandering about the neighborhood for some days, but probably could not, until now, muster sufficient courage to meet you."

"Bring the rascal here this moment."

The Lieutenant left the room, and almost immediately returned with the culprit. In the latter there seemed little change, save that he had grown haggard, as from hardship, and that the strange, hunted look had deepened in his eyes. But the Commandant, in his anger, noticed nothing of this, and burst out, harshly:

"So you are back at last. Where have you been?"

"Different places, Excellency. Sometimes here and other times in the south."

"With the Mexicans, rascal, of course! And what scheme of treachery led you there?"

Feodor's eyes flamed as he answered:

"Your words are hard, Excellency. I had no thought of treachery."

The Commandant was commencing an angry retort, when the door suddenly opened, and Captain Kotzebue entered the room, exclaiming:

"A thousand pardons, my dear Colonel, for the interruption; but, at the last moment before sailing, I chanced upon the memorandum for which we were searching only to-day, and as the wind is as yet a mere breath, I made an excuse for ——"

The speaker suddenly stopped. His gaze had fallen upon Feodor, who, with blanched face and glaring eyes, was hastily moving towards the door. In an instant Kotzebue flung himself in his path, crying aloud:

"God in heaven! 'tis Ouschendi!"

The Commandant started forward.

"Ouschendi!" he cried; "and who is he?"

"Once the favorite serf of Baron Moreff, but now for three years the blood of his master has been upon his hands," answered Kotzebue. "Colonel, my interruption was well timed. Feodor Ouschendi, you are my prisoner."

Feodor's eyes gleamed like those of a wild beast at bay, and his hand crept, furtively, to his breast; but the officers, discovering the movement, sprang upon him, and pinioned his arms. He raged and raved like a maniac, screaming:

"I had left the accursed land forever, and my life would have known no other crime. I have sought to expiate the deed. Why, have you no mercy?"

"Your mercy might have spared my murdered comrade's silver hair, Ouschendi," answered Kotzebue, sternly. "But words are useless. Your crime has overtaken you at last."

Soldiers, hastily summoned, now entered the room, and the wretched man was dragged, raving and cursing, to the doorway. There, for a moment, he ceased; and, turning his despairing eyes upon the Commandant, said, with a look of unutterable misery and bitterness:

"Do you wonder now that I cared not to meet the only witness of my crime?"

The next moment the door closed behind him, and he was hurried down to Kotzebue's boat, whither the Captain himself, after some further brief explanation to the Commandant, soon followed, and conveyed his prisoner on board the frigate, which immediately set sail. The settlers heard her parting gun with a thrill of horror, as they thought of their late comrade and the fate awaiting him; and when, later in the night, the waves rose, and, amid their sullen roar, a wild, thrilling scream seemed to rise from the sea and sweep by on the hurrying wind, the listeners crossed themselves, muttering that the wraith of the lost Feodor had given warning of his coming doom. But these ghastly fancies fled before the more horrible truth, when the morning sun, rising in majesty, shone down upon the wave-swept beach, where, with all the light washed out of his long, fair hair, and the brooding luster of his eyes forever quenched, while upon his nerveless wrists were the scars of the iron bonds he had broken only to die, by Feodor. They buried him upon the beach; and even at this late day, though the banner of the Czar has long since gone down from over the works which are now but moldering ruins, there are those who say that, on wintry nights, when the winds and waves are high, an unearthly scream rises above the rushing roar of the storm, like the dying cry of Ouscheeda.

Geo. Homer Meyer.

YOSEMITE.

"In the majestic sweep of glacial seas
Sequestered amid the silences,
Strange glories of the sun and of the snows
Gleam on my giant brows, undesecrate
Save by the wonders of Creative Love.
Unmatched in the world, I, consecrate,
Reign queen of solitude, and gaze, star-crowned,
Into infinity; from whose wide realms
Chant God's great harmonies. The burning morn—
Sweet solemn voices, spiritual as night,
Blazing its raptures o'er the fainting earth—
Sates me with splendor, till my thousand rills
With foam-fair fingers dash their arrowy spray
Across the radiance of my sun-lit heaven,
Veiling its brilliance. Morning's dewy mist
With its aerial web of shimmering light,
And evening shadows purpling in their gloom,
Shroud me anew with mystery. The awe
Of those who talk with God is on my steeps,
Dread, terrible, and lone. Invincible—
Reverberate furies of ten thousand storms
Thunder in vain around me. Age on age,
Cycle on cycle, have I, scatheless, reared
My crest amid the clouds! the circling skies
Sole witnesses." Judah's high altars were
The eternal hills. Is a new Sinai here?

Isabel A. Saxon.

STARTING A GRAVEYARD IN SELF-RISING.

Self-Rising is now a prosperous mining town in Arizona, nestling cozily among the sunny hills. It was a long time getting established as a permanent town. In its early years people lacked confidence in it. It had no graveyard. A good graveyard gives a town a solid aspect. It shows that people are settling there permanently. Business men, hunting for locations, would come and look at Self-Rising, and leave. It was devoid of that homelike cheerfulness which a graveyard flings over a town. Capitalists would not invest money in it. Capital is timid. It shuns a town which has no graveyard. The reason Self-Rising was for so long a time denied the comforts of a graveyard was because its first settlers came from a town about ten miles off, and, when they died, would return to the older town. This got to be a custom. All decent people wanted to be buried at the old town. Every one considered himself decent, though the weight of public sentiment might have been inclined the other way. The death of a man, as a general thing, is a matter of no particular moment to any one except himself, and he himself seems indifferent about it after he is dead. But in Self-Rising the death of a man involved others. There was the funeral to attend. It took a round trip of twenty miles to attend it. This gave the attendants ample time to think upon death—more, probably, than they wanted to use. Twenty miles of looking solemn had, after a while, its effect. The residents of Self-Rising began to wear a serious expression all the time, as if they were thinking about dying. It finally got so that the livery-man and the undertaker were the only persons in town who seemed to feel the genuine joy of existence. Business, too, was affected. Men had to spend too much time on that solemn twenty miles. Yet they felt a delicacy about refusing to attend funerals. The citizens of Self-Rising discussed the expediency of building a graveyard of their own. But when a man died, and it was proposed to start a graveyard by making *him* the corner-stone, his friends would object. They would say:

"Oh, he'll feel lonesome there by himself."

Then men who had the prosperity of Self-Rising at heart, and were anxious to shake off the twenty miles that were preying on its vitals, tried to hire a man to be buried on the outskirts of the town, as a starter. But, as it was necessary to die first, there was no great rush for the job. There were men in the camp who desired employment, but they were transient persons, that did not want to engage permanently. This job of starting a graveyard was offered as a steady one. Any man taking it, and giving satisfaction, would be allowed to keep it as long as he wished to follow the business. One day, while Self-Rising was still struggling with the twenty-mile problem, two roughs, new men in the camp, engaged in a desperate fight with pistols. Their forces were all slain. As they had no friends, and seemed unfriendly to each other, it was thought they would be good material with which to found a graveyard. They were buried on the edge of town, side by side. As they had fallen together in life, it was deemed meet that they should not be parted in death. A renewal of hostilities, on account of the closeness of their resting places, was not feared, as each seemed satisfied with the turn the fight had taken. No complaint. Men who had often traveled the twenty miles congratulated themselves on this foundation for a graveyard. They thought it would afford a rallying point for Self-Rising's dead. They mistook. An old resident would still drop off occasionally, but he would shun the new graveyard with the stubborn stiffness of a dead man.

By and by, a book-agent came into the camp. He was very persistent in soliciting subscriptions. The more a person endeavored to get away from the book-agent the more he got mingled and mixed up with him. If one tried to refuse to subscribe that moment he could feel, as it were, the book-agent beginning to wind around him—slowly, but surely. One morning that book-agent was found dead on a back street. It was thought that possibly he had met with foul play. His head was split open, and a bloody hay-knife was lying near his lifeless form. But the sections of his head had been stuck together again, seemingly to prevent suspicion, and make it look like a suicide. The book-agent was buried at the new graveyard. This made a third grave. Still, occasionally, an old citizen of the place would die, but his friends would not consent that he should be buried in the new graveyard. They were afraid the book-agent might hem him up in his coffin, where he could not help himself, and worry him for all time. A negro minstrel troupe came round to Self-Rising. When they opened in the evening, and began to get off their jokes, a very venerable man in the audience arose to his feet. He was ninety-two years old, and had spent three-quarters of a century in the East Indies, where he had drifted as a sailor-boy. He was indignant when he arose. He pronounced the minstrels a fraud; said he had heard those same jokes nearly a century ago, when he was a lad in Boston. The boys backed the old man up. A fight ensued. One of the minstrels was killed. He went to the new burying-ground. A lecturer visited Self-Rising to lecture on his travels in Australia. He never traveled more. Fourth grave. A great many kinds of people came to Self-Rising, looking around. Some remained, some passed on. A Freiburger came. He wore spectacles. The good people of the camp thought they had done nothing to deserve this visit. He said he had wandered all over the world. He didn't wander any further. During his life he had been useless, but in death he became handy for a fifth grave. His spectacles were suspended from a stick over his grave. Swinging in the sighing wind they gave a warning click. Still, no old-time inhabitant of Self-Rising was buried in the growing graveyard. A young man, beardless, and in his teens, came into camp. He was from the East, where he had been reading dime novels until he could stand it no longer, and had just buckled on two pistols and a long knife, and started to the West, to make life burdensome to the Indians. When he reached Self-Rising he had not seen any Indians, but had passed over some wild-looking country, had seen a bear's tracks and a dead coyote. He felt lonesome and timid, and was glad enough to get into the camp. He said he wished he was back home. He remained timid. A shock of an earthquake came one day. He was not expecting it. He fell to the earth. He never rose more. Fright. The sixth grave. His father came out and erected a tombstone over the grave. It was a stylish-looking piece of rock; had the figure of a lamb on it—one that looked sick and was about to die. That lamb took. The old citizens began to want to *rest* under the shadow of that tombstone. Time rolled on. They gathered around it, one by one, and each had a tombstone with a dying lamb on it. And now Self-Rising has as flourishing a graveyard as there is in Arizona. It is a source of pride to the people of the town. The arid south wind still whips the more arid hills in the vicinity of Self-Rising; the whirlwind lifts the fine sand into the thin air, and the ominous click of the Freiburger's spectacles goes on.

LOCK MELONE.

CARLYLE.

There were six of us there in the parlor.
We were talking of "culture" and "art;"
We exhausted Guido, Leonardo,
And we touched upon Kant and Descartes.

We soared upon Music's high pinions.
We descanted on Tennyson's style,
And were widely apart in opinions
Till somebody mentioned Carlyle.

Then three of them said he was "charming,"
And two of them said he was "grand,"
And I found my position alarming
When I asked, "Could they all understand?"

They declared him exceedingly simple,
If one's *comprehension* were clear;
And I caught the faint trace of a dimple
That redeemed a fair face from a sneer.

I left them extolling his grandeur,
And went to my room, where I wrote
A nonsensical extravaganza,
With the meaning entirely afloat.

It contained not the faintest suggestion;
It was turgid, obscure, and oblique,
But so solemn you'd swear, if not wisdom,
It was something exceedingly like.

I returned down the stairs, and I said,
"Don't allow the lamp to part us
Until first, with permission, I've read
This fine extract from *Sartor Resartus*."

I read it with slow declamation,
And I emphasized each empty clause.
They received it with loud acclamation,
And with most unstinted applause.

They said it was "grand" and "prophetic,"
They admired its profound, learned style,
And declared that where'er they had met it
They'd have known it was penned by Carlyle.

ICON O. CLAST.

DRUMS.

That bright May-day, months ago, while looking from my window on the procession which had formed to wreathe with flowers of remembrance the graves of heroes fallen in the war of the rebellion, all sorts of queer thoughts kept running riot in my head. They were memories rather than thoughts, and were called into life by the beat of the drum.

Not only that the martial music of the drums was such that it might have aroused the fallen brave from their gory beds, but the sound recalled to my mind other drums I had heard beaten, in different localities and under a variety of conditions. Those broad fields of glory, the Soldiers' Cemeteries, sprang up before my eyes, and I heard again the fife and drum that led the single file of soldiers who bore a sleeping comrade to his last repose. How many times, when out for an afternoon's drive in the vicinity of St. Louis, during the dark days of that unhappy time, did we meet such a *cortège*—impressive from its very simplicity. But of the poignancy of grief and the depths of sorrow which these little squeaking fifes, accompanied by the beat of muffled drums, will express, no one can have any idea, unless he has heard for himself.

How differently the drums, unmuffled, and in resonant tones, sounded when heading a new regiment that passed through the streets on their way from Benton Barracks to their first battle-field. Clear and sharp the fifes piped out their shrill notes, and the drummer-boys lustily beat their drums, as if they had no thought for the bullets that would soon whistle about their ears, and lay them low on the field. The most striking object in a photograph of the Antietam battle-field, taken soon after that fierce fight was the lifeless form of a drummer-boy, amid the slain, his poor dead arms still bent as if holding the drum-sticks—his drum, broken, lying a stone's-throw away.

With what deafening rattle the innumerable drums were beaten in the grand parade at the close of the war, in Washington, when Sherman's "bummers"—the *bona fide* article—brought up the rear of that almost endless cavalcade! Darkies and bummers, mixed, riding or driving before them mules and donkeys, on which were perched live specimens out of Noah's Ark, from a raccoon to a Thomas-cat! Such screeching of parrots and crowing of game-cocks, such bleating of young lambs and chattering of old monkeys, were never heard before nor since. They were all war-trophies, and so many proofs that the drummer-boy had "beaten" his way through the South with success.

No beating of drums ever excited the same feeling as the sound of the "long-roll" through the streets of Washington on the night of Lincoln's assassination. To those who were already asleep when the news of the tragedy became known—which it did about two minutes after the dread deed had been done—the sudden alarm must have been fearfully startling. Even to myself, who happened to be only a block or two away from Ford's Theater, one of a numerous party, this sounding of the general alarm had something terrifying, though apprised of the murder a moment before by a bare-headed, wild-eyed individual who rushed into the house, and threw open the parlor-doors without the ceremony of knocking or asking permission to enter.

A hollow mockery is the drumming of the little band at the head of recruits or regular soldiery on the march to a frontier post. Wearily they plod along through sand, dust, or mud, with the rain pouring or the sun blazing down on their drooping heads. Pretty soon a village or settlement comes into sight, and instantly the noisy taps of the drum-sticks and the ear-splitting squeals of the fife seem frantically to assert and insist that "there's nothing half so funny, nor so full of harmless glee, as the roving joyous life of a bold soldier boy."

Entirely different these same drums sound when the post or the camp has been reached, and the brisk tattoo seems to say, "Well, we're in an Indian country, and we've all got scalps to lose, but we'll keep a sharp lookout for 'Lo' by day and by night." "Taps" have a more quieting, reassuring sound; they say, "All safe; lights out; good night." In the morning when the sun rides high above the mountain that looks down on the plain, and guard-mount goes forward in camp, the drums seem to call out volubly to the rugged hights, "We're all here yet, and we all mean to stay, though a soldier's life in these parts is not so very gay."

What sort of a noise the drum makes when it sounds the call for battle when fighting begins in earnest, I don't know; I never made strenuous efforts to get near enough to learn. As a fear-inspiring instrument, the drum may be named when in the hands of the small boy, about Christmas time.

The drum, as an educator, is spoken of by Heine in his *Book le Grand*.

"*Parbleu!*" he says, "how much do I not owe to the French drummer who was quartered at our house; who looked like a devil, but was good as an angel at heart, and beat the drum so excellently well. It was a small, mobile figure, with a terrible black mustache, from under which the red lips pouted fiercely, while the black eyes darted hither and thither. Little boy that I was, I stuck to him like a burr, helped him to brighten his buttons till they shone like mirrors, to whiten his vest with chalk—for Monsieur le Grand was anxious to please—and followed him to the parade and guard-mount. There was nothing then but glitter of arms and merriment—*les jours de fêtes sont passés*. Monsieur le Grand knew but little broken German, only the principle expressions—'bread,' 'kiss,' honor;' but he could make himself very well understood on his drum. If, for instance, I did not know what the word '*liberté*' meant, he beat the 'Marseillaise,' and I understood him. Did I not know the meaning of the word '*égalité*,' he played the march, '*Ça ira! ça ira! Les aristocrats à la lanterne*,' and I comprehended.

"Once he wanted to explain to me the word '*l'Allemagne*,' and he drummed that all too primitive tone which we hear at country fairs, where they have trained dogs to perform, 'Dum, dum, dum.' It made me mad, but I understood him. * * I speak of the palace garden at Dusseldorf, where I often lay on the grass and listened devoutly when Monsieur le Grand told of the deeds of war the great Emperor, beating the marches which were drummed during those actions, so that I vividly saw and heard it all. I saw the passage over the Simplon, the Emperor in front, behind him climbing the brave Grenadiers, while the startled birds croaked overhead, and the glaciers thundered in the distance; I saw the Emperor, the flag in his arm, on the bridge at Lodi; I saw the Emperor in his gray cloak at Marengo; I saw the Emperor on his horse at the battle by the Pyramids—nothing but powder, smoke, and Mamelukes there; I saw the Emperor at the battle of Austerlitz. *Hui!* how the bullets whistled over the smooth ice plane. I saw, I heard the battle at Jena—dum, dum, dum; I saw, I heard the battle of Eilau, Wagram—but really, I could hardly bear it any more. Monsieur le Grand drummed so that my own tympanum was almost destroyed.

"While seated on the old bench in the palace garden, dreaming myself back into the past, I heard confused voices behind me, deploring the hard fate of the poor Frenchmen who had been dragged, during the Russian war, to Siberia, and held there as prisoners for years, although peace had been proclaimed, and who were only now returning home. When I looked around I saw them, these orphan children of glory. Through the rents of their tattered uniforms peered naked misery; in their weather-shrunk faces lay sad, deep-sunken eyes; and, though maimed, limping, and feeble, they still kept up a kind of military gait, and, strangely enough, a drummer with his drum staggered along at their head. With a secret shudder, I remembered the story of the soldiers who fell in battle during the day, rose up again at night, and, with the drummer at their head, marched toward their native town.

"Truly, this poor French drummer seemed to have climbed, half decayed, out of his grave; it was only a shrunken gray shadow, in a dirty, torn *capote*, a deceased yellow face with a huge mustache, which hung dejectedly down over his shriveled lips. The eyes were like blackened tinder, in which gleam but a few remaining sparks; but by a single one of these sparks did I recognize Monsieur le Grand. He recognized me, too, and drew me down on the grass beside him, and there we sat again, as in former times, when he taught me French and modern history on his drum. It was still the old familiar drum, and I could not wonder enough how he had protected it from the Russian grasp. He drummed again, as he used to, only without speaking. But if his lips were closely silent, his eyes spoke all the more, lighting up victoriously as he played the old marches. The poplars beside us trembled as the red 'Guillotine March' resounded. The struggles for liberty, the old battles, all the mighty deeds of the Emperor he drummed as of yore, and the drum seemed to become a sentient being, glad of the chance to express its inward delight.

"I heard again the thunder of the cannons, the whistling of the bullets, the din of battle; I saw again the death bravery of the Guards, the fluttering of the banners, the Emperor on his horse; but a sad tone gradually crept into the most exultant roll. From the drum there came sounds in which the wildest joy and the deepest mourning were strangely mingled; it was a march of victory and a funeral march at once. Le Grands eyes were ghostly wide open, and in them I saw nothing but a white field of ice and snow, covered with the dead; that was the 'Battle of the Moskwa.'

"I had never thought that the old, hard drum could yield such wailing notes as Monsieur le Grand now drew from it. They were beaten tears, and they sounded softer and softer, and, like a dull echo, broke the sighs from Le Grand's breast. And he himself grew weaker and more ghost-like; his withered hands trembled with the cold, he sat as in a dream, only stirring the air with his drum-sticks, and seemed to listen to voices afar off; and at last he looked at me with a deep—abyss-deep—imploring look. I understood him; and then his head fell on his drum!

"Monsieur le Grand never beat drum again in this life. Nor did his drum ever more utter sound. It should serve no foe of freedom for a slavish tattoo. I had very well understood the last imploring look of Le Grand. I drew the sword from my cane and thrust it through the drum at once." JOSEPHINE CLIFFORD.

"WHEN WITH A LINGERING ROSY LIGHT."

[*From the German of Emanuel Geibel.*]

When with a lingering rosy light
 The day descends into the sea,
Love, in the fragrant beechen shade
 Come wander forth with me.

Above us shines the crescent moon,
 Afar we hear the nightingale;
I press thy hand, I speak no word,
 To break the silence of the vale.

The highest bliss can find no speech,
 For maddest love is ever dumb;
A glance—a smothered sigh—a kiss,
 The wildest longing will o'ercome.

ALICE GRAY COWAN.

TO A HUNGARIAN MAIDEN.

Sweet friend, when I would speak to thee,
 I'd say less than my thought, or more,
Because your presence moves me as a sea
 By the waste woods and winding shore;
And many a point of ancient story
 Your glance to my swift fancy brings.
Such eyes, in days of Magyar glory,
Flashed from castles, weird and hoary,
 On armies led by hero kings.
O soul that hath had part in history!
(Pure women and heroic men lived there).
 O royal one! Daughter of fallen Hungary,
Thy life has been a star to common men,
 Full of rare sweetness, faith, and purity.

C. H. S.

THOUGHTS ON HOME.

Such is the patriot's boast, where'er we roam,
His first, best country ever is at home.

OLIVER GOLDSMITH.

Happy the man, whose wish and care
A few paternal acres bound,
Content to breathe his native air,
 In his own ground.

ALEXANDER POPE.

I knew by the smoke that so gracefully curled
Above the green elms that a cottage was near,
And I said, "If there's peace to be found in the world,
A heart that is humble might hope for it here!"

THOMAS MOORE.

If solid happiness we prize,
Within our breast this jewel lies,
 And they are fools that roam;
The world hath nothing to bestow,
From our own selves our bliss must flow,
 And that dear hut, our home.

NATHANIEL COTTON.

Around their hearths by night
When gladsome looks of household love
 Meet in the ruddy light,
There woman's voice flows forth in song,
 Or childish tale is told;
Or lips move tunefully along
 Some glorious page of old.

FELICIA HEMANS.

I'd kind o' like to have a cot
Fixed on some sunny slope; a spot
 Five acres more or less,
With maples, cedars, cherry trees,
And poplars whitening in the breeze.

'Twould suit my taste, I guess,
To have the porch with vines o'erhung,
With bells of pendant woodbine swung,
 In every bell a bee,
And round my latticed window spread
A clump of roses, white and red.

To solace mine and me,
I kind o' think I should desire
To hear around the lawn a choir
 Of wood-birds singing sweet;
And in a dell I'd have a brook
Where I might sit and read my book.

Such should be my retreat,
Far from the city's crowd and noise;
There would I rear the girls and boys,
 (I have some two or three.)
And if kind Heaven should bless my store
With five, or six, or seven more,
 How happy I would be! ANON.

A NEW SERIAL.

The editor takes pleasure in announcing a brilliant serial story commencing with the next number of THE CALIFORNIAN, and running through the remainder of the year, from the pen of Mr. W. C. Morrow, whose short sketches and stories in this magazine have attracted such wide and favorable notice.

THE CALIFORNIAN.

A WESTERN MONTHLY MAGAZINE.

VOL. II.—SEPTEMBER, 1880.—No. 9.

"TO THE VICTORS BELONG THE SPOILS."

It is one of the cherished theories of this Government that every citizen participates, by his vote, in determining its policy. Its policy, by reason of the diversity and perversity of human nature, is the subject of controversy. These controversies are molded into a greater or less degree of definiteness by political parties. Political parties are, therefore, the mouthpieces through which, and the instruments by which, the individual citizen impresses his views upon, and aids in shaping, the policy of the Government.

The ideal political party does not possess the essential attributes of permanent life, and, indeed, has no real fitness for a continued existence. It is essentially a temporary association of those who desire to carry into effect some proposed line of policy. It does not, like a church or religious sect, aspire to the noble task of "regenerating mankind." Its platform does not, like a religious creed, assume to embody a code of moral conduct, nor set forth a general or special "plan of salvation." Its constituents do not claim to be the "elect," and they have no right (though they frequently exercise it) to assert the "total depravity" of those who do not subscribe to their principles. The church was established for the exalted purpose of supplying to the world that wisdom which is supposed to emanate from "on high," and it may well claim the right to exist until salvation is vouchsafed to every unrepentant sinner. But no political party has ever attempted to formulate, and adopt as a platform, a complete system of government. Its mission is necessarily limited to solving and settling such immediate problems and short-lived issues as are constantly arising in the history of every government.

The true theory of a political party is, therefore, that it shall be an organized expression of public opinion on some present question of policy affecting the welfare of the State; that it shall dissolve as soon as the issue is settled which led to its formation; and that its constituent elements shall separate, and be at liberty to unite with opposing parties upon any new question that may divide the public mind.

But, strange as it may seem, such is not the theory, much less the practice, of the real political party, which claims to be, and is, in the strictest sense of the term, a permanent organization. It scorns the imputation of dealing simply with single issues, but assumes to possess a fountain of wisdom from which it may draw *ad libitum* for all future emergencies. It guarantees to its constituents that it has abundant skill and virtue to meet and successfully cope with any and every new issue that may arise. It tenaciously clings to its party name long after the issues which led to its formation have been settled, and rallies its followers with party war-cries that have long since lost their significance. Its party conventions are mighty convocations of politicians, who potentially dictate to the party masses principles to which they have never assented, or more frequently send forth weak, miserable, and deceitful platitudes, in the form of platforms, with which the party constituents are alike disgusted and indignant. It places in nomination, as "standard bearers," men who do not represent the principles of the party, or of whom the party masses have never heard. It then tyrannically cracks the party whip around the legs of the weak and cringing office-seeker, who hopes for party preferment, and relentlessly hurls the dread anathemas, "sorehead" and "bolter," at the recalcitrant follower who questions the infallibility of its party decrees. It promises offices to those who shall show themselves most diligent and successful in securing party majorities, and threatens dire punishment on those who, holding office, do not vote the party ticket. It makes good both its promise and its threat, by distributing to its party "workers" offices, clerkships, and even janitorships, as long as they hold out, and by summarily removing party opponents, or even party friends who have not shown sufficient zeal in supporting the party ticket, or alacrity in supplying places for party friends. It thus literally terrifies its adherents into supporting men and measures they would otherwise oppose, by sternly enforcing the rule that political tenure of office and hope of party preferment depend entirely upon rigid party discipline. The well schooled, "stalwart" politician is, therefore, as totally incapable of a manly and independent political opinion as a wretched, cringing old manumitted slave, whose servility clings to him after his shackles have been riven.

Most fitly, indeed, have these methods of enforcing party discipline, advancing party interests, furthering party ends, and perpetuating party power, been characterized by the humiliating term, "machine politics." The modern political party is more than a mere "machine." It is a huge car of Juggernaut, that periodically rolls through the length of this republic, ruthlessly crushing out all pure political motives, all disinterested political conduct, and all noble political action. The stench that rises from these crushed and mangled political sacrifices has poisoned the moral atmosphere, and inoculated corruption and fraud into the deepest veins and arteries of our body politic.

It would seem to be the all-important question, which should engage the alarmed attention of our statesmen, to ascertain, if possible, the cause of these monstrous assumptions of authority, these dread evidences of power and influences of corruption. But the difficulty is not so much in detecting the cause as in commanding the virtue to secure the remedy. The cause is already apparent. We have deliberately engaged in bribery, by bartering offices for votes. We have made politics a "trade," by giving to those who should most successfully engage in "organizing" party campaigns and "carrying" party elections the right to dictate and control party appointments, and have thus made the political parties, not the vehicles of enforcing public opinion on political questions, but mere bureaus for distributing minor offices. We have, in short, practically adopted that most vicious and damnable of political maxims, "To the victors belong the spoils," as the rule of conducting the civil service of this republic. We have engaged in this most degrading and revolting of all species of bribery until our moral sense is calloused and our moral vision blurred, so that we are alike blind to the evils and oblivious to the dangers that beset us. The two great political "machines" are about to be set in motion. At least one million office-holders—Federal, State, county, and city, including their wives and children—are, to-day, in breathless anxiety, fear, and suspense, lest the result of the November elections shall bring some great calamity upon them, in the loss of employment, income, and the certainty of a livelihood. On the other hand, another million, or, perhaps, more nearly two million, Federal, State, county, and city office-seekers, with their wives, children, and relatives, are secretly cherishing the hope and feasting upon the golden vision of a fat office, and a more easy and luxurious life. What a spectacle for a civilized country! What magnificent compensation for party zeal! What splendid pay for party work! What grand temptation to fraud, perjury, and ballot-box stuffing to the low, vulgar, and vicious elements, who are always "taken care of" by the shrewd and crafty political managers!

Who would naturally be the winners in such a race? Who would inevitably be the victors in such a contest? The fellows with brazen pretensions, brawny muscles, thick necks, and the other fellows with long purses. What disposition or taste could a modest, respectable, scholarly gentleman have to enter such an arena? What proportion of public attention could be directed to, or what genuine disinterested interest could be felt in, any political reform in the midst of such a low, vulgar, and contemptible bread-and-butter scramble? And yet we are in the midst of just such a contest to-day. Is it any wonder that we so often and so constantly hear expressions of doubt as to whether, after all, this republic is worth as much as we thought it was; and whether, after all, England, with her snobbery, her senseless titles, and foolish class distinctions, is not a safer, a better, and more desirable government than ours—recognizing, as it does, the fact that the ignorant and vicious are not fit to be trusted with the power of governing themselves, and that there must be a governing class? These doubts are expressed by people who have learned by experience that the political power of this country has gone out of the hands of the people into the hands of organized and corrupt political parties; and that these parties are managed by bad men who make politics a trade, and by political "bosses" who use them to keep themselves in power.

I have thus fully set forth what I deem to be the true province of political parties, and have alluded, in terms that may have seemed heated, to the evils which have been engrafted upon them by the "spoils" system—a system of conducting our civil service which is recognized by all thoughtful men as the greatest peril to the existence of this Government, and the most difficult question with which the future statesmen must deal. It will thus be seen that it is not so much the Government that needs reforming as the political parties that control the Government.

To reform a government is one thing; to reform a political party is quite another. We may reform the Government by the use of a party, but how can we reform a party? A party is presumed to be a mere temporary organization of people who think alike on some question of government policy, which will, if let alone, reform itself. As a matter of fact, however, it is quite a different thing. As now organized, it has all the strength and permanence of a government within a government. It is supported and maintained by a species of tax, in the form of assessments upon the salaries of the officers of the Government, the salaries being voted by the party managers who have control of the Government. It, therefore, draws its support almost directly from the Government, and has all the strength, and many of the functions, of a government. It is in no sense, however, democratic in its methods. It does not condescend to consult its members on matters of great party concern. All its important measures are concocted in secret party caucus. It is, in short, a tyrant of tyrants. It regards as the basest treason any attempt to reform its party methods, and deals with traitors in a far more effectual and terrible manner than our Government dealt with those who rebelled against it; for our Southern traitors, even the "Brigadiers," have been proudly elected, and have been honorably permitted to participate in the councils of the nation. But the party traitor, "sorehead," or "bolter," does not get off so easily. He is condemned to perpetual and ignominious banishment from party councils, to be scorned and sneered at by all good, well disciplined politicians. If, therefore, there is any one person in the world that the modern political party heartily hates, it is a "reformer." It never loses an opportunity to show its contempt for him, and for all reformers as a class. It is peculiarly fond of "practical" men, who have come up from the party ranks well schooled in all the cunning and craft of political wire-pulling, but has a mortal dread of scholarly men, who have been to college, or men who are suspected of having "theories." It has thus so fortified and entrenched itself behind party customs, usages, prejudices, and traditions, and has so perfected its machinery in all its endless detail of methods, that any attempt to attack or overthrow it is almost certain defeat.

Nor is there any inducement for these parties to reform themselves by giving up the control of the offices, for by so doing they would fall to pieces at once. There would be nothing to "rally" around. Take away the "spoils," and these high-sounding platitudes which are now marshaled in such formidable array as political platforms would sink into insignificance, and we should be surprised to find how little real difference there is between us.

The most tremendous evil of the "spoils" system is that it has so corrupted the parties that they do not reflect the opinions or sentiments of their constituents, but are constantly presenting to us false and fictitious issues, and not the real issues between the people. They deceive us, and lie to us, and make us think there are great differences, and that our opponents have committed, or are about to commit, some great political crime, which we must immediately prevent by voting the party ticket, when, in truth and in fact, there is no real difference between us at all, and our opponents are honorable gentlemen, but mere dupes like ourselves. These grave charges and counter-charges are made purely for effect, in order that our attention may be kept away from the real questions at issue, and from the specific details of corruption and bad government by which these parties are kept alive and permitted to thrive. Our voices are thus drowned by the loud noise which is constantly kept up about some imaginary danger from our opponents, if they should get into power. If we mildly remonstrate against these evils in national convention, we are sneeringly asked by some incipient statesman from Texas, "What are we here for, if it is not for the offices?" If we revolt against the tyranny of party management, and declare ourselves in favor of a reform in our civil service system, we are turned upon by the imperious Senator from New York with an allusion to Dr. Johnson's definition of patriotism, as "the last resource of a scoundrel."

Occasionally we are met by a condescending suggestion that the hope and reward of office form a sound basis of party strength and cohesive power, and create a healthy interest in public affairs. But all history teaches that political parties do not need artificial means of strength, and that cohesive power is the very kind of power they ought not to have. Party zeal is always strong enough, and party spirit always rises high enough, without the debasing incentive of plunder. As for interest in public affairs, we have always had quite enough, and too much. We are governed too much. We think too much about politics, and too little about art, literature, philosophy, our homes, firesides, amusements, and the things really worth thinking about and living for.

I presume it is not the province of this magazine, and I know it is not the purpose of this article, to trespass too broadly upon the debatable ground of party politics; but I cannot close this discussion without at least tracing the evils to which I have alluded to their true source. The responsibility of their continuance may be said to be in part common to all existing political parties. The responsibility of their adoption by the Federal Government rests alone with the Democratic party. To Andrew Jackson, the founder of the Democratic party,* must be awarded the unenviable, if not execrable, distinction of accomplishing at once the ruin and prostitution of American politics. It was he, who, under the advice and tutelage of Martin Van Buren, his Secretary of State, summarily ejected five hundred postmasters the first year of his administration; and it may, therefore, be truthfully said that the Democratic party was born and nursed into life by means of this most foul crime against purity, virtue, and good government. The celebrated maxim which I have quoted ("the spoils of the enemy belong to the victors") was formulated by Mr. Marcy, a noted New York Democratic politician of the Van Buren school; and it is, and has been, one of the "traditions" of the Democratic party. Never, in a single instance, in a Federal, State, county, or city election has it been departed from by the members of that party. Its adoption constituted, in a certain sense, an unpardonable sin, for it was one of those peculiar sins which its contemporaries and opponents were forced to adopt in self-defense. No party could afford to fight the Democratic party without offering its constituents, at least, as flattering inducements as those offered by the Democratic party to those who should vote and work for its party ticket. It became thus, at the instant of its adoption, a fixed and settled doctrine of American politics, to such an extent that it is known throughout the civilized world as the "American system." It is true, the Democratic party demands, in its platform, in the most savage manner, a thorough reform of the civil service; but there is no evidence that they have any higher idea of civil service reform than turning Republicans out of office and putting in Democrats. This is tacitly understood to be the meaning of that clause in their platform.

The Republican party came into power thirty years after the "spoils" system had been in vogue, and the political thought, habits, and morals of the American people had become fixed. In the magnitude of the impending peril to our national existence all lesser evils were forgotten. It found Democratic office-holders tainted with disloyalty, and many of them in open treason against the Government. It was, therefore, but natural that it should, at least, follow the usual custom, and make a "clean sweep" of all party opponents, especially in view of the fact that the great Democratic strict-construction doctrine of "State rights" had logically led a portion of the Democratic party into treason against the Federal Government, and had prevented a Democratic President from crushing it. Wars have ever been fruitful of corruption, and our war of the rebellion was no exception. The civil service became deeply tainted with corruption. Since peace has (fifteen years after the war closed) been finally declared, the Republican, and not the Democratic, party has shown symptoms of a genuine desire to divest itself of party patronage. It has twice, in national convention, rebuked the Conklings, the Camerons, and the Logans, who became identified with the "stalwart" school of "machine" politicians, and has chosen from among its ranks Presidential candidates, one of whom has shown a virtuous desire to improve the civil service, and has made his administration eminently a "clean" one; and the other of whom it is believed has the strength to combat and the wisdom to defeat any "Senatorial ring" that may be formed to crush him. To permit the Democratic party, therefore, to bring forth its ancient Jackson broom, with which to sweep out Republican office-holders, would subserve no possible good, but would, on the contrary, constitute the unjust pardon of a foul crime against the purity of American politics, for which the Democratic party deserves to die.

H. N. CLEMENT.

* Democrats were called "Jackson men" before they were called Democrats.

A TRAGIC STORY.

Over twenty years ago, during a visit to Damascus, I enjoyed the privilege of a personal interview with Abd-el-Kader. Although well advanced in years, he was still in the fullness of his powers, mental and physical. His form was as erect, his step as elastic, his eye as piercing, as when, twenty-five years earlier, he defied the military power of France. The following winter I spent in Algeria. I passed over most of the ground made memorable by the heroic struggle of the Algerian chieftain and his faithful followers against the invader. Everywhere I found the name of Abd-el-Kader spoken with admiration and reverence. He was regarded as the beau ideal of the hero, patriot, statesman. Even Frenchmen admitted that he was the bravest of men, fought nobly against fearful odds, and deserved a kindlier fate. Having seen the man, and heard something of his story from his own lips, I was anxious to know more of the cause he represented, the origin of the struggle, and the motive and methods of the French invasion. From copious notes taken at the time, but afterward consigned to the limbo of neglected papers, I give the following narrative:

A stirring story is that of the French conquest of Algeria—a story strangely checkered with glory and disgrace. We shall never have it told in all of its terrible fullness, since almost the only witnesses who can speak to us are Frenchmen, who would not willingly let the world know what atrocities have been committed in the name of military ambition. Some of the chief actors are still living, having achieved honorable fame in other fields; others, like Boyer, have gone down to dishonored graves, covered with undying infamy.

There had been long standing disputes between the Algerian Government and the "African Company," a half legitimate, half piratical concern, not unlike the East India and Hudson Bay monopolies. Nobody knew which was right, and nobody except the Dey and the Directors particularly cared. The one made large demands, which the other refused to pay. In 1817, one M. Duval was appointed Consul-General to Algiers, and began his administration by becoming the creature of the African Company, and ended by becoming the creature of the Dey. One sunny morning the Consul went to pay his respects to his turbaned Highness, and becoming either tedious, or impudent, or both, the latter, who might have had a quarrel with his favorite wife, or slept badly the night before, slapped him in the face with his fan. This was an insult not to be meekly borne. The indignant Consul struck his flag, and retired from a post which he had disgraced by his pusillanimity. France took fire at the insult offered to her representative, and a fleet sailed for Algiers. Certain demands made by the French Admiral were scornfully refused. A blockade ensued; it was raised; other insults were offered to the French flag; and, finally, Charles IX., who wished to divert attention from his tottering government at home, resolved upon the conquest of Algeria.

A force of sixty thousand men, commanded by General Bourment, sailed from Toulon, and landed fifteen miles west of Algiers, on the 14th of June, 1830. They were received by the Algerines, and a skirmish ensued, but without much loss on either side. In the meantime, the Dey of Constantine, with several thousand Kabyles, had arrived to aid the latter, and on the 19th a decisive battle ensued. The Arabs were defeated with terrible slaughter, and retreated to Algiers. The French, elated with success, followed close upon their heels. The city, strongly walled and defended by enormous fortifications, promised a sturdy resistance. The besiegers commenced operations under the Emperor's castle by erecting batteries and springing mines. Several spirited sorties were made, but with no considerable success. On the 4th of July the bombardment commenced in earnest; on the evening of the same day a breach was made, and on the 5th the French entered the city. The Arabs and Kabyles fought with great bravery, but the Turks fled in the thickest of the fight. The treasures of the citadel and the palace, to the value of many millions, were seized; the few fanatics who still resisted were put to the sword; the chief officers of the government were arrested; the Turks were ordered to depart forever; and the Dey, nearly ninety years of age, was sent a prisoner to France.

Algiers reduced, the French commander prepared to extend his conquests. Oran, and other seaport towns, speedily succumbed. Many of the petty chiefs of the vast interior gave in their adhesion without striking a blow, and the tricolor waved over the fortresses of Bougie and Bona. The conquest promised to be too tame for glory. But it is one thing to batter down the walls of cities, and quite another to conquer a people. The coast was subdued, but the vast interior was rebellious still. The Kabyles of the Atlas browbeat the garrison at Bougie under the very range of its cannon. The wild tribes of the Aures harassed their conquered brethren. The Dey of Constantine hurled insulting messages in the teeth of the French general. A large army was sent to chastise the insolence of the latter. Marshal St. Arnaud scoured the Grand Kabyle, pillaging, burning, and putting to the sword for a period of eighty days. The famous Boyer, whom the French soldiers themselves have surnamed "the cruel," ravaged Oran like a destroying angel. Constantine surrendered after two sieges, and the most frightful slaughter. The Kabyles became, for the moment, quiet; and the wholesome terror of Boyer effected its mission in the west.

But the conquest was not yet complete. There was one tribe which French craft could not wheedle and French bullets could not reach. These were the Riahs of the Auld, a hardy and defiant band who dwelt in inaccessible caverns. They had long harassed the conquerors, and Colonel Pélissier, afterward Duc de Malakoff, was dispatched to bring them under the common yoke. Being pursued, they fled to their caverns. Pélissier ordered faggots to be lighted and thrown into the mouth of their rocky retreats. He then caused a letter to be thrown in, offering them life if they would surrender. They answered that they would, provided the French troops should withdraw. This was refused, and more faggots were thrown in. Another offer of life by the French commander, which was disdainfully rejected. Fire was renewed and rendered intense. I leave a French historian to tell the rest of the dreadful story: "During this time the shrieks of the unhappy wretches who were being suffocated were fearful; and then nothing was heard but the crackling of the faggots. The silence spoke volumes. The troops entered and found five hundred dead bodies. About one hundred and fifty who still breathed were brought out, but most of them expired shortly after." The chronicles of the time inform us that this terrible fire was kept up for two whole days and nights, and that the rocks were cleft with the heat.

While French bombshells were exploding in the streets of Algiers, and French bayonets were cutting a bloody path to the citadel, a young poet was studying at one of the sacred schools. His name was Abd-el-Kader. He was an Arab by birth, and a Musselman by faith. Endowed with the enthusiasm of the child of genius and the hardy energy of the patriot, he resolved, young as he was, and dreamer as he had been reputed, to rid his country of the invader or perish in her cause. He had been an eye-witness of the downfall of the beautiful city, and had breathed his mingled rage and sorrow in lines of which the following is but a feeble translation:

"Oh! lament over Algiers, over its palaces,
Over its forts, which were so stately!
Oh! lament over its mosques, over the prayers which
were said therein,
And over the seats of marble
From whence gleamed the rays of Faith!
Oh! lament over its minarets, over the
Chants which were chanted from them,
Over the Tolbas and the schools, and those
Who read the Koran!
Oh! lament over the Zaanias, whose doors have been
closed,
And over the teachers who have become wanderers!
Oh! lament over its Kadis and its wise Muftis,
The pride of the city who made the Religion to pros-
per!
They are gone, forlorn and sad hearted:
They are dispersed among the people—the unfortu-
nate!"

He left Algiers, and went among the tribes of Mascara, by whom he was appointed Emir. His illustrious origin, his eloquence, his magnetic influence, soon gathered hosts around him. He inflamed the minds of his rude followers by his impassioned appeals, his poems, and his citations from the Sacred Books. He claimed descent from Fatima, beloved of the Prophet, assumed the gift of divination, and pretended to hold converse with Saints and the Father of the Faith. He soon became an oracle—was looked upon as one anointed from on high, who was to exterminate the infidels and restore the tarnished glory of Islam. Putting himself at the head of a force of twelve thousand warriors, he marched boldy against the enemy, with all the zeal of a fanatic and all the faith of a devotee. He laid waste their possessions; ravaged with fire and sword the country of the subject tribes; reduced in turn Arzew, Mostoganem and other important posts; drove the French garrison within the walls of Oran, and by a decisive battle on the banks of the Tafna, extorted a treaty investing him with the title of Sultan, and ceding to him the whole of the immense country between the mouth of the Chelef and the frontier of Morocco. This treaty, the concession of despair, the French perfidiously violated a few months after. Abd-el-Kader then literally "carried the war into Africa," by seizing important points, and pushing his conquests to the walls of Algiers. The tide of fortune which had borne him to the eminence of one of the most successful generals of modern times now deserted him. He was overcome by superior numbers, and sought refuge in Morocco. But it was a dangerous vicinity for so hardy a foe, and the French demanded, at the cannon's mouth, that the shelter he sought should be denied. He then fled to the desert, armed the rude tribes of the Sahara in defense of the True Faith, descended like a thunderbolt upon the French possessions, carried terror and carnage into the tents of the conquered tribes, and extorted another treaty, which his enemies broke on the childish plea that he oppressed the Arabs. Again he met reverses. His fortunes becoming desperate, he penetrated, in the capacity of a pilgrim, accompanied by a few followers, into the heart of the Grand Kabyle, and sought the alliance of those hardy mountaineers, traditional enemies of the Arabs, against a common foe. The words he addressed to those stiff-necked patriots are worthy of our own Washington:

"Know well," said he, "that if I had not opposed myself to the French they would, long ere this, have thrown themselves like a raging sea upon *you*. You would have seen what neither the times past nor the time present have witnessed. They have not left their country but to make yours enslaved. I am the thorn which God has placed in their side, and if you will aid me, I will cast them into the sea. But if you will not listen to my words, you will one day repent; but your repentance will be in vain."

They did *not* listen to his words; but the invader came ere they were aware, and the ruins of a hundred villages attested the truth of the warning.

There was nothing more to hope. What could mere eloquence and undisciplined courage effect against a hundred thousand bayonets? His strong points seized, his followers cut to pieces, his attendants bribed, hunted from village to village, from mountain to mountain, his retreat cut off, every hope of succor gone, the quarry fell at last; but it was not until he extorted, as a condition of surrender, permission to reside at Mecca or Alexandria—conditions which were granted in the letter and broken in the deed. After a treacherous confinement of some years, he was finally released, with permission to reside in Damascus.

And even yet Algeria was not entirely conquered. More than once since the downfall of Abd-el-Kader has the French power tottered, though sustained by a force three times as great as the standing army of the United States. The Arabs of the plains had succumbed, but the Kabyles of the mountains—a distinct and sturdy race, to whom war was a pastime and peace a drudgery—had not yet learned to bend their necks to the yoke. It took France twenty years to subdue them, while even yet outbreaks are not infrequent. Less than two years ago a serious insurrection broke out, which it took much treasure and blood to put down.

Injustice brings its own punishment. Rapine, spoliation, unholy conquest, sooner or later react upon the evil doer. Algeria, rich in resources, blessed with a genial climate and a fertile soil, has been a curse to France. It is a drain of many millions annually upon its treasury. It has required a large standing army to keep the conquered tribes in subjection. The colonists are neither contented nor prosperous; the natives have acquired many of the vices, with none of the virtues, of civilization. There is a blight upon the land. The iron has entered its soul. The Frenchman has established peace, but it is the peace of decay.

SAMUEL WILLIAMS.

FORGOTTEN.

Oh, my heart, when life is done,
How happy will the hour be!
All its restless errands run;
Noontide past, and set of sun,
And the long, long night begun:
How happy will the hour be!

Sunlight, like a butterfly,
Drop down and kiss the roses;
Starlight, softly come, and lie
Where dreamful slumber closes;
But Death, sweet Death, be nigh, be nigh,
Where love in peace reposes!

INA D. COOLBRITH.

HELEN'S SECRET.

A motherless girl of fifteen is the most utterly unprotected and desolate of God's creatures. Who should know that better than I, whose young life was wrecked for want of a mother's counsel when I needed it most? It may be I would have been headstrong and willful as other girls have been; it may be I would have taken my own way in spite of my mother's warning, and made her unhappy thereby; it may be I would have been just as selfish and unheeding and cruel to her as others I have seen; but, looking back upon that time, I only feel that my life might have been different if it had been guided into the proper channel by a mother's loving wisdom. But I was fatherless also, and was doubly deprived of that maturer knowledge and experience whereon I should have relied, and for lack of which I erred so fatally. I do not remember my father, who died when I was but a baby, and my memory retains only a faint and slowly fading portrait of her who was my mother. But those who knew her best trace some resemblance to her lineaments in myself, albeit I am smaller and slighter, and in the reproduction have failed to retain her beautiful brown eyes and golden hair, having instead eyes of questionable blue and hair as dark as evening's gloom. I was never remarkable for beauty, but at sixteen I possessed youth and health, the chiefest of attractions, and I was so light of heart that sometimes I recall those days with absolute pain, and wonder if the careless girl I remember could have grown to the woman I am.

There are pleasanter things in this world than living with relations, even when they are so nearly related as were mine, for I was brought up with the family of my father's sister. I was sent to school until I had attained a common, practical education, though I knew nothing of art or music, and but very little of books, for which I had a growing affection, secondary at that time, however, to many other matters of interest. I was not required to work, more than to do my share, which, in a household consisting of father, mother, and six children, besides myself, was not light. Neither was Aunt Janet shrewish, nor disagreeable, and I was not a Cinderella in any sense. She brought me up precisely as she would one of her own children, and saving the lack of an interest in me which led her to consult her own inclination rather than my welfare, I have no other than a feeling of regard for her; and I do not know, after all, but Aunt Janet would have done exactly the same had it been her daughter, instead of her niece, of whom she was making a well ordered disposition. But therein lies the difference, the sting of which is that mother would not have done so—she would have known and waited. But waiting was not to be thought of with one in my circumstances, and since I had an offer of marriage from a well to do farmer, Aunt Janet made up her mind for me without delay.

"I have spent all I am able to bring you up well, and there are my own girls growing up to take your place. It is not likely you will receive such another good chance of marriage as Ralph Harding offers you, and, indeed, a girl of your age ought to know her own mind if she knows anything, which, if she does not, the best thing she can do is to say 'yes' to some one who is able to take care of her, and has mind enough for both."

This was the burden of Aunt Janet's persuasions from the beginning of my early sixteenth summer, when Ralph Harding came to woo me, until I yielded to the pressure brought to bear upon me, and consented to take upon myself the burdens of wifehood ere I had well learned those which girlhood has to bear. I was in merciful unconsciousness of the trials I had yet to endure, and I was, moreover, in entire ignorance of the character of the man whom I was to wed in one short month. Ralph Harding was not disagreeable to me; I could admit truly that I liked him as well as any man I had met—but no more. He was just double my age, and handsome, with that mere physical attraction, which, if it has no soul attraction to match, grows repellent in time. I had not the time in my hurried state of mind, nor had I the subtile power of analysis which years of experience give, to attempt a study of his character. Learned, I knew he was not; and in after years I had ample time to discover that his stock-yard possessed much more attraction for him than the pages of any book. But he was well to do, as Aunt Janet said, and owned a handsome farm and well appointed house, of which I was expected to be mistress. I was never familiar with him, even in the days of our courtship, when one may surely be pardoned for all the foolish actions in which one may choose to indulge. Had I possessed any such desire, his haughty face and cold, black eyes would have chilled me into silence. But I was by nature both shy and reserved, and the qualities seemed to suit him well. He called me "Salome," without any prefixes, and in his absence addressed me in a brief note as "Miss Durant," and signed himself "Yours, etc." My ignorance of lovers' ways was only equaled by my innocence, or I might have resented such cool appreciation, but I had the feeling that resistance to his will would be useless.

One August morning we were married, standing calmly before the altar in our village church. I can recollect with vivid distinctness how the the fervid sun blazed on the fields outside, and how still the church seemed while we uttered our responses, and I wondered, with girlish carelessness, if the assembled company thought me fair of face under the crown of white blossoms. How still one's soul stands at sight of a child leaning on the crumbling edge of a precipice! But Salome Durant went over and down, and there was not one hand lifted to draw her back. How could I know that I was digging a grave for all the best and purest emotions of my womanhood? What does any girl of sixteen know of the birthright of her soul, the supreme necessity of assured love and faith in which she can repose in the years to come, and to secure which her heart should unfold as a blossom to meet the rays of the sun? O mother, mother! If God had only sent you to me with one sign; if you had but come to me in dreams, and whispered, "Wait!"

We did not go on a wedding journey. It was contrary to his desire, and he said he could not leave his business. So he took me home, and bade me become acquainted with my surroundings, for I was now Mrs. Harding and the mistress of his house.

"So sensible of him not to make any display," remarked Aunt Janet, with satisfaction.

As I did not know there was anything else to be done under the circumstances, I had no complaints to make, and obeyed his injunctions to the letter, inspecting the house thoroughly and criticising the one servant under my control. Thanks to Aunt Janet's preliminary training, I was able to do myself justice in the housekeeping department. My husband was not at first unkind; as long as I obeyed him implicitly he was satisfied. But the days soon came when my lonesome heart admitted to itself in secret that if this was all of life it was not very attractive. And how the years stretched out before me! After the first sharp realization of the narrowness and dullness of my life, I could not put the thought from me; and presently, instead of measuring time by the years still ahead of me, I fell to dreading the misery which could be crowded in the days. This state came upon me gradually, and it was not until I had been two years married that I fully realized the wretchedness of my situation. I think my husband began to dislike me because I did not bear him children, and after the first year of our married life he took but little more notice of me than he did of his dog, unless I displeased him. I don't know that I had expected anything different, but the inborn desire of every woman's heart for love and protection made me dissatisfied. At this juncture I had recourse to literature for amusement. I read every book that came in my way, and the gates of another world were opened to me. I declare that I did not neglect my duties to pursue that one pleasure of my life; I never heard my husband's step that I did not put away my book and willingly attend to his orders, but he may have thought I was deceiving him, for he came behind me one day, and, taking my book from my nerveless hand, threw it into the fire-place, saying sternly:

"You waste too much time with such trash. Have you nothing better to do than to sit hour after hour with a book in your hand?"

My heart rose up in my throat, but I remained silent through my utter fear of the anger in his eyes.

"Why don't you answer, you dumb thing? I might as well have married a block of wood. Speak!"

He raised his hand with a threatening gesture. From another part of the room his hound crawled to his feet, fawning about them with a visibly palpitating heart, uncertain whether the command was intended for him. He gave the animal a kick, which sent him whining behind my chair, never taking his eyes from my face.

"I did not suppose you cared," I answered, in a dull voice.

The hound crouched down on the skirt of my dress.

"Oh, you didn't," he sneered. "Well, I have this to say to you: I intend you shall employ your time more profitably to me than in reading novels. My mother used to sew carpet-rags when her work was done. You can do the same."

He turned on his heel and left the room, and his hound followed closely behind him with watchful eyes. I was never one of the women who could comfort themselves by weeping over their wrongs. Mine burned so deeply as to dry the fountain-head of my tears. Therefore, though I went silently about my allotted duties and employed my spare time in wearily stitching the dyed strips together, I was at heart rebellious and wicked. My reading had done me the harm to reveal to me what life ought to be, and how, instead of being the drudge of a man like Ralph Harding, I might have been an honored and happy wife. I think my husband felt the change in my disposition, for he took to watching me furtively thereafter. Under such circumstances, one cannot wonder that my aversion turned to absolute hatred. I tried to conquer it; I knew it was wrong and would lead to more misery, but once the truth was recognized by my soul it was too late to hide it. I set my teeth together with spasmodic force when I heard his footsteps approaching; I never lifted my eyes lest his own should read therein the expression of my aversion; my flesh absolutely writhed and shrank from his touch as if he were polluted, but I held myself in check, partly through fear and partly from necessity.

I do not know when the idea of escape first suggested itself to me, but, once entertained, it grew a part of my nature. I could not have endured the tyranny of the last two years of my married life if it had not been for the relief the idea afforded at the times when I had most occasion to hate him. It never occurred to me, as it might to some, to have taken his life. My disposition could not have entertained such a possibility, and all I contemplated was the putting of distance and silence between us. Even after the laying out of my plans, I foresaw that there was small possibility of my carrying them into effect under his watchful eye. I hardly dared to take the first step, for fear of discovery, which would only doom me to more degrading slavery. I realized the perils attending such a step, but imagination could not call up terrors enough to force me to live longer with Ralph Harding. For four deathless years I had borne in uncomplaining silence his arrogant selfishness, his brutal tyranny, and coarse sneers and jests. I was conscious that the level of his intellect was far below my own, and the feeling that I was his superior, in spite of his degrading insults, doubtless served to sharpen his anger. Possibly he felt that my dumb acquiescence was an aggravating assertion of my superiority to his jibes. When the time came that I found myself free from his hated presence, I felt thankful beyond expression that there was no child to be a bond between us. His child could have no part in my affections, I am convinced.

I do not know to this day why my husband was so short-sighted as to leave me to my own devices for a week. He never deigned to explain to me any of his actions. It was enough that he told me how to occupy my time during his absence, which might have been for years as far as I knew. But I was rejoiced at the opportunity.

"Now, remember, Salome, and do as I have told you, for if you do not I shall be sure to find it out when I get back."

And he might have added, "And woe be unto you if you dare to disobey me!" for his threatening glance betrayed it very clearly. I felt a defiant joy leap up within me as he departed without another word or glance. I would be free!—free at twenty after four long years of slavery! Free! when I should never have known at my age what it was to be otherwise. O God! the scars of my chains were so deeply marked that all the years of my life would not wear them out.

My first proceeding after my husband left was to give my assistant (what was I but a servant?) a week's holiday, telling her that I was going home to Aunt Janet for a visit. This was not likely to excite much suspicion—I had visited my aunt at rare intervals. When I had seen Sarah fairly out of the house, I attired myself in a plain and serviceable brown dress, and stored a few necessary articles in a small black bag, which had once belonged to my mother. The bag bore on its side the plain letters, "H. G." They brought another inspiration to me. It would not do to be known as Mrs. Harding; I would leave everything that did not belong to me, and the name was none of mine. Mother's name had once been Helen Gray—mine should be the same. To that I had at least the shadow of a right. When I left the house, I had not one article that was not lawfully mine; the clothes I wore were but a small part of my wages. Even my wedding-ring was left in the upper drawer of the bureau, but in my satchel I carried an old watch and chain and seal-ring that had been my father's, and some trifles of jewelry that had been keepsakes of my mother's for years. They would not bring much, but they would at least keep me from starving until I could find work.

I set out in the full blaze of a July sun, walking swiftly along till I reached the highway, my heart thrilling with conflicting emotions. I toiled on all the morning, and the dinner hour passed, but I could not bring myself to stop long enough to rest or refresh myself by the way. In the afternoon a team overtook me, and the driver drew up beside me.

"Will you have a ride, miss?" said a kindly voice.

My heart leaped with fear at being addressed, but I accepted his invitation, and climbed wearily to the high wagon-seat.

"You do be tired," remarked my host, sympathetically. "I'm glad I come along. How far might you be goin', miss?"

The word "miss" sounded oddly to my ears.

"I want to go to L—— to-night," I replied.

"Well, now, that's good. I be goin' there myself to sell this garden truck. We'll get to the city this evening; don't you worry."

And I didn't. We reached the city in the edge of the evening, and my friend put me off before a jewelry store, as I had requested. I could not get my supper till I had disposed of my father's watch and chain, for I had not taken one cent of Ralph Harding's money. I succeeded in obtaining sixty dollars for it; the jeweler said it was good gold, though rather light, but he did not refuse to buy it. With that sum I made my way to a railway depot, and entered the refreshment room, feeling faint for lack of sustenance. But I made a hasty meal, and, after payment, went to the office and purchased a ticket for a small station called Mount Pleasant; then sat in the waiting-room till the night express came in. I do not know why I chose Mount Pleasant for my stopping-place. I think the name gave me a sense of rest and quiet. I did not intend to bury myself in a city where I knew every effort would be made to find me. I had no very definite ideas of what I ought to do, but trusted to chance, in an idle, hap-hazard sort of way, that brought its own pleasure in the limits it allowed my vagrant fancy. The night express rumbled in, panted a few busy moments, and rattled away again with myself curled down in one of the seats in delicious idleness. When I reached Mount Pleasant, at ten o'clock the next morning, I found it a low-lying hamlet, hedged round by rolling hills; a sleepy place, only stirred to activity by the arrival and departure of the train twice a day. I alighted, and made my way to the small hotel, introducing myself to the landlady with a view to obtaining information concerning my surroundings. But my efforts proved futile. Did she know of any family who wanted a seamstress or housemaid? No; she didn't. Was there any chance to teach a small school in the district? She didn't know. Was there anything she thought it likely a young woman could be helped to which would enable her to earn her own living? She couldn't say now, really. After dinner I started out to prospect for myself. It did not take long to discover that the resources of the town were extremely limited. No one wanted assistance of any kind; in fact, the inhabitants were not disposed to earn their living by the "sweat of their brows," nor enable any one else to do so either. They did not care for educational privileges—were perfectly willing their children should grow up in ignorance. There was no demand for a seamstress; the fashions were of the most primitive kind. In short, I found myself at the end of a few weeks penniless and unemployed. I paid my last dime for some bread, which I put in my bag, and started out on foot. I left the town, which had been anything but pleasant to me, and struck off over the rolling hills in the direction of the country. I walked wearily past farm-houses and happy homes, but at none of them was there any place for Helen Gray. I suppose I was not in such apparent destitution that they thought of giving me alms, and the years of my life, if not of my suffering, were stamped so plainly on my youthful face that I was, doubtless, considered an imposter. At night I crept into a corn-field, and ate my last mouthful of bread in a sort of dull defiance of hunger. All through the long hours of that August night I crouched against the fence, sometimes watching far-off constellations as the stars wheeled slowly above me, and sleeping, brokenly, at other times with my head bent upon my knees. Yet not one thought of returning to the husband I had left ever crossed my mind even in my most wretched moment. I would have deliberately died by the road rather than he should have had my life at his disposal again. In the early dawn I gathered myself up and essayed to make a breakfast from the milky ears of corn near at hand. But a very little sufficed, and I proceeded slowly on my way. At noon I went up to a house that had a hospitable appearance, and asked to see the mistress. She came, hard-featured and shrewish, but I made one last effort. I took my father's seal-ring from my purse, and asked if she would buy it from me. I had no money, and wanted to purchase something to eat. She took the ring, looking at me curiously.

"I will give you your dinner for it."

"But, madam, it is worth much more than that," I objected, faintly.

"You will take that or nothing. I believe you have stolen this ring!" she said, sharply.

My fear and desperation lent me courage.

"Give me my ring! I did not steal it! It was my father's."

"How do I know that? You are well dressed for a beggar," eyeing me sharply.

I snatched the ring from her hard, cruel hand, and faced her in one flash of failing strength and pride.

"If you should live to be friendless and starving, may you receive as you have given!"

Then I never stopped again as long as my strength held out, being fearful that she would have me followed as a thief. I turned into by-ways and lanes; I wandered deeper and deeper into the wooded country; and by and by the sun declined and the trees threw long shadows across the road before my swimming vision. I saw a low cottage by the roadside—a haven of peace and comfort, with marigolds under the windows, and double red hollyhocks beside the gate. I put my hand on the gate and slowly opened it. At the creak it gave a woman came to the door, a broad, freckle-faced, fleshy woman, with her two red hands on either hip, and her sleeves rolled above a pair of stout arms. I dragged my feet to the doorway, and looked up at her.

"Could you give me—I am sorry——"

I put my hand out against the door-post to steady myself; everything was whirling round me. I gasped for breath, and cried out, wildly:

"O my God! I'm starving to death!"

Then I sank down in utter unconsciousness across the threshold.

I opened my eyes, at length, to find a dull light pervading the apartment in which I lay. I felt a delightful sense of rest and comfort. I was lying on a bed in the corner, and there was a low sound of whispering outside the door. I turned my head with a slight movement upon the pillow, and the woman I had spoken to looked in anxiously, but, seeing my eyes open, hastened to the bedside with a brightening face.

"Ah, shure, yer comin' to yer senses now, honey! I tought ye niver would spake another word, I did, as shure as me name's Kate Riley; an' I was just tellin' John he'd betther go for a docther; for truth I didn't know what in the wurrld to do for ye. An' how do ye feel, my dear?"

I smiled up in her comely face, and essayed to speak.

"I feel very comfortable, thank you," I said, weakly.

"Well, that's good. I've got some beef-broth handy by, an' I'll feed ye a bit, so ye'll feel betther."

She brought the bowl to the bedside, and held spoonful after spoonful to my famishing lips.

"Poor little thing! Why, ye were starvin' thrue enough. Whin did ye ate last?"

"I had some bread for my supper last night."

"An' nothin' the day? Why, God help ye, this isn't a haythin counthry, child!"

I confessed, between judiciously administered mouthfuls of beef-broth that was like nectar, a part of the true state of affairs. I never intended, from the time I left my husband's house, to tell any one that I had been a wife. But that I was homeless and friendless was perfectly true, and that I was forced to seek employment was excusable of one in my circumstances. My hostess listened to my account with the greatest attention and sympathy, and at its close said heartily:

"Poor girl! Put up yer ring an' bits o' jewelry. I've no use for 'em, widout I cud wear 'em on me nose, for divil a one cud I git on me big fingers! Yer welcome to stay wi' me till ye can do betther; an' as soon as yer able to work, if work ye must, why there's berries an' fruit needs pickin' down in the lot, an' John was scoldin' me this mornin' for bein' too lazy to help him. Now, honey, let me help ye up, an' I'll take ye to another room, where ye ken shlape till the sun stares ye out o' countenance. Come, now, not a word out ov' ye till ye've had a long night's rest."

The good soul put her two fat arms around me, and lifted me easily off the bed, assisting me to a small, clean bed-chamber, and bestowing me in the bed therein, talking cheerily all the while in the mellow brogue, which was a novelty to my ears. My slumber that night was deep and dreamless. When I awoke next morning I felt a new life thrilling through my veins. I dressed myself hastily, and went out in the garden. There was no one in the kitchen as I passed through, but the hands of the clock indicated eight as the hour of the day. There was a fresh coolness in the atmosphere, the skies above were blue and breezy, and the woods beyond the meadow looked delightfully green and mysterious. As I stood inhaling deep breaths of the free, fragrant air, Mrs. Riley came round the corner of the house.

"Good morning to ye, honey! Ye look as fresh as a bird, an' yer eyes are sparklin', so there's no need of me askin' how ye feel. John an' me had our breakfast long ago, but I've kept a bit hot for ye, so come along an' thry it."

Over the substantial breakfast which her kind thoughtfulness had kept warm we chatted confidingly. Mrs. Riley told me how "her John had taken the California fever, an' that nothing on earth would do him but he must sell the ould place next spring, and jine an emigrant train that was to cross the plains. An' if John tought best she s'posed she'd have to go wid him, seein' she couldn't be content to live widout him, though it would be hard to leave the place where she had buried her three children."

While the good woman was explaining the situation a thought flashed across my mind, born of my dire necessity, and I spoke at once.

"Oh, if you'd only let me go with you!"

"To Californy, Miss Helen! An' what ud ye do there?"

"It's a new country. I could find something to do—teach school, may be. And I have no home, you know, so I might as well be there as anywhere else."

"Thrue enough; but they say it's a rough place. But so far as that goes I don't see but what the wurrld's pretty much alike annywheres. An' it wouldn't be so bad for ye neither, for yer youth an' appealin' eyes 'd help ye out mightily."

"I wish you would let me stay and work for you this winter, Mrs. Riley. I can work, for all I look so small. And then in the spring I'd sell the things I've got for what they'd bring—only a little, perhaps—but it would help, and I would be so glad to go with you."

Perhaps she saw the passionate eagerness in my eyes; she reached her hand across the table and patted mine, with the cheery, half promise that she would see John about it, and he could tell me what to do. But my petition was not denied, and from that time I was included in their calculations, and I helped Mrs. Riley with such grateful zeal that she declared I left her nothing to do. The winter passed very slowly to my impatient heart, but monotonous as some of the hours were they never carried one regret for those that preceded them. I was happier than I had ever been since the time when my girlhood had been so sadly merged into wifehood.

With the first signs of opening spring the Rileys began to make preparation for the eventful and hazardous journey. The bargain for the farm was completed, and a white, canvas-covered wagon, drawn by two stout yoke of oxen, was purchased. Into this wagon was stowed all our necessary equipments. One day, being employed in rolling some small articles into a newspaper, preparatory to packing them, my eyes fell upon the following paragraph:

"By the collision on the Turin and Cairo Railroad yesterday morning, our respected townsman, Ralph Harding, Esq., lost his life. He was returning home from a trip to Cairo, whither he had been to make inquiries concerning his missing wife, whose mysterious disappearance several weeks ago has excited much comment. The body will be brought home to-morrow, for interment."

I looked at the heading of the paper. It was one published at my former home, and bore date of November 20th. I really think my first conscious feeling was one of relief that I could not be pursued and taken back by force. Ralph Harding was dead. With the realization of that fact came also the thought that I was a widow, and free to lead a new existence, if I chose. I would not alter my plans—it was too late, and I had no desire to do so. Neither would I fetter my soul with one cent of the money he had left. I do not think I meant to be hard-hearted, but I really could not feel the repentance I suppose I ought. I cut the paragraph out, and put it away, then went calmly on with my packing, curiously wondering whether he had been very angry when he found me gone, and wishing he had not met his death in searching for me.

In the last of April there came one bright day when we stored away in the big wagon our few remaining necessaries, and, climbing in, started forth on our long journey. We looked our last on the humble cottage with wet eyes, for it had been a home for all of us. After a few days' travel we found ourselves in line with a dozen other wagons, all journeying the same way, and we settled down to make the best of our circumstances. I do not like to remember the latter half of that journey. The hot, arid plains, bounded only by the eternal expanse of sky, which grew brazen with heat at the horizon, the scarcity of water, and the plenitude of dust, are a nightmare on my memory. When, at last, the welcome mountains were reached, we revived, and took a new hold on life. We camped under the wind-rocked pines at night, and gathered strength from the resinous balm of the pure atmosphere. By early winter we had reached a mining camp in the Sierra, where we decided to make our home for a while. Mr. Riley bought in with a hydraulic mining company, and his spare capital being thus invested, his wife eked out their income by starting a boarding-house. Of the two investments the latter threatened to pay the better, for "Mother Riley," as the cheery old soul was called, was a most indulgent landlady. I made it my business to gather the few children of The Forks together in a deserted miner's cabin, made habitable by the disinterested efforts of Mother Riley's boarders, and established a flourishing school. Miss Gray and her small flock were objects of eminent interest to the stalwart miners. Even to a person of my small consciousness, the curiosity with which I was regarded was very apparent. There was not, at that time, another unmarried woman in the whole settlement. Those who were willing to brave the hardships of a new country were women who had husbands and children, from whom they were not willing to be separated. But I was an anomaly, and to none, perhaps, more than to myself. I became used to the chivalrous speeches of the red and blue-shirted miners. They treated me very much as if I were a child, but with a protecting manliness which was far from being unpleasant. I felt an interest in them all, for the type was of that rude order of nobility with which new and dangerous countries are peopled. I was content, and, for the most part, tranquil, though called upon to pass through some strange experiences. I cannot tell why, but The Forks came to regard me somewhat as grateful patients might a hospital nurse, and many were the summonses I received to visit the dying beds of those whose loved ones were so far away that only the touch of a woman's hand could bring them nearer in imagination. I never refused, and usually set off provided with some delicacy from Mother Riley's store of invalid comforts.

One bleak afternoon in March there was a knock at Mrs. Riley's sitting-room door. She bustled to open it, and confronted a young man, whose anxiety was plainly evident in his face. He held his cap in his hand, and the boots into which his trousers were tucked were splashed with mud.

"I'm so sorry, Mrs. Riley, but I'm afraid Hamilton's going, and he wants Miss Helen to come down. It's awful weather for a lady to be out in, though."

"That is nothing, Mr. Stuart," said I, coming forward. "I'll go willingly, if he wants to see me. I can wrap up warmly, and wear overshoes. I'll be ready in a minute."

Henry Stuart's brown eyes looked down at me encouragingly as I clung to his strong arm and toiled along. We soon reached the cabin. Hamilton lay in the inner room, with his face turned to the door, and his hollow eyes brightened visibly as we came in. A tall miner rose up from the foot of the bed, and silently put another log on the fire. I sat down by the bed, in a wooden chair of rude manufacture, and took one of Hamilton's wasted hands in mine.

"What can I do for you, George? Mrs. Riley sent you down some of her precious blackberry cordial. Will you try it?"

"Good Mother Riley. I'm afraid it's too late. I thought I'd like to have you read and sing to me. It's hard to die, Miss Helen, without some good Christian comfort."

"I'll do anything you wish, George."

"Then read to me first—the old story, you know."

I turned the leaves of the pocket Bible to the divine chapters of the Crucifixion and the Resurrection. A peaceful smile hovered round his mouth when I had ended. Understanding the faint pressure of his fingers against mine, I sang some sacred songs for him. Henry Stuart sat silently at the window, and gazed out into the gathering gloom, while the shadows of night and of death folded the room in darkness, broken only by the fitful flickering of the fire. I do not know how long we sat thus. Henry rose at length, and lit the lamp. Then, with a slight exclamation, he came to my side, and put his arm around me hastily.

"Come, Helen. George is at rest."

It was true. His spirit had passed away so quietly that I had not known it, and only the pale clay was before me. I withdrew my hand from his stiffening fingers, and Henry led me into the next room, making a sign to the tall miner standing at the window.

"There's lights a-comin'," he said, moving toward the death chamber.

"Poor little girl, these scenes are too hard for you to witness," murmured Henry, pityingly, standing beside my chair, and stroking my hair with the gentlest of touches. I choked back my sobs as steps sounded outside.

"It's Big Ben and Riley. You will go back with him now, in time for a good night's rest."

They came in silently, swinging their lanterns ahead.

"Gone, is he? Poor boy!"

"He was a good chap. The boys'll turn out well to his send-off to-morrow, storm or no storm. He's always been a favorite o' the The Forks, an' we'll give him a first-class funeral," said Big Ben, solemnly, extinguishing his lantern.

"I don't s'pose I can do anny good by stayin', Stuart. There'll be more down presently. An', besides, my ould woman sent me afther the girl. Yer as well off widout her, now he's gone."

Together we started back through the storm and darkness, but I was absorbed in my own thoughts, and did not find the way long, though glad when the light in the window shone across our watery path. I went to rest that night, but sleep would not come to me. I was beset by a great temptation, and, alas! it gained the mastery over me. I knew—I could not but know—that Henry Stuart loved me. And I? What happiness had I known in my life that I should throw that chance away? I had only to put out my hand and take it. My life needed the completeness which his love would give. There was one thing tempted me. Once, in some light talk about futurity, he said a fortune-teller had predicted that he would marry a widow, and he had fought shy of widows ever since, for he had no mind that the prophecy should come true. The remark had recurred to me frequently, at different times, till it assumed more significance than he ever intended. But I hesitated to tell him of my past history while we were only friends, and I did not like to think of the effect the revelation might have on him. I could not bear that anything should come between us. He was so honorable and high-spirited, could he love a woman who had left her husband? There was no absolute necessity for his knowing. It was not in the remotest degree probable that he would ever find my secret out, and if I was not the innocent girl I seemed, God alone knows how passionately I wished I had been. It was my cruel fate to know more of life than I seemed to know, and infinitely more than I ever desired. How earnestly I longed to be pure, for the sake of his love; how degraded I felt myself to be as the hated memory of my husband rose up before me, brutal even in my dreams; how I wished that I might drink of the waters of Lethe, for my true love's sake, no one but myself can ever know. Next to being pure was to be thought so, and so I yielded to the tempter, and buried my secret in my own heart, resolving to keep it from Henry Stuart forever. Having put the past out of my sight, my spirits rose perceptibly. By the beginning of April I was able to resume my school duties, which the inclemency of the weather had for a few weeks interrupted. As I came home one evening, I heard Mrs. Riley's cheery laugh in the dining-room.

"What's the matter?" I asked, putting my head in at the door. Henry Stuart, in his sprucest attire, was standing by the window.

"Is that you, Helen? I was just afther tellin' Henry here what throuble I've been havin' wid them confounded grocery scales. I wint down to Bennet's two days ago, an' John persuaded me to git weighed. I knew he'd poke fun at me if I didn't, so I stheps on to the little table, an' brought the old thing down wid a whack. I weighed wan hundred and eighty-six pounds, if ye'll believe me! Well, I was jist mad, an' that's the thruth. Says I, 'Ye don't weigh fair, anyhow.' I come home, an' the more I thought about it the madder I got. So this mornin' says I, 'John, them scales lied. I don't weigh no sech amount. I'll not belave it till I go across to Gibson's an' thry his scales.' Well, John went wid me, and, as thrue as I'm sthandin' here, I weighed wan hundred an' ninety-seven! An' John, he says, 'Yer doin' well, Kate—'leven pounds in two days.' An' I come home madder nor I went away. Them grocers is cheats, that's my belafe. What d'ye think, Helen?"

I could not speak for laughter, in which she joined with hearty good will.

"Ye wouldn't think it was so funny if 'twas yerself, now, I'll be bound. Come, take Henry intil the sitting-room. Yer in my way here, an' them b'ys'll be chargin' in here fer their grub d'rectly."

Shrewd Mother Riley. Did she divine anything unusual from Henry's spruce attire? I led the way into the front room, shyly and silently. Henry was as ill at ease as if his new clothes were a misfit. So was I, for the matter of that, but, being a woman, had more adroitness in concealing it. He lounged about from one window to another, displaying his six feet of superb manhood to the most unconscious advantage. The first bell rang for supper. He gave a start, and turned his brown eyes on me appealingly.

"Helen," said he, helplessly drumming on the window-pane with the fingers of his right hand.

"Well?"

"Come over here a minute, won't you?"

I shook my head, with a mischievous smile.

"Too proud, are you? Then I'll come to you."

He crossed the room, and knelt by my chair, putting both arms around me.

"Helen, I know I'm not half good enough, but I love you very dearly. Could you ever care for me, little girl—even a little?"

"I'll try, Henry."

"My dearest! Will you be my wife—the only woman I have ever asked, or ever loved?"

Even in that supreme moment a sharp pang darted through my heart, as Memory held her mirror before me. I put it aside, as he gathered me in his arms and took his answer from my lips.

To say that I was blessed beyond anticipation in Henry's love would but faintly express the depth of my happiness. What if I did live in a house with three rooms, and not a single closet, and had my own work to do after we were married—was it not a home of love? We had a general wedding—it could not very well be helped, Henry was so popular. Harmony and jollity prevailed; toasts were drunk and speeches made, the only flag in town was strung across the street, and an anvil did duty for cannon. We were escorted to our domicile in triumph. It had been improved and enlarged since the bachelor days of Stuart and Hamilton, and nearly every miner in camp had contributed some article of furnishing, which collectively made a creditable *bric-à-brac*.

Five happy years rolled away, during which I had been steadily growing in womanly strength and independence. I was my husband's helper, not his slave. In the third year of our marriage our baby was born—a brown-eyed boy, whom I named Henry, also. The last gift of the God had come to make my life complete. Our boy was the image of his handsome father, and his small graces brightened every hour for us. We began to care more for riches—to lay them by for the time when our boy would need education. The mine paid a comfortable income, and by and by would sell for enough to start in business somewhere. We sat talking over matters after supper one cool evening in October. Our baby was asleep in his crib on the other side of the fire-place. Everything that occurred that evening is distinctly branded on my memory. When I rose to clear away the table, Henry insisted on helping.

"I'm not so ignorant as you might suppose," he said, looking at me across the dish-towel, with his head on one side; in proof of which he took up a cup, and proceeded to wipe it, cramming every inch of the dish-towel inside it, and then triumphantly twisting the wad round and round, in genuine man-fashion. I had a hearty laugh at his performance. I have forgotten how to laugh since. In the midst of our mirth there came a rap at the door. Henry sobered down, and went to open it. It was not usual for strangers to knock at the outside door of the kitchen, so I looked to see who entered. A man, tall, black-bearded, and hard-featured, with an exultant gleam in his wicked eyes, stood in the doorway.

"I've found you at last, curse you!" he said; and I knew Ralph Harding was before me. The blood froze in my veins.

"What do you mean, sir?" asked Henry, incensed at the form of his expression.

"Ask her—she knows!" pointing to me, with a cruel laugh.

"O my God! my God!" I groaned. It was too horrible! What had I done that I should be so persecuted.

"She's very much surprised to see me, no doubt. Why don't you explain, Salome? Shall I do it for you?"

With a sneer he turned toward Henry.

"This woman you have been living with for the last five years is my wife, Mrs. Ralph Harding?"

"Liar!" exclaimed Henry, springing at him with intent to throttle him.

They were powerful men, and well matched in strength. I threw my whole weight around Henry's neck, clinging to him despairingly.

"Don't kill him, Henry. It's true—what he says! O God, help me!"

Henry relaxed his hold, and staggered back. Harding looked on with evident triumph at a scene none but the arch-fiend himself could have enjoyed.

"Helen! Am—I—dreaming? Did—he—tell—the truth?"

"Oh, Henry, my darling! don't look at me that way or you'll kill me. I never meant to deceive you—I thought he was dead. Oh, I thought he was dead!"

"And you wished so, too, no doubt," said Harding.

"Yes!" I cried, desperately, turning on him at last; "I wished you were dead. I was glad when I saw it in the paper. You have been the cause of all the misery I ever experienced. I could endure your presence no longer, and I left you. I wish to God you had died before ever I saw you, Ralph Harding!"

His face was livid with rage.

"I don't understand, Helen. Were you ever married to this man?" cried Henry, sharply.

"My aunt induced me to marry him when I was only sixteen years old, and did not know my own heart. Life with him was torture, and when I was only twenty I left him, Henry."

"But you knew he was living!" said Henry, in a voice of agony which cut me to the heart. He tried to put me away from him.

"No, no! Oh, Henry, listen to me! I had not left him six months before I saw it in the paper that he was killed in a railroad collision. Oh, don't ever think I was so wicked as that. I supposed I was a widow!"

"Why, in God's name, didn't you tell me this before we were married!" he groaned through ashy lips.

"You said once you would never marry a widow, and I loved you so, Henry," I moaned, clinging to him. "Not a soul knew my history. I never thought of claiming one cent of his property even when I supposed I was his widow, I hated him so, Henry."

"Oh, Helen, I never thought you were deceiving me all these years!"

It was the only reproach he used, and, God knows, he had cause then. But I shrank away from him as if it had been a blow.

"See here, there's enough of this thing. You can't alter the facts of the case by talking. This woman is my wife. I have searched for her far and wide, but she was so devilish sly I never would have found her if I hadn't seen her in the street by accident. In spite of her kind wishes I wasn't killed. I'll make it up to her, never fear. Salome, you must go with me."

I sprang forward, catching Henry's arm again in terror.

"Never! Never! I would sooner die than live with you again! No power on earth shall make me. O God! Henry, save me from this man, or I will kill myself! I will! I will!"

I was wild with agony.

"Hush, Helen! You shall never go with him if I have to kill him to prevent it."

"There's two can play at that game!" said Harding, threateningly, making a movement to draw a weapon. In an instant Henry was upon him, and had thrown him down. Without knowing what I did, I sprang to the cradle, caught up the baby, and fled out into the darkness. With the speed which only terror can give I flew up the pathway to Mother Riley's, and burst in upon them with an ashen face and streaming hair.

"Holy mother! What has happened, Helen? Why are ye out wid that baby widout anything around him?"

She took the child from me to quiet it.

"Oh, go down quick, for heaven's sake! He's killing my husband!" I screamed, wringing my hands.

"Who's killing? Here, John! Ben! go down an' see! The poor thing's wild wid fear. Go on, boys. There's something wrong at Stuart's—murther or robbery."

Something wrong! I wonder how I lived through that awful night. How much one can endure and not die! Mrs. Riley hushed my boy to sleep, and put him to bed. A footstep sounded on the porch. I flew to the door.

"There now, Helen, don't look so terrifyin'. Henry's sent for ye. He was a bit hurted in the scuffle. The other feller got away; but we'll find 'im—we'll hunt 'im down like a dog in a ditch!"

I don't know how I got down the hill again. But my darling lay on the bed waiting for me, with a smile of the old-time light and love. I knew he was wounded unto death—he, brave and unarmed, had been cruelly cut down by a knife in Harding's hands. The ebbing life-blood had left him pale, but peaceful. I was too stricken to realise all that was passing.

"Come, darling, sit by me as you did by Hamilton. I thought that night that, if you were only beside me when I came to die, I would not find it hard. I want you to tell me all your sad story, dear—won't you?"

"Yes, Harry," and I told him as collectedly as I could the secret which had lain between us for so long.

"My poor Helen! If I had only known. You have not had a very happy life, have you?"

"I have been very happy with you, Henry."

"I like to hear you say that. Helen, I am going to leave you. You see it is, after all, the only thing I can do—for *he* is still alive. I have charged our friends to protect you from him. And if he ever should molest you again you have this safeguard—he is answerable for my death. Do you understand me, darling?"

"Yes, I know, Henry."

"I will leave you property enough to make you comfortable, and to bring our little Henry up carefully. He will be a comfort to you—something for you to live for. This is not all of life, dear love. If we were not to be reunited hereafter, how would you be recompensed for your cruel suffering here?"

"But how shall I live without you?" I broke out into one despairing wail.

"Don't, dear. Is it so hard? I wish I might have lived; but one of us had to die, and, perhaps, I am better prepared than he is. I did not try to kill him; only to defend myself. You will not let our boy forget me? I am tired—the end is at hand. Kiss me, Helen. The last! the last!"

I clung to him with kisses and despairing prayers. In vain! I could not hold him back. They lifted me, at last, in merciful unconsciousness from his side.

How many years have passed since that night? I do not know. I do not count life by the years any more. It will end some time—thank God for that! There is another Henry Stuart growing up beside me, brave and tender as his father was. The memory of his father serves for his model, and a nobler one he could not have. He is like his father in looks, too—just as tall and bonny. I am proud, with a lone mother's pride, of our son—Henry's and mine. I have never seen again the destroyer of my happiness. He has had years enough for repentance and remorse, which, if it has been bitter as my sorrow, is an atonement beyond any revenge I could desire.

May N. Hawley.

JOHN A. SUTTER.

Captain Sutter was the California pioneer *par excellence;* he led the way for all the others. He pushed his course over the plains and deserts in 1838, and after prospecting Oregon, the Sandwich Islands, and Alaska, settled in California in 1839. He was here to welcome Wilkes in 1841, and Commodore Jones in 1842; to fraternize with Fremont in 1844, and anticipate the deeds of Sloat and Kearney in 1846. According to the testimony of General Sherman, the United States are indebted to no man more than to Captain Sutter for the conquest of California. His experience as a soldier, the presence of his well stocked fort and granaries on the Sacramento, his great wealth, his hospitality, his fondness for adventure, his strong partiality for the American Government—all these circumstances combined to render his aid and influence in this connection of great importance. This is the principal event in Sutter's life, the one that invests it with the highest historical interest. The next one was the discovery of gold. The last one was the ungrateful act of the nation in depriving him of his property, in refusing him either restitution or compensation, and in permitting him to die in penury.

Sutter was born at Kandern, Baden, on the frontier of Switzerland, February 3, 1803. At the age of twenty he was graduated at the military academy of Berne, and entered the Swiss Guard of the French army as a lieutenant. He served in the Spanish campaign of 1823-4, and with Charles X., in the disastrous revolution of July, 1830. After the fall of the Bourbons he returned to Switzerland, and served a term of four years in the Swiss army, in which he rose to the rank of captain. In 1834 he emigrated to the United States, and settled at St. Louis; thence, in 1835, he removed to West Point, Missouri, in which State he became an American citizen. He remained there several years, driving a frontier trade in cattle. During one of his journeys to Santa Fé he heard such wonderful accounts of the Western Coast as rendered, to one of his roving and adventurous spirit, a further stay at West Point unendurable. In 1838 he set out with a trappers' party to the Rocky Mountains, whence, with six men, he crossed more than a thousand miles of deserts, tenanted only by wandering savages and wild beasts. Before the end of the year he had reached the upper Columbia, where Lewis and Clark struck it in 1805, and descended the river to Fort Vancouver. After resting from his long journey he made some efforts to proceed to Alta California, but he was diverted from this project by the promised advantage of a trip to Honolulu. Arriving at this place, he proceeded thence, on another commercial adventure, to Sitka, and finally to San Francisco, Alta California, where he arrived July 2, 1839. Sutter soon after established himself on the Sacramento River, near where the capital of the State now stands. With a liberal grant of land from the Mexican Government, and sufficient capital to stock it with animals, farm implements, seed, grain, and laborers, Sutter soon became a wealthy *ranchero*. His possessions included many thousand acres of land, of which 1,000 acres were in wheat; he had 8,000 head of cattle, 2,000 sheep, 2,000 horses and mules, and 1,000 hogs. He called his place New Helvetia, built a fort upon it to protect it from savages or revolutionists, opened his doors to all comers with hearty hospitality, and became the patriarch of the Pacific and the leader of its American population.

Barring some arrogance from Castro, a revolutionary Governor—whose pretensions Sutter had opposed, having vainly enlisted and led a company of two hundred men in favor of Micheltorena—he continued his patriarchal life until 1844. Then it was that Fremont came to New Helvetia, upon whose ramparts he and Sutter afterward raised the flag of the United States. Sutter had fondly hoped that this event would secure to him the possession of his vast domain under a strong and permanent government. It had precisely the opposite effect. It invited the emigration of Americans—that is to say, of men as well informed and as enterprising as himself. This weakened his influence, and from the lofty position of a patriarch among the Mexicans and Indians he fell to that of a mere landholder among the Americans. The envy and hostility which this position engendered ultimately led to the loss of his lands. But this was neither his first nor his only misfortune.

During the years 1845 to 1847, Sutter's principal occupation was the cultivation of his estates, which, for miles and miles along the Sacramento River, constituted one vast field of grain. His workmen were domesticated Indians; his overseers Americans and Europeans, squads of whom were now constantly attracted from the States to Sutter's Fort, the rallying point of emigrants to California. From this industry his gains were enormous. He sold grain to the Mexicans at San Francisco, to the Russians at Sitka, to the English at Columbia and Hudson's Bay Territory, to the Americans marching into the country from all directions. Sutter was rapidly becoming a millionaire, when, all at once, a great and singular misfortune happened to him. In 1847, after the Americans, under Fremont and Sloat, had deposed the Mexican authorities, Sutter had sent a party of men, under an overseer named Marshall, to explore the South Fork of the American River, and locate and build upon it a saw-mill. For the purpose in view this party had selected a nook in the mountains some fifty miles east of Sacramento, where timber was abundant, and the flow of water insured an adequate power. The land did not belong to Sutter's party—they had merely "squatted" upon it. All lands in California without specific titles now belonged to the United States. In this nook, which afterward received the name of Coloma, Marshall had thrown up a few rude dwellings, and commenced the construction of a mill and mill-race. For this purpose he had need to fell but a few trees in the vicinity. The remainder were reserved for the work of the mill. The village, the mill, the mill-race, the neighboring trees, have since all been destroyed—even the ground itself has been so torn and disfigured that to recognize it now is impossible. Man, in his search for gold, has no pity even for the earth that bore him. A single memento remains of this interesting spot; and if the citizens of California retain a spark of public spirit, this memento will never be permitted to leave the State. I allude to the late Charles Nahl's painting of Sutter's Mill, now in the possession of Mr. Julius Jacobs, of San Francisco. The mill and mill-race, the latter banked up with heavy timbers, is seen in the foreground. Near the mill in the background, is the home of Marshall, the overseer whom Sutter employed to construct the mill; to the left lies the village, interspersed with oak and pine trees; between the mill and the village lies a stream and clearing; and, behind all, rise the grand old hills that still slumber above this historic spot. The artist has turned every feature of the landscape to advantage, and his rare skill in grouping and coloring has lent it an attractiveness which is felt even when disassociated with the remarkable event that it commemorates.

I have talked with a dozen old pioneers, some of whom were with Marshall or Sutter at the time (Marshall was at Coloma, and Sutter at New Helvetia), and have endeavored to learn the true secret of the Find, but without success. Some of them say that Marshall found the first piece of gold; others that his little daughter found it; others, that Mrs. Wimmer, who provided meals for the workmen at the mill, found it;† and others, again, that Mrs. Wimmer's son found it. General Sutter himself once told me that Marshall was the finder, and, although Sutter was not on the spot at the time, I am inclined to believe this the true story; for, while still fresh, it must have been related to Sutter with great minuteness. It is, however, agreed on all hands, that, if Mrs. Wimmer did not find the gold, she was the first to determine its character. Woman-like, she put the doubtful nugget into a soup-pot, and boiled it. The result of that assay was to affect the fortunes of millions of people. Among others it affected Captain Sutter, for it made him a beggar.

The presence of gold in California had been suspected from very early times. Its existence in Lower California was known to Cortez, who fitted out a California gold-hunting expedition from Mexico in 1537, and secured some small quantities of the precious metal. In Alta California, gold was discovered by Drake in 1577-79. It is mentioned of this region by Loyola Cavello, a priest of the mission of San José, previous to 1690. Captain Shelvocke noticed it in 1721. Antonia de Alcedo speaks of large nuggets found previous to 1786-89. In 1837 a California priest endeavored to obtain English capital for working the placers. Some years afterward, Professor Dana noticed the gold indicæ. In April, 1847, Mr. Sloat communicated an article on the subject to *Hunt's Merchant Magazine*. Early in January, 1849, gold was found on Mormon Island, near Folsom.* But all these were either disconnected finds or mere indications. To suspect or find stray deposits of gold is one thing; to find it in such quantities that it will afford the basis of a vast industry is another. This is what Marshall found. His first nugget was not alone. There were millions of others near it, and tons of gold dust beside. A flask of the latter was secured and sent to Captain Sutter, at New Helvetia. While the Captain turned this momentous flask over in his hand, and, perhaps, innocently thanked God for this new stroke of good fortune, his workmen, who had caught an inkling of its significance, threw down their farming tools, stole his horses and cattle, and fled to Coloma. The Indians began to follow them, and before the good Captain had ceased turning over his golden flask, his estates had been robbed and abandoned. Scarcely two hundred Indians were left.

The news which came from the diggings every few days began to render Sutter's affairs somewhat critical. Gold had become more and more plentiful. The whole country was swarming into the placers. It was evident that his men would never return. Still he had enough of them left to harvest a very large crop, and it is the opinion of Mr. Huefner,‡ who was his man of business on the ranch at the time, that, had Sutter gone on with his farm work, the subsequent high prices of grain would have secured him a princely fortune. But this was not to be. Sutter, too, had caught the gold fever; and his remaining Indians were sent in charge of Mr. Huefner to dig for gold on the American River.§ Mr. Huefner informs me that this was

* For other references to early discoveries of gold in California, consult *Del Mar's History of Precious Metals*, pp. [illegible], and the authorities therein cited.

† It weighed about an ounce, and is still in the possession of Mrs. Wimmer, who recently offered it to the Pioneers' Society for $2,000. The absence of documentary evidence of its authenticity decided the Society not to entertain the offer.

‡ Recently expressed to me for the purpose of this article.

§ See for an instance of superior foresight on the part of Louis Peralta, of San José, *Del Mar's History of Precious Metals*, p. 306.

a losing enterprise. The Indians did not succeed in finding enough gold, or else, as he suspects, they embezzled a considerable proportion of the production. At all events, the cost of implements, provisions, and superintendence greatly exceeded the value of the gold obtained.

Meanwhile Sutter's vast fields of grain grew up, ripened, withered, rotted, and died. There was nobody left to garner them. The ranches were deserted. The fort began to fall into that decay which, to the disgrace of the State, marks it to-day. Once the patriarch of the Pacific, the possessor of a ducal domain, and an income that princes might have envied, Captain Sutter was rapidly traveling the road to indigence. He was robbed again and again. In 1849-50 a party of miners stole $60,000 worth of stock from him. Others cut down his timber and grass, and his lands were subsequently seized upon by claimants under new laws and new circumstances. Cities were built upon them. Pushing men had need of them, and in the race for wealth the claims of Captain Sutter to his own property were disregarded. His prior discovery and settlement; his title from the Mexican Government; his indispensable assistance in acquiring the whole territory for the United States; his princely hospitality which had fed thousands of colonists; his peculiar misfortune in having been the means of discovering the gold, and then of having lost, through this discovery, his mill, his workmen on the ranches, his animals, and his crops—all these things were forgotten. Selfishness and cupidity, under the euphemism of modern enterprise, had come to squat, like a poisoned toad, upon the patriarch's domain, and to efface the heroic deeds, the noble qualities, the rightful claims of Sutter.

His after life was uneventful. To say that he ran on the Whig ticket for Governor of the State in 1851, and afterward accepted from it the poor compliment of an appointment as General of Militia, is only to prove that he had fallen into a condition of extreme dejection and humility. He retired to his Hock farm, a small and undisputed possession on the west bank of the Feather River, and there for many years watched the wheat stalk and the vine as they annually blossomed and decayed, all to no purpose, as he thought, and directed the movements of his lawyers in a vain effort to recover his estates. It is needless to say that he did not succeed. The State, with a penuriousness that strangely contrasted with the tons of gold that it now annually threw upon the markets of the world, voted Sutter a pension of $250 a month; and so long as this was continued the brave old pioneer preserved his fortitude and sustained his hopes of restitution. When it was stopped he cursed the ingratitude which had pursued him, and left the State, as it proved, forever.

This occurred in 1868. From California Sutter repaired to Washington, there to sound in the cold ears of a distant government the oft-told story of his wrongs and his losses. It was here that I knew him—knew him only to love and respect him. His was a character at once grand and simple, at once enterprising and ingenuous. He continued a petitioner of the Government for twelve years—a petitioner whom people soon came to look upon as a celebrated somebody, from somewhere, who had a grievance which dated back into forgotten times; but what its merits were few ever knew or cared to inquire. The age—the miserably dishonest age—turned its back upon him and snubbed him. Disappointment and contumely, at length, did its work, and in the month of June, 1880, Captain Sutter, who was a Livingstone, a Cameron, and a Stanley combined, sank beneath his overwhelming burdens.

ALEXANDER DEL MAR.

A VALLEY OF VINEYARDS.

Standing upon an elevation above Napa Valley, and looking down upon the vine-clad hills and broad acres of waving wheat, we scarce can realize that only half a century has elapsed since the first white settler, George C. Yount, here located his claim. The land which now yields such abundant harvests, which to-day pours untold wealth into our coffers, was fifty years ago in the possession of the "red man." Valley and hillside were then alike one unbroken forest, a magnificent deer-park, dedicated to the use and abuse of the traditional Indian. Throughout the length and breadth of this fair land, the sole representatives of the "pale face" to be found were the Jesuits, who here and there established Catholic missions. The object of these missions was the conversion and education of the Indians. That success did not crown these labors, that this attempt to introduce civilization was frustrated by the want of appreciation on the part of the recipient of this benevolence, is hardly to be wondered at. At the date of Mr. Yount's advent among them (1831), it was estimated that there were from three thousand to five thousand Indians in Napa Valley. They were divided into six tribes: The Mayacamos, occupying the land near Calistoga; the Callajomans, on the Bale *rancho*, in the vicinity of St. Helena; the Caymus, on the Yount grant; the Napa, from which tribe the valley derived its name, occupying that land between Napa River and the city of that name; the Ulcas, east of Napa River, near Napa City; and the Soscol, in that locality yet known as the Soscol grant, now owned by Mr. Thompson. Of these six tribes there could not be counted in the valley to-day two score of representatives. They have been utterly, and, it must be confessed, shamefully, put to rout. However, we do not here propose to enter upon a discussion of the wrongs of the "poor Indian." The palpable injustice of the White Man must be forgiven, overlooked, forgotten, in virtue of the material benefit which has accrued therefrom to the world. The Indians throughout Napa Valley were commonly known as Digger Indians. The name was probably derived from the means adopted by them of obtaining sustenance. They lived upon the lowest possible grade of food, which they dug out of the earth. Why they should have resorted to this is a mystery, since that region abounded in food which might readily have tempted our nicer palates—game of various kinds, fish, wild berries, and fruits. No wonder that the Indian was constitutionally averse to labor, since Nature had so bountifully supplied him with all needful food and—clothing. More fortunate than are we, he could liken himself, did he perceive the analogy, unto the "lilies of the field."

Napa was settled, as was every other county in California, by people of every nationality under the sun. Across the Sierra they came—enterprising men, who saw before them a new Canaan, "a land flowing with milk and honey." Some fell under the trials of pioneer life; some attained wealth and power, only to see it wrested from them; some bequeathed to their children the lands of which they became possessed too late for their own enjoyment; but few, very few, are they who are alive to-day to tell the tale of the past. Our forefathers foresaw, in a measure, the results which must crown their labors, but little dreamed they of the glorious future which now dawns upon this valley. They could not predict the mine of wealth which has been developed by industry and perseverance.

Napa Valley, beautiful in itself, is rendered yet more so by its magnificent background. Nature has placed this "gem of the Pacific" in a rare setting. Completely encircled by mountains, it forms a natural amphitheater. Had Johnson selected this locality for his Happy Valley, even his genius would have failed to have imbued in Rasselas the spirit of discontent. Facing the valley as you enter it is Mount St. Helena, supposed to be an extinct volcano, four thousand three hundred and forty-three feet above the level of the sea. From an address delivered by General Vallejo several years ago, in Santa Rosa, we cite the following incident:

"In 1845 Governor Rotscheff advanced with a party of Russians to Mount Mayacamos, on the summit of which he affixed a brass plate, bearing an inscription in his own language. He named the mountain St. Helena, for his wife, the Princess de Gagarin. The beauty of this lady excited so ardent a passion in the breast of Prince Solano, chief of all the Indians about Sonoma, that he formed a plan to capture by force or stratagem the object of his love; and he might very likely have succeeded had I not heard of his intention in time to prevent its execution."

Mount St. Helena is the pride of the valley, and well it may be. At sunset it presents a gorgeous panorama of shifting color, a bewildering maze of brilliant effects. Like a magnet, its proudly lifted crest attracts to itself all the wealth of color with which Napa skies are so richly endowed. Through the greater part of the winter this mountain is snow-capped.

Napa is but one of the many valleys through the county. The mountains, which form its boundary line on the east and west, are intersected by *cañons*, which have been rendered very productive. The mountain land greatly enhances the beauty of the scenery. It is covered with magnificent foliage—trees of numberless varieties. Among them are conspicuous the oak, madroño, cedar, fir, and pine. The banks of all the mountain streams are fringed with the willow, the ash, gigantic brakes, flowering manzanita, and the California laurel. Descending into the valley we find an infinite variety of oaks, and here and there clumps of the stately madroño. These primeval beauties will not long be left to us, however, for the giant has been conquered by the dwarf—ignominiously put to route. Where the vintner plants his foot the woodman's ax is too surely heard.

Napa Valley is thirty-five miles long, and five miles wide—this at its widest point. It narrows perceptibly proceeding upward. Napa River follows the line of the foothills on the east. This stream, while extending the entire length, is, in certain localities, so extremely narrow that it seems presumptuous to claim for it the dignified appellation, river. It is by means of this river, and the copious mountain streams which traverse not only the main valley, but all the little ravines and *cañons*, that the land is irrigated. The county is small, but the fertility of its soil is unsurpassed. It boasts of sixty-four thousand one hundred and seventy-five acres under cultivation, thirty thousand five hundred and sixty-five of which are in wheat. The rich, arable lands of the valley are best adapted to the cereal crops, while the more gravelly soil of the foothills is reserved, though by no means exclusively, to the grape; but of this latter, more anon.

At first it was supposed that these hill lands were of no actual agricultural value. The mountainous belt, which has since been productive of enormous crops, was at one time only considered available for pasture land. "Further and further into new fields of utility the plow was pushed." Up the mountain sides sprung, as if by magic, orchards, vineyards, and even here and there a wheat field, until now the mountain lands are converted into beautiful homes—homes secured to their owners by unremitting toil, by perseverance and self-denial. We are constrained to say that in eight cases out of ten the men who have earned them are foreigners—Germans, Swiss, Italians—not native born Americans, and, in many cases, not even naturalized citizens. With their industry, their simple, frugal habits, they are wresting from our grasp the choicest gifts which God has given to man. We Americans do not understand the principle of economy, and, what is yet worse, we do not profit by the lesson taught us by our foreign brother. Here are men who, ten years ago, received laborers' wages at the cellars which they could to-day buy, did they choose. This suggests a query: Why do not our unemployed desert the sand-lot, and go to the vineyards? In this field there is no lack of work. In the St. Helena district alone, within a circuit of fifteen miles, there are twenty-three wine cellars and distilleries, some of these the most extensive in the State. Here the white man finds no Chinese rival. The work of wine-making is not intrusted to Chinamen. They are employed during the vintage to gather the grapes, and earlier in the season to do the hoeing and to burn brush; but the pruning, and plowing, and the wine-making itself, are done almost exclusively by white labor, which, in this district, commands from forty to sixty dollars per month.

Napa County rightly claims precedence for its agricultural advantages. Its peculiarly salubrious climate, and the adaptability of its soil, insure its crops almost beyond the question of a doubt. Of course they are variable, but utter failure never occurs. Of its varied features, all its manifold interests, it is impossible to treat in the space allotted to one article. The subject of Napa Valley—the history of its past, speculations as to its future—would fill a volume.

Let us turn to the interest at present paramount—grape culture. This is a subject of more than passing interest to the world at large, for the day is not distant when California will claim her right to stand upon an equal footing with the European wine States. She will undoubtedly rival, in maturity, those with whom she now, in infancy, competes. In proof of this statement, we recall an item, mentioned some months ago, regarding the shipment to Germany of a cargo of wine, amounting to one hundred thousand gallons, purchased in San Francisco by a Bremen firm. Of this amount a large proportion came from Napa Valley, the red wines of that valley having acquired a reputation unsurpassed by those of any other county. To-day the Zinfandel wine of St. Helena is accepted as a standard throughout the United States. In St. Helena we see the Gironde of America. The superiority of this locality for vine growing purposes is generally conceded. This district comprises about two thousand acres of vineyard, producing an average of three and one-half tons of grapes, or five hundred and twenty-five gallons of wine, to the acre. These wines are celebrated for their variety, their remarkable perfection, and at present for the high prices they command; also, for the extensive trade which they are now attaining in the Atlantic and Gulf States. It is estimated that one million five hundred thousand gallons of wine are made annually in Napa County. Last year's statistics will carry their own weight without any comment:

Wine Crop of Napa County for 1879, in Gallons.

CALISTOGA.	
L. Kortum	80,000
ST. HELENA.	
C. T. McEachran	3,500
Jacob Schramm	12,000
F. H. Rosenbaum	3,500
John C. Weinberger	40,000
John Laurent	50,000
Chas. Krug	175,000
Beringer Bros	75,000
Conrad Wegele	6,000
Berretta Bros	4,000
Chas. Lemme	12,000
Metzner & Co.	4,000
J. Haug	300
W. W. Lyman	4,000
Wm. Scheffer	120,000

E. Heymann	11,000
Sciaroni & Ramos	41,000
W. Degouy	50,000
T. A. Giauque	50,000
J. H. McCord	16,000
Trumpler & Leuthold	5,000
Salmina & Tassetti	35,000
Oscar & Schultz	2,000
OAKVILLE.	
H. W. Crabb	220,000
Brun & Chais	55,000
A. Jeanmonod	15,000
Debanne & Brassard	15,000
YOUNTVILLE.	
G. Groezinger	250,000
T. L. Grigsby	35,000
NAPA.	
G. Barth	90,000
G. Van Bever	62,000
G. Migliavacca	42,000
G. Pedrotta	10,000
Frank Salmina	4,500
Hagen Bros	15,000
J. J. Sigrist	15,000
S. A. Roney	3,000
Dr. Pettingill	8,000
Total for Napa County	1,553,000

Of these forty wine-makers but five are Americans. The rich valley land within the immediate vicinity of St. Helena, if full-bearing vineyard, is worth $300 per acre, the value decreasing on leaving St. Helena in either direction. Around Yountville it is worth from $200 to $250 per acre.

Having definitely determined upon the locality the vinter must next take into consideration what varieties of grape will best suit his purpose. The old Mission grape, a native of California, or, as some aver, brought here by the Missionary *padres* more than a century ago, is now in disfavor as a wine grape. It is invaluable for decorative purposes to those who cater to our romantic taste for legendary lore, but for the more practical purpose of wine-making it is discarded. However, it still holds its own with distillers. The high percentage of sugar which it contains, rating oftentimes as high as thirty-four per cent. to thirty-five per cent., renders it valuable in the manufacture of brandy. At this rate the substance contains twenty-five to thirty gallons of brandy to the ton of grapes. Eventually this special variety will, undoubtedly, be devoted exclusively to this purpose. The favorite wines grapes are the Zinfandel, Reisling and Chasselas. The Zinfandel is, beyond all question, the grape preferred among wine-makers for the claret wines. This grape is small, of a bluish black color, and grows in thick, heavy clusters. In certain localities it is most productive, very prolific, and regular in its production, being more impervious to the frost than are other varieties. Here be it remarked, that this dread enemy has, in a great measure, been conquered by a process of late discovery. When frost is apprehended its disastrous effect is averted by igniting barrels of tar, placed at intervals throughout the vineyards. The smoke arising thence warms the atmosphere to the extent of dispersing the frost. Those who were victims to the "black frost of '73," doubtless, now avail themselves of this "ounce of precaution;" but *revenons à nos moutons.* Why conjure up this dark phantom in our brighter days!

As the Zinfandel is preferred for red wines so is the Reisling for white. The wine made from this grape commands from eight cents to ten cents more per gallon than any other native wine in the market. It is comparatively scarce, but is now being extensively planted throughout the valley. Following upon these are the Chasselas and Berger grapes. These four varieties are used in the manufacture of champagne by our local manufacturers. For port and other sweet wines the Malvoisie and Burgundy are selected in virtue of their rich flavor, their juiciness, and the high per centage of sugar which they contain. For table grapes the Muscat, Tokay, and Black Morocco are extensively grown. The vintage of 1879 commands to-day the following prices: Reisling, 35c.; Berger and Chasselas, 25c.@30c.; Port, Angelica, Tokay, etc. (sweet wines), 60c.@70c.; Mission, 22c.@25c.; distilling wines, 18c.@20c. Unfortunately, there is now but little old wine in the market, unless that be taken into consideration which has been reserved by Mr. Chas. Krug, of St. Helena, for his Eastern trade.

To the uninitiated a few hints as to the mode of cultivation may prove interesting. Before planting a vineyard the land must be well prepared by thorough plowing, after which it is checked off in blocks, measuring six feet by eight feet, or, in some instances, six feet by seven feet. This is termed staking. At each of these stakes plant your cutting about twelve inches deep, two buds above ground. Second year, prune, leaving but one spur. Plow both ways; hoe between the first and second plowing; after which, run the cultivator through twice the same way. This process is to be repeated year after year. A vineyard does not begin to pay expenses until after the fourth year. A full bearing crop can not be properly anticipated until the seventh year.

The vintage begins in Napa about the first week in September. This last is by far the most interesting phase of the subject. Truth compels us to state, however, that the pretty pictures of rosy-cheeked, fantastically attired maidens, bearing on their heads, with artistic grace, baskets laden with luscious fruit—pictures from which most of us have received our impressions of "grape gathering"—are purely fancy sketches. At all events, the practical Yankee has divested our vintage of this charming feature, substituting in place of delicate women, whose physical organization renders them utterly unfit for such labor, strong men, whose backs are fitted to the burden of carrying the fifty-pound boxes into which the grapes are picked. These boxes are piled upon wagons, and thus conveyed to the cellars. Wine-making, in its various stages, is an interesting study in itself, not to be briefly touched upon; however. We cannot gather our grapes and bottle our wines with a single pen-stroke. The wines cellars in Napa Valley are constructed in accordance with the taste and wealth of the owner; consequently, we find an infinite variety of architecture. Some of these cellars are very elegant in structure and design. Those constructed of stone are especially noteworthy. Unquestionably, to the visitor, the cellars are the most interesting feature of the valley, especially if that visitor happen to be of the sterner sex. Every man considers it his bounden duty on visiting Napa to personally inspect one and all, if possible, of the forty wine cellars. Having so far listened to the dictates of conscience, he feels at liberty to satisfy his more æsthetic tastes; he turns his horse's head toward White Sulphur Springs. We will accompany him.

These springs, once California's most fashionable resort, can now be said to be in their halcyon days, the term considered in its literal sense. One by one, those who for more than half a score of years frequented this resort, have deserted in favor of the beach. It is still open to the public, but it is in vain we seek among its guests the old familiar faces. Monterey and Santa Cruz have undeniably robbed White Sulphur of its fashionable prestige; but until Nature withdraws the gifts which she has here scattered with so lavish a hand its glory will not have departed. Let the capitalist but wave his wand over these curative waters and their magical properties will at once be restored. The White Sulphur is, by far, the most beautiful *cañon* in the Mayacamos Range. It nestles in the bosom of the mountains, a little world within itself—a mimic stage whereon has been enacted many a scene from real life, drama replete with romantic incident.

Could we rightly interpret the significance of those waving branches which

"Speak not but in signs;"

could we force the confidence of that chattering brook, whose waters we know full well furnished accompaniment to many a love sonnet in the olden time; could we, in some mysterious way, become possessed of the talismanic leaf which rendered intelligible to the good children in fairy books the language of inanimate nature—who knows what secrets would be divulged? Who can say but that we would then hold the key to much that is problematical in the annals of San Francisco life?

Leaving the *cañon* (its manifold attractions of scenery and climate have been too often dilated upon to admit of recapitulation), we cross Edge Hill Creek, and turn to the right. Here we find some of the finest places in the St. Helena district—Edge Hill, Hillside, and Madroño Cottages. At this point we rein up in perplexity. Shall we attain the county road by way of the avenue, or go through the vineyards? The former affords a view of Mr. Lewelling's beautiful grounds; but by choosing the latter route, stopping at Mr. Pellet's, we obtain one of the finest and most extensive views which the valley affords.

It is utterly impossible to give even a glance at the many beautiful homes which add so materially to the charm of Napa County. To do so would be to wander up the mountain side, into ravine and *cañon*, over the hills to Pope, Chiles, Berryessa, and Conn Valleys. Where would our peregrinations end? When would we reach San Francisco again? It is too late in the season to start out on a summer's campaign. Nevertheless, we must stop one moment at Soda Springs, if only to say that we have tasted Napa soda as it bubbles from the earth.

This is a beautiful spot, its famous medicinal waters being but one of many attractions. The mechanical process of collecting and bottling these waters is extremely interesting. It is done so deftly, and with such astonishing celerity, that the men engaged in the operation seem themselves but automatons—a part of the machinery which they control. The buildings are of white granite, for the most part, overgrown with ivy. This gives to the place an appearance of antiquity, rarely seen in California. Located, as it is, on the side of a mountain, it is clearly discernible from the valley. A most glorious view is obtained at this point. As we stand here now, loth to descend from the mountain, a sense of awe creeps over us, which silences rapture itself. The valley is bathed in the golden light of the setting sun. The rosy clouds approach the blue mountain tops, imprinting a good-night kiss, and all fades away into the purple twilight.

SALLIE R. HEATH.

A STRANGE CONFESSION.

CHAPTER I.

On the 20th of June, 1878, about ten o'clock in the evening, a man and a woman were leisurely walking along St. James Street, in the quiet city of San José, California, when their conversation was suddenly checked by the smothered sound of a pistol-shot in a dwelling they had passed a short distance. It was on the north side of the street. There could hardly be a mistake in the house, as the one from which the sound undoubtedly issued was nearest the walkers, there being but few houses in that vicinity. They halted, listened some moments, and heard no other sound. The man suggested to his companion that they approach the house nearer. She hesitated some time, terrified more at the oppressive silence that followed the shot than at the probable existence of a tragedy; and then, receiving strength from the man's superior calmness, quietly consented, clinging closely to his arm. They halted at every few steps, and listened, but heard nothing. They stopped at the gate, and listened intently. Everything was quiet.

"Must have been in a back room," whispered the man.

"That sounded like a moan," said the woman, thoroughly frightened.

"Was it a man's voice?"

"No; a woman's."

They remained several minutes; to the woman it seemed an hour. Then they heard the moaning more distinctly.

"Call some help, Henry. Go in yourself—they are killing her."

"It is not a cry of pain," he said, quietly.

"What, then?"

"Anguish."

The only light visible was that from a lamp in the hall. The house again became perfectly silent. The man was about leading his companion away, when her quick hearing detected a sound. A nervous pressure of her hand on the man's arm caused him to listen. That which had attracted her attention was the soft creaking of shoes on the carpeted stair. She heard some one descending carefully and mincingly; then there was a short pause, the faint rattling of a small chain attached to the lamp, and in a moment the house was plunged in profound darkness. The creaking of the shoes was again heard as the unseen person ascended, the footfalls growing quicker as the top was approached, as though spurred by fright. This was followed by silence.

"It was a woman," whispered the man's companion.

"How do you know?"

"By the shoes."

"But how?"

The woman simply made a slight movement of impatience, and said nothing. They waited a short time longer, and then passed on. Said the man:

"I shall notify the police immediately."

Soon after they had left, the door of the house was unlocked and opened. A man walked softly out, carefully closing the door. He seemed to be an old man, for his step was heavy and infirm as he reached the walk. Still, his head was bare, and it was not gray. He tried to open the gate, but made a mistake in the latch side, and did not discover his error for some moments. When he gained the street he scanned it in both directions, and found it deserted. He walked toward the city, slowly and unsteadily, and with the labor of a man bearing a heavy load. Suddenly he placed his hand on his head, and discovered that he had forgotten his hat. He turned back reluctantly, gazed at the house, shivered, and turned again toward the city. An idea occurred to him, and, searching his pockets nervously and hurriedly, he found and drew forth a silken cap, which he placed upon his head, drawing the visor well down. He then proceeded.

There was a singular dogged determination in the man's movements. He carried his heavy burden fiercely and angrily, clinging to it while it crushed him; nerving himself to bear it safely to its destination; grinding his teeth and clenching his hands with bitter resolution. He had not the look of a man escaping—there was not the anxious, furtive look around; yet he feared the darkness. When he reached the lower corner of St. James Square, he hesitated to traverse the gloomy and dimly lighted distance diagonally across; but, gathering up the shattered remnants of his manhood, he braved the darkness, and passed through. With the same almost reeling gait he crossed First Street and entered St. John. As this street was poorly lighted, and without passers, he quickened his pace until he reached Market Street, where the light was better. To his left, about half the distance to Santa Clara Street, and on the opposite side of Market, was a two-story brick building, lighted up. It was the City Hall, containing the police station, with the prison in the rear. There were several pedestrians in that vicinity and on Santa Clara Street.

He was slowly crossing in the direction of the City Hall, when he hesitated, and then halted. However, after a moment he again went forward until he arrived at the entrance of the City Hall. He started to enter; then drew back.

"My God!" he groaned, and turned away.

His nerve had broken down.

He crossed Santa Clara Street, turned into San Fernando, and entered a drinking saloon.

"Give me some whisky," he demanded, in a calm, imperious tone, with an insulting manner, in a voice that implied a threat, in the way in which a dog would be commanded. The barkeeper meekly set before him a tumbler and a bottle. The stranger filled the tumbler to the brim, drank the contents, and refused the water that was offered him. As he paid for the drink, the bar-keeper said, pleasantly, as if to put him in a good humor:

"Pleasant weather we are having."

"Dry up!" came the reply, so suddenly, and with such fierceness, that the man behind the bar was confounded. The eyes of the stranger flashed, and he grasped the tumbler so threateningly that it seemed another word would send it flying in the face of the bar-keeper. The two men glared at each other, the one surprised and frightened, the other aggressive and terrible. The stranger's muscles slowly relaxed. He finally filled his glass, and drank again, and again, and again. Then he left.

The stimulus imparted by the liquor caused the blood to rush hot and thick through his veins as he stood for a few minutes in the shadow of a doorway—gave him strength and courage, brightened every faculty, made him a hero at heart. He looked at the street-lamps, at the stars, at the passers-by. He walked slowly toward the City Hall, pondering deeply.

It was with a firm step that he entered. He seemed a stranger to the surroundings. At the further extremity of the hall he found, to the left, an open door, leading into a room that was lighted, but vacant. A small door, opposite the entrance, confronted him. The upper half of it was glass, over which a shade was drawn. Posted above the door was a piece of card-board, on which was printed, "Police Station." He rapped, and the door was opened by a man between thirty and forty years of age, who surveyed him with a quick, searching glance. He politely invited the stranger to enter. The latter went in, and found himself in a very small room. It contained a desk, at which a young man sat, a safe, a stove, and two or three chairs. On the walls were posted several placards, offering rewards for the arrest of criminals, and photographs of other criminals on postal cards, with the offense and description printed alongside.

"Gentlemen," said the stranger, "who is in charge here?"

"I am," replied the man at the desk, with a look of deference at the older man, who said nothing.

"I have come to tell you something," said the stranger, somewhat confidentially, and with a little mystery and importance.

"What is it?"

"A crime was committed to-night——"

"On St. James Street?" This question came sharp and quick, like an explosion.

It greatly surprised and puzzled the stranger, and changed his manner. A strange dread succeeded his surprise.

"Has anybody—I mean have—have—has anybody been here?"

"I sent a couple of men to the house not long ago," said the elder man, who, until then, had been silent. "Maybe they'll fetch somebody."

The stranger was evidently embarrassed, and thrown from his reckonings. He reflected for a moment, and then his face cleared up.

"Do you know anything about it?" asked the man at the desk.

"Yes."

"What is it?"

"I came here for the purpose——"

"Well?"

"Of lodging information."

"Against whom?"

At this question the stranger wavered; and then, in a thick, husky voice, preceded by a harsh clearing of the throat, that sounded like the turning of a screw in a coffin-lid, he said:

"John Howard."

The officers wrote the name on a slip of paper.

"No middle name?"

"No."

"What is the charge?"

This was a terrible moment for the stranger. It might have recalled a ghastly picture, while it opened up a future full of revolting things; a fair name dragged in the dirt, scorned, spat upon, kicked into the gutter; a world from which the sun was blotted out; a maddened brain and a broken heart.

He wavered for a moment, but his determination was quickly restored by the gaze of the two men riveted upon him, burning him through and through. He dropped into a chair between the two officers, to hide the trembling of his knees.

"What is the charge?" repeated the man at the desk.

"Murder."

"E—h?"

The two officers were greatly surprised.

The stranger looked uneasily toward the door, and had the appearance of a man whom fear of some kind pursued; as though he dreaded something; as if he expected an accuser to rise through the floor and charge him with treachery. It was a frightened rather than a cowardly look; a dread of a calamity rather than an expectation of it.

"When did this occur?"

He reflected a moment, and then answered, deathly pale:

"About an hour ago."

"Did you see it?"

The question fell upon the stranger heavily, unnerving him. Struggling desperately to recover his self-possession, and rocking in his seat from side to side as though staggering under a stroke of paralysis, he glanced nervously from one of the men to the other, helpless, crushed, pleading. He did not answer the question. There was a strange hesitancy in his manner of imparting the information and lodging the terrible charge. His lips were glued together, and the men noticed that he shivered as with a chill.

"Tell us what you know about it? Whom did he kill?" This impatiently.

The stranger simply stared.

"Where is this man Howard?" asked the older officer, starting up angrily.

There was no reply. The informant looked up at him so vacantly that the officer became uneasy. He seized the stranger's arm and shook him. As though the rough touch had electrified rather than aroused him, he threw up both hands, grappled the air, and seemed like a drowning man catching blindly at whatever might save his life. He sighed brokenly, but the sigh changed to a gasp.

"Here! Wake up!" called the officer in a loud voice, again shaking him.

The vacant look continued. Said the officer in disgust:

"He's drunk."

This roused the stranger. As if just awakened, he asked faintly:

"What is it?"

"Has Howard left?"

The stranger shook his head, after hesitating some time with an effort to remember something.

"Where is he, then?"

His answer was a stare.

"In the name of God, man, what is the matter?"

The stranger did not reply. His stare relaxed, and his head fell upon his breast.

"Stupid drunk," remarked the man at the desk.

"Do you know him?"

"Never saw him before."

"It's about time for the men to be back, isn't it?"

"Yes."

There was a minute of moody silence. Then the older man asked a question that, all unwittingly to himself, had the effect upon the stranger of a knife in the throat:

"What is your name?"

"Hey?" asked the stranger, looking up, stupidly, the painful, vacant expression again stealing into his eyes.

"What's your name?"

"My name?"

"There they are, Chief," interposed the man at the desk as the footsteps of two men were heard in the hall.

Again did the searching, anxious look in the stranger's face assert itself as the two policemen entered the door. He peered behind them keenly and fearfully, but saw no one with them. He then sank back into his chair with profound weariness and exhaustion and a look of triumph.

"Well?" inquired the Chief, as he, too, saw that the men had no one in custody.

The two men were sore perplexed. Said one:

"Can't make head nor tail out of it."

"Where's the man?"

"What man?"

"That did the shooting."

"Oh!" The two men looked at each other, greatly embarrassed.

"Yes. John——" he had forgotten the name. Glancing at the slip of paper, he added, "Howard. John Howard."

"Why, that's her son."

"Whose son?"

"The woman that lives there."

"Well, where is he?"

The two men regarded their interlocutor blankly.

"He's gone," said one of them.

"Gone!"

"Slipped away. Jumped the town."

"Humph!" grunted the Chief. Then turning round to the stranger, he said:

"Your man has skipped."

His look was met by a meaningless stare.

"He killed his man, did he?" asked the Chief of the men.

"It was a woman."

"A woman!"

"Yes; young and pretty."

"Shot her, eh?"

"Right through there," said one of the men, as he placed his finger on the Chief's breast, a little below the left nipple. "It was the littlest hole I ever see; but the ball must a' went straight to the heart. There ain't no blood to speak of, except a little red stain on her corset, right around the edge of the hole. It must a' been a terrible small pistol, but it done the business up to the handle."

"The infernal coward!" muttered the man at the desk, who, it will be remembered, was a young man.

The Chief paid no attention to the interruption. He asked the men:

"Who's in the house with the body?"

"His mother and a young girl."

"Whose mother?"

"Why, the fellow that done the work."

"Yes. Well, what did she say?"

"She was so broke up and flurried, like, that we couldn't get much out of her. She was as crazy as ever I see a woman."

"Was the dead girl her daughter?"

"No. Just a friend living with them."

"Anybody else in the house?"

"Only a young girl—a niece, I think she said."

The Chief pondered a moment, and asked:

"About how old is this niece?"

"I should say about sixteen or seventeen. Maybe not so old."

"Humph! Well, what did the old woman say?"

"She kept ravin', and sayin', 'My poor boy! my poor boy!' And when I asked her where he was—I didn't know about his being a man, and stayin' there with her—she jumped up and stormed at us furious, and looked like a regular tiger; and said it was none of *our* business; that *we* needn't fret about him; that he was away off somewhere."

"She wouldn't give him away, eh?"

"No; she didn't—in so many words."

"And she never will," said the Chief, thoughtfully. "But I think we've got *that* game beat. And there's more ways to do it than one. You didn't search the house for him?"

"No, not exactly; we didn't know it was him that done it, you see."

"What was this young girl doing?"

"Oh, she's scary anyhow, and had fainted two or three times, and then came to, and was so dazed she didn't know anything. The old woman would be terrible cross with her, and then pet her and kiss her."

"Who are these people?—strangers, ain't they?"

"I guess they are. None of us ever heard of 'em before. I know the house was vacant a short while ago. I'll tell you, Chief, it's so late now we'll have to wait till morning before we find out anything, and watch the house to see if he comes out."

"It is too late to watch the house after you both came away, and left him every chance in the world to light out."

He said this somewhat reproachfully, and the two policemen looked ashamed.

"Say, my friend," said the Chief, addressing the stranger in a loud voice, as though he spoke to a deaf man, "did you see the shooting?"

There was only a vacant stare for an answer.

"Come! What do you know about it?"

Still there was only a non-comprehending, helpless stare.

"He's drunk," said the Chief. He seized the stranger's arm and shook him violently.

"Say! brace up! what is your name?"

"Hey?" came the pitiful, childish, meaningless query, asked as it would be by one half asleep to a question by some one existing only in a dream.

"What is your name?" The question was loud and imperative.

The answer came in a clear, and small, and meaningless voice, and in a purely mechanical way:

"John Howard."

Chapter II.

The officers were aghast. Certainly it was an easy capture. They led the prisoner, meek, and submissive, but shattered and trembling—drunk, it was thought—to the county jail, nearly three blocks distant, and locked him in a place reserved for the worst criminals. It was called the "tank," and consisted of an arrangement of six iron-lined cells, inclosed within four iron-lined walls, the cells occupying the center of the area. He spoke not another word, though plied with questions. He was in that condition of complete mental and physical collapse, when the last remnant of strength of whatever kind has been expended in the accomplishing of a great purpose. They left him, his white face pressed against the small wicket of his cell, staring blankly at the wall, which stared at him in turn, as blanched and meaningless.

The Chief did not share the elation felt by his men at the capture and its importance. He was gloomy and thoughtful, but he kept his trouble to himself. To the two men who had already visited the scene of the tragedy he gave this order:

"Watch the house until you are relieved in the morning. Arrest anybody going in or coming out, and one of you bring him to headquarters, while the other stands watch. Keep your eyes wide open."

The county jail is in the rear of the courthouse, which fronts upon First Street and St. James Square. After the policeman had disappeared through that gate of the Square which opens upon First Street, opposite the courthouse, the Chief, who was returning to the police station, halted, and listened until the footsteps of the men could no longer be heard. Then he retraced his steps, passed the courthouse, and turned into Julian Street, which is next to St. James on the north. He went down this street until opposite the house of the tragedy, and stood for some time looking at a lighted window in a rear room of the upper story. But the distance was too great for observation. He turned back toward First Street. On reaching this street he turned to the right, and had gone some distance, when he entered a yard in which stood a handsome dwelling, and rang the door-bell. The door was immediately opened by an old man in a dressing gown.

"You are sitting up late, as usual, Judge," said the Chief of Police.

"Ah, Casserly! Is that you? Come in, my boy; come in. Glad to see you."

This old man had been a jurist of some note; had been a judge until the infirmities of age demanded that his labors should cease; and had declined all honors and distinctions, preferring the quiet of his home and the company of his books. He was nearly eighty years old. He was of Jewish origin, as his name, Simon, indicates. He was a small man, with white hair, a clean shaven face, and stooping shoulders. In his face was the keen, bright look of younger days, tempered with the impress of profound thought and study. It was said that his knowledge of human nature was subtile and extensive.

"Now, Casserly," he said, as they were seated in his study, "something unusual has happened. And you always come to your old friend whenever anything troubles you. You know I am always glad to see you." He spoke with a cheery laugh, rubbing his withered old hands together in the friendliest manner.

He listened with absorbed attention to the Chief's recital, interrupting him frequently with pertinent questions. When it was finished he sat back in his arm chair, with closed eyes, tapping his forehead with his gold eye-glasses. After sitting thus for some time he said:

"Poor boy! poor boy!"

The Chief was surprised—almost startled.

"Poor *boy*, did you say, Judge?"

The old man nodded.

"It seems to me," said Casserly in a tone of deference, "that you might have said poor *girl!*"

"Why, Casserly?"

"She is the one who suffered."

"But suffers no longer, Casserly."

The Chief was thoughtful. The Judge added:

"It is the boy who suffers now, and more than the girl did in her death agony. He is with us and is one of us."

Casserly stood somewhat in awe of this old man's pity.

"What do you think of the case, Judge?"

"Very strange case, Casserly; very strange."

They sat in silence, the eyes of the Chief fixed steadily and hungrily on the old man's face.

"How old did you say he is, Casserly?"

"About twenty-five or twenty-six."

"Describe him accurately."

"Well, he's about five foot ten; weighs about a hundred and forty; broad-shouldered for a slender man; straight as an Indian; black hair and mustache; fair complexion; large blue eyes. He's as pale as death."

The old Judge nodded as each item of the description was called off.

"Casserly," he said, "a man at that age is both a man and a boy. It is the age when pride is stronger than at any other time in life, for it is tinged with heroism. But how can I tell, Casserly? I have not seen and studied him. You say he has white hands—you said so, didn't you?"

"No; I didn't say so; but his hands are small and white."

"Yes. Well, I knew it anyway. A man with such a face as you have described, and who has done what this man did in giving himself up to the clutches of the law, could not have hands that labor has stained and hardened. And he is pale. Then he is a student. You say he has not the appearance of a dissipated man—I think you must have said so, Casserly?"

"No, Judge," said Casserly, smiling; "but for a fact he has the appearance of a man who dissipates very little, if any."

"Then, Casserly," said the old man, "he is a hard student. Furthermore, he has—or had before this affair—a tremendous ambition. At the age of twenty-five, Casserly, there is all the will of manhood coupled with the heroic dreams of younger days, which may have been buried out of sight with other boyish follies, but whose ghosts linger about. It is the time in life when a man may undertake to do grand things; will sacrifice anything for his friend, or his father, or his mother, or the woman he loves."

This strange speech, which to Casserly's mind was entirely irrelevant, caused him to exhibit some surprise. Seeing it, the old man laughed.

"Why, you ought to know me by this time, and what a rambling, garrulous old man I am. I know what it is you come to ask me, Casserly."

"I beg your pardon, Judge, but I don't think you do."

"Oh, yes, Casserly. I know very well," and he laughed heartily.

"What is it, then, Judge?" asked Casserly, interested.

"In your old narrow, stupid way, that I can't rid you of, you want to know if the evidence is sufficient to convict. Own up to it like a man, Casserly," and he laughed quite heartily at Casserly, who laughed through his own confusion.

But Casserly was crestfallen. His deep regard for the power of the man who spoke to him, divining his thoughts, was strengthened.

"You are a great blockhead, my boy. You never get beyond the consideration that a man has committed a crime, and that he must be sent to jail—or hanged."

Casserly looked ashamed, and a little hurt. The old man noticed it, and good-naturedly said:

"But you are willing to learn, Casserly, and that is half the battle."

He became thoughtful again, and presently said:

"It is not sufficient to convict him, Casserly. The law throws great safeguards around a guilty man who protests his innocence, for it presumes that no man is guilty until he is proven so beyond a reasonable doubt, and the proof must be furnished by the prosecution. Still greater are the safeguards it throws around those who advertise their guilt, for the law then becomes suspicious. Of course, I except those cases where the plea of 'guilty' is made for manifest reasons—as, for instance, for clemency. The strongest motive in human nature, in its healthy condition, is self-preservation. There are three conditions in life in which this principle may be overshadowed. They are pride, despair, or religious fanaticism—all to an unnatural degree. By 'unnatural' I mean abnormal; for, as a matter of fact, there is no such thing as something unnatural in a human being. There are certain elements in his nature that are developed or suppressed by circumstance. Religious fanaticism may be termed the prolonged existence of emotional insanity. Now, these three conditions may be combined, in which case the result is generally incalculable, and can be foreseen only when we possess knowledge of a person's character and temperament, and in what proportions, and to what extent, the three conditions, or any two of them, may be united. So strong, Casserly, is this principle of self-preservation, that, even if it should be overshadowed to the extent of a desire for self-destruction, such overshadowing is only temporary. Give Nature time, and she will work it off as she would any other disease that may seem incurable, but that may not be so. There are few diseases of the heart but can be cured. To carry this idea a little further, Casserly, I believe that almost every trouble may be cured; and, if it is apparently not cured, you will find that another, and a more strange, condition has arisen. It is that, sooner or later, trouble will bring a relish of its own; and when this is the case, it no longer exists. I have seen people, Casserly, who hugged and nursed their troubles, and others who were rather proud of them. Take these so-called troubles away from them, and they would, indeed, be miserable; for by this time Nature has fitted the heart to bear the affliction, and to do so she had to remove the sweetness that happiness would bring to an untroubled nature. The law of adaptation applies even here, for, Casserly, life is for the greater part habit. It is hard to be without that to which we are accustomed, even though it be trouble. So trouble may be a consolation."

Casserly yawned. The old man continued:

"This young man has acted on impulse. Nature had not time to eradicate the disease before he took the fatal step of the surrender. The murder could not have been otherwise than the result of an impulse of some kind. But now watch the result. The time before his trial and possible conviction will be long and tedious, and the instinct of self-preservation may assert itself. Even this, however, is conditional. There is no rule that applies to human nature. Natures are so diverse. In no two is there the same combination of elements. If this man is actuated by pride, I should think, judging from his nature as I imperfectly understand it, that he may possibly assert his guilt to the end, and mount the scaffold triumphantly. If it is despair, he will fight for his life; for, with young persons, despair always yields to time, and hope, and love of life. If it is pride, he could hardly be guilty, or, at least, entirely at fault.

If it is despair, the chances are in favor of his guilt. If it is a mixture of both, he will take his own life, if the gallows is slow. But the question is too broad, the probabilities too numerous, and the evidence too slight, for us to draw an intelligent conclusion. I think the prisoner is an extraordinary man, Casserly—a man of invincible pride."

The old man again withdrew into himself, and, on emerging, continued:

"I suppose you understood my remarks on suicide to refer to this young man's evidently suicidal intent in his act of surrender."

"Yes," said Casserly; but Casserly was disposed to be accommodating.

The old man again reflected, and said:

"I think you displayed commendable forethought in one thing, Casserly."

"What was that, Judge?"

"Why, in the sending of those two men to watch the house."

Casserly looked pleased, and a gleam of cunning came into his eyes.

"I don't think you really dropped on what I did it for, Judge."

"Didn't I, though?" and the old man laughed heartily. "Why, Casserly, I can see through you as though you were a piece of French glass, if my old eyes *are* dim. The idea occurred to you that possibly this young man had surrendered himself to throw suspicion in the wrong direction, so that by the time he should have established his innocence the real criminal would be beyond the reach of justice. That was your idea, Casserly."

Casserly laughed.

"Do you think it a good one, Judge?"

"Oh, very good—in intention. It is of more importance than that, however, in preventing the flight of the young girl."

Casserly became very attentive.

"If this girl attempts to escape," continued the Judge, "depend upon it that her testimony would be fatal to young Howard. She could not tell a straight falsehood under the terrible ordeal of the cross-examination. But the mother—mark you, Casserly—the mother will have her tongue torn from her mouth before she will render damaging testimony against her son. Casserly, your mother died years ago, did she not?"

"I was too young to remember her."

"Then, Casserly, you do not know that a mother is the only friend in the world." The old man paused a moment, and then added, softly, "In the whole world, Casserly."

After reflecting longer, he said:

"Did he kill this girl in a fit of jealousy? I don't know. Had he betrayed her, and, through lack of love for her, by loving some one else more, killed her to hide her shame? I don't know. I have no idea. In any event, why did he surrender himself, when he might possibly have escaped? That is the great question, Casserly. It cannot possibly be answered now. But it is because either of pride or despair. This young man has charged himself with murder. Is his mother cognizant of it? Certainly not. Did she know that he had any such intention? Certainly not, or she would have followed him, clung to him, and prevented him. Very well. She knows he left the house soon after the murder. In fact, she seemed proud and triumphant that he was beyond the reach of the officers, as she supposed. There, Casserly, is ground for a terribly strong presumption of guilt. Terribly strong. What do *you* think?"

But Casserly merely shook his head helplessly.

"Terribly strong, sir, *I* think. There is another very curious circumstance. From what I can understand, he went into the office with great firmness—in fact, apparently laboring under very little excitement. Am I right?"

"Yes."

"But seemed to be greatly unnerved on learning that you had sent the officers to the house. Right again?"

"Yes; but I think it was the liquor."

"Casserly, Casserly!"

"Well, maybe not. And, now I think of it, he seemed anxious about their return."

The old man was all eagerness.

"Did he, eh? Then, Casserly," he said, somewhat excited, "he was fighting for time. For some reason he wanted to know the result of their visit."

His ardor suddenly died out, and he added:

"But there could be so many reasons for his wishing to gain time before he went too far. Yes, so many. Let that go, and let us analyze this matter of the surrender a little further. He did not advise his mother of his intention, for the reason that he knew she would resist it. He knew, furthermore, that his disgrace is her disgrace, and that, in addition to being disgraced, she will be broken-hearted. But hold! I am too fast. There are so few young men who know what a mother can suffer for her son. He may be such a man, but I don't think so. I contend that he is an extraordinary man. I think he is a man who would suffer anything for his mother, unless his whole equilibrium was destroyed. Now, by his act she will be disgraced and broken-hearted. Will she feel her disgrace, or care for it? No; for it will be swallowed up in love for the boy. I know these mothers, Casserly. In such a case as this they can baffle justice at every turn. Religion, pride, honesty, self-respect—all sink into insignificance when it comes to saving the life of a son. And they are wonderfully shrewd. There is not a flaw in their testimony. They can adjust great apparent inconsistencies the moment such are presented. They generally foresee and provide against them. I tell you, Casserly—you may think I am extravagant—but I know, I know."

The old man rose to his feet in his excitement, and continued:

"And she never loves him more than when danger threatens him, and the world is against him. A woman idolizes her son. She worships him. Yes, worships him—that's the word. She is faithful to him, if she knows he's a murderer. And, Casserly," he said, lowering his voice almost to a whisper, and shaking his finger in Casserly's face, "she will forsake her husband and her daughter, forsake heaven and earth, to save her son."

A tear glistened in the old man's eyes.

Casserly was greatly moved by this striking picture, and it filled him with uneasy forebodings.

"Casserly," said the old man, reseating himself, and as calm as usual, "this tragedy is mysterious. I can give you very little help now, for I have seen neither the man nor the mother. The great mystery lies in his surrender. While we are in a mood for speculation, let us form a theory—one based on the evidence before us. I am inclined to think that this boy is a law-student, and I'll tell you why: You think he was drunk. In any event, you detected the liquor, and you knew he had been drinking. He might have been drunk, or he might have been insane from despair, or he might have been acting a part. Had you thought of that?"

"No," replied Casserly, all attention.

"Well, it takes no great knowledge of law to know that a plea of insanity is the criminal's stronghold."

Casserly became intensely interested. The old man continued:

"Is it not possible that he preferred to take his chances with a plea of insanity, and give his surrender and conduct as an evidence of it, rather than to escape, and run the risk of capture, when the plea of insanity would have less weight?"

"By thunder! you have hit it."

The old man laughed softly.

"I have taken a good deal of pains with you to-night, Casserly. This case belongs to the State, and not to you. You have nothing to do with it."

Casserly, confused, looked appealingly to the old man.

"Ha! ha! ha! Casserly, I knew it all along. You want to work up the case, and become famous as a detective. You can't fool me, Casserly," and he enjoyed the joke immensely.

"Gracious!" he ejaculated; "it will soon be daylight. You have kept me up all night. You have a queer way of making me talk, Casserly, and there is never any stopping when I get started. I am a little anxious to know the result of the inquest."

Casserly rose to leave.

"Come again, Casserly, as often as you can."

If the truth must be told, the old man was flattered by Casserly's admiration of him and reliance upon him.

Casserly went directly to the police station.

"Well, Captain," he said, addressing the young man at the desk, who was Captain of the Night Watch, "is there anything new?"

"I should think so. There's the mischief to pay. Where have you been? I've had the town scoured for you."

"What is the matter?"

"Sit down, and I'll tell you."

The Chief drew up a chair, a look of anxiety in his face. The Captain commenced:

"Soon after Frank and Joe went down there, the old woman sneaked out of the house, peered around, and saw Joe across the street. He was kind of hidden, too, but she saw him anyhow. She called him over, and asked him if he was a policeman. He said 'yes.' Then she asked him what he was doing there. He said that was his beat. Then she wanted to know if he had seen or heard anything. He blurts out, like a fool, that her son had given himself up. Well, sir, Joe said that if that woman had been struck over the head with a club it couldn't have stunned her more. She staggered back and fell on the steps, but didn't say a word. He went into the yard and picked her up, and she was all weak, and her teeth chattered. After awhile she told him she was all right; that she was subject to dizzy spells. Then she sits very quiet, and says to Joe, 'Will you please, sir, go and send me a messenger boy? I want to let my daughter in the country know.' Joe studies a little while, he says, and then tells her he will; because the message might give something away, you see. So he calls Frank, and when the woman sees there are two of 'em she is all broke up again, but don't say a word. So Frank goes after the boy, and Joe stays. When the boy comes—he was riding a horse, mind you—the old lady takes him in the house and locks the door. 'All right,' says Joe, for he knew they were all in the house. Somehow it took the old lady a long time to write the message. The boy comes out, looking kind o' scared, and Joe says to him, 'What's the matter?' 'Oh, that's all right, Joe,' says the boy; 'I'm in a big hurry, and will tell you all about it when I get back.' Then he got on the horse and was gone like the wind. In about an hour another boy came out, crying. Joe thought it was the girl in disguise, trying to get away. He nabs her, because the clothes are too big, and give her dead away. But who should it be but the messenger boy?"

Casserly was aghast.

"And the other boy—"

"Was no boy at all, but the young girl. The old lady—she's a terror!—when she got the boy up stairs, put a pistol under his nose, and told him if he cried out she would shoot him like a dog. Then she made him take off his clothes, and gave him some of her son's to put on, and made the girl dress in the boy's uniform. The boy says the girl was scared, but the old lady made her drink some brandy, and made the boy tell Joe's name, and then took the girl into the hall and whispered to her. Then the girl went down stairs, and the old lady wouldn't let the boy go for an hour. She just sat there by the body, looking at the boy, and playing with the pistol, and didn't say a single word."

"Did you start any one after the girl?"

"Two or three; but it was so late in the night that nobody was out, and they came back without striking the trail."

"Did you telegraph?"

"No."

"How long has she been gone?"

"Over three hours."

"A big start, but we must catch her."

"But wasn't that a sharp trick, though?"

"Yes. I am afraid the woman is too much for me."

The Chief was silent a minute, and then said, reflecting on the words of the old man:

"It proves one thing, Captain."

"What is that?"

"Howard is guilty." W. C. Morrow.

DID DR. WHITMAN SAVE OREGON?

A reference to the Ashburton treaty, which occurs in an article, "How Dr. Whitman Saved Oregon," in the July number of the Californian, suggests the thought of how little may be understood of the nature of our treaties with foreign nations. The author of that article, in recounting the services of Dr. Whitman, imputes to him some influence in forming one of a series of treaties and conventions concerning the boundary of the United States; and without, apparently, having examined the subject, connects the settlement of the north-eastern boundary with the boundary of Oregon, when, in fact, they are distinct, and were settled by different treaties. The following are the facts relative to the Ashburton treaty of August 9, 1842:

On the conclusion of our War of Independence a treaty was held at Paris, November 30, 1782, when the *Provisional Articles of Peace* were signed, and the boundaries of the new power, so far as our possessions bordered on those of Great Britain, were defined as well as they could be without a more perfect knowledge of the geography of the region through which the line passed, but not "by metes and bounds" that could be understood by all. Therefore, in September, 1783, a second treaty was made and signed at Paris, called the *Definitive Treaty of Paris*, in which his Britannic Majesty acknowledged "the said United States" to be "free, sovereign, and independent States," and that he treated with them as such, relinquishing all claims to the government, and proprietary and territorial rights; and that disputes which might arise in future on the subject of the boundaries of the United States might be prevented, it was agreed and declared that the north-west angle of Nova Scotia should be at a point where a line drawn due north from the source of the St. Croix River should strike the highlands that divide the waters of the rivers falling into the St. Lawrence River and the Atlantic Ocean respectively, and along said highlands to the most north-western head of the Connecticut River; thence down the middle of that river to the forty-fifth degree parallel of latitude; thence due west on that parallel to the St. Lawrence River; thence along the middle of that river to Lake Ontario; and thence along the middle of all the lakes and rivers connecting, to the most north-west point of the Lake of the Woods; and thence on a due west course to the Mississippi River, down which river to the thirty-first degree parallel of north latitude the line extended, where it deflected to the east till it struck the Appalachicola River, and turned south again down that river to its junction with the Flint River, from which junction it turned straight east to the St. Mary's River, and along the middle of that river to the Atlantic Ocean.

So far, with the exception of the error of imagining that the source of the Mississippi was as far north as, and to the west of, the Lake of the Woods, there could be little or no trouble about determining the exact boundaries of the United States in 1783. The remainder of the line was from the point of beginning, at the head-waters of the St. Croix River, down that stream to its mouth in the Bay of Fundy. All the islands within twenty leagues of the shores of the United States, and comprehended between lines projected due east from the northern and southern boundaries already described, were to belong to the United States, excepting such islands as had previously been within the limits of Nova Scotia.

But the boundaries of the United States not being alone the object of the treaty, it was further agreed that the fishermen of our country should continue to enjoy the right, unmolested, to take fish on the Newfoundland Banks, in the Gulf of St. Lawrence, or at any other places in the sea where the people of either country had been accustomed to fish; and to take fish of every kind on such parts of the coast of Newfoundland as British fishermen should use, but not to dry or cure them on the island; and to be allowed to fish in all the bays and creeks of all other parts of the British dominions in America, with the liberty to cure fish in the unsettled bays, harbors, and creeks of Nova Scotia, Magdalen Islands, and Labrador, so long as they should remain unsettled; after which, the privilege should depend upon agreements made with the inhabitants or owners of the ground, which section of the treaty was one of great importance, particularly to the people of New England.

Nearly a dozen of years passed away, and there had been very little more discovered concerning the actual location of our northern line. But meanwhile the commercial marine of the United States was slowly growing in importance. Some small New York and Boston companies were sending vessels to the north-west coast of North America, to Africa, and to China, picking up cargoes in the Pacific to exchange for silks and teas in Canton, etc. One of these adventurous traders, who poked the nose of his vessel into almost every opening north of the forty-sixth parallel, was the first navigator to cross the bar of the Columbia River.

It was not in the nature of the British Government to view these ambitious efforts of the young republic without jealousy, and there arose some commercial questions that required settlement. Accordingly, a treaty was negotiated between John Jay, on the part of the United States, and William Wyndham, on behalf of Great Britain, called *A Treaty of Amity, Commerce, and Navigation*, signed at London, November 19, 1794, a part of which referred to our boundary, as follows:

"ARTICLE 4. Whereas, it is uncertain whether the River Mississippi extends so far to the northward as to be intersected by a line drawn due west from the Lake of the Woods, in the manner mentioned in the treaty of peace between his Majesty and the United States, it is agreed that measures shall be taken in concert between his Majesty's Government in America and the Government of the United States, for making a joint survey of the said river from one degree of latitude below the Falls of St. Anthony to the principal sources of the said river, and also of the parts adjacent thereto; and that, if on the result of such survey it should appear that the said river would not be intersected by such a line as is above mentioned, the two parties will thereupon proceed, by amicable negotiation, to regulate the boundary line in that quarter, as well as all other points to be adjusted between the said parties, according to justice and mutual convenience, and in conformity to the intent of the said treaty.

"ARTICLE 5. Whereas, doubts have arisen what river was truly intended under the name of the River St. Croix, mentioned in the said treaty of peace, and forming a part of the boundary therein described, that question shall be referred to the final decision of Commissioners, to be appointed in the following manner, viz.: One Commissioner shall be named by his Majesty, and one by the President of the United States, by and with the advice and consent of the Senate thereof, and the said two Commissioners shall agree on the choice of a third; or, if they cannot so agree, they shall each propose one person, and of the two names so proposed, one shall be drawn by lot in the same presence of the two original Commissioners," etc.

These Commissioners were to be sworn to make an impartial examination and decision of the question, according to the evidence. They were to decide what river was meant by the St. Croix of the treaty, and to append to their declaration the proofs, and give the particulars of latitude and longitude of its mouth and its source; when the decision made by them should be final. The Commissioners were to meet at Halifax, with the power to adjourn to any other place they might prefer; were to employ surveyors and a secretary, and otherwise to be furnished with every means of settling the question of the identity of the St. Croix River.

At the first glance this might seem an easy enough thing to do. But so it did not prove. The more knowledge the interested parties obtained on the subject the more doubtful they were of the point aimed at. Time passed on, and the United States purchased of France, in

1803, the Louisiana territory west of the Mississippi River, extending indefinitely north-westward, and adding a new feature to our boundary, in which Great Britain was interested. Then followed the war of 1812-14, and the second treaty of peace, signed at Ghent, in the Netherlands, December 24, 1814, by Lord Gambier, Henry Gaulburn, and William Adams, on the part of Great Britain, and John Quincy Adams, James A. Bayard, Henry Clay, Jonathan Russell, and Albert Gallatin, in behalf of the United States, and ratified by the Senate in February, 1815.

The fourth article of the treaty of Ghent referred to the boundary question. It recited that, whereas certain stipulations had been agreed upon by the treaty of 1783, concerning the islands that were to belong to the United States, and whereas the several islands in the Bay of Passamaquoddy, which was part of the Bay of Fundy, and the Island of Menan in the Bay of Fundy, were claimed by the United States, as being within their boundaries, and also claimed by Great Britain, as within the limits of the Province of Nova Scotia, in order to decide the matter two Commissioners shall be appointed, whose decision shall be final and conclusive. In the event of the Commissioners disagreeing, they should make reports, jointly or separately, in detail, of all the evidences and their opinions, and the reports should be submitted to some friendly sovereign or State, who should be requested to decide upon the differences, when the decision should be taken as final.

The fifth article of the treaty of Ghent provided, in the same manner, for ascertaining that point in the highlands lying due north from the source of the St. Croix River, which, according to the treaty of 1783, was to form the north-west angle of Nova Scotia; and also for ascertaining the north-westernmost head of the Connecticut River; and for ascertaining that part of the boundary between the source of the St. Croix and the St. Lawrence Rivers. Commissioners were at the same time provided for, to settle the line through the lakes and rivers from the St. Lawrence to the Lake of the Woods.

The Commissioners appointed to decide upon the proprietorship of the islands in the Bay of Fundy met in New York November 24, 1817, and awarded three islands in the Bay of Passamaquoddy to the United States, leaving the great Menard Island to Great Britain, which award was accepted, and on the 18th of June, 1822, all the islands in the chain of lakes and rivers were apportioned satisfactorily; but that part of the boundary in doubt, between the St. Lawrence and St. Croix Rivers, remained unsettled, though the Commissioners had met a number of times in New York in 1821, and though nearly forty maps had been made by the surveyors. The two points still in doubt were the north-west angle of Nova Scotia and the north-westernmost head of the Connecticut River.

It is not to be supposed that there was any real difficulty about the actual location of these two points. The difficulty was a diplomatic and political one entirely, and, to carry his point, the British Commissioner, acting for the British Government, insisted upon employing in the survey the geocentric method of ascertaining latitude, by which a difference of two miles was made in the location of the forty-fifth parallel, on which an important portion of the boundary depended. On the other side, the United States Commissioner adhered to the ancient survey made in 1774, and to the treaty of 1783, which was drawn up according to a map published in 1775. The two miles gained by the new survey placed Rouse's Point, with the entrance to Lake Champlain and the fortress erected there by the United States, on the British side of the line, which was clearly not the intention of the treaty of 1783.

In the meantime, however, new complications had arisen. The United States had, by acquiring the Louisiana territory, given alarm to Great Britain, who had designs on the north-west coast of North America. Astor, by his effort to establish trade on the Columbia River, had given still further alarm. Great Britain was well aware that the United States had pretensions in that quarter, which they were at some difficulty to maintain, an account of the occupancy of the country by the Hudson's Bay Company, but which, nevertheless, they resolutely asserted on every occasion when the subject was brought forward. In order to secure, if not the whole, a portion at least, of the west coast of America, this British Company pushed their explorations westward, keeping almost an even pace with United States explorers as to time and extent of discoveries. All these movements entered into the boundary question.

Great Britain had taken the position with regard to our rights to the fisheries on the Atlantic Coast, secured to us by the treaty of 1783, that we had forfeited them by the war of 1812, and had expressly refused to renew or recognize them by the treaty of Ghent. But the United States maintained that they were revived by the restoration of peace, and were of the nature of transitory rights in a judicial sense, which, oddly enough, meant a permanent right in the ordinary definition of the term. This matter, requiring settlement, was finally adjusted by the Convention of the 20th of October, 1818, which secured forever to the people of the United States the right to fish on that part of the southern coast of Newfoundland extending from Cape Ray to the Rameau Islands, on the western coast of Newfoundland from Cape Ray to the Quirpon Islands, on the shores of the Magdalen Islands, and on the coasts of Labrador, from Mount Joly to and through the Straits of Belle Isle, and northwardly, with the liberty to cure fish in the unsettled bays and creeks, as before enjoyed under the treaty of 1783, etc.

By this Convention the boundary question was so far settled as that a line drawn along the forty-ninth parallel, from the Lake of the Woods to the "Stony Mountains," was agreed upon as the demarcation between the territory of the United States and that of Great Britain. As to the territory beyond the Stony Mountains, concerning which the two powers held very contrary opinions, that was left for future consideration, and, by the terms of the Convention, was to remain free and open to either nation, without prejudice to the claims of their respective governments, for a period of ten years. No better understanding being arrived at during that period, this Convention was renewed, so far as the north-western boundary was concerned, until its final abrogation, and the treaty of 1846, by which the present limits were definitely fixed.

But to return to the proceedings of the Commissioners appointed to settle the boundary between the St. Lawrence and the sea. Great Britain, having made up her mind to secure every possible advantage, and the United States being equally bent upon not yielding one or two important points, which, according to the original survey could justly be claimed, Mr. Gallatin, writing to Mr. Clay, Secretary of State, in 1827, says:

"The only differences in the two constructions consists in that tract of land of about three hundred thousand acres, lying west of the north line (in the State of Maine), which is drained by the waters falling into the Gulf of St. Lawrence. Both constructions are admissible, and consistent with the spirit of the treaty of 1783, *the letter of which it is impossible to fulfill.*"

The difficulties experienced by the Commissioners arose from the wording of the treaty of 1783, which specified, as a part of the line, the ridge dividing the waters falling into the St. Lawrence from those falling into the Atlantic Ocean. Now, the only way by which an approximate compliance with the intent of the treaty could be arrived at was by assuming that the River St. John emptied into the ocean, though really it fell into the Bay of Fundy. The north line, which was to proceed in a straight course to the highlands before mentioned, crossed the head-waters of rivers running into the Gulf of St. Lawrence, instead of the ocean; and, in short, Mr. Gallatin said, not a single point could be found on the line, that, according to the words of the treaty, was on the highlands dividing the waters of the St. Lawrence from those falling into the Atlantic. The only ridge that would come within the meaning of the treaty was one between the streams that fell into the St. Lawrence River and the Gulf of St. Lawrence, but the treaty said nothing about the gulf. Other questions might arise, on attempting to compromise, with the States of Maine and Massachusetts and the Legislature of New Brunswick.

Not being able to come to any agreement, the Commissioners made their reports accordingly, and, after much careful negotiation, the matter was at length submitted by Mr. Gallatin and the English Commissioners, Charles Grant and Henry Unwin Addington, to William, King of the Netherlands, who on the tenth of January, 1831, made his award. But neither party being satisfied with the result of the arbitration, it was mutually rejected, and the matter relapsed to its former condition of doubt.

In all these years that the boundary question had been unsettled at both ends of the line across the continent, the United States had been growing in importance and strength, and were better able to insist upon terms than at the commencement of the controversy. Realizing this fact, Great Britain, while maintaining friendly relations, was sensitive to, and dissatisfied with, the attitude assumed by our plenipotentiaries regarding our pretensions on the Pacific Coast, avoiding a final issue, and depending upon some happy chance to secure the coveted prize of the Oregon territory.

But neither Government was willing longer to postpone the adjustment of the *north-eastern* boundary, when, in 1842, fifty-eight years after the independence of the United States, Lord Ashburton was sent on a special mission to the United States to prevent a possible war with this country, which was threatened on account of troubles between the two countries, growing out of the boundary question not only, but also out of some affairs of navigation, and the claim to the right of search of American vessels on the coast of Africa, which had long been a bone of contention. So serious were the questions to be considered, and so difficult of arrangement, that it was agreed between Lord Ashburton and Mr. Webster (who, though chosen Secretary of State by General Harrison, had been solicited to remain in the Cabinet under Mr. Tyler, and did so remain for one year after the other members had resigned) not to take up that of the Oregon boundary, but to be content if they were able to dispose of the others.

By these two diplomates, who were previously on friendly terms (Lord Ashburton having been in the United States, and Mr. Webster in England), the north-eastern boundary of the United States was finally settled by a treaty known as the Ashburton treaty, concluded August 9, 1842.

As is usually the case after a controversy so long continued, the critics on both sides were dissatisfied. In England the opposition party named the treaty the "Ashburton capitulation," while in the United States Mr. Webster was assailed for conceding anything in dispute. Those who knew the difficulties in the way of a perfectly satisfactory statement were pleased to accept the arrangement. The English Parliament, in both houses, thanked Lord Ashburton, and certainly Mr. Webster's part in the Ashburton treaty has been considered highly creditable to him.

That a private citizen like Dr. Whitman should have had any influence in determining questions that had baffled the skill of the greatest diplomatists for over half a century, is not susceptible of belief. He could say nothing they did not already know; and as to the folly said to have been contemplated by Mr. Webster, of "trading off Oregon for a cod-fishery," it will be seen by the treaties quoted, that the fishery question had been settled, as it was supposed, "forever," by the convention of 1818. It was, however, brought up again in 1852, after the Oregon boundary was settled, in order to force the United States into a reciprocity treaty with the British Provinces, when the United States secured greater privileges on the fishing grounds than they had before enjoyed; but which it is now said they are again in danger of losing.

So much for the origin and purpose of the Ashburton treaty. But there still remains the romantic, though unfortunately foundationless, story of Dr. Whitman's visit to Washington with a *political* purpose. Dr. Whitman left the Cayuse country on business connected with his mission early in October, 1842, and performed a tedious and remarkable winter journey to the States. The treaty he is said to have influenced was signed before he left Oregon, and he arrived at his destination in the following spring, after Lord Ashburton had returned to England, and about the time Mr. Webster retired from the Cabinet of President Tyler. He may have seen the great statesman, and may have given him his opinion of the Oregon country; but his doing so could not affect a treaty that was already made, nor one that was to be made, several years after, by different plenipotentiaries. Both Great Britain and the United States knew the value of the Oregon territory, and that was why it was so difficult for them to come to a settlement. Immediately after the Ashburton treaty, the negotiations concerning the "Oregon Question" were transferred to London, and there remained until 1844, when they were retransferred to Washington. Polk, who was a candidate for the Presidency, made the Oregon boundary the principal issue on which he was elected. It was Polk who set going the cry of "Fifty-four forty or fight," so popular at one time. Nevertheless, he very cheerfully signed the Oregon treaty of June 15, 1846, which made the forty-ninth parallel the northern boundary of the United States, west as well as east of the Rocky Mountains. As in the case of the Ashburton treaty, both governments were glad to be well rid of the controversy without a war. Perhaps no similar question was ever clothed with the real romance that has clung to and colored the Oregon Question. It less needs the adventitious aids of invention than any modern history. There was a good deal of the old adventurous and hardy spirit of the Spanish colonists of America in the deeds and discoveries of the rival nations contending for possession. That Dr. Whitman was, while "a soldier of the cross," equally fit to have been a soldier of the sword, there is no doubt. He was a valiant and true man, and would have scorned to claim for himself honors which he had never won. It, therefore, is no kindness to his memory to place him in a false position, from which the reader of encyclopædias could easily rout him. The author of "How Dr. Whitman Saved Oregon," is only one of a number who have given credence to this well-invented historical romance, without taking the trouble to look up his authorities. He is too good a writer to be so careless of his facts, and too sensible a gentleman not to be glad of being set right.

Mrs. F. F. Victor.

EARLY DISCOVERIES OF THE HAWAIIAN ISLANDS.

To the people of California the Hawaiian Islands have an especial interest, and the future relations of this charming group are likely to prove of great national import to residents of this entire continent. In geographical location they occupy a direct navigable line between the Pacific States of the American Union and the British colonies of Australia and New Zealand, as well as the rich and populous countries of Asia. Their natural position is a strong strategical point, highly important to the United States of America in the event of foreign war.

To the Christian philanthropist they have presented an interesting field during the labors of earnest American missionaries, sent out in 1819 by the American Board of Commissioners for Foreign Missions, and since maintained for over sixty years by expenditures exceeding one million of dollars, cheerfully contributed in the cause of human advancement. The success which has resulted from this national expression of Christian enterprise is known to all the world. The Hawaiian people are indebted to the American missionaries and American residents at their islands for their present advanced condition in general civilization, christian knowledge, constitutional government, wise and just laws, and even for the preservation of their national independence when formerly assailed by both France and England.

To the scientist they present many highly instructive natural records in the evolutionary history of the earth we inhabit, and their race and language offers an interesting ethnological problem. Many ancient records and prehistoric traditions, unless now carefully noted with a view of perpetuating testimony, will soon pass beyond the reach of future historians.

The beautiful and fertile group of tropical islands composing the Hawaiian Kingdom is situated in the North Pacific Ocean, between above the ocean level. When speaking the above names, each vowel is pronounced as one syllable, and the broad accent of European continental languages is given. British geographers formerly spelled these names phonetically, employing vowels as pronounced in English, which accounts for an apparent confusion when written by them—Owhyhee, Mowee, Woahoo, Atooi, etc.

By whom were these islands first discovered? The celebrated English navigator, Captain James Cook, visited them in 1778, and by him they were given the foreign name of Sandwich Islands, in honor of his patron, the Earl of Sandwich, at that time *First Lord of the British Admiralty.*

The honor and credit of having been the first European to discover this group of islands has hitherto been popularly accorded to Captain Cook. But it is now well known that the fact of their existence was ascertained by Spanish navigators more than two centuries before Cook saw them, and that knowledge carefully concealed from all other people by the Spanish Government, whose jealous and national policy was to selfishly prevent Spanish explorations and discoveries in the Pacific Ocean from becoming generally known. In the history of Captain Cook's third and last voyage it is related that the ships of his expedition, on leaving Christmas Island, steered to the north and westward, and on the 18th of January, 1778, at day-break, they first sighted one island, and, soon after, another. The first land-fall subsequently proved to be the island of Oahu, and the second, Kauai, both portions of the Hawaiian group.

Captain Cook anchored his ships in the Bay of Waimea, on the south side of the island of Kauai, and at that place his free and amicable communication with the natives first com-

may have drifted to Hawaii. Helmets, resembling in form those of ancient Romans, and feather cloaks, similar in shape to those worn in Europe in the seventeenth century, were also seen among the natives. Both articles, as it is now believed, were rude copies of some similar ones originally introduced among the islanders by shipwrecked Spaniards. No iron of any kind exists in the soil or rocks of these islands, and such pieces of iron, with a knowledge of their use, could only have come from some kind of foreign intercourse with a nation of civilized artisans.

From Kauai and Niihau, Captain Cook sailed for the north-west coast of America; and on his return from thence, in November, 1778, he discovered the islands of Maui, Hawaii, and other islands of the group. Captain Cook was killed by the natives on Sunday, February 14, 1779, at Kealakeakua Bay, on the island of Hawaii. He remarks in his journal as follows:

> "Had the Sandwich Islands been discovered at an early period by the Spaniards, there is little doubt they would have made use of them as a refreshing place for the ships that sail annually from Acapulco to Manila, and also by the English buccaneers, who used sometimes to pass from America to the Ladrone Islands."

Now, it is singular, and almost incredible, that Captain Cook should have had no knowledge of the existence of the Hawaiian group anterior to actually seeing them himself.

For twenty-eight years before Cook sailed from England on his last voyage of discovery, there had existed a work entitled "The History of Lord Anson's Voyage around the World, during the years 1741 to 1744. Edited by Richard Walter, Chaplain of H. M. Ship *Centurion*. Published in London. 1748." A copy of the first edition of the book is now to be seen in the Mercantile Library of San Francisco, California.

The *Centurion*, under Anson, sailed northerly along the west coasts of South America and Mexico, and on the way up captured several Spanish towns and merchant vessels; but being unsuccessful in meeting off Acapulco the Spanish galleon periodically sailing for Manila, the *Centurion* thence crossed the Pacific Ocean to Macao, in China; and from Macao she sailed to cruise off Cape Espiritu Sancto, Philippine Islands, where, in June, 1743, she fell in with the Spanish galleon, then *en route* from Acapulco to Manila; and, after a bloody engagement, Anson succeeded in capturing her, with the usual treasure and goods on board, to the value of over two millions of dollars. Several drafts and journals were also taken with the galleon, and thus came into possession of the British government as early as 1744. With them was a manuscript chart, drawn for the use of the Spanish General and Pilot-Major of the vessel. This chart contained all the discoveries which had, at any time, been made in the navigation between the Philippine Islands and New Spain, or Mexico; an engraved copy of which is given in the account of Lord Anson's voyage, inserted between pages 94 and 95, Book I., published in London thirty years before Cook's visit. The situations in the eastern part of the chart are, however, laid down ten degrees of longitude too far east, while the western part of the same is correct in its longitudes. To account for this singular error, it is conjectured that the galleon's chart above referred to was in two or more separate parts, as was generally the case with early Spanish charts of the wide Pacific Ocean; and that the English editor, or engraver, in joining them, mistook the divisions, by including a margin of ten degrees at the point of contact in mid-ocean.

In the galleon-Anson chart, we find delineated the following islands, with their Spanish names, previously given them by Spanish discoverers, laid down absolutely correct in latitude, and also in longitude if the ten-degree error above alluded to is allowed. These islands comprise a part of the Hawaiian group, and are truly described. No other land exists for ten, or even for fifty, degrees due east of them; neither is there any land to the west, in the same latitude, for a still greater distance. The islands are there named:

La Mesa, or the Table. The name is accurately descriptive of the island of Hawaii, with its high table land.

Las Desgraciado, or the Unfortunate. Probably so named by Spaniards, who may have visited the island and had some fatal encounter with its inhabitants. This island, called Mowee by Cook, is spelled Maui by the natives.

Los Monges, or the Monks. Three islands, lying near each other. Their native names are Molokai, Lanai, and Kekahelaua.

The islands of Woahoo and Atooi of Cook do not appear on this galleon's chart, but in some old Spanish charts they are laid down approximately correct. A table of situations, printed in Manila in 1734, by Cabrera Bueno, Admiral and Pilot-Major in the navigation between the Philippine Islands and Mexico, and published forty-three years before Cook's first visit and discovery, gives the positions of the Hawaiian Islands very nearly correct.

Spanish navigators in the Pacific were accustomed to reckon their longitude from the meridian of the Embocadero of San Bernardino, one of the Philippine Islands; thence counting and running eastward to the coast of Mexico, called by them New Spain.

It has been asserted by the Spanish authorities of Manila, that in the archives of the government at Madrid are to be found original charts of Spanish discoveries in the Pacific Ocean, made during the sixteenth and seventeenth centuries. And they show that "Gaetano," a Spaniard, discovered several of the Hawaiian group of islands, as early as the year 1542; and that "Mendana," another of Spain's navigators, discovered Kauai, the most western island of the same group, in 1567, or 235 and 210 years respectively before Cook's first visit.

In three maps, accompanying the geographical work of Charles T. Middleton, published in London in 1777, the year following that in which Captain Cook sailed on his last voyage, and during which he first saw the Hawaiian Islands, their Spanish names are given, and the group is laid down approximately correct in situation. This proves conclusively that the knowledge of them existed in England before any news of their discovery was received from Captain Cook's exploring expedition.

"Honest Bernal Diaz," in his "True History of the Conquest of Mexico," written in 1568, says:

"While Marcos de Aguilar had the government of New Spain, the Marquis de Valle (Cortez) fitted out four ships at Zacatula. The squadron was commanded by Alvarado de Saavedra, who, with two hundred and fifty soldiers, took his course for the Moluccas, Spice Islands, and China. He set sail in December, 1527 or 1528, and sustained many losses, misfortunes, and hardships on the way to the Moluccas Islands. I do not know the definite particulars; but three years afterward I met with a sailor who had been on board of this fleet, and who had told me of many strange and surprising things of the citizens and nations he had visited during his voyage."

From other sources we learn that but one of the four ships of the squadron above referred to reached her destination. The other three were lost on the way. Bernal Diaz further relates that

—"In the month of May, 1532, Cortez sent two ships from the port of Acapulco to make discoveries in the South Seas. They were commanded by Captain Diego Hurtado de Mendoza, who had the misfortune of a mutiny among the troops. In consequence thereof, one ship, of which the mutineers took possession, returned to New Spain, to the great disappointment of Cortez. As for Hurtado, neither he nor his vessel was ever heard of again."

To throw some light upon the probable fate of the missing ships referred to by Bernal Diaz, some traditions of the people of the Hawaiian Islands are herewith presented. Of these, the writer acquired reliable knowledge during his twenty-two years residence at these islands, which first began in 1825. They relate that, in ancient times, two foreign vessels were wrecked on the island of Hawaii (Owhyhee of Captain Cook), one on the south-west side, at Keei, near the Bay of Kealakeakua, not far from the place where Captain Cook was long afterward killed; and the other, on the east side at Kau, district of Puna. These events occurred during the reign of Kealiiokaloa, King of Hawaii. He was the thirteenth sovereign, anterior to the reign of Kamehameha I., who came upon the throne in 1792. If twenty years is reckoned as the average duration of life for each of these thirteen kings, we have an aggregate of two hundred and sixty years, which, deducted from 1792, gives the year 1532 as the approximate time of King Kealiiokaloa's reign, and also about fixes the date of the wreck of the two ships.

Therefore, it is highly probable that those vessels were some of the missing ones of the respective expeditions fitted out by Cortez in 1527 and 1532, for European vessels on the Pacific Ocean were comparatively few in those days.

Upon the island of Hawaii there is to be found at the present time a mixed race of people, whose ancient family traditions point with pride to some foreign origin. They are said to be the descendents of shipwrecked Spaniards, and the careful scrutiny of expert scientists tends to confirm this native tradition. They have sandy colored hair, and are of lighter complexion than the native Hawaiian race, who call them "ehus"—possibly a corruption of the Spanish word *hijos*. The Hawaiian language contains several words of unmistakable Spanish derivation. Other traces are perceptible in some of their customs and inherited ideas.

Another tradition is, that during the same king's reign (Kealiiokaloa) a boat came to Hawaii from *abroad*—that is, "from Tahiti or foreign parts," as expressed by the natives—in which was a foreigner of rank and importance. He remained there many years, and acquired great influence over the Hawaiians, by whom he was much beloved and regarded as a very high chief. He took for wife a native princess, and by her had posterity. After the lapse of several years he built a boat, and then embarked in her with all his family, and sailed for a foreign country, previously, however, giving a promise to return to Hawaii at some future time. It is conjectured that this important person may have been Captain Diego Hurtado de Mendoza, commander of the expedition fitted out by Cortez in 1532, and which Bernal Diaz, the historian, says was never again heard of after the mutiny on board of his ship, and the return of his other vessel to New Spain. This interesting foreigner, be he whom he may, was called by the natives *Olono;* and in process of time divine honors were accorded to his memory. When Captain Cook visited the island of Hawaii in 1778, he was believed to be the *Olono* of Hawaiian tradition, their ancient god, who had returned; and to Cook, it is well known, the natives paid divine honors—for receiving which that navigator has been highly censured by the Christian world. The discovery that he was really a mortal, when the natives witnessed his suffering by reason of a wound, was the immediate cause of their putting him to death.

Hawaiian traditions further testify to the fact, that during very remote times many boats or vessels, with white men in them, have, at long intervals, visited these islands. The crew of one such, it is said, remained permanently, and intermarried with native Hawaiians. In 1740 the King of Oahu, while in a canoe going thence to the island of Maui, saw a foreign ship at sea.

Many years elapsed after Cook's visit before Europeans again visited these islands. The celebrated French navigator, La Perouse, touched at them in 1786, as also did Portlock and Dixon, in the same year, with the British ships *King George* and *Queen Charlotte.* Captain Mears followed them in the ship *Nootka* in 1788. The ship *Eleanor,* of Boston, in 1790, was the first American vessel that visited the Hawaiian Islands; followed, subsequently, by several other vessels of that nationality, all of which were engaged in the lucrative fur trade of the northwest coast of America. In 1794, the American schooners *Jackall* and *Fair American* discovered, and were the first to anchor, in the harbor of Honolulu. Both vessels were captured by the natives, who massacred the principal part of their crews.

The American brig *Lady Washington,* Captain Kendrick, and the British ship *Butterworth,* of London, were at anchor in Honolulu harbor, July 4, 1794. During salutes being given by both vessels, in commemoration of American Independence, Captain Kendrick was struck by a hard wad fired from a gun of the *Butterworth,* and instantly killed.

In 1792, the islands were visited by Captain George Vancouver, commanding the British surveying vessels *Discovery* and *Chatham.* They introduced cattle and sheep, brought for the purpose from Monterey, California. Horses were first landed at the Hawaiian Islands by Captain Cleveland, in 1810, while in command of a Boston ship.

La Perouse, in the journal of his voyage, volume i., page 344, remarks, in regard to these islands:

"Their knowledge of iron, which they did not acquire from the English, is new proof of the communications which these islands formerly had with the Spaniards. It appears certain that these islands were discovered for the first time by Gaetan in 1542. This navigator sailed from Port Nativity, west coast of Mexico, latitude twenty degrees north. He stood to the westward, and having run nine hundred leagues in that direction, he fell in with a group of islands, inhabited by savages almost naked. The islands were surrounded by coral reefs. They afforded cocoanuts and other fruits, but neither gold nor silver. He named them King's Islands; and another island which he discovered, twenty leagues farther westward (probably the island now known as Kauai) he called Garden Island. It would have been impossible for geographers to have avoided placing the discoveries of Gaetan precisely where Cook has since found the (so-called) Sandwich Islands, if the Spanish editor had not said that those islands were situated between 9° and 11° of north latitude, instead of 19° and 21°, as every navigator would have concluded from the course of Gaetan. The omission of ten degrees may be a mistake in figures, or a political stroke of the Spaniards, who had a great interest a century ago to conceal all the islands of this ocean."

As a result of this carefully considered inquiry, directed to determine what European first discovered and landed upon the Hawaiian Islands, within the limited period accessible to existing traditional or historic testimony, it now appears that a British man-of-war, came, by capture, into possession of Spanish charts of the North Pacific Ocean, whereon their location was correctly laid down, at a time full thirty years before Cook's first visit, which may reasonably give rise to at least a possible inference that, before Captain Cook's departure from England, in 1777, some vague intimation of their probable existence and approximate situation may have directed his search to that particular spot.

The most interesting fact disclosed, however, is that they were sighted by Spanish navigators during the sixteenth and seventeenth centuries, probably as early as 1542; and to them is due the circumstance of their first discovery by any European nation.

HENRY A. PEIRCE.

IN A NEW ENGLAND GRAVEYARD.

Beside these crumbling stones—where saints of old
 Were laid to rest two hundred years ago,
 And where the quaint, still village, nestled low,
Lives gently 'mid its elms, and seems to hold
In thought the warning o'er this archway told,
 "*Memento mori*"—where the feet have trod
 Of later saints, akin to these in blood—
I think of *their* rest by the mart of gold,
The wild-pulsed city that the sea-winds beat,
 Where, on its bare, round hill uplifted high,
Far-seen from beating seas and eager street,
 Watching the graves where alien thousands lie,
A stark, lone cross—the dead about its feet—
 Lifts its white protest to the windy sky.

MILICENT W. SHINN.

OF WHAT WAS THE OLD MAN THINKING?

Alexis Steinhardt came from Germany when our republic was in its infancy. He had education and fortune—youth, too, and a certain degree of comeliness perhaps. He was making the grand tour of the world, as the finishing touch to the first chapter of his career. Those who knew him best believed him to be an undeveloped Goethe, and prophesied great things of him. In New Jersey he stopped at a farmhouse one night, and met his fate in the person of a young girl scarcely fifteen. She must have been remarkably beautiful at that age, if we are to credit the extravagant accounts of her loveliness still current in the present generation. I have her picture, taken at the age of ninety-three, and she was fine looking even then. No doubt her young husband was mightily pleased with his fair wife at that time. Keats says, "A thing of beauty is a joy forever." But that which was beautiful to my undeveloped taste a year ago is not so now. And who is to fix the standard of beauty, when we are so far away from its Divine Source, and when each day that carries us nearer flings doubts upon the previous day.

When Alexis Steinhardt married Elizabeth Ivan she seemed the realization of all his earthly hopes, the fulfillment of his life. He did not know how few of his hopes were earthly, nor how immeasurable the life he thought one frail being could fill. As time wore on her beauty ceased to surprise and delight him; her good qualities became an accepted fact. A fact once accepted claims no further attention. The "incessant soul" cannot stop to play watch-dog beside it; it goes on. He knew he had a good wife; he also knew (and for her own sake was glad to know) that she was adapted to the world she lived in. There was a constant ripple upon her surface, and her condition and surroundings sufficed her. In this respect she was widely apart from him. He could not confine his thoughts to the small duties that made the sum total of her existence. Not that he held them contemptuously; on the contrary, he was always ready to assist, but his heart was not in his hands for such a purpose. Of course, she soon discovered this, and laughed at his awkwardness, and went on loving and venerating him more and more.

In his youth he had been a brilliant and enthusiastic talker; as he grew older he became almost altogether silent. There was no suspicion of moroseness in his quiet demeanor, but an air of settled sadness. He had read once that Love, such as we poor mortals dream of, is an inhabitant of the skies, the fair being fluttering always above us to lure us up higher, and that the image we clasp in this world is but her projected shadow. His experience and observation were confirming him in many things he had read and seen unnoticed at the time. His travels had taught him that every phase of life is unhappy; that men in the mass are swamped in their own depravity. His great humanity stood in despair before this unalterable fact. He seemed to comprehend and feel the sorrows of the race almost as a God. His early dream of fame was gone. What cared he to scramble on to a pedestal, and call upon the multitude to applaud. Wealth had no allurement. Once he had desired money, that he might give; but presently he knew that nothing pauperizes a man, body and soul, like giving him that which he should create. Fictitious wealth is an impediment barring further progress. Wealth to be genuine must be wrought by its possessor—must be the outcome of the man. But then he saw the bar placed upon men, saw that the mass of them were enslaved, that no wealth producing genie could work through their hands until they should awake to a sense of their condition. Therefore, he smiled at the efforts of reformers, and knew he must wait the slow development of the centuries.

In the course of a few years he spent his inherited estate, and, by the advice of his wife's family, he went to Illinois, then almost a wilderness, where he preëmpted land. Their neighbors were few, and of the most primitive character. But this was nothing to him. He loved those rough-handed frontiersman and their honest wives better than any people he had ever met; not that he betrayed any affection, for he seldom even spoke to them. If he met them as he walked about with his hands behind him and his head down, he rarely lifted his eyes from the ground, and the nod he gave in passing was in gratitude for their friendly greeting, and not a personal recognition. And yet these people loved him, and felt a respect and veneration for him quite inexplicable to themselves. In these days he worked hard (and to little purpose) on his farm. He was subject to violent and prostrating headaches, and an hour's exposure to the sun would bring one on him. He bore it without complaint, and strove to work in defiance of it. This hurt his tender-hearted wife. She could not bear to see him in the field following the plow or harvesting the grain, with his cheeks blanched and his eyes filmy with pain. So she cast about in her mind for some other way of making a living.

Their farm lay along a large stream—one of the tributaries to the Mississippi. A few steamboats plied between New Orleans and St. Louis, then a town of about ten thousand inhabitants. Elizabeth Ivan came of a race of merchants. If she could only get some goods, and establish a store—this was her one thought. There was no store in that part of the State. Scarcely an article of imported goods ever found its way there. The women spun and wove wool and flax, and made all the household wear for their families. Two great difficulties faced her on the outset. She had no money to purchase her first stock, and, again, there was no money in the country to take in exchange. Insuperable as these barriers seemed, the feeling she had for her husband never for a moment permitted her to despair. Many a night she laid wide awake, with her face turned to him as he slept, listening to his quiet breathing, seeing by the light in her heart every line of his careworn features, feeling an intensity of desire to help him that she knew must eventually succeed, and that did succeed in time. They had a pair of horses and a wagon, the same that had brought them from New Jersey. She took these and her eldest boy, a lad of twelve, and started on a pilgrimage among her neighbors. She told them her plan. She wanted all the produce not used in their families, such as hides, tallow, lard, bacon, butter, eggs, wool, and flax. They were willing to let her have it. No doubt rascals were scarce in those times; at any rate, they trusted her fearlessly. She gathered up many loads of such articles as she knew to be convertible, and stored them in her house and barn until the day came when all her neighbors were to meet by appointment to aid in the construction of a raft. They were at "the Dutchman's" house a little after sunrise, and ready to begin. They felled logs, and built the "flatboat," as it was called, after which they stowed the goods upon it to the best advantage. Certain of the number then volunteered to go to New Orleans on this improvised boat with Mr. Steinhardt. They made the trip in safety, and brought back, by steamer, calicoes and other cloths, and groceries. This was the foundation on which a large fortune was built. Mrs. Steinhardt and her sons were salesmen and business managers. For a few years the profits were small and the work considerable, but, as people flocked into the State, and the land became appropriated, a town grew up and money flowed in. The old log house yielded its place to something far better and more elegant, and beautiful gardens were laid out.

All this time Mr. Steinhardt had been growing quieter. Of what was the old man thinking? He was not a reader, and what food for thought he may have had no one knew. He wandered about the house with his hands behind him, his intellectual face turned downward. When he raised it it startled one; it was as if a disembodied spirit had shape. Every one spoke of him as the "old man" now, though he was still young. His transparent body covered his spirit so thinly he created the impression of being near his grave. His life seemed adverse to his soul development. The winged Psyche began to show its iridescent colors through its thin shell long before it was permitted to go forth. Often as he walked about he would sing to himself in some foreign language (he spoke many), and we children would listen with absorbed interest to the unintelligible monody. It was about the time he was released from out-door occupation by the business capacity of his wife and sons, and before they were making anything but a bare living, that he *made himself a piano*—made every part of it out of such material as his circumstances and the neighborhood would command. It was a small instrument of only six octaves, perfect in all its parts, and of excellent tone. The case was of curly maple, polished like a mirror, and very beautiful. This piano was, perhaps, for twenty years the only one in Illinois, for the city of Chicago was not yet born, and the soil above the Galena mines was unbroken. People came thirty miles to see this "music box," and hear him play it.

Time wore on, and the frail man lived years and years longer than any one knowing him could have believed. Some of his sons married, branch business houses were established in different parts of the State. His daughters were educated in St. Louis, and made good marriages. The old man and his wife—now, alas, beginning to show the effect of the years—were almost alone in the house, when a visitor came to them, came to remain. Their youngest daughter was dead, and had bequeathed her only child to them. This pretty little creature, named Madeline, seemed to brighten Mrs. Steinhardt's life, and console her for the loss of her daughter. But her presence was an invasion to the old man. He had forgotten the ways of babies. Her inconsistencies astonished and unsettled him, her cries startled and annoyed him. He was nervous and anxious when in the same room with her—weaknesses the young lady soon discovered and treated with great indifference at first, but afterward with more consideration. The silent power of spirit over flesh asserted itself in time, and the little one began to love and reverence him; and many were the little arts she used in order to win his affection. His silence was a perpetual stumbling block to her; in vain she tried to lure him into conversation. Once or twice she climbed on his knees, and insisted on a game of "boo-heady;" she showed him her "itty toes," and invited him to play "piggy went to market." But nothing tempted him to an intimate acquaintance. Once the child was sick, and, as she recovered, her little face assumed, for a few days, a grave, melancholy apppearance; then he chanced to notice her, and spoke to his wife.

"Leezapet, tell me, who dot shild look like."

"Why, father," she said, stopping to think, "I do really believe she looks like you."

"Oh, Leezapet, she looks yust te ferry image of mine tear sister Regina. Mine shweet sister vot's peen in heaven dese vorty years. Mine Cot, Leezabet, dot shild must pe named Regina. Regina means somedings. Madeline is a voolish name."

And so her name was changed; but after this he took no more notice of her than before.

One day she stood by him looking at him with all her wistful soul in her blue forget-me-not eyes. It was evident she intended to come to an understanding with him—to compel an explanation. At last, with a dignity and repose that might command the respect of kings, she asked:

"Dappa, why don't oo ove Wegina?"

"You cry too much," he said.

A short time after this brief conversation Regina sustained a great loss. She left her beautiful wax doll sitting by the fire, and when she returned its face was terrible to behold. All its rosy flesh was running off in tears from its chin, and its appearance was ghastly in the extreme. When she saw it she uttered scream after scream, until her grandfather came into the room. Her cries, so shrill and ear-splitting, alarmed and vexed him. Any discordant noise set him trembling and angry; it was part of his misfortune that his hearing was too acute. When Regina saw him she stifled her cries instantly, with an effort so evidently painful the old man's heart stood still as he looked at her. Her little breast was heaving pitifully, and her face was agony itself. He went to her then and carried her out in his arms, striving to divert her mind from her doll, no difficult task for him. After that it became her habit to grieve over her losses silently; she cried aloud no more. And, presently, her grandfather became more dissatisfied with this expression of grief than with her previous noises. An awful look would come to his eyes to see her grieving silently, and once he told her to cry out loud, to scream and stamp, and be naughty like other children. It was evident he feared she would be like him, and for her own sake he hoped not.

Slowly the child grew in the old man's heart, but there were few evidences she received of it. He was still quiet, restless, and abstracted, wandering about all day and many hours of the night through the house, and garden, and deserted streets. What his secret thoughts were in all these years, who can tell? In the twilight the piano was opened and he played for hours at a time; not from printed music, but from his own mind and heart. He made the instrument express every passion and emotion. No doubt, to those who could understand, the mystery of his silence was revealed. Thoughts, beyond his power to clothe in the coarse garb of language, winged from his brain, draped in the gleaming tissue of subtle, enchanting sound. The little children of the village used to steal under his open window on the outside, and listen absorbed and noiseless. Sitting there, hand in hand, sometimes weeping from the irresistible pathos of the tune; sometimes glad, jubilant, glorious, careering heavenward on limitless waves of melody, we would sit while the evening dew fell damp and chill, and hear the old man interpret, not only his, but our own souls to us. We were in the budding period of life; we knew nothing of the obstructions that beset men and women on every side, that cripple their aspirations and crucify their faith. The condensing process of the years had not hardened our young bodies into prison houses for our spirits, and so we roamed free as air through worlds of enchantment, wherever the old man's tuneful fingers chose to lead. Our nursery tales grew upon our imaginations; they took form and substance. Aladdin's lamp led us through caves and aisles, sparkling with gold and jewels. We saw the fabled fountain whose spray was diamonds. The dark-eyed prince stepped out of the fairy tale with offers of love and constancy: "Half of my jeweled throne be thine forever."

But as we followed this impassioned guidance, our path zigzagged through hell as well as heaven. How often, in later years, have I tried to imitate him in such of his musical improvisations as were not too ethereal to bear "a local habitation and a name." How often have I tried to extract from the base notes the dull, hopeless, resonant wail of the ocean, as I have seen him do, while with his treble hand he wove a mist of dewy and gleaming sound, so tender, so bright, and peaceful, that, while it harmonized with the other part, it had the effect of rendering its despair doubly despairing. Even now it brings to my mind the picture of a foundering vessel, wave begirt, and the moon, careless in her proud beauty, trailing her robes through white billows of breaking cloud, above the waves and the doomed ship, like Fate, untouched by the suffering of this sad world.

As Regina grew larger a strange friendship sprang up between her and the old man. She would walk by his side for hours, never exchanging a word with him. But often when she was not with him he glanced around as if he missed her. She little imagined the hold she was getting in his heart. When she was about twelve years old her father came to see her, bringing his second wife with him. He had been married to this lady several years, but they had no children. As they saw more of the pretty Regina, they desired very much to take her to live with them. It hurt Mrs. Steinhardt to give her up, but she acknowledged her father's right. No one thought of consulting the old man, and he did not dream of losing his darling until the evening before her departure. Then his pale face turned deathly.

"Vat! Take mine leedle cal?" he said.

They went into lengthy explanations. He did not seem to hear them. Presently he went into the garden, as usual, and commenced his monotonous walk; but now his head was raised, and his wonderful eyes were fixed above.

The next morning Regina's father asked him if he was unwilling to part with her.

He shook his head.

"Take her avay. Dat is as it should pe. Let her pe clad unt young. Eart to eart, unt dust to dust."

The rest of the story is soon told. What was left of the old man's life seemed a lingering death. He never touched the piano again. He never mentioned the child's name. Her very memory appeared to have dropped away from him. In his walks, now gradually ceasing, his face was always turned upward. It was just three years after Regina went away that he lay on his death-bed. As he opened his eyes for the last time, and saw the one true and faithful friend of his life bending over him, he said:

"Leezapet, I voult ave died long dimes ago, put you held me. Alvays you vos coot, Leezapet. I voult stay mit you longer, put my pody is vorn oud. Vare ish ter leedle Regina?"

Regina was far away, at a fashionable boarding-school; and when he knew he would see her no more, he wept the first tears his wife had ever seen him shed.

And how did Regina feel when she learned the particulars?

O Youth! O Age! the *world* lies between you two.

Regina was taking her music lesson the next morning after the tidings reached her. Her dimpled hands trembled a little on the keys. Let us hope she had given a few tears to the old man's memory, even though all trace of them had vanished from her fair face in a single night. Madame Dupau observed that she seemed nervous.

"Oh, yes," she said. "I had unpleasant news from home. My grandfather is dead."

There was something like a sob in her voice, and Madame prepared herself to commiserate; but Regina went on:

"He was the queerest old man you ever saw. He looked just this way," puckering her pretty face all into wrinkles, and assuming the expression of an old, forlorn monkey.

Whereupon Madame laughed heartily, and Regina went on with her exercise.

HELEN WILMANS.

A MODERN AUTHOR.—"OUIDA."

The fact that every writer possesses a limited capacity, beyond which it is folly to endeavor to go, is one which has been demonstrated too often to admit of dispute. Bulwer, to be sure, wrote thirty-six novels, and retained to the last the power to enchain the interest, as well as to compel admiration for the beauty of his style. Nevertheless, his later works lacked the vigor of his earlier. Scott produced but nineteen novels, besides his poems, which were worthy of his name and fame. He wrote thereafter for so much per page, and every line shows the effort, thereby marring the beauty of his first books by the mediocrity of the last. Among our more recent authors, Mrs. Alexander contributed to the "Leisure Hour Series" five remarkable novels. We have read her sixth, and we sincerely hope that, for her own sake, she will be content to rest upon her laurels and not attempt a seventh.

"Ouida" is no exception to the general rule. Some years ago she set the world of light literature on fire by a number of rapidly issued novels. These, whatever may have been their numerous other faults, were eagerly welcomed by the great number of fiction readers as works possessing a certain feverish interest, and great finish and beauty of style. During the first six productions she fully sustained her reputation, but, upon the appearance of her seventh, plainly proved that she was a waning light. She evidently perceived the fact herself, for she thereafter adopted a new plan. Her next six novels were metaphysical productions—five hundred insupportably monotonous pages of reflections, dissertations, and descriptions of scenery, with the merest thread of a story to hold them together. Her books may be classified into three distinct series. *Granville de Vigne*, *Strathmore*, *Chandos*, *Idalia*, *Under Two Flags*, *Puck*, and her shorter stories, comprise the first and only series which can claim the merit of being interesting. After a lapse of some time she produced *Folle Farine*, *Tricotrin*, *Pascarel*, *Beble*, *Signa*, *In a Winter City*, and *Ariadne*. Although *In a Winter City* was issued before *Ariadne*, it properly belongs to the third and last series. In the latter, besides the last mentioned book, she has, as yet, favored us with but two productions—*Friendship* and *Moths*—and we devoutly hope that our patience will not be put to further proof. Had "Ouida" been satisfied with the fame which was hers when she finished *Puck*, her reputation in the world of light fiction would have been far superior to what it is now. Had she then been content to retire into obscurity she might have been able to impress her admirers with the belief that she did so from choice. And, had any one been so uncharitable as to suggest that she had "written herself out," there would, at least, have been no proof.

The novels of the first series are characterized by sustained interest, beauty of composition, and a peculiar descriptive talent. But they possess so many points in common that had each been published under a different *nom de plume* there could have been no hesitation in attributing their authorship to the same source. The first heroine, for instance, is invariably a wonderful beauty, in a voluptuous, dashing style—usually a "*blonde aux yeux noirs;*" is, with the exception of *Puck's* first heroine, a thorough woman of the world, an unprincipled coquette, and is possessed of all the frailties which "Ouida" is so inexorable in attributing to fashionable women of the upper ten thousand. The second heroine appears upon the scene some twenty or twenty-five years later, when her wicked predecessor has sunk into oblivion, her charms faded, and her fascinations a dream of the past. Now we have, with never an exception, the orthodox blonde of angelic type, whose innocence amounts to puerility, and who is childish in an insupportable degree. Writers who are the reverse of innocent themselves, in attempting to portray the innocent character, are apt to let their imaginations run away with them, and to produce something the reverse of natural—the very excess of exaggeration. On the other hand, in delineating the character of the unprincipled heroines, they are not so apt to overdo the matter, being more at home in the subject.

"Ouida's" men of this series are imitations of Bulwer's earlier heroes. They are very handsome and very fast; are possessed of all the vices of their sex, counterbalanced by all the virtues; and, carefully handled, are fascinating. When they are first presented to us they have usually reached the interesting age of thirty; are leading the reckless life of fast men of both worlds; commit deeds which make the hair of one of those worlds stand on end, and are the more admired and sought after thereat. They invariably fall in love with the seductive beauty, who is usually a married woman. Under her remodeling influence they do not improve. They take pride in being as lawless as men in civilized society well can be; commit all the extravagances ever known to man; run through their "hereditary acres" in a marvelously short time; become satiated with the world and with the woman of the black-eyed and golden-haired species; and, finally, either rush off to the wars to commit deeds of valor, or disappear altogether for a quarter of a century. At the end of that time they reappear on the surface of society, their fortunes renovated, a strict morality developed in their character, and fall in love with the baby-faced heroine of sixteen. The hero having now attained the mature age of fifty-five, it might reasonably be supposed that he would aspire to something above bread and butter. But "Ouida" knew men better.

Under Two Flags, although not her first production, is the finest of her works, and is, moreover, the purest in tone. There is little vice in it, but one love scene, and that her best, and the characters are forcibly drawn and not exaggerated. The greater part of the story is laid in Algiers, during the war between the inhabitants of that country and the French. The book, therefore, possesses something of historical interest. The little *vivandière* of the French army, Cigarette, is the center of attraction, and her heroic death gives rather a tragic tone to the story. The different scenes are forcibly and dramatically arranged.

Although "Ouida" manages to render her heroes fascinating through their very wickedness, in *Strathmore* she fails in making vice attractive, as Bulwer did in *Eugene Aram*. A more repulsive character than the former could not well be conceived. Uniting hardness of heart with all the vices common to mankind, he possesses the latter in such a cold, calculating degree, that all the efforts of his biographer cannot render him other than the most revolting of his sex. In addition, he shoots the friend of his youth, through jealousy; goes systematically and patiently to work to blast the reputation of the woman with whom he has been insanely in love, and whom he blames for the passions which prompted the murder; betrays a man, far nobler than himself, to the most horrible of living deaths, because he is so unfortunate as to possess the secret of that murder; and, finally, attempts to drown the aforesaid woman, when once more he has her in his power. With the exception of an occasional fit of remorse, Strathmore continues prosperous and unpunished to the end of the book. He becomes a shining light in the House of Commons, and, when he is as thoroughly steeped in wickedness as a man can be and go unhung, he marries the sixteen-year-old daughter of his murdered friend. Lucile, the child whom he honors with the remnants of what he is pleased to call his heart, is the very "sublimity of ingenuousness." She invariably speaks of herself in the third person when addressing her lord, says her prayers out loud on the balcony for the benefit of wandering, restless spirits, and worships her otherwise much feared and little loved husband to a degree which must have been extremely refreshing to that weather-worn veteran. The whole book is in the same absurd, impossible strain. The woman who developed all these evil qualities, who is represented throughout six hundred and eighteen pages as possessing not one redeeming virtue, and who, after Strathmore succeeds in hurling her from her position in society, becomes the most notorious woman in Europe, ending when youth and beauty have deserted her, by turning saint, and becoming a missionary among the wilds of America.

In vain "Ouida" endeavors to throw around Strathmore's vices the same halo of fascination with which she encircles her other heroes. He remains to the last the most selfish, egotistical, and brutal of men. The first portion of the book itself is interesting, but the latter part is too much drawn out, and its love scenes too endlessly repeated to render it otherwise than tiresome. The only really fine chapters in the book are those containing an account of a storm and shipwreck on the Welsh coast. It is in descriptive powers that "Ouida" excels, and these chapters, of which there are several, are rather poetical than otherwise. To quote a short extract:

"A wild night!

"A night to drown death-shrieks like the cry of a curlew, and play with men's lives as with wisps of straw. A night with black seas yawning in fathomless graves, and the hissing of the waters filling every moment that the thunder lulled. No rain fell; the air was hot and arid; the dense clouds looked to stoop and touch the waves where they rose, a mighty wall of water, mountain high; a darkness impenetrable brooded over land and sea when the lightning ceased for some brief seconds, and when it blazed afresh the heavens were filled with the flame, that lit up the white stretch of beach, the gray rocks that glittered, steel-like, in its light, the vast Druidic forests of the abbey, stretching westward, and the boiling, seething, roaring abyss, where the sea devoured its dead in the horror of night, to smile calm and sunny in the morning dawn when its cruel work would be done, and its prey rot below, with the sand in their eyes, and the salt weeds in their hair, and the nameless things of the deep creeping over their limbs—over the childish brow that had been flushed warm with sleep a few hours before, over the long, floating tresses that had been played with by a mother's hand, over the lips which had been sought in the bridal softness of a good-night caress. For the Sea is fellow-reaper with Death, and, like his comrade, spares not for youth, or love, or pity, for childhood's cry, or mother's prayer, or iron strength of manhood.

"It was a wild night. The wind rose in sudden blasts, swift and fierce as a simoom, sweeping down from the wooded hights of the ancient monastery over the darkness of the sea, and driving against each other the great masses of the clouds like armies hurled together. The deafening roar of waters met the thunder of the skies as they rolled back peal on peal; and in the lightning glare the solitary ship was seen, black and spectral, with sails rent away, and masts broken like willow boughs, flung from side to side, as a lamed bird is flung in cruel sport—now lifted on the crest of giant waves, now sunk from sight in the chasm of the closing waters—reeling, rocking, driven at the mercy of the winds, alone in the black, trackless waste of the Atlantic. The minute-gun was silenced now, or drowned in the tumult of the storm; but ever and anon from the tempest-tossed vessel there rose the shrill, piercing wail of perishing souls—the cry in which Strathmore had heard a voice as the voice of God, bidding him who had destroyed life save it. * * * * The moon was shrouded now in the dark clouds that were driven swift as the hurricane across the skies; but the almost ceaseless play of the lightning made it clear as day, and he saw the white faces of dead men rise up about him in the water, and the dark, floating hair of women's corpses was blown over his hands as he swam toward the wreck, through the seas which were strewn with the flotsam and jetsam of the shattered ship, and mounted with steady grasp the shelving, slippery mass, which was all that was left of the stately vessel that, when the sun had gone down, had been steering calmly before the wind, with white sails set, through a fair and balmy evening, over a laughing azure sea."

Modern rhetoric says that we must have but one subject in a sentence; but the passages are the more forcible from their very irregularity.

Her first book, *Granville de Vigne*, is interesting, well written, but entirely too long. The first heroine, for a change, is not only wicked, but coarse and vulgar, under a thin coat of varnish. De Vigne, the hero, and a gay young man of the world, falls desperately in love with this unprincipled individual, and, against the wishes of his friends, marries her. She informs him, immediately after the ceremony, that she is an old flame of his college days—the then apprentice of a milliner—has been adopted by a doubtful old lady of *ton*, who fell in love with her gambling propensities, and, finally, that she has entrapped him into marriage to revenge his former fickleness. "Striking himself wildly on the forehead," De Vigne rushes from the church. Being unable to repudiate his firmly tied *spouse*, he settles her in Paris, and goes to India to seek fame and oblivion at the point of the sword. After ten years' absence he returns to England, becomes the lion and darling of society, and falls in love with an obscure little artist. The latter, of course, does not know that he is already supplied with a partner of his purse, if not of his joys and sorrows. Neither does the world remember the fact of his marriage, "Ouida" having conveniently piloted its memory to suit the occasion. While he is still in a quandary, dreadfully in love, but not having as yet fully settled upon his course of action, the girl is suddenly kidnapped by one of his friends, elegantly known as the "Butcher." Not knowing what has become of her, but for various reasons believing her false, in a fit of desperation De Vigne exchanges his regiment for active service, and goes to the Crimea the next day. Here follow the finest passages of the book. In the vivid and stirring scenes of the Crimea, "Ouida" has full scope for her descriptive talent. Of course, all her heroes are in the Light Cavalry charge, and come out covered with wounds and glory. For the most part "Ouida" is faithful to history in her description of various engagements, but makes a mistake in laying the blame of this charge to Nolan's impetuosity, instead of to Lord Lucan's impatience and carelessness. Had the former survived the day, he might possibly have been locked up for disrespect to a superior officer, but as Lord Lucan was recalled from the Peninsula on account of this very charge, there cannot be much doubt as to whom the blame should be attributed.

Sabretasche, De Vigne's friend, is in much the same enviable frame of mind as the hero himself. Married in his youth to an Italian woman, who shortly after developed too strong an affection for one of her own countrymen, he left, but was unable to divorce her, having, unfortunately, no proof but his own convictions. Returning to England, he many years after, at the age of forty-five, falls in love with a young society belle. Having heard that No. 1 is dead, he is about to make Miss Violet Molyneux No. 2, when he is suddenly informed that his former spouse is still above ground. In this unpleasant turn of his affairs, he goes with De Vigne to the Crimea, and both unavailingly "rush into the jaws of death, into the mouth of hell." In the meantime, the ill-starred Alma escapes from her persecutor, the "Butcher," wanders into a forest, gets brain fever, is nursed through it in a woodman's hut, is visited by the wife of her "Sir Folko," as she calls him, is correspondingly depressed, but writes nevertheless to De Vigne, being anxious to clear herself from all blame. De Vigne gets the letter at the end of the campaign, goes to France, horsewhips the "Butcher," kicks him down stairs, and then proceeds to Fontainebleau, where his lady-love is staying. In the forest he meets his wife, for the first time since his marriage, and courageously resists a temptation to strangle her. He sees Alma, but is not much better off than before, not being able to marry her. At this important crisis his wife's first husband, who has been sojourning some years in Botany Bay, turns up, and relieves his unwilling successor of all further responsibility. Sabretasche returns after the Peace of Paris, picks up his wife dying one night in the streets, as she is reeling along in a blissful state of intoxication, puts her to bed, keeps a sharp eye on her until he is assured beyond a doubt that this time the breath is well out of her body, and straightway marries the much-enduring and long-waiting Violet. During the course of his wife's death-bed revelations, he learns that the heroine of the book, Alma, is his daughter. He thus has the felicity of becoming father-in-law to his most intimate friend and comrade, De Vigne, while Violet finds herself step-mother to her only rival in society, Alma Tresillian. These short summaries may serve to illustrate our novelist's general style. *Granville de Vigne* is exaggerated of course, but not so much so as *Strathmore*, and is interesting. It is beautifully written, and one of the Crimean scenes in particular would serve as a good subject for a historical painter's brush—that is, if his ambition lay in the blood-curdling line. It is after the evacuation of Sebastopol, and De Vigne and Chevasney are looking for their wounded and dying comrade, "Curly:"

"But we did not stay to notice the once white and stately city, now black and broken with our shot; we went straight on toward Fort Paul, as yet untouched, where stood the hospital, that chamber of horrors, that worse than charnel-house, from which strong men retreated, unable to bear up against the loathsome terrors it inclosed. That long, low room, with its arched roof, its square pillars, its dim, cavernous light coming in through the shattered windows, was a sight worse than all the falsied horrors of painter, of poet, or author; full of torment—torment to which the cruelest torture of Domitian or Nero were mercy—a hell, where human frames were racked with every possible agony, not as a chastisement for sin, but as a reward for heroism. There they lay, packed as closely together as dead animals in a slaughter-house—the many Russians, the few English soldiers, who had been dragged there after the assault, to die as they might; they would but have cumbered the retreat, and their lives were valueless now! There they lay; some on the floor, that was slippery with blood, like a shamble; some on pallets saturated with the stream that carried away their life in its deadly flow; some on straw, crimson and noisome, the home of the most horrible vermin; some dead, hastily flung down to be out of the way, black and swollen, a mass of putrefaction, the eyes forced from their sockets, the tongue protruding, the features distended in hideous grotesqueness; others dead, burnt and charred in the explosion, a heap of blanched bones, and gory clothes, and blackened flesh. Living men in horrible companionship with these corpses, writhing in torture which there was no hand to relieve, with their jagged and broken limbs twisted and powerless, were calling for water, for help, for pity; shrieking out, in wild delirium or disconnected prayer, the names of the women they had loved, or the God who had forsaken them; or rolling beneath their wretched beds, in the agony of pain and thirst which had driven them to madness, glaring out upon us with the piteous helplessness of a hunted animal, or the ferocious unconsciousness of insanity. We passed through one of these chambers of terrors, our hearts sickened and our senses reeling at the hideous sight, the intolerable stench that met us everywhere. We entered a second room where the sights and the odors were yet more appalling than in the first. Beside one pallet De Vigne paused, and bent down: then his dark bronze cheek grew white, and he dropped on his knee beside the wretched bed—at last he had found Curly. Curly! still alive in that scene of misery, lying on the mattress that was soaked with his life-blood, the wound in his shoulder open and festering, his eyes closed, his bright hair dull and damp with the dew of suffering that stood upon his brow, his face of a livid blue white: the gay, gallant, chivalrous English gentleman, thrown down to die as he would not have left a dog in its suffering. On one side of him was a black charred corpse, swollen in one place, burnt to the bone in another; the woman that loved him best could not have known that hideous mass. On the other side of him, close by, was a young Russian officer, just dead, with his hands, small and fair as a girl's, filled with the straw that he had clutched in his death agony; and between these two dead men lay Curly."

This book, I should have remarked, was written for the benevolent purpose of showing the folly of early marriages. "Ouida" gets very warm on the subject, and, evidently, is in earnest; but whether the present generation has profited by her advice I really have not it in my power to ascertain. I hope that I may not be pronounced satirical, however, if I further remark, that Mlle. de la Ramée no longer preaches the same philosophy. One's ideas on such subjects when in youth and when one has reached the *passé* stage are apt to conflict.

Puck—and here I am prepared for an exclamation of horror from all well regulated minds—*Puck* is, in some respects, superior to anything "Ouida" ever wrote. It is immoral, undoubtedly, and, with the exception of the last chapter, is not particularly interesting. Nevertheless, it contains more wit, and at times more pathos, than any of her other performances. It is written in her most sprightly, epigrammatic style, and displays that keen, analytical knowledge of the world, and of the faults and frailties of mankind, which is certainly hers in an eminent degree. Among the many forcibly drawn characters, that of the hero, Beltran, is the finest—is, indeed, the strongest she has ever created. With all his faults—faults which his other qualities more than redeem—he is, above all, a perfect and honorable gentleman. As "Ouida's" last brilliant effusion, *Moths*, is dedicated to "My friend, Algernon Borthwick, in memory of the days of *Puck*," it may reasonably be supposed that that gentleman is the idealized original of Beltran. "Ouida's" earlier characters are never life-like even when they are not overdrawn; we might live for a century and never meet one of them. In this very fact, probably, lies the secret of their success. We do not turn to fiction for instruction, or to have the every-day events of life, or the ordinary people we meet, analyzed and dissected by a clever novelist. We read to be amused, and to forget the monotony of life in the impossible day-dreams of well written, but nonsensational romance.

With the exception of *Bebée*, the only recommendation which the members of the second series can claim is, that they might possibly serve as guide-books for students of French and Italian scenery. *Bebée* is a pretty, simple little story, and possesses the merit of being short. For the rest, they are well written, excessively stupid, and are as impossible as the first series, without possessing their redeeming virtue of being interesting. In *Ariadne* she takes refuge in mythology, and in every other chapter gives us a page or two of her insipid little heroine and uninteresting hero. The rest are not worth particular mention. Some people affect to admire this series more than the first. But I strongly suspect that their admiration is based on much the same principle as that which induces them to admire ugly furniture—the uglier it is the handsomer it necessarily must be, and they are afraid of being pronounced uncultivated if they do not duly admire whatever rubs their sense of good taste the wrong way. Moreover, they probably think that, if "Ouida" could manage to spin out five or six hundred pages on less than no plot, the book itself must, of a consequence, be something deep and remarkable. In yielding compulsory admiration they mistake stupidity for profundity—that is all. The books of this series remind us of nothing so forcibly as of a frail, exquisitely cut cameo—a slight blow of the hammer and its utter nothingness and emptiness is revealed.

Of later years, either seeing the necessity for a change, or from motives of personal spite—probably a little of both—"Ouida" has come out with three satires on modern society, honoring many of her friends and acquaintances with an unenviable immortality. *In a Winter City* put Florence in a flutter of anxiety, which was lulled for a time by the appearance of *Ariadne*. But the security was premature. After a year or two *Friendship* appeared, and its principal characters were glad to retire into obscurity to escape the howl of derision set up by the circle in which they moved. Next *Moths* appears upon the scene, and many of its characters are known to be as true to life as are those of its predecessor. "Ouida" is a genuine product of evolution. In this, her last book, she is a little more stupid, a little more prolix, a little more overdrawn, a little more immoral than she has ever been before. The book is disappointing, moreover, for the opening chapters promise something sprightly, at least; but, alas! each one thereafter becomes more tiresome than the last.

If ever there lived such a perfect creature as Vere, we sincerely and devoutly hope that it may never be our fate to meet her. No wonder the world found her dull. "Ouida" endeavors to impress the fact upon us that, in her superiority of intellect and virtue, Vere "wrapped herself in cold reserve, and condescended not to please." But we are of the world's opinion still. If "Ouida" finds her interesting we truly hope that she will, in future, keep all such for her private delectation. Any efforts on our part to obtain possession will not be exhausting. In one respect, above all others, does "Ouida" show the decline of her powers—she can no longer create an interesting hero. They have all, of later years, been of the softer French and Italian type. On the whole, we may safely say that we prefer her former English ones in spite of their vices. Lord Jura, a Scotchman, is the nearest approach to her earlier creations, and is, moreover, the only respectable character in *Moths*. When we think of the five hundred and twenty-five pages of "agony long drawn out," through which Vere traveled in behalf of the singer Corrèze, we have less opinion of that heroine than ever. A more trifling, insipid, sentimental, "light of the boards," could not well be imagined. "Ouida" extols his nobility and self-denial by asserting that, when Vere was first united to her charming husband, Prince Zurnff, whenever that happy couple entered a city Corrèze immediately decamped. If we may judge by his subsequent performances, however, we may feel ourselves justified in suspecting that, if he had had much encouragement, he would have remained. We never before heard of a lover challenging a husband. Quite refreshing are the novelties in European life and manners which "Ouida" is so considerate as to occasionally offer to our sated senses.

We should like to see "Ouida's" circle of American acquaintances. Either it is limited to the very shoddiest class who go abroad, or, with her usual fine discrimination, she singles out and carefully delineates for our benefit the most reprehensible of the lot. Mrs. Henry V. Clams held America up to ridicule in *Friendship*. In *Moths* we are now introduced to Miss Fuchsia Leach, surnamed by H. R. H., "Pick-Me-Up," in delicate reference to the manner in which her father made his money. Her brothers, "Ouida" tells us, keep a scientific pork establishment "out west," where hogs are put in alive at one end of the machinery, and come out hams and bacon, thoroughly cured, at the other. For brilliancy of imagination, "Ouida" is certainly unrivaled. We have slang enough in California, heaven knows, but we are thankful, at least, that the choice and elegant sayings which enrich the conversations of Miss Leach have not yet reached us. As, for instance:

"'I surmise I'd best eat the curds while they're sweet. I look cunning, and I'm spry, and I cheek him, and say outragrous things, and he likes it, and so they all go mad on me after him'—meaning by her pronoun the great personage who had made her the fashion.

* * * * * * *

"'When I came across the pond,' she said to Vere one day, 'I said to mother, I'll take nothing but a Duke. Oh, you may turn up your nose,' continued Fuchsia, vivaciously. 'You think it atrocious that new folks should carry off your brothers, and cousins, and friends. Well, I'd like to know where it's worse than all your big nobility going down at our feet for our dollars. That's real mean. That's blacking boots, if you please. Men with a whole row of Crusaders at their backs, men who count their forefathers right away into Julius Cæsar's times, men who had uncles in the ark with Noah—they're at a Yankee pile, like flies around molasses. Waal, now, you're all of you that proud that you'd beat Lucifer; but, as far as I can see, there aren't much to be proud of. *We're* shoddy over there. If we went to Boston, we wouldn't get a drink outside a hotel for our lives. N'York, neither, don't think because a man's struck ile he'll go to heaven, with Paris thrown in. But look at all your big folks. Pray, what do *they* do the minute shoddy comes their way over the pickle field? Why, they just eat it—kiss it, and eat it. Waal, then, to my fancy there aren't much to be proud of, anyhow, and it aren't only us that need be laughed at.'

"'It is not,' said Vere, who had listened in bewilderment. 'There is very much to be ashamed of on both sides.'

"'Shame's a big thing—a four-horse concern,' said the other, with some demur; 'but if any child need be ashamed, it is not this child.'"

And so on, *ad infinitum.*

She is said to be an exaggerated portrait of some American girl whom "Ouida" has met. We sincerely hope, however, that the latter has confined herself to the truth in the matter of the fair "Pick-Me-Up's" nativity, for we should not care to claim her. She is pretty, "Ouida" acknowledges, in the piquant, highly-colored, *outragrous* American style. We would politely suggest that "Ouida" extend her observations before honoring our nation further. On the whole, however, we prefer Fuchsia Leach to Vere—she is less tiresome.

In these later books "Ouida" constantly intrudes her personality upon the public. The entire series are filled with protests against the unjust judgments of the world, upon which she never loses an opportunity to dwell. We are sorry that she has been a sufferer from the world's indiscriminating tongue, but we think that it would be just as judicious on her part were she not so constantly reminding us of the fact. If European society be what it is represented in *Friendship*, *Moths*, and *In a Winter City*, we would suggest that "Ouida" and the *News Letter* join forces and undertake its reformation. That of San Francisco may assuredly be considered a paragon of virtue beside it.

Probably the best thing about "Ouida's" books is their immorality. Do not start. We admit that it is very reprehensible in "Ouida" to have such a turn of mind. The effect, however, is superior to the intention. When we read a long novel, of a highly-strung moral and religious tone, we draw a long breath of relief at the end of so much impossible virtue; we are apt to seek out something rather wicked as an antidote. But "Ouida" gave us such an overdose, such a surfeit of her "fashionable vice," that, after we have waded through the average thirty-six chapters, we are thoroughly nauseated and do not want to hear of anything of the kind for a year at least. Not that she is ever vulgar; she is merely as insinuating and immoral as a writer well can be and still manage to preserve any decency. As some one said of Byron (and we hope she is duly honored by the comparison), she "smothers the dirt in a mine of gold." The "gold" consists of the pretty, well-turned sentences in which her wickedness is expressed, and her rhetoric is, in general, of the most approved modern school.

Seriously, she possesses some qualities which no one will gainsay her The composition of her books is exquisite; she still possesses the pen of a ready writer, and words, if not plots, are ever at her command. Her style, moreover, is all her own; among her many disciples none have been successful in imitating anything but her immorality. At times she is amusing, witty, and satirical; her books contain many clever truisms. She has evidently made human nature the study of a life-time, and is particularly well acquainted with all its weaknesses. She is an excellent, though merciless caricaturist, and we can well imagine the terror in which she must keep her neighbors. She must be as good as a recording angel—black or white, it is unnecessary to specify.

However, although she has made no little sensation in the literary world in her day, that day is already over. Every one has read her old books, and they will not stand a second reading. With the exception of the residents of Florence, no one cares particularly about her later ones. A generation or two hence and her name will be as completely forgotten as are now those of the authoresses of the last century, notices of whom we occasionally meet with in an essay or a memoir.

"Books, like everything else, have their appointed death-day; the souls of them, unless they be found worthy of a second birth in a new body, perish with the paper in which they lived."

FAG, M. P.

THE MISSIONARY OF INDEPENDENCE FLAT.

"Miss Parsons, have you heard the news?" cried Sally Fitch, bounding into her neighbor's kitchen one sultry July afternoon. "The minister's gone and brought home a new wife."

"No!" ejaculated Mrs. Parsons, as she turned a flushed face from the stove to confront her informant. "You, don't mean it, Sally? Do let's hear about it."

"I seen her and him both myself," pursued Sally, with a volubility that defied the shackles of grammar, "gettin' out of the stage in front of his house; and Kate Regan, she says he got married at the Springs, and wrote word to Miss Butler—that's his housekeeper, you know—to expect them to-day, and, sure enough, they've come. And she's awful pretty, too. She had up her veil, and I got a good look at her. But she's dressed all in black, not a bit like a bride. And Miss Butler was *awful* surprised, Kate says. You know he went to the Springs to see his sick aunt, or somebody, and then, all of a sudden, he went and married, without any notice at all. Miss Butler's sure he wasn't engaged when he left home. My, but won't church be crowded to-morrow! I know I'll be there, for one."

It needed a strong motive to fill the rambling wooden edifice in which the Rev. Cyril Noble was in the habit of conducting the weekly service, for the denizens of Independence Flat were not a church-going people, as a rule. The motive was not wanting on the Sunday following his return home, and the building was filled to its utmost capacity by a curious congregation, eager to satisfy themselves in regard to the outward appearance, at least, of the "minister's new wife." All they saw of her, however, was a girlish figure, clad in deep mourning; for, notwithstanding the oppressive heat, she did not once lift her veil, and disappointment was rife among them as they dispersed.

The minister's marriage had come about, as Sally had said, "all of a sudden," and in the briefest possible space of time after his arrival at a little watering-place, whither he had gone in obedience to the summons of a relative sojourning there in quest of health. Those who knew his calm, self-contained disposition, could not but marvel at the idea of his committing matrimony on such short notice; for, of all men living, he had seemed least likely to fall in love at first sight. It had happened, however, in this wise: He had reached the Springs just in time to perform the funeral service of a French gentleman, named Dubarry, who had died of heart disease at the only hotel which the place contained, and to administer what consolation he could to the daughter of the deceased, a beautiful girl, left alone, and apparently friendless, in a strange land. Though naturally neither susceptible nor romantic, his strong sympathy for the girl's forlorn condition merged, ere he was aware, into a warmer feeling, which led him to throw completely aside his usual habits of caution and reserve. He asked and won her consent to become his wife;

and, though aware that he was taking a precipitate, and perhaps imprudent, step, he was too deeply in love to allow the consciousness of his rashness to weigh heavily upon him.

"You can trust yourself to my keeping, Alixe?" he asked her, almost humbly, as if in apology for what she might deem his presumption in trying to win her confidence on such a short acquaintanceship; but whatever else she gave him or withheld, she had felt instinctively from the first that he was worthy of her trust.

So they were married within a week, and then went directly to his home. It was not a very lovely or inviting home to bring her to. He felt that strongly for the first time as he entered his own door with her leaning on his arm, and looked around at the prim cleanliness of the bare walls and stiff haircloth furniture, guiltless of cheerful coloring, or any attempt at comfort or grace. Mrs. Butler, his housekeeper, was a woman with the best intentions in the world, but her idea of the proper appointment of a room consisted in arranging each article of furniture as if it were on guard, the chairs with their upright backs against the wall, and every book upon the carefully dusted table placed at an irreproachable angle. Nor was the outlook from the front windows much more enlivening than the aspect of the interior. In front, a square inclosure, called "the garden," displayed a few melancholy shrubs, and a row of eucalyptus trees on the sidewalk raised straggling and wind-blown branches to the sunny heavens, as if imploring the boon of a shower to wash the dust from their leaves. In one direction, a straight, sandy street, with square, flat-roofed houses facing each other all the way, stretched as far as the eye could reach, and in another, a waste of sand was bounded by a line of low, barren hills, that shut out the neighboring country from view.

Perhaps Alixe was sensible of a contrast between her former surroundings and those to which she was now introduced, for a slight shiver passed through her frame, and an involuntary look of dismay crossed her face. As soon as practicable she went to work to alter the arrangement of things, and before evening she had, to use Mrs. Butler's phraseology, "the whole house out of sorts."

"If you'll believe me," said that good woman, when confiding her feelings afterward to a friendly gossip, "there wasn't a thing in a single room that wasn't put topsy-turvy and upside down. Even the parlor, that I've took such trouble to set in order day by day, though seldom used, was unfixed from one end to the other. She put the table slanting ways, and jumbled up everything on it; stuck the chairs all awry, some facing this way, and some that (think of the queerness of it!), and actually moved the best china vases off the mantel-piece, and hid them away in a closet. Then she closed the shutters, all but a little crack, just like it was a dungeon—said the glare hurt her eyes. I was a good deal put out, I am free to confess; but I guess she means well—she seems nice and pleasant mannered enough, though I should say she'd had a queer kind of bringing up."

Beyond this attempt to revolutionize the outward aspect of her new surroundings, Alixe betrayed no desire to interfere with the housekeeper's long established rule; indeed, she quickly settled down into a passive quietude that was almost like indifference; and Cyril, who watched her closely, began, by and by, to be troubled with a secret fear that he might have hurried her prematurely into taking a step which she was beginning already to repent of. Something more than this disquieted him: a curious reticence, a shadow of reserve that hung over all her actions and words, seemed to check the free outpouring of his own love, and to imply a want of the absolute confidence he craved from her in return. More than once, too, he had surprised her in tears, and his questioning failed to elicit from her any satisfactory reason for her emotion. And he, the quiet, self-disciplined man, who had through all his former life been wont to weigh in the balance of dispassionate judgment every impulse of his mind and heart, and yield to none that such judgment did not sanction, now found himself swayed by a passion of yearning and jealous tenderness that cast sober wisdom to the winds. He would watch her as she sat near him, sometimes, with a far-away, dreamy look in her eyes, apparently unconscious of his presence, and long, with an intensity that was actual pain, for the power to read her heart, and to assure himself of her real feelings toward him. He never put his questionings or doubts into words; he shrank involuntarily from a test which might—though the thought of such a possibility was agony to him—result disastrously to his hopes.

Going out one day to visit a sick parishioner, he returned unexpectedly, in quest of something he had forgotten, and found her reading a letter, which she crumpled hastily in her hand upon his entrance, while a deep blush crimsoned her face. Her embarrassment was too evident to escape his notice, and he stood still, regarding her with a beating heart.

"I have alarmed you, Alixe," he said, with a tremor in his tone that he could not suppress.

"No—oh, no," she faltered with increasing confusion. "I was only startled. I did no know you had come in."

He came nearer to her, reluctance to wound her feelings and a strong desire to satisfy himself contending for the mastery in his mind.

"You have a letter, I see," he continued; "may I ask from whom?"

"It is an old letter," she replied, looking down.

"A secret, evidently—one that I must not pry into," said Cyril, with involuntary bitterness. "Don't fear that I shall try to force it from you," he added, growing a shade paler, as he noticed that she held the paper more tightly, as if dreading that he might take it; and, turning abruptly away, he left the room. He went about his duties mechanically, feeling like a man dizzy from a blow, and unable to concentrate his attention upon anything. When evening came, he dreaded to return home, not knowing whether some terrible disclosure might not be awaiting him. To his surprise, as he entered the door, Alixe came to meet him; for the first time, she threw her arms voluntarily around him in a close embrace.

"Read this," she said, half inaudibly, "and forgive me, Cyril, if you can." She gave him the letter, and was gone.

There was need of forgiveness, then? He had not been mistaken. He opened the letter with trembling fingers, only to be completely mystified by its contents. It was a communication from a Mr. de Forest, a theatrical manager in New York, to Mademoiselle Dubarry, stating the terms of an engagement in which she was to play "Juliet" to the "Romeo" of a noted actor, and ending with a peremptory charge not to send any more excuses for her delay, which had already caused him much inconvenience, etc., etc.

What did it mean? Was she—his wife—an actress?

In feverish anxiety to sift the matter to the bottom, he sought Alixe, whom he found in her own room, crying as if her heart would break.

"I need an explanation of this," he said, authoritatively.

She gave him a frightened, piteous glance; then hid her face again.

"I knew you would despise me," she rejoined, amid her tears. "I did mean to tell you from the first, but you—you hurried me so: I could not find a chance; and it was all so sudden, it bewildered me. Afterward, I did not dare. I know you cannot forgive me; but oh, Cyril, in pity don't send me away!"

"I don't understand," said Cyril, passing his hand across his brow, as he sank into a chair. "Come here, Alixe, and talk to me plainly. Is this letter addressed to you?"

She made an affirmative sign without moving.

"Were you—did you go on the stage at that time?"

"Not exactly at that time; I was ill, and he got a substitute."

"You were a professional actress, then?" The words came with difficulty.

"Yes. Oh, Cyril—"

There was a silence.

"Come to me, I tell you, Alixe," he said, in a low voice, at last.

She rose humbly and stood at his side; he encircled her with his arm, looking searchingly into her face.

"If you had only told me this at first. You knew my whole life; I trusted you too fully to ask for an account of yours."

"I intended to do it; I never meant to deceive you. I don't know how I came to put it off. Of course, you would not have married me; but I did not realize then that I was doing you so great a wrong."

"I would not have married you! Perhaps I should. I cannot answer for my own heart. But it would have been better if I had taken you into my arms with an honest confession upon your lips. Oh, child, you have indeed done me a great wrong," said Cyril, in husky tones. "But as to your past life, that does not matter to me now; only no one—remember, no one!—must ever know of this. It is all canceled, as though it had never been. You are my wife; you are Alixe Dubarry no longer. I believe, as you stand here, that you will never bring reproach upon my name."

"There has never been reproach on *my* name; I will never bring it upon yours." She spoke proudly, but the next instant the remorseful humility of her manner returned. "Oh, Cyril, if I could only find words to tell you all my heart; but I cannot. I have never ceased to blame myself; it has been the misery of my life since I married you to think that I did not dare to tell you the truth."

"Were you so afraid of me, Alixe?"

"Yes, I was afraid; I felt that if you once got angry you could be so stern. And I thought—perhaps—you would send me away; and then I know I should have died of grief."

"Child, do you love me then?"

His whole soul leaped to his eyes, waiting for her reply. How often had the question trembled on his lips, and been forced back, unspoken.

For an answer she clung to him, her whole frame shaken with sobs; but in that mute answer he read the fullness of her love, and even his craving soul was satisfied. What mattered it to him what she had been? It was enough for him to know that now she was all his own.

"There will be no more concealment between us, Alixe," he said, solemnly, pressing his lips upon her bowed head. "Promise me that you will never let a shadow of doubt cloud my trust in you again."

"Never, Cyril, never. I promise on my sacred word."

The coming winter brought hard times, not only to the little town where the missionary lived and worked, but to the whole State. Work was scarce, and murmurings were rife among those who depended on the fruits of their labor for their daily bread. There was much distress at the Flat, and Cyril was kept busy enough with his efforts to alleviate it. His health, never strong, began at last to break down under the constant physical and mental strain; and there came a time when he felt the absolute need of rest, yet saw no way of obtaining it. Duty chained him to his post, and he toiled on, though half fainting beneath a burden which he was ill fitted to bear.

Alixe worked bravely to help him, developing qualities that astonished him; he had not dreamed that such strength of purpose and such power of self-sacrifice lay beneath her rather languid exterior. Hitherto she had taken no active part in the parish, and his people scarcely knew her. They learned to know her now, however, and to bless her coming, as they would have blessed the coming of an angel, into their poverty-stricken homes.

Cyril himself was very, very poor. His little income had dwindled down to a mere pittance, scarcely more than sufficient to keep hunger from his door; yet even out of this—his wife persuading him—he spared something here and there to supply a need greater than their own. Alixe did all the work of their household now; the faithful friend and servant, Mrs. Butler, they had been forced to send away. Her cheerfulness never flagged until he grew ill; then her courage began to ebb, though of this she gave no outward sign.

"You are my tower of strength, Alixe," he often said to her. How happy his commendation made her! Her whole soul was wrapped up in her husband now; truly "they love much unto whom much has been forgiven."

Sickness conquered him at last; he had struggled hard, but the adverse pressure was too strong for him to resist it further, and he was forced to succumb utterly. Fortunately, there did not seem to be danger in the attack; but it laid him prostrate, making him weak and helpless as a child.

"Has any letter come for me, Alixe?" he asked one day, when the usual hour for the postman's coming was past.

"No, dear; were you expecting one?" his wife rejoined.

"Don't you know my quarterly remittance is due? And we need it sorely just now."

"I dare say it will come to-morrow," said Alixe; and after that she kept watch furtively for the postman. Three days later he brought the looked-for letter, but it was empty. No remittance was coming yet; the missionary fund for this quarter was not large enough to answer all the demands made upon it, and Cyril, among others, would have to wait.

It was very hard; and the disappointment told heavily upon the sick man. He was not entirely without resources; he had a small sum, accumulated by careful economy, laid up in the bank for a rainy day; when this was gone, however, there would be absolutely nothing left for him to depend upon.

Alixe lay awake now every night, and thought, and thought, until her brain ached with thinking. Something she *must* do—more than she had already done—to help her husband; but what and how?

More weary days passed, and Cyril grew constantly weaker. A terrible fear began to creep over Alixe. What was the end of it all to be? Suddenly a bright thought occured to him. He remembered that in more thriving days he had lent some money to a friend who had come to him in distress. This friend had prospered since, but the loan had never been repaid. No doubt, if their necessity were made known to him, he would repay it without further delay, and this would relieve them of all present anxiety. The very dawning of this hope reanimated Cyril, and seemed to give him new life; it was, in truth, despondency more than bodily suffering that weighed him down.

"If I could only find a way to see him," he said. "Writing is so unsatisfactory; and, besides, I am not sure of his address. If I were in San Francisco I could easily find it out."

"Are you sure he is there?" Alixe asked.

"Yes; at least it has always been his place of residence, and his business is there. Oh, if I had but the strength to travel so far."

"But you have not, Cyril; you must not think of such a thing. Could you trust *me* to go? I would not be afraid."

Cyril at first vetoed the proposal utterly; but on thinking it over it gradually assumed a feasible shape. There was little risk in her making the journey alone, over a route frequented daily by hundreds of people; and, once in the city, her task would not be a difficult one. He wrote, with a feeble hand, a letter introducing her and explaining the purpose of her visit, and she set at once about making preparations for her expedition. Mrs. Butler was summoned, and she agreed to stay with Cyril and take care of everything until Alixe's return.

There are times when a vague presentiment of evil casts its shadow upon the mind, and dwells there, notwithstanding every effort of will and reason to banish it. Such a presentiment hung over Cyril on the night previous to his wife's departure, and so strongly did it affect him that he nearly decided to revoke his permission to her to go. He argued, however, against such folly, and partly succeeded in overcoming it before the moment came in which he was to bid her good bye.

Those words were bitterly hard to say—harden even than he had anticipated. Such was his weakness that he could not keep back his tears, though the parting was to be for so short a time.

"God bless and keep you from harm," he said as he kissed her.

And she answered, smiling, though her eyes were wet:

"What harm is likely to befall me, dear Cyril? I shall be quite safe."

"You will take care?" he asked; and even after she had reached the door, he called her back, and charged her again to let no harm happen to her. The shadow haunted him still, and it deepened when she was gone.

She had for a traveling companion a man whom she knew very well—a strict, upright churchman, one of her husband's most esteemed parishioners. She had been especially kind and attentive to this man's family when there had been sickness and distress among them, and he now made it a point of being especially kind and attentive to her.

"You are not afraid of being in the busy city alone?" was his question when about to part from her at her journey's end.

"Oh, no. When are you going back, Mr. Wise?"

"Day after to-morrow, I guess, Mrs. Noble. Will you be leaving so soon yourself?"

"Probably sooner. I shall leave to-morrow, if things turn out as I expect."

"Things don't turn out as we expect always, you know." Simple words, and containing as simple and homely a truth; but how often did they recur to her, almost in the guise of a prophecy, in days to come.

She sought, and found without trouble, the address of Cyril's friend, and a short walk brought her to his office—the office that had been his, at least. It had changed hands now, and a different name was over the door. Only a clerk was within, and, in answer to her inquiries, he informed her that Mr. —— had left for the East a fortnight ago, and did not expect to return.

"Can you give me his address?" asked Alixe.

"No, ma'am; I'm sorry I can't. Are you ill? Can I do anything for you?"

The clerk was little more than a boy, and had all a boy's freshness of sympathy for any one in trouble; and he was penetrating enough to see that his visitor's disappointment was of a more than ordinary kind. A deadly faintness assailed her for a moment, but she shook it off, and managed to swallow a little water from a glassful which the young man hastened to bring to her.

"No, I am not ill. I have been traveling, and am a little tired," she explained. "Many thanks. I am sorry I troubled you."

She went immediately back to her hotel, a very inexpensive one, in a remote location, and was going up-stairs to her room, when she met a person whom she instantly recognized, and whom, of all persons, she had least expected to meet again. This individual—a portly man, in broadcloth, with a fat face that ought to have been good-humored, but bore at present unmistakable signs of vexation—glanced at her, ran down a few steps, stopped suddenly, turned, and dashed up again, overtaking her just as she reached the first landing.

"Miss Dubarry! I *thought* I couldn't be mistaken. What extraordinary good luck. Bless me, who'd ever have thought that we'd meet on Western soil? Where have you been, and what have you been doing with yourself all this time?" he cried, extending his hand, on which a diamond ring glittered.

Alixe drew back. Somehow she was terrified at the sight of this man, which seemed to carry her suddenly back to the life of long ago.

"I am not living here, Mr. de Forest. I am only in the city for a few hours. I—please don't detain me. I am very tired, and must rest."

"Tired! You look tired enough," he said, with a glace of genuine pity at her haggard face. "I should say you were ill—or in trouble. Which is it?"

"In trouble," Alixe answered, bursting into tears. She was completely unnerved, and his compassionate look and tone broke down in an instant the barrier of her self-control. Besides, he had been kind to her in bygone days, and although she had shrunk from him in the first moment of their meeting, it seemed impossible now to reject the sympathy he was eager to offer.

"Oh, dear, this is sad!" he exclaimed; and he hurried her into a shabby little parlor, that was vacant, and there succeeded, without much difficulty, in extorting from her a partial explanation of the cause of her distress. Her true name and place of abode she carefully withheld.

"Lord! Lord! to think of your coming to this!" ejaculated Mr. de Forest, wiping his flushed brow with a cambric kerchief liberally scented with Maria Farina cologne. "But you don't mean that you've dropped your profession *surely!*"

"Oh, yes," Alixe hurriedly replied.

"No. Why on earth did you do such a thing? Anyhow, I have a proposal to make to you, which flashed into my head the very minute I I saw you; indeed, I may say, you appeared to me in the light of a complete godsend; for if ever there was a man in a quandary it's me, A. P. de Forest, at this present moment, and it struck me that nobody could help me out of it so well as you. I've got a term at the —— Theater, with *Romeo and Juliet* for the opening night, and this is the opening night, and my Juliet has gone and got ill. You served me so yourself, once, you remember. I'm always unfortunate with my Juliets; there's a sort of fatality seems to hang over them, some way. Now it used to be your best *rôle;* it's morally impossible that you should have forgotten it. There's a rehearsal at three this afternoon—plenty of time; and I'll pay you five hundred dollars, cash down, if you'll consent to fill the bill."

Five hundred dollars! The room seemed to reel before Alixe. She put up her hands. "It is impossible," she said, faintly. "Quite impossible."

What tempter was this who had risen before her?

"Why impossible? You know you haven't forgotten—you never could forget your Juliet to your dying day. And my offer's a fair one—you can't deny that."

"It is most generous," said Alixe, in a stifled voice. Five hundred dollars! In her present need it seemed a fortune.

"Just for one night, you know; no trouble about costumes or anything, and plenty of time to rehearse. And I'm quite sure you can't have forgotten," urged the manager. It was on this point that he laid most stress; probably, it was one on which he felt a little secret anxiety, notwithstanding his assurance to the contrary. How could she ever forget it, that old, familiar *rôle!* She had played it so many, many times; and some subtle influence seemed to transport her back now to the nights when she had listened, with natural exultation, to the applause her performance had called forth. For the moment she was Alixe Dubarry again, with old ideas, old associations all revived.

"It is impossible," she repeated, but in a vague, uncertain way this time, as if in a dream. Five hundred dollars—relief, restored health to her husband, now ill, perhaps dying, for want of aid; disobedience and treachery for one night—one single night; and he need never know, until she chose to confess, and would not his love for her condone the crime?

Crime! Was that a crime which would restore happiness to their home, and banish the wolf, Want, from their door? She would not compromise her husband's name or his honor by this one deviation from the path of duty. Why should she tell him that she had not obtained the money from his friend?

The manager watched her, with, at least, as much shrewdness as compassion in his glance; he saw that he was gaining the advantage over her, and resolved to follow it up. At heart he thought she would be a simpleton if she refused his offer, which was, undoubtedly, a more liberal one than he would have made to any lady whom he had not been anxious to assist. He had always liked her, this pretty, graceful little actress, who had never done discredit to her part, and never been unwilling to oblige; and the sight of her wan face and faltering movements touched his heart, remembering her, as he did, in better days.

He talked on, and she listened, and her replies grew weaker as the temptation waxed stronger—and then—

Yes, her consent was won. She would play "Juliet" once more—for the last time. And then she drove all thoughts of Cyril from her mind, and rushed with the excitement of delirium into the work before her.

It chanced, by rather a singular coincidence, that Mr. Andrew Wise, her fellow-traveler, had taken lodgings at the same hotel with herself. He was standing outside the door that evening when the cab arrived which Mr. de Forest sent for her; saw her, himself unseen, come out and enter it; heard the direction given, "To the —— Theater," and wondered at it; and finally, impelled by some reason which he could not define, determined to follow her there. There was something strange, it appeared to him, in the fact of his minister's wife going, under such unusual circumstances, to so unusual a place. He got a gallery ticket, and entered as the curtain rose upon the first act of the play.

Six months later a woman who had once been beautiful lay dying of consumption in a well-furnished house in the city. She was surrounded by every comfort, and received careful attendance from persons who knew her only under a fictitious name, as an invalid who had been placed by a physician in their charge, and who had endeared herself to them by her wonderful patience and humility, which shone like stars about her pathway, gaining constantly a purer luster as she neared its end.

There is a suffering so keen, an anguish so intense, that words are too feeble to portray the sharpness of the one, or measure the depth of the other; and tragedies that we do not dream of are being enacted in our midst every day.

Let us open this woman's diary and see what it contains. The entries are disconnected and incomplete, but sufficient to give us an insight into her inner life.

Here, April 13th, we read:

"I feel, with ever-increasing certainty, that my days are drawing to their close, and with this certainty the yearning grows stronger to be permitted to see *him* once more. To look into his eyes and know myself forgiven—to feel the clasp of his hand, the touch of his lips—nay, even to look at him from a distance. If he should count me unworthy of his touch, would be a happiness so great that I would bear it with me to my last hour, and cherish it amid the pangs of death. This silence, this utter estrangement, are insupportable. Was my sin, then, so great? Can tears and repentance never blot it out?

. . . .

"Since he came into his fortune he has caused me to be supplied with comforts, even luxuries, of every kind. He has not forgotten me, then. It is some consolation to be sure even of that. Perhaps he prays for me, too. Yes, I know he must, for he is a good man, and I need his prayers so much."

Then, under the date of June 10th:

"I had a fainting fit this morning, which Mrs. M——, my kind nurse, says was the result of extreme exhaustion. But it was not that which brought it on. I saw his name unexpectedly in one of the newspapers, and it seemed to drive all the blood to my heart and suffocate me. He has donated a large sum to a charitable institution in this city, and is doing much for the relief of the poor. He has a generous, princely heart, and could not steel it, I suppose, against any person who was not very wicked...... I wonder if any of the poor people at the Flat ever think of me? The days when I used to help him look after them seem to me now like a dream.

"Speaking of dreams, I dreamed last night that I was playing 'Juliet.' I don't know where I was, or anything about it, except that when I got through, there I saw him, standing and looking at me with such stern eyes. 'It was for your sake, dear,' I said to him; and then his sternness seemed to vanish, and he smiled. Does he believe, I wonder, that I *did* do it—that last time—for his sake."

Again, some weeks later:

"I have nearly come to the end of my little book. How straggling and odd my writing has become. He could scarcely read it, I suppose. I have a fancy that I should like him to have it after I have become only a memory to him. Only a memory—why, that is all that I am now. But he must not see it while I am here. Afterward, if he should read it, he would find out how dearly I loved him—how dearly......

"I had to stop there. It is useless to try......God bless you, my own,......forgive......"

And here the writing trails off into indistinctness. A few feeble, illegible strokes, and after that a blank page or two, are all that remain of the diary.

It never came into Cyril's possession. Perhaps it was as well that the misery of reading those pathetic scraps of longing and regret was not added to the misery which he already endured, and still endures.

He has no longer the burden of poverty to struggle under, for that was lifted soon after his wife left home, by the unexpected thoughtfulness of a distant relative, who bequeathed him a handsome fortune. He spends his money freely on everybody but himself. His own life is one perpetual round of self-denial, and no smile or look of gladness ever illumines his face. What memories have their hiding place down deep in his heart, what thoughts afflict him day by day and hour by hour, what woeful dreams haunt his brief seasons of repose—one may try to fancy, but can never know. If, in his rigid adherence to a fixed principle of duty, he has chanced to overstep that line where mercy ends, it is, perhaps, no fault of his. His own punishment is, at least, as severe as that which he has dealt out to another.

The world judges according to our actions, and its judgment is frail. It is good to believe that in a higher world our motives are balanced against our faults. Of sinning we have enough; but there is also repentance, and for repentance, forgiveness. And it may be that error is not always counted sin. Some day all shadows will be lifted, and error will be lost in the clear light of truth.

But in this life the shadow will never be lifted from Cyril's heart, which is desolate, like his home.

FANNIE M. P. DEAS.

A GLIMPSE OF MEXICO.

To the great body of Americans, our neighboring republic on the south is an unknown land, a *terra incognita*, concerning which vague and unsatisfactory ideas are entertained. Germany and France are farther from our shores, and Japan, Australia, and China are half way round the globe, but the average American citizen is better informed concerning these countries—their peoples and customs, their resources, geography, and political institutions—than he is regarding Mexico, with its long line of contiguous territory immediately to our south. Certain impressions prevail in which truth is blended with error; but the tendency is to exaggerate the bad and underestimate the good in the composition of our neighbor to such an extent that the truth itself is not clearly defined or appreciated. Romance has lent itself readily to the support of the prevailing misconceptions.

Somewhere down under the southern horizon is supposed to be a goodly land. The sunlight pours over it in a golden flood, and the yellow hazes of perpetual summer float in its valleys. Tropical forests reach away into the blue distance—the palm, the cocoa-nut, and the towering cactus. The yellow mango glistens among the dark green leaves, and olive-buds and orange-blooms load the air with their sweet odors. A thousand "strange, bright birds, on starry wings" flutter and carol amid the foliage. Valleys, rich in nature's gifts of wood and stream, plow green furrows through the land; blue mountains rise on either hand, and snow-capped peaks push their white tips up close to heaven.

Such were my preconceived ideas of the external physical aspect of this southern world before I had placed my foot upon its shore. But this was not all. At night I dreamed the moon came out and filled the valleys with mellow light. I could see tropic lakes, lying still, and deep, and clear, with the starlight reflected from their bosoms. The tinkling of soft guitars stole in and out upon the air of night. Dark eyes flashed from bower and trellised window, and the liquid music of the Spanish tongue was suggestive of limitless love, and life, and passion.

And then there was another picture. The women of this fair land were all beautiful and good; the land itself was God's own; but the men—the representative Mexican citizen—was a treacherous, bloodthirsty, stage-robbing, revolution-provoking individual. He dressed in a broad hat, a leather suit, sprinkled over with buttons and silver spangles, a pair of spurs and a gay *serape*. He was always armed to the teeth, and carried a long dark coil at his saddle-bow. He was graceful and polite, handsome, jealous, and lazy; quick to settle all disputes with knife or pistol, by fair means or foul, and finding the chief joy of his existence in inciting revolutions against the Government and waylaying the lumbering stage-coach. Watches were rare articles in Mexico. People seldom slept in beds, and the staples of diet were the traditional, historical, and long-suffering articles known as *tortillas* and *chile colorado*, or red peppers. According to this gratuitous estimate, feuds, anarchy, and civil disturbances lent a constant zest and romantic charm to first-class Mexican society, and the lover of excitement and adventure could find no finer field for the gratification of his tastes. But if I have since learned somewhat of the folly and extravagance of my early Mexican day-dreams, I fear there are others who still indulge them.

A few months since, a gentleman took his seat beside me on a westward bound train. He was well dressed and pleasant mannered, and talked intelligently upon the current topics of the day, both in America and Europe. I was congratulating myself upon having found so agreeable a traveling companion, when an allusion was made to Mexico, and, on learning that I had been there, he astounded me by requesting to be informed if Mexico was still a colony of Great Britain.

On another occasion, while talking with a Boston lady, a casual allusion was made to the revolutionary condition of our sister republic, when she turned upon me with the query:

"What about these Mexican wars? Are they constantly fighting among themselves, or with the surrounding nations?"

While I have no malicious purpose to subserve in thus poking fun at my whilom friends, I cannot avoid being reminded by their questions of the great ignorance existing in this country respecting our next-door neighbor. We often hear the remark made, and the newspapers are constantly repeating it, that we should have closer and more cordial relations with Mexico, politically, socially, and commercially. But here, as a general thing, the matter ends, and no one tells us just what is to be done to bring about so desirable a result. Nor is it a problem of easy solution. "San Francisco should control the commerce of the west coast of Mexico." Such is the stereotyped newspaper comment. How can this thing be accomplished? A satisfactory answer to the natural inquiry is not made. The political or international relations of our Government with that of Mexico should be more cordial and harmonious. Why is it not so? Nobody knows. The christian and enlightened people of the United States should exercise a moral influence upon the Mexican nation, such as should tend to elevate the masses of her population from the condition of ignorance and degradation into which they are now sunk. Is this force at work? And if not, why not?

I have not proposed, in this brief paper, to attempt a systematic answer to these questions, nor do I know that I could do so satisfactorily; but a residence of nearly five years in the Mexican capital, with exceptional opportunities for observing and acquiring information, has convinced me of the fact that the great necessity, the step which must precede all others in the bringing about of the most satisfactory relations, is a more thorough mutual acquaintance of the two peoples. They must learn to know each other's habits, wants, and modes of thought. They must get rid of old prejudices and misconceptions respecting each other, and take a charitable view of faults which are the natural outgrowth of ancient errors and superstitions, for which the present generation is not responsible. They should study the geography, history, political institutions, literature, and natural resources each of the other's country. In the United States the study of French and German in our schools should give way to Spanish, and, *vice versa*, the study of English should be made obligatory in the public schools of Mexico.

The process is a slow one. No sudden revolution of sentiment can be brought about in either country. The trade of Mexico cannot be appropriated in a day, or a week, or a year, nor can it be made manifest at once to the people of the two countries that their best interests are identical, and that fraternity is their best policy. This must all come about slowly and patiently. One need not, however, look far ahead in the history of this country to perceive the utility and the necessity of such a course. When increased railroading, telegraphing, and steam-boating facilities shall have brought the two nationalities into closer contact, those men who have been thus educated will have every advantage in all the avenues involving reciprocal interests, and the intelligent American merchant will know that in this way alone can he compete with his European rival.

Mexico is, in many respects, a most wonderful country. Taken as a whole, her climate, soil, and material richness are wonderful. Her history is wonderful and full of romance. Her mountain scenery is unsurpassed. Her people are picturesque and hospitable, and many of them live wonderfully close to nature. Her politics, not unlike our own, are often wonderfully mixed, and the customs, habits, and religion of her people are fruitful sources of wonderment to the stranger upon her shores.

Ex-Minister Foster, in his published letter of October 9, 1878, to the Manufacturers' Association of the North-west, at Chicago, in alluding to the natural richness of the country, and its admirable position for commerce between two oceans, makes use of the following language:

"No person can visit Mexico without being struck with its marvelous natural resources, its fertility of soil, its genial climate, and its capacity to sustain a large population and extensive commerce. The motto of its patron saint is a recognition of these gifts and capabilities: 'The Lord hath not dealt so with any nation.' ......It can produce all the coffee consumed in the United States. It has a greater area of sugar-producing lands than Cuba, and of equal fertility. Its capacity for the production of vegetable textiles is equal to any country in the world. Almost all the tropical drugs and all the fruits of the world can be cultivated successfully. Its varied climate admits of the growth of all the cereals of all the zones. Its ranges afford the widest scope and the best conditions for wool and stock-raising. And, most of all, skillful American mining engineers who have examined the matter, claim that its mineral wealth, yet hidden away in the recesses of its mountain ranges, is superior to that of California, Nevada, or Australia."

Covering altogether an area of about one million square miles, and extending as far south as the fifteenth parallel of north latitude, the soil of Mexico slopes gradually up from a tropic ocean on either side, until a vast central table-land is formed, ranging from four to eight thousand feet above the level of the sea. To this fact is due its varied climate and the limitless variety of its vegetable products.

Starting from the sea shore and directing his course inland, the traveler finds as he proceeds that he is gradually rising through the different gradations of the torrid zone and entering upon temperate latitudes. This he can at once detect from the decreasing heat, and, more particularly, from the change in the style of vegetation which surrounds him. A run over the railroad from the gulf port of Vera Cruz to the City of Mexico is a revelation to the intelligent stranger. This is the only completed line of railroad in the republic. The distance between the two points is about two hundred and sixty miles, the run being made in a little over eighteen hours. There is probably no road of equal length in the world upon which the traveler can pass so rapidly from torrid to temperate zone—from the region of the palm to that of the pine—and through so varying a panorama of wonder and beauty, as upon this Mexican road. Leaving the hot, fever-ridden sea coast at Vera Cruz, where death and the black *vomito* have maintained a reign of terror since the landing of the first Spaniard, your car rolls westward for a couple of hours over a level sand plain, covered with low, dense vegetation, interspersed here and there with giant trees, many of them leafless and apparently dead. The buzzard, or *zopilote*, as the natives call him, loves these solitudes, and countless numbers of them are forever perched along the naked limbs, or flapping curiously past your car window. From this low plain the road gradually emerges, the country begins to roll a little, the foot-hills draw near, the vegetation takes on another tinge and form, and before you can fully make up your mind to the change you are skirting the banks of a limpid stream, with picturesque hills on either side. The ascent is now rapid, and a charming panorama of mountain, stream, and *cañon*, with occasional glimpses of the Gulf of Mexico in the distance, is before you. Your car is headed bravely for the heart of the Cordillera, which rises, blue and mysterious, far above you; and now and then, as you twist and curve about the *cañons*, glimpses may be had from the car window of the white cone of Orizaba, which lifts its pale tip up so close to heaven that the Indians call it the Mountain of the Star.

The construction of this road, which is due to an English company, is one of the boldest of engineering feats. In addition to the natural difficulties to be overcome, the work was delayed and embarrassed, and the expense immensely increased, by the revolutions and civil disturbances which have so long distracted our unhappy neighbor. So great were the difficulties of all kinds which had to be surmounted, that this comparatively short road, which was commenced in the year 1837, was not fully completed until the year 1872, and the expense of the construction exceeded forty millions of dollars. It is the natural difficulties, however, which have been overcome by the skill of the engineer, which make this road remarkable. Mexico City is 7,500 feet above the level of the sea, but the road reaches at one point an elevation of about 8,000 feet. This elevation is not reached by slow gradations, but is overcome at once by a system of grades, and tunnels, and bridges, such as is not found anywhere else on this continent. The heaviest grades are on the eastern slope of the mountains. From a point forty-six miles below Boca del Monte, the summit station, there is a rise of 4,500 feet. From a point thirteen miles below this same station the rise is 3,600 feet. The larger part of this last mentioned rise is a continuous four per cent. grade. To better illustrate it, you are climbing the mountain in a car fifty feet long, the lower end of which is two feet below the upper end. The engines used on this road are English monsters of the Fairlie patent. They are double-enders, have two smoke-stacks and twelve driving-wheels, and weigh over sixty tons. The ease with which they handle a heavy train on a mountain side is admirable, but their complicated machinery makes them liable to get out of order, and American locomotives are gradually taking their place.

The scenery along the entire line of this route, after entering the mountains, is grand and picturesque in the extreme, the much admired views in the Sierra Nevada along the line of the Central Pacific Railroad sinking into insignificance in comparison and in thrilling interest. Your car twists in and out among the mountains, now on the verge of a dizzy precipice, now suspended in mid-air from a curving bridge over a foaming waterfall, and now diving with a wild shriek into the darkness of a tunneled ambuscade. The track on all sides of you seems to form a systemless labyrinth, and the whirling, changing vegetation all conspire to thrill with pleasurable excitement and interest. In a few hours' time you have risen from the region of the rice plant, the sugar-cane, and the orange to the wheat plains of the upper table-land, and the burning sands of Vera Cruz have been exchanged for the cooling shadows of Orizaba, with its crown of eternal snow. The verdict of all travelers who reach the City of Mexico is, that the ride over this road is alone worth the expense and the trouble of a trip to Mexico.

The Valley of Mexico itself has been too often described to warrant more than a passing allusion. Nature has been kind to this fair land, and the Valley of Mexico, with its lakes and streams and groves, is as beautiful to-day as it was when Cortez looked down upon it for the first time from the wooded hights of Ixtacihuatl. The lakes have receded somewhat, and the city in their midst has changed its smoking *teocalis* for a hundred gilded church domes, pointing skyward; but the sunlight and the mountains have lost no charm. To the southeast of the city, and at a distance of about fifty miles, rise the snow-capped volcano of Popocatepetl and its companion peak of Iztacihuatl, or the Woman in White.

The desire to ascend this volcano, and look down into its smoking bosom, early takes possession of the wanderer in Anahuac. The traditions connected with the spot, and the old Indian superstitions—of which Prescott has told us—the magnificent view to be had from the summit, and the novelty and adventure of the ascent, are powerful temptations to the average mortal from less favored lands to take his life in his hand and scale the snowy hights. A mountain is such a beautiful thing in the distance, so cloud-like and soft, that it is hard to believe that it is cold and cruel and fickle upon a nearer approach. But such must ever be the conclusion of those who venture high up into the snow wastes of a Mexican volcano. I was early taken with this wild love, and, in company with two others as deeply enamored as myself, took advantage of the first opportunity to make the ascent. We started, with our Indian guides, on the abrupt incline in the early morning, and for eight long weary hours struggled upward, through black volcanic sand, and over the slippery, treacherous ice, cutting our footsteps with a spade, foot by foot, as we advanced, until, exhausted and faint, at two o'clock in the afternoon we flung ourselves down at the outer edge of a great, black, smoking gulf, the crater of Popocatepetl.

This point had not been reached, however, without great suffering and distress. On nearing the crater we were met by the emerging sulphur fumes, which, together with the light air and intense fatigue, made sad havoc in our party. All ideas of sport had long since departed. Our heads seemed ready to burst with throbbing pains, and the cold was bitter and sharp when we stopped for a moment's rest. One of our number finally gave out, and was placed in the hands of two Indians, who literally carried him over the last few hundred yards of the ascent. The first view of the crater is startling. There is no preparation for it, nothing in sight to indicate its presence. You find yourself suddenly stopped on the edge of a wall of ice, and looking down into a smoking gulf two thousand feet deep. It is a perfect picture of death and desolation, and as you stand there, with throbbing temples, wonder stricken, the gloomy abyss seems still more death-like, from contrast with the beautiful world on every side of it. The form of the crater of this mountain is nearly circular—slightly elliptical, with the elongation extending from north to south. It is entered from the north, where the lip of the opening is lower than at any other point. Although in reality over three miles in circumference, its immense depth and abrupt sides make it appear much smaller; one might think that he could throw a stone across it. On every side the mountain rises to a sharp comb, bordering on this chasm, and in one or two places only is there sufficient room for a person to stand.

When all the stragglers had come up, a consultation was held, and it was decided that it was too late to go down that day, and that we must spend the night in the crater. Waving adieu to the world, we clambered down the wall of ice, and found ourselves on a narrow strip of warm sand, overtopping what is known as the interior lip. From this point there is a treacherous descent of seventy-five feet to the point where the wall of the crater becomes abrupt and perpendicular; and here, on an overhanging rock, is planted a rickety old windlass on which the sulphur-miners ascend and descend. The windlass is worked by hand. There is no cage or basket at the end of the coil. You are tied into a loop at the end of the rope, like a box of sulphur, and lowered away over the smoking abyss, the bottom of which is three hundred feet beneath you. One by one we were lowered over the precipice in this manner, and then commenced a most treacherous and difficult descent over the sloping pile of *débris*, from the base of the precipice, fifteen hundred feet down to the very bottom of the crater, where the only place of safety is to be found. We had hardly commenced this perilous descent when a tremendous report saluted our ears, and a hundred tons of rocks went crashing past us on the left and rolled into the bottom of the chasm. This was a mode of salutation that we had not anticipated, but it soon became evident that the ability to dodge rocks was the only guarantee of safety here. Owing to the alternate action of heat and cold, the sides of the crater have become completely rotten, and during the heat of the day immense quantities of rocks are constantly falling. Toward morning they freeze in again, and all remains quiet for a while. During the past twenty years many men have been killed on this spot by these avalanches of stones. In order to protect themselves, the sulphur-miners have built little huts in the crevices among the huge bowlders at the center of the crater. Some dying convulsion swelled up a little mound at this point, and only the larger bowlders, falling from the highest peaks, ever reach it. There is still danger on one side, however, from ordinary stones, and when that startling word, *piedras*, rings out through the chasm, the men come swarming out of the mines like a flock of quails, and hide themselves in well known places of safety. On entering the crater, no one escapes the dread malaria of the spot. Indian and White Man alike go down, with flying pains in the head, and a nauseating feeling at the stomach that is worse than sea-sickness. Conklin, of all our party, seemed most affected. He had strength enough to crawl to one of the huts, and there he sank down on a mat in an almost insensible condition. It was not long before the rest of us joined him, and then commenced one of the most unpleasant nights I ever spent. Seven of of us were confined in a space of about six by seven feet. It was impossible for any man to stretch himself out at full length. Nearly all of us were deathly sick, and combined with these discomforts was the constant fear of being crushed by the falling rocks. All night long they fell with fearful reverberating echoes from the surrounding cliffs. We were told that more than usual came down, owing to the fact that the preceding day had been a little warmer than common. In contrast with the booming sound of these flying bowlders, came the sucking, surging sound of the great *respiraderos* all around us. These breathing holes, or vapor-jets, are six in number. They are in constant action, and throw off immense quantities of smoke and vapor, with now and then a lurid tongue of flame. All the heat of the crater is not confined to these spots, however. Little jets of steam creep out from every crevice, all the rocks are warm, and it is impossible to find a place to lie down where you are not tormented by curling whiffs of sulphur smoke rising from the earth beneath you. Toward midnight I found it impossible to endure my cramped position in the hut any longer. Every muscle in my body ached, and, as sleep was out of the question, I gathered up my blanket and made my way out into the open air. A scene of the most weird and awful character presented itself. The crater seemed full of smoke. Detached clouds of vapor waved themselves back and forth along the cliffs like ghosts, and as I listened to the hoarse breathing of that mysterious power which I could not see, I thought of the wild Aztec legends connected with the spot, and, in my superstitious mood, I half believed that the restless spirits of their departed chiefs had risen to confront and haunt me for my intrusion into their dread abode.

Between two rocks on the southern cliff the moon looked down blood-red. I thought of eruptions and earthquakes, and although I knew the peculiar appearance of the moon was due to an optical delusion produced by the smoke, I could not divest myself of the feeling that I was treading on Plutonian territory, and that I might at any moment be shot out into space. Next morning every one was better, with the exception of Conklin. Noon came, and he revived a little, but this spell was followed early in the afternoon by another of the most alarming character. His face turned to the most ghastly color, his senses entirely left him, and he lay in the bottom of the hut like a dead man. It was impossible to get out now before morning, and, as we had no medicines or mode of giving relief, our anxiety was painful. The second night in the *infierno* was much the same as the first, with the exception that Thomas and I slept outside the hut. We had become indifferent to the danger from falling rocks by this time, and preferred the sky and the stars and the risk to the dismal interior of the hut. As soon as it was daylight, everything was made ready for our climb up into the world again. Conklin still lay insensible, and it was with heavy hearts that we carried him out and strapped him on the back of a stalwart Indian. To get him up those cliffs alive seemed an impossibility; but it was death to remain, so there was no choice. Inch by inch, and almost dragging him in some places, we got him up over the slanting *débris* to the foot of the perpendicular wall. It took nearly two hours to do that, and then, lashing him like a dead body to another Indian, he was hoisted up over the cliff. As the rope tightened on him, and he rose higher and higher, with head and arms dangling, there was not a man among us who expected to find him alive when he reached the top. In this expectation we were happily disappointed, however, for on reaching him we could still detect traces of life. Placing him in charge of two of the most trustworthy native mountaineers, we mounted the outer lip, and stood once more in the world. Never did old Mother Earth seem so beautiful. We felt as Lazarus must have felt when he rose from the grave; and when, a few hours later, we found ourselves down among the fragrant pines near the mountain's base, and our exhausted companion, revived by the fresher, denser air, opened his eyes with a look of recognition, we felt that our ambition for volcano climbing was abundantly satisfied.

Returning, however, from this digression, the question naturally presents itself: How is it that a country so rich in material resources, and so blessed by Nature with all that man desires to make him happy and contented, is so backward in the march of civilization, and so slow in developing its latent stores of material wealth? I think there is but one answer to this question, and that is the revolutionary condition of the country, and the absence of a firm, strong government to enforce law and order, and make life and property secure. Is there any excuse for this condition of things, and have Mexican revolutions, as a general rule, had any higher aim than plunder and the venting of a morbid spirit of unrest? I think I can answer affirmatively to both these queries. The population of Mexico is between eight and nine millions, three-fourths of whom are full-blooded descendants of the original Indian inhabitants. These people, after the Spanish conquest, and for nearly three hundred years, were ground down under the heel of a selfish and heartless despotism. The *peon* system was in full force—a system which, in its practical workings, reduced the condition of the masses to the level of slavery. Education was excluded, and priestly superstitions and tyrannies encouraged and fostered. The most oppressive trade laws and regulations were enforced, and the whole policy of the Spanish Government was directed toward crushing out the light, liberty, and manhood of an unfortunate people, and making them blind contributors to the wealth of Spain. As late as 1810, a Spanish edict was in force to the effect that the grape should not be cultivated in Mexico—that the colony should not compete with the mother country in the manufacture of wine; and it was the ruthless enforcement of this edict by the Spanish soldiery, who descended upon the vineyards of the priest, Miguel Hidalgo, and destroyed his vines, which induced the brave old man to raise his voice against Spanish tyranny, and on the night of the 15th of September, 1810, the first cry for Mexican independence was sent ringing through the land. The people did not know what it meant, but they knew that they were miserable and unhappy. They had heard of the Great Republic on the north, and that the people there ruled themselves and were contented and prosperous. Liberty was a soul-stirring word, and in their ignorance, poverty, and degradation, they felt its appeal, and rallied by thousands to the support of its standard.

Shortly before the death of the old hero, Santa Ana, I had the privilege of meeting him often in his rooms in the City of Mexico. He was cheerful and talkative, and loved to recall his early exploits and reminiscences of the first years of the republic. I can remember him distinctly as he sat one evening on his sofa in a dimly lighted room, with his wooden leg out straight before him, and his white, almost effeminate face beaming pleasantly on the circle of friends around him. His eye was black as a coal, and flashed with all the fire of youth when the conversation touched on any topic which pleased him. Some allusion was made to his early career in the dawning days of the republic.

"Republic!" he exclaimed. "I did not know what a republic was. A body of citizens came to me in Vera Cruz, and asked me to lead them in establishing a republican government. 'But what is a republic?' I asked. '*Viva la Republica!*' was all the reply they could make to me; and so we stumbled along in the dark in our efforts to make a government and free ourselves from Spain."

Mexico was not ready for a republican form of government when the cry for independence was raised, nor was she ready for it when her independence was achieved in 1821, nor is she, in fact, ready for it to-day. It cannot be denied, however, that the tendency from 1810 to the present time has been in the right direction. Although not prepared for republicanism, such republicanism as she has maintained is better than slavery, and the progress which has been made in many directions is most astonishing, in view of the difficulties of the situation. Every revolution, while it has decreased the material wealth of the country, has let in some light upon the people, and advanced some social, human, or political right. One by one the wrongs and abuses which had grown up in Mexico had to be met and overcome. The people were ignorant; the use of the elective franchise was unknown; there was no public press, nor way of molding public opinion; bad men were numerous, and availed themselves of the situation to plunder, and steal, and usurp power. There was but one recourse when a great wrong was to be crushed, and that recourse was to arms. Through the whole history of Mexico there have been zealous, honest, patriotic men struggling for right and their country's welfare. For many years the principal struggle was between the church and state, and it was an unequal struggle, for the church had wealth, and organization, and sympathy, and power. But the people triumphed, and the power of the church was broken forever. The result of this struggle was the Liberal Constitution of 1857, which is now the fundamental charter of the land. This document, which is modeled after our own, guarantees civil and religious liberty to all men, and, together with its accompanying liberal code of laws, is a giant stride in the march of progress. The *peon* system has been done away with, the liberty of conscience and the press proclaimed, the Jesuits banished, and schools and charitable institutions established in many parts of the land. My object in mentioning these things is simple. During the sixty years of Mexican independence she has been so busy getting rid of old obstacles and stumbling-blocks—such as our forefathers did not have to encounter in establishing this republic—that the progress actually made is remarkable, and deserving of praise and commendation rather than the contempt and indifference with which these struggles have generally been viewed. I would not defend all these revolutions, for many of them have been foolish—such as that of the chief, Marquez, recently in progress in northern Mexico, and the abortive attempts at insurrection which are now reported; but, viewed as a whole, I doubt whether the advancement already made by Mexico in all departments of civilized life could have been attained in the next fifty years without them.

There is, then, some excuse for the condition of anarchy which has prevailed so long in the neighboring republic. Nor is Mexico exceptional and alone in this respect. A glance back at the history of every European country will show that all have passed through the same experiences of civil turmoil and disorder before reaching a comparative state of tranquillity and prosperity. England has been no exception to this rule, and we in America to-day are enjoying the fruits and the benefits, in the shape of liberty and human rights, which resulted from each upheaval and civil disturbance of those unhappy times. Mexico has come later upon the stage, and when we consider the character of her population and the circumstances by which she has been surrounded, we believe she is entitled to a more charitable judgment from the civilized world.

A stable government is the object to be attained before prosperity of any kind can ensue. To the necessity of this proposition all intelligent Mexicans are wide awake, and the indications are that the time has arrived when this *desideratum* may be realized. With the exception of a few unimportant *pronunciamientos*, the administration of President Diaz, now in power, has maintained peace and tranquillity throughout the republic for nearly four years, and I fully believe that the day has gone by when any revolutionary movement can again overthrow the federal authority of the republic.

There is still much to be done before Mexico can enter upon the career of prosperity to which she is certainly destined. For the first time in her history she has reached a breathing place, and on looking about she finds herself impoverished, her credit gone, a heavy debt upon her shoulders, internal improvements of all kinds neglected, and her immense natural resources undeveloped. She looks to the outside nations, and particularly to the United States, to assist her through this crisis, by both moral and material support. Foreign capital is invited to come and open up her mines and hidden stores of wealth. She wants railroads and steam communication by water. It is true there is a fear at present of railroad communication with the United States. But is not this fear well founded? The Mexicans have not forgotten the history of Texas, and they know something of the grasping character of our countrymen. A railroad over the border will, they say, result in Americanizing the frontier States, and, in their present condition, they are conscious of the fact that they could not hold them. An honest effort is being made, however, to encourage commercial intercourse with the United States, and the Government of Mexico has done much more in this respect than has our own. There are now three lines of American steamships touching at Mexican ports, all of which receive a subsidy from the Mexican Government, but not a cent from the Government of the United States. These steamers would, in all probability, be withdrawn but for the aid thus afforded. If our merchants are really desirous of opening up more extended commercial relations with this country, would it not be well to call the attention of Congress to the matter, and ask for the expenditure of a reasonable sum annually in furthering this object? The judicious use of $150,000 a year would result in doubling the present means of communication with Mexican ports. And when we consider that larger sums are spent every year in maintaining steam connections with other, and perhaps less important and more distant, parts of the globe, it seems strange that the market at our very doors should have been so long overlooked.

Mexico wants to trade with us, but our merchants in opening up this trade must, if successful, operate in such a way as not to antagonize or violate the national feelings and the prejudices of a sensitive people. There are difficulties to be overcome, but they can only be overcome gradually and patiently. Nothing can be forced or done in a hurry. Reciprocity treaties, such as the existing one with the Hawaiian Islands, are impossible, and will not be considered, in Mexico. The Germans have shown themselves best adapted for this trade, and by their patient and persevering policy have fairly earned the monopoly of the commerce which they at present control. Mr. Foster, in his letter from which I have already quoted, in referring to this point, says:

"The Hamburg merchants establish their branches in various parts of Mexico, and send their educated youth out to serve an apprenticeship in the business, and to afterward assume the management of the branch houses. They become thoroughly familiar with the condition and practices of the country, and master the intricacies of the tariff and interior duties. Revolutions and changes of government do not disturb their equanimity. They become accustomed to 'forced loans' and 'extraordinary contributions.' Notwithstanding the irregularities of the custom-house officials and the embarrassments of the contraband trade, they keep the 'even tenor of their way,' and usually (though not always) in middle or advanced life are able to go back to Germany with a competence."

I have, however, already departed far from my original purpose in this paper. It was not my intention to dwell upon commercial topics. I wanted to say something more of the people of Mexico—their customs and habits. I had proposed to speak of their schools and religion, and the odd sights and experiences of a traveler in this interesting land. The Protestant missionary work in Mexico, the ancient ruins, that peculiar institution—a government pawn-shop, or *monte pio*—the floating gardens, Chapultepec, the bull ring, stage robbing, *hacienda* life, the *paseo*, popular amusements, and a hundred other subjects, each of which would merit a chapter in itself; all these must be passed over for the present.

It is in the city of Mexico itself that the best of everything Mexican is seen. Here is found education and refinement, a love for music and literature, fine schools and churches and philanthropic institutions. Many of the better classes of the people have traveled, and speak all the modern languages; and their professional men—physicians, lawyers, editors, and students—will rank favorably with those of any other people. The Mexicans are hospitable and exceedingly polite—two virtues, by the way, which cover a multitude of little sins, and which may be profitably imitated in America. The educated Mexican of to-day is a free-thinker on religious subjects. As in France, the tendency has been to go from one extreme to the other. The religious fervor or fanaticism of thirty years ago has given place to infidelity, atheism, spiritualism, and an absence of belief in anything. This applies, of course, to none but the educated classes. The great masses are still faithful to Mother Church. This Catholic religion of Mexico is a remarkable medley—a mixture of absurdities and sacred things. Such a thing as spiritual religion is unknown. The great body of the Indian population is as much in the dark to-day respecting the truths of the Christian religion as they were before the conquest. The church has been content to engraft a few of its forms upon the old Indian beliefs and superstitions, and the product is a condition of things found in no other country, Catholic or Protestant. In my excursions through Mexico I met many of the priests. They are generally jolly, good fellows, hospitable and kind, but almost as ignorant as their flocks. I once asked a good *padre* in an interior town, after returning with him from a religious performance:

"How is it that instead of playing with fire, and jingling bells, and bowing, and marching around, you do not get up once in a while and tell these people: 'It is wrong to lie; you must not steal; be good men.'"

But I saw that I had hurt his feelings, and got no reply save the characteristic shrug. The policy of the church, to hold the masses by amusing them, is fully lived up to in Mexico. There are many amusing forms and ceremonies of a semi-religious character. On Ascension Day, for example, every true and faithful son of the church considers it his duty to manifest, in some manner, his disrespect for the memory of Judas Iscariot. For this purpose every man, woman, and child procures a burlesque image, ranging in size from a few inches in length to immense figures six or eight feet high. These are all provided with a fire-cracker attachment, and when, on the day in question, the bell in the town announces that the hour has arrived for vengeance, every man touches off his Judas, and the poor fellow's effigy is blown into a thousand pieces. This performance is varied a little in different parts of the country. I remember on one occasion of being in a country village on Ascension Day, and of being startled by a wild shout from a hundred voices. On rushing into the street, I was surprised to see a frantic steer charging down the road at full speed, with the whole village at his heels, yelling and whooping like a band of wild Indians. Strapped fast to the back of the steer was a life-sized effigy of Judas Iscariot, and as it tipped back and forth, and the steer pitched and bellowed, and the effigy began to come to pieces, tossing an arm here, and a head there, the populace redoubled their shouts, and I have no doubt all felt satisfied that they had performed a good Christian duty, at the same time having lots of fun at the expense of old Judas for his crime of eighteen hundred years ago.

There is much to be done—there is much that we all can do, by extending our sympathy and charity—to raise these people to a higher plane of things. To know each other better must, however, precede all else, and the hope of exciting such desire on the part of my fellow countrymen has been the motive which has actuated me in the preparation of this paper.

D. S. RICHARDSON.

IF IT COULD BE.

If it could be as I dream
When the birds sing loud to the dewy morn,
And the wind comes up through the tasseled corn
Out of the ferny wood,
I should waken far in a glorious land,
Where the mountains, a gleaming sapphire band,
Stand in the sun's bright flood—
If it could be as I dream!

If it could be as I dream
When the maples wave their leaves in the sun,
And the shadows creep slowly, one by one,
Over the long green field,
I should walk in a busy, thronging street,
One would come that way, and our eyes would meet;
What would be then revealed,
If it could be as I dream!

If it could be as I dream
When the sunset fades, and the sky grows gray,
And the white moon sails on her silent way
Over a starry sea,
One would come again through the summer night,
And his eyes grow sweet with the old, glad light;
What would that meeting be,
If it could be as I dream!

JULIA H. S. BUGBIA.

A NEW ENGLAND FARM.

In a quiet country town of New England is a farm which used to be my earthly paradise. My own father's place was very pleasant in its way, but it called for a little too much work, from the time when a boy could ride a horse to plow out corn or follow the hay-cart with a rake. My grandfather's farm, on the contrary, was a place for infinite leisure and sport. The standing invitation he gave me was to "come down and do up the mischief." Then, too, there was the novelty of hidden nooks in house and barns, of unexplored meadows and pastures. Far up on the hillside the woodland lost itself in an unbroken forest, where the small boy could easily imagine beasts of prey. Under the scattering trees that fringed it, foxes had their holes by the side of a sheltering rock. Great was my admiration for the larger boy who could entrap them. Back of the farm buildings was a famous echo rock, from which, as I stood and shouted down the hill, my shrill tones were returned with startling distinctness. A log aqueduct brought down from the mountain the most delicious water, which poured with constant music into the great tub on the kitchen porch. Just back of the barns were giant walnut trees, whose nuts gave equal pleasure in the gathering and the eating, and whose fragrant leaves allured the swarming bees to new hives. A sturdy butternut helped to vary the entertainment of the winter evenings. Wide-spreading buttonwoods shaded the house in front, and offered pleasant loitering to the travelers on the high road. There was no cross-road near. One straight country street ran, with a few right-angled tributaries, for miles along the lower upland of the valley. This farm extended down to and across the river. Below the street were a garden and a barn, and in the high stone wall a wide gateway which gave entrance to the upper and the lower meadows. The upper meadows were safe from floods; but on their edge, irregular as the river-bank itself, though at a long distance from it, was a steep slope which let one down to the overflowed bottom lands. This slope was the favorite home of the burrowing woodchuck. In the lower meadows the patient swathman swung his scythe, knowing nothing of the modern mowing-machine. Thither the boys carried the forenoon and the afternoon lunch, to be washed down with copious draughts of cold coffee or molasses and water. If the mowing was beyond the river, there was a "pole" to cross—long, swaying, and seemingly perilous, with flattened top, but with no hand-rail. If the boy could not fare safely over, he must take his ducking in the shallow summer stream. At the river-bends, where the eddies had worn deeper hollows, were places for swimming and trouting. Beyond the bottom lands was another low upland, with a dismantled house, under whose steps a long "racer" had been seen to glide, in whose deserted chambers bats flitted at twilight. It was the haunted house of the farm. The whole estate contained only a little over three hundred acres, but to me it seemed almost a dukedom.

The farm buildings were ample and well appointed. Three large barns were filled to the roof with hay and grain, allowing stable room for horses and cattle. The sheep found shelter in additional sheds. An extra cow-shed and a cider-mill helped, with the two upper barns, to form a hollow square and keep off the northeast storms. The poultry had the range of the upper premises, but were forbidden to cross the street. Chickens in coops were placed in the garden below the street, to pick the bugs from the vines; but if an adult hen returned to her old cucumber ground, and would not be warned away, she went summarily to pot. The squealing pigs had a distant house of their own, with a huge kettle for boiling potatoes and apples. Near this building was a ribbed corn-crib. Farther on in the row, and nearest the house, were a wood-house, replenished from long piles of logs brought on sleds from the upper woodland, and a big tool-room, which was also a carpenter's shop. Here were fashioned ox-bows and yokes, ladders and gate-posts, bee-hives and barn-door buttons. Few things were needed on the farm which could not be made or repaired in that shop. The cider-mill challenged the boy's attention in the autumn, when apples were brought by the cart-load and dumped in huge piles on the ground, then carried in large baskets to the hopper, to be converted into pomace. The steady old horse turned the creaking mill. When the pomace was put into form and pressed, the sweet juice ran into tubs which invited sampling. Cups and glasses were a barbarism; the only proper instrument for tasting and testing was the long bright straw. No sherry cobbler was ever so delicious as that new cider. It was good sport to hunt hens' eggs, in obscure manger corners, on high hay-mows, or in the tall outstanding grass; to see the swarming bees settle on a limb of the near peach tree, and watch the process of hiving them; to ride on the high loads of fragrant hay; to trap the sly woodchuck, and see his grit as a prisoner; to follow the harvesters afield, and stack the clean oat-sheaves in "shocks," and to see the same oats fly from under the alternating flails. About the best fun of all was in the huskings on the great barn-floor. Here were at once activity and repose, individual excellence and social enjoyment. Every man had his stories to tell. The gray-haired grandfather recounted his early exploits, and told how his nimble feet used to trip those of heavier and stronger wrestlers. "Stand up a minute," he would say to his best hired man; and taking him by the collar and elbow he would illustrate his youthful "science," and send his man tottering across the floor. Hardly less was the sport of shearing-time, when the boys were allowed to hold the big shears and trim the sheep's fleecy legs. The shearing was preceded by a general sheep-washing, at the bridge on the nearest cross-road. It was "high jinks" for the boys to stand waist-deep in the water, pass along the swimming sheep, and give the larger lambs a useless bath by themselves. I need not speak of the search for the delicious wild strawberries, or the more profitable quest on the stony hillsides for the genuine New England huckleberries. Peaches grew well, in those past decades, in the fertile back-yard, and in many fields there were tempting crops of apples. That Seek-no-further was the best of its kind; that Roxbury Russet bore the soundest of fruit, which "kept" till June; that Blue Pearmain was the choicest in the region. In the cornfields grew fair broad pumpkins, pleasant to handle, and a treat for milch cows and fattening oxen. On one side of a high fence were piled the bright pyramids; on the other the jealous animals munched a broken segment and tried to thrust away their inferiors. What sleek looking cows and oxen those were! All well cared for and carded down, with brass buttons to blunt and embellish their horns. My grandfather had some of the best oxen in his neighborhood; with his elder son to manage them, his "Bright" and "Buck" would well nigh outdraw a span of Norman horses. When two or three yokes were put together, all but the stoutest chains would snap. A braying jack was kept below the street. Ranging the upper pastures was a troop of long-eared mules, from which the largest were taken every year and shipped to Charleston or Savannah. The "young stock" was carefully tended. A growing yearling or two-year-old, however, did not need the choicest timothy or herds-grass; what best suited his position was the coarse meadow grass. Sometimes he thought otherwise, and when the coarser fare was put into the out-door ricks he turned daintily away. My grandfather devised a method of treatment for just such cases: he went out a few times and drove the creatures all away from the ricks; then the forbidden fodder came to taste as sweet as clover, and the ricks were emptied.

I have not spoken of the house. It was a large farm-house, even for that region of large houses. It was once a country inn—a cool resort for the tired summer traveler, a gathering-place for rural recreations, a rendezvous for the militia-men on training-day. Two owners of the house were successively "Captains." The great memory of the place was the sojourn of Rochambeau and his French troops in the Revolutionary War; how they acted the fine gentlemen, were as merry as became their nation, danced gayly with the ladies, and made soft eyes at the eldest daughter of the house. She remained single through life, and in her later years was a helpless cripple; but her unbending dignity was graced and lightened by these youthful reminiscences. Her room—"Aunt Sarah's"—was the pleasanter of the two great front rooms of the house. The other was the parlor, and between them was a wide old-fashioned hall and staircase. There were but two rooms, also, in the rear of the main part—a dining-room of great length, and the family bed-room. I sometimes ventured into the latter, and was most of all interested in a little wooden bowl which held my grandmother's stock of pins. There were plenty of other striking objects in the room, but none which so impressed me as the pin-bowl. The dining-room had two fire-places, and a stately, solemn clock, full of mysteries. The long table was always populous, especially at Thanksgiving time. No cooking was like that of my grandmother's kitchen. The kitchen was large, of course; large enough for a wide fire-place, with its long swinging crane, its pot-hooks and huge andirons, and its high jamb whereunder a pretty large boy could stand to see how much he had grown the last twelvemonth. Big logs were laid on the fire, which like the temple-fires of old never expired. Lucifer matches were unknown; the coals of hard wood were carefully covered with ashes for the night. When we returned home after a two days' Thanksgiving visit, we repaired to the neighbors' to relight our household altar. My grandfather had an old saw about the kinds of wood to burn, that ran as follows:

"Chestnut wood is not so good
As walnut wood or oak;
But it will burn, and serve its turn,
And make a dreadful smoke."

At the kitchen table, early and late, sat the harvesters, including the men of the family. It was my great treat to sit there, too, and eat a bowl of fresh milk and the matchless rye and Indian bread. It was no easy matter to provide for that little farming community in the busy summer months. The early breakfast of the men, then the more leisurely one of the family; the lunches to prepare and send to the field, forenoon and afternoon; the double dinner, for out-door workers and in-door; the "tea" in the dining-room, and the men's supper in the kitchen; all this was enough to task the strongest and most ingenious housekeeper. There was never quite such another housekeeper as my stout, laughing, unwearied grandmother. None fared ill in her house; but children had dainty delights of their own. Luscious bread and butter, doughnuts just out of their savory bath, incomparable turnovers, draughts of fresh and creamy milk—these were but a tithe of the things by which she knew how to reach the childish heart. The home of these was the long, roomy "buttery," where dwelt essences and odors as from Araby the Blest. A second pantry held rows of mince pies and jelly tumblers, and cheeses—not from Araby, to my perverse taste. But I liked to watch the curds pressed into their round boxes, and to see the rims hardened and laid away in bright yellow rows. Pleasanter to see were the rolls of delicious golden butter, quickly and deftly shaped. Out on the kitchen "stoop" dropped the ever-running pipe of water from the hills: in this cool nook the curds were cut and the butter worked over.

The second story of the house was rich in bed-rooms; three had been made out of the long dancing-hall of the former inn. In one of these I was put to rest; and in the winter the cold sheets were made tropical by the long-handled warming-pan. Sweetest of dreams were those which visited that childish pillow. In the summer morning I looked out on the sunrise, the dewy clover, and the ripening grain, heard the larks at their matins, and drank in the pure fresh air. Of course, there was a garret in this large house, not a mere incident to it, but, to my boyish notion, its chief and crowning glory. Untold treasures were stored there; heir-looms from the past, and disabled implements or disused inventions of the present. There was the old-fashioned spinning-wheel, which could still whirl merrily around. There were the stately "fire-dogs" of a former generation. Great chests and boxes lined the sides of the room, and happy were the hours devoted to ransacking them. The garret was a boon inestimable for the children's rainy days. But there was a garret above the garret, a sort of third heaven, to which admission was rare. It was reached by a steep ladder, and had a floor of loose boards, and its own little window near to the apex of the roof. There were stored the most secret possessions of the house; walnuts and butternuts, bunches of seed sweet-corn, thyme and savory, and all "simples that have virtue" in domestic medicine. The cellar formed a fit foundation for so manifold activities. In it were the finer vegetables for the table. At the foot of the front stairway were rows of swinging shelves for the red and golden apples. Here was to be seen the base of the great stone chimney, which was strong enough to anchor a leaning tower. These immense chimneys took up no small part of the interior of the old-time houses.

Enough as to the farm and the farm-house. They were but the setting for their precious jewels—the human hearts and lives that found there a home. The head of the house was born on the spot, and was a genuine son of the soil. Modest, yet self-reliant, kind to all, but a sturdy supporter of justice, well balanced, full of uncommon common-sense, of strictest integrity, respected and loved by his neighbors, often an arbiter in personal differences, called not unfrequently to places of public trust, this plain New England gentleman was the type of a class that grows ever smaller in New England. It was from the best blood of the Puritans, and had the Puritan steadfastness and energy, blended with the old English heartiness and the true New English devotion to the welfare of others. Of my grandmother it is enough to say that she was a helpmeet for such a husband—self-forgetting, generous, lovable, sensible, beneficent. Her descendants rise up and call her blessed. In my humble opinion it is hard to find a finer type of character than that of this farmer and farmer's wife. But on the New England hills it is passing away. This very farm has been abandoned to another style of occupant. One of the sons, after some mercantile ventures and roamings, settled down at home, and toiled hard to relieve the hard-working sire. The younger daughter wrought with equal energy to lighten the in-door care. But in time the burden grew too great for them all, and they removed to a distant village home. Another son, to the grief of his father, who had thought his farm "large enough for both his boys," early broke from the trammels of so narrow a life, and found his vocation in our great metropolitan city, there to spend his life in active business and wide-reaching charities.

I lately passed the old spot, on the new railway skirting the hills. The house does not look as large as it used to; the trees are thinned and a little dwarfed. The whole valley is somewhat neglected and degenerate. So passes away the glory of many an old New England community. Foreigners come in to occupy the homes of the oldest families. But though these may have been displaced, their influence is not spent. In other villages and hamlets of other States, in thriving county seats and bustling young cities, in the great centers of trade and life, the New England blood is vital still, quicker than of old in its movement, responsive to the new demands of an age more alert, but hardly more happy, than that of the old-time New England farm.

MARTIN KELLOGG.

"WORDS, WORDS, WORDS."

The constant jealousy and care, not to name prejudice, of our careful speakers and writers, is not sufficient to prevent a constant incorporation of foreign and unusual terms into our daily speech. Sometimes these expressions are adopted to meet a real want, because, redundant as our English language is in words, we frequently find a lack of them to convey ideas in the shortest and most expressive manner. This want, I believe, is common to all tongues now spoken. Perhaps our own is more fortunate than any other in this respect, yet none are perfect. The English language, being one of sudden birth, compared to most others, took, in a very marked degree, the dress of its period, especially in nomenclature. Its origin was almost synonymous with what we may call a *renaissance* in science and the useful arts, which demanded scores and hundreds of new terms to define things which had no previous existence. I need not give examples to prove this. New names are added continually, and under the notice of every one. To qualify these new names we have several rules, such as etymological derivation, relevancy, custom, and so on; but first, I think, should be placed, whenever possible, relevancy to purpose or application—derivation and use both being transitory conditions, while relevancy is perpetual.

Our language possesses an advantage over all others now spoken, in the derivation of specific nomenclature. Being derived from a number of sources, and from tongues not generally understood by English-speaking people, names, as a rule, have no signification beyond the objects to which they apply. This is highly desirable, and, while seemingly an infraction of the rule of relevancy, it is not so, because a specific name becomes wholly relevant when it means one particular object, and nothing more.

In England, through the cause just named, there is, very happily, a nomenclature for places that is specific, because of this want of signification, and there is, for no assigned reason that I know of, a careful avoidance of names for towns and places that have other meanings. By examining a list of such names, in the *Postal Guide*, for example, it will be found that by our present English standard few of them have a meaning that appeals to our sense beyond the places themselves, although, to trace their origin, there may be found, perhaps in all cases, a distinct signification, the root of an adjective in Saxon, Scandinavian, Roman, or Keltic. The word "by," for example, from the Scandinavian "*by*," a village (used as a terminal in many English names, such as Witherby, Rugby, Derby, and so on), is traceable to a time when the Danes or Norsemen gave names that then had some meaning suggested by position, pursuits, or other circumstance in the towns or places. "Chester," a most common terminal for the names of English towns, is derived from the Roman "*castra*," a camp, and generally applied to places where military camps were maintained during the Roman sway in Britain. "Caster," in such names as Lancaster and Doncaster, has the same derivation.

At first thought it seems an easy thing to create names without general signification. This is, however, a mistake. It is not only not easy, but quite impossible, if we include the general adoption of such names. This is fairly illustrated in the fact that the more ignorant a people, and the poorer their language is, the more will they adopt names with a general signification. Of this we have a striking example in the North American Indians. Who has not laughed at "Sitting Bull," "Elk Slayer," "The Man who Grins," and so on?

In the United States our nomenclature is of the best and the worst. Not having the extensive store of strange tongues to draw upon that our English forefathers had, there has been a necessity, or, as we should say, a supposed necessity, for adopting names from our own tongue, and, in the greater number of cases, we have been singularly unfortunate in the selection.

Names drawn from the Indian tongue are beautiful, and are admired throughout the world. So, also, to English-speaking people, are names from the French and Spanish. Around San Francisco, for example, are villages and places with names that will go down to future generations with a "musical measure" that will have much to do with preconception of the places themselves. On the other hand, mustered among the beautiful Indian names in Nevada and Wyoming, we find those atrocious appellations printed by Mr. Bartlett in his *Book of Americanisms*—"Fair Play," "Red Dog," and "Hangtown," and others—which, let us trust, are ephemeral, and to pass away in time under an older and more orderly civilization.

The present purpose is, however, not to discuss nomenclature so much as the misuse and misapplication of terms, induced by circumstances that are peculiar to this country, and stronger on the Pacific Coast than elsewhere. There are various papers on "Americanisms" and American slang, several being in a late volume of the *North American Review*, by Richard Grant White, but so far as I know none touch upon the change of meaning of words from the old English standard, and, it may be added, from our own standard, which is the same. Among these is the term, "lumber," now applied constantly to all kinds of sawn timber, and even supplanting the hard timber, in some cases, by being applied to logs and standing trees, as well. The nature of timber traffic in this country demands two names, one for trees or logs, and another for sawn timber, such as boards, planks, and scantlings. Our trees are sawed in the forest, and the product comes to the market and is dealt in as "lumber." In Europe a timber merchant deals not only in sawn wood, but also in trees or logs, as we would say. The "manufacture" of square or sawn pieces is carried on where the material is sold to builders and others, so there is no complete division of the trade into separate branches requiring two terms. The wonder is, however, how the word "lumber" came to be employed. Its etymological sense does not suggest sawn wood any more than scrap iron, or marine junk; besides, it is a useful word in its true place, which we cannot well spare. Webster's Dictionary defines "lumber," "anything cumbrous and useless," and in that sense the word is employed in England, with a frequency, too, that proves how important a word it is in ordinary speech. "Timber," now going out of use in this country, is the old Gothic term meaning wood in all its forms, but especially when prepared or cut to dimensions. I say Gothic instead of Saxon, because the Gothic branch of the Germanic dialects is nearer a "base" than any other; for Saxon, or, indeed, any Germanic language, and the modern Scandinavian tongues, furnish a living source to which we may trace most of those old root-words that are generally called of "Saxon origin." "Timmer" in German and Swedish is the same as "timber." I may mention that in England, as well as in Northern Europe, sawn wood has names relating to its shape or dimensions, such as "boards," "deals," "planks," "battens," "scantlings," and so on, which seem to suit the purposes of commerce and speech much better than one general term of "lumber."

Calico—from Calicut, a town in India where the cloth was first made—means a plain white cloth of cotton. In England, and all countries where the trade in such cloth reaches, the term has this strict meaning; but by some freak, we in this country apply it to the printed web, and dub calico "muslin," a name belonging to a thin kind of cloth first made in, and taking its name from, Mossoul, a town in Mesopotamia. This crossing or shifting of terms is unfortunate, leading often to a misunderstanding in commercial transactions, and must in some degree prove an impediment in introducing American made goods, under these new names, into markets hitherto supplied by the British people. The word "guess," when employed for "suppose," is another departure from the true meaning and use of terms—one that often puzzles Americans when in England, because "guess" is much more frequently employed by English than American writers. An American traveler once said to me in Europe, "Why is it the English are always quizzing one about the word 'guess,' when I find it here three times in a London newspaper article?" He was by no means uneducated, but so long had he been accustomed to hearing and using the word employed instead of "suppose" or "think," that its true meaning had departed from his conception. Its constant and unnecessary use in speech in this country is an anomaly of the first order. We have "think," "believe," "suppose," "conjecture," not to mention "opine," that would do as well, leaving "guess" for undecided conjecture, its true sense, and almost opposite to "believe" or "think."

England being almost the only country with which comparisons can be made—the immediate source we may say of our language—custom there in the use of words should be regarded as a kind of authority; not because the custom is English, but because a stronger conservatism has more carefully preserved the true meaning and application of terms, or, to place it in other words, they adhere more closely to standards which are quite the same in both countries. This remark is especially true of the written language; for, in common speech, and taking even London in comparison, there is as much slang employed there as here.

One reason, and a strong one, that enables a closer adherence to the rules of language in England is that they are an older people, and have reached one stage in advance of us by the abandonment of what I will call exaggerative rhetoric. The plain, perspicuous style which Addison and the *Spectator* introduced has gone on increasing, and has in some degree reacted upon our own literature. If those moving harangues of Sheridan, Burke, Pitt, and Fox were delivered in the present House of Commons, the speakers would be "coughed down," or would have to speak to empty benches. This is a desirable reform, and to it, as before remarked, is due a more careful preservation of the meaning of terms. What the late Mr. Buckle called "the aspect of nature," considered as an element in controlling American speech, is alone enough to account, in a great degree, for our more tardy progress toward plain words and plain speech. All in our country is planned on a gigantic scale; new fields of boundless extent are continually being unfolded to our vision. Our language seems too poor in adjectives to meet the case. The terms "river," "mountain," "plain," and "lake" seem too contracted to describe what is far beyond those things in the old world, to which the same terms relate. The superlative degree alone answers for description, and from this, as well as other causes, comes an exaggeration that coins new terms and phrases, and alters the meaning of old ones. There is, moreover, a strange disposition among the vulgar to use new terms, whether more expressive or not. The singular of nouns becomes plural under this rule, and we hear that "the 'bellflower' is a fine apple," not meaning one particular apple, but such apples generally. We say, "Jones makes a good steam-engine," or there is no better "wagon" than that made by Smith; that a good "hat" is furnished by Brown; that Robinson "builds" a fine "suit." Such things are inexcusable, and merit the remark of Mr. Webster, who in his Dictionary says, in respect to the use of "guess" for "suppose," "such use is a gross vulgarism."

In contrasting our methods of speech with the English, the affix "er" demands some notice. This word, or affix, Mr. Webster informs us, comes from the Latin "*or*," meaning an "agent," and, if so, there is good ground for the American custom of applying it indiscriminately to persons or things; but I am inclined to doubt the correctness of this derivation, and think "er" is more nearly the Germanic personal substantive "*herre*," or "*herr*." In proof of this, I will point to the use of the term in England, where it is not applied to tools or implements, but to persons only. The affix is almost indispensable in speech, and it is a pity that we have not adopted the Latin "*or*" for inanimate agents, such as machines and implements —"grater," "mower," "scraper," and so on—keeping the Germanic personal substantive "er" for persons, as "baker," "reaper," "shoemaker." This would have avoided confusion, and our present use of the two terms, which is extremely irregular. For example, in iron works a certain machine for planing is commonly spoken of as a "planer," while another for drilling holes is not called a "driller," nor one for turning a "turner."

On some of the railway cars may be noticed a plate bearing an inscription to inform the reader that some one's "buffer," "coupler," and "platform" are patented. In common speech, and for technical use, these names might perhaps pass unchallenged, but mounted on a plate for the public to read, they can be relegated to the class to which Mr. Webster's "gross vulgarisms" belong.

Another suggestion may be made in respect to the words "use" and "employ." These are synonymous in ordinary speech, or, as we may say, "use" has taken the place of "employ," although the true sense of the terms points to the difference that what is "used" is consumed, as food, gas, fuel, and so on, while "employed" indicates a use without consumption. For example, we "use" soap and "employ" a brush.

A foreign gentleman, while attempting to learn English, once asked a question the simplicity of which, at first, caused him to be laughed at. He inquired, "When shall I say 'make,' or 'do,' in speaking English?" Several who were present each engaged to furnish an infallible rule, but the query was not solved. We say "make" a journey, not "do" a journey; but why? We "make" a mistake, or "do" a wrong, but why not "do a mistake," or "make a wrong?" The same gentleman, from some notes previously prepared, presented several other queries, only one more of which is remembered; namely, "When should one say, 'illegal,' 'illicit,' 'illegitimate,' or 'unlawful?'" Our divisions of these terms among classes of acts, or circumstances, is most confusing to one learning the language, and so far as I know lacks the warrant of any rule except common use. Mention was made in a previous place of a lack, sometimes, of terms in English expression. Such a want is the sole warrant for the introduction of foreign words in our literature, and this custom must be ascribed to the absence of synonyms or to pedantry—the latter generally, for that great master of English words, Thomas Carlyle, manages to do without foreign interpolations, when "he wants to." This I mention, because no one has ever wielded our language with such audacity, or forced ideas, as he has done, by a verbiage that claims our equal interest with the subjects treated. Two words only I will mention as wanting synonyms in English; there may be many more—scores, perhaps, but these will do as examples. "*Ennui*," in French, will, no doubt, at some future day, do duty in our tongue for a personal condition which it takes several English words to describe. The other is a very important word from the Swedish language, "*lagom*," meaning, as near as we can translate it, and imperfectly at that, "Just right," or "Just enough." Its frequent use in Scandinavian speech proves the value of the word.

"Either and neither," which are, in this country, pronounced with the two vowels as *e* long, e-ther and ne-ther, are, in England, called i-ther and ni-ther, the second vowel long. In respect to this, we read in Webster's Dictionary, that "analogy, as well as the best use, favors the first pronunciation;" a statement that may well be called into doubt. So far as analogy, we can do no better, certainly, than to compare with the German, in which an inflexible rule would make the second vowel long, and give us the English pronunciation. It is, moreover, more "congenial," if that term will apply; comes more natural, when once learned, and is adopted almost insensibly by persons who go to reside where this pronunciation is employed. As to use, Mr. Webster is certainly wrong, because the whole tendency and change is to *i* long—ni-ther and i-ther—while common use is, at least, equally divided among English-speaking people.

In Great Britain there are many dialects—English, Irish, Scotch, and Welsh, as principal. There are also the Yorkshire, Lancashire, Cambrian, and half a dozen others of more or less distinction. On the east coast, in places, Scandinavian terms are used to such an extent that a Swede, Dane, or Norwegian, who is ignorant of English, can, in many cases, understand the "drift" of a plain conversation. The Lancashire and Yorkshire dialects, which have been named as minor ones, have each large dictionaries; and a person, after living for years in London, Dublin, or Edinburgh, will be, for a time, confounded in parts of Yorkshire or Lancashire (Lancaster). These discrepancies, with the exception of pronunciation, do not exist among the educated classes; and the written language, except in a few names of things, is quite the same in all parts of the kingdom. These things I mention preparatory to a few remarks upon London pronunciation, which is generally conceded to be the most correct. English is certainly well spoken in London. Terminal syllables are more distinctly sounded, and the letter "r," the American shibboleth, is not formed in the throat, but with the tongue. In the "Cockney tongue," as it is called, there are some faults and variations from the acknowledged standard, even among educated people, which there is no parallel for in this country. I will mention two of them. The Italian sound of *a*, as in "bar, father, bank," is seldom heard. Instead, there is a sound not known in this country, and corresponding almost with the *ä*, or ä, in German; also, near the same as *e* short. Bank, for example, is Bänk, or Benk. Hat is pronounced hät, or het. While *a* long, as in mate, is sounded more like long *i*, or *ai*, perhaps; mate or gate is called mite and gite, or maite and gaite. The sound can not be fairly indicated by spelling, and must be heard to be understood. The second case is that of *o* long, as in "boat," "home," and so on. The American sound of *o* long, or, indeed, any sound of *o* long, whether in the Germanic or Latin languages, is beyond a Cockney's powers, and becomes nearly, but not quite, the Yankee "aou," as baout, haouse. This, like the sound of *a* long, can not be spelled, and is almost impossible for an American to imitate. The Southern negro pronounciation resembles it.

This essay is not presented as coming from a philologist, grammarian, or critic, even. The deductions ventured upon are drawn from personal observance. Perhaps something has been added to a subject which, unlike all others, is to be dealt with in a popular way only, if reform or change is to be expected.

J. RICHARDS.

AN EPISODE IN THE LIFE OF COUNT MORNY.

[TRANSLATED FROM THE GERMAN.]

The Crimean war was at an end. The Emperor Alexander was about to celebrate his coronation, and to place upon his youthful forehead the crown of Peter the Great, which, in descending from the proud head of the Emperor Nicolaus, had lost some of its bright jewels. The Emperor Napoleon III. stood at the zenith of his power, and, as it was always his policy to afterward make friends of those whom he had beaten—a policy which he later applied, at Villafranca, to the Emperor Francis Joseph, with peculiar success—Napoleon did his utmost to prove his kind feelings to the new Russian autocrat by sending a brilliant embassy to attend the coronation. He had appointed the clever Count Morny, the son of Queen Hortense and Count Flahault, his embassador to Russia; and without doubt there was no one more suitable for the mission—for Count Morny understood, like the grandseigneurs of the *ancien régime*, how to combine perfect elegance with the most lavish profusion; and this the Emperor's munificence enabled him to do. The Count was perhaps the most suitable person to insinuate himself into the favor of the young Emperor of Russia, and to impart to him the conviction that Napoleon was his best friend, and that Russia, forsaken by the Holy Alliance, could find no truer and better ally than Napoleon of France.

When Count Morny received his appointment the most particular instructions were given him concerning his demeanor at the Court of St. Petersburg. Napoleon communicated to to him all the reports of his secret agents, so that the Count had before him the principal personages of the Russian court as if in a *camera obscura*, and was as accurately informed concerning the scene of his future activity as if he had lived there for years. His carriages and his servants were ready, and he was instructed to depart the next morning.

When Count Morny left the Emperor, he entered his *coupé*, which was without coat of arms or livery, and drove rapidly along the Champs Elysées to the Barrière de l'Etoile, at which point he turned into the gateway of a charming hotel, built in a highly aristocratic style. Without uttering a word, he crossed the entrance-hall, passed the low-bowing servants, and entered a richly and elegantly furnished parlor, in which was a lady, who rose from her chair as he entered. In the dim lamplight which pervaded the room, this lady, who wore a simple dress of dark silk, made an almost youthful impression. Her face was fine and regular; her figure still full and graceful. Only the sharp lines around the mouth and eyes gave her a somewhat hard and severe expression, and showed that youth lay far behind her. Indeed, the Countess Lehon was certainly fifty years old, although she well understood how to destroy the traces of time in her appearance. People told of her—and perhaps they had ample ground for it—that in her early youth she had had particularly intimate relations with the Duke of Orleans, King Louis Philippe's son. Afterward, she had been the intimate friend and confidant of Count Morny; and the young Count Lehon, her son, who at that time was twenty and some odd years old, showed in his appearance a certain resemblance to the Emperor Napoleon's half-brother, who had just been appointed embassador to St. Petersburg.

"I come to take leave, my dear," said Count Morny, with chivalric politeness, kissing the hand of the Countess, "and to chat for a few moments with you, here at the most attractive center of charming Paris, before my departure to the country of the Muscovite barbarians."

"And Charles," asked the Countess, "my son; he will go with you?"

"The Emperor has refused it to me," replied Morny, shrugging his shoulders. "Prince Murat is to fill the place among my cavaliers which I had designed for Charles. The Emperor hopes to add, through this, more brilliancy to the embassy. It was impossible to influence him otherwise."

A bitter smile played for an instant around the lips of the Countess.

"Could not Charles," asked she, "have still found a place by the side of Prince Murat, if you had earnestly demanded it from the Emperor?"

"I tell you it was impossible," replied the Count. "You know that the Emperor is sometimes obstinate in trifling things; perhaps he fears the slanders of the Russian court circles, if Charles should appear there in my suite."

"I regret it," said the Countess. "He would have written to me—would have informed me of everything. You yourself," she added, with a touch of light mockery, "will perhaps not find time."

"Certainly I shall, my dear," replied the Count. "Although you must expect no long reports from me, I shall always find time, however busy I may be, to convince you of my unchangeable friendship. Yet a separation like that which is about to take place requires some precautions. You will be, when I am not here, without any direct protection, and you know that the Emperor has already several times made allusion to the papers which refer to the *coup d'état* and the time before it, and which are in your hands."

"They are well kept," answered the Countess, a peculiar flash sparkling from her eyes. "All your letters are preserved as my dearest possessions—among them, also, that in which you promise, as soon as circumstances admit, to give me your hand."

"That moment will soon arrive," replied Morny, with an expression of sincerest cordiality, "in which I can fulfill that promise, and give myself the highest happiness. The times till now have been so much disquieted, everything is not yet sufficiently consolidated, my own position is not yet firm enough, to think of a marriage. Lately the Emperor has several times hinted that it might be time for me now to establish my own house, and to introduce into it a lady who understands how to do the honors of a representative person. We shall speak again of this as soon as my mission is finished. Yet," he then continued, "would it not be better to destroy those papers before my departure, or, if we wish to preserve them for possible future events, which might, perhaps, be very well, would they not be safer in my hands than in yours?"

"They are perfectly safe with me," replied the Countess, firmly and severely, in a tone that convinced Morny that all further words on this subject would be in vain.

He changed the conversation. They chatted for an hour about this and that, and then he took leave with the cordiality of an old friend, in which a little of the lover's fervor seemed still to flame.

The brilliant festivities at St. Petersburg and Moscow began. The papers filled their columns with the descriptions of the magnificent displays at the coronation ceremonies at Moscow, where the Emperor Alexander had gone, accompanied by all the great lords of his empire and the embassadors of all the European powers. Count Morny outshone every one, through the richness and splendor of his carriages, his horses, and his servants. The taste and profuse luxury of his balls and assemblies were unequaled. He was the hero of the day. The highest circles of Russian society, following the example of the Emperor, bestowed upon him the most marked attentions. One day the papers spread the rumor that the French Coronation Embassador was going to marry a young lady from one of the first Russian princely families. When the Countess Lehon read this news, the paper dropped from her hand, wild anger flamed in her eyes; for some hours she remained locked in her boudoir. Afterward she showed herself in her splendid carriage in the Bois de Boulogne, smilingly returning the greetings of her acquaintances, and seeming not to perceive that these greetings were accompanied by ironical and inquisitive glances. The rumor mentioned in the papers was indeed true. Count Morny had understood not only how to outshine by his splendor the diplomacy of all Europe, and to convince the Emperor Alexander, as well as his ministers, of the sincerity of the friendship of Napoleon III., but the captivating charm of his person had won the heart of a beautiful Russian princess, whose inheritance counted into the millions; and the marriage, the celebration of which would also externally seal the new bond of friendship between Russia and France, was already sanctioned by Alexander II. and the Emperor Napoleon. Count Morny returned one evening from a magnificent festival at the Winter Palace, where the gracious distinction of the Emperor and the radiant glances of his betrothed, the beautiful Princess Sophy Trubetzkoi, had gratified his pride and filled him with happiness. On his table lay the letters from Paris. He indifferently threw aside some of them, to put in order the political dispatches for his secretary, when he suddenly stopped at the sight of a little envelope with an elegant seal, and opened it quickly. It contained only a few lines, in the hand of the Countess Lehon. These ran:

"SIR:—The papers speak of your marriage with a Russian princess. I request you immediately to have this rumor retracted. In case this is not done I shall be compelled to embarrass you and others by giving publicity to all your letters and papers, including those which concern the *coup d'état*, which, very fortunately, are in my possession."

The cheerful, happy smile disappeared from Morny's countenance; he bit his mustache, and angrily threw the note on the table. After some moments of reflection he seized his pen, and wrote on the margin of the little letter, which, like a sharp thorn, had suddenly thrust its threatening point into the rose-blossoms of his happiness:

"You must act quickly to avoid a great scandal."

He signed and put the whole in an envelope, to which he attached the great seal of the embassy, and wrote the address, "To His Majesty the Emperor." Then he called for his secretary, and ordered that a courier should immediately go to Paris to deliver this letter directly into the hands of his Majesty. Having done this, he went into the small dining-hall, where, every night at a late hour, the gentlemen of his suite were usually assembled to conclude the day with an informal supper, at which they communicated to each other their adventures in the field of diplomacy and gallantry. Count Morny was as cheerful as ever. His sparkling wit animated the conversation till far into the night, and nobody around him perceived the disquieting grief which troubled his heart.

The Emperor Napoleon had received the dispatch of his embassador at St. Petersburg. The courier had brought it in his traveling-coat from the station, and delivered it with his own hand. After reading this dispatch the Emperor did not send for his Minister of Foreign Affairs, but for M. Pietri, his Police-Prefect. Soon afterward the Chief entered the Cabinet. Napoleon gave him the paper, and asked:

"What is there to be done?"

M. Pietri, a man with the countenance of a hawk, with a broad, bold forehead, and crooked nose—a man who did not admit the existence of impossibilities—shrugged his shoulders, paused for a moment in reflection, and then said:

"That will be hard. The Countess Lehon is very smart and cautious. She will deny the possession of anything, and if one does not know exactly where she keeps those papers, forcible measures will be of no help, but only aggravate the scandal."

"No," exclaimed the Emperor, forbiddingly, "no force. And yet we must have these papers. It would be a European scandal, and Morny, who is in so many near relations to me, and whom I want, would be undone."

While the Emperor walked musingly up and down, and Pietri stood in meditation over the paper, the *valet de chambre* of his Majesty came in.

"A note to the Prefect," said he. "His secretary has brought it here because he thinks that the affair is of the highest importance and requires haste."

The Emperor made an affirmative sign, and while the *valet de chambre* withdrew, Pietri opened the letter, closed with the seal of the Police Prefecture.

"What is it?" asked Napoleon.

Pietri gave the Emperor the sheet. He read:

"M. PREFECT:—A true friend of the Empire considers it his duty to communicate to you that the Countess Lebon, on the tidings of the marriage of the Count Morny, has delivered all the papers to Orleans which the Count had left behind in Paris."

"It is too late," cried the Emperor, badly frightened, turning pale, and supporting himself by the back of a chair.

"This is a stratagem, sire," said Pietri, with a confident mien, after having reflected for a few instants. "The Countess Lebon wishes to give another direction to the search, and prevent measures from our side. If she had really given those papers to Orleans, she would not have written to the Count. She will not let the papers go out of her hands until she has either prevented the marriage or the wedding is performed."

"You believe so?" cried Napoleon.

"I am sure of it," replied Pietri. "Will your Majesty give me full power to treat this affair entirely in my own way?"

"Go," said the Emperor, "and act quickly. Yet, if it is possible, avoid any sensation."

"Your Majesty may be tranquil," replied Pietri. "I think I am sure of my point."

He hastened away. After half an hour, he drove to the hotel of the Countess Lehon, and while he was being announced to the lady of the house, six gentlemen, dressed in elegant style, entered the court, one after another, through the *porte-cochère*. The Countess received the Prefect with the most amiable smile.

"What brings the very busy Chief of the Police to a lady who is almost forgotten by the world?" asked she.

"An earnest matter, madame," answered M. Pietri, without any ceremony. "You have written this letter to Count Morny; you will comprehend that the Emperor cannot allow the carrying out of your threats; and I request you to immediately deliver to me the papers of which you have spoken."

The Countess sneeringly leaned back in her easy chair.

"That is a peculiar demand, sir," she said; "and to justify so peremptory a tone, one must possess more power than the Emperor, and more than all your police. I could answer you, that I possess no papers at all, that this was a mystification, but you would not believe me; therefore I tell you that I indeed am in possession of documents which are highly compromising to Count Morny, and to others, and which would at any rate prevent his Russian marriage, which is faithless and perfidious."

"It is not for me to meddle with Count Morny's conscience, madame," answered M. Pietri, coldly; "and if you refuse to deliver up these papers, which I ask of you in the name of the Emperor, I must for the present make you a prisoner in your house; although, as a matter of course, as long as it is possible, you will be treated with all that regard which your position may require."

"Those papers, sir, are in the hands of sure friends," replied the Countess Lehon, with an expression of haughty security. "As for the rest, do what you can, and can account for."

M. Pietri opened the door and gave a sign. One of the gentlemen who had followed him into the hotel came in.

"You will," said the Police Prefect, "not quit the room of the Countess; and take care that she neither removes nor speaks with anybody except in your presence."

The police officer bowed.

The Countess, as she looked at the two, mockingly, played with the tips of her slender fingers.

"I shall appear again after three hours," said M. Pietri, "in order to ask whether you have changed your mind, madame, and whether you have anything to say to me. If so, you can tell it to this gentleman, and he will communicate it to me."

He courteously bowed, as if an act of politeness had been spoken of, and went away. Out of doors he gave the rest of the officers the order to allow nobody to enter the hotel or to leave it. Then he asked after the young Count Charles Lehon. His *valet de chambre*—who had come, anxiously, into the ante-chamber of the Countess—led him to the apartments inhabited by the Count, who, however, already in the corridor, was hastening toward him, full of trouble and excitement.

Count Lehon—who, as we remarked, might at that time have been about five or six and twenty years old—showed in his elegant, pliant figure, and in his features, an unmistakable likeness to Count Morny. A certain childlike timidity was still visible in his face, and the glance of his eyes was gentle, thoughtful, and dreamy; his nature was just as delicate, sensitive, and susceptible as the Count's was cold, sharp, and impenetrable.

"For God's sake, sir!" exclaimed he, "what is going on here? You occupy the hotel. What has happened? What have you against us? Does the Emperor not know how much I am devoted to him, how much I am prepared to do for him—for him who has freed France from the revolution, and made her again great in Europe?"

"The Emperor knows your sentiments," said Pietri, earnestly; "and just for that reason, Count, he has given me the order to lead you immediately to him. He himself will impart to you what is the point in question, and you can be convinced that he will do everything to settle this painful affair—which indeed seems very intricate—as kindly as possible; and will do everything to keep, as much as he is able, at least from you, the consequences of your mother's behavior."

"But what has happened? What is the matter?" cried the young Count.

"Accompany me," said Pietri, "and you will learn all."

The young man tremblingly followed the Prefect into his carriage, and was driven to the palace of the Emperor, where both were admitted into the cabinet.

Napoleon looked up, surprised, when he saw the pale and excited young man enter his room with Pietri.

"Sire," said the Prefect, "Count Lehon is deeply moved at the measures which I have been obliged to take against his mother, and he wishes to assure your Majesty of his devotion. I did not consider myself free, until here in your Majesty's presence, to impart to him that the Countess has delivered documents of importance, relating to state affairs, into the hands of the banished Prince of Orleans—that is, to the enemies of your Majesty and France."

"O my God," exclaimed the young Count Lehon, "what a misfortune!" He covered his face with his hands and leaned against the door.

"Then it is really true?" asked the Emperor, with astonishment and alarm.

"It is true," said Pietri, while at the same time, with a light shake of the head, he gave the Emperor a sharp glance, "and your Majesty can conceive how painful this serious affair must be for Count Lehon, who is such a good Frenchman, and such an admirer of your Majesty."

"It is high treason," said the Emperor, over whose lips a fugitive smile passed, "which cannot occur without severe punishment."

Count Lehon sighed deeply and painfully; then suddenly he arose, and stepped before the Emperor, with joyful mein.

"No, sire, no," said he; "it is not true—it is a false accusation. It cannot be true, for until this morning those papers were in our house. I have seen them myself, and since then my mother cannot possibly have had the time to send them to London."

"The papers were there? You have seen them yourself?" asked the Emperor, after listening with attention, while joyful triumph lightened up Pietri's features.

"Yes, yes," exclaimed Count Lehon. "They were there. I have seen them. I came into my mother's room; she had opened the secret drawer in which she keeps the letters of Count Morny, and I saw her read attentively in the papers."

"If that be the case," said the Emperor, "the accusation which is made against your mother must be false. But why has she not told it? Why did she not show these papers? That would have been the best proof that they cannot be in London."

"The Countess Lehon," said Pietri, "does not know what is here the point in question. I have not thought it necessary to communicate anything to her, but have, first of all, only made sure of her person in the most discreet way."

"Oh," cried Count Lehon, "one must look after them. You will be convinced that the papers are there, under the picture of Count Morny, which is hanging in my mother's room. You must press sharply upon the nail which holds this picture. A cupboard in the wall, the casing of which is exactly joined into the tapestry, and which cannot be discovered by knocking, because a plastered wall covers it, will instantly be opened, and the papers will be found in it. Oh, sire, believe me that my mother, also, in her most violent anger against the Count, would never be able to betray your Majesty."

"You hear, Pietri?" said Napoleon. "I shall be happy if it be so."

"It is so, your Majesty," cried Count Lehon. "One must convince one's self. I, myself, will hasten to my mother, if your Majesty permit me."

"The affair is too serious, sire," said Pietri, "to allow any intercourse with the Countess before she is freed from the suspicion that rests on her. I am Police-Prefect, sire. To me every one, even Count Lehon, must appear under suspicion until the contrary is proved."

"You hear?" said Napoleon, kindly, to the young Count, who cast a glance full of terror on the Police-Prefect. "He is as cold as ice. He must be so. Well, I will keep you here, myself, as hostage, till the matter is settled. Write, here at my table, to your mother, and beg her to settle the matter on your account, because pride and anger might, perhaps, otherwise prevent her from doing so."

"Immediately, immediately," exclaimed the Count. "Oh, how gracious your Majesty is! How can I ever thank you for such consideration?"

He went to the Emperor's writing desk, and wrote a few lines, which he gave to the Police-Prefect, who then went away. Napoleon invited the young man to take a place by his side, and, with captivating amiability, absorbed him in a conversation, which made him almost forget the painful situation in which he found himself. M. Pietri drove back to the Hôtel Lehon. The Countess was lying on a lounge, reading, with apparent calmness and indifference, while the police officer was modestly seated near the door."

"Now," said the Countess, when M. Pietri entered, "the three hours have not yet elapsed. Have you yet convinced yourself that it will be in vain, if you intended to compel me, by a kind of modern torture, to deliver up documents which are in secure keeping far from here?"

"No, madame," said M. Pietri; "but I have to bring you this note from your son, who, moved by the kindness of the Emperor, beseeches you to put a stop to this unpleasant affair."

The Countess started up, frightened. Pietri gave her the paper.

"Oh," exclaimed she, with sparkling eyes, "they have ensnared the weak child. They think I shall yield to his demand. They think I shall forget myself, and sacrifice my revenge for the scrap of favor they have thrown to him. Never, sir, never!"

"Well, then," said M. Pietri, "so you have to blame yourself alone if I use force, and take a thing which you refuse to give me."

Pietri then quickly stepped up to the cabinet's wall, to where a picture of Count Morny, in a beautifully chased frame, was hanging. The next moment he had taken down this picture. A sharp pressure upon the nail that had held it, opened the panel in the wall. A small iron-safe stood in the dark hollow, lined with velvet. Like a tigress the Countess Lehon jumped up; she seized M. Pietri's carefully arranged side-curls with a tight grasp, and uttering an inarticulate cry of rage, she tore him away from the opening. In spite of this unforeseen attack, M. Pietri had already seized the strong-box, and thrown it to the officer, who had quickly approached.

"We have what we were looking for, madame," said he, removing her hand from his throat. "Every noise will be in vain, and will compromise only yourself. I beg you, therefore, to submit to the unavoidable."

"Ha, traitor!" cried the Countess, beside herself with rage, seizing a small Venetian dagger lying among her knick-knacks. She was about to rush upon the Prefect. But the officer quickly seized her arm, and pressed her wrists together, until she dropped the dagger. M. Pietri bowed to her very politely, and left the room with his companion. The Countess threw herself, sobbing convulsively, upon her lounge. The Police-Prefect returned to the Emperor.

"That is it; that is it," exclaimed the young Count Lehon, when he perceived the strong-box in Pietri's hands. "Your Majesty can well see that my mother is innocent. All the papers must be in it."

Pietri opened the cover; the Emperor eagerly seized the papers contained in the small box, and glanced over them, one after another.

"Is it not so, your Majesty?" cried Count Lehon. "Is it not true, people have maliciously accused my mother?"

"It was a vile imputation of her enemies," said M. Pietri, pressing the Count's hand. "All the measures are again recalled. Your mother is again free. I feel sorry for what has happened, but I could not act otherwise, and I hope that nobody has become aware of it."

The Emperor placed the strong-box, with a contented smile, on his writing-desk. "Go, sir," said he to Count Lehon, "and carry your mother my excuses. I have been happy to talk a little with you, and to convince myself how France is justified in reposing hope in such an excellent young man as yourself."

He gave the Count his hand, who, quite enchanted, left him, and hastened to his mother. He found her still sobbing, almost suffocated with anger.

"You have betrayed me," cried she to him. "These demons have understood how to use the child against his own mother, with their devilish cunning."

"I betray you, my mother!" exclaimed the young man, greatly surprised. "I have rescued you. I have defended you against a false accusation. I have proved to them that you were falsely accused."

The Countess looked full of astonishment at the gentle, smiling countenance of her son.

"You have bereft me of the weapon, my son," said she, at last, with emotion, "to punish that false, spiteful traitor, who forgets his oath, and gives up to a stranger the place which is due to your mother."

"Is not here the place for my mother?" said the Count, opening his arms, with radiant glances. "Can she find a place that is better and safer than the heart of her son?"

The Countess, for a moment, pressed her hands on her heart, but she could not resist the glance of her child; weeping, she sank into the arms of the young man.

The marriage of Count Morny was celebrated with much splendor. He led his young wife to Paris, into the magnificent Hôtel Morny, and the first visit which both paid after his arrival was to the Countess Lehon. The reception was warm. The Countess received the young wife like a motherly friend. Then she called for her son, and said:

"Forget never, Count Morny, that this child has a right to your friendship."

Morny embraced the young man, while his features expressed a tenderness of feeling which was usually foreign to him. His wife gave Count Lehon her hand, heartily. On the next day the *Moniteur* announced that Count Lehon had been nominated a "Knight of the Legion of Honor." Soon afterward he entered the State's service as Maître des Requêtes; and again, a short time after this, he was, through the influence of Government, elected as Deputy, and appointed a President to the Conseil-général de l'Aix.

A. WEISE.

NOTE BOOK.

THE CALIFORNIAN has now been running three-quarters of a year. From the issuance of the January number to the present time it has been met with words of encouragement and approval alone. Personal interviews, private letters, and the expressions of the public press have all bid us God-speed. The reception which the magazine has met proves that a field is open for it on this coast, and a glance at the pages of the various numbers reveals the existence of a local talent which, to many, was unsuspected. But it has been evident for some time past to those interested in the enterprise that, in disregarding the experience of all other publications, by fixing the price so far below that of other monthlies, a mistake had been made which, sooner or later, would have to be corrected. The large sums which have to be expended for paper, composition, press work, and the innumerable expenses of printing, issuing, and circulating a monthly magazine, which have, of late, been higher than for many years before, prevent the possibility of placing the publication on that high plane of literary and typographical excellence which its proprietors desire, without a change in the present price. The only alternative was one which the owners would not *for a moment* consider, that of deteriorating the quality and diminishing the quantity supplied at the existing rates. For some time, therefore, the only question has been, when shall this change be effected, and it has been decided, after consultation, that the sooner it is done the better. Commencing, therefore, with the first day of October, the price of the magazine will be advanced to thirty-five cents for a single number, and to $4.00 for the yearly subscription, the usual price for first-class monthlies. In order that there may be no dissatisfaction among those of our patrons who have not, as yet, subscribed by the year, THE CALIFORNIAN will receive yearly subscriptions at the old rate ($3.00) until the date fixed for the change in the price (October 1, 1880). No one, therefore, needs be affected by the change for the present year. With this change we expect to redouble our efforts to make the magazine worthy of the high favor with which it has been received, and are able already to promise new features which will make it more attractive than ever before.

IT IS A GREAT MISTAKE to suppose that the people of the Pacific coast are not a reading population. The number of books, periodicals, and papers annually sold is enormous. These range over the entire field of scientific, artistic, and literary thought. It is a greater mistake to presuppose an absence of literary talent here. The people are strong original thinkers. They wear no intellectual shackles. To an extent their isolated position exempts them from the mental impediments, the grooves and molds which inevitably prevent the freest expansion in an older community. Not to be vainglorious, the articles that have appeared so far in THE CALIFORNIAN illustrate this. Many of them have attracted attention in the East and abroad for the terseness of their style and the vigor of their thought. All that such a people require is a medium which shall not only reflect, but be a part of, the vigorous life which surrounds it—not in a feverish, sensational sense, but in that broad and comprehensive sense, which includes the whole gamut of human thoughts, impulses, inspirations. No man who wrote in deep sincerity the life of his age ever failed of recognition; and no magazine which truly embodies that which is best in a great people will ever fail of success.

THE EDUCATED MAN IN POLITICS is an individual much sneered at by the politician and much longed for by the citizen. There is no more urgent need in any popular government than that its best citizens, the representatives of its highest thought, culture, and conservative progress, should be brought to the front. The spectacle of an official devoid alike of education and native ability is not, unfortunately, rare. And, in a measure, the educated classes are to blame for it. One would suppose that those who, by their property or position, had the most at stake in the government of the county, State, or nation, would manifest the most interest in securing the purity of the same. But, as a fact, no class is so apathetic. It is next to impossible to rouse them to any interest in that which concerns them most of all. And, even if their interest be once aroused and they be induced to enter the arena, it is too frequently with an affectation of superiority, a disdain, Coriolanus like, of the people.

> "His nature is too noble for the world;
> He would not flatter Neptune for his trident,
> Or Jove for his power to thunder."

Now, if there is one thing which the average American citizen will *not* do, it is to hold a wax candle while some other citizen poses in the *rôle* of Virtue. And—right here—very many men mistake laziness for virtue. There is nothing that will thaw under the temptation of a little warmth so soon as ice. What we need is men of broad sympathies, discerning minds, quick purposes, and unfaltering wills. I can count a dozen men in my immediate neighborhood who ought to be governors, congressmen, senators. They are business men of ability, integrity, and success. They are appreciated by all who come in contact with them. Their opinions are listened to with respect, and any one of them in politics would be welcomed as a godsend. There are enough of them in the State to compel, by concerted action, honesty and genuine reform in their respective parties. But great numbers of them will not even go to the polls, and hardly any of them will take an active part in seeing that a proper ticket is nominated even in their own city or county. The results of such indifference are inevitable—the politician, the machine. Upon the indifference of the community the demagogue thrives. Who is to blame if the government suffers?—if incapable or unreliable men are chosen? The confusion of republican institutions has often been predicted—most eloquently of all by Macaulay—at the hands of the rabble. But in any fair contest between intelligence and ignorance, the latter must ultimately give way. Mind always controls force. If ever Macaulay's prophecy be realized, it will be not so much from the inability of the better elements of society to prevail, as from the imperturbable complacency and criminal neglect with which the ship of state is abandoned to whatever fate the winds and the currents may chance to bestow.

NOT ONLY do we require the active participation of educated men in our public affairs, but we need observers, scientific investigators. Mr. Henry George, in a recently published article, invokes with great force the assistance of the scientific method in inquiries into the labor agitation and kindred topics. This method should be applied to all social problems. Certain it is that denunciation and declamation effect little. No man can investigate who has prejudged. But a scientist, taking a deep interest in public questions, yet standing aloof from partisan activity, might discover many things which the combatants had overlooked, might trace causes where they saw only results, might find a remedy while they lamented over an evil. But such an observer must not be a mere theorist. He must see the world as it is, not as it might be. No man shall be our social physician who studies our organism from a chart. Society is the sum of men's prejudices, and one cannot be a reformer who fails to appreciate this. No reasoning will be so wide of the mark as that which proceeds from ideal premises. The scientific investigator, therefore, must possess a rare combination of qualities. He must be of the people and yet not of them. He must sympathize with their prejudices—for without sympathy no one can understand the truth which is in any idea—and yet he must not be influenced thereby. He must be able not only to observe, but to generalize. His mind must be both analytical and creative, radical and conservative, iconoclastic and protective. None other can interpret human nature, and none other can harmonize it. We believe that such an expounder will yet come. It is not conclusive against such belief that the physical sciences tend to "abstract" men, to make them incapable of appreciating such things as prejudice and passion. That result is an incident not to the scientific method, but to the matter studied. The facts of physical science are unvarying, rigid, unresponsive, unsympathetic. In many departments the disturbing elements are few; and even these, by further investigation, may be classified or predicted. There is no humanity, nothing individual, about physical science. The interest is purely intellectual, and it is for this reason that poets, who deal with the emotions, have so far given us more accurate ideas of our fellows than the men of science. There is more sociology in Robert Burns than in all the scientific books ever written. It is better that the science which investigates a rock should be as cold as its subject. But the science which investigates men must be warm. If it be not, the very difference between man and the rock may be overlooked. We must not hope to find our social scientific investigator among our scientists. He must be specially reared for his work. We cannot expect one whose training has been purely intellectual to accomplish it. What would be the value of John Stuart Mill's dissection of the French Revolution? Neither can we expect accurate generalizations from minds untrained to generalize. It is only very lately that men have commenced to study themselves. It is not wonderful that little has been accomplished. When specialists have devoted years to this field, we may hope that some man of acute sympathies, keen observation, and broad intellect may tell us what manner of men we are and how we can conserve our own highest and best interests.

A JUST CRITICISM upon a man of genius is a difficult and perhaps impossible accomplishment. Criticism observes rules, is conservative, is guided by experience, and forms its estimate by comparison with acknowledged criterions. Genius, on the contrary, breaks through all barriers, disregards all experiences, is entirely radical, and disarranges the most approved standards. Criticism runs in grooves, like the river; genius is comprehensive and illimitable, like the ocean. The former is forever fearful of overreaching its banks; the latter is impatient of restraint, and dashes impetuously against its rocky shore. Criticism points out the necessity of unities and combinations; genius violates them, and brings to view new beauties. Even while criticism protests, genius reaches down into some lowly place, and from out the poverty, and degradation, and, it may be, crime, brings such creations as "Little Nell," unsullied and pure, to the light. Criticism is stationary; genius is progressive. The face of the former is turned toward the past but the latter throbs with the life of the present. Criticism says, "It has never been;" genius speaks and *it is!* The former, therefore, can never grasp the latter. It may recognize genius, and thus be of benefit in exposing the spurious and detecting the genuine. But recognition was never analysis, and never can be.

THE OCTOBER NUMBER OF THE CALIFORNIAN will be one of the most attractive ever issued. The editor has been able to secure several articles of unusual interest.

SCIENCE AND INDUSTRY.

IS MATTER SIMPLY A MODE OF MOTION?

Science has already relegated to the domain of "motion" all such possibilities of sensation as light, heat, electricity, etc., which were formerly defined as imponderable matter; and now comes Professor Crooks with his alleged "fourth state of matter," involving conditions which seem to make it quite clear that not only gases, but even the most solid bodies with which we are acquainted, such as wood, stone, metals, etc., must also share the same fate, and be considered merely as different modes of motion. The Professor holds that a solid is simply an aggregation of molecules, "separated from each other by a space which is relatively large—possibly enormous—in comparison with the central nuclei we call molecules. These molecules, themselves built up of atoms, are governed by certain forces"—the chief of which are attraction and motion. Distant attraction is gravitation, but molecular attraction is cohesion. Both are independent of absolute temperature, but "the mass must be able to bear a reduction of temperature of nearly three hundred degrees before the amplitude of the molecular movements would cease." What would result from the arrest of these movements, and the actual contact of the molecules, is beyond our conception. All we know of matter is based wholly upon our experience of molecular movements. The atomic theory of matter was first announced by Boscovitch more than a century ago, and the idea that particles of matter are endowed with both attraction and repulsion, which is involved in that theory, has been held by scientific men in general until quite recently. When atoms "are said to touch each other they are by no means in actual contact, but separated by an insuperable repulsive force." This interval of separation may be the five-thousandth part of an inch, more or less. Within this interval, according to Boscovitch, if two atoms are brought a little nearer together they will attract each other; if still nearer, they will repel; "but no force, however great, can bring them into mathematical contact." The fundamental assumption was that matter does not continuously fill space. Faraday held that in regard to atoms and the intervening space, space alone is continuous. He further asked, Why assume the existence of matter independent of force?—and substituted the term, "center of force," for atom. Thus matter, in the ordinary acceptation of the term, disappeared entirely, to make room for the emanations of force, which fill the universe, and atoms to points of force-convergence. Of late the hypothesis of molecules and atoms has been greatly developed, and their size and motions mathematically measured. This need not be disputed when instruments have been devised by which one million lines can be drawn in the width of an inch, and each line distinctly seen by a microscope. In Boscovitch's theory there was no contact of atoms. By the theories of to-day they are constantly coming into contact and violent collision. What we call a solid is the *first* state of matter, and its molecules are in a constant state of activity. When the temperature of a solid is raised, these molecular movements increase in rapidity and extent of motion, until the mass becomes liquid. Then we have the *second* state of matter. A still further increase of temperature converts the liquid into a gaseous form, in which the molecules fly about still more freely, and we have the *third* state of matter. The gaseous condition is one preeminently of molecular disturbance, attended with constant collisions with each other and with the sides of the containing vessels. Now, if a gas is so rarified by an approximate vacuum that the collisions of the molecules in their flight are few as compared with the misses, the molecules will obey their natural laws, and move in *rectilinear* lines, like a flight of cannon balls directed to a distant object. This is called by Professor Crooks the *fourth* state of matter. The logical inference from which is that what we call matter, whether solid, liquid, or gaseous, is nothing more than the effect which the movement of the mass of molecules exerts upon our senses, as in heat or light. If we take up a drop of water, the movements of its molecules conveys to our mind the sensation of moisture. If we pick up a coin at ordinary temperature, the different motion of its molecules produces upon us an effect which we term metallic, and so on. If the temperature of the coin is raised, a corresponding effect is produced by the change of molecular movement. The Professor holds that the molecule, itself "intangible, invisible, and hard to be conceived, is the only true matter;" that the space covered by the motion of the molecules, which is the mass that we call matter, whether gaseous, fluid, or solid, "has no more right to be called matter than the air traversed by a rifle bullet can be called lead....... From this point of view, then, matter is but a mode of motion."

PROGRESS OF ENGINEERING IN AMERICA.

Until the close of the last century, natural power had ever been employed in its most primitive forms. Wind and water were the only motive powers called in to aid man in his labors; and the appliances to utilize them were of the simplest possible character. It is true, some great engineering works were undertaken and completed; but only at large expenditure of mere labor and muscle. But with the introduction of steam, in 1778, a new and wide field was opened up for the exercise of the genius of the engineer and mechanic. The invention of Watts was a triumph which set men to thinking, and its successful application contributed more to the prosperity and welfare of nations, and the advancement of science and mechanism, in the next succeeding century, than had been achieved by the united efforts of all previous time. Perhaps in no part of the world has it given birth to greater activity, or accomplished greater triumphs, than in the United States. At a late meeting of civil engineers in St. Louis, a very interesting paper was read by Mr. O. Chanute, summarizing the progress and wonderful growth which engineering has made in this country, and alluding to the high position which the United States has attained among nations. From this paper we briefly summarize as follows: In the matter of supplying towns with water, the application of steam as a power, and the improvements made in pumping machines, engineers have made a gain of fifty per cent. over what was accomplished twenty years ago. There are now five hundred and sixty-nine towns and cities in the United States and Canada supplied with water works, involving thirteen thousand miles of pipe, ten thousand of which is of cast-iron. Important progress has also been made in canal engineering; and we now have three thousand two hundred and fifty-seven miles of canal. Experiments are in progress in the way of steam propulsion which it is confidently expected will effect a saving of fully thirty-seven per cent. over present methods. In railways, Americans were among the first to appreciate Stephenson's inventions of 1828, and are foremost among nations in utilizing it. The United States leads the world in the extent of her lines, reaching eighty-six thousand miles; all Europe has but ninety thousand, and the balance of the world only twenty-five thousand. Our railroad engineers and locomotive builders lead all others. Our roads reach farther and cost less than any others, and our engines pull heavier trains and run more miles in a year, or during their life-time, than those of any other nation. The Pennsylvania Railroad was pronounced one of the best, if not the best, managed railroad in the world. [The present writer would name the Baltimore and Ohio as the only road whose management can be pronounced either equal or superior to that of the Pennsylvania.] In regard to bridges, there are now in the United States nine hundred miles of these structures—one-third of them stone or iron and two-thirds wood. [The East River Bridge, at New York, may be instanced as the boldest conception of bridge construction ever attempted.] The matter of river improvements is just now attracting much attention, and the fact is being realized that, until quite recently, but little has really been done in this direction. It has been demonstrated that the currents of the largest rivers may be controlled by simple brush dikes. [A complimentary reference to the recent work of our distinguished American engineer, Captain James B. Eads, at the mouth of the Mississippi, was received with loud applause. It may also be stated in this connection, that the brief utterances of Captain Eads, in regard to the work of observation in which he is now engaged in this State, gives evidence that his superior genius will eventually solve the most important and complex engineering problem which has as yet been brought to the attention of the people of California.] The movable dam on the Ohio—a French idea—has already proved a success, and the best engineering talent in the country is now engaged in effecting certain needed modifications, required to meet the peculiar nature and needs of our rivers. The recent improvements to navigation at Hell Gate and Flood Rock were referred to as great and novel feats of engineering. In telegraphic and gas engineering, we have made wonderful strides. In the former we lead the world. In the latter, since 1850, the number of companies has increased from fifty to nine hundred, with a capital of $200,000,000. In metallurgy, the increase of our blast furnaces is especially notable. In the amount of iron produced, we are next to England, Germany standing third. Our steel industry, which is now second only to that of Great Britain, will exceed that country in another year. Our increase has been fifty per cent. in two years. Our mining industry, especially in regard to the precious metals, is simply enormous. The petroleum industry was briefly alluded to. Our exports of that product are now the fifth on the list in point of value. In agricultural engineering, our progress has been truly wonderful, and before this all other branches become as dust in the valley. In the plow alone, the annual saving of labor in producing our crops amounts to fully $76,000,000 less than the same work would have cost thirty years ago. It is in ship-building and maritime trade alone that we have lost ground during the last two decades. This decadence is attributed to the war of rebellion, and to unequal competition with England in ship-building, and the superiority of iron over wood—an industry to which our engineers and capitalists have not given proper attention; but it was confidently predicted that in the early future we shall once more assume our proper place on the ocean.

THE NORTH POLE.

The most vigorous efforts to reach the North Pole, or to make any near advance to it by means of direct approach from any one given point, having all proved failures, a new plan of action has been suggested—that of reaching it much after the plan of a military investment. It is now proposed to establish a circle of permanent observing stations around the northern polar region. In the furtherance of this proposition, the Danish Government has resolved to establish a station in West Greenland; the Russian Government will establish two, one at the mouth of the Lena, and another on the new Siberian Islands. The United States has resolved to plant an observatory at Point Barrow in Alaska, and it is expected that Canada will occupy some central point on her arctic frontier. Holland has provided funds for a station in Spitzbergen, and Norway will select some point in the northern extremity of Finmark. In addition to these national undertakings, Count Wilczek will place a corps of observers upon Nova Zembla. The line of this circumvallation, by posts of observation, will not be far from four thousand miles in extent, along which the observers will be placed at an average of only about five hundred miles distance from each other. It is possible that this may lead to some plan of advancing posts, and keeping them up within supporting distances upon some more or less direct line. In this way, it is thought the Pole may be eventually reached, and the circumpolar regions explored, and mapped in aid of science, if not for the advancement of commercial interests.

CLOTH FROM THE DOWN OF BIRDS.

An ingenious Frenchman, M. Thierry Girées, has devised a method, and invented machinery, for the manufacture of cloth from the down of birds. The down may be worked either by itself or in mixture with wool, silk, or cotton. The goods produced, whether exclusively of down, or mixed with fibrous material, present entirely novel features and characteristics. It is found that the down, whether of the swan or any other bird, will take any shade of dye, from the most delicate to the deepest color. The cloth is very warm, more so than woolen, and may readily be made impervious to moisture. It has been found best, as a general thing, to mix the down with some fibrous material, and for most uses wool is preferable. In its preparation with wool, in order to make an intimate mixture, oleic acid is used, in certain fixed proportions, during the first stages of the manufacture—in sorting and carding. It is carded, spun, woven, fulled, and traveled down by special machinery, invented for the purpose by M. Cleres. The cloth is much like velvet; the "nap" of the mixed material, after it is finished, consists mostly of down. Shearing and dyeing is effected in the usual way, and, as already stated, this "down" cloth takes any shade of color. *L'Ingénieur Universel*, of July 2, gives an illustrated description of most of the machinery employed in this new article of manufacture.

INDUSTRIAL USES OF GLASS.

The industrial uses of glass, and especially its use as a material for construction, is attracting increased attention, both in this country and in Europe. The new process for toughening glass has greatly enlarged its sphere of useful application. But, as old as the knowledge of this material is, the various processes for toughening it are still in their infancy, and there is every reason to believe that great improvements may be looked for in the early future. One of the latest and most important of its industrial applications is that for millstones. The idea of its use for that purpose is said to have originated from the observations of millers that the finest flour has heretofore been manufactured from millstones capable of receiving the most perfect polish. This observation led to experiments with glass, grooved in the same way as French buhr-stones, which experiments have been attended with most marked success. Glass mill-stones grind more easily and evenly, and do not heat like other material; they are said to run perfectly cold. The discovery is pronounced one of the most valuable of recent years in regard to milling industry. The idea originated in Germany. Mr. Bucknell, a prominent English engineer, proposes to manufacture pipes for water, gas, and drains from toughened glass. Glass has also been successfully employed for railroad sleepers—the clamps and other metallic attachments being put in while the glass is hot and still plastic. As the degree of expansion of glass and iron is almost identical, there is no danger of cracking or breaking from that cause. The cost is also less than that for iron sleepers, which have been suggested as a substitute for wood. But the latest new application of this material is for the manufacture of types for printers' use. For such purposes, the glass is colored, for obvious reasons. Being much harder than type metal, it is not so readily worn or crushed out of shape. It can be cast in exactly the same molds as those now in use.

THE PHILOSOPHY OF DYEING.

A French expert has recently been making some very interesting experiments upon animal and vegetable substances, with the view of ascertaining how coloring matter is taken up by the substances which are being subjected to the dyeing process. It was found that the action depended largely upon the capillarity of the fiber or other substance treated. Microscopical examination of infusorial earth showed that the coloring matter entered the capillary tubes of the infusoria, and attached itself to the inner surface of the walls. So with fibrous material. The more fully the capillary construction was developed, the more perfect is the capacity of the substance to receive colors. This fact will be found of special importance in the art of dyeing, and affords an explanation of the reason why some substances receive dyes more readily than others.

ART AND ARTISTS.

THE ART ASSOCIATION.

Since, through the bounty of Mr. Lick, abundant provision has been made for the founding of a School of Industrial Arts, the question now arises: Which of our many wealthy citizens will step forward and add luster to their names by establishing upon a permanent basis the San Francisco Art Association, with its academy for the cultivation of the *fine* arts? During his life time, Mr. Lick was several times approached upon the subject, but without success. That gentleman regarded the higher cultivation of art as frivolous, and was not willing to admit the kinship between such and mechanic art. If the one is superfluous, why not the other, since the aim of each is to elevate and enlighten. Carpets have their uses—they add warmth to our dwellings; but looking at the question from Mr. Lick's practical standpoint, why should a rich and elegantly designed piece of tapestry prove more effective than woolen rugs or the old-fashioned rag-carpets of our forefathers? Practically, a bit of Sèvres china is not more useful than an ordinary porcelain mug, and a plain deal table will no doubt meet its requirements as effectively as if designed and carved most elaborately. But that gentleman was unwilling to consider the matter in this light. He could tolerate, and even encourage, beauty and elegance when combined with utility, but expressed little sympathy for that kind of art whose sole aim he claimed was to embellish. Fortunately, the greater proportion of the community entertain different ideas. They find food for thought, and endless pleasure, in the contemplation of beautiful and truthful portrayals of nature; and the picture, if faithfully executed, often proves more instructive than books upon the same topic. In fact, were it not for the remnants of ancient art still extant, little would be known of many of the earlier nations. If the one kind of art is essential or desirable, the other is equally so, and is entitled to all the encouragement the public can bestow upon it. The San Francisco Art Association was founded in the year 1871, comprising a very limited membership. Many of our most intelligent citizens early became identified with it, and by degrees it developed into one of the most popular societies in the city. Early in 1872 the present art school began its career under the auspices of the Association. The plaster casts donated by the French Government, together with an excellent collection of studies in the flat, purchased about the same time, supplied all that was requisite for the beginning of an art school. During the years that followed, the interest in the school increased, and much home talent has been developed, to say nothing of the benefit the school and Association have been to the community as regards the cultivation of taste, and as an educator in matters relating to art generally. At present, the school and Association occupy spacious and comfortable rooms, and the academy, under the management of Mr. Virgil Williams, has so extended its reputation that applications for admission to its benefits have been received from persons living east of the Rocky Mountains. Yet the school is much lacking in many essentials necessary to a thorough institution of the kind. The bare fact of its being dependent wholly upon the somewhat precarious receipts for tuition puts it out of the power of the directory to be rigid in its exactions as to ability, or even to dictate courses of study to students. The large rental, salaries for instruction, and other expenses to be met, entirely consume the receipts, and make it necessary even to solicit patronage. We believe our academy is an exception to all others in this respect. With us, the only qualification for admission seems to be the ability to pay the tuition, which is so high as to place the benefits of the school beyond the reach of many of our most worthy and talented youth. Tuition should be light, and a certain degree of proficiency should be exacted from every applicant. Then the art school would be regarded in the light of a benefactor to the community. The amount of money necessary to effect this would seem merely nominal to many of our very wealthy citizens, and, in addition to the great benefit it would extend to coming generations, would serve as a lasting memorial to the taste and bounty of the donor.

THE LICK BEQUESTS.

Among the few bequests and donations made by Californians for the public benefit, those of Mr. James Lick deserve to rank uppermost, both as regards the large sums bequeathed, and the variety and importance of the uses to which they are to be applied. Some time has elapsed since the death of that gentleman, but as yet we believe, little has been done by the trustees of the estate to put in operation the several institutions and charities covered by the will. Notwithstanding the disappointment the public feels at the protracted delay, the wisdom of the course pursued by these gentlemen cannot be questioned. Unfortunately, when real estate commanded much higher prices in the market the trustees were deterred by suits at law from disposing of the property, and since that time the constant decrease in value has served as an inducement to hold on to it in the hope of realizing greater returns in the future. To-day the property would bring hardly enough to meet the bequests. In addition to many munificent endowments for an observatory and telescope, public baths, asylums, and relief societies, the testator bequeathed $540,000 for the establishment of a school of mechanic arts, and $160,000 for statuary for the embellishment of the new city hall and Golden Gate Park. When these sums shall be forthcoming it is difficult to say, but the amount will be sufficient to establish an institution whose benefits cannot be computed, and one that will always be a source of pride to the community. Once established, other donations of money and appropriate objects will, no doubt, rapidly follow, as such has been the experience of similar institutions elsewhere. With the facilities a school of mechanic arts would afford our public, there seems to be no reason why California should not be able shortly to enter into direct competition with older communities in the manufacture of all objects of industry dependent upon a certain amount of knowledge and training in art. The field is almost unlimited, and the manufacture of such articles has proved highly profitable wherever it has been undertaken. As stated in a former article, France probably owes her greatness and prosperity to-day more to art and its application to manufacture than to any other cause. Anything that is "French" is impliedly artistic, and accordingly commands higher appreciation as regards taste and elegance than the products of other and less cultured communities, not to mention the vast sums expended in their purchase by outside nations. We believe the capabilities of the American people to be as great as those of any other, and having at our command all facilities for a thorough and proper cultivation of the arts, with material in abundance to work upon, there seems little doubt that eventually America will be able to supply its own demands as satisfactorily as do the French to-day. This will arrest the expenditure of the millions of dollars that annually find their way to alien purses, and it may not be preposterous to presume that among the other results of the Lick school even a Californian Worth may spring into being, whose ability as a manufacturer of artistic raiment will meet the demands of the most fastidious.

"COOKED" PICTURES.

In art vernacular the word "cooked" bears a meaning probably not likely to be understood by the general reader. As to its origin as an art term, or the appropriateness of its usage in the sense artists employ it, we are ignorant, though by custom it has long been adopted by the profession, and applied to those pictures, more particularly landscapes, in which the painter departs from the literalness of the subject, and, for the sake of effect or composition, transposes, or even rejects, certain objects, and sometimes introduces others, which add to the picturesqueness of the scene, and are consistent with nature, though they may not have actually held a position in the subject in view. Excepting in cases where it is the intention to make accurate portrayals of places of historical or other interest, the practice is regarded perfectly legitimate, and is indulged in by nearly all painters. It is rare to find in nature a subject that embodies all the elements of a picture. Taken in connection with its extended surroundings, no defects may be apparent in the subject, but when a certain portion of a scene, necessarily limited as to extent, is detached from its natural surroundings, it will often appear unsatisfactory as regards the composition of lines, disposition of light and shade, balancing of masses, or in some other respect that may detract from the picturesqueness of the subject. The experienced artist will often detect at a glance how the defect may be remedied, by some slight changes, generally in the foreground, and has no hesitancy in employing art as an auxiliary to nature. However legitimate the practice may be in landscape painting, we are much disposed to question its application to portraiture. There are few portraits not more or less cooked. For the caricaturist it is an easy matter to distort features, and render a face ridiculous, yet preserve the unmistakable likeness; and, on the other hand, the accomplished and skilled portrait painter can take liberties with nature, improve upon the features, expression, or complexion, and still preserve enough likeness to make his work acceptable. In fact, the latter faculty is one of the great secrets of success in portraiture. No one is so free from vanity as to reject a picture because it flatters him. With time, faces and forms change usually for the worse. Friends forget what we were, and credit us only with what we are. But the portrait stands as an enduring representation of whatever attractions one might once have possessed, and the more forcibly those attractions are delineated, whether real or fancied, the more prized becomes the likeness. As regards family portraits, of little or no interest to the public, one can forgive a want of truthfulness, but, unfortunately, few public likenesses are literally correct. A writer in the *American Art Journal* of July 17, under the heading of "Bad Art Tendencies," devotes considerable space to this subject. Speaking of Gilbert Stuart's portraits of Washington, painted in 1793, and which, to-day, are accepted as faithful portrayals, the writer says, "The artist thought it necessary to improve upon the original, giving posterity and the American people a portrait to be proud of." Washington, he asserts, "was a small man, with a peaked chin, a narrow and retreating forehead, with a face quite like ordinary mortals, and very unlike the one we see in the accepted portraits. Mr. Stuart broadened the forehead, gave a calm and serene countenance, and made the chin square and massive." He claims that the Houdon bust, taken from life, and not the Stuart improvements, convey a correct idea of Washington's appearance. The writer cites no authority for his statements, and, even though well founded, it will prove as difficult to persuade the American people to abandon their long accepted ideal of that great man as it has been to deprive Shakspere of the authorship of the plays. Nevertheless, that the practice of idealizing likenesses has long existed, and does yet at this day, cannot be denied. As examples, the same writer cites the portraits of Charles Sumner, the poet Bryant, President Hayes, and Justice Swayne of the Supreme Bench, painted very recently, and all of which will convey to posterity erroneous ideas of those great men. Not only does the painter of portraits idealize his subjects. Even the photographer has caught the idea, and, by skillful manipulation of the negative, can convert absolute ugliness into beauty, and substitute the roundness and freshness of youth for wrinkled age. When once a person has attained distinction, and become an object of national pride, it would seem that the desire to perpetuate his physical identity would outweigh his vanity. But such is often not the case, and if a reform is ever brought about in this matter, it will only be through the exactions of a jealous public.

BOOKS RECEIVED.

THE LIFE AND WORK OF WILLIAM AUGUSTUS MUHLENBERG. By Anne Ayres. New York: Harper & Brothers. 1880. For sale in San Francisco by Payot, Upham & Co.

This is one of the most readable pieces of biographical literature of the day. The style is easy, clear, and enticing. One reads because it is a pleasure to read. The narrative puts before the world the life of a pure, cultivated, and devoted soul. Born September 16, 1796, and dying on the 8th of April, 1877, he lived contemporaneously with some of the early and great men of the Protestant Episcopal Church in the United States, and did a work far beyond the average results of the best. Among the most widely known of his poems is the hymn, "I would not live alway." In a eulogy attributed to William Cullen Bryant, it is said of him, "Other men have accumulated wealth that they might found hospitals: he accumulated the hospital fund as such, never owning it, and therefore never giving it. The charitable institutions which he founded were to him what family, and friends, and personal prosperity, are to men generally; and dying as he did, poor, in St. Luke's Hospital, he died a grandly successful man." The founding of this institution, its management and success, was the crowning work of his life. In a note on page 18, is a bit of ecclesiastical history not generally known. It is said that "in the English prayer-book the 'Litany' follows the 'Collect for Grace.' The American revisers of the book placed it after the 'Prayer for the President,' which took the place of that for the 'King's Majesty.'" This was done, says Dr. Muhlenberg, as reported by Bishop White, that General Washington, not attending church in the afternoon, might hear the prayer in his behalf. His life was entirely identified with, and characterized by, Christian affections, schemes, utterances, and results. The poems he wrote, the educational and charitable institutions he projected and fostered into realization, attest how much a consecrated life may effect for human good. The book before us takes us most kindly into the quiet, but great, achievements of this Christian worker. All will feel encouraged to love the good and true, and to attempt the work and labors that proceed from love, after reading this portraiture of this good man.

REMINISCENCES OF AN IDLER. By Henry Wikoff. New York: Fords, Howard & Hulbert. 1880. For sale in San Francisco by A. L. Bancroft & Co.

Sketches of travel in autobiographic tints are rarely as inspiriting as these of the roving diplomatist, who stirs us by graphic views of provincial America and the shifting incidents and distinguished characters of half a century. The frank and genial personage who exhibits this panorama acknowledges three idols—the press, the drama, and the fair sex. These predilections might easily be divined. The hurried, slipshod style of the newspaper correspondent betrays itself, if there were no mention of James Gordon Bennett; theatrical affiliations are natural to one whose "chum" was the tragedian Forrest; while chivalrous devotion to the ladies finds attractive metal in the Countess of Blessington,

Lady Bulwer, and La Guiccioli of Byronic interest, but the greatest fascination in the fairy tiptoe princess, Fanny Ellsler, with whom the author embarks for America. And it is just here, as the episode becomes absorbing, that the book breaks off, with the provoking perverseness of a serial "to be continued." To the master-passions to which this industrious time-killer confesses may be added his intense delight in the lions of the day. This almost parasitical devotion of the Chevalier, as he has been familiarly known, to the reigning notorieties, brings us in perpetual contact with an incongruous, but interesting, list of celebrities, ranging from Andrew Jackson and Joseph Bonaparte to Fieschi the assassin and "Jim Crow" the minstrel. Armed with glowing letters of introduction, we are admitted into the most exclusive society; attached to legations, we shine at court receptions, and mingle in circles where "everybody is on the *qui vive* for a *bon mot*." We also accompany this restless wanderer while he skims the countries of Europe as he did his schoolbooks. Relics and ruins do not move him, though at Athens he uncovers the entire sediment of his classical reading. But he is fondest of the hum of great cities, the maze of London and the whirl of Paris, which, as the proverbial goal of the American, he is forever revisiting, and where he finds that antipathy to dullness which is the keynote of his entertaining book.

SAGE-BRUSH LEAVES. By Henry R. Mighels. San Francisco: A. L. Bancroft & Co. 1880.

One cannot read far into this little book without feeling that he has made a personal acquaintance. The author has left his breezy, cheery, vigorous personality upon every page. It is not a "bookish" book. It makes no pretensions and offers no apologies. Casting aside restraint, the author chats familiarly, coins words and phrases at will, and skips recklessly from topic to topic, always forcible and always in accord with the best instincts of the human heart. His vagaries and shortcomings are forgotten and forgiven in view of the sparkling good humor which bubbles up through the whole work, and one is prone, after glancing at the title-page, to keep on turning the leaves to the end. Henry R. Mighels was in many respects a remarkable man. He went through life with his eyes wide open. He saw much and felt much that most men neither see nor feel. He found beauty and food for reflection in little things, and few men could better invest such trifles with sympathetic interest. His love for nature was strong and genuine, and at no time is he more pleasing than while indulging some wildwood fancy. So this little book reaches us with an aroma of the sage-brush leaves and the mountain pine about it, and it will find its way to the hearts of hundreds of readers on this coast who knew and appreciated the author's sterling qualities, and who learned with genuine sorrow of his pathetic death.

A MODEL SUPERINTENDENT. A Sketch of the Life, Character, and Methods of Work of Henry P. Haven. By H. Clay Trumbull. New York: Harper & Brothers. 1880. For sale by Payot, Upham & Co.

A Model Superintendent is an admirable book for all Sunday-school workers, and especially for superintendents. Readers of the *Sunday-school Times*, who have been charmed by the terse, practical articles on the "International Sunday-school Lessons," from the pen of H. Clay Trumbull, will need only to know that he is the author to feel assured that the subject is worthy of public attention and has been ably presented. Both Mr. Trumbull and Mr. Haven were fortunate—the former that such a noble, unselfish, and useful life had been lived to furnish a theme for his pen, and the latter that such an able writer was found to tell the story of his life, and thus perpetuate his influence and his memory among men. The many who are seeking better methods of instruction are to be congratulated that so much valuable experience has been embalmed in these pages for their profit and inspiration. Certainly, none can read the story of this faithful life without the desire to emulate the example of him, who by "patient continuance in well doing" did so much for the good of his race. The value of the book consists largely in the fact that the methods proposed are not fanciful theories, but are those successfully tried by an intensely practical man, and narrated by an equally practical writer.

INDEX TO CALIFORNIA REPORTS. Vols. 1 to 53, inclusive. By Welles Whitmore. San Francisco: Sumner Whitney & Co. 1880.

The tendency of modern law-books is toward condensation, rather than amplification. When large libraries were infrequent, labored treatises were of great service to the practicing lawyer. But nowadays every lawyer has his library of greater or less extent, including at least the reports of his own State; and every city has its more extended law library, including everything which can be obtained upon the subject of jurisprudence. This facility of access to the reports has had its effect upon the literature of the law, and books are now prepared upon the assumption that all the practitioner desires is a reference to the cases under each point. Mr. Whitmore's book is a model in this respect. It is an index—as it purports—of topics, with the adjudications under each subject. It would be hard to conceive a better method for speedy reference to a desired authority. The work is accurately done, and within its peculiar field the book is entirely satisfactory.

AMERICAN PATRIOTISM. Speeches, Letters, and other papers, compiled by Selim H. Peabody. New York: American Book Exchange. 1880.

The compiler has collected with discrimination those speeches of the leading American orators which have become classic. The book commences with Samuel Adams (1764) and ends with Robert C. Winthrop (1876). We note some omissions, but find most of the Americans who really deserve the name of orators represented.

FRANKLIN SQUARE LIBRARY. New York: Harper & Brothers. For sale in San Francisco by Payot, Upham & Co.

No. 121.—*The Heart of Holland.* By Henry Havard. Translated by Cashel Hoey.

No. 122.—*Reata: What's in a Name?* A novel. By E. D. Gerard.

No. 124.—*The Pennant Family.* By Anne Beale.

No. 125.—*Poet and Peer.* A novel. By Hamilton Aidé.

APPLETON'S NEW HANDY-VOLUME SERIES. New York: D. Appleton & Co. 1880. For sale in San Francisco by J. T. White & Co.

Second Thoughts. By Rhoda Broughton. Vol. I.

Stray Moments with Thackeray. By William H. Rideing.

HARPER'S HALF-HOUR SERIES. New York: Harper & Bros. 1880. For sale in San Francisco by Payot, Upham & Co.

Roman Life in Ancient Rome. By Chas. G. Herbermann.

British and American Education. By Mayo W. Hazeltine.

KNICKERBOCKER NOVELS. New York: G. P. Putnam & Sons. 1880. For sale in San Francisco by A. L. Bancroft & Co.

Uncle Jack's Executors. By Annette Lucile Noble.

A Stranded Ship. A story of sea and shore. By L. Clarke Davis.

THE BACHELOR'S SURRENDER. Boston: Loring, Publisher. 1880. For sale in San Francisco by A. L. Bancroft & Co.

THE HISTORICAL POETRY OF THE ANCIENT HEBREWS. Translated and critically compared by Michael Heilprin. Vol. II. New York: D. Appleton & Co. 1880. For sale in San Francisco by J. T. White & Co.

THE LIBRARY MAGAZINE. Devoted to Select Foreign Literature. Vol. III. New York: American Book Exchange. 1880.

THE LIGHT OF ASIA. By Edwin Arnold. New York: American Book Exchange. 1880.

THE MANLINESS OF CHRIST. By Thomas Hughes. New York: American Book Exchange. 1880.

THE LEGEND OF ST. OLAF'S KIRK. By George Houghton. Boston: Estes & Lauriat. 1880.

OUTCROPPINGS.

HYMN TO NIGHT.

Stoop, O Night, from on high, bringing to me, fondly pressed in thine arms,
Of thy children but one, poppy-crowned Sleep, soother of day's alarms.

Lay his velvet-soft mouth close upon mine, hide with his hair my eyes,
Wave thy dusky, wide wings over us both, shut out the starry skies.

Press together the red lips of the wound draining my heart by day;
With impalpable threads, dreams upon reel, weave, while the shadows stay,

Such soft tissue of ease, rest for the warp, beautiful woof of dreams,
As shall bind up the hurt, stilling the ache, surer than Lethe's streams.

Send the visions that rise during thy reign up from the world below,
Through the ivory gate, scenes that my soul, waking, never shall know—

Blossoms of marvelous growth fragrant and fair, song that touches to tears!
Fusion of soul and sense, secrets of bliss, beings of brighter spheres—

For of the bitter days forced upon man large proportion is pain,
Too, too cruel our fate if in our dreams writhe our naked hearts again.

PHILIP SHIRLEY.

TWO CHAPTERS OF A LIFE.

"Going, going, gone!"

The auctioneer was a fine looking young man, and the melody of his rich, deep voice called in many a passer-by from the sidewalk. We are too late, as he has made his last sale for the day, and is just leaving the store. We can follow him, however, and see whither he goes so hastily. He soon turns from the busy thoroughfare into a quiet street, and, after walking several blocks, ascends the steps of a somber building, on the door of which is a large brass plate, bearing this legend:

"YOUNG LADIES' BOARDING-SCHOOL."

Not at all abashed by this impressive notice, he jingles the door-bell and serenely awaits a response. Being ushered into the parlor, he asks to see the Principal, who presently rustles into the room, the customary benignant smile wreathing her countenance. This smile extends beyond its accustomed limits at sight of the young man, and verges on to something like genuine cordiality.

"Mr. Channing, I am truly delighted to see you. You have been quite a stranger to us for some time. Miss Mary has been really alarmed about you."

"Quite unnecessary, I assure you, Mrs. Lake. Surely one of my vigorous frame should not cause any overweening anxiety. You don't notice any signs of a decline, do you?"

"No, I am glad to say, I do not; yet I cannot chide your sister for feeling a little uneasy when she does not hear from you for more than a week, and your boarding-house only a few squares away. However, I will go and announce that the cause of her trouble is in the parlor."

Soon after Mrs. Lake's departure, Mary Channing entered the room, and continued the lecture on her brother's long absence.

"Well, well, Mary," said he, at last, "I plead guilty. But I fear what I have come to say will not, under the circumstances, prove very acceptable. I have just received a call to go over to J——, and sell out a large stock of dry goods. A good commission is offered me, and I hope to make a neat little sum before I return. I shall be gone about three weeks."

"I should not feel your absence, so keenly Norton, if you would only be so gracious as to drop me a line occasionally, to let me know that you are in good health. You seem to forget that life in a boarding-school is not the most cheerful existence in the world; and, although Mrs. Lake, and in fact everybody here, is very kind to me, yet it is not at all pleasant to never get a glimpse of a home-face—the only one that is left me now."

There was just a dash of tears in her blue eyes as she said this, and her brother, fearing a calamitous conclusion to the interview, hastened to add a few comforting remarks, and by dint of some extravagant promises of future correspondence, averted the threatened "spell."

"By the time I get back from J——," he continued, "your course of study in this school will be completed, and then I propose that we spend the vacation at Aunt Martha's, in compliance with her long-standing invitation. We will just run wild in those glorious old hills. How I long for a breath of the fresh, country air! Walter Thorpe tells me he will be up in that vicinity about that time, and the amount of boat-riding and fishing, and erudite conversation that will be carried on then, will atone for all these shortcomings of mine. I think, when I return to the city, I shall at once open a law office, and quit my present business for good."

"I hope you will," said Mary; "for I do not like your present vocation, as you know."

"I know you are not partial to it, and I must confess that it has its objectionable features to me; but it pays well, and I manage to have some leisure time for study. Besides, it is an excellent drill in oratory. You ought to hear me argue a case with an obdurate bidder. I just fancy he is a juryman, and that the success of my case depends upon his purchasing the goods; and the way I pile up the evidence before him is appalling."

"I'm afraid you are a naughty boy," said his sister, fondly; "but if I ever hear of your swindling any customers, you may rest assured you will hear from me."

"It is getting dark," said Norton, "and I have to make some preparation for my departure to-morrow; so, good by. I will write more frequently in future."

Mary stood watching him from the window, and, as his manly form disappeared in the gathering dusk, her eyes filled with tears of pride.

"How noble he is!" she said. "He is the very prince of brothers."

Norton, meanwhile, was thinking of her. They were orphans, and she had that unbounded faith in his strong, independent nature which an affectionate child feels in its father. He had noticed how her cheek flushed at the name of Walter Thorpe. "Walter is an excellent fellow," he thought; "I know of no one I should prefer to him for a brother-in-law."

His thoughts were interrupted by an alarm of fire. He fell in with the crowd that always springs, like magic, into life at that dread cry, and soon reached the burning building. It was one of those wooden tenement houses, and the fire had made such headway before it was observed that the building was already reduced to a shell."

"There is some one in that third-story window," shouted a man, and instantly the gaze of the crowd was fixed upon the form of a little girl that leaned far out in the vain search for some means of escape. A ladder was hastily placed against the wall, but it was several feet too short.

"Drop from the window," they cried; but the bewildered child could not comprehend.

"A man could stand on the topmost round and reach her," said one.

"Too late," was the reply. "That wall could not support a man's weight."

Norton's lips paled, and his heart grew sick, as he heard the wretched child thus left to its fate.

"What if Mary should some day be deserted in this way!" he thought. "Oh, I cannot see her die without making an effort to save her."

Hastily muffling his face in his coat, he darted up the ladder. Half way up, he heard a warning crack, and, ere he could retrace his steps, the wall and part of the roof fell, and he was buried in the ruins. The child, being higher up than he was, fell directly in the center of the flames and perished. The firemen, who had just arrived, managed to fight their way to where Norton lay, and dragged him to the street.

"He is dead," said one.

"No, he has only fainted."

"Stand back and give him air," said another, pressing forward as closely as possible.

No one was able to identify him, and so his crippled and senseless form was carried off to the city hospital.

"Little girl, is this Fifteenth Street?"

The child screamed in terror, and ran across a vacant lot. The man staggered against a lamp-post, and groaned:

"O God, am I then so hideous!"

Ten years had passed since Norton Channing came out of that city hospital cruelly deformed by that terrible fall into the fire. During all those long years he had lived the life of a vagabond. His one aim had been to keep from his sister the knowledge of his misfortune. He had contrived to keep track of her without exciting suspicion. He knew that she was married to Walter Thorpe three years after the night of the fire, and that she was now living on Fifteenth Street. His eyes had been dimmed in the flames, and he could see distinctly but a short distance. Yet he had a vague hope that he might look upon his sister's face once more without her recognising him. A hot fever was burning in his veins, and he felt that he was sick unto death.

"Mary mustn't know," he muttered, feebly; "it would make her unhappy to hear of my misery. Better she should think me dead, as I soon shall be. No; Mary mustn't know."

As he staggered on he came to the gate which the child he had addressed had left open, as she ran through it to the house. She was now in the arms of her mother, who had been attracted to the door by her screams, and was now giving an excitable narration of her escape from a drunken man.

"There he is now, mamma."

Norton Channing supported himself against the fence, and turned his disfigured countenance toward the mother and her child.

"I would not harm you, little one, for all the world," he said, brokenly.

The mother's cheek paled at the sound of that deep voice, and she said, huskily:

"Who are you, sir?"

It was his sister's voice, and a great fear took hold upon him.

"She mustn't know. Mary mustn't know."

He made an effort to move away from the fence, but his legs tottered under him, and he fell senseless to the pavement. They carried him tenderly into the house, and summoned a physician.

"He cannot live," was the verdict. "His constitution was shattered by an accident ten years ago this evening. I remember distinctly: it was the first surgical examination I attended after beginning the study of medicine. I have often seen him wandering about the streets since. I wonder that he has survived so long; he must have often suffered from hunger."

"Walter, it must be Norton," said Mary, trembling violently; "It is just ten years ago that he left me so mysteriously. He must have been that unknown man we saw mentioned in the papers as having been injured while trying to save an inmate of a burning tenement house."

There was no lack of kindness now. The aching head was tenderly propped up on pillows, and the fevered temples bathed. After a few hours the blurred eyes opened wearily.

"Walter."

"Yes, Norton."

"Mary mustn't know. She must be happy. God bless her."

"Oh, Norton," said Mary, while sobs of anguish nearly choked her utterance, "why did you not come to me?"

"She mightn't have known me, you know," he went on, not heeding her question, "and I couldn't have borne that. I think I should have gone mad. Perhaps I am not quite right in my mind now. I sometimes think I must be mad; but Mary mustn't know."

After a little he grew more flighty, and imagined himself once more at his auctioneer's desk.

"How much for this bundle of hopes, gentlemen? No flaws in any of them. The hopes of a young man just starting into life—none other superior. How much for the lot? No bids? Too much of the article in the market already. Give us something else. Ah, here is a remnant, gentleman, the remnant of a life. How much for the remnant? Come, bid up, gentlemen. Start it at anything!"

"Nobody wants it," he added mournfully, and then suddenly, the poor, distorted face brightening, he cried, "What's that? A bid? Ah, going, going, *gone!*"

The tired head fell back heavily as the remnant was taken by the highest Bidder.

WM. A. CALDWELL.

MIDSUMMER.

Beneath the pines I idly lie,
   Content to breathe, content to dream,
Content to feel the days go by
With busy cares beyond, while I
   Lie still and watch the stream.

I hear the wild dove's cooing note;
   The ferns bend low, the insects call,
And, perched upon a little boat
That lies forgotten, from his throat
   A lark is praising all.

The stream runs gayly in and out
   Among the brakes; azaleas bloom.
And now I see a speckled trout
Above the pebbles dart about,
   And now I breathe perfume.

The sunlight falls in golden flakes
   Between the leaves that hide the sky,
And here, upon a bank of brakes
And starry pimpernels that makes
   This spot a poem, I lie.

Midsummer's hush is o'er the land,
   Midsummer's peace is in my breast.
"Within the hollow of His hand
He holds us!" and I understand
   That verse, in truth—and rest.

MAUD WYMAN.

WHY WOMEN SHOULD HAVE A COLLEGIATE EDUCATION.

A celebrated philosopher once said that the amount of civilization of any people could be determined by their appreciation of the ridiculous. The Tasmanian, the lowest species of the genus man, knows not what it is to laugh or smile. The Hottentot is equally ignorant. The Mongolian can get no further than a sickly grin. To the enlightened Caucasian alone is given the hearty, whole-souled laugh, the boisterous guffaw that expands the chest, and shakes the whole frame with merriment. Another philosopher would test a people's civilization by their religion, another would test it by their laws, another by their education. There yet remains a test as general as any we have stated, but in its application far more easy and simple—the domestic and political condition of woman.

The noble red man of this country will, day after day, ride his jaded nag with conscious pride and dignity, while his squaw wearily trudges after him on foot, carrying on her back the household effects which, happily for her comfort, are not very numerous. If there is agricultural work to be done, the squaw is the one that must do it; and if there are any domestic duties to be performed, the squaw is the one that must perform them. In short, the squaw must do everything except fight and drink fire-water—burdens which the noble warrior magnanimously takes upon himself. Progress is death to the Indian. The ancient Germans, even before the Christian era, were much higher in the scale of civilization than are the American Indians of to-day, and they treated their women with infinitely more esteem. Cæsar tells us:

> "Quum ex captivis quæreret Cæsar, quam ob rem Ariovistus proelio non decertaret, hanc reperiebat causam, quod apud Germanos ea consuetudo esset, ut matres familiæ eorum sortibus et declararent, utrum proelium committi ex usu esset, necne; eas ita dicere: non esse fas Germanos superare, si ante novam lunam proelio contendissent."

The Turks are by no means an enlightened people, and the Turks regard women as a species of cattle that must be penned in harems, as inferior animals without souls, as nuisances that must be tolerated because necessary to the existence of man. The esteem, or, rather, want of esteem, which characterizes the Chinese is too well known to require comment. The Chinese stagnate, and have been stagnating, for hundreds of years. The miserable condition of women in the early ages of Rome's existence is thus described by Gibbon:

> "A father of a family might sell his children, and his wife was reckoned in the number of his children, the domestic judge might pronounce the death of the offender; or his mercy might expel her from his bed and house; but the slavery of the wretched female was hopeless and perpetual unless he asserted, for his own convenience, the manly prerogative of divorce."

As civilization advanced, woman's condition was ameliorated, and in the most flourishing days of the empire she was accorded greater privileges than had been accorded to her by any nation in ancient times. Besides the rights of marriage, of divorce, of holding property, she could become a vestal virgin, and have showered upon her honors and favors which even the highest dignitary might envy. When Rome was an obscure settlement on the Tiber, woman was a slave; when Rome was the mistress of the world, woman was exalted and free. In this country, and in the leading countries of Europe, women have rights almost as extensive as those of men. They are respected, reverenced, and loved. The law acknowledges their equality in all things, except in a few political matters. The United States, and the leading countries in Europe (and their colonies), represent the highest civilization so far known to man.

We have taken our measure—the condition of woman—and, in a few instances, have applied it. It works wondrous well. We will always find the more barbarous, the more ignorant, the more degraded the people, the lower the condition of woman; the higher the civilization, the greater freedom and rights acknowledged and given as her just inheritance.

But is the better civil and domestic condition of woman due to civilization, or is civilization due to her bettered condition? Which is the cause, and which the effect? The answer is plain and simple. Her advanced condition is due to civilization; and civilization is due to her advanced condition. The effect, in turn, becomes a cause; the cause, in turn, becomes an effect. We have two forces acting and reacting on each other. Let us take one of these forces and make it stronger; let us improve a people's civilization, and very soon will be seen woman's condition bettered. Or, let us strengthen the other force; let us improve woman's condition, and surprising will be the progress of the people toward enlightenment. One way, then, to advance civilization is to better the condition of woman.

We believe that charity should begin at home. We believe that if we are to employ our time and energy in the cause of civilization, we should begin right here in our fatherland, and that we should not waste our efforts on a people whom we have never seen, and never wish to see. The civilization of the distant heathen concerns us not, and will not concern us so long as our services can be of the slightest benefit to our kindred. So, then, be it known, that when we speak of advancing civilization we shall confine ourselves to our own country and our own people. And the majority of our citizens need a higher civilization badly enough. There are the sand-lot orators, who, wielding the mighty weapons of flattery and vituperation, endeavor, under the guise of patriotism, to enrich themselves; there is the sand-lot rabble, who blindly follow the sand-lot orators; there are the men in high positions who embezzle the funds of the State; there are men in low positions who embezzle the money of the savings banks; there is a motley crew of such men in all kinds of positions, a crew so numerous that,

> "To count them all demands a thousand tongues,
> A throat of brass, and adamantine lungs."

And heaven only knows that true civilization in their case has many strides yet to make before it can ever come even within the most distant sight of the desired goal—the goal of such perfection as is possible to man. The great object, then, to be striven for is the moral and social improvement of our own people: not so much to make our educated and cultured men more learned and refined, but to bring the great body of our citizens up to the standard of our best and noblest men. We have our end now in clear view; let us see by what means it can best be attained.

As we said before, one way to advance civilization is to better the condition of woman. This is the general law, and this general law is the great principle that will guide us to the attainment of our end. Vainly does the miner attempt, with all the strength of his brawny arms, to move the boulder, which, from time immemorial, has securely rested on the mountain's side. He takes a lever, the rock gives way. Almost as vain would be our attempt to effect an improvement in man's moral and social condition by working directly on man. We take a lever; we take woman, and what was before a task almost herculean becomes now comparatively easy. Why woman should have such a tremendous power will be clear to every mind. She is the mother of the people. She raises up children in the days when their minds receive impressions, good and bad, which eternity cannot eradicate. She determines man's principles, sentiments, and religion. Who ever heard of an ignorant son reared by an intelligent mother? Ignorant men are the sons of ignorant women, and ignorance breeds vice and crime. We are, then, to effect our end by bettering the condition of woman. How shall we better her condition? By making her nobler, purer, more virtuous. How shall we make her more noble, pure, and virtuous? *By education.*

The great mass of our women are to-day in a certain degree and in a certain manner educated. To this fact is in a great measure due our present state of civilization. Were they not educated, this country could not boast of a republican government, but would rank somewhere along with China, Turkey, and Siam. We universally recognize the importance of intelligent women; hence, our primary schools, our common schools, our high schools, our universities, all equally open to both sexes. We all agree that women should be educated. But now comes the tug of war. In what should this education consist? How far and in what direction should this education go? Let us investigate the matter; a careful study may throw some light on this vexed question. As a general rule, the business of woman in this world is twofold—to get a husband, to be a good wife and good mother. There are exceptions to this rule. It is the destiny of many women to do more good on this earth by never entering into the bonds of matrimony. However, we shall not treat of the exceptions; it is the great majority that shall concern us. The education of woman, then, should so be directed as to qualify her to perform well her missions: she should be taught how to get a husband; she should be taught how to be a good wife and mother. Either of these studies is closely connected with the other, but intrinsically there is a wide difference. The one is the requirement of social laws, the other is the imperative law of nature. With primitive man the first is unknown, the second is bound up with his very existence. Since, then, it is not only a social requirement that woman should be a good mother, that she should rear her children in purity and virtue, and send forth into the world a new race of men and women, who should reflect with increased brilliancy her own greatness and goodness; since this is not only a social requirement, but the very law of nature, we must conclude that it is the most important of all her duties, and being the most important deserves the most attention. Hence would we direct the education of woman with an eye to this main end.

But is this the case to-day? Are women educated so that they can perform the duties of mothers as befits a high state of enlightenment?—or are they not, for the greater part, taught those things which will render them (according to their ideas) more successful anglers in the sea of matrimony—more liable to catch a husband? It is a lamentable fact, but nevertheless true, that such is their great aim nowadays. Of course, there are many exceptions to this, but we are dealing with the general mass. She is taught enough of piano, flattery, and singing to please the ear, enough of taste to so bedeck herself as to please the eye, enough of tactics to entangle the heart; all very good—fine accomplishments—but they do not fit a woman for the responsible duties of a mother. This is the radical defect in the education of our women. For the successful prosecution of her mission in life, most stress is laid on that which is of the less importance. Nearly all her time, energy, and ability are exercised for the successful prosecution of the business of getting a husband, while they should be exercised for the successful performance of her duties after a husband is obtained. Instead of being taught those flimsy things, generally called accomplishments, which are neglected and forgotten as soon as she enters into the state of matrimony, she should pursue those good, solid studies, which will not only materially effect her own improvement, and remain with her as long as life remains, but which will render her the best and most capable instructor of her children. What we mean by good solid studies can be summed up in one phrase—a collegiate education.

The opportunities which women have of obtaining such an education are much greater than the opportunities given to men. They are supported by their parents till married. Nearly all men have to begin the real struggle of life when they are yet mere boys. The young girl leaves the school or seminary at the age of sixteen or seventeen, and generally spends some four or six years in "society" before she marries. These four or six years are mostly occupied in talking gossip, and in reading countless volumes of trashy novels, which give her false ideas of the world, and altogether do her incalculable mischief—mischief which in many cases far outweighs the benefits she has derived from her schooling. It is this class of young ladies who so often give the newspapers food for articles on unequal marriages with coachmen, and scandalous elopements with unprincipled adventurers. So then, say we, instead of keeping girls at home after they leave the school or seminary, send them to the university. Never mind about their graduating, and being A. B.'s and Ph. B.'s; that is a secondary consideration. Let them take a special course in such studies as best suit their abilities and inclination. It is not the simple studies alone from which they will derive benefit; they will learn ideas and principles whereof before they had no conception. They will see what true education is, what true culture is. They will be imbued with that pure love of knowledge which will never leave them, and this pure love of the sublime and beautiful they will in after years instill into their children. Verily, a rich inheritance. Moreover, they will learn what the everyday life in this great world really is. They will come in contact with all kinds of young men; they will learn to despise the worthless and respect the good. The system of exclusive education of the sexes is becoming obsolete, as it should. "Seminaries for young ladies," where the young ladies must do only what is right because they have no opportunity of doing what is wrong, savors too much of the Oriental harem system. Throughout life there are temptations; we should learn already in our younger days to resist them.

To sum up, then, the influence of woman is the most potent means of advancing civilization. As the mother of our children, she is the molder of their character, the designer of their future career. To fit her for this highest of all positions she should be educated with a view not only to her own improvement, but to the great mission she has to perform in this world. Of vastly more importance is it that she should be able to take her little son upon her knee, and tell him why "fire burns," and "plants grow;" that she should be able to tell him about that great system which rules the "twinkling stars up above in the world so high," and to tell him of gravitation and electricity, and thus to create in his mind a just appreciation of the Almighty Power which made all things—of vastly more importance is it that woman should be able to do this than that she should be able to play Strauss's waltzes, or "The Return of Spring." We believe in the great refining effects of music, and painting, and fancy-work, but they are things of secondary importance, and, being secondary, should give place to the true education.

The impossibility, in the present state of human affairs, of educating all women up to the high standard is conceded; but such an education is within the easy reach of thousands, and, did this matter only receive a careful consideration, instead of forty or fifty young ladies in our State University at Berkeley, to-day, there would be as many hundreds.

SELIM M. FRANKLIN.

IN FLORA'S ALBUM.

Over her cradle the mother said,
"Now, what shall I name my little maid?
Would Lily, or Rose, or Violet
My bud of promise best beset?

"Nay, I will name her for all the flowers
Of wayside, or woodland, or garden bowers;
Then she may bloom at her own sweet will,
'Flora,' will match with my blossom still."

O wise young mother, to read so well
The secret only the years could tell!
For Lily, and Rose, and Violet
In her gracious maidenhood are met.

MARY H. FIELD.

THE AMERICAN NEWSPAPER.

During the past century, no other factor of modern civilization has so thoroughly kept pace with our national growth as the American newspaper. In no other of the learned professions has more advancement been made within the last two decades than in journalism. Time was when medicine, the law, and the ministry were considered the only professions of dignity and honor open for young men who had completed their college courses. Subordinate to these professions were those of teaching and authorship; but they were regarded rather as offshoots of the former than as separate and distinct professions. But journalism in America to-day stands the peer of any of the learned professions. It is demanding the brightest intellect, the broadest culture, and the best talent the land affords. To be at the summit of his profession, the journalist must be at once historian, scientist, politician, philosopher, and art critic; to some extent a lawyer and theologian, and, if not a physician, at least a metaphysician. There is no richer field for the exercise of industry and knowledge, nor for the display of genius and ambition. Its departments are varied and wide, and while few can hope to excel in all, any one of them will give ample scope and ample reward to him who pursues it with energy and devotion. To the youth thirsting for political fame, journalism offers a wider and freer field of action than the law. To the one longing for oratorical power, it shows in its ranks as bright examples as now exist in theologic or forensic fields of eloquence. To all who have literary ability, it has opened the gates of opportunity, and has dared to proclaim, and has proved, that talent is confined neither to age, condition, nor sex.

The origin, mission, and results of the American newspaper form a profitable theme for contemplation. One hundred and seventy-five years ago, the Boston *News-Letter*, the first periodical published in America, made its appearance. Sixty years rolled by, and the number of news and political papers had increased to ten. These were the germs whence sprang the best and most extensive system of journalism in the world—now numbering over eight thousand newspapers and periodicals, of which about ten per cent. are dailies. The mission of these early journals was mainly a political one. They strove to sow the seeds of independence in the minds of the colonists. How well and how nobly they accomplished their mission is evident to all. How marked the growth of journalism since the renowned Benjamin Franklin edited and published in Boston the little *New England Courant!* The mission of the newspaper of to-day is not solely what it was then. Instead of being, aside from their political nature, mere newsletters, containing dry and meager records of public occurrences, our daily and weekly journals are complete mirrors of all passing events. Their columns are also enriched with poetry, art, science, philosophy, and history, combining the fresh and varied literature of the present with the wisdom of the past.

The many departments of journalism give room for the exercise of almost every shade of literary taste. From the ponderous articles of the quarterly review to the crisp, racy items of the daily paper is a field boundless as varied. The magazine, while it is not, strictly speaking, a newspaper, still, from its close relation, demands passing notice. It is with us a fixed institution, furnishing room for deep thought and broad culture. Here the traveler, scientist, philosopher, and novelist, assisted by the skillful artist, portray in their most attractive forms the various things which serve to instruct and entertain the reading public.

The weekly journals form an important factor of the great system, especially the pictorials, where the pencil of a Nast, a Worth, or a Bellew stamps glory or shame upon the brow of many a man with the swiftness of lightning and the certainty of fate. The illustrations, combined with the comments on current topics and events, here form a system which leaves its lasting impress upon the mind of the most cursory reader.

The daily paper, in its columns, local, editorial, and corresponding, gives opportunity for the exercise of the bright, nervous, vigorous, reasoning, and descriptive powers, impromptu writing, and the development of sudden inspiration. And these writings are not unappreciated and laid away upon the bookseller's shelf, like the musty products of many authors' brains, but, in the form of news, and the discussion of passing events, are often read from one end of the land to the other, before the pen which inscribed those thoughts has long been dry. A pithy paragraph in the editorial column of a wide-awake newspaper thus often wields more influence than the most powerful plea from pulpit, bar, or stump. The daily appearance of the newspaper is now such an ordinary occurrence that its very commonness blinds us to the really wonderful nature of the event. In the newspaper all the momentous topics of the times are analyzed and discussed. The lightning is its fleet messenger, flashing through oceans, over mountains, rivers, and plains, news of the movements of commerce, the triumphs of invention, tidings of peace and war, joy and sorrow, prosperity and adversity—thus binding the world together in one electric bond of sympathy. There is something almost feverish in the speed with which news is sown broadcast at the present day. In Washington, during a session of Congress, at ten o'clock at night, some noted member of that body—a Booth, a Bayard, or a Blaine—rises to speak. For two hours, perhaps, he holds his auditors enchained with his eloquence. By midnight an editor sits at his desk, a few blocks away, with a digest of that very speech before him, to probe it with a keen lance of satire, or to laud it to the skies, as it may happen to clash or chime with his opinions; and, before daylight, damp from the press, the journalistic weapons smite either upon the head of the speechmaker or his political foes. Meanwhile, in a neighboring block, the sharp clicks of the telegraphic sounders are heard, as news of Congress and of the events of the day go flashing over the wires to North and South, to East and West, to cities near and far. While the nation lies slumbering, and the mantle of night covers the face of nature, the wires, as though gathering inspiration from the darkness, are throbbing with their electric freight, records of new-born events whose occurrence may please or grieve, may edify or astound, a mighty people. Men arise and take their news with their breakfasts, feeding both mental and physical at once. They devour the speeches of the Washington congressmen, doings of legislatures, reports of foreign wars, and of local intelligence, with the same avidity that they consume beef and bread. As a dessert, they turn to the editorial comments. The thinking and elucidating have already been done, and the result appears before the eyes of the reader in black and white. These are the ready-made opinions which he assimilates and believes to be his own, and which do, in reality, become his own by adoption. It is in such cases that the press assumes the office of the great molder of public opinion.

Americans are a news-reading people. One of the most encouraging signs of the times is the universal demand for newspapers among the laboring classes. The mass of news and information thus disseminated among the throngs acts like the wind blowing over the great lakes—ruffling and swaying the surface, thus bringing the water in better contact with the oxygen of the air, and keeping the entire body pure and wholesome. The results of the newspaper are that it educates the masses, fashions and elevates public opinion, and enlightens all. It is as indispensable to our institutions as oxygen to the lungs, or as sunlight to the eyes. In politics it is almost omnipotent; sometimes erroneous, sometimes spiteful, it might work serious mischief in some quarters were it not counteracted by truth from other quarters. But the spite and error in the few cases are largely overbalanced by the justice and reason in the many.

In full view of all the benefits of the press, people are occasionally seen who rarely miss an opportunity to carp at journals and journalists; people who have not brains enough to be properly termed cynics, but to whom the term "grumblers" will better apply. To these, we would say that the profession does not pretend to be made up of embodied perfections, and we will admit that there is much to be deprecated amidst the floating literature of to-day. But the counterfeit only proves the existence of something worth counterfeiting. The same is true in the other professions. For every shallow, useless, or vicious editor that can be pointed out, we can show you a corresponding legal pettifogger, a medical charlatan, a theological stick, or a superficial pedagogue. But the bright array of intellect in the journalistic galaxy is, in itself, proof that the attainments of the profession are high, and the rewards great. The road to political honors is as clear through journalism as through law, as is proved by the many journalists who have occupied, and do now occupy, seats in our American Congress and offices of foreign diplomacy. The only reason why there have not even more occupied high political office is because they rightly consider that to be a good journalist is, in itself, a greater honor and power than the possession of almost any office at the hands of the people.

Whatever opinions may be held at large concerning the character of James Gordon Bennett, Jr., of the New York *Herald*, there are few who will not concede the great benefits conferred on the world by that spirit of enterprise which sends a Stanley into the wilds of Africa, or a De Long to the ice-bound regions of the North, to explore and assist in the development of hitherto unknown regions. Carl Schurz, of the St. Louis *Post;* Bayard Taylor, of the New York *Tribune;* James Brooks, of the Portland *Advertiser* and New York *Express;* Henry J. Raymond, of the New York *Times*, and others, while journalists, probably wielded more influence, and did greater good than as recipients of some of the highest offices in the nation's gift. The names of Horace Greeley, of the New York *Tribune;* William Cullen Bryant, of the New York *Post;* William Lloyd Garrison, of the Boston *Liberator;* George W. Childs, of the Philadelphia *Ledger;* George D. Prentice, of the Louisville *Journal*, and many others of widely known ability and loyalty, will go down to posterity as illustrious examples of men who have left the world wiser and better for having lived and worked in it.

The newspaper is the nervous system of our body politic. It is our pride and boast that it is untrammeled. Let us in all cases uphold its liberty—understanding, however, that liberty is not to be construed into license or irresponsibility. When the press is fettered, public spirit must cease, for the great means of modifying individual opinions by each other would then be lost. As long as our press remains free from the restrictions imposed upon the press of France and Germany, so long will it be a check upon abuse of power and corruption in office; so long will rascality in high places quake for fear of exposure. Proportionately, there probably is no more corruption in politics to-day than there was generations ago. The means for ferreting it out and exposing it are only multiplied by this giant detective.

Our forefathers would doubtless have exhibited great incredulity had there been foretold to them the proportions the press of the present century would assume. We to-day might be just as incredulous were some seer to point out to us the growth for the next century of this mighty preserver of liberty. Whatever may be our doubts and fears for the future, it is a fact patent to all observing minds that there is little danger that this country will ever lose the first rank among the nations so long as the press continues to work in consonance with the best elements of civilization.

W. B. TURNER.

ODDS AND ENDS.

Our lives are full of odds and ends,
First one and then another;
And, though we know not how or when,
They're deftly wove together.

The Weaver has a master's skill,
And proves it by this token:
No loop is dropped, no strand is missed,
And not a thread is broken;

And not a shred is thrown aside,
So careful is the Weaver,
Who, joining them with wondrous skill,
Weaves odds and ends together.

DEBORAH PIOSLEY.

SENTENCES FROM RUSKIN.

Between youth and age there will be found differences of seeking, which are not wrong, nor of false choice in either, but of different temperament; the youth sympathizing more with the gladness, fullness, and magnificence of things, and the gray hairs with their completion, sufficiency, and repose.

Impressions of awe and sorrow being at the root of the sensation of sublimity, and the beauty of separate flowers not being of the kind which connects itself with such sensation, there is a wide distinction, in general, between flowering minds and minds of the highest order.

No merchant deserving the name ought to be more liable to a "panic" than a soldier should; for his name should never be on more paper than he could at any instant meet the call of, happen what will.

Childhood often holds a truth with its feeble fingers, which the grasp of manhood cannot retain—which it is the pride of utmost age to recover.

Wherever there is war, there *must* be injustice on one side or the other, or on both.

By far the greater part of the suffering and crime which exist at this moment in civilized Europe arises simply from people not understanding this truism—not knowing that produce or wealth is eternally connected by the laws of heaven with resolute labor; but hoping in some way to cheat or abrogate this everlasting law of life, and to feed where they have not furrowed, and be warm where they have not woven.

We have no right at once to pronounce ourselves the wisest people because we like to do all things in the best way; there are many little things which to do admirably is to waste both time and cost; and the real question is not so much whether we have done a given thing as well as possible, as whether we have turned a given quantity of labor to the best account.

In literary and scientific teaching, the great point of economy is to give the discipline of it through knowledge which will immediately bear on practical life.

PRESS OPINIONS OF OUR LAST NUMBER.

"This much, at least, is certain—no patriotic Californian can afford to be without his literary namesake."—*Argonaut.*

"THE CALIFORNIAN (a serial which more and more proves its claim to be no unworthy successor of *The Overland*) for August is, on the whole, an excellent number."—*San Francisco Bulletin.*

"It contains much that is good and promising."—*San Francisco Alta.*

"This home periodical is constantly improving and rapidly approaching the highest standard of American magazines."—*San Francisco Examiner.*

"It is a capital magazine, creditable to its editor and contributors, and a proud monument to the originality and culture of the Pacific Coast."—*Oakland Tribune.*

"We have received the August number of THE CALIFORNIAN, which is one of our most welcome visitors. The magazine contains something for every taste, and ought to be found in every household in the State."—*Oakland Times.*

"The stories, sketchy articles, and poetry, are varied and attractive, the usual departments are edited with ability, and altogether it is the best magazine published."—*Marin County Journal.*

"The August number of THE CALIFORNIAN has been placed upon our table, and it fully sustains the reputation of this very excellent monthly. THE CALIFORNIAN has become an institution on this coast, and is a publication we take great pleasure in recommending to our reading patrons."—*Weekly Sutter Banner.*

"The August issue of THE CALIFORNIAN is a particularly strong one."—*Santa Rosa Republican.*

"A credit to the Pacific Coast, and every family should have it."—*Winnemucca Silver State.*

"THE CALIFORNIAN.—This most interesting of all monthlies—especially to Californians—for August is before us. We always regret that we have not room in our columns to give a lengthy and deserving notice of this home book, made up mostly from home talent. Every family should have a bound volume of this literary gem in their library on New Year's day, 1881. Persons wishing to see a copy of the magazine can do so by calling at our office."—*San Joaquin Valley Argus.*

"THE CALIFORNIAN for August is received, and as usual is is filled with choice selections and interesting original articles. THE CALIFORNIAN is a Pacific coast magazine, and as such should receive a hearty support."—*Cloverdale Reveille.*

"Its contents are more than usually varied and interesting."—*Ventura Signal.*

"It is a credit to the Pacific coast, and any family without it is behind the times."—*Lake Democrat.*

"The August issue of THE CALIFORNIAN, published at San Francisco, is particularly attractive."—*Santa Ana Herald.*

"It is a good number, and shows a steady advancement toward the goal of literary perfection.......It is distinctively Californian, and as such has our warmest sympathies."—*Colton Semi-Tropic.*

THE CALIFORNIAN is growing among us. Its one hundred pages of choice reading should commend it to every reading household in the land."—*San José Mercury.*

"The August number of THE CALIFORNIAN is at hand, brim-full of good reading as usual. It ranks with the best magazines of the day. For sale at all book stores and news stands."—*Hollister Enterprise.*

"The bound volume which contains the first six issues of the new magazine, THE CALIFORNIAN, brings indisputable evidence of the quality and style of the publication. It is worthy of the Pacific coast, and should be liberally supported. The fact that the coming volume will appear in new dress is, in itself, an indication that popular interest is being secured. THE CALIFORNIAN is credited with being edited with ability, and the group of contributors is a capable one. The magazine is characteristic of this coast. It has local ideas and glimpses at local scenes, both in nature and the associations of our people. Thus the publication has the freshness of the Pacific Coast country upon its pages, and cannot but be agreeable to those who love the scenes and conditions in which they live and act. This freshness of its environment is reflected from the fabric of true culture and polite literature which occupy its pages. THE CALIFORNIAN has lived long enough already to show that it is worthy to be loved at home and admired abroad, and this reception, we believe, awaits its coming issues."—*Home Life.*

"THE CALIFORNIAN for August comes in freighted, like a Spanish galleon of the days of good old Padre Junipero Sera, with plenty of good things for Pacific Coasters, and everybody else......Capital stories and interesting literary articles are also included among the contents, and everybody should place himself on the subscription list forthwith."—*Gold Hill News, Nevada.*

"A capital magazine."—*Solano Republican.*

"THE CALIFORNIAN needs only to be read to be appreciated. The August number, just received, is especially interesting, containing instructive and entertaining articles from the pens of well known local writers. ......If you wish to subscribe for a magazine for your wives and daughters, you will find THE CALIFORNIAN will just suit you."—*Adin Hawkeye, Modoc County, California.*

"The August number of THE CALIFORNIAN is an improvement upon its predecessors, and is about as excellent a publication as one often has an opportunity to read. Some of the leading subjects treated of in this number are of great and absorbing interest, especially to Pacific Coast readers......THE CALIFORNIAN deserves a hearty support."—*Elko Post.*

"A SPLENDID MAGAZINE.—THE CALIFORNIAN for August is a superb number, though it seems to have breathed the political aroma of the atmosphere which surrounds us all, and it contains articles on affairs of state to which we readers of THE CALIFORNIAN have been unaccustomed. But they are quiet, dignified, impartial papers, and worthy of the magazine in which they appear. But the literary treat offered its readers is rare, and will delight all lovers of fresh magazine literature. We have not space to particularize, but suffice it to say that no preceding number excels it......The usual departments are continued, and made as interesting as ever. For sale at all book stores and news stands."—*People's Cause, Red Bluff.*

"We have just received the August number of the popular magazine, THE CALIFORNIAN. Its articles, covering such a broad scope of subjects, are particularly varied and interesting."—*Tehama Tocsin.*

"THE CALIFORNIAN magazine for August will give satisfaction to its increasing number of readers...... There is no magazine published more attractive to the people of this coast."—*Gilroy Advocate.*

"THE CALIFORNIAN, the only regular first-class monthly magazine on the coast, for August, has been received. It is, as usual, well filled with rich and racy articles from the pens of our best authors. Its contributors are mostly on this side of the Rockies, and are all good. This magazine should be in the house of every well regulated family in California. Send to THE CALIFORNIAN, 202 Sansome Street, San Francisco, and get it for a whole year. You will never regret the investment."—*Dutch Flat Weekly Forum.*

"It is an excellent number."—*Phœnix (Arizona) Herald.*

The August number of THE CALIFORNIAN is on our table, and is even more than usually entertaining. Exceedingly varied and interesting are its contents, contributed by some of the ablest writers on the coast."—*Lassen Advocate.*

THE CALIFORNIAN for August is the second number of the second volume, and in its new cover is much more attractive. Throughout the one hundred pages of reading matter, we have not noticed a single typographical error; and in its makeup, as well as literary ability, it continues to hold its own with the best. There are sixteen leading articles, any one of which is more than worth the price of the magazine."—*Medico-Literary Journal, San Francisco.*

"THE CALIFORNIAN for August is at hand, and a most welcome visitor it is. This number is replete with good things for the literary world..... It should find a place on the center-table of every household on the coast."—*State Line Herald, Oregon.*

THE CALIFORNIAN.—This magazine for August has been read with great satisfaction. People who fail to take the periodical miss a fine literary treat every month; and those people who subscribe for Eastern magazines in preference to this make a great mistake. Send for a specimen copy at least, to THE CALIFORNIAN, 202 Sansome Street, San Francisco, Cal."—*Independent Calistogian.*

"A credit to the Pacific Coast."—*Calaveras Advertiser.*

AUGUST CALIFORNIAN.—Each succeeding issue of THE CALIFORNIAN is looked for with marked interest, being always filled with a high order of literature. The August number before us is especially interesting. Each department of the magazine is evidently under the direction of the ablest talent in the Pacific Coast, and its whole make-up is the best evidence of its worth, is a credit alike to the proprietors as to our people, and well worthy of a liberal patronage."—*Bodie News.*

"Exceedingly varied and interesting."—*Susanville Advocate.*

"THE CALIFORNIAN.—The August number of THE CALIFORNIAN is at hand. It is like its predecessors, brim-full of choice matter......THE CALIFORNIAN is fast taking rank as the leading magazine, and is, to-day, the pride of all Pacific Coasters."—*Calendaria True Fissure, Nevada.*

"It is a good issue, and shows steady advancement."—*Alameda Encinal.*

"This western magazine has for its contributors some excellent writers, and the articles it contains are fully equal to those in the Eastern periodicals. It is a credit to the Pacific Coast, and we earnestly recommend this work to our readers in this section of the country."—*Burlington Daily Hawkeye.*

"An interesting number."—*Cleveland Herald.*

"THE CALIFORNIAN covers nearly a hundred pages of reading. The articles are mostly short and crisp, a great merit in a magazine as in a newspaper. Many of the contributors are women, some of whom write with much grace and force. There is the odor of the Pacific about the whole publication, which deserves to win its way to many Eastern homes."—*Philadelphia Chronicle.*

"Any family without it is behind the times."—*Plumas National.*

The following papers also contained long and appreciative reviews, from which we have not space to copy:

Democratic Standard, Eureka, California.
Woodland Democrat, California.
Ashland Tidings, Oregon.
Castroville Argus, California.
Salt Lake Herald, Utah.
Tuolumne Independent, California.
Nevada State Journal, Nevada.
Calaveras Advertiser, California.
Daily Junction, Ogden.
Watsonville Pajaronian, California.
Albany Register, Oregon.
Pacific Christian Messenger, Oregon.

Read the first item in the Editor's "Note Book" (page 276), and send in your subscription before the price is advanced.

THE CALIFORNIAN.

A WESTERN MONTHLY MAGAZINE.

VOL. II.—OCTOBER, 1880.—No. 10.

A WINTER IN BERLIN.—I.

I had a few months to spare for a vacation in Europe, but could not go over until late in October. At that season the current of tourists turns south from Paris, and distributes itself along the main lines of travel, through the south of France into Italy, where it eddies about Florence, Rome, and Naples, until the spring warmth turns it again northward. The more enterprising push on to Egypt and Palestine, though a few turn aside into Spain. It occurred to me that, instead of going over the Italian ground again, I would go this time in the opposite direction, and get a glimpse of another part of Europe; so, instead of following the crowd to the lands south of the Alps, I started for Berlin.

It was a chilly morning in the early part of November, 1879, when I left Paris. Occasionally during the day the fog lifted, and there were brief glimpses through the humid car-windows of the brown fields of northern France stretching away from each side of the road in long, narrow strips, and then of the villages and more variegated surface of Belgium. It was certainly a comfortless ride. As the early darkness came on, we changed cars at the frontiers, and the stiff uniforms of the railroad *attachés* and their harsh speech told us unmistakably that we were on Prussian territory. Cologne was soon reached, and a warm supper in the comfortable hotel in a great degree balanced the long account of the day's discomforts. A day in this quaint city, to look once more at the magnificent cathedral, and then I pushed on to my destination by the way of Hanover and Magdeburg. In a few days after my arrival in Berlin, through the assistance of a member of our embassy, I was enabled to find a home in a small German family. My hostess was the widow of a public official, who, in the course of a long and honorable career, had been enabled to give his family a social position, which after his death it was very hard for the widow to maintain upon the meager pittance which the Government doled out to her as a pension. The worthy Frau Geheimräthin, therefore, was glad to admit me as a member of her family. It may be as well to mention here that a "Geheimrath" is a privy-councilor, but at this day in Germany the title has become an honorary one, conferred by the sovereign upon meritorious subjects, and, according to the custom of the country, the wife is always addressed by her husband's title. I took possession of her two vacant rooms, and remained until the following May. For the time I was in every sense a member of the family, and I had thus a very favorable opportunity to see the interior of the life of middle-class Germans, and certainly the simple, unaffected hospitality, the culture and heart, which I met in the circle to which I was introduced, disposed me from the outset to be uncritical toward the features of the life about me which appeared strange.

My life during the winter was one of quiet observation, and as it may possibly be of interest to those who have not been in Germany to know something of its capital, I shall endeavor to summarize my observations and experiences.

By looking at the map it will be seen that the latitude of Berlin is a little north of that of London, and relatively to our own continent it is as far north as the northern point of Newfoundland, on the Atlantic side, and the northern point of Vancouver's Island, on the Pacific. The climatic conditions of Western Europe correspond more nearly in equableness to those of the western than the eastern parts of North America, and in a general way it may be said that the climate is what it would be if situated at a corresponding parallel west of the Rocky Mountains. The winter was very much like one in New York city, without, perhaps, the sharp and sudden contrasts one experiences there. There was considerable snow, and yet it was never deep, and I recall only a few days of good sleighing. During almost the whole of December the heavens were heavily overcast, and for weeks no ray of sunshine came into my windows. Daylight appeared toward nine in the morning, and the night settled down a little after four in the afternoon. Of course, the opposite extreme prevails in midsummer, when the long morning and evening twilight leaves not more than five hours of darkness—between ten and three o'clock. Great heat occasionally prevails in the latter season, but, taken altogether, the Berlin climate is more equable than that of New York, and less so than that of London. The Germans take many more precautions against the cold than we do, and than we deem necessary. A gentleman does not consider himself adequately protected for a street promenade in winter without a long overcoat, heavily lined with furs, with a huge fur collar up about his ears; in addition, he envelops his throat in numerous folds of a silk handkerchief, and finally stuffs his ears with cotton. In truth, the views and practices of the average German, with reference to fresh air, present some inconsistencies to an American, which certainly, at first view, appear hardly reconcilable, either with each other or with what we are taught to consider the fundamental conditions of sanitary well-being. Within doors he has a horror of fresh air. Closed double windows; every cranny through which a trifle of pure, unadulterated air can make its entrance carefully sealed; a hot, thick, steamy, and inodorous air; are to him the conditions of comfort. He revels in the stifling, tobacco-reeking atmosphere of the Bierkneipe, or popular concert-hall. When it was discovered that I habitually left the window of my sleeping-room open, even during the coldest nights, I was immediately warned that I was guilty of an indiscretion which would probably end in typhus fever. I was, however, so wedded to this bad habit, and took so much comfort in it, that I continued its practice, and, notwithstanding the ominous prediction, escaped any ill effects. And yet, while the German stews himself within doors, he will seize the slightest pretext, whenever the weather permits, to sit out in the open air. As May opens up, and even before the chill is out of the atmosphere, the restaurants and *cafés* place tables and chairs in such open spaces as they have about them, which are immediately put to use by guests, who linger over their beer late into the chilly evening. A bit of garden, with a scraggly tree in it, is an excellent stock-in-trade for a beer-house. I have asked several Germans to explain to me why their country people hermetically sealed their houses, and yet in the warm season counted so much upon the fresh air without, and they have invariably answered that it is because they have a great horror of draughts, and believe them provokers of rheumatic complaints, of which they have a great dread. The explanation, however, hardly seems adequate, because they will sit for hours out-doors in a chilly air that in any other part of the world would surely bring on the complaint they affect to fear so much.

In order to picture to oneself the situation of the chief city of the German Empire one must imagine a wide stretch of flat, sandy country, with a narrow, sluggish stream meandering through it, and on each side of this stream the crowded streets of the metropolis. This stretch of level surface, in fact, extends over the greater part of Prussia, from the Rhine to the Russian line, and north to the Baltic. This small river is the Spree. In a general way its course is from west to east through the city, expanding on the eastern side to its greatest width. It has one or two parallel branches, which have been widened and deepened into canals sufficient for the long, clumsy country boats to come up to central points in the city.

From an obscure fishing station on this river, established prior to the twelfth century, has grown a closely compacted city of over a million of inhabitants. The form of the city is substantially circular. If a line be drawn from north to south through the circle, the older parts of the city will lie to the east, and the newer to the west. Cutting the circle, in a line running east and west through its center, is the principal thoroughfare, known as the Unter den Linden, which extends from the old Schloss, on the east, to the Thiergarten, at the opposite extremity. This street is the pride of the Berliners, and their lounging place, but it cannot be said to present any especially striking effects. It is, perhaps, two hundred feet broad, but the stately lindens which are said to have once shaded its central walk, and which gave it its pretty name, withered and died as the pavements encroached upon them, and are now replaced by double rows of insignificant successors, which are only kept alive through persistent attention. The center is occupied by a broad foot-way, which has on one side a carriage-way, and on the other a horse-path. Outside of these, on each side, are the usual street-ways and sidewalks. At the east the Linden loses itself, when it crosses the Spree, in the wide space known as the Lustgarten, which was formerly a veritable garden, and also parade ground. On one side of this roomy square is the old palace, generally known as the Schloss; on another side is the Dome Church, where the imperial family attend divine service; and on the northern face the square front of the old Museum, with its broad flight of steps, stands forth with an air of aggressiveness. At the sides of these steps are the two magnificent bronzes which are so much copied in small—the amazon on horseback defending herself against a tiger, by Kiss, and the hunter on horseback combating a lion, by Wolff. Connoisseurs say that the Berlin Museum contains the best arranged galleries in Europe for the study of the development of art, in sculpture, painting, and engraving; but it has no works of special renown. Behind this building is the beautiful structure of the National Museum, where are the collections of modern art. Recrossing the bridge from this magnificent open space, and going westward, we come at once upon the Opera House, Emperor's and Crown Prince's palaces, the university, arsenal, and academy buildings. These are all clustered quite near to each other at the eastern end of the Unter den Linden, and are all exteriorly quite plain, looking more as if built for use than ornament. In the center of the Linden, directly opposite the Emperor's palace, stands the colossal bronze statue of Frederick the Great on horseback, towering up fully to the hight of the neighboring buildings. It is a wonderfully spirited and impressive bronze, and yet, withal, very natural. The shops of the Linden are in no way noteworthy, nor its architecture at all impressive. At the western end it terminates at the triple arch, which opens directly on to the Thiergarten. This latter is the public park of Berlin, and is certainly as charming as possible. It is about two miles long, and perhaps half a mile wide. Its charm lies in its extreme naturalness. It is merely a bit of wild woods, with carriage-roads, horse-paths, and foot-ways winding about among the trees. The natural undergrowth is left undisturbed. There is little attempt at artificiality, or, if there is, it counterfeits nature admirably. One can wander off into depths of wildness, ness of a surrounding city with its noise and turmoil is entirely lost.

In the winter I was accustomed to very often take long rambles into its remoter parts, and always with fresh enjoyment. The sharp, keen air braced one up for vigorous exercise, and it was exhilarating to tramp along the deserted winding paths, and look off among the dark-bodied trees, rising like mourners out of the snow. At times there were peculiar effects, when a sudden sharp, cold snap followed a moist day of greater warmth than usual, and the great arms of the trees, and every tiny branch of the bushes, were cased in icy crystals. Then the slant rays of the sun, gleaming through the frosty air, filled the silent aisles of the wood with multitudinous sprays of diamonds and pearls. But it is when the warmth of latter May comes that the exquisite beauty of this bit of nature is seen, for then it is turned into a sea of foliage of the most delicate beauty. This noble park is so near the populous parts of the city that it is easily accessible, and is consequently filled with people, on Sunday afternoons especially, and every fine day troops of children can be seen, with their nurses, reveling in the piles of loose sand which the authorities have very considerately placed in the play spaces for the particular delectation of the youngsters. Of the many public parks I have seen, I do not recall one which, to the pedestrian, is so attractive as this. I have heard ladies complain, however, that its drives are not extensive enough, and that, therefore, it is soon exhausted. Along the southern side of the Thiergarten is the Thiergarten Strasse, which is lined with villa-like residences, surrounded by gardens. Immediately south of this lies the fashionable quarter of the city, though it cannot be said that Berlin has any one quarter which is exclusively devoted to the residences of the wealthier classes. Just outside the north-east corner of the Thiergarten a new and beautiful quarter is growing up around the Königsplatz, which is also occupied by the upper ten. In the center of the *platz* rises a column, surmounted by a huge gilded figure with outstretched wings. This is the "Denkmal," or memorial column, recently reared, as expressed in letters of gold on its base, "by a thankful country to its victorious army." The fluted sides of the column hold cannon captured from the Danes, Austrians, and French, and the four sides of the spacious pedestal contain bronze reliefs of the principal scenes in the recent wars with those peoples. Near by is Kroll's summer theater, with its roomy gardens.

On the eastern side of the city the Friede-

der to accommodate that more populous quarter. Except in the center, in the part immediately around the Rathhaus, or city hall, the streets are broad and roomy, and there are plenty of open spaces. Great care is taken to keep the streets clean and well lighted. In the principal thoroughfares the gas-lamps are not above a hundred feet apart on each side, and are kept lighted all night, whether there is moonlight or not, so that one can walk about the city at all times of the night with a sense of perfect security, which is, perhaps, also aided by the presence of plenty of policemen in all directions. There is a certain monotony in the domestic architecture and coloring of the streets. Almost universally the dwellings are built alike, so that a description of one will answer, in the essentials, for all. Ordinarily, the house has a frontage of between fifty and sixty feet, and is, as we should say, five or six stories high, and in depth the main building will, perhaps, also be fifty or sixty feet, while wings will extend rearward on each side of a small open court, which lies like a well in the midst of the surrounding structure. A building of this kind will be made of brick, stuccoed, and usually painted a brownish color, and in a respectable quarter will be occupied by from twelve to sixteen families, and in the poorer quarters by many more.

Let us suppose we are entering one of these buildings to examine it. In the center, upon the level of the street, is the heavy double door. On the right, we see a little brass bell-knob, with the word "Portier" over it. This we ring, and in a moment the door opens, as it were automatically, with a slight spring. No one is to be seen, but as we enter we perceive on the right, near the level of the hall-way, a little window, through which a face is peering. This will belong to some member of the porter's family, who is taking an observation of the newcomer, and is ready to question him if his appearance suggests a doubt of his intentions, or to answer questions if desired. The corresponding apartments below the street level on the opposite side of the hall-way will probably be occupied by a small dealer in fruit and vegetables, or thread and needles. The stranger is thus constantly surprised in wandering through streets lined with elegant mansions, in which evidently the well to do classes are residing, at the incongruity of a series of shop-windows along the level of the street, with the miscellaneous display of small wares for sale, and by the signs of vegetable, meat, and other dealers. But to continue our examination. The hallway into which we have entered leads directly into the well-like court-yard already mentioned, and also to the rear stair-way connecting with several flats above. Before reaching this court, however, we notice on each side a flight of stairs ascending to the right and left. Let us take those to the right; those to the left would lead to flats and apartments corresponding to those we are examining, as the house is double. A half dozen steps brings us to a little landing, which serves for the suite of apartments—denominated the Parterre, corresponding to the French *entresol;* continuing up the polished stair-way to the next floor—the Erste, or *belle étage.* From the little landing we notice two double door-ways on each side, with a tiny brass plate on the wall by each, with the name of the occupant. Each is the entrance to a separate residence. In the middle of the door is a little bull's-eye, with an interior slide, which furnishes a convenient port-hole for observation of the visitor before the door is opened. If one should happen to call at an unusual hour, perhaps the lady of the establishment, unsuspicious of a friend at the unwonted time, will herself answer the bell; but she warily pushes aside the slide, and the waiting visitor will see an eye examining him, and then hear a rushing rustle along the hallway, and presently the red-faced *mädchen* will demurely answer his summons, and beg him to enter, and afterward the mistress will walk in with an air of having been entirely unconscious of his presence before the card was presented. Entering, we come into a narrow hall-way leading off to the right, which divides the reception and living-rooms—which look on to the street—from the dining-room, sleeping apartments, and the kitchen, in the rear. Such a flat will contain from six to twelve apartments, according to the magnitude of the building, with high ceilings and plenty of space. The same building will contain various grades of respectability. The Parterre and first *étage* may be occupied by a general, colonel, or baron; the second by a well to do merchant; the third by an officer of the civil service, whose income is modest, while the rear wings may be filled with the families of the less pretentious, or may be let out for furnished rooms. Toward the center of the city, where space is more valuable, one will see a conglomeration of family life and petty industries crowded into the same building, which is by no means agreeable to us, who are accustomed to the separation of business from domesticity. The floors are seldom carpeted, but are waxed, or sometimes varnished, with their nakedness relieved by a few rugs scattered here and there. There is a certain bareness and absence of the abundance of knick-knacks, elegances, and coziness of our American interiors, which convey an impression of indifference to show and display.

Evidently the German ladies do not devote as much time and attention to these minor graces as our women; possibly it comes from the general economical habits of the people, but more likely from the partial absence of the domestic life common with us. Whatever the cause, a German interior rather chills than attracts. In all the living-rooms one sees the tall porcelain stove, which is a fixture. These stoves give out a soft, agreeable heat, are economical, and require but little attention. Thus it will be remarked that each of these buildings is a collection of dwellings under one roof, very much concentrated, but yet each suite of apartments spacious enough for all reasonable purposes. Each building, as already suggested, is guarded by a porter, whose duty is to zealously watch the incomings and outgoings. The first impression is that there can be little privacy in such a method of living, but the contrary is really the case. I lived for six months in a building containing fifteen families, and never came to know the members of any of the others by sight, not even the one next adjoining on the same *étage*. One can therefore easily understand that Berlin, with over a million of inhabitants, covers much less ground than an American city of considerably inferior population.

In consequence of the flat surface on which the city stands, its drainage has presented some difficulties, but these have been overcome by a system of steam pumps, and I understand that now it is adequately sewered. As is well known, the successful termination of the Franco-German war, and the receipt of the milliards from France, excited a wild fever of speculation in Germany, especially in Berlin. Under its influence, the city received large accessions to its population, and new streets and quarters were rapidly built up. The reaction of 1873 burst the bubble, and ever since there has been the complaint of dull times common to all the rest of the world. Yet rents are not low, according to German standards, though moderate when judged by those prevailing in the large cities of the United States.

The impression which one receives upon a first acquaintance with Berlin life is that the people are rigidly governed, and that the military spirit is the dominant one, and this impression certainly deepened in me the longer I remained. It is true that just now the state of affairs is somewhat exceptional, as Berlin is subject to what is called "the petty state of siege." In the excitement which followed the two attempts upon the Emperor's life in 1878, the Reichstag voted a very severe law against the Social-democrats, which placed very arbitrary powers in the hands of the military and police authorities, and permitted the Government at its discretion to treat cities, either as in an actual state of siege, which would deliver the people entirely over to the military law, or as in the condition of petty siege, which gives the police certain exceptional powers of search, arrest, and banishment. Immediately after my arrival in my hotel I was presented with a printed form, on which I was requested to write my full name, family position, place and date of birth, profession, religion, where last from, and, in addition, had to submit my passport to the inspection of the police. This procedure was repeated when I removed from the hotel to a private family. In this way the police keep a record of the movements of every person in the city.

The whole life of Prussia is tinctured and impressed with the militarism, which has been its inheritance from the beginning. The drill-master has made his mark in all directions. Military order, rigidity, obedience, and in a degree its arrogance, control social movements and relations. One would not be surprised at any moment in the crowded streets to hear the order to "fall in," and to see the entire male population march off in regiments. I could well understand that it was a natural movement for half a million of armed men to pour across the Rhine within a few days after war was declared.

A glance at the map of Europe will show that the German Empire is a state without frontiers. On one side it is liable to be overrun by Russia, on the other by France, while in the south her jealous enemy, Austria, stands sullenly equipped for sudden war. The sad history of Germany shows that it has been made the battle-ground of Europe, and that her petty principalities have been the intriguing ground of the Great Powers. Prussia has finally grown to be the dominating force through her admirable military organization. It is before and above all else a military state, and has has been for two hundred years.

Professor Gneist, in the debate recently had in the Reichstag upon the proposition to increase the army, showed that in the time of Frederick the Great two-thirds of the revenue of his kingdom was consumed by the military organization, but that since then there has been a gradual reduction, so that, as he asserted, they ought to consider themselves peculiarly fortunate, because only one-fifth is now required.

With very few exceptions, indeed, the entire able bodied male population of Germany, between the ages of twenty and sixty, are soldiers, either in the active army or one of the reserve corps, and can be mobilized and made ready for attack or defense in a very short time. It is asserted that in the War Department are notices all ready to be sent, on the instant, to every man liable to service, calling him to his place, and the entire organization is so well coordinated, and the place of each man and each thing is so well arranged in advance, that it would only require eight days to mobilise one million of soldiers and put in line the immense material at the disposition of the War Administration.

At twenty years of age every man goes into the active army and serves three years, unless he has received a degree at a university, or has passed certain examinations, and in addition supports himself while in service—in which case he serves only one year, and is termed a "Freiwilliger." At the end of the three or one years' continuous service, as the case may be, the soldier goes back to civil life, and may pursue his vocation. Still, he remains a soldier. He is incorporated in the reserve, and must take his place in the ranks and serve six weeks in the year. He remains in the reserve four years, and then passes into the first van of the Landwehr for five years, and then for five years into the second van. He is at any time liable to be called on for active service up to his thirty-seventh year. After that he goes into the Landsturm, where his liability is to be called upon only for defensive warfare. Up to his sixtieth year he has a definite, fixed place in the military organization.

As is well known, the present effective system grew out of the complete break-down of the army at Jena in 1806. When Napoleon had completely subdued Prussia he hoped to render her in the future helpless, and so he imposed the condition that thereafter her standing army should not exceed 42,000 men, which, relatively to the armaments of the surrounding powers, was manifestly a bagatelle, but General Scharnhorst avoided the effects of this restriction by devising the present scheme, which in a few years gave the greater part of the population a military training; so that when, in 1813, following upon the frightful retreat from Moscow, the Germans rose against Napoleon, the Prussians were able to put a large and effective army in the field, and were further able, in conjunction with their allies, to retrieve at the sanguinary battles around Leipsic the disgrace of Jena. The Prussian system is simply the levy *en masse* and an equalization of the heavy burdens of war. Before its introduction the rank and file were exclusively peasants, and the term of service was ten years. These poor people were forced into the service and most brutally treated. The *burger*, or citizen, class was entirely exempt, and the nobility had the exclusive claim to officers' commissions. Even at this day, notwithstanding there is no legal exclusion of other classes, the officers are mostly noblemen or connected with the nobility. The career of arms is looked upon as the fit one for men of this class, and they are sufficiently numerous to largely monopolize its posts of honor.

The consumption of one-fifth of the annual revenue in army support, and in addition the withdrawal of nearly every active, capable man from productive pursuits for a period of three years, are certainly heavy burdens, but yet the Germans willingly submit to them, because they know that their national life and unity are held only upon this hard tenure. The productive power of the country is not only impaired by actual loss of time of the soldier while under arms, but also because of the additional loss of time which is suffered while the handicraftsman is taking up and again making himself expert in his interrupted calling. This last point was emphasized by the Opposition in debates upon the last army bill. On the other hand, the army is, in a good way, an educator. It takes the raw peasantry and young citizens and trains them to promptness, order, and obedience. The discipline is severe, as any one can see who has watched the recruits on the drill-ground, but it is not degrading or exhausting, and at the end of his three years the young man is intellectually and physically in better trim than when he entered the service.

That Prussia is a military state is impressed upon one at every turn. I recollect how strikingly it was symbolized to me one Sunday morning at the services in the Dome Church. The Emperor came into his *loge*. No other person was with him in his large compartment. Presently, when the clergyman commenced to read the liturgy, the congregation rose to its feet, and the old Emperor also arose and stood. His uniform was visible under the military cloak thrown back upon his shoulders, and he stood leaning upon the hilt of his sword, with his head inclined in prayer. It was a characteristic exhibition of the Prussian idea. In Prussia, the hand is always upon the sword, and God is worshiped according to the articles of war.

The other great factor in Prussia, and, in fact, in all German life, is the bureaucratic system. Personal government has always heretofore been the rule; the present attempts in the direction of a parliamentary *régime* are really as yet only tentative. There has grown up an elaborate civil and police service, which penetrates into all the relations of life, and has developed a system of "red tapeism" and rigid regulations quite appalling. The Prussian is, metaphorically speaking, marked and labeled at his birth, and he lives and dies and is buried according to a complex system of rules, to which he submits with admirable patience.

These two, militarism and bureaucracy, supplementing the natural sedateness of the people, and the absence of all street cries, which are strictly prohibited by the police, give to the external life of the capital an air of subdued formalism, which is quite in contrast with the exuberance of other great cities. The police are very numerous; there are above three thousand. If there is any gathering of a public character, the neighborhood fairly swarms with them. The authorities are evidently very much afraid of the populace. I was present at the unvailing of a statue of Goethe, in the Thiergarten—certainly a most peaceful and unexciting occasion, and there were not above a thousand spectators present; yet every approach was closely guarded by rows of policemen. I am sure there were five hundred of them about.

Officers of all branches of the military service are numerous in Berlin. They always appear in uniform, with sword at the side. The especial aim with the younger ones appears to be to get their trousers to fit as tightly as possible, and to compress their waists into the smallest possible compass. As a rule, they are fine, soldierly looking men, but one now and then remarks in the Unter den Linden a most attenuated pair of legs with a cavalry sword clanking alongside of them. The lieutenants furnish the dancing men of society. Military officers have certain privileges, such as non-liability to suit for debts. They also have the *entrée* to all public amusements at reduced rates. But, on the other hand, usage forbids them from appearing in any but the first places. For example, you will never see an officer in uniform in the parquette at the opera. With reference to debts, the unfortunate creditor can complain to the military authorities, and, if his debtor does not pay, he may be, and often is, compelled to leave the service. The pay is small, and few officers can subsist without private fortunes; consequently, the poor ones look about for rich girls to marry, and the latter are glad to respond.

The social hierarchy stands in about this wise in Berlin: First, of course, the imperial court and the upper aristocracy; then army officers of the upper ranks, and superior officers of the various branches of the civil service, together with the university professors. Next in order stand the lower military and lower civil officers; then the professions—lawyers, physicians, journalists—followed by bankers, and, lastly, wholesale merchants and large manufacturers. Here the line is drawn. Retail people, small manufacturers, and clerks are nowhere—are outside the magic circle. The foreign diplomatic corps, and also the leading artists and literary people, have the *entrée* into all circles.

A second lieutenant, or the holder of a Government office above a mere clerkship, has a better social standing than the enterprising merchant whose energy may be opening new fields of commercial enterprise in remote parts of the world. I am now speaking only of social conditions in the capital city. It is said to be otherwise in Hamburg, Bremen, Leipsic, and other cities, where commerce holds an honored place, but in Berlin one very soon discovers that the military and official classes, who lead society, look down upon the money-making part of the community in a contemptuous, patronizing way. I should not omit to mention a curious distinction, which is very carefully observed. A man distinguished as an artist, or in literature or science, or in any of the intellectual fields, no matter what his origin may have been, may be presented at court, but his wife, unless she be of noble blood, cannot be. It naturally follows from these social prejudices that the poor nobles, of whom there are crowds, and all others who can, are striving to get into military or official life, so that much of the energy, and even culture, of the community, is diverted from commercial and industrial pursuits. It is apparent that the peculiar military and political development of Prussia operates in a variety of ways to retard its economical advancement.

When we consider, also, that its broad stretches of flat country are by no means fertile, we need not be surprised that it is a poor country. Even in the capital, among all classes, the scale of living is lower, simpler, than in corresponding sections of society with us. It is noticeable in equipages, dress, and the table. Well to do Germans practice small economies which are unknown with us, and those who depend upon the limited salaries attached to Government offices content themselves with very plain living. Fortunately, there prevails a healthy social sentiment which does justice to those who are not ashamed to live in plain apartments, to wear plain clothes and eat plain food, if better cannot be afforded. Mrs. Grundy is not the terrible old female in Germany that she is in the United States. No amount of money will give a coarse-grained, ignorant man social prominence. It is true that mere birth furnishes advantages socially, which from a democratic standpoint seems absurd; this is the ridiculous side, but at the same time it must be allowed that the German soul does not go so low down in the dust before blue blood as does that of the average Englishman. The patent of German nobility descends to all the sons alike, and the natural result is that the land swarms with poor nobles, so that the very commonness of aristocratic clay has made it less precious in common eyes. It is quite common for nobles who have no property to drop the title and merge themselves in the common herd. What is called fashionable society is not materially different in Berlin, New York, or San Francisco. The same varnish is to be found in all. To see, know and comprehend the true social life of a people, to get the local flavor and color, one must go into the circles of the middle classes, and here the German character appears at its best.

The men of these classes are, as a rule, more carefully educated than their equivalents with us. They do not press into active pursuits so soon as our young men, and in every way their lives, their movements, and their thoughts are more deliberate. A German never seems to be in a hurry, and the first difficult lesson which an American must learn among them is to wait and be patient.

The politeness of the men to each other is rather punctilious; the fashion is to take off the hat with a formal swing, frequently reaching half way to the ground. Even when friends come together at the Bierkneipe, or in other social places, there is a careful observance of all forms of politeness. I have heard this formalism accounted for on the theory that, as the duel still prevails, men are always on their guard not to overstep the limits of strict good breeding. The men are loud talkers, and somewhat demonstrative, notwithstanding their phlegmatic demeanor; they are likewise capable of consuming innumerable glasses of white or black beer, and of smoking more vile cigars than any other people. The rule is to smoke everywhere; the exceptions are few. In a train of cars there will be one or two compartments with the notice, "Nicht rauchen;" if a similar warning is not visible in any place of public resort you will be sure to inhale the odor of cheap cigars. The popular concert-rooms become blue with tobacco-smoke, and toward the end of the performance one will be hardly able to distinguish the ghost-like figures of the musicians through the hazy medium. The men are also cultivated on more sides than with us, and while each one pursues his specialty with plodding zeal, he yet is not so apt to surrender his entire being to it, very often cultivating music or some of the sciences. Socially, the men assert their claims as lords of creation. They are formally polite to women, but not deferential. They seem to act upon the theory that every woman is guilty until she proves her innocence. The women accept a position of inferiority, and, as a German lady assured me, are satisfied with the manifold restrictions upon their liberty—simply, I suppose, because they never knew different conditions. The sexes are kept carefully separate from early youth up, and the boys of a family get the cream, while the girls must content themselves with the skim-milk. When a girl is marriageable, and attracts the attention of a marrying man, the latter seeks, either personally or through a friend, permission from the parents to pay his addresses to her; if his suit prospers they are betrothed formally by two successive announcements from the pulpit of the neighboring church, and frequently one will see in a newspaper a notice like the following, which I take from a daily journal:

> "The betrothal of our youngest daughter, Hedwig, with Mr. Carl Gothe, merchant, is respectfully announced.
>
> "EMIL MATZDORFF and wife (born Kuhl).
>
> "FRANKFORT, May 18, 1880."

The marriage may not follow for a long time, and sometimes the engagement is broken. If so, the announcement process, in case of a new betrothal, is repeated. The newspapers announce betrothals as marriages are announced with us. After the engagement, custom permits great freedom of intercourse between the lovers. The happy pair will often exhibit an effusive affection in public which is quite comical to the cold-blooded on-looker.

In the ordinary intercourse between the sexes, custom requires that the first greeting in the street shall come from the gentleman, and, if there is handshaking, he must first offer the hand. He has it in his power to drop or continue the acquaintance, as he pleases. An unmarried lady cannot take an unmarried man's arm in the street, unless she is betrothed to him, nor can she accompany him alone to any public place. In truth, unless ladies exercise the greatest discretion in ways that would never be thought of with us in her intercourse with gentlemen outside her own family, she is subjected to disagreeble suspicions. Nay, recently I read an article in a very widely circulated Berlin paper, in which the writer complains of the lack of politeness of German gentlemen toward ladies, and also states some of the observances required from a lady in public. It is improper for a lady to greet any but very intimate gentlemen friends heartily on the street, or to look back or around, or for two or more to stand talking together on the sidewalk, or for a young lady alone to stop and look in a shop window. The surface politeness, the hat lifting et cætera, of German gentlemen toward ladies, is demonstrative enough, but they will not put themselves out a particle for a woman.

After marriage the wife occupies a position a shade or two above that of an upper servant. If small economies are to be practiced, it falls to her lot to practice them. The husband must make a good appearance, even if the wife has to stay at home in plain clothes. She is expected to wait upon him assiduously. I have seen a loving husband, one who ordinarily was rather demonstratively so, call his wife from another room, and ask her to hand him a cigar or a glass of wine from the next table. His lordship would not take the trouble to rise from his chair and walk across the room. The lady of the house carves at table, and pours out the wine, and many wives perform menial services which our women of corresponding social positions would revolt at. A friend related to me an instance of a university professor's wife, who polished his boots every day. The male foreigner is generally, at first, very much embarrassed by the attentive ministrations of German ladies in social gatherings, but the noble animal, man, has, after all, such an innate sense of his own importance, that he very soon comes to take all these minor attentions as only his natural due.

The family tie, I think, is stronger than with us; the family clings longer together, and its members are more interdependent. It is often charming to see the genuine affection of children for their elders; there does not seem to be successive declarations of independence as children arrive near majority, as is too often the case with American youth. Birthdays are religiously observed. The odd theory prevails that one knows the birthday of each relative and friend, and yet it is impolite to ask them when the anniversary occurs. Consequently, if one has a wide circle of relatives and friends, he is obliged to indirectly ascertain the several birthdays, and then, perhaps, keep a record of them in calendar form. The correct thing is to send a bouquet, or a pot of flowers, with a card of greeting. My venerable landlady celebrated her seventy-fourth birthday during my stay in her family. I remarked that morning an unusual note of preparation in her apartments, and quite early she appeared in her best toggery. Cake and wine were placed on the table, and presently relatives, friends, and flowers in pots and bouquets, began to pour in. Very soon the windows were filled with blooming roses, azaleas, hyacinths, and May-flowers. Kindly greetings were extended by visitors, and cake and wine consumed. The old lady's face beamed with joy at these demonstrations of respect and affection. This irruption into the quiet house gave me the first intimation of the nature of the day; and in order not to be lacking in courtesy, I quietly slipped out and purchased a pot of blooming roses, which I sent with my card of greeting to the old lady, just as if I had known all along it was the festive day. The day closed with a grand family supper. It is also a very pleasant little custom for each one of a family, when he rises from the table, to bless the meal; and it is quite common for guests at a hotel, when they rise from the *table d'hôte*, to bow to those near and repeat the usual phrase, "Gesegnet die Mahlzeit." It is also common at private gatherings, when the company rise from the table, to greet each other with handshaking, and for relatives to kiss each other. Indeed, kissing is lavishly indulged in, but it always appeared absurdly comical when two strapping, bewhiskered fellows smacked each other, first on one cheek and then on the other.

W. W. CRANE, JR.

[CONCLUDED IN NEXT NUMBER.]

CRUISING IN A CHINESE MAN-OF-WAR.

In the summer of 1879 I was suffering from an attack of low fever, contracted in the low-lying districts surrounding Shanghai, where my residence was then situated, and deeming that a trip upon salt water might in some degree recuperate my health, I applied to my superiors for leave of absence. This was readily granted, and at the same time I was informed that one of the gunboats of the Foochow division, stationed at Ningpo, had just received orders to proceed on a cruise after pirates; also, to convey an official to form a new settlement upon a hitherto uninhabited island in the Chusan Archipelago; and that, if I liked, I might take a trip in her. Accordingly, I got my valise and blankets on board the steamer *Kiang Teen*, which belongs to the Chinese Merchants' Company, and which leaves Shanghai for Ningpo every alternate afternoon. Having secured a comfortable berth, I went up on the hurricane deck, to enjoy the cool of the evening, while proceeding down the Whangpoo toward the fishing village of Wonsung, where the river joins the mighty Yangtsze on its way to the ocean. The course of the steamer was difficult and tortuous, rendering it not an easy task for any captain, unless experienced, to safely navigate his vessel through the numberless sampans, cargo boats, and pleasure yachts that strove to pass across the bows. Nothing picturesque is presented to the eye along the banks of the stream, which are lined on one side with an expanse of reclaimed ground, about to be turfed over to form a promenade for the weary residents, to enjoy a whiff of cool air after the heated atmosphere they are subjected to during the summer. But we see long lines of wharves, at which huge steamers and ships, of all nations, are discharging their cargoes, and the stately buildings, residences of merchants who amassed a fortune in days gone by, prior to the opening of the Suez Canal and the completion of the telegraph to China. Alas! those balmy days are now departed forever. The great tea firm of Him Sun On know the price of Ningchows and Oopaks in London or New York as well as you do, and are not to be tempted with what you consider an alluring offer.

Steaming on, we pass the wharf of the China Merchant Steamer Company, whose fleet, traversing the coast of China, consists of not less than thirty-seven steamships, flying the dragon flag. Now we come in view of the buildings that are intended for the manufacture of cotton piece-goods on foreign principles, but which scheme has yet to be elaborated. On our right lie the British naval depot and a large brick structure, for tanning hides for export to Europe; also, a new dock, not yet completed, but which will, when finished, enable Shanghai to compete with Hongkong in docking large steamers.

We are suddenly startled by the gong signaling, "Stop the engine," and find that a sampan is right in our way, and the boatman, with the utmost *sang froid*, pulling leisurely, apparently oblivious of the fact that had the steamer struck his frail craft he would have been lost. He accomplished his object—to cross the bow—and then our captain sang out to him, "Oh, you scoundrel!" His smile was so simple and sarcastic as to dispel any wrath a person could entertain toward him. He simply replied, "Chin, chin, Captain," and paddled leisurely on.

We continued on our way down the river, passing Woosung, where we saw the British ship, *Iron Duke*, and the French war ship, *Armide*, and, dipping flags to them, steamed out upon the bosom of the great river. The evening being still sultry, after dinner the Captain and I indulged in our cigars until the bell gave us warning that it was midnight, when we retired to rest. At 5 A. M., I was awakened by the boy informing me that we were near Chên Hai, a town at the entrance to the River Yung, upon which the city of Ningpo stands.

At the mouth of the river a fort was built during the excitement occasioned by the Japanese invasion of Formosa. This fort may be safely pronounced the most formidable that China has erected. A short description may suffice. It is built of solid granite, covered with five-inch iron plating, and with a backing of teakwood and fir, so bolted together as to form a homogeneous structure. Its entire construction is upon foreign principles, and it is to the credit of the Chinese that they received no assistance whatsoever as to detail from any European. The whole erection of the fabric, from the foundation, which had to be blasted from the solid rock, to the topmost stone, was superintended by a mandarin named Lin, who studied the art from the various works upon fortification translated into Chinese. In form it presents a square, three sides facing the sea, and commanding the approach to the mouth of the river, and the fourth side constituting barracks and storeroom. The roof is concrete, and splinter proof. The mantlets are of iron, five inches thick. The fort proper consists of a double tier, the top tier retiring somewhat from the lower, and the whole face, being built at an angle, affords no surface for a shot to lodge in the batteries. The armament is four twenty-ton Krupp guns, breech-loaders, and six five-ton Armstrong muzzle-loaders; also, one long-range, fifteen-centimeter balloon gun, similar to those used at the siege of Paris by the Germans. The embrasures are solid iron doors, and, for the protection of riflemen, square towers, built of teak and armor plated, are erected at each end of the fort. Manned efficiently, it would be no easy task for any war ship to pass the mouth of the river.

Chên Hai boasts of owning a larger number of junks engaged in conveying merchandise up and down the coast, as far south as Foochow, and for fishing purposes, than any port in China. We steam through a narrow channel, between countless junks of various sizes, gaudy with green and red paint, tinsel, and gold, carrying on their sterns pictures of the tutelary deity of the Chên Hai prefecture, and the immense wicker-work basket, which, if the vessel is caught by a gale, is thrown to windward, and allows her to ride to the anchor easily. This fairway is kept clear only by the exertion of a foreigner, in the employ of the Customs service, who resides ashore, in a pretty little house, surrounded by numbers of mud houses and gray brick walls, but which has a pleasant look, with its veranda covered with vines. Still going along under easy steam, we see on both sides of the river, which is only half a mile broad, some things which, to a stranger, at first sight appear to be haystacks, but which we know to be ice-houses. Immense quantities of fish are caught in the Yellow Sea, in the district from Shanghai to Ningpo. In order to preserve the fish, ice is collected from the ponds and lakes around Ningpo, and stored for the fishermen's use. The cost is almost nominal. One picul (one hundred and thirty-three and one-third pounds) can be purchased for twenty-two to twenty-five cents, and, if plentiful, the figure is reduced to twelve cents, thus enabling all classes to use ice for household purposes in the summer.

We now come in view of the foreign concession of Ningpo, which may be aptly called an island, surrounded, as it is, by numerous canals and creeks, which form a connecting link with the great system of water-ways that extend throughout the empire of China. The trade of the port has year by year dwindled, so far as foreigners are concerned, to almost nothing—the whole of it, no inconsiderable item, having passed into the hands of the natives. There is nothing picturesque about the city of Ningpo or its surroundings. It certainly may be classed as one of the cleanliest cities of China. Passing the gunboat upon which I was to take passage, I hailed it, and found, shortly after the arrival of the *K'iang Teen* alongside the hulk, that the Captain's gig, pulled by six sturdy Amoy men, clothed in snow-white jackets and pants (similar in style to our man-of-war men's costume), straw hats, with black bands, upon which was printed, in gold letters, the name of the ship, and every bit as neat and clean as the eye or taste could wish for, was awaiting my orders. After presenting me with the Captain's card, the coxswain and the men took my baggage and quickly conveyed me on board the ship. At 3 P.M. steam was up, and we proceeded down the river, arriving at Chên Hai, where we anchored for the night. Early in the morning I was awakened by the noise of tramping feet upon the deck, and, upon rising, I found that a detachment of soldiers, to the number of five hundred and twenty, accompanied by twenty or thirty women, had come on board. These men were encumbered with rifles, bags of powder, umbrellas, rice-pans, dogs, paper lanterns, old cutlasses, etc., and such an incongruous amount of baggage and rubbish that it would require the practiced skill of an auctioneer to particularize.

They were to form the first settlers upon the island of Nan Teen, under the rule of an official duly appointed by the Governor of the Che kiang province. This gentleman, a jolly looking Chinaman, who, upon coming on board, was introduced to me by the Captain, immediately entered into a conversation with me, and asked me to breakfast with him, which invitation I accepted. As we were yet at anchor amid the fish boats, a fine supply of cod and sea-mullet was purchased, which, as I had been accustomed to the muddy-flavored finny specimens caught in the Whangpoo, I relished exceedingly. Having now received the stores of rice, salt fish, and cabbage for the commissariat department, and the tide serving, we lifted our mud-hooks at noon, and, steaming slowly and cautiously, almost threading our way through the numberless fish-stakes and nets that abound in the vicinity of the mouth of the river, found ourselves abreast of Tiger Island. A lighthouse, showing three sections of light, is erected upon this island. It serves to mark the entrance to the port, and is kept admirably served by the attendant keepers, two of whom are Manila men and the other four Chinese. As we were bound upon a search after two piratical junks, as well as upon a colonization commission, our orders were to proceed first to Chepoo Bay, distant from Chên Hai sixty-two miles, and there communicate with the mandarin in charge of two sailing war junks, whose force had not been sufficient to engage the robbers.

As the steamer proceeded at half speed among the islands, so as to arrive at Chepoo at daylight, I had ample time to enjoy the varied scenery that presented itself to my gaze—highly cultivated slopes, upon which were growing the cabbage plant, beans of every description, whose blossoms were exhaling sweet perfumes that reached us on deck as we wended our way quite close to the shore. Little cottages, belonging to the laborers, who, in nearly every case, were owners of the land they cultivated, were dotted here and there over the landscape. These then appeared to me, in the distance, to be well built habitations, but I found later, upon landing, that "distance lends enchantment," etc. The water is always smooth here, as it is naturally protected by the islands of the Chusan group, which act as a kind of breakwater against the influence of the monsoons. The passages, except the most intricate ones, are used by the coasting steamers in proceeding to and from Hongkong to the north, thereby saving some ten or twelve hours' run.

The sunset, gilding the waters, and here and there touching with its last rays the white sails of the innumerable small boats that came out of every creek and inlet on both sides of us, fell upon a scene that was unique and interesting. I was recalled from my admiration of the landscape by hearing the jabbering, in Chinese, of my military friend, as he asked me if I had any foreign food with me. Upon my replying in the affirmative, he coolly invited himself to supper with the Captain and myself. Now, the Captain, who had been living among foreigners from his fifteenth year, was used to our customs, spoke English with fluency, and was the first man who had left the Foochow training-ship to assume command of a Chinese gunboat. He not only navigated the ship by meridian, but was capable of working her by both stellar and lunar observations. He was well up in gunnery and all the practice of the English navy. He tried to enforce the discipline he had learned from his instructors, on board his vessel, and, I bound to say, he succeeded in a degree which astonished the soldiers, who treat their officers with familiarity and contempt.

The Captain's cook knew how to prepare food in foreign style; so, having ordered him to get supper ready, we invited our mandarin friend to partake. He made a very poor meal on account of his dislike to beef, which is seldom eaten by the Chinese middle or upper classes, and had it not been for the rice, cabbage, and bamboo shoots that formed part of our repast, he would have gone to bed supperless. However, with the aid of a bottle of brandy I managed to get him merry; and in the generosity of his heart he told me that if I wanted any land upon the island to let him know, and, although I was not a Chinaman, I could have the deeds made out in a native's name. As I didn't see my way clear to become a landed proprietor in that part of the empire, I declined his offer. We conversed for some time, till I told him that I wanted to go on deck, and get a little fresh air and enjoy my cigar. He gave his assent, and called to the servant to get his pipe ready, and I left him to smoke in peace.

It was by this time dusk, and, going up on the bridge, I found the Captain in close conversation with an old man, who, in his youth, had been one of the gang of rovers who plundered the junks as they pursued their way among the narrow passages that we were now traversing. He had been sent by the district magistrate at Ningpo to enable us to discover the haunts of the lawless crew whom we were searching, upon the old principle, "set a thief to catch a thief." There is hardly any twilight during the heated summer months in this latitude, and, darkness now coming on, it was deemed advisable, surrounded as we were by hidden dangers, which rendered it unsafe to proceed, to anchor, which we accordingly did. The scene on the deck of the *Foo Hoo* was very strange. Here was I, one foreigner, entirely at the mercy of six hundred Chinese. When I thought to myself how these people had treated my countrymen previously, I almost wondered that I could be among so many natives, and not a single word of disrespect or bad language uttered. Possibly, the fact that I spoke their tongue, and conformed, in a measure, to their peculiarities and ways, accounted for this; but it must be remembered that these soldiers were Hunan men, the natives of which province have always shown an inveterate hatred to Europeans, and have, whenever an attempt has been made by missionaries or travelers to visit their cities, displayed the greatest hostility. The men were grouped together in various attitudes about the deck, having their mats spread under the lee of the bulwarks, and, indeed, on every available spot they could find. Some were still smoking their last pipe before sleeping, and, in accordance with their usual habit, kept knocking their glowing tobacco ashes on the deck, marking it with little black spots, to the disgust of the quartermaster on watch, who, in vain, begged them to desist. The Captain and I had our beds made up in the chart-house on the bridge, it being too close and stuffy to sleep below, as the number of servants, cooks, pipe-bearers, and chair coolies attached to the *suite* of the mandarin were all quartered in the cabin. After chatting upon the capabilities of the new Krupp guns, and comparing their merits with the Armstrong, to which weapon my friend had a partiality, we thought about repose, and, turning into our bunks, sleep soon came to our weary eyelids.

I was disturbed by the morning gun, at 4:30 A. M., the echoes of which reverberated among the hills, startling the patient and hard-worked water buffaloes that were lazily chewing their cuds among the rank lush grass down toward the sea-shore. As we proceeded toward Chepoo, I went on the bridge, and was astonished to see the pass we were now entering. The water was seething and boiling all around us, and the current running at a terrific rate. In such a situation it was extremely difficult to steer the ship, requiring no less than four quartermasters at the wheel. On both sides of us rose precipitous rocks, covered from the base with verdure, amid which I noticed beautiful specimens of the Chinese pine, and here and there clumps of wild flowers. Our vessel was in such close proximity to the land on both sides that it would have been easy to throw a biscuit on shore, these being our only substitute for stones. The length of the pass is only about a quarter of a mile. Suddenly rounding a slight curve we came in sight of a magnificent sheet of water, almost circular in form, and completely land-locked. On our starboard hand was the town of Chepoo. Still steaming on we came abreast of the house of the mandarin, under whose beneficent rule the inhabitants rejoice. Two war junks, whose commander was to accompany us upon our expedition to the Archipelago, lay at anchor in the bay.

Everything being shipshape, at 10 A. M. the Captain, our mandarin friend, and myself pulled ashore in the gig, calling alongside the flag junk, whose men, seeing us approach, donned their uniforms, and hastily fired three guns in honor of the distinguished visitors, who happened to be of a higher rank than their officers. We found, upon inquiry, that their captain was awaiting our arrival on the shore, at the *yamun* of the magistrate, and, resuming our course, we arrived at the jetty, where a motley crowd of fishermen, boat-girls, and children, were assembled. Of course, being dressed in foreign costume, I was an object of curiosity to them. Some years had elapsed since they had seen a "foreign devil," the missionary that pays them a visit occasionally being clothed in native garments. Some few displeasing remarks were made by them, but were quickly suppressed by the underlings in the service of the magistrate. Sedan chairs had been provided to convey us to the quarters, but as we had only a short distance to go I proposed walking, so as to get a glimpse of the streets. The site of the town being on the slope of the hill, the ascent was thus somewhat difficult, but the Chinese had built steps to enable foot passengers to get along easily. Chepoo is essentially a fishing mart, and depends for existence on the fleet of junks that make the port a way station, on their voyages between Ningpo, Shanghai, and Tientsin to the north, and Wenchow, Taichow, and Foochow to the south. Nothing is to be seen in the main street but coir and bamboo ropes, anchors, native canvass, and all the necessary articles requisite for ship use. Here and there are dotted tea shops, where bargains for firewood, charcoal, or any stray flotsam and jetsam are concluded over a cup of hyson and dishes of melon seeds; and many a good round sum of Mexican dollars and silver bars has passed hands there in the good old days when Dent's and Jardine's fast clipper schooners came in with opium for sale.

The town is divided into two distinct parts, that to the north being inhabited by the natives of the Fohkien province, and to the south by those of the Chekiang province. The Fohkien population seldom intermarry with the Chekiang families, seemingly keeping aloof from intercourse, other than serious party fights over any wreckage that finds its way into the bay, at which times it becomes necessary for the war junks to interfere. They also enjoy a monopoly of the right to convey passengers to and from vessels at anchor. The boats used are identical to those at Foochow—sharp at the bow, and having a square stern, propelled, in nearly every instance, by women, one at the steer oar, and two sculling at the bow. Five cash (half cent) is the fare paid for their hire; and for a whole day's work to receive half a dollar is deemed good fortune.

After a walk of half a mile, we arrived at the mandarin's residence, where we received instructions for our guidance, and a system of ruses designed to be employed in the capture of the pirates. Their usual rendezvous was in a small creek about twenty miles from Chepoo Bay. It was agreed that, as the buccaneers had emissaries in the town to give them information, we were to keep our mission secret. The two native-built war junks were to sail to the northward on the evening tide, and when outside of the Chénmun Pass were to join us in Footow Bay. We were to take on board the old mandarin, commodore of the station, a native of Canton, whose face bore unmistakable signs of powder marks and scars, which gave rise to conjectures as to what his former vocation had been. It was confidentially imparted to me by the First Lieutenant of the *Foo Boo* that the gentleman had been in many a fight, and had captured many vessels, as leader of a gang whose depredations were at last so enormous that the Government deemed it policy to confer a button on him, and thus disperse the clique, rather than go to the expense of sending gunboats after them.

At daylight we got up steam, and found that our anchor was foul. This mishap delayed us nearly an hour, and before we got finally under way the sunrise was gorgeous in the east. Large masses of purple and orange clouds rolled over the tops of the hills, lending a softness to the otherwise tame landscape. Squads of laborers were going to their daily work in the fields, some to pursue their vocation of brick-making on the western shores of the harbor, some to gather the now fast ripening plums and apricots that the Chinese are so fond of when in a green state, and others, with their donkeys, to carry the spoils of the fish-boats to inland villages. The air resounded with the not over harmonious songs of the junk sailors, pulling up their sails or heaving their cumbersome anchors, to take advantage of the morning tide. Our pilot rushed up and down the bridge in an excited state, informing us that we must catch the tide in a particular channel, which he was bound to get through. Our two mandarin friends placidly seated themselves in the chart-room and conversed, while the Captain and I watched the ship as she pursued her course, at three-quarter speed, toward the southern entrance to the bay. If the entrance to Chepoo had struck me as being rather narrow, my surprise was changed to astonishment when I saw the place we were rapidly approaching. It was marked upon the English Admiralty Chart as impassable except for vessels drawing less than five feet of water. As our draft was twelve feet forward, and fifteen feet aft, and several nasty, black-looking rocks showed themselves right ahead of us, I felt alarmed, as also did our Captain. Upon expressing our fears to the pilot, he coolly said: "All proper: me savey; go full speed ahead." We shot through the gap at the rate of twelve knots per hour, and our ship, finding herself on the bosom of the Pacific Ocean, gave such a lurch and roll that it took me off my feet.

A number of junks were visible, sailing with the south-west monsoon on their way north. To the practiced eye of our ex-pirate pilot and mandarin, these were known to be Fohkienese vessels. We got close to one about eleven o'clock in the morning, and found that she was laden with poles for Shanghai. The method of carrying these poles is somewhat singular, and bears a close resemblance to our lumber-ships' deck-loads, except that the poles are lashed on both sides of the junks with immense bamboo hawsers, until the whole looks like a gigantic floating raft. Nothing is visible of the vessel herself but the four or five masts. Our guides questioned the sailors, and found that upon the day previous two piratical craft had been seen going in-shore among the islands distant fifteen miles to the southward, and answering in every description to those we were in search of. Accordingly, we again steamed landward, and heading for Footow Bay (so called from the summit of the island bearing a marked resemblance to the head of Buddha) to join our light-draught consorts, arrived there at 4 P. M., and found them snugly anchored. We took them in tow, and had scarcely rounded the cape before our attention was attracted by a cluster of boats, probably five or six in one spot, evidently so deeply absorbed in their labors that until a shot from our bow-gun aroused them to a sense of danger, they seemed quite unconscious. Immediately fifty or sixty men sprang from the vessel they had been pillaging, and, jumping into the small boats alongside, endeavored to reach their own two junks that were beating about in close proximity to the scene. Our armed boats were lowered, and pulled in company with the two war-junks—whose crews were supplemented by some of the soldiers we had taken on board—toward the piratical craft. Without any resistance—which, indeed, would have been in vain—the vessels were immediately surrendered, and, steaming toward them, we lashed one on each side and proceeded to make our way to Ningpo. The astonishment of the leaders of the pirates when they beheld our pilot and the mandarin was something laughable. They soon became friendly, however, and talked over old times, but they were careful in no way to criminate themselves as to the object of their attack on the junk that we had witnessed.

Arriving again at Chepoo, we landed our soldiers and the official in charge of them, and, wishing them a pleasant trip, resumed our return voyage. At Ningpo, where we anchored on the fourth day, we gave our prisoners over to the District Admiral, under whose kind administration confession was extorted from them. It appeared that on board the piratical craft traces of portions of the furniture of a foreign ship had been found; and although the men denied any knowledge of her name, they said the articles had been purchased by them on shore. Future search by one of the English gunboats solved the riddle. The table had been on board the British lorcha *Mandarin*, whose captain had been foully murdered by the crew, and the vessel and cargo, having been sent to the south of Shanghai, had been disposed of there. About five hundred and eighty Mexican dollars were also found on board the junks, and a quantity of clothing. Twenty-eight out of the sixty composing the crew had made their escape, to return once more to their old haunts. The leaders and the rest were sent to Hangchow, the provincial capital, for further trial, and I afterward saw in the Peking *Gazette* that ten of them were executed, and the others sentenced to a term of imprisonment for three years.

Thus ended my trip on the *Foo Boo*. The captain and officers vied with each other in showing me attention, and I was afforded every opportunity of observation. Were every commander in the Chinese navy as competent as Captain Lin Ko Chang, the Government might well be proud. It may be mentioned that the *Foo Boo* (literally, the happy rippling wave) is a brig-rigged man-of-war, with engines capable of driving her at the rate of over thirteen knots an hour. She is constructed of teak, armed with eight broadside Vavasseur guns, forty-pounders, breech-loading, and one bow-gun, throwing a shot of three hundred pounds. She was built in 1876, at the Foochow arsenal, and is numbered seven in the books of that establishment. On leaving her, I again took passage in the *Kiang Teen*, and arrived in Shanghai, safe and sound, after an absence of six days.

HENRY D. WOOLFE.

A STRANGE CONFESSION.

CHAPTER III.

On Saturday, the 21st, following the tragedy of Friday night, there was great excitement in San José. The earlier risers, through force of habit, glanced carelessly at the morning paper as usual, started at seeing the head-lines of the terrible affair, and then hurriedly and eagerly read the meager, but elaborated, account published. Many had already heard rumors, the story having gained some currency the night before; and these, more than the others, were eager to read it. As a general thing, people experience more satisfaction from reading the account of an occurrence, of which they have complete or partial information, than do those who have heard nothing. The facts were meager, for the reason that the reporters had been denied admission to the house. But in the name of all that should make journalism a builder up rather than a tearer down—the friend of the people rather than the devil's flag of truce, the shield of the innocent, the helpless, and the friendless, rather than the convict's winding-sheet—enough was said, and more. For the California news gatherer is, more strictly speaking, a news monger. He is nothing, if not "sensational." To be "sensational," one must have an imagination. To exercise the imagination, one must assume facts and build theories. In California it is considered necessary to exercise the imagination. The coldest thing in reasoning is this: that which is not a fact is a falsehood. There is no intermediate ground, no average. Consequently, a theory is a falsehood until it is established as fact. It is dangerous to publish theories where grave interests are involved. Perhaps the most sacred thing on earth is woman's honor; the next, human life. When the one is threatened, humanity revolts; when the other, nature is outraged. When by vague hints and surmises, and by wallowing in the blood that flows with crime, we conjure up visions of the lamp-post and a rope, we rob Justice of her balance, leaving her only the sword.

San José is a sleepy town, but it never takes a healthful sleep and wakes refreshed. It sleeps, quite truly, but with one eye open. This is done for fear a neighbor may do that which will pass unnoticed, in the dread that a scandal or a sensation may be overlooked. Likewise has San José some thrift. As an evidence of this, it is merely necessary to mention the fact that the noise of carriage-wheels may be heard at all hours of the night. It is not large enough to be a city, nor small enough to be a town. Being thus, it has nevertheless within its boundaries a peculiarly cosmopolitan population, in which the best and the worst elements of society may be found. In the former originate the scandals; in the latter, the sensations. Thus it furnishes within itself an almost endless round of pleasurable excitement, in which the flavor of the wine is mingled with the madness that it brings. Throughout the length and breadth of California, San José is the most delightful spot in which to live. Why should it not be? There is not a finer climate in the world; it has the College of Notre Dame, handsome church edifices, and the Normal School; the Alameda is the grandest drive west of the Rocky Mountains; and San José has the prettiest flowers and the handsomest ladies in all the State.

Crime has not been uncommon in San José. The Spanish bagnios of El Dorado Street, in days gone by, have seen more than one man put a knife into another's back, and the shadows that still darken San Pedro Street have their gloom intensified by the memories that linger there. But in the crime of the 20th of June, as the public understood it, there was that which stanched the blood that flowed in El Dorado Street, and threw a pall over the shadows of San Pedro. There was that in it which stirred stern natures and frightened the weak. It was that a strong man, in the full glow of youthful manhood, had confessed that he took the life of a girl. It was not unnatural that her dead body was sanctified by the tear that trembled in some mother's eye, and that for a shroud she wore the pity of the world. The manner of murdering her, it was thought, was so cruel, so heartless, so without the least element of manly strength and dignity, so degrading to the sterner stuff of which men are made, that it is no wonder a dangerous feeling commenced to grow.

When the great bell in the tower of St. Joseph's called the devout to early mass, there were already groups of men here and there, eagerly—some angrily—talking, and hopelessly hailing every passer-by for later news. Every man relied upon his neighbor, as is the case when a great calamity has fallen, or is about to fall. Strong natures thus crop out, and they are generally dangerous, but always welcome. Men demand a reliance upon something.

Casserly was at his post, not having slept, and busy arranging his plans. He had started the telegraph, and was determined that the fugitive, who carried justice with her, having kidnapped it, should be caught. Fearing another escape, he had put the mother under arrest, leaving her in the custody of an officer, by the body of her dead charge.

About ten o'clock, a citizen went to him at the police station, and desired to speak to him privately, there being a curious crowd in the room. Casserly followed him out.

"You had better keep an eye on the corner of First and Santa Clara," said the man.

"Why?"

"A considerable crowd is down there."

"Well, what of it?"

"Go and see."

The Chief went instantly. Arriving there, he found about a hundred men eagerly listening to a speech by a half drunken, tolerably well dressed man, talking half good-naturedly, half fiercely. The crowd was swelling rapidly. The Chief, seeing no occasion for his interfering, and curious to learn what the man was saying, stopped at the outskirts of the crowd and listened.

"I'll tell you what we did then," the man was saying. "As soon as the news was pretty well spread, we scattered handbills, calling for a mass meeting at twelve o'clock noon. In response to the call every store in Mobile was closed, and all the cotton brokers, commission merchants, and wholesale dealers turned out. We were five thousand strong. And we meant business. Then what did we do? Did we stand around with our mouths open and our hands in our pockets?—and snivel?—and cry?—and slink about like so many hounds? No, sir. The law can be outwitted, but the people never. When we open the jail-door, we give crime a relish of danger. Why was there a necessity for a Vigilance Committee in San Francisco? Because the law had failed. Very well. Then what did we do in Mobile? One man mounted a box, and made a speech that set them all on fire. They cried out with one voice, 'On to the City Hall!' But the Mayor had foreseen trouble, and had called out the militia. There were five splendid companies. By the time the crowd swarmed into Conti Street, thicker than bees and more hungry than wolves, the militia was drawn up in front of the City Hall with 'present arms' and bayonets fixed. The Mayor showed himself at an upper window of the City Hall, and shouted, and waved his hand, and made the crowd halt. Then he made a speech, insisting that the law should be allowed to take its course. But Conti Street is narrow; and the crowd continued to pour in from Royal, thirsting to be revenged for this outrage on humanity, and crowding onward those who had halted. At length the crowd stopped in front of the soldiers, densely packed. Then some man threw a stone; it struck the wall of the City Hall, and fell to the ground. The moment that followed was terribly quiet. Then another stone was thrown, and another. What happened then? A strange thing. You should know what it was. The order was given the soldiers to charge. They did charge, but they slipped their bayonets between the men of the mob, and nobody received a scratch. Not a shot was fired, not a bayonet-thrust was given. Do you think a soldier, with a spark of manhood in his heart, would have injured a hair of their heads? The crowd closed into the gap the soldiers had left, stormed the jail, and in less than thirty minutes our man was swinging to a tree. That is the way in which it should be done. But you are pale, and white-livered——"

His speech was suddenly checked by a powerful hand on his throat. In another moment, before even his instinct of self-defense could operate, he was thrown to the ground and quickly secured with handcuffs. Grasping the tendency of the speaker's words, Casserly had pushed his way through the crowd and seized his man.

Casserly was a man of prodigious strength. He was six feet in hight, and large and brawny—a Hercules. Prior to his advent in San José a year or two before his election to the office of Chief of Police, he was a boxing teacher in San Francisco. It was not known, however, that he possessed unusual strength and courage until the following remarkable occurrence rendered him conspicuous:

One evening, during a public speaking on Santa Clara Street, he was standing, with others, on a large box, the better to overlook the immense crowd and know how to act in case of a disturbance between political enemies. His head was thus brought within about two feet of an awning overhead, which was crowded with women. This awning was braced by iron rods, running horizontally from the outer edge to the wall. Some one suddenly exclaimed, in dismay:

"The awning is coming down!"

A glance showed Casserly that the rods were bending downward. The crowd fled from underneath, and a cry of terror arose. The box on which Casserly was standing was deserted, with the exception of one man. The glare of the torches revealed his face and form to the horrified gaze of the crowd. It was Casserly. Squaring his massive shoulders and bracing his powerful arms, he received the tremendous weight of the awning, and the women were saved.

Thereafter Casserly's strength and fearlessness were known; and there was considerable consternation in the incipient mob that witnessed his summary procedure with the man who sought to stir up bad blood by telling of the riot in Mobile. But this feeling gave place to anger. Some said:

"He had no business to interfere."

Others: "He's too fresh, anyhow."

And again: "Come on. We'll see fair play."

As Casserly rose to his feet, dragging the man up with him, he saw at a glance that the still rapidly increasing crowd was growing menacing. This roused the lion in him. He was a man to whom fear was absolutely a stranger. Holding his prisoner by the collar with his left hand, and pushing him as he would a feather, he backed to the wall, his eyes glaring and his nostrils distended.

Since Casserly assumed charge of the police department, he had shown an iron hand to the thugs and bravos who made El Dorado Street the stronghold of all the horse-thieves, highwaymen, and cutthroats, who had at intervals infested the greater part of the region between Los Angeles and San Francisco. He had already sent several to San Quentin, and the others feared him. Consequently, when this crowd, in which were many burning for an opportunity to take him at a disadvantage, saw that he was surrounded by a mob requiring little to render it dangerous, and that he was comparatively powerless, it spurred on the excitable and vindictive.

He was too wise to turn his back upon them. There is nothing keener or quicker than a Spaniard's knife. He recognized several friends in the crowd, and called on them for help; but they looked away, pretending not to hear—for Casserly represented the law, which might miscarry, and which was therefore looked on with disfavor. The crowd became insulting and aggressive, intimating that he had been bribed to protect the murderer. This caused him to turn a shade pale. At length, a brawny drayman suddenly seized Casserly's prisoner by the left arm, and by a violent jerk attempted to wrest him from Casserly's grasp. The effort failed, and with a blow between the eyes, powerful and quick, Casserly sent the drayman staggering back into the arms of his friends. This was the signal for the outbreak. The open space of some half a dozen feet between Casserly and the crowd was invaded. Casserly drew his club, and delivered a crushing blow upon an uplifted hand that carried a knife. This checked the crowd, and Casserly sounded his whistle. There is something appalling in the shrill sound of a police whistle. It is always a surprise, and sends a thrill through every fiber of the person more surely than does the warning of a rattlesnake. It is the voice of the law crying out for help against violence. The crowd fell back and melted away.

On the way to the city prison Casserly said to his man:

"I saved you from San Quentin."

"How?"

"By stopping you before you said too much."

The man hung his head in shame. Casserly won a friend.

But the popular thirst for revenge was not quenched. Rumors multiplied, and Howard was charged with nameless and revolting crimes in connection with the murder.

After locking his man in a cell, Casserly again went out upon the street. He was met near the door by an old man, who walked with a cane, and whose manner betrayed excitement. It was Judge Simon.

"Casserly," he said, "do you know what is going on?"

"I think it's not serious."

"Casserly! Are you blind?"

"No, Judge."

"Well, then, you *must* see that—"

"What?"

"—the people are rising!"

This brought Casserly face to face with the dreadful fact. He felt the blood tingling in his arms and hands. The weight of a world was on his shoulders, but he said, calmly:

"I will put them down."

He was the embodiment of the law, the fortress that guarded the inviolability of the Code. His body should stem the flood that threatened to sweep away the demarkations between outlawry and the sanctity of right. Like an oak that reared its head proudly when the sky was black with the gathering storm, he would stand proudly still, though torn from branch to trunk by the lightnings and dismembered by the winds. This one man against thousands felt in his right arm the strength of a legion, and said:

"I will put them down."

The manner in which he said this strangely reversed the relations between him and the old judge. He was a man of nerve; the other, a man of brain. The man who was helpless last night is master to-day.

Casserly led the old man into the office, sat down at the desk, reflected a moment, and asked:

"How do you word it, Judge?"

"Word what, Chief?"

It was no longer "Casserly," but "Chief."

Casserly paid no attention to the question, but wrote the following:

"OFFICE OF CHIEF OF POLICE,
San José, Cal., June 21, 1880.

"CAPTAIN HARVEY:—There is mischief on foot. They want to lynch young Howard. The Mayor is out of town. It is urgent that you quietly and immediately order your men to the armory. Will see you there.

"CASSERLY."

He sealed the note, and sent it by a messenger, with instructions to hasten.

"What was it, Chief?" asked Judge Simon.

"A call for the militia."

"Ah!"

He left the office, the old man following.

"What are you going to do now, Chief?"

"Strengthen the police force, and get the Sheriff to double his deputies."

"Ah!"

The two men had reached the corner of Santa Clara Street, when they were hailed by a man running toward them from the direction of El Dorado. He was about forty years of age, tall and gaunt, and dressed in clothes that were too short at the ankles and wrists. The bottom of his vest lacked some three inches of reaching the top of his pantaloons, and his suspenders were thus rendered conspicuous. His clothes were old, faded, and greasy. His arms and legs were very long. His neck was also of remarkable length; and his narrow, rounded shoulders, and his general appearance of being all neck, and legs, and arms, and hands, and feet gave him the aspect of a crane. As he ran, his legs flew promiscuously about, like the arms of a reaper. His face was long and narrow, and his eyes were small, and greatly sunken and crossed. Altogether, he looked villainous. He said to the Chief, with half closed eyes, and an air of portentous mystery:

"Things is bilin'."

"Yes?"

"You bet!"

"Where?"

"Right 'round El D'rader, thar, 'most to First."

Casserly betrayed no concern. "Sam," he said, coolly, "I advise you to go home."

"Why?"

"Because you might kill somebody, and that would start the whole thing."

The man vainly endeavored to conceal his pride, and, in a mysterious half whisper, said:

"'Feard it's too late, Chief."

"Why?"

"Look-a-here," he said, showing a cut in his vest.

"How did you get it?"

"A feller down thar, bigger'n what you are, any day in the week, was a-preachin' hangin' to the crowd, and I collared him, an' tol' him he was my pris'ner, when he outs with a knife and lets me have it here. But it wouldn't work on me—don't you forget it! I'm too old for thet kind of a racket, and I knocked it off this way, and then I put it to him as hard as I could send it with this!" Saying which, he drew a dirk-knife from a sheath. It was stained with blood.

The poor old Judge was so frightened at the ferocity of the man that he cautiously put Casserly between himself and possible danger, looking painfully anxious.

Casserly asked no more questions, and simply gave this strange advice:

"As you've started, Sam, you can kill a few more; it will help me out."

"I'll stay by you, Chief," and the man ambled away.

The old man asked:

"Who is that, Chief?"

"Sam Wilson."

"Rather dangerous character, isn't he?" the Judge asked, in a *nonchalant* manner, as if he were vastly accustomed to being thrown in contact with such dangerous men, and knew that they were harmless fellows—first-rate fellows, in fact—provided one knew how to manage them.

Casserly laughed.

"Don't you believe he did it, Chief?"

"No."

"Why?"

"Because I know him."

"You don't mean to say he's not a bad man, do you?"

"Yes."

The Judge was chagrined. Nevertheless, it was not until some time afterward, when he was surrounded by less exciting circumstances, that he realized the fact that he had made a mistake in reading character. Not yet entirely satisfied, he asked:

"Who is he?"

The laconic answer was:

"A chronic."

"But his vest was cut."

"He did it himself."

"And his knife was bloody."

"He stabbed a quarter of beef at a butcher's stall."

But "The Crane"—for that was his common appellation—was half right. The mob was gathering; and it was he who, by his exaggerations, and goings from one crowd to another, kept the fire burning.

CHAPTER IV.

The Coroner, having early Saturday morning received notification of the death, proceeded to the house about ten o'clock. He went alone. Idlers passed the house, gazing at it curiously, seeing nothing. The door and windows were closed. It was an unpretentious modern dwelling, two stories high, with a bay-window below, and another above, and a window and a small portico over the entrance. There are hundreds of such houses in San José. The sidewalk was shaded by a row of stately elms that extended the length of the block.

The approach of the Coroner sent a ripple of excitement through the crowd of idlers. The fire that was kindling in the heart of the city threw, as yet, no gleam there. When the Coroner arrived at the gate, he found himself a Stork wielding the scepter in a kingdom of Frogs, or a brevetted gnome at the head of an army of ghouls. Never before had he appeared so important in the eyes of the community.

One of the most prominent features of the prevailing popular sentiment in regard to the tragedy was the readiness to seize upon anything, whether fact or conjecture, that tended to throw light on the transaction. Then it is that the Coroner is of vast assistance to the newspapers. When the actors in such affairs are known, every detail of their history is analyzed with avidity. There is something tangible, which, however obscure, reveals more or less under the microscope of a great hunger for knowledge. But in this case the parties were strangers. They had moved to San José only a few days before, and had hardly been seen. That neighborly feeling which prompts a community to receive a respectable stranger, and which it shall not be intimated is tinctured with curiosity, had not exhibited itself. There had been no callers. No one knew of a skeleton in the closet. The desire, then, to learn more of the inmates of the house, and, above all, to arrive at the cause of the murder, amounted almost to frenzy. Those acquainted with the characteristics of a Californian mob will not think this statement is exaggerated.

Knowing the demand of the public for all attainable knowledge, the Coroner, always an important person on such occasions, was determined that he would unearth the mystery, so far as lay officially in his power, and receive the credit therefor. Thus he became auxiliary to Casserly. When he found, then, that a reporter awaited him at the gate, he felt that it was an attempt to wrest away his privileges.

"Doctor," said the young man to the Coroner, "the policeman refuses to admit me—the fool! He can't deny you. I will go in with you."

"Well, let me see," replied the Coroner. "He has orders from Casserly, I guess. I think it will be better for me to go in alone. She will talk more freely; and I can tell you everything I see and hear."

But the reporter, fully aware of the fact that no one can see and hear as well as a reporter, demurred. The Coroner insisted politely, urging his point—a good one—and the young man yielded. He knew there would be other opportunities.

The Coroner was named Garratt. He was short and stout, and had a round face and small eyes. He was as pompous as short and stout officials who have round faces and small eyes usually are. He rang the bell. A heavy step was heard descending the stairs. The door was unlocked and cautiously opened an inch or two, bringing to view one eye of the policeman. Then it was opened a little wider, and the other eye became visible.

"Good morning, Doctor. Come in."

"How're you? Anything new?"

"No."

"Where is the body?"

"Up stairs."

The two entered, and the door was again locked.

"Wait a minute," said Garratt. "Who's got the undertaking job?"

"Nobody."

Garratt drew a commission on such things.

"Is it laid out?"

"Yes."

"Who dressed it?"

"The old woman."

"That looks bad. She had no right to until the jury saw it. When did she do it?"

"'Fore I came in."

"All alone?"

"All alone."

"Looks very bad. Too much hurry."

The policeman's manner was in striking contrast with that of Garratt's. The former was serious; the latter, nervous and bustling. The policeman was fully accustomed to death and crime, but possessed that fine natural feeling of discrimination that told him the people with whom he had to deal were not ordinary. His manner showed respect, and some awe.

"Has nobody been here?"

"Two or three ladies wanted to get in, but I wouldn't let 'em."

"That's right."

"She wants to send for a Presbyterian minister, but there was nobody to go."

"No servant?"

"No."

"You might have got some one outside to go, but you did right. I will send now."

He opened the door, called one of the loungers he knew and sent him on the errand. Then the two went up-stairs.

There were four rooms on the second floor—two in front and two in the rear, with a hall the length of the latter, and between them. Each room had a door opening upon this hall. The doors were all closed. The policeman rapped softly at the first door on the left, and a woman's voice said:

"Come in."

He turned the knob carefully, as if afraid of waking some one, and opened the door in apparent dread that the hinges would creak. They entered.

It was a bed-chamber, neatly and almost elegantly furnished. There was a door communicating with the front room, which was also well furnished. The two windows of the rear room were open, and the fresh, sweet, bright morning sunlight flooded the room. Evidently it was a man's bed-room. The front room was a woman's. In the further corner of the room into which the Coroner was introduced, and to the left, with the head against the partition wall, was a bed, and on this bed was something entirely covered with a sheet. Sitting upright near the bed, and opposite the open communicating door, calm, proud, self-possessed, and extremely pale, was a woman of singular beauty. Her deathly pallor was rendered more striking by the black she wore. Seeing a stranger with the policeman, she rose with the air of a queen. She seemed to recognize instinctively in this stranger an enemy. She was about forty-five years of age, somewhat above the medium hight of women, moderately slender, but having full shoulders and a well rounded form. Her black hair was tinged with gray. The classic beauty of her face, the imperious dignity and the refined grace that accompanied every movement, the consciousness of power shown by her dark eyes, the calmness, the self-reliance, the courage, showed at once that she had descended from the Huguenots, and that her blood was blue. Her complexion was fair, her hands small. Her appearance gave evidence of the highest refinement, and of that large-hearted aristocracy that may yet be found in South Carolina and Virginia, but which is trampled down, lost, and forgotten in the jostling crowds that, covered with sweat, mount the golden stair of our Californian society.

"Mrs. Howard," said the policeman, awkwardly and embarrassed, "this is Dr. Garratt, the Coroner."

She bowed, and said, "I presume, sir, that you have come to hold the inquest."

"Not yet, madam; not yet. Haven't summoned the jury yet. Just came around to see how things are. Is that it?" he asked, nodding toward the bed and twirling his hat. His tone was heartless and harsh.

"Yes," she answered, and added, "will you be seated?"

The Coroner felt his brusqueness and inferiority. He sat down. She resumed her seat, and asked:

"Is it absolutely necessary to hold an inquest, Dr. Garratt?"

"Certainly, madam."

"I thought—I was thinking—that perhaps—"

"Well, madam?"

"—that by not holding the inquest it might be kept out of the papers."

"It is too late."

"Why?" she asked, quickly and anxiously.

"The papers are full of it."

This was a cruel blow. The woman's cheek mantled with shame.

"Already?" she asked, in a bitter tone.

"Yes, madam; here is the paper."

She received it with a hand that slightly trembled, adjusted a pair of gold eye-glasses that unsteadily reflected the light from the window, and proceeded to read. But she had undertaken more than she could accomplish; for at reading the startling head-lines her sight became dim, and she could not hold the paper firmly.

"Will you read it to me, sir?" she asked Garratt, handing him the paper.

He took it, intensely gratified, cleared his throat, and in a loud tone, cruelly emphasizing the words that ground into her heart, read the account. Every word burned as would a red-hot iron thrust into the flesh. Crushed though she was, there appeared her strong nature flashing angrily from her eyes. Every known detail was set forth—the circumstances immediately following the shot, as heard by the man and woman; the crime, so enormous and revolting, that, as a dispensation, heaven made the criminal to be his own accuser; his besotted and brutish condition; the flight of the girl, and the consequent evidence of an outcropping of natural and inherited proneness to crime; the arraignment before the people of the perpetrator, and of all who abetted him, or endeavored to shield him, or throw a stumbling-block in the path of justice; surmises, theories, and speculations; broad hints that summary measures should be adopted to prevent the cutting of so wide a swath of crime through a peaceful community—all cruel, all degrading, all prompted by the relish that it brings to tear out a human heart and feed it to the mob. When he had finished he looked up, and saw that her head was bowed.

"Is it all true, madam?"

This question acted slowly, but surely, like poison. Gradually recovering herself, she raised her eyes to his face. Her bosom heaved, and a tinge of color appeared in her cheeks. She rose to her feet, her face pinched, the muscles drawn, and the same dangerous look that her son had shown in the saloon flashing from her eyes.

"It is—*false*—sir!" she said in a low voice that faltered with emotion. "It is *false*—and, more—it is—*cowardly!*"

Instinctively Garratt rose nervously, and stepped back, his eyes fastened upon hers, which riveted his gaze. Then with a powerful effort she checked herself, turned away, passed into the adjoining room, turned the blind, and looked out. She remained thus a moment, and came back, her step growing unsteady as she reached the chair. However, she did not sit down, but stood against the bed, and with a trembling hand reached to pull down the sheet. But she broke down without disturbing it, withdrew her hand, staggered half backward, fell into her chair, covered her face with her hands, and burst into tears. Her heart was broken.

Still, she had a great work to perform, and the recurrence of a knowledge of it calmed and restored her. After the outburst her manner was entirely changed. The womanly grace, dignity, and tenderness reasserted themselves, but there was no trace of haughtiness. She decided upon a plan. "Doctor," she asked, "how were those presumed facts learned?—or do you know?"

"Oh, yes, madam," replied Garratt, his confidence in himself restored; "the greater part was learned from the officers." The policeman winced, and looked guilty. Mrs. Howard spared him by not looking his way.

"And then," continued Garratt, "there is a sameness running through crime that makes certain assertions always very near the truth."

There was a concealed insult in this, and the woman quickly detected it. "I would like to see the man who wrote it," she said.

"Why?"

"Because he wrote blindly."

"Well, then, if he is wrong, the courts will set you right."

"As I understand it, Doctor, there are some wrongs which the courts cannot rectify."

"Perhaps so—perhaps so."

The policeman had, during this conversation, sat uneasy, and finally said, in an apologetic tone, "There's a newspaper man at the gate."

Garratt darted a look through him. Mrs. Howard noticed it. Turning to the policeman, she said:

"Will you be kind enough to call him up?" and to Garratt, as the officer left without venturing another look toward him, "You officers hunt for crime. Newspapers seek, or should seek, to find the truth."

Garratt bowed, and smiled grimly. Mrs. Howard received the reporter so graciously that he was instantly at his ease, and he saw that he had to deal with a woman of superior intellect, intelligence, and tact. He explained that he had written the article; did so conscientiously, with the information he could procure; regretted that he had been unable, through her own and Casserly's refusal to permit an interview with her, to obtain her version.

"I see," she said, sadly. "I will now do all I can to assist you, and will give you all necessary information. You performed your duty, and I respect you for it. Come, and look at her," she said, going to the bed.

He stood beside her, as, with a firm hand, she entirely removed the sheet. It was a picture of rare beauty and sadness—a young girl, waylaid and strangled by Death on the high road to a future life that should have been full of years ripe with happiness; at the time when the sky should have been blue, and the air redolent with the perfume of flowers; when the storm should have passed mercifully over the lowly violet, and when the terrors of the Great Unknown should not have blanched the youthful glow that reflected the radiance of heaven.

She was arrayed in pure white. The face was mobile, and sadly sweet, betraying no indications of the death-pang. They all gathered around, awed and silent. Mrs. Howard, speaking in a low voice that might have touched a spring in the hardest heart, said:

"Her name was Rose Howard—a distant relative of my husband. He adopted her when she was quite a child, her parents having died. She was a gentle, sweet, unselfish girl; and I loved her as one of my own children."

She covered the body. She had gained a point—the reporter's heart was softened.

"The girl who left last night is named Emily Randolph. Her parents live in Ohio, and they sent her to me several months ago, for the benefit of the Californian climate. It was feared she had consumption. I lived in San Francisco until a few days since. As she did not improve in the harsh climate of that city, I came here to find a better. She is rather a nervous, weak child, and it was dangerous to allow her to remain during this terrible time. The manner in which I sent her away I am aware looks as if she knows something that I desire she should not tell. But I would not have her carried through the ordeal that I knew would be forced upon her, for her life is in my charge; and I knew that she would not be allowed to leave. If I disclose her whereabouts—even if I knew—she would be brought back; and I am unwilling that she, too, should follow this poor child to the grave."

Mrs. Howard ceased. Very little had been learned, and the reporter delicately waited until she should say more. Suddenly she became attentive to a faint sound from a distance, that floated through the open window. The men had not noticed it.

"What is that?" she asked.

"Where?" asked Garratt.

She went to the window, and looked out. People were running toward the city. The octopus was drawing in its gigantic arms to concentrate its strength somewhere. Leaving this window, she went hurriedly and nervously to the window of the front room, threw open the blind, raised the sash, and leaned far out, straining her eyes to see, if possible, what was the cause of the commotion. She was filled with an indefinable dread. Presently a man came hurrying along the sidewalk beneath the window. "What is the matter?" she asked him.

He halted, looked around for the voice, and discovered her.

"Haven't you heard?" he asked.

"What?"

"Of the murder?"

She was becoming sick and faint. She asked, "What are the people running for?"

"To see the fun."

"What is it?" she asked, breathlessly.

"Do you hear that noise?"

"Yes."

"That's the mob."

"Well, what then?"

"They are going to break open the jail, and take the cowardly murderer out, and hang him as high as Haman." And the man hurried on.

That was all. She stood petrified with terror. Then did the grand old heroism that warmed her blood break forth in all its splendor. She would throttle this giant who thirsted for the blood of her son, though he should be as strong as a hurricane, and as relentless as death. She sprang through the door, her look terrible. The policeman intercepted her as she made for the stair. She shook him off, exclaiming:

"I will save my boy!"

The bulldog of the law had said, "I will put them down;" the mother said, "I will save my boy."

She hurried down the stairs, opened the door eagerly, gained the street, and flew like the wind.

W. C. MORROW.

[CONTINUED IN NEXT NUMBER.]

AN AUTUMN DAY.

The earth lies wrapped in peace; upon her brow
The laurels of the fruitful year are pressed;
Triumphant and elate still seems she now,
As one who glad, yet weary, dreams of rest.

The sun, his useful ardor wisely spent,
Floods all the day with tender, mellow light,
That crowns, with smiling, well deserved content,
Sere reapèd meadows and gay wooded hight.

Upon the air's soft breath the gossamer
  Ghost of a blossom hither and thither flies;
All insect life, with plainly lessened stir,
  Pursues its little aimless industries.

Close by the fences, in still country ways,
  The plumage of the crimson sumac shines;
From tree and shrub with every zephyr sways
  The fairy drapery of scarlet vines,

As though the summer, when her reign was o'er,
  Fleeing, usurped and wounded, through the wood,
Added unto her giving one gift more,
  And glorified them with her own heart's blood.

Far out upon the little lake the trees
  Cast lengthening shadows; swaying branches nod
Unto their fair reflection; every breeze
  Kisses the glory of the golden-rod.

And over all the loving sky leans low,
  And seeing all the beauty mirrored there,
Itself most fair, smiles wonderingly, as though
  It had not dreamed the world was half so fair.

CARLOTTA PERRY.

A PRIVATE LETTER.

BERKELEY, Aug. 21, 1880.

My Dear Fellow-Being (— for really that is the only relation that gives me any right to address you), I was reading a story of yours the other day in a certain magazine, and was struck by a little mistake in grammar that you contrived to repeat a good many times. I knew you were a young writer, and it was plain that you were one of great promise; and it seemed to me a pity that a pen capable of such touches of the genuine literary power should slip into bad English, especially into a mistake so uninterestingly common, so newspapery, as it were, —a sin without any tang of eccentricity to spice it. Of course I feel a painful delicacy in convicting you of bad grammar, and I could n't think of speaking to you publicly about it. I would n't for the world have anybody know I meant you, not even yourself—for certain. That is why I write thus privately to you about it. Not that mistakes in grammar are such blood-curdling things, in themselves, but there is this harm in them: they catch the attention, and so distract one's mind from the real matter in hand. Have you never noticed how, when the eloquent B-an-rges is preaching, sometimes in the most impressive passage an unfortunate mispronunciation hits your ear and throws the whole train of thought and emotion off the track? Just so, my dear friend (for I begin to feel very good natured to you now that I am in the way of being abusive—there is a great deal of human nature in people), when I was reading your charming story, just as my feelings were beginning to kindle in that passage, you know, where——for the first time——with——, suddenly this grammatical blunder exploded under my rapt attention with a bang, and scattered my emotional tension to the winds.

Besides, there is the terrible *inference*. Don't you know how a bad slip in the refinements of English syntax, coming from some newly introduced person, and coming, too, with the fatal smoothness of habitual use, opens up to you in a second whole vistas of inference and of undesirable probabilities for an acquaintance? Just so you will be sending a manuscript some day to the Coastian, or the Scribbler's Magazine, or the Ocean Monthly; and the editor will pick it up from a two-bushel basket of such and his eye, flaming with the preternatural fires of haste and intellect, will snatch at a page or two of your trembling and otherwise innocen darling, and will pounce on this identical solecism. It will be enough for him; for the power of inference must needs be swift and savage in a hurried editor in prolific literary regions.

But you are impatient to know what all this is about. It is about the improper use, yea, the inveterate snarling up and inextricable entanglement of the uses of *shall* and *will*, *should* and *would*. "Oh," you say; "is that all! Why, everybody makes mistakes in *them*." No, in fact not everybody. You will find that our best writers never use these little auxiliaries improperly. Indeed, it is the absolutely perfect discrimination between such words, the subtle sense of the least delicate flavor or etherial aroma of difference between such impalpable significations, that gives one charm to their style. I admit, on the other hand, that occasionally the particular auxiliaries in question are maltreated by otherwise respectable writers. It is, in fact, an Hibernicism that has crept into use, in this country particularly. But it will be well for you and me to remember that only old and successful authors can afford to write badly.

Suppose, then, that once for all we look into this matter, and know the rights of these four small words. It is not difficult, but it will require a bit of research into English grammar. You hate grammar, I suppose? That is right. I never knew any one to love it: at least the thing that goes under that name in the schools. Of course no one can help liking the real study of grammar, the science of the subtlest workings of the human mind dealing with the symbols of expression; but few school-boys ever get a taste of that. They are dragged by the ear through such text-books as that of G–ld Br–n, and forever after hate every person and every thing that was ever associated with the subject—the desk at which they recited it, and the smell of the particular flower that came in at the window where they tried to learn it, and the teacher that drove them mad with the reiteration of its meaningless maunderings. You will hardly believe it, but there really are, though, of late, several grammars written by scholars, intelligible, sensible, delightful books. (Of course the School Boards have not introduced them: they only consider the bindings of books and their relative cheapness.) Such, for instance, are Prof. Whitney's "Essentials of English Grammar", and Prof. Bain's "Higher Grammar".

We will begin, then, by trying to forget all about the "Potential Mood" and other devices of Satan, found in the ordinary grammars, and go back to the origin of these four little "useful troubles", *shall* and *should*, *will* and *would*. You know that a thousand years ago, in good King Alfred's time, the English people spoke our mother-tongue in the form which we now call Anglo-Saxon, but which they themselves always called "Englisc",—"English", as it really was, only without the later accessions from the French, Latin, etc. In this original form of English the primitive verb had (besides our familiar imperative, infinitive, and participle) only two moods: the indicative, to express a *fact* (as, "*I was there*"); and the conditional (or subjunctive) to express an *idea* of a fact, merely conceived in the mind (as, "*if I were there*"). In the indicative, or fact mood, the tenses (there were only two, present and past; as, *am* and *was*) meant time: in the subjunctive, or idea mood (since mere mental conceptions are not tied up to time) they only meant different relations of doubtfulness (as, "*if ever I be king*", or, "*if I were king at any time*"). Take for example the statement of fact, "*it is wrong*": this is the indicative mood, and the present tense means present time, to-day. Or, "*if it is wrong*, he is not aware of it": this also is the indicative mood, in spite of the "*if*", because, although we do not assert it as a fact, we assume it to be a fact, for the time being, as you see by the conclusion; and accordingly the present tense means present time, as before. But suppose we say, "*if it be wrong*, he will not do it". This, you see, is the subjunctive mood, expressing a mere idea, as being possibly true; and the present tense does not mean time (it is future time, if any thing), but mere contingency. Again, take the statement, "*he was wrong*": it is indicative mood, stating a fact, and the past tense means past time, yesterday. Or, "*if he was wrong*, he has probably discovered it": this also is the indicative mood, in spite of the "*if*", because we assume the fact to exist, as the conclusion shows; and accordingly the past tense means past time. But suppose we say, "*even if he were wrong*, he would not discover it". This, plainly, is the subjunctive mood, expressing a mere supposition; and the past tense does not mean past time—indeed it may refer to any other time whatever except the past. What, then, does it mean? Do you not see that it means to throw the idea still farther away from reality than the present tense would do, implying that, while his being wrong is a supposition, it is an improbable supposition? And what more suitable for this meaning than to push it back into the past, where there can be no "if" or peradventure about things at all: where (as an old saying runs) "'tis as 'tis, and 't can't be any 'tis-er".

At this point, my dear young novelist (for that is what you are coming to, if the fates permit), you are beginning to suspect that you have been basely deceived. You began to read my letter with the alluring expectation of something genial if not absolutely frolicsome, and here we are in the thorny wilderness of——(we will not speak the loathéd word) the study that "teaches the art of speaking and writing the English language correctly". (As if it really ever did that! When everybody knows that *that* art, if learned at all, is learned at the breakfast table, and the mother's knee, and what we Californians still, by poetic license, call the "fireside". Then what is the use of all this long, —— ——? [Yes, I know you are calling it that.] Because there really are a few idioms in our much Hibernicized, and Scotticized, and Gallicized, and Missouriated and Downeasticized mother tongue, that cannot be known with perfect confidence without going to the very roots of the matter.)

Know, then, that *shall* and *will* were two Anglo-Saxon verbs (*shall* being of the form *sceal*, just as our word *ship* was originally *scip*, with the *c* pronounced as *k*). These were not auxiliary verbs, but genuine independent verbs; "*ic wille*" meaning "*I wish*", or "*I determine*", and "*ic sceal*" meaning "*I owe*", or "*I ought*". In the Anglo-Saxon version of the Parable of the Unjust Steward the question, "*How much owest thou?*" is rendered "*Hû micel scealt thû?*" This signification lasted to Chaucer's time, who writes, "that faith I *shall* to God". And Mr. Earle (in his "Philology of the English Tongue") says that in one of the old country dialects a child would still say, if asked to run of an errand, "I will if I shall": i. e. "I am willing to if I ought to."

These two verbs, to *shall* and to *will*, naturally came to be used very often with the infinitive mood (i. e. the noun form) of other verbs, this infinitive being the object of the mental act of *shalling* or *willing* (owing or wishing). For example, "*ic wille leornian Englisc*" meant "*I will to learn* (or, I will the learning of) *English*". Just so with *shall*: "*ic sceal leornian*" meant, "*I owe the learning*", or, "*I ought the to-learn*".

You see, therefore, the fundamental distinction between these two words (and it governs every case of their apparently arbitrary uses). *Shalling* involves the idea of influence or pressure or obligation, from without: *willing* involves the idea of self-determination, from within. This would be, if possible, still more evident, if I dared to ask you to plunge one fathom deeper into the inky sea of historical grammar; for the oracles of those abysmal regions tell us that the present, *shall*, is itself the past tense of an original old fossil verb *sculan*, meaning "to get in debt". (Grimm says, from an ancient present with the meaning "to kill": the past tense meaning, therefore, "I have killed and have to pay the legal fine.") The past tense signified, then, "I have got in debt", i. e. "I am under the pressure of an external obligation", or, "I owe". You perceive, now, the absurdity in the Hibernicism, "I will be obliged to refuse your request"; for this means, "I wish or will to be obliged to refuse it". What we desire to express is our being under the outside pressure of circumstances, so we say, properly, "I *shall* be obliged".

But, you understand, in such an example as this last, where hardly anything but mere futurity is expressed, we are outrunning the Anglo-Saxon usage. It was only in later times that this grew up. You can see how, since willing to do an act, and feeling a pressure to do an act, are both likely to result in the future doing of it, there would come about a habit of expressing mere future expectation by these combinations. And it soon came to be felt as an instinct of courtesy, in expressing a future act, to speak humbly in the first person as if about to do it because of outside pressure—"I shall do it", while the second and third persons are politely represented as doing it of their own free will—"you will", or "he will", do it. For instance, "I shall pay my just debts", is as if one said, "not that it's any virtue in me, but I must"; while, "you will pay your just debts", implies that of course you wish to, and would, whether compelled or not.

There are two apparent exceptions, but they are really only further illustrations of this original meaning of the words: in the interrogative form we use "*shall*" for the second person, because "*will*" would ask for consent or a promise; and in quotation we use "*shall*" for all persons, because the person is represented as speaking, and saying, in the first person, "I shall".

So much for expressing mere futurity: but, of course, where determination is to be expressed, the case is just reversed. Here the first person says, "I *will*", and the second and third are represented as dominated by this outside determination: "you *shall* do it", "he *shall* do it". (By the way, the phrase "I *won't*" is such an exceedingly valuable one, morally, that it is worth noting here that this is an abbreviation of a good old form, "I wol not".)

And now shall we briefly explore the matter of "should" and "would"? For, to tell the truth, since this is a strictly private letter, and you don't even know that it is you I am talking to, one may frankly say that in their usage, also, there were grievous wrongs

Mark you, then: this same "shall" had in Anglo-Saxon a past tense "*sceolde*", *should;* and "will" had a past tense "*wolde*", *would.* These, also, were at first not auxiliaries, but independent verbs, and meant as thus: "*ic sceolde leornian*", "I owed it (yesterday) to learn"; "*ic wolde* leornian", "I willed the learning of it". The same forms were used in the past tense (so-called) of the subjunctive, but here was expressed not a fact, but the mere mental idea of a fact; and the past tense meant not past time (future, rather, if anything) but doubtfulness. And soon, just as *shalling* and *willing* lost much of their independent meaning, and came to express mere futurity, so *shoulding* and *woulding* came to express merely doubtful or conditional futurity, and were used with other verbs as auxiliaries. The *indicative* past was lost, except in the single case of a statement like this: "He tried to prevent me, but *I would do it*"—where the past tense means past time, and the verb carries its original meaning. But the *subjunctive* past is the one we use so commonly and sometimes misuse so innocently. It occurs in conditional sentences, and the usage is different in the two clauses. For example, "If he should come, I should go". In the condition clause the usage requires "*should*" for all persons; in the conclusion clause it requires "*should*" for the first person, "*would*" for the second and third. That is to say, for any given person the same verb is used, in the present to express fact futurity ("*I shall go, you will go, he will go*"), and in the past to express doubtful futurity ("If it happened, *I should go, you would go, he would go*"). The same reasons of courtesy apply to the distinction of persons, as in the case of *shall* and *will.*

Here, also, there are two apparent exceptions. 1. We say, "I would if I were you", or "I wouldn't do that", using "*would*" instead of "*should*", because a flavor of its original meaning is what we require here, namely, wish or preference. And we say, "I would like to help you", using "*would*" instead of "*should*" for the same reason; for we mean, "I should wish (to like) to help you (if there were any use of wishing)". Just so we say, "I would he were here", which differs from "I wish he were here" only as being subjunctive (shown by the fact that the past tense does not mean past time), and so expressing only a mere idea of wishing, like "I could wish he were here (if there were any use in it)". 2. We say, "You (or he) *should* do it", meaning "You ought to". Here, also, the original meaning of the word is introduced. Only, one would expect the present tense, "*shall*"; but this had already been appropriated for the future. Besides, there seems to be an instinct to throw this idea into the subjunctive *past* (or past of unreality and timelessness), as we see by the equivalent expression "he *ought*" (which is the past of "*owe*"); or, better still, by a colloquialism which pushes the idea still farther off, into the past-past, or pluperfect, notwithstanding that the thought is still, if of any time at all, of *future* time,—"*he'd* (he had) *ought to do it.*"

But at this point you will doubtless throw down this unoffending screed, with the ejaculation that you knew *something* about it before, but now you are *all* at sea. Well, that is the danger of a little knowledge. But, my dear friend, if you will go carefully through Prof. March's Anglo-Saxon and Comparative Grammar, and Prof. Bain's Higher and his Composition Grammar, following them up with Prof. Lounsbury's History of the English Language, and will then confine your light reading for a year to the very best authors, rigorously eschewing all newspapers (except that exceedingly cultured and intellectual one whose editors may happen to be reading this remark), I promise you that you will then begin to be ready to enjoy entering on the study of these things.

Let us hear the conclusion of the whole matter, in a practical table (and, now I think of it, you might skip what you have read up to this point, and begin here).

For expressing mere futurity (the plural in all cases like the singular):—

I shall.
You will.
He will.

For interrogation as to mere futurity:—

[Am I going to?]
Shall you?
Will he?

For expressing determination:—

I will.
You shall.
He shall.

For expressing doubtful, or conditional ideas (future or timeless); in the condition:—

If I should.
If you should.
If he should.

In the conclusion:—

I should.
You would.
He would.

For expressing wish, or willingness, or preference, in this softened, semi-conditional form:—

I would (if I were you).
I would (like to do it).
I would (he were here).

For expressing duty, or obligation:—

I should (study, but don't want to).
You should.
He should.

Meantime, my dear young author, "*quid refert Caio utrum etc.*", that is to say, what difference does it make to Genius whether it speak precisely in the tongue of common mortals? I know that in point of fact you will always enjoy writing, and I shall always enjoy reading your stories: indeed, you *shall* go on writing them, and I *will* go on reading them, even though you should not use "would" as you should, or as you would if you should use "would" and "should" as Shakspere or Mr. Matthew Arnold would. E. R. SILL.

JOHN G. WHITTIER.

Mr. R. H. Stoddard has recently published a review of Mr. Whittier's poetry. Coming from so critical a pen, the article should be seriously considered; but as it does not give such an estimate of the Quaker poet's abilities as his many admirers could wish, I have been surprised that no one of these has taken up the cudgels in his defense.

It cannot be any breach of confidence to quote certain words of Mr. Whittier, written to me upon date of "Sixth mo., 26th, 1879," but written, certainly, without any reference to the then forthcoming review of Mr. Stoddard. He says, "I think, with thee, that a born Friend can best understand and appreciate the words of a Quaker writer." He knew that I had this birthright qualification, at least, and that my ardent love of his writings was the plea for an attempt to take his measure as a poet. Fortunately for me, criticism upon poetry and the poets is never so much to be desired as a generous appreciation; because poetry has a sort of higher law, to which the terrible critics themselves must occasionally bow, and a law that common people may successfully appeal to. The critics destroyed Keats, physically, but the people kept his literature. Let me take heart to declare a growing conviction among all classes that John G. Whittier is, of right, our national poet; and this in all deference to the claims put forth by the most ardent admirers of Longfellow and Bryant. If there be any competition, it does not extend, by general consent, beyond the honored three. Although there are many who have stepped within the charmed circle, it seems that they could not maintain their footing; but Longfellow and Bryant and Whittier have flooded the land with song for more than half a century, and the nation mourns when death breaks up such fellowship.

What constitutes a poet of the highest order? And what a national poet? And is the national poet of necessity the chief? These are topics for lengthy disquisition, accompanied it may be, nevertheless, by feeble argument; for did not Lamb and Hazlitt and Hunt give us essay after essay upon the English poets, only to confess themselves lost in the maze of beauty, and powerless to define? Criticism, even with these capable writers, was a generous and hearty discrimination, and not a cold-blooded dissection. Fortunately for the common people, again, it is posthumous fame that establishes the position of the poet. The people choose that generations shall read, and adopt, and reject, before the final verdict; the slighting of Milton and Shakspere, in their own times and by their own fraternity, is not exceptional—it is merely extreme. We may not understand the motives of an age that is past, but we can plainly see that in our own age the living, breathing presence of undoubted genius will prevent a full analysis of that genius, and delay the popular dictum. Now that Homeric Bryant has passed away, do we not feel more at liberty to enter our humble judgment?—and will not this feeling grow with time?

Milton said of poetry, that it should be "simple, sensuous, passionate." Leigh Hunt explained that Milton meant by "simple," unperplexed and self-evident; by "sensuous," genial and full of imagery; by "passionate," excited and enthusiastic. How thoroughly has Whittier fulfilled these conditions—the self-evident, the genial, the enthusiastic!

In the career that began with "Thanatopsis" and ended with a translation of Homer, we are presented with what arouses the intellect, and exalts and refines the imagination; but where is the enthusiastic? Where, indeed, the genial? And when are the sensibilities touched to the quick? There are seldom any tears for Bryant's page. Nor can I think—and let me express it with becoming modesty—that much of this deep emotion is kindled by the polished lines of Longfellow; though one may take sweet counsel from the "Psalm of Life," and hear the "Footsteps of the Angels," and sigh with sad Evangeline. Perhaps we may compare the harmonies of Bryant to those of the cathedral organ; the classic airs of Longfellow to the softest pleasings of Apollo's lute; and the melodies of Whittier to the sweetest intonations of the human voice.

In our enjoyment of the acting of certain tragedians, we listen, and look, and approve—we can find no fault. But there is something wanting to complete our satisfaction, and that is a thrill of sympathy between actor and audience—the magnetic recognition of the right, the

"Touch of nature that makes the whole world kin."

What we demand in the actor is still more imperative in the poet, whose works will exhibit him after he is dead. We insist upon his exciting our warmest sympathies at *unexpected moments*. The power to do this went far to make Burns the national poet, and it should not be wanting in ours. "The groves were God's first temples," and Bryant was a perpetual worshiper therein. Nature was his altar. But Whittier goes out from the Quaker meeting-house, with heart and soul on fire, to redress the wrong and advocate the right; to pour oil into the wounds of suffering men and women; to sing the songs that have moved, whether the singer would or not, the man of peace to fight and die; or, more glorious still, to suffer the tortures of adverse public opinion, and to live the martyr's life.

The very titles of the Quaker poet's songs are often suggestive of his oneness with the people—"Voices of Freedom," "The Prisoner for Debt," "The Reformer," "The Poor Voter on Election-day," "The Common Question," and, among the songs of labor, "The Drovers," "The Ship-builders," "The Shoemakers," "The Fishermen," "The Huskers," "The Lumbermen"—and however humble or rough the subject, it is clothed in a garment as of "white samite" by the tender hands of the poet. Neither race, nor color, nor condition, nor faith can blind his eyes to the fact of a universal brotherhood, nor keep his tongue from the incessant proclamation. There is the key-note to a popularity that will surely grow, for it is founded upon love and truth. Though by nature reserved, shrinking, sensitive as the mimosa, like the true reformer, Whittier knows no fear. He heeds nothing but the dictates of conscience. When he conceived that Webster had fallen from grace, he seized his pen indignantly and wrote:

"All else is gone; from those great eyes
The soul is fled;
When faith is lost, when honor dies,
The man is dead!
Then pay the reverence of old days
To his dead fame;
Walk backward with averted gaze,
And hide the shame!"

Our national poet must be one whose writings are thoroughly imbued with the spirit of reformation. Whittier's Quaker birth and education made him a reformer from the start. The pure and simple Quaker testimonies are the underlying principles of his works; and these are testimonies in favor of every great and wise reform. Let the reader recall the quotation from the poet's letter and he will pardon, what would otherwise be considered a digression, a few observations upon the sect that is small in numbers, but most influential in the shaping of our country's destiny. Laugh as we may at the Quaker eccentricities, the lives of these people are wonderfully consistent with their professions, and that when the finger of ridicule has been pointed at them from the foundation of the sect. These eccentricities, if that is the proper word, had often a sensible origin. The broad-brim was to be kept on the head, in season and out of season, as a perpetual protest against servility. Their use of "thee" and "thou" is grammatical; and the use of the plural form to an individual was an eccentricity of those who chose to flatter one man by addressing him as several. There is never a debt on Quaker church buildings, nor deserving poor among their congregations. They were the friends of the Indian; and, to this day, if the red man will not receive the messenger in drab, it is because he has forgotten the traditions of his forefathers. The Quakers were necessarily Abolitionists, and the friends of peace and of temperance. The Quaker system is as true a democracy as ever existed; for even their women preach and pray in public, and have a voice in the secular administration. In this school Whittier was born, and lives, and receives his inspirations.

Though he affiliated with ultra-Abolitionists, I cannot suppose that he was at entire accord with them. It is no attack upon their sincerity to call in question their fidelity to the cause of the Union; but of Whittier's fidelity to that cause there can be no doubt, else Dame Barbara would never have "snatched the silken scarf," to fling it forth with a royal will.

During the civil strife there were many of this simple Quaker faith whose patriotism so warred with their religious convictions that they were obliged to shoulder the musket, with other volunteers, and fight for humanity and the national preservation. It is necessary to keep steadily in view this peculiar religious education to comprehend the motives and the spirit of the man and the poet—*out* of the world, yet *in* the world; by his sect living apart, yet, through its tenets, wielding a powerful influence.

In his private life he is held to be modest, retiring, conservative; with his pen he is bold, uncompromising, radical. The purity of his printed page is the reflex of his daily life, the moral teaching an expression of the pious man. No matter how abhorrent sin may be to such a nature, the Saviour's teachings are abundantly shown in the lines to Burns—as graceful an offering as ever one poet made to another:

> "Sweet soul of song! I own my debt
> Uncancelled by his failings."

Criticism may find a line here and there which, by the rules of art, are faulty. There is not that invariable correctness of classic Longfellow: but is there not, generally, a true perception of English harmony? Well might he write in "The Poem:"

> "I love the old melodious lays
> Which softly melt the ages through,
> The songs of Spenser's golden days,
> Arcadian Sidney's silvery phrase,
> Sprinkling our noon of time with freshest morning dew."

We go to the poets Lowell and Holmes for a clear exposition of the peculiarities of the New England folk, and especially for the humorous side, but the power that is apt to centralize itself is not broad enough for the national poet. Whittier's "barefoot boy" is not a Yankee boy —he is the blessed little infantile tramp of the whole country. Maud Müller is as much an English girl as American; she is Anglo-Saxon. Yet Lowell, with all his descriptive power, could never have written "Snowbound." In this poem Whittier has chosen to be at home, in Yankeeland. And here Cowper could not be more graphic, nor Goldsmith more genial, nor Burns more domestic. The element of humor appears in it occasionally, which few poets of the first rank indulge in—their mission being too serious. Somewhat of the spirit of humor appears, also, in the "Negro Boatman's Song," but it is lost in the pathetic. In the poems descriptive of aboriginal life—in "Mogg Megone," in the "Bridal of Pennacook," in the "Truce of Piscataqua"—we meet with possible Indians, and not with unrecognizable creatures of romance, and we have local description as probable as it is graphic.

There is a very marked choice of Saxon words in Whittier's poetry—the short, simple words, that strike home; surely a necessity for our national poet. There is never an approach to mysticism, nor to any philosophy that the common people cannot understand. He is the poet for the people, as Lincoln was their spokesman. His views of life are encouraging. He "paints a golden morrow," and whenever a thanatopsis is presented, as in the poems, "My Soul and I," and "My Dream," I cannot but think that it has a wider spiritual significance than the "Thanatopsis" of Bryant. Milton's "simple, sensuous, passionate," as he applied the terms, are certainly applicable to "Maud Müller." The finest spirit of patriotism is revealed in "Barbara Frietchie" and in the "Centennial Hymn;" and in all the child literature of Wordsworth is there anything more natural and refreshing than the "Barefoot Boy?"

More than twenty-five years ago (I cannot now verify the date), an article upon Whittier's poetry appeared in one of the British Reviews, wherein the "Red River Voyageur" was characterized as a poem complete and finished in every respect. At that time, praise from English critics was not over abundant for literary efforts on this side of the ocean, so that our closest scrutiny of the mechanism of the poem, as well as of its poetic spirit, can be safely invited.

Turning again to Mr. Stoddard's review, it seems as if the critic, whatever his knowledge of the art of poetry, was disabled from judgment in this instance, because he is plainly not in sympathy with the sect to which Mr. Whittier belongs, else why, in that inexplicable parenthesis, does he state that the "New England Quaker of forty years ago was rather a tolerated, than a respected, member of the community." He does not see, apparently, that without the spirit of the Quaker testimonies there would have been no brave old "Barclay of Ury," and no picture of "The Meeting," such as Bernard Barton would have loved to show to "gentle Charles." I am not able to gauge the artistic merits of the "Voices of Freedom" (and it is plain that they were written before the maturity of the poet's powers); but if it is true, as

Mr. Stoddard says, that "they made no mark in our literature," let us be thankful that they have helped to make our laws.

There seems to me a remarkable sweetness in our poet's versification—something which is not to be confounded with the smoothness that belongs to Pope. This quality, and a rarer one still, a spontaneity of pathos, such as is apparent in the poems, "The Robin," "My Playmate," "In School Days," "Marguerite," and "Mabel Martin," call for special admiration. We look to our critic for his opinion of "The Tent on the Beach," and we find: "He added nothing to the poetic value of the tales themselves by this framework," in which they are set. This is the same kind of framework that Tennyson uses for his "Morte d'Arthur," and it is to be supposed that such conversational episodes highten our zest for the superior flights of the Muse. Again, Mr. Stoddard says, "His seriousness of soul, the intense morality of his genius, accounts, I think, for his defects as a poetic artist in such poems"—making a list, which ends with the "Pennsylvania Pilgrim." What new philosophy is this? Did Milton's seriousness of soul prove a stumbling-block? Nay, even Byron, it may be submitted, did his best when, shaking off the immorality of his genius, he wrote the sublime passages of "Childe Harold." Would that Bayard Taylor were living, "whose Arab face was tanned by tropic suns and boreal frost!" If we must yield to criticism, let it be fair and genial.

In closing this brief and inadequate paper, it is possible that the suggestions might be strengthened by calling attention to many other poems and ballads, the reading and re-reading of which would increase one's admiration for the poet's varied work. Certainly there should be mention of that musical and thrilling description of the Scottish maiden's hearing of the pipes of rescue, "The Pipes at Lucknow," but such enumeration, after a while, becomes wearisome, if not dictatorial, to the reader, who would prefer the selections that conform to his individual taste. It may be pertinent, however, and timely, to quote the "Centennial Hymn." Our poet, who in the prime of life went down into the very depths of sympathy for his country's humiliation, lives to see the triumph of the right, and, in his serene old age, to invoke that protection which alone can insure the perpetuity of the republic.

"Our Father's God! from out whose hand
The centuries fall like grains of sand,
We meet to-day, united, free,
And loyal to our land and Thee—
To thank Thee for the era done,
And trust thee for the opening one.

"Here, where of old by Thy design
The fathers spake that word of Thine,
Whose echo is the glad refrain
Of rended bolt and falling chain,
To grace our festal time, from all
The zones of earth our guests we call.

"Be with us while the New World greets
The Old World thronging all its streets,
Unveiling every triumph won
By art or toil beneath the sun;
And unto common good ordain
This rivalship of heart and brain.

"Thou, who hast here in concert furled
The war-flags of a gathered world,
Beneath our Western skies fulfill
The Orient's mission of good-will,
And, freighted with Love's golden fleece,
Send back its argonauts of peace.

"For art and labor met in truce,
For beauty made the bride of use,
We thank Thee; but withal we crave
The austere virtues strong to save,
The honor proof to place or gold,
The manhood never bought or sold.

"Oh, make Thou us, through centuries long,
In peace secure, in justice strong;
Around our gift of freedom draw
The safe-guards of Thy righteous law,
And, cast in some diviner mold,
Let the new cycle shame the old."

The fact that it is posthumous fame which establishes the position of any poet may be especially true of Whittier, because his vigorous defense of liberty, and reiterated abhorrence of slavery, both before and during the civil war, have prejudiced multitudes, and prevented their just appreciation. But when the mists of prejudice and the smoke of war have cleared away, posterity will see that his words are in unison with all that is noble in our Saxon being; that in his "Voices of Freedom" he has been true to the history of his times (uncompromising, he could pay a generous tribute to the memory of the slave-holder of Roanoke); and that these songs are merely variations of the same key of humanity that Milton sounded, and Cowper heard to sound again, and Browning chanted with her glorious voice.

JOHN MURRAY.

PENELOPE'S WEB.

"Mona, I leave camp to-morrow."

"Yes—?"

Reader, I leave it to you. Is there anything on earth more exasperating to a man than a woman's "yes," when punctuated by a simple dash? Followed by an exclamation, it conveys to the listener a faint conception of the speaker's frame of mind. It indicates surprise, and surprise too often betrays a carefully hidden secret. Interrogation implies a desire to learn more—invites confidence. The period carries with it at least this satisfaction: a definite understanding between the two parties has been attained, agreeable or otherwise, and there is nothing more to be said about it. But a dash may mean anything or nothing, as the case may be. Not exactly knowing what the case might be in the present instance, Henry Cameron mentally passed in review the possibilities and probabilities, and finally ventured a second remark:

"Is it your purpose that I shall go thence with my fate undecided? I have offered you my heart and hand, my home, my life—more than this is not in man's gift. Again I ask, Will you be my wife? Mona, I demand a definite reply. You *must* answer me, yes or no."

"*I must!* You rather anticipate your authority, Mr. Cameron."

A weak, pitiful subterfuge, and the girl felt it to be such the moment the words escaped her lips; but she would not gainsay them, even though she felt their import to be rightly conjectured. In these careless words Henry Cameron read his doom. The tender light died out of his eyes, leaving hard and cold the face a moment since glowing with passion. With a woman's unerring perception, Mona Calvert saw at a glance the construction which had been put upon her words. A brief silence ensued, broken only by the soughing of the pines in the forest, and the musical cadence of the ever restless waters, upon whose banks they were seated.

"Thank you for relieving my suspense." Bitter sarcasm lurked beneath the courteous words. The weapon did not fail to hit its mark. The girl quivered under the sting.

"I presume," the voice grew yet more bitter as he continued, "your decision is ratified by your conscience. One moment," he interrupted, as Mona's lips parted as if in protest. "There is an hour in woman's life when she resists man's authority only for the pleasure of being reasoned into submission; she rebels against his wishes only for the satisfaction of being conquered by him she loves; but unless she, herself, invests him with the right to control her actions, to attempt it were presumption—to succeed, tyranny. That you resent my assumption of this right has been rendered clearly obvious to me in the tone of your voice. I can draw but one deduction. Well, that dream is ended." He could not suppress the sigh which trembled on his lips; then, laughing bitterly, he arose. "How I must have bored you this summer! It is too late to make amends for that, but I will spare your further infliction," and, touching his hat, he left the spot.

He had barely turned when his steps were arrested by hearing a merry peal of laughter—clear, ringing, effervescent laughter—such as, falling suddenly upon the ear, would leave one in doubt whether, after all, it were not the note of some woodland songster, or an echo from the mountain brook.

All this time Mona sat coldly passive. Her effort to explain matters having met with a rebuff, she wrapped herself in a mantle of injured innocence, and deigned no reply to this outburst, which frightened, but at the same time amused her. She had just about made up her mind to accept, in all the dignity of pride, the situation as he had presented it, when she became forcibly struck with the ridiculousness of the whole scene. "The idea of a man's staking his life's weal or woe upon anything so mercurial as the tone of a woman's voice! What idiots men are, anyhow!" In this train of mental observation she chanced to stumble upon some reflection which appealed irresistibly to her risibles, and she laughed. This laugh had upon Henry Cameron's nerves—and muscles—the effect of an electric shock. Instantly he returned to the spot from which he had just effected an exit which would have crowned with laurels a tragic muse.

"What are you laughing at?" he asked, savagely. Had she considered the tone of his voice, she would have fled for her life, but, as it was, she merely replied, with absurd frankness:

"I am laughing at you."

"I am glad you find the subject so amusing," Cameron answered, wrathfully. "Mona Calvert, are you utterly devoid of a heart?"

"I never considered myself in an anatomical light. When I am sufficiently at leisure, I will make a diagnosis of my case. Should I then discover that the organ referred to is wanting in my composition, I will inform you."

She looked so exasperatingly lovely as she uttered these words that she well nigh maddened the man to whom they were addressed. This girl was a perpetual enigma to him. Now thoughtful, serious, and gentle, she seemed to him the personification of perfect womanhood; the next moment, wayward as a spoiled child, full of whims and caprices, she mocked his sentiments, defied his lightest wish, and pulled down, with a ruthless hand, his most cherished ideals. Ordinarily he could not himself have told in which of these moods he found her the most bewitching, but to-day pride and anger waged bitter warfare against love. He would not yield to the fascination. With keen intuition, Mona saw the conflict raging within his breast, and coolly decided the victory hers. She looked up into the dark face which lowered above her, and assumed an air of mock humility; but mirth crept out of the corners of her beautiful eyes, showed itself in the curving lips, and finally nestled contentedly in the dimpled cheeks. She had not uttered a syllable, yet she had succeeded in reducing to most abject slavery this man, who, a moment since, had angrily burst asunder the silken bonds with which she had held him enthralled. The smile on her face, like a ray of sunshine, had stolen into his heart, and scattered the clouds which had gathered, dark and threatening, on his brow.

"Would you like to know what I think of you, Mr. Cameron?"

"Yes."

Small encouragement, this, to proceed, but Mona was not a whit dismayed.

"I think you are a goose."

"You are at least frank in giving utterance to your opinion."

"Shall I prove it?" Without waiting for permission, she continued, "You make me a magnanimous offer, and then fly off at a tangent, not knowing whether or no I intend to accept it. Evidently you are afraid that I may be tempted, so avail yourself of the first loophole to escape. How do you know that I do not wish to be reasoned into submission?"

Her love of teasing, her saucy daring, had carried her too far. In an instant she was clasped to his heart. His kisses rained on her lips, and brow, and hair.

Mona was a natural-born coquette, but her coquetry had never exceeded the bounds of perfect propriety. She was not in the habit of having young gentlemen fly at her, and kiss her in this audacious manner. For a moment this proceeding startled her out of all self-possession; recovering it almost instantly, however, she freed herself from the clasp of Cameron's arms, and, drawing up to its utmost hight her slight stature, she said, her voice trembling with indignation:

"You have taken an unwarrantable liberty!"

"Forgive me. I have no excuse to offer, but that the temptation was too great for weak human nature. Oh, my darling, why cannot my love find an echo in your heart?"

He did not say that she had tempted him, but her own heart condemned her. Yes, with her lay the blame rather than with him. This thought silenced the angry words on her lips—the lips which he had kissed.

"Mr. Cameron"—it was a serious voice which spoke to him now—"I forgive you, inasmuch as I feel that I am, in a measure, to blame. I did not suppose that you would take my lightly spoken words *au grand sérieux*. You demand my answer—you shall have it. Shall it be final?"

There was no trace of gayety in the sober face uplifted to his. In the solemn brown eyes Cameron read that which made him answer:

"No; if you do not love me, I would rather wait a life-time to win you," without appearing to notice the inconsistency of this remark. It was but a few moments since he had *demanded* "yes" or "no." Mona continued:

"When camp breaks up my aunt and I are going to old Michelet's cottage—you know he is the camp dairyman who lives on the mountain-side. There we propose to spend the remainder of the summer. There you can come to me for your answer. Should I give it to you now, you would not be satisfied, for I do not love you, as I must love the man I marry. It is now July; when the grapes are ripe"—with a fearful grimace she bit one of the wild fox-grapes which hung over her head—"you can come to me, not before. Should 'absence make the heart grow fonder'"—the serious face relaxed into a smile—"then I will be your wife; but, understand me distinctly, I pledge myself to nothing. I shall answer as my heart dictates. Meanwhile, play that I am Undine, not yet possessed of a heart (though, I believe, a soul was the organ in which she found herself wanting), and who knows but that you may be the stranger knight to awaken it." Thus turning her serious words into merriment, the girl lightly sprang from the bank on to the little island in the stream.

A more exquisite personification of the fair being whose spirit she had evoked could scarcely be conceived. Over her soft gray robe, with artistic grace, she had festooned mosses of a lighter shade, caught here and there with bunches of maiden-hair and ferns. At her throat and belt were fastened clusters of the creamy azalea. This artistic blending of color could not but enhance the loveliness of delicately cut features, set in a frame-work of auburn hair. To complete the picture, this same hair should fall in waving masses to her feet, like a halo of glory; but our heroine was of a practical turn of mind, not given to incongruities. She did not propose to make a Miss Absalom of herself; so, before starting out upon her daily rambles through the woods, she took care to put her crowning glory out of harm's way—in other words, she wore it in a low coil, which, we are fain to confess, was exceedingly becoming.

Reclining upon her mossy carpet, peeping saucily at her lover through her tent of verdure, wild grape-vine, and starry clematis, she seemed to him to have become etherealized, to have lost her own identity, in the lovely vision which she herself had so daringly conjured up. He trembled lest the silvery brook, which separated his loved one from him, would become metamorphosed, would assume the portentous shape of the malicious Kühleborn, and spirit her away from before his very eyes.

"Could anything be lovelier than this sunset, auntie? I should think the utter impossibility of doing justice to these mountain sunsets would convert aspiring artists and poets into lunatics. I am so glad that I can just simply enjoy it all, without feeling the necessity of conveying to the world the extent of my rapture. How delicious is this breeze, after such a scorching day! This is my conception of *dolce far niente*. I hate the thought of going back to the city—don't you, auntie?"

"Well, no, Mona," replied Mrs. Haviland to the last question. "I cannot say that my enthusiasm borders on asceticism—but who is that on the trail?"

Mona looked in the direction indicated by her aunt.

"Apparently," said she, after gazing intently for a moment, "it is 'James's solitary horseman winding his way down the mountain pass.'"

Was the rose tint on the girl's fair cheek the reflection of the sun's last warm rays?

"Time and place certainly give plausibility to your conjecture," was her aunt's reply. This laughing rejoinder was succeeded by an exclamation of delight:

"Why, Mona, it is Mr. Cameron!" This gentleman had always been a favorite with Mrs. Haviland. She had long suspected his preference for her niece, but when camp life, with its manifold advantages, was productive of no visible result, she concluded he had received his dismissal. It was with real pleasure that she now saw him advance.

"I believe it is he," was Mona's comment.

Little hypocrite—as though she were not fully aware that it was he! Had she not been momentarily expecting him for a week past? The grapes were ripe.

Mr. Cameron, for he it was, now approached, with friendly greeting. A warm welcome was accorded him by both ladies. After seeing that his horse was properly attended to, and making arrangements with old Michelet for his own accommodation, he joined the ladies on the low balcony, his arms full of books and papers. From the depths of a capacious pocket he drew forth that luxury to country people, a box of French candy. They who have lived in the country, who have feasted for an indefinite period upon idealism and sentiment, alone can appreciate the exhilarating freshness which attends the influx of city life; they alone can know how replete with enjoyment is such an evening as our friends had in store for them. "How delicious this breath from the realistic world," as Mona laughingly expressed it—to her aunt's amusement, be it said. That lady could not but be struck by the girl's inconsistency, and sagely drew her own conclusions.

"Mona"—they are now in their old trysting place on the banks of Moore's Creek. They had sauntered forth after breakfast. Insensibly, almost unconsciously, their steps had led them hither, to "Undine's bower." In place of the mossy turf, which has disappeared with the fern and maiden-hair, is a carpet of pine-needles. The green canopy has been replaced by one of scarlet and gold, this the only perceptible change wrought by two months' time—"Mona, the grapes are ripe."

He whispered this, as though afraid of imparting the precious secret to the birds twittering in the boughs overhead.

It was after a brief hesitation that her reply was spoken:

"Mr. Cameron, I do not affect to misunderstand you. I will be your wife. One moment"—as he was about to give expression to the raptures which her words called forth. "Listen to me. I will be your wife; but I tell you frankly that the love I feel for you is not what I had hoped it would be. It is not that self-absorbing passion which I had imagined was the only form of true love. In my heart I believe that I love you, else I would never have given utterance to these words;

but"—her voice trembled perceptibly—"I am by no means sure. I have missed you; have longed for your presence. These signs might be rightly construed into evidences of love were it not that I have been strongly under the influence of association. How it would have been with me under different circumstances I cannot say. If you are satisfied—"

He did not allow her to say more. Folding his arms about her, he bent over the lovely face, and pressed upon her lips a solemn kiss. She did not resist his kisses now. It was his right; but there was a troubled look in the soft brown eyes, as he whispered:

"We will trust to time, my beloved, to intensify this love."

This their betrothal.

Days glided into weeks, weeks into months, and still Mona stayed on in the little cottage. Her lover chafed against the separation which this entailed. He was with her as often as practicable, but this did not satisfy his ardor. Finally, his patience was exhausted. One day he said to her:

"What in the wide world are we waiting for? Why should our engagement be a protracted one? Thank heaven, there is no obstacle to our immediate union."

"Yes, there is; a serious one."

Seeing in Cameron's face a look of absolute terror, she added:

"I will tell you a secret;" and, sinking her voice to an impressive whisper, she said, "I am writing a novel."

"Writing a novel," he echoed; "well, what has that do with the matter in hand?"

"Everything."

"I must confess that I am at a loss to see how. I did not know that the honor of marrying an authoress was in store for me; but since that is to be added to my other blessings, I will pay due deference to your literary proclivities; you shall immure yourself in books all through my business hours. I solemnly promise never to interfere, excepting when I am at home, and want you for myself." And he fondly caressed the beautiful head which he had drawn to his bosom.

"That just proves how much a man knows about housekeeping. I suppose, sir, in placing me at the head of your establishment, you expect me to be an automaton, whose sole duty in life is to entertain your lordship out of business hours, when you are at leisure to be entertained." He laughed at her indignation, vehemently disclaiming all intention of converting his wife into a butterfly.

"But," with mock seriousness, "you have not told me the name of your novel."

"I think," she answered, demurely, "I shall call it 'Penelope's Web.'"

"In the name of wonder, why?"

"Because I have attempted such a herculean task in trying to manufacture a hero. It is a kind of patch-work piece of business. I take a scrap of this man and a scrap of that, and weave them together, in the vain hope of making a perfect man; but, invariably, I have to ravel him out. Spite of everything I can do, he will have a made-over look. Anybody would know at a glance that he was made up of odds and ends. I am afraid the material with which I have had to work is at fault. Somehow, none of the pieces match, however perfect they may be in themselves. Now, can't you see how utterly impracticable would be my marriage at present?"

"I can not say that the obstacle appears to me overwhelming."

"Men are so obtuse!"—this with an indescribable air of resignation. "Listen to me. By chance I have stumbled across a hero in a degree *comme il faut*. So far, I have not had to insert a single patch, and my work is getting on famously; but the moment my Cæsar steps off his pedestal, and goes to fishing round in unheard of corners for the boots which he knows he put in their proper places, then I will be obliged to begin the raveling out process, and all my summer's work will have been completely thrown away."

"Mona, you are incorrigible. Wait until I get you back to the city; then I will marry you, in spite of yourself. Thank goodness, the rains will set in soon, and force you to leave this out-of-the-way place. Pope Valley is indisputably lovely, but it is too outrageously inaccessible."

After this every allusion to the subject of their marriage provoked from Mona some such ridiculous pretext for delay. Finally, Cameron concluded it was wiser to let the matter rest in abeyance until her return to the city. This event, joyously anticipated by the impatient lover, was now near at hand. The date of their departure was fixed for the first of November—it was now the last of October.

"Where is Miss Mona, Mrs. Haviland?"

"She is not feeling very well to-day, but I will tell her that you are here."

Mrs. Haviland was about to go in quest of her niece, when that young lady entered the room. Cameron advanced to meet her, with a melodramatic air.

"'If you have tears to shed, prepare to shed them now.' I have come to lead you out of your 'Happy Valley.'" The tender associations connected with this spot could not reconcile Cameron to the distance. It was with unfeigned joy he had approached the cottage, as he felt, for the last time.

Receiving no response to his laughing salutation, he looked up in surprise. An exclamation of dismay burst from his lips as his eye rested on Mona's countenance. He had not seen her distinctly until now. The usually radiant face was colorless. The dark circles about the eyes, the tightly compressed lips, betrayed intense suffering.

To her lover's anxious inquiry, she replied: "I have a terrible headache. I came in only to beg that you will excuse me to-night." Then, turning to her aunt, "It is nothing serious. I will be all right in the morning. All I want is sleep. Good night." As Cameron opened the door for her, she added, "I will see you in the morning."

At breakfast she joined them, asserting that she felt much better; but her looks belied her words. If possible, she was more ghastly white than when she parted from them the previous evening.

Turning to Cameron, as they left the breakfast-room, she murmured:

"Come."

Alone among the pines, he held out his arms to her.

"What is it, my darling?"

She shrunk visibly from the caress. With a feeble attempt at the old manner, she replied: "Oh, I am overworked. For two days past I've been busy raveling you out."

But the laugh accompanying these words died away in a sob. Then, without further attempt at restraint, she gave way to an *abandon* of grief. So alarmed was Cameron at this new phase in her character—he had never, until now, had a glimpse of the emotional side of her nature—that he scarce heard, much less understood, the import of her words.

"Why, Mona, what in the world has happened?"

"Henry Cameron, I have wronged you—not willfully, not deliberately; nevertheless I have done you an irreparable injury. I cannot be

"I do not ask for mercy; I do not expect forgiveness. Only let me prove to you that I was weak, not wicked."

"The usual plea. Well? I have already requested an explanation."

From his exceeding coldness she gathered strength. Passion would have unnerved her. She owed him a confession—a humiliating one. It was easier to confess to a judge than to a lover. Her voice trembled as she began:

"My novel was but a pretext to postpone the fulfillment of a promise which I should never have made. I thought the title would have suggested to you a hidden meaning. Like Penelope of old, I had recourse to this artifice to protract my decision, because"—her voice faltered—"because I dared not become the wife of another until positively assured that Ulysses could never return."

"Great God, Mona Calvert, are you a wife?"

The hard, set face was now livid with passion. He had sprung to his feet, as though stung by an adder.

As the force of these words dawned upon her comprehension (she did not consider how natural was the inference), the hot blood surged into the face which a moment since rivaled marble in its whiteness. She trembled in every limb, not from fear, but passion. Anger overmastered every other emotion. With flashing eyes, she exclaimed:

"How dare you insult me by such a question!"

The proud resentment in voice and attitude carried conviction even to this jealous man. It conveyed "proof as strong as holy writ."

"Thank God, in this I have done you injustice. Had you betrayed me to this extent——" He checked himself. "Please go on. I will not interrupt you again."

He resumed his seat, and bowed his face in his hands.

"To explain matters clearly"—her voice was less tremulous now—"I shall be obliged to enter somewhat into detail. Certain reminiscences are absolutely necessary for the elucidation of my story. My mother died when I was but an infant, leaving me to the care of my father and

shut himself up in his library. You can imagine, being an only child, how lonely my life was, or would have been, but for reasons which I will now explain." Her voice trembled slightly as she reached this point in her narrative, and a slight flush suffused the cheek, from which the unwonted color had faded out almost instantly. She paused an instant, then continued: "Adjoining our ranch was one owned by Colonel Leston. His son, Paul, notwithstanding that he was my senior by five years, was my constant companion. He was a thoughtful, gentlemanly boy, and my father gladly consigned me to such safe keeping.

"We were inseparable. When I could hardly walk, he, himself almost a baby, would put me on his pony and lead me all over the ranch. By him, who could scarce read monosyllables, I was taught to lisp the alphabet. Until Paul had attained his sixteenth year we studied together, my father our instructor, though, of course, he was far in advance of me. At this period Paul was sent to college. This my first grief; his rapture, of course, was unbounded; but I was heart-broken. In a perfect agony of tears, I clung to him. My tears and sobs were contagious. Holding me in his arms, he whispered: 'Don't cry, little sister, I'm coming back soon, and then what glorious times we will have.' Then stealthily brushing away a tear, he kissed me, and sprang into the buggy which was to convey him to the depot. I watched until a bend in the road hid him from my sight; then my tears broke out afresh. This our first parting. Before we met again a year had elapsed. Meantime, thrown entirely upon my own resources, I had unconsciously developed into a very dignified little woman. When we met, after our long separation, we were both strangely shy and awkward. I fairly quivered with excitement when I heard Paul's voice, but no woman of the world could have received him more demurely. I merely offered him my hand. He looked a little surprised, but made no comment. We had exchanged our last kiss. To dwell upon the incidents which transpired during this vacation, or in those succeeding it, would only weary you with unnecessary detail. Suffice it to state, that they were the 'golden milestones' in my lonely life. Paul still lacked a few months of being twenty-one when he finished his course at the University. His father was not wealthy. He had his own way to carve in the world. To do this he must leave home for an indefinite number of years. This he confided to me, his old play-fellow, the day of his graduation—the day which I had for years looked forward to as the acme of my felicity. In my childish ignorance I had fondly dreamed he would quietly settle down on the ranch. What profession he finally determined upon is of no import; enough, that after having been at home for a month or so, the day for his departure was fixed. It dawned. We were no longer children, and knew it. He never called me 'Little Sister' now. A year ago I resented this. His reply was: 'Once I regretted, Mona, that you were not my sister; now I rejoice that the same blood does not flow in our veins.' I looked at him wonderingly. I could not understand his meaning. Later the words recurred to me, and I, too, was glad. Through all of our separation we had never corresponded; both felt now that it was too late to begin.

"To conceal the emotion occasioned by the mere thought of his immediate departure, I assumed on this last day an unwonted gayety. I had become quiet only through force of circumstances. My real nature was not so. Paul, on the contrary, was extremely serious. Turning to me, suddenly, he said, 'Mona, would you be content with "love in a cottage?"' I knew perfectly well what he meant, but, with the perverseness of human nature, or woman nature, I answered:

"'No; I would not. I never could appreciate the sublimity of "Bread and Cheese and Kisses,"' and then I added, heaven only knows why, 'I do not think any man has a right to ask a woman to marry him until he can support her—not luxuriously, but comfortably.' This checked the words to which he was about to give utterance. I had deliberately sealed my fate. I knew it then; I know it now. Abruptly changing the subject, Paul said to me:

"'Why do you so often wear forget-me-nots?'

"I had a bunch of them in my belt.

"'Because they happen to be becoming to my style of beauty.'

"'A most potent reason. Did you ever hear the legend of this flower?'

"'No.'

"'"Once upon a time,"' he began, 'a pair of lovers stood upon a river's brink, even as we stand now on the banks of this stream; like this, it was overhung by a precipitous cliff. In a crevice of this smooth jutting rock the maiden spied a cluster of these same blue flowers,' touching lightly those I wore. 'She expressed a desire for them. Her lover forded the stream, scaled the precipice, and obtained the coveted blossoms. He had nearly made the descent when his foot slipped; he saw his imminent peril, and, throwing the flowers to his lady-love (we presume the current obligingly bore them to her), he called out: "Forget me not, dearest," and disappeared forever beneath the waters.'

"I made some laughing comment, to which he smilingly acquiesced; then, taking my hand in his, he seriously, almost solemnly, said:

"'Mona, I start to-day into the world in search of "forget-me-nots." Those I chance to find along life's highway I will send you from time to time; but if, more fortunate than the hero of our legend, I be spared to return, I will bring you some truly worthy of your acceptance; "forget-me-nots" that will fade only with life.'

"I understood him, and he knew that I did. This was all. This our last parting. A couple of months after Paul left home my father died suddenly, leaving me alone in the world. The rest of my story you know; how I went to my aunt, whose home is in San Francisco, with whom I have been ever since. Five years have elapsed since Paul Leston parted from me. I am now twenty-one; he left a child of sixteen. For three successive years I received from him an envelope, directed in his own handwriting, enclosing a spray of forget-me-nots; the post-mark, invariably, bearing the date of the anniversary of our last meeting." From these same post-marks I was kept informed as to his whereabouts. Other communication between us than this there was none.

"Upon the fourth anniversary this failed. The fifth brought me nothing. To say that I was faithful to him all this time were to say what is not true. Could I have learned anything of him through his father, I would gladly have sought the information, but, after my father's death, Colonel Leston had sold his ranch and moved I know not where. At first I was terrified by Paul's silence. I say silence, because this yearly token had spoken volumes to me. This feeling of fear was succeeded by one of doubt and distrust, and then came a sense of utter desolation and loneliness. Meantime, you came, and poured at my feet all your wealth of love. I schooled myself to believe that my childhood's dream was but an ideal. He was not bound to me by a single tie. Even had he married another I had no right to utter a word. Why should I waste my life in pursuing a phantom, when I might be cherished and beloved by a man who, for aught I know, is more worthy of my affection? Thus I unfortunately argued, you know with what result."

She paused, not knowing how to tell the rest, feeling that she was aiming a death-blow at the heart of the man who sat by her side so rigidly still.

"Yesterday I received this."

With trembling fingers she took from her pocket an envelope dated San Francisco. It contained a spray of forget-me-nots. They were scarcely faded; without the post-mark they would have carried their message: "Ulysses has returned—is already in port."

"This is my confession, Mr. Cameron." Her voice had sunk to a plaintive whisper. "I do not extenuate my fault—guilt I can not call it. I do not ask you to forgive me—only forget me."

It was a sad, wan smile which met her eye.

"Ulysses did not claim his rights, Penelope, until he had first matched his skill with that of the other competitors. Let us each have a fair chance. You cannot know what changes time has wrought in the character of this man, who was, when he won your heart, but a beardless boy; how can you tell whether you have interpreted aright this symbol?" pointing to the flower in her hand.

"Because the sight of this little blossom set every nerve to quivering, every pulse to throbbing. No, I will not add injustice to injury; even though this man should prove faithless, his image is so indelibly impressed upon my heart that it were sacrilege for me to accept the hand of another." The girl's face flushed as she uttered these words. She was conscious that it was a humiliating confession for a girl to make concerning a man who had never in words confessed his love. Cameron was quick to divine this thought, and he was struck by the brave humility which dared have faith in an unspoken pledge. Rising abruptly, he said:

"I will see you later."

She was alone with her thoughts; they shaped themselves somewhat in this wise: A woman's heart is an anomaly, even to herself. In listening to its dictates, she too often consciously, voluntarily, puts from her life's roses and embraces its thorns. Had she done this? Mayhap; she could not tell.

Hours afterward, when Henry Cameron returned to this spot, he found her lying within her bower. Like a child, she had cried herself to sleep. Trembling yet upon her lashes were the unshed tears. He bent over her and murmured low:

"Thou art now possessed of a heart, Undine, and it was I who taught it to vibrate to the touch of the 'stranger knight.'" A sad renunciation, this, of his own claim.

When she awoke he was speeding homeward. In her half open palm he had left these words:

"I cannot blame you. Farewell. H. C."

"Have you no word of welcome for me, Mona?—nothing to offer but this little, cold, passive hand?" He had come upon her suddenly, unannounced. Before she could realize his presence he had clasped her hand within both his own. There it lay imprisoned, like a snowflake—as white, as still, as cold. Recalled to consciousness by his words, she tried to withdraw it, but he held it faster yet.

"No, Mona; I have need of this hand. I have not finished with it yet," and he led her to the sofa. "Have you received my messages?"

"Yes."

She glanced furtively into the face of the tall, bearded stranger by her side. She did not venture a second glance. In the dark eye which met hers she saw that which made her heart beat as never it had beat before—that which made the color come and go in her face, like waves of rosy light.

"I have scaled the precipice; the prize—far too precious to intrust to winds and tides—I have brought with me. Will you wear it, Mona—a lasting symbol of the silent covenant between us?" And Paul Leston took from his pocket a tiny gold circlet; on the plain surface, in delicate tracery, was a wreath of pale blue forget-me-nots.

"Wait, Paul," as, reading his answer in her soft, luminous eyes, Leston was about to slip the ring upon her finger.

"No fear of 'bread and cheese' with our kisses, sweetheart; I left those adjuncts where I gathered this." The smile accompanying these words was reflected on Mona's face, but it faded away as she repeated:

"Wait, Paul."

Then, in the dimly lighted library, she told him all—the heart-ache, the doubt, the broken faith. She told him of the novel; she hated the thought of it now. She felt as though the web she had woven were a funeral pall for the noble man who had loved her; bravely she confessed all. When she had finished, Leston put his arms around her, as though to shield her from further temptation, and whispered:

"I was mad to have imperiled my chances thus. Forgive me, love, for exposing you to such an ordeal. I had no right to subject your constancy to this test. But I will insure myself against further risk." With a tender smile, he placed upon her finger a talisman.

Meeting Mona one evening, by chance Henry Cameron's eye fell upon this betrothal ring. Too readily he understood its significance. He checked the sigh on his lips and passed on. It would be strange indeed were there never a broken heart in this wide world—since it must be so, 'twere better a man's than a woman's—stranger yet to find perfect every web wrought of life's tangled yarn. SALLIE R. HEATH.

HENRY HUNTLEY HAIGHT.

In his "Data of Sociology," Spencer states that "ancestor worship is the root of every religion." To establish this theory he produces overwhelming evidence that primitive men of many races worshiped their defunct ancestors. This worship extended to strangers, and even to foreigners of marked ability; thus, "A temple was erected in China to the American filibuster, Ward; and in Benares, another to the English filibuster, Warren Hastings."

We have passed the stage of development where we deified the departed, but have not reached that where tombstones and funeral sermons tell the whole truth. The tendency to eulogize is not restricted to marble-cutter and parson. It has seized historian and biographer, also. Macaulay, in speaking of Middleton's "Life of Cicero," says:

"The fanaticism of the devout worshiper of genius is proof against all evidence and all argument. The character of his idol is matter of faith, and the province of faith is not to be invaded by reason. He maintains his superstition with a credulity as boundless and a zeal as unscrupulous as can be found in the most ardent partisans of religious or political factions. The most overwhelming proofs are rejected, plainest rules of morality are explained away, extensive and important portions of history are completely distorted; the enthusiast misrepresents facts with all the effrontery of an advocate, and confounds right and wrong with all the dexterity of a Jesuit; and all this, only that one man, who has been in his grave for ages, may have a fairer character than he deserves."

This tendency to hero-worship impairs, also, the judgment of contemporaries. Friendship, and even acquaintance, may unfairly affect the estimate of character. Propinquity alone is often a potent factor of error. Reputations, colossal to contemporaries, have shrunk perceptibly in the succeeding generation, and disappeared in the third.

Mindful of these sources of error, and believing that no investigation is worth pursuing except its object be to ascertain the truth, we give a brief outline of Governor Haight's life, and an analysis of his character. The paternal ancestors of Henry H. Haight, coming from England, settled in Salem, Massachusetts, more than two hundred and fifty years ago. Thence, leading westward the tide of New England emigration, some of the family reached Monroe County, New York, then on the frontier. There, in the city of Rochester, on the 25th of May, 1825, Henry Huntley Haight was born. His father, Fletcher M. Haight, had long been a leading lawyer of the county. His mother was a descendant of the Camerons of Lochiel.

At the age of thirteen young Haight was preparing for college at the Rochester Collegiate Institute. At fifteen, he entered Yale College as a freshman; at nineteen, and in 1844, he graduated with high honors. Throughout his collegiate career he held a high place for scholarship; and the contest between himself and his competitors for the highest honor, the college valedictory, was extremely close. His reputation as a scholar of great attainments was handed down to succeeding classes in college tradition long after he had graduated.

While in college his father had removed to St. Louis, where Henry was admitted to the bar in 1847. In 1849 he left for California, and in January, 1850, at the age of twenty-five, he commenced the practice of law in San Francisco. Associated with his father till the latter became United States District Judge for the Southern District of California, and afterward alone, and with different partners, Mr. Haight obtained and held a fair practice. While engaged in this pursuit he was nominated for Governor by the Democratic Convention, in 1867, and, in a spirited canvass, defeated the Republican candidate by a majority of over nine thousand. Prior to this time he had never held any political office, nor been considered an active politician, although he had always taken great interest in every important political question which arose.

During his term of office he showed himself honest, able, fearless, and independent—so independent that he alienated many political friends who had pushed his fortunes, and deemed themselves entitled to more consideration (some, perhaps, to more compensation) than they received.

His administration was pure and successful, but at its close he engaged in no further contest for office. He resumed the duties of his profession, without money, and hampered by a large debt, contracted while engaged in politics. Some little time elapsed before he regained his former practice, but eventually he obtained more, even, then before his accession to office. He labored at it unceasingly and with patient assiduity, down to the time of his death, and, during the later years of his life, with very gratifying financial results.

A few weeks prior to his death, he mentioned to the writer that he had labored so long and so assiduously that he felt the absolute need of rest, and was looking forward with great pleasure to a speedy release from the dry routine of business, and hoped for at least a year of relaxation and foreign travel. Obliged to forego this, he contented himself with a visit to the Eastern States, and, soon after his return, died quite suddenly at the residence of his physician, on the second of September, 1878.

Governor Haight possessed an equally developed and well balanced brain and a sound judgment, but he preferred to deal with principles, rather than facts. He took broad and comprehensive views of a subject, looking at it in all its relations. His mind was synthetic, rather than analytical. His mental perspective was perfect. The propinquity of an object did not deceive him as to its magnitude. When called to act in any matter where he was in possession of facts sufficient to guide his judgment, he decided promptly, and usually decided right. His temperament was so cool that he never lost his head, therefore he had always full command of his brain power; however novel, unexpected, and perplexing the circumstances which suddenly arose, he generally knew better, and sooner, than any one else, what should be done.

In unexpected political complications his advice was sought and relied on. In the trial of a case he showed no especial brilliancy. He was not a man to pluck victory from defeat, or to wring verdicts from an unwilling jury by the magnetism of his presence or the eloquence of his words. As a speaker, he was slow, and hesitated in selecting the word to express the shade of thought; but when an avalanche of unexpected evidence threatened to annihilate his case, no one could receive it with greater calmness, or plan more wisely to avoid its effect. When sudden election was to be made between irreconcilable theories of attack or defense, no one was more sagacious in counsel or prompt in decision. It has been said that he was irresolute and vacillating, and, therefore, unfitted for the executive chair. This is a mistake. It is inconsistent with his other traits of character. Nor was he a man to be cajoled or shaken from an opinion once formed. The true theory of his irresolution was this: He had no liking for matters of detail, and when called to examine them he invariably procrastinated. He delayed the investigation necessary to guide his judgment, and while he delayed he temporized with those awaiting his decision. He did not hesitate to decide on the facts when known. He never abandoned an opinion once formed. This neglect of matters of detail and fact sometimes entrapped him into difficulties in practice which many men of inferior ability would have avoided. The best proof of his brain-power is the ease and rapidity with which he could dispatch the matter in hand. Whether it was a brief, a lecture, or political platform, he would dash it off with no apparent mental labor. Once done, it required but little alteration or revision.

The greatest defects in his character, probably, were a want of system in the management of petty affairs—a thorough aversion to all matters of detail; hence, sometimes, procrastination in affairs most urgent.

His conscientiousness was one of his dominant characteristics. Whatever he believed his duty he would do despite all obstacles. This trait alienated from him those political friends who felt aggrieved that they could not control his actions. In religion an ordained Presbyterian elder, he was scrupulous in the discharge of the obligations of his creed, but most tolerant of the opinions of others. His private life was so spotless that in a campaign of great heat and bitterness no attack was made upon his character. He was wise, without guile; ready, but not impetuous; self-reliant, self-poised; in sudden adversities, undismayed; in counsel, sagacious; in the dispatch of business, rapid. Cultured, but not pedantic; moral, but not austere; religious, but not intolerant; amiable in disposition, genial in temperament, faithful to every trust, punctually discharging every obligation—he has left a record without a blemish. Whether he was a great man, as the world reckons greatness, it is too soon to determine. Altitude is best measured from a distance. To the State his life has been valuable, not only in the direct teaching of his example, but in demonstrating that the possession of integrity, purity, and honor do not decrease the availability of political candidates. This lesson of his life is especially commended to the attention of nominating conventions. It is on a point where doubts appear to have frequently arisen.

PHILIP G. GALPIN.

SOME INCIDENTS OF THE SEVEN DAYS.

We had been lying in the intrenchments thrown up after Fair Oaks for nearly a month, the monotony of our life being varied by an almost nightly alarm. There was nothing in front of our guns but a picket line, and it was a very uneasy picket, some three-quarters of a mile in advance. Let us take one night as a sample. We had sought our blankets soon after tattoo, with a fervent wish that those restless fellows would keep quiet for at least one night. It was a warm atmosphere, heavy with the rank exhalations of the Chickahominy swamps, and still, except for a low mutter of pent thunder. Toward midnight the report of a musket rang loud upon the heavy air, followed by another; and in less than a minute the rapid crack, crack, crack, and the fitful flashes piercing the dark horizon, where the tangled underbrush met the heavy belt of woods, showed that the picket line was thoroughly alarmed. Soon the flashes began to dart from the woods into the open, while from the brush came answering flashes, showing that our line was coming in. The first two or three shots awakened us. After waiting a moment to see that it was not an accidental shot, we seized our boots, and emerged growling at the "restless beggars that couldn't keep quiet at night." Having brass twelve-pound smooth-bore guns, not effective beyond one thousand five hundred yards at the best, we got out rather listlessly, as there was little probability that we would be wanted until the flashes began to appear in the open ground. Then we rushed, each officer to his section, and found the men who slept among the guns already at their posts. The "crack" had now become a crash, showing the reserves were in, when, from a neighboring embrasure, shot a stream of vivid light far into the night, and the sharp treble of the musketry was smothered by the roar of a heavy field-gun. Sparks of light darted with inconceivable swiftness across the open space, suggesting lightning-bugs, with super-insect velocity, and, just grazing the nearer flashes, drop among the flashes in the dark line of timber; and, as they seem to near the ground, the sparks explode with an intense flame, lighting up the dark trees for yards around. Pettit, the best gunner in the Army of the Potomac, is shelling the enemy's pickets over the heads of our retiring men, and so superb was his gunnery that I never heard of his killing a man of ours. Our troops would advance with perfect composure, with Pettit's shells just clearing their heads, and falling in death-dealing showers one hundred yards in front of them. The firing continued for some minutes. Then the crash subsided into cracks, with longer and longer intervals. The darting sparks became rarer, ceased entirely, and in fifteen minutes from the first gun silence and night had resumed their reign. This is, perhaps, repeated before morning. Multiply this by thirty, and you have an idea of life in the intrenchments. Then came Gaines's Mill, and through the numerous rumors and reports that fly around the neighborhood of a battle, we gathered enough to know that Porter had met with a heavy reverse. We were not surprised when one Friday night, about nine o'clock, we got orders to withdraw. Part of our battery accompanied the rear guard, and we spent Saturday in skirmishing and retreating. Evening found us at Savage Station, where a sharp affair took place. Nothing could have been finer than the charge of Sedgwick's Division of the Second Corps. Our guns were in battery in a plain, entirely open for nearly a mile, and the enemy in a heavy piece of woods at the extremity of the plain. It was after sunset, and rapidly growing dark. We heard a cheer behind us, and over our guns came a long line, its front waving and undulating as each regiment pressed forward. Maintaining a general alignment, on they went, at a double-quick, arms sloped diagonally across their breasts at what is tactically known as "arms, port," officers in front of the line pressing the eager men back with their swords. No need of file-closers to keep those men up. The hoarse cheer running along the line marked their advance, as they were lost in the creeping dusk, until, from the edge of the woods, came a sheet of flame. Without a pause the division threw itself into the fire. A few stragglers from one regiment appeared, but the line of fire went deeper and deeper into the forest, until the distant cheers and the sudden darkness that closed the scene told us that the enemy had abandoned the contest. Two guns were the trophies.

We slept soundly that night in spite of a heavy shower that came soon after the action ceased. I was aroused by an angry voice in the tone of energetic protest. Sitting up, and rubbing my eyes, I found that Captain H—— had just applied the toe of his boot rather sharply to a portion of Lieutenant K——'s anatomy, who, until that moment, had been peacefully sleeping by my side. Hence the protest; for although our worthy Captain was something of a martinet, and considered the instruction of four rather raw Lieutenants his most obvious duty next to looking after the welfare of his battery, he was not in the habit of kicking us. Said Captain H——:

"Gentlemen, excuse my abruptness; but I think if you will get up and take a look you will agree with me that this is no time for ceremony."

We got up and took a look. On either side of the battery, which was unlimbered and in position, was a long line which, at the first glance, seemed a line of battle lying down. A second look showed overcoats, blankets, knapsacks, haversacks, all the articles which strew the path of a retreating army just as their owners had left them, when they lay down upon the line which they had been holding the evening before. Not a living soul in sight, except our tired men stretched around the guns, and the jaded horses standing in the harness, which had not been taken off since they left the intrenchments. In the woods in front of us the rebel bugles were sounding reveille, and we could catch a gleam here and there where the level rays of the just rising sun struck the barrel of a musket, as a thin skirmish line moved cautiously from the woods. We spoke together.

"What does this mean, Captain?"

"It means, gentlemen, that the last of our army has been gone some hours."

It was true. The last brigade of our infantry had left about eleven o'clock, and the cavalry rear guard had followed soon after. We were alone in the presence of at least a corps of Lee's army.

"Mr. K——," said Captain H——, in the same calm and rather quizzical tone in which he had announced the situation, "hitch up your section as rapidly as possible and move by the flank, slowly, as if you were changing position, until you get on the road"—referring to the road to White Oak Swamp, known, I believe, as the Williamsburg Pike. "When you get on the road, take a gallop, and keep it as long as your horses can stand. Gentlemen, you will follow Lieutenant K——, a section at a time, and slowly, remember, until you get on the road. All depends upon the enemy thinking we are all here. That line of knapsacks may fool them."

We lost no time in hitching in and moving to the road. Lieutenant K—— had mounted his cannoneers on the ammunition chests. Captain H—— rode to the head of the column.

"Get off, every man," he ordered. "The horses will have enough to do with the guns."

"But, Captain," replied Lieutenant K——, "the men can't keep up."

"Mr. K——," said the Captain, "the men must take their chances. I must save the guns if possible."

We started at a fast gallop, the men running alongside as well as they could—and you never know how long a man can run until he is running for his life. Still, they soon fell behind in the two leading sections. Captain H—— remained with my section, which closed the rear, and we moved more slowly, allowing the rest of the column to get a long lead. Fortunately, the road was hard, sandy, and down hill, pretty much all the way. After going some distance, we heard an ominous sound, like the far-off tramp of horses. Captain H—— uttered one word—"Cavalry!"

It was that we feared. We could laugh at their infantry on that road. We concluded they had discovered the dummy line of battle, and started their cavalry in pursuit. Captain H—— halted my last piece, and fixed the prolonge. I mention this because it was the only time during the war that I knew of this being done. The prolonge was a stout rope, with a ring at one end and a toggle at the other. When not in use, it was coiled upon two hooks on the stock of the gun-carriage. When it was necessary to fire retiring, and the time could not be spared to limber and unlimber, the ring was put over the pintle-hook upon the axle of the limber and the toggle through the lunette, which is a hole in the iron plate that terminates the stock. Thus the gun was drawn with the trail on the ground, and could be loaded while moving, and fired without detaching the horses, the rope allowing it to recoil without injuring them. In this manner we went, with the trail bouncing over the ground, but still keeping a good trot.

The men of this section had kept up with the guns, while a majority of the men of the other sections had fallen behind, blown and exhausted by their efforts to keep up with the gallop. A turn in the road brought the welcome sight of White Oak Swamp, where our men were just throwing the last planks off the bridge. General Richardson had given us up, and was in a towering rage, for Captain H—— was his Chief of Artillery, and an intimate personal friend. Captain H—— always maintained that he was not notified of the movement; but an aid-de-camp of General Richardson said he awoke him at half past ten, and gave him his orders. As the officer was a man of undoubted veracity, it was evident that Captain H—— had awakened sufficiently to answer and then fallen asleep again—nothing strange, either, after a night and day of marching and fighting. It was a narrow escape.

Ten minutes after we reached the bridge, a considerable force of cavalry was reported on the brow of the hill above the swamp. Many of our men were missing, and we concluded captured; but they all came in—some by wading through the swamp. The cavalry had passed some. Too eager for the guns to stop and pick them up, the cavalrymen told them to go back and give themselves up, but they plunged into the woods as soon as the cavalry had passed, and finally straggled in.

We thought our labors for that day were over. We knew the removal of the bridge would block the pursuit for some hours, and we went into park on the side of the hill, above the bridge. The men threw themselves under the carriages to escape the fierce July sun, and in a minute were sound asleep. How long we slept, I cannot say. We were rudely awakened. Under cover of a piece of woods on the other side of the swamp, the enemy established four batteries, and opened one of the most rapid and accurate fires I have ever been under. Our position on the side-hill was untenable, and we lost no time in getting out of it. When I say no time, I mean as rapidly as could be done with men awakened from the heavy sleep of exhaustion, amid the shriek of solid shot, the smoke and noise of bursting shells, and the deafening report made by the blowing up of two limbers in a neighboring battery. We were soon ordered into a new position by General Richardson. The other battery had run away from their guns, which stood abandoned until near night. We had to bear the brunt alone. For nearly four hours we maintained this unequal combat—one battery against four. It seems to me there was not a minute during these four hours when you could not see in the air the little cloud of white smoke which marks the explosion of a case-shot, and, after the second of suspense, hear the whir of the leaden rain, or the harsher whiz of the jagged pieces of shell; while now and then, above all other sounds, would come the angry scream of the solid shot, as it flew over our heads, or sometimes struck, with that horrifying sound in which you hear splintered bones and mangled flesh. I could not but feel pity for the horses. The men were grand in their splendid energy. The figure of a No. 1—William Fleming, a hard-drinking, quarrelsome Irishman—is photographed on my memory. Stripped to his undershirt, black with the grim of powder and sweat, never in the fierce excitement of battle losing the mechanical accuracy of position which had made him the admiration of the recruit and the pet of the Chief of piece, sending his sponge to the bottom of the bore with his shoulders as square, and leaping out with as jaunty a step, and as knowing a toss of the staff, as if he were simply astonishing the last appointed second lieutenant. I ordered him relieved, and No. 2 stepped up to take the staff from him.

"To the devil with you!" shouted Fleming. "Bring me another bucket of water." For by that time the gun was so foul and hot that even his arm could hardly withdraw the sponge. Then, turning to me, he said:

"Excuse me, Lieutenant, but I'm good for an hour more, if you'll only make them loafers keep the bucket full."

But the poor horses stood with their heads hanging down, or lazily nipping the scanty grass; for they were thoroughly seasoned to fire, and hardly noticed it until one of those dull thuds would be heard, and you would see one horse of a team plunging madly or staggering wildly, or sometimes crashing down, an inert mass, as a solid shot tore through his entrails, while his mate would look at him wistfully, I even fancied sadly, as if he were saying, "What's the matter, old fellow?"

I was in the act of reporting to Captain H—— that one gun was so hot I was afraid to fire it, when a large piece of shell whizzed by me, and struck him in the thigh, breaking the bone. Lieutenant K—— assumed command. Twice did we fill our chests from caissons sent back for ammunition under this fire, until near dark we were relieved by Kinzie's battery of the Fifth Artillery. That night I was left with two guns to cover the retreat. Never mind the why and wherefore, it is not a pleasant thing to see the troops moving off and yourself left behind. It was rendered more unpleasant by the noise of axes and the glimmer of moving lanterns in the swamp, showing that they were repairing the bridge, and by the nervousness of the brigade commander who had the rear guard. About ten o'clock he could not stand it any longer, and we moved off. We came to where two roads branched, and he took the right hand one. One of my sergeants, who had been over the road with ammunition, said to me, "That's the Charles City Crossroad, and it goes right to Richmond." I rode to the head of the column, and told the Brigadier we were going right into the enemy's lines. He had asked my advice about the propriety of moving more than once, but I found that absence from the sights and sounds of the swamp had made him bold. He said:

"When I want your advice, sir, I'll ask for it."

"All right," said I; "you're going to Richmond."

I went back. In a few minutes the galloping of horses was heard in front, and several shots were fired. The brigade, which was composed chiefly of raw troops newly arrived, scattered, at the first shout of the enemy, into the woods on either side of the road. I was left alone on a narrow road, heavily wooded on either side, with a few rounds of canister, hardly a shell or case-shot in the boxes, and scarcely room enough in the road to unlimber. I didn't make any attempt. I was disgusted, and made up my mind to go to Libby, and get philosophical over it. While I sat there, along a road which intersected the road we were on, but which we had not seen in the darkness, came a battery, full jump, the carriages rattling and creaking. A cheery voice hailed me:

"What's that?"

"A section of A and C, Fourth Artillery," I replied.

"What in Hades are you doing there?" said the voice.

"Waiting to go to Libby."

"Fall in behind me," said he. "I've been in the same scrape in the enemys' lines. I guess we'll be all right now."

I fell in with alacrity. It was Battery C, Second Artillery, Captain James Thompson, a soldier and a gentleman. We went at a gallop for a mile or two, until the country lane became again a broad road, and we found ourselves in a hurrying stream of humanity. For several hours three columns, if you can dignify such confusion by any tactical term, poured alongside of us, now in the road, now in the fields, yet no panic, no rout, simply confusion incident to darkness, and the simultaneous actions that had been going on all day along the line of retreat.

A battery of the First Artillery halted that night in a little clearing. The men lay down, unhitching their horses, but leaving them in harness. The first sergeant, now an honored officer of the Third Artillery, told me he got up and walked toward one side of the clearing. He was halted, and turned back by a sentinel. Going toward the other side, he was again challenged.

"Who comes thar?"

The voice struck him. He replied, "Friend;" and said, "What regiment is that?"

The answer came, "Seventh Alabama."

"What regiment is that on the other side?"

"Fifth Georgia," replied the sentinel. "What battery is that?"

Here was a situation. The sergeant naturally didn't know the name of a battery in the rebel army. Hesitation would have been fatal. By a lucky inspiration he replied, "One of

Stuart's batteries," knowing that Jeb Stuart commanded their cavalry.

"Oh," said the other, "then you's a hoss battery!"

"Yes," said C——. "Good night."

He immediately awoke the Captain, who rather angrily said, "What the deuce is the matter now?"

"Excuse me, Captain," said the sergeant, "but we're camped between a Georgia and an Alabama regiment."

It is needless to say the Captain got up. Horses were hitched in quietly, and the battery withdrew from between the sleeping regiments, who never knew of the prize that was within their grasp.

Next morning brought us to Malvern Hill, and daylight brought order out of the confused mass. My friend, the Brigadier, had arrived, and sent an aid to order me to report. But as I had been ordered to report to him for a specific purpose, and that purpose had been completed, I refused to comply, and spent the greater part of the day looking for my battery. I heard it had been captured, and I asked Captain De Russy (Battery K, Fourth Artillery) to let me join his battery, as we had no food, forage, or ammunition. This was Monday morning, and I had not eaten a mouthful since Saturday afternoon. Late in the day, I found the battery down under Malvern Hill, on a little meadow. The first sight that greeted my eyes was half a dozen drovers, armed with sabres, pursuing a squealing porker; for, while the battle was raging on the hill, they were killing pigs and sheep that had been unanimously declared contraband of war.

Edward Field.

WHICH IS BEST?

Up to the stars yon mountain seems to rise,
And two are hastening toward its distant blue;
One ever keeps the far-off peak in view,
With silent resolution in his eyes.
The other longs to reach the mountain, too,
But oh, the sunshine is so warm and sweet,
The birds sing o'er his head, and at his feet
The blossoms smile through tender tears of dew.
At last they part, and when the day is done,
Upon the barren mountain, rough and steep,
One rests; and in the sun-warmed valley one;
And both lie down that night in peaceful sleep.
Choose, heart! Two paths there are—one toil, one rest,
And they are Love and Fame—but which is best?

Seddie E. Anderson.

"LIZ."

It was midsummer time in the heart of the Sierra. All the air was full of quivering heat, which fell upon the mountain side, withering the petals of the wild flowers, and forcing the ferns to bend their heads and drink from the clear streams that trickled down the slopes. The birds, overcome with the heat, were too indolent to sing; and only occasionally could one see the bright wing of the blue-bird or the red breast of the robin as it darted through the air, half eagerly, to snap at a fly asleep in the purple-and-white ceanothus thicket. The miners put down their picks and shovels to wipe the perspiration from their brows, then lay down to doze underneath the pine shade, for it was too hot for work. They looked longingly up at Sugar-loaf, whose summit, almost touching the clouds, seemed so inviting and cool. It stood, like a rock, boldly out in relief from the undulating sea of foothills covered with dry grass, and the sight was as tantalizing as the mirage of the desert to a worn traveler. The dust in the roads was yellow and thick; and when the stage made its daily entrances and exits into and from Nevada City, their leaders were obscured in a fine, penetrating mist of dust. It covered their flanks, until they looked as if they were emulating the poetical bee, who "powders his wings with gold." It settled over the passengers, until the most renowned physiognomist could not well have discerned a line of distinctive character in their dirt-grimed faces. Nevada lies in a gorge in the mountain, a town born of the mines, and of mushroom growth. All the heat was concentrated in that spot, and poured down in full vigor upon the rude cabins, scorching the leaves of a few preciously guarded rose-bushes in the gardens, even exhausting the energy of the hardy pioneers, who were content to sit indoors idly, while the chickens drooped about the yard and the ducks reveled in the waters of the ravine, which were very low and muddy, for the sun had drained it almost dry, and only a shallow stream flowed over the yellow clay.

While the men dozed, a young girl worked steadily, panning out dirt in the upper part of the stream, with her head bare, in the scorching sunlight. She was tall, and as brown as a berry. Her eyes were dark and expressive, and her rich auburn hair fell down her shoulders in unkempt profusion. Her shoulders were broad, but her face was young—the face of a child who had lived more in the years of her existence than was well for her. She looked as Joan d'Arc might have looked when she knitted in the cottage at Lorraine, while France lay bleeding, and the nameless ambition was stirring in her breast. Her feet were encased in an old pair of men's shoes. There was something pitiful about the expression of those shoes, supporting her slender, bare, brown ankles, which looked too slight to bear such a weight. They were aristocratic appearing shoes, but their original color was lost, for they were torn, patched, run down at the heel, the soles ragged; still, they possessed an air of gentility, as if they had seen better days. They turned up at the toes, as if they shrunk in disdain from their surroundings. They rolled over at the ankle, as if they shuddered at contact with bare flesh, and had been accustomed to silken hose. The tracery of arabesque patterns on their instep stood out clearly, and reminded one of Mrs. Skewton's frippery and artificial roses, after the decay of youth.

Liz did not mind the shoes, as she worked, only they were so large they impeded her progress, and gave her a sort of shuffling gait. She loosened the handkerchief around her throat, twisted her mass of hair carelessly on top of her head, tucked her ragged calico dress further up from the water, and shook her rusty pan to and fro, her eyes bent eagerly in their search for particles of gold, only occasionally glancing from her work at a figure sleeping under a tree near by and filling the air with a chorus of snores that reverberated through the mountains like distant growlings of thunder. His face, which was redder than the sun-burn, was shaded by an old crownless hat; his eyes were weak and sunken, his hair wiry and red, his clothes ragged and dirty; but he was a man of fine physique, marred only by a slight stoop of the shoulders.

"Well, Liz, what luck to-day? I see the old dad is quietly snoozing. It is a burning shame you are working out in this sun. It is hotter than Hades."

She blushed, as the speaker came in view from behind a clump of manzanita bushes, but answered:

"I'm sort of used to it. I can't get much blacker—and poor Dad's head ain't just right, you know, Dick."

Dick whistled significantly, but his countenance did not express much sympathy for the aforesaid head, for he thought, rightly, whisky and laziness were the things that were not "just right."

Dick Beech was one of the numerous crowd of young men who had drifted along with the tide in the early days, landed in California, and patiently sat down, waiting for Fortune to come to him, instead of troubling himself to search for her. He counted on stumbling on a big thing some day, so despised the humble panning for gold-dust, but somehow or other he always managed to obtain a share of the world's goods. He was looked up to as an oracle of learning by the simple miners; had befriended "Drunken Harry," as Liz's father was dubbed by his associates, and so had earned her eternal gratitude. She was not accustomed to being noticed, and did not court it, for the few women in town held up their skirts in pharisaical dismay when she passed near them. The daughter of a drunkard, a girl who could shoot a deer, ride a *bronco* like a man, and work in the diggings, was "a thing never dreamed of in their philosophy."

Liz was a waif. Motherless and alone, she had flourished like a weed in rich soil, and had grown into a tall, handsome maiden, defiant of the laws of society, "free as the mountain winds," a true child of the Sierra. The mountains were her idol, her sole companions, and she worshipped her dissolute father. His faults were only forces of circumstance to her, and she lived looking forward to a future when everything would be right. She had been taught a little by an old man named Hugo, who lived a hermit's life in a lone cabin, so she was not entirely ignorant; but Dick Beech was a revelation in her life. He belonged to a class she saw only in her dreams, and while she often treated him scornfully, as she did the rest, she reserved a higher place in her heart for him, because he had helped her father.

"I'm used to the heat," she said. "I like work, only there's nothing to pay for it to-day."

"Come, Liz. Your dad's asleep. Come sit in the shade. I want to talk to you."

She shook her head determinedly.

"I shall stay here all night, until I get something. When I make up my mind to do a thing I intend to do it, if it kills me."

"Dear, me! Heroism in calico. A new Judith—a coming Portia of the Sierra!"

"I am just Liz Byrnes. No fooling, Dick Beech," she said, stopping her work, her dark eyes sparkling, as if he had intended an insult.

"Well," he laughed, "don't show fight. It's honorable company I placed you in."

Then he stretched himself out full length on the dry grass, idly stirring the water with a stick, and regarding Liz curiously.

The sunshine brought out every tint clearly on the hillside—the blue-green of the pines, the purple-brown trunks, the gloss of the madroño leaves mingled with the emerald of the live-oak, and the mountains relieved dark against a sky of intense cloudless blue. The granite bowlders sparkled like monster diamonds in the strong sunlight, which beat down upon Liz's head, causing each hair to shine like a thread of gold. She would have well served for a model of the vestal Luccia as she raised the pan over her head to relieve her arms from their cramped, constant motion. Dick Beech lay there, listlessly watching, anathematizing her drowsy father, but never imagining that he might relieve her for a while.

"You will have a sunstroke," he said. "I insist upon you covering your head, or I shall borrow that inverted basket yonder Chinaman has on. Liz, do you know that you are very pretty?"

She opened her eyes wonderingly.

"You are as bad as the boys who call me names. I have never looked at myself."

"I wish I could paint you just as you are. Unfortunately, I have never learned how."

"These duds would be pretty things in a picture," she replied, touching them. "Why don't you go 'long and talk to Nancy Brown. I'm busy."

"Because you interest me, and she don't. I like you, Liz, just as I prefer a wild flower to a cultivated one. It's a matter of taste. I think we were intended for each other, and I love you, Liz."

She laughed, though her heart beat fast in happiness.

"I could work, and you be a gentleman. No, sir. I would like a man like old Hugo used to read of—a knight who would fight for me, go through everything for my sake, die, if need be—and kill bears," she said, merrily. "Dick, I heard about your hunt the other day. If I had had your chance, I would have shot him, instead of climbing a tree. I will love you on one condition: that you bring me a young grizzly for a pet."

"I don't care about sharing affections, and I am afraid the bear would be the strongest party. Liz," he said, suddenly, "one of Ham Jones's girls is going to be married to-night. Will you be there?"

It was intended as a Roland for her Oliver. She looked at him fiercely, her eyes snapping in anger.

"How dare you ask me? I am not good enough for them. Anyway, weddings are curious things. I see them dancing, kissing; in a year they fight like wildcats; then, two to one, they leave one another. It's like the game Dad plays, 'Heads or Tails.' I don't believe in weddings."

"But, Liz, suppose two people love one another?"

"Well, Dick, what is love?"

"That's a stunner. I don't know exactly. It's a kind of feeling when two people care for each other, and one can't live without the other. There was Abélard and Héloise, Romeo and Juliet."

Liz tossed her head scornfully.

"I can tell you it is always sorrow and trouble for one of them. I've seen too much of it. There was the baker's Lize. She was in love, and stepped around as if she was walking on eggs; but Tim married another woman, and, instead of eggs, the dust seems heavy mire, and now she is a poor, half-witted creature. That is what love does. Don't talk to me of that nonsense. Weddings and funerals are mighty like. Sometimes the first is a living death, the other a restful one."

A slight wind blew down from the summit of Sugarloaf, stirring the pines into motion, fanning the air, and creating a purer atmosphere. The evening shades were gathering, the color of the mountains changing to a golden purple in the setting sun.

Liz pulled down her sleeves, called to the figure underneath the tree, which grunted in reply, and, grasping a black bottle, started to its feet

The rags, unfolded, developed themselves into a resemblance to clothes, and a man rose, blinking in the light, with bloodshot eyes, and waited until Liz shouldered the pick, shovel, and pan; then lazily joined her. She whispered to Dick:

"Go. Dad can't 'bide you. He gets in such tempers sometimes he might hurt you."

So Dick obediently slipped back through the thicket from which he had come.

"Got anything to-day, Lazybones?" he growlingly asked.

"Not much, Dad," Liz answered, gently; for her voice always changed when she spoke to him, because she thought he was infirm, and she willfully closed her eyes on his imperfections. They walked together up the lonely path to their board shanty, which stood across the ravine opposite the town, in a grove of madroño trees; and no miner ever possessed such a rickety, desolate old cabin as "Drunken Harry," and, like its owner, it looked as if it was intoxicated and on its last legs. The planks were nailed on the frame unevenly, at a tipsy looking angle; the nails were half out, as if bound for a spree, and the shingle roof was patched in uneven heaps with cloth, boughs of trees, odd bits of lumber, and pieces of tin, until it appeared as if it were suffering from a mild form of delirium tremens. Handsome Liz looked as much out of her sphere in this hovel as a queen in a stable-yard, or a yellow primrose growing out of the barren rock-cliffs by the sea.

"Dad," she said, leading him in, "don't take any more of your *medicine* to-night—it makes you so cross."

"Shut up, girl; 'tend to your pertatoes. This is the stuff puts life into a fellow. When I feels sick or down sperited I jest takes a sip from this bottle," patting it affectionately; "then I feels straight, and says to myself, 'Harry, you're a gentleman.'"

Liz went into the house while he continued talking to himself in a maudlin way. She suspected the quality of the medicine, but would not say anything, because he was her father, and was the only person in the world near to her, the only one who had ever spoken kindly to her during the lonesome eighteen years she had lived in the world. The women in the town were unkind to her, and avoided her as they would a crotalus on the mountain rocks, so she lived a strange life, alone with nature and a drunken father. She had learned the lesson of silence, and however hard she worked, how heavy soever her burdens, she never complained.

"Dad, supper is ready," she called.

"Ugh," he growled; "a few ashy pertatoes."

"There's a bit of meat for you."

"That's well. Your pore dad's sick, Liz; you wouldn't take it from him, would you?"

"No," she replied, pushing the morsel toward him.

"I'm going down town; mind you keep close to the shanty. Got any dust 'bout you?"

She took the little she had found from her pocket, and looked at him beseechingly, laying her hand on his arm.

"Do you think, Dad," she said, looking up into his face, "that you need more *medicine*," slightly emphasizing the word. "This is all I have for bread, and we have no more in the house."

He pushed her roughly from him, and whined:

"You'd let your pore old dad die, and you'd never keer."

She handed him the pieces silently, and went out of the room, while he slunk down the trail quickly, toward the town, for his throat was dry and parched, burning for liquor to moisten and relieve it.

Tears gathered in her eyes as she watched his shambling figure disappear down the slope, but she brushed them away impatiently, and returned to the house to straighten up a bit, which did not take her long, for Liz had not been taught that great principle "which is akin to godliness."

She went out and sat down on a stump of a pine tree which stood near the door. The air was sweet and balmy, redolent with pine fragrance and odor of plumy buckeye blossoms. The feverish heat was gone. Nature's pulse beat faster, and a pleasing cool reigned over valley and mountain. Venus peeped over the tops of the pines, and peered down upon the girl sitting all alone in the forest. The new moon, bent like Diana's bow, shone in the skies, while all around clustered myriads of bright stars, like golden-winged bees round a wondrous tropical bloom. The lights twinkled down in the town like glow-worms' lanterns, and the breeze wafted up to the hights faint echoes of laughter and merry life. Liz gazed at the stars, and wondered "if beings who lived up there ever were poor and lonely as she was." Hugo had told her "they were other worlds," and she conjured up many fantastic fancies in her mind in regard to their inhabitants. "They were so bright, people must be happy there," she sighed. "There is so much misery here, I know the world can not shine like that."

Poor child, she had not learned that the deepest sorrow is oft concealed 'neath the most dazzling light.

She looked down at the town, and rebellious thoughts stirred in her breast as she thought of Dick Beech and his pretty speeches. Putting a shawl over her head, she concluded that she would go down and see the wedding, where she could see him also. She walked down the hill, crossed the narrow flume that spanned the ravine, and went to the house where the merry-making was. It was a regular miner's wedding. The fiddler was sitting on a chair, placed on an old dry-goods box, busily spinning off reels, Tom Tuckers, various medleys, and calling out, "Alaman right, alaman left." Some miners, who had slept in the day-time, were dancing in their very best style, cutting innumerable pigeon-wings, as they swung their partners. The windows were open, and Liz crowded close to the wall, watching Dick Beech eagerly, as he danced gracefully with the rural belles. Her eyes burned with jealousy as she watched him look at Nancy Brown with the same tenderness he had bestowed on her in the afternoon, and she felt as if she could gladly plunge a knife into Nancy's heart. "Indian blood flowed in Liz's veins," they said, and surely she possessed a haughty, deep, passionate nature that might well have descended to her from an Indian princess. She watched them as they played games and drank wine. The noise grew louder, the men more hilarious, and when the fiddler called out, "Salute your partners," they availed themselves of a liberal interpretation, and imprinted a rousing kiss on each buxom maid's lips. She did not know how long she watched, but the company showed signs of dispersing; so she stole away home. When she reached the bottom of the hill she noticed a light burning in the cabin, and her heart almost stood still, for she knew her father's moods were not pleasant after he had been indulging too freely in "medicine." As she came near she saw him walking back and forth, looking very savage, but Liz did not know what terror was; so she went boldly in.

"Where hev you bin this time o' night?" he growled, showing his teeth like a wild animal. "A pretty time fur an honest gal to be prowlin' round the country.".

He came near to her, raising his arm as if he would strike her, but she looked him steadily and defiantly in the eyes. "It's no matter; I am used to looking out for myself."

"A fine care you'd take. They are talkin' 'bout you an' that curly-headed, smooth-tongued chap down town; and I tell you, Liz Byrnes, ef I ketch him round here, I'll crack his head quicker than you ken say 'Jack Robinson.'"

She did not answer, only bit her lips to keep down the angry words.

"You defy me, do you. I'll show you."

Then, in a sudden fit of rage, he picked up a gnarled manzanita stick and struck her. Its aim was sure. It hit her on the shoulder, and the blood oozed through her thin calico gown. He looked at her as if half afraid. She started to speak. Her face turned deadly pale, while the red blood, slowly dropping, stained her dress. A look of hatred flashed in her eyes; then she turned away silently, wiped off the blood, while he went into the next room, as if afraid to meet her gaze. It was the first time he had struck her. He had cursed her, but the sound was familiar to her ears. And that one cut entered into her soul, and she felt she could never forgive him.

The next morning she went to her work as usual, but he sneaked off down town before she was up. The July sun had gathered a renewed force, but she worked sullenly on, only stopping once in a while to pour some water on her throbbing head. The heat was so intense a steam arose from her damp hair. She worked savagely, trying to stifle the bitter feelings in her heart, which hurt far more than the burning pain in her shoulder.

"Harry's Liz has struck a good streak to-day," the miners said, as she found an unusual quantity of dust, but she never heeded nor answered them.

Dick Beech sauntered down about the usual time in the afternoon.

"How does it go, Liz?"

She vouchsafed him no answer.

"Liz, what's the matter? Sulks to-day?"

Still no answer. She kept on steadily working.

"Don't be so hard on a fellow. It's so confoundedly hot, I wanted sight of you to refresh me."

She lifted her eyes for the first time, and looked at him with a peculiar searching expression, and answered:

"I should think you could find refreshment nearer home. Nancy Brown is good enough for some folks to look at."

"O jealousy, thy name is woman!" he laughed. "Why, Liz, your little finger is worth her whole body. But you know," he continued, stroking his mustache, "a fellow has got to have some fun. He can't sit in a corner. Some day, when I get rich, it will be different. What makes you look so fierce. I believe you would be equal to the Moor of Venice, if I loved any one else, and smother me like he did poor Desdemona."

"I could smother you, or kill you, Dick Beech, if you were false to me. I suppose I'm not good enough for the likes of you, but none of them will love you any better, Dick," and her expression grew tenderer as she said the words.

"I wish you didn't have such an awful temper."

And, privately, Mr. Richard Beech did think he was too good for poor Liz Byrnes.

They were attracted toward each other by the law of opposition. She was handsome and strong. He was polished and weak, and an ardent admirer of the beautiful, and kind to her; so she placed him in a niche of her heart, with her father, like the priests do the images of the saints in the cathedral, giving them each a shrine above the world below.

"What is that stain on your dress? It looks like blood. Has anybody hurt you?"

"No," she answered, looking away from him. "I only fell down on a stone and cut myself."

She despised a falsehood, but was too loyal to expose her old father, even to the man she loved.

"Liz, if it were not for your father, we would be married."

"Yes?" she said, drearily.

"But I could never stand him."

"The knights Hugo read of stood everything for the lady they loved. They killed giants, overcame dragons. They were strong to stand everything, and, Dick, they would have waited patiently, with brave hearts. Poor old Dad would not trouble you. I am proud of him. You don't know him as I do."

"In this nineteenth century, Liz, knights are not as plenty as blackberries. The Round Table is a romance, after all. Their wonderful Sir Launcelot and Galahad were not so fine, for they were human."

"But," she said, earnestly, the color creeping into her cheeks like the rosy alpen glow over summits of the mountains in the eventide, "people don't need to fight battles with their hands, old Hugo says. The beasts are in the heart we must conquer. Sometimes I feel as if a lion were caged in mine, and it's hard work to keep him quiet."

Then, as if half confused at her confession, she worked on.

"Life is long enough without so much trouble. I will see you again. I must go, for I have an engagement."

Liz nodded "Good bye" cheerfully, and her heart felt lighter as she went home in the evening. The cabin was deserted, no signs of her father anywhere, but she lighted a fire, and tried to cook an inviting meal. She waited for an hour; still he did not come, and, being tired from her work, she laid down on her cot, and fell fast asleep.

When she awoke it was dark, and the moon was shining in her face. She looked out of the door, down the long aisles of pines, but he was not there. The night was misty, so she thought she would walk down to the flume, where he usually crossed, and wait for him there. She sat there for hours, it seemed, until at last she saw his familiar form approaching. He was staggering more than usual. His gait was very unsteady. Liz rose, and called to him:

"Don't cross. Go up to the bridge."

But he answered her with an oath, and stepped on to the narrow inclosed flume, which was just the width of a plank. Liz started to go to him, but he waved his hands wildly, commanding her to "Go back."

Through fear for his safety, she obeyed. Her heart beat fast as she watched, with strained eyes, through the darkness, and saw his form swaying from one side to the other. The moon had gone down, and it was quite dark. She saw him stumble, and regain his balance. He reached the middle. She breathed more freely. He stopped, and commenced gesticulating. Throwing his arms up, he missed his balance, and fell; and Liz heard a sickening sound as he struck the rocks below. He groaned once, and all was perfect silence—a terrible quiet. She stood on the bank alone, as one petrified. She tried to move. Her limbs seemed bound with icy chains. At last she screamed, and scrambled down the steep declivity as rapidly as possible. Her cries reached the ears of a passing miner, and he hastened to the spot, and peered down into the darkness with his lantern. Liz was sitting there, helplessly holding her father's head on her lap, and beseeching him to speak. The man went to her, and felt old Harry's pulse.

"It's all up with him. Wait till I git some help. How did you find him?"

"Lying with his face in the water. But he is not dead. It was so shallow, and he has only one cut on his head. He is not dead, not dead," she cried, wildly.

The miner shook his head, and said, roughly, but kindly:

"I've seen 'em drown in an inch, when the jim-jams was on 'em, and it's as good to die by water as whisky."

Liz wrung her hands, but she could not cry, and her eyes burned like fire. The miner obtained assistance, and they bore the lifeless body to the cabin, and proffered their rude help, but she preferred to be left alone. There was no woman's hand to soothe or comfort; not one came near to whisper words of consolation to relieve her aching heart. She hoped Dick would come to her, but she was left entirely alone with her dead, and when the men came to bury him, they said:

"She was so white, it was hard to tell which was the corpse."

She grieved for him passionately, mourned because she could not tell him she forgave. Her pan lay idle in the corner; money was so little to her that she had no incentive to work; still, unless she roused herself she must starve. So she started out one afternoon more with the secret hope of seeing Dick than with any other object. She looked white and worn, a mere shadow of herself, walking in the sunlight, like some poor, lost soul, out of place in the world. She sat down on the bank, but a familiar whistle startled her, which brought the color into her cheeks.

"Hallo, Liz," he exclaimed; "so you have crawled out of your shell at last." His face had an uneasy expression. "I thought I wouldn't disturb you," he said, half apologetically. "I could not do any good, and I hate funerals, and such reminders. Now, Liz, what are you going to do?"

She looked at him earnestly, but he turned away, on pretense of plucking a cluster of manzanita berries that hung above his head.

"I—well—" he said, stammering; "the fact is, I'm too poor, Liz. We must wait for a while still."

A disappointed expression stole across her face for a moment; then she replied simply:

"I can wait, Dick."

O woman! thy faith is infinite, thy heart long enduring, long suffering; when love enters it is blind, and sees not fault or defect in the loved one—only content to be happy, even in waiting. Liz took up her work, and said to herself:

"I shall work for Dick; now I will have another object."

August, with its heat, passed by, and the few orchards were laden with ripe, red-cheeked peaches and golden pears, a fortune to their possessors in the early days of California, when peaches and pears sold for a dollar apiece. Gold was more plentiful than fruit. September breezes were cooler, and the young quail filled the *cañons* with the whir of their wings, and the dog-wood fruit clustered ripe and red as berries of coral, and the dry grass waved long and yellow in the sunlight.

One morning Liz went down town to obtain some supplies, for Dick had sent her some money as a present by a boy that day. She saw knots of men gathered in the street, discussing something very excitedly. She went into a store and asked:

"What is the matter?"

"They jest took Dick Beech up to the calaboose for stealin' Long Tom's pile last night, who lives above you, and they are going to try him right off. Better go down to the court-house. He is a triflin' sort of chap anyhow."

Liz put down her purchase, took up the money, and walked out. She saw a miner she knew.

"Is this true I have heard?" she asked.

"Bet yer, it is. There's bin lots of thievin' done here lately. I hope they'll string him up."

She turned away and followed the stream of men, women, and children who were running toward the large, wooden court-house. A crowd was already gathered there, the Judge seated on a platform, the prisoner on one side, the two attorneys on the other—miners who possessed a smattering of law, law suited to their prejudices, who were acting for the prosecution and defense. The Court preserved a semblance of order. The jury was impaneled, the men constituting it of course were miners, and their threatening looks toward the prisoner at the bar did not tend to reassure him. Liz stood in the back of the room, white as marble, listening breathlessly. Dick sat with his head bowed, trembling like a man with the ague. The prosecuting witness was called.

Long Tom shuffled up, attired in his Sunday best, a suit of butternut, which his hair and eyes matched exactly, proclaiming his descent, unmistakably, "from Pike County, Missoury." He appeared as uneasy as a young barrister wrestling with his maiden speech.

"Waal," he began, "I jest handed over the dishes and truck, fur Topsy, my dawg, to lick, when I thought uf somethin' I wanted down town, so I left my pile in an ole sack under the bed, some lumps and pieces of silver, 'bout a handful, I reckon. I was gone jest 'bout an hour. When I come in the bag was in the middle of the floor. I tuk it up and shook it. It was empty as Job's turkey, and I'd seen Dick Beech skulkin' 'round thar a while before, and no one else was near. I'd know that silver this side uf Halifax, cause I cut an X, my mark, on the four-bit piece."

Liz started, and looked at the money in her hand. There was the mark, ill cut and jagged, but plain as day. She closed her fingers tightly over the pieces, and a faintness came over her. She staggered, caught hold of a bench near, for now she knew Dick Beech was a guilty man, a criminal, and—she loved him.

Long Tom descended from the stand with a well satisfied air. The attorney for the defense spoke a few moments, evidently as a matter of form, for his arguments were weak and lame, showing his spirit was not in his work. The jury returned, and rendered their verdict of guilty. The Judge said:

"Prisoner at the bar, the court has found, when a man is guilty of the crime of theft, he should be hanged by the neck until he is dead."

Being prompted by a man standing near, he hurriedly added, "May God have mercy on your soul." This was a first case, and the honorable Judge was not quite posted.

"Do you know any reason why the law should not take its course?"

A hush fell upon the crowded room, and they looked intently at the prisoner, who never lifted his head. The flies buzzing in the sunshine on the window-pane were the only sounds that broke the intense silence. The expression on the faces of the people was as eager as that of the spectators in old gladiatorial conflicts, for the animal was rising in their natures, and they thirsted for blood. The Judge repeated his question. Dick lifted his head, looking haggard and appealingly toward the crowd, as if seeking sympathy, but there was none for the guilty in all those upturned faces. Before he could reply, Liz pushed her way through the crowd, and stood before the Judge, who regarded her sternly. Two bright spots burned on her cheeks. She looked straight at Dick when she spoke, and the people listened breathlessly.

"If it please your honor, I am guilty," she said, proudly, looking steadfastly at Dick. A gleam of joy and relief passed over his countenance. The color died from her face; a weary look came into her eyes.

"Does the man recognize this?" she said, holding out a few dollars in her hand.

Tom came forth. "Yes," he said, joyfully; "that's my mark. I could swear to it."

Dick covered his face with his hand, and would not look at her, but her eyes never left him, looking at him as if she could read right through his cowardly soul.

"I am willing to die, Judge; only let it be soon. You shall have the rest. Only let me speak once to this innocent gentleman."

Groans of derision burst from the crowd. A boy threw a stone, which struck her, but she stood there as if she had been a carved statue, and did not utter a word.

"Bad blood," "Bad stock coming out," she heard them say, and there was not one voice in all the town lifted in pity or sympathy for her.

"What you've got to say, say quickly," commanded the Judge.

She went to Dick, and whispered to him. He tried to kiss her hand, but she snatched it quickly away, rubbing it as if his touch contaminated it.

"You will find everything in my cabin to-night," she said, quietly, to the Judge. "I have nothing more to say. I am guilty."

Dick Beech walked out of the room a free man. He was pitied and praised, while she was reviled by every tongue, and he did not even say a word in defense of her. As the officer was escorting her to jail, they passed by a door of a saloon where he was in the act of drinking. The glass was raised to his lips. She merely glanced at him, but there was a world of love, misery, disappointment, and reproach in that single look. He let the glass fall. It shivered in a thousand atoms, the brandy stained the floor, and he went home to his room. Far sweeter and calmer was her rest, on the straw in a prison-cell that night, than his.

They mitigated the sentence, because she was a woman, but many long years Liz Byrnes expiated Dick's crime in the Nevada jail. He left the town. They said he prospered well in "Frisco," while she worked hard, endured patiently, for his sake. Surely, no human love could be greater than this, for she bore disgrace, was willing to suffer death, while he lived honored in the world. She was so young, it was pitiful. After her term was served, she went back again to the old cabin on the hill, an outcast, an object of scorn, to all the people; a martyr, a saint, in the eyes of the angels above.

She waited for him, hoping that he would come back to her some day, and she would forgive.

It was winter time, and the rain descended from the heavens in solid sheets. The winds swept around the mountain peaks like mighty monsters, seeking to wrest them from their foundations. The pines mingled their voices, and chanted a solemn requiem, while a torrent roared down the ravine in mad frenzy, dashing over rocks and leaping over bowlders.

Liz sat, with hands folded, watching the storm; but she was not afraid, though the wind threatened to blow down the crazy old shanty at every gust. Through the storm some one was beating his way to her door, and, as a fiercer blast blew it open, it drove a man, with dripping clothing, into the light.

"Tom," she asked, gently, "what do you want here?"

"Liz," he said, hesitatingly, "won't you shake hands with me? I knows all. Dick Beech is dyin' down at the tavern. He's told us," he said, wiping a suspicious moisture from his eyes. "You're an angel, Liz, which wimmen folks ain't often; but if ever there was one on airth, you're thet one, Liz Byrnes. He wants to see you 'fore he pegs out, the scoundrel."

"Is Dick Beech there?" she asked, excitedly.

"Yes. He came back a day or two ago. I never seed sich a change, and he desarves it."

"You shall not say anything about him," Liz retorted, angrily.

"They said he was doin' well," Tom said, "but it seems now he wasn't. It was well in drink, I 'spect. He got shot in a row at Black's saloon to-night, and he keeps callin' fur you."

She hastily threw an old shawl around her shoulders, and followed Tom. The rain and wind beat in their faces, but they kept steadily on, Tom holding a lantern before them, which illuminated the wet and slippery trail. At last they reached the saloon. It had seemed hours to Liz, who threw off her dripping wrappings, and went into the room where he lay dying slowly. Men were laughing, betting, drinking in the next room, for a human life was of little consequence to them.

"Liz," he said, feebly, raising up as she entered, "I knew you would come to me. Don't look at me so. It was that look that maddened me. It has haunted me so," he moaned, falling back on his pillow. "Only say you will forgive me. I have told them all. I would scarcely have known you, you are so changed. May I kiss you once, Liz, for I love you?" he said, looking at her wistfully.

She clasped his hands in hers, while a light, bright as a halo round the head of a saint, shone in her face.

"Yes, Dick, I forgive freely, freely, if you will only live! I don't care for those years, for my life was not meant to be like other women's."

The wind swept around the house like the wail of a lost spirit, and Dick held her hand in his, and smiled peacefully, for he was too feeble to talk any more. As morning neared, the storm died slowly away, the embers faded into ashes in the fire-place, and Dick's life ebbed quietly away. His soul was summoned before a Higher Tribunal. Liz sat there, motionless, by his side, through the long day, praying in her heart for death to be merciful unto her.

The Judge shook hands with her; the people crowded around, bringing offerings. They tried to make amends for their wrong to her, but she only said, wearily:

"It is too late now. It is all the same to me. When you could have been merciful you turned away. Now it is all over. Justice can never make amends for my suffering."

And then she said, softly, to herself:

"It was for his sake."

MARY W. GLASCOCK.

A SCRAP OF FRONTIER HISTORY.

It is probable that there is not on this continent a country possessing greater natural resources than the State of Sonora, Mexico. It has been celebrated for its wonderful mineral wealth from time immemorial, and the highest authorities are united in crediting it with agricultural and pastoral capabilities surpassing, perhaps, even those of California. Its native inhabitants are universally admitted to be brave, hospitable, and light hearted; overflowing with natural talent, fond of music, dancing, and the gentle and refining pleasures of social intercourse. But what a sad fate has fallen upon a country and people originally destined, apparently, to inherit a more than ordinary share of wordly prosperity: for it must not be forgotten that, in addition to the curse of revolution, which has blighted to such a terrible extent the whole of Mexico, and which even now threatens its utter disintegration and ruin, Sonora has suffered from an infinity of local disorders and accidents, from the many perils incident to a border State, from the raids of filibusters, the bitter quarrels and feuds of her own principal citizens, the antagonism of races, the insubordination of her industrious, but capricious, Indian population; and last, but by no means least, from the terrible, bloodthirsty, warlike, insatiable Apaches. Terrible, indeed, has been the desolation wrought by these inhuman fiends, the implacable foes of all peaceful industry, and the arts of civilization; and almost equally cruel and inhuman, it is sad to say, have been the reprisals which at occasional intervals have been meted out to them by an outraged and exasperated community. Before reading the terrible story which follows, it is necessary to picture to oneself the depopulated villages, the ruined *haciendas*, the deserted mines, the desolation and misery created by this dreaded tribe, and to remember that the war of civilized races against the Indians is a war of industry and intelligence against a nomadic people who have proved themselves, with a few rare exceptions, incapable of being elevated above a condition of barbarism; who require and demand not acres, or hundreds of acres, but countless thousands, to sustain each tribe; that the most enlightened and humane policy has hitherto wholly failed to convert them to the arts of peace; that the civilization of the entire continent is as desirable as it is inevitable; and that the passions of the savage nature which run riot in the contest awake, inevitably, the almost equally savage passions of the pioneers and frontiersmen, whose destiny it is to conquer or be conquered by them.

The town of Oposura is one of the oldest and most interesting in the State of Sonora. It is situated about forty-five miles to the west of Babiacora. In 1827, Babiacora was a town containing some three thousand inhabitants, three-fourths of the population consisting of Indians of the Opata tribe. It is situated on a table-land, about one mile from the river Sonora, which runs through the vale of Sonora, at that time one of the most fertile and beautiful districts of the State. Oposura, the ancient capital of the Opata Indians, contained, in 1827, upward of four thousand inhabitants, and was considered the prettiest and gayest town in that portion of the country. The river Oposura falls into the Yaqui River above Onabas. At that time the lands for a considerable distance below the town were divided among the inhabitants; the water from the river was carried through each lot by canals, so that vegetables, fruits, etc., were produced throughout the entire year. Each family grew corn, wheat, *frijoles*, sugar, and tropical fruits. Most of them had horses, mules, and an abundance of cattle feeding in the adjacent plains and mountains. Sixteen leagues to the north of Oposura is situated the mining district of Nacosari, to the east of which is Arispe, which, at the period of Colonel Bourne's visit, was a town of three thousand inhabitants. Adjacent to Nacosari there was at that time a beautiful vale, abounding with fig trees, pomegranates, peaches, and other fruits, together with a vast variety of ornamental plants and shrubs. Throughout this region, also, ran numerous canals, conveying water to every portion of the valley. This delightful spot was once the residence of a community of Jesuits. Ward, in his "History of Mexico," speaks of the ruins of a church and dwellings then existing at the upper end of the valley, and also the ruins of reduction works, even then so dilapidated that it was impossible to judge of their former extent, as "they had been abandoned upward of sixty years, and were entirely destroyed by the Apaches." And throughout the entire region of Oposura, Babiacora, and Arispe, as also far and wide in every direction, are still to be found the remains of once prosperous and productive mines, *haciendas*, and industries destroyed by the same ruthless hands. Many of these places, once so prosperous, are now mere deserts; and the entire country has been so repeatedly stripped and desolated that it is difficult to credit that it was once a garden spot of almost unequaled beauty.

In the year 1835, John Johnson, a native of Kentucky, resident in Missouri, then a very young man, resolved to move into Mexico. He finally settled in Oposura, and married there, shortly after his arrival, Delfina Gutierrez, a Mexican lady, born in San Miguel, north-eastern Sonora, but educated in Oposura. At this time the Apaches were ravaging constantly the north-eastern part of the State, the western portion being protected by Papagos, a tribe of friendly Indians, much feared by the Apaches. The head chief of the Apaches at that time was Juan José. He had been "raised" by the Elias family in Arispe, while it was still the capital of Sonora, and had received a fair education. It was one of his favorite practices to capture the mail-bags, more particularly, it is supposed, with a view to placing himself in possession of the information which they contained, of which he was not slow to avail himself. The next most influential chiefs were Marcelo and "Apache Guero." *Guero* signifies red, and is commonly applied to those persons in Mexico possessing fair complexions. Strange to say, such are by no means rare, for there is a *guero* in nearly every village or settlement throughout Mexico.

Juan José was a very sagacious, cunning warrior, as, indeed, many of the Apache warriors proved to be, to the sorrow of their enemies; but none among them had ever been so dreaded, so unscrupulous, so ruthless and terrible, as Juan José and his following.

It was at this time that the Apaches began to obtain their first fire-arms from the American hunters and trappers in exchange for horses and mules driven across the border from Sonora. Great was the indignation, and many were the protests of the settlers, but still the iniquitous trade continued until it became apparent that the Indians, who made war a profession, and who had vowed the extermination of their enemies, would soon be better armed than the *rancheros* and miners, or the residents of the towns and villages, who trusted principally to the military for protection against their savage foes. It is easy to imagine the uneasiness with which Johnson viewed this trade in fire-arms. It was his custom to make the journey to New Mexico and back once a year, engaged in the legitimate pursuit of a trader, taking out stock, and returning with assorted merchandise, such as found a ready sale in Oposura and the vicinity. A well armed party of the savages might, at any moment, ambush and cut him off during one of these expeditions, although this danger was little considered in comparison with the dread of Apache raids during his absence; for it was nothing uncommon for the savages, emboldened by the possession of fire-arms, to attack even the larger towns during the absence of the troops. Indeed, it was a favorite plan of theirs to entice them into the fastnesses of the mountains, and then to sweep down upon the undefended settlements, during which raids no mercy was ever shown to age, sex, or condition.

Johnson conceived and matured a plan for breaking up this dangerous trade, and at the same time striking a deadly blow against the Apaches. With characteristic reserve, decision, and originality, he determined to make use of the very hunters and trappers, known to have been engaged in the trade, against them, and he did not have to wait very long before finding an opportunity to carry his plans into execution. The Apaches had ravaged Noria, about thirty miles north of Oposura, killing and scalping men, women, and children, and applying the torch to everything destructible by fire. Johnson, whose place was headquarters for many of the frontiersmen, had at the time on his premises, or in the immediate vicinity, seventeen American hunters and trappers; and availing himself of the indignation created by this raid, so near home, he immediately made preparations for his long contemplated expedition, concealing his plans, however, and all but the immediate particulars necessary to its success. After examining with care the arms and ammunition of the Americans, he prepared a small pack-train, loaded with supplies, a selection of suitable merchandise, and a small howitzer, which he carefully concealed amid one of the packs, and taking with him five of his bravest and most reliable *arrieros*, he placed himself at the head of the party, and started on his perilous expedition. He struck the trail of the retreating Indians about a week after their devastating raid upon La Noria, and followed them fearlessly toward the very heart of the Sierra Blanca of Arizona, the headquarters of that portion of the Apaches. At the Presidio Frontera, he called on Colonel Narbona, a well known Mexican officer in command, a renowned Indian fighter, who urgently advised Johnson to return and abandon his expedition, as the Indians were known to be in the Sierra, well armed and in great force. They had between fifteen hundred and two thousand warriors, he told Johnson, available within a day's notice, and they would infallibly destroy him and his little command. Finding Johnson resolute, the Colonel said that he would have accompanied him with a hundred men—there being about a hundred and fifty at the fort—but that he considered the expedition entirely too rash.

The distance from the Presidio Frontera to the Sierra Blanca is some forty leagues. The Johnson party approached the foot of the Sierra the third day after leaving the fort. It was in the afternoon, drawing toward evening. They had traveled purposely without concealment. They could see the Indians telegraphing by fires from point to point, and knew they were concentrating to meet them. Juan José himself, at the head of a large force of warriors, shortly surrounded the little party, and haughtily demanded their business in the Apache country, to which Johnson artfully replied that he had been constrained to leave Sonora with his Americans on account of the approaching difficulties between the United States and Mexico. The quarrel with Texas was at that time at its hight, and war was actually impending. The raids of Juan José upon the mail-bags had prepared him to receive and believe this information, and he readily fell into the trap so carefully prepared for him.

Johnson announced it as the intention of his party to proceed to the copper mines of New Mexico, distant about a week's journey from the Sierra Blanca, and, asking for guides, proposed to give a portion of his pack, consisting of *pinole*, *panocha*, trinkets, and such provisions as the Apaches most coveted, in return for a guide to the copper mines, and the friendly services of the tribe. To this tempting proposition, Juan José consented, and the following day was appointed for the distribution of the supplies, and a suitable place was selected where Juan José proposed to assemble his followers, together with all the principal chiefs in the vicinity. The dreaded Apache Guero was appointed to superintend the division of the effects.

The same evening Juan José partook of some supper with the friendly trappers, and forgetting, in an exceptionally social mood, the Indian's habitual caution, he expatiated upon the cunning and valor of his principal chiefs, and pointed out with great pride to Johnson and his companions the Apache Guero, the Apache Negro, Marcelo, and others, relating at the same time their principal deeds of strategy and prowess. Strangely enough, but very opportunely as it happened, Johnson found among the Apaches, as prisoner, a young Mexican girl, made captive during one of the Apache raids. She was about twelve years of age, bright and intelligent, and remembered well the catastrophe which had left her the sole surviving member of her family. Johnson took compassion on her, and at once purchased her from Juan José. Scarcely had she joined the camp of the brave frontiersmen when she repaid her deliverers by informing them of the plans laid by the Apaches for the destruction of the Johnson party, which she overheard. The Americans were to be permitted to make the distribution of their effects the following morning, as agreed upon, after which the promised guide would be furnished to lead them—not to the copper mines, but to ambush and destruction—on the following day. A party of three or four hundred Apaches, then hunting in a suitable locality, had already been advised by swift runners dispatched for that purpose.

The place selected for the distribution of the goods and trinkets was a pretty little valley in the foothills adjacent to the Sierra. Here there was an opening, surrounded by a grove of oak timber and clusters of underbrush. Some large flat stones formed natural tables upon which the trinkets, etc., were artfully displayed by the hunters. In one of the clumps of underbrush, concealed by the pack-saddles, blankets, etc., lay the howitzer, loaded with double charges of grape and canister, and carefully trained so as to sweep with deadly effect the little opening within which it was foreseen the Indians would be crowded during the distribution of the pack.

Totally unconscious and unsuspecting, or perhaps thinking of the ambush prepared for the little party of hunters on the morrow, and of the second and final distribution of their goods which would then take place, came the Apaches, prominent among them, Juan José himself, Apache Guero, Apache Negro, Marcelo, Tutige, and other noted warriors. The Kentuckians, disposed apparently accidently, had in reality each selected his position with the utmost care, every trusty rifle loaded with the greatest precision, the powder-horn, extra bullets, and ready greased patches at hand; for the odds against them were fearful, and the slightest miscarriage would inevitably cost every man his life. No accident, however, intervened to prevent the complete success of the scheme. The Indians soon became completely absorbed in the distribution of the effects. The artilleryman in his ambush silently uncovered the howitzer, and watched the movements of the Apaches until an accidental grouping offered him the opportunity of firing among them with the most deadly effect. How many fell at the first discharge is not known, but this, terrible as it must have been at such short range, was only the signal for the still deadlier fire of the Kentucky rifles. Each hunter had selected his Indian, every one a chief or noted warrior, in accordance with a plan previously agreed upon. Thus fell at the first fire Juan José himself, Apache Guero, Marcelo, Apache Negro, and every brave of note of the band. The surprise was too complete for them to think even of rallying. Not one of authority sufficient to command them during such an extremity remained. Their arms had been left aside, with a few exceptions, the small number of Americans having completely deceived them, so that they had forgotten temporarily their habitual distrust and jealous precautions. Thus it happened that, despite their numbers, the panic was so great that flight alone was thought of. Immediately after the first fire, but before they could get out of range, another deadly volley followed them. Fifty-four were thus slain in a few minutes, and many more must have been wounded by the grape and canister from the concealed howitzer.

It was several years before the Apaches rallied from this terrible blow. Had it been followed up with vigor by the Mexican Government, the Indians might have been reduced to the last extremity, and the country spared many of the terrible outrages which subsequently ensued. But no steps were taken on the part of the Government. The Mexican officers and soldiers were jealous that a mere handful of men should have put the utmost efforts of their command to shame. But Johnson's principal object, the prevention of the sale of fire-arms to the Indians by the hunters and trappers, was most effectually accomplished, for the time, at least, as the Apaches were very careful thereafter not to allow any of them to approach sufficiently near for the transaction of business of any kind; and for several years the north-eastern portion of Sonora enjoyed comparative immunity from the dreaded foe.

Aurora, the young captive girl, returned with the Johnson party to Oposura, where she married into the Ramirez family. She died at Opata in 1879.

The people of Sonora were grateful enough to Johnson and his party, whatever may have been the sentiments of the military or the Government. They celebrated the expedition in a sort of ballad, probably of Indian origin, which, though destitute of poetic merit, may, perhaps, prove of interest to the curious or the antiquary.

It may still occasionally be heard, chanted in a peculiar monotone, on that distant frontier:

Versos Compuestos en la Campaña que Hizo Don Juan Johnson á la Sierra de Las Animas.

En esa sierra mentada
De las Animas, pasó,
Donde se llegó ese dia
Que Juan José Falleció,
Y otros en su compañia.

Fué infiel en su nacimiento.
Tuvó la fé de cristiano
Ese Judio falso y Tirano:
Su muerte fué en un momento,
Se lo dió un Americano
¿Donde se le iria el talento?

Don Juan Johnson apareció
Sin saber de donde venia,
Cuando él menos acordó
Ya estaba en la Rancheria.

Y Juan José, incomodado
Le habla con este destino,
¿Que andas haciendo tu aqui,
Si, por aqui no es camino?

Don Juan Johnson le responde,
De esto no tengas cuidado,
Yo voy para nuestra tierra,
Ya, no nos quiere este estado.

Juan José ha trato convida
Con un debido placer—
¿Americanos, amigos,
Traen pólvora que vender?

Don Juan Johnson le responde,
Yo voy para mi destino:
Es muy poco la que traigo,
Y es largo nuestro camino.

Juan José como-traicion
Trata de buscarle abrigo—
Donde quieres ir tan lejos
Quedate a vivir conmigo.

Don Juan Johnson le responde.
Si la polvora te apura
Me daras una mula
Que trajiste de Oposura.

A Juan José gusto el trato,
Y luego se dejó caer
Pues, como no sea mas de eso
Pronto la mandó traer.

Don Juan Johnson por cabal
Dice á Juan José valiente—
Determine del costal
Manda socorrer su gente.

Juan Diego, ese tatolero,
Nunca ignoraba la espera
Pero le trozo el martillo
Aquella fuerte cadena.

• • • • • •

The Johnsons are still living and flourishing in Sonora, and the descendants have proved themselves not unworthy of their sire. Don Manuel Johnson was killed March, 1872, at Culiacan, in fighting against General Marquez, who has been heard of recently in Lower California and Sonora. Johnson was Pesqueira's Chief of Cavalry, and displayed the most reckless and desperate bravery throughout the campaign. Don Ricardo Johnson, with whom many Californians are well acquainted, is the present head of the family. HENRY S. BROOKS.

EDUCATION IN JAPAN.

It is somewhat discouraging to find that our children in the schools are acquiring misinformation regarding a country so interesting and so important as Japan. All our geographies and maps must be changed. They have all fallen into the error, as have all our writers, without exception, of calling the main island Niphon or Nippon. There is no island having such name. *Dai Nippon*, or *Dai Nihon* (Great Japan), is the name of the empire—the entire Japanese Archipelago. The official name of the largest island, which we have been taught to call Niphon, or Nippon, is *Hondo.* The islands *Liu Kiu*, belonging to Japan, are marked Loo Choo on our maps. Yeddo, the capital city, should be written *Yedo.* It means "door of the bay," from *ye*, bay, and *do*, door. Still, this name has not been used either officially or popularly in Japan since 1868. It is called *Tokio* (*to*, east; *kio*, capital). *Tokei* is the spelling and pronunciation of those who affect Chinese learning. The name of the second city is *Ozaka* (accent on the first syllable). The name of the old capital is *Kioto*, not Miako, *miako* being a common noun. Hokoladi should be written *Hakodadi*, and Yesso, or Jesso, should be written *Yezo.* The sound or force of all the vowels and consonants in the Japanese names, as now written, is the Italian or European, the same as in the modern or Continental method of pronouncing Latin. These corrections are given by Mr. William G. Griffis, late of the Imperial Japanese College at Tokio (Yedo), and published some time ago in Circular No. 2 of our Bureau of Education, a very valuable document upon the present condition of education in Japan.

Mr. Watson, Secretary of the British Legation at Yedo, in his report presented to Parliament in June, 1874, gives a very interesting account of the working of the new system of European education inaugurated in Japan. This report is also published in the circular just mentioned.

It is doubtless quite generally known that Japan has "gone crazy" over Western science, Western education—Western civilization, in short—and has made the most unprecedented, most heroic efforts to Europeanize, or Westernize, the country. Emissaries have been sent to several European countries, and to the United States, to study Western institutions and report upon them. The result is most apparent in the school system, which has been entirely revolutionized in the greater part of the empire. The old system was that of ancient Greece: education was conveyed by men of learning to their individual followers. The Chinese classics dominated. The teacher, squatted on mats in the midst of his class, rarely numbering more than five or six, commenced with the first, and taught each in succession to pronounce the names of the Chinese ideographs—characters which stand not for letters, but words. Some ten thousand hieroglyphics had first to be learned by sound. Then they were shown to the pupils, and they learned them by sight. It was wholly a pouring-in system, tending "to magnify the memory of things imparted through the senses, and minify the reasoning power." This kind of school is still patronized by the ultra-conservatives, who affect Chinese learning, and believe it embraces everything necessary, especially the canons of the loftiest politeness, which is of primal importance in the eyes of most Orientals. Little was taught beyond reading and writing, and the committing to memory of volumes of the Chinese classics and ponderous treatises upon etiquette. "Mathematics was considered as fit only for merchants and shop-keepers." Yet nine-tenths of the Japanese could read and write, books were numerous and cheap, and circulating libraries were found in every city and town. "Literary clubs, and associations for mutual improvement, were common, even in country villages. Nevertheless, in comparison with the ideal systems and practice of the progressive men of new Japan, the old style was as different from the present as the training of an English youth in mediæval times is from that of a London or Oxford student of the present time." Thus writes Mr. Griffis.

In the reorganization of Japanese education a prominent part was played by the Rev. G. F. Verbeck, an American missionary. He won the confidence of the Government, and was appointed principal of a language school in Yedo. He had mastered the Japanese language, and became a general adviser and organizer in the new department of education, organized in 1871. The following year a scheme of national education was published. This divides the empire into eight educational divisions. In each of these there is to be a university, a normal school (for the training of teachers), schools of foreign languages, high schools, and primary schools. It is expected that the whole number of schools will be over 55,000; and the plan of education, together with the text-books and school furniture, will be that prevailing in Europe and America. Mr. Griffis says that during his five years of educational work in Japan he noticed everywhere, in traveling through the country, blackboards, chalk, slates, pencils, steel pens, iron ink, chairs, tables, charts, European or American text-books (translated), and "a host of new improvements, some diverging considerably from our models, according to native taste, fancy, knowledge, or means; but all tending to improvement, and of unquestionable advantage over those of old systems."

The Mikado, or Emperor, takes a deep interest in the new system of education, and the Empress is not behind him in enthusiasm. She lately visited a girls' school at Yeso (Yesso), and on that occasion had her photograph taken in a group, with the two Dutch ladies who have charge of the school. To those who know anything of the ideas of royal exclusiveness formerly held in Japan, this will appear very significant. The pupils of this school, numbering fifty-one in 1873, are being educated at the expense of the State. Four hours a day they study the branches of elementary European education under the Dutch ladies, and some hours more they pursue other studies under a master and two Japanese ladies. Their teachers pronounce them "intelligent, industrious, and promising." They wear our styles of shoes and stockings, but in other respects adhere to the native costume.

Since the promulgation of the new scheme of education in 1872, by the Imperial Government, there have been established in all, 5,429 schools; 3,630 public, and 1,799 private. The number of pupils receiving instruction in these is 338,463 males, and 109,637 females. Total, 448,100. This number does not include those attending the higher schools. Mr. Tanaka

Vice-Minister of Education in Japan, considers that 30,000 should be added to this number, making in all nearly 480,000, or about one in sixty-eight of the entire population.

The following is a translation of a certain portion of the scheme mentioned:

> "The education department will have sole control of the appropriation for the schools. It must be understood, however, that as education is for the benefit of the individual, the cost ought not to be paid out of the Imperial taxes, but should be paid by the people. At the same time, it is at present too early to throw the whole burden on them, and the Government will therefore assist.
>
> "The Government will, in no case, provide food and clothing for students. The only expenses which will be paid by Government, in whole or in part, are:
>
> "Salaries and expenses of foreign teachers.
>
> "The cost of building high schools, and that of providing books and instruments. The same rule will be observed for the middle schools.
>
> "Allowances to students in foreign countries.
>
> "Expenses in aid of the school district; to wit, 90 *yen* (dollars) per 1,000 of the population; or, for all Japan, the sum of 295,527 *yen*, 01.1 cents."

According to the new law, every child, male and female, must attend school long enough at least to complete the course in the elementary schools. This course embraces:

> "Spelling, writing, conversation, vocabularies, reading, morality, letter-writing, grammar, arithmetic, as far as division, instruction by lectures upon health, outline of geography, outline of natural philosophy, gymnastic exercises, singing (the last mentioned, not for the present)."

Among the schools for higher training at Yedo are the *Dai Gakko* or university, embracing several separate colleges for the study of medicine, jurisprudence, philosophy, and mining; also, a polytechnic college. Others, for veterinary science, commerce, and agriculture, also a college of arts, are to be added; the *Go Gakko*, a school of foreign languages; the *Shi Han Gakko*, or normal school, for the training of teachers; the high school for girls; several preparatory schools, and "certain establishments in connection with some of the public departments," which are designed for training in special sciences.

In the medical school or college of the university (*Dai Gakko*) the teaching is wholly conducted by German professors, without any interference of the Japanese authorities. In the preliminary department the readings take place in German by means of interpreters; in the college proper, among the more advanced students, without interpreters.

The *Shi Han Gakko*, or training school for teachers, was established to meet the demand anticipated for the fifty thousand schools which the Government counts upon establishing, as well as for the five thousand four hundred and twenty already existing in 1873. In this training-school the students are required, at a certain stage of the course, to take classes, teach and manage them, under the eye of their professors, "according to the discipline of American schools." As the students of this school come from all parts of the empire, most of them use provincialisms in speaking and styles of pronunciation differing more or less from the standard language of the capital; they are therefore thoroughly drilled in speaking, so that a uniform pronunciation may be secured all over the empire. The very best Japanese teachers are set over these young men, the foreign superintendent visiting the various class-rooms to see that the foreign methods and discipline are maintained. "No unnecessary talking, no awkward positions, no smoking, nothing that would be out of place in American schools, is allowed." The English language is not taught in this school, but several of our text-books are used, translated into Japanese, printed and bound in the Japanese style. Among these text-books are Willson's series of reading books, four in number; McNally's and Monteith's geographies; Robinson's series of mathematics, comprising arithmetic, algebra, geometry, and mensuration; Cutter's physiology; Willson's "Outlines of Universal History." More are to be translated, and the series, when completed, will comprise those in the average American high school.

The *Shi Han Gakko* has two departments, which may be called the theoretical and the practical. In the former, the young man is taught how to use slate, pencil, globe, map, phonetic and pictorial charts, blackboards, etc., just as a child would use them; in the latter he is taught, practically, how to teach and manage classes according to the methods of the best foreign schools. These classes are made up of boys and girls brought together for the purpose. Each student takes his turn in teaching these classes, a week at a time. "It is proposed," says Mr. Watson, "to increase, in a few weeks, the number of pupils, and to put fifty in a class, as in the primary schools of the United States. A new brick building, in foreign style, is also to be built. There will then be ten classes of fifty each, making five hundred in all." The young men acquit themselves with honor as teachers, and the progress already made is not only encouraging, but astonishing. The charts and translated books above mentioned are now manufactured by hundreds, and sent out to supply the new schools throughout the country.

The Government of Japan is organized on the departmental system, having a minister for each department. These departments are, foreign affairs, treasury, justice, education and religion, public works, imperial household, army, navy, and colonization. All these various departments employ a certain number of foreigners for educational purposes.

The Empire of Japan, in fact, is making gigantic strides toward the highest civilization. A spirit of progress informs and inspires the national heart; and the spectacle of a whole nation, characterized on our maps as "half civilized," casting aside time-honored traditions of exclusiveness and national superiority, and eagerly pressing forward into the grand army of reform, is one to gladden every heart possessing the least spark of natural nobility or fraternal love. How proud we ought to be, as a people, in being able to aid them in their grand work. How careful should we be to confess the errors into which we, a progressive people, have fallen, that they may avoid, as far as possible, the loss of time, money, and courage in learning merely to unlearn. The attitude of Japan to-day is wholly unprecedented in the history of the world. Never was the desire for learning, for high excellence in the mechanical arts, for the adoption of grand inventions, so general and intense in any country on the globe. So eager have the Japanese become for the acquirement of Western science and civilization, so impatient over the tedious waiting for the translation of scientific works, added to the fact that their own language contains no terms for expressing modern scientific ideas, that they have even proposed to adopt the English language as their own. This is probably wholly impracticable. In a country like Japan, women come to the front very slowly, and unless a majority of these should master the English, and make it the mother-tongue of their children, it is not likely that such an anomaly should happen as a national adoption of a new language.

Meanwhile, the work of education proceeds against many discouraging obstacles. Chief among these is the lack of adequate knowledge of the Japanese tongue on the part of the foreign professors. Lieutenant Brinkley, teacher of the artillery cadets in the naval college at Yedo, and "who takes rank among the very foremost foreign Japanese scholars," is of the opinion that there are not more than three or four among all the best English scholars in Japan "whose linguistic attainments could carry them over the language necessary to explain, say, the theory of variation." He is also of the opinion that it is impossible to impart extensive knowledge to Japanese students through interpreters employed by the Government. These are generally so deficient in moral courage that they will, in nine cases out of ten, "convey their own fortuitous ideas to the pupil," rather than confess their ignorance of what the professor is saying. Under such circumstances the teacher inevitably "lapses into practical demonstration and gesticulation;" and as these limits are soon reached, the "maxima of impartable theory lie within a very narrow compass." Mr. Brinkley attributes to this fact the opinion among Europeans that the Japanese mind is incapable of high mathematic attainments. He gives this an unqualified denial, "for, although he found it quite impossible, with all pains and patience, to impart mathematical knowledge through interpreters, yet he observed that that impossibility disappeared as soon as he was able to dispense with interpreters."

It does seem indeed lamentable that the Japanese, with their intense desire to acquire European science, should not be able to secure teachers who have mastered the language; but this is well nigh impossible. Mr. Watson speaks of the report that "a good Japanese grammar, by a native scholar," is in preparation. It is presumable, therefore, that none such exist, and, possibly, dictionaries of the language are also wanting. A good Japanese and English, and English and Japanese dictionary, with the English scientific terms explained, which have no corresponding terms in Japanese, is, evidently, greatly needed.

The Japanese Government appears to be generous in the matter of salaries to foreign teachers. The Circular of our Bureau of Education, from which most of the facts of this paper are taken, does not give the salaries of the foreign teachers at Yedo. As it is the capital, no doubt they are higher than at Yokohama, where they are from $600 to $1,200 a year.

Another serious obstacle to the progress of education in Japan upon modern methods, is the interference of the native officers *(yakunins)* of the Board of Education. It is in the schools of the capital that *yakuninerie* has "received its highest development and brought forth its choicest fruits." These native directors are accused of wishing to direct everything, even the choice of studies, when they are ignorant of what ought to be studied, of what the studies proposed are, and of the language in which those studies are taught. Mr. Watson, in his report, incloses a bitter article from the *Japan Mail*, criticising the conduct of native school officers. It is probable, at least, that there are two sides to this, as to all other questions.

The testimony regarding the mental and moral qualities of Japanese students is almost uniformly favorable. The Count de Beauvoir, a French traveler, and Mr. Pumpelly, of New York, who were employed a few years ago by the Japanese Government to improve the working of certain mines, both mention Takeda, a Japanese officer who had studied the Dutch language, and, from a description in a Dutch book, had constructed a very creditable blast-furnace, and made guns and rifled cannon. He had studied Bowditch's *Navigator* until he knew it by heart, and could calculate longitude from an eclipse; and yet he had accomplished this by the aid, solely, of a Dutch-Japanese and an English-Dutch dictionary! Mr. Pumpelly tell this story, and adds: "But this knowledge was purely mechanical. He knew nothing of mathematics from a philosophical point of view, though when he took up the study in this spirit he exhibited for the science a mental power which I almost envied him."

Another testimony is that the Japanese student is "bright, quick, eager, earnest, and faithful. He delights his teacher's heart by his docility, his industry, his obedience. In the course of five years the writer can remember no instance of rudeness, no case of slander, no uncanny trick, no impudent reply from any of his many pupils."......"Indeed, in all the gentler virtues, in abstinence from what is rude, coarse, and obscene, the average Japanese school-boy is rather the superior of his *confrère* in the west."......"In intellectual power and general ability we are very much inclined to believe that the average Japanese student is the equal of the average Western student. Even in the perception and conception of abstract ideas we are inclined to think him not inferior—provided his knowledge of the vehicle employed—*i. e.*, the language—is equal to that of his rival."

The same authority, a writer in the *Japan Mail*, says that to leave the boys of his native land who nourish their bodies upon beef, "and their brains with the ideas that have made England and the United States what they are," and to go among the quiet, docile students of these islands, is a rest to the worn teacher. The professional teacher goes to Japan with great expectations, and he is not disappointed. He finds there "as noble young men as ever thirsted for knowledge. He finds that he has only to point the way and his pupils follow. Their perfect trust and confidence in him are as beautiful as their diligence is commendable."......"Most of them, ever eager and insatiable after knowledge, remit no diligence, and yield to no despair."

Surely it must be a relief to the teacher, worn out with the rebellious physical energies of Anglo-Saxon students, to go among such as these. If they are half as bright and docile as they are represented to be, he will hardly complain that they lack independence and manly spirit. The Japanese boy's ideal of what is manly differs widely, no doubt, from that of "Young America;" but that of the latter cannot be the superior in all respects.

From every point of view the new spirit of reform born in Japan is as gratifying as it is wonderful. Not only in education, but in every thing else, it is manifest—in nothing more significantly than in the increased respect for the rights of women. Recent legislative enactments have annulled every kind of immoral contract, such as those by which, in thousands of instances, young girls were bound by parents or guardians to serve in brothels for a certain number of years. The severity of penal laws has been mitigated in a marked degree. The old laws forbidding the profession of Christianity are abrogated, or are practically a dead letter. Even the Japanese in the great cities and elsewhere are permitted to attend Christian churches without molestation. The banished Christians, thousands in number, have been sent back to their homes. Still the Government is determined that Christian doctrines shall not be taught by the foreign teachers in the schools. Mr. Watson learned, from a "reliable source," that the Government has resolved, while it will not interfere with private missionary enterprise in the empire, to refuse to employ any foreign clergyman as teacher in the schools. It appears, he says, "that some reverend teachers have been imperceptibly inculcating the doctrines of Christianity into the minds of their pupil."

Hence the binding resolution, in furtherance of which the Rev. Dr. Brown, of this country, and the Rev. Dr. Verbeck, who has done so much for the cause of education in Japan, have been removed from the post of teacher, and all the clerical teachers remaining in the schools have received notice of the termination of their engagements.

This seems a very severe act on the part of the Japanese Government, and it is at least possible that their suspicions in regard to the gentlemen already discharged are unfounded. The doctrines of Christianity might certainly be "imperceptibly inculcated," merely through daily reading in the schools that series of Willson's readers and the study of Wilison's "Outlines of Universal History." Moreover, what is more natural than that any Christian teacher, in answering some of the many queries certain to arise in any intelligent class about the meaning of what they are reading, might be obliged either to maintain a cowardly silence, or reply in a way easily construed as tending to "imperceptibly inculcate" his religious faith? Evidently, the foreign teachers in Japan are placed in a very delicate position, even where they honestly intend that their instruction shall be wholly secular.

Mr. Watson was informed by the native Vice-Minister of Education, Mr. Tanaka, that his Government intends to make education in the schools under its control entirely secular, "as far as is consistent with the fundamental tenets of the Shinto faith." This is the faith of the princes and higher classes. Its priests abstain wholly from animal food. It recognizes one supreme deity, inferior deities, and genii; and holds that the souls of the virtuous inhabit regions of light after death, while those of the wicked wander eternally through space, repelled by the heavens and the earth. No idols are used. This faith in Japan is often confounded with Buddhism, but they are distinct religions. Buddhism is the more democratic faith; and, doubtless, Japan will yet have as grave troubles about religious teaching in the public schools as have those countries they admire and emulate. But it is better to have faith that the good we see accomplished will increase and bear fruit after its kind. Certainly, if popular enlightenment can save a country from fatal errors in government, Japan is comparatively safe. There are other active educational influences at work in Japan besides the modern schools. Prominent among these are the press, the postal system, the railroad, and the electric telegraph.

In 1873, there were in Yedo eighteen newspapers; some published daily, others every fifth day. Of the daily papers, the average sale of copies of one was fifteen hundred, and of the two others eight hundred and sixty each; of the other fifteen, about two hundred copies. There is also a provincial press, whose power must be quite an important factor in the new civilization.

It has been said that the marvelous progress in civilization in a country like Japan is abnormal—a mushroom growth, likely to be soon followed by reaction, stagnation, and decay. But why should it be abnormal? Is it not rather an example of one of those *essors*, or leaps, which we are told occur in the growth of nations, as well as in plants and animals? In plants, this *essor* is exemplified in the germination and in the flowering; in the animal, in the birth and in the period of puberty. By these *essors* the most magical changes are effected; new functions are developed, and both plant and animal are born into a new life. In the life of nations, forces generate and combine slowly for years, until ripe for some grand *essor*. The invention of movable types, and of the steam engine, are illustrations of these grand leaps in the growth of civilization.

We have not heretofore known much of life in Japan—scarcely anything of great importance before our treaty with that country in 1859; but doubtless forces that we know nothing about were preparing the people for this great tidal-wave of reform which sweeps over and obliterates institutions and customs centuries old. Before the magical transformations now taking place in that country, more wonderful, a thousand fold, than anything that sage or poet has ever dreamed, the entire civilized world stands to-day in admiration and awe.

MARIE HOWLAND.

A TRIP TO THE SHOSHONE FALLS.

The existence of the Great Shoshone Falls of Snake River is known to but few people of the Pacific Coast, and a far less number have any definite idea of their exact locality. That a place abounding with so much grand and magnificent scenery, with so much picturesque loveliness, and so much wild beauty should rest in such obscurity is a mystery as unaccountable as it is strange. Were some artist to convey to his canvass one-tenth the beauty which Nature so lavishly bestowed, or some writer to devote the columns of a magazine to describing and extolling its splendor and grandeur, it would then become fashionable to visit the place, and no sight-seeing tourist would be satisfied until he or she had stood upon the brink of that deep, dark *cañon*, and beheld the sublime poetry of Nature which is everywhere there presented to view.

The falls—for there are a number of them—are located on Snake River, at a point ten miles north of Rock Creek Station, on the freight and stage road leading from Kelton, on the Central Pacific Railroad, to Boise City, Idaho, ninety miles north-west of the former place, and in about latitude 43°, longitude 115° west.

Snake River, for miles above and below the falls, flows through a deep, narrow *cañon*, from one-fourth to one-half mile wide; and its walls of dark basaltic rock rise vertically to a hight between two thousand and three thousand feet. From the brink of this *cañon*, the land runs back, level and smooth, for several miles, so that, standing a few hundred yards from the edge of the precipice and looking across the river, the range of vision passes entirely over the deep *cañon* and strikes the level land on the opposite side, and no trace or indication of the river is discernible. Go further back, however, and ascend the foot-hills to an elevation of one hundred or more feet above the level of the plain, and the dark outline of the river is plainly seen, winding its tortuous way through the arid plain like some monstrous serpent.

A party of three, on our return to Nevada from the Yankee Fork mining regions, allured by the glowing descriptions we had heard of the falls, determined to visit the place and satisfy our curiosity, although it involved several days' travel out of our direct course. We approached the river from the south, and, traveling along a sharply rounded point of table-land, drove our team to the very brink of the *cañon*. From this point, looking up the stream, we obtained the first view of the falls. For a mile or more above the falls, the channel of the river is plainly seen. It is not a wild, rushing torrent, beating and breaking and dashing against rocks and bowlders and the sharp angles of the bank, and foaming and frothing and fretting, as if anxious to escape to the level plain below, but a majestic body of water, one-fourth of a mile wide, with an average depth of fifteen feet, flowing, with not a ripple upon its surface, smoothly and tranquilly "on its slow, winding way to the sea."

The first obstructions which we see to this even flow are two immense bowlders, or columns of rock, which, standing abreast of each other across the stream, five hundred feet apart, divide the river into three channels. Swiftly flowing along the base of these barriers, the water, with a gentle bound, drops down a vertical fall of forty feet, when it again unites and becomes as smooth and tranquil as above. Thus flowing onward for five hundred feet, the waters are again divided into six channels by a row of bowlders of irregular shape, standing in a semi-circle about equidistant from each other.

Sweeping past these rocks, which seemingly attempt to stay its further progress, the water takes another bound, and leaps down a fall of sixty-eight feet, where, at the base, all the channels commingle together; but it is not so quiet and smooth and undisturbed this time. There is some fretting and foaming, some dashing and breaking of waves, for a short space, and then the current swiftly curves to the south wall, and gradually becomes more quiet. There can be no division of waters here; all must be united for the last grand leap. Seven hundred feet further on, and ere the foaming and fretting caused by the last fall has entirely disappeared from the surface, this mighty volume of water pours over a perpendicular precipice and falls vertically a distance of two hundred and sixty feet.

Our first object is to reach the base of the main fall, which does not appear to be more than a stone's-throw distant, but so winding and tortuous is the trail by which we descend that we traverse more than a mile before reaching the desired point. Securing our animals, and placing before them a good bait of hay, we commence the perilous descent; the Major leading the van, myself next, and the Doctor, with shotgun swung loosely over his shoulder, bringing up the rear. Down, down, we descend, following the zigzag trail over the great drifts of detached pieces of black lava rocks, which rattle and ring beneath the tread of our heavy-nailed boots like broken pieces of furnace slag; then passing down the craggy comb of a long narrow ridge, with yawning chasms on either side, our course turns abruptly to the right, around the sharp corner of a high projecting point of rock, and the pathway gradually becomes so narrow that there is barely room for a single person to pass. High above, to the right, towers lofty columns of rock, which threaten to topple over, and bury us beneath their massive weight; while to the left there opens a deep abyss, down which we dare not look from our dizzy hight. Emerging from this dangerous pathway, we come out on to a comparatively level and open piece of ground, whereon are growing a few tall and graceful cedars, whence we obtain another splendid view of the river bed, and the rushing, pouring torrents of water. Here, as the Doctor expresses it, we take a breathing spell. I have my fishing tackle with me in anticipation of good fishing at the base of the falls, but, unfortunately, have no bait. This want I make known to the Doctor, and soon his quick eye detects a carrion crow flying overhead, and within gun-shot range. (We had been told the fish would bite at any kind of fresh meat.) In an instant his gun is in position, and the report therefrom echoes and reverberates from wall to wall of the deep *cañon*, and, mingling with the roar of the waterfall, produces a strange, weird sound. Simultaneously with the report of the gun, the flight of the crow ceases, for the Doctor's aim is unerring, but, unfortunately, the bird falls into the river, just below the falls, and by the eddying current is carried to the opposite side. Scarcely has the echoing sound of the first shot died away when the second charge is fired; this time the crow falls into the stream, a few feet above the falls. We watch the dark object as it slowly floats down with the current. For a moment it seems to pause upon the very brink of the precipice, and then, with a sudden dart, it swiftly descends along the face of the flashing sheet of water, its dark color in strong contrast with the bright silvery whiteness of the pouring stream. Again we watch, and see the same dark object come to the surface of the boiling, seething whirlpool, hundreds of feet below, and float off down the river. A short distance along this strip of bench-land, and our trail leads down into a narrow, V-shaped gorge, with smooth, hard bottom, with nothing to afford a foothold, and becomes each step more steep and more difficult to tread. My fishing-rod of stout willow serves as an alpenstock with which I steady myself, and the Doctor, having discreetly left his shotgun in a friendly cluster of bushes, is now unincumbered, and with hands clutched against the smooth wall of the hopper-shaped crevice, is descending with a side motion; while the Major, who ever prides himself upon his military step and erect, martial bearing, with much humiliation is compelled to assume the same ungraceful attitude. A misstep here, and we would be precipitated headlong down the smooth wall for hundreds of feet, and, perhaps, landed in the foaming river below.

Suddenly the Major, who still leads the van, calls out, in tones of disappointment, that we can proceed no further, for our trail takes a sheer break off, and drops down vertically for twenty-five feet or more, and we cannot pass it without the use of ropes, and we have none. Still he is loth to acknowledge defeat, and, bending further over the precipice, again calls out, this time with exultation, "Yes, we can, for a tree has been dragged down, and placed over the break, and if we can only reach that we can easily get to smoother ground below;" and, with nerve and daring, he throws himself flat upon his stomach, and with arms and legs spread wide, imitates the motion of the crawfish down the steep, smooth rock, until his feet catch against the first limb of the tree. With words of encouragement he calls to the Doctor and myself to follow in the same manner. Our timidity almost forbids the hazardous venture, and but for his coaxing words and directions as to where to place our feet we would not have undertaken it. At the foot of the tree which, with its limbs running out at right angles with the trunk, serves the good purpose of a ladder, we find the gorge wider and less steep than above, and filled to a considerable depth with loose sand, which affords a firm footing, and in a few minutes we stand on the beach at the very base of the falls, with the cool spray dashing against our heated brows. In mute silence, and filled with awe, we stand and gaze upon the mighty volume of flashing, foaming, falling waters. It is near meridian, and the high south wall casts its dark shadows far out over the river; immense waves from the the whirlpool, caused by the pouring stream, beat and break around our feet, while the flying spray and mist completely drench our bodies.

No sound is audible above the thunder and roar and din of the waterfall, and the Doctor, realizing from his professional experience that it is no place for rheumatic persons to linger, gently pulls my arm, and we move off in silence farther down the stream, and out of reach of the flying spray. Soon the Major follows, and here, on a flat, shelving rock, which receives the warm rays of the sun through a rift in the high wall above, we find a comfortable resting place, from which a fine opportunity is afforded to study the physical details of the falls and their surroundings. The break in the bed of the river over which the water falls, is a complete semi-circle in form, with the arc curving up the stream, and, following the curve of the circle, is at least half a mile wide. From side to side the flow of water is of uniform depth and force, and as it pours in wavy, shimmering fleeces down the smooth, hard rock, it presents the appearance of great folds of snow-white, gauzy lace, gently swinging and vibrating in the soft autumnal breeze. From all along the base rise immense clouds of trembling, glittering spray, which gleam and flash through the rays of the sun, forming bright rainbow colors, that constantly shift and change. The basin at the foot of the falls stretches out in irregular shape, much wider than the bed of the stream above or below, and upon its surface great foaming waves roll and chase each other, and dash against the shore. So rough are the waters of this basin, which is a mile wide and two miles in length, that the Major, who has had some nautical as well as military experience, gave it as his opinion that no open boat could successfully ride its waves. The south wall of the *cañon*, under which we stood, is cut and grooved with deep indentations, at almost equal distances apart. These indentations commence at the apex of the wall, with light shallow furrows, that are hardly perceptible, and gradually deepen and widen, until near the base they become deep, broad gorges. Into these gorges the sand and *débris* have drifted from above, forming a good, strong soil, which, being protected from the hot, scorching sun, and moistened by the flying spray, produces a thrifty growth of cedars, around which twine, in graceful form, great lusty vines of the wild grape, now hanging full of long, slender bunches of unripe fruit. Interwoven with these cedars and vines is a dense growth of the hazel, alder, and maple, whose variegated foliage, with the gothic spires of rock towering high above for a background, forms a picture of exquisite beauty, in pleasing contrast with the awful grandeur of the river scene. The north wall, on the opposite side, frowns black and forbidding—no groove or indentation there. Its dark, columnar structure rises up thousands of feet, and against its base the waves of the basin lash with fury, and neither man nor beast dare attempt to approach the river from that side.

Between the base of the south wall and the edge of the water there intervenes a smooth, sandy, pebbly beach, from one hundred to two hundred feet wide. Upon this beach has been thrown, by the action of the waves, immense piles of driftwood, swept down the river from far above during high freshets. These piles of driftwood within themselves form a pleasing and instructive study. Here is the dwarfed and stunted cedar, which has come from a short distance above. By its side, and lying partly across it, is the slender trunk of the cottonwood, from some of the smaller tributaries, the gnawed ends of which clearly indicate the work of the industrious beaver. A few feet away is the gnarled and stubby nut-pine, from the foothills, with its spreading and crooked branches torn from the trunk. Reaching far along the beach is the gigantic form of the stately fir, that has been swept from some *cañon* high up in the Wind River range; and piled all around, in confused masses, are heaps of logs and chunks and limbs of every species of tree and shrub and bush that grows along the course of the stream, broken and abraded into all kinds of shape.

Nowhere in all this romantic spot has man marred the beauties of nature by his despoiling touch; no sickly sentimentalist has attempted to carve the name of any poet, author, hero, or divine upon any of these grand old walls, pillars, or columns; to none of these waterfalls, either great or small, has there been given a name, except the one general term, Shoshone—and he who stands here amid this awful grandeur, within this sublime temple of God, and does not feel his soul thrill, and his heart beat with a stronger emotion of love and reverence for the Great Jehovah, must be devoid of all the nobler impulses of humanity.

While the Doctor and Major are hunting along the beach for rare pebbles or curiously shaped pieces of driftwood, as *souvenirs*, I find a few grubs and millers under under a decayed log, with which I bait my hook, and in a short time pull from the stream a dozen or more silvery speckled trout. In the capacious pockets of the Doctor's hunting-jacket is found a small particle of salt and a few broken crackers, and it is but the work of a moment to dress the fish, and broil them upon a bed of burning coals; and upon our shelving rock, in the depths of the deep *cañon*, and within sight and sound of the mighty, roaring, thundering waterfall, we partake of our simple lunch with as much zest and relish as though we were feasting upon the rarest viands, served in the most approved style of the culinary art.

Fain would we linger amid these enchanting scenes, but the rays of the sun, now slanting from the west, warn us that time is passing, and we have much to see and many miles to travel before we find rest for the night. Ascending the narrow gorge, and climbing up the improvised ladder, which we find much less difficult to pass than in descending, we come again upon the strip of bench-land. Following this to the left for a few hundred feet, we turn down a smoothly rounded ridge of bare rock, which, in a short distance, abruptly terminates in a sharp, projecting promontory immediately over the falls. The scene from this point is not so terribly grand nor so awe inspiring as from below, but, mellowed as it is by touches of soft poetical beauty, it is more lovely to gaze upon. The sun now strikes directly against the broad sheet of water, forming a bright-hued rainbow, which hovers over the vortex below, and, in a graceful curve, spans the river from side to side. The lesser falls above, divided, as they are, into numerous channels, appear, in comparison to the great fall below, like miniature cascades, bounding and leaping over the rocks as though in mere playful wantonness.

After listening to some practical remarks of the Major, as to how this mighty power might be utilized and made subservient to the will of man, we again commence the ascent of the rugged side of the *cañon*, which we found not as dangerous as the descent, but far more toilsome. The Major, who is muscular and strong, relieves the doctor of his shotgun, and slowly we trudged on up the difficult trail. Will we never reach the top! A few more rests, a few more breathing spells, and we stand upon the edge of the broad plain, and within a few rods of our wagon and team. "Old John," who is ever on the lookout, catches sight of us as we approach, and utters a loud bray, as if to chide us, in his mule fashion, for leaving him to stand so long in the hot sun, and wage with his stub-tail an unequal warfare with the voracious flies. A drive of three miles up the river, along a smooth, sandy road, brings us to a point opposite the Little (or Twin) Falls. The river is here approached through what is called the Devil's Corral—and surely the whole English nomenclature could not afford a more appropriate name. Back, a little over a mile from the edge of the *cañon*, an immense chasm, or pit, has been cleft, or carved, in the solid rock, oblong in shape, two thousand feet deep and three thousand feet wide. The bed of this chasm is several hundred feet lower than the present bed of the river, which cuts across the lower end; and at one time it undoubtedly received the water of the stream, forming a deep lake, but now an immense bar, or levee, caused by the sands drifting from the plain above, has formed across the lower end, effectually barring the further flow of water; and what was inclosed at the time the bar was formed has long since been exhausted by evaporation.

The walls on each side, and at the outer end, are of the same black basaltic formation that characterizes the whole country hereabouts, and laid in layers, one above the other, their smooth, even surfaces standing perfectly vertical, and checkered and tesselated with almost regular seams, present the appearance of having been cut, and chiseled, and laid by human hands. Along the west side there runs a narrow ledge, which projects just far enough from the smooth wall to form a convenient roadway, and which has a very steep, but gradual, inclination from the crest of the wall at the outer end, until it strikes half way up the side of the sand-bar. This roadway is steep and narrow, but loose animals can with caution pass along it, and it is the only point for miles that cattle can approach the river for water. By an unlucky accident, the water in our canteen has leaked out, and our lunch of dry bread and fish produces an unusual thirst. Our animals are equally thirsty, for they have had no water since early morning; so, in a short time we have them unharnessed, and are hurrying down the narrow grade to the river. "Old John," who has fallen some distance behind, as is his custom on such occasions, calls to his mate in a deep, loud bray, but such an unearthly sound as it produces startles, and almost paralyzes, both men and beasts. The echo of that mulish bray rolls from side to side of the rock-walled cavern, echo answering echo with the most dismal and frightful sound. Is this a veritable pandemonium, in which are reveling all the fiends of the lower regions? Or are these dark, frowning walls pierced by a thousand unseen caves, in which are hidden wild beasts of prey, howling defiance at each other? The mules cower and tremble, and it is with difficulty that we lead them along the steep grade. All efforts at conversation are futile. The voice breaks into a guttural dissonance, no one sound being distinguishable from another, and all being finally lost in a hollow echo. Passing over the embankment of sand, and around a few jutting points of rock, we reach the river, and men and mules drink long draughts of the pure water.

Down the stream a few hundred yards we hear the roar of the cataract, and leaving the mules to graze upon the bunch-grass that grows along the river bank, we clamber down over immense rocks and bowlders that have slipped down from above, and in a short time we stand up on a rounded point immediately overlooking the falls. The river here is narrowed and compressed by the walls on either side to one-sixth its usual width; and as if to further compress the water, and force it through a channel as narrow as possible, an island of bare rock rises up in the middle of the stream at the narrowest point to a hight of thirty feet or more. The stream thus divided and narrowed, and the depth correspondingly increased, with a wild roar, plunges down a distance of eighty-two feet. The channel on the south side falls vertically, and the force of the current is so strong, that as the water rushes through the narrow chasm, it strikes the bed of the river several feet below the face of the precipice, thus forming a vast cavern behind the pouring sheet of water.

The north channel does not fall vertically, but rushes down the narrow gorge at an angle of near forty-five degrees in its furious course, throwing great clouds of spray high into the air. Jets of spray from each of these falls gleam and glisten in the bright beams of the evening sun, and sparkle like diamonds. A hundred feet or more below where the channels unite, and where the mist is in finer jets and less dense, the rainbow is formed in a beautiful curve, with each end resting against the black, smooth wall.

The Major expresses a strong desire to enter the cavern beneath the south fall, and behold the beauties there revealed, and commune with the river nymphs who make it their dwelling-place, and, with his usual daring and impetuosity, is soon sliding cautiously down the steep wall. The Doctor and myself watch his movements with bated breath, expecting to see him every moment lose his footing, and go dashing into the river. He reaches the edge of the stream in safety, and passes from our view behind the flashing sheet of water. In a few moments he emerges from the dark watery cavern, and beckons us to follow, but we know the consequences of entering there, and do not feel inclined to expose ourselves, in wet clothes, to the chilly air of night, which is fast approaching. The Major, when he again joins us, deprecates our want of nerve, and in glowing terms, depicts the varied splendors of the scene. The sun is near setting, and we hasten back to our mules, and lead them up the steep roadway. "Old John" is nervous, and continually switches his stump tail, for there lingers in his mule mind a faint memory of the terrible yells and sounds that smote upon his ear in descending this same spot, and it is with difficulty the Major holds him in check. Just as the sun is sinking behind the low horizon that stretches far away down the river we reach our wagon, and a two-hours' drive brings us to Rock Creek Station, where we find good cheer for ourselves and comfortable quarters for our animals.

ROBERT BRIGGS.

IN TWILIGHT WOODS.

Bird-songs grow faint with the sun;
  As the day fails in the west,
Each little fluttering one
  Creeps into his quiet nest.
Next, the pale dusk is a-quiver—
  Rose-songs forever are dear;
After this trembles a river—
  Stream-songs are gentle and clear;
Last, there is somewhat to shiver
  Down the swift pulse as a spear.
Faintly and far in the hills
There throbs a music of rills;
Fragrant and cool from the bay
The winds of the sea find way.
How dear is thy kindly mood,
Thou heart of the twilight wood,
When, shyly, in the twinkling skies,
The first star-blossom softly lies!

No more we hear faltering rills,
No more the low winds—we lie
As the pond-lilies afloat,
Motionless, under the sky,
On a blue lake of the hills.
And we rest with our faces
Deep-hid in the ferns and grass;
There, watching, at last we note
The dim world widen and shine,
Till, through the desolate places,
Dreams fair and immortal pass,
And the twilight grows divine:
The friends that we lost of yore,
The loved from the farther shore,
  Smile down in a trustful way;
They are not so very far,
More near than each gentle star,
  And sweet are the words they say
For us, whose rivers as yet run
Through night and day, 'neath star and sun.

CHARLES H. SHINN.

OUR ROAD-BUILDERS AND THE STATE.

It was a brilliant conception and a daring feat to fling a railroad entirely across the American continent. It ranks among the greatest of human achievements. Its equal exists not in all the world.

In any other country but ours the men who conceived and executed such a project would have been rewarded with both wealth and honors. England enriched and knighted Paxton for erecting the Crystal Palace in Hyde Park; France enriched and ennobled De Lesseps for reöpening the old Egyptian canal across Suez; Russia granted almost imperial distinctions to the Demidorffs for renouncing to the Government some mines, out of which they had previously made their own fortunes.

Some of these marks of national gratitude are unknown to our laws, which assume that every service may be adequately compensated with a pecuniary remuneration. If all rewards are thus to be commuted into one kind of reward, justice demands that the latter should at least be secured with a good title and permanent possession. If all public achievements, however great, are to be rewarded with money, the beneficiaries should at least be permitted to enjoy their reward in peace.

Such has not been the principle that has governed our dealings, the dealings of our national and State governments, with the builders of the great highway that connects California and the Mississippi Valley.

Before it was built we approved and offered great inducements to any one who should build it. We well knew the difficulties of the undertaking, and, so far as promises went, were liberal to profuseness, for we aimed at political and commercial advantages which the completion of the railroad could alone secure. One has only to read the debates in Congress during the progress of the original Pacific Railroad bills to be convinced of the correctness of these statements. We knew that the road had to traverse two thousand miles of desert, a blasted, withered solitude, destitute of wood and water, and as yet wholly unfitted for the occupancy of man. We knew that across this waste, over which a few savages held undisputed sway, there would need to travel thousands of emigrants to the Pacific Coast—men, women, and children—all of whom would be exposed to great privation and danger. We knew that to protect them and the vast possessions through which they would have to move, and the distant lands to which they were bound, we would be obliged to maintain forts and employ numerous bodies of troops. We foresaw that, with the railroad built, the many obstacles to this tremendous journey would disappear; that the emigrants would be conveyed safely and rapidly to their destination, and a portion of the troops dispensed with. Substantially, the only other route by which emigrants could reach the new Dorado was by the Isthmus of Panama, a route that involved two sea voyages in crowded steamers, and a land transit through fever-infected jungles. This route was dangerous, uncomfortable, and expensive; the time consumed was thirty to forty days; many vessels had suffered fire and wreck; hundreds of lives had been lost through accident, exposure, or disease; and the cost of passage varied from $200 to $500. By the railroad the trip from the Mississippi Valley could be made in five days at a cost varying from $50 to $100, the actual rates for many years past. We even calculated that in military and postal expenses alone the country would save many millions a year. Here was the calculation: Without the railroad, we shall need 75,000 troops to protect the emigrants, and to defend the trans-Mississippi, the Pacific Coast, and the frontiers. With the railroad, 25,000 troops would suffice. And in respect of the mails, a much greater weight of mail matter can be carried with greater safety and celerity, and at much lower rates. The economy in transporting the troops and mails, reckoned on the basis of 25,000 troops, and the small mails formerly carried by pony express, will amount to over $5,000,000 a year (the annual average cost of these services for the five years previous to 1862 having been $7,309,341; while it is now only $2,000,000). And this calculation does not include the economy of 50,000 troops, nor the greatly increased weight of the mails, nor of thirty days saved in time, nor of the improved condition of the troops upon arriving at their posts, nor of many other advantages, both military and military-financial.

All these we foresaw, and many others, and it is creditable to the sagacity of our national legislators and the press that their expectations in these respects have been fully realized.

They foresaw that vast tracts of desert lands, which were impossible of sale at $1.25 per acre, the Government minimum at that time, would readily sell at $2.50 per acre, the minimum since the railroad was built; so that, in fact, the Government could afford to give away one-half of the lands along the route, in order that the other half, which it retained, might be sold at double the price. They foresaw that, with the railroad built, no further fears need be entertained of the spread of polygamy in Utah, or of secession in California; that the trade of the Indies, of China, of Japan, of Australia, of the Sandwich Islands, of the coasts of Alaska, British North America, Mexico, Guatemala, Costa Rica, New Granada, Peru, Chili, and the islands of the Pacific, would be attracted toward our shores.

Besides these advantages, many others have been derived from the building of the railroad which were not foreseen at the time it was projected. We have found that the laying of connected lines of iron rails and of telegraph wires, protected by the railroad, is bringing about an equalization of climates between east and west, favorably affecting the distribution of moisture, and rendering the deserts less arid than before. We have discovered small oases, before unknown, scattered at long intervals on the desert, and susceptible, through the proximity of the railroad, of being turned to productive uses. We have been enabled, through the general increase of moisture and the discovery of these oases, to maintain vast herds of cattle upon plains that were previously unfitted for such a purpose. We have floated timber hundreds of miles in flumes to the railroad, and conveyed the timber by means of the road to points where it has proved of great advantage in colonizing and civilizing the country. We have discovered and utilized valuable mines of coal, iron, salt, borax, gold, silver, mercury, copper, lead, and many other minerals, few of which could have been utilized without the agency of the railroad. These have been opened and made to yield an enormous product.

Along the line of the road hundreds of towns and settlements have sprung up, whose population derive their entire subsistence from or through the road. For example, as Colonel Zabriskie informs us, in his recent letters to the *Alta California*, there were directly employed by the Pacific Railroad, in Placer County, during the year 1878, no less than three hundred and seventy-three men, to whom it paid $260,000 a year in wages, and in which it purchased $232,000 worth of timber. To cut this timber employed one hundred and three other men; to say nothing of those engaged in hauling it to the road, nor of those occupied in the general superintendence and service of the road, a portion of whom were obtained from the same county, nor of the share of construction and repair-money expended in this county, nor of many other means of support which the county derived from the railroad.

In short, this railroad has thrown open a great portion of this continent to settlement, and tended to render it fit for the abode of men; it has invited immigration from abroad, and conferred value to the extent of thousands of millions of dollars upon lands which before were inaccessible and valueless; it has brought all these lands under the operation of our Federal and State tax laws, so that now they yield to one or the other many millions of dollars a year in taxes; and it has paid for taxes upon itself up to December 31, 1879, over $3,000,000.

The industrial development brought about by the construction of this road is, perhaps, indicated in no more striking manner than by the fact that at the present time several overland roads are reaching their arms across the continent to claim a share of the vast commerce which the first road has begun to organize upon the plains, and to attract from the opulent countries that bound the western shores of the Pacific Ocean.

To those who would venture to construct the highway, which we expected would confer upon us a portion of these national advantages, we held out these specific pecuniary inducements: Alternate sections of land, and a loan of the Government credit for an amount estimated to be sufficient to lay the road-bed, including such profits as might be realized from the sales of these lands or the construction of the road.

Whatever may be thought of these inducements now, there were few who deemed it worth while to entertain them then. A good many prominent men had "talked" Pacific Railroad before it was undertaken, but there was no eagerness to undertake it—there was no competition for the subsidies offered by Congress. The difficulties were too great; the obstacles to be overcome were too formidable; the project, from any reasonable, any business-like point of view, was impracticable.

Nevertheless, there were some men, more adventursome or sagacious than the rest, who were willing to make the attempt, to brave the dangers and obstacles from which others had flinched, and to construct the great highway which promised so many advantages to the country. And not only did they succeed in this effort; they completed the road eight years before the time to which they were limited by Congress, and thus advanced by eight years' time the development of the entire country west of the Missouri River.

The reward which the undertakers of this great work looked for, the reward that furnishes he natural and proper incentive to all undertakings of a commercial character, the only kind of reward which the country could offer, the reward which it did offer to them, and the one which they declared themselves willing to accept, was wealth; and, taking into consideration the grandeur of the work they accomplished, the formidable character of the obstacles they had to encounter, and the public benefits which have resulted from the construction of the road, no fair-minded man can doubt that they fully and fairly earned all that they were offered, or that they received.

So far as the Federal Government is concerned, the reward due to the constructors of the Pacific Railroad has been paid, not, indeed, fully or unreservedly, nor with the grace that should accompany the performance of such an action, nor with the commendation that should follow the accomplishment of such an enterprise, or the fulfillment of such a trust as the undertakers of this road had fulfilled, but, after a fashion, coldly, grudgingly, and with reserve. This unhandsome policy of the Government was due to the following cause:

No sooner did the rapid progress made from time to time by the undertakers render it apparent that the road would be successfully constructed, than envy and detraction began to assail them. It was asserted that they had secured an over-favorable contract; that the amount to be loaned by the Government to help build the road was sufficient to both build it and equip it; that the dangers and obstacles to the undertakers had been magnified; that there was no fear of molestation from the Indians; that the Rocky Mountains were plains, and the Sierra easy of ascent; that wood and water could be procured almost anywhere along the route; that the lands were fertile, and the land grant had bargained away a domain as great and valuable as New England. In short, the men who first spanned this continent with a railroad were aspersed precisely like the man who first discovered it. When Columbus was ennobled and enriched for having discovered America, the envious and malignant proved that the discovery was valueless to the Spanish nation, and without merit to the discoverer. It was not the rich Indies, but a naked land, that he had found, and as for proving the rotundity of the earth, why, Thales had proved it twenty centuries before. Therefore, why reward Columbus? and, in the present instance, why reward Stanford and Crocker and Huntington, and the rest of the Pacific Railroad builders? This feeling and these arguments not only caused the Government to pay with reluctance the reward that it should have paid with alacrity—it led to other and much more important consequences. It created a prejudice against the railroad and all its operations. Although any man could have gone into the market, and can do so now, and buy its shares at or near par, it was characterized as an extortionate and odious monopoly, and treated as a public enemy.

Before proceeding any further in this recital, I desire to put an end to any false impressions that the ignorant or unworthy may put upon my motives. I am not interested in this road, nor in its promoters or stock-holders, past or present, nor do I know, nor have I ever known, any one of them. I have no business with the road. I have not been retained to make an argument in its behalf. I say these things voluntarily, because I believe them to be right, and because other public men have not had the courage to say them. I believe these road-builders to have been treated shabbily and unjustly, and I feel ashamed of my countrymen for having so treated them. Furthermore, I believe that in taking their cue from the cold attitude of the Federal Government in this matter, the people of this State—of my adopted State—have overreached the mark of prudence, and done themselves a great injury, which they cannot too soon hasten to repair.

Deriving strength from the influence which they had exercised with such success upon the Federal Government, and support from the popular passions which they perceived were being aroused on the subject, the enviers and detractors of the Pacific Railroad men now assaulted them through the press and on the rostrum, and, carrying the unthinking multitude with them, gained the Legislature and the Constitutional Convention, and grasped the power and the opportunities for which they had sought. These were to coerce, to bully, to blackmail, to bleed the railroad, and, failing in these, to legislate it into ruin.

Let us here review our own action—that of the people—in this matter. A great national road was constructed, and paid for, and, although we were proud of this road, and were always glad to come upon it, for we knew that it meant relief from privation and danger, and never hesitated to prefer it above any other means of conveyance, we envied the glory of its constructors, and coveted the wealth they had gained.

This wealth they had invested in a new project—one that reflects almost as much credit upon them as the other. With an enterprise that seems peculiar to them, they have quietly and rapidly constructed a railroad through the San Joaquin Valley, from Lathrop entirely through the State, to Arizona, and into the midst of that great mining region. Their design—their vast and bold design—is to connect together the Pacific Ocean and the Gulf of Mexico years before De Lesseps shall have pierced the Isthmus at Panama, or Commodore Ammen at Nicaragua. The new road is already beyond the Dragoon Mountains, and making two miles a day toward the waters of the Rio Grande. In the midst of this glorious work, when we, as a people, should be engaged in cheering them on toward its accomplishment, we have looked coldly on while they were being obstructed by legislative enactments and plundered by legislative highwaymen. Is this fair? Is it generous?

Let us view the matter from still another point of view—the point of view of the State, regarded as a single body politic—the State which has neither passions, feelings, nor sentiments, the State which has only interests.

Certain men, with wealth for their incentive, undertake a vast public work, which promises great benefits to the country at large and to this State in particular. They successfully accomplish the work, which proves to be of even greater benefit than had been anticipated, and succeed, though not without much trouble, in obtaining the wealth for which they had bargained. This wealth, together with other capital attracted toward them by their success, they invest in another public work, equally vast and promising still greater advantages to the country at large, and particularly to California, than the other. This work is little more than half accomplished when the State of California, in effect, says to them, "Stop! Free-trade is ended. Coercion begins. Facilities are unnecessary. Obstruction is desirable. Skill is worthless. Inexperience should rule. You shall hereafter charge only such and such rates; all others are hereby made illegal. You may not do this, nor that, nor t'other. The arrangements necessary to carry these provisions into effect will be made by an official who knows nothing about the matter." Is this just? Is it politic? Is it wise?

Its injustice and impolicy are too obvious to need argument; its unwisdom is evident the moment we examine the circumstances of the country and the operation of the laws which the State has recently enacted.

Take, for example, the circumstances of the great valley of the San Joaquin. The new road passes through this region, touches the coast at Santa Monica near Los Angeles, and thence plunges into the Mojave Desert, which it spans in order to reach the Colorado. There are six million acres of land within twenty miles of the railroad, as it traverses the San Joaquin Valley. Before the road was built, these lands could have been bought, for the most part, at one dollar an acre. To avoid dispute, let us say that they were all worth five dollars an acre, which is far above the mark. They are now worth from thirty to one hundred and fifty dollars an acre; let us say on the average forty dollars. Here, then, are over two hundred million dollars added to the wealth of the State and to its taxable resources.

These lands were practically unproductive before the railroad was built; they are now actually productive. This means that it pays a profit to cultivate them, and that this profit has been realized in spite of a railroad tariff which was declared by detractors and demagogues to be excessive and extortionate. Instead of regarding this increase of productiveness as the true criterion by which to estimate the influence of the road upon the prosperity of the country, the State listened to ignorant declamation, and passed a maximum law of freights and fares. This law provides that a road shall not charge a greater rate of fare for a shorter than for a longer distance in the same direction. For example, that if one dollar per ton freight is charged from Los Angeles, near which place there is schooner competition by sea, only one dollar can be charged from any intermediate station, although with the latter no such competition exists. The principle of this law is unjust, inequitable, and absurd. The railroad, in the pursuit of its welfare, will naturally limit itself to a rate of profits on the whole administration that will restrain competition from other roads; but in the subdivision of this general rate of profits it will and must charge more from one point than another, though the two may be equally distant. There are portions of a long line of railroad—many portions of this road—that will not pay any profit, indeed must be worked at a loss; for example, its long deserts and the mountain sections. The losses incurred on these portions must necessarily be made good from somewhat higher rates on others, and the latter will naturally be those points where ship or wagon competition is lacking. Again, a railroad can afford to carry cheaper for one man, who has large and regular quantities of freight to offer, than for another who has only small and irregular quantities.

This principle is ably sustained in Governor Stanford's letter to the Legislature of California, dated February 24, 1876. Says that experienced railroad authority, it has become a necessary principle "that each district penetrated by a railway should, as near as may be, pay its own expenses of traffic, without drawing upon some other more favorably situated region, offering large business, to assume an improper share of these expenses," and he instances a vast number of circumstances that determine the advantages and disadvantages of one district over another in this respect. Among these circumstances are competition by other railroads, or by other means of transportation, population, quantity and kinds of freight, frequency of handling, grades, climate, cost of labor, etc.

On the same principle, a sailing ship will sometimes carry one portion of her cargo at one-tenth the rates charged upon another; a steamship will carry emigrants at a loss, and make this good by means of extra charges upon the cabin passengers, whose patronage is gained through the influence exerted by the emigrants, or the popularity which their safe conveyance shall have earned for the vessel; a telegraph company will charge more for a message from Nevada than for one from New York, to California; a merchant will sell goods cheaper to one man than to another; a professional man will charge a higher fee to A than to B.

Suppose the Government attempted to regulate these matters, would not such interference be justly regarded as mischievous and intolerable?—and why so more in the case of a steamship or a private merchant than in that of a railroad? The principle is precisely the same. The fact that the merchant is a single person and the railroad company a combination of many persons, has nothing to do with it, and does not affect its soundness or relevancy.

Observe the operation of the contrary principle, which is embodied in the existing law, upon the circumstances of Los Angeles and Kern River. If the road carries freights from the former place where there is water competition, it is required by the law to carry them at no greater rates from the latter place, which is located more than one hundred miles from the ocean, and where there is none. Now this it cannot afford to do, because it would have to be done at a loss. It is, therefore, compelled to choose between renouncing the trade of Los Angeles, or that of the whole San Joaquin Valley. The result is that Los Angeles, the people of which city exhibited a very singular zeal in supporting this absurd legislation, have necessarily lost many of the advantages they otherwise would have derived had it not been for their persistent and needless antagonism.

In promoting a great object, such as the opening and settlement of remote regions, the distribution of population, the establishment of an important trade, or the publication of discoveries and inventions, it is sometimes necessary for the State to grant franchises, such as rights of incorporation, patents, copyrights, etc. It may not be good policy to grant such franchises if there is any other practical way of obtaining the object in view, nor is it good policy to grant them for too long a time; but once granted in good faith, justice demands that the State shall respect and sustain them, in order that the grantees may derive the benefits from them for which they risked their invention, enterprise, or capital. And I hold it to be quite as unjust—and, in the case of a State, unjust means unwise—to impair or invade the franchise of a railroad* after the promoters have risked their capital in its construction, as to deprive an inventor of his patent, or an author of his copyright, after the one has made public the secret of his mechanical device, or the other has committed his thoughts to print. If franchises are hurtful the State should not grant them, but if it does grant them it should protect them; for it is to be presumed that it derived advantages from them which it could not have obtained without them. Our State is still young in respect of its experience with railroads, as nobody is compelled by our laws to employ a railroad against his inclination or interest. The vast trade they have built up furnishes an overwhelming evidence of their usefulness. The State is greatly indebted to them, and is bound to become still more indebted, for the services which they can yet perform for it are very considerable. It will, therefore, have frequent occasion to deal with them; and it will be well for it to do so upon the same footing as experience has taught it to deal with other industrial and commercial organizations. The basis of this policy, like the basis of all State policies, should be truth and justice; and with these principles should be combined as much firmness, prudence, and sagacity as our legislators can command. It will not do to make bargains and then to back out of them by misrepresentation, detraction, or violence. No State can long survive which employs or encourages these methods; for their employment involves the demoralization of society and the destruction of credit.

That such has been the recent attitude of California toward the Pacific Railroad no disinterested and fair-minded man can well doubt, and the sooner it changes this attitude the better will it be for its own honor, prosperity, and safety.

ALEXANDER DEL MAR.

* A franchise, similar to that enjoyed by any railroad company under the laws of this State, may be obtained by any association of individuals upon payment of a nominal fee.

THE BATTLE OF THE WABASH.

A LETTER FROM THE INVISIBLE POLICE.

[The following letter was found on the top of Mount Tamalpais by a gentleman of this city, on the afternoon of the 24th of August, 1880, under these circumstances: The gentleman in question was one of a hunting party, and, having strayed from his comrades, and becoming weary, seated himself on a table-rock overlooking the Bay, San Francisco, and the Golden Gate. While there he discovered this manuscript letter neatly tucked away in a crevice of the rock. He retained it, brought it to the city, and kindly placed it at our disposal. It is written in a queer, wiry hand, scarcely human, while frequent erasures show that the work was, in a sense, incomplete. The only rational conclusion as to its authorship attributes it to the mountain gnomes, those invisible police that are said, by Spanish tradition, to frequent that peak on moonlit nights, and to whom the future and past are alike accessible. To the fact that they have no sense of the propriety of confining themselves, as historians, to the present and past, according to human conception, we are indebted for this view of the distant, but destined, future.]

TAMALPAIS, July 18th, 2080.

My Dear Sir: As you are now approaching the close of your course of comparative history, I deem it proper to give you, as apropos of this course, an account of the second great human inundation—the Americo-Mongolian conflict. The first instance of this kind, of sufficient magnitude to rank in our classification, was the overrunning of Southern Europe by the armed nations of the Northern Hive, which resulted in the intermingling, between conqueror and conquered, of national traits, customs, language, laws, and modes of thought, and which for centuries furnished the scientific searcher of historic truth the most inviting and fertile field. This letter is devoted to the second incursion of the kind, and which, alike in result, differs in method as widely as the customs and genius of another and far more enlightened age. The only part of this problem not yet solved by man, and which, from necessity, reaches out still further into the future ages, is that of race assimilation; for while many instances may appear of crossing, still, in no proper sense, is the end foreshadowed by the accomplished facts. I could, of course, give you this result as well as not, but I prefer to ground you well in the facts of the epoch closing with to-day, and leave your prepared and strengthened prescience to peer unaided into that following. I write from this date because, as past, present and future are to us the same—as we can, in fact, live in the future as well as the present—it is but a chapter of history written before, but as accurate as if written with all the events fully accomplished by men.

You remember that, while the Goths, Huns, and Vandals from the Northern Hive, and again, the Normans in England, at a later day, enforced their rule upon the countries they overran, the intellectual similitude of conqueror and conquered made possible a homogeneous amalgamation, which has not yet, and perhaps will never occur in America. The reasons for this may be apparent to you at the conclusion of this letter, after you have followed with me the successive steps by which the present result has been wrought out. Unlike, in this respect, all other events of similar character, we are to seek the cause of what we find, and what will probably be, in the peculiar character of the participants in this real drama. The Spanish conquests in America were unlike this, because accomplished by the old system of pure force, in which the modern and gigantic system of gradually undermining was entirely absent. Those were accomplished under the eyes of men who, impatient and fanatic, believed all things of like character should be done at once, and broken heads the only proper reply to protest, and who, short-sighted and unphilosophic, forgot that two or three centuries are but as so many days or years in the life of a nation. They obeyed the systems of their age, while it has been reserved for this more advanced epoch to accomplish more substantial results by those peaceful means, which, though they delay, gather a more abundant harvest. I tell you—which you should note and remember well—that only during the two centuries immediately preceding this date have any people completely thrown aside that low and petty exercise of impatient passion, and adopted that broader method by which whole races are now actuated, and the results of aggregated life accomplished on a grander scale. Up to this period, and still yet among the lower classes, the individual man has been a petty schemer, but only within this last epoch has the science of life and government been so well understood and carried out as to make of millions of men one great machine, well ordered and effective, working upon a general plan, and to a given end. In this attainment we are forced to accord to China the lead, not only in point of time, but also in the efficacy of execution.

We will now enter upon the discussion of the transition era--that period of time that constitutes the link connecting the old, and, we confess, the more narrow, system with the new and more comprehensive one—an era the like of which no human has witnessed. Discarding as arbitrary the reasons of other and similar human phenomena, and, as philosophic students of history, rising to an acceptance of the grander and broader considerations of life, we find, in the period of American history elapsing between the years 1870 and 2080, the most fruitful field of all past ages, the magnitude of which bristles with issues secondary, in their universal effect upon men, only to those immutable and jealous laws ordained by God.

The Spaniards in America engrafted themselves upon the country, and were soon lost in the preponderance of aboriginal blood. To-day those people are more Indian than Spanish. But this Mongolian question presents no such conditions. Being superior in numbers, and prevented, by precautionary considerations, from a free amalgamation with the white race—the negro becoming, in the clash of these Titans, nearly extinct--they have presented to us rather a pure problem of race contests. That conflict is now settled as to the industrial and political features of the country, leaving open and to be deduced as a corollary only those of social significance, and those which invest a contest of races for existence with considerations of future importance to universal history—that history that cares for no people, clime, or issue, which is cold, bloodless, pulseless, in its chronicle of the wrecks of time.

No better method occurs to me than to give you an account of my investigation of this problem. By the chronological reckoning common to our people, I transferred myself to the year 2078, and visited the haunts of man. At first, when I moved among the changed scenes of two centuries, I could scarcely make out what was presented before me. Cities had grown till their broad and far-reaching streets stretched away for miles; villages had become cities; rivers had, in many places, assumed the straightness of canals; while the whole face of the country, from San Francisco to Boston, was threaded by a net-work of railroad lines. The people had become numerous as the leaves of the forest or the sands of the shores; the wastes of Utah, Nevada, Colorado, and Arizona were populous with cities, and blooming with fields that smiled like gardens. The deserts of the alkali and sage-brush had disappeared, and in their stead broad fields of yellow grain waved in the sunlight to the rippling notes of the lark and the whistle of the quail. This way and that, toward every point of the compass, trains, laden with the treasures of commerce, thundered at the rate of one hundred miles per hour. The gas-light had disappeared from the streets, while the electric glow, soft as moonbeams, but brighter, flooded the nights; but upon the streets, as I gazed upon them, a million lights moved in a fire-fly dance, through the artificial gloaming, more numerous than the stars of the sky. Upon close inspection I found them to be bright little electric lights carried upon each hat—or whatever they used as a head-gear—that gave a far better light than the best street lamps of 1870, and which made an attractive scene when the thousands thronged the streets. Many changes had been produced since that year in the *personnel* of the citizens. The capital was at St. Louis, which city had no less than six millions of inhabitants. The population was still more motley than before, while the pig-tails were everywhere, and numbered about three of them to one white of all nationalities. The Pacific Coast had become one vast workshop of them, while a few negroes listlessly looked on at the thousands that held the cotton and rice fields of the South. Pig-tails were the style in San Francisco, while only an occasional white was met strolling along the long and busy streets. Most of the latest buildings were of Asiatic architecture, with the queer gables and pagoda-shaped tops, while blue and vermilion paints were over all. I was almost startled at the transformation. Crossing from Oakland by ferry to San Francisco, I observed that nine-tenths of the passengers and all the officers were Chinese, and that the only whites employed aboard were deck-hands. When I reached the wharf Chinese hackmen met me, chattering, and drove me away to a hotel. There the clerk was a Celestial, as were most of the guests. The dishes were of Chinese make, while their contents, at dinner, were equally Asiatic in quality, quantity, and service. Thousands of guests, in pig-tails, were in the corridors and halls. Going to the theater, at evening, I found the play in Pigeon English, to suit the cosmopolitan audience, but the boxes were all occupied by Celestials, glittering in silks and jewels. A Chinese mandarin occupied the bench in the City Hall, flanked by almond-eyed under-officials. I almost began to believe myself in China, till an American was brought in, and put on trial for shying a rock at the son of Honorable Ching Choo Fou

Lee, of Nob Hill, and I heard the venue of the complaint stated as San Francisco. The jury were Celestials, and the chicken's head was severed in the administration of the oath, as in the Flowery Kingdom. At the Exchange I found more of them; indeed, they had usurped every avenue held by the Americans two hundred years before, and had celestialized California.

That I might have an idea how these changes had been effected from a human standpoint, I concluded to refer to some noted historian, and get from him what were the views of men thereon. Upon inquiry of the clerk of the hotel, I was promptly referred to Professor Hap Lee, No. 1910 Canton Street. I set out, and soon found this was what had once been California Street, and that the professor's residence was an elegant stone mansion situated in the vicinity of where Mr. J. C. Flood, in 1880, contemplated erecting a residence—or, rather, as compared to this of the professor, a cottage. Fortunately, I found the professor at home, and was received in great state—not that he considered it was due me, but to himself, as the leader of social and literary *ton* in the city. Making known to him my wish that I desired a short *résumé* of the last two hundred years of American history, and that I had been referred to him as the most learned of living historians, he gave me, in substance, the following account, which, from its general accuracy, I incorporate in this letter:

"It has now been over two hundred years since our ancestors came across from the Flowery Kingdom on a whaling expedition, and arrived upon these shores to find this most beautiful land sparsely inhabited by aborigines of the race to which I presume you belong, I add with regret, to your shame. These people were very arrogant, and, for the times, wealthy; indeed, their wealth was barbaric, like themselves. They spoke a villainous jargon, that happily now is modified by contact with our superior tongue, and were egotistic to a painful degree. Our ancestors were poor, but noble, and finding here fair opportunities to better their fortunes, applied themselves to the task. Would you believe it, our ancient historian, Colonel Bee, who flourished about that period, writes that those benighted people looked upon rat fricassee, bird nest soup, and domestic chowder as objectionable dishes, and preferred their own odors to those of the Celestials? They were at first indulgent, merely laughing at the sacred Cuem, and vowed that 'John,' as they facetiously spoke of our sainted ancestors, wore their shirts outside their pantaloons. It is, my dear sir, difficult at this distance of time to perceive how such perversion of taste could ever have existed. These people, your ancestors, were sprung from a small tribe known originally as Diggers, as we learn from Colonel Bee, because they were all given to digging in the hills and mountains for precious metals. Our ancestors (may Buddha keep their eternal stomachs well regulated!) soon discovered that the aborigines, the ancestors of the present Melicans of this land, were loose and careless in their business, were scornful of small sums, and were never half satisfied with any enterprise that did not promise a million dollars in a few months; but they oftener lost than won. While all classes of Melicans were thus pursuing big sums, the despised 'John' set about procuring those occupations securing moderate but permanent incomes. Indeed, he not only made cigars, which were at first derisively called 'stinkers,' and did a great many other things, but even became servants in the houses of the wealthy. He was kicked, reviled, and metaphorically spit upon, but the sequel for the hundredth time proved to the world that persecutions of that character ultimately bless their objects as nothing else can. It is the healthy food of nature.

"It did not take 'John' long to get a footing, and no sooner was this realized than the barbarians became very jealous of him, and to such an extent was this jealousy developed into opposition that an agitator arose, one General Ker Nee, who incited a great deal of bitter feeling toward our slowly thriving ancestors. Indeed, he urged his followers on to kick the shins and pull the queues of our people, and even threatened to hang, burn, and torture them. Another of this city wrote many windy things against us, by which, it is said, his name was, about the time of his death, blown away in a fierce gale and lost. He even went so far as to advise the followers of General Ker Nee to burn a ship just arriving with more of the pilgrims from China; but as all those heroes knew this was intended only as wind, answered it in the same commodity, as it was cheap and plenty, but they did nothing beyond that he advised. General Ker Nee, however, raised a more serious gale at one time, and fiercely attacked some wash-houses, burned them, and kicked the inmates into the streets. He erected an altar to his barbarous principles at a place called 'Sand Lot,' which, according to the best authority extant, was situated across the bay, in the province of Marin, whence he made frequent incursions into the city. He and most of his followers, becoming enamored of that place, settled permanently over there some time afterward, and founded the city of San Conum (or some such villainous name), where they were buried after death. Indeed, the grave of the General is often pointed out near the crumbling walls of the old fort in which they resided, and over this grave still may be seen a monument, striped somewhat, like the poles barbers used in those days for signs, from which several learned men have concluded that he was originally a barber, but others as stoutly assert that it was in imitation of the court dress the General and his followers assumed when they went to reside at the fort. Why they should have shut themselves up there in such profound seclusion is a question about which history is not clear.

"While these things were being done, many of our people came over, despite this opposition, for they saw that the native barbarians were divided among themselves, and did nothing but talk and pass resolutions. It was very windy weather for many years; but our people were united for defense, which often is most effectual in an aggressive shape, and were assisted by a large number of more sensible Melicans who lived beyond the mountains, and who held to the theory that we had as much right here as they or any other people—that we were entitled to the benefits of a certain principle, that declared all men brothers, and God the impartial father of all. These were very sensible and good people, and though the Melicans of this coast had many conferences with those of the East, and urged upon them that our people were barbarians and heathens (just think of it!), it effected nothing. My dear sir, how singular it seems to us that in these conferences they urged against our ancestors as reasons for banishment only those things which we have for ten centuries considered our greatest virtues. They actually attacked our sacred religion, to say nothing of our customs, dishes, and the beautiful rites of our burial. They were, as I have said before, divided in council on the questions involved, and there is a tradition extant that this division was fostered by the sage Wing Ling, who demonstrated to those Eastern Melicans how they could become rich by perfecting a treaty between the United States and the Empire of China, and so pleased were they with the plan that they sent one Bullgamus to China, who accomplished the purpose for which he was sent. The Eastern men continuously afterward refused to adopt the mischievous distinctions urged by the red-handed Western barbarian, and called our people the down-trodden brotherhood. Indeed, it was a fortunate time for sowing these dissensions, as the men of the East had lately championed with success the same theories with regard to the negro, and were in that state of logic to readily accept and charge to the score of philanthropy the impression we wished to make. Our people still came in great numbers, and, when they arrived, paid no outward attention to the persecutions of the barbarians, yet they were prepared for any trouble that might arise. They had most of their trouble in this city, and were at one time prepared to cut the water-pipes and fire the town. It was then a small place of two hundred and fifty thousand people, a large number of whom were fancy but belligerent men, called Diddies, who came from some island in the Atlantic. Indeed, they went so far with their persecutions as to pass a law in their Congress prohibiting more than fifteen Chinese from landing on these shores from any one vessel; but our friends in the East, being powerful with the President, procured his veto of the bill, thanks to the money that section was making out of the Bullgamus treaty. At this General Ker Nee and others waxed wroth. They then sent delegates to the conventions of the two political parties that divided the sparse population of that day upon some question about the meaning of a certain paper, not now very clearly understood. The first one was held at the old town of Chicago, which is not far from the city of Kankakee, the delegation to which convention was headed by a fussy Israelite—some antiquaries suppose the same man whose name was blown away a few years afterward by a gale originating in his own windy writings. But be this as it may, he tried every way to get his anti-Chinese resolution in, but was squeezed out, and at last, to keep the Pacific delegation from going over to the other side, they put a cunningly contrived resolution in, that sounded like music, but had no tune. In fact, it meant nothing, and was so intended. Just here, permit me to add that a certain Ben Ah Butler, who was of some prominence in those days, wrote of these Eastern managers that they were the shrewdest men at doing things their own way, and pretending to do them the other, of all history, not excepting the family of Ah Gorham Lee, the founder of whose house was at that convention. He further tells a beautiful and moral story of one Konkerlin, a prominent member of that convention, who achieved notoriety by the wonderful and philanthropic feat of running five miles on a summer day to keep a man from shooting a poor German music teacher, and after he had appeased the irate gentleman, refused all refreshments, but consented to be ever afterward the friend of the family. I mention these things to show what powerful friends we had in the East at that period.

"Shortly afterward the other faction had a meeting at Cincinnati, which means *slaughter-pen* in the original Melican. Their resolution on the question was music with a tune; but we will pass this all, as one of the ephemeral evidences of the spirit of the age.

"Thus you will see, my dear sir, that events had considerably progressed in 1880; in the meantime, thirty-five thousand Chinese gathered in this city, and one hundred and fifty thousand were located west of the Rocky Mountains, though Consul Bee reported many less than that number. This gentleman was a man of far-seeing ponderosities, and saw clearly that, as an election for President was rapidly approaching, to report a falling away of Chinese residents and immigrants would practically take that question out of the contest, and relieve our Eastern friends of a great trouble that was gathering threateningly about them. You doubtless know how difficult it was for the profligate census-taking Melican to fail in making a full enumeration of our people, but it really turned out, the historian Ah Lee Kong gleefully reports, that not over half of the Chinese were enumerated. It has always been affirmed that there was what was called in the slang of that day a 'job' or a 'wash' (it has not been settled which) put up by one of the parties having the management of the census, and among whom most of our friends were to be found, and that they connived at this under-estimate, because it relieved their party of the burdens of substantial pro-Chinese tendencies. There were also other memorable reasons entering into this result, as was forcibly set forth on a memorable occasion by an Indian named Logan, a chief of the Illinois tribe, when he exclaimed, 'I don't owe posterity a d—d cent!' This is a proof, or, as the writers of that day beautifully said, 'The floating straw upon the current politique, directing the eager gaze of the inquiring student of social cosmics whither the festive stream of substantive events was meandering its murky tidal wave.' Those Eastern men cared nothing for our people, albeit they often spoke of the Rights of Man, Philanthropy, Man and Brother; and one, a poet-laureate by the name of Hayes, who in his time was much loved in several portions of the South, declared, in burning language, that this land was the asylum of the oppressed of all nations. Do I weary you, my dear sir, in dwelling on that ancient epoch?"

"No, your Excellency; I am deeply interested. But permit me to ask here what became of the descendants of the great General Ker Nee?"

"Well, sir, for the sins of the ancestor (which is authorized by the religion of the Melicans) they were all beheaded, in imitation of the bloody direction given by the General to cut off the sacred queues of our ancestors. The race became extinct. Years rolled by, and our people kept coming until they filled up this coast and passed beyond the mountains, then barren wilds, and poured into the cotton and rice-fields of the South. Then followed a long struggle with the negroes of that section, and, though the blacks wished to fight, and, as they brutally declared, 'feed our people to de cat-fish,' still our friends at the East sustained our people until the question was finally settled, one hundred years ago, and they still have possession of that country. From the first the aborigines showed a want of knowledge of our people that surprised us no little, but they failed entirely to see what was going on before their faces. Such was the almost incredulous egotism of those people, who popularly believed that one Melican was a match for ten 'heathens in any affair of personal daring. That they believed this is a matter for wonder, but such was the state of affairs, of which our people alone profited. They knew that China had a heavy population, but they mistook the situation by false estimates. True, some of their agitators, as early as 1879, pointed to the advantages we were obtaining over them in all the industries of the Pacific Coast, and, in a non-appreciative way, all the Melicans on this coast were unanimous in our denunciation, but they of the Eastern States did not feel, see, or, consequently, appreciate how unequally matched were their ill-fated brethren here. It was popular and customary to call 'John' a 'heathen,' and declare that a rat-eater was a fool; that one of their warriors was equal to ten of 'John;' but a curious fact is noted in the records of events found among the papers of Wong Fu Key, who lived here in 1881, from which we gather that the 'hoodlum' was nearly always whipped in the numerous physical contests of the day. This word 'hoodlum' is yet well known to our people, for you see he is here yet, in small numbers, 'tis true, but yet still extant. That was, I believe, the proper name of the larger part of the Melicans residing on this coast, as we who live see but few to whom the description of the great Wong Fu Key is not applicable. They knew that the Celestial Empire contained four hundred millions, but this odds they thought was offset by considerations of intelligence; nine thousand miles of ocean separating the two countries, with the then known and inferior appliances of navigation, in the glamor of their egotism formed the basis of a hearty contempt for the agitators. These latter in turn pointed to the fact that for thousands of years the Chinaman had been confined to his native land, and always regarded it as his home in life and after death. He had no navy in 1879, and but limited knowledge of the appliances of navigation and war, because those many centuries had been spent in ingraining into the national and individual character, by practice and descent, the true principles of economy, until he had the margin of life and death down to a few cents per day. This was true, and more. By this method was permitted the natural and utmost aggregation of population, made economy of utmost rigidity nature, taught patience and fanaticism, and prepared them to become the most apt and efficient imitators in the world. The exclusiveness maintained by the empire deprived the world of a knowledge of the vast wealth of China. About this time she began to borrow from other nations, and adopt, at small cost, as compared to the experiments they had been compelled to make in evolving them, those things soon to place her in the front as a maritime and military power. She had but followed on a grand scale the wisdom of the miller who dams up his water till he has enough to whirl his machinery successfully. She adopted the latest improvements in ships, and had arms the most effective on the globe, with armories and factories superintended by her own experienced workmen. She began to build vessels of commerce and war, and by 1895 was as well prepared for the competition on the water as any nation on the globe. It was during the fifteen years closing at that date that our Celestial Empire began to see, and our people to appreciate, that all this fuss and feathers against them was nothing more, and that the best field for substantial conquest and enlargement of the empire lay in this direction. The steps became apparent at once, that the Chinaman should become a citizen of the United States, so as to give him weight and influence. This was accomplished in 1890, and at the succeeding election in California the pro-Chinese ticket had seventy-four thousand majority. That frightened the opposition party, and it disbanded for want of leaders, no one being willing to arouse the certain political opposition of one hundred and fifty thousand voters, bound together by a common persecution and hope. So that party died, making its last fight in 1890, and so rapidly and to such an extent did this influence prevail that a Chinaman was elected a member of the Legislature in 1892, while in 1896 the same man, Wong Kiong Hop, became Mayor of San Francisco, that post of distinction being accorded by the affiliating party to secure the coalition. During all this time they were going into the South in great numbers, and becoming wealthy even more rapidly than on this coast. In that section their political advancement was clogged, and attended with much disturbance, to which 'John' only showed greater numbers and solid ranks. This produced a complete unification of the whites and blacks, for the first time in the history of that section. By the year 1900, they were strong enough to arouse an active opposition in New Orleans and other Southern cities, not entirely unlike that which had been experienced here. By 1925 they held much of the commerce and agriculture of the South, and had begun to establish manufactories for working up the native cotton into fabrics. It was this year that Wong Kiong Hop was elected to Congress from this State, having a short time before married a wealthy Melican woman. The imperial statistics now kept here show over one hundred Chinese as members of Legislatures, Mayors, Sheriffs, and in other important offices on the Pacific Coast, while an equal number held offices of similar importance in the South. During the following ten years nothing occurred to break the monotonous, but ever-increasing, growth of our power. In 1940 Wong Kiong Hop forced a rupture with the white political allies, and proclaimed himself candidate for Governor of California. This raised another bitter contest, but after the most active campaign he was elected over the combined white opposition, and all the offices of the State, with an insignificant exception, passed into Chinese hands. As the East cared but little for this section, they were not disturbed at this result, nor did the encroachments in the South cause them any uneasiness, beyond that of the growing manufacture of cotton fabrics, which they thought scarcely promised success. They cared nothing about the white or black Melicans of the South, as they could never agree. When one said yes, the other said no, and an affirmation on a proposition from one made the proposition all wrong for the other, for apparently no other reason than, as is usual, that the country was going to the bad under the other; while, from a standpoint of their joint interest, the country was going to worse than the bad under their silly sectionalism. And so the tide of events rolled on, the number of Chinese immigrants increasing each year, and no political party dared declare against it, on pain of Chinese opposition at the polls. The majority of these either stopped here or went into the South, as the policy was not to disturb the North by an inundation till the time came. I now pass over the next seventy-five years, in which this struggle went on, and come to the year 2000.

That you may fully understand the situation, I will beg your attention to a few statistics."

Then he arose, rapidly stepped to a book-case, took down a volume, and returned to his seat, which he drew to a center-table.

"You must know, sir, that, by this time, China had more merchantmen than all the navies of the world, peaceful and warlike combined, and a war navy double that of England, and ten times that of the United States. The white population of the United States was 49,430,000 in 1880. Here, sir, glance over these figures with me. In 1900, she had 80,437,249 whites. This rose in 1950 to 103,727,198, and by the year of which we are now speaking—2000—had fallen off to 91,200,473. Of blacks, in 1880, they had 4,327,341, which had gone down to 1,843,734 in 1900, and in 2000 to 320,453.

"As against this, we had, by the census secretly taken by the authority of the Imperial Government, in 1880, of Chinese in the United States, 203,730. It was in this year that we had demonstrated the foolishness of the opposition to us, and that the whites were practically tied, as to this question, by their own internal dissensions, and that leaders made promises and broke them, till, at length, the people had not faith enough to ask promises. Our people came, after that, in greater numbers. In 1890, they numbered 1,147,327; in 1930 we had on this coast alone that many, while in the whole country—let me see; yes, I have made the compilation on this fly-leaf—4,372,985. I take this year, 1930, because from then the influx became greater, swelling to the aggregate—not to weary you too much with detail—to 43,004,510 in 1965. That for 1980 showed an aggregate of 74,837,450. This was the era of greatest influx. In 2000, we had 90,374,001. A civil war need be mentioned only to say, that, during the time, the Chinese took firmer hold upon the country, and did little of the fighting. True, many of them were conscripted for military service, but their policy was not to fight, and they adhered substantially to it. In fact, they had a great advantage, as they were homogeneous, and threatened to join the other side if the conscription was forced, and this prevented its enforcement.

"Such indications will give you a true picture of the increase of population up to the year 2000. Now permit me to refer you to the statistics of 2070. There were: Whites, 71,052,903; blacks, 82,305; Chinese, 163,949,821; thus showing a majority of Chinese over all of 92,834,613. By reasonable calculation this number has now swelled to 100,000,000. The statistics of China show for that year a total of 405,987,489.

"During the earlier years social changes between the two races began to appear. Years of patient labor, with shrewd investments, had made some of our people very wealthy, and many built large and palatial residences in the most fashionable part of the city, furnished them after the most luxuriant American and European taste, and surrounded them with grounds that were models of art and beauty. Before this change our Consul at this place had been, a few times, invited to the houses of wealthy citizens to receptions, but it was always regarded as more official than social, and was confined to those in the diplomatic and consular service. This was first regarded as rather a favorable commencement, but after a few such events, when they saw that our representatives were men of fine, social culture, and, in every sense, socially the equals of those whom they met, this ceremony came to be considered the proper thing. It was an honor to have for an evening a representative of the Celestial Empire—the possessor of a pedigree that dated back two thousand years, a blue-blood among the blue-bloods. Indeed, we do not wonder at this when we remember that the American, while pretending pure democracy, in fact were socially aristocrats. By 'aristocrats' I may not exactly convey my idea, or faithfully portray the times to you. They affected the titled, and were quite snobby over any titled foreigner, or even over any of their countrymen who had attained eminence in public affairs. Particularly were they sweet (in the language of that day, which I culled from a wonderful work of the period, entitled, 'Good-bye, sweetheart, good-bye') on members of the English nobility, even worse than they are now; and to such an extent was this carried, that untitled strangers, feigning to be baronets, or even less dignitaries, in England, were admitted to the bosom of society, and lionized to a great extent, even without a demand for credentials. I once came across a curious story of such an event that served well to illustrate the peculiar receptive condition of society among those Melicans. A young lion, supposed to be an English noble, was found to be a plebeian, and was at once excluded from society; and yet this society would say that it received or expelled only on personal merit or demerit. You readily see if he were received on the claims of his personal merit his assumed title had nothing to do with it, so he was guilty of receiving nothing by false pretenses, and was certainly quite as good on matters outside of title as he was before. But they dismissed him, and shortly afterward fell into the same kind of snares. Any one who had official position saw the unmistakable tendencles of a growing social rank that seemed to attach to the office rather than to the person, while wealth, generally, was the 'Open, sesame,' to the patrician reception rooms. It became part of the social code, that with wealth the rule of presumptions attaching partly to persons was changed, and the person was not admitted because of positive personal qualities, but in the absence of insurmountable objections. As it was a matter of caste, it became quite easy to adjust the application of the rules of acceptance, so as to admit any desirable candidate with titles or wealth. This step from the acceptance of officials to that of the wealthy was easily taken, so potent had become the shekels of the wealthy in the social and matrimonial world. We have most abundant proof of this in the records of those times, kept by a prominent Chinese of this city, which makes mention of many notable invitations, and not a few communications of a tender character. As wealth had become, outside of official dignities, the only condition upon which the candidate for social honor received the highest preferment, young ladies who wished to hold their social guerdon, and who had admonitions of approaching bankruptcy, or who knew that they must bring money in the matrimonial market, or sink away from their former states, had strong temptation to fall into this trap set by commercial caprice. I have a curious relic of that age in the shape of a letter, which has been an heir-loom in my family for one hundred and eighty years. A brother of one of my ancestors, who was a dashing young fellow, with two millions of dollars, and well educated in the systems of both countries, was looking over his bank-book one day, when a letter was handed him."

Here the historian unlocked an *escritoire*, and took from an inner repository a faded envelope of tiny size and most exquisite shape, upon which was traced, in a delicate waving hand, bespeaking the gracefulness of the author, the name, "Mr. Ah Lee Tching, 1591 Dupont Street, City."

Taking the note from the aged envelope, and opening it, the following, in faded lines, but still beautiful, was read:

"CALIFORNIA STREET, City.

"DEAR MR. LEE TCHING:—You will, I know, pardon the boldness of this step, which would be unpardonable but for the motive that prompts it. My embarrassment will scarcely permit me to say what my heart is forcing from my lips; yet I must speak or die. I have met you, as you know, only twice, both times at Mrs. T——'s receptions at the Mission. Then the first time my heart went out to you, and ever since has known no man, no king, but you, in whom the happiness of my future is centered. Yes. *I love you madly!* Is this pleasant? Do you not find an echo in your own manly, noble heart for the maiden who loves you so tenderly? If you love me meet me on the incoming Oakland boat at 5 P. M., sharp, to-morrow. I will be alone. Devotedly, your own

"NINA ——."

The odors of roses that went with this little messenger, in that day of the long dead century, had ages ago taken wing, and gone to tell the listless airs the story of the maiden's devotion. The hand that penned it has been sleeping for a century and a half at San Mateo, from where, perchance, in each gloaming its spirit comes to listen to the moaning waves, and gaze across the tempestuous expanse of mysterious ocean toward the land that gave birth to the object of her love, where he, too, sleeps after the "fitful fever." Whether "Nina" was on the evening boat the next day, her little heart alternately trembling or standing still, as hopes and fears played shuttlecock with it, will never be known, as the naughty recipient of the missive was at that hour discussing boiled pig and rice, with fricasseed rat, and oblivious of the bright vision that so lately flitted across his life into the great world of the uncared for—like the low-voiced warbler that flits past us, to be lost in the darkness of the perfumed summer night of the south, with only one soft note of love and melody.

"I hear you ask," resumed the Professor, "whether the old system prevalent while our invasion was young, of leaving females behind, continued long. In answer, I have to give you a singular fact of natural history. For the most part during the eighteenth century few women came to America, but after that period a marked change took place. It was then safe to count upon a peaceful intercourse of the races, the prevalence of mere sentiment alone standing in the way, and as soon as the apprehension of massacres was dispelled it was far from difficult to get the ladies of China to come over. Indeed, considering the close margin of life then, and that for the last fifteen hundred years a falling off of laborer's wages five cents per day, although temporary, produced the worst possible effects of famine and pestilence, and that in America the Chinese laborer, who could not expect in his native land to make more than a bare subsistence, and was fortunate in doing this during his lifetime, could amass enough in a few years to be a well to do citizen in China, it is easily understood how women became anxious to come out in search of husbands. As soon, then, as the Emperor would permit, and peace here invited, they came over in vast numbers. As to the social status of those who came first, I am not prepared to speak, but it is reasonable to suppose that they were of the lowest walks of life, and were oftener immoral than otherwise. They were brought over by companies formed for the purpose, who paid the expenses of the passage, and furnished work till they could dispose of them as wives to some of their prosperous countrymen. They were subject to inspection and selection, 'tis true, much as is the horse in the market, the merchant charging the husband for transportation and other expenses, and a fee as profit. The Chinese who had been here for a few years gladly accepted the opportunities, and a brisk business was for many years carried on by those companies, under imperial charter. As in China, polygamy was practiced, the husband taking upon himself the evasion of the unjust and harsh Melican law against it. Thus the pure Mongolian race was rapidly propagated, and, with the rich and plentiful food of this new country, the birth-rate was largely increased among the Anglo-Chinese residents.

"While this was progressing it must not be supposed that our thrifty people did not to some extent amalgamate with the Melicans. At first the barriers of race were almost insurmountable, but thrift and prosperity, by attrition, gradually bore these down, so far as the lowest and the highest classes were concerned, and the amalgamation of blood began. It was fortunate that our people first reached and obtained a footing on the Pacific Coast, where race questions had never been prominent, and where nationalities of the white race were greatly mixed, and sharing all vicissitudes of fortune alike. Anywhere else in the United States more opposition would have been developed, but in the cosmopolitan population of this new West but little attention was paid to the first evidences of this tendency until they became sufficiently numerous and frequent to defy interference. One by one, through the two centuries that followed, these barriers were swept away, until, toward the close of the twentieth century, there was, in fact, none in public practice left, whatever may have existed as an abstract sentiment. Coupled with the natural laws was that prevalent sentiment among the Melicans of making money the standard of matrimonial acceptableness, and, as our people were frugal and industrious, they became wealthy, and could command wives from the native race with but little hinderance. As both races became very numerous, fortunes were less easily made, and this consideration pressed upon the natives with redoubled force, and became no inconsiderable influence in shaping this result. Now we come to a question of greater interest, from a scientific standpoint: What were the characteristics of the issue of this cross of races? As the supply of Chinese women was below the demand, they were always taken as wives by men of their own race, and the encroachments upon the whites were mostly for wives for Chinamen. Of course, in households thus composed of Chinese husbands and Melican wives, the husband ruled (and this could be done legally under Melican laws), and gave to it a predominant Chinese character. Meals were cooked and served, and all the social regulations were preserved, strictly upon the Chinese plan, both because of this law of man and nature, as well as its inherent superiority over the system of the wife's ancestry. There was given great preponderance to our ideas and civilization over the other during the formation period of the children's lives, and made them, in taste and sentiment, Chinese, even from their earliest infancy. Coupled with this was the advantage of engrafting upon a stock physically superior to ours, and hence it resulted that many of our most prominent men were of the light olive tints that resulted from the white mother's modification of the more pronounced type of the father. These children, being by culture more allied to our people, adopted our customs, and adorned our social circles, and made for us an additional link, still further obliterating the race barriers, and drawing the whites more toward us. Do not suppose for a moment that we were reciprocally affected in our distinctive nationalisms, for these we have ever, through all the centuries, kept unimpaired and unbroken. For this reason, also, the daughters, being, generally speaking, superior in physical beauty to the pure-blooded Mongolian lady, were much sought after, and popular as wives for the prominent and wealthy Chinese, and in but very few instances became wives for white men. On the other hand, white ladies had less opposition to the sons of this cross of races than to the pure-blooded Mongolian, both because of the white blood showing in the lighter tints, and also in obedience to that sentiment of race that made them half-brothers of their own great family. Without wearying you, my dear sir, you will from this readily see the drift of affairs, and understand how the increase of Mongolian population was so pronounced. All these people, having Mongolian blood in them, shared with us a common aspiration and a general sentiment of unity, growing in part out of the reasons and similitudes of condition. There are to-day among the Chinese in America quite four millions with an ancestry reaching back into both of these two great families of earth. This, however, is a clear Mongolian gain.

"There is now pending a Presidential election, and, for the first time, we have a Chinaman candidate—Honorable Hop Lee, the St. Louis billionaire. We are sure to elect him, and this the whites know. During the last forty years we have sent into New England and the North over thirty millions of our people. New England has lost her manufacturing trade, and they are so incensed at the shape of affairs that a war is imminent. The thing that annoys them most is a plank in the Mongolian platform, which I will read you:

"'403.—Recognizing their unfitness to exercise public power, from the abundant follies of which they have been guilty during the past two hundred years, we hereby declare the Melican unable to protect himself, unfit to exercise safely the elective franchise, and pledge the Mongolian party to the speedy disfranchisement of them, and the adoption of such other restrictive measures as may be necessary to properly secure to our people perpetual and permanent supremacy in this country in public and private affairs.'

"This, my dear sir, brings up the question squarely, and the issue is not doubtful. With a majority of Governors of our race, with the Senate, House of Representatives, and Supreme Court, and a majority of several millions on popular ballot, I can't see how we are to fail. In fact, they recognize this, and are preparing for war, still under the delusion that the hundred millions of odds in our favor cannot outweigh their valor. All this is anticipated, and we are prepared. Indeed, we have designed this event for twenty years, which is resulting as we wished and expected. Let me show you." And, taking me by the arm, he led me to a window, and, pointing toward a heavy, dark-hued house, rising over the others like a lofty mound on a plain, near where the Palace Hotel once stood, resumed: "You observe that heavy building? Well, in there are ten million rifles, of latest pattern, with a corresponding quantity of ammunition. This is alone for the Pacific Coast, but I don't see what we will do with them here. The hoodlum is a factor of the past, and the few still left will know better than to raise an arm. There are plenty of munitions of war in the East and South, and when the affair is precipitated they will see who make good soldiers. They have not, and cannot get, as many rifles in the whole Union as we have yonder. And then the Emperor of China will aid us. What can he do? This: We have this port, and he has already five millions of soldiers, with adequate transportation to put them across the ocean and into this port in three months from the time he hears of the beginning of hostilities."

Here he concluded, and I left him, with many protestations of thanks for his kindness. The following I write from personal observation during the period from this conversation to the hour in which I write:

The issue was squarely made, and war inaugurated without awaiting the election, which was completely overshadowed by the pending arbitrament of arms. The Americans had at last opened their eyes—who would not after reading that most explicit declaration in Section 403 of the Mongolian platform?—and over two millions of armed men were being rapidly mobilized in the great valley of the Mississippi. From every direction thousands of soldiers were being hurried toward the central position in southern Illinois. In the extreme South and on the Pacific Coast the Chinese forces completely overshadowed the whole country, and it was out of the question for substantial reinforcements to reach the Grand Army of Deliverance from either section. Still, in those remote and overshadowed portions no such excesses were committed by the Chinese as were expected—in fact, a profound sense of surprise existed at their moderation. Nearly three million Chinese were gathered in southern Illinois, under General Hop Wing. They were armed up to the highest achievements of art in firearms, for the most part with repeating rifles, fatal at the distance of two miles. As the Americans seemed to realize that the Mongolian ticket was irresistible, the pending election seemed to be forgotten in the more absorbing question of war. The appeal to arms was so manifestly the last chance that all eyes were turned to it, and about its issue all hopes clustered, the methods of peace being desperately abandoned for those of war.

The policy of General Phil. Schwartz, Commander of the American army, was to force the decisive conflict at an early day, while that of the Mongolian Commander was to temporize and delay till the column of two millions, hurrying from the Pacific coast, could reach the front. It was also made the wiser policy from the fact that five millions of imperial soldiers were *en route* from China to San Francisco, and expected to arrive within a month or six weeks. This immense force was being carried upon twenty-five hundred transports, convoyed by fifteen hundred monitors and improved gunboats, intending to protect the flotilla until its arrival in the Bay of San Francisco, and then pass rapidly around the Horn to blockade the Atlantic ports, to prevent assistance from their brethren of Europe reaching the Americans. It would take some time for this blockade to be effected, but it was calculated that this naval force could reach the Atlantic coast as soon as the land force from the transports could cross the mountains, with all their munitions of war, and join General Hop Wing at the front. Under the system of the art of war extant two hundred years ago, it would have been a grave question how this vast moving horde of five million soldiers could be provisioned during so long a march. They were, 'tis true, to march through a populous and wealthy country, but, from the nature of the passes, they marched along the same general route, and, under the old system, no country, however wealthy, could have supported them. This is true, even considering that they were Chinese, accustomed to live lightly, and perhaps the most frugally of earth, and that they could subsist upon much less even than the Mongolian soldier of America. I soon, however, saw that these reasons, however correct under the old system, had no application in this instance.

An American scientist some years before had analyzed food, and discovered the essential vital and life-sustaining element, and had succeeded in reducing the size and weight of a six months' ration to ten pounds, easily strung to the belt like the old cartridge-box. This the Chinese had adopted at once, as it was but a missing link for centuries in their system of economy, and the manufacture of food in this condensed form had become quite an industry. The Americans, as a rule, and a few of the wealthy Mongolians, for the mere gratification of the taste, now rapidly becoming disreputable, still loaded their tables with the dishes of old times. This was only, however, as a luxury, not a necessity. The discovery of condensing food seemed to have been the proper result of natural demands, and, when the masses adopted it, lulled to acquiescence by the anti-epicurean philosophers, in obedience to one of those great laws invariably controlling and adjusting supply and demand, a great dinner, such as any gentleman might every day give two hundred years ago, became a capital luxury that but few, even of the wealthy class, could continually indulge. This condensed food never administered to the taste, as a quantity as large as three compound cathartic pills of 1880 supplied the physical nourishment for an ordinary man for a day—even a soldier or laborer. This, then, explains the ease with which the maintenance and mobilization of such vast forces became comparatively easy. Every soldier of the Chinese Army of Invasion was provided with a kind of box, in size and shape, as well as mode of transportation, not entirely unlike the cartridge-box of 1880, in which were three thousand rations, for one man, of condensed food, which was enough to provision the army for a thousand days, or a little short of three years. Cooking utensils were entirely unnecessary, thus lightening baggage, which, with the absence of the provision commissariat, greatly lessened the impediments, and made movement easy and rapid. By a military bulletin, issued by the commanding General, Prince Ah Kio, son of the Emperor, I learned that this supply was calculated to last during the war. The water supply was still a great trouble, as formerly; so in this bulletin it was estimated that one million of this host would perish in crossing the arid plains lying between the Sierra and the Mississippi, as it was for the most part sufficient only for the sustenance of the inhabitants. It was still early fall when the vanguard of the first division of this grand army reached the Mississippi, and the almost innumerable host began defiling through the network of bridges prepared for their passage. Between them and the American forces, actively manœuvering to force engagements in detail, lay the native Mongolian grand army, two million five hundred thousand strong, while from the department of Kentucky and Tennessee nearly two millions were hurrying toward them to form a junction. The cities of Baltimore, Washington, Cincinnati, Memphis, and St. Louis were held by strong bodies of Mongolian troops, while from the latter place the Asiatic candidate for President, assumed the title of Chinese Viceroy, held his court, and issued orders in the name of the Emperor. Affairs were hastening rapidly to a final decision.

All efforts of the American commander, General Schwartz, to bring on an early engagement were fruitless. Almost every day battles were fought that, for numbers engaged and destroyed, were beyond parallel in modern warfare; still nothing decisive resulted. While forces enough to hold the ground were left in front of the Americans, flank movements, by heavy Mongolian forces, forced the Americans back, thus preventing the cherished wish of Schwartz.

Toward the latter part of the fall of 2081 the grand army of invasion completed a junction with the concentrated native Mongolian forces, and lay encamped in several counties in lower Illinois. This had been effected, and the ground held against the Americans, at a loss of half a million Americo-Mongolians, and to the Americans of little over half that number. General Schwartz seemed now in a dilemma, not certain whether to hazard a general engagement, or retire, and again try to beat them in detail. His army, now concentrated to the utmost, consisted, by report of the War Department of October 29, 2081, of 4,374,320 infantry, 97,342 cavalry, and of 18,240 field pieces. General Hop Wing had under his command, within the limits of ninety miles, 13,200,450 infantry, 173,000 cavalry, and 37,004 field pieces. On the 3d of November, while General Schwartz was still deliberating upon his plans, General Hop Wing advanced in thirteen columns to the attack, and moved rapidly on, so that on the 5th the advanced guard of the army encountered the American outposts, bringing on an indecisive engagement that lasted till nightfall. It was now too late to expect anything but a decisive engagement in force, so the night was spent by both parties in bringing up forces and arranging detail. Early next morning the conflict was taken up where left off the previous evening, the Chinese attacking with great fury, and sustaining heavy losses, while column after column was thrown in by both armies on the wings of those already engaged. All that day the battle raged with fury. The night of the 6th of November was spent, as the preceding one, in preparation for the grand attack of next day. The sun had scarcely risen on the 7th, when 8,000,000 Chinese were hurled, with fixed bayonets, upon their adversaries, to be met with a fire more destructive than the day before. This line of on-rushing heathens extended from the Wabash River across the rolling hills and valleys for nearly eleven miles, and were met by the intrenched Americans along the entire front. All day the conflict raged, while the smoke rose like a vast cloud-column wavering in the thunder-riven air, and cast a shadow of dim sulphurous twilight over the field, through which lurid volley-flashes, swift-dashing squadrons, and reeling, shattered columns could be dimly seen. The Americans were everywhere able to repulse the charge with greater loss than they sustained, and were congratulating themselves with assurances of victory, when the roll of platoons to the right rear aroused them. A column of 2,340,000 Mongolians had swept rapidly around their flank and was swinging to the American rear, where they encountered the division of General Smith, who was moving up to support the extreme right wing. This movement was, of course, checked, and a desperate fight then began on that part of the field.

The division of General Smith now reached from the Wabash River on his right to the right of the main line, reaching from a point on the river four miles below, and extending westward at an angle of about forty degrees—the Chinese closing in on them from two sides of the triangle, the third being formed by the deep and swollen Wabash. Under the repeated charges of Ah Ping, commander of the flanking column, and harassed by the Chinese cavalry, General Smith fell slowly back, resting his left on the right of the original American line of rifle breastworks, while his center and right were slowly borne back, forming a V, with the angle continually growing smaller. By nightfall, the two American lines were within two hundred yards of each other, back to back. General Schwartz had looked in vain for some hours for an opportunity to retreat, and had made several concentrated charges to that end; but no opportunity was presented, or, if presented, was such as to appall contemplation in view of the fearful sacrifice now certain. The die of destiny was now cast; the flanking column, with an irresistible rush, pressed General Smith back on General Schwartz's line, and the Americans were surrounded. Though the Mongolian hosts passed through the American lines and into each other, they seemingly took no notice of it. Night had fallen, but the battle went on. Charge after charge rolled up against the thinned Americans, only to grapple a while, and retire shattered and bleeding. Toward midnight a heavy snow-storm set in, the fleecy particles filling the air with whirling sheets of ice. Through all the long night the din of battle fell upon the ear, and when day dawned, struggling through the storm, the partial lull of an hour gave way to the wildest fury. With the first gray of dawn, the long, yellow-uniformed hosts moved with yells and fixed bayonets, when the white flag arose over General Schwartz's line. The only response it met was a roar, like the bellowing of a storm-lashed ocean pouring its high waves among rocks, and the attacking column fixed bayonets and moved forward. One, two quick volleys from the now desperate Americans strewed the ground with them, and with wild cries, smoke, snow, and unutterable confusion and fury, the three lines closed.

The sun was high in the heavens when the conflict ended. The American army had passed from earth, while about their couch of death lay five millions of dead and wounded Mongolians. But few of the Americans were taken prisoners, and they were afterward placed in slavery by especial imperial command.

Thus was fought the great battle of the Wabash. The grand American army was exterminated. Then the smaller bodies of soldiers all over the country disbanded, or were furiously attacked and dispersed to meet no more, while a reign of horror, unknown even under the rage of Huns, Vandals, and Goths, spread all over the land. The mild policy advocated and practiced before by the Chinese had subserved its end; now dawned a different day under the changed rule. From the Gulf of

Mexico to the St. Croix, from Boston to San Francisco, the flames of unbridled passions rioted upon defenseless people; each midnight sky photographed in its angry reflections the conflagrations of a thousand cities. The blow was decisive; the Republic fell on the Wabash, broken into a million fragments; her people passed into Asiatic slavery. The fruit-time of folly had come. By vice-regal order, rapine, murder, arson, and all the devils of human passion were to be unrestrained for a hundred days. Revolting at this sickening corollary of a people's folly, I turned away, murmuring to myself, When will the world learn that milksop philanthropy is not statesmanship?

LORELLE.

SCIENCE AND INDUSTRY.

NOTES ON THE FORMATION OF COAL.

It is well known that the coal-beds had their origin during the vast vegetable growths of the carboniferous age. The carbon and bitumen of that rank vegetation, which escaped ordinary decay, were undoubtedly solidified into coal, but by what particular process this was brought about is a matter in regard to which scientists differ. The coal of recent formation is not regarded as a true coal. It is rather of the nature of fossilized vegetation. There is no sign of vegetation in pure coal, while the lignites present unmistakable indications of vegetable fiber. The inference is that the component parts of true coal have been expelled from vegetable and animal matter by heat and pressure, in the form of oil, and afterward solidified into coal. A German scientist, Moses Zweizig, has recently published some interesting notes in this connection, from which we condense as follows: The enormous oil deposits of the carboniferous age resulted not only from resinous vegetation, but also from the countless myriads of marine animals which accumulated in connection with vegetable matter, in localities and under conditions favorable to such results. When these oil deposits were subjected to the proper conditions of heat, evaporation, and pressure, the coal-beds were formed, more or less bituminous, according to the degree of heat and other conditions to which they were exposed. In some cases these oil deposits were so sealed between rocky strata that no solidification could take place, and the oil has remained to this day. From these reservoirs we are now deriving the coal oil of commerce. The best anthracite coal contains about ninety per cent. of carbon; the oily cannel coal was evidently formed with very little heat; the ordinary bituminous with more; while the hard anthracite has been subjected to such a degree of heat as to render it nearly a pure carbon, like the residuum from the ordinary distillation of crude petroleum. Oil, being lighter than water, it readily accumulates on the surface of lakes, and, on long exposure, it forms a sheet of bitumen, or pitch, which in winter is hard, so that a man can walk on it with safety. There is such a lake on the island of Trinidad, and similar lakes are known to exist in other volcanic regions. Hence, during the periods of vegetable and animal oils, and of extraordinary volcanic activity, producing, no doubt, an abundance of oil directly from mineral sources, it is reasonable to suppose that immense bodies of water were thus covered to a great depth with plastic coal. The time of such formation necessarily corresponded with a period of volcanic inactivity. While forming, the sheet may have been occasionally sprinkled with a slight shower of ashes, causing an impurity in the coal; and a rent in the sheet, caused by contraction, may account for the fact that the miner sometimes suddenly loses the vein, and must grope for it through the rock. When volcanic action revived, the greatest imaginable changes must have taken place to account for the strata of rock overlying the seam. Between some of the seams the stratum is over two hundred feet thick. Showers of ashes or streams of lava may have sunk the sheet to the bottom, when, during the next period of inactivity, another seam may have been formed, to be submerged in like manner, but perhaps with a stratum of only a few feet in thickness.

SPECTRUM ANALYSIS.

Notwithstanding the good work which the spectroscope has done in some directions, and although its delicacy and accuracy seems to be well established in qualitative analysis generally, but little success has thus far been attained in its application to quantitative analysis. The principles which form the basis of these two processes are quite dissimilar. Qualitative analysis by the spectroscope is accomplished in the following manner: When an element is subjected to the heat of the electric spark, it is volatilized, and emits rays of certain colors, or, more correctly speaking, of certain wave-lengths. These wave-lengths are always the same in color and position on the spectrum for the same element. No two elements show the same wave-length, or color and position. When a compound body is thus subjected, each element shows its own proper lines, so that we can determine, at sight, the name of the elements of which that compound body is made up; but we cannot, by this method, determine the *relative proportions* of the different elements in the compound body. To reach that end, which is quantitative analysis, a different method is required. The principle which forms the basis of the method as usually employed was first noticed by Mr. Lockyer, and may be stated as follows: When a powerful induction coil is used for obtaining the spectrum of any mineral body, if the distance between the electrodes is gradually increased, certain of the lines of the spectrum break in the middle; and on still further increasing the distance between the electrodes, the lengths of the broken spaces in the spectrum lines are proportionally increased, until the lines themselves finally disappear. The most elaborate experiments in this direction, and after this method, have been conducted by Mr. W. C. Roberts, of the London

Mint, and by Mr. A. E. Outerbridge, of the Philadelphia Mint. Their experiments were undertaken with the special view of employing spectrum analysis for assaying the precious metals; but the results, as reported by each of these gentlemen, are quite unsatisfactory, and the method, founded on Lockyer's discovery, is pronounced "defective in the extreme." Mr. Outerbridge found that while the spectroscope was very sensitive to pure metals, a comparatively large quantity of gold might be present in an alloy, and the spectroscope fail to indicate even its presence. This same want of sensitiveness holds good of other metallic alloys. On this finding, Mr. Outerbridge pronounces the spectroscope impractical for assaying purposes. Messrs. John Parry and Alexander E. Tucker read a joint paper before the English Iron and Steel Institute, in May last, on the application of the spectroscope to the analysis of *iron* and *steel*, in which they came to conclusions very similar to the above in relation to the precious metals. They say: "Theoretically, a well focused spectrum of steel should be an unerring index to its composition; this is partly true in practice, but it is not, in our experience, absolutely so." They further report, that spectra of pure iron, chrome steel, Siemen's steel, and pig iron, etc., have, in some of their experiments, failed to show the presence of bodies which further research has proved to exist. Several reasons are given by Messrs. Parry and Tucker why this should be the case in their experiments with iron compounds. First, the number of lines due to iron is so great—from 100 to 150—that they overlap, in the lines due to other bodies, in the small spectra of only two inches, which was the largest they could obtain with the apparatus they used. Second, the intensity of light due to the mere *traces* of bodies may not be sufficient to record lines on the photographic plate, which was used instead of a screen. Third, because of the variation in the volatility of the elements and, therefore, the necessity, but impossibility, of any variation of the intensity of the spark to conform to the requirements of the different elements of any given compound. From the above it will appear, that there is need of enlarging our chemical knowledge in regard to spectrum analysis before it can be made fairly practical in the way of analysis, or absolutely reliable for even determining the bare presence of all the different elements in any given compound.

NEW USES OF THE TELEPHONE.

According to a statement in a leading technical journal, it appears that there is good reason for believing that the telephone may soon supersede cupellation in the assay office, at least to some extent. Professor Roberts, the chemist of the London Mint, has recently discovered that equal and similar volumes of various metals and alloys have each a different and constant effect upon an electric current flowing around a coil. If two coils are connected by a wire, and a piece of silver alloy of known weight and fineness is placed in one of them, a disturbance of the current is produced, which may be correctly indicated by an attached telephone. Now, if another piece of silver alloy of equal weight and fineness be placed in the other coil, the equilibrium of the two coils is restored, and the telephone is silent. But if the second piece of silver varies either in weight or fineness from the first the telephone instantly detects the fact. Hence, it is easy to comprehend how, by the use of standard alloys, the telephone may be employed as a reliable and ready substitute for the slow and tedious process of assaying. It is proposed to give the first practical test of the value of this discovery by employing it in determining the fineness of silverware, which has hitherto been done only by scraping, or boring, oftentimes manifestly to the permanent injury of the ware subjected to that process. Its use in readily determining counterfeit coins will at once suggest itself. But little is probably known as yet in regard to the adaptability of the telephone. Its employment in thermometric experiments, and its use in almost indefinitely extending the sense of hearing, are but the beginning of its possibilities. It will, doubtless, eventually prove capable of being utilized in many other and now most unlikely ways.

THE MECHANICS' FAIR EXHIBITION.

The modern "Industrial Fair" is now regarded as one of the greatest moral forces that ever impelled humanity in its rightful career of progress. In no other way than by this grand mode of object-teaching could such new and extensive fields of practical action have been opened up as have been improved during the past half century. A community of interest and thought has grown out of these industrial exhibitions, which has pervaded the whole civilized world with a new and healthy impulse in the direction of the beneficent arts of peace, in disseminating more widely the knowledge and spirit of trade, and in giving capital a more secure basis of investment, and labor a more constant field for employment. In short, the legitimate mission of these exhibitions—whether county, State, or national—is the unity of mankind into one great industrial brotherhood. The series of exhibitions, culminating with the one which has just closed in this city, has not been without their due influence for good. In passing through the pavilion, as we have often done during the past month, our attention has been arrested by quite a number of new and valuable inventions and improvements in almost every department. We regret that space will not admit of a full description of each; but as it is, we can only make the following brief reference: In the way of machinery we have, first, several additions to our mining appliances—Huntington's oscillating stamp-mill, Bruckman's combined crusher and pulverizer, Waugaman's dry separator, Goss & Adams's improved ore-feeder, and Dodge's rock-breaker. We have also, in the line of new machinery, an important agricultural invention in the way of an improved elevator and feeder for threshing machines by Byron Jackson; a new safety clutch for elevators by R. E. Hendrickson; a valve cut-off by A. O. Gale; and a washing machine, of novel construction, by Freiloer & Mahler. Another new invention, and one which added quite a novel feature to the pavilion, was an automatic railroad signal, to give warning of an approaching train, so that tracks and switches may be in readiness. We also noticed an improved hat-rest for opera houses, and other places of public assembly; an improved wire cushion for billiard tables; a novel device, whereby a bed is made, by a slight manipulation, to assume the character of a parlor organ, etc.

ART AND ARTISTS.

POPULAR TASTE.

Some time ago a wealthy San Franciscan, who had just returned from abroad, was boasting of his success in having procured, at very moderate rates, a choice collection of foreign pictures. He admitted his inability to judge of merit in works of art, but was perfectly satisfied with those he had procured, and proceeded to relate his method of obtaining them. It was his custom while in Paris to visit regularly places where pictures were sold, especially at auction. As the crowds came in he observed closely before which pictures they most congregated, and, after listening to their comments, if favorable, he marked upon his catalogue the pictures under consideration, with the intention to bid upon them. Since it was his wish to purchase cheaply, of course the greater number and more meritorious of those selected fell into other hands, yet he secured between thirty and forty works for the embellishing of his Californian home. Notwithstanding our lack of faith in the excellence of this manner of securing a gallery of pictures, we gladly accepted an invitation to view them, hoping to find evidences of higher general taste among the French people in matters of art than we believe to belong to the masses in general in other localities. It is a commonly expressed opinion by many people of intelligence the world over, that the masses are, after all, the best judges of merit, whether in music, literature, the drama, or art, as applied to painting and sculpture. Being unfamiliar with the processes by which certain results are produced, the methods employed have, of course, no place in their reasoning, but their conclusions are based entirely upon results attained. If a play be absorbing, and the parts acted with spirit, the production is at once pronounced a success, and the general verdict is that the author is entitled to distinction. The popular writer is pronounced the great writer, and the painter whose pictures excite the greatest general interest is, in the opinion of these intelligent gentlemen, the one upon whom the laurels should be heaped. Having reached this conclusion, they are content to go no further. They find in it consolation for the fact that their judgment differs, in many instances, very materially from that of so-called connoisseurs and professors. They attempt to make no distinction between peoples, and taste, as a result of more or less education, is by them completely ignored. They believe in inherent capacity, and cite themselves and the community in which they live as an evidence of the correctness of their views. Ask one of these gentlemen if he considers the popular test an infallible one, and he will unhesitatingly answer yes. Yet he will make no attempt to explain the fact that in his own community, "Under the Gaslight," or some equally sensational play, will draw crowded houses for weeks, while a Shakspearean representation is withdrawn from the boards after three nights, for want of patronage and popular appreciation. He will hardly claim that the "Arkansas Traveler" or "Ten Thousand Miles Away" are among the greatest musical productions, notwithstanding their popularity, and if asked to explain why Mr. Hopps's sign, representing a party of emigrants crossing the plains, attracts more admirers among the masses than the best picture ever painted by Hill or Keith, will only shrug his shoulders, and reaffirm his faith in the popular judgment. Absurd as this statement may seem, it is true in regard to a large number of our most respected citizens. Upon visiting the collection brought from France, it would be useless to say we were not disappointed. Though showing more or less skill, the pictures belonged to what the French call the "*bourgeoise*" order, and what in our own country are designated "pot-boilers"—showy, sensational subjects, gayly painted, and intended to captivate the uncultured, and keep the pot boiling, while artists devote their time and care to more serious works upon which to base their claim to distinction in their profession. As a people, the French, perhaps, show a greater aptitude for art than any other. This doubtless is owing to the greater facilities they enjoy for its study and cultivation. From infancy their thoughts are more or less associated with art. Their capital is the art center of the world. Their galleries are more numerous, and comprise many of the greatest works of ancient and modern times. The very atmosphere they breathe seems to be impregnated with it. Yet none perceive more readily than they the distinction between cultivated and uncultivated taste. If one of our intelligent citizens were to assert in their presence the belief that a community of Americans, who, until recently, had never seen other than very mediocre pictures, and who possessed no knowledge of the possibilities of art, could pass intelligent and just criticism upon pictures, he would at once become an object of ridicule. That picture making is a science, as well as an art, is yet to be learned by many; and that knowledge is as essential to a proper appreciation of the arts, as it is of the sciences, will be admitted by all who have given the subject the attention it deserves.

THE OBELISK.

No doubt, ages hence, when London bridge shall be in fact a thing of the past, and the crumbling remnants of St. Paul's shall stand a stranger in their own land, surrounded by a new civilization, overtowered by hitherto unknown types of architecture, a curious fragment from the forgotten past, the wanderer to the continent of America will be astounded to discover upon that distant shore a towering monolith, so distinctive in character as to defy all reconcilement with surrounding objects. Grave treatises will be written by the sages of that time to account for the strange similarity existing between this and other monuments still extant in the ancient kingdoms of England and France. Like fragments will be found on the northern coast of Africa. Papers will be prepared and read before the learned societies of the day proving its Egyptian origin, and indulging in novel speculations as to what special time in the world's history the Pharaohs issued their mandates from an American throne. That the children of Thebes and Memphis were a powerful and aggressive people, and had at some time, lost to history, overrun the world, will be proved in many an earnest debate by these lasting monuments. Before that time, be it understood, history will have repeated itself. Empires, kingdoms, and republics will have grown, flourished, and disintegrated. A new Genghis Khan will have arisen, and, dividing his mighty forces, will have advanced East and West, sweeping the world of its ancient civilization, using our libraries to heat their baths, as did the conquerors of Alexandria; or burning them on the highways, to destroy all traces of a false religion, after the manner of zealous Christians. When all this shall have been accomplished, the obelisk recently landed in New York will then become the possessor of a secret to which that of the Sphinx, were it known, might appear commonplace. All the pleasantry and satire expended by our contemporaries upon the harmless stone will have perished with the story of its transportation, and the Alexandrian obelisk will stand a perpetual puzzle. We do not insist that events shall transpire exactly as above foreshadowed. Probably they will not; but to make a rather sudden transition from fancy to fact, we confess ourselves much at a loss to comprehend why there is so much apparent opposition, or, at the least, ridicule, expended by some of the Eastern periodicals upon this interesting and, no doubt, valuable monument of early Egyptian art, to say nothing of its historical associations. The expenditure of the $100,000 for its purchase and transportation may be begrudged by some of those who contributed nothing to the fund, but the large number in this country interested in archæology who have not the time or means to bestow upon lengthy journeyings to gratify their taste will welcome its arrival, and view it with interest. Having no antiquities of our own, the American is more disposed to appreciate those of other nations; and it would seem that all should feel interested in procuring as many such objects as possible for their edification and instruction. Indeed, in our opinion, the only regret to be felt is the denuding a country of these interesting monuments of her past history, and disassociating them with the scenes of the events they record. Sometimes, however, as with the Elgin marbles, their preservation depends much upon a transfer of ownership, and where such is the case, we hope America will secure her full share.

NEW PICTURES.

As a rule, our artists seem reluctant to place upon view many new pictures. The various places of exhibition contain mainly works with which the public are already acquainted, though at Morris & Kennedy's, on Post Street, several new pictures are to be seen that are deserving of special mention. Among these, Mr. Perry's small picture of a sleeping babe is particularly attractive, as well for the simple, quiet composition as excellent quality and rich, unobtrusive color. Mr. Hahn has also two small pictures, companion figures, representing two types of girlhood engaged in domestic pursuits. They are drawn with Mr. Hahn's usual care, and painted in his best style. The public are already so familiar with this artist's work that it requires no special recommendation. Those interested in the doings of our absent artists will be gratified to find at the same place specimens of the later work of Benoni Irwin and Thaddeus Welch. Both of these gentlemen have been abroad for several years, and their pictures show marked progress. Mr. Irwin's "Surgical Operation," after Rembrandt, is regarded as an accurate copy of that famous, though by no means enticing, subject, and will be of special interest to those unacquainted with the original. The "Lady with a Guitar" is more pleasing, and deserves careful study. The figure, draped in Spanish costume, with black veil and rich dark-toned dress, sits in profile, relieved against a dazzling yellow background. The free and skillful handling, fine harmonious coloring, and accurate preservation of values will at once impress the spectator. Mr. Welch's picture of "The Shoemaker" is a surprise to his friends and those acquainted with this artist's former work. He had, previous to his departure, become so identified with landscape painting that it is difficult to reconcile him with the painter of the excellent *genre* picture now on view. The subject is a homely though picturesque one, and is painted with such fidelity to nature as to cause one to forget his whereabouts, and imagine himself actually in the presence of the hardworking, unshaven old cobbler, who, seated before his littered bench, with greasy cap and apron, is engaged upon the shoe of a young girl who quietly watches his movements. The old interior, with soiled walls, well used stove and utensils, littered floor and benches, and large glass window, through which one sees the sunny street, with its shops and pedestrians, and, above all, the cobbler himself, almost challenge criticism. Shoes of all conditions—new and old, large and small, masculine and feminine, patrician and plebeian—strew the table, cover shelves, floor, and benches, each one with its story, and painted with the utmost faithfulness. The picture is so well composed, the painting so excellent, and the drawing and modeling in every other respect so accurate, that one is at a loss to decide whether the peculiar enlargement of the cobbler's feet and many of the shoes strewn round, is the result of accident or intention. Notwithstanding this apparent defect, the picture cannot fail to interest and command the admiration of all who see it.

MECHANICS' FAIR EXHIBITION.

The display of pictures at the Mechanics' Fair, just ended, in general excellence probably surpassed any recently held in that connection. With very few exceptions, the pictures were old to our San Francisco public, but many of these are sufficiently good to excite fresh interest with each exhibition—more especially those of Rosenthal, and some of the works of many of our home artists. Undoubtedly the best picture in the exhibition, from the standpoint of the artist, is "The Awakening," by J. G. Gony, an importation of the late W. C. Ralston, and now the property of Messrs. Hagerman and Haquet. It represents a nude woman, just awakening from slumber. The accessories are so simple, and so subordinated to the figure, that the picture resolves itself simply into a splendid study of the female form. The former, however, are so admirably painted, and so rich and harmonious in color, that to our mind they constitute the chief excellence of the picture. The figure is gracefully posed, the drawing faultless, and the flesh-coloring good—the whole, in fact, presenting so much realism as to have aroused much vigorous opposition from a good portion of the community, and much comment *pro* and *con* from our leading press. The opposition became so strong that the management was at length induced to veil the picture, and finally adopted the rather questionable plan of leaving the matter of its exhibition to the wish of a majority of visitors upon a fixed evening. Mr. Guay's picture is, to our mind, a simple portrayal of one of God's most beautiful creations, executed so skillfully as to command approbation as a work of art. It would have excited no comment whatever in a French gallery, unless it be for its excellence, and certainly is no worse than many of the productions of the famous English artist, Etty. We believe that the true lover of art and nature can gaze upon it as enthusiastically and admiringly as upon any other beautiful natural object, and not for a moment entertain a question of its propriety. A simple, guileless nature could certainly study its beauty of line, delicacy of modeling, its lights, shades, and half-tones, the masterly treatment of the flowing hair, and the elegantly painted accessories, without the least fear of contamination. Indeed, so much depends upon the character of the spectator that it is difficult to establish any fixed rule of propriety in the matter. The question simply resolves itself into one of custom and training. In our country, or in some parts of it rather, we are unaccustomed to such exhibitions, and are a little puzzled to know how to behave in their presence. We can certainly dispense with them; and as a simple act may become evil by the construction we choose to put upon it, it is perhaps well to retard the introduction of such works until our community is better prepared to receive them.

BOOKS RECEIVED.

A History of Classical Greek Literature. By Professor J. P. Mahaffy, Trinity College, Dublin. New York: Harper & Brothers. 1880. For sale in San Francisco by Payot, Upham & Co.

This is a work in two generous duodecimo volumes by an author who had already gained a good repute. Not to mention other productions, his "Social Life in Greece" met with a very favorable reception not many years ago. Now he appears in the more critical *rôle* of a general historian of the wide range of the classical Greek literature. The undertaking was a large one, and, as these volumes show, it was not rashly entered on. The field was an open one: for since the elaborate work of Colonel Mure, and a translation of K. O. Müller, supplemented by Donaldson, no English author had given a connected view of the results of the later investigations. It was time for some competent hand to present the freshest fruits of modern research, and lay before the English-reading public "a prospectus of Greek literature as a whole, of its life and growth, and of the mutual relation of the authors whom younger students read in accidental and irregular order." In executing the task thus described Professor Mahaffy treats only of the classical Greek writers. He resolutely closes the list of poets with Menander, and of prose writers with Aristotle and the lost historians of the fourth century B. C.; thus ignoring the productions of the critical Alexandrians, though giving account of Theocritus and others of the so-called Alexandrian school. As a needful introduction to the earliest Greek classics, he treats of the rise of epic poetry, and the succession of prevailing forms. Lyric poems must have antedated the extant epics. All other styles, together with many epics that preceded Homer, were utterly supplanted by the superior Homeric epics. Each prevailing type then ran its full career till it was worn out, the lyrical returning afresh after the epic, to be, in turn, overshadowed by the dramatic. As to Homer, Professor Mahaffy holds a position midway between the extreme German skeptics and the strong English conservatives, like Mure and Gladstone. He is a chorizontist, believing that the "Iliad" and the "Odyssey" were from different authors. He thinks, with Grote, that an Achilleid was the core of the "Iliad," but supposes the overlying portions to be, not from an original Iliad, itself a unit, but a concrete from various hands. Among the early rhapsodists who composed and recited heroic lays, and wandered from court to court, "one, called Homer, was endowed with a genius superior to the rest." Probably his superiority, like Shakspere's, was not fully appreciated at first; but succeeding generations of listeners gradually recognized his excellence, and then his work was extolled and enlarged. Various episodes were added, and some glaring inconsistencies attached themselves to the older poem. "When the greatness of the 'Iliad' had been already discovered, another rhapsodist of genius conceived the idea of constructing a similar but contrasted epic from the stories about Odysseus and Telemachus; and so our "Odyssey" came into existence." With all his fairness, we think Professor Mahaffy fails to bring out the force of the chief objection to all the theories of a patchwork Homeric authorship; viz., the necessity of supposing that many, or several, poets of such magnificent gifts, should work in such perfect harmony. We are thankful that, in protest against the destructive German critics, Professor Mahaffy does leave us a Homer; but he gives us still too many Homers. By his own assertion it is not easy to pick out the inferior work of the interpolating and supplementing rhapsodists. The German critics can in no wise agree in their specifications. If there was a series of these mightiest of the world's poets, would they work in just the same vein, or would they differ as Æschylus, Sophocles, and Euripides differed in tragedy, or as Plato and Aristotle differed in philosophy? In an appendix, Professor Sayce treats of the Homeric problem from a linguistic point of view. He certainly does make it appear that the language of Homer may be called a mosaic; but the blended Æolic, Ionic, and Attic elements may prove rather an inevitable contamination by transmission than an original diversity of workmanship. Passing over Professor Mahaffy's interesting account of the chief lyric poets, we note his estimation of Æschylus as not only first, but chief, of the tragic three. A still greater claim is put forth by our critic. He says, "So long as a single Homer was deemed the author of the 'Iliad' and the 'Odyssey,' we might well concede to him the first place, and say that Æschylus was the second poet of the Greeks. But by the light of nearer criticism we must retract this judgment, and assert that no other poet among the Greeks, either in grandeur of conception or splendor of execution, equals the untranslatable, unapproachable, inimitable Æschylus." Professor Mahaffy almost reverses the usual judgment as to Sophocles and Euripides, claiming for the latter more tragic power than is wont to be conceded to him. "He was, doubtless, an inferior artist to Sophocles; he was certainly a greater genius, and a far more suggestive thinker." A full account is given of the prince of comic writers, Aristophanes. The "New Comedy," in which Menander stands preeminent, is treated briefly, and somewhat unsatisfactorily. As Professor Mahaffy's first volume is wholly taken up with the Greek poets, so the second is devoted to the Greek prose writers. This entire separation of prose and poetry is in imitation of recent German authors, and has decided advantages. It keeps the two pictures as distinct as their subjects are unlike. Introductory to the account of Herodotus is a chapter on the early use of writing, the influences of religion and philosophy upon literature, and the dawn of history. Between the great historians Herodotus and Thucydides we have the figures of the early philosophers, the Sophists, Socrates, and the earliest Greek orators; between Thucydides and Xenophon come Plato and the pre-Demosthenic orators; after Xenophon, Demosthenes and his contemporaries; after Demosthenes, Aristotle, the wayward and wonderful genius, on whom even the brilliant and more wonderful Plato could not impress his own image. We could wish that the historians, the orators, and the philosophers had been kept more distinct in Professor Mahaffy's vivid picture of the Attic golden age. For one thing we have especially to thank him. He has not confused his account by a mass of dry details, but has preserved a proper historical perspective. The really great figures in this greatest of the world's literatures stand out in just proportions. The criticism is at once sympathetic and independent. The narrative is uniformly interesting, and often charming. Frequent allusions to recent writers seem to link the ancient world to the modern. Throughout these volumes we find a breadth and suggestiveness of treatment stimulating alike to the scholar and to the thinker. We commend Professor Mahaffy's work to all intelligent readers who do not wish to be ignorant of the most intellectual and the most original people ever projected into the great drama of human thought and human activity.

THE LIFE AND LETTERS OF HORACE BUSHNELL. New York: Harper & Brothers. 1880. For sale in San Francisco by Payot, Upham & Co.

A little over thirty years ago a small volume dropped into the religious circles of New England, made up of a dissertation on language, and three discourses delivered on important public occasions, the whole bearing the title, *God in Christ*. The subject was well fitted to seize the mind for which it was meant with power. The thought was a trifle nebulous, perhaps, but warm with an intense vitality, while the style was electric in every touch. The heresy hunter scented fine game in the book. An ecclesiastical trial soon widely advertised the "bane" and the author. The latter was saved from the stake by a qualified acquittal, which still left an appetizing suspicion hanging over his orthodoxy. Another volume, *Christ in Theology*, soon followed, aiming to more fully explain and clear up the positions of the author. This failed to dissipate the suspicions of the more sensitive. But it was now evident that a new light had come to view in the theological heavens—more than a transient meteor; but was it a star, or only a comet "trailing its evanescent glory across the sky?" The theological students and younger men in the ministry read the new thinker with avidity, and from this early taste many of them came to look for any new paper from the same hand with something of the eagerness with which the novel-reader hastens for the latest outcome from his favorite author. *Sermons for the New Life* appeared in 1858, original enough in thought to take them entirely out of the traditional dullness of sermon literature, rich in the suggestions of a profound and varied experience, and breathing withal a spirit so saintly, so almost pietistic, that the sensitiveness of the orthodox was greatly allayed, and they concluded that this phenomenon, were he star or comet, had better be left to go on undisturbed in his own orbit. The next year came his *chef-d'œuvre*, *Nature and the Supernatural*, designed to make clear the harmony between "science and religion, reason and revelation, nature and the supernatural." This work had long engaged his mind, and he had found time to nearly complete it during a year spent here in California in quest of health, in 1856–7, at which time the Trustees of the College of California (afterward transformed into our State University) tendered him the Presidency of that institution. This honor his love for the church over which he had been settled as pastor, in Hartford, Connecticut, for more than twenty years, constrained him to decline. His teeming brain afterward tossed to the reading public half a dozen octavos on miscellaneous subjects, largely "the literary by-play of a laborious profession," as he calls one of them, in which, notwithstanding great and growing physical infirmity, his amazing versatility seemed to spin off the "plus energy" of his mind. Meanwhile he had serious work on hand. In elaborating his *Nature and the Supernatural*, another theme opened to his view, which he made his next great labor. The fruit was *Vicarious Sacrifice*, which was given to the world in 1866.

In this he claims that the atoning sufferings of Christ were no appeasing compensation thrown to angered Justice as an equivalent for the penalty of sin, no mystic device to liquidate the claims of law by putting the innocent under pain for the guilty, but the simple duty of the Sufferer in fulfilling his mission to an evil world; that in this simple fidelity to his own aim, even to the bitter end, he wrought out a divine manifestation of love to the unworthy, which is the mightiest of all influences, under well known laws of impression, to break down enmity and win love, and so "ingenerate" the spirit and life of the Sufferer in the hearts of those who are won by his self-sacrifice. This view startled the orthodox friends of the author again not a little, but it was so manifestly a step out of the realm of theological fictions, and what F. W. Robertson had before characterized as "the wonderfully unreal interpretations" of Christ's sufferings, that many of his opponents even more than half acquiesced in his new position, and large numbers of young men went wholly with him. In great feebleness of body, he supplemented this work, nine years later, by another, entitled *Forgiveness and Law*, and then the busy pen grew silent. He died at Hartford, where he had so long labored, February 14, 1876, at the age of seventy-four. Dr. Bushnell has assured his place in history. In his outward life there was nothing especially remarkable. It has hundreds of parallels. He will live in his writings. He founded no sect, had the basis of no new philosophy, lead no reform, discovered no new truth or principle in theology; yet so thoroughly did he enstamp the doctrines of his own class of religionists with the originality of his genius that it amounts to a revolution in religious thought. He touched the creed with his diffusive thought, and lo! it is another thing. It can never again be what it was. Probably no man of his generation has so profoundly affected and changed the current views of religious truth and experience in orthodox circles as he.

Yet it must be confessed that the influence of Dr. Bushnell is not likely to fall with power outside the circles of religious orthodoxy. His genius was versatile, acute, penetrative, intense, rather than comprehensive. He complained that Emerson tired him. He burlesqued the metaphysicians, although he found his richest author in Coleridge, the most metaphysical of all English minds. He was a little ostentatious of his claim to hold essentially with the old orthodox thinkers. He broke with none of their assumptions respecting the fall and moral state of man, miraculous inspiration and revelations, special providences, and specific creations—just the assumptions that the researches of modern scholarship and the demonstrations of natural science have brought into most serious question. He discarded the idea of evolution in its scientific form. To him, every shape of life was a separate and specific creation. Christianity was the coming of God into nature from without, instead of the outcoming of divine forces that had been working progressively forward from the beginning of creation—a miracle flung into human history by the arbitrary act of Deity. "Coming into nature from without" is his own phrase to designate the way the "Christian scheme" was given. The following words from *Work and Play*, p. 271, sufficiently indicates his idea of creation:

"There is one great fact...... that the animal races certainly were not created originally as germs, but as full-grown bodies; for how could the races of birds, for example, begin at the condition of eggs, with no parent bird to hatch them?—and how could the young of other animals be kept alive without their dams to feed them? In all of which it is clear, beyond a question, that *trees* and full formed living bodies were created first, and had the priority of all the sperm-cell and germ-cell operations. The mere mineral world, uninhabited as yet by living creatures, could not compose the germs of anything; and as the animal races certainly did not come out of germs originally, we naturally believe that all creatures of life, animal and vegetable, began as creatures in the full activity of life."

This was printed in 1864, and one finds no hint that he ever felt constrained by later developments of science to reconsider this position. From such a point of view it was impossible that he should do much toward the solution of the most vital questions between science and religion that press the mind of this day—he never came up to them. His effort in *Nature and the Supernatural*—wonderfully ingenious in thought and rich in style as it is, and hailed by many as the finest defense of the Christian system since Butler's *Analogy*—by reason of starting from this unscientific assumption, must be counted as already superannuated: a brave old ship thrown high ashore, able to yield rich stores to any one who will take the pains to pay it a visit, but not able to carry any across the seas it was built to sail. But his writings, so far as they move in the sphere of religious thought and experience, promise to long remain among the most inspiring and helpful to be found in the lore of the Christian church.

This *Life and Letters*, prepared by the daughter of Dr. Bushnell, aided by very able friends of his, brings out the man in vivid relief. Its six hundred pages might have been condensed somewhat, perhaps, without material loss, but affection and admiration can be pardoned for finding it hard to omit. Besides, the minute study of such a figure pays. The part of the biographer is done with no little artistic skill. In the quotations, freely indulged, from the writings of the subject, the reader gets a taste not only of his vigorous thought, but feels the stimulus of one of the most unique and quickening styles to be found in modern literature.

THE FATE OF REPUBLICS. Boston: Estes & Lauriat, 1880. For sale in San Francisco by A. L. Bancroft & Co.

The plan of this book is quite simple, and the author has not found it needful to add a word of preface. The undertaking is to sketch, very briefly, the nature and fate of every republic named in history, extinct or now existing, and to apply the results of the inquiry to a study of our own national problems. No one will deny that the idea is a good one. The book is neither unreadable nor lengthy, and as it lacks depth and originality, and shows withal from time to time some good sense, and is written clearly and with manly earnestness, it ought to find its way to a large and respectable public. The causes of the downfall of republics in the past are set forth briefly and plainly, though the author's competency to treat historical questions at first hand would be more than doubtful, if he made any claims to such competency. He does not, however, and his collection of data leaves, after all, a tolerably clear, though of course very inadequate, total impression of the life of republican institutions. An account of existing republics, compiled in like manner and joined with some speculations about the future, forms the transition to the most important part of the book—the discussion of the supposed securities and existing perils of our own republic. The precise point of view of the author upon a number of important questions is kept out of sight. One even has some doubts as to his religious opinions. When speaking of the trust of many in Providence as the guardian of America, he very solemnly remarks that, though "there is no difficulty in discovering and tracing remarkable providences" in our country's annals, yet "the student of history everywhere meets the startling fact that the era of providential interposition, after a while, in case of nearly every nation, gives place to the era of at least apparent providential desertion." He further adds that "the day may dawn when a monarchy will result in the greatest good to the greatest number. Then, if that day come, God will not longer interpose to save the republic, but will order its overthrow, and in mercy permit a monarchy to be established by those who have skill and daring sufficient to undertake and accomplish it." Whence it appears that our author's Providence has a preference for the strongest party, and and for the most skillful and daring leaders. Surely our trust in such a Providence will need very little proof, and furnish very little comfort. This remark, and the dedication of the book to General Grant, as to the fittest earthly defender of our endangered republic, would put a suspicious reader upon his guard, lest the author might be inclined to make game of him now and then, using some especially subtle irony. A glance further convinces, one, however, that this old soldier—for such he declares himself to be; viz., an officer in the

Northern army during the Rebellion—lacks, among other things, the sense of humor, and can introduce a chapter on the dangers of Popery with an enumeration of the cases where true prophets of coming evil have been disregarded, beginning with Demosthenes and continuing even until now. This chapter on Popery is decidedly the weakest in the book, as the one on national government, and on the conditions under which alone a republic can be stable is, though very brief, in our thinking, the very best. The author's conclusion, in the last chapter of the book, after speaking of "Political Evils," is that the only thing that can save the United States from the fatality of historic republics is "biblical Christianity among the masses of the people." His own faith seems to be, indeed, somewhat clouded, for he speaks a moment after of "the invisible forces of the universe, sometimes called God, which countenance nothing but righteousness," an expression whose origin and drift every one initiated will comprehend forthwith. But his hope as to the social effects of "biblical Christianity" is only weakened by his *fear* that the people will not be governed by it. With this bible-faith, as he holds, we could "disband our army, extend our territories, get rid of tramps, be safe against invasions, insurrections, and usurpations," and, in brief—so we judge our author's meaning—see the roast pigeons come flying lovingly into our mouths. But the author has little hope that we shall be fortunate enough to see so happy a result. We are too unbelieving.

Samuel Lover. A biographical sketch, with selections from his writings and correspondence. By Andrew James Symington, F.R.S.N.A. New York: Harper & Brothers. 1880. For sale in San Francisco by Payot, Upham & Co.

This little book is a tribute of personal friendship. It is rather a compilation from the works of the author than an attempt at a biography. In the two hundred and fifty-six pages which it covers, there are upward of sixty selections from Lover's stories, novels, and songs, besides about twenty of his letters. While several of these quotations are quite brief, the longest covers thirty-nine pages of the book. They are strung together upon a slender thread of narrative, so slender, indeed, as to leave a certain sense of incompleteness in the performance of the task. The author has chosen to present Lover to the reader rather through his own writings than by writing about him. Perhaps this was in a measure due to the fact that his life was an uneventful one. But when we learn that the man was a successful miniature painter, an etcher, a novelist, and a musical composer; that he has written several songs which are familiar, the world over, as household words, and that his dramatic talent was such that, like Charles Dickens, he could enchant audiences by reading and reciting selections from his own writings, we feel that we should be glad to know more of the man himself than can be acquired from this "life-sketch." Such versatility of talent, accompanied by evidences of success, rank Lover as an extraordinary man. His name would be preserved through the instrumentality of either "Widow Machree," "Rory O'More," "The Bowld Sojer Boy," or "The Low-backed Car" even without the aid of his more ambitious, and possibly less enduring, productions. As the author of *Handy Andy*, he earned for himself a distinct and well defined position among writers of fiction. His sketches of Irish and American character, and his humorous stories, place him before us not only as an acute observer, but through and by means of them we are enabled to estimate the genial temperament and happy nature of the man who could devise so much amusement for himself and others from the eccentricities and whims of those with whom he came in contact. The author expresses in his preface the desire that "Lover's exemplary perseverance, courage, reverence, conscientious, patient goodness, and hopeful, buoyant brightness, may in some degree influence despondent toilers, young or old, who, it may be, are now in these hard times wearily fighting the battle of life." It is in this spirit of reverence for his friend's memory that he has approached his task. The abundant quotations of Irish stories, sketches, and ballads render the book readable and entertaining. It is put forth with the expressed intention of supplying the public with a "shorter life of Lover" than that already published by Bernard, and it is, perhaps, from the necessities of the situation that we rise from the perusal of the book with a feeling that, after all, our desire for knowledge of Lover himself is not fully satisfied.

An American Dictionary of the English Language. By Noah Webster, LL.D. Revised, enlarged, and improved, by Chauncey A. Goodrich, D.D., and Noah Porter, D.D., LL.D. Springfield, Mass.: G. & C. Merriam. 1880. For sale in San Francisco by Payot, Upham & Co.

The man whose necessities limit his library to one book should get Webster's Unabridged Dictionary. It would be difficult to conceive of a more perfect work than the new edition of this great conservator of the English language. As there is nothing for which men have more frequent use than language, and as there is nothing less frequent than its accurate use, it follows that there can be no book of reference of greater value than one which is an acknowledged standard by which we can regulate our daily speech. Elsewhere in this number Professor Sill speaks of the "terrible inference" which "a bad slip in the refinements of English syntax, coming from some newly introduced person, and coming, too, with the fatal smoothness of habitual use, opens up to you in a second." Many times, persons, from mere carelessness, permit themselves to use colloquialisms which expose them to ridicule, as well as to the "inference" of ignorance and essential vulgarity. Hence we say, that there should be no better thumbed book than one's dictionary. It would be an invaluable habit which would regard every word with suspicion until its lineage and its social position among its verbal contemporaries were fully established. To one who has impartially examined the merits of the different dictionaries there can be no question that Webster's latest unabridged edition is far in advance of any similar work ever published. It is more complete and satisfactory, more accurate and authoritative than any of its competitors. It is abreast of the times, and contains a supplement of nearly five thousand new words, with their definitions. The new pronouncing biographical dictionary at the back contains the names of about ten thousand noted persons, with their nationality, occupation, and the dates of their birth and death. There is also a valuable vocabulary of the names of noted fictitious persons and places; there is a list of Scripture proper names, with their pronunciation; a similar list of Greek and Latin proper names; an etymological vocabulary of modern geographical names, and a pronouncing vocabulary of the same; a list of common

English Christian names; quotations from foreign languages; abbreviations and contractions; arbitrary signs; the metric system of weights and measures; and a classified selection of pictorial illustrations. While many of these features have appeared in former editions, several are new, and all are brought down to the latest date. The body of the work is also illustrated by numerous designs. The definitions and the spelling are such as are sanctioned by the best usage. It is no disparagement to other publications to say that, as a monument of learning and accurate industry, this latest unabridged edition stands unparalleled.

CONGREGATIONALISM. The Congregationalism of the last three hundred years, as seen in its literature, with special reference to certain recondite, neglected, or disputed passages, with a bibliographical appendix. By Henry Martin Dexter. New York: Harper & Brothers. 1880. For sale in San Francisco by Payot, Upham & Co.

This bulky, but elaborately wrought, work its author styles an "episode." Dr. Dexter has for the last fifteen years been recognized as a chief authority in the history of that peculiar form of ecclesiastical polity which came to America in the *Mayflower*, and which had much to do with shaping the civil polity, first, of New England, and, subsequently, of our whole country. Many years since, Dr. Dexter began to collect material for a thorough history of the Plymouth Colony, and is still working industriously in that direction. Meantime, in this episodic way he issues this tractate of 1080 pages, designed to serve as a sort of thesaurus, or guide-book, to the literature of Congregationalism during the past three hundred years. The main text of the work occupies 716 pages. To this follows an appendix of 286 pages, giving the titles of 7,250 books and pamphlets, together with the date at which each was published. These are all works illustrative of the history and character of Congregationalism. Apart from all questions of purely denominational interest, the volume throws much light upon the early history of New England. It is a work of immense research, and is deserving of praise, at least, as a guide-book to future students and writers of American history. It is a good service rendered not only in its special line, but in the line of general history. There is a wide field open to similar thorough workers in other directions.

AMERICAN ART REVIEW. Devoted to the Practice, Theory, History, and Archæology of Art. San Francisco: A. L. Bancroft & Co. 1880.

This monthly publication, which has now reached its ninth number, is devoted to the general development of art, but its special feature is announced to be "a series of original painter-etchings by American artists." One advantage which a magazine that produces etchings has over one that publishes engravings, is that in the former case the plates are the work of the artist himself, without the intervention of a middleman, or engraver. Such etchings are in no sense a reproduction, but are the direct work of the master-hand. The publication before us is certainly one of the most perfect of its kind, and those interested in American art have reason to congratulate themselves upon its success. Among the artists who have contributed, or have promised to contribute, original etched plates are A. F. Bellows, J. Foxcroft Cole, Henry Farrar, J. Appleton Brown, Edwin Forbes, R. Swain Gifford, Peter Moran, James D. Smillie, J. W. Champney, Wm. M. Chase, F. S. Church, Samuel Colman, F. Dielman, H. F. Farney, J. M. Falconer, George Inness, L. S. Ipsen, John La Farge, Walter F. Lansil, Mrs. Anna Lea Merritt, Charles H. Miller, Thomas Moran, Walter Shirlaw, George H. Smillie, J. R. Tait, and F. P. Vinton. We give these names, which will be recognized as those of leading American etchers, to show the high standard at which the *Review* aims. Plates are also promised from Unger, Flameng, Rajon, Greux, Leibh, Meyer, Forberg, and other renowned European artists. Although etching is the principal feature, it is not by any means the only one of this charming work. Engravings, heliogravures, wood-cuts, photo-engravings, etc., are given in profusion, and with the most accurate art. In addition, a number of able articles are given each month from the pens of critics of ability and reputation. As we have turned over the pages of the several numbers, we have been particularly struck with Mr. Bellows's exquisite little etching, "Mill Pond at Windsor, Conn.," in No. 7, and with Mr. Wm. Unger's "Wallachian Team," in No. 9. No. 6 contains a fine head of Sir Gilbert Scott, by Mrs. Anna Lea Merritt; also a suggestive plate, "Travellers before an Inn," by Mr. Unger. Karl Hoff's "In the House of Mourning," in No. 8, is a powerful and touching embodiment.

FRANKLIN SQUARE LIBRARY. New York: Harper & Brothers. 1880. For sale in San Francisco by Payot, Upham & Co.

No. 126—*The Duke's Children.* A novel. By Anthony Trollope.

No. 127—*The Queen.* By Mrs. Oliphant.

No. 128—*Miss Bouverie.* A novel. By Mrs. Molesworth.

HARPER'S HALF HOUR SERIES. New York: Harper & Brothers. 1880. For sale in San Francisco by Payot, Upham & Co.

No. 141—*The National Banks.* By H. W. Richardson.

No. 142—*Life Sketches of Macaulay.* By Charles Adams.

SPORTING ADVENTURES IN THE FAR WEST. By John Mortimer Murphy. New York: Harper & Brothers. 1880. For sale in San Francisco by A. L. Bancroft & Co.

AMERICAN MANUAL OF PARLIAMENTARY LAW. By George T. Fish. New York: Harper & Brothers. 1880. For sale in San Francisco by Payot, Upham & Co.

BUNYAN. By James Anthony Froude. New York: Harper & Brothers. 1880. For sale in San Francisco by Payot, Upham & Co.

CHAUCER. By Adolphus William Ward. New York: Harper & Brothers. 1880. For sale in San Francisco by Payot, Upham & Co.

ODETTE'S MARRIAGE. A novel from the French of Albert Delpit. Translated by Emily Prescott. 1880. Chicago: Henry A. Sumner & Co.

THE BALLET DANCER'S HUSBAND. Translated from the French of Ernest Feydeau by Mary Neal Sherwood. 1880. Chicago: Henry A. Sumner & Co.

HER BRIGHT FUTURE. A novel. 1880. Chicago: Henry A. Sumner & Co.

OUTCROPPINGS.

WATCHING THE BELLS.

'Tis Sabbath evening, and the hour of worship is at hand;
Deep lies the silence, like a kiss of God, upon the land.

I stand within a valley; and, on either side, the towers
Lift up their heads, and listen for the coming of the hours.

On yonder dusky dial now the pointer creeps apace;
It stands upon the minute, like intent upon a face.

See yonder huge, dim shadow rise athwart the shutter bars,
Like the dark brow of a prisoner lifted upward toward the stars!

It stands aloft upon the dusk, as if to hail the skies;
But silence, like a mighty hand, upon its black throat lies—

A moment only, and its voice in billowy clamor breaks,
And on the drowsy, twilight air a long, deep answer wakes.

Now, in yon open tower, I see the bell begin to move,
The rising of its ponderous rim against the sky above.

It cries out wildly to the night, as 'twere a naked soul,
And through the hollows of the hills its dying echoes roll.

But in that grim and lonesome tower, with windows through the stone,
Why sleeps the great cathedral bell, and keeps the hush alone?

It wakes—it stirs; with hollow rush, and parting of the night,
It hurls its huge bulk to the sky, and fills the tower with fright.

It speaks, and all the rest are still; it sinks, but thunders yet—
It speaks again, and in the vault the mighty peals have met.

Paul Pastnor.

WALT WHITMAN AGAIN.

In the July number of The Californian appeared an article entitled "Satin *vs.* Sacking." In it the writer pitted the extreme of two distinct styles—Whitman's and Fawcett's—against each other. In one, the writer aimed to clothe his thoughts in cheap, badly fitting garments, full of rags and patches, until an idea looked like "Topsey," with her head thrust through the bottom of a gunny sack. In the other, we find thought—such as it is—arrayed in a masquerading costume, all glittering with tinsel and dazzling with color, but, for the life of one, the character of the thing inside cannot be even so much as guessed at. Either of the two will attract attention anywhere. One is as diffused and elaborate as the other is clumsy and tedious. It is, perhaps, out of place to criticise adversely the writings of a man who gives satisfaction to thousands of people, but hardly more so than to eulogize one whose writings thousands could not be hired to read.

It has become fashionable for Americans to vastly admire anything which they have never read.

Walt Whitman has gained great notoriety "because he got out of the common rut." On the contrary, he remained persistently in the commonest rut he could find. His admirers lay great stress upon the fact that his writings are "absolutely without art." Now, what would these people think of their upholsterers and crockery men, if they insisted in bringing chairs without finish, or plates unglazed? We are told to abhor art in nature, and who does not? But poetry is not natural, never was, and never can be. It is artificial in all its aims, and stilted and unreal in its construction. We despise art when applied to the mathematically trimmed box-wood trees seen in the gardens of San Francisco, because such art cannot impress us as does a natural landscape in the Sierra; but, at the same time, we want the tiles in the walk regularly laid, and the posts of the porch perpendicular. An elegantly furnished room, beautified by art, is preferable to a log cabin, with a pool of stagnant water just before the door. One is all art, and the other absolutely without it, like Whitman's poetry. Of course, these comparisons indicate extremes, but not more so than *Leaves of Grass* and *Phantasy and Passion*.

Whitman apparently labors to acquire as much pure and simple clumsiness as possible in his versification. He describes the visit of a runaway slave to his house as follows:

"The runaway slave came to my house and stopped outside,
I heard his motions crackling the twigs of the wood-pile,
Through the swung half-door of the kitchen I saw him, limpsy and weak,
And went where he sat on a log, and led him in and assured him,
And brought water, and filled a tub for his sweated body and bruised feet,
And gave him a room that entered from my own, and gave him some coarse, clean clothes;
And remember perfectly well his revolving eyes and his awkwardness,
And remember putting plasters on the galls of his neck and ankles.
He stayed with me a week before he was recuperated, and passed North.
I had him sit next me at table. My firelock leaned in the corner."

The above gives the details of a very touching picture. Nothing can be more beautiful or poetical than the melting of human sympathy for the alleviation of distress. The meter employed is that in which Longfellow has written much, and is something which the ear soon tires of. It is simply prose, cut up into certain lengths, and the reading of it, with its monotonous pauses, and regularly recurring accents toward the close of the line, after a time sounds like a boy hammering endlessly upon a drum. It has justly been compared to an auctioneer reading off the inventory of a grocery store. If in such versification a line is reached which is too short or long, or the accent is in an unfamiliar place, it is like an oasis in a desert. Those who assert that they like such poetry would choose a rough charcoal sketch in preference to a finished painting. Let us look for a moment at Whitman's opposite, Poe.

Here is a fair refrain of his studied art, taken from the "Haunted Palace:"

"Banners yellow, glorious, golden,
  On its roof did float and flow
(This—all this—was in the olden
  Time long ago);
And every gentle air that dallied,
  In that sweet day,
Along the ramparts, plumed and pallid,
  A winged odor went away."

It is not hard for one to imagine Whitman rendering the above something like this:

On the roof of the castle yellow banners floated, and glorious and golden banners—
It was a very long time ago that all this happened—
And the airs that came over the white ramparts at that time
Had wings to them, which took away a very sweet smell.

Speaking of animals, Whitman merely remarks that he would like to live with them, and enjoys looking at at them:

"I think I could turn and live with animals, they are so placid and self-contained;
I stand and look at them sometimes half the day long."

Lytton paints a finished picture from the same scene, where he writes:

"From the warm upland comes a gust, made fragrant with the brown hay there.
The meek cows, with their white horns thrust above the hedge, stand still and stare.
The steaming horses from the wain droop o'er the tank their plaited manes."

Here are some strange passages from Whitman in which strange mixtures occur:

"A child said, What is the grass? fetching it to me with full hands,
How could I answer the child? I do not know
What it is any more than he.
I guess it must be the flag of my disposition, out of hopeful green stuff woven;
Or I guess it is the handkerchief of the Lord,
A scented gift and remembrancer, designedly dropped,
Bearing the owner's name some way in the corners,
That we may see and remark, and say, Whose?"

The idea that it is the "flag of his disposition, out of the hopeful green stuff woven," makes a peculiar combination of the raw and the manufactured article in one metaphor. If the child had brought him a tuft of sheep's wool, he might, with the same propriety, have designated it as his shirt. He next thinks it must be "the handkerchief of the Lord," as if Divinity sometimes had a bad cold, and needed to use a handkerchief. If such poetical license is to be allowed, the ownership of cravats, paper collars, towels, and blue neckties will next be attributed. Such lines only lower the plummet of bathos to the lowest depths. The idea of the Lord's name being worked in the corner, that the finder, seeing, may vociferate, "Whose?" is still more absurd. If the name were there, why in the name of all that is good should the finder say "Whose?" He goes on to say:

"Tenderly will I use you, curling grass;
It may be you transpire from the breasts of young men;
It may be if I had known them I would have loved them;
It may be you are from old people, and from women,
And from offspring taken soon out of the mothers' laps ·
And here you are the mothers' laps.

"The grass is very dark to be from the white heads of old mothers,
Darker than the colorless beards of old men,
Dark to come from under the faint red roofs of mouths.
Oh, I perceive after all so many uttering tongues,
And I perceive they do not come from the roofs of mouths for nothing."

Now, if one should take the last stanza of the above, and read it to a crowd of a dozen people, the reader would wait a long time before the listeners agreed as to what it means. What is meant by the remark that the grass did not come from under the roofs of mouths for nothing? Grass does not, as a rule, "transpire from the breasts of young men," or the "white heads of old mothers."

The author himself is utterly at a loss to render his meaning intelligible, for he writes:

"I wish I could translate the hints about the dead young men and women,
And the hints about old men and mothers, and the offspring taken soon out of their laps."

I have seen these lines somewhere, but cannot now positively state that they came from Whitman's pen. They are certainly in Whitman's style:

"There are times when at midnight I feel a great stillness,
And I like to feel it, too, because it helps me brood never."

Contrast this with the master tones of Prentice:

"'Tis midnight's holy hour, and silence now is brooding like a gentle spirit
O'er the still and pulseless world."

Perhaps many who find beauties in Whitman will charge others with overlooking them. Jewels have before now been found in ash-heaps, but all people are not expected to be possessed of the patience necessary to insure finding them. SAM DAVIS.

THE FOUR BULLWHACKERS OF BITTER CREEK.

Perhaps every person who is somewhat advanced in life can remember some incident of his early years which he would really like to forget, something that resulted from the freshness and vast inexperience of youth. I remember one which I have spent a good deal of time trying to forget. Just before the Union Pacific Railroad reached the Bitter Creek country, I made my first overland trip to the Pacific Coast. I staged it from the then terminus of the Union Pacific to the Central Pacific, which was pushing east. The stage broke down on Bitter Creek, and the passengers had to walk to the next station. I grew tired of walking before I reached the station, and coming, late in the afternoon, to where some teamsters were camped, I concluded to stop with them for the night. On asking their permission to do so, they assented so heartily that I felt at home at once. Life in the West was something new to me. I was young and buoyant, and just out of college. I was fond of talking. I thought it would be novel and delightful to sleep out with these half-savage ox-drivers, with no shelter but the vaulted, star-gemmed heavens. There were four teamsters, and as many wagons, while thirty-two oxen grazed around in the vicinity. Of the teamsters, one was a giant in stature, and wore a bushy black beard; another was shorter, but powerfully built, and one-eyed; the third was tall, lank, and lame-jawed; while the fourth was a wiry, red-headed man. In my thoughts I pitied them, on account of the hard life they led, and spoke to them in a kind tone, and endeavored to make my conversation instructive. I plucked a flower, and, pulling it to pieces, mentioned the names of the parts—pistil, stamens, calyx, and so on—and remarked that it must be indigenous to the locality, and spoke of the plant being endogenous, in contradistinction to exogenous, and that they could see that it was not cryptogamous. In looking at some fragments of rock, my thoughts wandered off into geology, and, among other things, I spoke of the tertiary and carboniferous periods, and of the pterodactyl, ichthyosaurus, and dinotherium. The teamsters looked at me, then at each other, but made no response. We squatted down around the frying-pan to take supper, and as the big fellow, with his right hand, slapped, or sort of lamped, a long piece of fried bacon, over a piece of bread in his left hand, sending a drop of hot grease into my left eye, he said to the one-eyed man:

"Bill, is my copy of Shakspere in yo' wagon? I missed it to-day."

"No. My Tennerson and volum' of the Italian poets is in thar—no Shakspere."

The lank looking teamster, biting off a piece of bread about the size of a saucer, said to the big man, in a voice which came huskily through the bread, "Jake, did yer ever read that volum' of po'ms that I writ?"

"No, but hev often heern tell on 'em."

"Yer mean 'Musin's of an Idle Man,'" spoke up the red-headed man, addressing the poet.

"Yes."

"Hev read every line in it a dozen times," said the teamster with the red hair; and as he sopped a four-inch swath, with a piece of bread, across a frying-pan, he repeated some lines.

"Them's they," nodded the poet. "The Emp'rer of Austry writ me a letter highly complimentin' them po'ms."

"They're very techin'," added the wiry man.

I took no part in these remarks. Somehow I did not feel like joining in.

The wiry man, having somewhat satisfied his appetite, rolled up a piece of bacon rind into a sort of single-barreled opera-glass, and began to squint through it toward the northern horizon.

"What yer doin', Dave?" asked the stout man.

"Takin' observations on the North Star. Want to make some astronomical calkilations when I git later Sechrymenter."

"Well, yer needn't ter made that tel'scope. I could er tuk yo' observations for yer, bein' as I haint but one eye."

"Git out thar, yer durned ole carboniferous pterodactyl," yelled the lame-jawed driver to an ox that was licking a piece of bacon.

"I give a good deal of my time to 'stronomy when I was in Yoorup," remarked the tall man.

"Over thar long?" asked one.

"Good while. Was Minister to Roosby. Then I spent some time down ter Rome."

"Rome!" exclaimed the lank individual. "Was born thar. My father was a sculptor."

"Good sculptor?"

"Yes."

"Well, one wouldn't er thought it, to look at yer."

"I never was in Yoorup," remarked the one-eyed man. "When I occypied the cheer of ancient languages in Harvard College my health failed, and the fellers that had me hired wanted me ter go ter Yoorup for an out, but I concluded ter come West ter look——Hold up thar, yer infernal ole flea-bitten ichthy'saurus," he bawled to an ox that was chewing a wagon cover.

I felt hot and feverish, and a long way from home.

"I got ready once ter go ter Rome—wanted to complete my studies thar—but give it up," said the one called Dave.

"What for?"

"They wanted me ter run for Guv'ner in Virginy."

"Yer beat 'em?"

"Thunder, yes."

"Why didn't yer stay thar?"

"Well, when my job as Guv'ner give out they 'lected me 'Piscopal Bishop, an' I hurt my lungs preachin'. Come West for my lungs."

"Found em?"

"Well, I'm improvin'."

I did not rest well that night. As day came on, and the men began to turn over in their blankets and yawn, the tall one said:

"Hello, Bill. How yer makin' it?"

"Oh, I'm indigenous."

"An' Dave?"

"I'm endogenous."

"An' you, Lanky, yer son of a sculptor?"

"Exogenous."

"How you feel, Jake?" inquired one of the three who had responded.

"Cryptogamous, sir, cryptogamous."

I walked out a few steps to a little stream, to get a drink. I felt thirsty, and I ached. Then I heard a voice from the blankets:

"Wonder if them durned ole dinother'ums of ourn are done grazin."

Then a reply:

"I guess they've got to the tertiary period."

I walked a little piece on the road, to breathe the morning air.

I kept on. LOCH MELONE.

AFTER THE SEASON.

Fade, flowers—droop, trees—in ozonic heat;
Glare, pavement, in the sun;
What matter dust and scorching street!
The season's course is run.

The noisy roll has ceased at last;
The blossoms, balconied,
That dust has choked, and crowds have passed,
Have withered, drooped, and died.

No evening crowd round Mayfair's doors;
No Kensingtonian hum;
No languid waltz on polished floors;
No ball, no rout, nor drum.

But where reviving breezes blow
On purpled heathery hill,
Or where the virgin-peaks of snow
Worn minds with beauty fill,

London has fled; and, still the same
At rest or on the wing,
Dresses and chats, and loves and hates,
In autumn as in spring.

London has fled; but yet amid
  The heat and poison air
Three millions linger — never rid
  Of labor, famine, care.

Three millions who, in den and court,
  Hid from God's wind, God's sun,
Pine for air fresher, purer thought,
  Or end lives scarce begun.

No glimpses of green waving trees
  For them, nor dewy grass;
E'en Nature's ripeness brings disease
  And death to them, alas!

So time for some in sadness flows;
  To some in perfumed ease;
God grant His pity unto those—
  His patience give to these!

LAURA WILLEY.

ANNOUNCEMENT.

THE CALIFORNIAN has now been running three-quarters of a year. From the issuance of the January number to the present time, it has been met with words of encouragement and approval alone. Personal interviews, private letters, and the expressions of the public press have all bid us God-speed. The reception which the magazine has met proves that a field is open for it on this coast, and a glance at the pages of the various numbers reveals the existence of a local talent which, to many, was unsuspected. But it has been evident for some time past to those interested in the enterprise, that, in disregarding the experience of all other publications, by fixing the price so far below that of other monthlies, a mistake had been made, which, sooner or later, would have to be corrected. The large sums which have to be expended for paper, composition, press-work, and the innumerable expenses of printing, issuing, and circulating a monthly magazine, which have, of late, been higher than for many years before, prevent the possibility of placing the publication on that high plane of literary and typographical excellence which its proprietors desire, without a change in the present price. The only alternative was one which the owners would not for a moment consider, that of deteriorating the quality and diminishing the quantity supplied at the existing rates. For some time, therefore, the only question has been, when shall this change be effected, and it has been decided, after consultation, that the sooner it is done the better. Commencing, therefore, with the first day of October, the price of the magazine will be advanced to thirty-five cents for a single number, and to $4.00 for the yearly subscription, the usual price for first-class monthlies. In order that there may be no dissatisfaction among those of our patrons who have not, as yet, subscribed by the year, THE CALIFORNIAN will receive yearly subscriptions at the old rates ($3.00) until the date fixed for the change in the price (October 1, 1880). No one, therefore, needs be affected by the change for the present year. With this change, we expect to redouble our efforts to make the magazine worthy of the high favor with which it has been received, and are able already to promise new features which will make it more attractive than ever before.—[*Reprinted from last month.*]

A LITERAL MEXICAN.

One of our Eastern exchanges tells this story: Wickedly anxious to obey orders to the letter was a Mexican taking the stand, in a New York police court, as a witness in an assault case. Having informed the Judge that he spoke English, he was told to state what he knew of the affair in question. Thereupon the prosecuting attorney, an Irishman by birth, quite unnecessarily intervened with:

"Ye understand, sor, that ye are to go on and state to the coort what ye know about the case in your own language."

"You want me to tell the story in my own language?" asked the witness.

"Yes, sor, I do," replied the lawyer.

The Mexican began: "Este mujer queria a mi casa—"

"What is that ye're saying?" exclaimed the attorney.

"I am speaking in my own language, as you requested me to do," was the reply.

"I didn't mane for ye to spake your own language when I said for ye to spake yer own language," exclaimed the legal gentleman. "Can't ye spake to me as I'm spakin' to ye?"

"I can try, sir," said the Mexican; and he went on with his story thus: "Well, thin, yer Honor, this man and this woman kem to my house, and says the man to the woman, says he, 'I want to spake wid ye,' says he—"

Here the indignant examiner broke in with: "What do ye mane by spaking in that way?"

"Shure, sor," responded the witness, "ye axed me to spake in the language ye use yourself, and shure I'm thryin' to oblige ye."

Then the Judge thought it time to interfere, and bade the Mexican talk English.

"With pleasure, your Honor," said he. "I should have done so at first, but the learned gentleman seemed rather particular in regard to the language in which he wished me to give my evidence."

This is the last number before the price is advanced. Read the announcement on this page, and send in your yearly subscription before the first day of October, so as to get the benefit of the old rate.

UNDERSTOOD.

In the gloaming
  Love is born,
When the roaming
  Sun is gone,
When the starlight casts its shade
On the lover and the maid,
  As they sit
  With wistful eyes,
Silent in their sweet surprise.

By the token
  Understood,
Though unspoken
  Be the word;
By the trembling, conscious air,
As it bends to stroke their hair,
  Two shall plight
  With wistful eyes,
Clasping hands in sweet surprise.

THE CALIFORNIAN.

A WESTERN MONTHLY MAGAZINE.

VOL. II.—NOVEMBER, 1880.—No. 11.

THE NEW NAPOLEON.

Last spring I received a letter from the editor of the chief London magazine asking me to write him an article to be entitled "A Week in Wall Street."

I knew nothing whatever of Wall Street then. I resolved, however, to oblige my friend. I went into Wall Street at once to get the desired information and experience.

This was six months ago. I have just got back. I have not yet written a line of that article. But I have material enough to write a book bigger than Macaulay's "History of England." I know all I want to know about Wall Street. And, if you will pardon the digression, I may add that I am getting bald-headed.

The first thing I did was to climb into the gallery of the Stock Exchange, and look down into the den of two thousand "bulls" and "bears" that were growling, howling, roaring, and bellowing there. I have been in Bedlam, and I have presided at a Democratic State Convention. But I never saw or heard anything like this. I said to myself, "This thing cannot go on long. This thing must stop before night. These men will kill themselves. This thing will burst, explode of its own internal fury." But I looked up and read the legend above the President, "Founded in 1742," and then concluded that it would still go on.

Then I went to a broker whom I had met at the Union Club, and told him what I wanted to learn. He kindly took hold of the tape which continually streams out from the "ticker," as the little wheel of fortune is called, which constantly records the rise and decline of stocks, and tried to explain all about it.

I found it impossible to get interested. There were about two hundred different names of stocks on the list. These were represented by one, two, or three letters, or figures, or some sort of abbreviated word that I could not understand or distinguish, and I was constantly getting confused.

Around this "ticker" gathered and grouped a knot of eager, nervous, and anxious men. Ten, fifteen, or twenty at a time would clutch at the tape, as it streamed out with its endless lines of quotations, and mutter to themselves, jabber at each other, swear like pirates, drop the tape, and dash away. Others would dart in, clutch the tape, swear or chuckle, as their fortunes went, wheel about, give orders to their broker to buy or sell, as they prophesied the future of the market; and so it went on all day from ten till three, when the battle was ended by the fall of the hammer in the Stock Exchange.

When I tell you that there are more than five thousand of these "tickers," or indicators, you can form some idea of the magnitude of the business. If we give ten men to each "ticker," you have the spectacle of fifty thousand stalwart men standing there holding up a little dotted string, waiting, hollow-eyed and anxious, on the smiles of fickle fortune. To this fifty thousand you may add two thousand brokers. You must give each broker, at least, five clerks, office boys, and messengers, which swell the list ten thousand. To this sixty-two thousand you can safely add two hundred thousand speculators on the outside. So you have a total engaged in this gambling of more than a quarter of a million.

The stock broker is not necessarily a rich man. He must, of course, have a seat in the board, which costs about twenty thousand dollars. But other than that he requires little more than an office, and an indicator, or "ticker." He takes the stock which he buys for you to his bank, and borrows the money which he pays for it. But they do not long remain poor if they have a fair patronage, for their commissions are enormous, double their old price, and they have no risks whatever. They rarely deal in stocks themselves, and they are careful to have plenty of "margin" for their own protection.

Of the broker I am bound to say that I believe him honest, and not void of all conscience. Besides, I found him, as a rule, a well read, well traveled gentleman. They chronicle fewer commercial failures by far than do the merchants of the great city of New York, and they rarely figure in the courts.

But to return to my subject. Finding but little interest in this great maelstrom of excitement without taking part, I, under the advice of my broker, bought a little Wabash. I bought Wabash because it was the first stock on the list which I could distinguish from the mass of two hundred names. And I came to remember it because I had been born on its banks, as it were. Indeed, on the very banks of the Wabash River I have seen my father furrow the field for corn in the spring, while my mother followed after, dropping the corn in the furrow; while three little boys toddled after, myself of the number, and covered the grain that lay in the little squares of the mellow earth. And so it was with a touch of tenderness that I bought Wabash, and became one of the eager party holding on to the tape—watching, waiting the turn of fortune's wheel.

She did not betray me. My stock began to move upward from the first. It was not so dull now. How interesting it all was! I called the click of the "ticker" the pulse and heart-beat of the nation. If the land was healthy and prosperous, the pulse beat high and buoyant. If the land was threatened with drought, short crops, or misfortune of any kind, the pulse was low, feverish, and dull. It was like a poem.

I had now an interest in the prosperity of the land beyond a sentiment. I was a part owner in the one hundred thousand miles of railways in America. From that day forth I studied the geography of my country as never before. My little up-town room in the fourth story was lined with maps of American railways. In less than a week I could quote the opening or closing prices of half the stock on the list.

How patiently I held on to the tape along with the other timid and hopeful little lambs! We would exchange opinions, encourage each other, and lay great plans for the future. We became very confidential, our little knot around that "ticker;" and when one of our set lost money he had our honest sympathy. They were pleasant days, these first, for stocks went up steadily, and it seemed at last, when and where I had least expected it, I was to make a fortune without either care or toil. I am perfectly certain that in those few weeks I grew to be a better man.

At last I closed out. I had in my hand more than ten thousand dollars. I had not invested so many hundred. What scribe had ever been so fortunate! Stocks still advanced. It seemed as if they would never stop going up.

I sat down and tried for days to decide what to do. Coolly, deliberately, and after as much and as mature thought as I am capable of, I went back to Wall Street with my money. I had no use for ten thousand dollars. I had great use for fifty thousand. I hug myself in satisfaction now, to remember that I thought not so much of myself as of my friends at this time. I could get on with that sum well. But away out on the great gold shore of the vast west sea I wanted to build a home—a city. I would gather about me the dear spirits of old. In some sweet spot where there were woods and cool waters, a warm sun and prolific soil, we would meet and build a city—a city of refuge—where every Bohemian might come and have a home, rest, peace, plenty, so long as he or she should live or care to stay. I even drew up a plan of my city, and framed a few brief laws for its government. I named it Utopia.

On returning to Wall Street, I chose three different brokers—one a "bull" house, one a "bear" house, and one a "conservative" house. By this I hoped to get all sorts of opinions. I got them.

With my "bears," I sold St. Paul short. There was talk of rust, grasshoppers, rains, floods. St. Paul would tumble to the center. It had already advanced from eighteen to sixty-nine. I sold at sixty-nine, seventy, and seventy-one.

With the "bulls," I bought Pacific Mail. No danger of grasshoppers on Pacific Mail. No drought, no floods or rust! Pacific Mail had fallen from sixty-two, and would surely go back up to eighty. I bought Pacific Mail and sat down to wait for it to go up and St. Paul to go down.

Things began to move my way. I began to work vigorously on the plans for my city. I had arranged to bring my dear old parents away from the Far West wilds of Oregon, where they had dwelt for a quarter of a century. They had never seen the great city. Now they should see it, hear the mighty preachers, and sail on the Atlantic.

How life widened out! I had an interest now in every ship that sailed. The flow of money to or from the land was to me of vital concern. All commerce was as rich with interest to me now as the poetry of Homer. At ten o'clock sharp I found myself holding on to the tape, waiting to see if I had grown richer or poorer through the night. All day, till the hammer fell, I stood with my finger on the pulse of commerce.

I ought sooner to have mentioned that, from the first day there, I found that the stock dealers did not so much inquire after the weather, the probable ill or good fortune of ships, the growth or failure of crops, floods or fires, as after the movements of one certain man—a small, dark, silent man; modest, unobtrusive, even a timid, and shy man, to all appearance; yet a man who held their whole world in his single right hand.

"Gould is selling!" The street trembled, and stocks fell two, three, four points in an hour. "Gould is buying!" The street started up, and stocks rose accordingly. Every rumor, good or bad, came coupled with the name of Jay Gould, and he was held responsible for all that was done; while, in truth and in fact, this man, nine cases out of ten, neither knew nor cared how the market was going.

Never was a man so bitterly abused. I seek in vain for the mention of one word of praise, or even respect, for Jay Gould during my half year in Wall Street. Perhaps I am too much given to shouting for the bottom dog in the fight; but this persistent and bitter abuse begot in me an interest in this singular and silent little man, and I began to study his life, and look into his mighty enterprises. I found them so vast, so grand, so far reaching and splendid as to be almost incomprehensible. Certainly no Napoleon ever had half such a brain. And yet, for all this, I never heard a word of admiration. Every man in Wall Street seemed to be so bound up in his own petty losses or gains that Gould was looked upon as a kind of thermometer that marked the rise and fall of stocks. "An inspired fiend," is the highest praise I heard for him. Day after day you could constantly hear such expressions as these: "Some one will shoot that —— before he is a year older," "Well, he will never live to enjoy it," "Let him look out what he is about," "They fixed Fisk, and he was a stronger man than Gould;" yet very tranquilly the dark little Napoleon passed on through it all, as if utterly unconscious of these mutterings, and utterly careless of what men thought or did. Of course such coolness and courage as this appeals to a man from the Pacific, and my interest in this man constantly increased.

I may mention here that I did not find the average stock speculator much of a man. Quite unlike the grand old California gamblers of our first days, I found them a sober, cold-blooded, calculating lot. And here let me call attention to the gulf that lies between the stock speculator and the legitimate railroad man. Let the line between them be not forgotten. The one is to be shunned, dreaded, despised. The other is to be respected, admired, sympathized with. The one, with a force of a quarter of a million strong men, lives in luxury and gives to the world not so much as one grain of wheat.

This quarter of a million brokers and professional stock speculators live on the fat of the land; and yet, all together, they never give to the world so much as one lucifer match. They are camp-followers who plunder the dead.

But the great builders of railways are quite another quality of men. Although railroad builders are often, much too often, speculators also.

Gould is preëminently a builder. He is not a man who tears down. If ever his hand touches a railroad, it seems to start at once into life, although it may have lain rusting and rotting in its grave for years. If ever there was a man inspired for any special work, in these later days, Jay Gould seems to be that man. You may study the map of Europe and comprehend the sudden movements and colossal combinations of the First Napoleon, if it be possible. Then turn to America, and see what this man has done and is doing here, and you will find that his achievements far outreach those of the great Emperor.

When I first traveled through Europe, I found I had to have a passport for almost every one of the thirty petty states. This was expensive and troublesome. But now Bismarck and the Emperor have tied all these together, and the world calls them great.

A few years ago the railways of the West lay in broken bits and fragments; one at war with the other, cutting each other's throats, and maintaining standing armies of presidents and officers on enormous salaries, all of which the farmer had to pay for.

Jay Gould reached out his hand, remodeled all, consolidated all, swept the standing army out of existence, and gave the farmer a road that took his produce to market for less than half the former cost

Bismarck, with a million men, tied Germany together, and the world applauded, although he did deplete the treasury and double the taxes.

Here a single man, assaulted on all sides by the abuse of enemies and feeble detractors, without a dollar, except as he could make it out of his scheming brain, has united and bound together railways, and established systems which are ten-fold more important, every one of them, than the unification of the German States; and, instead of doubling the taxes, he has doubled, trebled, quadrupled the taxable property of the countries wherein he has wrought. He has given employment to perhaps a million of men in building and maintaining and reconstructing these railways; and, what is most important of all, so reduced tariffs that the farmer can now ship his grain at a rate that must soon make him a wealthy man.

Take, for example, what is now called the Wabash system. A little time ago the stock was selling at half a cent on the hundred. The old iron rails were rusting away, and the whole concern was bankrupt. Now, steel rails, thousands of additional cars, and like new equipments generally, blossom all along the two thousand miles now consolidated and merged in one corporation. And, with this new life, new towns are going up all along the lines. Truly it may be said of this man that he has built as many cities as some men we call great have destroyed.

I have mentioned the Wabash system only because it is the most familiar to me, and hence I know that, under the presidency of Solid Solon Humphreys, it must continue to flourish like a bay. Just as much might safely be said of railways away down in Texas, out on the plains, and even in the Mexicos, that have been built or called back into life by this little king of American enterprise.

But perhaps I ought to draw the line here. I do not know Mr. Gould, and he very likely may take umbrage at what I have said; but I should think that one who has borne so much abuse ought to be able to bear this much well earned praise from one who admires pluck and achievement, and dares applaud.

And now, right here I want the reader to stick a pin, and ponder well this one idea: Great-brained men are to be born to us here in America. What shall they do? Hew each other to pieces, as in Europe? Nay. I trust we have grown beyond the age of barbarism.

What shall we do with our Napoleons? I should say, recognize them when they come. I should say, in the first place, let us get rid of that brutal idea which we have inherited from Europe, that it is a nobler thing to burn a city than to build a city.

I should say that, instead of bowing down before an effete nobility of Europe, and repeating their comings and goings in our present day, we should give some solid recognition to the great world-builders in our midst.

I should say that, instead of fawning upon our own few Generals who made their little reputations by tearing down, we ought rather to forget them, and remember those who build up.

And if the prophesied day of universal peace is to come, it will come in this way. When a great-brained and ambitious man springs up among us, he will do, or undertake to do, that which is deemed greatest. And if the public heart is so coarse and uncultured as to still cherish the old idea that it is greater to destroy than to create, then he will destroy. Let greatness be measured by the solid good a man does to the world. He may be selfish in his work; he may be utterly so. Man is by nature that way. That does not make the substantial benefits less.

Measured by this standard, which I feel is the right one, I should say that this man, Jay Gould, is not only the most colossal figure in America, but in all the world.

It is a grand thing to fight for one's country. But it is a grander thing to make one's country worth fighting for.

This is the idea I should like to impress upon every young heart. It is such an easy thing to be a butcher. But it takes time, and kindness, and skill, and refinement to raise the flock for his shambles.

Our new Napoleons are to imitate this one. They are to understand that he who strikes one blow toward building roads that tap the flow of golden grain to Europe contributes something toward enriching his own land, and also toward feeding the hungry of the old world.

Of course, I know nothing of the inner life of my hero. I do not desire to know of it. The perpetual abuse of enemies has made him singularly alone and exclusive. Yet I am told that his home-life is most perfect and sweet, and that his sons are growing up to be men of great taste and culture. One thing we do know, however--that to the suffering South, Kansas, and other places, he has, in the most unobtrusive way, sent more solid help than any one man besides in the world. Fancy any old world Napoleon heading a subscription list!

To have learned what I have of the magnitude and importance of this new Napoleon's work, knitting the lakes to the gulf, the Atlantic to the Pacific, the North to the South, in a network of steel that nothing can ever break—this was worth my half year in Wall Street.

Wall Street? How did I come out? Oh! Well, I was short of St. Paul and long of Pacific Mail. I expected Pacific Mail to go up and St. Paul to go down. They did, and I had twenty-one thousand dollars. But that was not enough to build a city with. I held on.

One day it was rumored that the rust was not so bad in St. Paul after all. It began to start up! Pacific Mail began to shoot down. It was said the Chinese had established an opposition line. I tell you it takes a big man to sit on two benches at a time. Ten to one he will spill himself between the two just as sure as he attempts it.

I sold some St. Paul and bought more Pacific Mail; but all to no purpose. They kept right on. Then I got out of Pacific Mail at the lowest figure it touched, and bought Wabash. I began to flounder, and got frightened. I sold and bought, and bought and sold. I frequently saw in the papers that I was getting rich in Wall Street, and kept on working like a beaver. The end was only a question of time.

One day my broker took me by the sleeve, and led me like a lamb as I was aside. My fun was over. And Utopia is indeed Utopia.

No one with so little money ever entered Wall Street under better advantages. All men were kind and good. I think no man there ever attempted to mislead me. But it is simply impossible to make money there, and keep it. Let me mention here that during my six months there I paid my brokers in commissions eleven thousand four hundred and twenty-five dollars! These commissions alone will devour any possible profits.

Of course, it is not a pleasant thing to admit oneself beaten. But if this brief history of my venture in this dangerous land will diminish at all that tired and anxious army of tape-holders who waste their shekels, their days, and their strength in vain waiting—why, I willingly bear the reproach.

And, after all, I lost but little, having but little to lose. And I learned so much, having so much to learn. JOAQUIN MILLER.

THE CHINESE ARMY.

Looking at the relations at present existing between Russia and China, the present seems opportune to give a brief description of the Chinese army. Much has been written about the capabilities of the soldiers of the Celestial Empire, but should Colonel Gordon, who is now in China, be engaged by the Government to remodel the army, no doubt the task which the Russians have set themselves to accomplish would not prove so easy as they expect.

China, like other countries, has its War office, but the care and vigilance of this department is exercised, not only on behalf of the land forces, but, in addition, it has the control of naval affairs. Its duties are multifarious. The charge of the grain transport, the security of river embankments, the overlooking of the being controlled by the viceroys of the respective provinces, the duties of the Chinese Board of War, in comparison with those of similar ministries in foreign countries, are much circumscribed.

And now a word concerning the bannermen. In the year 1643, when the present Manchu dynasty conquered China, a force of soldiers was established, consisting entirely of Manchus and Mongols. These troops were arranged under eight banners, *pukki*. These banners were further subdivided into two wings or divisions, the first, third, fifth, and seventh banners constituting the right wing; the remainder the left wing. Each banner is distinguished by a triangular flag of yellow, white, red, and blue for the troops of the left wing; and the

comes within their charge. The number of bannermen in Peking, under pay, is estimated, inclusive of the before mentioned divisions, at eighty thousand men, as it is the policy of the reigning dynasty to exercise a kind of espionage over the various high officials at the provincial capitals. There is a Tartar General commanding the garrison, which consists of bannermen and their families. Special quarters are assigned to them, to isolate them, as it were, from the Chinese inhabitants; but, despite the precautions taken to insure their loyalty and purity of descent, they have mixed and intermarried among the citizens, and adopted the Chinese language, manners, and customs. As soldiers these men have become useless, and their maintenance costs the Government large sums of money. They are seldom called upon to drill, either at Peking, or the outstations. Receiving but small pay, they are permitted to engage in any occupation or traffic. Their allowance from the throne is paid to them in rice or grain, by a system of orders upon the imperial granaries, which orders they sell to the highest bidder. The arms in use among the banner force are swords, bows and arrows, spears, and a few muzzle-loading rifles.

The regular army of the capital consists of natives of the provinces of Chihli and Shantung. The infantry is constituted as follows: Four battalions of eight hundred and seventy-five men and officers, each armed with muzzle-loading rifles of Russian manufacture (these battalions are well acquainted with European tactics, each man having received instruction at Tientsin before proceeding to join the force); one battalion, or cadet corps, under the authority of the *Hei wu fu*, or Court of the Harem (it is composed of five hundred young men, and their arms are bows, arrows, and spears); three battalions of eight hundred men each, mostly armed with matchblocks, swords, and shields. The Prince of Chun, father of the present Emperor, has a body-guard of two hundred men, armed with various Chinese weapons.

The cavalry are mounted upon stout, wiry Mongolian ponies, supplied to them from the imperial stud grounds. There are also five divisions of one thousand men each, armed with Enfield carbines, Chassepôts, and spears.

The artillery consists of twenty-four field guns, nine and twelve-pounders (two horses and six men being attached to each gun; the guns are mostly brass, smooth-bore, of Russian manufacture), and six Armstrong breech-loaders. The necessary instruction for working the guns was given to the sergeants attached to them. They, in their turn, served to drill the men forming the force. Beside these foreign guns, a brigade of one thousand men use the obsolete swivel-gun, fired from a bench, or tripod, and carrying a ball weighing from four ounces to a pound.

A camp is in existence at Hai Tien, in the vicinity of the summer palace of Yuen Ming Yuen, composed as follows: Three battalions of infantry, each eight hundred and seventy-five men, armed with Remington rifles; two thousand cavalry; one battery of field artillery of four twelve-pound guns, and one howitzer battery of four guns. These troops, which are all foreign drilled, are composed of native Chinese alone. They are kept as a sort of reserve in the event of an attack on the capital.

The available force for the defense of Peking numbers:

Infantry	10,000
Cavalry	5,000
Artillery (with 30 guns)	1,750
Bannermen	80,000
Total	96,750

Within eighty miles from Peking, is the city of Tientsin, the residence of the Viceroy, Li Hung Chang, the joint commander-in-chief of the Chinese army. The troops at Tientsin are a large body, and may be said to be mainly composed of men from Anhwei, a province of Central China, the home of the Viceroy. With few exceptions the whole of the officers commanding the force are natives of this province. Owing to this fact, the Central Government at Peking have some reason to fear a popular *émeute* in favor of Li, and, as a rule, adhere to any decision or conform to any suggestion he may make. The garrison is quartered in and around the city, in camps surrounded by high walls, and strongly fortified. At each angle of the structure, Armstrong, Krupp, and Vavasseur guns are mounted. Their size varies from twelve to forty-pounders. At the more exposed positions, such as over the gates, Gatling guns and mitrailleuses are to be found. Within the inclosures there are mud huts built for the soldiers, and wooden buildings for the officers. The most rigid discipline prevails. Opium smoking is punished, on the second offense, by cutting off an ear; on the third offense, the remaining ear, and should the person be detected a fourth time, he suffers the death penalty. Women are forbidden to enter the camp, and gambling is also prohibited. The drill of infantry and artillery is upon the German method throughout. The cavalry force still adheres to

of the English method, learned by a few of the officers some years back. The total force at Tientsin is as follows:

Infantry	35,000
Artillery	8,000
Cavalry	2,000
Total	45,000

The arms used by the infantry are of various patterns—Enfield muzzle-loaders, Snider, Winchester, Remington, Chassepôt, needle-guns (German pattern), Albini, and a few repeating rifles. The artillery are armed with Armstrong, Krupp, Bochüm (Broadwell's principle), and Vavasseur nine and twelve-pounder field-guns. Ten batteries of Gatling guns and French mitrailleuses serve for this arm of the service. The cavalry are armed with Sharp's repeating carbines and lances.

At a distance of twenty-five miles from Tientsin, the Viceroy caused a large walled military city to be erected, in 1876, upon the banks of the Peiho. The occupants of this place number:

Infantry	50,000
Artillery	5,000
Total	55,000

They are in every respect similar to the Tientsin garrison, both as regards discipline and arms. Since the year 1865, European drill instructors, of various nationalities, have been engaged in teaching the Chinese foreign tactics; and those men who showed in any way a proficiency in their attainments were dispatched to various points, where garrisons existed, to impart the knowledge acquired. The German successes in 1870 led the Viceroy, Li, to adopt the tactics then used by the Prussian army. A sub-lieutenant in the German army, who was well versed both in Infantry and artillery drill, was engaged. After a service of ten years, during which time he made the Chinese acquainted with the science of artillery and with field duties, he has returned to Europe.

Traveling southward, we come to the treaty port of Chefoo. Here, again, a Prussian officer is occupied in drilling the soldiery. The number of men of all branches of the service at this post is:

Infantry	15,000
Artillery	2,000
Total	17,000

At nearly every treaty port, a garrison of foreign-drilled troops is maintained. The figures nese army are only approximate, as each viceroy has the immediate control of the soldiers in his province, and a larger number exists on paper than is actually available. The actual command, as to the movements of the men, is vested in the *Tsung Ping* and the *Titu*, or the commander-in-chief and brigadier-general of each province. Each battalion carries a number of triangular flags bearing the surname of the general in command of the division, so that a major portion of the force, when seen on review or escort duty, is turned into flag-bearers. Owing to the lax system of payment prevailing, numberless grievances have to be heard, and risings among the soldiers are numerous and frequent.

The real standing army of China, in which is comprised the soldiery of the treaty ports, provincial capitals, customs barriers, and guards at the high officials' *yamens*, are known as the *Luh Ying* or green banner division. They render purely nominal service, leading a lazy life, and engage, under the cognizance of their commanders, in trade. Should the general commanding, or the viceroy, order an inspection, they are drummed together to pass muster. The viceroys and officials have of late years made extensive purchases of foreign breech-loading arms and artillery of modern construction. It may be safely asserted that nearly every pattern of rifle is in the hands of the Chinese troops; but by far the greater portion of the army have the Remington rifle. Owing to its simplicity, accuracy and simple mechanism, it is the favorite arm. The artisans at the arsenal near Shanghai and Tientsin turn out, by the aid of machinery, about five thousand rifles weekly. The various gunmakers of Europe and the United States have agents in China, who are pressing the respective qualifications of the rifles in their charge upon the officials. Winchester, Sharp, Albini, Snider, Chassepôt, and German rifles may be seen in the service, but the Remington has the lead in point of the number in use. The ships comprising the Shanghai and Foochow squadrons are all armed with this gun.

The artillery in use is also of a mixed kind; some of the batteries being composed of brass smooth-bores, and others of Armstrong muzzle and breech-loaders, and a few Krupp and Gatling guns. There are no cavalry stations at the southern ports whatever. The officers of the army are all mounted, and carry the short curved sword as a defensive weapon. During actual warfare the commanding officers generally are in the rear of the army.

In case of service proving too arduous, or the

any brigandage or insurrection, there are in the empire a number of disbanded soldiers. Their services were in requisition during the late rebellion, and they gain a livelihood by hanging around the mandarins' residences. These soldiers are called *Chwang Yung*, or braves. When no longer required they are disbanded. These gentlemen are the principal actors in any agitation against foreigners, and are to be hired for any purpose whatever. The best men for soldiers that China can boast of are natives of the province of Hunan, Honan, and Anhwei. They form the major portion of the army of the north-west. Averaging five feet in height, they are strongly-built, and are capable of bearing great fatigue and hardships. These men have always received great attention in Chinese military circles, as they are considered very brave. As to the qualifications of the officers of the army, the old-fashioned trials of strength, sword and spear exercise, are still in vogue in the service; but a number of young men who have received, and are receiving, instruction in Germany, France, and England, and who have also profited by the lessons of instructors in China, have changed, and will doubtless improve and regenerate the tactics of the army.

Turning to the army in Kansuh and North-west China, under the command of Tso Tsung Tang, we find, according to the latest advices, that it consists of about one hundred and eighty thousand men—one hundred and fifty thousand infantry, twenty thousand cavalry, and ten thousand artillery. The best guns are in use in Kansuh. Krupp mountain guns, siege guns of twenty and forty-pounders, and Gatling guns are to be found. Here, again, the infantry are armed with Remington and Martini-Peabody rifles, and the cavalry with Remington revolvers and Sharp's carbines. The munitions of war are in great quantities, and supplies to the force are constantly on the road from Shanghai, Nanking, and Tientsin arsenals. This body of men is in a good state of efficiency. The only drawback to warfare in China rests on the vile roads, want of bridges, and slow means of transport; and this state of affairs is extremely apparent in North-west China, where mountain passes and gorges are numerous. Should Russia attack the Chinese in this quarter she will find her work difficult. The passes can be defended by good men to the last extremity.

The number of foreigners engaged in China consists of one German at Chefoo, one German at Shanghai, one Frenchman in the North-west, two Englishmen, one at present traveling (General Mesney), and one at Formosa; but a large [illegible] tionalities, are in the employ of the Imperial customs, whose services are available at a short notice. The capabilities of the Chinese as to their soldierly qualities may be summed up briefly. The history of Colonel Gordon's small force during the Taiping rebellion plainly shows that if they are properly armed, trained, and led by officers enjoying their confidence, they furnish material for admirable soldiers. Frugal and temperate, hardy and enduring, they undergo hardships and privations without complaint. With men like Gordon and Giquel to lead and spur them on, they make formidable soldiers. The total of the Chinese army may be put down as follows:

Infantry	320,000
Infantry in the North-west	150,000
Cavalry	80,000
Cavalry in the North-west	20,000
Artillery	20,000
Artillery in the North-west	10,000
Total	600,000

This strength, by calling out the braves, can be at any time brought to a total of one million men. The army of the north-west is now receiving reinforcements from the south, and a large number of troops will be massed upon the Mongolian frontier to repel any attack made in that quarter. In addition to the above force there are upon the inland waters of the empire about two thousand small sailing gunboats, each armed with one gun and manned by twenty-five or thirty men. Their discipline is lax, but their services might possibly be available in war time. They are principally employed in the suppression of smuggling, in conveying native officials to and fro, and convoying powder and warlike stores into the interior. Their locomotion is effected by a large striped blue and white sail, and also twelve or more oars, or long sweeps. The pay of these men is very small, being at the rate of two or three dollars a month, but this is eked out by making the most out of any unfortunate that comes into their clutches. At every *lekin* (inland-tax) station, two or more of the boats are to be found, to aid the officer in charge in his collection.

What the ultimate position, or *personnel*, of the Chinese army may be in the future, if drilled by such men as Colonel Gordon, it is difficult to surmise; but there is no doubt of the fact that, until a uniform method of arming, drilling, and general equipment is established throughout the empire, in lieu of the present system, which permits each viceroy to adopt his own ideas of military matters, the Chinese army, taken as a whole, cannot cope with Eu- [illegible]

OPPORTUNITY.

This I saw once, or dreamed it in a dream:—
A child had strayed from out the palace gate
Far up a meadow slope, led on and on
By butterflies, or floating thistle-down,
Till now he played close on a precipice,
And stretched to reach the rolling globes of down
As they sailed out across the dizzy gorge.
A laggard saw him from the distant road,
And thought, "No use for me to go—too late:
Had I but seen him ere he reached the verge,
Or if it had been yesterday—just there
I stood, and flew my goshawk: 'tis too late."
He twirled his scarf, sighed, hummed a foolish tune,
And turned, pitying himself without a chance
For great emprise, and idled on his way.
A whole hour passed: the daughter of the king
Suddenly saw the boy, still at his play,
(For every blue-eyed flower had smiled its best,
And beckoned, nodding to him, to hold him back),
And flew and saved him, clasped upon her heart.

And this I saw, or dreamed it in a dream:—
There spread a cloud of dust along a plain;
And underneath the cloud, or in it, raged
A furious battle, and men yelled, and swords
Shocked upon swords and shields. A prince's banner
Wavered, then staggered backward, hemmed by foes.
A craven hung along the battle's edge,
And thought, "Had I a sword of keener steel—
That blue blade that the king's son bears,—but this
Blunt thing—!" he snapt and flung it from his hand,
And lowering crept away and left the field.
Then came the king's son, wounded, sore bestead,
And weaponless, and saw the broken sword,
And ran and snatched it, and with battle-shout
Lifted afresh he hewed his enemy down,
And saved a great cause that heroic day.

E. R. SILL.

A STRANGE CONFESSION.

CHAPTER V.

It has already been stated that the jail is in the rear of the court-house. The south wall is a few feet farther south than the line of the corresponding wall of the court-house. This is the strongest county prison in the State, and is so penetrable, if due precaution is exercised. It is approached by a passage-way some thirty feet wide, between the court-house and the St. James Hotel. On the north side of the court-house is a narrower passage. Running out in a straight line from the rear wall of the court-house to a fence inclosing the back-yard of the

twelve feet high. It extends in a similar manner northward from the court-house, thus barring on both sides the only approaches there are to the jail. Behind this wall is the outer yard of the jail. In the wall north of the court-house is a large double door, seldom opened. The approach to it is rarely used. The wall on the south (next the hotel) has two doors—one, rather small, for persons, and the other for wagons. The prisoners are never admitted into the outer yard, for the wall inclosing it could not have been intended to afford security of any kind, unless to prevent the passing of anything through the grated windows of the jail by persons outside.

The inner court of the jail, in which the kitchen and pump are situated, and where the prisoners are frequently admitted to find sunlight, is upon the north side of the jail, and is surrounded by a high brick wall. The eastern wall of this court faces the rear of the court-house, and the western wall forms one of the four sides of the Big Tank.

There are four entrances to the jail confines—the main entrance, through a hall that leads to the jailer's office; a door on the south side, opening into the jailer's apartments; a heavy iron door that communicates between the inner court and the outer yard; and another that is never used, and the existence of which is known to but few. This door fills an important part in this history.

Criminals held for minor offenses, and women, and insane persons awaiting examination by the Commission of Lunacy, are placed in the large, well aired compartments in the second and third stories. Those charged with or found guilty of graver crimes are placed in one or the other of the two divisions of the Tank. This latter is a prison of remarkable strength. It is divided into two compartments—the Little Tank and the Big Tank—separated from each other by a wall about thirty feet high, that reaches a roof lighted through corrugated glass set in iron. The walls surrounding the whole are made of brick, and are thick and massive. Imbedded in the center of the walls, and running their entire length and hight, is a network of heavy iron bars, crossed and riveted. It would require a persistent bombardment with artillery to demolish such a wall; for, if the brick should be thrown down, the iron would stand.

Both the Little Tank and the Big Tank are arranged on the same plan. The former contains four cells, and the latter, fifteen. The description of one will apply to the other, with the exception of this difference in the number of thieving, or rape are assigned to the Little Tank. The four cells in this are in two rows, back to back, the rows being separated by a narrow passage (for ventilation and drainage), strongly grated above and at either end. The cells are eight feet by nine, seven and a half feet high, and are covered with heavy granite slabs. In the rear wall of each is a small grating, to admit air. The doors are made of heavy plate-iron, doubled and securely riveted. In the upper part of each door is a small wicket, that closes with an iron shutter opening outward and barred on the exterior. Sometimes a prisoner is favored by being allowed to attach a string to this shutter, that he may close it at his will. When once closed, he can not open it. Surrounding the group of cells is a wide passage. Prisoners are generally permitted to exercise in this area, but are always locked in their cells at five o'clock in the afternoon, when supper is served.

Each Tank has a door communicating with the jailer's office. These doors are secured by a heavy grating that opens inward upon the Tank, and a solid plate-iron door that opens into the office. Neither Tank has a window.

In the arrangement of this costly and secure prison there is a single defect—another door in the Little Tank, a superfluous and unnecessary thing. This is the door that is never used. The wooden wall that blocks the entrance to the outer yard of the jail is but a portion of a wall that runs almost entirely around the jail, Tanks, and court, the only discontinuation of it being the court-house wall.

The court-house and jail run back in the direction of Market Street about half the depth of the block. The wooden wall behind the jail forms the rear inclosing fence of several yards, belonging to cottages facing on Market Street.

One more fact must be mentioned as showing the absurdity of an attack upon the jail. The court-house is two stories in hight. To each story there are eight windows looking down upon the approaches to the jail. These windows are provided with iron shutters. Four men, armed with rifles, could have been stationed at each of the thirty-two windows. Furthermore, the windows of the St. James Hotel could have been similarly filled with men; and in addition to all this, armed defenders could have occupied the windows of the jail that peered over the wall, and could have swarmed behind the parapet of the jail.

Taking all these facts into consideration, it is not idle to assert that it would have required extraordinary strength and determination to make the jail disgorge in open fight.

Chapter VI.

Where the common rabble, armed with stones and axes, will succumb to organized resistance, the cool foresight and calm resolution of the better element, when it engages with the rabble in the accomplishing of a purpose, presents an appalling picture. The latter uses the former as a tool. There is a twinge of conscience, a nervousness resulting from revolting manhood, that causes the finger to tremble which pulls the trigger on a dauntless breast, actuated in design by an honest desire to make crime a terror—to invest it with horrors that the scaffold renders comparatively tame. Summary punishment is more effective as example than that born of the slow incubation of the law. The law is the servant of society. As such, it may be betrayed, cheated, bribed. This is a possibility inseparable from a condition of servitude. The master lays down rules by which the servant is to be guided. When great urgency is required, he thrusts the servant aside and does the work himself, because it is his own affair, concerning him vitally.

The officers of the law had, on this occasion, arrayed against them a far more dangerous element than bravery. It was cunning. They did not dream of that; for who ever knew a mob that displayed cunning! It is a flood, rushing blindly on, crushing, drowning, sweeping away, until stopped and hurled back upon itself by a mountain; depending alone upon its momentum.

It was about noon that Casserly found himself powerless. He was compelled to admit it. With that self-consciousness of superior power that raises up a commander, Casserly felt his strength, and assumed control of the defense. It is true that the Sheriff was the proper guardian of the jail; but, though a man of sufficient nerve for ordinary occasions, he was inferior to Casserly in qualifications for generalship. He cheerfully, therefore, placed himself and his twenty deputies at Casserly's command. The captain of the military company did not even ask a question as to Casserly's authority when ordered to guard the approaches to the jail.

Casserly had attempted to disperse a second mass-meeting, held at the corner of First and Santa Clara Streets. He knew that many were armed. Indignation and excitement ran at a high pitch, increasing with the mob. Casserly burst into this crowd, scattered the men right and left, and plowed his way through the stormy sea of humanity, ordering the rioters to leave. him, for he was feared. He pushed a speaker from a box, and mounted it.

"Go to your homes!" he shouted. "I promise you that Howard shall receive the full penalty of the law. What are you about to do? Are you devils, or men? If there's a brave man in this crowd, I challenge him to mount this box and stand beside me, my companion in the preservation of the peace."

Not a man moved. All remained sullen.

"Then, if you are cowards, there may be some honest men among you. I will give the first honest man one minute to start for his home."

He held his watch in his hand. A half minute rolled by. No one stirred.

"A half minute has gone."

The second-hand rapidly marked thirty seconds more. Still no one moved.

"You are a set of cowards and outlaws. In five minutes I will charge you with the militia, twenty sheriffs, and thirty policemen. I give you fair warning. There's not a blank cartridge in the lot."

This caused a howl of mingled curses and hisses to rise from the mob. Casserly's position was perilous. He choked down his choler and chagrin, descended from the box, and slipped away.

Then it was that Casserly saw he was powerless on the street. He would immediately concentrate at the jail, and, armed and intrenched, defy the mob, were it ten thousand strong.

During this time the unusually large force of policemen had not been idle. The majority were men who had never served in that capacity, and were, consequently, more zealous than prudent. They mingled with the mob in sets of four. Several times had they attempted the arrest of the more turbulent individuals of the riot, but as often were their prisoners rescued.

Shortly after Casserly left the box, two sharp taps of the fire-bell were heard. Every policeman suddenly disappeared. It was the signal to concentrate.

Then Casserly resorted to a ruse that deserved success. If he could introduce a sufficient counter excitement there was a possibility that by the time it should die away the spirit of outlawry would have had its back broken. He sent a man to a barn near Market Plaza, with instructions to fire it. The barn was dry and inflammable. In a short time dense volumes of smoke were seen in that quarter of the city. Market Plaza is about as far from Santa Clara Street on the south as is the jail on the north. The fire-alarm was sounded, and the engines tore noisily through the streets, deadening the wavering of the crowd, and a few boys left for the scene of the fire, but the ruse failed; the mob could not be diverted from its object.

In his heart, Casserly did not wish to avert the attack. When he threatened a charge, it was far from his intention to make one, and thus precipitate a collision in which the law would be the aggressor. He felt perfectly secure; and it was only an over-estimate of his power that had led him into the error of thinking to intimidate the mob, and quell the riot in its incipiency. His grounds for security were these: In addition to the militia (a company numbering some sixty men), the deputies, and the policemen, there were many volunteers, including nearly all the city and county officials; and the constables had multiplied themselves, after the manner of certain infusoria. In this way there were about three hundred men gathered together to protect the jail—all fully armed with rifles, shotguns, or revolvers. With the exception of a few blank-loaded guns held convenient, each barrel of every shotgun was loaded with three and a half drachms of powder and twenty buckshot—loaded to kill. At close range the shotgun is the most deadly of weapons. Suppose, then (reasoned Casserly), that by some improbable turn of events the mob, numbering nearly two thousand, should overpower the resistance, what would result? Nothing. The outer wall might be torn down, the jail might be invaded, but the impregnability of the Tank was an insurmountable obstacle. No axe, nor sledge-hammer, nor crowbar, nor file could effect an entrance to this stronghold. There would be no time to employ blasting-powder. But might not the jailer be robbed of his keys? Certainly not; for Casserly had taken charge of them, and concealed them. He had cause afterward to regret this, as the sequel will show. Thoughtful as he was, he could not foresee everything.

The mob soon found itself moving by impulse upon the jail. Strange to say, although it had no plan, no organization, it was controlled and sustained by a few stern men, who, by going hither and thither, assiduously aggravated the spirit of outlawry that animated nearly every breast. The mob had no plan, but it had an object—to take the prisoner from his cell, and hang him. This lack of preparation and organization was not accidental, as will presently appear.

The mob rolled along First Street toward the jail, with shouts, cries, and curses. It maintained solidity, as contact sustained courage. When it arrived at the court-house, everything seemed deserted, and nothing appeared to prevent a consummation of the deed. Nevertheless, a few knowing persons detected one suspicious circumstance. The great iron sliding-doors at the entrance to the court-house were drawn and barred. The thirty-two windows—and especially the sixteen on the side next the hotel—had their iron shutters nearly closed, leaving an opening only a few inches wide. Through these interstices nothing could be seen in the darkness of the interior. The building was wrapped in gloomy silence—an unusual occurrence, and one that boded danger.

All the attention of the mob was directed to the passage between the hotel and the court-house, for the reason that it was the wider and the first arrived at.

With the exception of a space of sufficient width to admit a carriage, there are chains stretched, from post to post, across the entrance to this passage. They were probably placed there to protect the grass and shrubbery occupying the ground not taken by the graveled drive. Now, that portion of the chain fence, always left open for carriages, was on this particular day closed. This fence was by no means a trifling obstacle to the mob. There were two chains, one below and the other above, the upper chain striking a man's leg just above the knee. The chains were not stretched taut, but hung rather loose, making a treacherous object over which to step, especially if the least haste should be exercised. The posts were large, and were sunk deep in the ground, which is paved with asphaltum, and the chains were strong.

The mob halted in front of the court-house, and endeavored to organize, but no leader showed himself. After some minutes of loud talking, and hurrying to and fro, about seventy men, armed with axes, formed in front of the fence of chains.

Then the great iron door opened sufficiently to permit one man to pass out. Casserly advanced alone and undaunted. He crossed the broad stone floor, shaded by the stately Corinthian columns of the piazza, descended the steps half way, and stood upon the granite landing there. He removed his hat, and raised his right hand high above his head, palm outward. This gesture and pose, in which respect was indicated by the bared head, and attention demanded by the uplifted arm, sent silence through the crowd.

"Men," said Casserly, his voice penetrating to the farthest limits of the densely packed throng, deep, powerful, and deliberate, "you are about to attempt...a deed...of violence and bloodshed. Are you...mad? You would... vindicate justice by...trampling it...under foot

Leave the law...to take its course. I speak to you...as a friend. And I give...this...solemn ...warning...once...and for all: That if you enter...that passage...the roof of yonder jail ...and these sixteen windows...will pour down upon you...volleys of leaden death...that will strew the ground...with your...dead bodies... and render...your firesides desolate...and your children...fatherless. Heed that warning. Go quietly...to your homes. If you...disregard it ...God have mercy...on you! I will do...my duty."

Having finished, he watched the effect. An awful silence followed.

At this moment, when the conflict might have been averted, and when order seemed about to be restored, a man was seen running along the street, bearing aloft a large piece of canvas, stretched upon a frame. The profound silence that prevailed allowed his voice to ring through the throng like a bell, as he shouted:

"Read! read! read!"

All eyes were turned upon him. The canvas bore this startling announcement, in large letters, daubed hastily with a marking-brush—coming from none knew what source, nor by whose authority:

"At nine strokes
of the Fire-bell
Howard will be hanged."

The man continued to shout: "At nine strokes he will be hanged! Read! read! At nine strokes! Hanged! hanged!"

What did it mean? Perhaps nothing. Men stared at it. Many shuddered. There stood the jail, and in it was the murderer. The mob had only this to do: to crush the shell, take out the kernel, and roast it. Perhaps the notice was intended to impart zest to the undertaking, to pour oil upon the fire that was threatened with being smothered by Casserly's broad hand. The man was surrounded.

"What do you mean?" was breathlessly asked by a hundred voices.

"Read! read!"

He said nothing else. Casserly's countenance betrayed the deepest astonishment. He stood as if petrified, yet his mind was actively searching the darkness for a solution of the mystery. It would have been utterly useless for him to attempt the capture of this man, who was buried and crushed by the crowd that packed around him.

While attention was thus diverted from Casserly, a man with a furtive, frightened look, panting, exhausted, and covered with perspiration, tunneled his way a short distance toward Casserly. Finding that he could proceed no farther, he picked up a small stone, wrapped a narrow strip of paper around it, inclosed this in a larger piece, making the whole firm and solid, and threw the ball at Casserly. It struck one of the stone steps behind Casserly, and bounded to his feet. At first he thought it was a missile, but the fact that a paper ball should strike with such force attracted his attention, and he picked it up. He removed the outer covering, secured the narrow slip, and read the following, written hastily with a pencil:

"Keep them at bay thirty minutes longer. If necessary, give them a volley of blank cartridges. Above all, we warn you, in the name of the people, not to harm a hair of their heads. If they crowd past you, let them attack the jail; you know it can't be broken open. By that time we will come to your assistance.

"A HUNDRED CITIZENS."

Casserly was sore perplexed at the appearance of the mysterious notice; he was troubled at reading the note. He was in utter ignorance as to who was the sender, and why it was sent. His anxiety amounted almost to despair. Was it a trick? The jail certainly was strong enough to resist an attack; and, after all, it would be terrible to sacrifice human life in the manner contemplated by him. If it was a snare, what was to be gained? The note said, "It can't be broken open." No one was more fully aware of that fact than Casserly, and the strength of the jail was increased a hundred fold by Casserly's muskets.

He turned, and disappeared through the door, which closed behind him, swallowing him up. Then he reflected seriously. Perhaps the note came from friends, who were organizing; but why was no name signed? He saw that his position was a grave one. He resolved to follow the advice of the note to this extent: he would fire blank volleys, and, if that failed, he would occupy the windows in the rear of the courthouse, and with powder and ball prevent the demolition of the jail. For (he reasoned), admit that the man is deserving of death, is that a circumstance to be taken into account in this emergency? No. The grand idea, that preponderated against all others, was the prevention of an outrage upon the sanctity of the law. Casserly was a conscientious officer—if, in all truth, there is such a thing. There is no popular idea so erroneous as that an officer of the law is the servant of the people. He is the under-servant of the law, which is the real servant of the people. In other words, he is a bloodhound employed by the law. The law is just; it is the concentrated wisdom of ages. Sitting only in judgment, not in condemnation—searching neither for crime nor for virtue, but waiting patiently until it shall be called upon to decide what is right and what is wrong—it scorns to be called by any other name than Justice. Between the law and its minister there is this difference: the law presumes innocence till guilt is proved; the officer acts on the presumption of guilt till innocence is established. The law is the theory; the officer is the practice. Why is this? The answer is simple: the law is wise, the officer is something less—he is merely human; the one has intelligence, the other a heart; the one is devoid of pride and vanity, the breast of the other rankles with these infirmities. The officer, being less honest than the law, betrays it to society and his own vanity. It is pride that leads him to seek conviction rather than justice. The modern district-attorney is the most striking example of this incongruity between the name and the thing, the idea and the reality. He draws his salary in the name of justice, but secretly looks upon it as blood-money. But the officer's aim is to hang according to law. In this lies his pride, and to this end will he exert his energies. Consequently, although he will preserve a malefactor from the jaws of a hungry mob, he will the next moment cheerfully adjust the hangman's noose under a proper judicial edict.

Some time was required to relieve the mob of the dampening effect of Casserly's terrible warning and the surprise of the mysterious notice, and it saw death lurking behind the iron shutters of the sixteen windows. The moments flew rapidly. The air seemed stifling with the sickening odor of warm blood. The advance was finally made upon the fence of chains. The upper front window was flung wide open, and Casserly again appeared to give a final warning; but before he had time to utter a word, a shot was fired from below, full at his breast. It was the first shot of the conflict. The ball struck that side of the double shutter that opened toward the jail, glanced upward, and buried itself in the window-casing, leaving an elongated grayish spot on the iron shutter. It had passed within six inches of Casserly's head. It was too late to say anything more. Casserly closed the shutter. The battle had opened.

The cowardly shot and Casserly's retreat had the effect of counteracting all hesitancy on the part of the mob, which yelled wildly, and which began to condense and to press forward. The men with axes occupied the front, but their ranks had been decimated by Casserly's impressive warning; their places, however, were immediately filled by men armed with all manner of strange weapons, snatched hastily here and there. The gradual rising of excitement and the increasing noise showed that the lion had couched to spring. The front advanced, pushed from behind, furious, loud, and bloodthirsty. The chains were reached. Forty or fifty men attempted to step over, but the crowding from the rear caused some of them to lose their balance, and others tumbled over them, tripped to the ground; the crowd pressed on, not allowing sufficient time for those in front to clear the treacherous barrier of chains.

At this moment, when this unforeseen accident had caused some confusion to arise, a paper ball suddenly flew from the window that Casserly had recently vacated, struck the hotel, bounded into a small tree near the barrier, and fell at the feet of the mob.

"I wonder what this is," said a rioter, stooping to pick it up.

His hand had not reached it when there came a terrific crash from the sixteen windows; the paper ball was a signal. Casserly had poured his fire into the mob. The effect was wonderful: the mob fell back upon itself, crushing and grinding, howling, cursing, and paralyzed with terror; the wildest confusion reigned.

Presently, however, it was discovered that not a man had received a scratch. Many who were fleeing in wild dismay checked their flight. After some delay order was restored; but there was an absence of that reckless and fearful determination that had heretofore characterized the attack. Men sustained and encouraged one another by incendiary utterances. The crowd, which had been scattered over a large area, embracing the greater part of First Street, between St. John and St. James, again began to assume close order and to concentrate toward the front. One man, who had dropped his axe, more hardy than the others, advanced stealthily to recover it; but a single shot, the ball from which struck the pavement at his feet, caused him to beat a hasty retreat. The shot was aimed to miss.

Then came a reaction—one quite natural, and that might have been expected. The terror inspired by the blank volley gradually gave way to anger. The idea diffused itself that Casserly was endeavoring to frighten men as he would children. Manhood rebelled against such indignity. The impression took root that Casserly dared not fire upon them; that the stake for which he played did not warrant a wholesale slaughter. Casserly knew the man was guilty, and that he deserved to suffer the direst vengeance of outraged society. Casserly was but as other men; he also had a home, was an integer of society; he should naturally concur in steps taken to remove a cancer from the body politic. Therefore, while, for the sake of decency, he ostentatiously interposed his opposition to irregular chastisement for a heinous crime, he must at heart have sympathized with this movement, which met no hinderance elsewhere. By this course of reasoning, the mob was led into a serious error.

The crowd again bubbled and seethed, its venom returned. Much valuable time had already been lost.

Two men were standing in St. James Square, anxiously watching the result of the attack, and pale with expectation. One of these was Judge Simon. He remarked to his companion:

"They are preparing to renew the attack."

"It is terrible!"

"See! They are advancing again."

"My God!"

"Casserly will shoot them down like dogs."

"Do you think so?"

"I know it."

They stood thus, painfully absorbed in the preparations for the second advance. Suddenly Judge Simon violently started, the pallor of his cheeks changing to the hue of death.

"Listen," he said, hardly above a whisper.

"What is it?"

"One."

"One what?"

"Two. The fire-bell."

"What can it mean?"

"Three. Hush."

"Must be another ruse of Casserly's."

"Four. Perhaps."

"Maybe they have stolen Howard from the jail—"

"Five."

"—and hanged him—"

"Six."

"—as the notice said."

"Seven."

"That's only six."

"Seven, I tell you! Eight."

"My God! What is it?"

"Nine."

They waited in breathless silence for another stroke. They listened in vain. Had Casserly in reality acted on the notice, and, to mislead the mob, sounded the alarm that tolled the death of Howard? The alarm had risen above the tumult of the riot. The mob was stupefied, but uncertain. It groped in the dark, fearing treachery, yet hopeful that the bell had clanged out the alarum of the people's vengeance. A loud cheering was heard in the direction of Santa Clara Street. It flew from mouth to mouth, entered the mob, and was there taken up and swelled a thousand fold. It scattered the mob like a fire-brand among wolves. The attack was abandoned, and the cry went up up from two thousand voices: "The murderer is dead!"

All eyes were turned upon a ghastly spectacle, that displayed its hideousness under the very eyes of the riot. A body swung by the neck from a beam that ran out horizontally from the ridge of the roof of the old San José Theater. This building is situated on First Street, near the corner of St. James. It is an old barn-like wooden building, erected about twenty-five years ago by James Stark, the actor. It was the first theater built in San José. It was a famous place of amusement in bygone days, and many actors of renown have trod its rattling boards. It is now used for a carriage factory. The old planks are overlapped—the way in which houses were built in early days—and in some places they are warped and twisted with age. It is not more than three or four hundred yards from the court-house. Hence, the body, that swung so limp and helpless, was in plain view of the mob, which rushed pell-mell to the scene.

There it hung, slowly turning from side to side. The head and face were entirely concealed by a cap, or cowl. The body was neatly dressed in black. A rope was wrapped around the legs, and the arms were pinioned to the sides by another rope that encircled the body several times. Two placards were attached to it—one upon the breast and the other upon the back. They were made of large pieces of white pasteboard, with irregular letters daubed upon them, large enough to be read a considerable distance, and each bearing this notice:

"Howard, the Woman-Murderer."

The placard upon the back was secured by a string passed through the upper edge, the loop being thrown around the neck. That upon the breast was differently attached, and in a manner so cruel, so revolting, that upon seeing the sickening spectacle a shudder ran through the crowd. It was pinned to the breast with a hunter's knife, driven straight in to the hilt.

At the moment when Judge Simon's companion suggested that the sounding of the bell was Casserly's ruse, the latter remarked to a friend:

"That is very strange."

"It is."

"It must be somebody's ruse to draw of the mob."

The man looked knowingly at Casserly, and said: "I suppose you did it."

"I did not."

Casserly heard the cheering, and his heart sank as the cry arose that the murderer was dead. He was greatly alarmed when he saw the crowd melting away, and his doubt changed to certainty when a man came running back from the crowd in front of the hanging body, and gave Casserly the news. It was a terrible surprise, though he was almost prepared to hear it.

But after reflecting a moment, Casserly's face brightened. All was confusion in the court-house. The guard had abandoned the windows, and flocked around their leader, who said:

"Somebody has fooled the mob."

"How?"

"I'll bet a hundred dollars it's a stuffed figure."

This set them all to thinking.

"I'll bet another hundred dollars," continued Casserly, "that Howard is in the Little Tank."

This was a doubt easily set at rest. Casserly proceeded to the jail. On being admitted, he asked the jailer hurriedly:

"Where's Howard?"

The jailer, evidently surprised, replied:

"Why, in the Tank."

"Are you sure?"

"Certainly."

Casserly unconsciously drew a deep breath, greatly relieved.

"Do you know," he asked the jailer, "that it is reported he is hanged?"

"No."

"A man has just told me that he saw the body."

"Impossible. But let's go into the Tank, and see."

Casserly retraced his footsteps into the court-house, procured the keys, and returned.

Before opening the door of the Tank he asked, as if desirous of leaving no possible room for doubt:

"Did you hear any unusual noise in the Tank?"

"I heard him call out once, and would have opened the door, but you had the keys. The voice was very faint, but I'm almost sure I heard it."

Casserly swung open the plate-iron door, and looked through the grated door. He saw nothing. Then he inserted his face in a depression made in the grating inward, to allow one a larger perspective. Still he saw nothing. Howard was in his cell, doubtless. As he unlocked the grated door he asked the jailer:

"Did you lock him in his cell?"

"No."

Casserly entered, followed by the jailer.

"Number 3, ain't it?"

"Yes."

Casserly went straight to this cell, the door of which was open. The prisoner was not within. Casserly called: "Howard!"

His voice reverberated from wall to wall, but no answer came. Then was Casserly thoroughly alarmed. Hurriedly and anxiously he ran from one cell to another. All were tenantless. The two men stared at each other, blank astonishment being depicted in their faces.

"Where is he?" asked Casserly.

"I don't know."

"You *must* know."

"Positively I do not."

They glanced around upon the walls, and reflected upon the impossibility of scaling their smooth surfaces. Even should this be done, the roof remained, and it was intact.

Then did a suspicion, that had been growing in Casserly's breast for the last few moments, take shape; and, with a steady look upon the jailer in a manner that admitted of no trifling or equivocation, he asked, sternly:

"Where is that man?"

"Upon my honor, I do not know."

Casserly nodded. His tone was quiet, but it indicated danger.

"Did you leave him in here?"

"Yes."

"When did you see him last?"

"About two hours ago."

Casserly again nodded, and asked no more questions. The jailer, stung by the look of suspicion that Casserly did not attempt to conceal, said, with great earnestness:

"I tell you, Casserly, that I don't know how he left this Tank. It is a terrible mystery."

"Doubtless," replied Casserly, calmly.

Suddenly Casserly noticed the small door in the south wall of the Tank. This door, like the other, was doubled, having a grating opening inward, and a plate-iron door opening outward. They were both closed. He approached closer, to examine them. He seized the grating, which yielded and swung open. He then pushed upon the solid door, and it opened. He turned upon the jailer, who stood petrified with astonishment, and, with raised voice and glaring eyes, he demanded:

"How is this?"

The jailer could not reply. He was stifling. Casserly stepped into the yard, followed by the jailer. He saw several footprints on the ground. Following them around the corner of the jail, he found an opening cut through the wooden wall. Sick at heart, Casserly again turned upon the jailer:

"How came that door unlocked?" he demanded, angrily.

"I don't know."

"Where did you keep the key?"

"I didn't know there was a key. The door has been locked ever since I took charge, nearly two years ago. I never heard of a key."

Casserly turned to leave, without saying another word. He met Judge Simon in the yard. The old man asked, in a deprecating tone:

"Casserly, how is this?"

Casserly merely shook his head.

"There is a terrible report on the street about it, Casserly." Casserly's look was inquiring, but his tongue was silent. "I don't believe it, though," continued the old man. "It is too horrible—too unnatural."

Casserly's interest was aroused. "What is it?" he asked.

"Why, Garratt told me that he saw a woman helping the mob to hang the poor boy."

Casserly's look betrayed some surprise. The old man approached closer, and whispered in Casserly's ear:

"He said he recognized in that woman—"

"Well?"

"—Howard's own mother."

Casserly almost staggered under this revelation. His strong nature was shattered. Crushed and humiliated, and almost overpowered by this mountain of mystery that bore him down, he entered the court-house, cheated at every turn, and outwitted like a fool.

W. C. Morrow.

(CONTINUED IN NEXT NUMBER.)

WRINKLED SIRENS.

It is not pleasant, but really lamentable, to acknowledge, first, that sirens have wrinkles; second, that the world is fairly crowded with wrinkled sirens. But the language of facts is incontrovertible; wrinkled sirens exist; there are plenty of them; there is a reason why they exist, and there is a remedy for them. Education, as all the world will admit, ought to have two ends. It ought to develop strength and to supplement weakness—especially with wrinkled sirens. What is good, it ought to make better, and what is wanting, it ought to supply. Some principle of this kind practically obtains in the education of boys; why not with girls? Not only are the strong points of a boy's abilities and character carefully noted, and afforded fair fields of exercise, but his deficiencies also, his stupidity in one or other line of study, his bodily indolence or awkwardness, his cowardly, lying, or cruel propensities—all are noticed by his tutors, and due efforts are made to counteract them.

But in the case of girls, only one of these two ends of education is commonly pursued. The peculiar gifts of women, their affectionateness, piety, modesty, and conscientiousness, their quick apprehension, and brilliant intuition, their delicacy of sentiment, and natural love for poetry, music, and all things beautiful—all these qualities are drawn out by the education usually given to them, to the very utmost of the teachers' powers. But the equally ordinary defects of women—their wrinkles, if you please—their bigotry and superstition, their hastiness and superficialness of judgment, their morbidness of sentiment, their lack of sustained ardor for solid study or abstract thought—all these deficiencies are usually left at the end of the most elaborate female education very much as they were in the beginning. It is seemingly taken for granted that, while every defect or wrinkle in man is more or less capable of cure, of being ironed out, in a woman it is hopeless of remedy. Perhaps the cause of this anomaly is a lack of faith in the possibilities of human nature; but I shall not now inquire too deeply into these causes. Perhaps the associations of ideas of what we most love in woman with so many of woman's weaknesses has endeared the weaknesses themselves, even as some one has said that the silliest custom and wildest belief, which had once been associated with our religion, became dear and venerable in our eyes. In any case, the true faith in womanhood must needs include the conviction that the weaknesses—physical, moral, and intellectual—so often attached to it, cannot truly be an integral part thereof, and that, to relieve it from them, would not be to take aught from its beauty and its charm, but, on the contrary, to increase them.

But before following out this line of thought, it is needful to meet, at the outset, an argument which, whether plainly expressed or silently understood, actually bars this whole road of progress in the feelings of thousands. Hunyan's Apollyon no more "straddled all across the way of life" than does this argument the life for women. Briefly, it is this: The end and aim of a woman's life is to be beloved by a man. But men love the weaknesses of a woman rather more than her strength. This fact raises more than half the antagonisms in man to the claim of the ladies struggling for a Sixteenth Amendment to the Constitution. It makes men crowd the theater to witness "Miss Multon," or "Hamlet," where Ophelia passes in review, rather than go and listen to Portia. It was the myriad-minded Coleridge who said, "Every man would desire rather to have an Ophelia for a wife than a Portia." "Therefore, it is vain to seek to banish feminine weaknesses, for, by so doing, we are depriving the spider of its thread."

To this simple syllogism I have two answers. The first is, that if some men, and even a majority of men, prefer a colorless Ophelia to the rich, brave nature of Portia, yet the one man who prefers Portia is a million times more worthy of love, and more qualified to make a wife happy, than the ninety and nine who prefer Ophelia. Secondly, I am prepared to maintain, that no outward gain whatever is equal in value to the inward gain of a healthy and vigorous frame, a highly trained intellect, a calm reason, a wealthy memory, well ordered passions, and a heart lifted to the love of all things good and holy. Make a comparison between a woman, as a wife, like this, and one ignorant, silly, full of pitiful vanities and ambitions, a prey to her own temper and jealousies, and may a man not parody Solomon's proverb, "Better a solitary life where wisdom is, than a house full of children and folly therewith."

More than half the weaknesses of women are the results of that imperfect physical health and vigor, that *petite santé*, to which their habits commonly consign them from childhood, and which also they inherit from valetudinarian mothers. The other part of these weaknesses appears to be only the natural complements of their best qualities. Of the first of these classes I shall now speak.

There is something radically wrong in the present state of things which makes the whole upper class of the female sex—the sex least exposed to toil or disease—very little better than the inmates of a convalescent home. Few ladies are able to do any real work of head or limb for a few days consecutively without breaking down deplorably. The chance of a wetting in a shower, which ought to hurt them no more than it hurts the roses, is a serious source of alarm to their friends. This state of things cannot be remedied in one generation; but it will never be remedied at all by a few fashionable calisthenics. Perhaps the hints I propose, or rather the remedies for wrinkles, may shock many lady readers, but they are remedies which will appeal strongly, if prejudice is not allowed to block up the way of approach. In the first place, the ladies of our best society on the Pacific Coast, like those of New York, London, and Paris, do not go to bed early enough. It should be the *habit* to retire at half past ten, and this, as a habit, is absolutely invaluable to vigor, freshness, and eyesight. If you do not want this vigor and freshness and clear eyesight, sit up until midnight, and your wish will be gratified. Another typical female defect, and source of wrinkles, is eating too little solid food—eating too much such rubbish as sweets and pickles, hot cakes, pastry, and drinking only water or tea, whereby a healthful appetite is spoiled. Nothing like this will force a woman to the habit of falling back on nervous excitement, for want of natural strength. It would be a great blessing to women if they were more, as men are, sensible of imperious hunger and thirst, and desire for sleep, and less able to draw on their nervous capital when their daily income of strength is exhausted. One of the sad results of society swagger or ostentation is the checking of the appetites of young girls, and causing them to dwindle into what vulgar people consider "genteel" proportions. The remedy for this is to commence at once to treat defective table duty not as a feminine grace, but as a disagreeable, ghoul-like phenomenon. With its many evils and absurdities, it may be questioned whether some pounds of superfluous adipose matter be not, on the whole, a pleasanter burden than a perpetual dyspeptic pain in the side. Naturally, exercise follows here. Nobody wants ladies to train like pugilists, but the truth is that, however good and wholesome exercise may be, its occasional taking can never make a thoroughly healthy woman. It is the whole twenty-four hours which need to be spent healthfully; not one hour of vigorous exercise and ten of sitting in overheated rooms, or walking in thin shoes on cold pavements. Of the two kinds of strength, muscular strength and brain strength, it is the latter which it most concerns our women to obtain. But the training for strength of brain includes a certain, although secondary, degree of muscular training also. What a miserable sight is that of a man of great, perhaps feverish, mental activity, who has accumulated hoards of learning, and is full of generous aspirations, but whose narrow chest, and drooping and rounded shoulders, sunken cheeks, and over-lucent eyes betray that the fleshy pedestal on which his soul is standing is crumbling beneath him. How almost invariably such a man's thoughts come to us tinctured with sickness; how, in matters of judgment, he is apt to lack ballast, to be carried away by prejudice, to waste moral energy on trifles, to ignore the common principles which determine the action of healthy human nature. We pity these things, and deplore them as exceptional failures when we see them in a man, but when we find them in a woman—much more frequently—why do we not attribute them to the same cause of unequal development of mind and body, and not, as we do, take them for granted as weaknesses inherent in the feminine nature itself. A perfect woman, in the physical sense, is no more crotchety, and credulous, and prejudiced, and vehement about trifles than a well constituted man. Some one has said that the belief in the gloomier doctrines of theology is inseparable from a bad liver.

It would be a curious table which gave the proportions between dyspepsia, headaches, tight lacing, and narrow chests, and the belief in certain follies, and the general instability of character and temper which have made women, for ages, the butt of masculine cynicism. Exercise is, no more than food, a thing to be taken and profited by *vi et armis*. The child who should be compelled every day to swallow a breakfast and a dinner composed of objects disgusting to it, would never be expected by any sane person to thrive thereon. But it is often assumed that the same child will obtain all the benefit of exercise if obliged to walk solemnly up and down a lawn or path for so many hours, or to perform calisthenic exercises in a dull schoolroom. This is an error. Exercise, especially in youth, must be joyous exercise, spontaneously taken, not as a medicine, but with the eagerness of natural appetite. Supreme among all penny-wise and pound-foolish policies, is that which grudges a girl of fourteen a rough pony, or a patch of garden, and lavishes on her, four years afterward, silks and jewels, and all the costly appurtenances of fashionable life. How is it that Harriet Hosmer became the woman of whom America is so proud, England so fond? Because her father taught her to shoot, to ride, before Gibson taught her to model "Sleeping Fawns;" because she possesses physical strength, energy, and joyous animal spirits, faculties that win every prize and charm every heart.

Naturally, this topic leads me to that of dress, which is certainly the great stumbling-block in the way of exercise. To advise a lady to dress herself with any serious eccentricity from the prevailing fashion of day and class is to advise her to incur a penalty which may very probably be the wreck of her whole life's happiness. Men sneer at a woman so dressed, and, perhaps, allow themselves coarse jokes at her expense. But it is only the fault of public opinion that any penalties at all follow innovations, in themselves sensible and modest. To train this public opinion by degrees, to bear with more variations of costume, and especially to insist upon the principle of fitness as the first requisite of beauty, should be the aim of all sensible women. I ask any sensible woman if anything is in worse taste than to wear clothes by which the natural movements are impeded, and purposes, of whatever sort, thwarted. Ladies laugh at a Chinese woman's foot, and call the practice of making it small very cruel and barbaric, yet it is not one iota more so than wearing long, trailing skirts, when a woman wishes to take a brisk walk, or to run up or down stairs; no more barbaric than to wear bonnets which give no shade to the eyes under a summer sun, or pinching the feet into thin, tight boots, which permit of fatal damp and chill, and cramp the limb into a pitiful little wedge of flesh. Not one Pacific Coast lady's foot in five hundred could be looked at if placed in an antique sandal.

The sooner our women learn that there is no such thing as perfectly idle health, or perfect health without hope, the better. Lives which have no aim beyond the amusement of the hour are inevitably, after the first few years of youth, valetudinarian lives. Women occupy themselves with their own sensations, and quack themselves, and fix their thoughts on one organ or another, until they can bring disease into the soundest part of the body; and all because, four-fifths of the time, they are idle dawdlers. There must be work, and there must be freedom for women, if they are ever to be really healthful beings. If the weaknesses of women, which arise from imperfect bodily health, were removed by better systems of diet and exercise, and hopeful employment maintained for a generation, what weaknesses would remain? I believe there would be few beyond those which may be reckoned as the natural defects or wrinkles, the complementary colors of their special merits. Women are capable of the most intense personal affection; therefore they are liable to neglect abstract principles, and to regard persons too exclusively. Women are tender-hearted and merciful; therefore stern justice and veracity have less than due honor at their hands. Women have brilliant intuitional powers, and think with great rapidity; therefore slow processes of argument are distasteful to them, and their judgments are hasty and often erroneous. All these, and sundry weaknesses besides, are easily explicable. Are they irremediable? Surely not.

Men also have defects and wrinkles. They are strong, therefore rough; resolute, therefore cruel; slow of judgment and often stupid; prone to exact justice and vengeance, therefore apt to forget mercy and charity. We do not take it for granted that men cannot become gentle, and nimble-witted, and tender-hearted, because the opposite faults are well nigh natural to them. Still less do we cry out that they will lose some of the charms of their sex, and become effeminate, because they correct their defects or smooth out their wrinkles.

To recognise an error is already half way to remedy it; and if the parents, and educators of young girls, will look straight in the face the defects and wrinkles to which they are prone, and, instead of taking them as matters of course, will set about resolutely to remedy them, the victory is secured.

It ought to be a very evident truth that, while studies which women most need in order to correct their weak proclivities are commonly denied them, they are, on the other hand, overworked with wretched attempts to acquire a multitude of things rather calculated, than otherwise, to increase their defects. Real art, real music, real painting, real sculpture are magnificent gifts and graces, noble educations for both mind and heart; but the mock-music, mock-drawing, and mock-painting of young ladies to whom the simple groundwork—not to speak of the meaning and grandeur—of their art has never for an instant been revealed, can these be called elements of education? They are elements of nothing but pretentiousness and false taste. I have faith in a coming Arcadia, when our women will expand with a physical and mental beauty hitherto unknown; when they will acknowledge these defects and wrinkles as such, and correctable, and not mere little womanly *péchés mignons*, that cannot be cured. Meanwhile, it is the duty of all parents, teachers, and writers to set themselves resolutely to the work of that complete education which shall no longer consist merely in making what is good better, but also in changing what is bad and weak into what is good and strong; an education which shall give our girls their just social, moral, mental, and physical power by securing that genial play of natural spirits which is their great, and sometimes their almost mystical, prerogative; and also by fixing them upon solid ground of purity and principle which prevails with the best of our men. Our girls have the future of American society in their hands, and they need all that belongs to them to keep and to exalt their powers.

BOYNTON CARLISLE.

A GRASS-WIDOW.—SHE TELLS HER OWN STORY.

Dear Liz:—I have just read your letter. I larf, I do. I larf good. Oh, what a girl you are! Bound for glory through the medium of a yellow cover, are you? Well, sail in; I shall never overtake you, because I am not traveling in that direction.

Do you know, Liz (you invited my confidence), that I am the biggest fool outside of Bedlam? A motley fool, as Shakspere says; a durned, complicated fool, as Sut Lovengood expresses it; a piebald, pinto, Dolly Varden, and measly fool. Put all these adjectives in, and even then you will hardly get the true inwardness of my idiocy. And what do you think I've been, and gone, and done? But I won't tell you just yet. I want to give you some idea of my physical state, hoping it may palliate the absurdity of the rest of me. You know the physical is the foundation of the mental and moral, and if it gets into a shilly-shally, slip-shod, weak-kneed condition, the whole superstructure begins to wiggle and lean. I know I am not well. It don't agree with me to be shut up within four brick walls, where the sun never shines, and I have turned pale, and my hands and feet are always cold. Therefore, I have lost my attitude of proud(?) independence, and find myself in a leaning posture, ——— ——— ——— ——— ———. You can fill in the space with the simile of the vine yourself. And so—I wonder if I had better confess my weakness, or squnch up this piece of paper, and throw it in the waste-basket. No, I'll tell you, if it bursts my corset-lace. I might as well come to the point at once. I have fallen in love.

The cat is out of the bag at last, and a wretched looking specimen it is.

Now, if my "sweetness" would only make love to me after the fashion of the average male creature, I should be cured of my infatuation in a week. But here is a sort of double, back-action, ten-donkey power Rochester, and he can't treat me mean enough to do his feelings justice. And the result is, I find myself thinking about him night and day. What perverse animals we women are! A certain amount of kicking seems indispensable to our happiness.

What makes me madder than any thing else is the fact that this individual has literally nothing to recommend him to my interest but the fact that he has fenced himself in against me. Victor Hugo defines man as the animal that laughs; hand my name down to posterity for defining women as the divinity that climbs.

Climbing—that is it. I am climbing every moment of my life, either in imagination or reality; climbing the fence Mr. Taft has built about himself. I am like a mouse that prospects with untiring zeal the vulnerable spot in the trap for the morsel of cheese that seems so tempting. But, mind you, the mouse acts on her best judgment, while I have learned, from a previous experience, that after the first bewitching bait there is nothing but starvation.

For I tell you, Liz, that love don't last after marriage.

And, great heavens, who would want it to? It is the most tormenting of all infernal conditions that ever was hatched. It binds you neck and crop to one idea; you cannot get away. You are staked out with a short halter, and all you can do is to wind yourself up into tortured, complicated knots and snarls in never-ending variety.

There are but two happy moments in the whole experience. The first is when you cut loose from your senses and drop in. There is a dare-devil recklessness in this species of abandonment that challenges all heaven for competition. Then follows the double-distilled quintessence of purgatory (label it with a word of four letters and pass on) into which you are submerged; and presently this flood flows off, and you crawl forth to the light of day weak, helpless, feeling like a drowned rat, but *happy;* mind that, Liz, happy at last just to be out of torment.

AND AS LIKE AS NOT YOU'LL TAKE THE DIVE AGAIN IN LESS THAN A YEAR.

I tell you, my girl, I stand dumbfounded before this last sentence; I give myself up for a hopeless case. And it isn't me alone; it is you, it is every living soul all gone to the "demnition bow-wows" in one line of small caps. All hopelessly insane, and no keepers to take care of us.

Now, of all the "aggerawations" connected with this blarsted, humbugging life this is the darndest.

And this lover of mine; lover, indeed—ha! ha! If you could hear that laugh it would curdle your blood, it is so bitter and wicked. Well, then—Mr. Taft—he's a homely little villain, and as for sense he don't begin to be my equal. (*Mem.*—A man don't need sense if he will carry around a little private bulldog in his disposition with which to bark at the women out of his eyes.) I have never heard Mr. Taft make but one attempt at a laugh, and that was when he had said something particularly cutting to me; and oh, what a laugh! It went off like a bunch of damp fire-crackers. There may be other laughs where that came from, but surely it was the pioneer of its tribe, and broke its brambly way as an advance guard. He has no wit, and no appreciation of it in others, and you know, madam, that is my strong suit. But Mr. Taft—O, heavens! he's as dry as Mark Twain's last joke, and as depressing in his influence as the funny column in the newspapers.

He is a lawyer. I said he was homely, but that cannot be. There is dignity and character in his face, and reticence, and modest self-respect. Worth makes weight; and it seems as if he had absorbed some special privileges in specific gravity, and could hold down the beam against any other man. In appearance he is short and stocky—not fat, but full; and as he wears his clothes tight, and very fine and fashionable, he is a regular little brick. He stands square on his dew-claws, and has the finest walk of any man in the city. He clips it off down street like a small stern-wheel steamer. He "squabbles" all my admiration of handsome men by being so much handsomer than the handsomest of them without any beauty at all. He is on the shady side of forty, I think; but you know I was not a spring chicken myself, until I got released from my hated marriage and went back on my age. But there is something about Mr. Taft—a cool alabaster polish—that seems widely removed from the heat of youth. Let me see what it is. He seems automatic, as if the Lord had not made him; as if he had accreted his existence from some other source, to show the Lord what could be done without his assistance.

I was in his library one day, and then I could understand him better. There was all the dry, rubbishy books on law that ever were written. Volumes and volumes; Chitty and Blackstone, and Wawkeen Miller, and all the rest. And there were safes, and holes innumerable full of paper bundles, and these were cases he had had, I suppose. Now, my little man is a digest of all these books. He has fed on them; they are incorporated in every atom of his body. He is a man made out of the raw material of books, and informed, and vivified, and set in motion by their contents. The ten pounds or so of original man-material which he brought into the world has served as stock on which to graft a cutting of law; and the cutting has absorbed the original until there is nothing but law in the whole concern.

(*Mem.*—Can he love a woman, I wonder? Is it in the soul of the law to implant such a passion?)

Yes, Mr. Taft is a book-worm. 'Way back in the home nest, I remember, we brats found a book-worm one day, and dissected it under a microscope; and it was full of "chawred up paper," as we told mother afterward, who was in the habit of spanking us when our scientific investigations took a cruel turn.

It was an unfortunate thought, this of the book-worm, coming to me in his library as it did, for I was instantly filled with the idea that he, too, was filled with chewed up paper. Indeed, it seems likely, and if so I am sure the pieces were chewed up by rule and red lined on the edges; also, that they are packed in according to the most perfect method, all the space being fully occupied. His appearance bears me out in this. His form is so plump, and his skin so creamy fair. He is just as compact as he can be; and his actions, though rapid, prompt, and graceful, seem to be by rote. He has a set *répertoire* of movements, and when he gets through them he is wound up and goes through them again.

I cannot tell you what intense curiosity I have about him. His simplest acts are full of interest for me. If I hear his name but mentioned, I can feel my ears prick up and set forward instantly. No matter how dead I may be in every other direction, I am all alive Taftward.

MURDERATION, Liz! Think of a woman of my bitter experience coiling up all her logic against marriage and going over to the demented majority! I wonder if I am fool enough to marry him. There is another question of graver import, poking its head high above this one, and goggling at me with the round, unmeaning eyes of Minerva's bird; and that question is, *whether he is fool enough to marry me!*

There is a sign on the hall-door of his rooms, high up, "C. L. TAFT." And you don't know what fascination the name has for me. All the letters are square-built and stocky, like the man himself; and they are plump, as if stuffed with cut paper. There is another sign, farther down the hall, with the letters carved bodily out of the solid board; and a window in the background, the light of which shines through the open spaces. I have my own opinion of the person represented by this name. I do not know him, but I am sure he is too spiritual to succeed in this wooden world, and had better be transplanted to his heavenly home. I shiver as I look at the intangible representation, and turn to my comfortable, earthly letters, so suggestive of life and warmth. Now, imagine me secretly looking up at this door, like Hope gazing upon the overhanging cross in the chromo we see everywhere; or maybe it is Faith, or Patience, or Charity, or some other female representative of some special virtue. I have no memory for anything now—I am daft outside of Taft. Well, I gaze on these magical letters. They are all Greek to me except the last word. I wonder what the C stands for. I run through the whole range of names—Charles, Clarence, Clement, Conrad, Carl, Claude, and all the rest down to Caleb. I always stick on Caleb, with a wretched conviction. I hate the name—it is simply awful; and I feel it is part of the infamous luck tracking me through life that this man's name should be Caleb. If ever you have a doubt of anything, Liz, no matter how wide a range it may take, from despair upward, be sure and hitch on to the lowest round; then, if you find yourself mistaken, it will be because there were invisible rounds below the range of your utmost dread, and all you will have to do will be to unhitch and descend. So I feel sure, if this man's name is not Caleb, it is something worse. Then I go to the L, but I can make nothing of it. It is as inscrutable as the Sphinx. It has not even the semblance of a countenance to give it expression. Just two little sticks and a small triangle. Are these symbols, and have they some cabalistic meaning?

Come to think about it, this is the first time I have written you since I came here to live. I am copyist in the office of Lehang & Morgan; and Mr. Taft's rooms are just across the hall from ours. Both my employers are kind to me, and Mr. Morgan would be in love with me if I would let him. But who wants what they can have. Give me the pleasures of the chase—give me something to overcome. I want to break down barriers. I want to climb into somebody's pen; (I just "clim" out of one, but don't mention it.) I am like a breachy ox—it makes no difference which side of the fence I am on, I must jump it.

Lawyers are a new revelation to me. From the nature of their profession, they are secretive. They question, and cross-question, and hunt for motives, and trust no one. At least, this is true of Mr. Taft. He can no more comprehend my frankness than he can fly. I am a perfect enigma to him. He continually probes the undertow of my character for what does not exist. He smells dead men's bones, and means to drag them to the light of day. Our conversations are made up of questions on his part, and answers, dodges, evasions, and all sorts of whimsical lies on mine. He is unconscious that the strongest point in his social life is an interrogation point.

The knowledge he has of men and women has been gathered from law-suits. He fights shy of the "softer" sex, and only knows them in the witness-box. He keeps a kind of secret, detective watch over me, and does not suspect that I know every move in his game better than he does. Little he dreams that the concealments of the wise are open proclamations to the foolish. If I look at the clock, and afterward put on my hat, he is sure I have an appointment with some one, and would bet on its being a man. I can read all this, and much more; he is as open to me as I am shut to him. I am glad to be an object of interest to him on any terms, and find no fault with the situation.

I have written enough to show you that he has no appreciation of me. What is there to appreciate? Something, perhaps; I hardly know what. But I tell you, Liz, the cussedness so apparent on the surface of my kind of women is only an effervesence, that purifies the current below. Keep my tongue still, and, if I should escape explosion, I might pass for a reasonably good woman. However, it matters little what people think so that one really is the best she knows. And, as for me, I have love and pity; I hate selfishness and hypocrisy, and would like the privilege of speaking the truth. The necessity of concealment from the strictures of social enactment makes me mad. What person, or number of persons, have the right to extort a lie from an honest soul? I want to live out the best there is in me, and the world won't let me do it.

And Mr. Taft's treatment of me shows that he is ignorant of the existence of such feelings; and he regards their careless and whimsical outcropping through my talk as a covering to something I wish to conceal. This phase of our doings pains me, and puts it in my head that I am possibly barking up the wrong tree for a man.

I don't know where this thing will land me. Shouldn't wonder if there were breakers ahead. I'll write again soon.

As ever, your friend,

CATHERINE ELLIS.

[At the time I received this letter, I had not seen Kate Ellis for several years. I had written to her on hearing of her being in San Francisco, and the foregoing is the reply. We had been girls together, and I could not forget the charm of her society. She was so strong, so loving, so pitying, so hopeful, so original, and so unconventional. The irrepressible quality of her spirits, her frank jollity and her laugh, which was music and sunshine, with a touch of pathos, would ring through my memory as often as I thought of her. Her married life had been wretched, and she had lost her only child. This quite crushed her for a time; but the years had brought healing, and Kate was herself again. It was only a short time until I received her second letter.]

Dear Lizzie:—How good you are to write me so soon, and how you *do* write. If I know anything about it, you will make your mark in literature yet. Now, Liz, aren't you ashamed to talk of obstacles? What is an obstacle but something to climb over? One goes to sleep on a smooth road. So much for that nonsense. And what did you say about failures? Don't you know that a failure is just a door shut in your face; some other person's door at that. When you reach your own door, it will open to you. And you are borrowing trouble about these things. Read Emerson; come up into the over-life, and discard both hope and fear.

So much for hard sense. And now, Presto, change!—and enter Mr. Taft with his train of vanities, and, prominent in that train, myself. I have been getting paler every day since I came here, and yesterday I invested the whole amount of ten cents in rooge—how do you spell it?—r-u-ge?—r-u-s-h-e?—r-o-g-u-e? Well, take your choice of these spells, and if you don't get the right one it is your bad spelling, not mine. Now, this roo—*truck* just sets me up and makes my looking-glass a greater attraction than ever.

OH, I HAVE A THOUGHT! Quicksilver is a little world by itself, and revolves on its own axis. Quicksilver made into mirrors demands more quicksilver made into vermilion; and vermilion demands more mirrors. Here is perpetual motion at last, turning on the pivot of woman's vanity, and promising to endure forever.

But, to go back before this last world was discovered, if I am half as handsome as I think I am, I don't see how Mr. Taft can resist me. Now, listen to this description: My hair is a lovely auburn. I assisted it in its transmogrification from its original mud color by a little preparation known to the Initiated. It is cut off in front, and tortured into crinkles that fall low on my "alabaster brow." My lovely eyes, so soft and yet so bright, so liquid in their light, like stars that gem the night, look out from beneath this frizzled mass like the innocent peepers of a poodle dog. My features, though somewhat irregular, harmonize as a whole, and the result stands before you—a perfect creation, an unexceptionable piece of loveliness, a cameo struck whole from the great divine source of Beauty. So much for *me*.

Now, if people cannot see how beautiful I am it is their loss, not mine. "Beauty is in the eye of the beholder;" and if the beholder is blind, does that mar the fact? Therefore, I warn you against that little touch of sarcasm in the laugh with which you greet this description, madam, lest you fix upon yourself the imputation—*devoid of taste*.

I stopped this letter here yesterday, for an accident happened to my darling. No—a darling, though not mine. He slipped on the steps and sprained his ankle. It is an awful sprain, almost a fracture. I heard his quick step past my door; then I heard him fall and ran to him. He was holding on to the banisters, trying to get up stairs when I saw him. I made a swoop downward, like a hawk on a June-bug, and "lit" close by him. He smiled when he saw me, and as I caught him about the waist he laid his arm over my shoulder and yielded to my assistance. But it was no use; he could not bear any weight on the injured limb, and I had to call help and have him carried up to his room. His pain was intolerable. In spite of his evident self-control, the groans trembled through his white lips. My heart was torn at the sight. I sent for a doctor, and then I took off his shoe and stocking, and pressed and chafed his delicate white foot and ankle—how lovingly and tenderly, he may never know. But it did him good; his face relaxed, and his breath came easier.

Say, Liz, I don't believe he wears more than No. 4 shoes. I wear No. 5 myself, though I never owned it before. The two things I have lied about with unswerving persistence and mulish perversity are my age and the size of my feet, and I don't believe it is in the power of the gospel to save me on these points. There is no doubt but the first thing I shall do when I enter the next world will be to order a pair of shoes too small for me, and exchange them with the under-clerk surreptitiously. Now, I always hated small feet in men, until I saw and handled this beautiful little foot of Mr. Taft's; and then my ideas underwent a change. And why not, even on rational principles, leaving my love-lorn condition out of the question. Beauty is beauty wherever you find it. So I wipe out another prejudice, and am all the more free for it.

Since I wrote you before I think I have made some progress in the pursuit of Mr. Taft's heart. I don't know, but I think he is more familiar with me, though familiar is too strong a word.

A few days ago I was in his room, and he began asking me questions as usual, and they took a personal turn. He asked how long I had been in the city?—where I came from?—was I Mrs. or Miss Ellis?

"And so you have been married?" he said.

"Yes."

"And have had children."

"Yes."

"Are they living?"

"No."

"How many had you?"

"Six."

"Six? Is it possible?"

And indeed, Liz, I suppose it *was* possible; but you ought to have seen his look of astonishment. I was transfixed by it. But I never was with him ten minutes that he did not put me in the witness-box.

"How long were you married?" was his next question.

"Five years."

"Five years and six children? Explain."

Oh, but I had to think fast. "Twins and triplets," I said.

"Two births."

"Yes."

"That only accounts for five."

"I said five."

"You said five years and six children."

"You are wrong; I said six years and five children."

"Let it go at that, then. Was your marriage one of love?"

"No."

"Did you marry for money?"

"No."

"For a home?"

"No."

"Will you mention the consideration that induced you to take so momentous a step?"

"I wanted to see how I would look in orange flowers and a bridal veil."

"Couldn't you have hired a costume and found out?"

"But I wanted the sensation."

"And so you were married six years?"

"Five years."

"Are you positive?"

"I should think I ought to know. I was there."

"And how many children did you have?"

"Six."

"Are you positive?"

"I counted them every night when they came home."

"And you always made out six?"

"Always."

"Suppose the number fell short, what did you do?"

"Borrowed one of a neighbor."

"Do you know what I think of those children?"

"No."

"I think they were all borrowed, Mrs. Ellis."

And then he took up his pen and began to write one of those interminable briefs. Why briefs, in the name of Moses? This was a hint for me to leave, and, as a natural consequence, I didn't want to. I was standing all this time, and he was sitting at his desk. He wrote pages, and still I stood there. Presently he looked up, and said:

"How long did you live with your husband, Mrs. Ellis?"

"Fifteen years."

"Ah! and how many children had you?"

"One."

"You have been awfully bereaved since I heard from you last."

"Bereaved indeed, Mr. Taft. Six children could have filled my heart no more perfectly than did my one little daughter that died so young."

I felt my voice tremble, and he glanced away a moment, only to turn his calm eyes upon me again. He had seen tears in the witness-box a thousand times. He knew their analysis—salt, sodium, and water.

"And so you were married fifteen years; and where is your husband?"

"I am a widow."

"Is your husband dead?"

"Yes; and glad of it."

"You or your husband?"

"I, of course. I haven't heard from him since."

"Did he treat you badly?"

"Horribly."

"And you?"

"I kept even. I squared accounts with him every day."

"Did you sue him for a divorce?"

"No, he sued me."

"On what complaint?"

"That I failed to provide for him."

"And he got a divorce on that ground?"

"He might have done it if he had not died."

"And where is he now?"

"In Arizona working a gold mine."

"What did your divorce cost you?"

"Nothing as yet; I am to pay the bill when I marry again."

"What bill."

"For the tombstone."

"Is it a large one?"

"Yes, very. I wanted it large, for fear he might claw out and come back again."

"I don't refer to the tombstone; I refer to the bill."

"Oh, yes, the bill for the tombstone was very large."

"Drop the tombstone, and tell me about the bill for the divorce. *I* am more interested in that."

"Ah! That was a different bill altogether. His name is Bill Wilson. He is the man my husband was jealous of."

"That was before he died."

"No, afterwards."

"Mrs. Ellis, you can be excused."

"My name is not Mrs. Ellis; at least, not that I know. Don't a divorced woman take her own name again?"

"As a rule, madam, she takes some other person's—Bill Wilson's, for instance."

Then, Liz, he rose to his feet, and bowed, to signify that the interview was ended; whereupon I walked round the desk, and sat down by him, just as he was reseating himself. And now, mark my words, I saw an unmistakable flash of pleasure in his face, but he stifled it instantly, and turned toward me, cold and impassive.

In the meantime, I was making myself quite comfortable. I put my feet on the rungs of his chair, adjusted my overskirt, and smiled on him *bewitchingly*. Don't dock that word of one particle of its strength. I mean it. I was in my most dare-devil mood, and did not care where it led.

Truly, the allurements of the chase are wonderful. Heigh, ho, tantivy! Put in the yelping of the dogs, the tooting of the horns, the reckless speed of the sportsman, and the poor little hare almost run down, and you have the situation.

Oh, men! men! if you knew as much about women as I do, your power would be unlimited. This is an apostrophe—not intended for the ear of any male biped that lives. Could I be so base as to give away my own sex by showing our enemies that their power lies in their indifference to us?

I am afraid of making my letter too long by recounting any further conversation with Mr. Taft. It lasted an hour; it was sensible and sincere on both sides. As I got up to leave the room, he raised with me, giving me his hand, and so we walked, still holding hands, to the door, where he bowed me out, with the rarest smile that ever illuminated a face.

I wish I could go and take care of him as he lies in the next room suffering, but I dare not do it.

[And so ended the second letter, which aroused my curiosity not a little, and caused me to look forward for another. But it was two months before I heard from Kate again. Then she wrote:]

Dear Lizzie:—If you are waiting for the conclusion of my romance to make a magazine article out of, just write—The heroine, after hanging suspended by the slender thread of hope for eight mortal weeks, fell into the dismal abyss below, from which she finally crawled out bruised, sore, and miserable, but game still; and has now resumed business at the old stand of Lehang & Morgan.

That is enough. That is all there is of it.

When I met Mr. Taft after his accident he spoke to me with much restraint; and at each subsequent meeting his manner was cooler and cooler, until the sight of him sent my heart below zero, and chilled the very marrow of my bones. He has learned to hate me, Lizzie. No doubt my preference for him, so boldly manifested, disgusted and alarmed him. There is a paragraph going the rounds of the papers about some woman who chloroformed and married a man in spite of himself. I'll bet she was a grass-widow; and I'll also bet that if Mr. Taft has read it he has the same conviction.

O miserere! my jokes on this subject turn on dry hinges, and creak dolefully. I suppose he has seen too much of the ugly side of married life from his numerous divorce cases to take the risk of marrying; or, perhaps, he cherishes ideas of marriage with some beautiful young girl, and resents the encroachments of a poor faded thing like me.

At all events, it is over, and I am free again. I don't mean that my heart is free, for I love him better than ever, but I mean the danger of marrying is past, and I think I ought to be glad of it. I have done something, however, that had better been left undone. I have written him a note. I am forced to meet him in the hall, and on the stairs, several times a day; and at last these meetings actually frightened me, his face was so stern and cold, his manner so repellant, his hatred and disgust were so visible. I could not bear to remain in the house. So I hunted another place, but without success. At last, utterly discouraged, I wrote him something like this:

"*Mr. Taft:*—You treat every one with politeness but me. I don't know the cause of your evident dislike, but think you are afraid to treat me kindly lest I should prove troublesome to you. Whether this assumption on your part is correct or not, I resent it all the same. And since it costs you such an evident effort to speak to me, I will excuse you from speaking any more.

"C. Ellis."

I left this in his room one evening, and went home with a heart as heavy as lead. Going up Clay Street hill on the cars, the moon shone high above the domes and spires of the city so beautiful, so serene. I don't believe she cares whether school keeps or not; she takes no interest in stocks; the banks can break as they please, it don't disturb her. In this respect she and I are Siameses, but we differ in other particulars. For instance, she is satisfied with the lonely royalty of her position, which I am not. She has no thought for any other moon of the male persuasion, in which she also differs from me.

BUT, AFTER ALL, IT IS BECAUSE THERE IS NO OTHER MOON ON HER BEAT.

Now I think of it, I am positive that, if there was another, and if she is of the female sex, as represented (alas! on no better grounds than her changeableness), no amount of centripetality, centrifugality, polarity, and the rest of it could keep her in her orbit twenty-four hours.

Bah! She's a humbug, "Chaste!" "Vestal!" She's an old maid from circumstance, and not from choice.

I went to my own room, where I battled with myself all night; but it was no use. In the morning I was as blue as the picked shank of an old turkey-hen, with a face as long as three rainy days.

By the way, Liz, he who laughs gives, and the world is richer for it. The next morning, as I meandered down street to my office in this most wretched mood, I passed a little rusty looking man in the door of a poor habitation, singing a bewilderingly joyous carol, just like a bird. A neighboor looked out of another door and said:

"Hello, Jack! You're happy this morning, ain't you?"

Then Jack laughed—such a laugh; as happy and natural as a child. He didn't seem to need anything to laugh at, but just laughed because he was "laffy;" and I laughed too. The clouds vanished from my sky, the stiffening came into my back, and I went sailing down to Sansome Street as breezy as a nautilus. Therefore I say, he that laughs gives, and the world is better for it.

But presently the prison-house of four bare walls closed around me, and the Taft influence pervaded everything again. I long for sunshine and music more than I ever did in my life. I think they would cure me, bodily and mentally.

I am too far gone in this folly even to hold myself up to your ridicule. Poking fun at the "Widder" Ellis is dull work. I am getting sorry for the poor thing. Do you remember the old fairy story, in which the king lost his wife, and in the violence of his grief beat his head against the wall five days? I never could imagine what good it did him under the circumstances; but I would have faith in the remedy if applied to myself.

You don't know how much I regret having written that note. Mr. Taft takes me at my word, and speaks to me no more. And yet there is something in his manner, or the atmosphere about him, that makes me think he has me on his mind.

When I wrote that note, it was in a desperate attempt to end my love and suspense. I thought if he ceased to speak to me I should soon become indifferent. But it is not so. He enslaves my thoughts to a greater extent than before—for now I am sick, *sick* for even the cold greetings I used to get. As I look back from the iceberg on which I am wrecked, I seem to see in all our previous intercourse the flowers and sunshine of the tropics. I have ruined even the small hope I had. I have no alternative but to grin and bear it. I am glad I had not the power to hurt him as I hurt myself.

I would not tell you all this, dear Liz, but that I must tell some one. Oh, if my baby had only lived, as an outlet to her foolish mother's heart, I should have escaped this. And yet yet what *she* has escaped by dying!......

How different the effect of the sights on the streets now and three months ago! I was out at the park one day when I was happy and hopeful, and I shall never forget my feelings. Under the influence of the pure, vital air, the trees and flowers, the fountain, with its arching rainbow, together with the sight of temple, dome, and minaret, and the music that spiritualized it all, I went into a strange mood. "I saw men as angels walking." Every living soul was idealized, each after his or her own type. All had come up out of their baser lives into a semblance of that which was angelic within them. Even the hard, ugly clothes of men and women lost angularity, and flowed in graceful outline, and blended in harmonious color. But nothing can describe the children. They were angels—angels swinging, angels floating on the lake, angels in goat-carriages, angels in the gymnasium, angels swarming everywhere. If ever I go to Heaven, I shall see no sight more truly angelic.

I doubt if the man who said, "Beauty is in the eye of the beholder," knew half the meaning of what he said. Beauty is forever unfolding out of the commonest things to him whose soul unfolds to meet it. And LOVE is the unfolding power.

I learned enough in that day to know that perfect love, reciprocal between God and man, can renovate this world in an hour.

And, for the first time in my life, I raised to the conception of how the beautiful, golden-haired Nazarine, child of the sun as he was, for the love of a fallen race renounced the shining halls of his native Heaven, to walk with bleeding feet the hills of Judea, with none for his companions but fishermen and harlots.

So I sat for hours looking upon the scene, the passing crowd, the angelic children, all from some exquisite retirement of soul, with one thought undulating upward like a prayer: Most sweet and pitiful!—most sweet and pitiful!—behold these ruins and restore.

[After this letter, which I have left unfinished to avoid one of Kate's sudden transitions from the sublime to the ridiculous, it was weeks before she wrote again. But the letter, when it came, was Kate all over; and I submit it, as I have all of them, without change. I hold that our style of writing has grown so fossilised through the formality of set phrases that it is becoming impossible to express much diversity of character through it. And I both hope and believe that the literature of the Far West, by the unfolding of native talent, will break up the rules of long established usage, and inaugurate a style so elastic as to meet the demand of even the most extravagant originality, and that, too, without degenerating into coarseness.]

Dear Lizzie:—It has been a long time since I wrote you, and a sorry time, too, though that is forgotten now. Why, it was only yesterday I thought I could never write another line to any one.

What are we to think of a sentiment that enslaves us like love? I believe it is a disease, and expect to see it handled as such by practicing physicians before long. The way science is advancing, it will hardly be a hundred years until we shall see flaming placards announcing to the love-lorn the curative properties of "The World Renowned Anti-magnetic Obfusticator," or "The Chain Lightning Exterminator," warranted to abolish the necessity of suicide by restoring to a healthy condition the victims of this awful malady.

In this emergency, however, while the world waits its development, we must use such palliative remedies as we find at hand; and at the present time, THE ONLY ANTIDOTE FOR LOVE IS MARRIAGE. And I am going to be married to Claude Lorraine Taft. (Out upon Caleb! Didn't I tell you his name wasn't Caleb?)

I have been almost sick, and altogether maudlin and idiotic for two months, and getting weaker and paler from confinement and much writing, until I can hardly climb the stairs. Yesterday, just as I reached the top of the second flight I turned dizzy. I sprang forward to avoid falling back, and as I did so a door opened, and a quick step approached. I can't tell how I knew it was Mr. Taft, for my senses were leaving me, but I did know it in a kind of dream-like way, and I knew he caught me as I fell. My next recollection, in a state of semi-unconsciousness, was of being on the lounge in his room, and feeling his arms around me. My senses were wrapped in a heavenly languor, from which the slightest effort would arouse them. Every moment I became more and more alive to the tender names he was calling me; and presently, when his lips pressed mine with a touch of velvet, I felt the dimples twitching in my cheeks, and knew I could hoax him no longer. I opened my eyes laughing, to see such anxiety, such love as I never saw before. I raised my arms, they were like lead, but I got them round his neck, and drew his head down to mine, and as the strength returned I smoothed his hair, and petted him up like everything. By the way, his hair is *mighty* thin on top, and he hates it, too—a fact that at once disproves my chewed paper theory.

Don't imagine that he exhibited any weakness or discomfiture. He was master of the situation, and faced it like a—lawyer. He said he had a plea to make against me, and asked if I was ready to defend myself. Then he waited a moment, and as I did not answer, he told me that as I was too timid to speak in my own defense, he would speak for me. (Think of my being too timid, Liz. However, I was glad he thought so.) He said that when there was no one employed to defend the plaintiff the Court appointed some one. And as he was the Court and the whole caboodle (only he didn't use that word) rolled into one, he would not only stand for the prosecution, but would appoint himself on my defense, too. Then he made love to me in the queerest way, using any amount of law terms. And I tell you, no matter what *any* body says about the law being dry and musty—it is just *delightful*, "and make a note on it" for private reference.

But, Liz, the trial was not conducted as fairly as one would expect from a man of his irreproachable standing; and there is no doubt some foundation for the accepted theory, that the practice of law demoralizes men to a certain extent. Only enough, perhaps, to make them perfectly angelic in some cases. For though guilty of nothing but folly, the verdict went dead against me, and I was sentenced to life-long imprisonment in the arms of complainant, and remanded to prison immediately.

Now this is all. And if you want to make a magazine article out of it just change the names and go ahead.

One word in explanation, however. Mr. Taft had firmly resolved never to marry. He had seen too much of the ugly side of married life to risk it. And in the interval he was separated from me by his hurt he gathered moral force to renew the resistance he had begun and abandoned on our first acquaintance.

The wedding will take place in a few weeks. I will notify you when the day is appointed, and shall hope to see you at that time.

As ever, your loving friend,

CATHERINE ELLIS.

[This ended my correspondence with Catherine Ellis, for the next letter that I received was signed with a different name.]

HELEN WILMANS.

RUSSIAN RELIGION AND RUSSIAN GOVERNMENT.

During the summer of 1877, when I accompanied the Russian Army of the Caucasus as a correspondent from Armenia, I had an opportunity to become familiar with the religious sects which have been sent in exile to the Caucasus. To give an account of those sects is quite beyond the powers of anybody who is not master of the Russian tongue. Even to one possessing this qualification, it is no easy matter to make a complete study of the doctrines of those sects, for the reticence of their members is so great as to have kept even the Russian Government in ignorance of much that it would gladly know. Certain facts have, nevertheless, been definitely ascertained, and others which are current seem sufficiently supported by the joint testimony of several witnesses to merit a reproduction in print. It is thus possible to ascertain the bearing of the sects toward the Established Church, from which they have revolted, although for a minute study of their dogmas, their church service, and all the details of their spiritual government, the materials are insufficient. It will, nevertheless, be seen that there is, perhaps, nothing in the Caucasus, apart from the treatment of the conquered tribes, which throws so much light on the policy and tendencies of the Russian Government as the religious sects which have been sent thither in exile.

These sects are three in number, and are called the Molokans, the Doukobortsi, and the Scoptsi. Far above the other two stand the Molokans. Their creed is principally distinguished by a rigid adherence to the moral teachings of the Bible, and a rejection of all the ceremonials and the idolatry of the Russian Church. In the home of an Orthodox Russian, Byzantine pictures of saints stare at one from every corner; with the Molokans they are never to be seen. The Molokans also dispense with priests, and the simplicity of their service is almost Puritanic. They are notorious for the sobriety of their lives and the uniform honesty of their dealings. I can testify, from my own visits to their villages, that I have never seen greater cleanliness and neatness of dress among any peasant population. In comfort and in cheerfulness, their homes give evidence of an order of living wholly unknown to Russian peasants. To step from the barbarism of Armenia into one of their villages is like getting back again to civilization; and even Tiflis, with all its attempts to be thought European, can offer nothing comparable to the delightful freshness of a Molokan village. The people constantly impress one as men who have learned to hold religion and conduct in mutual counterpoise, so that their daily lives are, in large measure, a realization of all that their religion urges them to follow.

The Doukobortsi resemble the Molokans in setting aside the ceremonies and priestcraft of the Orthodox Church, while they attach great importance to the moral teachings of the Evangelists. They reject the doctrines of the Trinity and of the divinity of Christ, and they forbid oath-taking and military service. Civil marriage is common, if not universal, among them, and many communal institutions exist, which it would be interesting to describe if I had been able to gather information enough to render the description trustworthy. The head of the sect is a woman, but the precise authority she exercises seems a matter of doubt.

The Scoptsi, or self-mutilators, found their religion on the necessity of avoiding the lusts of the flesh, and pretend to have discovered in their interpretation of a Biblical text,* divine authority for the means they take to secure this end. Emasculation is the indispensable condition upon which their creed must be accepted. With those who have suffered thus early in youth the features take a cast which at once distinguishes them from all others—a skin like parchment, colorless, without a beard, and without eyebrows. The voice, too, has the shrill pitch of the eunuch's. When a new member is admitted to the sect he has a choice between the "great seal" and the "small seal." The first is said to involve the complete act of mutilation, the second the simple act of deprivation. Few men who have arrived at maturity survive the first operation, but in case of death they are at once elevated to the rank of saints. No sect in Russia is so rich as this. The interest of its members seems to have concentrated itself in an almost miserly love of money-making, which, however, is always directed to the ends of their religion. Thousands of roubles are known to have been paid to a single man for his adoption of the faith. The Scoptsi are also by far the best organized sect in Russia. At times the members have been so unexpectedly shielded from the penalty of the law that it was suspected by the Russian Government that their organization resembled that of the Free Masons. With these, however, they have nothing in common. The sect is governed by twelve apostles. Who they are, and where they reside, is a mystery known only to the highest members of the sect. When one of them addresses a gathering, his identity remains concealed from all but the select few. Some years ago it is related that an officer of the Russian army undertook to ferret out, on behalf of the Government, the secrets of this sect. For two years he acted as a peddler in that part of the Caucasus where its members are most numerous, and sought, by selling wares in their villages, to attain to a degree of intimacy which would disclose to him the veiled points in their religion. But, inasmuch as he was unwilling to join the sect as a regular member, all his efforts proved vain. Returning to Russia, he continued his investigations there for some time with no better result. But as he was once passing the night in a small inn, he heard two men in the room next to him talking of a forthcoming meeting of the Twelve Apostles, which was to be held on a certain day in Siberia. The officer started in all haste for the town designated. He discovered where the conference was to be held, and made arrangements with the military for the seizure of all its members. But by this time the Apostles had got wind of his plans, and when the capture ought to have taken place all but one were found to have disappeared. Il-

* See Matthew xix. 12.

ness had prevented the flight of the single one that remained. He was seized and cross-examined. He admitted at once that he was an Apostle of the sect, but all threats of exile and of physical torture, in case he should refuse to disclose the names and residence of the others, only elicited the reply that he was bound to secrecy by the holiest of oaths, which death itself could not make him renounce. A curious seal ring was found on his finger, and when asked whether it was the mark of an Apostle he admitted that it was. But at the same time he assured his captors that it would be vain for them to use it as a clue to the eleven, since, now that he had been seized, five hundred of his sect would wear the same ring on the morrow. The whole inquiry ended in nothing new being discovered, and the Apostle was exiled to the Caucasus. Thither, in the neighborhood of Poti, all the discovered members of this sect are sent. So numerous is this colony of exiles that those of military age alone form an entire battalion in the army. For obvious reasons they are thus kept separate from the rest of the troops, for, in spite of the hideousness of their religion, their abundance of money often makes easy converts among the needy and uneducated.

Though condemned for propagandism to exile in the Caucasus, it is not to any peculiarities of that region that Molokans, Doukobortsi, and Scoptsi owe their origin. The members of these sects exist all over Russia. Nor are they alone in their heresies. Various sects, like the Jumpers, make their religion an excuse for the wildest erotic excesses. Others combine dances with their religious worship. After prayer, a sort of orgy begins with shouts and dancing, and is prolonged until the worshipers faint away, or fall down foaming at the mouth. At such moments, they are supposed to have visions and direct communication with the Deity. Siberia, which, like the Caucasus, has been chosen as a home for religious exiles, includes, among other heretics, the sect of the Self-burners, who, on having a vision, shut themselves up in a house, and burn up themselves and their families. Lately, several hundred people are said to have destroyed themselves in this way on a single day.

It would be interesting to trace the upgrowth of these various sects, to learn under what circumstances they had their origin, and by what line of persuasion their founders made converts. But for such an inquiry the historical evidence is wanting. In the absence of documents relating to their past history we need not, however, be debarred from inquiring what circumstances contribute to make their further development a possibility to-day. For they are a living element of Russian life. They make converts, and are punished by the Government. The Church and the police are solicitous about them. We may seek, therefore, not unprofitably, to determine what elements of Russian society are to be held accountable for their progress.

The cardinal fact common to all the sects is their utter renunciation of allegiance to the Established Church. Let the Russian religion, therefore, be our first object of comment. The Russian State religion is Christianity reduced to fetich worship. It is a pyramid of ceremonials, gaudy with much tinsel, but resting on no moral foundation. To live life nobly is no part of its teachings. It concerns itself with death, and its priests insist that its ceremonies are to be observed for the sake of God's favor in bestowing the ultimate reward of the kingdom of heaven. The sole ground for doing right, or for abstaining from evil, is made the hope of heaven, or the fear of hell; and the chief duties of the good churchman are to propitiate saints, to bow and cross himself devoutly before their images, which confront him in every room of every house, to observe the appointed fasts, to be duly shriven, to receive communion, and to pay his priest the fees he exacts for false certificates that all these duties have been performed. In short, by its appeals to purely selfish instincts in man—his desire to be protected from harm while alive on earth, and to be blessed with immortal happiness thereafter—the Russian religion makes itself preëminently the creed of a people among whom civilization has made little growth. Far different from this is the version of Russian orthodoxy which is found in the rhapsodies of Pan-Slavonian dreamers. But the fact stands unaltered, that its inculcation of the essentially Christian privileges and responsibilities dwindles into nothing by the side of the tremendous importance attached to the talismanic virtue of mere ceremonial. The Russian of the highest society bears the mark of this teaching not less plainly than the lowest peasant. The one, when a sudden thunder-clap rolls overhead, uncovers and crosses himself quickly to keep off the devil. The other, whom education has taught that the formal observances of his Orthodox Church are more Asiatic than European, professes to have discarded them altogether; but let the occasion arise, and he will prove that, with his religion thrown overboard, he has yet held fast to superstitions which would do no discredit to an age of necromancers and witchcraft. He agrees, too, with the peasant in the contempt with which they both treat priests. It is a sorry comment on the influence of the Russian Church, that its priests should be tabooed by good society for the unpardonable crime of not being *hommes civilisés*, and at the same time be used by peasants as the constant butt of homely and proverbial satire. But, best of all, in illustration of the thoroughly external relation of Russian religion to Russian life, is the readiness not only to accept, but also to give up again, successive European theories of morality and of unbelief, which has been for more than a century a prominent national trait. This shows more clearly than anything else, not only that the Russian Church has failed to make good its own claims to permanent acceptance, but also that it has been no result of its teaching to awaken in its followers any lively sense of the function of religion as a power over conduct, rather than as a mere formula of thought which may be set aside whenever a fresh one comes into fashion.

These characteristics of the Russian religion cannot, however, alone be held responsible for the number and the peculiarities of Russian sects. It would be unwarrantable to affirm that it is a tendency peculiar only to the Russian Church to separate religion from conduct, and degrade it to the level of a profitable investment, which not only involves no interference with the impulses of our daily lives, but also secures to us an ample return of happiness in the future. The creed which permits sins to be wiped out by confession and by the propitiation of saints, through church offerings and payments for masses, presents perfectly parallel features to those of the Russian Church. If numerous instances may be cited of Russian thieves going to church to pray for some saint's aid in an act of some contemplated robbery, offering in return a certain share of the plunder in the shape of tallow candles, it is yet equally true that similar incidents are not infrequent in Spain, Italy, and South Germany. It is accordingly not in the absence of a moral content to her religion, a feature shared in common with Russia by other countries, that we seek an explanation of that extraordinary upgrowth of sects which Russia possesses alone.

The two great facts in this matter of Russian sects are their peculiar character and their great number. What has led the Russian people to profess doctrines so nonsensical, and often so abominable? And why has the revolt against the Established Church, of which each sect furnishes only a different example, taken so many various forms, instead of concentrating itself in one grand movement, like the Reformation? The answer to these questions lies not only in the characteristics already ascribed to the Russian religion, but also in the peculiar circumstances under which that religion has grown up and exerted its influence. The Russian Church has never, like the Roman, been a repository of the best culture. The Russian despot early perceived the inconveniences to foreign States arising from temporal pretensions of the Holy See, and wisely determined that his own Church should never attain to such intellectual enlightenment as might prove dangerous to his sovereign will. To keep the clergy ignorant, as it is to-day, has always been the policy of Russian rulers. A further step toward the execution of this plan united the heads of Church and State in the single person of the Emperor, and thus effectually put religion under Government control. But if Russia was thus deprived of a Pope, it was nevertheless taken care that she should enjoy all the blessings of infallibility. To do no more thinking than the Government prescribes has always been in Russia an essential quality of the good subject; and so rigorously has the necessity of thus accepting opinion on authority been enforced, that it may be said to have become the characteristic feature of the national mind to be utterly incapable of independent thinking. It is to this worst form of ignorance, an incapacity of judgment, that I have little hesitation in attributing the success which the promoters of the more obnoxious of the Russian sects have had. All the sects, whether for better or for worse, agree in regarding religion as something more than a mere observance of ceremonials, which is to secure immunity from punishment and rewards of happiness in the future. Whether we turn to the disgusting doctrines of the Scoptsi, or to the admirable lives of the Molokans, we find in each case that the religion holds forth its rewards only in return for a certain order of living. It has, in short, joined to itself a morality and imposed on its followers a responsibility. This one feature of the sects has enabled them to claim the attention of all those whom the emptiness of the Orthodox creed no longer satisfied; and it is not surprising that the Russian, with his long training in ignorance, when called for the first time in his life to pronounce upon a religion with a moral content, often proves incompetent to discriminate between the morality that rests upon a rational basis and that which is but the offspring of a diseased fancy.

We may thus set down a long training in ignorance, and a consequent incapacity of judgment, as the principal reasons for the successful diffusion of absurd and disgusting doctrines among the Russian people. It remains, however, to pass beyond the character of the sects, and to explain why they have sprung up in such number and variety. That the multitude of sects have never been able to unite and form a common body of dissenters seems to me to result simply and inevitably from the fact that the Russian Church and the Russian Government are both under the single headship of the Czar.

To this assertion, that the head of the Government is also the head of the Church, the average Russian is never tired of replying that the only real head of the Church is Christ. This sounds well; but to those who would convince themselves of the truth of the matter, we recommend, once for all, the following pregnant passage, from Mr. Wallace's *Russia*, to be read and pondered. The author is discussing the relation of the Synod, the supreme ecclesiastical body, to the temporal power, and proceeds:

"The Synod is not a council of deputies from various sections of the Church, but a permanent college, or ecclesiastical senate, *the members of which are appointed and dismissed by the Emperor as he thinks fit.* It has no independent legislative authority, for *its legislative projects do not become law till they have received the imperial sanction;* and they are always published, not in the name of the Church, but in the name of the Supreme Power. Even in matters of simple administration, it is not independent, for *all its resolutions require the consent of the Procureur, a layman nominated by his Majesty.* In theory, this functionary protests only against those resolutions which are not in accordance with the civil law of the country; but as *he alone has the right to address the Emperor directly on ecclesiastical concerns*, and as *all communications between the Emperor and the Synod pass through his hands*, he possesses in reality considerable power. Besides this, he can always influence the individual members by holding out prospects of advancement and decorations; and if this device fails, *he can make the refractory members retire*, and fill up their places with men of more pliable dispositions. A council constituted in this way cannot, of course, display much independence of thought or action, especially in a country like Russia, where no one ventures to oppose openly the imperial will. * * * If a bishop sometimes complains to an intimate friend that he has been brought to St. Petersburg and made a member of the Synod, merely to append his signature to official papers and to give his consent to foregone conclusions, his displeasure is directed, not against the Emperor, but against the Procureur. He is full of loyalty to the Tsar, and has no desire to see his Majesty excluded from all influence in ecclesiastical affairs; but he feels saddened and humiliated when he finds that *the whole government of the Church is in the hands of a lay functionary, who may be a military man, and who certainly looks at all things from a layman's point of view.*"

The italics are mine. Few, I presume, except the sentimentally insane, can read this extract without disgust at the monstrous absurdity of pretending that Christ, and not the Czar, is the only real head of the Russian Church. A more perfect device for giving over the Church, bound hand and foot, to the imperial will, it would be difficult, indeed, to imagine. As a matter of fact, the complete and absolute union thus indicated of the temporal and the spiritual powers is one of Russia's most potent instruments, both in foreign conquest and in home administration; and has been, also, the chief means of fostering the upgrowth of the multitude of religious sects.

Therefore, while Russian ignorance, fostered by the Government and the Church, is to be held responsible for the unworthy character of many of these sects, we must turn, as I said before, to the power derived by the Church from its union with the State, for an explanation of their number and variety. In this result, however, it is not to be denied that ignorance, too, has had its share; for the Russians have never yet known clearly enough what they wanted to unite in any one movement for attaining it. The Roman Church had sowed the seeds of enlightenment so abundantly among men that, when at length it began to look upon knowledge with suspicion, the growth which its own hands had implanted could no longer be arrested. It was thus, in large measure, the result of its own acts that those who revolted from its authority were able both to guide their revolt by intelligence, and to find intelligent followers for its support. But no similar educating capacity on the part of their national church has ever prepared the Russians for union in one common movement of reformation, and the revolts from the Orthodox church have taken all the directions that ignorance could dictate.

Far more potent, however, than ignorance, in making a common movement of dissenters impossible, is the influence already indicated. United with the State, the Russian Church has always had the State's strength to back it. Jealousy of a rival creed could thus always be followed by an immediate exercise of this crushing power. The State, which, for the sake of controlling any dangerous pretensions of ecclesiastics, had united *one* church with itself, would naturally be led, by the same policy, to stop, by all means, the troublesome upgrowth of another; and the consciousness of having this force at its command would leave the Established Church always free, in the treatment of its rivals, to despise inquiry into the merits of their doctrines, and to put them out of existence on the mere ground of rivalry alone. As a matter of fact, the mutual action and reaction of these two tendencies of the Church and the State have combined to produce as perfect a system of intolerance as one could readily imagine. A few illustrations will suffice to show how the Government forces the people to be religious in the Orthodox fashion.

By the law of the land all children of Orthodox parents are bound to remain members of the Orthodox Church. No Orthodox parent has a right to bring up his children as members of a different communion. Violation of this renders the parent liable to criminal punishment and exile for propagandism to Siberia. If one of the parents is Orthodox and the other a member of another church, all the children must be Orthodox. If neither of the parents is Orthodox, while at the same time each is a believer in a different creed, it is not for them to say to which of the two faiths their children shall conform. Orthodox they must be by the State's command. In this respect the offspring of parents of different heterodox creeds are treated precisely as illegitimate children, who must all be Orthodox. Terrible as these infringements upon personal liberty may seem, they are supplemented in actual practice by subterfuges which make them even more monstrous. For fear of desertions from the Orthodox faith, it is specially enacted that the minister to whose church defection is made shall be held personally responsible. If he be found guilty, for example, of having allowed an Orthodox Russian to take part in his service, he receives a warning for the first offense; for a recurrence of it, he is temporarily suspended from his office; and if it be again repeated, he is deprived permanently of the right to preach. No such penalties, however, need be dreaded by the Orthodox pastor when a member of some heterodox communion strays into *his* fold. In accordance with the Russian elastic and reversible scheme of justice, the heterodox Russian who receives the sacrament from the hands of an Orthodox priest becomes thenceforth, willingly or unwillingly, Orthodox forever. The same result befalls him on whom the right of extreme unction is performed by Orthodox hands.

A shocking instance of this happened to a Russian within my own circle of acquaintance. The man, an officer in the Russian army, and of distinguished family, was stricken down with a fever while serving in Siberia. He finally became delirious, and the doctors pronounced the case hopeless. Nobody happened to know that he was a member of the Lutheran Church, and the priest sent for was Orthodox. That priest, in spite of the explicit injunctions of his Church, administered the sacrament to a man who was out of his mind, and then performed the right of extreme unction. A few hours afterward the crisis of the fever passed over, and the patient gave evident signs of recovery. The priest at once proclaimed to the neighborhood that, with God's help, he had wrought a miracle. Be that as it may, the officer steadily improved in health, and was strong enough after some weeks to start for St. Petersburg. Mark, now, what followed. In going one day into the Protestant church, of which he had long been a member, he was greeted by his pastor with the request that he would leave the church, and not bring with him the penalties which fell upon every heterodox preacher who ministered to the Orthodox. On demanding, in astonishment, an explanation, he was informed that the account of his miraculous cure had been sent to the Synod, which had warned his former Lutheran pastor that the man was thenceforth Orthodox. In vain he protested that he had always been a member of the Lutheran Church, that he had never voluntarily altered his faith, that the sacrament and extreme unction had been administered to him when he was unconscious. It made no difference—Orthodox he must be for the future; and a direct appeal to the Czar only elicited the reply that his Majesty could not interfere with general regulations of the Ecclesiastical Synod, which had already received his imperial sanction. With such power as this wielded by the Church, it ceases to be a wonder that the Russian heterodox sects have never united in a common movement. Far more wonderful is it that dissent has ever been able for one moment to assert itself.

This much of the doings of the Russian Church must suffice to show how intimately the study of the dissentient sects is connected with an understanding of the tendencies of the Government. For, though it is to the ignorance and the intolerance of the Church that the sects and their characteristics are directly to be attributed, it is nevertheless the Government which, by its policy, has kept the Church ignorant, and the Government which, by its force, has given that ignorant Church power to carry out its will. No better than the rest, the Russian Church takes its place with all the other tools by which the Russian despot's work is done. A religion without morality, a press without liberty, generals without generalship, and officials without responsibility to the people whose affairs they manage, make up a sum of evils great enough to set a whole nation clamoring for justice. But people do not clamor in Russia. They know too well the bourne from which no clamorer returns. Nineteen years ago the Emperor emancipated the *bodies* of some millions of his subjects; but he forgot the equally important duty of emancipating their *minds;* and so the poor beings still continue to be thought for, not thinking—subjects, not citizens. Compared with the decrepitude of Turkey, we are bound in justice to concede to Russia that superiority which belongs to a nation that contains, and has already given good evidence of, capacity for progress. But, measured with Western Europe, Russia cannot escape being put in the category of semi-civilized States.

ALFRED A. WHEELER.

SHE KNOWS.

Who is it is so pretty
That she can't be named,
And who so naughty, naughty,
She should be ashamed:
Who is it has a hundred beaux?
A little, wicked sprite
Of torment and delight—
She knows—she knows.

Who is it that does fly me
Fleetly as a fawn—
First lures me to pursuing,
Then is instant gone:
Who changes every wind that blows?
A fickle, elfin creature
Of crazing form and feature—
She knows—she knows.

For whom is all my sighing
Through the lonely night;
For whom is all my pining
Through the hours of light:
Who never lets my heart repose?
A certain wayward maid
No mortal can persuade—
She knows—she knows.

But how shall she escape me
If I, bold, pursue?
And should I overtake her,
Then what will she do?
What under heaven do you suppose?
The little angel sinner—
The very mischief's in her—
She knows—she knows.

JOHN VANCE CHENEY.

MINING IN THE SKY.

Homer is a mining district in the Sierra Nevada Mountains. The name is not a classical compliment to the locality. There is no tradition current that the poet was born or reared in either of the district camps. Nor is it said that he sought inspiration amid the grand scenery in this section of the Sierra main range. The Homer of Homer District was its reputed discoverer. He had no poetry in his soul. He had an eye to business. He studied nature for a practical purpose. Mythology was not in his line. He wanted no literary bonanza. He looked for gold, of which he stood in great need, and found it free and rich. He was simply a prospector, and a simple prospector. As a natural result, he disposed of his mining interests for ready cash. Then he sped to San Francisco for rest and recreation, and was ruined. The last of a series of sprees left him a poor man. He defied poverty—with a pistol. Less than six months after the location of Homer the locater met death by his own hand. Such is the tragical interest attaching to the district.

History has in this case furnished another example of its power of repetition. Prospectors, like many inventors, are not only mere children when manipulated by men of the business world, but are apt to lack the mental stamina necessary in the man who successfully stands prosperity. Homer had the shrewdness to sell some of his rich claims, where others in his position might have wasted their opportunities. Prosperity led him into the excesses of dissipation, and adversity, which followed closely, impelled him to self-destruction. The lucky prospectors of the Pacific Coast have enriched men and communities. The successful prospectors, those who have reaped an adequate, lasting profit, are so few in number that it is even difficult to find one in a mining community. Prospectors who have just missed a fortune, who view their misfortune philosophically, and who have a strong and abiding faith in the future, are to be seen in every camp. Each prospector is a success in his own estimation. His failure to find a rich ledge is a freak of fortune. Luck is against him. Luck will change with time. If he were not sure of ultimate success, if he did not feel that wealth awaited him, if he did not thrill with an eager expectation almost unknown in the haunts of civilization, he would soon tire of the dangers and hardships peculiar to prospecting, and take to the herding of cattle, the hewing of wood, or the drawing of water. Prospecting has a fascination for the ignorant and intelligent alike. It requires no special education to appreciate the value of the precious metals.

By a curious anomaly the popular qualifying adjective used among prospectors in speaking of luck applies with equal facility to good or bad luck. It is a strong adjective and would offend polite ears. There is no offense in leaving the matter to the imagination of the reader. Therefore, I adopt that course.

Homer District is one hundred and seventy miles east of San Francisco, and thirty miles south-west of Bodie, and embraces within its limits portions of two or three of the many lateral spurs or ridges on the eastern slope of the Sierra Nevada range. It is directly west of Mono Lake, from which it is distant seven miles, and its western boundary is the south-eastern corner of Tuolumne County. The summit of the range at this point forms a dividing line between Mono and Tuolumne Counties. Waters flowing east are in Mono; those flowing west are in Tuolumne. The trend of the range on the boundary line is about north and south.

I was at Bodie in the month of July, and an enthusiastic friend assured me that it would be rank treason to the mining interest if I did not accept an invitation to visit Homer. The acceptance was forthcoming. We left Bodie at the break of day. The sky was still spangled with stars, the air was fresh and cool from the effects of a bath taken the preceding evening, and every indication pointed to a pleasant and dustless ride. The town of Bodie was quiet. Several stragglers, more or less hilarious—the tailings, so to speak, from saloons and gaming dens—were moving about the main street in an aimless way. Otherwise there was no animation save that we imparted to the town, as we passed through the leading thoroughfare on our buckboard. My companion was a gentleman who has fought the Apaches and the Sioux with Crook, who has seen rough times in the mining camps of Idaho, Nevada, Dakota, and California, who has climbed the Alpine glaciers, and whose geniality is bright and cheering as sunshine. On the score of a long and intimate acquaintance I call him Joe.

It was our intention to breakfast at a station due north of Mono Lake, and distant about fifteen miles from Bodie. The grade of the road was in our favor most of the way, the horses were in fine condition, and we bowled along at a lively gait. For a few miles the scenery was tame and devoid of interest. The road wound about hills of volcanic rock, principally trachytic lava, which was black, or of a rusty brown color, and looked as if the life had been burned out of it. Scattered over the hills were low, scraggy nut-pine trees, so twisted and dwarfed as to excite special sympathy. These scrub pine trees are very independent. Give one a crevice for a beginning, and it will overcome all obstacles. Sympathy appears to be wasted on the nut-pines, after all. Yet they look lonesome and forlorn enough at times.

Our course drew us toward Mono Lake, and once we were within two miles of its northern shore. The lake is most striking when seen from a distance. The chemical properties of the water give the surface a glassy smoothness. The rugged, rocky islands rise from their aqueous setting like huge cameos, and terminate in jagged peaks. The great expanse of water extends fourteen miles east and west, and nine miles north and south. The country immediately north and east of the lake shows no timber belts, and seems, at first glance, an arid waste. Closer inspection develops elongated patches of green north of the lake, which, in some instances, are continuous for miles, and seemingly reach the lake shore. These intruding patches, or panels, are ranches beside the streams flowing from the mountains to the lake. West of the lake are black lines of timber, which extend far into the mountains. Above the timber the mountains are naked, until the caps or mantles of snow are reached. There is no regularity to the snow-line. One tall peak may show the slightest suspicion of a cap, set well to one side, and worn rather jauntily, while a lesser peak will be covered by a mantle of spotless white, extending far below the general line of snow. The Sierra Nevada Mountains have a very disorderly look in the Mono Lake country, and afford many evidences of a topographical spree. The elevations are dissolute. You see, at a glance, that they have been out all night. The peaks crowd each other. It is as if each peak were trying to rest on its neighbor, and all were experiencing a still, solemn drunk. Looking into the crowd of mountains west of the lake one sees every description of elevation. There are short mountains, stout of build, and round and full as a well nourished alderman. There are symmetrical mountains which arouse admiration by the beauty of their outlines. There are tall mountains which imperatively command attention. To the northwest is Castle Peak. It belies its name when viewed from the east. We could see no towers. It rises bodily to the hight of thirteen thousand feet, but has no unusual contour. Tracing the range south, Mount Lyell, Mount Dana, and Cathedral Peak are easily distinguished from the numerous lesser elevations. Mount Dana pushes nearest to the sky. The altitude of this peak is thirteen thousand two hundred and twenty-seven feet, and its pinnacle is seven thousand feet higher than Mono Lake. The peaks named, and others of minor note, are tipped with snow, and patches of snow, resembling fragments of frosting from a wedding cake, cling to the broad sides of the mountains, far below the pinnacles, and stubbornly resist the summer sun. The lake in the foreground, with its volcanic suggestiveness, and a chain of extinct volcanoes, with truncated cones, a few miles to the south, made a lasting impression on my mind. The lake and volcanoes told of a convulsion of nature which must have been sublimely terrible to leave these lasting evidences of its work.

Professor Whitney, who critically examined the volcanoes south of the lake, furnishes the following statement in his *Geology of the Sierra Nevada:* "The highest of the volcanoes was ascended, and its sides found to be covered with loose ashes, lying at as steep an angle as the material would allow, mixed with fragments of volcanic rock of various kinds, especially of trachyte. The broad top was found to be of a light gray trachyte, with about twelve sharp knobs rising around the outside, apparently the remains of the lip of the ancient crater. Obsidian and pumice are abundant on the top and sides of the cone and over the plain beneath. The soil, or ashes, of all these cones is intensely dry and pulverulent, so that a man sinks into it over the ankles at every step; yet it supports in places a stunted growth of trees and shrubs, and even herbaceous plants. It is evident that but little rain ever falls here, as the sides of these cones are so little washed, the material of which they are composed being of such a character that they could not long retain their present form except in a very dry climate. These cones rise to the hight of from nine thousand two hundred to nine thousand three hundred feet above the level of the sea, and the highest is about two thousand seven hundred and fifty feet above the level of Mono Lake."

The station where we halted for our morning meal consisted of a tent and a small shed. The tent was partitioned into three small rooms—

one for sleeping purposes, one devoted to cooking and eating, and the third and last, though not the least important, contained a rude counter, a barrel of whisky, a tumbler, and a bench. The station people were two in number. First in order was a buxom woman, on the shady side of forty, whose ruddy cheeks, numerously dimpled chin, and general amplitude of person contrasted favorably with the barren country about the place. Second, and decidedly subordinate, was a man, the husband of our hostess, who promptly complied with the pointed requests of his superior officer. Joe had said it was a nice station to patronize, especially as it was the only one on the road, but he had also remarked that the bouncing and blooming female in command possessed a leading characteristic of her sex, in that she was not averse to homage from the men. Joe had traveled the road before, and knew whereof he spoke. The delicate task of dispensing honeyed words fell to me. Joe held that compliments from a stranger always had the greatest weight with the ladies. I naturally deferred to his judgment, experience, and years. We asked for something to eat, and the good woman said that she had nothing to offer us but bacon. I threw out a guarded compliment to the scenery in that neighborhood as a feeler. In a moment potatoes were found. I spoke of the tasteful arrangement of the tent interior, ascribed the pictorial decorations to her rare but truly feminine appreciation of art, and finished my offering with a really bright and witty saying I had heard in the Bohemian Club Rooms at San Francisco. The effect was magical. Eggs, milk, butter, coffee, and canned fruits were produced in bountiful profusion. It was such a clear case of cause and effect that I began to feel a slight alarm. I feared that our amiable hostess would try to delay our departure until she had ice-cream or a sybaritic luxury to offer. So we paid our bill—a ridiculously reasonable charge, by the way—and ordered our team to the door. As we were starting, our fair and flustered entertainer said, in reply to a farewell remark, "Oh, yes, gentlemen, it is lonesome way out here, especially for us. We have known better days. We once kept a beer saloon in Reno." And then she sighed, the good old soul, and we rode away.

We passed by the old Mono and Dogtown Diggings, once rich and profitable, but long since abandoned, and in two hours were at the entrance of Mill Creek Cañon. The *cañon* is in Homer Mining District. It cuts the main range at right angles. Mill Creek is formed by cascades and rivulets falling from the snow-clad mountains at the head of the *cañon*. In the bed of the *cañon* it is a picturesque stream, shadowed by tall trees and mountain shrubbery, often divided by huge granite bowlders, and rich in the music of rushing waters. Where the course is clear, the creek hurries forward with the gentlest murmur. Rocky obstructions and the prostrate trunks of trees induce a ceaseless roar, mingled with splashing, and force the waters into a mass of foam. In places, indeed, it is a passionate mountain torrent, and presents a dangerous aspect to the intending forder. After leaving the *cañon*, and in its passage over the open plain to Mono Lake, it is quiet and decorous. The entrance to Mill Creek Cañon shows glacial action in interesting and instructive forms. On the north side of the *cañon*, and at its very mouth, is a perfect terminal moraine, from which more or less *débris* has been washed out on the plain by later action. This moraine is best described as a long, low, though clearly defined, mound, crescentic in shape—the snout, as it were, pointing toward the plain. Its length is apparently three thousand feet, and its greatest width three hundred feet. On the south side of the *cañon*, and at an altitude of fifteen hundred feet above the level of Mono Lake, are two lateral moraines, lying parallel to and within a short distance of each other, which are as perfect in their way as the terminal moraine. The lateral moraines are two thousand feet long and two hundred and fifty feet wide. They lie on the side of a mountain, and have a north and south course. And between the westernmost moraine and the peak of the mountain is a large glacial valley. Above the latter moraines the mountain side is torn and twisted. Here it was that the glacier expired. Here was the final struggle. The path of the glacier is traced for miles into the range. The glacial *débris* and eroded rocks, and the basined lakes of Mill Creek Cañon clearly show the line of movement. Professor Joseph Le Conte has studied the glacial ruins on the eastern slope of the Sierra to good purpose, though his reports, so far as I have observed, do not relate to this particular locality. Anterior to the discovery of gold on Mill Creek, the *cañon*, being distant from routes of mountain travel, was a *terra incognita*.

Our road led us to the north side of Mill Creek, and involved fording. The stream had a width of twenty feet, was about three feet deep, and ran like a mill-race. We placed our feet on the dash-board, above the reach of the raging torrent, and dashed across in safety. There is exhilaration in fording this creek. There is also cool dampness. This dampness reached the seat of the buckboard, and evoked from Joe a frontier exclamation befitting the occasion. The road is in the bed of the *cañon*, and so near the creek that the sound of the moving waters is seldom absent. As we rode along the *cañon*, on an easy grade, its walls rose higher, and were more precipitous. Trachyte was succeeded by bands of micaceous granite. This granite was destined to give way to the metamorphic granite adjoining a belt of diorite. In the metamorphic granite and diorite the gold ore is found. The pine, cedar, fir, and tamarack trees became more abundant. The rocks were more rugged. The scenery was wilder. The mountain faces were seamed and furrowed, and inspired veneration. A flood of sunshine poured into the *cañon* and glorified its beauty. The soft air, laden with the bracing odor of the balsamic pine, the ceaseless sound of the rushing waters, and the countless charms of countless views, stimulated our enthusiasm to the utmost tension. Every stride of progress revealed fresh and striking features in the landscape. The mountainous walls of the *cañon* were ever showing new profiles, new stratifications, and new colors. Four miles from the entrance of the *cañon*, we reached Lundy Lake. It occupies a glacial basin the full width of the *cañon*. The creek flows into the lake from the west and out of it on the east. Lundy Lake is a gem of the Sierra Nevada. Though less than half a mile wide, and only one mile long, it has a distinctive character never known in mere ponds. The maximum depth of the lake is said to be two hundred and fifty feet. The deep channel is on the north side, and far below the road winding around the mountain. With varying depths, the tints on the surface change. The crystal water is light blue where shallow, dark blue where deeper. At the point of greatest depth it is a jet black. Stately trees encompass the lake at present. But the woodman is ruthless. Picturesqueness is a luxury which he cannot always afford. Tall, straight trees represent so much lumber to him. So down come the trees. Some have come down; others are coming. He has his eye on them.

After a brief halt at the lake, we rode on. Pine, fir, and cedar trees were more frequent, and increased in size. Groves of mountain aspen also bordered the road. Near the western shore of the lake is the mining camp of Lundy. It consists of a few brand-new cabins, and is supposed to have a future. The character of that future remains to be determined. I hazard no prediction. The site is in a grove of noble trees, and has many other attractions. At this stage of developments it is impossible to give the position of Homer's leading mining town. There is a wide difference of opinion on the subject. One day last winter an enterprising prospector, who had tired of "herding a stove"—*i. e.*, sitting about the fire in a bar-room—determined to locate a town-site for himself. So he slipped off on his snow-shoes, and worked his way up the *cañon* to a spot he deemed favorable for a thriving town. Stakes were procured, and before night he had a town laid out on the snow. The depth of the snow was thirty feet. Local report says that several of the lots were sold. I cannot vouch for the sale. But it is a fact that the spring thaw left the town-site in the air. The *cañon* narrowed to a point at the bottom. This narrative is related with great unction by the people of Homer. I heard it several times during my visit, and as some one had stated the particulars in Bodie, and Joe had given me a detailed account of the same matter during our ride, the novelty of the whole business came to be charming toward the last.

We pushed forward, over a rough and rocky road, by a mountain swamp, through a mountain meadow, and into the camp of Wasson. Lundy and Wasson are a mile apart. Each has its advantages and disadvantages, and both are ambitious. Neither has a graveyard, though Lundy has already been the scene of one or two fatal discussions. The tradition is said to be popular among miners that the pistol and knife advertise a camp, and are powerful promoters of mining development, and they are also credited with the belief that no camp can attain a healthy state of activity without a graveyard. I trust that Homer will have little use for graveyards. I hold the courtesy and hospitality of the people in grateful remembrance. Among the more pretentious residences in Wasson is that of Mr. C. H. Nye, who accompanied Homer in his early prospecting expeditions in this section. Mr. Nye is directing hydraulic operations in the bed of the *cañon*, and is confident of success.

A short distance beyond Wasson we drew up the team on a rocky bench, and abandoned ourselves to the view. On either side of the *cañon* the cleft range rises boldly to hights varying from two thousand to three thousand feet. Each mountain face is stained, and scarred, and channeled. The discoloration of the rocky surface imparts an antique appearance to the mountains. Without the seams, the scars, and the stains, the scene could not reach its hoary grandeur. The signs of age are all essential. They invest the towering rocks with a tangible sentiment. Striping the mountains, in a northerly and southerly course, are ledges of gold-bearing ore. These ledges, or the croppings thereof, are followed, with the eye, up each side of the *cañon*, from the line of the float rock, bordering the creek, to the apparent summits of the mountains. The *cañon* is a mining cross-cut worthy of old Dame Nature. But practical views and impressions are speedily dispelled by grander sights. Whirling through narrow gorges about the head of the *cañon* are cascades rivaling, in flawless beauty, the towering snow-capped peaks. Two long and prominent cascades arrest attention as the chief features of the spectacle. We hear no rush of the waters. At first glance the cascades look like serpentine bands of crumpled snow. The scene is suggestive rather than satisfying. We see the Promised Land, but are not there. We hurry forward, exchange our team for a couple of trusty riding mules, and soon gain a knobby ridge which fairly commands the cascades. The ridge abuts against the wall on the north side of the *cañon*. Old and gnarled trees, sole survivors of a grove of mountain monarchs, shade us from the searching sunlight, and the drooping branches are rustic frames for many gorgeous vistas. Dashing down the lofty and precipitous mountain which walls the *cañon* on the west, and following a sinuous channel in the north-west corner of the *cañon*, is a foamy torrent, now a fall, and again a cascade, which is continuous in its series of falls and cascades, for a distance of four thousand feet, and has a descent of two thousand feet. For one thousand feet the angle is not less than seventy degrees. The volume of water in this cascade is eight hundred miner's inches. Such is the North Fork of Mill Creek. It seems to issue from a crevice in the rocks. Its real source is a chain of lakelets far back in the mountains. North and south of the North Fork are minor cascades—threads of silver winding down to the main creek. In the southwest corner of the *cañon* is the Mill Creek Cascade. The main source of Main Creek is a chain of lakelets eight thousand feet west of, and two thousand feet above, the point in the *cañon* where the junction with the North Fork is accomplished. Eight thousand feet of cascade and fall! A continuous line of sparkling foam! It whirls hither and thither, plunges over the face of a precipice, dashes through the rocks, but is foam from the time it leaves the lakelets till it disappears in the *cañon* bed. The flow of water in the main fall is three thousand miner's inches.

We viewed the cascades from other positions of vantage, and never knew a feeling of weariness. These grand works of nature,

> "With grace divine imbued,
> Bring to their sweetness no satiety."

We lingered around the cascades for some hours, and until the time at our disposal was more than exhausted, and then rode down the *cañon* to the Homer mill-site, which is eight thousand four hundred and fifty feet above the sea level. The creek is too strong for fording in the vicinity of the site, and has been bridged. We crossed the bridge, and headed our mules up a crazy trail on the south side of the *cañon*. The trail winds through a gorge, several hundred feet wide, which we crossed and recrossed constantly in making the ascent. It was like tacking against a sharp head-wind. Still there was no monotony in the trip. Joe was chipper, and cheery, and full of anecdote. He told how several animals had fallen from the trail to the bottom of the *cañon*, and in other ways contributed to the cheerfulness of the occasion. The trail is worn through loose float rock, and has a width of six inches. The mules did not mind the narrowness of the trail. They leisurely walked to one side of the gorge, sniffed the overhanging rock, gathered their feet in a bunch, like the trick horse in a circus, turned slowly and deliberately around, and walked off on a new tack. The angle of the gorge for the first thousand feet is thirty-two degrees. The tunnel of the Homer Mining Company is in this gorge, entering the mountain one thousand and fifty feet above the level of the creek directly below. The southern boundary line of the Homer mine, on the summit of the mountains, has an altitude of eleven thousand three hundred feet above the sea level, and is two thousand eight hundred and fifty feet above the level of the mill-site. Near the mouth of the Homer Company's tunnel is the canvas tent which sheltered the *employés* of the corporation last winter. The situation is airy and has a good view. These are its sole recommendations. After a general examination of the surface rock, which entailed hard scrambling, and a walk through the tunnel, drifts, and crosscuts, we seated ourselves on the dump, and were content to remain quiet for a while. From this hight the features of the *cañon* bed were seen in miniature. It was like looking through an inverted opera-glass. Men were dwarfed into specks, tall trees became low shrubs, and the houses were proportionately insignificant.

During our brief interval of rest a prospector drew nigh, with his jackass, and came to a halt. The mining prospector has been the hero of song and story since the days of less recent California. Romance demands him, and he always takes the form required by the exigencies of the plot. He stands on a lofty eminence, and is the central figure in a grand scene. His soul is stirred to its inmost depths. The nobility of his nature asserts itself. He is inspired. The wanton breezes play with his curly locks, and ever and anon caress his marble brow. He speaks not. He is posed to represent an apotheosis of mankind. He stands there, in the story, a very god.

Our visiting prospector was not of the romantic class. He was low of stature, rough in dress, smoked a short and very black pipe, and spoke with a strong brogue. He stood beside the neatest little jackass I ever saw—a perfect love of a jackass, to borrow a society phrase, with coquettish ears, soft, dreamy eyes, and fawn-colored hair. The prospector had a grievance. He was verbally consigning himself to the place Bob Ingersoll pronounces a myth. And all because of the jackass. He swore copiously, not at the animal, but in its behalf. The animal listened patiently, attentively, and with apparent appreciation. When the man paused for want of breath, the animal waved an ear or two, and blinked. He was such a mite of a jackass, and his ears were so long and ponderous that the movement of an ear to and fro was a compliment not to be lightly considered. It transpired that the prospector and his pack animal were just returning from a trip which had been curtailed by the sudden illness of "Moriarity." "Moriarity" was the jack. "Moriarity" had presumably eaten an assayer's outfit. Nothing weaker than acid could have given "Moriarity" such a bad case of colic. At all events, "Moriarity" was a very sick jack. Never was jack nursed more tenderly. Delicate attentions were lavished upon him. He was coddled, and fondled, and a dose of medicine was administered. He voiced no protest. He had no complaint to make. But he could not conceal his anguish. His broad, intelligent face was wrinkled, his eyes were fireless, and he was unsteady of limb. His sweet patience was inexhaustible. As I gazed on him I was impelled to the reflection that "the shallow murmur, but the deep are dumb." "Moriarity" was finally tucked away in an improvised bed. There are so many ordinary jacks in the world that a superior jack is not very soon forgotten. The warm attachment existing between "Moriarity" and his owner aroused my curiosity. I had witnessed the noble fortitude of the jack under trying circumstances. Hence a desire to learn something of his history. I asked the prospector a few questions, judiciously prefacing my inquiries with a few complimentary remarks about jackasses in general, and his own in particular. He agreed with me that people could grow very fond of these animals. I do not give his exact words. His ideas serve the purpose. He proceeded to say that one could not learn to love a jackass unless a close intimacy existed between the two. No man entertained the same feeling for all jacks that he did for one or two, or a select few. Every jack who was not ugly or ill bred was liable to have friends and admirers. Some jacks, like some individuals, never were appreciated. A good deal, of course, depended upon the society in which a jack was thrown. That sick jack, that diminutive creature, climbed up the face of a precipice with a pack, weighing two hundred and fifty pounds, on his back. *He* was both handsome and good. He never strayed from a camp, and left his owner in the lurch. On the contrary, he always kept a close watch on his master's movements. "Ivery night," continued the prospector, now thoroughly enthused, "he comes to me siveral times, whin I'm shlaping, and sniffs me blankets to see if I'm gone or no. He's the nicest baste in the woruld, and me frind." The prospector left us, and other subjects came up for discussion. Still, it was a long time before I could dismiss the jack from my mind. I could not help thinking of the place he occupied in his master's affections. I wondered if the feeling was reciprocated between master and jack. And then I mused upon the multitude of jackasses who do not know when they are well off.

Lake Cañon is the second natural cross-cut of Homer District. It opens from the south side of Mill Creek Cañon near Lundy, and has a north-easterly and south-westerly course. It is smaller than Mill Creek Cañon, but of equal importance as a mining proposition. The south fork of Mill Creek, a chain of lakes, and a cascade, descending almost vertically a distance of seven hundred feet, are among the scenic effects of Lake Cañon. Mining in the Lake Cañon section has reached a high altitude, higher than the Homer. The croppings of the May Lundy mine are eleven thousand three hundred and thirty-five feet above the sea level, and the tunnel of the May Lundy Mining Company is only two hundred and eighty feet lower. Several other companies are at work near the May Lundy, and with flattering prospects. The gold of the Homer District mines is rich and clean. Bodie gold is really an electrum of gold and silver. Homer gold is the genuine article. It is the gold that lured the argonauts to California. The proportion of silver in Homer gold is one dollar in seventy-five. The great hight and precipitousness of the Homer Mountains will not interfere with the development of the mines. The tunnel system of works facilitates exploration. Mill Creek Cañon, where most of the milling will be performed, is from seven hundred to eight hundred feet lower than Bodie, is accessible by an easy grade, and abounds in timber and water. With the aid of tramways, the ores can be easily and cheaply transported to mill. Few districts in the world can boast of such abundant facilities for mining and milling. Time and work must determine the value of the district as a grand mining proposition. A prophecy would be out of place here.

Homer was discovered on the twenty third of August, 1879. Systematic operations were not begun until late in the fall, when the Homer Mining Company started their tunnel. The district was buried in snow during four months of last winter. Hardy miners ventured out now and then and walked to Bodie on snowshoes; but these trips were necessarily rare. They came to be regarded as perilous after the travelers had returned once or twice with frozen ears and hands. The few people who wintered in Homer assuredly had a rough experience. They lived principally on a certain sort of faith and hope. Subsistence on such a diet requires a heroism which we seldom see outside of a mining camp.

My last view of Homer was in the gloaming. The mountains loomed up grand and gloomy, then slowly faded away. Memory treasures the Homeric scenery. Where is the artist who will transfer to canvas this marvelous illustration of the heroic and picturesque in mining?

W. M. BUNKER.

A WINTER IN BERLIN.—II.

The Germans are considered to be a more sociable people than the English or Americans, but I think this is a mistake. They are gregarious, but in one sense not as sociable; that is, they are fonder of being in crowds than our people, but it seemed to me that intimate home visiting is not so common. The average German is very fond of going with his family to the popular concert-room, or garden, and there, seated about a table, the women will knit and the men smoke; very likely supper will be eaten, and certainly all will imbibe indefinite quantities of beer; friends will speak to each other, the women will indulge in *klatsch* (gossip), and there will be a great quantity of bad tobacco smoke floating in the air. On warm Sunday afternoons the families will go in crowds into the Thiergarten, or to Charlottenberg, or Potsdam, or some other of the suburban resorts, and enjoy the fresh air, sunshine, and also the inevitable beer; but home intimacies and visiting are much less common than with us. A person may have a wide circle of acquaintance, and yet never go into their houses, nor see them in his own. Of course, in a large community there is not complete uniformity in this regard. I give merely the very distinct impression which I received of this extreme gregariousness, and yet lack of home sociability. This gregariousness manifests itself, also, in the numerous *Vereins* everywhere to be found. Every trade and pursuit, and one may say, idea, has its "union."

Through the kindness of a German lady I was enabled to take part in some characteristic Berlin social gatherings. This particular company called itself the *Montag Gesellschaft* (Monday Society), though why was not apparent, as it came together only at odd intervals. It was chaperoned by a few middle-aged ladies. There were usually present sixty or seventy persons, young and matronly ladies, army officers, and civilians of the better classes. Each one paid four marks (one dollar) for the invitation ticket. The assembly was held at some well known hotel. As soon as the company was present, usually about eight o'clock, it sat down to dinner. Each gentleman was expected to order a bottle of wine, which was extra. An hour and a half was consumed at table. Germans are loud talkers, and before the end there would be a tremendous uproar in the room. When it was time to adjourn the elderly gentleman presiding arose, and proposed the health of the Emperor, which would be drank standing, accompanied by a chorus of enthusiastic *hoch, hoch's*. The ladies and gentlemen then passed into an ante-room, and drank their coffee while the tables were being cleared away. After which dancing commenced. The favorite dance is the waltz. The same piece of music was played for a half hour at a time; the dancers whirled around the room two or three times, and then sat down to catch their breath; in a little while the same dancers, however, each with a different partner, would be off again in the dizzy whirl at a very rapid pace, and so on to the end. The theory seems to be, to get as much exercise in a given time as one can with as many partners as possible. The young officers are the model dancers, and naturally the favorites with the girls. These dashing young bloods and elegant partners relieved the fatigues of the vigorous dancing with occasional glasses of beer. At these particular *Gesellschafts* there were usually present four or five *attachés* of the Chinese Embassy in full national costume, and it would have harrowed the soul of a Kearneyite to see the amount of attention they received from the women. I could see that the envious young gentlemen secretly thought also that the Chinese "must go." A stranger in Berlin, and, in fact, in every town, immediately remarks the vast number of beer and wine shops and restaurants. In Berlin they are in every quarter of the town. They are of all shades of excellence and badness, from Poffenberg's, on the Unter den Linden, down to the "Fruhstück Lokal," in the remote *strasse*, where droskymen and laborers regale themselves. My first conclusion was, that the entire population ate and drank in these places, but a longer acquaintance with the habits of the people disabused me of this hasty impression. The explanation of the support which these resorts must necessarily receive in order to make a tolerable profit finally dawned upon me when I learned more of the habits of German men. Every German, no matter what his calling, has his wine or *bier kneipe*. This is a public house to which he resorts every evening, and passes two, three, or more hours, as the case may be, in the circle of his chosen friends, drinking, smoking, and chatting. As the customary dinner is early, he will frequently take his supper there, and he will probably, evening after evening, year in and year out, frequent the same *kneipe*, meeting there always the same companions. The merchant, the lawyer, the doctor, the literary man, the mechanic, the laborer, each has his *kneipe*, where he meets congenial society. I have been told that there are Berliners who have no *kneipe*, but they must be classed among the eccentrics. The wives, therefore, never expect their husbands to pass the evenings at home, or, at least, the entire evening.

As to whether German women are better educated than our own women, with corresponding opportunities, I must confess I am in doubt, principally because, from American ladies long resident in Berlin, I have heard quite conflicting opinions. Averaging their opinions, and supplementing them with my own observation, I am inclined to think that the German women are better linguists and musicians, but not as well up in other branches. You will hardly meet a lady of any pretensions to good training who cannot speak more or less English and French; and, in several instances, I have been very much surprised at the accuracy of their English, both in speaking and writing, and also at the breadth of their reading in English literature.

Those who know the Berlin women in the best circles say they are bright, intelligent, and intellectual; and it may be said of all their countrywomen that they have a strong tendency to sentimentalism. They do not "come out" as early as our girls, and are not as self-dependent or self-adapting. Beauty of face is not the specialty of the Berlin women, though one often sees very good figures. I remember making this reflection at the annual subscription ball at the Royal Opera House. This was an occasion when one could see together an excellent representation of Berlin society, called out by the fact that the Emperor, Empress, and the Imperial Court were present, and came down on the floor. Of course, in so large an assemblage there were beautiful faces, but they flashed upon one in the throng as rare surprises; plain, good-natured features, and ample, well fed figures, were the normal types.

Like most men, when the intricacies of a woman's toilet come in question, I can only give impressions, and these were that the dressing was rich, but by no means elegant; in truth, rather unartistic, but diamonds, pearls, emeralds, amethysts, and all sorts of precious stones sparkled upon the persons and dresses of the greater part of the ladies in dazzling profusion. The men of the Court are generally good looking, manly fellows; but the women! Perhaps the less said the better. There was one, however, fresh and charming—the young daughter of the Crown Prince, the Princess Saxe-Meinegen. And so at the opera or at the theater, one may search long through the crowded audiences for really pretty faces; the æsthetic soul hungering for beauty or brilliancy must content itself with the homely, good-natured, bread-and-butter style of visage. The *penetralia* of German households are not as cleanly or orderly as might be. In truth, the godliness which goes along with cleanliness is too often lacking, where the critical eye of the passer-by cannot penetrate. In houses of the more recent construction are bath-rooms, but I am disposed to believe they are more generally used as waste or servants' rooms than for their intended purpose. In houses more than ten years old, I doubt whether such a necessary appendage can be found. A significant fact is that the linen goes to the laundry only at intervals, very often, of six months, quite commonly of two and three. On these occasions, the laundry-woman appears and carries away the loads of material, frequently to some suburban establishment. Possibly the system may have its advantages, but certainly one's impressions would be that it is more labor and patience saving than nice. It was some time before I I could make my washer-woman understand that I wished her to come once a week. She evidently could not comprehend its fitness, and I am sure at last put it down as the absurd, though profitable, habit of a foreigner, who could not be expected to know better.

The only serious meal in a German family is the dinner, which ordinarily comes between half past one and three o'clock. The banks are closed between those hours, and active business is largely suspended. Deliberation and time are given, not so much to the actual consumption of the dinner as to quietude afterward. If the food is bolted rapidly, the German insists upon plenty of time to digest it. He therefore sits long at the table, and sips his wine or beer, and afterward, over his coffee, smokes his weed. In all this he extracts more real, solid, reasonable satisfaction out of one dinner than an American will out of a dozen. Judged by our standards, his table habits are rather gross. Men and women shovel their food into their mouths very commonly with their knives, edge inward, and generally there is a slobberiness which is not agreeable. At a *table d'hôte*, or dinner party, the din of voices becomes extraordinary; for the people talk loud and all at once. If it is trying to the lungs, no doubt it is good for the digestion. At a *table d'hôte* there are three things which a German gentleman almost invariably does. First, when he enters the room he takes out a small pocket-brush and carefully brushes his hair; secondly, he produces a large, bright-colored silk handkerchief, and blows a bugle-blast; and lastly, at the end of the repast, he calls for a candle and lights his cigar, without consulting the preferences of the other guests. This, however, is not to be taken as an exhibition of selfish, bad manners. On the contrary, he is performing merely a social function, which presumptively is pleasurable to everybody; for the smoking habit is so common that the non-smoker is rather in the attitude of one who should apologize for his lack of culture, and therefore should pay the penalty of his defective development by quietly withdrawing or suffering in silence. The other meals cut only a secondary figure, and are often eaten in a scrambling fashion, here and there as it may happen.

I doubt whether the mysteries of German cooking are comprehensible to the Anglo-Saxon mind, or permanently endurable by the Anglo-Saxon stomach. In order to obtain that peace of mind which is absolutely necessary to aid the digestion of the compounds which daily come upon the table, one must not seek to comprehend.

Is there not a close relationship between the methods of cooking of a people and their intellectual and moral development? Cannot the positive, practical directness of the Anglo-Saxon mind be connected with their plain, succulent, unmistakable roasts and chops?—or the grace and artistic sense of the French referred to their delicate *ragoûts* and sauces?—and the cloudy, self-evolving philosophies of the Germans to their incomprehensible mixtures of fish, flesh, fruit, and vegetables? Or would a closer analysis show that the reverse process works out food preparation from innate characteristics?

The fundamental principle of German cookery is to mix together as many incongruous things as possible. My countrymen have a special talent, recognized the world over, for inventing mixed drinks, but his combinations pale before those of the Germans in mixed cooking. That compound which is so toothsome to a German, a herring salad, is concocted from sixteen different articles. A German beefsteak is made of hashed meats, rolled into a ball and fried. What they call roast beef is a chunk of meat boiled a while and then baked; it usually looks like a lump of india-rubber. With the meats is always served a *compote*, made of stewed or preserved fruit. The vegetables are deemed at their best when they are floating in grease. Sausage, however, is the great national delicacy. It is produced in great varieties of size and quality; and the sausage shops of Berlin are the most elegant in the city. The German family table, with its mysteries and abominations, is the severest trial which the American has to undergo who submits himself to the domestic life of the country. My estimable landlady modified her culinary practices somewhat to suit my fancies; yet six months of effort failed to reconcile me to the strange diet. I have met with a few Americans in Germany, a long time there, who first endured, then pitied, then finally embraced the execrable cookery; but, as one might suspect, they have in a degree become denationalized.

In Berlin, however, one is not obliged to suffer this daily martyrdom; there are a few good restaurants, like that of Poffenberg, or the Kaiserhof, or the Hôtel de Rome, where one can fare sumptuously and in a civilized way, and, for those so inclined, there are a few very good *pensions* which adapt themselves to our ways of living.

However, the clothes a people wear, the houses they live in, the food they eat, and the special social customs they exhibit, may, perhaps, be put down simply as surface characteristics, which, among European peoples, are not widely different.

We may also go further, and say that, in a general way, their several civilizations are all developing upon the same lines; but these are generalizations too broad to be satisfying. Inside of these lines we see that each is developing a special nationality—a life of its own, which gives it national individuality. We see a special national mind, which makes the German one, the Frenchman quite another, and the Russian yet a distinct third. The German type, though an old and well defined one, has met obstructions to its unification, which are only now, in this generation, being overcome. The oft quoted lines of Arndt,

"Was ist des Deutschen Vaterland?"

and the enthusiastic response of this song, that it is

"So weit die deutsche Zunge klingt,"

which expressed merely an aspiration when written sixty odd years ago, is now rapidly taking form. The unification of North Germany is the most remarkable event in Europe since the disappearance of the first Napoleon from the scene. This unification is working in all social directions. Berlin, therefore, as the chief city of the new empire, has become the political center of the continent, and the new influences at work are drawing to it not only the political, but also the social, intellectual, and artistic forces of the empire. Heretofore the small States—the "Residenz" towns, dispersed in twenty or thirty little States—divided these forces. Weimar, as we know, became a literary, and Dresden and Munich artistic centers, and the universities, also, scattered at many distant points, formed scientific and philosophic centers. These little capitals were also, each in its degree, centers of special aristocratic and social influences, but since the political unification the best social, intellectual, and artistic life of Germany is slowly, but surely, being drawn to Berlin. Weimar, Dresden, Stuttgard, and even Munich, are losing their earlier glories. The change is not a rapid one, and it will probably be a long time before Berlin becomes to North Germany what Paris is to France. Already political opinion takes its direction from the capital, and, naturally, its newspapers are assuming greater prominence than ever before.

One of the features of the former decentralization was that the ablest journals were to be found in the smaller cities, and at points remote from each other, and this is the case in a degree still. The Cologne *Gazette* and Augsburg *Allgemeine Zeitung* are yet leaders; nevertheless, it is plain that the metropolitan is growing at the expense of the interior press.

Mark Twain, in his recent book, *A Tramp Abroad*, referring to the newspapers of Hamburg, Frankfort, Baden, and Munich, as correct types of the German press, says they are deficient in everything that makes a newspaper attractive. If that is the case as to those particular journals (and as to that I cannot say), certainly those of Berlin cannot be dismissed in such a depreciatory way. There are a great many of them, of all shades of opinion and ability, and representing all sections of society. In the matter of the primal requisite of a daily journal, news, they are far superior to the French, and almost equal to the best English and American papers. Apparently they do not expend as much money and energy in collecting news, nor are they so anxious for the earliest and first information, no doubt because the German readers are not as eager or exacting in this regard as ours are. The most influential are the *Nord-deutsche Allgemeine Zeitung* (said to be Bismarck's organ), the *Vossiche Zeitung*, the *National*, the *Preussische* or *Kreuz-Zeitung*, the *Tageblatt*, and the *Fremdenblatt*.

A small newspaper, called *Das Kleine Journal*, founded the winter I was in Berlin by Dr. Strousberg, who is somewhat notorious for his connection with railroad schemes in Russia, and his bankruptcy and subsequent trial, became immediately a great success. It sells for five pfennings, or one and a quarter cents, and contains not only a full summary of the current news, but also has very good editorials. I have seen in it original correspondence from San Francisco, and editorials about California affairs. Perhaps the *Tageblatt* may be taken as a fair specimen of a Berlin daily. It is said to have the largest circulation. I have before me the number for May 21, 1880. It consists of sixteen pages, each page about three-quarters the size of one of the San Francisco *Evening Bulletin*. I should say that, taking into consideration differences in size of page and type, the *Tageblatt* contains matter equal to at least ten pages of the *Bulletin*. Of the sixteen pages, five and a half are given up exclusively to advertisements. The upper parts of the first and second pages are devoted to political editorials and political news, the lower to a chapter of a *feuilleton*, and theatrical and musical news; the third page contains a letter from Hamburg, news from various points of the empire, with long lists of changes in civil and army offices; the fourth page has local news; the fifth contains local news, and has also reports of judicial proceedings and of a sitting of one of the municipal councils; the sixth contains a very full and detailed statement of the prices ruling at the money exchanges of Breslau, Hamburg, Frankfort, Vienna, Amsterdam, London, Paris, St. Petersburg, Bremen, Cologne, Antwerp, Glasgow, and Liverpool, followed by half a page of advertisements; the seventh has telegraphic news from various parts of Europe; the eighth is composed of advertisements; the ninth has political editorials and some paragraphs of theatrical news; the tenth and eleventh contain telegraphic correspondence from St. Petersburg and London, a letter from Bromberg, telegrams from Munich, Brussels, and Vienna, local news, and a report of the proceedings of the Prussian Landtag. One column of this and the following page are taken up with very full and detailed reports of the markets for various kinds of goods in all the commercial centers of Europe, and also in New York and Rio Janeiro, followed by a report of prices ruling in the Berlin exchange the previous day of over seven hundred different stocks or shares, and winding up with a barometrical and thermometrical report from all parts of Europe. The last four pages are filled with advertisements.

The news of all kinds is full and detailed. This paper has morning and evening editions, and is sold to subscribers at forty-three cents a month; single numbers sell on the street for two and a half cents. It is equal to any paper of its class in the United States, and very much superior to the average of our daily press both in tone, style, and matter. In the *Vossische*, *Nord-deutsche Allgemeine*, and *National* are articles admirable for their range of thought, knowledge, and moderation of tone. As to style, they cannot ordinarily be praised; it is strangely involved and slovenly. The student of German at home, who thinks himself well up in the language because he can read Goethe, Schiller, or Heine readily, will find himself, to his surprise, very much at fault when he goes to Germany and takes up the daily paper. It is like going from the open, sunny fields into a dense forest, with tangled undergrowth.

Every calling or pursuit in Germany which finds expression in words seems to have a style, or want of style, of its own; it is only the purely literary person who cares to cultivate the art of expression for its own sake. There is, consequently, a philosophical, an official, a scientist, a newspaper, and a literary style, and that of the newspaper is certainly one of the most obscure; the aim of its writers seeming to be to give in one sentence the main thought, with all its possible shades, exceptions, and qualifications, with the nominative at the beginning and the verb as far off toward the end as possible.

I have been surprised how well the better Berlin papers are up in American affairs. They keep their readers informed about all occurrences of importance going on in our midst. Even the various phases of the Kearney agitation, of our local political movements, and of the Chinese question were well understood and discussed by them. With reference to American news they are better informed, and give fuller information than the English journals. Those, therefore, who characterize the German press as behind the times are themselves lagging in the rear of the facts.

It is very easy for the traveler hurrying through a country, who is, perhaps, either only partially or not at all acquainted with the language, and who has casually glanced at one or two newspapers, to generalize and summarily condemn the whole press of the country as deficient; and then it gratifies our national pride to think we are in advance of those decaying old communities.

The Berlin press lacks, it is true, somewhat of the push of our best papers in the gathering of news; its leaders certainly lack the literary finish of our best; but, on the other hand, the news is carefully collated and arranged, the thought of the articles is elevated, and the "interviewer" and sensational reporter are carefully excluded.

It is said that the Berlin press is controlled by Jews, and that they are corrupting public opinion. During the winter I was in Berlin there arose a violent controversy over the Jew question, as it was styled, which called out newspaper articles, pamphlets, and speeches from many prominent men all over Germany, and was heard of in other parts of Europe, and also on our side of the Atlantic. The substance of the charge against these people, when stripped of the profuse verbiage in which it was couched, was that they used the daily press to decry old German ideas and traditions, and especially to sneer at and secretly undermine evangelical religion. There was a grain of truth here in a bushel of chaff. It is largely true that the Jew element is active in the press, and this because it is a large and rich element in the community. It is said there are over forty-five thousand Jews in Berlin alone, and that one in every ten of the educated men of Prussia is of that extraction. The skeptical tone of the press is merely a reflex of that of its readers. The pride of the Berliner is that his city is the home of free thought; that all shades of belief and unbelief receive respectful hearing, and can freely seek out its circle of sympathizers. The undoubted tone of intellectual Berlin is skeptical, and the prudent Jew who owns or writes for a newspaper knows on which side his bread is buttered.

The prevailing religion is the Lutheran. I attended very many services in different churches during my stay, and always, with one exception, found them poorly attended, and mostly by women of middle age. Ordinarily not many men were present. The exception was the little, old-fashioned church formerly in charge of the celebrated Schleiermacher, and now under the sacerdotal care of Pastor Panck. He preaches every two weeks, and the edifice is filled to overflowing with the gentler sex, who evidently admire the pastor greatly, for he has sympathetic earnestness, and a clear, deliberate eloquence, which is more of the heart than the head. On the intervening Sundays there is a beggarly array of empty benches. The Catholic population have a grand, roomy edifice, modeled after the Pantheon at Rome, the Church of St. Hedwig, which is usually quite well filled.

Fortunately for the Germans, they never accepted Calvinism and its depressing austerities. Consequently, with both Protestants and Catholics, Sunday is a feast and holiday—a day when rational enjoyment can supplement religious exercises.

Church services usually begin at ten o'clock. Most of the shops are closed during the entire day, though a few open after the close of the religious services. Work and business generally cease, and the people give up the afternoon and evening to enjoyment. In winter the numerous popular concerts begin as early as four o'clock in the afternoon, and at the theaters it is quite common to have a concert from four or five until seven, and then the usual performance. These places are always crowded on this day, and the eating, drinking, and smoking of the festive populace goes on simultaneously with the strains of Wagner or Strauss. In the warm days of May, and in summer, the Thiergarten and Charlottenberg are filled with promenaders, and the out-door concerts are crowded. The charming Zoölogical Gardens are then also filled with spectators. Sunday afternoon is also the favorite time for family visiting.

The churches, except one or two of recent construction, are exteriorly of little architectural merit, and internally are as uncomfortable as hard, straight-backed, uncushioned seats can make them. In winter they are badly heated; a horrible chill pervading the atmosphere. The clergyman preaches his sermon from a little round tub of a pulpit, perched up on the side of the wall, like a bird's nest against a barn, so that one must almost dislocate his neck to keep him in view. One is almost disposed to think that the effort was to make the place of worship as uncomfortable as possible; and certainly a regular attendance in any of them evidences unusual religious ardor.

Socially, the clergyman is respected; but his office does not at all put him in the social foreground. Of course, if he indicates superior talent, he makes his weight felt, and will take corresponding rank among his fellows; but, from what I learned, I should say that he has not the social estimation that our clergymen have merely from their calling.

Perhaps it goes without saying that the Germans are a musical people; and one is, therefore, not surprised at the number of musical entertainments in Berlin. Music fills a large space in all social enjoyments. You will hardly meet a man or a woman who is not an instrumentalist, or who cannot sing. Leipsic claims to be the musical center. Its conservatory and its *Gewandthaus* concerts are world-famous. But now both Stuttgard and Berlin are disputing its long-time supremacy, and those competent to judge believe that the ultimate leadership will fall to the metropolis. Certainly the musically inclined can get their fill there. During the winter, there is not an evening when one cannot hear music of the highest order. There is continued succession of concerts at the Singakadamie. The Royal Opera gives performances nightly; and, in addition, there are concerts by specialists. The popular concerts are almost without number, especially on Sunday and holiday evenings. Wagner's music is much played; and those who, like myself, cannot at first appreciate it come soon to like it after hearing it performed by large, well trained orchestras. Those who are fond of choral singing find an exquisite treat in that to be heard every Sunday morning at the Dome Church, rendered by a choir of boys. But the characteristic popular concerts are those at Bilse's, and which are given every evening in the year—in winter, until May 1st, at his hall on the Leipsiger Strasse, and in summer at the magnificent Palm House, at Charlottenberg. To hear a Bilse concert at its best, one must go on Sunday evening, and go early in order to secure a place in the *Saal*, which is the most democratic but best part of the house. The concert usually begins at six and lasts till ten o'clock. There are four parts, with intermissions of about fifteen minutes; so that the hearer gets three hours of music for an entrance fee of nineteen cents. If you take a seat at one of the tables, you are expected to order at least one glass of beer or a cup of coffee or chocolate, which will cost a few cents more. For this trifling fee, one can have an evening of excellent music, very nearly, if not quite, as well rendered as at a concert of Thomas in New York, where one pays a dollar and a half for a seat. This *Saal* is long and wide, and is filled with small tables, and as the evening progresses their occupants will be eating and drinking and smoking, and all chatting, during the lulls between the pieces, in loud confusion; and very soon a cloud of bluish tobacco smoke will float up into the high spaces between the upper tiers of boxes. If one does not care to sit at one of the tables in the *Saal*, he can find a seat in the balcony for thirty cents, or he can have a roomy *loge*, with seats for ten persons, for one dollar and a quarter, in addition to the entrance fee of nineteen cents for each person. It is quite common for a party of ladies to go alone and occupy one of the tables in the *Saal*, and knit and take supper. Down below is a huge restaurant, called the "Tunnel," which is always crowded during the intermissions. There are seventy performers, all good instrumentalists, who occupy a platform at the farther end of the hall. As I said, these concerts are given every evening in the year, and it was always to me a matter of wonderment how any man could arrange three hundred and sixty-five different programmes. I happen to have one of these programmes by me, and it is a fair sample of the average. There are three numbers from Wagner—the "Overture to Rienzi," the "Trauermarch," from the *Götterdämmerung*, and the "Evening Star Song," from *Tannhäuser*; also from Schubert, Haydn, Strauss, Rossini, Meyerbeer, Rubenstein, Liszt, Gounod, Doppler, Verdi, and Berlioz. I noticed when I was there, and it was pretty often, that two or three things from Wagner would be given, and they were always much applauded. During the winter, Edward Strauss brought his orchestra up from Vienna, and drew crowded houses during the short time he remained in Berlin. He played his own and his brother's compositions almost exclusively, and their exquisite rendering almost lifted the audience to their feet and sent them whirling off in the enchanting mazes of the dance. It was a treat to watch Strauss. He stood facing the audience, violin in hand, and would, rather impassively, lead through the prelude. But when the music moved into the swell of the dance, he commenced to play with a movement that undulated gracefully in accord with the rollicking harmony, seeming to move the melody along and make himself part of it. I remember that, in response to an *encore*, the band struck up the "Blue Danube Waltz," and notwithstanding it is old, and has been played to death upon pianos and hand-organs, the rendering of the opening bars was so charming that the audience spontaneously broke out into rapturous applause. There is an excellent musical conservatory at Berlin, under the leadership of Joachim, and, in addition, multitudes of opportunities to study music inexpensively.

Berlin has also many excellent theaters; but one must be well up in the German language to enjoy a German play. The *Schauspielhaus*, as it is called—that is, the Royal Theater—is subsidized by the Government, and presents standard plays in the best manner. The Germans possess an excellent translation of Shakspere's drama, by Schlegel and Tieck, and they are as frequently played as upon our stage; and, though I am not prepared to say that they are better appreciated than with us, yet I am inclined to think they are more enjoyed. On Shakspere nights, the Schauspielhaus is always filled, though the pieces will be rendered only by the usual stock company. If one wishes to see comic opera well played in the true, rollicking spirit, he must go to the Friederick Wilhelmstädtisches Theater, north of the Unter den Linden. At Kroll's, on the beautiful König's Platz, there is ample garden space, which in the summer evenings is a veritable fairy scene of brilliancy; here good operas are given during the warm season. Spectacular pieces prevail at the Victoria. The Louisenstadtisches also does considerable comic business of the operatic style. Far over in the north-eastern part of the city is the Ostend Theater, a really excellent establishment. Then there are the Wallner, the National, the Residenz, the Belle Alliance, and the Wilhelm—all good theaters. If one wants to go alone, without his wife, and see broad fun, he will find his way to the Variété, or the American, or the Flora, or the Walhalla. There are other theaters of a cheaper order; in fact, I believe there are, all told, twenty-three theaters, not concentrated, but scattered all over the city. The acting in the better class places is very good, and the scenery and stage effects excellent. The companies are all very much larger than ours, and when it is necessary they crowd the stage with characters. Especially is this the case at the two royal establishments. I remember in the second act of *Tannhäuser*, the ample stage, in the scene in the hall of the Wartburg Castle, was filled with a crowd of magnificently dressed guests; certainly one hundred and fifty persons were on the scene.

The performances commence early, and are out early, usually beginning at seven, sometimes at half past six, and ending between half past nine and ten o'clock. The theaters fail, in comparison with ours, in the interior decorations. They are, in this respect, plain and somewhat dingy. There is a parquette, also open balcony seats in a portion of the first tier opposite the stage, but the sides are taken up by various sized *loges* and boxes. With such a variety of places, there is a corresponding variety in the entrance prices. In the Royal Theater there are nine different prices, ranging from one dollar seventy-five cents down to twenty-four cents; in those next in rank the parquette price will be seventy-five cents. At the Schauspielhaus, when a piece is popular, it will not be played every night until it ceases to draw, but it will be repeated only once, and if very popular, possibly twice, a week. Every evening there is a change of programme, and often two or three or more popular plays will be going along at the same time. I was told that one reason for this daily change is because there are a great many regular subscribers for seats, and many who subscribe for one or more specific nights in each week. On Sunday morning the newspapers give the programme for the ensuing week at the Opera and Royal Theater. It is not uncommon for a lady, and it is quite frequently the case for two ladies, to go to either of the royal establishments without a gentleman escort. There is very little display in dressing at any of the places of amusement. At the Opera and Royal Theater the ladies go without bonnets, otherwise the toilets are as usual, only that conspicuousness seems to be avoided.

It may be premature to say that Berlin is also gradually assuming the position of art center of the empire. The partisans of Munich, Dresden, and Dusseldorf, will not admit that such can possibly be the case, yet it seems to me that art cannot resist the centralising tendencies which are gradually drawing the genius and talent of the country in all departments to the political metropolis. In the National Museum are a few good pictures, and many of the good, ordinary, second-rate kind. I have been surprised at the exceedingly meager display of passable paintings, outside of this collection, reachable by the general public.

German artists are conscientious, painstaking—in truth, almost oppressively so; but they absolutely fail in that subtle artistic sense which is native to the French, and which puts something into their pictures which is seen and felt, but cannot be closely analyzed. However, I say this with some hesitation, because it is counter to what American artistic friends in Germany, in whose judgments I have confidence, have insisted with emphasis in disputes we have had upon this question. They admit that the French are greater masters of *technique* than the Teutons, but insist that they have not so much expression—that there is more artificiality and surface work, and less soul. After all, one must at last fall back upon one's own tastes, and, fortunately, the ranges of art are broad enough for each one to follow his own bent without quarreling with his neighbor. The sculpture in the National Museum is of a much higher grade than the painting. During the winter, a magnificent group in marble, Prometheus chained to the rock, was placed in the lower hall, and was always surrounded by crowds of admirers.

The old Museum, as I remarked, has no exceptionally fine paintings, but it is so arranged as to make it, probably, the best gallery in Europe in which to study the history and development of art.

The Berlin University, though relatively a modern foundation, has become not the rival, but the equal, of that of Leipsic. It was established by an edict of Friederich Wilhelm III., in 1810, and the first year had four hundred and fifty students; now there are more than three thousand. Among the earlier professors were Fichte in philosophy, Schleiermacher in theology, Savigny in jurisprudence, and Niebuhr in history. At present it has a corps of remarkable men, among whom are some whose fame extends over both hemispheres—Gneist in jurisprudence, Dubois-Raymond in physiology, Virchow in pathological anatomy and histology, Helmholtz in physical science, Von Freitscke and Droysen in modern history, Mömmsen in Roman history, Held in political economy, Lepsius in Egyptology, Curtius in Greek and Roman archæology and Greek history, Grimm in the history of German art, besides a host of others distinguished in their several specialties. The university buildings are on the north side of the Unter den Linden, nearly opposite the Emperor's palace, and are roomy, but rather dingy and gloomy.

If one is passing between eight and nine o'clock in the morning, he will see the little court-yard abutting on the street filled with young men walking up and down, many of them munching a modest breakfast of sandwiches. These young gentlemen are awaiting the commencement of the lecture hours. A visitor is at liberty to enter any of the lecture rooms, and listen to a single lecture, though, of course, if he attends regularly, he must be entered as a student. There are, however, public lectures delivered by many of the professors, which any one can attend for a very small fee.

During the winter of 1879–80 there were between fifty and sixty American students—fine, representative young men, who were there for work, and not to play.

One is constantly meeting on the streets young men with great scars seaming the left side of the face in all directions. These youngsters are members of the dueling corps, who have been through the farce of a student duel. This absurd caricature of a genuine affair of honor still prevails among a limited number of students, and these prudent swash-bucklers get a cheap reputation for valor among the girls and their silly comrades. Once in a while an American is tempted to make a fool of himself by joining one of these dueling, beer-drinking corps, but I am glad to know that they are exceptional cases. It is said that there are various devices, such as introducing red wine or raw meat into the wounds, to magnify the scars. The dueling custom, fortunately, is dying out in the universities. It has degenerated to such depths of nonsense that certainly it must eventually die of ridicule. This would have been its fate long since were the Germans more susceptible to ridicule.

The universities are powerful factors in the political and social life of Germany. On the political side their influence is deeply felt, through the vast army of civil servants who carry on the administration of a Government which reaches and regulates the innermost relations of the citizen's life. All the members of this beaurocracy, except of the lowest grades, are university men. Moreover, there is a rich literature in speculative politics emanating from university professors, and in practical politics, in the representative bodies, the Landtag and Reichstag, Gneist, Virchow, and Treitscke are prominent men. It cannot be denied, however, that the tendency is to produce *doctrinaires*—men who have worked up to their own satisfaction certain theories, which they insist upon seeing carried out to their logical consequences—and, considering this, it is not strange that *cathedrâ* socialism is a university product. On the social side, the university gives a peculiarly intellectual tone to Berlin, which may be characterized as boldly speculative, and, withal, rich and varied. A man or woman may think or believe what he or she pleases, and meet with no cold social reception, if outside the common current.

The military element, which embraces largely the aristocracy and the conservative classes, and their hangers on, and is a dominant power, is not in accord with the university element. The champions of brute force look with disdain upon the professorlings, as they designate them, as bookish theorists, and yet there is no army in the world where book-knowledge earns a better reward than in that of Prussia. The hostility necessarily grows out of the fundamentally opposite tendencies of the two pursuits. University life infallibly leads to free thought, to independence, to mental (if not actual) insubordination, and to individuality. Military life, on the contrary, always tends to restricted thought, unquestioning obedience, strict subordination of both body and mind to another, and the sinking of the individual in the regiment.

Bismarck and his sect are also very much of the same mind as the army men; and this is by no means strange, because all his successes and all his policy stand upon the unsparing use of military force. Under these circumstances, Berlin is not socially homogeneous, but has its distinct circles, which only touch each other upon their outer edges.

During the winter there were sessions of four different representative political bodies—the Landtag, which is the lower house of the Prussian Parliament; the Herrenhaus, which is the upper chamber; the Bundesrath, which is the assembly of the representatives of the different States comprising the empire, like our Federal Senate; and the Reichstag, which is composed of the direct representatives of the entire body of the German people throughout the whole empire. I visited all of them except the Bundesrath, which does not hold open sessions.

The appearance of the members of all these bodies was very much like that of our House of Representatives; though, perhaps, there was a larger proportion of elderly men. In the Reichstag, the four hundred members were crowded together on seats behind narrow desks, very much like a lot of schoolboys. In front of, and just below, the presiding officer is a tribune, from which the member speaking addresses the house, though a member has the privilege, if he desires, to speak from his place. To the right and left of the tribune are double rows of narrow desks, at which the members of the Ministry sit. The current business of these several bodies goes along much more quietly than with us. When a proposition is up for discussion the President of the body announces that Herr So-and-so has the word; thereupon the gentleman named walks up to the tribune, delivers his speech, and retires. During its progress, perhaps there will be short, sharp expressions of approbation, or the reverse, from different sides of the chamber; then the Chair names another member whose turn has come, and so on until the debate is closed.

I was present at the debate upon the proposition of the Government to increase the army.

All the principal members—among them Count von Moltke, Benningsen, Reichart, Gneist, Eulenberg, and the Social Democrats, Liebknecht and Hebel—spoke. General von Moltke, though eighty years of age, stands erect, and speaks in a clear, direct, and forcible manner. The prevailing style in the oratory was quiet and undemonstrative, and the entire discussion, extending over two days, upon a project which was of great interest to a tax-ridden people, and which was attracting attention all over Europe, was conducted in a peculiarly quiet way.

It is apparent that among the body of the people there is not much political activity. The day of great organized political parties has not yet arrived. The Reichstag is split into many fractions, none of them at present of any great vitality, and Bismarck seems to use one or the other, or several together indifferently, as it suits his purpose. Ministerial responsibility is unknown, and parliamentary government is as yet in the experimental stage.

It is difficult, without a close following, to understand the aims and significance of the different political parties. In a general way it may be said that the Center comprises the Ultramontane, or clerical Roman Catholic, members. The Conservatives are composed of the Junkers, or country squires, and those who are averse to liberalism and all new-fangled ideas. The National Liberals, until recently the controlling party, are believers in a free parliamentary government, coupled with German unity. Of the two, they place a higher value upon unity, looking upon a firm knitting together of all parts of the Fatherland as the first and essential step toward true political freedom. This party stood heartily by Bismarck, until he began to abandon free trade and coquette with the Ultramontanes, when it showed symptoms of splitting up, and at present is in a critical condition of uncertainty.

The Fortschrittpartei is composed of advanced liberals, who insist always not only upon representative parliamentary government, but also upon a strict ministerial responsibility, and likewise upon guarantees of personal liberty, such as those of our Constitutional Bill of Rights.

The Free Conservatives constitute a fraction which I confess I do not know where to place. As far as I can understand their aims, they constitute a roving force of emancipated, old-style Conservatives who are inclined to liberalism, but yet somewhat afraid of it. In addition to these, are the Social Democrats, with, as yet, only a few members, though behind them is really a very large constituency, and two or three Poles, and a member or two from Schleswig-Holstein, who stand always in the attitude of protestants against the absorption of their countries into Prussia; and in the same category must be placed the representatives from Alsace and Lorraine.

During the period of my stay Bismarck only appeared once in the Reichstag, and then very unexpectedly. He remained only long enough to deliver a short, bitter speech, berating the Ultramontane Center, and then as suddenly departed, so that I did not have an opportunity of hearing the great man, much to my regret.

I cannot conclude the recollections of my pleasant winter experiences in Berlin without speaking of the American colony there. It was small, less than a hundred and fifty in number, made up of a very few permanent residents, some ladies there for artistic or musical work, some with their families for purposes of instruction, and the American students at the University. Every one was there for some distinctive object aside from mere amusement. Paris absorbs the idlers and mere pleasure-seekers among our countrymen who visit the continent. Naturally, from his official position, and yet more from his national reputation and personal qualities, Hon. Andrew D. White, the American Minister to Germany, is the central figure of this little colony, and most worthily and efficiently represents our country at the German Court. The traditions of our diplomatic service fortunately reserve this post for a man of scholarly reputation; and certainly Mr. White is a fit successor to Wheaton, Bancroft, and Bayard Taylor, and his accomplished wife and daughter are excellent representatives of our best American social culture. At Mr. White's receptions and dinners, one could meet many of the representative men in German literature, art, philosophy, and politics; such men as Auerbach, Richter, Knauss, Meyerheim, Treitschke, Gneist, Curtius, Lepsius, Mommsen, Lasker, and many others. The Rev. Dr. Thompson unfortunately died a short time before I reached Berlin, and consequently I was denied the pleasure of his acquaintance. He was foremost in the little American colony, and his loss is still deeply mourned by its members. From Germans who were personally acquainted with him, I learned that during his residence of five or six years in Berlin, he had attained a recognized position of honor among its intellectual leaders as a man of learning and ability, and had made himself generally known and beloved among the people. W. W. Crane, Jr.

ALBUM VERSES.

Side by side in sun and shadow,
Underneath the self-same sky,
Walk we in the self-same pathway,
Though the days and years go by.
All the blossoms and the bird-songs,
All the hill-slopes in the sun,
All the shine of far-off waters,
Are the same for every one.

Walk we side by side together,
Far apart as sun from sun;
Though the world we see together
Be the same for every one,
Yet the soul-world where each walketh
Never foot of other knew;
Dumb to others all its bird-songs,
All unknown its sacred blue.

If with loving search and faithful,
Following the far-off light,
Still we seek for truth and beauty,
Still we keep the path of right,
Heart to heart we know together
All the world, about, above—
All the sacred hights of Duty,
All the holy sky of Love.

MILICENT W. SHINN.

FISHING ON THE WINNIE-MAME.

The shadow of Mount Persephone still hung over a pretty bend of the Winnie-mame, or Mc-Cloud river. A grateful shade would last for an hour or more ere the river bank and middle distance of the mountain faded away in that indescribable grayish-white haze that heralds the first shaft of sunlight.

The hush that awaits day affected even the party of trout-fishers who came quietly down the bank to the boat that grated on the pebbly shore under the great oak, whose branches swept the water. When all were ready, a gentle push sent the craft swinging slowly out into the eddy with her load of earnest workers. Gliding a few yards up stream, cautiously turning into a current that shot them down with lightning rapidity, then another skillful maneuver, finished the Z shaped course, and landed them across the river in a little mooring between two rocks.

Wire cage, fishing lines, rods, and bait were ready. A hook of flies peeped out of one pocket, but the old boatman had no faith in them for this particular spot at this time of year. It was cool and early, and when each one had selected the deep, dark pool, behind a rock or under the shade of bushes, where he hoped for bites, the calm of great expectations in the fishing line settled on the disciples of Isaak Walton. The deep shadows on the mountains, the half-awake looking house over the river, an Indian paddling a canoe just above the rapids, the far-away bark of a shepherd-dog, and the tinkle of a cow-bell up some *cañon*—these were the only sounds that broke the stillness of the morning air. After a while all is still, and fish after fish is taken as the party settle themselves down to work. The graceful bend of a rod, and the taut line, followed by the sudden glimpse of a trout swung ashore, show where one fisherman has hidden away. Just the broad-brimmed hat of another peeps over a low bush. Two men and a little girl make a fine picture on that broad, flat rock. The child, with the unconscious instinct of appropriating everything, has thrown aside her own hat, and sheltered her head with one of he great "umbrella" leaves, as she calls them, the green scollops framing the little gypsy face with piquant grace. It is the *saxifraga peltota*. The Indians call it *tortis*, and eat the stems as we do rhubarb. In very shady places along the river bank these leaves attain a circumference of ninety inches.

Syoo-lott (Indian name), or trout, large and small, with the magenta stripe down their silvery sides—how one's mouth waters to think of them broiled and well seasoned! When we go camping we will show you how they can be cooked in hot ashes. If a *wye-dar-derk-et* comes up on the hook, it is a great prize, for one is seldom found so far south in the river. Up near Horseshoe Bend, sixty miles to the north, the campers bring in two-pound beauties, ornamented with spots, which are deep salmon-colored on their backs, fading almost to a pink on the sides. The Indian name is pretty, but some one once said that they looked as if they wore "Dolly Varden" dresses, and this name has clung to them ever since. They are very dainty eating.

Plenty of white fish come greedily for your bait, but the innumerable little bones are an objection. Suckers we don't want. The mud or bull fish are a nuisance to the fisherman. Only about four inches long, they take the bait in their great, ugly mouths with such vim that you cannot but feel annoyed at the extra little jerk you give your rod, thinking of the fine trout which you expect to whisk up out of the water. Don't throw it back, for it will eat up the salmon eggs in spawning time. Even the Indians won't eat the ugly thing. They call it *chatt-all-us*.

Our lines are not for salmon, so we don't cast them far out, where their jumping and splashing is scarcely heard above the roar of the rapids.

"Why, we have caught more fish than that," said one, as the floating cage was opened for a finny member.

"Oh! There is a hole in the wire, and the small ones are going out as fast as we put them in."

The box is lifted on the rock, and the fish squirm out in all directions.

"Catch that big one going off the rock," exclaims the little girl, as she makes a jump for the shining wriggler; losing her footing, and, against her will, hastening to make the acquaintance of the little water-ousel (*sour-sinny*, as the Indians call it) that has been bobbing around under the water in search of a breakfast. But a strong hand grasps her dress with, "Shure, and ye most went after him yerself, that."

The hooks were soon baited with the tempting red salmon eggs, and another breakfast was well under way, when a most impatient exclamation startled the fishers, and there, sure enough, on the other side of those bushes, sat that "respectable tramp," so much a part of the scenery, with his Rip Van Winkle clothes, that he looked like the stump of some dead tree. This time he held in his hand a broken fishline, not a decayed gun. Away went that provoking salmon—line, hook, and all—after "Rip" had stolen out so early, and played with that fish for nearly an hour.

"Come over and breakfast on our trout," was all the consolation he got from the boat-load, as they pulled up the rapid stream, and soon disappear on the other bank.

Another salmon must pay for the loss of that fine fellow; and pulling a bit of jerked venison and a cracker from his pocket, our piece of scenery went to work again, fishing and eating. One hour—two hours passed. The sun arose higher and hotter. The Indians became curious. A white man sitting there in the hot sun, fishing for the fun of it, when there was plenty of fish at the house, was something that they, with their dislike of unnecessary exertion, especially on a hot day, could not understand. So old Mum-dal-muk sculled himself across the river to see the *ti-patoo* (white man) land the big salmon that was on the end of the line that wound up and ran off the little clicking reel. Nearer and nearer the salmon came to his destiny, now sulking down in that big hole, where he may stay fifteen or twenty minutes; again making a desperate effort for liberty, and starting up stream, but showing signs of fatigue, and coming slowly to the surface, flapping his tail out of the water with a good-bye sort of an air. Now, reel him up, and keep the line tight. The hook is strong, and the fisherman has a firm hand on the rod. Spasmodic twitchings, faint squirms of the body, a gentle wiggle of the tail—the line is winding around the reel slowly but surely, bringing him in to a good landing-place. The dip-net is ready. But he is not caught yet, for buzz goes the reel, and the line flies out yards down stream. Mum-dal-muk, in evident disgust, says, "Indian fish to-night—come;" and, stepping into the canoe, goes back, probably, to expatiate on the folly of the white man, who works so hard for one fish.

It was the last effort of life on the part of the salmon, for soon after he was wound in with little trouble, and a quick dip landed the eighteen-pounder safely in the meshes of the net. "Rip" and his prize are soon seen crossing the dam, but he stops, apparently interested in something going on among the Indians. Catching up a big hat that lies, for convenience, anywhere on the porch, and with curiosity for a companion, we saunter down to the dam. Con-choo-loo-loo, Ki-o-cha, and a number of Indians seem to be the actors; and as we round the old dead tree, and step on the narrow plank of the dam, our right hand involuntarily seizes the little fence of poles and grape-vines, for we seem about to rush through the wooden grating in the water with the hurrying stream.

At this instant a long black stick shoots into the water, very like a pitchfork with long, slender candle-extinguishers on each point. These caps are about four inches in length and an inch around at the base, made of wood, and tipped with a splint of the deer's shin-bone, which is sharp and strong. The whole is smeared with tar; then each end of a two-yard rope is fastened into the side of each cap. The middle of this rope is firmly attached, with slack-line by a slip-noose, to the handle of the spear, about half way up. When thrust into the fish, the spear goes with such force that it pierces through; the little caps come off the two prongs and turn, and the fish swims clear of the spear, held only by the rope, that tightens on the handle with the strain. This spear mutilates the fish, but secures many more than could be taken with hook and line. The Indians have, however, a bone hook, without a barb, that they used long before white men came among them. The steady hands and sure aim of the Indians made them very successful. The poor luck of the white men, as each in turn tried his hand, raised a grunt of contempt among the natives. All along the dam the spears flew fast. A little Indian boy cuts a stout willow stick, and, stringing a couple of fish, slings it over his shoulder, to the utter disregard of his clothing, and trudges up the hill to the Chief's wigwam, just in sight. In a short time he is back, followed by a squaw, and together they carry off the fish. If we were to follow them home, we would find the eaves of the hut, the branches of the trees, the rude fence, and every place where a fish could be hung, ornamented with dripping salmon, opened, cleaned, dressed, without salt, and drying, soon to be packed away for winter use. The roe, a special luxury, is carefully hung up by itself to dry.

Tramping up the river one day, we thought we saw a small wigwam built out over the water, and connected with the shore by a narrow walk of small sticks laid across two long poles, like a narrow-guage corduroy road. Closer inspection proved it to be one of the Indian salmon spearing houses. Over a swift, deep riffle, two stout poles are driven into the river bottom, meeting at the top, cone shaped. Around these a kind of basket frame-work is made, the whole thickly thatched with willow-brush, that falls to the water and runs up several feet above the apex. The poles from the land, being fastened to the frame and covered with sticks, help to make a floor in the side of the house nearest the shore. The other half has no floor. The Indian crawls in through a small opening from the narrow walk, stretches himself on the platform, which is a foot above the water, and there awaits, spear in hand, for his salmon. The hut being about six feet high, gives him plenty of room to raise the spear; and the only light in the dim, shady place, coming up through the water, enables him to see clearly to the bottom of the river. This is a cunning invention of their own, generations old. We are not so enthusiastic as the scientific fisherman, and, as the sun is blazing away at one hundred and thirty degrees, we pick out all the shady paths, until we find ourselves on the porch, sheltered by hop-vines, quite content to wait until after sunset, and see the white men haul the seine down on the "fishing ground," as a pretty little half-moon stretch of pebbly river-shore was called.

The gray rocks were still in a blaze of sunlight glory. The shadows had come down the western hills, crossed the river, and just frowned on Joaquin's wigwam, when a voice sang out, "Fishing ground!" The path lay across the house-yard, over the shady kitchen porch, past the bunk-room, and out of the little gate. From there the ground sloped to the level of the river. A rise of land lifts us to the stage-road, and in sight of a little house built close to the hill. We rest a moment, and sing out, "Hallo, artist!" as we catch sight, first of a hat with a blue ribbon painted on it, and then of the genial face of the wearer. We move aside to let a couple of savage looking Indians pass on horseback, and, a little farther on, step over quite a stream of water that comes tumbling out of one end of a long, queer looking structure, built under a hill, like a miniature snow-shed on stilts. This is the old trout-hatching house; and the volume of water that runs through it from the hillside spring, and falls out of the other end, has made for itself such a robber-looking retreat under those big trees that we wonder if the barrels back in the shade are part of the spoil.

A natural rocky gateway seemed to form an entrance to the fishing ground, which just then presented a lively scene. The big boat was partly drawn up on the shore. A little Indian boy in it leans far enough over the bow, that bobs up and down in the shallow water, to make you think that a ducking would do his small hands, face, feet, and clothes lots of good. Some distance back from the water's edge, a number of Indians and white men are unwinding the great seine from the skeleton windlass where it was put to dry the night before. The old horse stands near the pulley, ready for work.

On the northern point of the little half-moon, under the shelter of two trees, ash and fig (the latter a lonely stranger, standing on historic ground), was a roomy arbor, open to the river, so thoroughly shaded that the rows of tin pans on the shelves shone like silver in the dim light. This was where the eggs were first put after having been taken from the fish to be hatched artificially. To sit on the platform that extended out over the water, and fish for trout, was happiness.

The southern point of the curve darkened off into black oaks and alders. Here some campers had built a fire, and, leaving the kettle of water to boil, they joined the fishermen, to lend a hand, and get a fish for their evening meal. The nets were now piled up on the stern of the boat, and the long ropes lay on the sand. The oarsman takes his place, and rows up stream a short distance, and turns; then the man at the net throws the folds into the water, one great lap at a time, while the boat is making a sweeping circle in the river. Twenty white men and Indians have hold of the two lines, and the old black horse stands ready to add his strength. The net is out. The boat comes in, having described a great circle. An Indian secures it as the men jump ashore and help pull in the net. And now all is excitement. The horse staggers off; the men shout and tug at the rope; the river foams with the struggles of the fish; the dogs rush wildly into the water. Nearer and nearer the great net of fish comes to the shore. "Rip" and the party of manning fishers have a hand on the ropes, and are "in at the death." Then comes the distribution. Those suitable for spawning are placed in the "fish corral," fenced off in the river by the arbor. Others are thrown back in the water. The Indians take what fish they want, and pitch them upon the sand, where little black-eyed fellows dart around with clubs and knock them on the head until dead. The campers have their fish, but it is getting late in the season, and the fishermen won't eat them; so none go to the house. Joe comes down from a rock, where he stood counting, and watching with quick eye, the number of salmon that went into the *corral*, back in the river, or on shore. The net is pulled up on the sand, straightened out, and wound around the wheel, where little Indian boys have been playing and swinging for the last hour. The squaws get up from around the little fires, where they were quietly looking on, pick up a fish or two, and trudge up the various trails to their *rancherias*. The Indians string a dozen or more of the fish on a pole, two of them taking it over their shoulders. Jim rides the horse home, and the rest of the men talk over the big haul as they look around to see that nothing is left small enough for an Indian to steal, and then start for home through the stone gateway.

"Pretty good haul. Hope for more next week. Will make two or three hauls in an evening then. Too many grilse. Not many for the *corral*. Did you see that deformed one? Regular curvature of the spine. Coming down to see the Indians swim and dive for fish to-night? They generally go in about eleven. Have some kind of an outlandish name for the performance. Think it sounds like *noo-ri-noo-pee*."

The voices die away in the distance. The artist lingers on the way, and his eye wanders over the river, and up the dark, ravined hill, where bright stars seem to be shining among the trees. These wild firesides are all pictures to him. Then he dreams over the scenes of the day, and longs for eleven o'clock, that he may have another view for his imaginary canvas.

Bright bonfires blazed along the river's edge, between the fishing ground and an old encampment, lighting up the dark river and gloomy mountains with weird glancing specters. Picturesque groups of swarthy Indians, clad in bright colors, held council. Little arbor shelters had been built, and many small family camp-fires winked around rocks and trees. There is little preparation for the swim as yet, for the moon still hangs just above the hill. Ancient custom and superstition call for a starlight night. The squaws seem to be preparing little delicacies for the feast in the way of roasted acorns, salmon-berries, and manzanita-berry soup. At last the moon has gone, and the few *ti-patoos*, or white men, are now interested in watching a powerful dark fellow, who is preparing a torch, some seven or eight feet in length, and half a yard or more in circumference, made of innumerable pieces of *checker-chute*, or pitch pine, bound together. This man seems to be the chief of the fishing swim, and a few words from him bring some ten or fifteen Indians from the darkness of a group of trees, each with a small lighted torch in one hand. The leader enters the bushes, two others following, one holding at each end of a net, some nine feet long. Behind them come men with stout clubs. Then follow the men with long twigs of willow, stripped of their leaves, made very limber by twisting, one end being fastened around the left wrist, the other end held in the left hand, thus making a strong loop on which to string the fish. The business of the remainder seems to be to make as much noise as possible by splashing the water, talking, and shouting. The bushes close behind them as they pass up the shore a little distance to a favorable place to enter the water.

Here they throw all the little torches in one pile. When a good blaze has sprung up the great torch is lighted, and soon the Indians below gather near the water to see the brilliant light that comes bobbing up and down over the rapids, steadied by the left arm of the swimmer, while he guides himself with his right. The force of the current carries him along with little effort on his part. The torch buoys him up, for the greater part of it is under water. The blaze, just over the swimmer's head, gives a ghastly appearance to the upturned face that ducks under the water every few moments to wash off the falling sparks. After him come the whole band, yelling through the foam, frightening and dazzling the fish with the disturbance of the water and the bright glare of the torch, which lights up everything for yards around. The men with the net disappear, as they swim right into the midst of a dark pool of salmon. The mouth of the net is closed, and three salmon floundering in the meshes, are soon dispatched by blows upon the head. Holding the mouth of the net slack, other hands take out the fish, passing them to the Indians with the willow slings, on which they are soon strung through the gills. Indians who can carry a torch successfully, or dive with the net and bring up the most fish, are held in great respect. For these accomplishments the Chief, Jim Marshall, takes the palm.

On the bronzed fishermen swim for another dark pool, the fish flapping all around them, and knocking against their bodies. Occasionally a man is bitten as the fish dash along, spasmodically opening and shutting their mouths. It must be remembered that all these maneuvers take place in a snow-fed stream, rushing impetuously in a descent of nearly fifty feet to the mile. To dodge the rocks in the rapids, and to dive in almost bottomless holes, requires both expertness and fearlessness.

Soon they have passed the encampment, and voices are heard nearly a third of a mile down the river. Only fifteen minutes have passed since they entered the water, and now they come up the shore with their dripping trophies. Tossing them to the women, they gather around the big bonfire to rest a moment and get warm. But the excitement urges them on, and again they are battling with the water and fish. Their voices ring out over the roar of the rapids. The old Chief Con-choo-loo-loo sits by the fire. Men, women, and children cast fanciful shadows, as, more or less occupied, they moved around, preparing the feast. The fish come in fast now, and count up into the fifties.

After the divers and swimmers have returned for the last time, and are seated in posts of honor, high revelry holds sway. The shore is crowded with figures. "Rip" and the artist look on. The Indian whose contempt for the man with the salmon-rod was so expressive in the morning, stands by and points in triumph to the great strings of fish, saying, "Indian get many fish," little understanding that it takes generations for a people to become inured to such severe enjoyment, and not at all convincing the white man that his way was not the best.

The fires die down; the blaze goes out; sparks smoulder and blacken; the noise grows less; dogs snatch up the remnants of cooked fish and hurry after the darkening shadows. It is long after midnight, and the fishers, civilized and uncivilized, lie wrapped in sleep.

LUCY SARGENT.

THOMAS CARLYLE.

Thomas Carlyle, the sturdy and combative Scotsman, on whose shoulders the mantle of John Knox seems at times to have rested—the lover of strength, the foe of sham, the prophet of labor, the upholder of heroes or those whom he thought were heroes—is well worth the appreciative study of each earnest soul. Called by turns the "Chelsea Sage," the "Modern Diogenes," the "Last Roman," the "Censor of His Age," Carlyle has been a problem for thinkers, and a point of attack for hosts of critics, who have called his philosophy unsound, and his use of language absurd. *The British Review*, in speaking of *Sartor Resartus*, once said that it "would probably prove an interesting book if it were only translated into English." It moves me to laughter to imagine the sort of a reception Carlyle, the cavernous-browed, must have given that particular number of *The Review*.

Hardly another author, living or dead, English or Continental, is more difficult to rightly consider. Almost against our wills we are led into partisanship. This man is no smooth dreamer nor idle rhymester. About him there is nothing *dilettante*. He holds his pen as a spear, he wields it as a dagger in the front of battle, nor is he content unless blood follows the stroke. The iron of the old Crusaders runs fierce in his veins; to write a book is to plan and win a battle. About such a man there is much to study, much to approve, and somewhat to condemn. His life is open to the world, as much, at least, as any man's life can be. We, in some measure, may, if we will, comprehend the ruggedness and inborn honesty in the very nature of Carlyle. Perhaps we shall even understand his environments, trainings, and struggles against the various devils which do so encompass our poor humanity with their pestiferous suggestions.

We cannot begin better than by a short account of the chief steps in Carlyle's career, which we may now consider as practically finished, his race being nearly run, and his last book, probably, published.

In Dumfrieshire, Scotland, there is a little village, called Ecclefechan, a pretty enough place, having rounded hills near it, and streams flowing incessantly past. Here, in 1795, Thomas Carlyle was born in a farm-house, and here he spent the earlier years of his life. His father was a shrewd and fervidly religious man, and a lineal descendant of the Scotch Covenanters. We cannot doubt that the sifting and vivifying of the old records, which gave us, years after, Carlyle's *Life of Cromwell*, had its roots in the training of his boyhood and in the traditions of his Puritan home. We shall fail to do Carlyle justice, in considering the events of his literary career, unless we clearly realize that the roots of his character cling fast to the primeval granite of one of the most reserved and earnest races the world has ever known, and that the surroundings of his earlier life only deepened the solemnities which were to him inseparable from human existence, and which, indeed, only made that existence the more divine.

Throughout Carlyle's works are glimpses which we may confidently accept as autobiographic. Often, in his riper years, when he has been smiting the Philistines, and tearing, with sardonic laughters and wild sarcasms, the follies, fripperies, and foolish sentimentalities that cloud, stain, and too often destroy earnestness, he will break off sharply, as in the midst of his crusade, and, remembering some scene of his childhood, will recall it with pathetic and wonderful tenderness. Of the nature of such a reminiscence is this, from his *French Revolution:*

"In the heart of the remotest mountains rises the little Kirk—the dead all slumbering round it, under their white memorial stones, in hope of happy resurrection. Dull wert thou, O reader, if never in any hour (say of moaning midnight, when such Kirk hung spectral in the sky), it spoke to thee things unspeakable, that went to thy soul's soul."

Glimpses like these show us the meditative lad, Carlyle, lying beside the rills that flowed beneath the Scottish pines; climbing the peaks to watch sunset and sunrise, with their unapproachable glories; following the sowers in the newly plowed fields, over ridge and hollow, till through the soft twilight the moon rose and the stars shone—yea, Sirius, in his "chains of sidereal fire."

The earlier chapters of *Sartor Resartus* are full of such autobiographical glimpses. We may, if we try, read between the lines much that it concerns us to know of his desultory habits of study, of his omniverous reading powers, of his perplexing doubts, and his fits of gloominess. At the age of fourteen he entered the University of Edinburgh, but he was soon at war with the system of education in vogue there, which he pillories, long after, in terms of unlimited denunciation. He says that what he gathered by unguided browsings among the books of the great library was all for which he had need to be grateful to his Alma Mater. This sturdy, stubborn country lad, who had few acquaintances, and almost no friends, was a mystery to his teachers, and by no one, at that period, helped in any effectual wise. He asked too many questions, and despised "straw logic" with too bitter a contempt. He was not a lad to be taken up, petted, flattered, introduced into society, put forward on public occasions. Evidently it would have been as much as one's life was worth to have suggested such a thing to young Carlyle, who studied and read as he chose, heaping unmeasured criticism upon his luckless preceptors.

After leaving the University, yielding to his father's long cherished desire, Carlyle essayed theology, with a view to the Presbyterian ministry. It could not be. Fever paroxysms of doubt overwhelmed him. In the black midnight, in dark and whispering ravines, beside the pallid breakers, shut apart from other men, alone with himself and with the Mystery of the Universe, he fought the same fierce battle which comes, sooner or later, to each one of us poor wanderers in the wilderness, girt round by desert tribes and desert hunger, but haply driven by swords of flame, led by pillars of cloud. Long afterward, Carlyle, in remembrance of his own perplexities, wrote:

> "What the light of your mind, which is the direct inspiration of the Almighty, pronounces incredible, that, in God's name, leave uncredited. At your peril do not try believing that."

The result of his self-examination was that he decided not to enter the ministry, and he became for some years a school-teacher. Soon he began that study of German authors which led him into writing as a business. He first studied Schiller, of whom he published a biography. This was in 1824, and, in one remarkable chapter, this young man of twenty-nine describes the dangers, difficulties, and advantages of the literary life.

After this *Life of Schiller* was published it was translated into German, with a commendatory preface from Goethe. For some time previous Carlyle had been studying Goethe, in whose writings he found, with an intense rapture, that his own griefs and battles had been known by others, and had by others been conquered. So, after all, he took heart, and went forward, past the lions of doubt. And I count it as one of the proofs of the essentially sound character of Goethe's work that this strong, defiant, and earnest young man found comfort and help therein.

The year 1826 brought a new era. Carlyle was married to one who was in every respect a worthy companion for him, and together they began the beautiful work of building a happy, untroubled home, which result is the flower and crown of Saxon civilization. His wife owned a small estate in Galloway, among the granite hills and black morasses. Here, within sight of the Irish Sea, in a region mainly pastoral, yet relieved by occasional fields of rye and barley, by trim white cottages, and by softly flowing vales, is the small estate of Craigen-Puttoch. *Sartor Resartus*, written here, is full of bits of descriptive scenery, which evidently apply to this place. Carlyle and his wife studied and read much. They took long rambles over the wind-blown hights, above the scintillant summer sea, and the strength and freedom of this life went into the books he wrote.

While, however, he was at work on *Sartor Resartus*, Carlyle continued his German studies. Essays appeared in the reviews on "Novalis," "Richter," "Heyne," "The Nibelungen Legends," "German Playwrights," and similar topics; and also a noteworthy essay on Burns. By these earlier essays, now collected under the title of *Miscellaneous Essays*, the world became aware that, somewhere in the wilderness, a man who had the audacity to have ideas of his own had begun to utter his message. Here was a great, shaggy-haired young Scotsman, and it was hard to know what to do with his wild enthusiasms, his whirlwinds of prophecy, his bursts of unextinguishable laughters, his white heats of indignation. But he wrote after his own fashion, in his little Craigen-Puttoch cottage, and German writers never had a more appreciative critic. In his studies of Goethe, "Mephistopheles" is an endless source of wonder and pity to Carlyle.

> "Poor devil," he says, "he is the natural, indelible deformity of wickedness. To see falsehood is his only truth. For him, virtue is some bubble i' the blood. It stands written on his face that he never loved a living soul. Coming forward, as he does, like a person of breeding, and without any flavor of brimstone, he may stand here in his merely spiritual deformity, at once potent, dangerous, and contemptible, as the only genuine devil of these later times."

But no man ever becomes very famous by merely writing of other men's work. Sainte-Beuve and Taine came the nearest to that. It is creative work which is the need of the world. So, while Carlyle was pursuing his German studies, he was putting into shape the essential particulars of his own philosophy. He wrote some poetry also, and it has true melody and quaintness. It may be doubted whether it were not in some measure a mistake for a man with such poetic fire to confine himself so entirely to prose; though, truly, his best prose has all the march and melody of an epic, and the Craigen-Puttoch book, nursed in those desolate wilds, was a grand step forward. It was *Sartor Resartus*, one of the great prose works of the century, and one of the books whose reading has marked, and will continue to mark, an epoch in the life of many a young and earnest soul.

Sartor Resartus, more nearly than any other of his works, represents Carlyle in the flush of his magnificent prime. A great, stormy, and passionate soul struggles therein for utterance, even through clouds and thick darkness; he grapples with those eternal questions of life, death, matter, spirit. No more awakening and eloquent contribution to metaphysics was ever penned by mortal man. As all deep and great spirits must, he approaches the high mysteries of the Infinite and the Eternal with awe unspeakable. Carlyle reverences, as realized human ideals, two things strongly: First, the *Church*, in its widest and most reverential sense; secondly, the *Kingship*, in its earliest meaning, when the strongest were chosen and obeyed. Glimpses of these two fundamental truths—the Church, the Kingship—we obtain in *Sartor Resartus*, as of snow-peaks seen through the deep forests; and the second of these—hero-worship—was destined to grow out of its proper proportions, and, alas! overshadow, in Carlyle's philosophy, other quite as essential matters.

But let us see if we can understand *Sartor Resartus*. The best passages are full of resonant music, whose forceful pulses thrill heart and soul. I remember once reading portions of this book to a group of rugged miners, resting from their toil. We were in a deep ravine in Northern California; a turbid river swept by; a yellow cliff of gravel, to which a few silver pines yet clung, rose abruptly three hundred feet above our heads. I had been wandering among the rugged peaks for many happy hours. I found these miners preparing for dinner, and shared their simple meal. Then they asked me what book I had; and so I read to them what Carlyle says about the dignity—nay, the absolute necessity—of work, and also that superb passage, which I would I had space to quote in its completeness, wherein "Teufelsdröckh" moralizes on the spectacle of a great city by night. These hardy, busy miners did not call Carlyle obscure, but were moved by his force, eloquence, and massive severity.

It has been said that *Sartor Resartus* was a "pantheistic" book; but Carlyle himself would be the first to deny that. It is, in the character of its philosophy, somewhat related to Kant, and also to Hamilton; but it utters forth some fundamental truths which neither Kant nor Hamilton had expressed. The central thought is this: that matter, all material things—yea, time and space themselves—are but the veils, the garments, the vestures, the habiliments of SPIRIT, which latter only is alive, all else being dead utterly. Here I must quote his words:

> "To the eye of vulgar logic, what is man? An omnivorous biped that wears breeches. To the eye of pure reason, what is he? A soul, a spirit, and divine apparition. Around his mysterious Me there lies, under all these wool-rags, a garment of flesh (or of senses) contextured in the loom of heaven, whereby he is revealed to his like."

There is nothing mystical about this. It is a simple statement of a fact, and the proposition carries its own evidence with it. Carlyle sees poetry in the commonest object about us, and finds something to study everywhere. Each one of his books is full of examples of this admirable faculty.

As I consider this subject, I am impressed with the belief that a distinguishing mark of the few men who have conquered new realms for the human mind consists in their sense of and delight in the mystery which abideth in common things. That certain men lived here once, but are not now visible; that other men are here now, but after a while—how long we do not know—will pass out of sight; that we are "such things as dreams are," and "are cut down as the grass;" that we tread the same earth as our fathers trod, and are moved by like passions; that Homer, for example, was once so intensely alive, and is now, strangely enough, but unrecognizable dust—all these things are inexpressibly wonderful to Carlyle. Solomon and Shakspere, two of the profoundest writers the world has known, are never tired of this mystery. It haunts them day and night, as a wonderful reality, as part of the Order of the Universe, and they love to speak of it. With Carlyle, TIME and SPACE are the two infinite marvels, and he says many noble things about them.

In *Sartor Resartus*, plainly visible to men, were the most passionate ardor, the most cutting sarcasm, the strangest diversities, contradictions, and absurdities. This was no smoothly finished book, written easily, with desire to please the "upper ten," and fashioned according to the schools; it was a great and living Voice, deep as a bugle-blast, loud as the sound of many waters. A son of the people spoke to the great heart of the people, and, despite its many imperfections, this strangely fascinating, noble, and original book became a classic of our English language. This new Elijah, this fire-hearted Prophet of Horeb, brings not "a gospel of despair." The book itself, full of pulses of strong life, is sufficient denial. It is the story of a pilgrimage. Teufelsdröckh crosses deserts of despair, cold winds of doubt in starless nights encompass him, but he clings fast to an all-embracing desire for truth—truth divine. So he conquers fear, he tramples Tophet under foot, he faces vast life and vaster death—at first with grim, fire-eyed defiance, afterward with new faith and love. Then he finds what he calls the Sanctuary of Sorrow, and he knows its divine patience, and knows, also, that true living begins only with renunciation. Then follows this passage, the flower of *Sartor Resartus*:

> "I see a glimpse of it," cries he, "elsewhere. There is in man a higher than love of happiness; he can do without happiness, and instead thereof find blessedness. Was it not to preach forth this same higher that sages and martyrs, the poet and the priest, in all times, have spoken and have suffered, bearing testimony, through life and through death, of the god-like that is in man, and how in the god-like only may

he find strength and freedom? Which God-inspired doctrine art thou honored to be taught, O hearer?—and broken with manifold, merciful afflictions, even till thou become contrite, and learn it? Oh, thank thy destiny for these; thankfully bear what yet remain; thou hadst need of them; the self in thee needed to be annihilated. This is the Everlasting Yea wherein all contradiction is solved."

And so, with this quotation we leave *Sartor Resartus*. Carlyle's next work was *The French Revolution*. The histories of this great event, which toppled the thrones of kings, and shook the foundations of society, were, when Carlyle began his work, a mass of contradictions. He tore them to pieces, in vivid analysis, the fruit of months of painful patience, and he painted a new picture of this volcanic outburst. Let us see how it was done. He tells us of the meaning of the French Revolution; he describes Sans-culottism, that portentous, inevitable end of so much; that danger of modern society; that rebellion and victory of unimprisoned anarchy against worn-out authority. As we read his pages the past becomes real. In this book there are three parts, three scenes in the tragedy—the Bastile, the Constitution, the Guillotine. Not a word is out of place. The mere index of one of Carlyle's books gives a sense of his power. The chapter on the storming of the Bastile has been called as stirring as one of Homer's battles, and his pen-pictures of the leaders of the Revolution are startling. We see blear-eyed, woe-stricken Marat; we hear the leonine roar of beetle-browed Mirabeau. So the story goes on, storm following storm, and tragedy succeeding tragedy, until it is a tale of woe unutterable. Carlyle never pauses, he piles simile on simile, hight on hight. His voice is deep with tears one moment; the next, cries of death and war ring in our ears. When he wishes to describe the passions of the Revolution he speaks of winds "raising the sands of the desert, and whirling them around in Sahara waltz." It is a grand similitude. The millions of France were whirled in an atmosphere of hate, terror, ambition, frenzy, and no lesser comparison could describe the portentous spectacle.

Carlyle's next works were *Chartism* and *Heroes and Hero-Worship*. The first of these is strongly in sympathy with the laboring classes. He at this time believed in universal education, though not in universal suffrage, nor had he yet begun to condemn machinery and this industrial age. *Chartism* is, therefore, chiefly interesting because it shows that at that time he had faith in the ultimate teachability of the masses. *Chartism* abounds in weighty sentences which we of California should study and heedfully cherish. He says, for instance:

"What means this bitter discontent of the working classes? Is the condition of the laborers wrong; so wrong that rational workingmen cannot, will not, and even should not, rest quiet under it? Or is the discontent itself mad, like the shape it took? Not the condition of the working people that is wrong; but their disposition, their own thoughts, beliefs, and feelings that are wrong?"

In another passage, while urging a strict poor-law, he eloquently says:

"Work is the mission of man on this earth. A day is ever struggling forward; a day will arrive in some approximate degree, when he who has no work to do, by whatever name he may be named, will not find it good to show himself in our quarter of the solar system; but may go out and look elsewhere—if there be *any* Idle Planet discoverable."

In another noble sentence, he says:

"To this English People in World History there have been—shall I prophesy?—two grand tasks assigned. Huge-looming through the dim tumult of the always incommensurable Present Time, outlines of two tasks disclose themselves: the grand Industrial Task of conquering some half or more of this terraqueous planet for the use of man; then, secondly, the grand Constitutional Task of sharing in some pacific, endurable manner the fruit of said conquest, and showing all people how it might be done."

In *Heroes and Hero-Worship* we find the same general views as those advanced in *Chartism*. Carlyle insists upon it that it is safe to appeal to men's nobler nature. This is peculiarly a book for young men. They can best appreciate its kindliness, its sympathy with the best men of every age, its fire of eloquence, and its zeal of enthusiasm. Herein the convictions of *Chartism* are developed; the only person worthy of respect is he who can and does command others.

Next comes *Past and Present*. This is a leaf from English monastic life in the twelfth century, and it describes with homely vigor the career of Abbot Sampson. The gist of *Past and Present* is a sort of hero-worship again. Find your best men, set them at work, and obey them with child-like faith—that is the lesson which Carlyle would have us learn.

After this Carlyle began one of his three greatest works. His next book was of the nature of a revelation. In order to show what he did we must remind you that Covenanter's blood flowed in Carlyle's veins, and John Knox was one of his heroes. Now, in the slow and yet persistent progress of the English people there are a few epoch events which gleam forth as stars. The bold barons at Runnymede are deathless, heroic figures; Armada days, when the brave islanders defied the galleons of Spain, are ever memorable; but of no less importance was the Puritan Revolution, the days of Pym and Hampden, of sturdy Parliament and pusillanimous king, of psalm-singing Roundhead and roystering Cavalier. It is one of the classic periods of English history. But, before Carlyle wrote his *Life of Cromwell*, this man, one of the leaders of a great people, was as one lost from record. His real life was not known; it was buried in rubbish-heaps, and only third-rate compilers had ever written of Cromwell. Cautious David Hume said that a collection of Cromwell's speeches would pass for one of the most nonsensical books of the world. Carlyle, as if in sheer defiance, took old records, fragments of letters, piles of public documents, long mouldering in silence, and with and for these he lived, month after month, until he had made once more audible the voice of one of earth's great men. Cromwell had been dumb for two hundred years, but now he forever speaks, and Carlyle's life of this noble Englishman is one of the most unassuming and eloquent books of modern biography. Through every line there beats the sturdy English heart. This land of Cromwell, Milton, Shakspere, is Carlyle's mother-land; if he denounces, it is as a prophet, with sorrow in his voice. This earnestness, rising at times to positive inspiration, makes the *Life of Cromwell* a landmark and beacon. It is a chapter of true history; a leaf of the universal gospel.

Hitherto we have seen Carlyle strong and stern enough, but nevertheless hopeful, and, on the whole, with wise and right views of life and living. When he finished his *Life of Cromwell* he was about fifty years old. His life so far had been a succession of hard battles and of glorious triumphs. Development followed development until he stood easily in the front rank of living writers. In his best moods he appealed strongly to the conscience and reason of men, and his constituency was constantly widening among thoughtful persons everywhere. It is a pity he could not have gone on in the same brave, patient way. But, from this time onward, Carlyle's obscurities of style increased; he had less patience with stumbling men, less belief in humanity, more bitter, and often cruel, sarcasm; in short, he became more and more a prophet of evil, less and less the leader of the highest hopes of men. I do not say that so great a change was at once visible. Carlyle's writings were still at times powerful for good; they still abounded in brilliant and noble passages, well worth the study of any man. But, on the whole, there is a decadence, mournful enough to those who have thrilled at the divine beauty, the divine ardor of the work of his young manhood. We can sum up Carlyle's mistake at this era in one sentence: Fault-finding in excess. He became a Radamanthine judge of the faults and the follies of his brother men. His quaint, rich humor, whose unexpected scintillations, in the midst of philosophy and analysis, often convulse the soberest of readers, becomes, in his later years, more stilted, more *bizarre*. His laughters, once so rich and infective, degenerate into unhealthy spasms. We are told that all this was the result of dyspepsia, to which grim demon Carlyle had become a slave. But this is not the whole reason. In Carlyle's scheme of philosophy there is a flaw. His brilliant conception of hero-worship, at first helpful, became wrenched out of its proper place, and finally led him into the chief errors of his later writings. We must not forget that blind hero-worship is a double crime. The essential postulate of hero-worship is hero-accountability. Our fit leaders must be purer, stronger, better, nobler than other men.

It is pitiful enough to see some of the persons whom Carlyle beatifies in his later works. There is Frederick the Great, a man by nature of a low order, a cruel, dangerous, unheroic man, whose seisure of the province of Silesia from a friendly nation and from an unprotected queen, will ever remain as one of the cruel and evil deeds of the age. This indefensible act brought on a general war in Europe. Said Macaulay, with a keen sense of justice:

> "On the head of Frederick is all the blood which was shed in a war which raged during many years, and in every quarter of the globe."

The seizure of Silesia unsheathed the scalping-knife along the frontiers of New England and New York, and our heroic fathers, pressing into the wilderness to lay the foundations of States, knew the terrors of midnight torch and creeping assassin—because this princely robber stole Silesia! For this reason the conscience of humanity revolts against Carlyle's deification of Frederick. Yet we must not deny the force of his battle-pictures, the clearness of his explanations. He makes the earlier history of Prussia as clear as a modern story. He does this by his vivid and accurate use of language, and by his own earnestness and constructive imagination. Of course we admire the pluck and energy of Frederick, but no one can call him a real hero, such as those whom Carlyle chose in his younger days.

Next in the descending scale of Carlyle's works came the *Latter Day Pamphlets*. In these he returns to social and political topics. We can, therefore, accurately measure the extent and nature of the change which has come over his philosophy. In the works of his young prime he declares that he has faith in humanity, faith in the great middle classes, faith in education, and he shows a healthy sympathy with those who are striving to carry their share of the world's burdens. In the *Latter Day Pamphlets* he calls the people "Cadarene swine," forever incapable of choosing right, and devil-driven into the sea. He does not any longer have faith in constitutional government. He even hints that an absolute monarchy is our only hope. This era, he says, is an age from which all virtue, courage, nay, even cleanliness, have departed, and society is nearing the Falls of Niagara. He sits in his little Chelsea cottage, a lonely old man, determined to bear faithful witness against this degenerate age. We still find fervid passages, his pages are still attractive, but somewhat of their earlier beauty has departed.

With deepest delight we therefore turn again to the resonant sentences of his earlier manhood, when he went forth as a young Viking to sail the seas of literature, to plant his flag on islands before unknown, to give battle with many a pirate ship, and to unsheath his sword in every deserving cause. With endless delight we return to *Sartor Resartus*, *Cromwell*, *The French Revolution*, *Past and Present*, and *Earlier Essays*. Here are well-springs perennial for all thoughtful men, not merely now, but also forever. So long as men live on this brown earth of ours, so long will the rugged and stormy eloquence, the grand invective, the sublime, prophetic ardor of this modern Elijah, this son of the desert and the wilderness, be strong to warn and strong to inspire. "Gird up your loins," so cries this fire-eyed prophet. "Gird up your loins, and quit yourselves like men."

As I read Carlyle I forget the mistakes and the harshness of his later days. I only remember with what courage he set his lance in rest, and how many altars of evil this Paladin overthrew, and against the ancient summits of how many wrongs he hurled his Thor-like hammer. Thomas Carlyle, despite all his faults, was a true helper of the children of men, was a brave, aggressive soldier in the endless war between darkness and light—so he will not be forgotten. He put his soul into accord with the nature of things, and, even in this complex, doubting, and troublous age, he did, in some wise, find expression. Therefore his life and his books are gifts unspeakable, and the gray granite of Carlyle is one of the foundation-stones of modern English prose.

CHARLES H. SHINN.

A MINER FROM ARIZONA.

She had met him in the hall twice before that day—unmistakably a fresh arrival, dressed, from the hat to the boots, in new store-clothes, bought ready-made, without much judgment or taste as to fit or material. When he walked it was with a deliberate, rather shambling, but by no means heavy step; when he stood still it was with feet wide apart, and a general air of surveying a big stretch of country around him, calmly expectant, half alert, half indifferent—too discreet to court danger, but conscious of the power to do it battle. Not an old man, and a handsome man withal, his beard blanched from exposure more than age, and the lines in his face speaking of hardships and much solitary life.

He had planted himself with his back against the balustrade surrounding the stairway, and waited for her approach, without the slightest tone of disrespect, but evidently with the intention of addressing her. Such a hungry, longing look as there was in his large eyes of bluish-grey—such an expression of being lost and alone here, in the large, strange city, more than ever he had been on his wildest, most solitary prospecting trip. Uncovering his head, he said:

"Excuse me, madam" (which proved him a Southerner—a Yankee would have said, Miss), "but I have seen you several times since I came here, and don't know any one else to ask: Is this this really the Worthington House, or not? I can't get any kind of satisfaction from the lady I rented my room of."

"This is the Worthington House; yes, sir.

"How comes she to say, then, that she is not my old pardner's wife? Old Worthington told me, years ago, that if I ever came to San Francisco, I must stop at his wife's fine lodging-house, on Kearny Street. The house is fine enough; I haven't seen anything finer in Arizona"—a humorous smile lit up his face—"but that"—indicating the parlor with a bend of his head—"ain't old Worthington's wife, and I know it."

"You are right; the present landlady purchased the place of Mrs. Smith, who bought out Mrs. Worthington several years ago. Perhaps Mrs. Ward feared to lose you as a roomer if she disclosed the fact at once that she was an utter stranger to Mrs. Worthington, or any one connected with her."

"Reckon I'll stay here now," he decided, after meditating, "seeing that I've got comfortably fixed, and found some one to talk to. You are the lady that paints the pictures?" pointing to door at the end of the hall, where a sign announced that portraits were painted in oil and water-colors. He moved slowly up to the door and contemplated a number of small portraits, mostly of actresses in elegant costumes, which were displayed in one large frame. He regarded the bright, graceful figures for a while, and then turned to his amused companion.

"What's the reason," he asked, with blunt directness, pointing with his finger to the frame, "that these women, and most all the women I see on the street, have got such bright, pretty dresses, and things on them, and only you wear a black gown like that? I didn't hurt your feelings, did I?" he asked, apprehensively, as he saw the laughing hazel eyes suddenly droop, and tears gather on the long lashes. "Indeed, I didn't mean to—and you so kind to me. Why, I'm not fit to be a white man," he continued in self-abasement; "I'm worse than an Indian to go and do such a thing as that."

"I know you did not mean to give me pain," she replied, softly. "How could you know? It was my little sister who died about eight months ago, and I am wearing mourning for her. Don't you understand?"

"Where is your mother?" he asked presently.

"Dead," was the reply.

"And your father?"

"He died two years ago in Napa. He failed in a quicksilver mining enterprise, and died of a broken spirit, I think, rather than a broken heart."

The hungry look in the man's face had changed to one of intense curiosity. He was not yet satisfied; it was, perhaps, the old prospector's instinct that urged him to push investigations further. Perhaps, too, he had never struck just such a "lead" before.

"Brothers?" he continued the examination.

"None," she answered, smiling in spite of herself. "No relatives in the world that I know of, and no friends—at least none in this part of the world."

She had opened the door to enter her studio, but noting the face of her new friend fall suddenly back into the old dreary expression, a quick pain touched her heart that any being should be more forlorn than she herself had been.

"Come into my studio," she said, "and I will show you my little sister's picture—painted by myself, from memory."

There were different pieces leaning against the wall in various stages of progress and completion—simpering faces of fat old dowagers, toned down into something like humanity by the touch of a genial brush; faces of lovely women, and handsome bearded men; but on an easel rested a flower-piece, the creamy yellow and velvety red of the rose mingled there with the sky-blue of the forget-me-not. A reflection of the warm, rich coloring seemed to flash across the stranger's features as he planted himself in front of the picture.

"My stars, but that's fine!" he exclaimed, with quite unlooked for animation. A rapid, half contemptuous glance swept the line of portraits. "I shouldn't bother with these things if I could paint like that," pointing to the flowers.

A weary sigh escaped the lady's lips.

"I paint those flowers only for recreation; the portraits pay better, and are a surer source of income to me."

He cast a keen look around the room. It was plainly furnished, though tastefully decorated.

"Must cost lots of money," he said, "although it's only a back room."

"No doubt the landlady has made him sensible of the value of a front room," she commented, inwardly. Then she said:

"Not that so much; but I still have debts to pay, contracted during the lingering illness of my poor little sister. Afterward I can indulge my own taste more than at present."

She pointed to a miniature suspended near the easel—a small body, but a head of ideal beauty.

"Was she a cripple?" he asked, hastily.

"Helplessly so. I lifted her from the bed to the lounge, and back again, to the day of her death."

"And now mourning for her like that! She must have been no end of trouble and expense to you."

She looked at him a moment, with gentle pity in her eyes.

"Have you never had any one to love—any one whom you had to care for? Don't you know that it is the purest joy we can find on earth to know that we are all in all to some one who is entirely dependent upon us—"

She hesitated and blushed. What right had she to be lecturing this man, a stranger to her?

He had regarded her silently, and with a new light breaking in his eyes.

"You're a mighty good woman," he said, with his usual directness. "Seems to me you are like my mother."

"Where is she?"

"Dead, I reckon."

"And—allow me to return some of your own questions—have you no other relatives?"

"Yes, dozens. Brothers and sisters—some in Arkansaw and some in Texas, some in the 'Nation,' and some back in Georgy, whar we were all bo'n." He had imperceptibly fallen into his native dialect during the recount. Recovering himself, he went on, as if in half apology, "But I never hear from them nowadays. The half of them may be dead for all I know."

"And you are on your way now to hunt up as many of them as you can still find?"

"Oh, Lord, no!"

It was said with such sincere horror that she repressed a laugh with difficulty.

"I came in from Arizona to see what I could do here with several mines I have in the Territory; some of them terribly rich, too. If I can sell, or only bond, them before I go back, I don't care if I buy half a dozen of your pictures myself. Flower-pictures, I mean," he added, hastily. "I don't want any of the old women you've painted here."

There was no use struggling any longer; she must laugh, in spite of herself—the merriest, heartiest laugh she had indulged in for many a long day—while he stood by, calm and unmoved, neither offended nor roused to join in her merriment.

"I mean what I say. My name is Calhoun Kendal," was all he felt called upon to offer as voucher of his honesty of intention; "and if I sell only one or two of my claims, I shall have money enough to buy stacks of such things."

"Which will be very fortunate for me," she replied, gayly. "And as you are to be a patron of mine, I cannot do less than invite you to visit my studio whenever you feel inclined. I shall always be glad to see you," she added, with sweet sincerity.

Then he made her a short bow, and left her to work on her portraits with what relish she might. One thing is certain—the lady with the most pugnacious nose had that aggressive feature of her face softened into comparative loveliness in the course of the afternoon; the artist seemed to paint something of her own beauty into the picture.

Margaret Benson's sitting-room adjoined her studio; and she belonged to that large class of much-to-be-pitied San Franciscans who go, day after day, to eat their solitary meals at a restaurant. Not but that San Francisco restaurants are good. Let him who dares find fault with any of our "peculiar institutions"—but it does seem a very undomestic manner of living. Flushed with triumph at having accomplished that much dreaded and dreadful nose, Miss Benson took up her hat and wrap and started in search of her unsociable dinner. On the stairs she overtook her new friend, who stood still, to give her the opportunity of passing by or addressing him, as she might choose.

"One more unfortunate, going in quest of dinner?" she asked, laughing. "Come with me, if you have not yet established yourself permanently at any one place. I know they make you pay three times as much as you ought to at the place where you have been in the habit of going."

"How do you know where I have been in the habit of going?" he asked, with a quick, suspicious look, which one would have hardly sought for in his face.

She did not notice it. "I have not the remotest idea where your haunts may have been, Mr. Arizona," she answered, with comical gravity. "I only hazarded that opinion on the strength of the general appearance of things, and as the result of my own keen observation." And when they had finished their very comfortable dinner, he was free to own that her "keen observation" had not misled her.

Mr. Calhoun Kendal was not an idle man, by any means. Of the different mining properties which he owned, some alone and some in partnership with others, a number were almost sure to find a market in San Francisco, he thought, though it was "mighty slow work," as he often complained. It always seemed a relief to him to find an asylum in the studio of Miss Benson; and the lady herself, as well as those who happened to be sitting for portraits, were equally entertained by the man who could tell of "hair-breadth 'scapes," and incidents in which the romantic and horrible were strangely blended. He soon came to be a well known figure, and the wonder among her lady patrons was that Miss Benson should not induce him to sit for his picture. So much character in his face, they said, and altogether so striking a head, with the flowing beard, and the high, furrowed brow. But he would not listen to any proposal tending in that direction. He didn't want to be made a figure-head, he told her in confidence, one day. She might paint as many flower-pictures as she wanted to for him, and he'd buy 'em all some day, when he had sold a mine; but face-pictures!—no, not for him.

Some days his hopes ran high in regard to these mines, and other days he seemed discouraged and hopeless of doing anything with them.

"You see," he explained to her, "those strikes that were made by myself when out prospecting all alone I could sell or bond at low figures, and make something at it, but places that three or four of us together took up have got to be held at higher figures, or neither of us make a cent. Now, these fellows, my pardners, have put this thing into my hands, and, of course, I'm not going back on them. If I can't sell or bond something for them, I'm not going to bond or sell anything for myself alone—and that's just how matters stand."

"And did you go through the country alone—all by yourself? Where did you get anything to eat? How did you keep the Indians off? You could not fight them single-handed, could you?"

He answered her questions in rote, and conscientiously:

"Yes, I went through the country alone frequently; and sometimes, if I thought I had found a pretty good showing, I rigged up a tent with blankets or branches, and stayed while my provisions held out, if there was water and feed for my mule, when I had one. Sometimes I footed it, and then I carried what grub I could, and went back to some settlement for more when it gave out. I never fought a large number of Indians single-handed but once. I was living in a shanty in the mountains, and discovered about thirty Indians prowling around early one Sunday morning, when I peeped through a chink in the wall. One of them came up near enough for me to take aim at him through a small opening by the fire-place, and he jumped into the air with a yell, and fell down dead. The rest seemed to think there was a whole garrison concealed in the shanty, and they made off, leaving the dead one behind. Then I went out, dug a hole, tied a rope around the Indian's neck, and dragged him into it. After that I saddled my mule, went to Tucson to get my grub for the week, and looked around to see if I could discover more of them skulking among the timber."

She had clasped her hands in horror. The thought of the dead Indian, dragged along by the rope around his neck, made her shudder with terror.

"But were you all alone—no other human being near?" she persisted.

"There was a cat—as smart a cat as ever I saw. She liked fresh meat best, but as the supply was short, I used to shoot game for her, and she knew whenever I took up my gun early in the morning, before going out to work, that the game was for her. You should have seen her watch, and bring in the rabbit, or squirrel, or birds I shot! It was just fun."

"And the Indian—did you stay there, where you had put him into the ground?"

"Certainly. It is much safer prospecting near a dead Indian than a live one."

A horribly prosaic being, she called him, with a little shiver, and so utterly devoid of sentiment or romance, but with such uncompromising honesty of purpose that all his faults and peculiarities vanished, in her eyes, before his good qualities.

He seemed best satisfied when they were alone, and she worked at the flower-pictures. He followed every move of her hand, and wondered how human fingers could perform such deft and delicate work. His own hands were singularly awkward. There was nothing they touched or lifted but was set down awry or bent, and whatever could possibly be broken by contact with the ground was sure to find its way there out of his hands. In fact, he liked best to hold quiet possession of a comfortable corner of the lounge, to which she was in the habit of bringing him the paper he wanted to read, the glass he wanted to drink from, or the fruit she always had ready for him to eat. To her it seemed so much less lonesome since she had some one to provide for again, while he followed with his eyes her every step and motion when attending to his comfort, as though he meant to paint her from memory some day, as she had painted her dead sister.

They went out together sometimes, though he said that an hour's sight-seeing made him more tired than a month's prospecting, but if any show were brought to him, he said, he didn't object to looking on. It was the procession in celebration of the national holiday he was speaking of, and he was not a little proud of his front room on this occasion, as it looked out on Kearny Street, and he could solemnly invite Miss Benson to see the "show" from his windows. But if the sun of the Arizona deserts had never caused him discomfort or a headache, the sun of San Francisco, glittering on the polished steel of the unstained arms of the war-like militiamen, caused him great discomfort and a most distressing headache. Without the slightest regret at losing so fine a sight, Miss Benson instantly drew the blinds, and made the patient recline on a lounge. Then she went to her landlady's kitchen, prepared a cup of strong tea, and, between keeping ice-water on his head, and compelling him to drink his tea black and without sugar, she restored him to his usual health in an hour or two. While he lay on the lounge his eyes followed her, as usual, in spite of all she could say to the effect that the eyes must be closed to drive off a headache.

"But I can't see you, then," he protested; and as she was about to change the wet cloth on his forehead, he suddenly seized her hand, and pressed it to his lips.

"You are a mighty good woman," he said, simply. Our friend was not the man to lift his fancy to the hight of "an angel." "I can't think why you should be so kind to me. Nobody ever has been before."

"Just for that reason," she replied, with a pitying look at the hard, weather-tanned hands.

"I am going to work now in earnest," he said the next morning, stopping to look in on her before he left the house. "I want to know whether I'm going to be a rich man for the rest of my life, or a poor one, and—act according. If these capitalists here want any of my mines, they will have to say it pretty quick, or I'll go on to New York with them."

Margaret wished him the best of luck for his day's work, and could not prevent the rich blood from showing clear and rosy in her delicate face.

For a week or two it seemed doubtful whether he would retire on a hundred thousand dollars or go back to Arizona "dead broke." Then he came home one day to pack his valise (he had never owned a trunk in his life), and start back for Arizona to consult his different "pardners" in regard to their willingness to consolidate some half dozen of the mines, as he had just "struck" a number of moneyed men who would incorporate as the "Kendal Consolidated" under certain conditions, and give stock equal to $50,000 to each partner for his share and claim.

"Shall you be gone long?" Margaret asked, with a slight tremor in her voice.

"From six weeks to three months. Shall you be here when I return?"

"Yes."

"I'll buy those pictures if I come back with money," he said, taking a last look around the room, and he turned to go.

For two months she heard nothing from him; then a slow step came up the stairs one day and approached her room. She sprang to open the door to a mixture of dust, sun-burn, and flowing beard, her face flushed and her eyes sparkling.

"Welcome home!" she exclaimed, with a thrill of delight in her voice.

"Powerful hot down there," he said; and he quietly dropped into his old corner of the lounge. "Looks like home here," he continued, after a pause; "and you are certainly the best woman in the world," as she approached him with a glass of cool water and took his hat from his hands.

Mrs. Ward had already heard of his arrival, and hastened to inform him that his old room would be vacated and ready for him in half an hour. And before a full hour had passed it seemed to them all that he had been gone only since yesterday.

His trip had been successful, he told Margaret, and the Kendal Consolidated had been incorporated during his absence. He could have returned in a month's time, if it had not been that he wanted to relocate, for himself, a very good prospect he had come across years ago, and which would be valuable now in view of the railroad to be built through Arizona.

Early the next morning he visited the office of the Kendal Consolidated, and seemed to have grown an inch or two while there. He had met so many people at the office who were eager and anxious to see the Mr. Kendal who had discovered the great Kendal mine. It chimed in well with the interests of the directors that the name and fame of Mr. Kendal should not be hidden under a bushel; and the Secretary had not only told him that the stock already sold higher than they had expected it to go, but had undertaken to bring him together with parties who would take his last location off his hands without once looking at it.

"I'm a rich man now, sure; and as big a man as any in the city."

Margaret laughed, as she had laughed at all his oddities since she had known him. The next day, however, when he returned from "our office," and told her of a fine young man to whom he had been introduced, and who was to take him to his father's house, she did not laugh.

"Has a sister, he says—a nice young gal that he wants to introduce me to."

She looked at him in an odd, startled sort of way. Not that any eccentricity of orthography or grammar in his speech could have surprised her, however; she had grown accustomed to that. When he really left the house that evening to pay the visit, she was a thousand times more lonesome than she had been during all his stay in Arizona. Long after ten, when she heard his step on the stairs, she hastily turned off the gas, but listened at the door. Yes, his step halted there before he passed on to his own room.

In the morning she was at work on a portrait, but laid it aside for a "flower-picture" when Mr. Kendal came in to sit with her a little while.

"Fine gal, that sister of young Driscoe's," he broke out, as enthusiastically as was possible for Calhoun Kendal. "Our Secretary said he would introduce me to some high-toned people, and he kept his word. Highly respectable family. The mother wears a real point-lace cap and tucker—or whatever you call it; and the young lady was dressed the prettiest I ever saw. Very stylish, and the last *mode*, Dick says—that's the boy's name. Live in good style, too—very genteel house and elegant bricky-brack furniture, and all that."

Margaret listened in surprise to words which she knew had not belonged to her friend's vocabulary till within a day or two; but Mr. Kendal talked on, regardless of the girl's silence.

"We're all going to the theater—the old lady, Dick, Sadie, and the father, too, I reckon. I didn't see much of him, though; guess he hasn't got much to say. Wanted to go to-night, but Dick says we must go respectable, and I must get a black dress-suit first. He's going to take me to his own tailor; guess he'll fix me up pretty fine. Of course, I want to look respectable when I escort a stylish young lady. I just wish you could see her—she's a *mighty* pretty gal. But, here—I'm doing all the talking. Have you nothing to say?"

Mr. Kendal, of the Kendal Consolidated, was not very quick of perception, or he would have observed that the hand holding the brush had trembled so that that little implement of art had to be laid aside, and a pair of wax-white hands lay idly folded in the girl's lap. But suddenly he was struck with the stillness pervading the whole form, and he bent forward to look into her ashy face.

"What's the matter?" he asked, in alarm. "Are you sick, or in pain? You look fit to die."

"What difference would it make to any one?" The words were uttered below her breath; yet Mr. Kendal's somewhat dull ears had caught their import.

"Why, Margaret," he stammered, shocked at the sudden change in her being, "how can you talk like that? You know I would give half the money I've got, and run a hundred miles without stopping, to see you relieved or cured if you were sick. Shall I go for a doctor, or call Mrs. Ward?"

"No, no." She looked full into the large, honest eyes, bent upon her with such a genuine expression of concern. "It was only a sudden faintness, and will pass in a little while. Go to your office now, and I will rest a little."

But if Margaret had hoped for an hour to herself, she had made a miscalculation. Mrs. Ward said she had orders not to leave Miss Benson alone, as she came in. "And I'm to send for the best physician, and he is to prescribe the most costly drugs; and I'm to take Miss Benson out in a carriage, and I'm to hire a nurse, a parson, a circus-band, and a barrel-organ—all to restore the health and cheer the spirits of Miss Benson. Precious Miss Benson! She will be wrapped with gold-cloth and hung with diamonds pretty soon," Mrs. Ward added, laughing heartily at the recollection of Mr. Kendal's concern.

Margaret smiled, but with pale lips. "An excellent man is Mr. Kendal, and a true friend."

He would not even go to look after his black suit in the evening, he was so glad to find Margaret better, and was overjoyed to find her at her easel again early the next morning. She had left the door open for him purposely, and now, while they were both commenting on the form just springing into life on the canvas, a voice outside, inquiring for Mr. Kendal, attracted their attention. The servant dusting and brushing in the hall approached the door, followed by a young man, who very unceremoniously looked into the room over the domestic's shoulder, and did not even wait for Mr. Kendal to invite him to enter.

"These your rooms, old fellow?" he asked, without seeming to notice the other inmate.

"This is Miss Benson's studee-o. Miss Benson, allow me to introduce Mr. Briscoe. Miss Benson is my oldest San Francisco friend, and a great artist. I consider it a favor to be admitted here, and am sensible of the privilege granted me to watch so highly gifted a lady practicing her art."

If the lance was somewhat unwieldy which the knight of the sun-browned hands was breaking in the cause of chivalry, his friend understood that it was meant to rebuke the lack of courtesy and deference shown a lady, and Dick Briscoe was quick to take the cue.

"Ah! beg pardon," contracting his eyebrows, as though the light from the one window might have blinded him. "Happy to meet Miss Benson—a friend of yours and an artist. Beautiful!" he exclaimed, standing before the flower panels on the wall. "How Sadie would admire those! We must ask permission of Miss Benson to bring my sister in to see them some time," he said, alert as usual, turning to the honest Arizonian, whose face was relaxing at the praise bestowed on his friend.

The new black suit was sent home to Mr. Kendal in due time, and he presented himself to Margaret in his fine array on the night of his visit to the theater with the Briscoe family.

"Do I look respectable in my new clothes?" he asked.

"Eminently so," was the truthful reply, "but I liked you far better in the more unconventional dress you wore when I first saw you."

"These don't feel so comfortable, either," he admitted.

Mr. Kendal was charmed with his glimpse of what he considered fashionable life, and he went in pursuit of it to the church or the theater with equal gusto. As a crowning piece to his stylish outfit, he had purchased a black cylinder hat, to the amazement of Dick Briscoe himself, who came to conduct him to the church where the Briscoe family rented a pew.

"Ain't it rather a bore, though?" he asked, considerately.

"Well, yes," Mr. Kendal admitted, cheerfully; "but then, you know, a black silk hat *is* the most respectable kind of a hat to go to church in, after all."

"That's so," assented the accommodating youth, and moving his own tile a little to one side, he stepped to the window to conceal a smile. He himself had put the "respectable" wrinkle into his friend's head, but this was out-Heroding Herod. However, if his Arizona friend was pleased, why should he object?

"I've done it," exclaimed Mr. Kendal, rushing into the studio one morning, sinking into a chair, dropping his tile, and wiping his heated brow on a scented pocket-handkerchief. "I've talked to her father—she said I might last night, at the theater. I am going up to see her this afternoon, to tell her that he's willing."

Margaret wished him joy, and the happy man started on his visit at the earliest proper moment. Dick Briscoe himself opened the door for him, and led him into the parlor, where Miss Sadie received her elderly lover without any attempt at coyness. He was bewildered a moment by her beauty and seductive smile, but after the first confusion he timidly approached, and laid his hand on one of the long braids of yellow hair that fell gracefully across her shoulder. "My stars," he gave word to his admiration, "I never before knew that you had such a beautiful head of hair."

"No, by Jove, nor I," chimed in Dick, who had posted himself on a sofa opposite to the lounge on which his sister was airily seated, evidently for the purpose of enjoying Sadie's first reception of an accepted lover.

"You, Dick!"

With a single cat-like spring she was beside her brother, shaking him by the arm, and threatening him with her pretty little hand.

"Let me alone," he protested, choking with laughter. "Mr. Kendal, call her off. She hates me for being in the room. I'll go now," and he rushed out, leaving Sadie to her adorer.

Of course Miss Briscoe was pretty, very pretty, with bright black eyes, and a full suit of fashionable yellow hair, bewilderingly arranged, and a form as lithe and swift in its motions as that of a panther or a cat. There was something audacious about her, that had at first astonished and attracted the unsophisticated man, while the petted-child air she could assume had made him long to stretch out his hand and caress her as he would a playful little kitten. That the young lady had been christened "Sarah" in her infancy detracted nothing from her good looks, but she hated all who ventured to be familiar with her original name.

If there was any change in Margaret Benson, Mr. Kendal did not notice it; he still came into the "stodee-o," but it was generally only to tell of some new excellence or beauty he had discovered in his *fiancée*, or to draw comparisons between the female portraits there and Miss Sadie Briscoe—always, of course, awarding the palm to that young lady.

"How old are you?" he asked of Margaret one day, after he had been confiding to her his discovery of some new merit in his betrothed.

"Twenty-five—nearly twenty-six," was the composed reply.

"My stars! Why, that's what we call an old maid in my country."

"I am afraid it is called so here, too," she assented, smilingly.

"Now Sadie is only seventeen—and she says she has always wanted to find in the man she loved one who would be companion, husband, and father to her at the same time." (The truth of the matter was that Miss Sadie had passed her second decade; "but," as she said to brother Dick in confidence, "the old fellow wants a young wife for his money, and I think I'll fill the bill.")

One morning shortly after breakfast Mr. Kendal was seized with one of his sudden headaches, and remembering Margaret's former kindness he saw no reason why he should not again appeal to her Samaritan qualities. She darkened the room, bathed his head in ice-water, and was making all preparations she thought necessary, when Dick Briscoe, not having found the Arizonian at the Kendal Con. office, came to inquire into the cause of his absence.

"You can't think how good that woman has been to me," said the patient, when Margaret had left the room, "and she knows just what is good for me when I get sick."

"But how do you think Sadie would like it if she knew of Miss Benson's coming into your room when you are sick?"

"I should think very poorly of any woman who was too nice to take compassion on a fellow-being when sick," Mr. Kendal declared.

Mr. Dick made a note of it. "But she might be jealous," he suggested, insinuatingly.

"Sadie jealous of me?" A pleased smile broke over the Arizonian's face. "But she need not be jealous of Miss Benson, I'm sure."

Dick seemed so concerned for Mr. Kendal's health that he made him promise not to leave the house till he should call for him; and though the patient had recovered within an hour or two, he kept his word scrupulously and to the letter, and did not leave the house.

Early in the afternoon there was a faint rustle of silk along the hall by Margaret's room, and directly the door of Mr. Kendal's room flew open, and a dazzling array of wavy yellow hair, fleecy lace, and glittering jewelry rushed into the outstretched arms of the happy man.

"Oh, what a dear little puss you are," he said, after she had breathlessly related how Pa and Ma [it was "the old man" and "the old woman" between Sadie and her brother in private] both believed her gone to the matinée, and how shocked and grieved they would be if they knew that dear Brother Dick had consented to her prayers, and had brought her to see her dear suffering darling.

"How can I ever show dear brother Dick my gratitude?" and he held out his hand to that noble young man, who had discreetly turned to the window till the first transport should have subsided.

"Ah! but you wicked, naughty man had a strange lady tending you, when you knew that I would gladly have braved everything to come to you if you were sick. Where is the wretched woman that dared to take my place? Let me see her at once."

More delighted than he wanted to own, her lover assured her that she should not only visit the "studee-o" of the lady, but that he had a surprise in store for her there; and he marshaled the brother and sister across the hall. With due pride he introduced his betrothed to the tall, self-possessed woman at the easel, who received her visitors pleasantly, inquiring of Mr. Kendal about the pain in his head.

"And now for my surprise," said Mr. Kendal, as Sadie was complimenting Miss Benson on the different flower-pieces by her hand. "Them's all mine"—waving his hand toward the pictures, and forgetting his grammar in his anxiety to give his beloved pleasure. "Miss Benson has been a long while painting them for me, and the price is no object, as they are to be a present to you, my dear."

Miss Briscoe quickly raised her eyes to Miss Benson's face. Had this handsome woman really never fascinated her husband *in spite*? And had Miss Benson never tried to secure the prize for which she herself had so eagerly striven? There was a flush on Margaret's face, and Miss Sadie eyed her keenly; but after a moment the glittering black orbs drooped involuntarily before Margaret's clear hazel eyes.

"I shall prize them so highly," Miss Sadie said, sweetly, "both as a gift of Mr. Kendal and as the work of a true artist."

But once in Mr. Kendal's room again, she stamped her pretty little foot in uncontrollable passion.

"You shan't have that old maid come into your room any more—I won't have it—do you hear? I am jealous, you know," she continued softly, when she saw the look of displeased surprise in his face. "If I didn't love you I wouldn't be jealous of you—would I?"

He answered the argument with a kiss, and Miss Sadie returned to the attack. "Who is your friend, anyhow? You say she has no relatives, no friends, earns her own support, and lives here all alone? H'm—I don't think that is strictly respectable, and I don't know that Pa would approve of my marrying a man who was intimately acquainted with such a person."

"I am sure," her lover cried, in alarm, "I mean to do nothing to hurt your feelings, but Miss Benson is really the best woman—"

Miss Sadie made the spring at him which she often made at her brother, and which Mr. Kendal thought so charming.

"But I tell you I'm jealous, and never want to hear the woman's name again."

She stood on tip-toe before him, and made playful attempts at choking him.

After a while they passed out through the hall together, and Margaret, lonesome and forgotten in her room, came to her door as the party began descending the stairs to the street. Just then a gentleman met and passed them, looking around in the corridor to read the different signs. Without a glance at him, Margaret drew back into the room, but the gentleman had caught sight of her, and hastened to her door before she could close it.

"Margaret—Miss Benson!" he exclaimed, extending both hands, while Margaret, opening wide the door, looked searchingly into his face.

"Philip!"

Her surprise brought the red blood to her face, leaving it all the more pale the next moment.

"And is this your—your home?" he asked, looking around the room he had entered.

"My studio, home—what you will," she answered, with an attempt at firmness and cheerfulness.

"Oh, Margaret, poor child," he cried, pityingly, "don't try to make me believe you are happy and contented. I saw the pain and heartache in your face before you knew who I was."

She had dropped her head on her arm, which rested on the table beside her, and sobbed like a tired child. He laid his hand on her soft hair a moment.

"Could you find no way of communicating with us? Only two months ago I heard of your father's death and—and misfortune. We were losing ourselves among the pyramids of Egypt when Providence sent a fellow Californian in our way, who spoke of it. We started home at once, I by the most direct route, but my mother was compelled to return by way of Paris. The Lord only knows what extravagances she has been indulging in—spangled dresses and red shoes, for aught I know."

Margaret smiled as the image of Mrs. Dufresne, grand and calmly dignified, arose before her.

"As well Semiramis or Zenobia in frizzled hair and a Dolly Varden."

"Well, whatever she brings, you may depend there will be something to replace this black gown of yours."

"A terribly ugly dress this, is it not?" she asked, bitterly. "It has cost me many a pang."

"You have had great trials, but your friends should not have allowed you to remain alone here, brooding over the past and its irrecoverable losses."

A harsh word arose to her lips.

"I could find no friend after poor papa was dead. I doubt that I would have had the courage to write to your mother, if I had known where to address you."

"So hard has the world dealt with you? Ah, well, mother will be here soon now, and you shall forget all coldness and unkindness. I am to put mother's own house in order for her, and I will have to go to Oakland to-morrow, and talk my prettiest to the Elliotts, to induce them to give up the next two years' lease. You know we were to have been absent for five years. Then we must refurnish the house. I shall depend a good deal on your assistance, and altogether on your taste. And, by the way, there you have four pretty flower-pieces to decorate the walls of your *boudoir*."

"They are not mine any more. They are sold." Her lips trembled, and he looked compassionately into her white face.

"Yes, it must be hard to part with, for money, what has grown dear to us and a part of us in its very creation."

She hid her face in her hands, and he looked on in distress a moment, till he gently tried to remove them.

"Why, Margaret, girl, is there any other sorrow in your heart than what I know of? Tell me of it. You know you may confide in me."

She brushed the tears from her lashes.

"There, I am better now, and shall never again be lonesome and forsaken. I know you will always be to me a true friend—a kind brother."

Philip Dufresne started.

"Yes," he said, after a pause, "your best friend, I hope, always."

Mr. Kendal had parted with the brother and sister Briscoe at the next street corner, and they pursued their way home.

"I say, Sal——" began the graceless brother.

"Shut up, you imp. My name is Sadie," interrupted the sister.

"Oh, bother! I say, I had a great mind to try this afternoon how far the gratitude of my prospective brother-in-law would bear stretching. I'm in a tight place, and the old man can't be stirred a peg. What's a fellow to do?"

"At any rate, not to blackmail Mr. Kendal," returned Miss Sadie, indignantly.

"Not, at least, till you are fairly married to him, you mean, Sis. I am certainly entitled to some acknowledgment for the way I fished him up for you?"

He spoke with the most injured air, as if his claims to having captured some highly valued, but dangerous, wild animal, had been disputed.

"Don't I tell you you shall have all the money you want as soon as I am married? Don't you go and break up this whole thing now by your greediness."

"Greediness!" he repeated, more injured than ever. "If I had had as many rings and bracelets and watches given me as you, I wouldn't talk of greediness in others."

But they made peace before reaching home, each recognizing the necessity of keeping up amicable relations with the other. The peace was of short duration, however. Miss Sadie, dressing for a drive with her lover the next day, missed a pair of heavy gold bracelets, his gift, from her toilet-table. She stormed down stairs to the sitting-room, where young Dick held sole possession.

"My bracelets!" she gasped.

"What's the matter with them?" he asked, with ill-assumed indifference.

"They're gone—stolen."

"Chinaman took 'em?" the brother suggested.

"No, he didn't," she protested. "I'll not stand this, Dick. I want my bracelets back."

"Oh, bother your bracelets! Tell the old codger the Chinaman took them, and make him bring you some more." And, picking up his hat, he left the house.

Philip Dufresne, having settled matters with the lessees of his mother's house, had insisted on Margaret's active assistance in putting the same in order. Upon Mrs. Dufresne's arrival she took Margaret away from her lodgings at once, much to the surprise of Miss Sadie Briscoe, who heard of it through brother Dick. This young gentleman had been assiduous in his attentions to the Arizonian of late, and, visiting him almost daily, had seen and heard of the friend who had attended so constantly on Margaret.

"The Dufresnes?" Miss Sadie asked between surprise and envy. "Miss Benson's friends? Why, you said she had no friends. The Dufresnes are immensely wealthy, and the Philip Dufresne of whom I know is a tall, handsome, dark-eyed man. But that old maid need not try for him. He could marry the handsomest girl in San Francisco."

"Miss Benson is not the woman to 'try for' any man," Mr. Kendal protested, so sharply that Miss Sadie fell from one surprise into another. Altogether this had been an uncomfortable interview. The Chinaman had been accused of stealing the bracelets, and duly discharged from service; but the lover had failed to bring her a new pair since.

In her new-found home, all that tender kindness could suggest was done to make Margaret forget the past few years of her life. In her solicitude, Mrs. Dufresne spared herself neither fatigue nor trouble, insisting on visiting theaters, concerts, opera—places of amusement to which Margaret had long been a stranger. Philip's eyes always lighted up with a strange flash when she declared, however, that to her no place seemed so pleasant as her present home—that she was never quite happy away from it. The place was worthy her admiration—grand old trees shutting it in from the street, while a terrace, bright with conservatory and gay-blooming flowers, overlooked the blue lake, and a smooth lawn sloped down to the water's edge.

Mrs. Dufresne had always had a mother's fondness for Margaret, and her affection had not changed. But Philip Dufresne would not be satisfied with a sister's love from the girl. Margaret's nature was too transparently truthful to conceal from Philip's eye the sore spot in her heart; but Philip knew that time would heal what he hoped had been only a bruise—never a wound.

Fourth of July, 187–, was to be celebrated with unwonted splendor; and Mrs. Dufresne was not too fashionable to insist that they celebrate the day by viewing the procession to take place in San Francisco. Philip was instructed to secure a front room on the line of march, their plan being to cross the bay in the morning, watch the procession, take lunch, and return to Oakland some time in the afternoon. To Mrs. Dufresne's chagrin, Margaret wore a somber black dress on the morning of the Fourth, though, as Philip had predicted, there had been divers dresses for her among those sent from Paris. Margaret's face was paler than it had been for some time.

"Are you sick, child?" she asked Margaret, in great alarm. "Had we better stay at home?"

But Margaret insisted that she wore the black dress only because it would surely be cold in San Francisco on the Fourth of July; and they set out for the boat, where they were joined by more friends. It was a merry party that proceeded to the city together, and just enough to fill both windows in the room. Philip left the ladies to themselves, when he had seen them all comfortably seated—Margaret alone insisting that she wanted no seat by the window, but preferred standing behind Mrs. Dufresne's chair, and looking over her shoulder. Perhaps it was as well that Philip had left the room—Margaret could not have hidden from his keen eyes the tears that coursed slowly down her cheeks and fell on the bouquet of white roses she held in her hand. Shout after shout went up from the street, as the long, showy train passed by; band after band clashed out its music—loud martial strains, or gay rollicking airs. To Margaret alone the music was playing only dead-marches and funeral-hymns; for she was burying her dead to-day—deep out of sight—for ever and for aye. And as her tears fell faster, the white roses in her hand drooped and withered, as her head was bent over them, for she had decreed that the sorrow and the tears should be buried with them to-day, where eye nor memory could ever rest on them again.

Strangely enough, on the boat, homeward bound, Philip's eye fell first of all on the white roses in her hand. They were out on the guards together, and he was trying to shelter her from the cold wind that blew on the bay.

"What a sorry bouquet to carry to Oakland," he suggested.

"It is not going there. I was only waiting to reach the middle of the bay, so that it would not drift back to San Francisco." And, turning, she flung the flowers into the water.

"Let us go in," she said; and she laid her hand on his arm, with a touch that thrilled him strangely, when he looked hastily into her smiling face.

The cold wind that blew on the bay did not reach the shore. The closing day was warm and balmy in beautiful Oakland, and Margaret came to the dinner-table in white, with scarlet flowers at her throat and in her hair. Mrs. Dufresne was delighted with this change from her morning's costume, and Philip's eyes spoke volumes of thanks. After dinner, when she had sung Mrs. Dufresne's favorite airs, Margaret passed quietly out to the moonlit veranda, and Philip was soon by her side.

"Will you walk with me?" he asked. And she silently laid her hand on his arm.

The lake beneath them glittered in the moonlight, the air was heavy with the odor of jasmine and heliotrope; from the open windows floated the soft strains that Mrs. Dufresne was calling forth from the grand piano, and all around seemed harmony and peace.

Philip's step grew slower.

"Margaret, you will give me my answer now—this night."

She bent her head, but the moonlight betrayed the flush on her face:

"And it is—yes!"

She did not release the trembling hand he had seized, and he drew her to his bosom and held her in a close embrace.

"My darling," he murmured, "it was so long to wait."

"You knew my heart, Philip," she answered softly.

"As true and faithful a heart as ever beat in woman's breast," he said, earnestly. Then he drew her into the house. He knew how his mother longed to clasp her to her breast as her daughter.

Days of busy preparation followed for Mrs. Dufresne, who often declared, in comic despair, that she must apprentice her son to some trade in San Francisco to keep him away from under her feet in Oakland.

Margaret did not forget her old friend, Mrs. Ward; many a lovely bouquet of Oakland flowers graced her center-table. Mr. Kendal was married, and young Mrs. Kendal, in answer to a protest against her extravagance, had said that, "as she had married the old fellow for his money, she wanted the pleasure of spending it."

Philip Dufresne had always liked the honest-hearted miner, and did not lose sight of him altogether. Soon after his own quiet wedding he brought distressing news to Margaret about their old friend. He was greatly harassed in mind and pocket by the pranks of his worthless brother-in-law, for the young gentleman had carried his operations into strange territory after appropriating as much of his father's funds as he could lay hands on. Strangers were not as lenient as his father and his brother-in-law, and it required large sums to cover the boy's criminal acts and save the family from disgrace. Mr. Kendal looked disheartened, Philip said, and had declared that a hundred such mines as the Kendal Con. could not keep his wife and her brother in pocket-money.

Sitting by the window one bright summer morning gazing idly down the well-kept walk, Margaret was startled to see their old friend enter the gate. She hastened out to meet him, extending both her hands. He looked so forlorn and wretched that it made her heart ache.

"Welcome, Mr. Kendal!" she cried cordially, and at the sound of her voice he looked wistfully up into her face.

"Oh, Margaret—Miss Benson—Mrs. Dufresne—what a blind fool I have been! I deserve all my trials. I am not fit to be a white man—I'm worse than an Indian."

She smiled in spite of herself at his favorite form of self-revilement; but she brought him into the parlor and seated him by the window, speaking to him cheerfully to dispel his gloom.

"It's no use," he said; "I have come to bid you good-bye. You are the only friends I ever had here—you and your husband."

He was going back to Arizona, he went on to say, for he was almost beggared, and was of no more use to himself or his young wife. With empty hands he would never return to her, for there were only slights and reproaches for him in his own home, though his fortune had been sacrificed to gratify his wife's whims and save her brother from prison. His fingers strayed nervously through his grizzled hair, while he spoke, and idly plucked at the tangled beard, and altogether he was the picture of a man who saw only desolation and a waste before him, where he had spent his life's best strength to build him up a blooming Eden.

Looking upon him, a great pity flooded all the woman's heart, and she knelt beside him and held the poor awkward hands in her own, speaking words of comfort and sympathy that filled the man's soul with peace, made him feel fresh hope, and called back something of his old energy.

Margaret would fain have detained him till her husband came, but Mr. Kendal said he would bid him good-bye at his office, and, softened and cheered, he went out from her presence.

Months later, Philip laid his arm tenderly around his wife's shoulder, and bade her read a paragraph he had marked in the paper:

"The body of a man supposed to be the once famous Mr. Kendal, the discoverer of the mine known by his name, was found on the Gila Desert, some ten days after a severe sand-storm had been raging there. The theory is that he had been laboring under an aberration of the brain, consequent upon great disappointment in finding mines he had meant to relocate taken up by other parties—otherwise he would not have started across the desert without other water supply than a small canteen, which was found by his side empty."

Margaret's head sank on her husband's shoulder, and he turned to kiss away the tears that hung on her dark lashes.

"O faithful heart!" he said; "most tender of women and truest of wives—I thank God that you are mine."

JOSEPHINE CLIFFORD.

A DEAD RIVER.

I plowed in my fields in November,
For the rain, like a dream, came at night,
And lo! where none could remember,
Deep buried and hidden from sight,
I uncovered the bed of a river
That laughed like a maid in the sun
Ere its heart-beats were silent forever
And its musical life-stream had run.

I sit in my cheerless November,
And the past, like a dream, comes at night,
And lo! where none can remember,
So deep is it hidden from sight,
I uncover my grief for a maiden
Who laughed, river-like, in the sun
Ere her heart-beats were hushed in my Aidenn
And her musical life-stream had run.

CHAS. H. PHELPS.

CLIMATIC STUDIES IN SOUTHERN CALIFORNIA.

It seems to be a fact that misapprehension of the peculiarities of climate and of the agricultural capacities of Southern California is more marked among the people of the upper portion of the State than among residents of the East. Odd as the fact may seem, there is yet a certain reason for it. To the inhabitant of the Eastern States, Southern California is simply a new region, where, he has heard, his harsh winters are unknown, and where the orange flourishes as in its native home. When he reads of it, it is the account of men who have gone with eyes free from any preëxisting prejudice, and have told what they saw. Of the people of Northern California, however, comparatively few have ever visited the southern portion of the State, while they have learned just enough of the climatic peculiarities of the coast to know the general law that rainfall diminishes as you go south; and observing that the average annual rainfall of Sacramento is eighteen inches, while that of Stockton, upon the south, is sixteen and eight-tenths inches, and that in the Tulare country, which is still farther to the south, it has decreased to only six and a half inches, they reason that as what is distinctively known as Southern California lies yet beyond those lands of steadily failing moisture, it must be still more arid. They have not stopped to inquire whether there may not be other influences at work changing or suspending the action of the law.

For a proper understanding of the climate of Southern California, it is essential that the general climatic laws of the whole State should be studied. The most strongly marked feature in the physical geography of California, and the one which at once catches the eye of the observant traveler, is the fact that its mountains, for hundreds of miles, run parallel with the coast, and that there are two of these great chains, one rising abruptly almost from the sea-line, like a long wall, with only here and there a shallow coast valley, as at Santa Cruz, lying outside of the range and facing directly upon the ocean. This is known as the Coast Range. The other is the great uplifted crest of the Sierra Nevada, which, for hundreds of miles, in unbroken chain, forms the horizon line upon the east, crossed only, at long distances, by some rugged pass, leading to the interior basin of the continent.

This range, with its great altitude, its heavy snows, and its immense condensing power, is the source of all the important rivers of California. From it come the Sacramento and San Joaquin, with their tributaries, and in Southern California, the Los Angeles, the San Gabriel, and the Santa Aña.

These two ranges of mountains divide the lands of the State into two classes of widely different climatic features—the humid coast valleys, lying outside of the Coast Range, facing upon the ocean, and marked by a comparatively great precipitation of moisture and slight evaporation; and the more arid interior valleys, lying between the two ranges, and characterized by just the reverse—a light rainfall and an excessive evaporation.

The great interior basin of California, the Sacramento and San Joaquin, together with several smaller valleys, as the Santa Clara and Napa, formed by a local splitting of the coast mountains into two ranges, drains outward to the ocean through the gap which forms the inlet to San Francisco Bay, while through the same gap flows back the cool air current which gives the daily sea-breeze to these valleys.

The winter rain-current, which is a south-westerly wind blowing in from the sea, has to cross this Coast Range before it can reach and water the dry interior valleys. According to a well known law, it parts with much of its moisture in climbing the elevation, giving a climate upon the ocean face of the range damp and foggy—home of the redwood and the fern, both of which are types of vegetation flourishing only in a comparatively humid atmosphere. After crossing this range, the rain-current, thus deprived of a large portion of its moisture, passes on to give a lighter rainfall upon the level plains of the interior, until it reaches the tall line of the Sierra, where, with the cold of a still greater elevation, the remaining moisture is wrung out of the clouds, giving precipitation largely in excess of that which fell in the valleys; and again we find forests of dense growth, yet of a type that does not, like the redwood, need the constant humidity of the ocean air, which, after the winter rains have ceased, rolls in a daily fog to the seaward face of the Coast Range. How thoroughly the Sierra has accomplished the remaining work of condensation is shown in the almost hopeless aridity of the plains lying eastward from its base, and to which the now desiccated rain-wind next passes.

This winter rain-current in its sweep inland passes over the crest of the Coast Range in a more or less continuous sheet; yet, like a vast aerial river, which it is, it avails itself of every break and depression of the range to pour through in still denser volume. And it is opposite these breaks and depressions of the range that we find the line of greatest rainfall in the interior valleys, as the lower and more humid portion of the current has at these points been able to reach the interior without having its moisture wrung out in crossing the range. It is in this way that the Sacramento country, with its river-valley leading out to the ocean through that break in the Coast Range which forms the entrance to San Francisco harbor, has a greater rainfall and a more humid climate than the plains which lie behind the range. Whoever has stood and watched the evening fog roll in at the Golden Gate, seeking, like a river flood, first the lower level of the water-ways, and then the broken passes in the hills, will readily understand how the south-east currents of the winter obey the same general law.

The comparatively great rainfall of the country north of the Sacramento, as contrasted with the plains upon the south in the San Joaquin and Tulare country, is to be attributed to the same cause; for while the main volume of the rain-current entering through the break and the adjacent depressions of the range west of San Francisco Bay, and then, following the water-level back to Sacramento, keeps on with its original north-easterly sweep to the section north and east of the river, any portion of the current seeking to turn aside to the level plains upon the south must double back upon itself, and struggle against the drier portion of the same south-west wind, which has, in the general sweep, after losing a large portion of its moisture in crossing, forced its way over the higher line of the same Coast Range south of San Francisco, and passed on directly inland. Hence the rainfall of the country north and east of Sacramento increases, while upon the South, although the land drains by the same outlet to the sea, it steadily diminishes.

The working of the same law may be seen, although upon a more limited scale, in the smaller valleys which surround and drain into San Francisco Bay. Napa Valley, lying upon the north, with its mouth opening at an acute angle toward the incoming rain-current of the Golden Gate, hardly knows what it is to have a failure of crops through lack of moisture; while Santa Clara Valley, upon the south, and opening out toward the north, rather in the direction toward which the rain-current is going than toward that from which it is coming, has a much lighter rainfall, and suffers from drought more frequently. The lower and moister stratum of the rain-current, entering at the Golden Gate, in order to reach the Santa Clara Valley would have to double back upon itself, and battle with the direct current from the south, which, after parting with enough of its moisture to water the Santa Cruz country, has already forced itself, a partly desiccated wind, over the mountains of the Coast Range through what is known as the Santa Cruz Gap.

The influence of the Coast Range upon the climate of the interior valleys is felt in still another way: by obstructing the inward flow of the daily sea-breeze, with its moister air, its lower temperature, and the frequent night fogs, evaporation in these valleys goes on with scarcely a check the moment the rains are over, and so the water that does fall is more quickly dried up.

The direction of the two ranges, the Coast and the Sierra, also has its influence, and that far from a favorable one, upon the climate of these valleys; for by their course from north to south they leave the country open to the full sweep, both winter and summer, of the harsh, dry north wind, while the chill which comes with this wind in winter retards and checks vegetation during the first three months of the rainy season, and to that extent practically shortens what might otherwise be the season of most rapid growth.

If one were asked how the physical features of California might be changed to give a moister and more productive climate to the interior valleys, he would probably reply:

(1.) Drop the Coast Range of mountains down until it is practically obliterated. By doing this the great winter rain-current would be no longer obstructed in its landward flow, neither would it be robbed of a portion of its moisture, as now, before it had fairly left the coast line, and so precipitation would be increased. Also, with this barrier removed the ocean fogs would no longer be walled out, but would pass inward over the land, and add their portion of moisture, while by giving the humid ocean air ready access, in the shape of these fogs and the damp, cool daily sea-breeze, evaporation would be checked, and a dry, hot air no longer greedily suck up the surface moisture of the soil.

(2.) Keep up the elevation of the Sierra, but bring it slightly nearer to the coast, so that it may condense all the moisture possible from the rain-currents, and its melting snows and its rivers may be available for irrigating the plains lying between it and the ocean.

(3.) Wall the land in upon the north-west with mountains, so as to shelter it from the drying winds that now sweep over it, in winter checking and retarding, by their chill, the growth of vegetation, and in summer parching it up and blasting the tender grain.

(4.) If, in addition to these changes, the winter could be made slightly warmer, so that vegetation should not be retarded by the cold, then the whole duration of the rainy season would be a period of growth, and so the season practically lengthened.

In making the reply thus itemized under these four sections, one would be describing exactly what has taken place in Southern California.

Out of the broken confusion of the Tehachape and Tejon Mountains, where the Sierra and the Coast Ranges seem to become inextricably entangled, the Sierra at length emerges, and, skirting the Mojave Desert upon the west, turns eastword under the local name of the Sierra Madre as the northern wall of the Los Angeles and San Bernardino country; then turning again southward along the western rim of the Colorado Desert, goes on to form the backbone of the peninsula of Lower California. A stray fragment of the Coast Range rises again for a while, under the name of the Santa Monica Mountains; joins the dividing ridge between the westerly plains of the Los Angeles country and the San Fernando Valley; breaks down entirely where the San Fernando Valley opens into the Los Angeles, giving outlet to the Los Angeles River; then rises as a low, irregular range of hills between Los Angeles and the San Gabriel country—hills having an elevation of only two or three hundred feet; breaks down again completely after a few miles, where the broad valley of the San Gabriel comes out from the Sierra, irrigating with its waters the fertile, low-lying lands of El Monte and Los Nietos; then the hills rise again as a broken range, gradually attaining to a hight in scattered peaks of one or two thousand feet, but torn asunder where the Santa Aña, coming from its source in the San Bernardino portion of the Sierra, and watering upon its way the San Bernardino and Riverside countries, bursts through to the lands of Santa Aña and Anaheim and the coast plain, and on to the sea. Beyond, this broken, wandering remnant of the Coast Range becomes again, but this time hopelessly, entangled with and lost in the Sierra. This breaking down of the Coast Range throws the whole valley system of Southern California, known collectively as the

Los Angeles country, open to the sea, making it practically a vast system of coast valleys, with the Sierra as a background; and it is to be classed with the Humboldt and Santa Cruz countries in climate, but from the sheltering mountains and the more southern latitude milder in temperature, and in extent upon an infinitely larger scale. About three thousand square miles of level valley land open out to the sea at this point. The sharp trend eastward of the coast line south of Point Conception also brings the sea nearer to the Sierra, making its influence more felt, while the deflection of the Sierra from a north and south direction to almost due east turns it into a huge barrier, raised directly across the path of the cold north wind, which sweeps the upper portion of the State. Under the shelter of its peaks, ranging in elevation from six to eleven thousand feet, these southern valleys nestle, looking from the snow-clad crests above them out toward the warm southern sea.

There is something about the coast south of Point Conception which reminds me always of that land of the Lotus-eaters,

"Wherein it always seemed afternoon;"

something in the smoother heaving of the waters, the softer sky, the milder breezes, and the dreamy haze that lingers tenderly about the dim outline of the distant mountains.

I well recollect my first trip down the coast; it was upon the *Orizaba*, thirteen years ago. We left San Francisco, sailing out into the fog and the cold north-west wind that whistled drearily through the rigging as we turned southward. All day it chased after us, as, with overcoats tightly buttoned, we shivered about the decks. All night it drove us on. The next day, about noon, we rounded the lighthouse and fog-bell of Point Conception. It was like the transformation scene in an Oriental tale of magic. Almost in a steamer's length we had passed from the fog-bank into sunshine. The cold wind died away. The rough tossing of the ship changed to a gentle rocking upon the glassy swell. And hour after hour we coasted along a shore, such as those tired wanderers drew nigh who sailed on and on in the hush of the afternoon toward the "hollow Lotus-land." And then, just at daybreak the next morning, we rounded a high headland, and all one dreamy forenoon lay at anchor in the roadstead of San Pedro, gently rocking upon the lazy swell that rolled slowly in from the south.

I have never forgotten the picture. Hour after hour I lay watching the green of hill and plain, stretching away league upon league to the great white line of the Sierra; watching the green of the long, heaving billows rolling in from the southern seas; watching the gulls idly circling about the ship; gazing down through the transparent waters at the strands of trailing seaweed waving gently about the keel, and at the fish lazily basking amid the floating leaves. And over all, though it was only January, a glow and a glory of sunshine, such as northlands may dream of, but never know.

The exemption of Southern California from the working of the general law of a continuously diminishing rainfall, and an even more arid climate as you go south, lies in the fact that it is essentially a coast country, and not a continuation of the San Joaquin and Tulare Valleys. The mountains which shut those valleys off from the sea are, as already shown, broken down and lost in Southern California. The tendency to a reversion to the interior type is seen, however, in the San Fernando Valley, which is partly shut off from the ocean by the Santa Monica Mountains, belonging to the coast system. The tendency is seen only by a comparison with the great open valley system, which is not so shut off. Even in the San Fernando Valley the elevation of the Coast Range is so slight, and the breaks so open, that the only result is to shelter it partially from the fogs and give a somewhat drier air and higher summer temperature. The shelter is only enough to make this valley the most noted wheat region of Southern California; not enough to rank it with the parched and unreliable San Joaquin and Tulare plains.

The Mojave Desert may be looked upon, not as the geological, but as the climatic, southern continuation of the great interior valley of California.

The following tables, giving the temperature and humidity, month by month, of Sacramento and Los Angeles, are compiled from the last published annual report of the United States Signal Service:

MEAN TEMPERATURE FOR EACH MONTH, FROM JULY, 1877, TO JUNE, 1878.

Month.	*Sacramento.* Degrees.	*Los Angeles.* Degrees.
July	75.7	71.1
August	73.0	70.1
September	72.6	69.8
October	62.7	63.4
November	53.9	62.1
December	47.8	55.3
January	49.0	54.1
February	51.0	54.6
March	56.5	55.8
April	59.8	58.0
May	60.4	62.0
June	73.0	64.7

Number of days at Sacramento with temperature above 90°, 55; highest temperature recorded, 103°.

Number of days at Los Angeles with temperature above 90°, 4; highest temperature recorded, 93°.

HUMIDITY.

Month.	*Sacramento.*	*Los Angeles.*
July	43.0	61.8
August	46.0	64.5
September	43.0	62.1
October	40.0	67.4
November	72.0	46.5
December	74.0	56.4
January	70.0	61.0
February	80.0	69.3
March	74.0	72.7
April	65.0	60.8
May	57.0	70.4
June	53.0	72.0
Annual mean	61.3	64.5

AVERAGE ANNUAL RAINFALL.

Sacramento, 18 inches; Stockton, 16.8 inches; south end of San Joaquin Valley, 6.5 inches (these three measurements are taken from the official report of the State Engineer, 1880); Los Angeles, 17.97 inches (average for the last eight years, as shown by rain-guage kept by Mr. Ducommun, at Los Angeles).

A comparison of the foregoing tables shows Los Angeles to possess, as contrasted with Sacramento, an atmosphere warmer and drier in winter, and cooler and moister in summer, while the table of precipitation shows the average annual rainfall of eighteen inches at Sacramento diminishing as you go south, in accordance with the law already mentioned, to 16.8 at Stockton, and in the Tulare and Kern Valleys, still farther south, to only 6.5 inches. Yet at Los Angeles, in Southern California, it has suddenly risen again to 17.97 inches, almost the same as at Sacramento. The cause of this has already been explained in the first part of this article.

The warmer winter in Southern California, as compared with the more northern portion of the State, and the greater exemption from cold, drying winds, make this amount practically equivalent to a larger rainfall in Upper California, as vegetation is not so much retarded by the cold of December and January, but the whole of the winter becomes a growing season. The growing season is also prolonged by the fogs and humidity of a late, cool spring. The heat of summer sets in late. The season is several weeks behind that at Sacramento. Almost nightly, until July, a heavy fog rolls in, wrapping the more open portions of the country in a cloud of mist—at times almost a drizzling rain—which does not lift until several hours after sunrise.

The daily sea-breeze, only slightly obstructed by the low fragments of the Coast Range, finds its way to all portions of the system of valleys, saving them from the excessive temperature and the rapid evaporation of the Sacramento and San Joaquin country. Winter flannels are only changed to a lighter summer flannel. In eleven years of residence at Los Angeles I doubt if I have worn a linen coat upon an average five days a year; many years I have never had one on at all.

Another factor enters into the problem of the climate of Southern California. The influence of the Sonora summer's rain current is sensibly felt everywhere south of the Tehachape Mountains.

Rains are common in all the mountains of Southern California during the summer months, with a moist, cloudy air in the valleys. Three seasons in eleven years I have seen heavy rains of several hours duration, extending all over the valleys, in July and August. During these months of every year thunder-storms with often vivid lightning can be seen, sometimes daily, following along the line of the mountain chains. These summer rains help in a measure to keep up the volume of water in the rivers for irrigation, while all over the valleys the moist air which the rain current brings is instrumental in materially checking evaporation. The summer has little of the harsh dryness of the climate in the northern portion of the State. The humidity of the atmosphere is shown by the great fleecy cumuli, which float slowly across the sky like the summer clouds of the Eastern States, and by a peculiar softness of air resembling much the balmy mildness of the Mediterranean.

This soft, moist air admits of the raising of one product not elsewhere extensively cultivated in California. Here, as in the Mississippi States, corn is the staple crop, its broad, green leaves luxuriating in the warm air in which it delights. So the rank growth, and the rich, juicy green of the orange and fig leaves, show the mildness and the humidity of a climate which to them is home.

The drainage from the watershed of the Sierra, which stands as a huge background to the whole system of valleys, affords an unusually abundant supply of water for the purposes of agriculture. Over much of the land a double crop is raised—small grain without irrigation in winter, corn by irrigation in summer. Besides the three principal rivers rising from the Sierra—the Los Angeles, the San Gabriel, and the Santa Aña—each *cañon* for a hundred miles gives its small brook, and the underground flow is so great that the number of flowing artesian wells is estimated in the State Engineer's report at nearly one thousand. The *cienegas* are also a peculiar feature of these valleys. The underground flow from the Sierra here and there comes to the surface, making stretches for miles of moist land, green with grass in the driest part of the summer.

The broken, hilly Coast Range, lying at the verge of an upland plain between the Sierra and the sea, affords innumerable natural sites for extensive reservoirs for the storage of the winter floods, thus saving the winter water for summer irrigation. Many small reservoirs have been built upon this upland plain, and in the hills. The city of Los Angeles has commenced a series of such works, the largest finished covering some sixty acres. These southern valleys are by far the best watered portion of California, while the extensive use of water for irrigation is reacting upon the climate, making it still more humid.

The peculiarity of the physical character of the country which has been described, the practical obliteration of the Coast Range, and the facing of the high Sierra directly outward to the ocean, gives rise to one type of climate not elsewhere found in the State. It is not the climate of the Coast Range; neither is it the climate of the Sierra. It is a climate produced by giving the daily sea-breeze of the Coast Range to the Sierra. It is a climate which can hardly be described. The peculiar charm of it must be felt to be understood.

Along the base of the Sierra back of Pasadena, on eastward back of San Gabriel, past Cucamonga with its noted vineyards, above Pomona, and on beyond San Bernardino, growing warmer as it recedes eastward from the sea, is a belt of foothills above the fog line, facing out toward the noonday sun, looking down across the plains, and the hills of the Coast Range, upon the warm southern sea, and yet fanned daily by an ocean breeze that has no harshness. I do not say that there is no more perfect climate than this belt affords, but I have never seen one. The Southern Pacific Railroad upon its way to Arizona skirts the foot of this belt for a hundred miles.

This, however, is only one of a number of climates developed. There are local peculiarities which one would not suspect until after actual residence. Along certain lines lie what might be termed wind-belts. These are caused by the breaks in the Coast Range of hills. The night fogs also are more apt to follow certain well defined courses; and in the winter frost has its sections of preference, while other portions of the country escape entirely. There is a varied choice of climates within a comparatively limited area. Within three hours by rail one may have the fresh air of the sea-side at Santa Monica or San Pedro, with surf-bathing and a temperature always cool, even in the warmest days of summer; or, passing inland, the grass lands and dairies of Compton and Westminster, or the corn lands of Los Nietos and the region about Anaheim; the milder but still essentially coast climate of Los Angeles City; then, passing within the line of the Coast Range, the still more sheltered San Gabriel plains, where the orange best flourishes; the inland wheat-fields of San Fernando Valley, resembling somewhat the climate of the great interior valley of the San Joaquin; then the warmer raisin lands of Pomona and Riverside; the long fogless belt of the Sierra foothills; and beyond, the alfalfa lands of San Bernardino.

And still beyond, a hundred miles inland over the open valley from Los Angeles, is the San Gorgonio Pass, land-marked from the Colorado to the sea by the twin peaks, San Jacinto and San Bernardino, with snowy crests rising ten thousand and eleven thousand five hundred feet above the plain. Here the Sierra breaks down, forming the only natural pass in all its long chain, the grassy plain, without even a dividing crest, swelling and rolling through at an elevation of only two thousand nine hundred feet, a natural gateway for the southern transcontinental roads upon their way to the East. Beyond, is the great mystery of the rainless desert.

J. P. WIDNEY.

THE CHILDHOOD OF CHARLOTTE BRONTE.

During the brief literary career of this noted authoress, few personal details ever came to the knowledge of the public. A curate's daughter, a governess, a small, shy woman, living lonely among bleak moors in a sad parsonage, nursing sisters who died early, and were buried under her windows—these were all the facts that she had seen fit to communicate to the world.

In all her books, there is nothing whining or sentimental, although much that is morbid; they seem to appeal to the reader with a mute pathos; and he knows that, under the story he reads, another story is written. Miss Bronté resembles Henry Fielding in this respect; not more entirely did he put himself into his stories than did she. There are few eminent authors of whom the world will ever know as much as it does of Miss Brontë; for few authors, when they have spoken for themselves in their works, have ever such a friend to write their biographies. Mrs. Gaskill has written many a page, but she has never told a tale more tragical than the life of Charlotte Brontë. She was born in the year 1816, in the little, dreary town of Haworth, which is built upon a steep street, among the sad moors and barren hills of Yorkshire. Her father was curate of the parish; her mother came from Cornwall, and never returned thither—a mild, pious, gentle woman, who bore her husband six children in rapid succession, then died; and lived only in their vague memories and nursery traditions. So early the home seemed to be cleared of the only gracious influence which might have modified the hard life of the children. The Rev. Patrick Brontë was an Irishman, and a very remarkable character. He makes a kind of grandiose impression whenever he appears; a vast, savage nature, an abortive Titan. Mewed up in the moors, at a time when Yorkshire was the roughest part of England; relieving his anger by firing off pistols in rapid succession at his back-door, stuffing the hearth-rug into the fire until it smouldered away, or sawing away the backs of chairs, riding and walking about with a loaded pistol, which was his inseparable companion, cutting his wife's silk dress to shreds, putting the gay shoes of his children into the fire, feeding them upon potatoes because he wished them to be hearty, and to have no high-flown notions—the Rev. P. Brontë, with his fierce, passionate, nature, was not likely to be the most tender of parents, when dyspepsia set in, and he resolved to eat alone in his room, which he did to the end of his life. But, with all these savage traits, he had a wild love of nature; walked far and wide, in all weathers, over the heaths; was faithful in visiting the sick, diligent in the care of the schools, and was evidently a greatly misplaced and wasted force in the humble curacy of Haworth.

While the dyspeptic father was firing pistols out of the back-door, and eating alone in his study, the mother was dying slowly of a cancer, and the house on the very edge of the graveyard was hushed.

The children had few books—their father would foster no nonsense; but Emily read aloud the newspapers, and they discussed the comparative merits of Hannibal and Bonaparte. They gave preternatural answers to their father's preposterous questions; and when he asked his youngest girl, Annie, what such a child most wanted, she, instead of reveling in childhood, answered, "Age and experience."

The gentle mother died, and then began the reign of an aunt, with strong prejudices and a distaste for Yorkshire, who went clicking up and down stairs in pattens, lest she might take cold, and at length took her meals also in her bedroom. The children recited to their father, and browsed upon all sorts of books; but at length the two eldest were sent to a school at Cowan's Bridge. Here they were starved and stunted, exposed to every hardship and disease, with all the heartless cruelty of charity institutions. The story of their sufferings is piteous; it is as sad in the history as it is in the burning, indignant description of the school in *Jane Eyre*. Maria, the eldest, died in consequence of this school, and Elizabeth contracted the disease which soon swept her after. The father removed them from school, and an old servant, Tabby, came, at this time, full of all kinds of traditional lore, for which she found delighted and enthusiastic listeners in the girls. There was a brother, Branwell, also, a weak, fascinating, brilliant character, self-indulgent and idolized by his sisters, and so winning in his ways and conversation that he was always summoned to the village inn when the passing traveler wanted amusement.

The talent of the girls began to display itself in domestic literature. They wrote every kind of work, and imagined an island, and had each their heroes among the living and eminent Englishmen of the time. Wellington was Charlotte's hero. He occupied her imagination, and all her contributions to the mimic domestic magazine were purported to be written by "Lord Charles Albert Florian Wellesley."

In 1831, Charlotte was the eldest living child; very small in figure, calling herself "stunted," with soft, thick, brown hair, and eyes of a reddish brown. The rest of her features were large and plain, and she was altogether very quiet in manners and quaint in dress. She then went to school to a kind, motherly woman, Miss Wooler, and amazed all the girls by knowing a great deal less and a vast deal more than they did, by being moody and silent, then by repeating long pages of poetry, and declining to play ball. She would stand on the play-ground and look at the sky and the shadows of the trees, and talk politics furiously; or frighten the poor little girls out of their poor little wits by telling horrible stories as they lay in bed at night.

But the girls loved her, and Miss Wooler loved her, then and always afterward. After a year she went home again, and lived in solitude, passing her time in drawing, reading, and walking out among the moors with her sisters, and devising plans with them for the education of their brother, who was finally destined for a painter. The three girls grew up together—Charlotte, sad, shy, and religious; Emily, with a suppressed vehemence of nature, and very reserved; Annie, the youngest and mildest of all. They were what their parents and their life had made them. Inheriting the paternal strength with the mother's gentleness, a youth, bereaved of childhood, had passed in solitude and gloom.

GERTRUDE HARROW.

ORPHEUS AND EURYDICE.

A GREEK MYTH AS RELATED BY THE CAHUILLA INDIANS OF SOUTHERN CALIFORNIA.

A great pestilence had destroyed the people; only an old woman and two children—a boy and a girl—remained. When they grew up, the man proved himself a great hunter, and the girl, who possessed remarkable beauty and a lovely disposition, an adept in all household arts. In time they married, and now the old woman, fancying herself neglected, plotted against the life of her foster-daughter. Twice she failed in her attempt, but the young wife, aware of her design, apprised her husband, and told him that should she be slain in his absence, her soul would notify him of the fact by dropping tears upon his shoulder. One day, while hunting, he received the fatal sign, and hurried home, but ere he could execute vengeance on the hag, she transformed herself into a gopher, and burrowed in the earth, where she had concealed the body of her victim.

For three days and three nights he lay upon the grave, lamenting the loss of his love, nor tasted he of food or drink throughout that weary vigil. At last he perceived a small whirlwind arise from the grave and disappear. Soon a second arose and moved toward the south, gradually augmenting in size as it progressed. This he followed, and, passing over a sandy plain, perceived that it left foot-prints; then knew he that it was indeed his wife. Redoubling now his efforts, he gained upon the apparition, and, addressing it, was repaid by hearing the voice of his love reply, "Return, O my husband, for where I go, thither thou canst not come. Thou art of the earth, but I am dead to the world." Nevertheless, impelled by his great love, he insisted on following, even to the world of shades; and at last, moved by his entreaties, she consented, but cautioned him, "Forget not that no earthly eye may ever again see us!"

They passed over a great sea, and entered the realm of ghosts. He saw here no form, but heard myriads of voices, sweet as the tones of zephyrs, breathed lightly o'er Æolian strings, addressing his spirit-guide:

"What hast thou here, sister? It smells of Earth!"

She confessed that she had brought with her a mortal, her husband, and begged that he might be permitted to stay. She rehearsed his mighty deeds and many admirable qualities while on earth; but all in vain. Again were the voices heard, still musical, but now stern and threatening in their tones.

"Take him away!" they said. "Guided by love he comes, and love pleads his cause; love is all-powerful on Earth, but earthly love avails not in the courts of Heaven!"

Abashed by the evident displeasure of these invisible ones, she still braved their anger, and pleaded for her love. She dilated on his many virtues and his great skill, until at last, despite their assertion "that love availed not," the spirit-guard relented, and he was allowed to make exhibition of his acquirements, with a view to his possible admission. He was required to bring a feather from the top of a pole so high that the summit was scarcely visible; to split a hair of great fineness and exceeding length from end to end; to make a map of the constellation known as the "Lesser Bear," and to indicate the exact location of the North Star. Aided by his wife, he succeeded in accomplishing all these tasks to the satisfaction of his examiners; but, in a trial of hunting, failed utterly, the game being invisible. A second attempt resulted as before, and he had become discouraged, when his wife advised him to aim his arrows at the beetles which flew past him in great numbers.

Acting upon her instructions, each beetle, when struck, proved a fat deer; and so many did he slay that the spirit-voices commanded him to desist. They then addressed his wife, who was yet to him invisible. "Sister," they said, "thou knowest none who enter here return again to earth. Tucupar (heaven) knows not death. Our brother-in-law hath done full well, yet mortal skill may not avail to win a heavenly prize. We award him the guerdon,

Love, chiefest of earthly blessings, in thy person; yet only on one condition."

Then, addressing the husband, they said, "Take thou thy wife. Yet remember thou shalt not speak to her, nor touch her, until three suns have passed. A punishment awaits thy disobedience."

They pass from the spirit-land, and travel in silence to the confines of matter. By day she is invisible to him, but at night, by the flickering flame of his camp-fire, he perceives her outline on the ground near by. Another day he remains faithful to his instructions, and by the evening blaze her form appears more plainly than before. The third day has passed, and now, behold! the amorous flame leaps forth to greet her, recumbent by his side, radiant with beauty and health, and restored, as he fondly believes, to him and love.

But, alas! one-half the lurid orb of day yet trembles, poised on the western verge, as with passionate vehemence he pronounces her name, and clasps to his faithful heart—not the form of her he loves, but a fragment of decayed wood.

Heart-broken and despairing, he roamed the earth ever afterward, until at last the spirits, in mercy, sent to him their servant, Death, who dissolved his mortal fetters, and carried him, rejoicing, to the bosom of his love.

J. ALBERT WILSON.

NOTE BOOK.

WE ARE IN RECEIPT of several numbers of the *Kieler Zeitung* containing a pleasant and appreciative review of the article in the August number of THE CALIFORNIAN upon Fritz Reuter. A former number of the *Zeitung* had contained a similar *critique* upon the article upon Klaus Groth, Ditmarsch, and Plattdeutsch, in the February issue. As to the essays themselves, the author did not, and does not, claim more for their merit than that they were mere rough suggestions to cultivated Americans as to a new and fertile field in literature, which might be entered upon with a certainty of acquiring pleasant and healthful ideas in consonance with English and American tastes of mode and thought. But we are glad that the appreciation which was shown for both Groth and Reuter in the articles in question has aroused a warm feeling of friendliness in the bright and cultivated town of Kiel, which feeling seems to have been enhanced by the fact that it was a genuine American, and not a stray naturalized German, who ventured an English encomium upon the Plattdeutsch lyrist and pastoral writer, Groth, and upon the prose-sketch writer, Reuter. We of California are intensely material in our wishes and aims; but if our hungry ambitions seem too absorbing, it is not because we wish to underrate culture and æsthetical pursuits. The man whose fortune lies on a gambling table, no matter how much of an art-enthusiast he may be, can have but a careless eye for the Venus of Milo while the *croupier* is extending his rake. So it is with the Californian. "Give me a fortune," he cries, "and I will be a willing disciple." But while the fortune is delayed, while his life-ship is still at sea, he is impatient of the sound of the philosopher's voice or the music of the poet; and it does not add to his good nature to be asked to winnow out the fallacies of the one or the false notes of the other. But for all our materialism and money-greed, we still can find points of sympathy with Kiel. We are a sea-port; so is Kiel. We are almost daily startled with the thunder of naval salutes; the streets of Kiel are alive with bluff naval officers. We, too, have a university; for is not Berkeley just at our elbow to teach us grammar and spelling? We have a different climate, it is true—a sort of matronly, middle-aged summer, in lieu of the wintry gusts of the Baltic. But sometimes differences only emphasize sympathies. We found one Tory Englishman who thought there were too many liberally educated men in Schleswig-Holstein. We wish he could see the same fault in us. But all this is away from what we wished to say, which was to assure our Kiel friends of our distinguished regard, to wish long lives to its academic and naval gentlemen, and to hope that its poesy and its Holstein roses may blossom forever.

IF ANY ONE IN THE WORLD IS TO BE PITIED it is the man who has "lost his grip." Go along the street any fair day and you will see him leaning against the railing in the sunshine, with a discouraged expression in his face, looking helplessly at the busy throng as it surges by. Draw near to him, and you will find him communicative. All his barriers of reserve have been broken down these many years. He will take it as a favor if you speak with him. He has a sort of apologetic appeal in his voice that makes you pity or bully him, according to the style of man you are. He is doubtful of himself even in the commonest matters. His only hope of prosperity is to lean on some one, just as he leans against the railing in the afternoon sunlight. His opinions are all supplemented with, "Don't *you* think so?" If he has anything to do, there is a premonition of failure in every gesture as he sets about it. His whole manner is a mute protest against your reposing too much confidence in his ability to accomplish anything. But speak of the past—then he will talk bravely enough. He will entertain you by the hour about his palmy days, how he had the finest store in the wholesale quarter, how he was the leading spirit in the great wheat deal fifteen years ago, how he was this, that, and the other—always in the past. Every one who now has money made it by a trick of subterfuge that he can tell, with some asperity, the secret history of. You may learn from him of more skeletons that grin in costly closets than repose in the most populous necropolis. Ten to one he knows the prices of all the stocks that are listed on the boards.

He will confide to you where the next "deal" is to be, lamenting, rather suggestively, his need of the little sum which would enable him to participate. Day after day he grows more seedy, more dependent, and day after day the brave, noble woman at home puts forth more resolute exertions. His children grow up with an air of made-over gentility—a little graceless, it may be, and hardly realizing the fond hopes that are built upon their future. By and by it is all over, and perhaps the tired couple rest as peacefully under the weeds and wild flowers as does the millionaire in his sarcophagus. It is an inspiring sight—this world of ours—as it rolls on to its splendid destiny. But how many pitiful, tearful things it carries with it!

THE OTHER SIDE OF THIS PICTURE is the man of resolution, erect, undaunted; as Emerson puts it, "the man whose eye meets yours." In a recent conversation, a friend, who had amassed wealth, attributed his success to the fact that he looked always forward and never backward. "When any venture goes badly with me, and I am convinced that it is a loss, I turn my entire attention to the next thing in hand, and waste neither energy nor time on what is gone. I am convinced that this habit has benefited me to the extent of thousands of dollars." This man has preserved not alone his fortune, but his cheerful, happy disposition and vigorous will by this simple maxim. If there be in the broad universe a spectacle truly worthy of admiration, it is the human being who is not

> "a pipe for Fortune's finger
> To sound what stop she please;"

who is not elated by prosperity nor downcast by misfortune; who is conscious of his own strength, but not arrogant; who is brave, yet gentle; intelligent, yet not pedantic; self-contained, yet not reserved; charitable and not profligate; who can stand without humility before a king and without pride before a peasant. Such a man, moving in the serenity of conscious power, leaning upon nothing, depending on no one, is his own best and ever present inspiration. He has that best of gifts, the power of rising superior to things external to himself. For no truth is more unchangeable than that the world is different to every person; that it is to each just as it appears through the lens of self. The earth is a goodly frame or a sterile promontory, as one or another may look upon it. The perfume of the daisy is imprisoned in the song of Burns. To Byron its fragrance would have been unnoticed. If it be true, therefore, that to each his own being is the universe, why should one stand abashed in the presence of another, save that his sphere of existence is more contracted, more incomplete? One may have a million dollars, and yet his world may be so small and mean that his mind cannot stand erect in it. Another may have only his strong arm and his clear vision, and yet the sun shall not penetrate so comprehensive a domain as his thought. If we could only realize this, that a man is neither worthy nor unworthy, noble nor ignoble, by virtue of anything external to himself, some of us would not cringe so much, and none of us would ever bully another.

APROPOS OF MR. BOYNTON CARLISLE'S ARTICLE in the present number, there is one aspect of the question of the education of the female sex to which, perhaps not inappropriately, he might have alluded. Was it not Prescott who told of the great Aztec seminaries of learning, where young women, after years of instruction, were finally graduated in the mysteries of feather-work? One can hardly help smiling at the time and pains which were spent upon this useless accomplishment. But have we no feather-work accomplishments in our day? How many millions a year do we spend in teaching girls music, talent or no talent? All over this broad land—from ocean to ocean and from lake to gulf, as our stump-orators say—young women are practicing with a persistence which would be praiseworthy if it were not painful. Apostrophizing England, Webster said that her "morning drum-beat, following the sun and keeping company with the hours, circles the earth with one continuous and unbroken strain of the martial airs of England." But Webster's drum-beat has given way to the five-finger exercise, and the martial airs are replaced by the incessant invocation of the "Maiden's Prayer." In hundreds of families, where it is hard enough in all conscience to provide the necessaries of life, an additional point is strained that the daughters may learn music. There is no parallel in history to this devotion of an entire sex to a single study. The results ought to be marvelous. *And yet the world has never produced a single great musician of the female sex.* There is no counterpart to Mozart, Mendelssohn, Beethoven, Handel. Not a great piece of music to-day bears the name of a woman as its composer. It may be assumed that if the male sex had devoted itself with such unanimity to the study of one science or art, it would have abandoned it upon finding its efforts so utterly fruitionless. I am not one of those who believe in the inferiority of women. In many respects they are decidedly our superiors. But I see nothing but folly in this music-madness. Out of every hundred thousand persons, perhaps one may be born a musician. It may be that this estimate is too liberal. Now, there are families in which every daughter is laboriously instructed in music. Is it any wonder that these girls never get beyond a point at which it is useless to themselves and tedious to their friends? Suppose the thousands of young women of the United States were to take the millions of dollars and the countless hours which they annually expend in this non-productive manner, and devote them to any science—to geology, which they could study on every hillside; to botany, which they might learn in every garden; to chemistry, to zoology, to astronomy, to any one of the great departments of physical science—can any one doubt that the result would be more profitable both to themselves and the State? For here is the difference: one must be *born* a musician, and Nature, in her excessive frugality, decrees that these births shall be rare. But the great book of science lies unrolled, so that any person who has intelligence and application may read. Some of the most valuable discoveries, some of the most invaluable observations, have been made by amateurs. With the leisure which most ladies have, with the same means now expended in making them indifferent musicians, they might be admitted into the *arcana* of the most beautiful sciences. Any one can appreciate what the effect would be upon the general intelligence of the people, if the female half of the entire population, or even the proportion now studying music, were to apply itself with the same assiduity and quickness of perception in one of the directions indicated.

SCIENCE AND INDUSTRY.

WHAT MANUFACTURING INDUSTRIES CAN DO FOR A CITY

Few people fully realize the importance of manufacturing industries in building up a city; but the forthcoming census report, which will be more complete in industrial statistics than any which has preceded it, will furnish a mass of facts in that direction which should be carefully studied by all interested in the building up of our great commercial and industrial centers. We are already in possession of a few isolated returns which it may be profitable to consider. Take, for instance, the town of Paterson, New Jersey. Less than twenty years ago it was comparatively a small place, of little industrial importance. A few enterprising gentlemen, impressed with the idea that there was an important future in this country for the silk business, resolved to take hold of that enterprise, and fixed upon Paterson as their center of operations. The result has far exceeded their anticipations, and to-day there are not less than sixty flourishing silk manufactories in that city, besides locomotive works and other industries, which support a population of over sixty thousand souls. The silk industry belongs to a class of manufactures which, until recently, has been thought to be beyond the reach of American enterprise and skill. But facts within the last twenty years have proved that there is nothing dependent upon the skill of man which is impossible to American artisans when properly backed by commensurate capital. Philadelphia has probably manifested more enterprise in this direction than any other city in the Union, and is destined to become the greatest manufacturing center in the world, if, indeed, it has not already attained to that eminence. The census which is now being taken will show that the annual value of the manufactures of that place will reach a grand total of over [illegible]. The capitalists of that city are fully alive to the importance of providing ample employment for all competent skill that presents itself for that purpose. Many similar illustrations might be cited of what may be done when there is a will and a united effort on the part of combined labor and capital to make each help the other on a liberal basis. It is to be hoped that the citizens of San Francisco will profit by the lessons which are being taught by the incoming census returns. There is no city in the world which has a greater future before it if we only profit as we may by the advantages within our reach. The times just now are propitious. As a State and as a nation, we are on the eve of an era of prosperity such as perhaps has never before been witnessed in the history of American industry.

A NOVELTY IN LOCOMOTIVE BUILDING.

The first really radical change in locomotive building since the days of Stephenson is now in process of being carried out at the Grant Locomotive Works, in Paterson, New Jersey. When it is completed, this queer looking machine will present very much the appearance of a locomotive turned up side down; for the machinery and one set of wheels will be on top of the boiler, instead of under it or at its sides. There will be two pairs of driving wheels, but, instead of having them follow each other, as in the usual construction, one pair will be on top and resting upon the rims of the other. What are usually the rear wheels will be the upper ones, and they will turn in an opposite direction from that in which the engine is going. This upper pair will act as friction wheels upon the rims of the lower pair, which rest upon the rails. The object of this novel construction is to increase the speed of the locomotive without increasing the motion of the piston. As is generally known, all devices hitherto employed to gain speed have depended either on an increase in the size of the driving-wheels or the number of strokes of the piston, to both of which methods there are practical objections. This device is intended to utilize in the locomotive the familiar principle in mechanics of gaining speed by making a larger wheel drive a smaller one. Speed in this case being the object, the loss of power involved is of but little consequence. The upper and larger wheel is driven by the piston. The friction is secured by causing much of the weight of the engine to rest upon the upper set of wheels. The boiler will be carried very low, and it is claimed that the locomotive will run steadier, and with less oscillation of either piston or engine than is involved in the present mode of construction. It is expected that this will be the fastest locomotive ever placed upon a railroad track.

REPRODUCTION OF SPEECH BY A BEAM OF LIGHT.

One of the most interesting papers produced at the late meeting of the American Association for the Advancement of Science was read by Mr. Alexander Graham Bell, well known from his connection with the telephone, in which that gentleman gave an account of an invention which Mr. M. S. Painter and himself had perfected, and which, in its accomplishments, rivals in marvelousness either the telegraph or the telephone. This invention consists of an exceedingly simple device whereby articulate speech may be readily transmitted over long distances, without any wire connection whatever, simply by the use of a ray of light. The instrument by which this is accomplished is called a "Photophone." The steps which led to the invention, and the progress thus far made in reducing it to practice, were most graphically told and illustrated by Mr. Bell, and may be described as follows: Take an ordinary telephone circuit; remove the metallic transmitting disk, and substitute in its place a similar disk of mica or very thin glass, such as is used for covering microscopic slides; let this disk be silvered so as to make a mirror of it. Remove the receiving disk from the opposite terminus, and substitute in its place a disk of selenium. Now remove the connecting wire between the two termini, and so place the receiving disk that a strong beam of light—either sunlight or artificial light—may fall upon it. Let the reflected light be so received by an intervening lens that it may pass in a direct line of parallel rays to the receiving disk of selenium. Everything is now in readiness, and the speaker may proceed as with an ordinary telephone. The action of the voice upon the back of the receiving disk or mirror puts it in vibration, and produces a series of pulsations in the beam of light similar to the pulsations produced by the voice in a current of electricity with which a telephone wire is charged. These pulsations of light produce the same effect upon the sensitive selenium receiver as do the electric pulsations upon the ordinary telephonic receiver, and the articulations of the voice are as faithfully reproduced and heard in the one as in the other.

ELECTRIC IRON.

Nature truly "works in mysterious ways her wonders to perform." Among the many mysteries of Nature, few appear more mysterious to us than the fragments of meteoric iron which so often "come down" to us from the immensity of space. Where they come from, or how they have been elaborated, who can tell! One thing, however, we do know—that in meteoric iron we have the nearest approach to perfection in that metal that the utmost ingenuity of man can devise; and we may also in this, as in numerous other instances, learn that the hight of human endeavor should in all practicable cases be in imitation of Nature's processes. That electricity has something to do in bringing these meteoric masses into the condition in which they come to us, seems to be more or less apparent. To prove this, small masses of pig-iron have recently been subjected to long continued electrical action with most remarkable results. Mr. James Barrett, an English gentleman of Kentish Town, North Wales, has furnished a photographic illustration of such action, which affords a practical illustration of the power of electricity to effect most remarkable results in this direction. The surface of this specimen is shown to be most unmistakably in the transition stage of passing from common pig-iron into a metal more highly refined than has ever before been seen in any other specimen of iron alloy, except that of undoubted meteoric origin. It is also claimed that this specimen "depicts what, without explanation, would be a riddle as puzzling as any which the Sphinx of the Thames embankment could propound, did it indulge in problems; and challenges attention toward the solution of one of the most important questions of the day." As to the question of costliness, it may be remarked that the production of electricity on a large scale, in localities favorable for cheap water-power, involves almost unlimited possibilities; and when electric iron can be produced in merchantable quantities, no other kind of that metal will be able to compete with it in price.

A NEW MECHANICAL MOTION.

The invention of "a new mechanical motion" is reported, designed for working metal, wood, or stone into irregular forms and surfaces, which have heretofore been reached only by hand labor and the graver's tool. The agent is described as being applicable to a perpendicular, reciprocating, rotary, or spiral motion. The tools, which are of various shapes, according to the nature of the work required, are caused to strike very rapid blows—from six to eight thousand a minute—and are said to produce certain new and useful results heretofore impossible to be effected by any known machinery. It is claimed that many classes of useful and ornamental work, hitherto done by hand at great expense, may be wrought out by this new device with great rapidity, beauty, and accuracy, even with the unskilled labor of boys and girls. The machines are applicable alike to the finest work in gold and silver, or to large masses of iron, wood, and stone, over which latter the cutting-head moves with the majestic and irresistible power which belongs to the most ponderous class of machinery in modern machine shops.

A NOVEL PROJECTILE.

An officer of the British army, in the last number of *Macmillan's Magazine*, gives a detailed description of a novel projectile which he has devised to meet the peculiar conditions involved for penetrating the monitor type of war vessels as now constructed, upon which solid shot can produce but little effect. The new projectile has a dish-like form and rapid vertical rotation. The rotation is imparted by a "catch" near the muzzle of the gun, which gives to the projectile a twirl as it leaves the barrel. This catch may be applied to any ordinary smooth-bore. The projectile simply rolls out of the gun with great initial velocity, unretarded by rifling or a column of packed air before it, as is the case with ordinary missiles. Such a projectile will maintain its line of motion like that of an advancing velocipede wheel, and when it strikes the sloping side of an armored ship, from which a solid shot would glance doing little or no injury, the whole momentum of this shot would be brought to bear like a circular saw, cutting its way through any armor which a ship could carry.

REVOLUTION IN TELEGRAPHY.

Mr. House, the well known telegraph inventor, is said to have devised a new instrument for transmitting, receiving, and recording, which works automatically, and by which messages may be transmitted at the rate of from two hundred and fifty to three hundred words per minute. Such an instrument, if practical, must work quite a revolution in telegraphy, as by the best instruments now in use forty words per minute is considered quite rapid work. It is also claimed that messages can be sent by this new instrument for one-tenth the cost involved in the use of the instruments now employed. As it works automatically, a large portion of the force now required in large offices can be dispensed with. This fact will not make the new instrument very popular with telegraph operators.

HOT POLISHED SHAFTING.

The effect of polishing iron at an elevated temperature is very generally known. It is that which gives to Russia sheet-iron its peculiar blue finish. A magnetic oxide, adhering firmly, is superficially formed, and renders the metal much less liable to oxidization than sheet-iron as ordinarily made. This principle has recently been applied to the manufacture of polished shafting. It is claimed that a peculiar process is employed, which yields important advantages, but only when the best of raw material is involved. This latter fact, of itself, it is further claimed, furnishes a guarantee against inferiority in shafting turned out by this process.

ART AND ARTISTS.

FASHION AND ART.

Fashion after all has its advantages. In addition to the opportunity it affords the rich to distinguish themselves from their fellows as possessors of the means necessary to keep pace with its vagaries, and also to the benefits derived from its constant changes by merchants and those interested in the manufacture of the various articles subject to its whims, it likewise indirectly, and perhaps inadvertently, contributes to the development of many of the useful arts, and even the sciences. Were it not for fashion, however, probably that much laughed at word, "culture," would not have lost its true significance, and become among journalists a by-word of affected superiority. The rage for all kinds of learning classified under the general head of culture has so possessed some sections of our country that its influences are extending to all classes, often to the disparagement of other and more important duties. This rage is, probably, a fashion of the day, and will, no doubt, run its race, as do all others, but will leave its good effects behind, and result advantageously to the people and to the development and appreciation of many subjects which otherwise would have long remained unrecognized. Among the most conspicuous fashions of the day, outside of those relating to personal adornment, is the so-called rage for art, pictorial as well as decorative. A certain knowledge of art is fast becoming essential to the establishment of any claim to accomplishment. Our youth, principally of the gentler sex, devote a certain portion of their time to its cultivation, either in the academies or through private instruction. Elementary instruction is given in many of the public schools, and a visit to any pretentious household will reveal the productions of amateur aspirants to this kind of distinction. Among the wealthy, also, one's standing is more or less dependent upon the amount of appreciation and patronage he bestows upon the arts. In new communities, where wealth is by no means synonymous with culture, much of this kind of appreciation is feigned, but constant association with objects of beauty and taste is sure in time to engender a real appreciation for such objects. Indeed, pictures are regarded quite as essential to the well furnishing of an establishment as is the library—though unread; and the host, however deficient in such likings he may be personally, at once recognizes the wants of his many friends, and endeavors to supply this demand upon his munificence. In other words, it is the fashion to do so, and fashion is an exacting mistress. What pictures to buy and in what manner to select them seems to be a difficult problem for many to solve. None like to betray their ignorance in such matters, and from a fear of such exposure hesitate to buy any works by an artist not of extended reputation. With unlimited means this can be effected, and perhaps accounts for the fact that some of our most wealthy citizens limit their purchases to foreign productions. Some take pleasure, it is true, in associating their pictures with the various places in which they were purchased; however, in one instance, a wealthy Californian identified his pictures, not by subject or artist, but by the prices paid for them in Rome, Florence, and Paris. Not unfrequently men are found who possess both a knowledge of art and the means to gratify their taste. It is a pleasure to visit their galleries. One is sure to encounter excellent work, often of men whose names are not familiar to the public, and their collections are not so much characterized by a long list of prominent names attached to mediocre pictures, as by a display of genuine merit, in which the pictures themselves, and not the names, prove the attraction. Such men are never at a loss to know what to purchase. They can detect excellences as readily in a local studio as in the Salon, and to them belongs greatly the credit of encouraging and developing the growth of art in their respective communities.

PRETTY PICTURES.

If the views of artists could be arrived at, no doubt it would be found that, almost without exception, they would prefer to have the word "pretty" dropped entirely from the art vocabulary. So-called pretty pictures are frequently to be met with, and with some painters possibly that same quality is the object for which they strive. Where such is the case, however, it is usually an effort on the part of the artist to meet the exactions of an uneducated taste. Although it is the desire of most painters to produce an agreeable, if not beautiful picture, the existence of so many other qualities essential to a good picture, and which so greatly outrank in importance the mere prettiness of subject, causes the painter to regard the word "pretty," when applied to his production, in an unfavorable light. Did those who employ it so freely but know how, as an art-term, that word is regarded by artists and connoisseurs, the expression would be rarely heard in the gallery. Its use argues either the inability of the speaker to detect the greater excellences in a picture, or that there is a lack of those excellences. Either of these conclusions is anything but gratifying to the artist who has bestowed his thought and study upon the subject. Pictures rarely depend for their attractiveness upon the prettiness of objects employed. Often objects that are regarded ugly or uninteresting in nature, when portrayed upon canvas prove most pleasing. This simply shows the distinction between prettiness and picturesqueness, a distinction many fail to recognize. Probably, in nature, no more beautiful animal can be found than a nicely groomed, finely shaped horse, with his glossy coat and elegant proportions. But on canvas, the neglected, worn out old stager, with shaggy hair, drooping head, and all the evidences of neglect, at once impresses the beholder as being the more impressive and interesting of the two. Likewise, a tottering shanty, with broken chimney, unhinged doors, stained and moss-grown roof, and neglected surroundings, although repulsive to many in nature, when conveyed to canvas surpasses, as a picture, the cleanly painted house, with well kept lawn, and all the appliances and conveniences of a complete and desirable home. Indeed, the more of rugged, careless nature the subject embodies, and the less of trimness, prettiness, and precision, the more valued and interesting it becomes as a picture. The artist usually endeavors to make choice of such subjects. His aim is picturesqueness, not prettiness. Having employed his art in its composition, his knowledge in its color and *technique*, and his skill in its manipulation, he presents his work for view, and invites intelligent criticism upon its merits and defects. If, after all this, the beholder is simply impressed by prettiness of subject, it is easy to imagine the chagrin of the painter, who, however, would prefer to attribute the lack of appreciation of his work to want of knowledge on the part of the spectator, rather than to a lack of those higher and more essential qualities for which he has striven. Indeed, next to having the observer remark upon the beauty or elegance of the frame that surrounds his picture, before passing upon the picture itself, probably nothing is more distasteful to the earnest and ambitious painter than to hear his picture called pretty.

JAPANESE PRECEPTS.

Outside of the many and peculiar characteristics of the Japanese, resulting from an isolated civilization, by which they are so markedly distinguished from the other peoples of the world, we now and then discover motives and thoughts in their lives which go to show their general kinship and common origin with the rest of us. Indeed, some of their notions are rather a refinement upon our own, especially as regards pictures and the manner of viewing them, which we gather from certain precepts published some time since in the *Art Interchange*, and said to be the discovery of a Boston paper. The article says: "The Japanese are fond of pictures and ornamentation in their dwellings, but they do not, as we do, have a great many things exposed to view at once. One or two pictures, a *fungus*, and a hanging basket, or a bracket serve for a time, when these are laid away, the pictures being rolled up, and their places are supplied by other things. But if a visitor expresses a liking for such things they will bring out quantities for his inspection. They enjoin the following good rules for looking at a picture: You must not look at it on a dark day, nor a cloudy day, *nor* when it is so cold that your breath will form a mist before you; nor must you look at it when you are ill, or cross, or unhappy, lest these circumstances influence your opinion. You must not unroll it, so as to see the artist's name, at first, but study it at leisure, so as to judge impartially of its merits."

THE POTATO AS A CLEANSER.

In an article entitled "Picture Cleaning and Restoring," published in the *Art Amateur*, some time since, the potato was made to figure conspicuously as a cleanser of pictures. The fact is entirely new to us, and will, no doubt, be of interest as well as value to many artists and owners of pictures. The writer, after describing the process of removing varnish from the face of the picture by means of friction produced by rubbing the finger over the surface, says: "If it is the object merely to clean its surface, a little lukewarm water may be best applied with a sponge until the water ceases to be discolored. If then the varnish still presents an appearance of dirt, take a potato, and cutting it in half apply the fresh portion to the varnish, and by a series of circles all over the surface, completely rub every part. Apply again the lukewarm water until it shows no taint of dirt. Should, however, the picture continue to exhibit traces of dirt, pass a sponge dipped in warm beer over it. Then, after it has become perfectly dry, wash it with a solution of the finest gum dragon dissolved in pure water." After pictures have become thoroughly hardened, and before the application of varnish, the writer says: "The application of a potato, as before shown, should always be resorted to, to remove the exudations of the oils which rise to the surface, as well as the dirt collected, and this simple process will be sufficient to clean nine out of ten modern works. Artists will also find the use of the potato most valuable before commencing the progressive steps of their work, as it gets rid of that annoying greasiness which causes the newly applied and wet paint to run, after the manner of water upon a tea-tray. It ought to be remarked that the cleaning of a picture that has been varnished and one that has not undergone that process are two different things. Liberties may be taken with the former which would prove fatal to a picture not thus protected. In either case, as a preliminary experiment, the potato may be applied without fear of injury, provided that the moisture left by its juice is removed from the unvarnished picture. Many finished oil paintings collect upon their surface what is termed "bloom," which in many instances entirely obscures the beauty of the work, and several receipts have been given for its removal; but all of these, or nearly all, are only temporary cures, the bloom returning, sometimes with greater depth and opacity. Here again the potato is said to be the best remedy, if not an entire cure. Apply it as before, wash off with clean cold water, and then wipe the surface of the picture with a little sweet or nut oil on a silk handkerchief until perfectly dry."

BOOKS RECEIVED.

THE LIGHT OF ASIA, OR THE GREAT RENUNCIATION (Mahâbhinishkramana). Being the Life and Teaching of Gautama, Prince of India and Founder of Buddhism, as told, in verse, by an Indian Buddhist. By Edwin Arnold, M.A. New York: American Book Exchange. 1880.

The tendency of contemporary thought to freedom in religious ideas is peculiarly well adapted for the favorable reception of a work devoted to the life and labors of a great moral teacher. Mr. Arnold, the editor of the London *Daily Telegraph*, has seized upon a fortunate moment to present to the public his views of a religion embraced by three hundred and seventy millions of people. The poem is a religious epic of exceeding interest, having nothing of the irksomeness that is apt to be found in works devoted to the elucidation of a religious belief. In eight books, the birth, the youth, the renouncing of royal station for a hermit's lot, the studies and the teachings of Gautama, the founder of Buddhism, are told. In keeping with that characteristic of the Hindu mind that loves to deal with the wonderful in the tangible and intangible, that surrounds all its imaginings with a warmth and richness born of a tropic clime, the advent and the stay of the Buddha have been entwined with tales of celestial demonstrations and superhuman power. Many of these tales the poet has introduced into his poem, and rightfully so, as enabling one the better to compare the treasured legends of this with those of other faiths. Buddhism was an outgrowth of Hindu thought and feeling, rebelling against the rigid doctrines of Brahmanism. Like the latter, it was founded on the theory of the transmigration of souls, from which it sought a release. The end of both faiths was an escape from a ceaseless birth and death. But the means of attaining this end, and the end itself, were different. Brahmanism sought a final absorption in the soul of Brahma through a life of asceticism, self-torture, and exposure to the elements. Buddhism taught that Nirvana, a never ending peace, was assured to all who would practice self-control and universal charity. The one extended its consolation to the outcast, the poor, to the Sudra as well as to those of the higher castes; the other reserved its benefits for those of the three higher castes alone. The one was founded on a moral code equal to any the world has ever seen; the other took its origin in the interpretation of the phenomena of nature, and was preserved in formalities.

This moral code, and the lofty character of its framer, are the theme for the poet's contemplation. Into four parts the unfolding of this subject resolves itself—the birth and youth of the Prince; his life in that golden home, where "love was gaoler and delight its bars," comprising the awakening to the sense of a people's misery, and the renunciation of his existence of ease; his wanderings, studies, and final learning of the truth; and the truth itself, the doctrines of Buddhism.

To have accomplished the task of presenting in a clear form the meaning of Buddhism, to have selected from the immense mass of writings upon this subject such matters only as are of general interest and importance, evince no ordinary ability as a compiler. But the author has done far more than offer for our consideration a skillfully arranged condensation of Buddhist teachings. With the knowledge of a scholar versed in the religions of the Orient, he has combined a power of poetic expression of the highest order. Never unmindful of his theme, he has called to its adornment all the wealth the East, rich in scenery and in idea, can afford. To highten the dramatic effect of the whole, the early pages are devoted to a minute and glowing description of the glorious station and worldly happiness of Gautama, surpassing even the conception of ordinary man. The Indian home, "where skill had spent all lovely fantasies to lull the mind," the *nautch* girls' dances, the music whispering through the blooms, the chime of ankle bells, the essences of musk and champak, that drowsy led the soul of the prince to sleep, unthinking, by his queen, Yasodhara, are sharply brought in contrast with the yellow robe, "the scanty meal, chance-gathered from the charitable," the couch of grass by night, the homeless and lonely lot of the hermit, self-imposed, to find a refuge for suffering mankind. This dramatic effect is most intense in the fourth book, recounting the struggles of the prince between his love for his wife and the blissful existence he had led, and the call of duty to leave all these, to wander a beggar in the search for truth. Not only is the scene of the renunciation very powerfully drawn, but it is itself the summit of a climax, for which the mind is prepared by the thrilling meeting of the prince with the "old, old man, whose shriveled skin, sun-tanned, clung like a beast's hide to his fleshless bones," with the pest-stricken wretch, and with the crackling, crumbling body on the pyre. These are not the only instances in which the author has demonstrated his appreciation of situation. The whispering of the Devas, the gods of the air, upon the silver-stringed gourd placed carelessly on the sill of his marble palace, that rouse to action the listless prince; the muffled tramp of snowy Kantaka, bearing his master beyond the iron gates, that, ponderous, rolled back silent; the weird and dazzling vision of the ten chief sins, the tumult of whose rout stirred not a leaf of the sacred tree whereunder Buddha sat, attest a high dramatic power.

Aside from the strictly didactic element of the poem, the exposition of Buddhism, to which the limits of this notice do not permit us to advert with any carefulness of criticism, that wherein this production excels is in its completeness and in its unity. It is the story, fully and finely narrated, of the life and labors of one man; all things bend and are made subservient to the illustrating of this life and labor. From the birth to the death, each incident that may serve to interest or to instruct us regarding the subject of the song is faithfully portrayed. There are no digressions which are not of importance, either as explaining the customs of the Hindus or as furnishing an allusion to the older Brahmanical teachings wherewith to compare the gradually forming doctrines of the new faith. It is the oneness of aim conspicuous throughout that enchains the attention and carries one irresistibly along. Grand as is the conception of this work, its execution bears it suitable company. A love for the Indian people and a reverence for the lofty character of the Sakyamuni have inspired and guided the poet in the accomplishment of his undertaking. To cite illustrative lines of different beauties which characterize the performance would be to quote the bulk of the poem. The noticeable features which distinguish the excellent in literature will be found on almost every page of this production: the intelligibility of its figures, the grace of its diction, the aptness of its expression, the variety of its ideas, the purity of the style, the admirable adaptation of the verse to the subject, and to the land where the scene is laid, more firmly impress one the longer and the oftener he reads. The descriptions, both of nature and of architecture, are admirable for accuracy of detail and for the suggestiveness of the whole. The pictures of "the stainless ramps of huge Himala's wall" that "led climbing thought higher and higher until it seemed to stand in heaven and speak with gods," and of the dawn that sprang with Buddha's victory, when in the east,

> "Flamed the first fires of beauteous Day, poured forth
> Through fleeting folds of Night's black drapery,"

and

> "Far and near, in homes of men there spread
> An unknown peace,"

are masterpieces of landscape painting in poetry.

The harvest scene in the first book, the golden home in the second, the sleeping company of the Indian girls, and the matchless steed, white Kantaka, in the fourth book, are all admirable for force and naturalness. The "old, old man" is a realistic figure, haggard and wan with years. It evinces the bard's command of the horrible. Beautiful and artistic as are these passages, they do not rise too noticeably above the general excellence of versification and of description with which the poem is characterized. This is evidenced by reading these more striking lines separated from the context. Their full grandeur is not appreciated unless one turns to them from some ordinary reading, or from one's ordinary occupation. To approach them by the pathway of the the poem itself, is to be brought nearer by its general elevated tone. This test establishes not only the sublimity of the grander parts, but also the superiority of the whole.

The refinement of the author's mind is made manifest in countless exquisite figures wherein the meaning sought to be illustrated is perfectly disclosed. One looks for metaphors, similes, and apostrophes in every poem, but is always more or less taken by surprise by the effective use of "apt alliteration's artful aid." Of the many alliterative passages, that in the eighth book will serve as an illustration — the doctrinal part, referring to

"The mighty whirling wheel of strife and stress
That none can stay or stem."

The earnestness of the poet in pressing upon the attention the principles of the faith he is elucidating is not his least observable characteristic. It has not been attempted to enumerate all the allusions to the doctrine of the transmigration of soul, but we call to mind the scene, in the second book, of the former life of the Prince, when he won from the jungle's monarch his Yasôdhara, who was then a tigress, he a tiger. An existence as a fisher-lad is also told; and then there come the illustrations of the belief drawn from the grain of rice that shoots a green feather, gemmed with fifty pearls, and from the ripples following ripples of the river flowing to the sea, to steam unto the sun, to fall and flow again.

In a word, Mr. Arnold, out of his love for the task which he has assumed, has surrounded its accomplishment with the faithful elaborations of the student, and with the elegance of the poet. To say that his work will live long in the literature which it has enriched is to state what is manifest to all. The merits of a poem, complete in its conception as a whole and perfect in the execution of its details, would assure its preëminence in any language. It is, however, the new avenue of thought which has been opened through its means that confirms its lastingness. Beauty without purpose, or richness without aim, may accomplish nothing more than temporary brilliancy; but with purpose, beauty and richness become glorified. *The Light of Asia* has revealed to the attention of a reading world a truth long hidden in its ignorance of India. It will excite to the contemplation of a moral excellence existing in a land where immorality is popularly supposed to grow rank. And, by inciting to a study of the merits of other religions, it will enable the Christian the better to appreciate the perfection of his own.

A SELECTION OF SPIRITUAL SONGS, WITH MUSIC. For the Sunday-school. Selected and arranged by Rev. Charles S. Robinson, D.D. New York: Scribner & Sons. 1880.

Spiritual Songs for the Sunday-school is the latest work of Dr. Robinson, and is a charming little book which commenced its useful career in July last. It is certainly not little in the sense of insignificance, for the volume shows in every feature the utmost care, taste, and knowledge. The publishers call the attention of the "Christian public" to this new enterprise, but we hope that the field of this collection of refined words and superior music will be broadened to the notice of *all* cultivated people, that they may appreciate what a stride is here made in the general direction of progression. It contains no painful incongruities, as is too often the case with religious song-books. There are no sickly sentimentalities set to boisterous, rollicking tunes. It is evidently not intended to inculcate into the minds of little children monstrous absurdities instead of pure simple religion. There is no extreme sensational music about it. The words contain the element of the truest purity and child-like simplicity, without descending to weakness and senselessness. The music is of a high order, without becoming too difficult and complicated. The words and music are devotional and appropriate (the latter a rare quality), and at the same time they are made attractive, as they should be. The book contains new and beautiful songs, and retains many of the best old ones, that will always be loved for their associations and their real worth. Altogether, this work seems to be a perfect thing of its kind. At all events, it is elevated far above the dust of commonplace.

DREKA'S DICTIONARY BLOTTER. A combination of word-book and a blotting case. Philadelphia: Louis Dreka. 1880. For sale in San Francisco by Doxey & Co.

This combination of dictionary and portfolio is neatly and conveniently arranged. It has attached a vocabulary of words in ordinary use, a list of synonyms and of common Christian names. It is handsomely bound, and is both elegant and useful.

We have received the following publications, several of which we shall review in a future number:

MR. BODLEY ABROAD. With Illustrations. Boston: Houghton, Mifflin & Co. 1880. For sale in San Francisco by A. L. Bancroft & Co.

MY COLLEGE DAYS. By Robert Tomes. New York: Harper & Brothers. 1880. For sale in San Francisco by Payot, Upham & Co.

THOMAS MOORE, THE POET; HIS LIFE AND WORKS. By Andrew James Symington. New York: Harper & Brothers. 1880. For sale in San Francisco by Payot, Upham & Co.

GEORGE BAILEY. A Tale of New York Mercantile Life. By Oliver Oldboy. New York: Harper & Brothers. 1880. For sale in San Francisco by Payot, Upham & Co.

WHITE WINGS. A Yachting Romance. By William Black. New York: Harper & Brothers. 1880. For sale in San Francisco by Payot, Upham & Co.

HARPER'S HALF-HOUR SERIES. New York: Harper & Brothers. 1880. For sale in San Francisco by Payot, Upham & Co.

No. 143. — *Republican or Democrat.* A Retrospect, with its Lessons for the Citizen of 1880.

No. 144. — *Modern France. 1814-1879.* By Oscar Browning.

GUIDE TO COLORADO, NEW MEXICO, AND ARIZONA. San Francisco: A. L. Bancroft & Co. 1880.

FRANKLIN SQUARE LIBRARY. New York: Harper & Brothers. 1880. For sale in San Francisco by Payot, Upham & Co.

No. 134.—*Clear Shining after Rain*. A Novel. By C. G. Hamilton.

No. 135.—*Pride and Prejudice*. A Novel. By Jane Austen.

TIT FOR TAT. A Teutonic Adventure. By the Marchioness Clara Lanza. New York: G. P. Putnam's Sons. 1880. For sale in San Francisco by A. L. Bancroft & Co.

HINTS FOR HOME READING. A Series of Chapters on Books and their Uses. New York: G. P. Putnam's Sons. 1880. For sale in San Francisco at Doxey's.

THE STILLWATER TRAGEDY. By T. B. Aldrich. Boston: Houghton, Mifflin & Co. 1880. For sale in San Francisco by A. L. Bancroft & Co.

POLITICAL AND LEGAL REMEDIES FOR WAR. By Sheldon Amos, M.A. New York: Harper & Brothers, Franklin Square. 1880. For sale in San Francisco by Payot, Upham & Co.

OUTCROPPINGS.

NOVEMBER.

From out October's funeral pile,
I saw an old man rise and smile,
Scattering the Past's bright leaves the while,
And lo! it was November.

The mellow air chilled at his breath,
The lingering flowers shrank low in death,
And streamlets silent grew, beneath
The stern brow of November.

He scattered snow; he pelted sleet;
He pinched the little frozen feet,
Whose owners limped along the street,
Crying, "O cold November!"

He brought an anguish, none can know
Save those who taste the cup of woe,
And see its full brim overflow
In that dread month, November.

Onward he marched, with ruthless tread—
Shrub, flower, and leaf, he crushed them dead,
And whirled them high above his head,
Shouting, "I am November!"

I saw him on Sierra stand,
From east to west stretch forth his hand,
And marked the greetings of the land,
That dreaded not November.

The thirsty hills sent up a shout,
And valleys all their joy rang out;
The mists encompassed him about,
And welcomed in November.

"Oh, bless the land to which I bring
The joys and fruits of early spring;
Where herdsmen smile, and plowmen sing
The beauties of November!"

Thus spake the sage, and sat him down
Upon the hills, all seared and brown,
Weaving a green enameled crown—
The first gift of November.

I saw him weep sweet tears of bliss,
As grass-blades sprang his feet to kiss,
And birds in their full happiness
Caroled throughout November.

He brought the fatness from on high,
That falls from cloud and dewy sky;
And earth held high a revelry,
And joyed throughout November.

MARGARET A. BROOKS.

A PEEP AT HARVARD.

While mixing ingredients for the legal cauldron five or six years ago at Harvard, glimpses of that lofty chief of the colleges were gained, which, though lacking the high colors of romance, may perhaps deserve to be termed interior views of an ancient institution. Possibly, too, the interest of these impressions may be enhanced by the circumstance that the University was then rapidly becoming representative and cosmopolitan, by breaking from the traditions of the past and taking all knowledge for its province.

Yet during this period of fermentation created by the inauguration of the new *régime*, the students clung to their wonted ways. They might still be said to be characterized by the rarity of the "grinders" or workers, and the abundance of prodigal drones. This contrast between the army of idlers and the handful of studious slaves of the lamp, though perhaps not more marked than in most of the older colleges of the country, has given emphasis to the charge that Harvard is a rich man's university. Despite the protestations of the unpatriarchal President, fortified by statistics, it must be admitted that well-lined purses are the rule, that plutocratic tendencies prevail, and that loss of caste would follow the custom, inaugurated elsewhere, of paying one's way openly by manual labor. But there is another reason why so many frequent the Castle of Indolence. It is very hard to win honors, and the picked few who try for them, and who are really men of superior mold, effective writers, and thorough investigators, are looked upon not as leaders, but as mere drudges and bookworms; while it is easy, with the aid of cramming under private tutors, to get the degree, and so the many have enough time for recreation and pleasure—athletics and *opéra bouffe*. Hence, it is only during lecture-hours, where the listless listeners share the objections of Faust to note-taking, or in the cramped, sepulchral library, that there is any lack of activity. There is no sign of stagnation in Boston at the hostelry billiard-table, where the humorist said the University was located, and the opening scene of Harvard stories is laid nowadays; along the river, where the boat-crews are practicing; or in the fields, where the latest variation of foot-ball is in vogue; or, in winter, at the bowling-alley of the gymnasium; or, at evening, in the theaters, where the sons of culture are given standing-room at reduced rates, and wildly applaud the blonde burlesq-

ters, but yet are not quite as privileged as their more decorous German brethren, who, without charge, may "enter Paradise," and freely mingle with the kid-gloved gods of the gallery.

No wonder that the ruling spirits are a cynical set, discarding all flowers of speech or arts of oratory, and tabooing all "sentimental extravagances." Little would they heed if you rapturously unfolded their points of vantage. Speak to a group of them on the subject: point out that they dwell in an idyllic country-town, yet were within half an hour's call of the famed city of the books; that they were privileged to dine in a cathedral and room in high-storied brick buildings, whose alcoved windows looked upon avenues of elms, and whose sturdy walls were flanked by like edifices that made up the "Red Republic of Letters;" that they could jostle famous poets and authors at every step, and stroll past historic houses and monuments, which visitors from afar delighted to gaze at.

To this assemblage of blessings they would oppose a host of evils, and hint that your views were rather "rosy"—or, perhaps, in honor of the college color, they might call them "crimson." Yes, they would say, it was pleasant to be located in placid, leafy, romantic Cambridge, a town almost entirely inhabited by Harvard graduates, and to be ruled by the foster-sons of their own college, but it was hard that even when the faculty were willing to drop compulsory morning prayers, these overseers should be compassionless and force the poor students to trudge to chapel at early morn in the wintriest weather (not to speak of being forced to swear that they had listened to a sermon nearly every Sunday). This was particularly consistent in an institution professing to be non-sectarian, though it did have an ecclesiastical seal, a hymn-like college air, and a Divinity School with Unitarian tendencies. Yes, they would admit it might be well to have notables like Ralph Waldo Emerson around, if the Sphinx of Concord had not become a source of discord, and, forgetting his transcendental theories, raised up his voice against Tyndall and Spencer, and insisted that scholars should freeze in the cause of religion.

Of course, it was pleasant to take one's meals in a stately edifice, even if it was top-heavy and ill proportioned; to look up at the high-arched ceiling, with its vista of broad beams, and at the great stained-glass window, flooded with richly colored sunshine. Truly, only an altar and an organ were wanting to complete the illusion that this was a grand temple of worship. It was inspiring, in the cloister-like vestibule, to note the memorial wall-tablets of war heroes, and, within the hall, to gaze at the busts and portraits of presidents, founders, and benefactors. It was companionable to sit down to dinner three hundred strong, even though stared at from the gallery by fair but curious visitors, and to chat about easy courses of study while drumming for the dilatory waiters. It was encouraging to obtain, at panic prices, an abundance of fresh milk, thin slices of coarse-grained roast beef, pursuant to contracts made with fellow-graduates, and other light dishes prepared in immense ovens, on a gigantic scale, and at ruinous figures; but all this was hardly substantial enough to sustain even feats of culture or literary flights, much less boating and base-ball; and the hungry student, tired of that unending series—pudding and pastry, baked beans and brown bread, cracked wheat and soft mush—might sigh, as in the ballad, for an occasional taste of juicy steak and pigeon-pie. True, most of the buildings that inclosed the college yard were lofty, and had Revolutionary associations, but they were erected before comfort was invented, and were chilly, dismal dormitories at the best, with all the ancient inconveniences; supervised, besides, by those prying proctors, who would not wink even at a harmless display of fireworks. Of course, this last mentioned system of having a brood of spying students as inspectors finds its original in the English universities, as do other features favored by the ruling powers. As for the students, they largely affect English ways, especially imitating the muscular type made familiar by "Tom Brown." Though the usual appurtenances of the gay, unstudious Harvard man are ulster, fur-cap, cane, and small dog, yet the style of the English swell is extensively copied. "Dundreary" is everywhere, with his suit of checked tweed, his hair parted in the middle, his stare and eye-glass, his hesitating speech and everlasting drawl. This fashion is largely due to the influence of vacation visits to Great Britain. Indeed, the shadow of Oxford and Cambridge, of late more visible than ever, is seen in the establishment of fellowships for the support of the resident graduates, and for those sent abroad, as well as in various details of organization. Still, the great molding influence is that of the German universities; witness the discarding of text-books, the flexible elective system, and the management of the professional schools. The Teutonic importations do not include, however, the salutary plan of wandering from university to university, which is, perhaps, hardly as practicable in broad-acred America, land of long distances, and in which Harvard would be unwilling to take part except as a receiver of pilgrims. Dueling has likewise been given the cold shoulder, but drinking-bouts are not unheard of; and though the medieval songs which Longfellow has repeated in his "Hyperion," or the beer-laws, which Mayhew has copied, are unknown, still merry gatherings are held in a cave-like cellar, where the glasses clink to the melody of "Riding in a Sleigh," or "Married to a Mermaid at the Bottom of the Deep Blue Sea." Yet there is no sign of the classical banquets so enticingly pictured in "Fair Harvard," nor even of the mock examinations of Freshmen, or the shin-shattering football "rush." Certainly the times have changed, when hazing, and Junior exhibitions, and burlesque programmes, and nearly all dangerous practical jokes have disappeared; and those who would make night hideous, and yet escape exposure in court, must run the gauntlet of the vigilant policeman who guards the college grounds. The result is that the freaks of the turbulent are confined to such pranks as sending newcomers to Longfellow's house to get registered, wittily marking the college walls, or pointing out as the college shoe-black the eccentric Professor of Greek, Evangelinus Apostolides Sophocles, who claims descent from the author of the *Antigone*, and has the face of an ancient and venerable philosopher, but the gait and dress of Don Quixote's famishing scholar.

A special favorite of the students is the cranky-minded Daniel Pratt, who calls himself the Great American Traveler, is of the mountebank stripe, and writes for organs of the "bum," bearing such strangely suggestive names as *The Lunatic* and *The Volcano*. He visits all the New England colleges and delivers incoherent harangues to the students, passing around a sadly battered hat for contributions. Lank, mole-eyed and wind-dried, he stands under a spreading chestnut tree, amid the jubilant and applauding students, and heaps together long, involved, high-sounding sentences, uttered in piping tones, and when at a loss bridges the gap with some such favorite word as "palladium" or "vocabulary."

That the spirit of mischief finds such harmless vents is greatly due to the decline of the class spirit, caused by the largeness of the classes, which are of such extent that, especially under the separative influence of the elective system, members of the same class may not even know one another by sight. The chief promoters of comradeship are the clubs, which are not mysteriously secret, as the Greek-letter societies never flourished at Harvard. Only on class-day do old feelings of antagonism undergo a mild revival, when each class squats in a circle on the ground, whoops for itself, and indulges in the gruff, Harvard cheer, "the barking 'rah, 'rah, 'rah," then rises, and, in the dance around the liberty tree, forms a swaying ring, which finally becomes torn apart in the struggle to break through the ranks of the other classes. Pleasant indeed is this gala holiday of memorial leaves and blossoms, class odes and ivy orations, of "teas" and "spreads," glee songs and merry dances, illuminated grounds, laughing girls in swarms, and other festive features. It quite dwarfs Commencement, which has no longer the peculiarities of a country fair, but is sedate and stately, with essays on the speculations of the speculative, and addresses that have the flavor of English after-dinner speeches. This final gathering would be dreary enough if it were not for the unsteady stragglers who have indulged too freely in the worship of the punch-bowl, and the line of graduates in procession, headed by the tottering veterans, all singing, "Carry me back to Ole Virginny," with such a comical, stress-laden prolongation of the "Oh!" at its third repetition in the chorus. But it is a happy day for the usually grave Senior, walking about with a contented smile, and waving his ribbon-tied diploma in token of emancipation.

NATHAN NEWMARK.

DAYBREAK IN THE COUNTRY.

Still night, and all the earth lies hushed and calm,
For Nature's breath scarce stirs the drooping leaf;
But now the stars flash out in sad alarm,
Then, pale as daybreak comes to ease their grief.

And, paling still, they softly hide away;
Nor dare remain, and yet as loth to go.
All fearful lest they meet the coming day,
All fearful lest their flight be still too slow.

Oppressive then the gloom and hush. The night
Seems blacker, colder, stiller than before.
And then the East, with fingers deft and light,
Draws shyly back the curtain from her door.

And Dawn peeps out with merry laugh, whose ring
Awakes the land. The cock begins to crow;
The linnets waken, start, and straightway sing;
The wild sweet roses, wet with dew-drops, blow.

The air comes laden with the scent of hay—
So sweet, one almost sees the new-mown sheaves;
And cow-bells lightly tinkle far away,
And happy voices float up through the leaves.

The sun has kissed the land, and all below
Seems fresh and pure. And this the linnets hear:
A cheery "Good day, Hem," "Good morning, Joe,"
As flushed with hope the glad new day draws near.

MACH WYMAN.

"CAMARADERIE."

Rather lengthy word that, but we have nothing in English that expresses quite the same thing. Comradeship approaches the thought, but it is an awkward word, and the old phrase of "good-fellowship," though it be good honest English, comes not so glibly from the tongue as the Iberian phrase; so we'll e'en let it stand as the title.

Many of us began to experience this feeling in the days that are so often termed, gushingly, the "days of innocency"—just as if there were not as much "pure cussedness," according to weight and strength, in the boy of twelve years as there is, proportionately, when there are twenty additional years piled upon his head. Yet these small twelve-year old imps show a strange, and on the whole unselfish, delight in each other's society. Every school has its Damon and Pythias in bobtail coats; and if they do punch each other's little bullet-heads once in a while, always manage to make up again, and take solemn oath and covenant "not to tell;" and, to the credit of honest *camaraderie*, one is happy to say this vow is more often kept than the vows they are so profuse with about ten years after. The satisfaction taken by the small boy in the mud-holes and marbles, kites and kicking-matches, is just as real, and as keenly felt, as any that comes to him after his coat-tails have lengthened, and a mold started on his upper lip. To the student of humanity, it is amusing to note the solemn earnestness of two urchins over the games that are their business in life, and the eagerness of discussions over matters that we older boys feel to be the veriest trifles. And yet we cannot but feel that the pursuits of the small wretches, screaming "Knuckle down!" on our sidewalks, with their grubby little paws eagerly working, and their dismal little trousers coated with mud at the knees, are just about as respectable, and are doing as much good in the world, as those of the men who tear up and down Montgomery Street, stock-gambling. Should there be any vote asked for as to the superior cleanliness of the Montgomery Street hands, it would not be best to institute discussion. That would surely make visible the deeper grime on the souls of the adult dwellers on the *pavé*, provided they are credited with the possession of such useless appendages.

The passion that forms the stock in trade of our novelists and poets is entirely distinct from *camaraderie*. All the halo thrown over it by genius, and the universality of its being experienced by mankind, like measles or whooping-cough, only prove that it is involuntary and selfish in its nature. All classes of humanity—divines, lawyers, money-grubs, convicts, doctors, and even stock-jobbers—are, or fancy they are, in love at some part of their lives. But there is only once in a while a real comrade.

The early settlers of this State know something about *camaraderie*. The tramp across the plains in the early "fifties" brought out the qualities of your fellow-travelers beyond cavil, and happy was he who found a true comrade.

One of these comes to mind just now—a slender, handsome boy, with straight Greek face, and eye like blue steel; one whom stampedes did not discourage nor Indians terrify; who rode with head erect into the wild storms of the Platte River, and growled not at the thirst and dust of the terrible Humboldt Desert. When fever laid its hand on us, who so quietly thoughtful as our comrade? Under no other guard slept we so securely in those all too short summer nights. But the fine young face was never covered with the full beard of manhood. Stormy Hatteras took him to its depths, with hundreds of others, in the ill-fated steamer *Central America*.

Camaraderie is not "exigent"—it does not require that one be on a perpetual strain to entertain one's company, by incessant fire of gabble, until you feel talked to a mere empty husk, and are mentally out of breath; or, what is nearly as bad, to be overwhelmed by an avalanche of words, even if sparkling with wit, or full of good sense and reason, when one is not "i' the vein."

Sidney Smith said one of his best things when he spoke of "eloquent flashes of silence," though only *camaraderie* can truly appreciate "golden silence."

One of my best comrades was a man so deaf that one had to raise the voice to a perfect war-whoop before it would penetrate the dull ears. But this man heard with his eyes; large dark eyes, watchful as the eyes of a Huron, and gentle as the eyes of an antelope.

Ah! the solid comfort in a stormy day, when our cutties sent a fragrant cloud to the ceiling, each poring over his book! Ever and anon an outstretched forefinger would point out some sentence of Carlyle, like printed electric light; or the deaf man's *staccato* ha! ha! ha! would burst forth in recognition of the stinging dissections of Thackeray.

But best of all was a long summer-day's ride. Then the watchful eyes noted every play of light and shade in the breeze-tossed foliage, saw all the color-glory of the flowers, and fairly glowed with delight over a troop of fussy, graceful quail, skittering along the roadside. The eye and hand of an artist, a brain stored with the thoughts of the best English writers, and the gentlest heart that ever beat—this was my deaf comrade.

Camaraderie does not always approximate in age or intellect. As a Scot would say, "I forgathered wi' a bairn just noo." It was on the overland trip; a bonnie four-year old boy, with hair like corn-silk, and merry blue eyes, a pair of roguish lips that prattled or kissed all day, and when the lips were settled into their Cupid's bow, and the merry blue eyes veiled, no prettier picture of sleep was ever seen.

How many times, when I entered the pretty Oakland home, came the coaxing request, enforced by a pair of chubby arms about my neck, "Won't you take me for a little trot after dinner?"—said little trot being a solemn promenade, adapted to the pace of a very short pair of legs. Many were the hours we spent looking over the bright waters of the bay, or lounging under the dark shadows of the live-oaks. And the meerschaum smoke, mingled with patter of little feet and the prattle of a sweet baby-voice, made those hours hours of rest. Never failed to come the words, "Didn't we have a good time crossing the plains?" "Didn't we shoot at a mark in the desert?" "Didn't I scare that Indian with my pistol?" This last valorous feat was the making a Piute buck, standing by the track, dodge his head to escape the deadly fire of Boy's little toy pistol out of the car-window.

Dear little comrade! As he grows up under the live-oaks, may he continue as charming a comrade as the four-year old boy. But this growing up is risky work.

There is right good *camaraderie* in a horse. Something very touching in the patient glance of his eye—a sort of dumb remonstrance against harsh usage. It seems to say, "I can't talk to you, but I'll do as well as I know how."

The horse cannot go into convulsions of joy, as the dog does; cannot grovel at our feet, making spasmodic bounds to attract notice—acting like an Oriental before his tyrant. Yet is the horse a thoroughly good comrade, when well treated. The lightest pressure of the heel, or the touch of the reins, communicates our wishes as if he were part of the nervous system of his rider.

A little Black Morgan was my comrade crossing the plains in '53; and though he was a wild and unbroken colt when I bought him in Indiana, it took us only two weeks to become thoroughly acquainted, and when I pastured him in the Santa Clara Valley, after he had borne me across the continent, he would come half a mile at the sound of my whistle. His faith was so great that, though the sight of the yeasty surf at the Cliff House made him snort and tremble, without a blow he bore me to midsides in the tumbling billows; but I must say he seemed delighted to get away from the beach.

Years after I bought another as like Morgan as could be, and have kept him until the wrinkles are gathering about his eyes; and he has become very waywise, and will let another trot by him without going into a paroxysm of cantering. Yet we have been comrades over hundreds of miles of the worst roads in the world—so good a comrade that only death shall part us. In the morning, when after an early breakfast the meerschaum tastes the best, there is real enjoyment to loiter out to the stable and stroke the mottled coat. The soft brown eyes come round with a gaze of lazy content, the black nose pokes about after the hand to be patted and patted—all quietly and entirely unlike the passionate welcome that the dog gives.

Avaunt! small boys, dogs, horses, and masculine comrades! *Place aux dames!* Dare we consider whether genuine *camaraderie* can exist between woman and man? Doubtless it may exist, because nothing seems to be impossible where humanity is concerned; but its existence is very rare, and takes place only when the natural endeavor to please—the feeling of gallantry on the part of the man and the desire to render herself pleasing on the part of the woman—is entirely out of the question, from relationship or circumstance. Then there may be a real feeling of *camaraderie* between man and woman. Perhaps there is no more beautiful example of true *camaraderie* at its best than the relationship between an aged husband and wife, who have outlived all other feelings but that the existence of each to the other is about all there is left of life. There is no more necessity for any effort to be pleasing. Each one has become part of the other in thought and action. Nay, the expression of two aged faces is often singularly alike—so much so as to give the idea, at a superficial glance, that there is a resemblance of feature.

There is also a quiet understanding between some brothers and sisters which is wonderfully restful and soothing. The small talk of society is entirely unnecessary; conversation is just the thought that springs up fresh and free and is uttered without having to review it in the mental chambers to see how it will look exposed to the air. There is no human intercourse more free from all selfish feeling than the relations of brother and sister who are good comrades. Even the devotion of maternal love in all its beauty and unselfishness cannot be separated from the feeling of possession. "My child" is mingled with every emotion.

Quiet sympathy and unselfishness are the main ingredients of true *camaraderie*. Happy are they who can inspire the feeling.

W. H. WOODHAMS.

QUITS

One pleasant afternoon in the summer of 187-, a party of young people were enjoying themselves upon the broad *azotea*, or flat roof, of a well to do foreigner in the city of Mexico. It was a feast-day, and the people were in the streets. A holiday air hung over the city, and the valley was lovely in the brown haze which stretched away, over lake and wood, to the far-off snow-peaks. Dancing had been going on upon the house-top; but, as the day wore away, and the old Mexican musician began to nod over his harp, the young people turned their attention to other modes of amusement. Among those present was a handsome young Canadian, who, on some pretext or other, had drifted away from his northern home, and was now permanently located in the Mexican capital. For convenience, we will call him the Doctor. He was the life of every social gathering, a favorite alike with ladies and gentlemen, and withal a most lovable good fellow. In thus alluding to him, I am saddened by the reflection that he afterward came to a most untimely death, his young life being destroyed by the accidental discharge of a pistol in the hand of a friend.

The wall of an adjoining house rose above the roof on which our party was located, and its blank exposure was broken in one place by a small window which overlooked our position. This window was heavily barred with iron, as are all Mexican windows, and it apparently led into an unoccupied room—for no one was seen to look out, although we had been frolicking beneath it for several hours. It was when the dancing was nearly over, and we were about to go down, that the Doctor approached me and proposed that we should practice throwing a knife against the wall referred to. He, by the way, was an expert in such things, and could send his blade singing through the air and stand it quivering in the wall with unerring precision. I, on the contrary, had no practice in this doubtful accomplishment, and not only failed four times out of five to strike my blade into the wall, but my throwing was so wild that I finally managed to toss the knife against the window, where, glancing from one of the iron bars, it fell inside with a rattle and a crash, and then all was still.

For a moment we all stood speechless in contemplation of the probable mischief which had been done; but as no one came to the window, and all remained quiet inside, we concluded that the room was empty, and thought no more about it.

The next morning I was sitting alone in my office, when a servant entered and placed a note and a parcel upon my table, and stated that he was told to wait for a reply. The name signed to the note was strange to me, and a hasty glance showed that the writer was, or pretended to be, the occupant of the room into which my erratic knife had flown. He stated that on the previous evening he was sitting, with his wife, by the table, reading, when his window was suddenly broken in, and the knife—which he inclosed—struck the lady upon the temple, inflicting a painful wound. He had made inquiries, and learned that I was the assailant, and as he was desirous of knowing what motive I had for the assault, he took this means of finding out. Furthermore, he wished to say that he was not actuated by curiosity alone in making this inquiry. My act was not a thing to be lightly overlooked, and unless I could make a sufficient explanation, he should demand the personal satisfaction which one gentleman never refuses to another. The note was courteous, but very firm and as its authenticity was corroborated by the presence of the knife, and I felt myself to be clearly in the wrong in the matter, I did not hesitate as to my action, but replied to it at once, explaining the circumstances of the accident, and assuring him of my regret at its occurrence. I stated that I would call, with his permission, to make my personal apologies to him and to his wife, and that I was ready and willing to make such reparation as I could for my carelessness. I told him, and with truth, that I would have called before, but for my impression that the room was unoccupied, and that no harm had been done. This note I sealed and sent back by the servant, who had been waiting.

It may be well to remark just here that the *code duello* is in full force among the upper classes of our sister republic, and that desperate encounters are of frequent occurrence. Foreigners are often forced to adopt this mode of adjusting personal grievances, and any disposition to avoid responsibility is sure to be followed by social ostracism. As will be seen, I took advantage of this fact, a little later, to further a purpose of my own.

Several hours after dispatching the note which I had written, my friend Pythias sauntered into the room and flung himself lazily upon a lounge. He had been with us the evening before on the *azotea*, and knew of the knife accident. I told him what had happened since, and handed him the note which I had received. He took it, and pretended to be deeply interested; but there was something in his manner which was not entirely natural. His acting was not good, and it suddenly flashed across my mind that I had been made the victim of a practical joke. I accused him of it; and, after trying for a few minutes to evade me, he acknowledged the truth of my suspicion. As I had surmised, the Doctor was the prime mover in the mischief. He had managed somehow to obtain the knife from the vacant room, where I had thrown it, and then, calling together a number of the boys, had proceeded to write the note, in choicest Spanish. Pythias described to me the hilarity which my reply had created, and finally acknowledged that he had been sent around to spy out the land, and see how I took it, and that the boys were awaiting his return and report at the Iturbide.

I was not so much angered as mortified at the trick which had been played upon me, and for some time was at a loss how to proceed. An idea at length occurred to me, and I sat down and wrote the following note:

"*Dr.* ———:

"SIR:—I have just learned of the deception which you this morning practiced upon me. Your joke is no joke; nor will I permit such liberties to be taken with me. I demand of you personal satisfaction, or such immediate and full apology for your *insult* as my friend Pythias may consider adequate.

"I am, sir," etc.

Pythias entered heartily into my plan, and undertook to deliver the above note, and to act as my second in the proceedings. It was agreed between us that no explanation by the Doctor should be considered "adequate," and that a meeting should be brought about. In order to have no hitch in the programme, we sent for a friend of the Doctor, whom we knew he would call upon as his representative in case of serious difficulty. This gentleman consented to play a part in case he was selected; and thus we laid the scheme for turning back upon the Doctor the joke which he had initiated.

It will not be necessary to describe here the consternation which my note caused in the little circle waiting at the Iturbide. Nor can I stop to speak of the negotiations which preceded the final meeting. It is sufficient to say that the terms proposed by my second were so exacting, in fact, so humiliating, that a man of spirit, as the Doctor undoubtedly was, could not accept them. Not wishing to fight, and sincerely regretting his action, the poor fellow's position was most unhappy, and I several times found myself on the point of relenting before the climax was reached. Pythias, however, and the few conspirators who were with us, including the Doctor's second, insisted on seeing the fun out, and so "darkened counsel" and confused the intercourse of the two principals that a reconciliation seemed impossible, and the Doctor felt bound to meet me in deadly combat.

Everything was done expeditiously and quietly, and it was arranged that the meeting should take place in the woods of Chapultepec, in the early dawn of the following morning.

Promptly at the hour, I was on hand, accompanied by Pythias and a young Mexican physician who had been let into the joke. The Doctor, with his two friends, arrived a few moments later, in a coach, and all dismounted in an opening in the wood. The huge trees trailed their long white moss down over our heads, and the scene was impressive, even to those of us who knew it was to be a farce. To the Doctor, however, it was a serious matter, and his admirable deportment under the trying ordeal inspired us all with the deepest respect. I wanted to go up and throw my arms around him and cry "quits," but the others prevailed upon me to refrain, and so I let matters take their course. The ground was quickly measured, pistols prepared, and, taking our positions, we both fired promptly at the word. With an exclamation of pain, I sank to the ground, and the Doctor, after standing a moment like one petrified, was hurried into his coach by his seconds and driven away. As soon as the coach was out of sight, I arose from the ground and went back to the city. The pistols, as the reader will readily understand, were loaded only with powder. The poor Doctor was, however, not yet out of trouble. Thinking he had killed me, and fearing prosecution, he hailed an outgoing stage, and, saying a hasty good-bye to his friends, went over the mountain—sixty miles—to Cuernavaca. Here he proposed to conceal himself until he could learn the extent of my injuries, and decide upon the proper course to pursue. I was not disposed, however, to let a matter go further in which I already felt myself to be more than even. That evening a special coach rattled out of the city, and sped swiftly southward toward the Cuernavaca grade. Pythias, the Doctor's friends, and all the boys were aboard, and here and there were stored suggestive piles of good things—champagne baskets and portly flasks.

It was midnight when we clattered into the dark, rambling old town of Cuernavaca, and our coach brought up with a flourish in front of the principal *mesón*. To find the Doctor was an easy task, and, late as it was, we dragged him out of his bed and carried him, in a semi-nude condition, half way across the town to our quarters. The sleepy guards thought at first that a band of *pronunciados* had invaded the town, and proposed to lock us all up, but a few silver dollars quieted their suspicions, and we were left to our own devices. None of us slept a wink that night, and the dilapidated crowd which reached the capital on the following day was a sad commentary on the wisdom of our years. The Doctor was satisfied, I am sure, and from that time forward I never knew him to perpetrate a practical joke.

D. S. RICHARDSON.

FROM THE GERMAN OF EMANUEL VON GEIBEL.

O Thou, before whose mighty power
  The storms abate, the sea grows calm,
On this wild heart Thy blessings shower
  And heal it with Thy peaceful balm!
This heart, with all its restless longing,
  That once inflamed, too fiercely glows—
Itself and others sadly wronging,
  Its erring love but grief bestows.

Oh, save it from wild passions burning,
  Its wishes ever restless play,
Its wandering love for aye returning—
  Be Thou its love, its hope, and stay.
Then free of earth with doubt and sorrow,
  With joys and fears so quickly past,
'Twould hail with joy the blessed morrow,
  And then be calm and still at last.

T. B.

UP VESUVIUS.

"See Naples and die," is an old saying. See Vesuvius and prepare to die, is the thought we would express after having climbed its steep cone, and looked into its fiery mouth. For many years we had wished to see Italy, its cities and sunny skies. At last we have our wishes realized, and here from our casement we can look out on the city of Naples, the lovely bay, and Vesuvius smoking in the distance. Naples has a population of over four hundred thousand, and is full of life and stir. The streets, though many are mere alleys, are well kept. Our hotel, the Washington, is homelike and tidy, and the view from our window is unsurpassed. The building seems to stand in the very center of the horse-shoe curve of the bay, and we can hear the waves as they come rolling in from the distant sea, dashing over the Molo, or quay, beneath our window. The city extends far around the curve to our right. To the left is seen Vesuvius, with its cloud of smoke by day and its fiery stream of lava by night. Pompeii lies sleeping at its feet, while, farther on, is Sorento, its walls gleaming white in the midst of green foliage; and directly in front lies Capri, behind which the sun, like a golden ball, is sinking.

We reached Naples in the evening, and agreed to make the ascent of the mountain the next day, if possible; for during the rainy season in Italy every sunny day must be improved. Morning comes, and with it some clouds. However, we decide to run the risk of being caught in a shower, and at eight o'clock our party of seven start. We have a large carriage, drawn by three horses, and we are bound for a good time. Our route lies through the heart of the city, and then extends out through the poorer quarters and suburbs. We pass whole families out of doors—the women sewing, knitting, or pulling flax, the men working at tailoring; while many children are tumbling over each other, with but little of this world's goods upon them. In many instances women are standing on the streets combing their long black tresses, to which they pay much attention; but their garments are ragged and covered with dirt. Immense quantities of macaroni, drying on poles in the sun, are seen on either side of the street. Occasionally, the beggars run after us, but not to annoy us, as we had been forewarned. Children, dragging old men after them, follow the carriage, talking in their noisy way, and trying to awaken our sympathies by sham crying, but when a laugh from us shows them we see the deceit, they good humoredly return it, and soon leave us for other victims. We dare not open our purses, or even give them a centime, otherwise there would be no escape for us. We soon reach the gate of the city, where we find our Italian guide waiting, who tells us it will not rain enough to mar the pleasure of the day. Horses are therefore ordered for the ladies of our party, to meet us at the Hermitage.

Soon after leaving the gate, the road gradually ascends, and we wind in and out over the lava beds, which have been accumulating for hundreds of years. The view we have at this point is charming. Below lies Naples, the sun lighting it up like a beautiful picture. The blue waters of the bay meet the horizon beyond the rocky peaks of Capri, while plain and mountain extend far away to the east. As we still ascend we find lava formed into most uncouth shapes, resembling all kinds of animals. There are acres of this lava; the walls on either side the road, and the road itself, are made of it. Little farms and vineyards, green and flourishing, extend to within a mile of the cone. These vineyards yield the grapes for making the famous wine called "Lacryma Christi," much used in Naples. The Hermitage is a dilapidated stone building, where travelers usually leave the carriages and take saddle-horses to ride to the foot of the cone. It is two thousand feet above Naples, and we have been three hours in reaching it. Our guide soon arrives with the horses, and while preparations are being made for our horseback ride, the court-yard, filled with Italians, dressed in all sorts of colors and styles, chatting, singing, and quarreling it seems to us, they are so noisy, makes a scene certainly novel, if not entertaining. It is raining, so we decide to eat our lunch, as our guide tells us it will soon clear away. We warm our hands over the fire in the open brazier; then, going out, we mount our steeds. They are neither young nor handsome, but fair specimens of Italian beasts, poor and poorly cared for. Now the fun begins. Every man and boy in the yard wants to go—either to lead the horse, carry our wraps, or hang on to the tail of the animal. However, Potazoli, the guide, succeeds in driving all off except those we need. We find several parties *en route*; among them English and Russian ladies who think nothing of walking the entire distance. It is a pretty sight—the horses carefully picking their way over the rough road, the guides, dressed in odd colors, walking by them, carrying bright wraps, while they chatter like a flock of birds. Before us rises the dark mountain; behind us we can still see the beautiful bay and city, shaded by dense clouds, while a rainbow spans the valley. The halt is about a mile farther on than the hermitage, and seven hundred feet above it. Here we dismount, and again have a noisy time with the guides. We soon arrange with them, however, according to our own terms. One lady is seated in a chair fastened to two poles, and is carried by four men, while one man assists each of the rest. Our guide throws a strap over his shoulder, to which we cling while he pulls us up as best he can. The cone rises fifteen hundred feet above where we leave the saddle-horses. It is composed of slag and loose ashes, making the road very difficult to travel. We frequently stop to rest; and, as we look back and around us, we think of the horrifying times of 1869, when the lava spread over a distance of two miles, and in some places was thirteen feet in depth. After an hour's climb, our guide suddenly turns and says, "Crater there." We have reached the summit of the cone. The dense smoke from the crater hides everything from view, while the fumes of sulphur are almost suffocating. We stand, as it were, upon the rim of a huge bowl sunk into the top of the mountain, with here and there a piece chipped out. Looking back we can see the path up which we have come, through the dense smoke. On the other side of the rim, our way leads down to where the stream of lava silently flows along, and at last finds an opening in the bowl through which it winds its way down the mountain. Suddenly the guide takes us by the arm and almost carries us down a steep, rough place, shouting as only an Italian can. All about us smoke is issuing from the hot ashes, and, as it lifts away a little, we can see the dim forms of those who have preceded us standing by the side of the wonderful stream. On one side, the rocks are yellow with sulphur. In the distance, we can hear the boom of falling stones thrown out from the mouth of the crater. Now and then a report like that of a gun reaches us. It is the cracking of the lava, as it cools. It has commenced to rain, and as the large drops fall on the red-hot lava, the noise is like the hissing of a thousand serpents. The dim forms of the Italians, seen through the smoke, look like so many imps of darkness, as they jabber and stick their long wooden forks into the lava to burn coins. One can easily imagine how a Dante or a Michael Angelo could paint the infernal regions. The noise, the smoke, the steam issuing from the crevasses, the hissing of rain as it falls on the lava, the cracking of the rock, the little handful of people who have come from countries far remote from each other to meet for a moment in this hollow of the earth, and, above all, that slowly creeping, red-hot stream, steadily making its way down into the valley, present a weird and sublime scene, and awakens strange thoughts difficult to express. The atmosphere is filled with sulphurous gases, and, as the thick clouds are settling down around us, we decide to go—for, grand and sublime as the place is, it would be neither safe nor comfortable to pass the night in. We remain as long as possible, however, listening to the falling rain, and the terrible boom from the crater, a hundred yards away. The climb out of the crater is exceedingly fatiguing, but when once on the rim the descent is quite easy, as we go down a steep side of the cone, where the slag is soft. We then mount our horses and ride to the Hermitage, through the falling mist. After resting a few moments, we drive home, glad of the rest and quiet of the night. Whenever we look back we see the fiery monster, while ever and anon the sky is ablaze with light, reflected from its red mouth. We feel we have had a glimpse into one of the secret places of the Most High. We have seen one of His wonderful works, and know something of the might of His power.

J. L. H.

Naples, Italy.

WORDSWORTH.

Many a man considers his fitness for the teacher's profession demonstrated by his unfitness for every other calling. Reasoning somewhat after the same fashion, Wordsworth, not feeling good enough for the ministry, doubting his ability for the law, unwilling to incur the dangers of the army, and wisely concluding that he could not succeed as a politician, determined to be a poet. "Poeta nascitur non fit," we confidently quote; but here we have an example of one who was made, not born, a poet, and it may be worth while to try to discover by what magic he gained his high rank among English poets.

He was a fair scholar, but not a distinguished one, and his most ardent admirer never claimed for him dramatic power. His gift of language was so feeble and his imagination so barren that he was always heavy and sluggish in conversation, while not even his profound self-love could blind him to the fact that he had no wit. He flattered himself, however, that once in his life he had really produced a joke, and from the shouts of laughter which invariably greeted him when he repeated it he concluded that it was a good one. Once, when he was living at Grasmere, a peasant woman asked him if he had seen her husband. "My good woman," he replied, "I did not know you had a husband." And this rare joke the great poet of nature and the poor repeated to the end of his days, never suspecting that he had been guilty of a gross impertinence to a stranger.

But if we look in vain for the things we are wont to admire in other poets, we equally miss their vices from his character. Impertinent and obtuse he might be, but honorable and manly we know that he was. He could not, like other poets, touch every deep and passionate chord of the human heart, but he lived a stainless life. His own shadow falls darkly across pictures we would gladly see in the full light of the sun, but it is the shadow of one who sought God through Nature. He was not strong enough to stem the tide of German pantheism, but with it he clothed what otherwise might have been a spectral theism.

His views of the nature of Poetry were certainly unique. He says, "She can boast no celestial ichor that distinguishes her vital juices from those of Prose; the same human blood circulates through the veins of them both." He expressly says that the language of common life only should be admitted into poetry, and should be used in the same way as it is in prose so far as the meter, which forms its only distinguishing mark, will allow. To illustrate his meaning he published his early poems, courting not the praise, but the scorn of critics, of whom he says, "They will look around for poetry, and will be induced to inquire by what species of courtesy these attempts can be permitted to assume that title." How, indeed? we exclaim after toiling through them. Like other muse-struck boys, he pined and drooped and besought others to leave him to his grief at fifteen, and at eighteen had so far recovered as to write an interminable account of his "Evening Walk," interspersed with descriptions of female beggars and crowing cocks. This he dedicated to a young lady. He tunes the pipe of Pan, and sings such thrilling strains as this:

"The mountain raven's youngling brood
Have left the mother and the nest,
And they go rambling east and west
In search of their own food."

Not much "celestial ichor" there surely, but quite enough to keep the meter warm. He becomes a gentle monitor, as we hear from his own lips:

"And gently did the Bard
Those idle shepherd boys upbraid,
And bade them better mind their trade."

In his deep love for the innocent and helpless, he pauses to watch a little girl feed a pet lamb its supper, and describes the process for less favored mortals. Space forbids the transcribing of more than one specimen couplet:

"The lamb, while from her hand he thus his supper took,
Seemed to feast with head and ears, and his tail with
with pleasure shook."

He devotes ninety stanzas to the moonlight ride of an "Idiot Boy," who eventually came out nowhere, and did nothing; and while dizzy with soaring so high, he wrote "The Mad Mother," who expresses her appreciation of nature's harmonies in the couplet:

"I'll teach my boy the sweetest things,
I'll teach him how the owlet sings."

Then he labors through four long cantos to set before us in a vivid light how much William Wordsworth suffered when "The Wagoner" was caught in a storm, fell in with tramps, stopped at an ale-house, made himself drunk, and was discharged. He paints Peter Bell, and his patient donkey, so much wiser than he, in brilliant colors.

Having followed our poet thus far in his mad career, with bated breath and anxious minds, a world of care is lifted from our hearts when, at the age of thirty-two, he marries a sensible woman, who brings his soaring muse back to earth, and curbs his wild fancy for the rest of his life.

In the poems of these later years he ceases to appeal to the imagination only, and, addressing himself to our intellects and moral natures, is more interesting to most readers. To this period belong "The Egyptian Water Lily," "The Borderers," "The White Doe of Rylstone," "The Headland of St. Bees," and his epic. The first cannot fail to please, for we stand again in the courts of Arthur, by "Caerleon and Usk," and with us are Merlin, Nina, "benign enchantress," Launcelot, and Guinevere, Gawain, and Galahad; and the lesson we learn is that one of the might residing in a pure and stainless heart, which comes down to us through the ages with the gleam of Arthur's virgin shield. But we turn away disappointed, for the past has not been so rich as we expected. We cannot admire Galahad as we feel we ought, we care less for the fair stranger than we hoped to, and Mage Merlin has withered in our sight. "The Borderers" is a drama, and doubtless would have succeeded had it possessed a plot and some dramatic interest. As it is, we admire unselfish Idonea, and pity her generous but very verdant lover. At the head of Wordsworth's writings, both in his own estimation and that of others, stands "The White Doe of Rylstone." Not for beautiful pictures, nor strong and grand characters, nor high waves of feeling, but for its subdued undercurrent of thought, its patient endurance, its still waiting, its meek suffering, it touches us in our best and most quiet moments. Among his shorter pieces, none is marked by purer feeling or more graceful expression than "The Headland of St. Bees." His epic is a tedious and unfinished work concerning the growth and progress of his own mind. Of this poem his biographer remarks, "In point of fact, the one element of greatness which 'The Excursion' possesses indisputably is its heaviness." It abounds in fine passages and noble thoughts, but, like the dictionary, is somewhat tedious when read by course. If, then, we seek the causes of Wordsworth's success, we find them not in his poetic genius, for he had drunk neither at the Urdar fount nor

Helicon's spring; nor in grace of expression, for even "The White Doe of Rylstone, his masterpiece, is full of inaccuracies of expression; nor do we find it in the power of his thought, for he was shallowness itself, compared with Coleridge, Pope, Goethe, and a dozen others. We must conclude, then, that we have here an example of that reverence which the world pays to a good man as such; and his fame goes far to prove that we are a conservative people—very apt to think as our fathers did, especially as we, most of us, leave the reading of Wordsworth to our fathers to do, though the fathers do very little of it.

M. E. TEMPLE.

WOULDN'T PAY FOR BREATHING THE AIR.

Bill Smedley was resting his left foot on the top of a beer keg, in front of a saloon in Butte City, Montana, the last time I saw him. On his bent left knee he rested an elbow, thereby arranging his arm so as to support his chin, which rested in his hand. His clothes were well-worn, with here and there a rent. His hair stuck out through a hole in the crown of his hat, while the great toe of his right foot peeped forth, ruddy and cheerful, from the boot. The whiffs of smoke, drawn from a short, black pipe, curled lazily from his lips. His eyes were half closed and dreamy. His thoughts were in dreamland. Bill had experienced the ups and downs of Western life, had been rich and poor by turns, and was now very poor. He had grown philosophic, and looked at things in a way different from what he had in his youth, when life's pathway smiled to him and seemed rose-garlanded.

"Hello, Bill! Been looking for you," said the tax-collector, coming up. There was no response. He repeated, "Bill, hello!"

"Well?"

"Want to collect your tax."

"Hain't no property."

"Well, pay a poll-tax, anyhow."

"Don't own no pole."

"A poll-tax is a tax on yourself, you know."

"I ain't property."

"But the County Court levied this tax on you."

"Didn't authorize 'em to levy any tax on me."

"The law does, though."

"What if it does? 'Spose I'm goin' ter pay for breathin' the air?"

"Still, you are one of us. You live here."

"I didn't bring myself into the world."

"You exercise the privileges of a citizen: you vote."

"Don't want to vote if you charge for it."

"Don't you want a voice in the election of officers?"

"No. If there was no officers you wouldn't be here consumin' my time."

"The schools must be supported. We must educate the children."

"If you do, they won't work."

"There are other county expenses—paupers, and so on. If you were to die without means, you would want us to bury you."

"No, you needn't."

"Why, you would smell bad to the people."

"I kin stan' it if they kin."

"I will levy on your property," said the officer, growing impatient. "I will hunt it up."

"I'll help you. I want to see some of my property."

The officer moved on rather abruptly, while Bill continued, as if musing:

"Let them fellers have their way, and they'd make life a burden. Want to assess my existence; want to charge me for enjoyin' the bright sunshine; ask me to pay for beholdin' the beautiful landscape; charge me for lookin' at the grass grow an' the rose unfold; charge me for watchin the birds fly an' one cloud chase another."

The eyes continued to blink dreamily. The wreaths of smoke reached up in graceful spirals toward the blue dome. The footfalls of the tax-collector grew absenter and absenter.

LOCK MELONE.

HE RESEMBLED THE OLD MAN.

One of our exchanges has the following: A good story was yesterday told at military headquarters about young Jesse Grant, who has just returned to Galena from the West. Jesse went through a number of Arizona mining towns, and was given some prominence. At one place, a big, burly, profane, and dissipated miner, who had sold a six-hundred dollar claim, and was in town having a high old time, took a drunken notion to distinguish himself by thrashing young Grant, who is small, and of light build.

The big miner came up the street, cursing as he came, and swaggered into a restaurant, where Jesse was sitting, and, approaching a young and well dressed man, but evidently a native of those "diggings," who was at a table near the entrance, he slapped him heavily on the shoulder and exclaimed:

"Look byer, youngster, how many bits to the dollar?"

The stranger addressed quietly laid down his knife and fork, deliberately eyed the intruder for a full minute, and suddenly resolved himself into an Arizona whirlwind. All in the space of a second or so, the big miner was knocked down several times, stood upon, sat upon, his clothes partially torn off, and, with both eyes closed, dazed and bewildered, was thrown into the street.

The stranger quietly returned to his knife and fork, and the miner remarked, as he picked himself up and peered curiously into the door:

"Durned ef the youngster don't resemble the old man."

SEND US ITEMS.

Our aim is to make "Outcroppings" a light and pleasing corner of the magazine, and we should be glad if our readers would send us from time to time, briefly and pithily told, such humorous incidents as may come under their observation.

THE CALIFORNIAN.

A WESTERN MONTHLY MAGAZINE.

VOL. II.—DECEMBER, 1880.—NO. 12.

SAVONAROLA.

This article is intended to present a memorable movement in the Roman Catholic Church—a reformation of morals, preceding the greater movement of Luther to produce a reformation of both morals and doctrines. As the representative of this movement I present Savonarola, concerning whom much has of late been written—more, I think, because he was a Florentine in a remarkable age, the age of artists and of reviving literature, than because he was a martyr, battling with evils which no one man was capable of removing. His life was more a protest than a victory. He was an unsuccessful reformer, and yet he prepared the way for that religious revival which afterward took place in the Catholic Church itself. His spirit was not revolutionary, like that of the Saxon monk, and yet it was progressive. His soul was in active sympathy with every emancipating idea of his age. He was the incarnation of a fervid, living, active piety amid forms and formulas, a fearless exposer of all shams, an uncompromising enemy to the blended atheism and idolatry of his ungodly age. He was the contemporary of political, worldly, warlike, unscrupulous Popes, disgraced by nepotism and personal vices—men who aimed to extend not a spiritual but temporal dominion, and who scandalized the highest position in the Christian world, as attested by all reliable historians whether Catholic or Protestant. However infallible the Catholic Church claims to be, it has never been denied that some of her highest dignitaries have been subject to grave reproaches, both in their character and their influence. Such men were Sixtus IV., Julius II., and Alexander VI.—able probably, for it is very seldom that the Popes have not been distinguished for something, but men, nevertheless, who were a disgrace to the superb position they had succeeded in reaching.

The great feature of that age was the revival of classical learning, and artistic triumphs in sculpture, painting, and architecture, blended with infidel levity and social corruptions, so that it is both interesting and hideous. It is interesting for the triumphs of genius, the dispersion of the shadows of the Middle Ages, the commencement of great enterprises, and of a marked refinement of manners and tastes; it is hideous for its venalities, its murders, its debaucheries, its unblushing wickedness, and its disgraceful levities, when God and duty and self-restraint were alike ignored. Cruel tyrants reigned in cities, and rapacious priests fattened on the credulity of the people. Think of monks itinerating Europe to sell indulgences for sin; of monasteries and convents filled, not with sublime enthusiasts as in earlier times, but with gluttons and sensualists, living in concubinage and greedy of the very things which primitive monasticism denounced and abhorred. Think of boys elevated to episcopal thrones, and the sons of Popes made cardinals and princes. Think of churches desecrated by spectacles which were demoralizing, and a worship of saints and images which had become idolatrous—a degrading superstition among the people, an infidel apathy among the higher classes; not infidel speculations, for these were reserved for more enlightened times, but an indifference to what is ennobling, to all vital religion, worthy of the Sophists in the time of Socrates.

It was in this age of religious apathy and scandalous vices, yet of awakening intelligence and artistic glories, when the greatest enthusiasm was manifested for the revived literature and sculptured marbles of classic Greece and Rome, that Savonarola appeared in Florence as a reformer and preacher and statesman, near the close of the fifteenth century, when Columbus was seeking a western passage to India; when Michael Angelo was molding the Battle of Hercules with the Centaurs; when Ficino was teaching the philosophy of Plato; when Alexander VI. was making princes of his natural children; when Bramante was making plans for a new St. Peter's; when Cardinal Bembo was writing Latin essays; when Lorenzo de Medici was the flattered patron of both scholars and artists, and the city over which he ruled with so much magnificence was the most attractive place in Europe, next to that other city on the banks of the Tiber, whose wonders and glories have never been exhausted, and will probably survive the revolutions of unknown empires.

But Savanarola was not a native of Florence. He was born in the year 1452 at Ferrara, and belonged to a good family, and received an expensive education, and was destined to the profession of medicine. He was a sad, solitary, pensive, but precocious young man, whose youth was marked by an unfortunate attachment to a haughty Florentine girl. He did not cherish her memory and dedicate to her a life labor, like Dante, but became very dejected and very pious. His piety assumed, of course, the ascetic type, for there was scarcely any other in that age, and he entered a Dominican convent, as Luther, a few years later, entered an Augustinian. But he was not an original genius, and a bold and independent thinker like Luther, so he was not emancipated from the ideas of his age. How few men can go counter to prevailing ideas! It takes a prodigious genius and a fearless inquiring mind to break away from their bondage. Abraham could renounce the idolatries which surrounded him when called by a supernatural voice; Paul could give up the Phariseeism which reigned in the Jewish schools and synagogues when stricken blind by the hand of God; Luther could break away from monastic rules and papal denunciation when taught by the Bible the true ground of justification—but Savonarola could not. He pursued the path to heaven in the beaten track, after the fashion of Jerome and Barnard and Thomas Aquinas, after the style of the Middle Ages, and was sincere, devout, and lofty, like the saints of the fifth century, and read his Bible as they did, and essayed a high religious life; but he was stern, gloomy, and austere, emaciated by fasts and self-denial. He had, however, those passive virtues which mediæval piety ever enjoined—yea, which Christ himself preached upon the mount, and which Protestantism, in the arrogance of reason, is in danger of losing sight of—humility, submission, and contempt of material gains. He won the admiration of his superiors for his attainments and his piety, equally versed in Aristotle and the Holy Scriptures. He delighted most in the Old Testament heroes and prophets, and caught their sternness and invective.

He was not so much interested in dogmas as he was in morals. He had not, indeed, a turn of mind for theology, like Anselm and Calvin; but he took a practical view of the evils of society. At thirty years of age he began to preach in Ferrara and Florence, but was not very successful. His sermons at first created but little interest, and he sometimes preached to as few as twenty-five people. Probably he was too rough and vehement to suit the fastidious ears of the most refined city in Italy. People will not, ordinarily, bear uncouthness from preachers, however gifted, until they have earned a reputation. They prefer pretty and polished young men with nothing to say but platitudes or extravagances. Savonarola seems to have been discouraged and humiliated at his failure, and was sent to preach to the rustic villagers, amid the mountains near Sienna. Among these people he probably felt more at home, and he gave vent to the fire within him and electrified all who heard him, and won the admiration of the celebrated prince of Mirandola, so that his fame spread rapidly, and he was recalled to Florence, 1490, and his great career commenced. In the following year, they pressed in such crowds to hear him that the church of St. Mark, connected with the Dominican convent to which he was attached, could not contain the people, and he repaired to the cathedral. And even that spacious church was filled with eager listeners—more moved than delighted. So great was his popularity, that his influence correspondingly increased, and he was chosen Prior of his famous convent. He now wielded power as well as influence, and became the most marked man of the city. He was not only the most eloquent preacher in Italy, probably in the world, but his eloquence was marked by boldness, earnestness, almost fierceness. Like an ancient prophet, he was terrible in his denunciation of vices. He spared no one, and he feared no one. He resembled

Chrysostom at Constantinople, when he denounced the vanity of Eudoxia and the venality of Eutropius. Lorenzo de Medici, the absolute lord of Florence, sent for him, and expostulated and remonstrated with the unsparing preacher—all to no effect. And when the usurper of his country's liberties was dying, the preacher was again sent for, this time to grant an absolution. But Savonarola would grant no absolution unless Lorenzo would restore the liberties which he and his family had taken away. The dying tyrant was not prepared to accede to so haughty a demand, and, collecting his strength, rolled over on his bed without saying a word, and the austere monk wended his way back to his convent, unmolested and determined.

The premature death of this magnificent prince made a great sensation throughout Italy, and produced a change in the politics of Florence, for the people began to see their political degradation. The popular discontents were increased when his successor, Pietro, proved himself incapable and tyrannical, and abandoned himself to orgies, and insulted the leading citizens by an overwhelming pride. Savonarola took the side of the people, and fanned the discontents. He became the recognized leader of opposition to the Medici. He became a politician as well as preacher, and virtually ruled the city.

The Prior of St. Mark now appeared in a double light—as a political leader, and as a popular preacher. Let us first consider him in his secular aspect, as a revolutionist and statesman, for the admirable constitution he had a principal hand in framing entitles him to the dignity of statesman rather than politician. If his cause had not been good, and if he had not appealed to both enlightened and patriotic sentiments, he would have been a demagogue, for a demagogue and a mere politician are synonomous, and a clerical demagogue is hideous.

The political career of Savonarola commenced with terrible denunciations, from his cathedral pulpit, of the political evils of his day, not merely in Florence, but throughout Italy. He detested tyrants and usurpers, and sought to conserve such liberties as the Florentines had once enjoyed. He was not only the preacher, he was also the patriot. Things temporal were mixed up with things spiritual in his discourses. In his detestation of the tyranny of the Medici, and his zeal to recover for the Florentines their lost liberties, he even hailed the armies of Charles VIII. as deliverers, although they had crossed the Alps to invade and conquer Italy. If the gates of Florence were open to them, they would expel the Medici. So he stimulated the people to league with foreign enemies in order to recover their liberties. This would have been high treason in Richelieu's time, as when the Huguenots encouraged the invasion of the English on the soil of France. He was a zealot, and carried the same spirit into politics that he did into religion, such as when he made a bonfire of what he called vanities. He had an end to carry—he would use any means. There is apt to be jesuitism with all men consumed with zeal, determined on success. To the eye of the Florentine reformer, the expulsion of the Medici seemed the supremest necessity; and if it could be done in no other way than by opening the gates of his city to the French invaders, he would open the gates. Whatever he commanded from the pulpit was done by the people, for he seemed to have supreme control over the people, gained by his eloquence as a preacher. But he did not abuse his power. When the Medici were expelled, he prevented violence. Blood did not flow in the streets. Order and law were preserved. The people looked up to him as their leader, temporal as well as spiritual. So he assembled them together in the great hall of the city, where they formally held a *parlemento*, and they reinstated the ancient magistrates. But they were men without experience. They had no capacity to govern, and they were selected without wisdom on the part of the people. The people, in fact, had not the ability to select their best and wisest men for rulers. That is an evil inherent in all popular governments. Does San Francisco or New York send its greatest men to Congress? Do not our cities elect such rulers as the demagogues point out? Do not the few rule, even in a Congregational Church? If some commanding genius, unscrupulous, or wise, or eloquent, or full of tricks, controls elections with us, much more easily could such a man as Savonarola rule in Florence, where there was no political organization, no caucuses, no wire-pullers, no other man of commanding ability. The only opinion-maker was a preacher, who indicated the general policy to be pursued. He left elections to the people. And when these proved a failure, a new constitution became a necessity. But where were the men capable of framing a constitution for the republic? Two generations of political slavery had destroyed political experience. The citizens were as incapable of framing a new constitution as the legislators of France after they had decimated the nobility, confiscated the church lands, and cut off the head of the king. The lawyers disputed in the town hall, but accomplished nothing.

Their science amounted only to an analysis of human passion. All wanted a government entirely free from tyranny, all expected impossibilities. Some were in favor of a Venitian aristocracy, and others of a pure democracy; yet none would yield to compromise, without which no permanent political institution could ever be framed. How could the inexperienced citizens of Florence comprehend the complicated relations of governments? To make a constitution that the world respects requires the highest maturity of human wisdom. It is the supremest labor of great men. It took the ablest man ever born among the Jews to give to them a national polity. The Roman constitution was the fruit of five hundred years' experience. Our constitution was made by the wisest, most dignified, most enlightened body of statesmen that this country has yet seen, and even they could not have made it without great concessions. No *one* man could have made a constitution, however great his talents and experience—not even a Jefferson or a Hamilton—which the nation would have accepted. It would have been as full of defects as the legislation of Solon or Lycurgus or the Abbé Sieyès. But one man gave a constitution to the Florentines, which they not only accepted, but which has been generally admired for its wisdom, and that man was a Dominican monk. The hand he had in shaping that consitution not only proved him to have been a man of great wisdom, but entitled him to the gratitude of his countrymen as a benefactor. He saw the vanity of political science, as it then existed, the incapacity of popular leaders, and the sadness of a people drifting into anarchy and confusion, and, strong in his own will and his sense of right, he rose superior to himself, and directed the stormy elements of passion and fear. And this he did by his sermons from the pulpit, for he did not descend, in person, into the stormy arena of contending passions and interests. He did not himself attend the deliberations of the town hall. He was too wise and dignified a man for that. But he preached those principles and measures which he wished to see adopted, and so great was the reverence for him that the people listened to his instructions, and afterward deliberated and acted among themselves. He did not write out a code, but he told the people what they should put into it. He was the animating genius of the city. His voice was obeyed. He unfolded the theory that the government of one man, in their circumstances, would become tyrannical, and he taught the doctrine, then new, that the people were the only source of power—that they alone had the right to elect their magistrates. He therefore recommended a general government, which should include all citizens who had intelligence, experience, and position—not all the people, but such as had been magistrates, or their fathers before them. Accordingly, a grand council was formed of three thousand citizens, out of a population of ninety thousand who had reached the age of twenty-nine. These three thousand citizens were divided into three equal bodies, each of which should constitute a council for six months, and no meeting was legal unless two-thirds of the members were present. This grand council appointed the magistrates. But another council was also recommended and adopted, of only eighty citizens not under forty years of age—picked men, changed every six months, whom the magistrates were bound to consult weekly, and to whom was confided the appointment of some of the higher officers of the State, like embassadors to neighboring States. All laws proposed by the magistrates, or seigniory, had to be ratified by this higher and selecter council. The higher council was a sort of Senate, the lower council were more like Representatives. But there was no universal suffrage. The clerical legislator knew well enough that only the better and more intelligent part of the people were fit to vote, even in the election of magistrates. He seems to have foreseen the fatal rock on which all popular institutions are in danger of being wrecked—that no government is safe and respected when the people who make it are ignorant and lawless. So the constitution which Savonarola gave was neither aristocratic nor democratic. It resembled that of Venice more than that of Athens, that of England more than that of the United States. Strictly universal suffrage is a Utopian dream wherever a majority of the people are wicked and degraded. Sooner or later it will plunge any nation, as nations now are, into a whirlpool of dangers, even if Divine Providence may not permit a nation to be stranded and wrecked altogether. In the politics of Savonarola we see great wisdom, and yet great sympathy for freedom. He would give the people all that they were fit for. He would make all offices elective, but only by the suffrages of the better part of the people.

But the Prior of St. Mark did not confine himself to constitutional questions and issues alone. He would remove all political abuses; he would tax property, and put an end to forced loans and arbitrary imposts; he would bring about a general pacification, and grant a general amnesty for political offenses; he would guard against the extortions of the rich, and the usury of the Jews, who lent money at thirty-three per cent., with compound interest; he secured the establishment of a bank for charitable loans; he sought to make the people good citizens, and to advance their temporal interests as well as spiritual. All his reforms, political or social, were advocated, however, from the pulpit, so that he was doubtless a political priest. We, in this country and in these times, have no very great liking to this union of spiritual and temporal authority. We would separate and divide this authority. Protestants would make the functions of the ruler and the priest forever distinct. The Popes themselves were secular rulers, as well as spiritual dignitaries. All bishops and abbots had the charge of political interests. Courts of law were presided over by priests; priests were embassadors to foreign powers; they were ministers of kings; they had the control of innumerable secular affairs, now intrusted to laymen. So their interference with politics did not shock the people of Florence, or the opinions of the age. It was even imperatively called for, since the clergy were the most learned and influential men of these times, even in affairs of State. I doubt if the Catholic Church has ever abrogated or ignored her old right to meddle in the politics of a State or nation. I do not know, but I apprehend, that the Catholic clergy, even in this country, take it upon themselves to instruct the people in their political duties. No enlightened Protestant congregation would endure this interference. No Protestant minister dares ever to discuss political issues from the pulpit, except, perhaps, on Thanksgiving Day, or in some rare exigency in national affairs. Still less would he venture to tell his parishioners how they should vote in town meetings. In imitation of ancient saints and apostles, he is wisely constrained from interference in secular and political affairs. But in the Middle Ages, and the Catholic Church, the priest could be political in his preaching, since many of his duties were secular. Savonarola usurped no prerogatives. He refrained from meeting men in secular vocations. Even in his politics he confined himself to his sphere in the pulpit. He did not attend the town meetings. He simply preached. He ruled by wisdom, eloquence, and sanctity, and as he was an oracle, his utterances became a law.

But while he instructed the people in political duties, he paid far more attention to public morals. He would break up luxury, extravagance, ostentatious living, unseemly dresses in the worship of God. He was the foe of all levities, all frivolities, all insidious pleasures. Bad men found no favor in his eyes, and he exposed their hypocrisies and crimes. He denounced sin, in high places and low. He did not confine himself to the sins of his own people alone, but of princes and in other cities. He took in all Italy in his glance. He invoked the Lord to take the Church out of the hands of the devil, and to pour out his wrath on guilty cities. He throws a gauntlet of defiance on all corrupt potentates. He predicts the near approach of calamities. He foretells the certainty of divine judgments upon all sin. He clothes himself with the thunders of the Jewish prophets. He seems to invoke woe, desolation, and destruction. He ascribes the very invasion of the French as a just retribution. "Thy crimes, O Florence! thy crimes, O Rome! thy crimes, O Italy! are the causes of these chastisements." And so terrible are his denunciations that the whole city quakes with fear. Mirandola relates that, as his voice sounded like a clap of thunder in the cathedral, packed to its utmost capacity with the trembling people, a cold shiver ran through all his bones and the hairs of his head stood on end. "O Rome!" exclaimed the preacher, "thou shalt be put to the sword, since thou wilt not be converted. O Italy! confusion upon confusion shall overtake thee; the confusion of war shall follow thy sins, and famine and pestilence shall follow after war." Then he denounces Rome: "O harlot Church! thou hast made thy deformity apparent to all the world; thou hast multiplied thy fornications in Italy, in France, in Spain, in every country. Behold, saith the Lord, I will stretch forth my hand upon thee; I will deliver thee into the hands of those that hate thee." The burden of his soul is sin—sin everywhere, even in the bosom of the Church—and the necessity of repentance, of turning to the Lord. He is more than an Elijah; he is a John the Baptist. His sermons are chiefly drawn from the Old Testament, especially from the prophets when they denounced woes. He is stern, awful, sublime, like them. He does not attack the polity or the constitution of the Church, but its corruptions. He does not call the Pope a usurper, a fraud, an imposter; he does not attack the office; but, if he is a bad man, he denounces his crimes. He is still the Dominican monk, owning his allegiance, but demanding the reformation of the head of the Church to whom God has given the keys of St. Peter. Neither does he meddle with the doctrines of the Church; he does not take much interest in dogmas; he is not a theologian, but he would change the habits and manners of the people of Florence; he would urge a reformation throughout Italy of morals; he sees only the degeneracy in life; he threatens eternal penalties if sin be persisted in. He alarms the fears of the people, so that women part with their ornaments, dress with more simplicity, and walk more demurely; licentious young men become modest and devout; instead of the songs of the carnival, religious hymns are sung; tradesmen forsake their shops for the churches; alms are more freely given; great scholars become monks; even children bring their offerings to the church; a pyramid of vanities is burned on the public square. And no wonder! A man had appeared at a great crisis in wickedness, and yet when the people were susceptible of grand sentiments—this man, venerated, austere, impassioned, like an ancient prophet, like one risen from the dead, denounces woes with such awful tones, such majestic fervor, such terrible emphasis, as to break through all apathy, all delusions, and fill the people with remorse, and astonish them by his revelations, and make them really feel that the supernal powers, armed with the terrors of Omnipotence, would hurl them into hell unless they repented.

No man in Europe at the time had a more lively and impressive sense of the necessity of a general reformation than the monk of St. Mark; but it was a reform in morals, not of doctrine. He saw the evils of the day—yea, of the Church itself—with perfect clearness, and demanded redress. He is as sad in view of these acknowledged evils as Jeremiah was in view of the apostacy of the Jews. He is as austere in his own life as Elijah or John the Baptist. He would not abolish monastic institutions, but he would reform the lives of the monks—cure them of gluttony and sensuality, not shut up their monasteries. He would not rebel against the authority of the Pope, for even he supposed he was the successor of St. Peter, but he would prevent his nepotism and luxury and worldly spirit—make him once more a true servant of the servants of God, even when clothed with the insignia of universal authority. He would not give up auricular confession, or masses for the dead, or prayers to the Virgin Mary, for these were indorsed by venerated ages; but he would rebuke a priest if found in unseemly places. Whatever was a sin, when measured by the laws of immutable morality, he would denounce, whoever was guilty of it. Whatever would elevate the public morals he would advocate, whatever the opposition; and his morality was measured by the declaration of Christ and the Apostles, not by the standard of a corrupt age. He revered the scriptures, and incessantly pondered upon them, and exalted their authority—the ultimate rule of all holy living, the everlasting handbook of travelers to the heavenly Jerusalem. In all respects he was a good man—a beautiful type of Christian piety, with fewer faults than Luther or Calvin, and as great an enemy as they to corruptions in State and Church. He denounced them even more fiercely and passionately. Not even Erasmus pointed out the vices of the day with more freedom or earnestness. He covered up nothing; he shut his eye to nothing.

The difference between him and Luther was that the Saxon reformer attacked the root of the corruption, not merely outward and tangible and patent sins which everybody knew, but also and more earnestly those false principles of theology and morals which sustained them, and which logically pushed out would necessarily have produced them. For instance, he not merely attacked indulgences, then a crying evil, as peddled by Tetzel and others like him, and all to get money to support the temporal power of the Popes, or build St. Peter's church, but he would show that penance, on which indulgences are based, is antagonistic to the doctrine which Paul so forcibly expounded respecting the forgiveness of sins and the grounds of justification. And Luther saw that all the evils which good men lamented would continue so long as the false principles from which they logically sprung were the creed of the Church. So he directed his giant energies to reform doctrines, rather than morals. His great idea of justification could only be defended by an appeal to the Scriptures, not the authority of councils and learned men. So he made the Scriptures the sole source of theological doctrine. Savonarola also accepted the Scriptures as Luther did; but Luther would put them in the hands of everybody, of peasants even, and thus instituted private judgment, which is the basal pillar of Protestantism. The Catholic theologians never recognized this right in the sense that Luther understood it, and to which he was pushed by inexorable logic. The Church was to remain the interpreter of the Scriptures—I mean its doctrinal and disputed points. Savonarola was a churchman. He was not a fearless theological doctor, going wherever logic and the Bible carried him. Hence, he did not stimulate thought and inquiry like Luther, nor inaugurate a great revolutionary movement, which would gradually undermine papal authority and many institutions which the Catholic Church indorsed. Had he been a great genius, with his progressive proclivities, he might have headed a rebellion against papal authority, which upheld doctrines that logically supported the very evils he denounced. But he was contented to lop off branches; he did not dig up the roots. Luther went to the roots, as Calvin did, as St. Augustine would have done had there been a necessity in his day, for the theology of St. Augustine and Calvin is essentially the same. It was from St. Augustine that Calvin drew his inspiration next after St. Paul. But Savonarola cared very little for the discussion of doctrines. He probably hated all theological speculations—all metaphysical divinity. But there is a closer resemblance between doctrines and morals than most people are aware of. As a man thinketh, so is he. Hence the reforms of Savonarola were temporary, and were not widely extended, for he did not kindle the intelligence of the age, as Luther did, and those associated with him. There can be no great and lasting reform without an appeal to reason, without the assistance of logic, without conviction. The house that had been swept and garnished was reëntered by devils, and the last state was worse than the first. To have effected a radical and lasting reform, Savonarola should have gone deeper. He should have exposed the foundations on which the superstructure of sin was built; he should have undermined them, and appealed to the reason of the world. He did no such thing. He simply rebuked the evils, which must need be, so long as the root of them was left untouched. And so long as his influence remained, so long as his voice was listened to, he was mighty in the reforms at which he aimed—a reformation of the morals of those to whom he preached. But when his voice was hushed, the evils he detested returned, since he had not created those convictions which bind men together in association; he had not fanned that spirit of inquiry which is hostile to ecclesiastical despotism, and which, logically pushed out, would subvert the papal throne. The reformation of Luther was a grand protest against spiritual tyranny. It not only aimed at a purer life, but it opposed the bondage of the Middle Ages, and hence all the superstitions and puerilities and fables which were born and nurtured in that dark and gloomy period, and to which the clergy clung as a means of power or wealth. Luther called out the intellect of Germany, exalted liberty of conscience, and appealed to the dignity of reason. He showed the necessity of learning in order to unravel and explain the truths of revelation. He made piety more exalted by giving it an intelligent stimulus. He looked to the future rather than the past. He would make use, in his interpretation of the Bible, of all that literature, science, and art could contribute. Hence, his writings had a wider influence than could be produced by the fascination of personal eloquence, on which Savonarola relied, but which Luther made only accessory.

Again, the sermons of the Florentine reformer do not impress us, as they did those to whom they were addressed. They are not logical, nor doctrinal, nor learned, not rich in thought like the sermons of those divines whom the Reformation produced. They are vehement denunciations of sin; are eloquent appeals to the heart, to religious fears and hopes. He would indeed create faith in the world, not by the dissertations of Paul, but by the agonies of the dying Christ. He does not instruct. He does not reason. He is dogmatic and practical. He is too earnest to be metaphysical, or even theological. He takes it for granted that his hearers knew all the truths necessary for salvation. He enforces the truths with which they are familiar, not those to be developed by reason and learning. He appeals, he urges, he threatens; he even prophesies; he dwells on divine wrath and judgment. He is an Isaiah foretelling what will happen, rather than a Peter at the Day of Pentecost.

In his oratorical gifts he was transcendent, the like of which has never before nor since been witnessed in Italy. He was a born orator, as vehement as Demosthenes, as passionate as Chrysostom, as electrical as Bernard. Nothing could withstand him. He was a torrent that bore everything before him. His voice was musical, his attitude commanding, his gestures superb. He was all alive with his subject. He was terribly in earnest, as if he believed everything he said, and what he said were most momentous truths. He fastened his burning eyes upon his hearers, who listened with breathless attention, and inspired them with his sentiments. He made them feel that they were in the very jaws of destruction, and that there was no hope but in immediate repentance. His whole frame quivered with emotion, and he sat down utterly exhausted. His language was intense, not clothing new thoughts, but riveting old ideas—the ideas of the Middle Ages, the fear of hell, the judgments of Almighty God. Who could resist such fiery earnestness, such a convulsed frame, such quivering tones, such burning eyes, such dreadful threatenings, such awful appeals? He was not artistic in the use of words and phrases like Bourdaloue, but he reached the conscience and the heart like Whitefield. He never sought to amuse. He would not stoop to any trifling. He told no stories. He made no witticisms. He used no tricks. He fell back on truths, no matter whether his hearers relished them or not; no matter whether they were amused or not, he was the messenger of God urging men to flee as for their lives, like Lot when he escaped from Sodom.

His manner was as effective as his matter. He was a kind of Peter preaching a crusade, arousing emotions and passions, and making everybody feel as he felt. It was life more than thought which marked his eloquence—his voice as well as his ideas, his wonderful electricity which every preacher must have, or he preaches to stones. It was himself, even more than his truths, which made people listen, admire, and quake. All real orators impress themselves, their own individuality, on their auditors. They are not actors, who represent other people, and whom we admire in proportion to their artistic skill in producing deception. These artists excite admiration, make us forget where we are, and what we are, but kindle no permanent emotions, and teach no abiding lessons. The eloquent preacher of momentous truths and interests makes us realise them, in proportion as he feels them himself. They would fall dead upon us, if ever so grand, unless intensified by passion, fervor, sincerity, earnestness. Even a voice has power, when electrical, musical, impassioned, although it may utter platitudes. But when the impassioned voice rings with trumpet notes through a vast audience, appealing to what is dearest to the human soul, lifting the mind to the contemplation of the sublimest truths and most momentous interests, then there is *real* eloquence, such as is never heard in the theater, interested as spectators may be in the triumphs of dramatic art.

But I have dwelt too long on the characteristics of that eloquence which produced such a great effect on the people of Florence in the latter part of the fifteenth century. That ardent, intense, and lofty monk, who filled the cathedral church with eager listeners, world-deep like Dante, not world-wide like Shakspere, was not destined to uninterrupted triumphs. His career was short. He could not even retain his influence. As the English people wearied of the yoke of a Puritan Protector, and hankered for their old pleasures, so the Florentines remembered the sports, and spectacles, and *fêtes*, of the old Medician rule. Savonarola had arrayed against himself the enemies of popular liberty, the patrons of demoralizing excitements, the partisans of the banished Medici, and even the friends and counselors of the Pope. The dreadful denunciation of sin in high places was as offensive to the Pope as the exposure of a tyrannical usurpation was to the family of the old lords of Florence; and his enemies took counsel together, and schemed for his overthrow. If the irritating questions and mockeries of Socrates could not be endured at Athens, how could the bitter invectives and denunciations of Savonarola find favor at Florence? The fate of prophets is to be stoned. Martyrdom and persecution, in some form or other, are as inevitable to the man who sails against the stream, as a broken constitution and a diseased body are to a sensualist, a glutton, or a drunkard. Impatience under rebuke is as certain as the operation of natural law. The bitterest and most powerful enemy of the Prior of St. Mark was the Pope himself—Alexander VI., of the infamous family of the Borgias—since his private vices were exposed, and by one whose order had been especially devoted to the Papal Empire. In the eyes of the wicked Pope, the Florentine reformer was a traitor and conspirator, disloyal and dangerous. At first he wished to silence him by soft and deceitful letters, and tempting bribes, offering to him a cardinal's hat, and inviting him to Rome. He refused alike the bribe and the invitation. His Lent sermons became more violent and daring. "If I have preached and written anything," said this intrepid monk, "heretical, I am willing to make a public recantation. I have always showed obedience to my church; but it is my duty to obey God rather than man." This sounds like Luther at the Diet of Worms; but he was more defenseless than Luther, since the Saxon reformer was protected by powerful princes, and was backed by the enthusiasm of Northern Germans. Yet the Florentine preacher boldly continued his attacks on all hypocritical religion, and on the vices of Rome, not as incidental to the system, but extraneous—the faults of a man or age. The Pope became furious, to be thus balked by a Dominican monk, and in one of the cities of Italy—a city that had not rebelled against his authority. He complained bitterly of the haughty friar, who rebuked him and defied him, to the Florentine ambassador. He summoned a consistory of fourteen eminent Dominican theologians to inquire into his conduct and opinions. He issued a brief forbidding him to preach, under penalty of excommunication. Yet Savonarola continued to preach, and more violently than ever. He renewed his charges against Rome. He even calls her a harlot church, against whom heaven and earth, angels and devils, equally brought charges. The Pope then seized the old thunderbolts of the Gregories and the Clements, and excommunicated the daring monk and preacher, and threatened the like punishment on all who should befriend him. And yet Savonarola continued to preach. All Rome and Italy talked of the audacity of the man. And it was not until Florence itself was threatened with an interdict for shielding such a man, that the magistrates of the city were compelled to forbid his preaching. And the great orator mounted his pulpit for the last time, March 18, 1498, near four hundred years ago, and took an affectionate farewell of the people whom he had led, and appealed to Christ himself as the head of the Church. It was not till the preacher was silenced by the magistrates of his own city that it seems he rebelled against the papal authority, and then not so much against the authority of Rome as against the wicked shepherd himself, who had usurped the fold. He now writes letters to all the prominent kings and princes of Europe to assemble a general council; for the general council of Constance had passed a resolution that the Pope must call a general council every ten years, and that, should he neglect to assemble it, the sovereign powers of the various states and empires were empowered themselves to collect the scattered members of the universal Church, to deliberate on its affairs. In his letters to the Kings of France, England, Spain, and Hungary, and the Emperor of Germany, he denounced the Pope as simonical, as guilty of all the vices, as a disgrace to the station which he held. These letters seem to be directed against the man, not against the system. He aimed to his ejectment from office, rather than the subversion of his office—another mark of the difference between him and Luther, since the latter waged an uncompromising war against Rome herself, against the whole *régime* and government and institutions and dogmas of the Catholic Church; and that is the reason why Catholics hate Luther so bitterly, and deny to him either virtues or graces, and represent even his death-bed as a scene of torment and despair—that pursuing hatred which goes beyond the grave, like that of the zealots of the Revolution in France, who dug up the bones of the ancient kings from those vaults where they had reposed for centuries, and scattered their ashes to the winds.

Savonarola hoped the Christian world would come to his rescue, but his letters were intercepted, and reach the eye of Alexander VI., who now bends the whole force of the Papal Empire to destroy that bold reformer who had assailed his throne. And it seems that a change took place in Florence itself in popular sentiment. Hostile parties obtained the ascendancy in the government. The people—the fickle people—began to desert him; and especially when Savonarola refused to undergo the ordeal of fire, one of the relics of mediæval superstition, the people felt that they had been cheated out of their amusement, for they had waited impatiently the whole day in the public square to see the spectacle. He finally consents to undergo the ordeal, provided he may carry the crucifix. To this his enemies would not consent. He then laid aside the crucifix, but insisted on entering the fire with the sacrament in his hand. His persecutors would not allow this either, and the ordeal did not take place. At last his martyrdom approaches. He is led to prison. The magistrates of the city send to Rome for absolution for having allowed the Prior to preach. His enemies busy themselves in collecting evidence against him, for what I know not, except that he had denounced corruption and sin, and had predicted woe. His two friends are imprisoned and interrogated with him, Fra Dominico and Fra Salvestro, who are willing to die for him. He and they are now subjected to most cruel tortures. In the agonies of body his mind began to waver. His answers are incoherent. He implores his tormentors to end his agonies. He cries out, with a voice enough to melt a heart of stone, "Take, oh, take my life." Yet he confessed nothing to criminate himself. What they wished him especially to confess was that he had pretended to be a prophet, since he had predicted calamities. But all men are prophets, in one sense, when they declare the certain penalties of sin, from which no one can escape, though he take the wings of the morning and fly to the uttermost parts of the sea. Savonarola thus far had remained firm, but renewed examinations and fresh tortures took place. For a whole month his torments were continuous. In one day he was drawn up by a rope fourteen times, and then suddenly dropped, until all his muscles quivered with anguish. Had he been surrounded by loving disciples, like Latimer at the burning pile, he might have summoned more strength, but alone, in a dark inquisitorial prison, subjected to increasing torture, among bitter foes, he did not fully defend his visions and prophecies, and then his extorted confessions were diabolically altered. And that was all they could get out of him, that he had prophecied. In all matters of faith he was sound. The Inquisitors were obliged to bring their examination to an end. They could find no fault with him, and yet they were determined on his death. The Government of Florence consented to it, and hastened it, for a Medici held the highest office of the State. Nothing remained to the imprisoned and tortured friar but to prepare for his execution. In his supreme trial he turned to the God in whom he believed. In the words of the dying Xavier, on the Island of Shan-Shan, he exclaimed, "In te domine speravi, non confundar in eternum." "O Lord," writes he, "a thousand times hast thou wiped out my iniquity. I do not rely on my own justification, but on thy mercy." His few remaining days in prison were passed in holy meditation. At last the Papal Commission arrive. The tortures are renewed, and also the examinations, with the same result. No fault could be found with his doctrines. "But a dead enemy," said they, "makes no more wars." He is condemned to execution. The messengers of death arrive at his cell, and find him on his knees. He is overpowered by his sufferings and vigils, and can with difficulty be kept from sleep. But he arouses himself, and passes the night in prayer, and administers the elements of redemption to his doomed companions, and closes with this prayer: "Lord, I know thou art that perfect Trinity, Father, Son, and Holy Ghost; I know that thou art the eternal Word; that thou didst descend from Heaven into the bosom of Mary; that thou didst ascend upon the cross to shed thy blood for our sins. I pray thee that by that blood I may have remission for my sins." The simple faith of Paul, of Augustine, of Pascal! He then partook of the communion, and descended to the public square, and was led, while the crowd gazed silently and with trepidation, to the first tribunal, with his companions, where he was disrobed of his ecclesiastical dress. Then they were led to another tribunal, and delivered to the secular arm; then to another, where sentence of death was read, and then to the place of execution—not a burning funeral pyre, but a scaffold—which, mounting, composed, calm, absorbed, he submitted his neck to the hangman, in the forty-fifth year of his life—a martyr to the cause of Christ, not for an attack on the Church, or its doctrines, or its institutions, but for having denounced the corruption and vices of those who ruled it—for having preached against sin.

Thus died one of the greatest and best men of his age, one of the truest and purest whom the Catholic Church has produced in any age. He was stern, uncompromising, austere, but a reformer and a saint—a man who was merciful and generous in the possession of power—an enlightened statesman, a sound theologian, and a fearless preacher of that righteousness which exalteth a nation. He had no vices, no striking defects. He lived according to the rules of the convent he governed with the same wisdom that he governed a city, and he died in the faith of the primitive apostles. His piety was monastic, but his spirit was progressive, sympathizing with liberty, advocating public morality. He was unselfish, disinterested, and true to his Church, and his conscience, and his cause—a noble specimen of both a man and Christian, whose deeds and example form part of the inheritence of an admiring posterity. We pity his closing days after such a career of power and influence. But we may as well compassionate Socrates or Paul. The greatest lights of the world have gone out in martyrdom, to be extinguished, however, only for a time, and then to loom up again in another age, and burn with inextinguishable brightness to remotest generations, as examples of the power of faith and truth in this wicked and rebellious world—a world to be finally redeemed by the labors and religion of just such men, whose days are days of sadness, protest, and suffering, and whose hours of triumph and exaltation are not like those of conquerors, nor like those whose eyes stand out with fatness, but few and far between. "I have loved righteousness, I have hated iniquity," said the great champion of the mediæval Church, "and therefore I die in exile."

In ten years after this ignominious execution, Raphael painted the martyr among the sainted doctors of the Church in the halls of the Vatican, and future Popes did justice to his memory, for he inaugurated that reform movement in the Catholic Church itself which took place within fifty years after his death. In one sense he was the precursor of Loyola, of Xavier, and Aquaviva, those illustrious men who headed the counter reformation; Jesuits, indeed, but ardent in piety, and enlightened by the spirit of a progressive age. "He was the first," says Villari, "in the fifteenth century, to make men feel that a new light had awakened the human race, and thus he was a prophet of a new civilization—the forerunner of Luther, of Bacon, of Descartes. Hence, the drama of his life became, after his death, the drama of Europe. In the course of a single generation after Luther had declared his mission, the spirit of the Church of Rome underwent a change. From the halls of the Vatican to the secluded hermitages of the Apennines this revival was felt. Instead of a Borgia there reigned a Caraffa." And it is remarkable that from the day that the counter reformation in the Catholic Church was headed by the early Jesuits, Protestantism gained no new victories, and in two centuries so far declined in piety and zeal that the cities which witnessed the noblest triumphs of Luther and Calvin were disgraced by a boasting rationalism, to be succeeded again in our times by an arrogance of skepticism which has had no parallel since the days of Democritus and Lucretius. "It was the desire of Savonarola that reason, religion, and liberty might meet in harmonious union, but he did not think a new system of religious doctrines was necessary." The influence of such a man cannot pass away, and did not pass away, for it cannot be doubted that his views have been embraced by enlightened Catholics from his day to ours—by such men as Pascal, Fénelon, and Lacordaire, and thousands like them, who prefer ritualism and auricular confession, and penance, monasticism, and an ecclesiastical monarch, and all the machinery of a complicated hierarchy—all the evils growing out of papal domination—to rationalism, sectarian dissensions, irreverence, license, want of unity, want of government, and even dispensation from the marriage vow. Which is worse, the physical arm of the beast or the maniac soul of a lying prophet? Which is worse, the superstition and narrowness which excludes the Bible from schools, or that unbounded toleration which smiles on those audacious infidels who cloak their cruel attacks on the faith of Christians with the name of a progressive civilization, and so far advanced that one of these new lights, ignorant, perhaps, of everything except of the fossils and shells and bugs and gases of the hole he has bored in, assumes to know more of the mysteries of creation and the laws of the universe than Moses and David and Paul, and all the Bacons and Newtons that ever lived? Names are nothing. It is the spirit, the *animus*, which is everything. It is the soul which permeates a system that I look at. It is the devil from which I would flee, whatever be his name, and though he assume the form of an angel of light, or cunningly persuade me, and ingeniously argue, that there is no God. True and good Catholics and true and good Protestants have ever been united in one thing—*in this belief*, that there is a God who made the heaven and the earth, and that there is a Christ who made atonement for the sins of the world. It is good morals, faith, and love to which both Catholics and Protestants are exhorted by the Apostles. When either Catholics or Protestants accept the one faith and the one Lord which Christianity alone reveals, then they equally belong to the grand army of spiritual warriors under the banner of the Cross, though they may march under different generals and in different divisions, and they will receive the same consolations in this world, and the same rewards in the world to come.

JOHN LORD.

A BRIEF VISIT TO CALCUTTA.

Of all places to approach by water, there are few, if any, so dangerous as Calcutta. I discovered this not only by personal observation, but heard that opinion expressed by navigators of forty years' experience. For more than a hundred miles from the shore, the water is discolored, almost to muddiness, thus denoting the presence of sand-bars and other sunken dangers. A chart of the place exhibits long lines of sand-bars shallowly covered with water, and between them the water is sufficiently deep for navigation. Numerous vessels are lost by running on a bar and toppling over to either side. What is complimentarily designated the "Pilot Station," is merely two brigs, each bearing about fourteen pilots and their assistants, cruising about for incoming steamers and vessels in order to supply them with pilots. Until one of these indispensable gentlemen is secured, the captain of a ship, perceiving that she is in shoal and treacherous water, far out of sight of land, navigates his craft in fear and trembling. As the vessel in which I was a passenger approached, a cannon was fired from a pilot-brig as a signal for her to be hove-to, as she was in a position of considerable jeopardy. Then a pilot and his assistant came on board, the duty of the latter being to constantly heave the lead and report the depth of water, a proceeding probably nowhere else necessary more than a hundred miles from shore. As only sky and water are visible, the most experienced pilots have but the lead for their guide. As the land is neared, the dangers augment, and no fewer than thirteen light-houses warn from as many perils. In respect to this and other details, I would observe, once for all, that I am speaking of matters as they existed when I made my visit, some seventeen years ago. The land being extremely low near the shore, it is not perceptible at any considerable distance. Sangor Island, near the mouth of the River Hoogly, is the first object of interest seen. It is a boat-shaped place, full of jungle, which is infested by tigers. There is a light-house there, which is surrounded by a high wall to protect the keeper, his family, and domesticated animals from those beasts of prey. Long before the shore is sighted, birds fly around the ship. They are thin, emaciated creatures; they move languidly through the air, as becomes beings in such a debilitating climate; their wings seem scarcely able to keep them afloat in the atmosphere; they appear as if they would every moment drop into the sea, and they seek the upper spars and rigging of the ship for rest, where they can be easily caught if their capture were worth the trouble. All up the Bay of Bengal, I frequently observed water-snakes swimming alongside the vessel. The birds mentioned I found to be a fair indication of much of the animal life—not excepting man—of India; that is of languor, laziness, and a disrelish for exertion. The climate, of course, is the cause of this, as it is irksome to be active under the blaze of a tropical sun, and when, night and day, one's body is in a chronic state of perspiration.

To persons who visit the Orient for the first time, there are objects of interest or curiosity, but not always of a pleasant character, on all sides. Calcutta, as the reader is without doubt aware, is situated on the east side of the River Hoogly, about one hundred and twenty miles from the Bay of Bengal; but such a hundred and twenty miles to travel! I counted more than four hundred human corpses floating past the ship. They were all the bodies of Hindoos, some of whose sects cast the remains of their relatives into the sacred waters of the Ganges, one of the affluents of which is the Hoogly; others of the sects burn their dead, and yet again others bury them after the Christian fashion. The pilot, probably reading disgust on my face at the sight and smell of the putrifying bodies, perpetrated what may have appeared to him a witticism, but to me it seemed of rather a grim and ghastly character. He remarked:

"You evidently do not like the smell of boiled meat. Wait until night, and you will get the the odor of roast for a change."

Sure enough, when the ship was anchored for the night, large fires were perceptible on the shore, and the smell of charred bones was wafted by the breeze to our olfactories. Human remains were being incinerated. Such was my initial experience of India, "the brightest gem in the British crown." It took our ship, although assisted by a powerful tug, three days to travel the hundred and twenty miles from the mouth of the Hoogly to Calcutta. The reason of this is that there are certain sand-bars in the river which can be crossed only at full tide. Having crossed one of them, the tide has probably become too low by the time the next one is reached, and another full tide has to be waited for. We did not travel by night, but anchored. The arms and legs of dead bodies were constantly getting foul of the anchor-chains, and had to be cast off with a boat-hook. At some places the Hoogly is not twice the width of Market Street; at others it is a mile or more wide, and the current frequently runs at the rate of eight miles an hour. While at anchor, waiting for the tide to rise to enable us to cross a sandbar, four of us went ashore in a boat, and had some excellent sport shooting alligators. Going on shore is not unattended by danger. On the west bank of the river I observed a monument, which the pilot explained to me was a cenotaph which had been erected to the memory of two young lovers. They had met casually as passengers on board of a ship bound from London to Calcutta, and during the long voyage of four months had formed a matrimonial engagement, and were to be united on their arrival in India. While the ship was at anchor in the Hoogly the couple conceived the idea of having a ramble on shore, and the captain placed a boat and crew at their disposal. As a long time elapsed without the return of the lady and gentleman to the boat, the sailors instituted a search for them, and at length discovered shreds of their clothing and traces of blood and struggling. Both the lovers had been killed by a tiger. Their friends erected the cenotaph mentioned.

While casting into the sacred rivers the remains of relatives is the funeral rite of some of the Hindoo sects, yet it cannot be doubted that many women are drowned for infidelity. Byron mentions this mode of getting rid of refractory or unloved wives in another part of the world, where he makes Gulnare say:

> "When wearied of these fleeting charms and me,
> There yawns a sack and yonder rolls the sea;"

and he adds in another place:

> "Morals were better and the fish no worse."

The tug which towed our ship up the Hoogly was a curiosity in its way, or, rather, those on board were. The crew were so numerous that they literally swarmed, like bees in a hive, upon the deck. They appeared to be a crowd of Lilliputians, and forty or fifty of them pulled a rope that three or four Europeans or Americans could easily have managed. The little steering-wheel was handled by four of these apologies for men, two on each side, although the wheel of a craft six times the size is usually manipulated by one British or American sailor. It may be remarked, *en passant*, that the young men are so small in stature and beardless, and so effeminate in feature, it is extremely difficult to tell them from the women except by their dress. This is of the scantest description, and only sufficient to comply with the commonest demand for decency, but the women wear calico dresses reaching nearly to the ankles. On looking at such beings it ceases to be a wonder that Lord Clive, with seven thousand English troops, dispersed hundreds of thousands of them.

Before proceeding as far as Calcutta, all vessels anchor at a place called Garden Reach, four miles from the city. The locality is celebrated as the site of the magnificent palace of the dethroned King of Oude, who was pensioned by the British Government with $600,000 a year. At the time of my visit the *effete* old monarch was in his dotage, and amused himself, like a child, by playing with dolls and other toys. In his harem there were a vast number of imprisoned beauties, guarded with great strictness. Our vessel anchored in front of the palace grounds at nine o'clock in the evening, and the captain informed me that it would not be safe to land and attempt to reach Calcutta until the following morning. But it went against my grain, after a long sea voyage, to remain another night on board when I was within four miles of my destination. The pilot's assistant, a fine, muscular young fellow, over six feet tall, whispered to me to ask the pilot's consent for him to accompany me on shore, as it would be comparatively safe for two to go together. The permission was readily accorded, as the pilot and I had become great friends during our three days' acquaintance. He had primed me with advice and recipes to guard against contracting that terrible complaint, cholera. I was to eat no fruit for several hours before sleep. This was easy to comply with. I was to drink so much brandy every day. This was also comparatively easy to do. I was to keep out of the sun. This was difficult. I was to avoid certain quarters of Calcutta. This was likewise difficult, as I desired to explore the entire city. On the whole, however, I got on very well—that is, I escaped the scourge. The pilot's assistant, who had armed himself with a heavy stick, and I, were put on shore in one of the ship's boats, and we evaded the customs officers, it being illegal for a passenger to land until the ship had been inspected. We were not so fortunate, however, in eluding the palace guard, one of whom challenged us as we passed through the royal grounds, which we could not avoid doing. My companion's only reply was to knock the sentry down, and then he exclaimed to me, "Now let us make fast time to the main road." This we did, and fortunately found a *gharry*—a public hack, drawn by two ponies—as if there to order, and in less than twenty minutes we were in front of Wilson's Hotel in the "City of Palaces." During our quick drive I discovered that the pilot's assistant's offer to accompany me was not wholly disinterested, for he informed me that he had been only a few days married, and was anxious to get home to his wife. All my efforts, therefore, to secure his companionship for a two or three hours' ramble over the city before retiring to bed, were futile, and he remained with me only long enough to join me in my first dose of the medicine prescribed by the pilot.

I had scarcely registered at the hotel when a young Hindoo, after having made a respectful *salaam*, placed a letter in my hands. It was a recommendation from his last employer. On informing him that I did not require his services, he replied that every guest at the hotel engaged his own servant. This was news to me, and I was not slow to discover that there really was something in the proverb, "Live and learn." On questioning the hotel clerk on the subject (the caravansery was the leading one of the city), he told me that for my extra comfort a special servant would be necessary; that there were many services which I would need that the ordinary help of the house would not consider it their duty to perform, etc. Well, finding it proper when in Rome, or, rather, in Calcutta, to do as Calcutta does, I employed the young Hindoo. The wages which he demanded appeared to me, as Mark Tapley would say, "ridiculously small"—three rupees (about a dollar and a half) a month, without board or lodging, as he found himself in everything. I made up my mind that I could stand that, although it subsequently transpired that my new retainer did not give me more than two hours of his time daily. He refused to accompany me to stores to carry home a few small purchases. All he did was to bring me a cup of coffee at five o'clock in the morning, to prepare my bath (an indispensable necessity in that climate), to offer to act as my *valet* when dressing, a service I dispensed with, and to stand behind my chair and wait on me at meals. After he had prepared my bath, about five o'clock in the morning, I did not see him until breakfast time, nine o'clock; after that not until *tiffin* (lunch), at one, and then not until dinner, at seven, which was the last I saw of him for that day.

To return: On the night of my arrival it occupied only a few minutes to register and secure the services of Selim, my Hindoo servant, when I sallied out for a couple of hours' solitary stroll by the light of a full moon. It was then about ten o'clock, and, judging from the numbers on the streets, I perceived that in such a climate it was pleasant to turn day into night and night into day. It would be tedious and uninteresting to give an analysis of my feelings on finding myself for the first time in a city of such historic interest, every street and square of which has a story that has been narrated by Macaulay and a thousand other gifted writers. I concerned myself, however, with the practical present rather than with the glorious and inglorious past, and without particularly speculating on the future. I saw a great deal to condemn, and also not a little to admire, during my first night in the city, and had plenty of food for reflection on my return to my rooms, while vainly for many a long hour in the oppressive heat wooing sleep "to weigh my eyelids down and steep my senses in forgetulness." Until nearly morning I found slumber to be out of the question. One might, like Elaine,

> "Now turn to right, and now to left,
> And find no ease in turning or in rest,"

an experience which is, probably, not uncommon. I found that it was only between the interval of coffee and a bath at five in the morning and breakfast at nine that I could enjoy any sound repose. Mosquito-bars have the effect on me of making, or appearing to make, oppressive weather doubly oppressive; yet without them it would be simply impossible to remain in bed in Calcutta. Not mosquitoes alone, but insects of many kinds, from one to three inches long, join in a night-long serenade, and, if possible, feast on one's blood. I subsequently discovered that sometimes the plague of insects was so great that it was out of the question to play billiards, on account of the impossibility of keeping the board free of the little pests, which constantly turned the course of the balls.

On the morning following my arrival I found that the ship had come up from Garden Reach, and was moored opposite the city. One of the sailors had been stricken with cholera, and was a corpse before sunset. This was by no means cheering, and the matter was not mended by a gentleman observing to me, "We are never wholly free from cholera here, but this year it is more prevalent and fatal than usual, and new-comers are more frequently attacked than those who are acclimated." It began to dawn on my mind that I had made a slight mistake in visiting Calcutta, and I at once paid devoted attention to some of the medicine recommended by my friend, the pilot, with a flask of which I had prudently armed myself. I soon learned that the best French brandy was the almost general *panacea*, both as a preventive and a cure for cholera. During an attack of the disease there were mixed with that liquid, camphor and Jeremy's sedative preparation of the tincture of opium, and exterior applications were used. It was not long before I became satisfied that errors of diet and other imprudences were the main causes of attacks of this complaint, and in a few days I ceased to feel any solicitude on my own account. I received another lesson, worth narrating for the benefit of others, during my first three or four days in Calcutta. After the long voyage, I had, of course, a large number of articles for a laundry. Selim informed me that men did all the washing there, and that he would find me a man for the purpose. I did not then, as I do now, know that nearly all Hindoos are innately and instinctively thieves. When a worthy appeared to take my clothes away he asked me to count the several kinds of articles, which I declined to do, as involving too much trouble. He knew he was dishonest, and he expected me to treat him as such. I made the mistake of not doing so. When he returned, professedly with all the clothes laundried, I perceived by the bulk that not half of them were there. He stoutly protested that he had brought back every article, but on my threatening to call in a *chokeedar* (policeman), he said he would bring the rest of the clothes, if I would wait a few minutes. I kept what he had brought, and he soon returned with about as much more. Again I threatened him with a *chokeedar*, when he departed and brought more of my clothes. This proceeding was gone through four times, and as I had not counted the articles given to him, and could not prove that he had not returned all, I paid him. The charge was moderate enough: two rupees (about a dollar) a hundred pieces, or a cent a piece, counting large and small promiscuously. My impression is that Selim was "in cahoot" with the laundryman, for when I refused to count the pieces before letting them be removed, I noticed that the two men exchanged meaning looks.

As the design of this paper is to chronicle some of my personal impressions during a short visit to Calcutta, much space cannot be given to a history or description of the city. Space will not permit of it; nevertheless, a few facts in this connection will not be out of place. Calcutta takes its name from Kali Ghutta, the *ghaut*, or landing-place, of the Goddess Kali, wife of Siva, and was founded by Job Charnook, an agent of the East India Company, in the year 1690. It is a city of Hindoostan, capital of the Province of Bengal, and is the metropolis of British India. It is the seat of the supreme government of the country, and the abode of the Governor-General. To him the Governors of Madras and Bombay are subordinate. About the period of my visit the population of the city was 377,924, of whom 239,190 were Hindoos, 113,059 Mohammedans, 11,224 Europeans, 11,036 Eurasians (as the offspring of a European father and a native mother are called), and 681 Jews. The population of the city and suburbs was 616,249. The number has since vastly increased, the population of the city alone in 1872 being 447,601. Calcutta extends for about six miles along the east bank of the Hoogly, and the width is about two miles. Fort William, in which the white inhabitants took refuge during the Sepoy rebellion in 1854, is a little south of the city, and is the largest fortress in the British dominions. It cost $10,000,000, and can accommodate a garrison of 15,000 troops. In times of peace its garrison is one British and two native regiments. Between Fort William and the city is the Maidan, a beautiful park, and the Esplanade, fronting which is the palace of the Governor-General. Calcutta is divided into what is called the Northern, or Native District, and the Southern, or European District. What is termed the Chowringee is the native or "Black Town," constructed, for the most part, of mud or bamboo cabins, and narrow, dirty streets. In this quarter one occasionally observes an idol of wood or plaster set up in the street. The houses are high, and loop-holed in the upper stories, and stores are on the ground floor. The European houses are built of brick and stucco, and are generally detached, and have spacious verandas. What strikes a new arrival as exceedingly singular is the position in which large numbers of the private residences are built. I cannot better describe it than by stating that the position is reversed from the way of placing houses in the United States and Europe. The stables and other out-offices front the street, and the main building faces an inner court or garden. This is for the purpose of securing coolness and shade in the family apartments, but the effect is anything but beautifying to the public thoroughfares. The principal structures are the Government House, the town hall, the mint, the cathedral, the Hindoo College, and the hospital. The Asiatic Society has a valuable museum and library of Oriental manuscripts. There are several educational institutes, the Hindoo, the Madriassa or Mohammedan, the Sanscrit, and the Fort William Colleges. What is designated the Strand extends southward along the river, forming the favorite drive of the European and wealthy native residents. For about an hour before sunset, and for some time afterward, the Strand presents a very animated appearance, and reminds a person of Rotten Row, Hyde Park, London, during the evening hours. All the wealth, beauty, and fashion of Calcutta may be seen in elegant equipages of all kinds. On many of the carriages there are six servants—three on the box and three behind—dressed in gaudy colors, the men in the rear waving fans over those in the body of the coach, to keep them cool and to drive off the insects. There everybody goes to see everybody else, for not to be seen on the Strand is to be out of the fashionable world of Calcutta. But, indeed, the crowd is motley enough. The flash turnout of the wealthy courtesan whirls past the carriage and outriders of the Viceroy, and the stanhope of the rich *parvenu* heads off the brougham of the Chief Justice.

Viewed from the river, which varies in width from a quarter to three-quarters of a mile opposite the city, Calcutta may appear to merit its magnificent appellation of the "City of Palaces," but it did not give me that impression while perambulating its streets. The Chowringee portion of the place is positively forbidding in its appearance, and is little more than what might appropriately be termed an exaggeration of our Chinatown, and about as offensive to eyes, ears, and nose. But, indeed, the high-sounding title of "City of Palaces" is not claimed for the whole metropolis, but only for that portion of it which commences at the Maidan and extends a certain distance northward. A street of sixty feet in width intersects the city parallel to its greatest length. The Esplanade is ornamented with a statue of Lord Hardinge. Both the Sikhs and the Chinese have places of worship in Calcutta, and the Martiniere, as it is called, is an institution for the education of the poor of both sexes, founded under the will of Claude Martin, who amassed a colossal fortune in the Orient. Each of the squares incloses a tank near the middle, with a planted walk surrounding it. I was naturally curious to behold the celebrated "black hole," in which, although not twenty feet square, nearly one hundred and fifty human beings were crowded for a night, and from which most of them were taken dead in the morning; but I found that it had been filled up, and that the post-office occupied the site.

The water is deep enough—from six to seven fathoms—in the Hoogly, opposite Calcutta, to afford anchorage to ships of fifteen hundred tons; but, on account of hurricanes, vessels are generally also moored to the shore as a precautionary measure. The landing-places are called *ghauts*. The city is supplied with water by tanks—of which there are about a thousand—in which the periodical rainfalls are collected. The water is delivered to the citizens by means of leather bags. Filling and carrying these afford occupation to a vast number of laborers. Soon after sunrise and before sunset they may be seen at this occupation, and doubtless earning fair wages according to the low scale of remuneration in the place. All efforts to procure water by boring have failed, and there are no mountains or hills where reservoirs could be constructed, and whence aqueducts could convey water to the city. The water of the Hoogly, which is very muddy and impure, is extensively utilized. I observed sailors filling ships' barrels and tanks from this source; but, even for culinary purposes, water in which numberless human corpses were floating would not be particularly desirable. Water is somehow conveyed to fountains at the corners of the principal streets, and just before and after sunrise an early riser may witness the native population going through their ablutions.

Calcutta has the largest commerce of any city in Asia, and commands the entire trade of Bengal. All the way from the Nepaul frontier the skins of tigers and other wild animals are sent for sale to Calcutta, as well as live beasts for exportation to menageries in Europe and America. The shipping of the ferocious brutes is a very exciting scene, especially when it is accomplished by the puny men described, and who are childishly afraid of the quadrupeds. The Hindoo has an instinctive dread of a tiger, on account of the blood-curdling stories which are constantly narrated of the havoc caused by this terror of the jungle. Nor is the fear groundless, as it is computed that six hundred persons are annually killed by tigers. The "man-eaters," as they are termed, are usually old tigresses, that find it easier to capture a man than a deer; but, besides this, after having partaken of human flesh, they prefer it to any other. But the more legitimate subjects of export than wild animals and their skins are indigo, opium, sugar, saltpeter, rice, raw cotton, raw silk, piece goods, lac, hides, etc. The climate is favorable for such productions, while it is decidedly unhealthy for man. In summer—termed so *par excellence*, because the weather is a few degrees warmer than the so-called winter—all who can afford to do so leave for the mountains. Lord Eldon, who was Governor-General during my visit, died there before I left. While the office, next to that of Lord-Lieutenant of Ireland, is the greatest in the gift of the Queen, yet few noblemen desire the proud position a second time, and many have requested an early recall. The climate is so excessively debilitating and enervating that only the strongest desire for gain or glory can induce a person to remain in such a place. The rainy season lasts from June to October, and the average rainfall is sixty-four inches. Vultures, kites, crows, storks, and a bird called the adjutant (not adjutant-general, although adjutants are very general in Calcutta) by day, and foxes, jackals, and wild dogs by night, act as public scavengers. The streets of Calcutta swarm with crows, which are as much encouraged there, and are more effective scavengers, than our imported English sparrows here. While in Calcutta I heard an amusing incident narrated in this connection. The crows, besides scavengering, were apt to poach on forbidden ground. Much to the annoyance of a monkey—whose chain permitted him only to ascend and descend his pole and to go a couple of yards from it—his food was constantly stolen by crows. One day he placed his dinner at the foot of the pole, and then lay down near it as if he was dead, but doubtless keeping watch from the corner of an eye. It was some time before the crows were deceived by the cunning monkey, but at length one ventured to approach the forbidden fare. Quick as thought the monkey grabbed the crow, and completely plucked it alive, except that one long feather was left at the end of each wing. During the operation the other crows set up a terrible chatter, but this did not disconcert Jocko, who made a clean job of it. At last he released the plucked crow, which was able to walk to its companions. The sequel of the story is that the monkey's triumph was complete, and his food was no more pilfered.

During the warmest hours of the day nearly all business is suspended in Calcutta. The merchants take their *siesta* after the Spanish fashion, and very generally transact their affairs in the morning and evening. Even at these times locomotion by palanquin is adopted; and, as the languid-looking bankers and others lie stretched at full length in the ungainly looking vehicles, they appear to a stranger like patients being borne to a hospital. For my part, I could never bring myself to enter a palanquin, as to me it had a hearse-like appearance, and I had, moreover, an aversion to lie on the same cushions which had probably been reclined on by promiscuous thousands. It seemed to me a most favorable place for contracting the cholera, and therefore I preferred to employ my natural means of locomotion, or to hire a *gharry* if I desired to go a considerable distance. One morning, while considering how I could most pleasantly pass two or three hours, I was glad to see my friend the pilot. His class in Calcutta was, under the rule of the East India Company, superior to the same class anywhere else, for their salaries were very large, and only those who had received the education of gentlemen were licensed. Hence, when the British Government took the place of the Company in the management of India, it was stipulated that under the new *régime* the pilots should maintain their old *status*. My friend had been in the employ of the Company, and afterward, when I became acquainted with him, was in the service of the Government

In many ways he was useful and entertaining to me during my brief stay, and on this occasion he invited me to visit his bungalow, which was a few miles from Calcutta. Unlike most East Indians, his robust frame and stamina appeared to defy the effects of the trying climate. He lived highly, and seemed to scorn to take extra precaution against contracting the great disease of the country. I found, however, that he was no mere theorist regarding the advice he had given me as to the best means to keep the cholera at arm's length, for he was one of those physicians who swallow their own medicine. If a liberal imbibition of French brandy was a *panacea* against the disease, he certainly deserved immunity from it, as he backed his advice to me on the subject with very systematic example. Less than an hour's ride brought us to his bungalow, which was in every way constructed for coolness and comfort. Like nearly all bungalows which I subsequently saw, it had only one story, and was entirely surrounded by a veranda. The windows were small, the rooms large, lofty, and airy, and the inevitable *punka* kept the air in motion. Near the veranda, the shrubbery grew tall and luxuriantly, and as it grows nowhere else than in India, and afforded a delightful shade in itself and to the residence. While waiting for *tiffin*, I was, in the spacious garden, initiated into the mysteries of many tropical plants and shrubs which I had never seen elsewhere, even in hot-houses. In my friend's wife and grown daughters I had an opportunity of judging for myself in regard to what I had often heard and read of East Indian ladies, and of European ladies who had gone to reside in the Orient. A comparatively brief residence there renders the freshest and rosiest complexion colorless, or waxen-hued. The ruddiest face cannot long resist the climate, and does not regain its color on a return to England. In India, the blood appears to be thinned, and never to be restored to its normal condition. For the reasons stated I was informed, and, indeed, I saw for myself, that nearly all the society ladies in Calcutta painted. They have to do so, or to be content to look as pale as ghosts. My visit to the bungalow was my first experience of the suburbs of Calcutta, and the trip was in all respects delightful and instructive. It may be mentioned that bungalows for the accommodation of travelers are erected on all the principal roads of India. The rent of one is usually a rupee (half a dollar) a day, and parties who do not bring their provisions with them can generally find plenty, and native cooks, in the vicinity of the bungagalows. It is astonishing what long journeys persons accomplish in palanquins by day, and resting in bungalows by night. Four natives will carry a man at the rate of six miles an hour; and, with relays of carriers, great distances are soon traversed. How men who live almost exclusively on rice — their religion prohibiting them from eating animal food, or anything that ever had possessed animal life—can all day toil along with the poles of a palanquin on their shoulders in such heat, is surprising. But speaking of sects that think they can pass through the world without partaking of animal food, I may observe, in passing, that a wealthy Hindoo is said to have been driven to self-destruction on being shown, by the aid of a microscope, all the animal life there was in a single drop of the water of which he had been drinking.

Society in Calcutta is very convivial, and much hospitality prevails among the few white inhabitants. The Governor-General and his wife, of course, lead society there, and an introduction to them, and an attendance at the Viceroy's *levées*, are indispensable as passports over the thresholds of the *ton*. But a laudable common sense prevails in the matter of dress or costume. In such a climate it would be extremely uncomfortable to wear a dress-suit of broadcloth at a party. Gentlemen, therefore, who dine, say, with the Viceroy, appear in the reception room in full evening dress, but before entering the banquet hall they repair to an adjacent apartment, and change the heavy claw-hammer or swallow-tail dress-coat for a white linen jacket, so that the guests present an appearance not unlike that of the waiters in some of our restaurants. This arrangement may not be strikingly picturesque, but it is sensible and comfortable. Those in attendance on the Prince of Wales during his Indian tour complained bitterly of the martyrdom which they endured by having constantly to appear in his presence in full regimental uniform. While he himself dressed as lightly as possible, as was befitting in such a climate, he gave no such privilege to his staff.

One of the "sights" of Calcutta is the Botanical Gardens, which are situated on the west side of the Hoogly, opposite the city. They are said to be more opulent in all that relates to horticulture than any other gardens in the world. Here, in the wildest luxuriance, in the open air, grow flowers, plants, and shrubs which in most other latitudes can be reared and nurtured only in hot-houses. From the seed onward, everything that grows is rapidly forced by the heat into maturity, and attains robust development. It is in these gardens that is found the largest banyan tree in existence, under the foliage of which, it is said, a whole regiment of soldiers can camp. Serpents here are more plentiful than agreeable, but they create no alarm, as, unless when trodden on or otherwise molested, they seldom make an attack. The gardens are extensively patronized by the inhabitants, and junk-like rowboats on the river do a thriving business in transporting visitors to and fro. When I crossed the Hoogly to see the gardens, I tendered a half-sovereign (about $2.50) to the boatmen from which to take the fare, and, to my surprise, they received it with reverential awe. They gave me the correct change in rupees and annas, but I was subsequently informed that the money would be all lost to them, as they would bury the gold piece. Gold is one of their gods, and to save it from pollution, they put it out of sight in the ground. I never afterward tendered any but silver money in Calcutta. Gold there is not in currency, although some of the banks will receive it on deposit or give rupees in exchange.

Hotel life in Calcutta is very pleasant, although it is shared in almost exclusively by the sterner sex, except in the case of "transients." The guests consist largely of British army officers on leave, and their society is very agreeable and instructive to new-comers. Whatever faults Americans may have to find with English officers, one thing is certain, namely, that the *curriculum* through which they must pass, and in which they are examined, insures their being scholars, and, with very few exceptions, they are gentlemen. Hence, there are no more pleasant parties than their mess dinners. The officers of English regiments in India received both British and Indian pay, and most of them having also private means of their own, were thus enabled to live in good style. Indeed, in the three great cities of British India—Calcutta, Madras, and Bombay—the society of military officers, their wives, and families, may be said to be the best. At the *table d'hôte* of the hotels there is little restraint, and the guests speak to one another as they would at a private table. Late arrivals do not at first take kindly to Indian curries; they would appear to be an acquired taste. They are no more like so-called curries made in Europe and America than coffee is like champagne. After a short residence in India, foreigners acquire a great relish for curries, and would not consider the breakfast or the dinner table complete without one. It is singular, but true, that the best French cooks in vain essay to make a curry as it is made in India. Not even royalty itself, in Europe, with all that it pays for its *cuisine*, can command one of these dishes as it is prepared and served in Calcutta, unless it is made by an imported Hindoo cook. This was discovered by the Prince of Wales during his Indian tour, and hence he took to Europe with him two native cooks, expressly to make curries. It is not only that they are much hotter than those dishes made in the temperate zones, but there is a deep mystery in the compounding or mixing of the multifarious ingredients. I have ever found that the warmer the countries which I visited, the hotter were the condiments and spices used in cookery. There is true philosophy in this; in warm weather a person perspires far less after a warm than a cold drink. In connection with this subject it may be remarked that, among the white population in Calcutta, there is not that desire on the part of families to live and board at hotels, or in suites of apartments in private houses, that there is in this country. Every lady there likes to have her own city residence or bungalow in the country. It is true that domestics are obtained for a "song," in Calcutta, but such servants! Twelve of them may be had for the wages of a European or American cook or housemaid; but the latter will do as much work and not consume as much food as the dozen. The one who opens the door for visitors will do nothing else; so with respect to the one who makes the beds; the person that cooks the food will not wash the dishes, and so on. Housekeeping in Calcutta is therefore no sinecure for a lady; she must be a good general in order to secure efficiency and to promote discipline among her army of domestics.

Not my least pleasurable excursion was that which I made to what is known as "The Seven Tanks Villa," because there are that number of tanks in the gardens, four miles from Calcutta. The proprietor was a wealth *rajah*, who invariably received and treated foreigners with great hospitality. While driving to the place in a *gharry*, the coachman asked me if I would like to see a troupe of Indian jugglers perform, as there was one in sight. On my replying in the affirmative, he drew the vehicle up on a pretty plot under the shade of some banyan trees, and waited for the conjurors to arrive. The strollers numbered eight, four men, three young and attractive looking women, and a little girl. The snake-charming portion of the performance I cut short, as there seemed to be no mystery about it, but the clever tricks which they exhibited appeared almost miraculous. I have seen J. H. Anderson, who called himself the "Wizard of the North" (but whom an English paper facetiously dubbed "the Wizard of the North and by East half East"), Jacobs, Herman, Heller, and others exhibit, but their deceptions and illusions, as they impressed me, were not comparable to those of the strolling band of Hindoos referred to. The latter, moreover, performed their marvelous tricks without tables full of traps and springs, and other apparatus and appliances, which are employed by European and American conjurers. I thought that if some enterprising European or Yankee would only take those Indian jugglers to the Old and New Worlds, there would be money in the speculation. But there were difficulties in the way, one being that a person cannot take a native from the country, be it only for the purpose of making and cooking curries, without giving security to the Government for his return. Besides, the natives, when taken to Europe, are very apt to die or become incapable from cold, and require to be treated as hot-house plants. The juggling performance lasted for more than an hour, and cost me a rupee (half a dollar), probably the cheapest entertainment ever given for the money where the audience, or, rather, spectators, consisted of only two persons, myself and the driver. We then proceeded to the Seven Tanks Villa, and I thoroughly inspected that palatial residence and grounds. The greatest object of interest was, probably, the picture gallery, which contained works of high art, chiefly imported from Europe, and which only considerable wealth, aided by sound judgment and good taste, could have procured. Carriage riding in Calcutta is not an expensive luxury. On this occasion I had the *gharry* and driver over five hours, and it cost two rupees ($1).

On my return to the city an unpleasant surprise, but one not unusual in Calcutta, awaited me. I received a note to attend the funeral of a gentleman with whom I had dined the previous evening. Seven o'clock is the usual dinner hour at hotels and private houses. I had seen him only a few hours before, in high spirits and apparently perfect health, presiding at his table and entertaining a large party in all the honest pride of hospitality. Early next forenoon he was a corpse, stricken down by cholera. Yet he had been what is called acclimated, a fact in which I learned to put little faith as a safeguard against the treacherous disease.

In Calcutta Sunday is particularly dull and monotonous. The latest services are held in most of the churches at eight o'clock in the morning, in some of them at nine. The heat would render midday services almost intolerable. It requires no little ingenuity to avoid suffering from *ennui* on the Sabbath. The slight mental effort required in reading causes a person to perspire as much as physical labor with a spade in a garden does in an average European or American climate. For my part, I suffered less from the heat while strolling about on the shady sides of streets than I did while perfectly quiescent; and seeking repose at night, when it was not procurable, was, perhaps, the most wearying ordeal of all. As regards theaters and other public amusements, they have never been much of a success in Calcutta. While I was there a troupe of American negro minstrels were performing, and the perspiration made great white streaks through the burnt cork on their faces. If during what is known as "the fan season" most of the theaters are closed in the United States, the reader can imagine how it must be in a city where the "*punka* season" prevails all the year round, although, of course, some months are warmer than others—that is, those months when the sun is north of the equator, for Calcutta is just on the border of the northern tropics.

I had intended to go overland from Calcutta to China, but not being a salamander, I gave up the idea after three months of purgatorial existence in the former place, as I was persuaded that the journey would be very exhausting, and even hazardous. India's story is a great one, especially from the time of Aurungzebe; and the military glory of Lord Clive and the civic rule of Warren Hastings have invested the Orient with peculiar fascinations for all lovers of the marvelous. The extraordinary wealth, too, of the country, in gold, silver, diamonds, and pearls, has ever made it magnetic for fortune-hunters; but, to my mind, the climate is an insuperable bar to comfortable or healthy residence there. Shakspere, in one of his extravagant metaphors, makes Troilus say of his loved Cressida:

> "Her bed is India—there she lies a pearl."

This and all the rest of it are very pretty, especially when read about in a temperate zone, for assuredly, after one visit to Calcutta, distance will evermore "lend enchantment to the view." If, in one sense, my not proceeding overland to China was a disappointment, I had my compensation in my return to Europe by way of the Cape of Good Hope, as the Suez Canal was not then quite ready to be opened for navigation. Going by the Cape, however, I had an opportunity of calling at St. Helena, and visiting the Briars, Longwood, and Napoleon's grave. But of these things I must not now speak, as they are foreign to the subject of this article.

R. E. DESMOND.

A DEAD FRIEND.

This dead man, soon to seek oblivious earth,
Was loyally my friend, and loved me well.
For him no shadow of blame that could repel
His reverence, in my honored life had birth.
Like some famed knight, admired for brawn and girth
By the young warrior eager to excel,
Ideal in his fond soul I seemed to dwell,
The exemplar and high paragon of worth!
Now deeply, while I linger where he lies,
A burdening shame upon my bosom weighs....
Perchance he is watching me, in calm surprise,
Far from the turmoil of terrestrial days—
Piercing my faulty spirit with the gaze
Of supernatural and clairvoyant eyes! EDGAR FAWCETT.

THEIR GREAT SCHEME.

This story has a moral; but what it is, I don't know. So the best I can do is to tell the facts, and let some one else search for the moral; though I do not really suppose there is any one in the world who can find it.

The scheme began with the conversation between the Professor and young Socrates, on their way to the Doctor's. That is, it is fair enough for all practical purposes to say that it began with that; it really began in the characters and circumstances of the eleven people who dined that day at the Doctor's, and those, of course, began in remote hereditary influences and ancient chains of events that, for their part, began in Eternal Cosmic Forces, and the Unknowable First Cause, and all that sort of thing. I mention this only to show why the moral is so difficult to find; I cannot be expected to go back so far, and will begin the story only a few hours before the Professor and young Socrates had their conversation—that is, with Penelope.

Penelope came to the Doctor's early, about the middle of the afternoon, and brought her Kensington work. She had been invited to dinner only, but she had known Mrs. Doctor long enough and well enough to warrant an occasional liberty. Nevertheless, Mrs. Doctor sometimes had moods in which she resented intrusion; therefore Penelope apologized.

"I came over, Mrs. Doctor," she said, "because I was possessed with such a loathing of my room, and my work, and everything I should have been doing, and everybody I should have been seeing, that if I had stayed there till six o'clock I should have come here in such a state of malignity that you would have sent me home for fear I should poison the soup. So I came to get civilized a little before dinner. I'll sit up to-night and finish my work."

Now, many ladies in Mrs. Doctor's place—especially if they had known, as she did, that Penelope's gloomy disposition and situation were the sequel of a very sad love-story—would have said, caressingly, "Why, you dear girl, of course you must always come right here when you feel blue."

But Mrs. Doctor had always thought it wrong in a girl to let her life be spoiled by a love affair; and though she said sometimes to the Doctor that she was "very sorry for Penelope," she had been known to say, when the young woman was unusually provoking, that she "had no patience with her." Moreover, she had her own troubles that she thought about a great deal more than about other people's love affairs. So what she did say was:

"But it was hardly right, Penelope—though I'm glad to see you—to leave work to be done late at night. You know what the Doctor thinks of your working so late."

She said it kindly, laying down the long white ruffle she was hemming, and looking at her visitor with a smile, instead of speaking icily, with her eyes on her sewing; so Penelope knew it was one of the afternoons when she was welcome, and felt a little pathetic pleasure. She leaned back, with a *nonchalant* laugh, in her chair on the opposite side of the bay window.

"Oh, it's a choice of evils. When I am detesting the work most thoroughly I can only trick myself into doing it by putting it off till the very latest minute, and then letting myself be frightened into it. Do you know what I'm doing now? Designing pictures for tailors' advertisements, and labels for the canning establishments."

Mrs. Doctor sewed with indignant energy.

"Penelope, why in the world do you keep at such pitiful work, when you are capable of so much better? You know the Doctor has the highest opinion of your abilities, and you have plenty of opportunities to get into worthier work, if you would only exert yourself to follow up your chances."

Penelope shrugged her shoulders a little and smiled.

"I haven't the energy. And why should I? I don't care for fame; and I don't care for money, unless I could get it without having to work or to meet people—and you know I should have to do both about as much in the highest walks of art as in the lowest. I don't enjoy most of my fellow-beings."

"Well, sometimes I don't," said Mrs. Doctor, with an air of exceptional candor. "But I don't think it's right. It's only when I get to worrying about things, and one ought not to do that, you know."

"How *is* the Doctor's health, now?" said Penelope, with perfect comprehension, willingly changing the subject. She was not much interested in her own affairs, and had long got over expecting sympathy in them. Mrs. Doctor, from different motives, was also generally very reserved about hers; but she was in a confiding mood this afternoon. So the two women sat, and stitched, and talked, one on either side the recess between the lace curtains and open window, where the great yellow jasmine shook its flowers in on the carpet. Notwithstanding Penelope's pride in the burlap and bulrushes—at that time something quite new and interesting in art—the olive-green leaves and brown heads grew slowly, for all her motions were a little languid and indifferent. If Mrs. Doctor had been thinking about Penelope she would have noticed, looking across at her, that she was getting somewhat angular in form and face at twenty-five, and that her forehead was distinctly crumpled, and her eyes, though clear, quite without brightness; and she would have remembered that, seven years before, Penelope had been one of the most eager, quick-motioned girls, with the most shining eyes and the happiest voice in California. Penelope, on her part, was surveying Mrs. Doctor, knowing that the little, carefully dressed lady, with her intense face and collected manner, lived and went about, rose up and lay down, in one absorbing idea—and that idea was the Doctor. She sat and listened, with a half-sarcastic, half-sympathetic interest, wondering if it ever occurred to Mrs. Doctor that it might be worse to have no husband at all than to be anxious about one.

"The Doctor is certainly growing feeble, and he knows it. It chagrins him not to be able to do all he once could, and he will do more than he ought to dream of. 'Let me work out the dregs of life that are left in me, and then die and done with it,' he says. Not that he finds any pleasure in it; indeed, his profession becomes more distasteful to him every day. I feel sure he would recover his health and spirits if he would only stop short and rest; but he can't feel so, and he wants to do all the good he can before—well," with a change of voice, "'before he dies,' is the way he puts it. It seems as if I should go wild with anxiety."

It was five o'clock when the Doctor came in with Honora, whom he had picked up on the way. Honora had no more than had time to go home and dress after school, and was very tired, though she carried herself straight, and only showed weariness by her eyes, and by being quite silent. The Doctor was evidently tired too, and dispirited; he looked pale, and talked with Penelope and Honora with an evident effort. His wife, though she hardly appeared to glance at him, knew at once that some disagreeable event of the day was weighing upon him. It was no unusual thing, in his present physical and mental state, for little annoyances, or even the necessary discomforts of his profession, the sight of disease and pain, to wear upon him cruelly. As he sat now, sidewise in a large chair, with one arm thrown upon the cushioned back (looking, indeed, rather saintly, with the low western sunlight shining full through the window around his fine, thin features), the three women noticed, two with friendly regret, and one with a death-like pang, that he was growing gray and stooping, and seemed even frailer than usual.

A half hour later, the Professor and young Socrates came down the walk, between the tall rose-bushes dripping with crimson petals. Socrates was talking fast, as usual, and Penelope, turning a little away from the rest, laid her cheek against the high back of her chair, and watched the two approaching, listening, with her look of pleasureless amusement about the corners of her mouth, to Socrates's monologue that came in through the open windows.

"But as to Brook Farm experiments, it would be, of course, easy to apply the same destructive analysis to them as to all ways of practically acting on a theory. You know it is a commonplace of 'exact thought' (if I may be permitted to use a phrase after Mallock has handled it), that any theory of life whatever, followed rigidly to its logical ultimata, would produce inaction. Even if one takes the liberty to *assume* an object in life, and (as of course he will do in this century) makes the 'Improvement of Humanity' that object, he has to look at a very narrow circle of sequences (I say *circle*, or, better, *sphere*, and not *line* of sequences, intentionally) to feel sure that any one course is more adapted to his end than another. It hardly needs any doctrine of evolution to illustrate that we subserve universal ends equally well by success or failure, by action or inaction (a point in which mysticism and positivism touch). Yet it would be only a childish loyalty to one's own convictions that could make one act upon them by abjuring action—a logical suicide, as you see. One may surely be permitted to choose whether, being bound to serve medical science, he will serve it as the cadaver on the dissecting table, or as the young ignoramus with the scalpel. Therefore, I should not think of considering the usefulness of Brook Farm experiments in the light of these ultimate philosophical considerations."

At this point, the Doctor, at the open door, interrupted with his pleasant greeting. The Professor's grave face, as he came in, wore still a trace of slightly amused interest. He did not lack as many years of sixty as Socrates did of thirty, and the young man's manner of instruction to him was not quite the right thing. Not but what he knew perfectly well that Socrates was much cleverer and profounder than he; but he did not consider it any object to be so clever and profound, and did not believe that Socrates would consider it one when he grew older. So he submitted to being patronized with a grave amusement, not devoid of admiration, but not devoid, either, of a paternal pity for the misfortune of an intellect that drove a young man into the hot pursuit of fundamental verities.

Later, when the guests were all present, Penelope, standing in her forlorn black silk by Honora in *her* forlorn black silk, glanced about the room, while Honora examined the bulrushes.

"'Les Miserables!'" she said, with a cynical smile.

They did not look very miserable. Amabel and Junius were talking with the Lawyer, whose face was lighted with satisfaction as he watched Amabel's; her pretty blue eyes were bright with enjoyment, and Junius's boyish laugh broke out every few minutes. The Editor stood talking to Isola, who sat on the piano-stool, in profile, and touched gay little chords, with one hand, as a sort of running accompaniment to her remarks. The Doctor was laughing, too, as he talked with his old friend, the Professor, and Mrs. Doctor was evidently entertained by Socrates (whom the Doctor considered a very remarkable young man).

"The Doctor looks badly, to-day," Honora answered, speaking a little stiffly, because she did not like Penelope's cynical manner. "He ought to give up his profession, if he could only be persuaded to."

"He has the obstinacy of a gentle nature—as formidable a thing as the 'wrath of a patient man.'"

"I think he would be willing enough to give up his profession if he could afford to travel, or find some pleasant occupation," Honora said.

Penelope did not answer, and Honora, sitting down, began to look over the magazines on the table by which Penelope was still standing. The Doctor had crossed the room to speak to Junius, and the young fellow had turned a little aside from the group, and, sitting sidewise on his chair, and resting his folded arms on the back, was looking up into the Doctor's face. The light had instantly faded out of his own face as he turned away from his sister and the Lawyer, and without the veil of animation he looked less boyish—even, indeed, worn and anxious.

"No, sir," he said, "I don't seem to get ahead any. If I could once get the mortgage cleared off, Amabel and I could work along, and take care of the little ones; but it drinks up all I can make the farm pay to keep the interest down, and support us all. We are both pretty green, you see; father's and mother's sickness was so sudden that Amabel had no more time to get the hang of housekeeping than I of farming. She's wild to earn money, but she has her hands more than full, cooking, and scrubbing, and sewing, and sending two chicks off to school, and looking out for another all day—fingers to tie up, and faces to wash, and aprons to mend, and all that. It's hard luck for a slip of a girl like her, and she hardly gets time to look at her books, or her music, or painting; but she's clear pluck. What hits me especially is that the mortgage was put on to send me through college; and that rather binds me to send my little brothers through, when it comes their turn."

"But you're hurting yourself, my boy," the Doctor said, putting a thin hand for a moment on the young fellow's shoulder, and looking kindly down into his face. "Do you know how worn out you are looking? Isn't it false policy to struggle with the mortgage? Wouldn't it be better to sell out, take what is left, and start afresh?"

"Yes, if Amabel and I were all. But it would break up the family, and we can't consent to board the infants out and let them grow up hit or miss. There's only one thing: we might sell out here, and go away back, on Government land, and fight it out. We could manage to teach the chicks, but it would be rather rough on the whole five of us to take to the woods that way. Still, we've talked of doing it."

"I thought you liked pioneering."

"I do," said Junius, eagerly. "I like roughing it, and I should enjoy taking up new land, if only I could have enough of my friends along to make a jolly crowd. If I could get up a colony to go into the thing, Amabel and I wouldn't hesitate a minute."

Penelope, standing by the table, and absently fingering the burlap, caught a few fragments of this talk. She turned to Honora again:

"Honora, does the world look bright to *you* to-day?"

Honora lifted her tired eyes from the pictures in her hand.

"Bright! I am fagged out with this endless teaching. It is such a routine. In one of these graded schools you are just a cog in a machine. You don't seem to accomplish anything—begin each year just where you began last year. The children lose their individuality to you, and the school-room gets to be just a great whirling mechanism, that tortures your nerves like the noise of a factory. I suppose it's because I'm tired; but, Penelope, I dread every night to have morning come. I don't feel that I'm doing any good, either; I have no faith in the system. Children should be taught in small numbers, and in close personal relations with their teachers. The school should be something like the family?"

Penelope looked down at Honora's face a few moments; then she said, with a glance at Isola's profile:

"What has happened to Isola?"

"Why?" said Honora, quickly.

Penelope smiled slightly.

"Socrates told some one that I have a vulture's scent for trouble. Do you think that I can't see that she is perfectly wretched? Listen to the affectation of that laugh. Notice the constant supervision she is exercising over the corners of her mouth—that is, if we may judge the invisible corner by the visible. And don't you hear her fingers put a tone of incongruous melancholy into those ostentatiously gay scraps every time she is off her guard?"

Honora sat for a few moments looking at Isola; then she looked at Penelope.

"Her mother is in town," she said.

"Indeed!" cried Penelope, with a tone of genuine pity.

"It is one of the most pitiful things I ever knew," Honora said, warmly. "There she is, with beauty and intelligence and education that fit her for any society, and eager to associate with the very best, and her mother's disgrace, and the lowness of all her family and connections, hold her down hopelessly."

"If she had never educated herself, and never learned that there is a world different from that she was born into, she wouldn't now be struggling and panting to enter it, and smarting with a sense of being shut out," Penelope said, reflectively. "Her only chance is to cut loose entirely from her own people. They would be rather relieved to be rid of her, I fancy."

"She would gladly do that if she had an opportunity to go to some remote place under favorable social auspices, but she knows too much to throw herself among strangers unbacked."

"She will wait a long time for such an opportunity to come and knock at her door," said Penelope, with the bitter edge back again in her voice.

Honora did not answer, and their hostess's invitation to the dining-room prevented any further talk on the subject. The same eleven now seating themselves about Mrs. Doctor's table had often before found themselves grouped together. They had all lived for a number of years in Oakland; most of the younger ones had been to school together, and their parents and the older ones had been friends in New England. All except Isola were of much the same sort of blood. There were even such distant relationships among them as are apt to exist among any people of the same caste whose race has lived in the same section for generations. They were all exceptionally well educated and intelligent, had tastes in common, and could all talk well about these tastes. It was their community of extraction and antecedents that had thrown them together in Oakland; and their habit of attending or shunning the same concerts, lectures, and the like, and in every way living by much the same standards of taste, had kept them together, and without any deliberate choice on their part, had made them quite familiarly acquainted. School acquaintance had brought Isola into the group.

"What were you and the Professor discussing as you came in, Socrates?" said the Doctor, with an absent-minded air, due to the demand that the process of carving made upon his attention.

"Brook Farm, sir," said the young man, looking up with the smile of one who foresees a chance to defend a thesis hovering on his lips. "We were hardly discussing, however, for we were agreed in a decided fancy for that phase of fanaticism."

"The Brook Farm idea," said the Doctor, punctuating his remarks by pauses according to the exigencies of the carving, "has always been rather a pet of mine. Nothing in that line has succeeded yet, but I have a notion that the failure has been because of blunders in carrying out the idea, not because the idea itself is a blunder. I believe something will be made of it yet."

"I have a great deal of faith in it," said the Professor, in his slow, grave way. "It seems to me a more hopeful way of regenerating society to keep separate and pure some little reservoirs of mental strength and moral purity, whence streams may flow out to cleanse the world, than to let our pure waters be dissipated over the whole barren surface or lost in muddy pools."

"The little leaven is usually leavened by the whole lump," Penelope added to his closing words.

"For that matter," said Socrates, "you can hardly isolate your leaven beyond the danger of being lumped without cutting off the lump's chance of being leavened. And I don't imagine the Zeitgeist is to be much helped or hindered by such devices. But though there may be no good in it, there certainly is no harm; and the thing does seem to me in harmony with the best intellectual life of the time."

"It would be a life that had its pleasant points," said the young Lawyer. "If the company were well chosen one would escape the beasts that we are always meeting in business and society, and could enjoy the luxury of loving humanity at an endurable distance from it."

The Lawyer was more conspicuously aristocratic than the others, had traveled in Europe, and used English slang without an effort. He addressed himself especially to Amabel, by whom he sat. Indeed, he had gone directly to her on entering the house, and had not quitted her side since; the Editor, who had been talking with her before, had found himself imperceptibly elbowed out of the conversation, and had withdrawn to the piano and Isola, and had looked distinctly miserable ever since. Mrs. Doctor had inferred from the constant and evidently pleasant companionship of Amabel and the Lawyer that they ought to be seated together; Penelope, who had no interests of her own, and consequently saw an inch deeper than Mrs. Doctor into the few interests of other people that she roused herself to think about, saw that Amabel and the Editor were quite as happy together as Amabel and the Lawyer. But since the Editor's practice, when any one tried to "cut him out," was to retire from the contest in proud wretchedness, while the Lawyer's practice was to himself perform the "cutting out" operation with easy assurance, underlaid by dogged determination; and since "nothing is so successful as success," and every one helps the winning party, it naturally resulted that Amabel never fell to the Editor's lot except when the Lawyer was absent. The girl herself liked and admired both young men, and could hardly have told which she liked better. In a deliberate choice, she would perhaps have felt that the Editor was a more congenial friend; but she had been of late, without choosing, or even realizing it, so much more in the Lawyer's company that she had a hundred little things in common with him, more than with others, and was getting into the habit of turning to him with remarks or questions, quite unconsciously to herself. Certainly, absorbed in her brothers and her daily anxieties, she was not in love with either young man; but because a girl of twenty is not in love with one or two men, either of whom satisfies her mind and heart, it does not follow that she will not be, in a month or a year. Whichever of the two succeeded in placing himself first before the waking eyes of her womanhood stood as good a chance as ever man stood of having her love; and they both knew it. Penelope suspected it, too; and, with her own old hurt aching, remembered that the two young men had been dear friends for years, and said bitterly to herself, "Tragedy ahead."

"A party that would go and start a Brook Farm somewhere on Government land would be just the thing for you and me, Mab, wouldn't it?—that is, if they would take us in," cried Junius, breaking in with his fresh young voice on the trains of thought that the Lawyer's look at Amabel had started in at least three minds.

"The great difficulty," said the Editor, without lifting his eyes from his plate, and using a sullen tone that was neither characteristic nor becoming, "the great difficulty would be in selecting the right people to form the party. It's a familiar saying that Brook Farm failed because those who undertook it were not adapted to the life. I should go further, and say that it could not succeed unless all the members of the party were bound by genuine personal affection."

"If society could be broken up into isolated groups, and every soul in every group had every one in the world that he very much loved or liked associated with him in a family-like intimacy, and every one else shut out—why, the ideal life would be achieved at a stroke," Penelope said, sadly enough.

The Doctor looked at her with a pointed cheerfulness that meant reproof more than sympathy for her melancholy tone, as mothers assume an especially sprightly manner by way of pleasantly reproving crying children.

"No one has to reform society at a stroke," he said. "One enterprise of the kind is all any one need have on hand. No doubt the difficult point is to secure just the right membership; but it isn't impossible because difficult. Our present party, for instance, could carry out such a scheme—we know each other, could work together well, are intelligent and practical and not fond of promiscuous associations; we could share work and property without ill feeling; we have no faults unknown to each other that could come to light and upset our calculations—"

He stopped, with voice suspended, to indicate an indefinite list of other qualifications. He had spoken merely for argument; but Junius put down his knife and fork and cried, impetuously:

"*Well—why not?*"

They looked at him and laughed a little. So abject slaves of habit are modern men and women that not one of them thought of any such breaking of bonds as a serious possibility. But in a moment the Editor said, in that peculiar laughing tone that is meant to pass off one's remarks as a joke if they do not meet favor, yet to allow them to stand as serious earnest, if they do:

"When I was traveling on horseback *for The Trumpeter* I met a man at Red Bluff just starting to join his family at a dairy ranch in the mountains. It was August, and the plains were fearful; the thermometer at a hundred and ten; dry northers coming down over miles of plain, loaded with gritty dust; plain itself as barren as shoe-leather, except for the dusty oaks; sky so murky you couldn't see a horizon. So I accepted his invitation to go with him and make my way through to the Coast. We went through a purgatory of dust and heat, and then came to—Paradise, I think. Between two high peaks, topped with eternal snow, was a green valley of delightful temperature, full of delicious streams and springs from the snow-cap. So far as I could judge, the soil was excellent and varied enough for all sorts of products—a sort of Swiss Family Robinson's island, in fact. The wild-flowers, the waterfalls, the forests of shrubs and trees, you may imagine as wildly as you can, and you will hardly do justice to the reality. It was not so much a valley as a little plateau among mountains—a 'bench,' as they call it—and was open in places to a view over a perfect sea of mountains. From the western side of the great snow-peaks, you could see the Pacific. My hosts drove their cattle up in late spring, when the pasturage failed below, and made butter and cheese all summer, and when the rains began returned to the lowland, to be within reach of a market. I came back in October; the valley was still lovely, and I found many others as paradise-like." He paused a moment; then, looking at Amabel in spite of himself, went on, "They were Government land."

No one spoke. Each realized that the last words were a proposition. The Professor looked serious; the others glanced round the table, each ready to dismiss the idea with a laugh if it seemed to strike the rest as preposterous; and then, seeing his own state of mind reflected in their faces, each was suddenly smitten with a wonder whether there might not be something in it. Then Junius broke out again:

"Well, why not? There isn't one of us here that has anything to prevent, and we all have bothers we'd be glad to get away from. We are smart enough to raise our own corn and potatoes, and leave money out of the question, like savages or pioneers. It would be a regular lark!"

"To shuffle off the coil of nineteenth century life, and return to the simplicity of primal man, yet keeping the wisdom of modern man; to be children of Mother Nature again, bringing back to her lap the gifts of wealthy but hard-hearted Stepmother Art—you are right, Penelope, it is the ideal life," the Doctor said, thoughtfully.

"Why not put it as a formal proposition?" interposed the Professor. "Will the eleven now present, or any portion of them, agree to be the nucleus of a select colony to begin life on ideal principles, in some suitable spot? I, for one, am so convinced of the wisdom of the scheme that I put myself down as the first."

There was silence, while each one consulted his inner consciousness. They had not taken it in earnest until the Professor's note-book came out and received his name. Even Junius, now it had become so serious, paused to revise his conclusions. Amabel looked across the table to him, and their two pairs of frank blue eyes met, with that look of full sympathy and trust that neither, as yet, could give to any third person. Both were young and fresh-hearted enough to be willing lightly to throw aside everything and begin life on a new basis; both realized the escape from present troubles that the plan would offer; both loved nature and a free, simple life, and the death of their parents had gone far enough into the past to cause only an undercurrent of sadness, over which their young buoyancy reasserted itself. They both flushed with excitement.

"Will you go, Mab?" the boy cried.

"Oh, yes, I should love to dearly," she answered, and the sweetness of her voice made the schoolgirlism even graceful.

The Lawyer looked down gently at her sweet, eager face. He was young, not yet thirty, and the world was before him; but he had not the ambition which would make retirement from the world seem intolerable to most young lawyers. His tendency was rather to indolence and indifference than to professional ambition; he had a comfortable property, and the profession was more a gentlemanly device to save him from mere dilettantism than anything else. His real employment was the enjoyment of life according to the very highest methods; as his tastes, both moral and intellectual, were fine, and well trained, he made this employment highly praiseworthy, and even included a good deal of philanthropy in it. He had a distaste, however, for most human beings, which, added to a healthy liking for nature and woodcraft, and for new experiences, made him not at all averse to a few years of sylvan retirement with a select company. Moreover, he had for Amabel the irresistible passion to which such a temperament seems prone—a passion whose impulse is more to possess and enjoy than to idealize and revere, and which is an absorbing restlessness until possession is achieved. Under the stress of this feeling, he would not have hesitated at anything that kept him near Amabel. The Editor, on the other hand, had ambitions and aspirations, and could be quite friendly with people who said "presume;" but he cared far more for Amabel than for all his ambitions and aspirations, and was ready enough to relinquish them to follow her. Most of all, his suffering under the process of being "cut out" had risen to such a pitch that the thought of joining a colony that included her, provided it excluded the Lawyer, was like a prospect of exchanging hell for heaven. It was with the thought that something might prevent the Lawyer joining them that he had made his suggestion about the mountain valley.

Isola grew a little pale. Out of the despairing shame she had been oppressed with, a door seemed suddenly opened to her greatest desire. The acquaintance of these people had never secured her the recognition that they themselves had from others; outside this little group, and even to a certain extent inside it, she was looked upon more as its *protégée* than its friend. She knew that not one of them could have sent her to his friends in New England with just such a letter as he would have given Penelope or Honora; any introduction would have to either hide or condone her antecedents, and her sensitiveness even exaggerated the disadvantage that would be. But a few years in this select colony would partly supply the lack of antecedents, and partly do away with the need of them.

Penelope looked around the familiar faces, and her own softened. They did her some injustice in thinking that it was merely brooding over her old troubles that had spoiled her life, and in saying, as Socrates did, that being broken-hearted was Penelope's profession. It was, in truth, not more the primary hurt than the unnatural conditions of loneliness and lovelessness it left behind that had crushed heart and hope and gentleness out of her. She belonged to that type of women who find life intolerable unless it holds at least one loving companionship; having this, all the many interests of living are real, in the light of it; without this, they are empty and tiresome forms. As a wife and mother, she would have been rarely happy and lovely. Left alone as she was, her sense of being unprotected by any near love, of having no resource or stronghold, amounted to positive despair. Life and society gave her the sort of overwhelming but unaccountable terror of a nightmare; the universe seemed full of an inimical spirit, between which and herself she longed to interpose some love, given and received. Early in her loneliness she had tried to cling to one and another of her acquaintances, to keep off the horror of her desolation; but she had learned now that they all had their own near loves and near interests, from which she was excluded, and that she only made herself disagreeable as an acquaintance by trying to be anything more. So she had settled into a prevailing mood of hopeless endurance, varied by periods of positive horror at her own desolateness, and secretly thought of suicide as a probable ultimate resource (she had found that to think of it openly disgusted people). The Professor's proposal now came to her like a hope of home. She saw that the close association of the colony would put them into almost family relations; she would have a home, a family, and her "ain folk" once more. She looked around the table, and her heart went out hungrily to these old friends; she felt a glow of affection toward them, a sense of being among her own, a belief that they belonged to her and she to them, creep through her, like returning warmth after long numbness; she was conscious, with a surprise so great as to be not unmixed with dread, that her pulse was beating once more with a long-forgotten hope and eagerness.

There was one moment for all these various thoughts, and then the Lawyer, speaking so close on Amabel's exclamation that it sounded like a corollary, said:

"Put my name down."

Amabel's eyes, returning from her brother, met his, with a frank exchange of pleasure. The tension of the Editor's lips and eyes grew a little more rigid; but he said nothing. The Lawyer looked across at him.

"You'll go, of course, old fellow?" he said, cordially, even affectionately; yet there was an undertone of reserve in his voice at which the overstrained sensitiveness of the other winced.

"Yes; he may put me down," he said, with some hesitation, and so low and constrained a voice that several of the company wondered whether the Editor was not growing disagreeably moody.

The Doctor looked across at his wife, smiling, but with a wistful look in his eyes.

"What do *you* think of this bold scheme, my dear?"

"I think it a most excellent plan," she said, decidedly. "I approve of our joining them."

There was a little pause of surprise, during which they all went a stage further in realizing that the matter had become serious; for Mrs. Doctor was practical and conservative, and they had expected her to dismiss the idea with quiet contempt. But it was life or death to her to detach her husband from his profession; and no other consideration weighed with her for a moment. He looked at her surprised and amused. Then he said:

"Very well."

"Good!" cried Junius, in tones little below a shout. "Valuable allies! And now we shall feel quite safe about having measles."

"Put my name down," said Penelope, smiling at the boy quite warmly and naturally for her.

"Honora?" asked Mrs. Doctor, looking kindly toward her. Honora was apt to wait to be asked before she spoke.

"Yes," she said, without hesitation, "I shall be very glad to go."

"And Isola?" the Professor asked, holding his pencil ready for the last name.

Isola bowed her head.

They gathered in a close group in the parlor, and discussed it all with an eagerness that remotely imitated that of a group of school-children planning a picnic.

"We are casting down that idol of the nineteenth century, division of labor," said Penelope, sitting on the arm of a stuffed chair.

"Thank heaven for that!" cried the Doctor. "No, Socrates, don't mention evolution, nor specialization of function, nor Herbert Spencer. Let us be ichthyosauri, if we like."

"Can any fellow here, except me, milk?" called Junius, both hands on his sister's shoulders. "Or hoe potatoes? I shall have to teach you all. The chicks can get better teaching among all these wise people than in the public schools, Mab. By the way, we must have chickens."

"And cows"

"And a dog."

"Horses, of course."

"And all the pianos, violins, pictures, and painting traps owned by the company collectively."

"How about books?" said Honora. "Shall we each carry our whole private store, or no duplicates among us?"

"Oh, by all means, let us have private property in such things," said the Professor, anxiously.

And Penelope added, with decision:

"There should be private property in books and clothes."

"We can transfer our small accumulations of *bric-à-brac* to the wilderness," suggested the Lawyer.

He addressed himself, as usual, to Amabel, but Junius, looking over her shoulder, took the remark to himself, and responded:

"And Penelope can decorate our log-cabin with bulrushes."

"It will be good to work in the new, clean earth, out in the sunshine and pure air," the Doctor said.

"And delightful to cook, all of us women together, like sisters," Penelope said, wistfully, "and no dreadful servants, nor artificial relations with any one."

"There will be good botanizing."

"And geologizing."

"And shooting and fishing."

"We can write magazine articles."

"And books, and Penelope shall illustrate them. Socrates shall work out his system of philosophy in peace, and the Editor shall write novels, and Amabel poetry."

"We can visit the haunts of men for days or weeks when we feel inclined, and get the new books, and see the new pictures, and so on.

And one of us, on horseback, can get the mail weekly."

At last they sat down, one by one, and listened to the Professor, who was beginning systematically:

"The first thing to be done is to decide whom we shall ask to join us, and then to appoint a committee to select a site. As we do not remain near a city, but, considering perfect isolation and virgin nature essential to the ideal life, constitute rather a colony than a company like that of Brook Farm, it is probably understood that each one will wish to add to our number those who are nearest in affection to him."

"None of us but Isola have any family on this side of the continent, except for Amabel's little brothers and Honora's mother," Mrs. Doctor answered.

Isola said nothing, but Amabel and Honora spoke together:

"Of course my babies must go."

"Mother will be very glad to go."

"Now," said the Professor, adding the four names to his list, "let us not be precipitate in further selections, since we have agreed that the membership of the colony is the most vital point. Would it not be well to ballot on nominations?"

"But," said Honora, "one of us might blackball some one whose presence was essential to the enjoyment of another of us."

"In that case," said Mrs. Doctor, with precision, "if the one who wishes the member wishes him so much as to be unhappy without him, and the one who objects would not be made unhappy by his presence, the objector should yield, and *vice versâ*."

The Doctor laughed, and put his arm around his wife.

"That is, we need shades between blackball and whiteball."

"Well," said Junius, "if we're going to do it up so brown, Amabel and I will get a lot of marbles, assorted shades, to express a whole assortment of likes and dislikes, and we can ballot with them next time we get together."

"It sounds ridiculous," Penelope said, while the others laughed, "but we are all agreed that everything depends on a perfectly congenial membership. We don't want to take in any one who will make any one else uncomfortable, nor leave out any one whose absence will be felt as a loss."

"Very well," the Professor answered, "we will ballot according to Junius's suggestion."

It was morning when they met a few days later—a sunny Oakland morning, when even the cypresses and blue-gums do their best to look happy. Nine of the party sat, with a fine disregard of passers-by, on the Doctor's front steps, waiting for Junius and Amabel. There were brown birds twittering in the cherry and acacia trees of the garden; the two diagonal paths that converged from the front corners of the Doctor's quarter-block, and met in a curve before the steps, were bordered with tall pink, and crimson, and yellow roses, and an enormous group of shining white lilies stood opposite the steps, and filled the air with sweetness. Presently Junius drove up, and while he tied his horse, Amabel came down the walk, looking like a combination of rose and lily herself. The Lawyer sprang up, and met her half way to the steps.

"Here they are," she said, enjoying her office; and she sat down on the lowest step and poured the marbles from a bag into her lap. "These are bright red—that means a burning desire to have the candidate with us. You must vote *that* when you want us to know that you can't be happy without him. And these white ones mean that you would like very well to have him, and have no objections. And here are some gray ones—they mean that you'd *rather* he wouldn't come; by that, if anybody else wants him *very* much (and votes red, you know), you withdraw your objections. And then these black ones mean that you can't bear to have him with us. Junius tried to make me get ever so many more. He said four colors couldn't express all the shades of feeling. But four express all we want them to."

"Then a black ball overrules a white one, and a red one overrules a gray," the Lawyer said, smiling into her eyes. "But what if black and red meet—Greek to Greek?"

"Oh, it won't happen," the Doctor said. "It would be a very unlikely chance. Our tastes in people agree pretty well. Gray and white are more likely to join battle, but we can arbitrate between those mild enemies, especially as we are behind the candidates' backs."

"Unless we should ballot on ourselves, to make sure that the present party is satisfactory to all its members," the Editor said, drearily.

"Oh, *of course* we all want each other to go," cried Amabel, with charming fervor.

The Professor looked thoughtful.

"It might be well. In case there should be any inharmonious feeling among us, it would be well to know, and possibly to rectify it. At all events, it would look better, as a matter of form, to be able to say to those who join us later that all have been balloted on in the same manner. Suppose we begin our ballot with the eleven present."

The Doctor brought a cigar-box, and fitted an immense paper funnel into a hole in the lid, "to make the ballot secret," he said.

"Who comes first on your list, Professor? Yourself? Oh, begin with some one else. Junius and Amabel next."

"Oh, don't vote on us first," cried Amabel, suddenly bashful.

"The Lawyer comes next," said the Editor, with an abruptness that made his voice sound unnatural.

"The Lawyer it is, then."

One by one, with much merriment and much pretense of secrecy, they put their hands inside the funnel, and let the hidden marble drop. Only the Editor dropped his as quickly as possible, without looking at any one, and sat down again, behind them all.

They crowded together eagerly, to see the lid raised, and there was a good deal of laughing and joking among them. Suddenly there was silence, and they looked at each other in dismay. Several gray balls and a black one lay among the white ones in the box.

The Lawyer's handsome face blackened with a look that made Amabel shrink, as he reached for his hat; but as he met her eye, his expression changed, and he sat down silently.

The balloting went on in silence and excitement after that, and in a sort of dismay, that grew deeper after every ballot. When the last one had been taken, they all stood and looked at each other in silence.

Not one of the eleven, except Amabel, had escaped black or gray balls!

They stood dismayed, seeing their air-castle falling about them. They all saw the full significance of it. If they, so well known to each other, so congenial in tastes, so agreeable to each other as acquaintances, could not be content in closer relations, who could? Curiously enough, though each one had been aware of his own private dislikes, they were amazed at the aggregate result. They had not dreamed that others had similar private dislikes. The Doctor was the first to speak.

"Such is life," he said, with a weary laugh, gathering the marbles into their bag. "We have been playing with marbles again, like any other babies."

Then Penelope picked up her hat from the step.

"Good-day," she said, putting it on.

She walked down the path, between the roses, looking older than ever (she had been looking young again, these last few days). And all the way down the street to her boarding-house, and all day, at her tiresome work, the thought of that one unfailing last resource, that she did not dare to speak of for fear of disgusting people, was more closely present with her than it had ever been.

The rest, following her example, dispersed silently and coldly. They never mentioned Brook Farm again. Indeed, they did not meet as much, nor as cordially as before. There was an uncomfortable consciousness among them. No one dared to ask another what his ballot had been, nor even to say: "I voted white for you," lest an evasive answer should show that a frank, "So did I for you," was impossible. Only the Lawyer, a few days later, had the courage to say:

"You voted white for every one, I suppose, Amabel?"

"Except red for my brother," she said; and he answered:

"But I voted red for you."

The rest remained always in a somewhat distant and embarrassed state of feeling toward each other. They came in time to think of the whole affair with mortification, as though they had been guilty of a very wild and childish freak.

That is about all there is to tell, for the rest was only what necessarily had to follow. The Doctor died, as every one knew he would; and his wife, utterly crushed in health and spirits, and sunken into settled melancholy, will not long survive him. Penelope still wavers between the idea of suicide and that of adopting a baby. The baby would be pleasanter in some respects, but she is a strong believer in heredity, and cannot quite make up her mind to take the risk; besides, she has grown too old-maidish to like the trouble of a child. Isola, willing to go anywhere away from her home, is teaching school in Modoc County. Honora has broken down in health, completely worn out with teaching, and she and her mother, both invalids without means, are at their wit's end to live. Of course Amabel married the Lawyer; he is most tenderly devoted to her, and she makes him very happy; and if he, perhaps, lives more for his enjoyment of her than for hers of him, why, it does no harm, for she is entirely satisfied with him, and never questions whether another might have revealed to her deeper depths of happiness in married life, and a more profoundly satisfactory love. If his moral fervor and loftiness falls in any way short of hers, she does not suspect it, for he makes a conscience of her, so far as his intercourse with her is concerned; and he exerts himself, for her sake, to succeed brilliantly in his profession. Junius has sold the farm, and studies law with him; and the children live with them, which Amabel considers very generous on her husband's part. The Editor left the State as soon as the engagement was announced, and has now a position as newspaper correspondent in dangerous places, such as Central Africa, Afghanistan, or Dulcigno. As for the Professor, he is a little older; and Socrates, in the intervals of "pot-boiling" work, pursues indefatigably the fundamental verities, and enjoys life pretty well, on the whole.

MILICENT W. SHINN.

THOREAU IN BOOKS AND IN THE WOODS.

The fame that ripens after one is gone is better than that which runs with his life—is more permanent, because it is sifted of all caprice. There is a better perspective than when the personality of the individual was so much in the foreground. Shakspere, Milton, and Bacon have a grander presence in the world, a more potent influence now than when they were in the ranks of the living. The Egyptians tried their great men after death, to find whether they were worthy of the highest honors of sepulture. In a critical age like this, crucial tests are applied by the many rather than the few. And in no age of the world hath there been a more discerning judgment touching what is worthy of eternal remembrance than now. If one speaks to the multitude it may be for the day; at best, only a few will remember so much as an outline of his thought. A few more will remember that they were wrought to a pitch of enthusiasm, but by what magic they cannot now tell. And so many an orator lives only in tradition, which becomes fainter every year. As the years go by, and personal recollections are lost, there is a bolder questioning. Why was this man so obtrusively in the foreground of human vision? What did he do? Where is the fine gold of his life hidden?

There have been painters who lived in garrets, and yet painted for immortality. When they were gone, every canvas on which they had laid a color became infinitely precious. There is a resurrection to life which follows hard on death. It is necessary that some should not wait for the verdict. If it be a favorable one, it is enough perhaps that they hear it announced in the next world; though it does not mitigate the pinch of poverty in this, nor help one's credit with the banker. Turner died with a studio full of paintings, and hardly more than a local fame. It was Ruskin who anointed the eyes of his countrymen until they finally beheld in his works the master, than whom there hath been none greater in modern times. His crudest sketches and drawings were eagerly sought. Gold was not so precious as some scrap on which had been traced the scant lines of this man of genius. When Hawthorne died his fame was secure. It had been well enough assured while living. But the diaries and note-books of this man, who once had such a small reading constituency, are eagerly sought and read. Of the two volumes which Thoreau published before his death, neither brought him fame nor money. We shall hear presently what he has to say of his authorship and its fruits. It is possible he had some presentiment of his posthumous fame. He had been long reading in the open book of Nature. He read where other men saw nothing but inexplicable mystery. To him it did not seem long that the acorn became an oak, with repose and majesty, in a thousand years, so that it was an oak at last. He had a kind of Brahminical wisdom, which bred in him great patience and calmness of soul. He lived and wrought as one might who expected to look upon his work a thousand years hence. Yet he had no overwhelming sense of a mission. Finding himself in the world, he chose to look sharply into it, and find out if possible if there might not be some revelation, something which he could interpret to his own soul, and one day interpret to others. And what prefatory interpretation can be more healthy than this?

"Man's art has wisely imitated those forms in which all matter is most inclined to run, as foliage and fruit. A hammock swung in a grove assumes the exact form of a canoe in the water—broader or narrower, and higher or lower at the ends, as more or fewer persons are in it: and it rolls in the air with the motions of the body like a canoe in the water. Our art leaves its shavings and its dust about; her art exhibits itself even in the shavings and dust which we make. She has perfected herself by an eternity of practice. The world is well kept; no rubbish accumulates, the morning air is clear even at this day, and no dust has settled on the grass. Behold how the evening now steals over the fields, the shadows of the trees creeping farther and farther into the meadow, and ere long the stars will come to bathe in these retired waters. Her undertakings are secure, and never fail. If I were awakened from a deep sleep I should know which side of the meridian the sun might be by the aspect of nature, and by the chirp of the crickets; and yet no painter can paint this difference. The landscape contains a thousand dials which indicate the natural divisions of time; the shadows of a thousand stiles point to the hour."

There was this striking difference between Hawthorne and Thoreau. The former had such a morbid spiritual nature that a critic has aptly termed it a miasmatic conscience. There is a night side of moral, as there is of physical nature. It is not good to look upon either too long. If one were never to see humanity except in prisons and hospitals, with the ghostly shadows of it at midnight flitting in and out, he might give all this a terrible sharpness of definition as an expert. And so while Hawthorne dealt largely with an unhealthy moral anatomy, Thoreau dealt with the healthy naturalism of woods, mountains, lakes, and rivers. He was a poet without measure or rhythm, a naturalist without a single dogma of science. He sought in the forest a higher companionship than could ordinarily be found among men. He was not averse to society, only he wanted the best. This high eclecticism has led to many misjudgments. He has been set down as a misanthrope, a recluse, as one fleeing to the wilderness to escape the temptations and burdens of society—an ascetic from choice and a hermit from the mere love of solitude—whereas, none of these assumptions were really true in whole or in part.

At the recent term of the School of Philosophy at Concord, among the more miscellaneous readings and conversations was one given by Professor Blake, from the unpublished manuscripts of Thoreau. A synopsis of the estimate there made might well be set over against that which Lowell made in an hour when a clearer critical discernment had left him:

"It appears that the current notion of Thoreau is about as distorted as could be possible. He was the kindest of men, with as acute sense of the rights of others, and in all social relations was guided by a fine instinct of courtesy. This often would compel acquiescence in opinion or action that jarred with his convictions, and being a man who, above all things, lived by his convictions, he was driven to avoid whatever might thus compromise himself with himself. No one could more highly or closely value human intercourse, but a certain moral exclusiveness narrowed him to a limited circle of friendship. He often refused to see people because he could not honestly talk to them. Without vanity, he had a large pride and an equal obstinacy; but the pride, it is told, was of the kind which always marks strict moral fidelity to self, and the obstinacy simply expressed intelligent conviction tenaciously held. Perhaps, on the whole, Thoreau lacked flexibility. There was in his mental, as in his physical build, something angular, and this came prominently forth on occasions. For he had more than the courage of his opinion, as is commonly said of strong-willed men. His opinion was himself. * * * There was just one thing Thoreau would not do, and to understand this is, probably, to understand his life. He would not compromise individual virtue. The notion of anything short of the finest integrity gave life a bad odor, and he would not have it. His sensitiveness was as great here as with most men in the matter of honor and cowardice, and the fine edge of his character did not blunt under the wear of circumstances, as most commonly happens in the world. The story of the Journals, as read here in Concord, with the story of his life by those who long knew him, all point very clearly to one solution of Thoreau's attitude toward organized society: it was neither iconoclastic nor whimsical, but simply expressed private incommensurability with the average taste in ethics and character."

And so this man went back to the simplicity and truthfulness of nature. It was essential that he should stand well in the court of his own conscience. There have been pure and holy men in cloisters and convents, and there have been such in the cloisters of the woods. Some there are who obtain a beatific state, fighting face to face with the foe. They blaze their way to heaven by the scars inflicted on themselves and humanity, as a sturdy pioneer blazes a trail through the forest. It is a flesh-and-blood conflict. These men of brawn make good martyrs. John Brown argued with a rifle in Kansas. He proposed to strike the fetters off four millions of slaves with a lot of antiquated pikes and rusty muskets. He blazed his way, using just the kind of force which was used a few years later with more success. He was the most fitting martyr of his times. Thoreau was the first to greet him as such. He would have accepted the same fate gladly, if that had appeared to him a duty. He had the firmness of moral fiber which would not allow him to retreat from a position where his conscience had led him; and so, having refused to pay taxes on one occasion, because he would not pay tribute to a slave-holding power, he went to jail. There he writes: "I saw that if there was a wall of stone between me and my townsmen, there was a still more difficult one to climb or break before they could get to be as free as I was."

Let it be set to the account of personal sacrifice that he was a celibate, not from choice; but it coming to his knowledge one day that the love of his brother had taken the same direction as his own, he silently retreated, sealing up his own affection so that no secret choice of his should ever cast a shadow on another. He would not accept gifts nor live on the bounty of his relatives. He paid his way with scrupulous exactness, but he took good care to see that the cost of living should be reduced to the lowest farthing. "I am convinced," says he, "that to maintain oneself on this earth is not a hardship, but a pastime, if he will live simply and wisely, as the pursuits of simpler nations are still the sports of the more artificial."

Our modern civilization runs largely to sumptuous dishes and costly raiment. It sets up conventional standards of living, many of which are absurd. It makes life an expensive business, reducing the problem to bread and butter, laces, ruffles, and much fragile crockery. There is a freshness in the philosophy, even if it be old, which teaches how little is necessary to meet the real wants of life. There are some truths which have been so long buried that if once exhumed, they seem altogether new to the world. One must have the courage of strong and high conviction to be free anywhere. Thoreau chose his freedom not from selfish or ascetic considerations, but because he sought a nobler exaltation. If any wanted his companionship they must go where he went. "Of course," he writes, "you will be glad of all the society you can get to go up with. It is either the tribune on the plain, a sermon on the mount, or a very private ecstasy still higher up. Use all the society that will abet you." It is not at all strange that one with such an ideal should find the best, and be at his best, by going apart somewhat from the world. If he find his best society in brooks, in mountains, rocks, rivers, forests, and birds, why should we quarrel with him? And if one attains to a noble simplicity and elevation of life in that way, hath he not for the time chosen wisely? Therefore the poet-naturalist went to the woods, and, in a sense, discovered a new world, so near to him, so remote to all not of his following! There is a hint of the future direction of his thought in this utterance, made long before he went to live on the margin of Walden Pond:

"The wilderness is near, as well as dear, to every man. Even the oldest villages are indebted to the border of wild wood which surrounds them more than to the gardens of men. There is something indescribably inspiriting and beautiful in the forest skirting, and occasionally jutting into, the midst of new towns, which, like the sand-heaps of fresh fox-burrows, have sprung up in their midst. The very uprightness of the pines and maples asserts the ancient rectitude and vigor of nature. Our lives need the relief of such a background, where the pine flourishes and the jay still screams."

We know in what spirit Thoreau went to the woods by such expressions as these:

"Men nowhere, east nor west, live yet a natural life, round which the vine clings, and which the elm willingly shadows. Man would desecrate it by his touch, and so the beauty of the world remains veiled to him. He needs not only to be spiritualized, but *naturalized*, on the soil of earth. Who shall conceive what kind of a roof the heavens might extend over him, what seasons minister to him, and what employment dignify his life? Only the convalescent raise the veil of nature. An immortality in his life would confer immortality on his abode. The winds should be his breath, the seasons his moods, and he should impart of his serenity to Nature herself. Such as we know him, he is ephemeral, like the scenery which surrounds him, and does not aspire to an enduring existence. When we come down into the distant village, visible from the mountain-top, the nobler inhabitants with whom we peopled it have departed, and left only vermin in its desolate streets.

"We need pray for no higher heaven than the pure senses can furnish, a purely *sensuous* life. Our present senses are but the rudiments of what they are destined to become. We are comparatively deaf, dumb, and blind, and without smell, or taste, or feeling. Every generation makes the discovery that its divine vigor has been dissipated, and each sense and faculty misapplied and debauched. The ears were not made for such trivial uses as men are wont to suppose, but to hear celestial sounds. The eyes were not made for such groveling uses as they are now put to and worn out by, but to behold beauty now invisible. May we not *see* God? Are we to be put off and amused in this life, as it were, with a mere allegory? Is not Nature rightly read, that of which she is commonly taken to be the symbol, merely? When the common man looks into the sky, which he has not so much profaned, he thinks it less gross than the earth, and with reverence speaks of the 'heavens,' but the seer will in the same sense speak of the 'earths,' and his Father who is in them. What is it, then, to educate but to develop these divine germs called the senses?—for individuals and States to deal magnanimously with the rising generation, leading it not into temptation—not teach the eye to squint nor attune the ear to profanity?"

Disappointed men have sometimes fled to the woods because the world had got the better of them. But Thoreau went there for greater sweetness of life. He would get the better of the world by some years of non-conformity. He was only twenty-eight years old when he began his experiment at Walden. It lasted two years. In this voluntary isolation, it is doubtful if any other years of his life were more fruitful. The Brook Farm experiment was tried about the same time. The aim was not dissimilar—freedom from many petty burdens, self-improvement, elevation of life, plain living, and high thinking. A majority of the Brook Farm phalanx were known to Thoreau. Hawthorne, his friend, was there for a time. The former might have had a pardonable pride in the consciousness that his experiment was the more successful. There was no bankruptcy. He had lived for a few shillings a week in a cabin made with his own hands, had planted and cultivated a garden, cooked his own food, had been thoroughly master of times and opportunities. Hawthorne found occasion to write an ideal story, founded on supposed incidents at Brook Farm. Thoreau wrote a thoroughly realistic account of his life at Walden. The poet-naturalist did not go to the woods to write fiction. He would tell what he knew, and nothing more. He could no more garnish it with a tale than could John Muir his account of the glaciers of Alaska. The same transparent sincerity, simplicity of life, honesty of statement, and sharpness of insight distinguish both. As a mere matter of living, aside from the opportunities of study and observation, there was not much in the Walden experiment. Many a pioneer miner in this State has lived as frugally, and accepted ten-fold more of privation. The naturalist was a prince in his cabin. The miner was not. The thousand small particulars which Thoreau records have the spirit and freshness of a child-nature. They are a part of his discoveries. When the naturalist enters his world of observation nothing is trifling or unimportant. John Muir devotes a paper to the description of that lonely bird, the water-ousel, whose habitat is about the foaming cataracts, far up the mountains. Thoreau knew the cry of the loon better than the voices of men. Not a bird twittered in the forest that he did not know its name, its time of nesting, and how its callow brood were fed. Squirrels came at his call; even the foxes came with stealthy tread to the door of his cabin. The partridge beat his tattoo on the dry log hard by, and the whippoorwill furnished his vesper hymn. The whir of the night-hawk was to him a familiar and grateful salutation. He could determine the four points of the compass by scrutinizing the bark of a tree, and he knew the time of night by looking up at the stars. His sense of smell was so acute that he could in that way recognize the approach of persons to his cabin; and his hearing was more acute than that of the most cunning Indian. He had trained his senses to see God in the reign of law about him. He found not a dissonant world, but one of order, of revelation, and of glory. There was not a leaf, a blade of grass, nor a wild flower that he did not know in its botanical relation, and did not recognize as having some ministry for him. The world was palpitating under his feet with life, and the fragrance of the sweetbrier, the birch, and alder was purer to him than the incense offered in any temple. With what grace could he say to a friend, "If the day and the night are such that you greet them with joy, and life emits a fragrance like flowers and sweet-scented herbs, is more elastic, starry, and immortal—that is your success."

Whatever of sternness there was in his nature was born of simplicity, of transparent honesty. He was an unconventional man. The richness of his nature did not come from overmuch flesh and blood, but rather from an elimination of all the grossness of sense. Christopher North, Thackeray, and Dickens could drain a bowl of punch or sing a humorous song with a rolling, rollicking exuberance; while Thoreau would have reached a better exaltation by drinking spring water from his bark cup, or in listening to the song of a thrush in the thicket. The wild grapes, which the autumnal frost has flavored, may be better for the poet than the full flagon of wine. The gross feeders and heavy drinkers may be mellow men, but they have little converse with the gods. The man who has a high ideal standard of taste, of touch, of perception, and of interpretation, will always have something of remoteness about him. He does not touch humanity at all points, nor indeed at many, because the plane of his life is above theirs.

There was also in Thoreau's manner of life, for a time, a wholesome satire on the more vulgar uses of wealth. The rich parvenu delighted in fast living. He demanded consideration not for what he was in himself, but for what riches he had gained by hook or by crook. If he had kept a pot-house or had been a soap-boiler, he was only the more importunate and the more imperious in his demands for distinguished consideration. He aspired to give law to society. He established standards of living, of dress, of domestic expenditure. He delighted to have his dwelling described as a "palatial residence," and the attire of his wife at promiscuous jams, minutely described in the flash papers of the day. It came to be a proverb that rich men's sons of this class never amounted to anything. The exceptions were painfully rare. The young cubs differed only from the parent stock in that they had smaller abilities to create wealth, and greater facilities for spending it. They lived faster than their fathers, and reached the goal sooner. Society of this sort has been sadly in need of a pungent satirist for a long time. Since the issue of the *Potiphar Papers* there has been no one to turn these vulgar phases to wholesome public account. In such a social and intellectual atmosphere as that about Concord, society of this sort could have no admission. It could have none in many of the social centers of New England. The aristocracy of intellect and scholarship was the only legitimate one there. If it had some blue blood, it was gentle and considerate. It was quick to recognize talent, genius, and scholarship, and was constantly making recruits from the brighter young men and women of the day. It was in vain that Dives left his card or drove his four-in-hand furiously along the avenues. There was no golden key which could force admission. Thoreau went in as one of the elect. He met Emerson, and Channing, and Alcott, and all the choice spirits, on ground which was common to him as well as to them. If one cannot live on the rarified atmosphere ten thousand feet up the mountain side, he had best betake himself to the valley. Men who dwell on intellectual hights live apart. So did Thoreau and so did Hawthorne. They had a small following, but it was select, critical, and appreciative. It is larger now. Of the latter it is much to say that, as a master of expression, his rank is at the head of all American authors. Of Thoreau, Higginson, the most discriminating of his judges, says that "he wrote the only book yet written in America that bears an annual perusal." How slowly does immortality ripen! Thoreau lived to see only two volumes published, his *Week on the Concord* and *Walden*. These brought him neither fame nor fortune while living. Four or five other volumes were subsequently published, including *The Maine Woods*, *A Week in Canada*, and *Cape Cod*. Of the thousand copies of his *Week on the Concord and Merrimack Rivers*, his publisher returned him seven hundred unsold copies. That was Thoreau's introduction to authorship. Higginson recently copied from his unpublished diary the following comment on this venture. It has in it the undisturbed calmness of a philosopher, and the tender, self-revealing spirit of a child:

"For a year or two past Munroe has been writing from time to time to ask what disposition should be made of the copies of *A Week on the Concord and Merrimack Rivers* still on hand, and at last suggesting that he had use for the room they occupied in his cellar. So I had them all sent to me here, and they have arrived to-day by express, piling the man's wagon, seven hundred and six copies out of an edition of one thousand which I bought of Munroe four years ago, and have been ever since paying for, and have not quite paid for yet. The wares are sent to me at last, and I have an opportunity to examine my purchase. They are something more substantial than fame, as my back knows, which has borne them up two flights of stairs to a place similar to that to which they trace their origin. Of the remaining two hundred ninety and odd, seventy-five were given away, the rest sold. I have now a library of nearly nine hundred volumes, over seven hundred of which I wrote myself. Is it not well that the author should behold the fruits of his labor? My works are piled up in my chamber half as high as my head, my *opera omnia*. This is authorship. These are the works of my brain. * * * I can see now what I write for, and the result of my labors. Nevertheless, in spite of this result, sitting beside the inert mass of my works, I take up my pen to-night to record what thought or experience I may have had with as much satisfaction as ever. Indeed, I believe that this result is more inspiring and better than if a thousand had bought my wares. It affects my privacy less, and leaves me freer."

The best prose pastoral, and the best volume of out-door philosophy, which has yet been produced by any American author, had its origin in the little hut by the margin of Walden Pond. Thoreau declared that men at present have only rudimentary eyes, and he went to improve his in the woods. He had found a place where he could sit and stand without the aid of a furniture warehouse. He thought it would be a good thing if a sacrament of purification were observed every few years, and all were compelled to bring forth their rubbish and burn it. He thought that might be the "outward and visible sign of an inward and spiritual grace." But the thrifty housewife really has a domestic sacrament once or twice a year, when the whitewash, scrubbing-brushes, and dusters become the instruments of purification. It is a pity that so much rubbish survives. Probably no one ever thought more meanly of himself than when he saw his furniture, rubbish, and *impedimenta* carted through the streets from one domicil to another. Had heaven frowned upon him, that so much trumpery and wreckage had accumulated? The symbolical renewal of the world is by fire. The general conflagration is coming, and there is a small sect which figures out the day and the hour. There are good reasons for hoping that the time for a grand clearance will not be extended. Seeing that the world is mortgaged for more than it is worth, it might be a good thing if fire, in some way, could work a general defeasance.

Thoreau said that at Walden he lived as far off as many a region viewed nightly by astronomers. He lived in what he termed a new and unprofaned part of the universe. This ideal remoteness suited him only for a time; but it was when his mind was most fruitful. His isolation was more constructive than real. He did not wholly drop association with his kind, for he went to the village post-office twice a week, and could never quite exclude from his hearing the gossip of the town. After a hard day's work, it may be very restful to blow soap-bubbles with the children. After reading a chapter of the Vedas in his cabin, Thoreau was not averse to seeing how the society-bubbles were blown, though he refused to furnish wind or take his turn at the pipe. It was no part of his plan to drop his relations with society, though he took good care that it should not impose any of its arbitrary customs upon him. He only changed his relations for a short time to see if there was any more rational and wholesome way of living. He would know more of dumb and inarticulate nature; and to know this he must be brought into closer relation with it. He had little relish for artificial music, but when the needles of the pine trembled to the vibrations of the far-off bell he was glad for the revelation, holding that the wood-nymphs made the responses. But his gentle cynicism got the better of sentiment when he thought that the music of some young people who had come to serenade him, was akin to the music of a cow. The hooting of an owl he thought was truly Johnsonian; but he did not object to the serenade. He maintained that the *tronk* of the frog, as he leaned his drooling chin upon a leaf for a napkin, was truly aldermanic.

Thoreau adopted a maxim of Oriental philosophy, "Renew thyself each day; do it again, and again, and forever again." He rose early and bathed in the pond as a part of his religious exercises. But that was no more than the most grasping miser of San Francisco did who plunged, every morning, winter and summer, into the salt sea. Refusing to pay a shilling for admission to the cemetery of his ancestors, he attempted to scale the walls. The man of ten millions saved his shilling, but soon after it cost another shilling or more to carry him legitimately through the gates of that ancient cemetery. Hydropathic religion is liable to wash out. Certain it is that it never changed a mean character into a noble one. What a health-giving spirit there is in this declaration:

"The morning, which is the most memorable season of the day, is the awakening hour. Then there is least somnolence in us, and for an hour, at least, some part of us awakes which slumbers all the rest of the day and night. Little is to be expected of that day, if it can be called a day, to which we are not awakened by our Genius, but by the mechanical nudgings of some servitor—are not awakened by our own newly acquired force and aspirations from within, accompanied by the undulations of celestial music instead of factory bells, and a fragrance filling the air—to a higher life than we fell asleep from; and thus the darkness bear its fruit, and prove itself to be good no less than the light. That man who does not believe that each day contains an earlier, more sacred, and auroral hour than he has yet profaned, has despaired of life, and is pursuing a descending and darkening way. After a partial cessation of his sensuous life, the soul of man, or its organs, rather, are reinvigorated each day, and his genius tries again what noble life it can make. All memorable events, I should say, transpire in the morning time and in a morning atmosphere. The Vedas say 'all intelligences awake in the morning.' Poetry and art, and the fairest and most memorable of the actions of men, date from such an hour. All poets and heroes, like Memnon, are the children of Aurora, and emit their music at sunrise. To him whose elastic and vigorous thought keeps pace with the sun, the day is a perpetual morning. It matters not what the clock says, or the attitudes and labors of men. Morning is when I am awake and there is a dawn in me. Moral reform is the effort to throw off sleep. Why is it that men give so poor an account of their day, if they have not been slumbering? They are not such poor calculators. If they had not been overcome with drowsiness, they would have performed something. The millions are awake enough for physical labor, but only one in a million is awake enough for effective intellectual exertion, only one in a hundred millions to a poetic or divine life. To be awake is to be alive. I have never yet met a man who was quite awake. How could I have looked him in the face?"

Thoreau took a poet to board for a fortnight, and mentioned that he brought his own knife, although the host had two in the house. But never more than one or two of his guests were bold enough to stay and eat his hasty pudding. While making it they saw the crisis approaching, and stole silently away, as if the house might be shaken to the foundations. When a hermit-philosopher came to talk with him of an evening, he said the conversation expanded so that it racked the whole house, and he had to calk the seams afresh with oakum. He knew pretty well the character of the visitors who called at his house in his absence, divining the number, sex, and tastes, even when no other card was left than a leaf pinned on his door, or by some odd arrangement of the primitive furniture. He was more careful to note the threnody of a song-sparrow in the early spring, and the chit of a blackbird, than the conversations of his guests. He affirmed that solitude was wholesome. But that, after all, would depend upon environment. Solitude is not wholesome in a dungeon, although it might be in a garret on a rainy day. Thoreau had never found a companion who was so companionable as solitude. But Daniel Webster once wished an antagonist who had maligned him, no greater punishment than that he should be left to the solitude of his own company. No doubt, the best thinking is done in a solitary way; but then, one may be as much alone by mental abstraction as if there were not another in the universe. And this isolation may sometimes be as complete on the thronged street, or in the great congregation, as it could be in the heart of the primeval forest. Profound thinking demands a condition of temporary seclusion. But the noblest acts are wrought out face to face, and where the dust and grime of the world is thickest. There must be broad-shouldered men, with blood and brawn enough at times, to enforce some high thinking with the battle-ax and the broadsword. If all men went to the woods to browse on birch and wintergreen, no university training could save the world from lapsing into a savage condition. Indeed, there is never more than a thin partition between an unlettered and a lettered savage. A civilized dog, if left long in the woods, will fraternize with the wolf. There is some wildness in the blood which classic culture never wholly tames. Thoreau himself, who loved the Greek better than his mother tongue, by long isolation, might one day have fraternized with the Indian in his war-paint, so that one could not tell which was the wisest, or which the most profound philosopher. Society, says our author, is commonly too cheap. True enough. And the way to make it dearer is not wholly to desert it, but to enrich it by toil and sacrifice and all noble living. The man who has done most for society never finds it cheap. Never did a brave man fighting for his country think, when the struggle ended, that he had one scar too many. Thoreau found two years at Walden enough. He had the honesty and courage to go back and say so. How well he puts the case for his life in the woods:

"We need the tonic of the wilderness—to wade sometimes in marshes where the bittern and the meadow-hen lurk, and hear the booming of the snipe; to smell the whispering sedge, where only some wilder and more solitary fowl builds her nest, and the mink crawls with his belly close to the ground. At the same time that we are earnest to explore and learn all things, we require that all things be mysterious and unexplorable—that land and sea be infinitely wild, unsurveyed and unfathomed by us, because unfathomable. We can never have enough of Nature. We must be refreshed by the sight of inexhaustible vigor, vast and titanic features—the sea-coast with its wrecks, the wilderness with its living and decaying trees, the thunder-cloud, and the rain which lasts three weeks and produces freshets. We need to witness our own limits transgressed, and some life pasturing freely where we may never wander."

After a critical reading of Thoreau's works, one can hardly escape the impression of a certain incompleteness about the man. There is hardly more warmth in him than there might be in an iceberg. He lacked the better qualities of humor as much as Hawthorne, and is said to have eliminated many sentences from his manuscripts lest there might be found lurking in them a humorous suggestion. The sayings are oracular, and are frequently tinged with an Oriental philosophy, which was much affected by him in the later years of his life. He narrowed the range of his observation by going apart from the world, and so cherished, for a time, a kind of indifferentism about its good or evil fortunes. He had a microscopic power of vision, and when it was turned upon the smallest object he saw all there was of it, and vastly more than common men had ever seen. The faculty of looking into the soul of things was developed in Thoreau beyond that of other men. He was wide-eyed in this respect, and piercing in his vision. It was never arrested by the husk, the rind, or the sham. His rustic neighbors called him the "terrible Thoreau," partly because of his remoteness, and partly because he was ever seeing so much where they were seeing so little. His learning seemed to them occult, mysterious, and supernatural. The great man in a rural community may often be a small man in the world. Thoreau's physical cosmos was Concord, with a radius of a dozen miles. When he became known in the commonwealth of letters the world was not too large for him. It is said that half his manuscripts remain unpublished, and their publication is eagerly anticipated. After such a lapse of years, so much could not be said of any other American author except Hawthorne. Time and fire try every man's work, of what sort it is. Irving grows smaller in the perspective of thirty years; but Thoreau does not. He came and went silently. It is the sure indice of a great character that the world is ever learning something about him, and is ever eager to learn. He has not been exhausted. He was a discoverer, and the world as yet has had only a few hints of his discoveries. By this test, Napoleon III., in narrating the battles of Julius Cæsar, was not so great a man as Thoreau describing a battle of red and black ants in the woods at Walden.

The line of his thinking was luminous and clean cut. With his wonderful vividness of expression there is always a degree of reserve, a hiding of power. He was not a broad-shouldered man, taking kindly the burdens of the world. Yet he seemed capable of absolute self-negation at times. There was ever a wholesome fragrance about his life, as of balsam and the wild spices of the woods. He never looked upon the night side of nature. For him there was no night at all, but the night was ever as the day. Lowell, in a captious and deprecating criticism, says that Thoreau saw only the things he looked for. Fortunate he who can see as much! The rudimentary eye is still in many of us, and even that is sometimes overgrown by the cataract. A recent critic in *The Cornhill Magazine* is more appreciative, but in combating Thoreau's philosophy misses the man—the real essence of his life. It is remarkable that both of these critics dwell so largely upon surface excrescences, and concern themselves so little with what was vital in his character and work. The pulp of the fruit is often under a rough exterior. Why should we quarrel with the shell? Going beneath it, we find a man of transparent purity, of singular genius, poet, naturalist, revelator, savage, scholar, a philosopher without a school, a religionist without a creed, and so rare a man withal, that his successor hath not made his appearance in a quarter of a century. W. C. BARTLETT.

MISSION SAN GABRIEL

The circling hills, and a sunny reach
Of sloping plain on the east, that each
Fair morning of the summer day
Wakes to the earliest glancing ray
Of dawning light from beyond the crest
Of snow-clad peaks, whose solemn rest
Is like to God's! And, looking down
With a rugged, stony, lifeless frown,
Upon the north is a lonely wall
Of storm-beat rock, so grim and tall
You backward bend to lift your eyes,
And lift, and lift, to the far-off skies.

And the rocky wall, with changeless face,
Looks down alway upon the place
Like the stony face by the Pyramids,
Whose staring eyes, beneath their lids,
Behold the palms of the ancient Nile,
And deem the years but a little while—
The years of the nations come and gone,
The years that knew Creation's dawn.
A little while? The ages dead
That come and go o'er the hoary head
Are a breath but spent, or the meteor's light,
To the weary length of the endless flight
Of times and times, since the Sphinx's face
Its birth-hour knew.

Ah, yes! the place—
I half forgot. No pyramid
Is standing here, but an orchard, hid
In trailing vines, and a fragrance sweet
That floods the air of a village street;
A winding lane that twists and turns,
With babbling brooks and graceful ferns,
Beneath the shade of the sycamores;
And the flashing water leaps and pours
Its mimic flood in the tiny brooks,
Where, between the leaves, the sunlight looks
With laughing glance in the shallow pool
By pebbles lined—so fresh and cool
That the mocking-bird, for very joy,
Pours out its soul, like a romping boy
Let free to toss in the waving grass
Beneath the trees.

I turn and pass
Adown the ways of the quaint old streets,
Where red-tiled roofs and gables greet
My sight from the trees and tangled vines
Whose festoons break the sunlier lines
Of house and street; and the fig trees' green,
With purple fruit, and the nectarine,
And the peaches' down, and, back of all,
Orange and lime in solid wall
Of green and gold, and the deeper sheen
Of the orange broke by the fresher green
Of lemon boughs; and then I hold
My hat in hand, for, stained and old,
Before me stands, with its sleeping dead,
A time-worn church.

I bow my head
As humbly to the cross on high
As the brown-skinned native passing by.
Though not my church, it is still to me
A church of my God, and the cross I see
Is mine—is mine by the tortured face
That knew its pain, yet knew no race,
Nor tongue, nor kin, nor ban that stood
To part the ways of our brotherhood.

A quaint old spot! And the summer day
Goes slowly by, and fades away.
And still I linger, and watch the saints
And the martyrs, decked with their gaudy paints,
And the red-tiled roof, and the toppling wall,
And talk with the gray-haired priest of all
The long, long years that have come and fled
O'er the Mission Church and its sleeping dead.

And the *padre* sits, with his snow-white hair,
On the rawhide seat of his easy chair,
While the curling smoke, with a lazy grace,
Rolls up from the lips o'er the calm old face.
"Señor," he says, and he sips his wine,
The ruby juice of the Mission vine;
"Señor, the walls of crumbling clay,
And the red-tiled roof, where the shadows play,
And the *padre* old, with his whitened head,
And the Holy Ground, with its silent dead,
Only are left of the Mission here,
Señor," he said, and an unshed tear
A moment hung on the trembling lid,
And then by the thin old hand was hid;
"Señor, the red-tiled roof will fall,
And the rains will wash the crumbling wall,
And the *padre* old, with his whitened head,
Will lay him down with the sleeping dead;
And the busy plow will leave no trace,
With its cruel share, of the dear old place,
Nor the grass-grown mounds, where in the deep
Evening shadows the crosses keep
Their silent guard o'er them who sleep.

"Only, may be, when the broken tile
Is turned to light, for a little while
Will the plowman pause, and gazing stand,
With sweaty brow in his horny hand,
And wonder where are the hands that wrought
And labored here—and were then forgot.
Señor," he raised the old gray head,
"Señor, the Lord will find His dead."

I turn and stroll through the fallen gate
Of the Campo Santo; and in the late
Glimmer of starlight I can see
Shadow of tower and orange tree

Touching the grave-stones tenderly.
Above a fallen stone I stoop
And part the poppies that curl and droop
Over the graven lines. I spell
Slowly the fading words that tell
Age and a name, and then a tale,
Tersely written: "A MUERTE FIEL."

Father Francisco, with tottering tread,
Is walking the orange path—his head
Bent o'er his beads. "Padre," I ask,
"Tell me the tale." He ceases the task
Of counting the beads of his rosary,
And this is the tale that he tells to me:

"It was many a year ago,
Many a year of joy and pain—
For seasons came and seasons go—
And Carlos the Fourth was King of Spain."

So spake the Padre's gentle tone;
He crossed himself. "Peace ever be
To her in her grave! She sleeps alone,
Faithful to death."—"Ah, yes, and he?"

"The tale I will tell. 'Twas told to me
When first I came to the Mission here
Long years ago. Yon orange tree
Was then a twig. Señor, I fear

"The tale may tire you, or may seem
A simple thing. We live alone
Our quiet lives, until we dream
Our Mission to a world has grown.

"It was many a year ago,
Many a year the grass has lain
Upon her grave: I only know
Carlos the Fourth was King of Spain;

"And yet the flag of his Majesty
Was flaunting wide on the Spanish Main;
And from Orizaba to the sea
Was never a league of Mexic plain

"But called him lord. Señor, I pray
My old man's talk you will pardon me.
Much years I have. Señor, to-day
Is not as the olden time."—"And she?"

"Ah, yes! She loved: a simple love
Of village maiden, leal and true;
As guileless as the moaning dove,
Her God and truth she only knew.

"He sailed away to the seas, for he
Of other race and other clime
Was born and bred. Señor, to me
'Tis passing strange. May be my time

"Too much I've lived in the cloister's cell.
'Tis strange to me, the maiden heart;
I read it not. I only tell
My simple tale. Señor, no art

"Have I to wonder learnedly
Of maiden loves. I only know
He sailed away upon the sea.
Señor, 'twas long, long time ago.

"And still she loved; and still the days
They came and went; the winter's rain,
The summer's green, the autumn haze."—
"And he?"—"He came not more again.

"Señor, long years I linger here
Among the hills. The Mission bell
Is to me as the drawing near
Of Heaven's music. And I tell

"The passing years as one his beads,
With heart still lifted heavenward—"
"The tale?"—"Ah, pardon! Little needs
That more I speak. A young life starred,

"And that was all. Some spoke of death,
And ships long lost in unknown seas;
And others spoke with bated breath
Of vows forgotten soon; but these

"She would not hear; she only shook
Her head alway with a smothered pain—
And still a hope was in her look.
And the years went by, but never again

"That ship came back. Señor, she sleeps
Long years at rest. Perhaps 'twas well—
His love for the sad the good Lord keeps.
Pardon, Señor; 'tis the vesper bell."

The sun has crept low in the west
And hangs a moment on the crest
Of treeless hills; the shadows dim
Of rugged rocks, so strangely grim.
Have wrapped the *cañons* in their fold
Far up the mountain slopes, and hold
The gloomy depths in stern embrace.
A moment, on the Padre's face
The sunlight falls. It crowns the hair
With gleams of gold so strangely fair,
I gaze in wordless wonder.

Hark!

A tender music in the dark
Swells on the air; the night is sweet
With melody. The village street,
And hill, and plain, and leafy dell,
Are hushed to peace beneath the spell
That trembles from the vesper bell.

VESPER HYMN.

Gently fall the shades of even;
One by one the stars appear.
Turn from earth to thoughts of heaven—
For the angels hover near.

Gently fall the shades of even;
Toil and strife and labor cease,
Darkness bringeth earth near heaven;
And the angels whisper, Peace!

"Padre, I go." I bowed my head.
"Pax vobiscum!" he gently said.
And the sun went down; and darkness came
From out the east, and the west aflame
With dying light.

Once more I said,
As a monicot softly I bowed my head,
"I go, O Father! Bid me peace!"
And he gently prayed, "May the Lord give peace!"

J. P. WIDNEY.

IN THE COURT-ROOM WITH RUFUS CHOATE.

Ready to enter the arena of life and bear my part in its struggles, I had a great desire to adopt the legal profession, and in my enthusiasm on the subject became much interested in the celebrated man who is the subject of this sketch. My particular recollection of him was in connection with the celebrated criminal trial, in Boston, of Albert J. Tirrell, indicted for the murder of one Maria Bickford. Annis Merrill, Esq., now a resident of San Francisco, was the junior counsel associated with Mr. Choate in the case.

The murder alluded to was discovered in early morning, the inmates of the house having been aroused by the smell of fire. The house was filled with smoke. The fire, which was found to be in a store-room adjoining the apartments of Mrs. Bickford, was soon extinguished. The body of Mrs. Bickford was found in her room with the throat cut from ear to ear, the wound evidently having been inflicted with a razor lying beside the body. Articles belonging to Tirrell were found in the room, and he was known to have occupied the apartment that same evening. He had been traced from the house, at about four o'clock in the morning, to a livery stable, where he hired a team to convey him to the town of Weymouth, some twelve miles distant. All traces of him were then lost, and nothing was heard of him until his arrest in New Orleans, some months afterward.

The case was tried in Boston before three venerable judges, in the year 1846. The opening plea, or argument for the defense was made by Mr. Merrill in a speech of marked ability; but the public indignation had been aroused, and was so intense that there seemed no chance of escape for the prisoner. Indeed, it seemed a hopeless case, and the meshes of the law seemed to have woven themselves around the victim, defying the skill of attorneys to set him free.

The fact that such eminent counsel as Mr. Choate was engaged in the case gave it a peculiar significance, and created an interest in the trial that otherwise, perhaps, would have passed by like many others, scarcely known outside the court-room. I think I shall never forget those days spent in the court-room, spell-bound by the magical influence exerted by Mr. Choate. I longed to be a member of that jury, that I might be a privileged person in court, and attend the trial throughout its whole length, and watch with interest the management of the case in the hands of this eminent lawyer, assisted by his able associate. Mr. Choate seemed from the first to have a feeling of confidence that he should win that jury in spite of the army of evidence which had accumulated against his client, and which seemed to others to preclude any hope of acquittal. To me, the whole interest in the trial was centered in Mr. Choate. He was enthusiastic in his devotion to his duty, and full of surprises and tactics that taxed the ingenuity of the opposite counsel to its utmost. The District Attorney entered the court-room each morning laden with the calf-bound literature pertaining to the law, for he could not tell what moment he might be called upon to interpose the text of the law, and cite its precedents, to counteract or demolish the positions taken from time to time by his wily opponent.

Unlike most lawyers of the present day, who usually desire their client seated at their side, where they may hold frequent consultations, Mr. Choate is said to have had very little personal intercourse with his clients in criminal cases. In the trial of Tirrell, as Mr. Choate came into the court-room, on the first day, his eye wandered restlessly over the assembled audience till it rested at last upon the prisoner in the dock. He deliberately walked over to his side, and in a few quiet words announced himself as his defender, never speaking to him again during the trial; and it is even said this meeting in court was the first one between them. Mr. Choate entered the case by interesting himself greatly in the selection of the jury. He measured his men as though desirous to learn, if possible, their weak points, or, perhaps, their eccentricities of character, to discover how each might be influenced by his arguments or his eloquence. His dark, lustrous eye seemed to read the innermost thoughts of the different candidates for the jury-box as they presented themselves. As he wound up his questions to jurymen, in a solemn, slow-spoken style of manner, his long finger pointing directly to the party spoken to: "Have you any scruples, sir, regarding the death penalty?" he fixed his eye upon the juror to note particularly the *style* of his answer. A frown, or an almost imperceptible shake of the head with its shock of black curly hair, as he conversed with his associate counsel, indicated plainly enough that a juryman under discussion between them would not answer. It seemed to be his first care to obtain a whole jury according to his wishes; failing in that, to make sure of his influence over enough of its members to make a respectable division of opinion, and, consequently, a disagreement. This, it may be said, is true of all lawyers; but, with Mr. Choate, the tact displayed in selecting jurymen was very noticeable. There was no better judge of human nature than he. He seemed determined to make sure of his men before trusting them with issues so important to his client. He studied the jury throughout the trial, and was always a quiet observer of the effect of each bit of evidence on them. Before a trial was concluded, he had learned the peculiar characteristics of each, and in his address to the jury endeavored to so adapt himself to each as to convince him, if possible.

The case proceeded slowly. The jury at last selected, the District Attorney opened the case, and the witnesses were called. Those who seemed of little importance were not detained long upon the stand by Mr. Choate, and the sarcastic smile that played around his features as such witnesses resumed their seats, seemed to indicate that he felt no misgivings as to his ability to demolish their simple testimony before the jury. His tactics and his dissecting knife were reserved for the principal witnesses. With a polite deference to the bench when checked by the Judge, he nevertheless handled an opposing witness in such a manner that nothing but the plain truth, without equivocation, would avail to prevent his utter demoralization. A stubborn or a contumacious witness was handled without gloves, and was always forced to yield. He took very copious notes, seizing his pen with an eager clutch as some important bit of testimony was elicited, as if eager to jot it down while it was *hot*. It was quite evident from the first that he had his plans made and his method of defense mapped out, but these were only developed late in the trial, a fact which disturbed his opponents sadly. When the Government rested its case, it was impossible to know, from anything that had dropped from his lips, what would be the nature of the defense. The opposing counsel groped in the dark, annoyed by the confidant manner of Mr. Choate and his associate, and counseled together in the vain attempt to discover what tactics the enemy would adopt. To a spectator like myself, it was interesting to watch the attorneys on either side as each new feature of the trial developed itself. Mr. Choate seemed to be the aggressor, and his opponents were kept on the alert continually to counteract his moves in this game of life.

Newspapers, reporting the case from day to day, commented freely upon it, and when the Government rested the case it seemed as good as decided, and the gallows-tree began to cast its ghastly shadow across the path of the prisoner. It had been incontestably proved that Tirrell was present on the eventful night; that he had been seen to leave the fatal room at an early morning hour; in fact, proved as clearly as circumstances could prove it, that he committed the fatal deed; and a hopeless task seemed to be imposed upon the eminent counsel for the defense to unwind the network that had closed about the prisoner.

Mr. Choate never for a moment showed the least appearance of discomfiture. Frequent were the consultations with his associate as the time drew near for him to unfold his plans and state the nature of his defense. The public press had conjectured in vain on the subject, and a death-like stillness prevailed in the courtroom as Mr. Choate arose, ran his long, skinny fingers through his curly locks, unconscious of the unusual gaze fixed upon him, and with fire flashing from his eyes, announced to the court and jury, with an earnest voice, that his defense was *somnambulism*—that his client was a *sleep-walker*, had been so from birth, and that he was prepared to prove, beyond the possibility of a doubt, that Terrill had committed the deed, if he committed it at all, in the unconsciousness of sleep.

No smile of sarcasm wreathed the faces of opposing counsel, for Mr. Choate laid down his points with such vehemence and such a confidence of success that his opponents felt there was work before them to controvert a position which Mr. Choate had been fortifying, unconsciously to them, from the very first. Witnesses were called in rapid succession to testify to the strange conduct of the prisoner on many occasions—that he was accustomed to make strange noises and groans, both loud and distressing. Those that saw him on that eventful morning testified to his strange conduct and conversation. One witness affirmed that at the stable referred to he had to take hold of Tirrell and shake him, to *wake him up*. No cross-examination seemed to shake faith in the credibility of any one of these. Aware of its singular character, Mr. Choate seemed determined, if possible, to convince court and jury and spectators of the validity of his defense by the cumulative testimony of great numbers of reputable people.

As the evidence in the case was concluded, and the day arrived for the arguments of counsel, the court-room was crowded with the representatives of the bar, and others eager to hear Mr. Choate in his appeal to the jury. I shall never forget the scene, or the thrill of excitement with which all were more or less filled, as, standing erect, his coat buttoned and his hand thrust in his breast, the great advocate first took a calm survey of each of the twelve faces before him, his eagle eye darting from one to another, while a solemn stillness pervaded the court-room. Even the staid and sober judges leaned back in their cushioned chairs, and gazed with interest upon the scene. Mr. Choate seemed at first a little nervous, and even timid, as he arose to speak. Whether this was assumed or not, he did not come before the jury with the air of a braggadocio, or one confident of his abilities; and the listener to his first utterances would even have pronounced him apprehensive of results. He commenced his address by calling the attention of the jury to the solemn character of their deliberations. After fixing their attention, he opened his case. Argument, raillery, sarcasm, pathos poured from his lips. Skillfully avoiding anything that appeared like an attack upon their judgment or good sense, he strove in the outset to win their favor and confidence. I have heard it said of Mr. Choate that he considered the first moments before a jury as the all-important moments. Their interest in the case, and their eagerness to hear and know the line of defense, are early exhibited; and if you fail then you will never win them at all. It was quite apparent that it was Mr. Choate's plan to get control of his jury early, and he availed himself of such weapons as argument, anecdote, and jest. He seemed fully to believe every word he uttered, and his air of sincerity carried conviction to his hearers. Before a jury Mr. Choate was perfectly at home, after getting into the midst of his argument; and he was acknowledged one of the ablest of criminal advocates. The jury fairly hung upon his words, often leaning forward in their seats in their desire to hear. He went rapidly through the evidence in the case, throwing suspicions on the testimony of witnesses for the Government, alluding in no mild terms to the infamous character of these witnesses; and after long speaking, which it would seem might exhaust the speaker, if the jury showed symptoms of fatigue he aroused them by playful extravagances; he indulged in witty allusions, he told some humorous story, always bearing upon points at issue, or he purposely thrust his lance at opposing counsel, provoking a little war of violent words, till he had succeeded in arousing the tired jurymen to a listening attitude. Mr. Choate always endeavored, if possible, to make his speech before a jury without an adjournment of court intervening. He preferred to say all he had to say at one sitting, as his arguments were to be carried in the mind throughout his whole speech. He knew when to stop. He knew in just what condition of mind to leave his jury. His eye wandered from one to another, and he would often address himself to an individual who seemed indifferent, till he had secured his attention, continually varying his moods to suit the temper of his audience. He related stories of the freaks of somnambulists. When he was wrestling with a strong or telling point in the argument, and wished to fix it particularly in mind, his gestures were violent, he seemed beside himself, and as he came down with a thud upon his heels, he carried the impression to the hearts of the jury that he himself felt the truth of what he uttered. When battling a point that told against his case, he skillfully led away the mind from contemplation of it in its inimical aspect, painting it in colors of his own, and fixing the attention on his own interpretation. His quick eye detected at once a point gained, and he followed up a home-thrust till he was sure of his man. During his address to the jury, he gave proof of his great command of language, fanciful and poetical. He held his audience spell-bound. He quoted from books bearing on the matter of somnambulism, told stories of cases of the disorder that were serious or fatal in their issues. Throughout his long address, the same stillness pervaded the court-room, crowded to its utmost capacity.

The jury were out a little more than two hours, and as they came into court, and were polled by the clerk, I watched carefully the face of the great advocate. Except a little tremulousness of the fingers, no trace of excitement could be observed. The quiet of the court-room was painful, as the clerk put the usual question:

"Gentlemen of the jury, have you agreed upon a verdict?"

"We have."

"What say you, gentlemen—guilty or not guilty?"

"*Not* guilty."

The words were scarcely uttered when Mr. Choate ran both hands through his thick hair, and seemed to breathe a sigh of relief. He felt himself a victor, but there was no shaking of hands, no jubilant smile, and no self-satisfaction apparent. He seemed like a man who *knew* it could not be otherwise. The prisoner was afterward tried for arson, committed in connection with the murder, he having been indicted for both offenses. Mr. Choate defended him in this case also, but had little difficulty in securing an acquittal after the experience of the murder trial. Tirrell was completely at the mercy of Mr. Choate, who held his life in his hands. I verily believe no one else could have secured the verdict.

It is difficult to give an idea of the style and method of this eminent lawyer. He was guilty of no pettifogging, of no underhanded attempts to get the better of his opponents. With him it was a fair fight for a verdict. A full court-room always attested the opinion entertained by the members of the bar, and the public generally, of his great abilities. Since his day few men have arisen who could command an equal share of popularity. In fact, the practice before a jury is quite different from that of the olden time, and much of the honorable dealing of earlier days has departed. However, I am not writing to moralize, but simply to record a reminiscence of a great lawyer.

J. S. BACON.

A STRANGE CONFESSION.

CHAPTER VII.

It had come about in this manner: When Mrs. Howard, bareheaded, her eyes glaring, and her cheeks flushed, arrived at First Street, Casserly was standing upon the steps, addressing the mob. Frenzied with a desire to do whatever might be done—whatever human ingenuity could suggest to do, whatever a mother's heart could urge should be done—she tunneled like a mole through the dense mass of humanity that separated her from Casserly. She would become Casserly's ally. She would choose between the mob and the scaffold—anything, everything, to gain time. But her strength failed. She was rudely handled, and once she cried out with pain. Seen thus frantic, she was taken for one of the mob.

"Here is a woman," cried a man. "Make way for the woman!"

"A woman! A woman!" arose the shout. "A brave woman! Should we hesitate when a woman sets the example? Make way there! She will help us to hang the scoundrel. Hurrah for the woman!"

She turned like a lioness, and writhed in agony. It seemed that her eyes would burst from their sockets. At this they shouted again. Oh, that she were a man—that she had a knife to plunge into two thousand hearts at once, that the blood might flow around her to the waist, and that she might drink it, and lave in it, and think it rarer and sweeter than the nectar of the gods! Was it as great a mother's heart as thine, O woman, that looked upon the Crucifixion with but a tear upon the cheek? Misguided woman! You should have been as noble as the women of the Ganges, who cast their offspring into the jaws of crocodiles.

She choked down the words that clamored for utterance. Bruised and sore, her hair disheveled, her clothing torn, she turned back, and gained the outskirts of the mob, her heart bursting and her brain on fire.

"O God!" she prayed, unconsciously and silently, "that the sun should shine upon such a scene—that the earth did not quake and the heavens turn black! Oh, that the world might be rent with thunder and lightning, and bolts of death hurled by a million gods upon this gigantic pack of bloodhounds. Give me strength, O God! Arm me with the instruments of thy vengeance. Save him—save him—save him!"

She trembled in every joint. As she was mentally casting about for means to avert the impending catastrophe, an unfortunate woman, standing near her at the corner of St. James Street, approached her with a reeling gait. This woman's eyes were bloodshot, and a course leer darkened her features. Turning upon her, Mrs. Howard asked, in a voice so husky and shattered that it could hardly be recognized as a woman's, "What are they going to do?"

The woman winked knowingly, and replied, "I know."

"Will they break open the jail?"

The woman shook her head.

"Then they can't take him out," exclaimed the mother, triumphantly.

"Oh, but they can."

"How?" was the startled inquiry.

The woman simply shook her head. This so exasperated the mother that she clutched the woman's arm with nervous strength, and demanded, threateningly:

"What do you mean, woman?"

The strange woman was in that state of intoxication in which Indiscretion opens readily the cage-door of Secrecy. It is a good plan not to impart secrets to people who drink. The woman asked:

"Do you want to see him strung up?"

The mother, with that quick power of divination possessed only by women, and suppressing the revolting effect upon her nature of the cruel question, replied, with every trace of excited color fading from her face, "I do."

"Truly, now?"

"I would pull on the rope. I would put a knife into his heart. Let me see him."

And, indeed, she looked so terrible at that moment that the strange woman was thoroughly frightened, and stared as if she saw a specter.

"Do you know anything? Tell me," cried the mother.

"Oh, don't look that way. You frighten me."

"Tell me, I say. Tell me."

"Come, then."

They turned into St. James Street, and proceeded toward Market. It was soon evident that the strange woman regretted what she had done, and in order to disembarrass her conscience, she retreated into the stronghold of women, and begged:

"Do you promise solemnly that you won't give me away?"

"Yes."

Thus they reached Market Street. The woman halted at one of the cottages in the rear of the jail. A butcher's cart was standing on the sidewalk, quite close to the gate. It was covered with a cloth top, that concealed the interior. The driver was none other than the Crane, who quietly sat with the lines in hand, and his ugly knees nearly under his chin, the seat being low, and the Crane's legs being very long. Besides, his long back was bent, and his neck was stretched forward, so that his face appeared almost between his knees, which were separated, that the view might not be obstructed. There was an air of such profound self-importance in his face that if the fact had been heralded from the house-tops that the Crane knew a secret worth knowing, it could not have been plainer. If anybody had doubted for a moment that he was a dangerous man, and one whom it would be rashness to trifle with, it was necessary only to look at him, and see the invincible determination in his face, to have arrived at the conclusion that he was the most dangerous and reckless man in the world. And yet the Crane was not a bad man at heart, though he had been heard often to say that he had rather be a bad man than no man at all, like some people he knew; and even while he would on all occasions protest that he was not a dangerous man (unless it was in a good cause), and that he would shield with his strong right arm the weak and down-trodden (unless they were in the wrong, of course), he was, nevertheless, quite solicitous that extravagant ideas of his recklessness and courage and general depravity—such as is consistent with the vagaries of knight-errantry—should prevail. It gave him tone, he thought, and standing in the community. It made him a man feared of cowardly men, dreaded of bad men, respected of good men, and honored and worshiped afar of women, like a star. Rough and uncouth as he was, and devoid of every trace of refinement or education, he was contented with himself, as such men generally are, and even congratulated himself that he was himself, and not somebody else; for if he had been some one else, he could not have lived in such close communion with so dangerous and so reckless a man. At times he would relate the most blood-curdling stories of his past life—times when he would shoot at the drop of the hat, for the merest quibble in conventionalities; how he could get the drop on a dozen men at once, who were covering him with revolvers; women, who would act in the most unaccountable way, when he had given them no encouragement further than to barely speak to them, and whose husbands and fathers and brothers he respected too deeply to play them the villain. These stories he would retail to young girls and timid women, with the strictest injunction not to repeat them; and they would soon thereafter be discussed in mean little drinking saloons, and laughed at over a glass of beer. Thus the Crane was quite a character in town, and afforded no little amusement to the *coteries* of the saloons and engine-houses. But that the Crane had ever been guilty of a wrong, that he had ever killed a man, that he had ever brought desolation into a quiet and peaceful home, nobody ever believed. It sometimes happens, however, that people walk in their sleep, and that, while thus walking, they carry their dreams into action. The records of the penitentiaries, as well as those of the insane asylums, show that persons who dream a great deal—especially in daytime—may walk in their sleep, and sleep in their walk, and live among dreams and fantasies until their lives are colored with their dreams.

The Crane did not notice the women, so completely was he absorbed in his own reflections. Mrs. Howard's companion pointed down an alley running through the yard, and said:

"That's the jail wall—that high fence."

"I see."

A man was working vigorously at this wall, cutting a hole through with an auger and a saw. Three or four other men stood near, urging him to make haste. The roar of the mob in the next street deadened the noise they made.

"Who are they?" asked the mother, breathlessly.

The woman regarded her with a knowing leer.

"What are they doing?" cried the mother, choking with terror.

"Well, you know," answered the other, confidentially; "they've got the key—to the side door—of the Little Tank—where he is locked up—and they'll take him out—and—"

"And—what, woman?"

"—hang him."

The mother shuddered. This new danger was more startling than the other, for it was the work of cool and cowardly and silent determination—like the crawling of a snake that coils to spring. Her knees trembled, and the ground swam before her. Should she inform the police? No; for she could not approach them. Even should she succeed, her son would still be in the clutches of the law, and under the shadow of the scaffold. There would be time to raise the alarm, she thought, when a desperate resolution that she formed should fail of effect. It was evident that this part of the mob was working secretly, and that it was the intention of the men to hang him quietly, while Casserly was engaged in front.

"Let's help them hang him," said the mother.

"Oh, I couldn't," replied the woman, her eyes dilating with horror.

"Then, I will."

"How can you! How can you! Oh, you cruel, cruel, cruel woman! You are a bad, wicked woman!" cried the poor creature, her cheeks ashen with terror. Then she covered her face with her apron, and went into a house, crying bitterly.

Mrs. Howard approached the men with a firm step, and a strange light in her eyes.

"I want to pull on the rope," she said, almost choking.

The men regarded her with looks of astonishment.

"Go about your business," said one, firmly and kindly. "This is no place for a woman."

"I *shall* stay. Didn't he kill a woman? Oh, let me help you!"

Then the men looked serious. Naturally, a woman should have even a greater interest in this matter than a man. In any event, if a woman demanded vengeance, it was but right that a morsel of the feast should be set before her, garnished with choice ends of hemp, and sauce made of tears and blood.

"What would you do?" they asked.

"Anything—anything!" she cried; and her eyes suddenly glittered as the thought occurred to her as by inspiration: "Give me a knife; a long and sharp one; and I'll show you what a woman can do!"

"Would you?"

"Try me!"

"Here; take this one."

He handed her a long, keen hunting-knife. She received it, her hand slightly trembling; carefully examined the edge and the point, and placed it in her bosom, leaving the handle visible.

"You are a brave woman."

She made no reply. A brave woman, indeed!

"I'll tell you when to use the knife. You may help us, if you will."

The man who addressed her was evidently the leader. At the termination of this conversation the opening in the wall had been made. One by one the men crawled through. However, the last man experienced some difficulty in clearing the passage, by reason of a bulkiness about the waist which did not correspond with the general proportions of his body, as if the crime he contemplated settled in that portion of his person, producing inflammation. The leader, who had passed through, laughed softly at his embarrassment.

"Jim," he remarked, "it clings about you as though it had a fondness for you."

"Like a boa constrictor," suggested another.

"Is it crawling toward your neck, Jim?" asked a third.

The man did not seem to enjoy these jokes. The leader asked, "How long is it, Jim?"

"Fourteen feet."

"Pretty long, isn't it?"

"No; six for the drop, six for the stay, and two for the knot."

"Then you allow nothing for the guy."

"We can spare a foot of the knot."

"So? Inch and a quarter, is it, Jim?"

"No—inch."

"Inch! Why, inch and a quarter is regulation."

"Different States use different sizes. Tyburn has—"

"Listen!"

"It's nothing."

"But inch and a quarter is better style, Jim."

"Well, this will hold a hundred and fifty pounds on a six drop, without a fray."

"But there's no danger, anyhow. He won't drop, but will simply swing." This sagacious remark was made by one of the men, who had hitherto been silent, and it settled the question in favor of the rope.

The mother had, in the meantime, passed through the opening the last, and listened quietly to this conversation, which had been carried on hurriedly and in low tones, while the leader inserted a rusty key in the iron lock.

"Suppose the lock is stuck with rust," he suggested.

In fact, the key had already failed to turn. He removed it, and peered into the lock. Then he reinserted it, and tried it again, his face reddening with the effort he made, and again failed. At this he cursed.

"Are you sure this is the key?" he asked of one of the men.

"Certainly; I've had it ever since I was deputy here."

Another man stepped forward, inserted the barrel of his pistol in the key-bowl, and, with the powerful leverage thus obtained, turned the great key. Then they pulled upon the door by the key, but it required the united efforts of three men to force the door to yield. The grated door confronted them. This was unlocked and opened with ease.

The mother stepped backward toward the wall, and said in a low, earnest voice:

"I'll not go in till you bind and gag him. Be sure and gag him. Tell him you are friends, and then secure him; but don't hurt him—don't hurt him!"

They regarded her with some surprise and disgust. "Oh," she said, "I am brave;" and she drew the knife.

Hearing the noise, the prisoner, who was lying down in his cell, thinking the jailer was entering, remained quiet, until he saw strangers at his cell door. The light was very dim within to those who had left the bright day without; but they saw a tall young man, standing upright, and looking steadily at them. In his look there was no trace of fear, or suspicion, or surprise. He surveyed them calmly, and said nothing.

It was a momentary question with the leader whether he would take his man within the cell, or call him out. Certainly the latter course was the better, by reason of his advantage of sight in the darkness of the cell. But he did not require an invitation, for he stepped out, bareheaded and erect. He was extremely pale, but calm and collected; and it seemed that prison-damp had already stamped its greenish hue upon his face.

"Hello, my young friend," said the leader. "Keep quiet; we've come to take you away. Do you know what is going on?"

"No."

"There are two or three thousand men out there looking for you."

The opening of the prison-door had admitted the tumultuous noise of the riot; and this explanation of the leader was all that was necessary.

"What do they want?"

"To hang you."

This terrible news sent a shock, hardly perceptible, through the prisoner's frame; but he was immediately calm again, apparently susceptible of no emotion whatever. There was in his conduct something that needs to be mentioned. It was utter indifference of self. This is a condition of human nature that physicians hail with delight, but preachers dread and struggle against. In the one case it is life; in the other, death. Perhaps, if the truth were known, indifference, in its various forms of recklessness, carelessness, or what not, would be found at the root of every crime. Desperation is nearly like it, and suicide is synonymous with it. And doubtless there is not a single passion or sentiment but that, when stirred to its lowest depths, or expanded to its fullest limits, brings us all to this.

But, after all, is it not a kind of selfishness?—an egregious, overweening selfishness?—an utter disregard of whatever disastrous effect it may have on those near to us, and dear to us? As John Howard was indifferent, he was fearless. Perhaps if he had not been the one, he would not have been the other. Recklessness is another name for bravery.

"We have come to save you," continued the man. "But you'll have to do as we say. We must bind you and blindfold you. We are your friends. I know you are desperate, and may resist those who would save you. Submit quietly, then, and don't force us to extremes."

The prisoner regarded them with absolute contempt. They were not men of his class. He felt, in his blindness, a superiority to them in every element of manhood. Besides, he was possessed of that spirit of perverseness which was necessarily a concomitant of his present disposition—a spirit which, in kings, as history records, has more than once foundered an empire He said nothing, but assumed a defiant attitude; and, as the prospect of a struggle opened before him, he seemed to awake from his lethargy, eager to create danger where it might not exist, and to meet that danger with desperate calmness and resistance, if by so doing he could intensify it. So, be on your guard, gentlemen of the mob! You have against you one unarmed man, while you are five and armed to the teeth; but, for all that, have a care! The cause of a desperate man is to him a righteous cause. The eyes of the prisoner flashed, and his muscles knotted.

"You fool!" exclaimed the leader—a powerful man—as he sprang upon the prisoner.

But he found a strength equal to his own, and an agility that far surpassed his. The prisoner grappled with him, twisted him like a reed, and dashed him to the floor. The four other men encircled him. He struck right and left, and sprang about like a panther, now getting in their clutches, then slipping dexterously away and tripping them. It was a quiet struggle. Some blood was beginning to flow from blows he had struck like thunderbolts, and then they overpowered him, and bore him down, his muscles violently quivering with the superhuman strength he put forth in resistance. Then, as his breast heaved with rage, nature asserted itself, and he uttered a piercing cry of despair.

Quiet there, boy! You have a friend without, whose horrified glance has followed every movement; whose heart is bursting for you—a friend truer than heaven, boy, for she will never desert you.

The men were muttering curses, as they pressed him upon the floor. The mother rushed into the Tank. A cruel sight there awaited her. One man was binding his feet, another his hands, and a third was thrusting a gag into his mouth.

The woman crept forward and peered into her son's upturned face. It was the cry that aroused her, but he could utter no sound now. Acute suffering appeared about her eyes and mouth, and raised great ridges in her forehead; while the intense pain the prisoner experienced from the gag, which was thrust far down, made the tears start to his eyes, and his features twitch convulsively. He saw her, and recognised her. Through all his suffering there appeared unbounded astonishment, and a look so intense that it pierced her heart like a knife. It was an appealing look—a look of deprecation—a look of supplication—that went down into her very soul, and stirred up all the mother there. Angered and excited, the man who managed the gag thrust it still farther down, and the pain was unbearable.

"You are pressing it down too hard. Stop! you hurt him," exclaimed the mother.

"What!" replied the man, angrily. "We want no chicken-hearted women here."

With that he gave the gag another thrust, and the prisoner writhed in agony and cast an imploring look upon his mother, while his face became discolored with suffocation.

Suddenly, overcome by an impulse that nothing could restrain, maddened and furious, the woman drew the knife, and, with distended nostrils and grinding teeth, struck desperately and with all her strength.

"Take care there!" cried one of the men as, with blanched face, he caught her arm and stared at her. "If that knife," he continued, slowly and threateningly, "had come down it would have gone into—the wrong man's back."

He held her firmly; her muscles relaxed; her face became crimson. Then he released her arm, which fell limp to her side.

"I was excited," she stammered.

"Be more careful in future, then."

They loosened the gag, dragged him out, and placed him in the bottom of the butcher's cart.

"What are you going to do with him?" asked the mother, with tremulous voice.

"We'll string him from the beam of the old San José Theatre."

He heard this, lying within, but not a groan escaped him. Since the gag had been released, he had remained perfectly quiet and submissive, trusting all to his mother. She felt this, and it strengthened her.

"Let me and the driver hang him alone."

"Why, the Crane would faint."

At this, the insulted Crane peered around, and looked quite desperate and dangerous. The mother's quick glance drilled him through, and a look of satisfaction, tinged with a single bright ray of hope, lighted up her face. She urged the point so strenuously, and seemed so determined to take a prominent part in this fearful avenging of outraged society, that the men, who really dreaded the consequences of their contemplated act of violence, finally yielded, and threw the rope into the cart. Men must be in great numbers to retain for any length of time the fury that leads to the lamp-post, unless sacred rights of their own have been invaded.

Before climbing upon the seat the woman said, "Gentlemen, you have done me a great favor. We may meet again."

She was perfectly calm, and the men saw she was very handsome. They told her they would be in the street to see the hanging. Afterward, when they had more time for reflection, they wondered why they had taken a woman into the crime; and one man even went so far—and they laughed at him for it—as to say that somehow or other he had a faint remembrance that the prisoner and the woman resembled each other. As they were driving away, she asked:

"Gentlemen, who are you?"

A quick look passed from one to another. The leader replied:

"A hundred citizens."

Casserly went immediately to the scene of the hanging. Despite the immense throng that crowded the street, a great and oppressive quiet was over all. Strong men looked at the hanging body, and went away, sick and faint.

A man was ahead of Casserly, for when the latter reached the spot, this man, all alone, stood upon the platform beneath the beam. He placed one arm around the body and held it, while he cut the rope. Whether it was accidental or intentional, he allowed the body, when the rope was severed, to slip from his grasp and fall over the railing. It struck the ground with a dull thud, almost at Casserly's feet. A horrified shivering seized the crowd. Casserly stepped forward, knelt beside it, placed his hands upon it, and then hastily rose, his face crimson with rage.

"Casserly," said Judge Simon, laying his hand timidly on Casserly's arm.

"Bah!" exclaimed Casserly, with profound disgust.

"What's the matter, Casserly?"

"He's gone! That thing is stuffed with straw!"

CHAPTER VIII.

They found the mother at her home, sitting quietly beside the bed on which her dead charge lay. Her toilet was perfect. As Casserly, accompanied by Judge Simon and the Coroner, entered, she rose with the old queenly grace and dignity, and invited them to seats, which she placed for them, with an unconsciously sweet and winning manner that impressed Judge Simon very strongly. He could not realize the fact that this was the woman of such desperate courage and cunning, so calm was she, and so soft of step and graceful of manner. But he saw what Casserly could not see, that there were deep cares and anxieties in her face; but they were almost hidden from view by a look of triumph, which glowed with suppressed intensity.

As Garratt was the only one with whom she was acquainted, he introduced the others. Casserly felt very ill at ease. The woman's tenderness and refinement placed a barrier between him and her, while they drew Judge Simon toward her, and he became her friend instinctively. Casserly's awkwardness seemed to him to obtrude itself, and proclaim itself aloud, that she might see it the more easily, and scorn him for it. He was a kind-hearted man—brutality was foreign to his nature; for, had he been otherwise, he could not have perceived the difference. With things that came to his understanding by mental processes, he was slow of comprehension, but of whatever came by way of the heart, or feeling, or whatever may be termed the finer instincts of human nature, he grasped the meaning readily. Knowing what she had done, and what she was capable of doing, Casserly felt himself a great child in her presence. He had not yet a sufficient knowledge of criminal matters to know that a woman may outwit the shrewdest detective skill, where a man would be caught in the simplest snare. Is there in this fact the shadow of a possibility that, as hypocrisy and cunning go hand in hand, women are naturally greater hypocrites than men?—or, perhaps, more successful in hypocrisy? Casserly was learning, however; but still, had he been a greater rascal he would have been a better detective.

Casserly and Judge Simon had settled between them these propositions: That the young man's flight was, under the circumstances, no further evidence of his guilt; that, after all, he was, possibly, not the real criminal. Then, assuming that he was not, who was? Evidently the fugitive girl, or the mother herself. It appeared as reasonable to suppose that Howard would sacrifice himself, if need be, for the one as readily as for the other—provided he loved the girl, or, provided further, that he did not love her, but loved the girl who was dead, and cared no longer for his own life. Thus it will be seen that unless some starting-point could be discovered, there was no foundation whatever on which to build a theory, and they were as far from the truth as ever. One gloomy fact stared Casserly in the face: the crime must be ferreted out. It seemed a hopeless undertaking unless the girl could be found. Every effort had been put forth to secure this end. Constables, sheriffs, policemen, in addition to thousands of persons who constituted themselves detectives wherever the news had penetrated, were watching closely and carefully. There is a kind of glory attaching to participation in the capture of a criminal that makes every man, woman, and child an informant to the death on an unfortunate fellow-being; and yet, but point to blood on the informant's hands when the deed is done, and you horrify him. It is there, however, in ugly patches, covering the hand and arm to the elbow, constantly defiling with its loathsomeness everything pure that it touches, crying aloud with a hundred thousand tongues the old, old story of inhumanity. Here is one definition of "Society must be protected": vindictiveness must be satisfied.

It had become a fixed idea in Casserly's mind, under Judge Simon's instruction, that the girl must be found—that possibly she was the criminal.

The inquest remained—and who would testify? The mother. The whole case was in her hands. She could make any statement of alleged facts that suited her ends. It even seemed that the white sheet covering the lifeless girl was the window to the secret chamber in which the mystery was concealed; that the folds, which were very plainly visible, composed the sash, and that the panes had been very thickly coated with white paint, that no glance could penetrate.

"Madam," said Casserly, "where is your son?"

He knew well enough that he was wasting words. She replied:

"I do not know."

"Is he the guilty party?"

She betrayed no excitement, nor surprise, nor anoyance, but trifled with some ornament upon her wrist, and did not raise her eyes or answer the question. Casserly waited some moments. At length she asked:

"He said he was, I believe?"

"Yes; but he did it in such a way as to leave some doubt about it. He did, however, madam, in a moment of excited passion—and, besides, he was under the influence of liquor—say something that forces me to do a very disagreeable thing."

He paused. She continued to play with the gold ornament, and seemed to take no interest whatever in his recital.

"There are, besides, some corroborative circumstances. While he was sitting with me in the police office the confession was on his tongue, but I unconsciously broke it off by telling him I already knew of the affair, and had sent two officers to the house. Now, he did not complete his confession until the officers returned, for he evidently expected some one with them."

Still she continued to play with the bracelet, and did not raise her eyes or say a word.

"Madam," he continued, "why did you go so quietly down those stairs and turn out the hall lamp?"

She raised her eyes, and regarded him long and earnestly. She must have felt surprise at this revelation, but she did not exhibit any. Her look was one of calm and forgiving reproach, and it had a powerful effect upon Casserly, who felt that it said: "Poor fellow, you are trying to do your duty, but you are beyond your depth. I, a woman, am deeper than a thousand like you, Casserly. You are a mere boy, Casserly, and I really wish you were older, that you might be on a footing with a woman. Would you tear the secret out of my heart, Casserly? Would you put a mask over your stupid soul, and become a burglar, and, armed with a jack-knife or a nail, essay to penetrate through a wall of steel and stone a hundred feet in thickness?"

"Do you decline to answer the question, madam?"

"Mr. Casserly, what do you expect?"

"The truth."

"Ah!" and she dropped her eyes, and resumed her toying with the bracelet.

"Casserly," said Garratt, "it seems to me that one thing is quite plain: if Mrs. Howard believed her son innocent, she would not have effected his escape, but would have trusted to truth."

"But what about accomplices?" asked Casserly, looking steadily at the woman.

To his utter surprise, when he thought this shot would strike straight home, she remained perfectly quiet. After reflecting a moment, Casserly asked, "Did the dead girl love him?"

"Oh, yes. They were brought up together from childhood. A sister could not have been more tender than she, nor a brother more considerate than he."

"You misunderstand me, madam—purposely, I fear."

"Indeed, Mr. Casserly!"

"I did not mean the love of a sister."

"Oh, I could not see into the poor child's heart."

"But you know, madam."

She simply shrugged her shoulders. Thus was this painful conversation kept up at some length, and nothing was learned.

"Madam," said Casserly, at last, "I referred just now to a painful duty I had to perform. I must arrest you."

She did not raise her eyes.

"On suspicion," continued Casserly.

She gave no evidence of emotion.

"You must come with me to the jail."

She quietly rose from her chair. It seemed that she was not near so strong as she was, for there was a slight tremulous movement of her knees. But her face was very, very calm—so quietly at rest that it was painful to look upon. There was not a thought in her eyes. Even the look of triumph had faded away or had died, and was buried in her heart as a grave. Thus looks the loving wife when she receives the first blow in cruelty from her husband. It was the old look of friendlessness with which her son had peered through the grating of his cell at the blank wall beyond. There was no appeal—only rest, absolute rest, and nothing more, and much like the rest that death brings. But death were far better than the calm which, in life, causes such a look as that.

She mechanically put something on her head, and then, as she was about to pass through the door, she bethought herself, and went back to kiss the dead girl.

"Will you take care of her for me?" she asked, in a voice that was all a mother's.

"Certainly, madam," replied Casserly.

Then she remembered something else, and stepped before Casserly, facing him. In a very sweet and winning and submissive manner, as a sick child who takes his bitter potion with a smile, she held out her hands together toward Casserly, and said, softly and kindly:

"Here. You always handcuff them, don't you?"

Casserly's face flushed crimson.

"Not you, madam, not you," he said, hurriedly, as he gently pushed her hands aside and led the way.

What, Judge Simon! Is that a tear on your withered old cheek? Fie on you! There, brush it away quickly, sir, for some one may see it.

Chapter IX.

It is quite beyond the power of this old-fashioned history—and, by the way, as it *is* old-fashioned, it is often inclined to be pedantic, in quite a droll manner, as old-fashioned things and people generally are—to state with any certainty that Emily Randolph, the fugitive girl, was pretty; and in this assertion an attempt is made to lay aside all taint of pedantry. But, from an old-fashioned standpoint, and on antiquated grounds, and by rules so antagonistic to this age of advancement that they never saw crinoline nor *crême de lis*, it will be stated that she was very pretty indeed—that is, she was plain, which in one sense means about the same thing. It is a common expression that such and such a woman is so "homely" that it—the "homeliness"—must cause her physical pain. On the same principle, beautiful women must live in a state of physical ecstasy; and they generally do. But it is a law of our nature that we tire of extremes, as we see them to be such from our standpoint; and carrying this idea a step farther, are there not times in the life of a beautiful woman when she deplores her own comeliness, as plain women fret over their plainness? The sum total of life is an average. In it there are not separate columns for love, and for sickness, and for sorrow, and for joy; but Time strikes a balance, which is the result of all combined. Wealth in one direction is poverty in another; poverty in one direction is wealth in another. If your appearance, young lady, is in easy circumstances, your disposition also is very apt to be. You had better be an humble violet than a rose with a thorn. For when a handsome woman has outlived her beauty, it is too late—too late—to learn charms and graces of the heart.

Emily Randolph was a violet—a very sweet and tender violet. There was in her appearance such an appeal to stronger natures that any great tall man, with broad shoulders and the strength of an ox, would feel an impulse to stand between her and the rough buffetings of the world, and with his strength turn the storm aside as if it were a bagatelle. When this should be accomplished, his next impulse would be to address her by all manner of senseless pet names; and then take her for a stroll, and be very wise and very fatherly; then he would buy for her some sweetmeats at a confectioner's, and leave her at her door, a virtuous and self-contented man. When he would awake in the morning, it would be to two facts—first, that it was broad day; second, that he was desperately in love with her.

As a rule, brunettes are small, and sharp, and quick, and—treacherous; while blondes are generally large, and handsome, and slow, and good-natured.

There are not many men and women in the civilized world who have not been boys and girls—barring the generation that is just approaching maturity. When thus of tender years, there are very few who did not, on some bright day, see sparkling in the grass, a short distance away, the rarest and most brilliant diamond in the world. Then it suddenly disappeared, as the line of light was lost; but the eager child sought the ray again. He moved his head to the right, to the left—now up, now down—until he found it. Keeping his head quite steady, that he might not lose the ray again, he crept cautiously forward, being compelled to bring his head nearer and nearer the ground, until he was forced to fall on his hands and knees, and thus crawl onward until his face was almost in the grass. Then he reached out and caught up the precious gem, to find that it was only a very mean and ugly little piece of glass. Had he been older, he would have known that diamonds never glitter in their natural state, and that he might walk over acres strewn with them, and never know one was there. Somebody once said that this is a world of disappointments; in reality, it is a world of childish ignorance.

Emily Randolph was a blonde; but she was quite a small and fragile blonde, as if her sire apologized for her complexion. She was twenty years of age, though she looked younger, and was made up of the most demure little womanly ways, and the most charming little affectations, and the most feminine graces. She seemed quite a child; but, at the same time, you would not have been one whit surprised to see her wearing spectacles and a cap, and having several of her grandchildren climbing all over her.

Yet, with all her loveliness, the men who could appreciate and love her are rare. John Howard was such a man.

On the third day after the riot, she was walking alone in the terraced grounds of a comfortable home at Santa Cruz. The owners of the place were old friends of Mrs. Howard, who had sent her thither. The girl was in profound ignorance of the startling events that had transpired in San José. She did not know, even, that Howard had surrendered himself, nor that his mother was in prison; for she had borne a hastily written note to Mrs. Howard's friend, telling him earnestly to conceal from the girl all knowledge of transpiring events; so that when, in her deep distress and anxiety, she begged for tidings, they told her to be patient—that all would come right. On her own part, the child, in strict obedience to a solemn injunction from Mrs. Howard, refused to say anything whatever of what she might have known about the tragedy. Rather than divulge this knowledge, she would have had her tongue torn out, after so solemn a request. She had been kept very close in the house, and sometimes seemed impatient of restraint, and expressed some wonder that she was treated thus. Nevertheless, they guarded her closely; for, from what they learned from Mrs. Howard's note and from the newspapers, her testimony would tie the rope around John Howard's neck.

It is true that they did not press her with questions, for they dreaded the result; but it is equally true that a little pardonable curiosity—especially as the whole matter was shrouded in such deep mystery—prompted some members of this quiet family to leave the way open for any hint that she might drop. Still, she religiously held her tongue.

And it was noticed that she was very sad and gloomy. At times she would start from her sleep with a piercing scream, and cry, "John!" in the most pitiful, pleading voice. But on other occasions she was quite calm, and always bowed down with grief.

On the third day—Tuesday—she was walking alone on the terraced grounds, and, feeling weary and lonely, seated herself on the steps leading to the first terrace from the street. Thus concealed from the house, she was dreamily looking over the town, and watching an engine that moved up and down upon the railroad. Mingled with the noise it made, came faintly the roar of the breakers.

Suddenly her heart leaped violently to see a man in imminent danger of being run down by the engine. However, he stepped from the track just in time, receiving no other injury than the maledictions of the engineer. In her anxiety, she stood straight up, and ran down the steps to the gate. Tender-hearted as she was, she would have been the first to reach the mangled body. By some special providence, there sometimes seems to be a great amount of heart in very small bodies.

The man evidently saw her, for he came straight toward her. Then she was embarrassed, and turned to leave. What was her astonishment to hear the man call:

"Miss Emily!"

Greatly startled—for the man was a stranger—she turned around to look at him, and found he had arrived at the gate.

"Did you call me?" she asked, timidly.

"Yes. I have something to tell you."

"About—about— Who sent you?"

"Never mind that, my child; don't be alarmed—I'll not harm you."

In truth, the man's face bore a kindly look that reassured her.

"Do you know what terrible things have happened since Rose Howard was killed?"

The girl became as pale as death.

"No," she exclaimed. "They—they—never told me."

"You didn't know John Howard was arrested for the murder?"

Her eyes opened wide with astonishment; and the man saw that the beating of her heart, as he entered the gate, was so violent that the throbbing was painfully visible in her throat.

"Arrested!" she exclaimed, hardly able to control her voice. "Arrested! What do you mean!"

"It is the truth, my child. Now listen carefully. He denied it, but after a time, when he thought he was going to be lynched by the mob, he admitted that he knew who did commit the murder."

She regarded him with so much pain and astonishment that he almost wavered from his object. He drew a paper from his pocket, on the back of which, folded, was printed in black type the word:

"WARRANT."

"He told who it was," continued the man. "I advise you to make a full confession, and keep nothing back. It will go easier with you. You are so young, and such a child—"

He was startled at her appearance. As the meaning of his terrible words dawned upon her, her eyes flashed with indignation and anger. Then this look faded away, and gave place to deathly pallor.

"Tell me all about why you did it, and how. It will be far better for you. You no doubt had good cause. Tell me."

She was becoming very weak and faint.

"Did he tell you that?" she asked, in a choking whisper, no longer able to speak aloud.

"Yes. Tell me all, now."

She looked around in a frightened, uncertain way, and her bosom heaved, and her breath came in gasps. Then she sank down upon the steps, and crouched down very low and humbly, and sobbed as though her heart were broken, murmuring convulsively between her sobs:

"Oh, John, how could you! How could you, John!"

"My child," said Casserly, kindly, "keep a brave heart, and tell me all."

But she continued to sob, and could say only, "Oh, John! How could you, John!"

"You must come with me, my child. Keep a stout heart now, like the brave little woman you are. I hate to do it, but I must arrest you for the murder of Rose Howard."

"John! John! how could you, John!"

He picked her up gently, and led her up the steps to the house. She sobbed all the time, and clung closely to his arm, as if he were her protector, and the only friend she had in the world. This nearly broke Casserly's heart.

As the evening train bore them to San José, Casserly imagined he heard a hundred voices—some in heaven, and some under the ground, and others far, far away—crying in despairing, heart-broken tones:

"How could you, John! Oh, John, how could you!" W. C. MORROW.

[CONTINUED IN NEXT NUMBER.]

THE VOYAGE OF JUAN DE FUCA A FRAUD.

In the memorable canvass which resulted in the election of President Polk, the title to Oregon and its area entered largely into the speeches of political orators. The shibboleth of Democracy was "Fifty-four forty or fight." The writer, then a youth, zealously espoused the opinion that the United States was the sole owner of *Oregon*, north to the Russian line. A few years later, Oregon became his adopted home.

The ideas formed during youth, amid the excitement of political contest, were intensified in their Americanism by subsequent reading of speeches in Congress, the more dispassionate State papers of the able negotiators, and numerous works upon the Territory; in short, the writer was a thorough disciple of the *ultra* American view. The faith was abiding that the Spanish claim, by right of discovery to the north-west coast (of which the United States had become assignee, by the Florida Convention of 1819), reached north till it met the Russian line.

Among the discoveries accepted as established was that Juan de Fuca, in 1592, while in the service of Spain, had entered what is now known as the Strait of Juan de Fuca. To a resident upon Puget Sound, how pride-provoking the thought that the country had been visited by white men away back in those primitive years! Thus the impulsive impressions of boyhood, educated as years advanced by an American system of reading, matured into *belief*, rounded into the *conviction* of manhood. To the writer, Juan de Fuca was a hero, a discoverer of unknown lands and seas; his voyage a reality—a valuable *fact* supporting territorial right. The Treaty of Limits, of June 15, 1846, did not fully determine the Oregon boundary. While there remained matter of controversy, a too natural prejudice against yielding territory to a rival nation reconciled a continuance of such belief. Until 1872, when Emperor William finally traced the north-west boundary between the United States and Great Britain, De Fuca's claim continued to be relied upon despite its inconsistencies. Through all those years—a generation almost—it had proved a pleasure to champion the so-called Greek pilot and his voyage; to claim credibility for his voucher and journalist, Michael Lock the elder, he who had been English Consul at Aleppo and enjoyed the intimate friendship of Richard Hakluyt, the distinguished geographer and naval historian. The belief, strengthened by the desire, was entertained that the inland waters of Washington Territory had been visited in the sixteenth century by a Spanish expedition; that through such discovery Spain had acquired the sole right to the region and had transferred such right to the United States, thereby fortifying the claim of the latter in its controversy with Great Britain. Hope, stimulated by national bias, was the "wish" becoming "father to the thought," and it proved all-sufficient to cause credence in Lock's story.

But truth, the great iconoclast, asserts its prerogative; relentlessly it demolishes the idols of youthful fancy as it sweeps away the ideals of manhood. The test of Pacific Coast history has been its very uncertainty, amounting in several instances to mystification. The doubt which surrounds the names, *California*, *Oregon*, and *Juan de Fuca*, illustrates this feature. Who will dissipate the spell and say where and when originated and what signify the names California and Oregon? Spanish words which compound into a "heated furnace," or "big ears," were not ascribed to the respective regions by Spanish geographers, nor were such peculiarities of climate or appearance of natives by them chronicled. The world has not yet learned the etymology, origin, or meaning of either word. Associate "big ears" with Bryant's immortal line, "Where rolls the Oregon," and how quickly the mind in disgust is reminded that "ignorance is bliss." Knowledge at once would banish all the poetry from Bryant's beautiful thought. No; rather "Oregon" remain meaningless than to be a synonym to call to mind the chief peculiarity of a very useful animal. Nor is it likely to be known why Lock's Greek pilot transmitted his euphonious name of Apostolos Valerianus into harsh and grating Juan de Fuca.

That story of Lock, that pretended voyage to the Strait of Anian, for whatever purpose invented, has run its course. At birth discredited, after the lapse of two centuries, when almost forgotten, the story was resuscitated. At the close of the eighteenth century there were those ready to reconcile discrepancies, to explain away inconsistencies, to claim that the voyage and its hero had been entities. In the present age, as knowledge and science assert their mastery, fabulous claims cannot stand in the light of investigation. Juan de Fuca, as a historic character, and his alleged voyage, have again returned to share the fate to which many consigned them at the origin of the story—to companionship with the mythical Strait of Anian and the fabulous voyages claimed to have been made through it from the Atlantic to the Pacific Ocean.

The *hope* that such strait existed stimulated voyages of discovery to the North Pacific. Lock's narrative had an influence. There were many geographers and navigators who credited the claim of De Fuca, who more firmly believed in the existence of the Strait of Anian, who accepted as probable the location he had assigned. Doubtless, it proved an agency which contributed to science, which added geographic knowledge. Its greatest *prestige*, perhaps, accrued from the fact that the illustrious Captain Cook considered it quite worth while to seek for the strait in the latitude in which De Fuca's story had placed it. As no strait was there found, importance attached to Lock's account by Cook denying that any strait existed where De Fuca had alleged it was. Cook at least conceded that the voyage possibly had been made, and that there was no physical reason why the story should not be believed. The idea upon which the story was founded, interoceanic connection, had lived until the British Government resolved to ascertain its truth or falsity. To that end was selected the most distinguished geographer of that day, England's most intrepid scientific navigator. Along with him were Burney and Vancouver, who early afterward acquired a fame almost equal to that of their illustrious chief. Despite Cook's weighty contradiction, navigators still wistfully looked in that vicinity for the supposed strait. Within a decade from the time Cook had seemingly forever set at rest De Fuca's claim, Berkly and Mears gave to it renewed vitality by establishing the existence of the large arm of sea a single degree of latitude north of De Fuca's location of the Strait of Anian. Mears not only attested his own faith—he vouched for the truthfulness of Lock's account, the integrity of De Fuca's claim. He redeemed from obloquy the name and voyage of De Fuca. He proceeded to examine the waters and adjacent shores, and volunteered the statement, "Juan de Fuca was the original discoverer of the strait." Exulting that he had found what had escaped the observation of Captain Cook, he controverted that great authority. Generously he acknowledged his faith in Lock's Greek pilot. He says: "We arrived at the entrance of the great inlet, which appeared to be twelve or fourteen leagues wide. From the mast-head it was observed to stretch to the east by the north, and a clear and unbounded horizon was seen in this direction as far as the eye could reach. The strongest curiosity impelled us to enter this strait, *which we shall call by the name of its original discoverer, John de Fuca.*"

A broad arm of ocean within a degree of latitude of De Fuca's alleged Strait of Anian was, to say the least, a remarkable coincidence. Take into consideration such coincidence, the early date of the voyage, the rude appliances likely to have been on so small a vessel, his own want of scientific qualification, the narration made in a foreign tongue to a foreigner, who afterward published a translation, and there is much to account for that narrative finding believers after Mears's voyage had been published. This tribute of Captain Mears contributed greatly to strengthen De Fuca's claim. It was the acknowledgment by a navigator of a rival nation present in those seas, then disputing the pretensions of Spain, based upon priority of voyages to those coasts. Mears, in the nomination by him of the strait, asserted that De Fuca and his voyage were verities. At the close of the eighteenth century Lock's narrative found a voucher in an intelligent officer of the British navy. Mears renewed the assertion that there is upon the north-west coast of America an inlet of sea, which Lock referred to, and which, in honor of its "original discoverer, has been named the Strait of John de Fuca."

At the very threshold of the nineteenth century that voyage became a factor in the controversy as to the ownership of Oregon. English authority in 1596 asserted that the voyage had been made in 1592. When the strait had acquired a fixed location upon the map of the world, English authority proclaimed that its original discoverer had been Juan de Fuca, while serving Spain. Its political importance hinged upon "whether Sir Francis Drake, in 1579, had reached the north-west coast of America in 48° north latitude, or whether he had, upon reaching 43° north, then turned southward;" for it must be remembered that the two contemporaneous publications of Drake's piratical cruise thus differ. On the authority of *The World Encompassed*, the name of the former, Great Britain attempted to break the entirety and force of Spanish claim (urged by the United States) to a high northern latitude, by claiming that Sir Francis Drake, in 48° north, discovered and named the coast *New Albion*. Now, if Drake's highest northing was 43°, as stated in the *Famous Voyage*, and the name *New Albion* was ascribed by Sir Francis to the bluff shores adjacent to the Bay of Sir Francis Drake, and De Fuca, in the Spanish service, did sail inland in the strait bearing his name, then the Spanish claim, under which the United States were asserting right, was good by virtue of De Fuca's discovery to the territories lying upon that inland sea.

At this day it will not be gainsaid that De Fuca's alleged voyage, based alone, as it is, upon English authority, is quite as believable as that Sir Francis Drake saw any part of the north-west coast north of 43° north latitude. Interest or national prejudice having ceased to cloud the result of investigation, those cobwebs which, as a gauze, cover, but fail to conceal, the reality of fact, are brushed away, and truth appears. The respective claims of Great Britain and the United States now adjusted, it is no longer of practical moment whether there ever was such a personage as Juan de Fuca, or whether such a voyage was made.

Lock's narrative, so often referred to, aptly illustrates the period in which it was penned. Its reproduction may, perhaps, amuse, its crude ideas of geography invite reflection. Here it is, as extracted from the *Pilgrims*, published in 1625, by Samuel Purchas:

ORIGINAL ACCOUNT OF THE VOYAGE OF THE GREEK PILOT, JUAN DE FUCA, ALONG THE NORTH-WEST COAST OF AMERICA IN 1592.

A Note made by me, Michael Lock the elder, touching the Strait of Sea commonly called Fretum Anian, *in the South Sea, through the North-west Passage of* Meta Incognita.

When I was at *Venice*, in April, 1596, haply arrived there an old man, about sixty years of age, called, commonly, *Juan de Fuca*, but named properly *Apostolos Valerianus*, of nation a Greek, born in *Cephalonia*, of profession a mariner, and an ancient pilot of ships. This man, being come lately out of Spain, arrived first at *Leghorn*, and went thence to *Florence*, where he found one John Douglas, an Englishman, a famous mariner, ready coming for *Venice*, to be pilot of a Venetian ship for England, in whose company they came both together to *Venice*. And John Douglas being acquainted with me before, he gave me knowledge of this Greek pilot, and brought him to my speech; and, in long talks and conference between us, in presence of John Douglas, this Greek pilot declared, in the Italian and Spanish languages, thus much in effect as followeth:—

First, he said that he had been in the West Indies of Spain forty years, and had sailed to and from many places thereof, in the service of the Spaniards.

Also, he said that he was in the Spanish ship which, in returning from the Islands *Philippinas*, towards *Nova Spania*, was robbed and taken at the *Cape California* by *Captain Candish*, Englishman, whereby he lost sixty thousand ducats of his own goods.

Also, he said that he was pilot of three small ships which the viceroy of *Mexico* sent from *Mexico*, armed with one hundred men, under a captain, Spaniards, to discover the *Straits of Anian*, along the coast of the *South Sea*, and to fortify in that strait, to resist the passage and proceedings of the English nation, which were feared to pass through those straits into the *South Sea*; and that, by reason of a mutiny which happened among the soldiers for the misconduct of their captain, that voyage was overthrown, and the ship returned from *California* to *Nova Spania*, without anything done in that voyage; and that, after their return, the captain was at *Mexico* punished by justice.

Also, he said that, shortly after the said voyage was so ill ended, the said viceroy of *Mexico* sent him out again, in 1592, with a small caravel and a pinnace, armed with mariners only, to follow the said voyage for the discovery of the *Straits of Anian*, and the passage thereof into the sea, which they called the *North Sea*, which is our north-west sea; and that he followed his course, in that voyage, west and north-west in the *South Sea*, all along the coast of *Nova Spania*, and *California*, and the *Indies*, now called *North America* (all which voyage he signified to me in a great map, and a sea card of mine own, which I laid before him), until he came to the latitude of 47 degrees; and that there finding that the land trended north and north-east, with a broad inlet of sea, between 47 and 48 degrees of latitude, he entered thereinto, sailing therein more than twenty days, and found that land trending still sometime north-west, and north-east, and north, and also east and south-eastward, and very much broader sea than was at the said entrance, and that he passed by divers islands in that sailing; and that, at the entrance of this said strait, there is, on the north-west coast thereof, a great headland or island, with an exceeding high pinnacle, or spired rock, like a pillar, thereupon.

Also, he said that he went on land in divers places, and that he saw some people on land clad in beasts' skins; and that the land is very fruitful, and rich of gold, silver, pearls, and other things, like *Nova Spania*.

And also, he said that he being entered thus far into the said strait, and being come into the North Sea already, and finding the sea wide enough every where, and to be about thirty or forty leagues wide in the mouth of the straits where he entered, he thought he had now well discharged his office; and that, not being armed to resist the force of the savage people that might happen, he therefore set sail, and returned homewards again toward *Nova Spania*, where he arrived at *Acapulco*, anno 1592, hoping to be rewarded by the viceroy for this service done in the said voyage.

Also, he said that, after coming to *Mexico*, he was greatly welcomed by the viceroy, and had promises of great reward; but that, having sued there two years, and obtained nothing to his content, the viceroy told him that he should be rewarded in Spain, of the king himself, very greatly, and willed him, therefore, to go to Spain, which voyage he did perform.

Also, he said that when he was come into Spain, he was welcomed there at the king's court; but, after long suit there also, he could not get any reward there to his content; and therefore, at length, he stole away out of Spain, and came into Italy, to go home again and live among his own kindred and countrymen, being very old.

Also, he said that he thought the cause of his ill reward had of the Spaniards, to be for that they did understand very well that the English nation had now given over all their voyages for discovery of the north-west passage; wherefore they need not fear them any more to come that way into the *South Sea*, and therefore they needed not his service therein any more.

Also, he said that, understanding the noble mind of the queen of England, and of her wars against the Spaniards, and hoping that her majesty would do him justice for his goods lost by Captain Candish, he would be content to go into England, and serve her majesty in that voyage for the discovery perfectly of the north-west passage into the *South Sea*, if she would furnish him only one ship of forty tons' burden, and a pinnace, and that he would perform it in thirty days' time, from one end to the other of the strait, and he willed me so to write to England.

Substantially, the *entire* claim of De Fuca has been here presented. Here is the only evidence upon which rests his alleged discovery. The voyage—how and when performed, the result, the treatment by his alleged employer, the explanation of too early presence thereafter in Venice, the alleged repudiation of the claim for service urged at Mexico and Madrid, are made the foundation of appeal for English aid. An attempt to excite British jealousy against Spain, and an invoking of sympathy for losses sustained by De Fuca at the hands of Sir Thomas Candish, the renowned English pirate, upon whom the honors of knighthood had been conferred for his successful ravishment of Spanish commerce, are the stimulants upon which Lock and De Fuca, both or either, expect profit. But Lock's story was not extensively credited. Like other narratives of voyages to the unknown North Pacific in search of the Strait of Anain, it kept alive the idea that the great *desideratum* in navigation and commerce might be realized—that a strait of sea existed connecting the two oceans, furnishing a direct transit across the North American Continent. The absence of records in Spain or Mexico to corroborate Lock's account serves to discredit it. In 1584, Gali, returning from Macao to Mexico, approached and saw the north-west coast in a high northern latitude. In 1596, Viscaino (in three vessels), after most extensive preparations for a North Pacific exploration, sailed as far north as La Paz, when he ingloriously returned, the voyage proving a signal failure. Is it not singular that De Fuca in 1596 (though not published till 1625), should claim that he had *piloted* a few years previously an expedition consisting of *three* vessels, which was a failure? No other similar expedition left Mexico about that period, and this unsuccessful voyage of Viscaino was the year when Lock alleges he met De Fuca at Venice. Between 1584 and 1596, we have no record of any Spanish expeditions being fitted out in Mexico for the North Pacific. Again, it was in 1588 that Candish burned the Spanish galleon *Santa Alta* off Cape San Lucas. De Fuca claimed to have lost sixty thousand ducats by that disaster. Had a person who made the discovery or voyage that De Fuca claims to have made been a passenger on the captured ship, the world would have some authentic record of such fact. But as it is, the fact that between 1588 and 1596, no Spanish expedition sailed from Mexico, it follows that he did not serve as pilot, nor as commander. Had any Spanish voyage resulted in so important a discovery as Lock describes, it would have been entirely unnecessary for Lock to repeat it as derived from a stranger on the streets of Venice. It is simply impossible that Juan de Fuca should have sailed from Mexico in

1592 to the strait upon which Mears conferred his name.

The inconsistencies of the account are patent and glaring. Had De Fuca ever seen the strait, or its shores, or its native population, he never would have dictated the fable which Lock has fathered. The configuration of the land, the number of the natives and their attire, the gold, silver, and pearls, the width of the strait, its extent, shore line, indeed no peculiarity therein ascribed to the inlet, can now be identified in the Strait of Juan de Fuca and its surroundings. Modern geography brands as false every feature of the Lock description; thousands of living witnesses attest that it can have no application to the shores of the Strait of Juan de Fuca, or to the natives of northern Washington or Vancouver's Island. The English Government paid no attention to Lock's appeal in behalf of his hero, his so-called Greek pilot, who had lost his ducats. Mentioned only by contemporary writers, without additional particulars to corroborate it until Cook's third voyage in 1776, no steps were taken to inquire into its probability. Authorities entitled to high consideration have treated it as a fabrication; and now it is of no moment whatever whether Lock invented the whole story, or whether he and Juan de Fuca were *confrères* in a projected raid on the English exchequer.

For a third of a century accepting as true, yet doubting—always unwilling to deny, ever trying to reconcile and believe, because territorial claim was confidently asserted by able authorities upon the *basis* that De Fuca made the voyage, but, above all, because a national prejudice, mistaken for patriotism, dictated such belief—the writer continued satisfied in his educated faith that Mears acted justly when he awarded to Juan de Fuca the honor as "original discoverer" of the strait. But dogmatism is unpardonable in the light of investigation. Truth compels the conclusion that Lock's narrative refutes itself, because:

(1.) Of palpable discrepancies as to time, geography, physical features of the country, and the number, clothing, and wealth of the natives.

(2.) De Fuca could not have escaped from Candish in the captured *Santa Aña*, in 1588, and have been pilot and commander of the voyages narrated. Nor could he have tarried so long at Mexico and Madrid, and reached Venice in 1596.

(3.) Concurrent history negatives, the mercenary motive taints, the whole story.

(4.) As Mexican and Spanish authorities assert no claim to the discovery, it is impossible that such expedition could have sailed from Mexico or under the auspices of the Spanish authorities.

However reluctantly, necessity demands that the "original account of the voyage of the Greek pilot Juan de Fuca along the north-west coast of America in 1592" should be denounced as a fraud; that such "voyage" is a fit companion of those of Gaspar Cortereal, Lorenzo Ferrer de Maldonado and Admiral Pedro Fonté.

Whether Lock fabricated the story, and what was his purpose, or whether the so-called Greek pilot imposed upon him, will never be learned. To-day the only tenable view is that the Strait of Juan de Fuca was first seen by white men in 1787, and that the party who saw it was the crew of the long-boat of the Austrian East Indiaman *Imperial Eagle*, commanded by Captain Berkly. D. S.

AN UNKNOWN TURNING-POINT IN THE DESTINY OF THE REPUBLIC.

There are in the lives of all nations certain pivotal points at which destiny seems to pause and rest the future in the hand of one man. Happy the nation which at such a moment finds at its service a man strong and true! The press dispatches of March 2d of this year briefly chronicle the passing away of such a man:

"Death of Dr. William Maxwell Wood, Surgeon-General U.S. Navy, yesterday, at his residence, Owing's Mills, Baltimore County, aged 72."

This man came from oblivion to do his duty and sink again into oblivion. Mark how his hand gave an impulse to the whole Republic! And yet the utmost endeavors will keep his memory green only a day or two. His country even now does not know him.

It is only recently that Great Britain has turned her eager eyes exclusively upon India, and withdrawn her watchfulness from North America. The teeming mother has sought everywhere for footholds for her children. She grasped at Yucatan, Louisiana, Texas, and Oregon. With jealous hunger she hovered over California, waiting to pounce upon it. Texas won an independence, and was melted into the greater Republic. This brought our frontier to the Rio Grande. Great Britain, in behalf of her citizens holding Mexican bonds, was at this time negotiating with Mexico for a mortgage on California, as security for these bonds. The plan was for England to enter into possession and pay the bonds. That this occupancy meant final possession was probably well understood by the Mexicans, for the negotiations were long delayed. Whatever the cause, the delay occurred, and the consummation was never reached. Why it was never reached is capable of exact demonstration. Dr. William Maxwell Wood rebuffed Great Britain, and snatched the morsel from her mouth.

Draw the mind back to 1846. Then Oregon was a wilderness, and California a waste of Mexican ranches. There were yet no overland stages, no Panama mails. Almost the only communication with home was afforded by one ship relieving another on the Pacific station. Men in responsible positions on the Pacific groped desperately to feel the movements of the rulers on the Atlantic. Dr. Wood was Fleet Surgeon of the Pacific fleet at this time. The frigate *Savannah*, sloops *Cyane*, *Warren*, *Levant*, the schooner *Shark*, and the store-ship *Erie*, made up our little squadron. The British had a fine fleet in the same waters—two fleets, in fact, a small one at the mouth of the Columbia River, and a large one, under Admiral Seymour (flag-ship *Collingwood*), off Mazatlan. This latter fleet made it its business to shadow the American fleet and narrowly watch all its movements.

The American commander, Commodore Sloat (flag-ship *Savannah*), at this time was lying off Mazatlan. So the rival nations set their ships of war to watch the rich prize, but with this difference: The British Admiral had perfect communication from Tampico to Mazatlan. His country, friendly with Mexico, strained every nerve to keep him informed. At the first gleam of war he was to snatch California to blaze upon the crown of our mother-land. On the other hand, Sloat was in the dark about everything. Mutterings of threatened war with Mexico reached his ear in that vague way that only hundred-tongued rumor can whisper. The lying dame whispered, too, of war with Great Britain. All knew that England was smarting under her failure to get Texas. All were aware that Mexico and the United States were chafing on the Rio Grande. Yet no one knew anything positively of what was occurring or what had occurred. So the two fleets watched each other and California. In 1842, Commodore Ap Catesby Jones had seized California for our Government, but he had not been sustained, and he had involved the country in difficulty. This made Sloat anxious and cautious. Dr. Wood himself mentioned to Sir Thomas Thompson, commander of the British frigate *Talbot*, the fact that there was rumor of war between the United States and Mexico. Sir Thomas positively assured Dr. Wood there was and could be no truth in such rumors, as he would receive any such news far in advance of other sources. Dr. Wood sadly knew this to be true. At about this time Dr. Wood was relieved by Dr. Chase, as Fleet Surgeon, and he prepared to return home. He voluntarily undertook to carry through Mexico (a rumored hostile country) dispatches to the home Government. It was a country of intense bitterness at the time, productive of assassins, so that this undertaking was more than duty; it was patriotism. The letter of transmittal accompanying these dispatches is as follows:

"[No. 47.] FLAG SHIP SAVANNAH,
Mazatlan, April 30, 1846.

"SIR:—I forward this by Dr. William Maxwell Wood, to whom I have given permission to return to the United States at his own request. He came out as Fleet Surgeon of the squadron, and some time since was superseded by Dr. Chase. Dr. Wood is a gentleman of observation and intelligence, speaks and reads the Spanish language, and will, in passing across the country, undoubtedly acquire very valuable information for the Government, and I refer the Department to him for information I have communicated to him verbally, which I did not think safe to trust in my letters across this country. I have the honor to be, very respectfully, your obedient servant, JOHN D. SLOAT.

"To HON. GEORGE BANCROFT,
"Secretary of the Navy."

It will be seen by this that in going through hostile Mexico Dr. Wood carried his death-warrant in his pocket. The most honorable belligerent in the world, on discovering this letter in his possession, would have hung him without a trial.

Hostilities began on the Rio Grande April 25, 1846, by the capture of Captain Thornton and his detachment, including Lieutenant Hardie (afterward the rebel general). A few days after this event (May 8th) Palo Alto was fought, and on May 9th the Mexicans were defeated at Resaca de la Palma, and on May 13, 1846, the United States formally declared war against Mexico. Now, on May 1, 1846, Dr. Wood, armed with his hazardous dispatches, set out from the post of San Blas to return to the United States by going through the national heart of Mexico—the City of Mexico itself—his only companion being Mr. Parrott, United States Consul at Mazatlan, who was returning home on account of bad health. No one who has slowly jogged over the dusty way, and under the pale blue sky of that tropic region, but can let his mind revert for a moment and see again the cactus, the chaparral, the low red hills, the blue mountains, the luxuriant Eden valleys of that five days' ride from Mazatlan to Guadalajara. Few ever measured the lengthening miles with as anxious hearts as did these travelers. Guadalajara had forgot its flowers, and birds, and bursting vines. The whole city was wild with the news—war! war! The hot rumors were blowing thick from the Rio Grande. As may be imagined, Dr. Wood did not now court observation. He hastened to a *hacienda*, or inn, and went at once to his room. The adjoining room was separated from his only by a thin partition, and was occupied by some Mexican officers of rank. He overheard their violent talk and hot discussions, and the facts he learned were startling. Hostilities had begun on the Rio Grande. He heard them reading an account of the capture of Captain Thornton and his dragoons. Dr. Wood immediately procured a Mexican newspaper with a full narrative of the affair. This sufficiently corroborated in outline the facts he had so fortunately overheard from better authority. There was no doubt now. He was in an enemy's country, and was the bearer of hostile dispatches. It was a moment of extreme peril to an American officer. But it was a moment of destinies. It was one of those pregnant pivotal moments alluded to. And fortunately the great republic had in this far-away spot one citizen who was not even thinking of personal safety, but was coolly revolving plan after plan to aid her. Sloat must know this news before Seymour, or California was lost. But how?—how? Dispatches were to go forward, and dispatches were to go back. Information was to be collected for the Government, and information was to be sent for the Government. Dr. Wood, notably a cool man, of large intelligence, looked at his problem as a statesman and as a military man. He knew as well as any the importance of this news. He was learned, far-sighted; and even then was looking to the future of our country. Fortunately his personal courage was such that he was not hampered by a single thought of danger. He wrote a full account of all he had overheard. He recorded the facts told and the views expressed by the Mexican officers. He translated the newspaper accounts. When he had finished he inclosed the whole to Commodore Sloat. This packet he took to Mr. Parrott, who, from his large commercial relations in Guadalajara and Mazatlan, was enabled to procure a courier without exciting suspicion. This courier, ignorant of course of the news he was bearing, but stimulated by the offer of a reward at the end of his journey, rode night and day till the packet was delivered at Mazatlan, and thence immediately transmitted to Sloat. A thrill of excitement ran through the whole squadron, among those who were permitted to know the news. The *Cyane* and *Levant* slipped out of the harbor, under secret orders, for Monterey, and the rest of the squadron was held in readiness to act instantly on any further information which might be received from the comrade who was in the very center of the enemy's country.

Dr. Wood had now done all that could be done. He was in the midst of enemies, and had hostile dispatches on his person that would give him short shrift if they were found. He knew, as a military man, that his safety lay in surrendering himself to the authorities. But his dispatches were of vast importance to the Government. If he could safely traverse Mexico, he would have information that would be invaluable to the country. This debate never passed through Dr. Wood's mind. With calm serenity, he knew no alternative, but posted on to the City of Mexico itself. How often have I heard that ride described. His only companions were the picturesque villains who acted as postilions and guides. How the mules were urged to the utmost! How the horses foamed, and the yellow dust rolled heavily up on the sultry air!

Here we have come to our episode.

In 1832 Dr. Wood was surgeon of a twelve-gun schooner, cruising in the gulf. A man-of-war of the existing Mexican Government committed an act of piracy upon a United States merchantman. The schooner captured the offender off Tampico, in view of five consorts. But the Captain of the Port of Tampico was a Baltimorean, a townsman of Dr. Wood, and was aboard his ship at the time. He was by a *ruse de guerre* decoyed aboard the schooner, and held there until the desired capture was completed. From that time till he met him in the City of Mexico, fourteen years later, Dr. Wood had not heard of his Tampico townsman. But, while on this perilous journey, this friend came up to the Doctor in a hotel in the City of Mexico. They looked at each other; the recognition was instant and mutual. The Captain said, gravely:

"You took me prisoner once, and I have *you* now."

The Doctor was startled, but, affecting indifference, made some light reply. The Captain took him to his own room and told him he was disgusted with the Mexican Government, and would never take part against his own country. The streets of Mexico were rife with war news.

Resaca de la Palma and Palo Alto had been fought, and Dr. Wood heard, with bitterness, the newsboys calling out exaggerated accounts of "Overwhelming defeat of the North Americans." But his Tampico Captain was an intimate friend of Torel, the Mexican War Minister, and he told Dr. Wood these accounts were all false, published to deceive the people. The flower of the Mexican army had been annihilated by Dr. Wood's own life-long friend, Zachary Taylor. Surgeon Wood, through this channel, every night learned the discussions of the Mexican Cabinet, and received, as it were, from the Minister of War himself the latest secrets of the campaign and of the national policy. All this information, together with his own observations, Dr. Wood promptly transmitted to Sloat, through the Mexican mails, under neutral cover. On the receipt of this, which at the time was characterized as "vital" and "all-important" information, Sloat himself put to sea, and joined the *Cyane* and *Levant* at Monterey, where, on the 7th of July, he raised the stars and stripes and formally took possession of California. Admiral Seymour arrived one day later, and was terribly chagrined to find that he had been outwitted, that American patriotism had been superior to his carefully laid plans, and that California was lost to Great Britain forever.

While residing in the City of Mexico, and hanging around the doors of the Cabinet, Dr. Wood, with an unnecessary audacity that is inspiriting, determined to visit the stronghold of Chapultepec, which is one of the outposts to the City of Mexico. He actually inspected the entire fortification, and made notes and drawings. While doing so he aroused the suspicions of a German, an officer in the Mexican service, who closely questioned him, but, taking advantage of the German's imperfect knowledge of English, Dr. Wood succeeded in deceiving him, and yet, as the Doctor himself stated, "without any sacrifice of literal veracity." I remember the close of the conversation was something as follows:

Mexican Officer—"I believe you are an American."

Dr. Wood—"My dear sir, can't you understand that I use *English?*"

Saying which, he coolly turned and walked away.

Believing now that it was no longer safe to remain in Mexico, and convinced that the chances of arrest or assassination were becoming greater, Dr. Wood determined to return home. But before starting for Vera Cruz he compiled his entire knowledge and information as to affairs in Mexico for the use of the Government. This packet he sent through the mails to a German friend in Vera Cruz (a neutral, of course), with directions to forward it to some reliable citizen of the United States for the use of the Government, if the packet were not called for in a certain number of days. But, by great address, Dr. Wood reached Vera Cruz in safety, and had the pleasure of reclaiming his packet in person. Vera Cruz was blockaded by our own fleet, but by the kindness of a neutral captain, Dr. Wood at last was sent out to the fleet as officer of one of the neutral boats. None but the brave can appreciate the exultant bound of the heart he must have felt, as, with dispatches all safe, he stepped aboard the flag-ship over which streamed the American flag, and on whose deck were none but friends. Dr. Wood, as bearer of dispatches, was immediately sent home in the steamer *Mississippi*, and he proceeded at once to deliver in person his information to the Secretary of the Navy, who tendered him the highest expressions of praise and gratitude, and *ordered his expenses to be refunded him!* Neither Congress nor others ever gave to this voluntary service a place in history or a mark of appreciation. And the man who was brave enough to so serve his country was modest enough to believe he had done only his duty. Hon. S. R. Mallory, Chairman of the Senate Committee on Naval Affairs, wrote as follows:

"Every intelligent mind must at once appreciate the importance of the service which you have rendered the country, and your personal hazard in traveling through the heart of the enemy's country, communicating with your military superior, and furnishing him with *the sole and otherwise unattainable information upon which he based the acquisition of California.* The importance of this acquisition can best be estimated by asking ourselves what would have been our national position in the Pacific and upon the Oregon frontier had Great Britain, instead of ourselves, acquired permanent possession of it. I have always contended that its acquisition constitutes one of the navy's strongest claims upon the gratitude and fostering hand of the nation, and this chapter in its history, furnished by your own service, but strengthens this conviction. But how are you to be rewarded for it? That is the question. Swords and brevets were scattered without number upon many who rendered far less service. I cannot at this moment make any distinct suggestion to you as to your mode of proceeding to obtain that to which I deem you honorably entitled, by a national recognition, by some substantial token of your valuable services, but I can promise you my aid, whatever it may be worth, to the attainment of such recognition."

But Dr. Wood thought it was not his place to move in such a matter, and the subject was never brought before Congress.

Commodore Sloat, under date of March 20, 1855, wrote as follows:

"I am most happy to acknowledge the very important services you rendered the Government and the squadron in the Pacific under my command, at the breaking out of the war with Mexico. The information you furnished me at Mazatlan from Guadalajara (at the risk of your life) was the only reliable information I received of that event, and which induced me to proceed immediately to California, and upon my own responsibility to take possession of that country, which I did on the 7th of July, 1846.

"I have always considered the performance of your journey through Mexico at that time as an extraordinary feat, requiring great courage, presence of mind, and address. How you escaped from the heart of an enemy's country, and such a people, has always been a wonder to me, and has been so characterized by me upon all occasions.

"Very truly your friend,

"JOHN D. SLOAT.

"DR. WILLIAM MAXWELL WOOD, U. S. Navy."

We have come to our conclusion. It is this: Commodore Sloat never received any information but that furnished him by Dr. Wood. Had Dr. Wood not done this at the risk of his life, Admiral Seymour would certainly have seized California; for Sloat dared not act except upon positive information, and even had he suspected Seymour's design, he could not have frustrated it. California even then was meditating separation from Mexico and union with Great Britain. Had Great Britain by any means once secured possession of this coveted prize, certainly we would have lost the State. The port of San Francisco, controlling the Pacific, would have been British. Then the natural possibilities of our destiny loom up too vast to be discussed. The war with Mexico might have become a war with England. The war of the rebellion might have become the war of Southern Independence. The present is real, but while rejoicing in it it is fitting to give a thought to the one hand that did its utmost to model the present, be that utmost much or little. No recognition ever came from the Government, and will now never come, for its servant is dead. But, far from being disheartened by this lack of reward, it will be well for the youth of to-day to pause, and find in the consciousness of patriotic duty well and nobly done that best and truest reward, the plaudits of a self-approving soul. C. E. S. WOOD.

NOT A SUCCESS.

"MY DEAR TILLY:—I congratulate you upon having left the city, upon being once more near to Nature's heart. What a strong, insatiable embrace she has! If you are fit to love her, she never lets you forget that brown breast of hers. Standing in our town-garden these spring nights, the earth-odors madden me, the solemn brown hills attract and taunt me as they loom lonely and unpolluted above the ignoble, little, new houses huddled in the valley between me and the hights. A light burns in each small, square window, but suggests none of the amenities of home—only brutish fatigue and offensive odors of strong foods. All the courage it takes to live dies in me. I think with intense longing of our days in the woods, not so many years ago. Walking home in the wind, I stop on the hill and watch the water, barred out on this side by the low-lying blonde sand-dunes, carrying the vessels gayly out to sea, bound on their different courses, and, like Wordsworth, I choose mine and fancy her name and port, and wish that I were upon her deck. My dream is not of a ship laden with precious things for me, coming home "shoals and quicksands past," but of one under whose sails I might be carried into far, strange harbors. The Nile's reeds rustle, and the lizards sun themselves all day on the ruins of the old cities of Ceylon, but the keel of that ship has never been laid.

"You do not blame me for wishing for a longer tether, do you? I feel so lonely in the state of life unto which it has pleased God to call me, as the dear old catechism says. There was a sad, strange poet who told how he stood in a pleasure-garden watching a poor swan dragging itself painfully about in the dust by the side of its tank, which was dry. Sometimes it stretched its long neck toward the sky, as if it asked for rain. So exiled and so ungainly I seem, and imagine other circumstances under which, in my own element, I might feel less weary revolt against the monotony of day after day, less like

> 'Sailors forgotten on a desert shore,
> The captives and the conquered.'

"It is not living, it is only dull endurance: to be always 'a bitter weed growing outside the garden wall, all day straining my eyes to see the blossoms within as they wave their crimson flags to the wind. And yet my dark leaves pray to be as glorious as the rose; I try to bloom up into the light.' That is Adah Menken. You should read her *Infelicia*, if you can find it. Poor Mazeppa! she had a strong heart, and genius of a better sort than was required for the piquant exhibition of her person and giving her bouquets to her horse to eat. Her prose poems are hysterical at times, but they are human, some of them heart-breaking.

"Tell me of your own loves, dear, but do not ask for mine. Like poor Clairon in the play, Shakspere, Wordsworth, Swinburne are my lovers; experience and ambition my shrines. Whether I shall ever offer up there anything more precious than a great dumb agony, I have no courage to ask. This misery and thirst are nothing new; they have grown with my growth, and strengthened with my strength. I look all along my happy, riotous childhood, and my sheltered, love-lighted girlhood, for the source of the intolerable yearning that devours me; but it is only in my own wild, bitter, selfish heart: it is not to be subdued, and haunts me like the memory of a paradise known and lost, toward which I struggle still, blindly. Forgive me my long, egotistical prosing. You will never ask me to write about myself again, will you? It is only to you that I have ever so spoken. Don't preach patience and self-control at me. I am tame. Modern life is the black dose that Fate, like a mythological Mrs. Squeers, of uncompromising appearance, stands pouring down our unhappy throats, to deaden the angelic appetites we may have brought from heaven for the few nectarine flavors there may be floating over the earth for Nature's unspoiled children—a homely version of *surgit amari aliquid*. But I am not one of those favored ones; my device is Meg Merrilies's 'gape, sinner, and swallow.'"

The letter I was reading ended thus, without date or signature. It seemed to me a morbid, wretched affair enough, and yet somehow honest, the confidence of such genuine unhappiness that I felt guilty at having read it, for it was written to Miss Lewburd, who had tossed it to me across a heap of grass, with a brief command to peruse it. We—that is, a party of summer friends who had convened for the month of June at the Lewburds' comfortable country house—were lying upon the lawn, *sub Jove* entirely, for there were no trees, our heads or elbows pressing deep into mounds of newly cut grass. The afternoon post had just come in, and all were interested in their letters, so I made no remark, but sat looking at the prospect and turning the letter slowly between my fingers, when a small rustle attracted my attention, and I found Miss Lewburd seated by my side.

"I want to talk to you about that letter," she murmured confidentially. "You pretend to read character and to study people; how old do you imagine the girl is who wrote it? If she were not a friend of mine, wouldn't you guess a hundred and fifty just from what she says?"

"Never," said I, shaking my head; "rebels are young, especially rebels feminine; this is a precocious one, I grant you."

"When you laugh like that, I hate you," cried Miss Lewburd, vivaciously.

Whereupon I became grave.

"Is her family very poor?" I asked, returning to the letter.

"Well off, I fancy. She never could dress herself decently, but everything she had was all right," was the lucid reply.

"She was a friend of yours at school, I infer," said I.

"Neil Frankland! Rather. Why, I loved that girl so that I used to think I never could love a man half so well."

"Do you think so still?"

"I never acknowledge when I change my opinions," said Miss Lewburd, casting down her eyes. "But I want to know if you can make out what she means? I never read her letters through. Does that make sense to you?"

"Oh, yes," said I, half absently, looking at the folded letter.

"What do you suppose makes her write so?"

"If she were a young man, I should say that she was kept too close; as that is not a valid excuse for a young lady's *ennui*, I presume she writes for effect, or lacks occupation, or has had a hard flirtation and singed her wings," I ventured to say.

"No, indeed," replied Miss Lewburd, eagerly. "You saw what she wrote when I asked her about her love affairs. Wordsworth, indeed! There's a magnetic, fascinating idol. He wrote Songs of Seven, or some such thing, didn't he? It was about some cottage people in a graveyard, any way. You needn't laugh; I despise poetry. But, truly, Neil doesn't like gentlemen at all, and she's not a bit a girl gentlemen would like."

"What did you call her a minute ago?" I asked.

"Her name is Mary Neil Frankland, but she has an elder cousin with the same name who lives in the same city, so they call my friend by her middle name."

"Is she pretty?"

"Not a bit. You might like her eyes, perhaps. You'll think I'm not talking very nicely about my best friend. She *is* awfully clever, and never gives up the people she likes, no matter what they do—there!"

"Tell me when you answer that letter," said I, as we rose to our feet and went toward the house; "I have something to say to her."

Later, at the end of Miss Lewburd's response, I wrote, "*Race de Caïn, cœur qui brûle, prends garde à ces grands appétits*," and told Miss Lewburd to preserve my *incognito*, and say nothing about how the postscript came to be added. A year passed, and my father's fortune became a wreck. My best plan appeared to involve a change of abode to a distant city, whither I departed, armed with letters from my friends to several people in my new home. One was to Albert Neil Frankland, and my destination was, in effect, the native place of Miss Lewburd's remarkable correspondent, as I recalled. This, then, was either the father or uncle of La Menken's admirer.

Mr. Frankland proved to be the young lady's father. She was one of several, brothers and sisters; a tall, pale, quiet girl, whom I never should have dreamed the author of the letter I had read had she not said, as I took my leave of her:

"I have never had an opportunity, Mr. Craven, to thank you for classing me with the children of Cain. May I do so now?"

Miss Lewburd had betrayed me, as I might have known she would do, but there was no time to shift the responsibility; so I said:

"I should like to talk over that little episode with you, since you have not forgotten it."

"When you please," she answered, laughing.

Before I took the liberty of scolding her a little for her morbid views, I studied her somewhat. She was certainly indifferent, rather patronizing without knowing it, to many of the persons who frequented her father's house, and I was forced to confess that they were hardly the sort of people likely to fascinate one of her temperament. They were quite as little attracted toward her, and at all social gatherings she wore a listless, good-naturedly tolerant air, most original for one of her age and sex. She treated me well from the beginning, and as I watched the cool patience with which she lived a life totally distasteful to her, as I knew by her confession to her friend, I began to take a deep interest in her. We had a long conversation at last, in which I tried to be neither prig nor preacher, but to tell her, from a strong friendliness I entertained for her, the danger of nursing discontent, and the uselessness of trying to plunge our eyes into the fog that surrounds certain aspects of life, while right around most of us there is a bright, every-day sunshine, in which we are called upon to perform little necessary every-day duties, and we had best leave the solution of the enigmas to—a—the course of time—the future, I concluded, somewhat lamely as I felt. She shook her head impatiently.

"It is a consciousness of imprisonment, a sense of strong wings that cannot unfold; it is *le cœur qui brûle* that some of us must carry from our cradles to our graves."

Then she added, smiling:

"And if we perform our little duties punctiliously, and try to escape from none of our responsibilities, and defy no prejudice, and submit to all conventionality, may we not remark to a trusted friend that that burning heart in us swells and aches with the pulse of a new spring, without getting such a reprimand from Mr. Berkeley Craven?"

One afternoon, as I was walking on the beach, I came upon her reclining on the warm white sand, while a few paces off one of her young brothers threw sticks in the water for a Newfoundland dog. I sat down beside her. We had come to know each other very well.

"Are you unhappy?" I asked her, abruptly.

"Very happy," she replied, while the tears welled slowly into her eyes. "Here, on the shore, happier than anywhere else."

"I have caught your restlessness," said I, looking out to sea. "But I am not resigned to bear it as you do, and it takes something more than a rolling surf to console me. I miss something from every hour that I don't spend with you. I know it is your presence that I want. You must care for me a little when I love you so well. I know you think this is a weary world, but I would try to make it better worth enduring, if the endeavor of a whole lifetime goes for anything."

I raved a while, not knowing what I said, but she kept her face studiously turned from me and was silent.

"Will you let a man cut his heart out before you, and never even look at him?" I cried at last, indignant at her impassivity. Then she turned slowly toward me—but who could bring himself to tell in what words the woman he loved confessed that she gave her heart into his keeping!

Is it individual perversity or universal human nature that intensity of response to feeling deadens or tranquillizes the challenging outburst? It was the self-imposed, inflexible law of Neil's life to hold in tyrannical subjection every strong inclination and emotion of her nature, so that, long as we were friends, I had not the least suspicion of her love for me until I told her of my own. After that, I learned little by little into what her imagination had deified me. I felt the awe of her absolute devotion that falls upon a son when he first realizes the sacrifices of his mother. The little jealousies and fevers of a lover were out of place in the presence of such worship, but all the rapture and impulsive transport of a new passion were at rest in me, too.

We were married, and lived quietly, but very happily. I felt that I had begun the world aright, with a true wife by my side to fill the void in my life and hopes, and give strength and purpose to my work. Neil's affection was not a thing of the nerves or of words. She really lived for me and for our home. I was poor, though I meant to be rich for her sake some day, and she accepted the sort of existence I had to give her without actually appearing to notice the difference from her father's household arrangements. She was loyal to me, even in the small matter of gently refusing the incompatible invitations and costly presents which her relatives showered upon her. They understood her, and ceased to hold out to her the temptation to divide her allegiance to me, but I doubt if they loved me the better therefor. I have called this a small matter, but I have seen a woman literally kill her husband through cruel humiliation, by living sumptuously more than half her time at her father's house, and coming to his with discontent, disdain, and patronage. The poor wretch labored overmuch to coin his brain for the insatiable vulture-Venus, and it went to ashes in the crucible. I chafed at our circumscribed hospitality, but Neil answered me that for her at least it was a glad escape. She said, I believe truthfully, that she regarded visitors from the outside world as an interruption and a slight discipline. The few friends I brought to our table were men upon whose sincerity I could rely. I knew they took pleasure in my society and cared for it, without caviling at the absence of choice dishes and wines, and a retinue of attendants. Neil's *ménage* went like clock-work. There were no *contre-temps* but those made by my own impatience, and I had them explained to me, and repented and was forgiven later, when Neil ended by saying, with a short laugh in which there never seemed any gayety:

"Trust me, Berkeley. I shall always do you credit."

Only one thing made me angry—she was so orientally submissive when my friends were with us. She never spoke except when directly addressed, and then without enthusiasm or challenge; nor did she ever discuss them after their departure, or speak of them at all, save collectively in reference to prandial arrangements.

"I don't like an *empressée* hostess," I expostulated once; "but there is a happy medium."

"Ah!" she sighed, laughing, "I wish it were not so, but I can calculate to a nicety just what each one will say, and when I look at them they seem to have '*connu*' written all over them. They would put me to sleep if they were not your friends. Since they are, let me be civil, not unnatural. Don't require the impossible, Berkeley; indeed, I have no *brio*."

And the gay good-nature in her voice deepened in her earnest eyes to the yearning look of love that never failed to disarm my trifling dissatisfaction. She was always busy. Even at night, she brought her interminable sewing under the lamp, unless I expressly banished it. It seemed unsuitable work for her, though she was a good needle-woman; and it irritated me to see her stitching. One day when I had leisure, and she looked tired, we took a long walk among the hills, changing as they did at last to sand-mounds, fluttering and shifting along under the wind, seeming alive as they basked in the sun an hour, with those tigerish bars of iron-dust on their backs. At last, sheltered from the sea-breeze, which had brought a fresh color into Neil's pale face, we lay reclined under some little oaks. I was smoking and looking at the land-view, while Neil read Swinburne's essay on Blake. How well I remember it! I interrupted her to ask her if she thought she read as much as formerly, and she told me carelessly she imagined so. When I looked at her again she seemed to be studying me intently over the top of her book. We ate some great Italian chestnuts, and as we talked the conversation turned upon Miss Lewburd. She was married, it appeared, but was anything but happy, her husband proving a drinking good-for-naught.

"Dear little, unbalanced, wild, pretty creature," said Neil, with a burst of adjectives most unusual with her. "How dearly I loved her, and how much I wish I could help her now!"

"Do you know," said I, "that I once had a vague, conceited idea of trying to make Miss Lewburd care for me. Only fancy if she had come out here to be poor with me."

"She might have been very different under those circumstances, and shown courage and strength of character," replied Mrs. Craven, judicially. At this I laughed uncontrollably, and betook myself to the composition of some doggerel celebrating Matilda's volatile inconstancy:

"Yes, I know, my child,
We have dreamed it so
Far inland, of white sea-sand
And a strong tide's ebb and flow.

"Under hot faint skies,
How I longed to be!
Fields of grain and wild-birds' strain
Satiated me.

"And your little heart,
Fierce if fleet as flame,
Felt brave to dare and strong to share
My life, or wild or tame.

"So far in the past!
Could you look with me
Between those knolls, where the surf rolls,
And hear the roaring sea.

"What a weary sigh!
Comic-piteous eyes—
You would say, 'Is this the way
An artist's life-time flies?

"'No gems nor gaslight glare,
No low-voiced flatteries?
Not a love like heaven above
Atones for lack of these.'"

"You are unjust to her," Neil persisted, as she read these absurdities. "Dear girl! I mean to write to her to-night."

One day, soon after this, I was in Mr. Frankland's office, when he developed to me a plan he had of visiting Europe and the Holy Land, and perhaps India, with his wife, his unmarried daughter, and, "if I could spare her," Neil. Absurd as it may seem, his words depressed me terribly. I had no grievance, nor *ennui*, nor bachelor proclivities to make me rejoice at the prospect of my wife's absence. She was my comrade, and I could not do without her. Mr. Frankland said we must talk it over together, and settle how it should be; and I went home moody and out of spirits. Neil forbore to question, but did a great many cosy little things for me which I knew she would not have done unless she had fancied me disturbed. The climax was reached when, in the evening, she played some waltzes and marches which she had acquired *peine forte et dure* because they were favorites of mine. She was naturally about as musical as Memnon before the dawn.

I told her at last what her father had unfolded to me that day. There came a glad, free look into her patient eyes that gave my heart a hard wrench. I don't know what it might have stung me into saying had she not spared me all pains by remarking, tranquilly, as she took up her work:

"Of course you told him I should not go."

"Of course I told him nothing of the kind," I exclaimed. "It's been the dream of your life to see the very places Mr. Frankland means to travel in, and you would be a strange person if you did not embrace your only opportunity of realizing it. For it is your only one; the Prophet knows I shall never have the means to show you anything but dry daily bread."

She put her work aside, and came and stood before me, looking down, and without a tremor in her voice, and with that little laugh that was worse to hear then than any sob, she said:

"My dear Berkeley, if I cannot see those places with you, it is the same to me as if they did not exist. 'My Italy's here.' Don't look so wretched. You don't want me to go, I suppose." I stood up, and threw my arm about her.

"Neil," I said, a little chokingly, I fear, "I sometimes feel as if the whole purpose and bent of your life were thwarted even more by me than by your circumstances before we were married. It haunts me with a vague remorse that you act a part for my sake every day, and that it is too hard for you, and now that you are giving up the only thing you care for because you are tied to me, I could tear myself for very rage. Can you forgive me that I have condemned you to such a miserable fortune?"

"My life thwarted! What big words for me. And fancy your remorse being only vague when you think I act a part every day. I should say it was time for lively dissatisfaction. Oh, Berkeley, did you think I had a mission, like Mrs. Jellyby, that I am too conscientious to fulfill at the expense of your comfort?"

She smiled brightly at me, but I saw her face through a sudden mist in my own eyes. I could not think of any compensation in my power for her sacrifice. Our pleasant, quiet life remained uninterrupted until shortly after Mr. Frankland and his party sailed, when Miss Lewburd descended upon us. Mrs. Lewburd she was now. She had divorced her unpleasant lord, and resumed her own name. There was trouble on both sides, but he made no objection to a separation, was the rumor that floated out to us with her. A wealthy relative, dying soon after the catastrophe, had left her a well invested sum of money, which to her, unincumbered with children, was a fortune. I came home one evening to find the fair lady enthroned in the parlor, with evident intentions of dining with us. She was very much changed from the flighty little gossip whose tirades had so often amused me in days gone by. She had dyed her soft, light hair a golden red, and wore it in hard, gummy rings around her forehead and in front of each ear. She was painted and powdered like a fourth-rate actress; her voluminous skirts filled our little rooms full, and she kicked them into place as unceremoniously as a heroine of *opéra bouffe*. She seemed to stand a little in awe of Neil, to whom she talked sentimentalities about the past that made me quite ill. She appeared to excite herself at will, and to be hard and reckless purposely to contrast with her affectionate reminiscences. Her voice was loud and slangily reverberating, her vocabulary in no way improved, and her conversation "all a wonder and a wild desire" to appear something that she was not. She had picked up the cant phrases of scientific atheism, and played with the great doubts of the age like a cat with a ball of yarn, making the same egregious snarl.

When Mrs. Lewburd had departed I permitted myself to criticise and abuse her with the greatest freedom, when, for the first time, I saw Neil thoroughly roused and angry. She defended "Tilly" warmly, reminded me of how much "sorrow" the woman had seen, to what depraving influences she had been exposed, and told me some rubbish about her good heart and true nature under a tawdry exterior.

"What on earth brought her here?" said I, discontentedly.

"My letter," replied Neil. "She said that in all her troubles, when the world was so unkind to her, not one of the girls of our set, who had promised to stand by each other always, held out a hand to her. I didn't ask her to come out here, you know, but only said that through all changes I was as firmly and truly her friend as when we were school-girls. She said that when her troubles came she turned so joyfully toward the one place where she felt there was a welcome for her. As for her appearance and manner," my wife continued, in a tone of conviction, "they are exactly what all men admire and pursue, wherever I have been able to observe. She is dashing, coquettish, self-possessed, and a brilliant conversationalist."

"She's not my sympathy, unmanly though the confession may make me appear," said I, laughing uneasily as I felt my temper going. "Seriously, I dislike the woman, and I hope you will see very little of her. She has money and any amount of chee—, self-possession, as you say; so I think you can afford to let that wonderful loyalty die a natural death."

I did not insist upon the discontinuance of the intimacy, hoping my wife would come to see the matter as I did; she had never differed with me in matters of moment. The two friends met every day, either in my house, or in Mrs. Lewburd's rooms at the hotel, but I felt I owed Neil some forbearance, and did not remonstrate again. At last it was town talk that Mrs. Lewburd was compromisingly intimate with a handsome, scoundrelly "loafer," for whom gentlemen felt a thorough contempt. This I could not bear to tell Neil, she really seemed to care so much for her friend; but I again dissuaded her very strongly from being seen with Mrs. Lewburd, and from receiving her. At the heels of this attack on poor "Tilly," I was attacked myself by something like swamp fever, which pierced all my joints with pains, as if I had been racked. Neil nursed me night and day, even lifting and turning me upon my pillows, because she was gentler than any attendant. She was never downcast nor foreboding, but through long, sleepless nights, and wretched, restless days, her wonderful verbal memory seemed inexhaustible of poetry and songs, and the famous chapters of the Bible. There was something soothing and sympathetic in her very silence, and my every fancy was anticipated by her, until, the heavens be praised, I was convalescent. The rheumatism was not yet out of my ankles, and it would be a week or two before I could venture out into the blessed sun, when one day Neil came into the room where I was sitting reading, and said:

"I think you can spare me to-day. I have arranged everything for you to lie down when you are tired, and Tilly has come with her horses to take me driving."

"Has she brought Vernon Spencer with her?" said I, contemptuously.

"Who is Vernon Spencer?" said Neil. "But to answer your question, no; she is alone. You have no objection to my going, have you?"

I was determined she should not be seen with Mrs. Lewburd, so I said:

"I shall not be a tax upon you much longer, Neil. I suppose it is a crime to be ill, but neglect will not hasten my recovery. It is in your own interest not to abandon me altogether, quite yet. I shall be well the sooner."

She was gone before I finished speaking. I heard the front door close and then a heavy fall in the hall. I sprang up, but my weak knees held me pinned. They brought Neil into the room insensible, and I cried over her like a baby. The doctor told me that she was worn out, but that as I was well now, she could rest. I was at work the sooner for not having her to spoil me; being nursed for hire is not to be protracted for any pleasure there is in it.

Natural sleep, and a few days resting on the sofa, were all Neil's splendid constitution required to rally; and, one night, when a basket of flowers came, bearing on the card, "With Tilly's love," I told my wife the stories current about her friend, and how it was neither lawful nor expedient that her intimacy with such a person should continue.

"And leave that wicked man to lose her, body and soul, without giving her a word of warning!" cried Neil, with flashing eyes.

"And leave that thoroughly corrupt woman to go to the devil her own way," said I.

"My little friend," murmured Neil, leaning her face over the flowers, "my poor, weak little girl, who knows no more of the cruelty of the world than ——"

"Than you do," said I, exasperated. "Now, hear me; I must insist that you drop Mrs. Lewburd's acquaintance. If she pursues you here, give orders that she is not to be admitted. If you feel indebted to her, I will make her a present, but all connection between you must cease here and now."

Neil never spoke a word, but she looked a good deal. The next morning, by one of those infernal accidents that come to destroy the best *finale* man ever planned, before the servants could have orders not to admit Mrs. Lewburd should she call, the lady presented herself, in review order, to take Neil to lunch with her. I received her. My resolution was taken. I told her firmly that henceforth my house would not be open to her, that she was no friend for my wife, and I intended them to meet as strangers from that day. I told her that she must see how difficult this was for me to say, but she knew best if I were not justified in saying it. She looked frightened and disconcerted, made an attempt to speak, but appeared unable to articulate a word; then she rose and left the house without uttered remonstrance. Neil and I had a bitter quarrel, that ended in granite silence; but at last, as I sat one day thinking of all she had been to me in the past, I determined, after a sharp inward struggle, to submit my pride, and ask her to forgive the slight I had put upon her friend, and demand a reconcillation. She was very generous, and I did not fear a repulse, nor martyred looks, nor anythink that sours a pardon. I finished my chat with the Captain of the *Swallow*, whose vessel was off on a three years' cruise in the Indian waters that afternoon, went home, though it was early, and found that my wife had gone out. There was nothing strange in the circumstance, yet a hideous gaingiving turned me cold. In my room I found this note from her:

"You have relented already, dear Berkeley, and I do not need to tell you how deep and hard to bear alone my repentance has been. Relying really upon your magnanimity, dear, I have gone to her, to my friend. Her husband has tracked her here, in hopes to extort money from her. I doubt if he can do worse than annoy her, but she fears him terribly, and has sent to beg me to stay with her until to-morrow morning. She is alone in the world, with no one to take her part. Can I selfishly shake her off when she appeals to me, just because the world has slandered her? Your own heart cries out, no. Then good-bye till to-morrow morning.

"NEIL."

"By heavens!" I cried, crushing the paper in my hand, while the blood surged into my face like a tide, "she has defied me. My commands are no more to her than my wishes. She will compromise herself as she pleases? So be it. That to-morrow is a distant one when she sees my face again. I will give her cause not to forget this day."

I was beside myself with anger..

I sent some clothing forward to the wharves, borrowed money of a capitalist with whom I was on certain terms, and sailed on board the *Swallow* that evening for the Malay Peninsula.

The voyage made me old. There are no words to describe the variations of feeling to which I was a prey—the bitter remorse, the forced self-justification; but when I reached the East my mind was made up that it was better for us to be parted a while—it was always so. I should write her all particulars, and what her own plans had better be. Her family would be returning, and in a year, perhaps, we, too, might come together, older, and sobered, and better controlled. I joined a naturalists' party to visit the islands of the Malay Archipelago, and in Sumatra was ill for many months of coast fever, with only a little thief of an Arab to pull me through. I longed for home and Neil. The large, rich life of those volcanic seas only deepened the weariness it should have consoled. There was nothing for it but to make the speediest journey possible back to the United States.

I stood at last, with a throbbing heart, before my own little home. During my long absence I had received no communication from my wife nor from her relatives, yet I had no misgivings about my welcome.

A slatternly girl opened the door, and, before I could speak, nodded rapidly, saying:

"Oh, the gentleman to be measured. Miss Frankland expects you, sir, up-stairs."

And, preceding me, she ushered me into what had been my own room. By the window, Neil sat, sewing. The woman left us, and, with a hoarse cry of apprehension and appeal, I held out my arms to my wife. She slowly raised her eyes. O God! In those glorious eyes there was not one ray of recollection as she scanned my sun-burned face.

"Sit down, sir," she said, quietly. "In one moment I can take your measure. You are not the gentleman I expected. Did Judge Russell recommend me to you?"

"Don't you know me?" I asked, frantically. "Neil, I have come back to be forgiven. Forget what your people have taught you to think of me. I have never loved you less for a moment."

She seemed to fear me, but that terrible strangeness did not fade from her eyes.

"Who are you?" she asked, haughtily.

"Do I need to say? O my love! I am your miserable husband, Berkeley Craven."

She laughed a little.

"I am sorry you are miserable," she said, "but I have no husband, and I must insist upon being called Miss Frankland by you."

I came a step nearer, and looked yearningly in her face. She stood up and pointed to the door."

"You must go now," she said, decidedly.

A great dread was wrenching at my heart. I asked her for Judge Russell's address, and she wrote it upon the back of a card advertising her as a shirt-maker. Going from one to another, I unraveled the mystery of what was to me the tragedy of my whole life. For three days after my departure, Neil had been like one distracted; and at last, when my registered name was found, and she knew that I had left her, the shock, combined with her exhaustion and long self-repression, had resulted in brain-fever, from which she had arisen perfectly forgetful of me, of her marriage, of all but the haunting consciousness of a rooted sorrow. Her father had died abroad, and her mother and sister returned to find that the estate had melted away in the settlement, and now they were taking scholars. Neil seemed to understand their position, but any intellectual employment distressed her since her illness; so, with the influence of her father's friends, she had taken up her present occupation. She clung to our little house as her home, and they rented two of the sunniest rooms for her. She was fading rapidly; was unfit for any work, especially for the confinement of sewing, but she would not relinquish the pleasure of adding something to the family treasury. I determined that she should have rest; and, braving the black looks and hatred of her family, bent my pride to persuade them of my affection and repentance, and to beg that my wife should be given back into my keeping. I took what employment I could get—not elevated nor elevating—and put my poor girl into more secluded and commodious rooms; and, with a physician's aid, strove to bring her back to life and memory. She seemed to know that she could not live long, but deprecated whatever was done for her, imagining all to be the work of her mother and sister, and they never tried to make her comprehend my return; but I waited in patience, with an aching heart. At night, when she slept, I used to sit by her bedside, watching her by the pale lamplight. She was worn and wasted, and the heavy shadow of grief lay on her purple eyelids. One night as I lingered near her, and it was almost dawn, she awoke, and our eyes met.

"You know people say shells echo with the lost sea," she said, quietly, as if we had been talking. "My mind echoes with such a sound; it is the voice of some one I have lost. Is it my father's voice that I hear chiming always in my ears, eager and imperious? And in your face there is a look I have only observed lately, when you come to sit by me, that reminds me of some one I have seen before. Who is it? Who can it be?"

I fixed her eyes with mine. I willed her to know me, now at this supreme moment, with the passion of prayer.

"Look at me," I whispered, bending over her.

A strong shudder ran through her frame; she recoiled, putting up her hand as if to ward off a blow, and then bent her eyes upon my face with a terrible frown.

"You have been here a long time!" she gasped, seizing her head hard in her hands. "And I could not—wait, wait one moment—it is all coming back to me. Ah, Berkeley! my husband."

She strained me to her in her emaciated arms. I laid her down dead.

She lies there among the red flowers that she loved so. "The white wreaths make me cold," she once said. "When I am dead at last, bury me with red flowers, half-faded, fiery blossoms, full of bitter summer."

The fine lips press restfully upon each other, the shadowy lids, so slow to close in sleep, are quite drooped. And the great, true heart is still, and the flame of the abounding life that I had so prodigally wasted, burned out as consumed with desire of Death's strange eyes.

And I rave impotently, O my well beloved! while your untamed, long-imprisoned soul rejoices to spurn its cage and be at liberty. You have been stretched out upon the rack of this tough world, but the torture is over. The cry of my heart is as old as the sin of the world: "My punishment is greater than I can bear."

PHILIP SHIRLEY.

THE ANCIENT GLACIERS OF THE SIERRA.

All California has been heavily glaciated, the broad plains and valleys so warm and fertile now, and the coast ranges and foothills, covered with forests and chaparral, as well as the bald, rocky summits of the Sierra Nevada, swelling high in the cold sky.

Go where you may, throughout the length and breadth of the State, unmistakable evidence is everywhere presented of the former existence of an ice-sheet, thousands of feet in thickness, beneath whose heavy folds all the present landscapes have been molded; while on both flanks of the Sierra we find the fresher and more appreciable traces of the individual glaciers, or ice-rivers, into which that portion of the ice-sheet which covered the range was divided toward the close of the glacial period.

No other mountain chain on the globe seems to be so rich in emphatic, well preserved glacial monuments, easily seen by anybody capable of looking. Every feature is more or less glacial. Not a peak, ridge, dome, or mere rock, *cañon*, lake-basin, forest, or stream, but in some way explains the past existence and modes of action of flowing, grinding ice. For, notwithstanding the post-glacial agents—the air, rain, snow, frost, rivers, etc.—have been incessantly at work upon the greater portion of the range for tens of thousands of stormy years, each engraving their own characters more and more deeply over those of the ice, the latter are so enduring and so heavily emphasized, they still rise in sublime relief, clear and legible, through every after inscription, whether of the mighty avalanche, the torrent, or universal, eroding atmosphere. To-day, in higher latitudes, the great glacial winter still prevails in all its cold, white grandeur. The unborn landscapes of North Greenland, and some of those of our own Alaska, are still being fashioned beneath a deep, slow-crawling mantle of ice, from a quarter of a mile to more than a mile in thickness, presenting noble illustrations of the ancient condition of California, when all its sublime scenery was sealed up, or in process of formation. On the Himalaya, and the mountains of Norway and Switzerland, and on most of those of Alaska, the ice-mantle has been melted away from the ridges and table-lands, where it was thinnest, thus separating it into distinct glaciers that flow, river-like, through the valleys, illustrating a similar past condition in the Sierra, when every *cañon* and valley was the channel of an ice-stream, all of which may be easily traced back to where their fountains lay in the recesses of the alpine summits, and where some sixty-five of their topmost residual branches still linger beneath cool shadows.

The transition from one to the other of those glacial conditions was gradual and shadow-like. When the great cycle of cold, snowy years—called the glacial period—was nearly complete, the ice-mantle, wasting from season to season faster than it was renewed, began to withdraw from the lowlands along the base of the range, and gradually became shallower everywhere. Then the highest of the granite domes began to appear above the icy sea, and long, dividing ridges, containing distinct glaciers, between them. These glaciers at first remained united in one continuous sheet toward the summit of the range for many centuries. But as the snowfall diminished, and the climate became milder, this upper ice-sheet was also in turn separated into distinct glaciers, and these again into smaller ones, as one tributary after another was cut off from its trunk and became independent; while at the same time all were growing shorter and shallower, though fluctuations of the climate would now and then occur which would bring the receding snouts to a stand still, or even enable them to advance for a few tens or hundreds of years, when they would again begin to recede.

In the meantime the plants were coming on, the hardiest species establishing themselves on the moraine soils and in fissures of the rocks, pushing upward along every sun-warmed slope, and following close upon the retreating ice, which, like shreds of summer clouds, at length vanished from the new-born mountains, leaving them in all their main telling features nearly as we find them now.

It will be seen, therefore, that the lowlands near the level of the sea, and the foothills, and the tops of the highest domes and ridges, were the first to see the light, and therefore have been longer exposed to post-glacial weathering. Accordingly, we find that their glacial characters are more worn and obscured than those of the higher regions, though all are still legible to the patient student.

GLACIER PAVEMENTS.

By far the most striking and attractive of the glacial phenomena presented to the non-scientific observer in the Sierra are the polished glacier pavements, because they are so beautiful, and their beauty is of so rare a kind, so unlike any portion of the loose, earthy lowlands where people make homes and earn their bread. They are simply flat or gently undulating areas of solid granite, which present the unchanged surface upon which the ancient glaciers flowed, and are found in the most perfect condition in the sub-alpine region, at an elevation of from eight thousand to nine thousand feet. Some are miles in extent, only slightly interrupted by spots that have given way to the weather, while the best preserved portions are bright and stainless as the sky, reflecting the sunbeams like glass, and shining as if polished afresh every day, notwithstanding they have been exposed to corroding rains, dew, frost, and snow for thousands of years.

The attention of the game-seeking and gold-seeking mountaineer is seldom commanded by other glacial phenomena, as moraines, however regular and artificial in form, or *cañons*, however deep, or strangely modeled rocks, however high and sheer; but when he comes to these bare pavements he stoops and rubs his hand admiringly on their shining surfaces, and tries hard to account for their mysterious smoothness and brilliancy. He may have seen the winter avalanches of snow descending in awful majesty through the woods, sweeping away the

that stood in their way like slender weeds, but concludes that this cannot be the work of avalanches, because the scratches and fine polishing striæ show that the agent, whatever it was, moved along, and up over the rocks, as well as downward. Neither can he see how water may possibly have been the agent, for he finds the same strange polish upon lofty, isolated tables beyond the reach of any conceivable flood. Only the winds seem capable of moving across the face of the country in the directions indicated by the scratches and grooves. Even dogs and horses, when first led up the mountains, study geology to this extent, that they gaze wonderingly at the strange brightness of the ground, and smell it, and place their feet cautiously upon it, as if afraid of falling or sinking.

In the production of this admirable hard finish, the glaciers, in many places, bore down with a pressure of more than a hundred tons to the square foot, slipping, and pressing, and planing down granite, slate, and quartz alike, and bringing out the veins and crystals of the rocks with beautiful distinctness. Most of the granite below the sources of the Tuolumne and Merced is porphyritic, the feldspar crystals in many places forming the greater part of the rock, and these, when planed off level with the general surface, give rise to a beautiful mosaic, and when the sunlight falls upon it the multitude of starry crystals shining at different angles make a blaze of white beams, as if the ground were covered with burnished silver.

The brightest and most elaborately finished of the Sierra landscapes lie on the headwaters of the Tuolumne and Merced, above Yosemite Valley. The mountains, both to the north and south of this region, were, perhaps, subjected to about as long and intense a glaciation; but, because the rocks are less resisting, their polished surfaces have succumbed to the attacks of the weather, leaving only here and there small, imperfect patches. The lowest remnants of the old glacial surface are about from three thousand to five thousand feet above the level of the sea, and thirty to forty miles from the axis of the range, on the west flank. The short, steeply inclined *cañons* of the eastern flank also contain enduring mortoned bosses, and sloping aprons, brilliantly striated and finished, but these are far less magnificent than those of the broad western flank.

Perhaps the one best general view of these brilliant landscapes, that is easily accessible, and comprehends specimens of all the more striking of the glacial characters, is to be had from the top of a lofty conoidal rock that I have called the Glacier Monument. It is a majestic monolith of porphyry, about fifteen hundred feet high, situated on the left bank of the ancient Tuolmune *mer de glace*, a short distance to the north of Cathedral Peak. At first sight it seems absolutely inaccessible, though a good climber will find that it may be scaled on the south side. Approaching it on this side, you pass through a beautiful spruce forest growing on the lateral moraine, catching glimpses now and then of what appears to be a perfect cone of granite, towering to an immense hight above the dark evergreens; and when at length you have made your way across the woods, wading through thickets of azalea and ledum, you step abruptly out of the tree shadows and leafy, mossy softness, upon a naked curve of porphyry, that forms the base of the monument, which is now beheld unveiled in all its grandeur. Fancy a well proportioned monument, of comprehensible size, say eight or ten feet high, formed of one stone, exquisitely finished, and set, not in a graveyard, but in a wild pleasure-ground. Now, magnify it to a hight of fifteen hundred feet, retaining its simplicity of form, and fineness, and brilliancy, and fill its surface with crystals; then you may have some conception of the rare beauty and sublimity of this ice-burnished cone, one of the noblest monuments of the glacial period to be found in the range.

In making the ascent we find that the curves of the base rapidly steepen, but the feldspar crystals, two or three inches long, having offered greater resistance to atmospheric erosion than the mass of the rock in which they are imbedded, have been brought into relief, roughening the surface here and there, and offering slight footholds, while some of them have been weathered out altogether, and rolled to the bottom, forming a glittering ring around the base. And it is interesting to observe that, after the outer layer of crystals, whose upper surfaces formed part of the original glaciated surface, have been weathered out, the lower layers, as they successively come to the surface, unprotected by the glacier polish, have but little superior power of resisting disintegration, and, therefore, the whole surface is subsequently weathered off at about the same general rate.

The summit of the monument is burnished and scored like the sides and base, the scratches and striæ indicating that the mighty glacier of the Tuolumne Basin overwhelmed it while it lay dark and steadfast beneath the crystal flood, like a bowlder at the bottom of a river. How enormous the pressure it withstood! Had it been less solidly built, it would have been carried away- ground into moraine fragments, like the adjacent rock in which it lay imbeded; for it is only a residual knot, brought into relief by the removal of the less resisting rock about it

—an illustration in stone of the survival of the strongest and most favorably situated.

Hardly less wonderful is its present unwasted condition, when we contemplate the long, dark procession of storms that have fallen upon it since first its crown rose above the icy sea. The whole quantity of post-glacial wear and tear it has suffered has not degraded it a single inch, as may readily be shown by measuring from the level of the polished portions of the surface.

A few erratic bowlders, nicely poised on the rounded summit, tell an interesting story, for they came from the alpine peaks twelve miles away, drifting like chips on the frozen sea, and were stranded here, while their companions, whose positions chanced to be above the slopes of the sides, where they could not come to rest, were carried farther on by falling back on the shallowing ice.

The general view from the summit consists of a sublime assemblage of ice-born rocks and mountains, lakes and meadows, and moraines covered with forests and groves—hundreds of square miles of them—builded together into one of the brightest and most openly harmonious landscapes to be found in all the range. The alps rise grandly along the sky to the east, the gray pillared slopes of the Hoffmann Range toward the west, and a billowy sea of shining montoned rocks seem, from their peculiar sculpture, to roll on westward in the middle ground. Immediately beneath you are the Big Tuolumne Meadows, eight miles long, with an ample swath of dark, pine woods on either side, stretching east and west, enlivened by the young glistening river that is seen coming fresh from its fountain snow, tracing the lowest portion of the ancient Tuolumne *mer de glace*, which, during the snow period, was lavishly flooded by many a noble affluent from the ice-laden flanks of Mounts Dana, Lyell, Maclure, Ord, Gibbs, Conness, and others that are yet nameless. The *mer de glace* thus formed was over four miles wide, and poured its majestic outflowing current full against the end of the Hoffmann Range, which divided and deflected it to right and left, just as a river of water is divided against an island that stands in the middle of its current. Two distinct glaciers were thus formed, one of which flowed through the great Tuolumne Cañon and Hetch Hetchy Valley, while the other swept upward for five hundred feet in a broad current across the divide between the basins of the Tuolumne and Merced, into the Tenaya Basin, and thence down the Tenaya Cañon into Yosemite Valley.

The map-like distinctness and freshness of this glacial landscape cannot fail to excite the attention of every beholder, no matter how little its scientific significance may be recognised. These bald, westward-leaning rocks, with their rounded backs and shoulders toward the glacier fountains, and their split, angular fronts looking in the opposite direction, explained the tremendous grinding force with which the glaciers passed over them, and also the direction whence the glaciers flowed; and the mountain peaks around the sides of the upper general Tuolumne Basin, with their sharp, unglaciated summits and polished, rounded sides, indicate the hight to which the glaciers rose; while the numerous moraines, curving and swaying in beautiful lines, mark the boundaries of the main trunk and its subordinate tributaries as they existed toward the close of the glacial winter just before they vanished. None of the great commercial highways of the land or sea, marked with buoys and lamps, fences and guide-boards, is so unmistakably indicated as are these abandoned pathways of the vanished Tuolumne glaciers.

I would like now to offer some nearer views of a few characteristic specimens of these old dead ice-streams, which have exerted so profound an influence on the scenery of the mountains, and concerning which so little is generally known, though it is not easy to make a selection from so vast a system so intimately interblended. The main affluents of the great Merced glacier are perhaps best suited to our purpose, because their basins, upon which their histories are vividly portrayed, are more approachable to the general traveler, and are comparatively well defined. They number five, and may well be called Yosemite glaciers, since they were the agents by which beauty-loving nature created the grand valley, grinding and fashioning it out of the solid flank of the range, block by block, particle by particle, with sublime deliberation and repose.

The names I have given them are, beginning with the northmost, Yosemite Creek, Hoffmann, Tenaya, South Lyell, and Illilouette Glaciers. These all converged in admirable poise around from north-east to south-east, welding themselves together into one huge trunk which swept down through the valley, filling it brimful from end to end, receiving small tributaries on its way from the Indian, Sentinel, and Pohono Cañons; and at length flowed out of the valley, and on down the range in a general westerly direction. At the time that the tributaries mentioned above were well defined as to their boundaries, the upper portion of the valley walls, and the highest rocks about them, such as the Domes, the uppermost of the Three Brothers, and the Sentinel, rose above the surface of the ice. But during the valley's earlier history, all its rocks, however lofty, were buried beneath a continuous sheet, which swept on above and about them like the wind, the upper portion of the current flowing steadily, while the lower portion went maring and swedging down in the crooked, dome-blocked *cañons*. Every glacier of the Sierra fluctuated in width and depth and length, and consequently in degree of individuality, down to the latest glacial days. It must, therefore, be borne in mind that the following descriptions apply only to their separate condition, and to that phase of their separate condition that they presented toward the close of the period when most of their work was done, and all the more telling features of the valley and the region adjacent were already brought into relief.

THE YOSEMITE CREEK GLACIER.

The broad, many-fountained glacier to which the present Yosemite Creek Basin belonged, was about fourteen miles in length by four or five in width, and from five hundred to a thousand feet deep. Its principal tributaries, drawing their sources from fountains set far back among the northern spurs of the Hoffmann Range, at first pursued a westerly course; then, uniting with each other, and absorbing a series of short affluents from the western rim of the basin, the trunk thus formed swept around to the southward in a magnificent curve, and poured its ice over the north wall of Yosemite in cascades two miles wide.

This broad and comparatively shallow glacier formed a sort of crawling, wrinkled ice-cloud, that gradually became more regular in shape and river-like as it grew older. Encircling peaks began to overshadow its highest fountains, rock islets rose here and there amid its ebbing currents, and its picturesque banks, adorned with domes and battlements, extended in massive grandeur down to the brink of the Yosemite walls. When the long winter had nearly passed, the main trunk, melting and ebbing from season to season, at length vanished altogether in the sunshine, and a multitude of waiting plants made their way into the new grounds prepared for them.

In the meantime the chief Hoffmann tributaries, slowly receding to the shelter of their fountain shadows, continued to live and work independently, spreading garden soils, deepening lake basins, and giving finishing touches to the sculpture of their fountain rocks. At length these also vanished, and the whole basin is now full of light. Forests flourish luxuriantly upon its ample moraines, lakes and meadows nestle everywhere amid its shining rocks, and a thousand gardens, filled with the fairest flowers, are blooming along the banks of its streams.

THE HOFFMANN GLACIER.

The short, swift-flowing Hoffmann Glacier offered a striking contrast to the one just described, both in appearance and manner of working. The erosive energy of the latter was diffused over a wild field of sunken, bowlder-like domes and ridges. The Hoffmann Glacier, on the contrary, moved right ahead on a comparatively smooth surface, making a descent of nearly five thousand feet in five miles, steadily contracting and deepening its current, and finally thrusting itself between the Yosemite domes in the form of a solid wedge of ice.

The concentrated action of this energetic glacier, combined with the Tenaya, accomplished the greater portion of the disinterment and sculpture of the great Half Dome, North Dome, and the rocks adjacent to them. Its fountains, extended along the southern slopes of the Hoffmann Range, gave birth to a series of short, fan-shaped tributaries, separated from each other by picturesque walls, that are built of massive granite blocks, bedded and jointed like masonry.

The story of its death is not unlike that of its companion, already described, though the declivity of its channel, and its uniform exposure to sun-heat, prevented any considerable portion of its current from becoming torpid. It was first burned off on its lower course, slowly withdrawing, and lingering only well up on the mountain slopes, beneath its fountains, to finish their sculpture, and encircle them with a zone of moraine soil for forests and gardens.

The gray slopes of Mount Hoffmann are singularly barren and forbidding in aspect, but the traveler who is so hopeful as to ascend them will find there some of the very loveliest of the Sierra gardens. The lower banks and braes of the basin toward Yosemite are richly planted with chaparral, which yields a lavish abundance of bloom and berries, and is, therefore, a favorite place of resort for bees and bears, while the middle region is heavily wooded with silver-firs. Nowhere in all this wonderful region will you find more beautiful trees and shrubs and flowers. Nowhere will you find the cold traces of glaciers more warmly clothed with life and light.

THE TENAYA GLACIER.

The Tenaya Glacier was rugged, and broken up with yawning crevices and ice-falls, on account of the extreme hardness and solidity of the ridges it had to pass over.

Instead of drawing its sources directly from the summit of the range, it formed, as we have seen, one of the outlets of the Tuolumne *mer de glace*, issuing from this noble fountain like a river from a lake, two miles wide, about fourteen long, and from five hundred to fifteen hundred feet deep.

In leaving its source, it first flowed upward about five hundred feet over the divide between the waters of the Tuolumne and Merced, into the basin of Lake Tenaya. Hence, after contracting its wide current, which had been partially separated in crossing the divide, and receiving a strong affluent from the fountains about Cathedral Peak, it began to move with renewed vigor, pouring its massive flood over the south-western rim of the Tenaya Basin in splendid cascades. Then, crushing heavily against the Cloud's Rest ridge, it curved toward the west, compressed and welded its creviced current, and bore down upon the Yosemite domes with its whole concentrated energy.

Toward the end of the ice period, while its Hoffmann companion continued to grind rock-meal for coming plants, the whole trunk of the Tenaya Glacier became torpid, and vanished, exposing wide areas of rolling rock-waves and glistering pavements, on whose channelless surface water ran wild and free. And because the main trunk vanished almost simultaneously throughout its whole extent, we, of course, do not find terminal moraines curved across its channels; nor, since its banks are, in most places, too steeply inclined to admit of the deposition of moraine matter, do we find much of the two main laterals. The lowest of the residual glaciers belonging to this basin was developed beneath the shadow of the Yosemite Half Dome. Others were formed along the base of Coliseum Peak, on the south side of Lake Tenaya, and along the precipitous wall extending from the lake to the Big Tuolumne Meadows. The latter, on account of the uniformity and continuity of their protecting shadows, formed moraines of considerable length and regularity, that are liable to be mistaken for portions of the left lateral of the main glacier.

The pathway of this grand old glacier is noted for the depth of its *cañon*, the beauty of its lakes and cascades, and the extent of its resplendent glacier pavements.

THE SOUTH LYELL, OR NEVADA GLACIER.

The South Lyell Glacier was longer and more symmetrical than the last, and the only one of the Merced system whose sources extended directly back to the main summits on the axis of the range. Its numerous ice-wombs, now mostly barren, are ranged side by side in three distinct series, at an elevation of from ten to twelve thousand feet above the sea. The first series on the right side of the basin extends from the Matterhorn to Cathedral Peak. That on the left extends through the Merced group, and these two parallel series are united by a third, which extends around the head of the basin in a direction at right-angles to that of the others.

The three ranges of summits in which these fountain-wombs are laid, together with the Cloud's Rest ridge, nearly inclose a rectangular basin, that was once a massive *mer de glace*, leaving an outlet toward the west opposite to the most fruitful of the fountains. The grand trunk glacier, lavishly filled by the tributaries derived from these numerous ice-wombs, was from three-fourths of a mile to a mile and a half wide, fifteen miles long, and from one thousand to fifteen hundred feet deep.

After flowing in a north-westerly direction for a few miles, it swerved to the left, and poured its shattered cascading current into Yosemite Valley between the Half Dome and Mount Starr King.

Could we have visited Yosemite Valley at this period of its history, we should have found its ice cascades vastly more glorious than their tiny water representatives of the present day. One of the grandest of these was formed by that portion of the Lyell Glacier that fell over the shoulder of Half Dome.

This glacier, as a whole, resembled an oak, with a gnarled, swelling base and wide-spreading branches. Picturesque rocks of every conceivable form adorn its banks, among which glided the numerous tributaries, mottled with black and gray bowlders, from the fountain-peaks, while ever and anon, as the deliberate centuries passed away, some dome raised its burnished crown above the ice to enrich the slowly opening landscape.

The principal moraines occur in short, irregular sections, scattered along the sides of the *cañons*, without manifesting subordination to any system. This fragmentary condition is due to interruptions, caused by portions of the sides of the *cañons* being too steep for moraine matter to lie on, and to the breaking and down-washing of torrents and avalanches, while the obscurity resulting from these is still further augmented by forests and their underbrush, making a patient study of details indispensable to the recognition of their real unity and grandeur.

The left lateral of the trunk may be traced about five miles from the mouth of the first main tributary to the Illilouette Cañon. The corresponding section of the right lateral, ex tending from Cathedral tributary to the Half Dome, is more complete because of the evenness of the ground. A short side-glacier came in against it from the slopes of Cloud's Rest; but, being fully exposed to the sun, it was melted long before the main trunk, allowing the latter to deposit this portion of its moraine undisturbed. Some conception of the size and appearance of this fine moraine may be gained by following the Cloud's Rest trail from Yosemite, which crosses it obliquely and conducts past several sections made by streams. Slate bowlders may be seen that must have come from the Lyell group, twelve miles distant. But the bulk of the moraine is composed of granite and porphyry, the latter derived from Feldspar and Cathedral Valleys.

On the sides of the moraines we find a series of terraces firmly expressed, indicating fluctuations in the level of the glacier, caused by variations of snow-fall, temperature, etc., showing that the climate of the glacial period was diversified by cycles of milder or stormier seasons similar to those of post-glacial time.

After the depth of the main trunk diminished to about five hundred feet, the greater portion became torpid, as is shown by the moraines, and lay dying in its crooked channel, like a wounded snake, maintaining for a time a feeble squirming motion in places of exceptional depth, or where the bottom of the *cañon* was more steeply inclined. The numerous fountain-wombs, however, continued fruitful long after the trunk had vanished, giving rise to an imposing array of short residual glaciers, extending around the rim of the general basin a distance of nearly twenty-four miles. Most of these have but recently succumbed to the new climate, dying in turn as determined by elevation, size, and exposure, leaving only a few feeble survivors beneath the coolest shadows, which are now completing the history of the South Lyell Glacier, one of the clearest and most symmetrical sheets of ice-manuscript in the Sierra.

THE ILLILLOUETTE GLACIER.

The shallow glacier that filled the Illilouette Basin more resembled a lake than a river of ice, being nearly half as wide as it was long. Its greatest length was about ten miles, and its depth perhaps nowhere much exceeded eight hundred or a thousand feet. Its chief fountains, ranged along the west side of the Merced group, at an elevation of about ten thousand feet, gave birth to fine tributaries that flowed in a westerly direction, and united in the center of the basin. The broad trunk at first flowed north-westward, then curved to the northward, deflected by the lofty wall forming its western bank, and finally united with the grand Yosemite trunk, opposite Glacier Point.

All the phenomena relating to glacial action in this basin are remarkably simple and orderly, on account of the sheltered positions occupied by its ice-fountains, with reference to the disturbing effects of larger glaciers from the axis of the main range earlier in the period. From the eastern base of the Starr King cone, you may obtain a fine view of the principal moraines sweeping grandly out into the middle of the basin from the shoulders of the peaks, between which the ice-fountains were laid. The right lateral of the tributary which took its rise between Red and Black Mountains measures two hundred and fifty feet in hight at its upper extremity, and displays three well defined terraces, similar to those of the South Lyell Glacier. The comparative smoothness of the uppermost terrace shows that it is considerably more ancient than the others, many of the bowlders of which it is composed having crumbled. A few miles to the westward, this moraine has an average slope of twenty-seven degrees, and an elevation above the bottom of the channel of six hundred and sixty feet.

Near the middle of the main basin, just where the regularly formed medial and lateral moraines flatten out and disappear, there is a remarkably smooth field of gravel, planted with *arctostaphylos*, that looks at the distance of a mile or two like a delightful meadow. Stream-sections show the gravel deposit to be composed of the same materials as the moraines, but finer, and more water-worn from the action of the converging torrents issuing from the tributary glaciers after the trunk was melted.

The southern boundary of the basin is a strikingly perfect wall, gray on the top, and white down the sides and at the base with enduring snow, in which many a crystal brook takes its rise. The northern boundary is made up of smooth, undulating masses of gray granite, that rise here and there into beautiful domes, dotted with junipers and fringed around their bases with pine and silver-fir; while on the east tower the majestic fountain peaks of the Merced group, with wide *cañons* and *névé* amphitheaters between them, whose variegated rocks show out gloriously against the azure sky.

The ice-plows of this charming basin, ranged side by side in orderly gangs, furrowed the rocks with admirable uniformity, producing irrigating channels for a brood of wild streams, and abundance of rich soil adapted to every requirement of garden and grove. No other section of the Yosemite uplands is in so perfect a state of glacial cultivation. Its domes, and peaks, and swelling rock-waves, however majestic in themselves, are yet submissively subordinate to the garden center. The other basins we have been describing are combinations of sculptured rocks, embellished with gardens and groves; the Illilouette is one grand garden and forest, embellished with rocks, each of the five beautiful in its own way, and all as harmoniously related as are the five petals of a flower. After uniting in the Yosemite Valley, and expending the down-thrusting energy derived from their combined weight and the declivity of their channels, the grand trunk flowed on out of the valley without yielding much compliance to the crooked *cañon* extending from the foot of the main valley proper. In effecting its exit, a considerable ascent was made, traces of which may still be seen on the abraded rocks at the lower end of the valley, while the direction pursued after leaving the valley is surely indicated by the immense lateral moraines extending from the ends of the walls, at an elevation of from fifteen hundred to eighteen hundred feet. The right moraine was disturbed by a large tributary glacier that occupied the basin of Cascade Creek, causing considerable complication in its structure. The left lateral is simple in form for several miles of its length, or to the point where a tributary came in from the south-east. But both are greatly obscured by the forests and underbrush growing upon them, and by the denuding action of rains and melting snows, etc. It is, therefore, the less to be wondered at that these moraines, forming so important a part of the chips derived from the valley rocks in the process of their formation, were not sooner recognized.

The ancient glacier systems of the Tuolumne, San Joaquin, Kern, and King's River Basins were developed on a still grander scale, and are so replete with interest that the most sketchy outline descriptions of each, with the works they have accomplished—the mountains they have brought into existence, the *cañons* they have furrowed, the rocks they have crushed, and worn, and scattered in moraines—would fill many a volume. Therefore, I can do but little more than invite everybody who is free to visit these interesting regions and see for themselves.

The work of glaciers, especially the part they have played in sculpturing the face of the earth, is as yet but little understood, because they have so few loving observers willing to remain with them long enough to appreciate them. Water rivers work openly where people dwell, and so does the rain and the dew, and the great salt sea embracing all the world; and even the universal ocean of air, though invisible, yet it speaks aloud in a thousand voices, and explains its modes of working and its power. But glaciers, back in their cold solitudes, work apart from men, exerting their tremendous energies in silence and darkness. Outspread, spirit-like, they brood above the long predestined landscapes, working on unwearied through unmeasured ages, until, in the fullness of time, the mountains and valleys and plains are brought forth, channels furrowed for the rivers, basins made for the lakes and meadows and long, deep arms of the sea, soils spread for the forests and the fields—then they shrink and vanish like summer clouds.

JOHN MUIR.

"UTOPIA."

The incidental mention in a rambling article recently published in THE CALIFORNIAN, of a desire to found a new city or community somewhere in the warm and roomy South-west, has brought upon me a deluge of letters.

No man who is much in earnest in this world can have either time or inclination to answer the chronic letter-writer of America. He or she is the most prolific growth of this great land. Idle-handed and empty-headed, this creature, which cheap postage and thin education has made possible, is the nuisance of the nineteenth century.

But among all these letters there are half a dozen, at least, from earnest, honest, and thoughtful people, and these letters, so far from vexing me, give the greatest encouragement—not from what they say, propose, or promise, for they are mostly merely brief inquiries, with here and there a thoughtful suggestion; yet the *fact* that so many solid minded men and women are in sympathy with an enterprise of this kind shows not only its need, but that it can succeed.

I do not count Brook Farm at all a failure. Indeed, I am almost ready to reckon it the greatest success ever achieved. I know it is the custom to say that such minds as those of Fuller, Hawthorne, Ripley, Dana, Curtis, and so on, conceived Brook Farm. I think it more correct to say that Brook Farm gave us Nathaniel Hawthorne, Margaret Fuller, George William Curtis, Dana, Ripley, and on through the catalogue of the greatest, purest, best brain of America.

There are a dozen reasons why this little community, so far as the "business" of it was concerned, came to an end. Plant a pine under the shadow of an oak, and it will die, although the pine be the statelier tree of the two if it can have the sun. This new city must be planted out, by itself—far out, where there is room, and in the warm sun, and in the prolific soil of another land than New England. And in another land, not only because of the richer soil and the warmer sun, but because the cardinal points must be diametrically opposed to the one hard, dominating idea of Yankee character, if it is to flourish long and do any great good upon earth.

I respect her money-getting—her hard, cold soil and climate have crystallized it. And money-getting, up to a certain point, makes greatness. But the sinews of war are not war itself.

And it is to be admitted that in all her money-getting this little land of granite and ice has brought more renown to the Republic, and done more solid good to the world, than all the other States of the Union.

But that is not the proper line of argument. Consider, rather, if she has done so much with all her hard opportunities, what is it she might not do if she had the ample leisure which the Community proposed would afford her children?

I will now briefly set down some of the cardinal ideas involved in this new establishment. It is the briefest and best way to answer these letters. The writers of those among them stamped with sincerity will be satisfied. As for the others, it does not matter.

In the city of London there is one man in thirteen at work. It takes the other twelve to stand over and watch that one man, and keep him at work.

This is a startling statement, but if you will consult statistics you will find it is the cold, frozen truth.

The city of Paris is even less industrious than London. The population of New York is so migratory and unsettled that there is no means of finding out just how idle she is, but it is safe to say that here there is not more than one man in seven or eight at work.

So you see that in the great cities of the world there is an average of about one man in ten obeying that great primal command, that by the sweat of your brow you shall eat your bread.

But how this one man has to work! Stand by and see him down in the dirt and muck, or see him pausing wearily on the pavement. He is in rags. He is filthy. His face is dirty. His hands are hard. His heart must be hard. His face is haggard and brutal. He does not lift his eyes. He works doggedly on. This man has not had enough to eat. That little tin bucket held his dinner. His *dinner*, mark you, my Lord Mayor and ladies and gentlemen, who would be miserable at missing a hot plate of soup, hot fish, hot meat, warm delicacies, and wine at *your* dinners! And yet you have not one of you done a stroke of real work in all your worthless lives.

This laborer, look at him again! He is a brute. You have made him a brute. You keep him a brute. His children will be brutes. Sometimes he lifts his eyes to the sun. May be he has been thinking. But he shakes his shaggy head, and his eyes droop, and he clutches again the pick-handle. There is no escape, and he knows it. The master is noting him. The police are eyeing him. You are all watching him. He must keep at it, ten, twelve, fourteen hours every day. You have tied him up, chained him, bound him tighter than ever slave was bound in savage Rome. Yes, right here, in the heart of your great Christian city.

One would think this strong man would climb out of the pit he has dug in the street to fix the gas or water-pipe or pavement, and run, and run, and run, for liberty, for life. But where would he run to? Right into prison. And so he holds on to his pick. He will climb out wearily when the sun goes down, take up his dirty coat in his dirty hands, and drag himself doggedly home. Home! He will kick his wife for the wrong that you have done him—you, whom he cannot reach. Then he will get drunk as he gets older and weaker and pains creep into his marrow, for he must have something to keep up his strength. Then he will kick his wife again. And what wonder! He is desperate, reckless. He must strike something, what matters it whom or what? He will kill her finally, for this wrong that you have done him. Then you will arrest him for murder. You will put him in prison, and, for the first time in his life, give him enough to eat. Then you will try him for murder. Then you will dress him up, for the first time in his life, and hang him. And what cares he? You have only taken him out of that grave in the street, and put him into another.

But suppose some one man out of the eight idlers had gone and got down into the pit with that poor laborer, and done half his work? Suppose that *three* of them had gotten into the pit, and left the poor man but one-quarter to do? He would have been a man. He would have lived a man, and died a Christian gentleman.

Secondly: Shut a man up in prison, and the average man will walk from six to eight hours daily. He will do this year in and year out, unless he be put to work there, for he must have exercise. In other words, a man must and will have some some sort of physical effort every day.

Now, what we must get at in order to bring this half civilized age out into full sunlight, where it may have some possibility of development, is to give this strength, this wasted physical force, some proper direction and application.

Statistics show us that there is only one man in seven or eight at work, so far as we can learn. Of course, in the provinces and fields they are more industrious than in the populous centers, but, for the sake of the proposition, we will say about that number.

Well, physical science, as well as observation, proves that these other seven absolutely need the exercise of honest toil, and will take it in any form or action, even if fenced up in prison, to the extent of about six hours a day.

These two facts are the foundation-stones on which to build this new community. The proposition, you observe, is not at all new. It is the old problem of the distribution of labor.

I believe it is pretty generally conceded by thoughtful men that our civilization is not, with all its culture, ease, and refinement, a towering success. And men are constantly hewing off corners, in the impossible effort to fit the divine doctrines of Christ into a life of idle luxury.

A hundred thousand honest clergymen climb into their pulpits every Sunday morning, perfectly conscious of the great unevenness—yes, I think unevenness is the word—of life, as laid out before them in the present form of civilization.

They charge you that by the sweat of the brow you must earn your bread. And yet they know perfectly well that the one effort of every parishioner before them is to avoid the primal curse—to get hold of money and loaf, and let the other fellow sweat *his* brow.

And this brings us back to that other old biblical truth, that money is the root of all evil.

Now, my plan is to have no money, or, rather, to have no rich man, no poor man, no individual property; but a city – a rich city, if God should so favor it—but a city in which every man there could lift up his face and say, "I own just as much, and no more, of this city, as the richest man in it. I helped make it, and it is mine."

Would you mind inquiring for a moment why men want money? To me the bravest and the greatest man in all history is Alexander the Great, and the grandest act in his life—in fact, the one act which illuminates it like a sunrise—was his behavior at the battle, or, rather, after the battle, of the Granicus. The spoils were enough to enrich an empire, but he gave away all to his generals and his soldiers.

"And what have you kept for yourself?" asked one.

"Hope!" answered Alexander, with his face lifted toward Indus.

Now, if a man could be brave—I mean morally brave, for, after our civil war, I don't think physical bravery need ever be questioned any more among Americans—all the time, and have plenty of faith and hope, he need not have much money to be happy. But man at heart is cowardly and weak, and he grows to be afraid he will come to want. He feels that he must have money, must build a wall of gold between himself and the possibility of want. And this is particularly the case with old men. As a man gets old and weak he often becomes very mean. It cannot quite be said that all old men are misers. But it can be asserted that all misers are old men.

The most common excuse that a strong man in his prime gives for his desire to get money is the wish to provide for those dependent upon him. A laudable desire indeed. And no doubt the man giving this reason is perfectly honest, and believes that he has this high and unselfish motive only. But, unfortunately for the solidity of this reason, we find the man who has not one relative dependent upon him just as eager to get money, just as mean-handed in keeping it.

No, the fact is we are all moral cowards. We are not only afraid to be poor, but, under our present form of society, we are ashamed of it. We even lie, and pretend to be rich.

Well, now, let us quit our city for a moment, and imagine ourselves established in a little new-built city, on a wooded and watered slope of the Sierra.

Let us suppose that we have everything there that heart can desire; that we have helped build this city; that we are part owners of it, and shall continue to be so long as we live or choose to remain there; and then let us ask ourselves what use we would have for money.

Of course, the force of habit, the hard, vulgar custom of clutching at every cent we could snatch from our neighbor might cling to us for a time. But you can see that the backbone of the desire to plunder our fellows would be broken; and knowing that for all life we would be provided for, and our children after us—why, the soul would grow good, and strong, and unselfish; and we could turn our splendid strength to higher and holier purposes than man has known since Adam's fall.

Before considering how this city is to be built, maintained, and governed, I wish you might have to shut up your book, turn down a leaf, and first imagine the happiness of a city where the only inequality is that which God himself has given to the minds and bodies of men—an inequality which is rather a difference of color or form than inequality. Just as a man arranging a garden would have red flowers, white flowers, huge or small, fragrant or fine to see; all unlike, all unequal, but all and each in time very good and to be desired.

Oh, the heart-burnings to be escaped in such a place! Consider how the rich man's neck would unbend; how the poor man's back would straighten till he stood up, straight and tall, as God first fashioned him.

Now, is this Community possible? It is as simple as is the opening of a farm in Colorado or California. I know some people will smile. Some may mock. But the world moves!

It is idle to expect any great capitalist to embark in this. The world has plenty of philanthropists; but they seem to me to prefer building a hospital to put a man in when he gets hurt, rather than put forth a little finger to help him from getting hurt at all.

But when one constantly has all this North Pole nonsense thrust in his face, millions thrown away, sending good, live men to perish up there in the cold for the sake of an uninhabitable land and sea, while we have so much untouched land here, which half a world might be made happy on, it seems as if there might be one man in the world who has faith enough in human nature to give it a chance out in the roomy West. But perhaps not. And since the enterprise has not money for its object, it very properly ought not to ask money to begin with. Bricks without straw? May be. But when you consider how Salt Lake City sprung up in the desert, without a penny, with only a pick and shovel in the hands of its builders to begin with, and with the millstone of polygamy about its neck all the time, you ought not to despair of this enterprise if it is worthy. And it is worthy, and it will succeed, without any man's help, if only a few brave, patient, and faithful souls begin it.

I once belonged to a little association formed solely for this purpose. Nearly ten years ago we talked this over and over in London. The idea has deep root there. We used to turn our faces toward our imaginary "Utopia" as a sort of Mecca of the club. And then we would fall to quoting "The Ancient Mariner." For you know Coleridge very nearly came over the sea for this same purpose.

Finally, when the King of Italy confiscated the property of the Church, and offered the monasteries for sale on easy terms, all of a sudden our ideal object seemed about to become a fact. Some members of our club chanced to be wintering in Rome, and one of them bought a large estate, with a city already built, down below Naples.

What a happy and hilarious party we were that rode down to take possession of the old haunted convent and half deserted city on a hill! We were going to invite all the Bohemian world. There should be no houseless wanderers any more. Here were houses enough certainly to shelter all the poets, painters, and musicians out of doors. We were going to lead a river from a neighboring mountain down through the streets of this deserted and dirty old city, and wash it clean for the first time in a thousand years.

But we soon discovered that the place was stricken with fever. And that was why it had been so long deserted. The people had died! Only a few miserable monks in brown, who rather preferred death to life, and the hideous marsh-buffalo, groaning and wallowing through the mud-lakes under the hill—these seemed to be the only satisfied inhabitants of the whole region; and finally, with the fever in every one of us, we went back to Rome and gave it up, satisfied that our only fit field of operations was in young and healthful America.

But our enterprise had created some stir in the Eternal City, and soon after our return the King gave us an audience. His Majesty was over kind, and tried to encourage us to go on. But our bright young leader was still very ill, and hardly able to get out, and we had but little heart left. He died soon after, and as the hot weather came on the others of our party scattered like birds, going whither each one's fancies or fortunes led or allowed, in search of health; for we were all suffering more or less from the malaria—and we never met any more.

A few years after, I laid my plans before the Emperor of Brazil. He was at first enthusiastic, and generously offered all the land required. At a subsequent interview, while insisting on giving a large tract of land, he quietly hinted that I had better bring all the people I wished to embark in the enterprise from my own country. I saw clearly that he had little faith in the work. And perhaps he was quite right, so far as his own people are concerned. The luxurious South American certainly possesses but little of that Spartan self-denial required to establish a community of this sort.

The enterprise was abandoned this time, not at all because of the Emperor's indifference, but largely because just about that time the British Government had to send out a ship to bring home certain colonists, who had, from a failure of crops and other misfortunes, become destitute and dissatisfied. Clearly, the climate and fates were against it here. Besides, as this is to be an experiment, it ought to be set up and maintained right in the current and under the eyes of the world, so that whatever good it brings forth might be made apparent and encourage other like Communities to spring up over the earth. There are to-day, scattered all over the United States, nearly half a hundred "Communities," of various kinds and qualities. But they are nearly all hampered and bound down by some sort of hard and narrow doctrinal point of religion. And then they all are devoted to getting money, just the same as are individuals. One of these Communities furnishes the canned fruits of the world, and accumulates great wealth. Another one makes the famous Shaker rocking-chair. But none of these societies make any claim to superior culture, either physical, mental, or moral. And certainly they are made up, as a rule, of very melancholy types of humanity.

Perhaps the most intelligent and deserving of all associations of a coöperative sort in America is that of New Rugby, established by Tom Hughes, M. P. But let it be borne in mind that all these Communities, whatever their tenets, pretensions, or pursuits, are all getting on well, getting wealthy—are content and happy.

Remember our object is not to make money. Our aim is solely and simply to make men. The first thing to be thought of is perfect physical development.

No man should be permitted to commit suicide. If he must kill himself he ought to do it instantly, however, and not by slow degrees, during which time he begets his kind, bequeathing his disease and his weaknesses.

And so no man or woman should be permitted to do one stroke of work more than is needful for the healthful development of the body. To do more is to injure God's image, and outrage heaven. But only think how many millions have to do this every day as society is now organized—or do worse. I think I have explained that every man must have a certain amount of exercise. Let this exercise be taken at the plow-handle, the carpenter's bench, or anywhere, or in any way that a man may choose to work, just so much as his health may require, and no more, and we have the solution of the whole matter. Let *every* man do four hours' work each day, instead of every *eighth* man doing sixteen hours' work; and see how much more work would be done! And only consider what a strong and mighty race of men would spring out of the earth!

This would be one of the cardinal aims of Utopia. We would put physical culture first, because nature has put it first.

I know the theologian who follows the pale light of his midnight lamp down to the very edge of his grave, and thinks he is doing God's service in the act, would place moral culture first. And I know that the nervous and hollow-breasted student, who forever holds a book before his eyes and shuts out the sight of heaven, would place mental culture first. But I tell you that moral culture and mental culture are only handmaids, waiting meekly and dependent entirely upon physical perfection.

Give me a perfectly healthy man who sleeps well, and I will trust him utterly. And only think of the boundless possibilities of such a culture!

Poor man! For many, many thousand years a slave to his fellow-men, and even now a slave to himself. For the past half century, the horse has had some opportunities to show the blood that is in him. But man has never had any opportunity whatever. Give him half the chance of a horse. Let him forget for half a century the slavish habit of money-getting, even in our little colony as contemplated, think of his body, his mind, and his Maker, and there would be race of gods upon earth. For surely man is as capable of culture and development as the horse, the ox, the rose bush, or the pear tree.

Of course, it is repulsive to think of training up a man's body as you do that of the lower animals. But when that training leads up through pleasant paths, by the founding of cities such as I have dimly sketched, and hewing out ways for the weaker world to come after, then the idea becomes beautiful and poetic.

And here, in this simple and unselfish life, woman, for the first time in all history, would have perfect development of soul and body, and so take that higher plane to which she was born, standing midway, as it were, between God and man.

To get back to the hard practical fact of this city-building, let us consider how poor men are to accomplish it. Simply enough. You only need to begin. And you are really more in need of *men* than money. I mean strong, broad-browed men—men full of faith and hope and charity. For I care not how much money be embarked in the enterprise, if you do not have good, patient, moral, high-minded, and unselfish men and women to begin with, the undertaking will have but a brief and inglorious existence.

Some rich men proposed to me the other day that I should go out and locate this city, and they would furnish all the men and money necessary; and if the community failed of its purpose, it could dissolve and become a settlement, just like any other frontier town; and they would hold the deeds to the lands thus made valuable, and so, even at the worst, secure to themselves great profit.

This smell of money is so rank! Besides, when I do embark in this, if ever, I shall burn my ship; there will be no contemplated turning back. Better to go right out, one or two or three strong, and somewhere on a green and watered slope of the mountains, remote from settlements, but not too far from railroads, build a camp-fire, mark your bounds upon the land, proclaim it yours, and so begin.

You will have a sufficient following, I think, and very soon, if you once go rightly and bravely to work. The first things to be considered must be health and beauty in the location. The great men of the earth have grown up with the mighty mountains at their back and the plains for a play-ground.

Only to think of locating a city on a high watered and wooded slope, ten thousand miles to choose from, with only health, comfort, and beauty to be considered!

Never yet has been a city located with such high privilege. They have all been built subservient to commerce, to money-getting. Every city in the world save the two theocracies, Jerusalem and Salt Lake City, has been laid out and built by some marshy and sickly boat-landing, or railroad center, to oblige commerce and to make money, without any regard to health, comfort, or beauty of location whatever. And beauty is such an ally of goodness.

Of course you must have plenty of farming land at hand, rich and well watered; mountains for sheep, and plains for cattle. And then you should have mines, where surplus, new men could be set to work to take their three or four hours' exercise daily, until they could be fitted into any other place or employment, should they prefer it.

Either by ignorance or accident, I find that about one-half the world has got into the wrong box. Just about half the people you meet are dissatisfied with the calling in which they are engaged. All this is at once to be set at rights here, and every man, woman or child is to do just what he or she chooses to do in these few hours of exercise they must take.

Our agreed plan in London was to begin with at least fifty strong, and money enough to build a few substantial houses, and stock our lands with cattle, sheep, and horses, and to also plow and sow as much land as would furnish our few men their required exercise in caring for it.

We, of course, expected our members to double, treble, quadruple right along year after year, after we once got fairly to work and the world came to understand our high aims and the health, happiness, delights of our new life.

Our purpose was to admit every man, woman, or child who came to us after we were once fairly established; though it was settled that great care would have to be shown in getting in good material for the keel and main timbers of our ship at the start, so as to maintain a high and artistic level.

Any one coming to us was to have a place at the common table at once, where we all ate together in a great hall, with music and merriment, as if each day was a gala-day. He was to have clothes if he were naked, just as good as the best of us. He was to be permitted to choose his kind of work, either cook, herder, hunter, dishwasher, or what not; and he was to take his exercise at that kind of employment, and from that moment be a part and equal owner of that city and all its property, its peace and happiness, so long as be chose to remain a part of it.

These men held that there is no really bad man on earth in his right senses. Crime, they said, came of disease of mind or body. But in our model city we would live so healthily and happily that there would be disease of neither mind nor body. And so there would be no crime.

For my own part, I am quite certain that every creature does the very best he can with the light and opportunities given him. I admit there are many great fools. But no man is wicked at heart who is healthy in mind and body.

Many of us are bent and ugly in mind and form, I know. But there is all the time an effort, a feeble effort—I know sometimes, a pitiful effort—to stand up straight. Trample on a plant, throw rocks and rubbish on it, crush it; yet it will try to struggle up toward the sun; it will creep up on its broken joints, peep up through the rocks and try to get straight and look as pretty as it can. Well, man is just like that. Give him a chance. He is at least as good as the plant under your feet.

All religions were, of course, to be tolerated, even encouraged. But it was agreed that we should have but one temple of worship; that this great temple in the center of the city should be lecture hall, church, music hall, theater, and general center for all public purposes. The question of religion was counted the hardest problem of all. But it was hoped that the various denominations would finally melt into a sort of liberal Christianity, where the services to be held regularly on Sabbath days would be composed mainly of lectures on religious subjects.

Our government, of course, was to have been that of the land. But, under and subject to this, we planned a sort of patriarchal system of directions. Yet one great object was to avoid all laws and rules as far as possible; for, as we considered that laws are made only for the punishment of the vicious, we hoped to never come in contact with them.

Early marriages were to be encouraged. And we hoped to establish such a high moral sense among our people that divorces would never be required or desired. The children were to all be brought up as one happy family —all alike and equal.

The ground-plan of our city was not unlike a wagon-wheel. The temple was to be the hub, with all the streets running to this great center, like the spokes of the wheel. And all were to live inside of this city, where sociability could be kept up and encouraged; for the isolated farm-house is well known to be a melancholy place, and often the scene of selfish and unmanly tyrannies. The English, with all their boasted baronial independence, look with singular favor on the social life of the peasant just across the channel. It may not be generally known that there is not a single cottage or isolated farm-house in all France. The Frenchman is too sociable for that, and will group his home close to that of his neighbors.

Such were some of the general ideas advanced in planning this new city, in the old world, now nearly ten years. Do not quite despise them; for the best of them came from the brightest minds of that time. And all were meant for the good of man.

Emerson has said it takes a great deal of time to be polite; and yet every gentleman is by nature very polite. Well, every man ought to have time to be a gentleman. This he would have in our Utopia: time to be good and great.

It was agreed among us that nothing should be written or said on this subject till something had been done. But, alas! the years have slipped through our fingers; two of the warmest supporters of the scheme have gone on to that grander City of Rest; the others are scattered over the world; I am growing gray, and nothing at all is done. And so I give these suggestions to you, lest we all die out, and the very idea of our great enterprise, of which we all hoped so much, should die out with us.

JOAQUIN MILLER.

AN EVENING WITH WINTOON INDIANS.

While angling for salmon and trout during a vacation, last summer, on the Cloud River, in Shasta County, I had an opportunity of seeing a Wintoon Indian make a fire by the friction of two pieces of wood. The process adopted by him differs in some particulars from that used by the savages of other countries. It will be of interest to the archæologist who desires to preserve the evidence of all the habits and customs of man in his original savage condition, and may be of service in showing some shipwrecked mariner how easily fire may be made where he can obtain two pieces of dry wood.

Word came to the United States Fishery that there was to be an Indian dance that evening at the upper *rancheria*, which is a beautiful spot on the right bank of the Cloud, about five miles above the fishery. Just before sunset, with two companions, I crossed the river in a dug-out, where we found the trail. The weather was perfect. The sun had descended below the hills that guard the western bank of the river. The narrow valley and its cold, hurrying stream, fringed with alders and azalias, were sinking into shade and seemed hushed to sudden silence, broken only in the still reaches and quiet pools by the occasional heavy splash of a salmon at play, or the sudden leap of the hungry trout intently busy in making entomological collections from among the ephemera, caddice and other flies, that spring into multitudinous and joyous existence under the magic wands of the long shadows creeping over the water. Our trail led along the east bank among the talus from Mount Persephone, whose gray limestone summits tower three thousand feet above the river. Our path was in the shadow of the opposite hills; but, a few hundred feet above us, the setting sun was bathing the somber rocks on our right in purple mist, while the loftier peaks stood out against the deep blue sky-like minarets burnished with refulgent gold.

After passing the cliffs, the trail led through groves of mingled oaks and pines self-planted on the benches above the river. How few Californians know that the particular region of the foothills of the Sierra in which both oaks and pines intermingle, is blessed with a more delightful and health-giving climate than any other portion of the State. The shadows now more rapidly darted up the mountain sides, and we were soon in the gloom of the forest, and found it difficult to keep our way. This trail is the only one near this bank used by the Indians in going up and down the river. Without doubt it has been used for thousands of years; yet in all this time it has never occurred to one of them to remove from it a fallen tree, or roll away a bowlder. I wondered, as we stumbled on in the dark, whether man, when first emerging from his original, savage state, commenced by the domestication of animals, cultivating the soil, or by clearing a path from his cave to the forest where he killed his game. The Wintoons have not yet arrived at any of these stages of civilization. They have no domestic animals other than the horse and dog, obtained originally from the Spaniards. The nearest approach to cultivation is not connected with a supply of food, but with intoxication. All of their camps are "kitchen-middens," in a state of slow but constant accretion, and the soil about them becomes very rich.

Wild tobacco (*Nicotiana Bigelovii*) grows sparsely in favored spots on the hills near the river. When, by accident, the seeds are carried to the rich and prolific soil of these kitchen-middens, it grows with added vigor to increased size, and is much prized by the Indians for smoking. To the civilized smoker of tobacco it has an intensely vile flavor, and is exceedingly nauseating and stupefying. When the plant makes its appearance above the ground in the spring they frequently loosen the earth about it with a sharpened stick, and pile brush about each plant to prevent it being trodden upon or injured. It has not occurred to them that the seeds could be saved and planted. While cultivating no food plants, they guard with jealous care particular oaks of the species *Q. Chrysolepis*, *Kellogii*, and *Brewerii*, and all the prolific nut-pines (*P. Sabiniana*), as these supply them a large amount of food. They are learning that the hog of the white man is their great enemy—that he eats the acorns as they drop from the trees, that he destroys the grass in the small valleys, the seeds of which they gather, and that he roots up and eats the camas (*Camassia esculenta*) and other bulbs, that yield them food when the salmon have returned to the ocean.

Filled, as these people are, with the densest ignorance and the most weird and mythical superstitions, they yet have, in all that relates to their supply of food, a knowledge of the natural history of their immediate vicinity that seems wonderful. No fish or crustacean of the river, no reptile, no animal or bird, no tree or plant, but has a name; and every child is taught these names, and given the knowledge of what can be used as food and what would be injurious.

In about an hour we arrived at the Government trout ponds, but found all the attendants had left for the dance, except an Indian with his canoe to ferry us again across the river. The village was about a mile above the crossing. On arriving we found a great many families had gathered, coming for many miles up and down the river. There were, probably, three hundred and fifty, of all ages. We learned that the dance and gathering was an annual meeting, partly religious, and that it is given as an expression of gratitude for the return of the salmon to the river.

The *rancheria*, or village, is on the right bank of the river, at a beautiful bend, where the water sweeps around the base of a mountain. From what could be seen at night, the spot had been occupied by the Indians for ages.

In the center of the *rancheria* was the *temescal*, or sweat-house. It was constructed by digging a large circular, basin-shaped hole in the ground, four or five feet deep. Around the edge of this hole large posts are sunk, about five feet apart, and which extend upward to the top of the ground. In the center are planted four large trunks of trees, with the original limbs upon them, extending a few feet above the surface. From these four trees stout limbs of trees are laid, reaching to the posts at the edge. These limbs are fastened firmly by withes to the branches at the center-trees. The whole is then thatched with pine and willow brush, and covered with a layer of earth about a foot in thickness. The entrance is a long, low passage, and is made by driving short, thin pine posts side by side, about three feet apart, and covered in the same manner as the house proper. To enter, one has to stoop quite low, and continue in this position until he comes into the sweat-house. We entered. All about us, crowded together, were the Indians, squatted on the earth, the males in the foreground, and the *mahalas*, or squaws, with their pappooses, in the rear. In the center a low, small fire was burning, quite near to which sat the caller of the dances, smoking a pipe which looked like three large wooden thimbles placed inside of each other. This he held perpendicularly in the air, with his head thrown back so as to allow his lips to inclose the mouthpiece. After puffing three or four times, he passed it to others of the crowd. Some of the Indians had similar pipes, but, so far as I could see, this one was the largest and finest.

Directly opposite to the entrance, there had been a kind of fence erected, behind which the dancers were getting ready. We did not have long to wait, for soon the caller commenced yelling, and all the eyes of the audience were turned toward the dressing-room. Out came the Indians—seven men and about fifteen *mahalas.* The men were naked, except for a girdle of eagle feathers about their loins and a narrow band of woodpecker feathers about the forehead. The latter is very handsome, and brings a good sum when sold. In their hands they carried long, thin reeds, covered with small, fine feathers, which they blew as they ran around the fire, stamping the ground. The women wore calico dresses of bright colors, and in their hands carried grasses, which they held up. As the men ran, the women formed a half circle about them, turning from side to side, all singing in a monotonous, low tone. They were accompanied by the musicians, who consisted of three men—one blowing a reed, one pounding on an old tin pan, and the other striking a split stick against a piece of wood. The time was perfect, and it was astonishing with what rapidity the men dancers got over the ground. They put their whole strength into the dance, and keep it up for an hour at a time, only stopping at intervals to get breath and hear comments on their performance. When the dance is finished, the men cast off the feathers and run naked, reeking with perspiration, and plunge into the river, the water of which is rarely warmer than 45° Fahrenheit.

It is usually those who are sick who take part in the dance of this kind, and this treatment is supposed to cure; but, as a remedy or luxury, it seems to have been in universal use among all the California Indians.

While the monotonous dance was in progress, we left the sweat-house, and, meeting Sarah, the daughter of the old Chief Consolulu, I asked her to tell her father that I wanted him to have an Indian make a fire as it was made before white men came to the country. Sarah is one of the few members of the Wintoon tribe who have any knowledge of the English language. When a child, she was taken to live with a family at Shasta. In a few years she became homesick, and longed for the companionship of her own people; for their wild, free life, and for the mountains where she was born. So Sarah turned her back to civilization and its constraints, and joined her people, that she might live as they live, and share their joys and privations. She retains, apparently, but little evidence of the attempt at civilization except her Christian name and some knowledge of the English language.

After long negotiations, and the exercise of considerable diplomacy, an Indian came to me, bringing his beaver-skin quiver, filled with arrows. From among these he took a dried branch of buckeye (*Æsculus Californica*) about as long as the shaft of an arrow, but much larger at one end. From his quiver he also produced a piece of cedar (*Librocedrus decurrens*). This was about eighteen inches in length, an inch thick, and two inches wide in the center, but tapering to a rough point at each end. Its general appearance might be described as boat-shaped. In the center of this piece of cedar, on one side, he had made a circular hole a quarter of an inch deep, with a piece of obsidian, and from this hole he had cut a channel extending to the edge of the wood. He now gathered a handful of dry grass, and some fine, dry, powdered wood from a decayed pine. Each end of the boat-shaped piece of cedar, with the side containing the hole and channel uppermost, was placed on a couple of flat stones and held firmly by another Indian. The dry grass was piled loosely under the center, and on it was scattered the fine powder of the decayed wood. The fine powder was also scattered in the channel leading to the hole in the center of the boat-shaped piece of cedar. He now took the branch of buckeye and placed the largest end in the circular hole, and, spitting on his hands, commenced revolving it back and forth rapidly between his palms, and at the same time bearing down with considerable force. This constant exercise of pressure, while revolving the buckeye, caused his hands to be rapidly shifted to the lower end of the stick, when he would remove them to the top again and renew the process. At the end of five minutes he was perspiring from the exercise, and no fire had been produced. He stopped a few seconds and said something. I asked Sarah to translate his speech. Sarah told me he was saying, "Fire, why don't you come to me now as you did when I was a boy?"

This he repeated several times, and commenced work again. In another five minutes smoke made its appearance where the two woods were in contact. In a few seconds the powdered dust of the decayed wood took fire, and the fine coals communicated this fire to the dust in the channel, and rolled down to the dust scattered on the dry grass. He now took the bundle of grass in his hands, and, carefully blowing upon it, soon created a blaze. Meanwhile, a great many of the Indians came out where we were, and crowded about us, and seemed to take great interest in the proceedings. All manner of questions were asked of us, and translated by Sarah; among which were:

"Where you come from? Don't white man have any more matches?" or, "You like this way better than white man's way?"

The buckeye is very much harder than the cedar; and I find it is the invariable custom among savage people, in making fire by friction, to use woods of different texture and hardness.

As soon as the fire blazed the crowd went back into the sweat-house, and we with them, but only to remain a short time, as it was already midnight, and we had a long distance to travel. Soon we were on our way to the fishery. As we were crossing the river, the moon came over the mountains and shone down upon us. We made a weird looking picture in the canoes, with an Indian at each end, paddle in hand. As the first gray streaks of dawn appeared in the north-eastern sky, we arrived at the fishery.

GEO. H. H. REDDING.

QUESTIONS.

Were I a bird to fly unto thee
In the wild weather, the wind and rain,
Beating my wings at thy window-pane,
Wouldst thou thy casement open to me?
In thy soft hands were I nested warm,
I should forget the cold and the storm,
Sheltered with thee.

Or, wouldst thou cold and unheeding be,
Turning to leave me affrighted there,
Fluttering, throbbing, in mute despair?
Then, thou no pity showing to me,
Fainting I'd fall in the stormy night
Dead 'neath thy casement's mocking light,
Driven from thee.

Were I a leaflet to float to thee,
Drenched with the dews of the morning sweet,
Lying in sunshine, low, at thy feet,
Wouldst thou not, tenderly lifting me,
Keep me to prove to the Winter snows
That the dead Summer had her rose,
Cherished by thee?

Or wouldst thou, finding no joy in me,
Leave me to perish beside thy way,
A little rose-leaf, withered and gray—
O my heart, unremembered to be;
There in the sunlight moldering to lie,
Crushed by thy feet as they hurried by,
Forgotten by thee!

JULIA H. S. BUGEIA.

NOTE BOOK.

WITH THIS NUMBER, THE CALIFORNIAN completes its first year and its second volume. We trust that our readers have not wholly failed to participate in the pleasure which we have had in our efforts to make it worthy of their perusal. Monthly magazines occupy a growing, rather than a contracting, place in modern literature. They have crowded the old-fashioned review to the wall. They are progressive, alive. In their pages appear the latest and best productions. Whatever proves worthy is afterward preserved in book form; the rest is allowed to perish. The magazine, therefore, is a sort of literary sieve, giving to the public the fine and sifted flour. Within certain recognized bounds there is great room for difference and individuality in a monthly. It may be local or cosmopolitan, purely literary or general in character, sectarian or non-sectarian, partisan or judicial, radical or conservative. It has been the aim of THE CALIFORNIAN, in a broad sense, to be what its name implies. Without provincialism, it has desired to be the exponent of the life which surrounds it, to be worthy of the resolute men and women who give to that life its vigor and its fascination. Doing this, it has also sought to be pure in spirit, to dwell upon the higher and better plane of human thoughts, sympathies, and emotions. It is for the reader to say how far these efforts have been successful. We would like each reader to answer this in his own mind. Accompanying this number is an index for the entire volume. It represents what we have accomplished, and we are willing to be judged thereby. Does it redeem our promises? Is it fairly a credit to the magazine? Is it reasonably an earnest of as good or better work in the future? Is it, or is it not, a good thing that such work should go forth to the world to offset the representations or misrepresentations that of late have been so frequent in regard to our Californian life? We request you to answer these questions for yourself, and to apply any test which you may deem reasonable for their solution. So far as patronage is concerned, we have met with a generous welcome. Starting at an inauspicious time, THE CALIFORNIAN has yet made an auspicious beginning. The subscription list and the sales at retail have been fully up to expectations. The advertising department has been liberally patronized. About to commence our new volume, it is with better assurances than ever before. That there is a field for a monthly upon this coast has been fully proven. It only remains for THE CALIFORNIAN to continue to show itself worthy of its opportunities. And, with the same generous response on the part of the public, those connected with the magazine pledge their best efforts toward the accomplishment of that result.

GENEROSITY IS THE CHEAPEST OF VIRTUES. In many cases it is almost synonymous with selfishness. If one has plenty of money, it is so easy to be generous. It involves so little trouble, so little personal exertion. Persons given up wholly to their own enjoyment, to their own pleasures even at a disregard for the comfort of others, often pride themselves on being generous in money matters. The little courtesies of life they never observe. The delicate forbearances of a nobly generous and unselfish spirit are unknown to them. They are loud in their opinions, domineering in their differences, headstrong in their resolutions. They make way with their elbows. And yet they plume themselves upon being free-handed "good fellows;" and so they are, by a money standard. But any virtue that measures itself by such a standard is base. The very giving of such men is selfish. They give for the pleasure it confers on them, not for that which it confers on the one who receives. True generosity shrinks from offering money, save in emergencies; is delicate in attentions; is considerate and forbearing; puts not itself forward, but yields precedence; and never gives itself patronizing airs, which destroy the grace of the most welcome gift. In truth, there is not one man in ten thousand who knows how to give a present — nor one woman in as many hundred. We are all so awkward when we try to be graceful; and so bungling when we try to be gracious.

IT IS A FINE THOUGHT OF EMERSON'S, that one ought to attain the full stature of his being in one place as well as in another; that one ought not to say, "I would be better, or of more consequence, if my life had been cast there instead of here." It involves the same old lesson of neglected opportunities. One's environment has really little to do with any real greatness there may be in his nature. Washington was great in an untrodden wilderness; Burns was great in an obscure cottage; Shakspere, in a play-house. One of the most famous of the German philosophers is said never to have traveled more than thirty miles from the little town where he was born. Emerson himself lives apart from the highways of the world. The truth is just here, that, let any man fix his ideals high; let him scorn meanness, affectation, hypocrisy; let him cherish sincerity, honesty, truth; and let his life represent, with singleness of purpose, some lofty principle, and, whether the world knows it or not, that man is great. If emergencies come, as constantly they do, all turn to him. There is no truer natural test than the instinctive dependence of weak natures on a strong one. It is useless to shift location. If we are unworthy in one place we will be unworthy in another. If we are not entitled to the favorable judgment of the world we shall not get it by a change of venue. Fix your mind upon any really great principle of life, and then ask yourself what better occasion could you have for its exercise than is presented to you every day. It is useless to go hunting opportunities as Don Quixote did. They come thick and fast around you. And, for that matter, opportunity never yet made any man great. It is always the man who lifts opportunity into eternal fame. It is a pitiful excuse, this plea that we would accomplish something if we were only somewhere else. I know of no idea which deserves a wider recognition than that here, in this present environment, in this living, throbbing present, is our supreme opportunity.

SCIENCE AND INDUSTRY.

SOMETHING NEW ABOUT THE FORMATION OF DEW.

We are all familiar with the bright, transparent beads of water formed upon grass and other kinds of vegetation during the clear and still nights of summer and autumn. This water is known as "dew," and the generally received theory of its formation was first clearly set forth by Dr. W. C. Wells, a physician of London, in his famous *Essay on Dew*, first published in 1814. This essay still continues to be the standard authority on the subject, and, so far as the writer is aware, nothing further new or of special interest in this connection has found its way into any standard publication up to the present time. Dr. Wells's theory, as is well known, sets forth that dew is a deposit of invisible moisture from the atmosphere upon surfaces, the temperature of which is lower than that of the surrounding atmosphere. The deposit formed in a warm day upon the outer surface of a pitcher of cool water is due to the same law. But now comes Mr. J. U. Lloyd, with a series of articles in the *Christian Standard*, of Cincinnati, commencing with July 24, 1880, in which he admits that the idea is beautiful and the theory true to a certain extent, but denies that all the moisture thus observed is derived from the atmosphere. He holds that there are two kinds of dew, derived from entirely unlike sources, and which, when separately collected, show entirely different chemical characteristics. The one, when deposited from a pure atmosphere, is almost pure water, while the other, although collected from vegetation exposed in the same field and to the same atmosphere as the first, contains so large an amount of sugar (glucose) as, in some instances, to be quite perceptible to the taste. Mr. Lloyd says he had noticed that on certain species of grass dew is found in the evening in drops upon the tip end of each thrifty blade, before the remainder of the blade is moistened, and before there is moisture upon the surface generally of any vegetation in the vicinity; that these drops are continually falling off, from their accumulating weight, and are constantly being replaced by other drops at the same point. It was evident that these drops were not condensed from the atmosphere. He noticed that while one species first shows the drop upon the tip of the blade, others were covered with beads of moisture simultaneously along the entire edge of the blades, while still other herbs and leaves remained perfectly dry or exuded moisture from their entire surface. He asks, "Can this variation be explained by any law of radiation?" and answers the question in the negative. He argues, both from observation and reason, that dew proper is deposited from the atmosphere, according to Dr. Wells's theory, but that the drops formed at the tips and edges of certain grass blades and leaves, as above, are *exuded from the plants*. The sugar found in such drops is the surplus of that which is formed in the upward passage of the fluid, and which, not being appropriated by the plant, goes to waste in solution with the exuded water. Hence the familiar fact that cattle prefer grass which is, or has recently been, wet with dew (exuded moisture)—it is sweeter than that which is more dry. The term, "honey dew," is frequently applied to a moisture which sometimes attracts bees and other insects by its peculiar sweetness. There seems to be a great difference in the amount of water exuded by different plants. "Blue-grass" is especially noticeable for the rapid formation of drops on the tips of its leaves. The plant commonly known as "Indian turnip," the large-leaved species of Caladium, or "Elephant's Ear," etc., are also specially noticeable. He also holds that this excreted dew is greater in quantity than that which is condensed from the atmosphere. The philosophy of this exudation may be condensed from one of the Doctor's papers, as follows: The rootlets of each clump of grass, or of each shrub or bush, are constantly absorbing from the earth water charged with such mineral ingredients as are needed for the growth of the plant, and the grass blades and leaves are continually exhaling the surplus water into the atmosphere. The cells of the plants seize upon the nutritive principles, appropriating them to their support and growth. The surplus, or depleted water, escapes, in the day time by insensible evaporation, but during the night, when but little or no evaporation takes place, this moisture accumulates upon the leaf surfaces, and becomes visible. In some plants it exudes mainly from a few comparatively large microscopic openings in the tip of the leaves, as in blue-grass; from others along the edges; from others still, evenly over the entire surface. The latter, for evident reasons, is more generally confined to wooded plants, with leaves and branches. These deductions, the Doctor avers, are the result of extended observations, sometimes carefully conducted with chloride of calcium and bell glasses, and by other means. The question here raised is certainly a very interesting one, and will no doubt be speedily confirmed or exploded. It is given in these columns for what it is worth, as an interesting item in the progress of scientific investigation.

THE WORK NOW BEFORE ASTRONOMERS.

Professor Asaph Hall, in an address before the astronomical section of the American Association for the Advancement of Science, which lately held its annual session in Boston, gave an admirable outline of the present status and future prospects of the work before astronomers, which we briefly summarize as follows: An accurate knowledge of the proper motions of the fixed stars, and of the great changes of light and heat among them, can only be attained by long continued and laborious observations made through centuries yet to come. Hence, the observations of to-day should be carefully divided up and made so accurately that the astronomers of the future may rely with confidence upon the results of the labors of their predecessors to detect and measure changes which take place only during the lapse of ages. Similarly prolonged observations are also needed for the full development of the secular changes in our own solar system. With the exception of Neptune, the *orbits* of the planets are already quite well determined; but in many other respects much is yet to be learned. In the case of Saturn, all the tables are in error; but these errors are supposed to arise from some defect in the theory of that planet. The lunar theory is still an unsolved mystery, and all the lunar ephemerides are affected with empirical terms. The observations of the fixed stars are of the highest importance, since they are the fundamental points on which our knowledge of planetary motions and even the motions of the stars themselves depend. Previous to the present century, but little work had been done on double stars. In this field, although the work is simple, the observations should be made with great care and accuracy. The astronomer, above all other scientists, should have patience in his work, and be content to allow future generations to reap the reward of his toil. The physical theories of the universe, of which modern popular science is so productive, are generally worse than useless, notwithstanding he who rants freely about the nebular hypothesis is often considered one of advanced astronomers of the day. A good observation of the smallest double star, or of the faintest comet or asteroid, is worth more than all such vague talk. It is only about forty years since a stellar parallax was first measured, and then the most powerful instruments were employed. Much remains to be done in this direction. Photography, which has rendered good service in descriptive astronomy, does not admit of the accuracy of measurement required for stellar work. The determinations of the motion of stars toward or away from the sun are so discordant that no confidence can be placed in the results thus far obtained. It is hoped that some of the large instruments now in course of construction may throw more light upon this obscure subject. Argelander and his assistants completed their great catalogue of 324,198 stars in 1861. It is a work of great value and should be extended to other parts of the heavens. By taking account of a large number of stars, it may be possible to determine the motion of the solar system in space. Very few American observatories have been established for the purpose of doing purely scientific work, for they are generally built in connection with some college, and are the product of some local enthusiasm, which builds and equips an observatory and then leaves it helpless for support. The Professor remarked, in closing, that the present and prospective means for placing instruments at elevations of eight, and even ten thousand feet, will doubtless result in much good. At such altitudes, we may be able to do, with small apparatus, work that under ordinary conditions requires much more powerful instruments.

IRON-CLAD STEEL—A NEW MANUFACTURE.

A product of iron and steel, of a novel character, has recently been turned out at the Norway Iron Works, of South Boston. This new manufacture is called "iron-clad steel," from the fact that the steel in the mass is perfectly inclosed by a thin coating of soft iron. This inclosure is effected by first constructing a box of iron, which is filled with plates or bars of steel, an iron cover put on, and the whole subjected to a high heat until it becomes a solid mass. The walls of the iron box are then welded to the steel which has been placed within them, by being repeatedly passed through rollers until the mass has been drawn out into the desired shape of square, flat, or round bars. The most curious feature of the process is the fact that the iron and steel keep their places relatively—the iron constantly outside the steel, no matter how much it is worked, provided it is not cut. It may even be drawn out into an iron-clad wire, as gold is made to cover copper or brass while undergoing a similar manipulation. The advantage of the process is said to consist in the fact that the steel thus clad with iron is less subject to decarbonisation in the various processes of being worked up for use. After an instrument has been prepared, the iron can be readily removed, if desired, by the file or emery wheel, and a more perfect steel be produced. It is already being made into horse-shoes, and will be tested for other uses, as time and circumstances may suggest. The article is controlled by a patent, which belongs to the company above named, which is now engaged in the experimental work of introducing this new article of manufacture.

NEW OBSERVATIONS IN STELLAR PHYSICS.

Professor E. C. Pickering, of the Harvard Astronomical Observatory, has recently made a most interesting discovery, which is regarded as second in importance only to the revelations of the spectroscope, in regard to stellar physics. He has ascertained the fact that when a prism is placed between the object-glass and eye-piece of a telescope, the *light of a star* is drawn out into a continuous band, but when directed to a *planetary nebula* the light is collected into a star-like point, without any appearance of a band; hence, the astronomer is thus able to distinguish at once between a star and a planetary nebula. Immediate use was made of the new device, with most satisfactory results, as four other objects were soon discovered which are distinctly recognized as new planetary nebulæ. In addition to these, still another object has been brought to notice, which presents the appearance of two star-like points within a single continuous band. This is different from anything previously observed, and is regarded as an important object for investigation. Astronomers will look with much interest for further developments by means of this simple, but important, modification of the ordinary telescope.

A LIGHTNING FLASH.

All the more ordinary effects of "lightning" may easily be reproduced by artificial means, but on a very small scale—how small may be readily inferred from the fact that a three foot spark is considered a long one, even from the most powerful machines, while it is quite certain that lightning-flashes in the clouds, or from one cloud to another, often exceed a mile in length, and sometimes extend to four, and even five miles. The destructive power of a spark from a machine or from a lightning-flash in the clouds is proportioned to the distance over which the spark or flash will move. When a tree is struck by a violent discharge, a large portion of the trunk is usually split into fragments. A more moderate discharge simply ruptures the channels through which the sap flows, and a tree is often thus killed without any visible or external evidence of damage. This result is due to the sudden vaporization of the sap. In the first case the heat is so great and in such volume that the vaporization takes place with the suddenness due to the burning of an explosive compound, and may be illustrated by the violent action produced by pouring melted iron upon so small a quantity as only a few drops of water.

TRANSFORMING SOUND INTO LIGHT.

M. Trève has described to the French Academy of Sciences an experiment with an apparatus which he calls a singing condenser, by which he believes he effects the transformation of sound into light. When a current of electricity is brought to bear upon his condenser a sound is produced, which he attributes to the vibrations of the air in the condenser, produced by the shock of the electric current. Reversing this experiment, he placed the condenser in a Geissler tube, and brought the two poles of the electric current to bear upon the condenser through the electrodes of the table. The tube was then connected with an air-pump. The condenser sounded as usual when the current was directed to it under the ordinary atmospheric pressure; but when the air was withdrawn the sound became more and more feeble, until, as a vacuum was produced, it ceased entirely, and a clear, bright light appeared, sparkling like pearls, from the leaves of the condenser, quite unlike the ordinary pale, vague light of the Geissler tubes.

ART AND ARTISTS.

PICTURE SUBJECTS.

It has now become a recognized fact among artists that, for exhibition purposes, the larger and more important the canvas and subject, the greater likelihood there will be of its attracting its due amount of appreciation from the public. There is, no doubt, reason in this, especially in the larger exhibitions, where the exhibits extend into the thousands, as is the case annually in the Salon, and the more important exhibitions of the great European cities. There is so much to be seen, and the visitor's time is usually so limited, that he finds himself at a loss where to begin and how to bestow his time to the greatest advantage. Some consult the catalogues, and devote themselves principally to the contemplation of the work of those whose reputations are fully established. Others enter the gallery, and by a general, comprehensive glance, select those works whose power of color, composition, or subject are most apt to arrest the attention. By this course, all the more quiet and modest works—and, in many instances, most meritorious and carefully studied—are overlooked, and the artist who has perhaps devoted a year or two to the careful working out of his theme, has the mortification to see it entirely passed over, while other works, solely on account of their size or some striking feature, excite general comment. This accounts for the fact that the Salon in particular presents annually such startling subjects, in the way of tragedies and nudes. Few French artists expect to sell their exhibition works. They use the Salon as a means of advertising, and choose subjects in themselves striking, handling them in the most forcible manner their skill will permit, merely to bring themselves before the public and upon which to build a reputation that will serve them in the disposal of their other productions. Even in our local galleries, there is an acknowledged advantage in large over small pictures. When the exhibit is limited, large pictures are sure of good positions on the line, and the desire of the hanging committee to produce an agreeable *tout ensemble* often leads them to select the larger canvases as nuclei about which to group other works. This, in effect, often gives undue importance to such pictures, and is sure to redound to the advantage of the artists who produce them. The time is rapidly approaching, however, when the public will be more exacting, and will be guided in its judgment and approval more by truth and fidelity to nature, without regard to subject or size, than to any external factitious advantages. This brings us to the character of subjects generally treated by our California landscape painters. Probably few, if any, countries present the variety and beauty of subject for the painter afforded by our coast. For grandeur and massiveness, the Sierra will meet the demands of the most aspiring. The less rugged, but more picturesque, coast range, with its beauty of lines, running streams, and rich masses of foliage, present a class of subjects peculiarly and distinctively its own. The broad plains of the interior, dotted with oaks and cottonwoods, green and literally carpeted in the spring time with most brilliant patches of wild-flower coloring, and, later on, reduced to the somber, arid, and yet rich russets, browns, and soft, neutral grays of midsummer, afford subjects strikingly in contrast, and each abounding in beauties of their own that cannot but impress the lover of nature. Our sea coast is bold, rich, rugged, and in picturesqueness not easily surpassed. Indeed, the artist has but to express his wish, and Nature stands ready to more than meet it. We sometimes feel disposed to raise the question whether Nature has not been too bountiful toward the artists of California, and if, in her indulgence, she has not spoiled rather than benefited them. They have so long feasted upon the grand and massive that they no longer have a relish for Nature in her quiet and more lovely aspects. Every spring we read of long pilgrimages to the Sierra and Oregon in search of subjects for pictures, yet a half hour's walk in any direction from our metropolis reveals subjects that Corot and the great French landscape masters would grow enthusiastic over. We are reminded of this more particularly from having a few days since looked through the album of Mr. Latimer, one of the most promising of the students at the art school. Mr. Latimer is a careful draftsman and industrious worker, and has been filling his portfolio with drawings of bits of nature found in the neighborhood of Oakland and Alameda. His subjects are well chosen, and are highly picturesque, and reveal the existence of a class of subjects not hitherto treated by our Californian artists. Lying only an hour's ride from their studios, and with nature continually before them, some of our artists could in a few hours' time produce much more valuable and meritorious work, of a fresh and interesting character to the public, than could be evolved from the labors of the studio in as many days. Better a truthful portrayal of minor subjects than faulty delineations of massive subjects, valuable chiefly on account of their remoteness.

THOMAS NAST AND THE FRENCH SCHOOL.

A glance at many of the more recent numbers of the publication to which Nast usually contributes shows very plainly the influence of foreign training upon some of its pictorial contributors. We have for so long a time identified Nast with this periodical, and *vice versâ*, that it is difficult to reconcile one's self to the changed appearance of the paper since it has passed so extensively into the hands of other artists. Indeed, Nast may be said to have made it. The well known caricatures of this artist that have for so many years appeared, and the plain, frank individuality that characterized them, became as recognized features of that paper as the title-heading itself. Acknowledging Mr. Nast's great ability as a caricaturist, and the valuable service he has rendered both the paper and the various causes he has espoused, we are somewhat at a loss to understand the reason for his being supplanted to so great an extent in the later numbers. Rumor has it that certain political differences between proprietor and artist constitute the cause; but whatever it may be, the public greatly misses the artist's handiwork, and will continue to do so, notwithstanding the excellence of later contributions. As a caricaturist, Mr. Nast is difficult to excel. Though his work can hardly be called artistic, there is a force, directness, and unmistakable meaning to every line which stamps its superiority, and appeals at once to the understanding of the masses. With little attempt at composition, and less at movement or foreshortening, it seems to be the aim of this caricaturist to crowd as much meaning as possible within a given space. When figures do not suffice, inscriptions are inserted in every available space, combining letter-press with the pictorial, and producing a sort of compromise between the two, which strictly belongs to neither, but which is, for the purposes intended, of great force. Mr. W. A. Rogers's "Change in the Cabinet," in a recent number, shows much more of the artist, though, as is to be expected, his attempt at the pictorial places his work a little above the appreciation of the masses, and deprives it of that simplicity which is sometimes essential to the popular understanding. His drawing is good, and his grouping effective, and the variety of pose and expression gives his work a value above that of merely a political cartoon. In "Waiting for the Signal," a drawing by Thulstrup, the influence of the French school is more apparent than in any of the others. Were it not for the English inscriptions, one might almost imagine himself inspecting a plate from one of the modern French periodicals. The deep, flat shadows in juxtaposition to broad, simple lights, is a favorite method of treatment with many French artists, and bids fair to become popular with our own. The return of so many of our youth from foreign art institutions, with foreign ideas, will no doubt greatly influence the character of American illustrations; and it is not without regret that we look forward to the time when many of our homely and faulty, yet nevertheless cherished, notions of pictorial art will be supplanted in our own land.

A RISING CALIFORNIAN ARTIST.

Three pictures are exhibited by Messrs. Morris & Kennedy which are well worthy of attention, both from their intrinsic merit and from the fact that the painter of them is a Californian. They are the work of Mr. Thaddeus Welch, who, we understand, left San Francisco to study in Europe some seven years ago, and is at present in Paris. We have seen the works of many young Americans who have studied abroad, but we do not remember to have seen many which so completely justify the painters of them in having gone abroad as do these of Mr. Welch. It is too often the misfortune of young Americans in Europe to find that they have learned the language of color without having anything to say in it. They have learned painting, but have nothing to paint. Mr. Welch, however, shows in his pictures that he has studied the technical side of his art, not for its own sake, but chiefly and rightly as a means of expression. His three pictures all indicate that the workman has passed his apprenticeship, and feels an easy confidence in handling his tools. But, above and beyond this technical skill, they indicate gifts in the painter which will make us watch his development with the greatest interest. His subjects and his treatment of them show a wide sympathy with man and nature. There are two landscapes and one interior. Of the landscapes, the first represents a lonely, thatched farm-house, in midwinter. Snow covers everything, and the chief aim of the artist has been to depict the frozen necessity of winter, binding house and field. This he has well succeeded in doing; and the cold birds on the fence, and the on-coming gloom and storm, and, into the midst of it all, the men leading off their harnessed horses, all heighten the effect. The second landscape is a delightful pastoral. On a little hillside, divided by a stream which makes a passage just wide enough for us to look through and see that the city lies far away, a number of sheep are grazing, watched by two boys. It is just after lambing-time, and the lambs follow their mothers. Nobody who had ever observed the lives of sheep could fail to recognize this picture's truth to nature. There, in a delightfully cool shadow in the foreground, lies one ewe resting; near by stands another, whose ears some anxiety for its lamb has pricked into alertness; a little way off, a ewe is giving suck to its lamb, and the little fellow, down on his fore-knees, shows all his satisfaction in his vibrating tail; other ewes graze on the hillside, and the impatient ram is moving among them. The charm of the picture is complete. This sweetly depicted bit of country life shows a deeper feeling for nature than we have noticed in the work of any young American. It has a touch of pure poetry. The third of Mr. Welch's pictures represents a shoemaker at work in his shop. He sits facing the window, against which the snow is piled up from without, and in front of him is his work-bench, covered with all his tools. He is repairing the shoe of the little girl with the red shawl around her head, who stands at his left. The theme is humble, but not too humble for Mr. Welch's sympathy and loving treatment. He evidently believes in the dignity of work, however humble; for into this picture he has put qualities which make it an important revelation of his strength and vigor as an artist. It is altogether the most powerful of his three pictures, and leads us to expect great things of Mr. Welch. We shall look forward to the appearance of his future works with much interest, which, we doubt not, will be shared by many of our readers.

BOOKS RECEIVED.

HISTORICAL STUDIES OF CHURCH-BUILDING IN THE MIDDLE AGES—VENICE, SIENA, FLORENCE. By Charles Eliot Norton. New York: Harper & Brothers. 1880. For sale in San Francisco by A. L. Bancroft & Co.

This most delightful book, with its vivid pictures of the three great Italian republics, each at the heyday of its life, makes us feel proud of the achievements of American scholarship. Its author, Mr. Charles Eliot Norton, a near relative of that distinguished scholar, George Ticknor, whose memoirs were published four years ago to the great pleasure of the literary world, sustains and amplifies his relative's fame. The intimate friend of Carlyle and Ruskin and Burne Jones in England, and of Lowell and Longfellow and Emerson in America, Mr. Norton has shown, in studies of Dante, of Turner, and of William Blake, the rarest sympathy with genius. But he has chosen lately to express himself less through direct communication with the public than through personal contact with the students of Harvard, where, as professor of the fine arts, he has been for the past five years, according to the general testimony of recent graduates, the most potent source of culture within the university. We are, therefore, especially grateful for this present book, which we have no hesitation in pronouncing the most important contribution to an intelligent appreciation of the spirit and work of the church-builders of the middle ages that has appeared since Ruskin's *Stones of Venice*. Books there are in plenty which measure these same cathedrals of Venice, Siena, and Florence by rule of thumb, and set forth their dimensions; but Mr. Norton's work differs from all of these in the noble and scholarly manner in which he unfolds, in vivid pictures from contemporary records, the conditions of life which made the building of such cathedrals possible. Architecture, no less than music, or poetry, or painting, is the expression of the thoughts and feelings of the nation that creates it; and he is but a beginner in the study of it who has not passed from the study of dimensions to an inquiry into the causes which give a nation once, but not again, the power to express itself in architectural forms of supreme beauty. For the satisfaction of such an inquiry, Mr. Norton's book is a treasure-house of materials. Opening with a preliminary account of the state of Europe after the disruption of the Roman Empire, it proceeds to describe the upgrowth of the new order of society, in which Christian piety and civic pride became the most potent directors of national energies. Successively in Venice, in Siena, in Florence, the building of their great cathedrals during the twelfth, thirteenth, and fourteenth centuries, is depicted as the monumental expression of their piety and their patriotism. The charm of the narrative cannot be transcribed. In temperance of statement, in grace and strength of diction, in unerring appreciation of all that is noblest in thought, word, and deed, the book is beyond praise. It has, too, that freshness of originality which results from the fact that the author has searched the very archives of the cities themselves. He is thus able to present minutest and most instructive details as to the methods adopted for securing the best work, and in following his descriptions we see the progress of the building and hear the comments of the citizens. But, above all, the book is remarkable for the power of sympathetic imagination which pervades it from beginning to end and makes us feel, when Mr. Norton writes of Venice, or Siena, or Florence, that he is alternately Venetian, Sienese, Florentine, himself. It is difficult, for example, not to believe that Brunelleschi was his personal friend. We close this book with two thoughts in mind. The first connects itself with our pitiable, half-finished city hall, and suggests how much our own republic might learn, even in mere business (about which we Americans think we know so much), from the practice of those little republics in Italy six hundred years ago. Our second thought is of Harvard, and we congratulate that university on the possession of such a man as Mr. Norton for the elevation of its youth.

To the publishers of this book we can give no higher praise than that the beauty of their printers' work is in every way worthy of the contents.

POLITICAL AND LEGAL REMEDIES FOR WAR. By Sheldon Amos, M. A., Barrister at Law, late Professor of Jurisprudence in University College, London. New York: Harper & Brothers. 1880. For sale in San Francisco by Payot, Upham & Co.

Sheldon Amos is a philanthropist. His thoughts and his writings turn to the alleviation of the sufferings of mankind, to their moral advancement, and to their lasting good. That he should direct the attention of the world to the possibility and means of attaining peace among men is eminently characteristic of his philanthropic spirit. His *Political and Legal Remedies for War* opens in a chapter devoted to an inquiry into the probability of reducing the frequency of wars, and into the possibility of a permanent peace. Having pointed out that peace among nations is not wholly fanciful, he then examines the causes of wars, with the view of averting them by removing or lessening these causes in the future. In the third chapter the means of lessening or removing these sources of discord among peoples are treated politically, and in the fourth chapter, legally. It is seen that the author's handling of his subject is logically planned.

Mr. Amos does not pretend that there are no reasons for fearing that war may still have a long tenure of existence, but, as an international lawyer, whose duty he believes it to be to hasten, if possible, a day of permanent peace, he summons the following illustrations from the past in support of his faith "that some day war between civilized States must become obsolete:" Private wars, judicial combats, and dueling have vanished or are looked upon with reproach; the character of war is changeable, justifying the belief that it is likely to be as impermanent an institution as those which have passed away; and civilized States evince a growing desire to reduce such features of warfare as are least in harmony with the demands of the current civilization. In maintenance of the same view, the awakening among the people of the earth that wars are an evil, is dwelt upon —a feeling strengthened by popular education, by popular interest manifested in social questions, by the manifest burden of an expensive military establishment, and by the horrors of actual warfare, exposed through the medium of the war correspondent, and through books, that picture the real meaning of a conflict between nations. The spread of liberalism, the rise of philosophic schools, teaching peace, and the influence of religion, all culminating in the modern development of an international association for the settlement of disputed questions, encourage one in the hope that permanent peace may be attained in the future, and invite to the study of how this much to be desired end may be assured.

To enumerate all the causes of wars would entail the task of reciting all the reasons alleged therefor upon the occasion of a declaration of war, as well as the underlying, but unmentioned, springs of discontent. The author has preferred to mention all the general possible causes, with the view of ascertaining which of them are the least remediable. Among these causes are the antagonism between a nation's external relations in respect to its boundaries and treaty engagements, and its internal growth making these relations more and more irksome; hereditary jealousies and antipathies among States; the disposition of the more powerful States to intervene in the affairs of the less powerful; the traditional systems of foreign policies, ill adapted to the changes in international relations; the absence of an international morality, induced by an artificial national "honor;" standing armies, fostering the idea that war is a necessity; and the unsettled condition of international law. These various causes are honestly discussed, and the thoughts which they suggest are succinctly stated. From time to time the possible measures of relief that might be adopted are briefly mentioned, as in anticipation of the more elaborate consideration of these remedies.

The chapter devoted to the political remedies for war is the most entertaining, as well as the most suggestive, in the book. Therein is set forth in what respects nations, in their relations with one other, might avert the resort to arms. In illustration of the positions taken, the author reviews many of the most noticeable instances in modern diplomatic intercourse. A comprehensive review of treaty stipulations and international correspondence, made for a guide to future negotiations, cannot but prove interesting. In elucidation of his argument, the principles of intervention and non-intervention are explained—a question of exceeding interest in view of the pending struggle between Chili and Peru and Bolivia, the particulars wherein treaties might be improved are pointed out, the history of the balance of power theory is told, the doctrine of neutralization is stated and approved, the growth and constitution of the large standing armies in Europe are considered statistically and historically, and the policy condemned, and the resort to international congresses for the settlement of disputes is discussed in the light of reason and example, the circumstances under which they are likely to prove useful being defined. These are the respects wherein political remedies are deemed to be available in reducing the frequency, and ultimately paving the way to the abolition, of war. The legal means operative for the same beneficial ends are found in the systematizing and codifying of international law so far as is possible, and in reforms concerning the operations of war as it affects the trade of belligerents and neutrals, and concerning the laws of war as they bear upon the manner in which it is conducted.

All these delicate questions of international relation are candidly raised and considered. Although it might seem that a work of this nature would be too technical for ordinary perusal, its clearness of arrangement and of statement combine with its historical allusions to make it a valuable addition to the general library. The subject is in every sense a live one, and this, with Mr. Amos's evident earnestness, commends it. It is not sufficiently elaborate to make it a text-book—such was not the design; and this fact, no doubt, will greatly tend to its wider introduction among the people at large, whose passions, prejudices, and opinions the author considers an important factor in the continuance or cessation of wars.

Ultima Thule. A new volume of poems, by Henry Wadsworth Longfellow, with a new portrait of Mr. Longfellow. Boston: Houghton, Mifflin & Co. 1881. For sale in San Francisco by A. L. Bancroft & Co.

The Iron Gate, and Other Poems. By Oliver Wendell Holmes, with a fine new steel portrait. Boston: Houghton, Mifflin & Co. 1881. For sale in San Francisco by A. L. Bancroft & Co.

The names of Longfellow and Holmes have been so long and intimately associated with whatsoever things are pure and admirable in American literature that any new volumes from them have an assured appreciation and welcome. With Emerson, they are the survivors of an age, rather than a school, to which we are indebted for nearly all the contributions which will probably survive the close of the century. There are few poets that have enjoyed a continuous popularity for so extended a period as has Longfellow. Without great originality or intensity, there is, nevertheless, an even purity and sweetness in his poetry. He does not express the thoughts that a few men feel and throw down to the world; he brings up the thoughts which all men feel into the chaste atmosphere of his refined verse. Hence, the commonest man may say: These are my thoughts, clad in a better garment than I could have provided. Holmes, perhaps, has less of this universality in his poetry, but he has a distinctive field, which no one has ever occupied more gracefully.

Bricks Without Straw. A Novel. By Albion W. Tourgee. New York: Fords, Howard & Hulbert. 1880. For sale in San Francisco by A. L. Bancroft & Co.

This book is a sort of logical sequel to *A Fool's Errand*, by the same author, written with a political object, and so to be taken *cum grano salis*. Aside from the evidences of the haste made to get the book upon the market during the election excitement, the work is well done. The field is a vast one. It involves a conflict of races, and we know no better presentation of the subject than this book, if it can be borne in mind throughout that it is the brief of an advocate, and not the dictum of a judge.

The Code of Civil Procedure of the State of California. By Nathan Newmark. San Francisco: Sumner Whitney & Co. 1880.

English Men of Letters. Edited by John Morley. New York: Harper & Brothers. 1880. For sale in San Francisco by Payot, Upham & Co.
Byron. By John Nichol.

Franklin Square Library. New York: Harper & Brothers. 1880. For sale in San Francisco by Payot, Upham & Co.

No. 139.—*Lord Brackenbury.* A Novel. By Amelia B. Edwards.

No. 141.—*Just as I Am.* A Novel. By Miss M. E. Braddon.

No. 142.—*A Sailor's Sweetheart.* By W. Clark Russell.

Harper's Half-Hour Series. New York: Harper & Brothers. 1880. For sale in San Francisco by Payot, Upham & Co.

No. 141.—*The National Banks.* By H. W. Richardson.

New Colorado and the Santa Fe Trail. By A. A. Hayes, Jr. New York: Harper & Brothers. 1880. For sale in San Francisco by A. L. Bancroft & Co.

The Worst Boy in Town. By the author of *Helen's Babies.* New York: G. P. Putnam's Sons. 1880. For sale in San Francisco by A. L. Bancroft & Co.

The Flight into Egypt. A Narrative Poem. By Thomas E. Van Bebber. San Francisco: A. L. Bancroft & Co. 1880.

Methods of Teaching. A Hand-book of Principles, Directions, and Working Models for Common School Teachers. By John Swett. New York: Harper & Brothers. 1880. For sale in San Francisco by Payot, Upham & Co.

History of the English People. By John Richard Green, M.A. Volume IV. New York: Harper & Brothers. 1880. For sale in San Francisco by Payot, Upham & Co.

Judge and Jury. A Popular Explanation of Leading Topics in the Law of the Land. By Benjamin Vaughan Abbott. New York: Harper & Brothers. 1880. For sale in San Francisco by Payot, Upham & Co.

The Hour Will Come. A Tale of an Alpine Cloister. By Wilhelmine von Hillern. From the German, by Clara Bell. New York: William S. Gottsberger. 1880. For sale in San Francisco by A. L. Bancroft & Co.

A First Italian Course. Containing a Grammar, Delectus, and Exercise-book, on the plan of Dr. William Smith's *Principia Latina.* New York: Harper & Brothers. 1880. For sale in San Francisco by Payot, Upham & Co.

OUTCROPPINGS.

A BOSTON SYMPOSIUM.

At an entertainment, lately given in this city, there was introduced an imaginary dinner, given in Boston upon the occasion of the two hundred and fiftieth anniversary of its settlement, at which many noted authors were present by proxy, others being represented by suppositituous letters. Mr. W. D. H-w-lls presided, and, after brief opening remarks, introduced Dr. O. W. H-lm-s, who talked delightfully of his early recollections of Boston, and concluded with the following poem:

BUNKER HILL MONUMENT AND THE OBELISK.—A DIALOGUE.

The Monument.

Respected monolith, pilgrim to our shore,
How could you enter at the Castle Garden door
When Boston's seaward gates were open wide,
Inviting you to enter and abide?

Here is the home of Light and Knowledge,
"The General Hospital," and Harvard College.
Every citizen's a philosopher, or poet,
And yet so modest that he scarcely seems to know it.

Here they lunch on protoplasm, dine on trilobites,
The very boys leave marbles, tops, and kites,
On lofty themes to hold discourse, and high debate—
The Nebular Hypothesis, Free Will, and Fate.

How different in the Knickerbocker city, given up to
Mammon,
Where speculation 's everything, and *culchaw* gammon!
What, in such a place, is the sculptured story
Chiseled on your sides in days of Egypt's glory?

They will vote the "marks" and "scratches," past all
divination,
Then—send to Boston for an explanation.
Therefore, pull up stakes at Central Park,
And come this way, first-cousin of the ark.

In Boston Common, on a grassy mound,
Near "The Long Path," with elm trees all around,
There may you stand and point the sky
Through coming ages to the passer-by.

Professors grave, with spectacles on nose,
And doctors wise will stand about in rows,
Young ladies "eye-glassed," erudite, and literary,
Careless of fashion, but profound, and philosophic, very,

Will gather round in groups, in learned theories prolific,
To discuss, in Sanscrit tongue, each hieroglyphic.

But I, the granite shaft which rests on Bunker Hill,
Four times your stature, and far grander still,
I, who have given you this cordial invitation,
Must also urge you to be mindful of your station;

I, who came from Quincy granite stock,
Of course could never recognize Egyptian rock.
So, if you come this way, you'll promise, "will yer,"
Never to presume to be familiar?

For, passing by my vastly higher station,
There is a matter which affects your reputation:

At home they call you Cleopatra's needle, I believe,
After a woman whose character, I grieve
To say, was never good; and thus you're blasted hither,
Because your name's connected with her.

I'd have you know that Beacon Hill society
Is conducted on the strictest of propriety.

The Obelisk.

I, the brother of the pyramids—
I, who was old when Homer sang,
And past my prime when Persian host
Ravaged the fair land of Egypt—
I, that stood watch and guard beside
The temple-door for two thousand years—
I, who have seen nations rise and fall,

Religions born and grow, flourish and decay,
What to me is time, or space, or place?
In this fair garden of the West
I stand, and shall stand, when
Other Goths and Vandals come from afar,
To sweep away a race enfeebled by luxury and vice.
And you, my stony friend, have stood
Against the northern blast these *fifty* years—
A moment in my existence.
For every year of your brief time,
Take half a century from mine,
And I should ante-date the Cæsars then.
Your lofty column, stone added to stone,
Aspires to the stars. So Babel's tower,
Another "hollow mockery," arose on yesterday;
And to-day none but I, and the Sphinx,
Who will not speak, could tell the spot.

And now, in closing, let me catch your rhyme,
To tell you that you're hardly for all time.
Although you are so grim and stolid,
You're a hollow shell, while I, like Dixie land, am *solid.*

The following letter was then read:

C-NC-RD, September 10.

DEAR MR. H-W-LLS:—I think it was Æschylus, who said that a man's home is his castle. I am so fortified in mine, that not Boston, nor the farthest Ind, shall draw me from it.

What's Boston to me, or I to Boston, that I should dine for her?

From a sufficient hight, all towns appear alike. Boston is great; but there was another Athens.

Glory not in that wherein you differ.

Individuality is no ground for pride.

Towns are one, as man is one, and a pint cup may have no more moral character than a boned herring.

I honor Boston too much to flatter her.

Fools like flattery, and Boston is no man's fool.

Rude truth is a better, if less palatable gift, than flattery, and Boston is on the earth, after all.

She has been a reformer, but many a reformer perishes in his removal of rubbish, and that makes the offensiveness of the class. Let her be indifferent to sneers, and indignant at flattery, and she shall attain the highest.

I wrote a little poem a number of years ago, that many people have, I am told, been unable to comprehend. They have thus (unconsciously, no doubt), greatly honored me; but, as a concession to feebler powers, and as a tribute to Boston, I have slightly reformed it, and trust that, as amended, it may prove more intelligible. Very truly, R. W. EM-RS-N.

BOSTON.

The town of life, the town of life,
I see thee pass
In various guise—
Wise and foolish
Solemn and gay,
Strong and weakish,
Lofty and mean—
Protecting right and hating wrong;
Temperate of all but tongue,
And the inventor of the game,
"Overboard with tea," we name;
Some I see, some I have guessed,
They laughed from east to west;
Little Boston least of all
Among the legs of her guardians tall,
Walked about with a puzzled look.
She by the ear dear Nature took;
Dearest Nature, strong and kind,
Whispered, "Darling, never mind!
To-morrow they will wear another face,
The founder thou I—these are thy race."

Mr. H. W. L-ngf-ll-w then read this historical account of the naming of the city:

BOSTON.

Should you ask me why this meeting—
Why this celebration, banquet?
Why these essays, speeches, letters?
Why these frequent iterations,
"Culture," "Boston," "education?"
I should answer, I should tell you:
In the land of Massachusetts—
Massachusetts, or the "Red Hills"—
Is a famous, favored city,
All whose sons are of the wisest,
All whose daughters of the fairest,
All whose people are so cultured,
Educated, and fastidious
That they cannot help but show it
When they meet with other people.

I should answer, I should tell you:
We have met on this occasion
By our words and deeds to fitly
Celebrate the anniversary
Of the founding of that city,
Of the settlement of Boston.

Ye who love old Massachusetts—
Love her notions and her people,
Love her freedom of opinion,
Scientific and religious,
Covering all denominations,
From the strictest orthodoxy
To the wildest of free-thinkers;
Holding orthodox conclusion,
That the fall of tempted Adam
Through succeeding generations
Curseth all mankind in common,
From the old and hardened sinner
To the infant in the cradle,
To the doom of condemnation,
Burning, horrible, and endless;
Holding, also, skepticism
And the Nihilist's negation,
Doubting, scoffing, unbelieving,
Save in bald annihilation—
Listen to our feeble tribute
To the pride of Massachusetts,
Boston, pride of Massachusetts.

Ye who love the dear old Bay State—
Love the logic of her wise men,
That, from premise once adopted,
Reasons straightway to conclusion,
Never heeding consequences;
Love the meekness of the fathers
That so mildly taught the Quakers,
That so gently drove out witches,
And so kindly dealt with Baptists—
Listen to our praise of Boston,
Boston, pride of Massachusetts.

Ye who love this famous city—
Who believe, without a question,
All ideas worth the knowing
Germinate in Boston Common,
Beacon Street, and Harvard College;
That their origin and being
Are within the city's limits
Or immediate surroundings;
That as to a wheel the hub is,
So unto the world is Boston;
Who believe that this the hub is
Of the wheel of thought and culture;
That the spokes of thought run outward
From this hub to the circumference,
Making all revolve around it,
Guiding all things from that center,
Holding still at proper distance
Outside fellows that surround it—
Listen to this song of Boston,
Boston, pride of Massachusetts.

Would you learn the early story,
How they named this fairest city?
What the name of Boston meaneth,
Which hath now become so famous?

Listen, then, to the tradition,
For the history of this city
Older is than all her wise men,
And may look into the dim past
Full two hundred busy summers.

Very wise and very skillful
Were the founders of this city,
And, with clear, prophetic reason,
They foresaw that in the future,
As they looked down the ages,
That the city which they founded
Was predestined to be greater
Than all others round about it—
Greater far than other towns, the sea—
And from Lynn to Quincy
Should be ruler of the seacoast;
So they had a celebration,
First a long and grand procession,
Numbering more than forty persons;
Then they gathered round the table,
Ate their baked beans and their brown-bread,
Had the first great annual dinner,
Which thenceforth became the custom
From that day unto the present.
When the brown-bread and the baked beans
Were removed from off the table,
Long they sat in solemn conclave,
Much as we are now assembled,
And discussed the mighty question
Of the city they had founded:
What should the most fitting name be?
Some insisted, as the ruler
Of the country round about it,
That its name express *the master*.
Others said this wondrous city
Shall rule chiefly through its culture,
By the force of its example,
By the setting of the fashion
In religion, science, morals,
Doctrines, politics, and manners,
And the name should be expressive
Of the style, the mode, the fashion.
Then at last one of the wise men
Said unto the striving factions:
"Let the name, then, be expressive
Of the thought ye each contend for.
Does not 'boss' express the master?
Is not '*ton*' the ruling fashion?
Let us name the city Bos-ton."
And the wise men all consented.
This the origin of Boston,
Boston, pride of Massachusetts.

J—q—n M-ll-r read this poem:

WELCOME, SIERRA!

I leap to my saddle; the world is grown weary.
 The dust of your cities lies thick in the way;
I wave you farewell, my heart it is cheery—
 The splendid, far peaks, they beckon and sway.
But dearer than all is the voice of the prairie,
 The swift antelope, the brown wolf at bay.
Oh, build with the eagle, far up in his eyrie,
 Where scented pines are stately and gray;
Oh, follow the hunt on the boundless savanna;
 Be strong as a god; go, pluck of the fruit
Of tropical suns, of palm and banana;
 Know warm life's redness—drink deep and be mute,
And worship free Nature. Yes, lie on the sand
 By ultimate seas of the sun-down West,
And plow not, nor reap not, nor trouble the land
 With houses and building; dream dreams, lie at rest
From tempest and fret, from spoiling and scorn;
And find ye the kingdoms of kings new-born
In untraveled lands.
 Lo! I shall do this;
I shall turn me from men; shall pierce, as of old,
My snow-clad Sierra, my limitless wold;
Shall climb the fierce peaks of my ridged Andes,
And shape the loud songs of my buccaneer seas;
Shall steer down the billow, when swift sunlight glances
 On dark tropic isles, deep-hid in blue seas.
You green-girdled islands, your master advances,
 And mocks at his cares. Free! utterly free!
There brave brown monarchs, in dark nights of hail,
Stand tall by the palms, and stately, and fair.
Our broad-breasted men by their Argonaut sail,
 Their horse-leather hands grip fast to the oar;
We turn from dead empires, we carry the freight
 Of kingdoms to be on some virginal shore.
Lo! fervid, and grand, and far as a star,
The passionate peaks of that island are
White and chill while the cold moon rides
Through cloud-land rivers in flowing tides;
Chill and white they jostle the stars,
And look into heaven, and carry the scars
Of red lightning-bolts.—Now, that is the land
To covet and take, know war and know love,
 And everything else that lies upon the sun.
 But what is it all when all it is done,
Save a weaving of shadows that others have wove?

Mr. J. G. Wh—tt—r's contribution was as follows:

A—— y, 15th, 9th mo., 1880.

DEAR FRIEND:—I thank thee for asking me to be at the dinner, upon the 250th anniversary of Boston's settlement; but thou must pardon me that the quiet of my home is more to my liking. I would not have thee think that I do not love Boston, and am not proud of her; and to show my respect for her, historically, and for those who so well represent her now, I send with this a few verses. I am thy friend,

J. G. WH—TT—R.

BOSTON.

1630.

Behold a sterile, cheerless shore,
 On Massachusetts Bay—
Three peaks to heav'n proudly soar,
 And wait the coming day.

At last they come—the favored few
 Who plant an empire vast.
"They builded better than they knew,"
 When here their lot they cast.

In time, a hamlet greets our sight—
 And then a growing town,
With beacon lifted on the hight
 Which now proud structures crown.

1776.

When Folly ruled the mother land
 Here Liberty was born,
Where Faneuil Hall, its cradle grand,
 Salutes the coming morn.

No tyrant's power the chains could weld
 To bind those heroes brave.
No awe of mighty hosts withheld
 The tide that onward rolled,

Till scattered colonies unite,
 And form a nation strong,
Which, seeking freedom in their might,
 Dispelled the power of wrong.

1844.

Again, brave Boston lifts her voice,
 And speaks in thunder tone;
The slave whom freedom shall rejoice
 No more with chains shall groan.

Once more is heard in Faneuil Hall
 A proud and lofty strain—
Proclaiming liberty to all,
 From Florida to Maine.

The fire, then lit, ne'er ceased to glow,
'Till slavery's power was dead,
And shameful wrong, and blighting woe,
No more their venom shed.

1880.

And now, old Boston, proudly turns
To view the vanished years;
Upon her altars incense burns,
For bright their course appears.

She ne'er has sought the approving word
"From Mammon's crowded mart,"
But spirit calls she hath preferred,
And found the better part.

Ne'er may she fall from that proud hight,
Her sons have nobly won,
But, true to freedom, truth, and right,
Complete the work begun.

Mrs. A. D. T. Wh tn y offered as her tribute the following:

FANEUIL HALL'S LAST NIGHT ASHORE.

[A Novel in 250 Chapters. Dedicated to Boston.]

Chapter I.

You see Faneuil was such a serene, fidgety boy, a Janus-headed boy, looking all ways at once, and never twice in the same direction.

His father, old Hall, was a near neighbor to old South Church, and Hall's folks had arrived that very night, and we were all sitting out on the lean-to porch, hanging over the gooseberry patch, and watching the dear gooseberries as they waved up and down in the moonlight, and smiled up into our answering faces.

It was all there: the gooseberries, the heavenly harmonies of the squash-vines, running up their octave, clear into a diminished seventh of cranberry pie and quince marmalade. And when Faneuil slid down from the lean-to shed and disappeared among the gooseberries, how little we thought that his garden sass would before morning be waiting for him on the other side!

When he came back he said:

"Why heavenly harmonies?"

"Faneuil," said I, "a parable is something that acts as if it wanted to fit somewhere."

Why did nobody tell us, as we sat on the lean-to shed, that Faneuil was so soon to be translated into another type?

But we ate and drank, and not only that, the moon went down, and the pretty beryl-green face of Faneuil began to be illumined with a light that never was on sea or land. "Patience Strong's Outings" were exceeded by Faneuil Hall's Innings (of gooseberries), and before morning he could be heard away up to Faith Gartney's saw-mill, where the Real Folks had just washed their dishes, and sat down to their Kensington work.

"Well," said Emery Jane, the next morning when she heard of Faneuil's death, "he's made up of carpet-rags, anyhow, and the piecin' and the weavin' 's left to ourselves. The type is where the trouble comes in, and everybody must look out and grab all the bright pieces he can. In the kingdom come, everybody'll get credit for his own rags."

If Faneuil Hall had not evaporated, where might his everlastingly infinite littleness have been now? That is the strangest part of it, that his spirit has spread out into the infinite circumference of the big unknowable what-do-you-call-it, and is enjoying the true inwardness that only hot biscuit and green gooseberries could give him here below.

After the funeral, we sent for South Church's folks to come over. Old South took the big rocking-chair that stands in the East-west window, and said that he thought that in the great inexpressible hereafter there would be rocking-chairs for all hands.

"Yes," said the minister, "the true meaning of a rocking-chair is known only to the faithful few, who have had the light of experience to guide them."

Patience Strong answered that she thought that on the other side there would be no sharp corners of Eastlake furniture and *bric-a-brac* pianos, "for," said she, "we shall then be abstract impossible nonentities, expressive only by the moonshine which shineth more and more unto the perfect day.

End of Chapter I.

Mr. J. R. L w ll, being unable to attend, sent a Biglow paper:

TO BOSTON.

An' so yu're goin' to celebrate the day
When them old Pilgrims lit on Boston Bay!
Wal, what's the use? They didn't know, I guess,
That anybody'd think they'd ought to bless
Them for it, or make a big to-do an' show
When they'd ben dead two hundred years or so.
But I'm thinkin' in these degen'rit days
Yu're allers huntin' suthin' up to praise;
An' I believe it's nothin' but the fun
You spect to have—that's why the thing is done.
Yu're 'mazin' fond of allers rampin' round,
Makin' speeches, and sech like noisy sound.
When I 's a boy they didn't use to think
They could afford to spare the time to wink.
We used to work the year around, 'cept trainin'
And July Fourth, unless we'd git the grain in
When it rained, or looked kinder's though it might,
Which it gen'rally did, just out of spite.
But now you copy furrin' ways and fashions
An' I don't see how you arn yer rations.
I don't b'lieve yure's honest as yure fathers
Or you couldn't never spend such slathers
O' money. But 'tain't no affair o' mine—
I don't like your vittles or your furrin wine.
But I jest tell you, 'tain't no kinder use,
An' I've sot my face firm 'gainst such abuse.
'F you want to git together now and spout,
I don't see why it can't be done without
Spendin' so much money that you might use
In doin' suthin' useful. I refuse
To go to your darned old spendthrift dinner,
But send you this t' kinder sorter winner
Out the grain from 'mongst the pile of chaff,
If there's any there, which I guess 's more'n half
Doubtful. I don't see no solid reason
Why you celebrate. If this is treason,
Make the most on't, for I don't care a snap
If you get mad; an' if one thumpin' rap
Could knock the conceit (that, certain, you have got)
Clean out, you'd then be quite a tol'ble lot.
You may think this ain't so very civil
But's better'n all your etarnal drivel
'Bout Boston's bein' so 'mazin' smart a town.
Why, there's hull lots o' places takes you down—
More houses, more folks, more everything but brass.
Out West I don't b'lieve you'd hardly pass
For much of anythin' but a village.
They've got parks that they reserve from tillage
Bigger than all the towns you've lately jined
Thinkin' you could all creation blind,
And make 'em think you'd grown so awful fast
Since Uncle Samuel took his census last.
I guess I'd better stop, I'm gittin' riled.
But there's lots o' poets'll treat you very mild,
An' say you beat all holler anythin' out;
But 'tain't best to allers have such praise 'bout
You're perfect, which is very scarse below,
An' 'fore you git it you've a piece to go.

HOSEA BIGLOW.

P. S.—

I guess, come to cool, I've been kinder rough,
But then, you know, kind hearts is often gruff.
You see I'm gittin' sorter old and cross,
And I forgit I hain't no right to boss.
I'd really like to see you all, I swow!
And if I didn't have a job that now
Keeps me over to one of the neighbors,
I would come right down—I would, by jabers!

Mr. Br-t H-rte sent from across the Atlantic the following:

BOSTON.

On the south fork of Yuba, in May, fifty-two,
  An old cabin stood up on the hill,
Where the road to Grass Valley lay clear to the view,
  And a ditch that ran down to Rock's Mill.

It was owned by a party that lately had come
  To discover what fate held in store,
Who was working for Brigham, and prospecting some,
  Which the clothes were well cut that he wore.

He had spent all his fortune to buy this old hut,
  For he never could bear a hotel.
He refused to drink whisky or play poker, but
  He was jolly and used the boys well.

In the long winter evenings he started a club,
  To discuss the affairs of the day.
He was up in the classics—a scholarly cub—
  And the best of the talkers could lay.

He could sing like a blue-jay, and played on the flute,
  And he opened a school, which was free,
Where he taught all the musical fellows to toot,
  Or to join in an anthem or glee.

So he soon "held the age" over any young man
  Who had ever been known on the bar;
And the boys put him through, when for sheriff he ran,
  And his stock now was much above par.

In the spring he was lucky, and struck a rich lead,
  And he let all his friends have a share.
It was called the New Boston, for that was his breed,
  And the rock that he showed them was rare.

When he called on his partners to put up a mill,
  They were anxious to furnish the means;
And the needful was turned into his little till
  Just as freely as though it was beans.

Then he went to the Bay with his snug little pile—
  There was seventeen thousand and more—
To arrange for a mill of the most approved style,
  And to purchase a Sturtevant blower.

But they waited for Boston a year and a day,
  And he never was heard of again.
For the lead he had opened was salted with pay,
  And he'd played 'em with culture and brain.

Moral:

Now this incident shows—I'd like to explain—
  This yere culture is not all you need;
And that *smart* men, who confidence easily gain,
  You must *watch*, or they'll *prey*. That's their creed.

M-rk Tw—n, selected for the historian of the occasion, produced the following:

I presume I have been asked to give my remarks a historical turn because of my well established reputation for veracity. It proves the Master of Ceremonies a discerning and appreciative party, for history is what I am particularly strong on. My mind, what there is of it, is judicial and calm. If I have a fault—which I don't acknowledge—it is that I am too conscientious, too single-minded in my devotion to truth. I am simply incapable of embellishment, and in this brief historical sketch I shall unfold a tale as plain and unvarnished as a New England bean-pole—but not so long. In the year 1620, the good ship *Mayflower* ran aground on Plymouth Rock. She had a miscellaneous cargo, largely composed of Bibles and old arm-chairs. Her commander, Governor Carver, was an exemplary citizen, but was addicted to the habit of repairing to the depths of the forest primeval and shooting at glass balls. Soon after the settlement of the *Mayflower* on the aforesaid rock, three brothers of an enterprising spirit pushed on to a small peninsula on Massachusetts Bay, and concluded there to squat. They squatted. There were three slight hummocks on it, and with the same tendency to magnify the importance of everything belonging to or connected with them that still marks their descendants they called them mountains; and the eldest brother, who was slightly classical and also a Dutchman, wished to call the settlement Tremont, but the youngest brother had a prophetic soul (inherited from his uncle), and a fine appreciation of that force in the use of language that people who can't use it now call "slang," and he stood out for calling it the Hub Town, and finally belted the other brother, who was referee, with a hymn-book, and carried the day. There are other legends, but this is the frozen truth. It was so known for a hundred years, until at a town meeting, held early in the eighteenth century, it was proposed to cut out two letters for the sake of euphony, and call it Boston. The argument was not favorably received, but when some mathematical chap demonstrated that the cost of writing those two letters, in ink and goose-quills, would be two shillings and fourpence to each head of a family—provided he lived a thousand years—there was not a dissenting voice. It was the first solid vote in history. The same principle defeated a proposition to survey the town, and establish straight streets therein. The expense, two pounds three and ninepence, was deemed a wicked extravagance, as long as the cows had already laid out the paths "for nothin'." But what possessed those cows, infirm of purpose, to meander around that peninsula in such a ridiculous manner, is too many for the present historian. The principal recreation in those days was the gathering of the fathers in the evening to watch the mothers milk the erratic cows, the spot most frequented being subsequently called Milk Street. This was before our esteemed friend Miss Anthony was born. Her gentle voice had not been raised for suffering woman, and it was pretty hard papers for the old girls. The Pilgrim Fathers had much to bear, but the pilgrim mothers could give them points and discount them on trials; for, in addition to all the troubles that the fathers had, they were called upon also to endure those disagreeable old codgers themselves. This is not original, but my publishers have issued an injunction against my saying anything original except by subscription. No one can doubt the patriotism of our forefathers. How it must have hurt their feelings to have chucked that tea overboard—to see it wasted! They had several nice skirmishes in Revolutionary time, and fell back in good order when they couldn't make the other fellers. A monument was erected on a hill; but whether the fight was on that hill, or the monument is on the other, has never been settled. I cannot dwell on this fascinating theme. Boston is now noted for culture and baked beans. The view from the State House, on Beacon Hill, is the finest in the known world. I have surmounted the Pyramids; I have waved the American flag from the summit of the Himalaya; I have gazed from the Tower of Pisa; I have stood by the tomb of Adam, and wept; but never—no, never—have my feelings been so stirred up—so churned, so to speak—as when I corkscrewed my way up to that giddy eminence, and allowed myself to drink in the entrancing loveliness of the frog-pond on Boston Common.

G-l H-m-lt-n and H. H. offered bright and effervescing tributes, which we regret our inability to secure.

Miss S-s-n B. Anth-ny declines to furnish any report of her remarks, which were very spicy, and produced a profound impression.

It is not a matter of surprise that the Rev. E. E. H-le has had no opportunity since the dinner to write out his interesting response, which was marked, as usual, with originality and versatility.

PUBLISHERS' DEPARTMENT.

EXTRAORDINARY INDUCEMENTS FOR THE NEW YEAR.

With this number THE CALIFORNIAN completes its second volume, and, encouraged by the success which has met their efforts, the publishers beg to return their thanks to the reading public, and to promise renewed efforts for the future.

It has been their aim to publish a monthly which should be distinctive, original, healthful, progressive; to make it a pleasure to the readers and a credit to the Coast. In this, all circumstances considered, they claim to have succeeded; and, with a continuance of the appreciation already shown, they promise for the future even a greater degree of improvement than in the past. For the coming year, desirous to meet the public half way, the publishers announce three unusually liberal offers, from which subscribers are at liberty to choose.

FIRST OFFER.

FOUR VOLUMES FOR FIVE DOLLARS.

We have on hand a limited number of sets of THE CALIFORNIAN for 1880.

From this date *till the first of January next*, provided said sets shall hold out, we offer to supply for ONE DOLLAR (to every new subscriber who pays four dollars in advance before said date to THE CALIFORNIAN, at its office in San Francisco, for the year 1881) the entire twelve numbers for 1880, in addition to those of 1881 as they come out.

THIS MAKES TWO YEARS' SUBSCRIPTION TO THE CALIFORNIAN FOR FIVE DOLLARS (regular price, $4 per year.) By accepting this offer you will have THE CALIFORNIAN from the commencement—four handsome volumes of the latest and best literature.

SECOND OFFER.

SPECIAL INDUCEMENTS TO CLUBS.

Every one who subscribes to THE CALIFORNIAN has it in his power to induce several of his friends or neighbors to subscribe.

We have decided to offer special rates to those who desire to get up clubs, so that the magazine shall come cheaper to each member of the club.

Observe that the larger you make your club the greater the reduction to each one.

CLUB RATES.

(1.) To a club of TWO new subscribers for the year 1881, we will send THE CALIFORNIAN for $7.60, instead of $8.00, the regular price (being $3.80 each).

(2.) To a club of THREE new subscribers for the year 1881, we will send THE CALIFORNIAN for $11.10, instead of $12, the regular price (being $3.70 each).

(3.) To a club of FOUR new subscribers for the year 1881, we will send THE CALIFORNIAN for $14.40, instead of $16, the regular price (being $3.60 each).

(4.) To a club of FIVE new subscribers for the year 1881 we will send THE CALIFORNIAN for $17.50, instead of $20, the regular price (being $3.50 each).

(5.) To a club of SIX new subscribers for the year 1881, we will send THE CALIFORNIAN for $20.40, instead of $24, the regular price (being $3.40 each).

(6.) To a club of SEVEN new subscribers for the year 1881, we will send THE CALIFORNIAN for $23.10, instead of $28, the regular price (being $3.30 each).

(7.) To a club of EIGHT new subscribers for the year 1881, we will send THE CALIFORNIAN for $25.60, instead of $32, the regular price (being $3.20 each).

(8.) To a club of NINE new subscribers for the year 1881, we will send THE CALIFORNIAN for $27.90, instead of $36, the regular price (being $3.10 each).

(9.) To a club of TEN new subscribers for the year 1881, we will send THE CALIFORNIAN for $30, Instead of $40, the regular price (being $3 each).

The money in every instance must accompany the names.

We will send the magazine as above to one address or to several, as may be desired. It is not necessary that all the club should be in the same locality.

THIRD OFFER.

LIBERAL PREMIUMS TO THOSE WHO WILL PROCURE US SUBSCRIBERS.

Many of our readers, without leaving their homes or incommoding themselves, can procure many new subscribers, and to such we offer the following liberal premiums.

Observe that the more subscribers you get the larger the premium for each one.

PREMIUMS.

(1.) To any one who sends us the names of TWO new subscribers for the year 1881, accompanied by $4 each, we will allow 40 cents.

(2.) To any one who sends us the names of THREE new subscribers for the year 1881, accompanied by $4 each, we will allow 90 cents.

(3.) To any one who sends us the names of FOUR new subscribers for the year 1881, accompanied by $4 each, we will allow $1.60.

(4.) To any one who sends us the names of FIVE new subscribers for the year 1881, accompanied by $4 each, we will allow $2.50.

(5.) To any one who sends us the names of SIX new subscribers for the year 1881, accompanied by $4 each, we will allow $3.60.

(6.) To any one who sends us the names of SEVEN new subscribers for the year 1881, accompanied by $4 each, we will allow $4.90.

(7.) To any one who sends us the names of EIGHT new subscribers for the year 1881, accompanied by $4 each, we will allow $6.40.

(8.) To any one who sends us the names of NINE new subscribers for the year 1881, accompanied by $4 each, we will allow $8.10.

(9.) To any one who sends us the names of TEN new subscribers for the year 1881, accompanied by $4 each, we will allow $10.

TO THE ONE WHO SENDS US THE LARGEST LIST OF NAMES OF NEW SUBSCRIBERS, ACCOMPANIED BY THE AMOUNT OF THEIR SUBSCRIPTIONS, BEFORE THE FIRST DAY OF FEBRUARY NEXT, WE WILL PAY $25, IN ADDITION TO HIS PREMIUMS.

This last offer is one at which not only grown people can make money, but we commend it especially to boys and girls. Get your parents to subscribe. Get your relatives to subscribe. Get your friends to subscribe. Try every one you know. This is a splendid chance for you to make money in your spare hours. Don't take "No" for an answer.

OUR ADVERTISING DEPARTMENT.

THE CALIFORNIAN prints each month a limited number of advertising pages. It is the only first-class literary magazine published west of the Mississipi Valley, and reaches thousands of households all over the Pacific Coast. Instead of being cast aside as soon as read, THE CALIFORNIAN is carefully preserved, is passed from hand to hand, thus giving advertisements a great degree of prominence and a very wide circulation. Its advertising pages are few and well displayed, and the magazine carries a degree of influence very favorable to advertisers. It is a standard medium, and care is taken that no questionable advertisements shall be admitted. Instances are not wanting in which advertisers have been richly repaid in patronage drawn to them by reason of their business announcements in THE CALIFORNIAN. And it is proper to say here that our readers who desire to purchase will do well to deal with those whose advertisements they find from month to month in THE CALIFORNIAN, as, from the care taken, only reliable and responsible houses are admitted.

HOW TO SEND MONEY.

The safest and best way to send money is by express, post-office order, or draft on San Francisco. We will not be responsible for money sent in an other way. Address

THE CALIFORNIA PUBLISHING CO.,

(P. O. Box 2,319.) 202 Sansome Street, San Francisco, Cal.

www.ingramcontent.com/pod-product-compliance
Lightning Source LLC
Chambersburg PA
CBHW031935290426
44108CB00011B/564

* 9 7 8 3 7 4 2 8 0 0 4 4 2 *